Under the editorship of **LEONARD CARMICHAEL**

- Vice President for Research and Exploration,
  National Geographic Society.

- Formerly, Secretary, Smithsonian Institution;

- President, Tufts College;

- Director, Tufts Research Laboratory of
  Sensory Psychology and Physiology.

PSYCHOLOGY

The Fundamentals of Human Adjustment

FIFTH EDITION

NORMAN L. MUNN

The University of Adelaide

HOUGHTON MIFFLIN COMPANY / BOSTON
New York / Atlanta / Geneva, Ill. / Dallas / Palo Alto

*To my wife Barbara, and
Henry, Wesley, Ronald,
Barbara, Alan, David,
and Normajeane,
I affectionately dedicate
this book*

EDITOR'S INTRODUCTION

The publication of William James's *Principles of Psychology* in 1890 was certainly one of the greatest events in nineteenth-century psychology. James had labored for twelve years on this work, and it gave order and coherence to the whole subject as it was at that time. For many reasons this work of genius can never be duplicated, but the need for such a work is at least as urgent today as it was seventy-five years ago. In this fifth edition of *Psychology: The Fundamentals of Human Adjustment* Norman L. Munn has, in the editor's opinion, done an outstanding service for our day in meeting the same objectives that made James's book so valuable in his.

The first edition of Munn's *Psychology* appeared in 1946. It was an immediate success because of its remarkable and far-ranging scholarship and its lucid, vivid style. I well remember the thrill that I had in editing that first edition. From the beginning I felt certain that it was a great contribution to knowledge as well as the work of a true teacher. I experienced the same deep satisfaction in editing the second, third, and fourth editions.

Now I can say that this fifth edition not only brings its reporting of research up to date, but in conception it is better than any of its predecessors. This is a result of more than a quarter of a century of work by an able scientist. In preparing each new edition of his books, Dr. Munn reads diligently and discerningly the vast outpouring of research publications that have appeared since previous editions. Then he does not merely "cut and paste," he rewrites. As a result, the total number of pages in the present edition is not increased, in spite of the large amount of wholly new material that it contains. Dr. Munn never forgets that each new student can master only limited amounts of information in a single course.

It should be emphasized that this is a book that teaches. Dr. Munn's objective has been to produce a book that will present to the student, in a single volume, the full spectrum of the modern scientific study of human behavior. Toward this end, the book has been organized and developed to employ all the aids to instruction that have proved useful with previous editions in the author's own classes and in the classes of many of his colleagues. Thus the student who begins his study of modern psychology with this fifth edition is fortunate.

The editor has spent much of his life as a psychologist not only in teaching and research, but also in university administration. In the latter capacity he has necessarily thought much about the general objectives of higher education in America. Today it seems clear that each university student should learn how to explore in depth by himself any topic that becomes important to him currently or in later life. He should learn, too, all that he can about what man has done and thought in the past; but in addition he should certainly learn what scientific procedures have revealed about the bases of human behavior and the laws governing mental life.

That Dr. Munn's *Psychology* is ideally suited to assist in achieving this last objective is apparent. Moreover every topic in the book is presented in such a way as to suggest how those who wish to can learn more about it. The student will discern, for example, that the study of mental life is related to the general study of biology. Thus the fifth edition can make a real contribution to the general education of the student. At the same time it is an excellent introductory book for those who expect to take additional courses in psychology or to do their major undergraduate work in this challenging and important field.

In the editor's opinion it would be a great underestimation of the present edition to think of it only as a good college textbook. This it surely is, but like the earlier editions it is also a substantial contribution to knowledge. I am often asked the question: "What is the contemporary state of scientific psychology?" I always answer by suggesting a reading of Munn's *Psychology*. This is a volume that every thoughtful undergraduate will want to add to his permanent personal library. Its scholarship, its clear, crisp style, and its outstanding glossary will make it an authoritative reference long after undergraduate days have been left behind.

Leonard Carmichael
Washington, D.C.

PREFACE

In this edition, as in those which preceded it, I have sought to provide a representative survey of modern scientific psychology. My efforts have in general been guided by the view that an understanding of scientific psychology contributes to a well-rounded education. I have also aimed to give the student an understanding of psychological processes in himself and other people, to suggest how this knowledge may facilitate his personal adjustment, and to point out some significant applications of psychology in the professions, in business, and in industry.

My use of the earlier edition in teaching American and Australian students revealed many ways in which it might be improved. Students, colleagues, and other users of the fourth edition also gave me the benefit of their experience by making constructive criticisms and suggesting improvements. I have taken cognizance of these in preparing the present edition. The chief reason for a new edition, however, is the rapid advance that psychology is making in many areas covered by an introductory textbook. My survey of the psychological research since I wrote the last edition has demonstrated the need for significant revisions in almost every area. Some deletions were shown to be necessary because recent research has sometimes failed to support earlier findings. In addition to revising material already in the text and deleting parts of it, there was an evident need to include much that is new. Overall, however, this revision has resulted in a considerable page reduction, without omission of any important topic dealt with in the fourth edition. Most of this reduction was accomplished by (1) doing away with the previous part arrangement, with its sometimes lengthy introductions, (2) rewriting some topics so that they could be dealt with in a single chapter instead of two or more, and (3) eliminating repetition in text and illustration legends. The latter revisions not only reduce redundancy but also require more careful study of the illustrations.

Beyond this general face-lifting, there has been a detailed reappraisal of every discussion from the standpoint of how well it reflects the outcomes of recent research and theoretical considerations. In order to keep abreast of developments in psychology and the related fields of physiology, neurology, and genetics, it has been necessary to rewrite many sections of the former edition and to introduce such topics as split-brain research, the role of RNA in retention, the genes and DNA in heredity, thermoregulatory behavior, the role of the amygdala in emotion, social influences in emotion, stress under field conditions, the influence of early experience on various psychological processes, voluntary control of individual muscle units, the role of awareness in learning, statistical learning theory, probability discrimination, contiguous conditioning, short-term memory, the stopped image and perception, the moon illusion, cognitive dissonance, collective problem-solving, ergonomics, and automation, to mention only a few of the additions.

Users of the earlier edition will observe from the present table of contents that one chapter has replaced a two-chapter introduction on the scope and methods of psychology. The new chapter on the human organism has a developmental introduction excerpted from the former chapter on individual development. Other portions of the earlier developmental chapter now appear in various topical contexts: development of the self in the personality chapter, conceptual development in the chapter on thinking, and so on. The first of the chapters concerned with individual differences now includes the statistical supplement that was formerly part of the appendix. A second chapter deals with the origins of individual differences in heredity and environment, with some attention given to the maturation of sensorimotor functions and the influence of early experience on these functions. Intelligence now is discussed in a single chapter, in place of two as before. There is now only one chapter on basic aspects of motivation. It includes both physiological motivation and motives which stem from socio-cultural influences and personal experience. The former chapter on emotion has been modified extensively to reflect some recent experiments on stress, aggression, and anxiety. Discussions of neural aspects of emotion are also brought into line with current findings. The chapter on conflict and adjustment has not been greatly changed over the former chapter on frustration and conflict. It does, however, take cognizance of some interesting recent research on voluntary control of individual muscle units. The two chapters on personality have been reduced to one streamlined version which includes some new information on the self concept and on the influence of infant care on development of personality. The discussion of learning has been greatly modified. Elementary aspects are now dealt with in a single chapter which has a better integrated discussion of conditioning and other aspects of the learning process than appeared in the two former chapters. A large amount of new research is represented. The chapter on foundations of learning has been rewritten to provide a more meaningful treatment of learning theory and the research on which this is based. Certain aspects of contiguity are taken into account and there is a brief discussion of statistical learning theory. Memory and forgetting are still treated in a single chapter, revised to include new material on short-term memory, the memory trace, and other aspects of retention. Thinking again has a single chapter devoted to it. This incorporates some new findings on reasoning and creative thinking. Closer attention is given to Piaget's contributions in this area. The chapter on communication and language has undergone relatively little change. It does, however, include some new material on language development and on the social implications of word usage. Sensory processes are now given one chapter, emphasizing the encoding and decoding aspects of sensory information, with less attention given to the more formal experimental studies of sensory experiences. The discussion of theories of color vision has been revised to encompass new findings on the cones and related retinal structures. One will observe that the chapter on attending and perceiving has been partially rewritten to incorporate a great deal of new material which stems from research on stopped images, stimulus homogeneity, the moon illusion, and other aspects of perceptual experience. The present chapter on social behavior includes new material on cooperative behavior and collective problem-solving, as well as a discussion of the concept of cognitive dissonance and related research, with special reference to social roles and role conflict. The final chapter, again dealing with human efficiency, includes a somewhat condensed treatment of aptitudes and some consideration of such new topics as ergonomics, automation, and the psychological problems of man in space.

The glossary has been expanded to include terms that are used for the first time in this edition. A new manual for students, entitled *Psychology in Review*, has been prepared by professors Dodge and Peter Fernald, which includes programmed material.

The illustrations have come from many sources, which are acknowledged at appropriate places in the text. The various original drawings were done by John Awtrey, Elmer Smith, Frank Nicholas, Lilli Mautner, Austin Stevens, Jane Pitts, and the Hagstrom Company. I want to express my indebtedness to them and also to Rosamond Vaule and Susan Darby, of the publisher's Educational Art Department, for the helpful way in which they have followed up my suggestions regarding illustrations.

Dr. Leonard Carmichael's editorial criticisms and suggestions have once again served to improve the quality of this text. I am also indebted to Robert C. Rooney, the Houghton Mifflin editor responsible for translating the manuscript into a printed textbook, and to his able assistant, Diane Gibson. Their sympathetic understanding of my educational aims and their ability to transfer these to the printed page are very much appreciated.

My colleagues in the Department of Psychology have made many useful suggestions, and one of these, Peter Delin, not only helped with the proofreading, but also pointed out many ways in which my presentation could be improved. I am also indebted to the staffs of the Barr Smith and Medical Libraries of the University of Adelaide, who helped me to find material not otherwise available. The Adelaide College of Education provided me with photographs for the recognition memory test.

My wife, beyond being a constant source of inspiration, has helped in ways too numerous to mention.

Norman L. Munn
Adelaide, South Australia

TO THE STUDENT

Your experience and behavior have much in common with the experience and behavior of other people. Even your problems of adjustment — the frustrations to be overcome, the aspirations to be achieved, the emotions to be controlled, the personal and interpersonal conflicts to be resolved — are shared by many others. So look upon this as a book about yourself — not as a treatise on some hypothetical human being. While studying it, ask yourself continually, "How does this apply to me?" Remember, too, that the study of psychology can give you insight into the conduct of other people. It should increase your understanding of why they behave as they do and, through this understanding, improve your ability to predict, perhaps even control, their behavior. Applications of psychology in the home, in the classroom, in the professions, in business, in industry, in warfare, and in the perpetuation of peace are focused primarily on the prediction and control of human conduct.

Observe that each chapter has a summary which brings its contents to a sharper focus. You may find it profitable to read this summary first, then reread it after reading the chapter. This suggestion is made in accordance with the principle that ideas are most readily conveyed to others when you tell them what you are going to tell them, tell them, then tell them what you have told them.

Students are often confused by a profusion of names and dates which serve to identify the author's sources. My policy has been to mention very few names in the body of the text, and then only the names of people who are historically important or especially identified with certain theories. Most of these names occur in the first chapter, which is an historical introduction to psychology. Following the custom of many currently used textbooks, quotations and passages dealing with particular researches to which I have referred are identified by a small superscript number. If you wish to identify the person whose contribution is involved, turn to the Reference section of the Appendix, where you will find the author, the source, and perhaps notes and other references. Do not try to memorize such information. These references and notes will be useful to you, however, in tracking down relevant information for term papers or other reports.

This course will add immeasurably to your vocabulary. All major psychological terms are defined in the Glossary. If you find a term whose meaning is not sufficiently clear from the definition given in the text, or from its context, turn to the Glossary for help.

There is another source of guidance and supplementary instruction available to you in the form of a manual, entitled *Psychology in Review*. It has been prepared to help you get the most out of studying this book. A prominent feature of the manual is its inclusion of some programmed material on each chapter of the text. This is designed to provide an efficient and interesting way of mastering basic concepts.

You will observe that each chapter of the textbook ends with a list of books and some notes about each. These books are relevant to one or more topics in the chapter. They are, of course, not listed with the idea that students will necessarily read them. They are included for the convenience of those who wish to delve more deeply into a topic or to get reference material for term papers or other reports. The books listed are among the most recent in the respective areas. Most have appeared within the last decade.

CONTENTS

PSYCHOLOGY

The Fundamentals of Human Adjustment

1

The Science of Psychology

*T*here are many false notions about psychology and psychologists. One of these is the belief that psychologists can read one's mind or estimate one's character at a glance. Another misconception is that they are authorities on such things as spiritualism, mental telepathy, and fortune-telling. Psychologists are, in fact, often called upon to explain how a currently famous "mind reader" does his tricks or how a certain astrologer could have predicted some historical event.

One often meets people who assert that they are themselves psychologists. Why? Because they are "observers of human nature" and can "sum up people" at a glance. One well-educated man known to the writer felt that he could tell whether or not a person is narrow-minded by noting the distance between his eyes. Some claim that they can discern dishonesty from shifty eyes, or from the inability of a person to look them steadily in the eyes. Such claims come from an honest misunderstanding of what psychology is and can do.

There are also many people without scientific training who make a dishonest living out of a gullible public by setting themselves up as psychologists. These "psychoquacks" will study a person's head, his facial characteristics, the date of his birth, or his handwriting and then, in accordance with their own particular theories, tell him what his capacities are, the sort of person he should marry, or how he should plan for his future.

Members of this "psychological underworld" have been known to offer courses in psychology by mail and to give a "doctor of psychology" degree for a price. There is, in fact, no legitimate doctor of psychology degree. Psychologists have degrees like other scientists, degrees granted by reputable universities.

Even apart from honest misconceptions and psychological racketeering, the terms "psychology" and "psychological" are often used in a very loose way. One hears people speaking about "the psychology of the French," "the psychology of the fraternity man," or "the psychology of the industrialist." One also hears of the "psychological moment" to close a deal, or to make a proposal. These terms are used with little or no regard for the actual nature of psychology.

Psychology is a science and the properly trained psychologist is a scientist, or at least a practitioner who uses scientific methods and information resulting from scientific investigation. ■

BEGINNINGS

Psychology did not begin as a science. Rather, it started in primitive mysticism, became a branch of philosophy and then, after more than 2000 years, finally achieved status as a science. All the other sciences had a similar transition: from mysticism through philosophy to separate development as scientific disciplines. Psychology, the youngest of biological sciences, began its separate development less than 100 years ago.

This transition from primitive mysticism to scientific psychology is interesting in itself and for the understanding that it provides of how psychology became what it is.

☐ Our primitive ancestors asked questions about the nature of the world around them and these questions led to the development, finally, of such sciences as astronomy, physics, and biology. Their questions about themselves, especially about their experiences and behavior, led to mental philosophy, and finally to the science of psychology.

If we may judge from the ideas of people who live in primitive tribes today, our remote ancestors were mystified by dreams. They wondered why their sleeping life brought them adventures in far-away places, the defeat of their enemies, and achievement of other desires, such as the capture of suitable mates. Waking experience was only slightly less mystifying. What was it that looked out of one's eyes, heard through one's ears, and felt through one's skin? Why was man sometimes impelled to break the taboos, like running off with another man's wife? What made a man tremble when he wished to appear brave? And what caused his actions to be stilled forever?

Many primitive peoples answered such questions by supposing that there was a man within man — an invisible, ethereal creature who, except during dreams and death, was imprisoned within the body. For them, the mind was this ghostly image of man himself. But theirs was a poor explanation of experience and behavior, for the inner man was no less a mystery than what he was supposed to explain. What was "he" like? How did "he" get there? How did "he" do the things attributed to him?

Some of our modern ideas of mind, as well as the term *psychology*, come to us from Greek philosophy. Plato (427–347 B.C.) was interested in how one's mind (in the shape of ideas) controls conduct. But the substitution of "mind" or "ideas" for the "inner man" still left us with mysteries. A more modern note was introduced by Aristotle (384–322 B.C.) when he claimed that mind is a function of body processes. He implied that to understand experience and behavior one would need to study the body functions which produce them. Ideas had a place in Aristotle's mental philosophy, but they were thought to come from the influence of the environment on the sense organs. He taught that environmental objects activate the sense organs, which then transmit the effects of such stimulation to the heart. Here, he believed, they leave impressions which are the source of ideas. Ideas acquired in this way could be combined. They were the source of conscious experiences, and they provided the control of behavior which was so puzzling to earlier thinkers.

Aristotle's concept of mind as a function of body processes was an important step in the direction of making psychology a biological science. One could not observe an invisible inner man, quite obviously; nor could he observe ideas as such. He could, however, observe and study what the body did and how this was related to its structures and its physiology. An eventual outcome of such study was the discovery that it is the brain and not the heart that plays a key role in determining the nature of conscious experience and in controlling behavior.

Dissection of the human body was prohibited until around 300 B.C. For about 500 years thereafter, culminating in the physiological researches of Galen (approximately 130–200 A.D.), much was learned about the construction of the body and its mode of operation. But Descartes (1596–1650) was the man who again brought new insights of importance to modern psychology. He thought of the body as a complicated mechanism which could be activated by light, sound, and other aspects of the environment (stimuli) without the participation of any immaterial, inner substance. Judged by what we know today, Descartes's was a crude and very inadequate model of body functions; but his emphasis on the importance of such functions in the control of behavior took root and greatly influenced the development of psychology, and the coordinate sciences, physiology and neurology. □

These were some of the events leading up to the development of psychology as a science. But what is science? ■

THE NATURE OF SCIENCE

The essence of science, from the standpoint of the scientist himself, is "a disposition to deal with the facts rather than with what someone has said about them."[1]* This means that the scientist must observe for himself and that what he observes is the primary basis of his speculations and conclusions. The importance of observation for science is brought to a focus in the following story from Francis Bacon, a leader (1605) in the history of scientific investigation.[2]

□ "In the year of our Lord 1432, there arose a grievous quarrel among the brethren over

* These numbers designate references listed in the Appendix by chapters.

the number of teeth in the mouth of a horse. For 13 days the disputation raged without ceasing. All the ancient books and chronicles were fetched out, and wonderful and ponderous erudition, such as was never before heard of in this region, was made manifest. At the beginning of the 14th day, a youthful friar of goodly bearing asked his learned superiors for permission to add a word, and straightway, to the wonderment of the disputants, whose deep wisdom he sore vexed, he beseeched them to unbend in a manner coarse and unheard-of, and to look in the open mouth of a horse and find answer to their questionings. At this, their dignity being grievously hurt, they waxed exceedingly wroth; and, joining in a mighty uproar, they flew upon him and smote him hip and thigh, and cast him out forthwith. For, said they, surely Satan hath tempted this bold neophyte to declare unholy and unheard-of ways of finding truth contrary to all the teachings of the fathers. After many days more of grievous strife the dove of peace sat on the assembly, and they as one man, declaring the problem to be an everlasting mystery because of a grievous dearth of historical and theological evidence thereof, so ordered the same writ down." □

The youthful friar of this story was enunciating the fundamental principle of all science; namely, to seek the facts rather than depend upon authority or upon sheer speculation.

The scientist does not, however, collect all and sundry facts, even within the field of his major interest. Like the disputants of Bacon's story, he begins with questions. These are questions which, to him, deal with issues of importance. He then looks for relevant information. If appropriate data have not already been reported by other scientists, he may carry out his own observations. These may be focused upon objects or events which occur naturally, as in the case of a geologist examining rocks or a biologist studying the migration of birds. Wherever possible, however, a scientist observes under controlled conditions. He varies aspects of nature and records the results. Early physicists, for example,

varied the frequency of vibrating strings and observed that, as more vibrations per second were produced, the pitch of the resulting sound became higher. They were then able to formulate a general law governing the relationship between frequency of vibration and pitch. Without experimental observation this would have been impossible.

In carrying out his observations, experimental or otherwise, the scientist is not trying to prove something. He is impartial. He seeks information and, if the facts gathered upset a pet theory, then the theory must be discarded or at least modified to correspond with the facts.

Findings are not accepted by scientists unless they can be verified. This means that others must be able to repeat the observations and obtain the same results. The law of vibrating strings mentioned earlier was not accepted until others repeated the experiment and observed the reported relationships.

Thus scientists look for information with which to answer significant questions. Where possible they experiment. They do this because empirical information is most conducive to the discovery of lawful relations and because the results are verifiable. As scientific observation proceeds, many seemingly disparate phenomena are found to be interrelated. Increasingly comprehensive formulations are therefore developed. It is then possible to predict and even to produce events not previously observed. Such formulations made possible the first atomic explosion and the launching of an earth satellite. Scientific prediction occurs on a much less spectacular scale whenever a geneticist, mating animals with different characteristics, is able to say what the offspring will be like with respect to these characteristics. It is also evident when a psychologist is able to say that the illumination of a room must be increased by at least one per cent before it will be experienced as brighter, or when he says that 95 per cent of a group of flight candidates with a particular score on a battery of special tests will become pilots.

The rest of this chapter is designed to clear up misconceptions about the nature of psychology, to show how it became a science and to indicate, in an introductory way, the present scope of its investigations. ■

ORIGINS OF SCIENTIFIC PSYCHOLOGY

We have said that psychology is a biological science and the reason for this is that its observations relate to living organisms. Psychology is, in fact, one of several biological sciences, each distinguished from others through its concern with some special aspect of living things. The distinguishing feature of psychology is that it observes and attempts to understand the *behavior* of organisms. It is concerned primarily with their responses to the world around them.

Man is not only a biological organism but also a social one. His behavior is modified by and in turn modifies the behavior of others. Psychology is therefore a social as well as a biological science. It must take account of the fact that human babies are dependent upon others for survival and that, during this dependence, their ways of behaving, including their language, are imposed upon them, wholly or in part, by their elders. As a result, they come to act less like animals and more like human beings. Psychology must also consider collective behavior, as when human beings act in groups of various kinds.

Since the behavior of human beings is grounded both in biology and in social interaction, psychology is often referred to as a *biosocial* science. The appropriateness of this designation becomes increasingly apparent as psychologists penetrate the intricacies of human behavior.

☐ The word *psychology* was actually derived from two Greek words, *psyche* (soul) and *logos* (discourse). Psychology, or "mental philosophy," was thus literally a study of the soul. The term "soul" did not at first have religious implications such as it has today. For some it was an inner flame, for some a form of motion, and for others a function of body processes.

About 400 years ago mental philosophers began to translate *psyche* as "mind" and psychology was then defined as "the study of the mind." This definition continued in use until the present century. It was eventually replaced by the definition of psychology as "the science of behavior." ☐

The emergence of psychology as a science of behavior had certain antecedents in the older sciences of physics and physiology as well as in efforts of Wilhelm Wundt (in 1879) to establish psychology as a science of conscious experience. Physicists discovered the relationship between sensory stimulation and such elementary experiences as "sensations." Sound sensations, for example, were found within limits to depend upon the frequency of sound waves — the higher the frequency, the higher the pitch. Color sensations were observed to depend in certain ways upon the wavelength of light (Figure 1.1). At the same time as physicists were focusing upon features of the physical world, physiologists were turning their attention to the sense organs and brain, which, when stimulated, gave rise not only to sensations but also to reflexes and other aspects of behavior. These achievements, especially with respect to sensation — something very close to the interests of mental philosophers — suggested that psychology might itself become an experimental science. In fact, a physiologist (E. H. Weber) and a physicist (G. T. Fechner) are sometimes credited with having founded the science of psychology, because they demonstrated methods of measuring and formulating relationships between the intensities of stimulation and the intensive aspects of experience.

☐ Weber's studies led to an important formulation known as Weber's Law. The general question to which he sought an answer can be stated quite simply: "How much must intensities of stimulation differ before one can notice the difference?" Take the lifting of small weights, for example. Suppose that you lift one weight, then a second weight. How much heavier (or lighter) must the second be before a difference is felt? After many experiments, with the second weight sometimes equal

again, 1/30th of the standard. This fundamental principle holds, with some limitations, in vision and in other senses, although the particular fraction depends upon the sense involved. With respect to illumination, for instance, a just noticeable increase in brightness requires 1/100th of the illumination with which one begins. In extending Weber's procedures for measuring the relation between external stimuli and conscious experience, and in developing a more precise mathematical formulation of such findings, Fechner felt that he was studying the relation between mind and body. □

The actual founding of psychology as a separate science, with its own department in a university, is credited to Wilhelm Wundt (Figure 1.2), who had been known earlier as

● 1.1

Newton Experimenting with a Prism. Although philosophers had debated about the explanation of color experiences, Newton's observations demonstrated for the first time that white light is composed of various wavelengths and that these provide the stimulus variations which underlie the experience of color. That is to say, certain wavelengths give rise to red, others to yellow, still others to blue, and so on, as shown in a spectrum. This is further illustrated in Plate 9. The illustration is based upon an old woodcut. (Bettman Archive)

to, sometimes lighter than, and sometimes heavier than the first weight, Weber was able to formulate his law. He had discovered that a just noticeable difference in weight is a constant fraction of the first of the pair of weights compared, i.e., that which serves as the standard in a series of judgments. In the case of lifted weights, this fraction was 1/30. Thus, if one lifts 30 ounces and then 31, the second feels heavier. But if the second weight is only 30.5, one cannot observe this difference and they both feel equally heavy. Suppose, however, that the standard weight is 90 ounces. How heavy must the second be if one is to feel it as heavier? The answer is 93, or,

● 1.2

Wilhelm Wundt. The laboratory founded by Wundt in 1879 trained many of the early experimental psychologists, including several who established similar laboratories in America.

a physiologist and philosopher. Wundt had seen the fruitfulness of experimental procedures in physics and in physiology, where many of the problems dealt either with stimuli basic to human experience or with the underlying structures and functions of the organism. What impressed him especially was the success of Weber and Fechner in formulating lawful relations between intensities of stimulation and the corresponding experiences. Such findings seemed to refute the widely held view that since mind could not be measured, psychology could never become a science. Now it seemed apparent that mind, or conscious experience (regarded by Wundt as synonymous with mind) could indeed be measured. The result was that in 1879 Wundt opened a psychological laboratory at the University of Leipzig and began offering advanced degrees in psychology. Young men and women from all over the world came to Leipzig to study the new science. Many of them later founded laboratories of their own and, through their research and writing, achieved world-wide distinction as psychologists.

The aim of the new science, as Wundt envisaged it, was to analyze conscious experience into its elements, much as the chemist analyzes matter. The nature and intensity of stimulation was controlled with suitable instruments. But the basic information, the data for analysis, came from what the stimulated person said about the resulting experiences. He was to describe these as they occurred. Such description requires introspection, or inward observation, as when we note that something tastes sour or that a musical note is pleasant. However, those who engaged in what Wundt called *experimental introspection* had been trained to analyze experience as it occurred under the controlled conditions of the laboratory. Their analysis was to be carried out in a purely impersonal manner. At least this was the aim of their training. Wundt referred to the new science first as "physiological psychology" and later as "experimental psychology."

The major emphasis in Wundt's laboratory was on sensations and more comprehensive sensory experiences called *perceptions*. However, there were also attempts to measure emo-tional feelings as well as images and ideas. Observations were later extended to experiences involved in motor reactions. Conscious aspects of thinking were also studied. But Wundt was not content merely to analyze and describe conscious experience. He also wanted to know the underlying biological structures and functions.

Because of its preoccupation with the conscious aspects of human life, psychology was at this time defined as "the science of conscious experience" and anything which did not lend itself to investigation through experimental introspection was thought to be outside its sphere of interest. Nevertheless, the infant science soon outgrew such limitations.

Even within the general area which Wundt first mapped out for scientific investigation there was a broadening of scope. Attention gradually shifted from descriptions of conscious experience to investigations focused upon the use of sensory and perceptual processes in the initiation and control of behavior. Indeed, work in this area still goes on. Scientists in various fields, especially physiology and neurology, share the psychologist's interest in such processes. Moreover, the findings in this and related areas of psychology have had great practical significance in industry and the armed services, since the design of equipment which men are called upon to operate must take into account their sensory and other capabilities.

New areas of investigation

While Wundt and his associates studied conscious experience, others were opening up new fields of investigation. A German philosopher named Herman Ebbinghaus began the experimental psychology of memory. He attempted to answer such questions as: How do we remember? What makes us forget? What are the most efficient procedures for memorizing? Such questions had always engaged the attention of mental philosophers. Now, instead of merely talking about them, or depending upon what some authority like Aristotle had said, Ebbinghaus tried to answer them experimentally. He memorized verses of poetry and meaningless groupings of letters

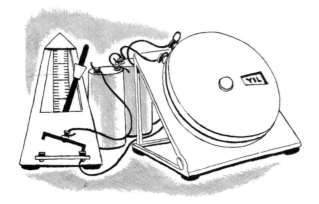

● 1.3
A Memory Apparatus. This early apparatus (Ranschburg's) exposed one nonsense syllable at a time. Rate of exposure was controlled electrically with a specially constructed metronome.

called *nonsense syllables* (Figure 1.3) and he did so under conditions designed to provide answers to his questions. One can see here an interesting shift in emphasis. Instead of describing conscious experience, as Wundt had done, Ebbinghaus was concerned with how well the learner could repeat what he had memorized. This was an emphasis upon behavior; more specifically, language behavior.

The results of these investigations on memory were published in 1888. Some of Ebbinghaus' questions were answered. Some results raised additional questions, and various extensions and modifications of the methods developed by Ebbinghaus were soon being used to answer these. In fact, this is another area of psychology in which research continues, and with outcomes of practical as well as scientific significance. Findings on memory are of obvious value in education and they comprise an important aspect of the area now known as *educational psychology*.

• *Learning.* Research on memory was important in opening up the whole field of learning to experimental investigation. When we memorize, we are usually learning verbal material such as words, numbers, or other symbols. Thus research on memory is largely concerned with what has been called *verbal learning*. Very soon after Ebbinghaus' pioneer research in this more restricted area of learning there developed an interest in so-called *motor learning*, where, although verbal aspects may be present, emphasis is on overt acts like hitting a target or, at a more complicated level, typing or playing a musical instrument. As in the case of research on memory, pertinent questions which investigators attempted to answer had to do with how learning occurs and how one may increase its efficiency. Such research is more vigorously pressed today than ever before; its outcomes are of obvious value in education and in various other fields of everyday life. Industrial psychologists, for example, often have as their major responsibility the efficient training of workers in the specific skills which modern industry requires.

• *Individual differences.* Another area of investigation, the results of which were to have scientific as well as practical value, both in education and elsewhere, was that dealing with individual differences. Weber, Fechner, Wundt, Ebbinghaus, and their fellow investigators were concerned with the study of *processes* (sensation, perception, memory, learning) and in discovering general principles pertaining to these. They paid little or no attention to the fact that there are individual differences in sensitivity, in memory, and in learning ability.

□ Individual differences had not completely escaped observation. The early Greeks discussed such differences and Plato made much of them in his *Republic*. They had also been noted in astronomy. Many years before Wundt's laboratory was opened, a noted astronomer had discharged his assistant for perceiving the transit of stars across the hair of the telescope nearly a second later than he himself perceived it. Another famous astronomer, seeing a reference to this earlier incident, decided to compare his own reports on such transits with those of fellow astronomers. There were marked differences, even among these experts. Such a difference came to be called the *personal equation*. □

Although individual differences had been observed and discussed by philosophers, astronomers, and others, little of scientific importance had been concluded. At the time

Wundt was starting his laboratory at Leipzig, however, an Englishman named Francis Galton began to study individual differences in body measurements and, more or less incidentally, in such psychological functions as sensitivity and imagery. His primary purpose was to trace the hereditary origins of such differences.

These earlier observations of individual differences, especially Galton's, inspired J. McKeen Cattell, an American student in Wundt's laboratory, to undertake an extensive study of individual differences as such. The differences studied were in such things as vision, hearing, memory, and speed of reaction (Figure 1.4). The instruments and materials used to measure such differences came to be called *mental tests*. These were not intelligence tests in the modern sense, but they foreshadowed present-day tests and especially the aptitude tests now so widely used to select persons for various occupations.

One outcome of these studies was the development of statistical methods for analysis of individual differences. Statistical analysis not only revealed norms (such as averages) but also the extent to which individuals differ (variability) and relationships (correlations) between differences in one area (for instance, body build) and in another (such as personality).

Intelligence tests of the kind in use today were devised and first put to practical use early in this century. The pioneer intelligence tester was a French psychologist named Alfred Binet, who used his tests to decide whether or not a child had sufficient mental development to profit from normal schooling.

• *Observers and subjects.* We have seen that scientific psychology began by studying aspects of conscious experience and that, as new investigators entered the field, its scope was broadened to take in memory, the learning process, and also individual differences. In the course of these developments there was a gradual shift of emphasis from descriptions of conscious experience to observations of behavior. Those who studied memory and other aspects of learning were concerned more with *what was done* than with associated experiences. Even the name given to those who served in psychological experiments indicates

• 1.4

An Early Form of Chronoscope for Measuring Reaction Time. This is the D'Arsonval chronoscope. The subject was seated with the response key in his hand. When the experimenter struck the top of the table (or the subject's hand) with his key, he gave the signal for response and simultaneously caused the chronoscope pointer to engage with a clockwork device. It then swept the dial once per second. As soon as the subject squeezed his key, a circuit connected with a magnet was closed, thus disengaging pointer and clockwork. Since the experimenter's signal activated the pointer and the subject's signal stopped it, the elapsed time, read in 1/100-second units, gave the latter's speed of reaction. (After Binet)

this shift. Wundt and his followers called the person who introspected an *observer*, the reason being that he observed his own experiences and reported them to the investigator. Later psychologists, and especially those who were not so much concerned with conscious experience, were themselves the observers. They observed behavior. Those who memorized, learned the skills being studied, and took mental tests were then referred to as *subjects*. Today the term *subject* is in almost universal use to represent an organism, human or animal, studied by the psychologist. ■

THE INFLUENCE OF EVOLUTIONARY BIOLOGY

The idea that man is the end product of developments initiated in lower organisms and that his structures as well as his behavior are foreshadowed in the structures and behavior of prehuman animals is ancient. It appeared in Greek philosophy. Several philosophers of the eighteenth and early nineteenth centuries also held this view. Thus the concept of evolution, although popularly attributed to Darwin, did not in all respects originate with him.

The prevailing opinion in Darwin's day was that each species had an independent creation. The idea that one might have changed gradually into another was talked about, but there appeared to be insufficient supporting evidence. In reality, many facts were available which, if their significance had been realized, would have made a strong case for evolution. Some of these had been known for a long time. Others were observed by Darwin himself. Darwin's major contribution, however, was to synthesize these facts; to show their relation one to another. The result was a factual basis for evolution. Darwin then formulated a theory designed to explain evolution. This is the theory of natural selection. It calls attention to wide variations in the structures and reactions of a given species. It makes a point of the struggle for existence, a struggle which leads to the survival of relatively few. It argues that survivors in this struggle are the fittest, i.e., those with variations which adapt them most adequately to their environment. The poorly adapted perish and have no offspring. Survivors pass their desirable characteristics to offspring through heredity. The theory supposes, moreover, that this process, carried on over millions of years, led to the appearance of such distinctly different organisms as, for example, cats, monkeys, apes, and men.

□ Darwin's theory of the survival of the fittest through natural selection proved highly controversial. The argument as to *how* evolution occurs still goes on. Nevertheless, as we shall observe shortly, Darwin's views played an important part in the development of psychology as a science of behavior.

By demonstrating the factual basis of evolution and by suggesting how organisms may have evolved, Darwin took the evolutionary concept out of the sphere of pure speculation and placed it in the area of natural science. Indeed, the publication in 1859 of his *Origin of Species* was a major step in the history of scientific biology.

In the course of his research, Darwin made some historically important observations on emotion. These were brought together in his *The Expression of the Emotions in Man and Animals*, published in 1872. Darwin's main thesis, supported by an accumulation of evidence, is that many human emotional reactions are meaningless unless viewed as carry-overs from our animal ancestors. During intense rage, for example, men tend to bare their canine teeth. This is for them a useless reaction. Then why do they do it? Darwin pointed out that when this occurs in animals, it serves to frighten the object of rage and also to bare the teeth for action. Although the reaction is useless to us, we inherit it, much as we do our useless appendix. □

By pointing out that man's psychological as well as structural characteristics evolved from those of prehuman organisms, Darwin directed psychological attention to animal behavior. Psychologists as well as biologists began to investigate so-called instincts. These are complex unlearned behavior patterns. Examples are: a spider spinning its web in a certain pattern characteristic of the species; a wasp paralyzing a caterpillar and depositing its eggs on the animal; or a bird building a nest which typifies its species. The question then arose as to whether man has instincts. This is still a controversial issue and we will discuss it later in this book.

Out of an interest in animal behavior came studies of sensory processes and learning ability in animals. These began with such questions as: At what level of evolution does consciousness appear? How do the conscious experiences of animals compare with those of man? Do animals have anything resembling human intelligence? Are they capable of reasoning?

The first attempts to answer such questions used a procedure referred to today as *anecdotal*. Naturalists gathered stories about the behavior of animals, usually pets of the informants, and arranged these systematically in such a way as to demonstrate the evolution of intelligence. Such stories are, of course, unreliable. The owner of a pet, like the parent of a child, is not the best judge of its intelligence. Moreover, human beings have a tendency to anthropomorphize — to humanize, or see human traits in animals. This is well illustrated in an ancient Chinese story.

☐ Chuang Tzu and Hui Tzu were standing on a bridge across the Hao River when Chuang said, "Look how the minnows are shooting to and fro! How joyful they are!"

"You are not a fish," said Hui. "How can *you* know that the fishes are joyful?"

"You are not I," answered Chuang. "How can you know I do not know about the joy of the fishes? . . . I know from my own joy of the water." ☐

Still another difficulty with anecdotes is that the unscientific observer, in his effort to tell a good story, often exaggerates. Science cannot rely on such evidence. Its observations must be systematic, they must be impartial, and they must be verifiable. For these reasons, anecdotes were soon replaced by experimental investigations designed to answer specific questions about animal intelligence.

Does an animal sense the various aspects of its environment, like colors and sounds? Methods of answering such questions involved a discrimination technique, a simple form of which is shown in Figure 1.5. How does one animal's intelligence compare with that of another? This question was answered by using tests of learning ability, one of which is shown in Figure 1.6. Here the comparison was in terms of how many trials an animal required to learn and how many errors it made.

☐ The question of how to get inside the animal, so to speak, and study his conscious experience has never been solved. We can tell whether or not an animal responds to aspects of its environment like colors and sounds. We do this by studying its discriminative behavior. But we cannot answer such questions as what

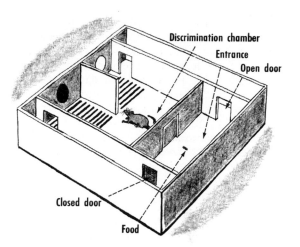

● 1.5

An Early Form of Discrimination Apparatus. When a hungry animal enters the discrimination chamber, it is confronted by two stimulus patterns (in this case, a white circle and a black circle). In front of each pattern is an electric grid. Suppose that the investigator decided to reward response to white and to punish response to black. Now, if the animal goes to the white area, it proceeds along the side alley and back to the entrance, where a small food pellet has been placed. If the animal goes toward the black, on the other hand, it receives a shock through the floor. Moreover, if it continues, it does not have access to the food. This means that it has to come back and correct its response. On the next trial, the white area may be on the left. It is alternated from right to left in accordance with a chance sequence. Thus, the problem must be solved visually and not by going in a particular direction.

animal consciousness is like, nor even whether it exists. Therefore the question as to where consciousness first appears in evolution cannot be answered. Anybody who undertakes to describe animal consciousness is making inferences based upon the animal's behavior. His inferences are necessarily anthropomorphic; that is to say, interpreted and described in human terms, as in our Chinese example. ☐

This inability to describe the consciousness of animals handicapped a group of

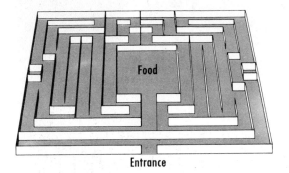

● 1.6

An Animal Maze. This was the first maze used to study learning in white rats. A hungry rat placed in the entrance received food when the center was reached. In successive runs an animal tended to reach the center more quickly and with fewer entrances into blind alleys. Finally the path was run without error from entrance to center. This maze, the prototype of many others, was used by Small at Clark University in 1900.

psychologists calling themselves "functionalists." Whereas Wundt and his followers had been trying to describe conscious experience, and of necessity only at the human level, these psychologists thought that it should be studied from the standpoint of how it helps in adjustment. They argued that when consciousness evolved, it may have had survival value in the struggle for existence. In learning a motor skill, they said, we are at first clearly conscious of our activities. Then, as the habit approaches perfection, consciousness recedes. Eventually we may perform the habit without any conscious attention to what we are doing.

However, the functionalist position was weakened by the difficulty of studying conscious experience while one has his attention on what he is trying to learn and by the impossibility, as indicated above, of knowing if and when consciousness enters animal life.

Later functionalists, as we shall see, paid less attention to conscious experience and came to focus on the environmental and organic conditions associated with efficient learning. Their work on the learning process, in both animals and human beings, laid a founda-

tion for other important developments in psychology. Like the work of Ebbinghaus on memory and of Cattell on individual differences, the study of learning processes in animals and human beings came to have great practical significance, especially in education.

Although evolutionary biology turned the attention of psychologists to animals and lessened their preoccupation with analysis of conscious experience, not all research, even with animals, had evolutionary implications. It became evident that the structures of other mammals were similar to our own in basic details and that such subjects could serve as valuable aids in investigating the relation between brain processes and behavior, the role of glandular processes in motivation, and fundamental aspects of the learning process. Many investigations can be carried out with animals which would not, for ethical and other reasons, be possible or practical with human subjects.

But even apart from this, animal research has often provided insights into the nature of fundamental psychological processes and has suggested more fruitful ways of studying human behavior. Sources of information have been opened up which were once thought to be available only through introspective approaches. We shall see later that modern theories of learning have grown out of work with animals and that their hypotheses are frequently tested through experiments on animals. Here the relative simplicity of animals is helpful rather than otherwise. This is because it is usually more fruitful to begin with simpler organisms than to begin with those that are infinitely complex, like human beings. A medical student begins by studying and operating on simpler creatures like dogfish and cats. The builder of skyscrapers begins with simpler projects. Similarly, the investigator of learning begins with the simplest forms of learning, and these are found in lower animals. With them the investigator cuts below the ideals, purposes, attitudes, and culturally conditioned complexities of human behavior in order to learn what he can about the foundations that we share with other organisms. He feels that he will then be in a better position to

• 1.7

Dr. Arnold Gesell Testing a Baby. The dome was devised for one-way vision, so that observers could see the baby without being seen themselves. Movies of the children's reactions are being made. These are then analyzed frame by frame to discover age changes in behavior. (Photo, courtesy of Edmund B. Gerard)

understand the added complexities of human behavior. ■

BEGINNINGS OF CHILD PSYCHOLOGY

It is a curious thing that the scientific study of child behavior is only of recent origin. Philosophers had talked about the importance of childhood in determining the nature of the adult and poets had written about it, but systematic study of psychological processes in children did not begin until late in the last century.

□ Two parents, including Charles Darwin (1877), published infant biographies. Preyer's (1882) *The Mind of the Child* was written by a father and observation was limited to one child. Although restricted in these ways, this was a careful study dealing, for example, with reflexes, sensory ability, emotional development, and thought processes. It is, in fact, a landmark in the history of child psychology.

Like anecdotes in animal psychology, child biographies gave way to systematic observations. Experimental methods came to have an important place in such studies and these methods were often similar to those already found so fruitful in the investigation of

animal behavior. This is not surprising when we consider that infants, like animals, are incapable of providing introspective data. Even from children old enough to speak, introspective information is, to say the least, of very limited value. □

When child psychology got under way there soon developed an interest in such questions as: What reactions are usual, or normal, or to be expected at given age levels? Research designed to answer such questions is often referred to as *normative*, a search for norms. Intelligence tests such as those which originated in France (p. 11) were normative but confined largely to memory and reasoning. They were, of course, designed for school children. They did not tell how a baby of three or six months, or of two or four years should be reacting. Nor did they deal, in any direct way, with sensory, perceptual, and motor development.

The first extensive developmental schedules designed to tell parents what children usually do at various age levels from birth grew out of research conducted by Arnold Gesell (Figure 1.7) and his associates at Yale University. Various test situations, calling for response to such objects as dangling rings,

15

cubes, and mirrors were used at the early age levels. At later ages the tests involved observations of language and social behavior. Large numbers of children were tested. The chief outcome of this research was a detailed catalogue of the responses to be expected at successive age levels. Over and beyond its scientific value, information like this is of obvious value to pediatricians, educators, and parents.

Sigmund Freud (1856–1939) and later psychoanalysts claimed that childhood experiences leave an indelible impression on adult personality. Freud emphasized experiences associated with sexual development. Others stressed the importance of frustration and insecurity in childhood, with or without sexual overtones. Regardless of such differences among them, these men helped to turn the spotlight on childhood and, more specifically, on parent-child relationships and other aspects of family life. This approach supplemented and rounded out, as it were, the approaches to child psychology that we have already considered. Moreover, the influence of childhood on adult personality became an interdisciplinary problem, bringing about cooperative studies among psychologists, sociologists, and anthropologists. The latter were led to investigate how methods of child-rearing characteristic of different cultures (such as Samoan, Hopi Indian, and Eskimo) influence the personality of adults. ■

CONCERN FOR THE INDIVIDUAL

Psychology, as we have considered it so far, was especially concerned with what might be called purely scientific or theoretical issues. This was true despite the fact that many outcomes were later applied in education and in everyday life. Some psychologists even argued that psychology should remain in the "ivory tower." They felt it to be a science and not a technology. These men emphasized the study of such processes as vision, perception, learning, memory, and thinking. Their aim was to discover the psychological characteristics of men, animal species, or children. Even those interested in individual differences concen-

trated on aspects that were more or less abstract, like the range of differences, general tendencies, relations between differences in one trait and those in another, and the hereditary bases of differences.

Individuals, as such, are unique, while science is customarily concerned with trends or general principles. Nevertheless, because they dealt with human beings, psychologists were soon involved in problems of individual adjustment. They then encroached on the educational sphere more than ever. And they also became involved in a province which had been traditionally a medical one. The eventual outcome was *clinical psychology*, involving the study and correction of behavior problems.

Normal and abnormal people

When attention was turned to individuals in terms of helping them solve their problems, the question arose as to the meaning of "normal" and "abnormal." Where to draw the line between normality and abnormality is still controversial and it will be discussed in the chapter on personality. However, some people deviate so far from the customary patterns that there is no question about their abnormality. These are the psychotic, the neurotic, the feeble-minded, and those who experience exceptional trouble in adjusting to educational and other aspects of their environment.

The psychotic

Psychoses are serious mental illnesses. Those suffering from such illnesses are known today as psychotic or, to use a medico-legal term, "insane."

☐ Psychotics were once thought to be possessed of the devil and were thrown into dungeons and mistreated in various ways to "drive the devil out of them." Physicians paid little attention to insanity, for medicine was concerned with the treatment of ills of the body and not with the manifestations of demons. Psychology was still mental philosophy and not involved in such problems. Pinel, a French physician, is credited with having changed the attitude toward insanity. In his opinion, insane people were ill rather than wicked or possessed, and should be given humane treatment. Accordingly, when he became, in 1794, superintendent of a "lunatic" asylum in Paris, Pinel's first act was to unshackle his charges and take them out of the dungeons, in which many had been locked for years. By treating them as human beings, Pinel was able to restore many to sanity.

Because of Pinel's influence and that of other enlightened physicians, the last 150 years have seen a markedly changed attitude toward insanity. The insane (psychotic) are now regarded as mentally ill rather than possessed or lunatic (influenced by the moon) and what were once "lunatic asylums" have become mental hospitals. At first there was only custodial care in such hospitals, but today there are treatments designed to cure the patient so that he can again take his place in society. □

The scientific study of psychoses came about as a result of the changed attitude toward these disorders. As soon as the idea of demonic possession was given up, and psychotics were regarded as ill, medical men began to observe psychotic behavior, to classify its varieties, and to seek the real causes. They found that some such disorders result from destruction of brain tissue associated, for example, with untreated syphilis and with the ravages of old age. Such disorders are now classified as *organic psychoses*. Certain other psychoses appeared to have no such organic basis, but to result from deranged habits of thought. Because they were due to abnormal functioning in what was apparently a normal brain, these were called *functional psychoses*.

The study and treatment of psychotics developed as an aspect of medicine. But psychology, being a science of behavior, is concerned with both the normal and the abnormal. In fact, the breakdown of a mechanism often tells us a great deal about its nature. If one discovers the causes of breakdown, moreover, he may be able to repair the damage, or even to prevent it. Prevention of behavior disorders is, in fact, the chief function of a field of psychology now known as *mental hygiene*.

The neurotic

Behavior disorders classified as neurotic (or sometimes *psychoneurotic*) are milder and also much more frequent than psychoses. It is seldom necessary to institutionalize neurotic people. Moreover, their disorders are, so far as we know, all functional.

There are different kinds of neuroses and we have all seen one or more examples in people around us. Neurotics having a functional disorder referred to, in general, as *hysteria* may suddenly become blind or deaf, lose feeling in their limbs, become paralyzed, or forget who they are. Today, as we will see in Chapter 9, there are more specific names for hysterical disorders. Other kinds of neurotic behavior include unreasonable anxiety, compulsions to commit certain acts, and preoccupation with bodily aches and pains. These are also considered later. Hysteria has had such historical significance, however, that we now confine our attention to it.

One reason for calling hysteria a functional disorder is that its symptoms can be produced during hypnosis. The hypnotist merely tells his subject that he is paralyzed, for example, and the suggested symptom is thereby produced. Another reason is that such symptoms as the above may disappear during hypnosis. The hysterically blind see, the hysterically anesthetic feel again, and the paralyzed limb moves as suggested.

□ Although it had been practiced for centuries, hypnosis first came to scientific attention when something akin to it was used by Mesmer in 1766 to remove neurotic symptoms. Mesmer applied magnets to his patients and their symptoms forthwith disappeared. He discovered later that magnets were not necessary; that passes made with his hands, along with suitable suggestions, were sufficient. His method, known as "Mesmerism," soon came into ill repute. There were various reasons for this, one being Mesmer's claim that a sort of "animal magnetism" passed from him to his patients.

In true hypnosis the patient is put into a sleeplike trance. This procedure was, in fact, first called "neurohypnology" meaning nervous sleep. About a century ago, when medical men were using hypnosis to produce anesthesia, many patients underwent painless surgery (even amputation of a limb) while hypnotized. But after anesthetics were discovered, hypnosis was seldom used.

The use of hypnosis in studying hysterical behavior was revived late in the last century by a French neurologist named Charcot, who believed that hysterics alone could be hypnotized. Others did not share his view. They reached the conclusion that any person can be hypnotized provided he gives his consent and follows closely the instructions of the hypnotist. The latter view eventually prevailed. It appears that Charcot's subjects were selected and hypnotized by his medical assistants and that in order to guarantee a good demonstration, they provided him with known hysterics. Of chief importance in this connection, however, is the fact that two men who were to become leaders in the study of neurotic behavior came under Charcot's influence. One of these was Janet, who introduced the concept of personality integration. He pointed out that neurotics tend to be divided within themselves, as it were, whereas normal people represent an internal unity; that is to say, they are *integrated*. The other man who came under Charcot's influence at this time was the young Viennese neurologist, Sigmund Freud, whose ideas about childhood experience and personality have already been noted. □

Freud began by hypnotizing his patients, who often recalled events, desires, and fears which went unrecognized in their waking lives. They were not aware of these before being hypnotized and they did not remember them when brought out of the trance. Nevertheless, these unconscious residues of earlier experiences were believed by Freud to account for neurotic behavior.

The idea that behavior is influenced by events of which we are not conscious was revolutionary. Wundt had claimed that psychology is the science of conscious experience. Now Freud was saying that there is an unconscious realm which introspection cannot reach and which, nevertheless, plays an important role in human life. In addition to this

revolutionary idea Freud introduced a new type of psychotherapy to be called "psychoanalysis." This made no use of hypnosis. Hypnosis was dropped for several reasons, the most important of which had to do with the fact that a person does not usually remember anything that happens while he is hypnotized. During the trance he may recall disturbing past experiences and even have an emotional upheaval while doing so. Recall of disturbing experiences and release of "pent-up emotion" offer some relief to the patient. But Freud felt that it would be much better if his patient could recall and give vent to emotion while fully aware of what he was doing. Under these conditions he would be more likely to remember what had happened and thus receive greater benefit from it. Therefore Freud adopted his *free association* technique in which patients said everything that came to mind while relaxing on a couch. They also talked about their dreams and used these as points of departure for free association. During many sessions, sometimes over a period of years, the patient's "unconscious" was emptied out, so to speak. The outcomes of this procedure were studied and evaluated as a basis for understanding the patient's problems and suggesting ways of adjusting to them.

While using his approach to neuroses, Freud very soon reached the conclusion that these disorders result from frustrated sexual desire, or from anxieties associated with sexual functions. He pointed out that we are taught from early childhood not to talk about or even think of sex. Failure to observe these teachings is followed by shame. Because we are taught that sex is shameful, we repress experiences and thoughts associated with it; in other words, we put them "out of mind." As a consequence, Freud claimed, we eventually lose awareness of them.

Freud wrote extensively (see Figure 1.8) and his methods and theories have had a marked influence upon psychology, medicine, and various spheres of everyday life, even literature and art. It should not be assumed, however, that all of Freud's ideas are scientifically sound. He developed several ideas about neurotic and normal personality which,

• 1.8

Freud Reading the Manuscript of his *Outline of Psychoanalysis*. This picture was taken in July 1938, when Freud was 82. As indicated earlier, he died in 1939. (Sigmund Freud Copyrights Ltd.)

because they are based primarily upon observations of abnormal people and appear to rest upon insufficient proof, are without adequate scientific demonstration. Many feel that Freud overemphasized the influence of sex in human life, and some of his fellow analysts differed from him in this regard. He may be credited, nevertheless, with having shown the determining influence of urges unknown to the individual and especially of urges derived from childhood experiences. The latter suggestion, as we have already seen, had a marked impact on child psychology.

Although Freud was especially concerned with understanding and helping neurotic people, his observations and concepts have influenced other areas of psychology. This, as we will see in later chapters, is most apparent in the study of motivation and personality. Many commonly used terms in these areas, like "unconscious motivation" and "repression," stem from Freudian psychoanalysis.

The feebleminded

Intelligence tests were first used to keep mentally incompetent children out of the French school system. Behind this there is a long history which culminated not only in the development of intelligence tests but also in the establishment of psychological clinics to help the feebleminded and other handicapped people.

Until fairly recent times, the feebleminded, like the psychotic, were mistreated to "drive the devil out of them." No more than custodial care was provided, and even that was of the poorest imaginable kind. Eventually they were given better care and efforts were made to understand the nature of their disorders and how best to educate them.

☐ The limited educability of feebleminded children was revealed in a study which, at the time, received its motivation from broad philosophical issues. A philosopher named John Locke (1632–1704) had claimed that the human mind at birth is a *tabula rasa*, a blank sheet. This was a radical idea, for Plato and others had assumed that certain ideas are inborn; that is, present in the human mind from the start. Locke's *tabula rasa* concept meant that ideas, rather than being present at birth, are derived from experience. The

Seguin's Formboard. The child is timed while he places the blocks in the proper holes. (Pix Inc.)

implication of this doctrine for education seemed clear. Anybody could be made intelligent by presenting his senses with the right ideas in sufficient number. This theory induced Itard, a teacher of the deaf, to attempt the education of a "savage" boy who had been found living in the woods like an animal.

When discovered in 1798, the boy was believed to be around ten years old. He walked on all fours, ate like an animal, and made unintelligible sounds. Itard devised various ways of bringing ideas to the boy and he kept up his efforts for five years. During this time there was some progress. The boy learned sensory discriminations, to recognize some objects, to speak a few words, and to read and write a little, although with poor understanding. He also learned various motor skills. But, despite such progress, Itard's pupil did not rise above the level of feeblemindedness. Was this because he was innately deficient? Or was he normal at birth, but handicapped by years of animal-like existence? These questions could not be answered. Thus the controversy which started this investigation was not

resolved. Nevertheless, Itard had stirred up an interest in the feebleminded and suggested that, even if one cannot educate them into normality, they can be educated to a degree.

One of Itard's followers, a man named Seguin, devised methods of training the mentally handicapped. When he went to the United States in 1848, he helped establish special institutions for the care and training of the feebleminded. Seguin's formboard (Figure 1.9) is still widely used, along with others of which it was the prototype. It is useful in testing children as well as feebleminded or illiterate adults. □

The first clinic for the study and treatment of mental and other handicaps was opened at the University of Pennsylvania in 1896 under Witmer's direction. Today psychological clinics are found throughout the world. In the United States alone there are now more than 10,000 clinical psychologists. These are working in clinics for adults as well as children. Many are in school systems, colleges, the Veterans Administration, the Armed Services, and mental hospitals and homes for the mentally retarded. Many work in close cooperation with psychiatrists.

Psychiatrists and clinical psychologists

Psychiatrists and clinical psychologists are jointly concerned with psychotic and neurotic people. The psychiatrist is a physician with an M.D. who specializes in psychological problems and is also qualified to prescribe drugs and other medical treatments. Some psychiatrists are also psychoanalysts, receiving this designation because they specialize in the use of psychoanalytic procedures.

The clinical psychologist is usually a Ph.D., although he may also have an M.D. His major training and clinical experience are in psychology, with emphasis on behavior disorders. He may be accredited by a national or state board in clinical psychology.

In dealing with severe cases of mental illness such as psychoses and some neuroses, clinical psychologists work closely with psychiatrists. Customarily, their function here is to administer and evaluate psychological tests, thus facilitating diagnosis. In certain circumstances they engage in psychotherapy with their clients or patients.

Less serious behavior disorders, including problems of school or home adjustment, are usually dealt with in a psychological clinic. Here the clinical psychologist, although he works in close cooperation with medical doctors, is himself responsible for nonmedical aspects of diagnosis and therapy. If the clinical psychologist suspects the presence of a psychosis or of some glandular or other organic disorder, he sends his client to a physician for medical diagnosis. Medical doctors, when they come across nonpsychotic behavior disorders and problems of adjustment, refer their patients to a clinical psychologist. More serious disorders are referred co a psychiatrist.

The growth of psychology as a science was greatly dependent upon the development of research methods adapted to the solution of its special problems. We shall now consider some of these. ■

HOW PSYCHOLOGISTS GET THEIR INFORMATION

Whatever his special field of interest may be, a psychological investigator is systematic in his approach. He begins by asking questions which appear significant to him, in view of what is already known. Some questions are theoretical in nature, such as: "What is thinking?" "Why do we forget?" "Is there a relationship between body build and personality?" Other questions are practical, referring to the solution of immediate problems like the reduction of accidents, the prevention of delinquency, or the more efficient teaching of some special skill. If the investigator is interested in development, animal or human, he will look for trends, and the questions he asks will be of this nature: "At what level of animal life does reasoning appear?" and "How does childhood experience influence adult intelligence?" The clinical psychologist deals with such questions as how to aid Mary Smith in her efforts to cope with personal problems — perhaps she is troubled by excessive shyness, scholastic difficulties, or family adjustment.

The investigator does more than ask questions. He also looks for the answers. Instead of appealing to authorities or engaging in unbridled speculation, he examines what other investigators have discovered. If the relevant information has not already been found, he gathers the facts himself — going, as it were, to "the horse's mouth." Sometimes the answers to his questions come from systematic observation of behavior that occurs naturally. The nature of anger outbursts in children requires a description of such outbursts as they occur naturally, and of the events preceding them. In studying the development of locomotion in children the investigator is again usually dependent upon what might be called "naturalistic observation." Animal behavior that occurs in a natural habitat, like the migration of birds or the mating behavior of fish, is likewise observed and described without the intervention of the investigator in the behavior itself. But even the naturalistic observer may, at times, introduce conditions designed to reveal the bases of naturally occurring behavior. The studies illustrated and described in Figures 1.10 and 1.11 are good examples not only of intervention but also of the sort of information revealed by it. Pure observation indicates, for example, that the blind avoid obstacles; but only the introduction of experimental controls tells us that they do so through echolocation, the perception of reflected sound.[3] Likewise, naturalistic observation reveals the complex pattern of mating behavior in a stickleback, but experimental intervention alone can show us precisely what stimuli control such behavior.[4] When naturally occurring behavior is not the investigator's particular concern, he may study behavior experimentally, in the laboratory. He is interested in such questions as: "What stimulating conditions elicit the behavior in question?" "How does the behavior vary when stimulating conditions are varied?" "What is the relationship, if any, between one aspect of behavior and another?"

Experimental research

Experimentation is of basic importance in any science, for it allows maximum control

| A | B | C |

- **1.10**

Perception of Obstacles by the Blind. Blind people have remarkable ability to perceive silent obstacles before making contact with them, yet they do not know the basis of this ability. There have been many theories, the most prevalent being that the blind have an unusual sensitivity of the facial skin and nerves which enables them to sense pressure changes as the obstacle is approached. This is the theory of "facial vision." A relatively simple series of experiments settled the issue. It demonstrated, in the first place, that seeing subjects who are blindfolded can also avoid obstacles, although not as accurately as the blind. In the second place, it showed that covering the skin with felt (**A**), thus removing the possibility of "facial vision," did not seriously interfere with perception of obstacles. Although this research discredited the aforementioned theory, it still left unanswered the question, "How do they do it?"

Earlier research with bats had demonstrated that they emit vibrations of higher frequency than the human ear can pick up, and that these vibrations, reflected back (sonarfashion) from obstacles, enable them to fly in the dark without hitting anything. This suggested that blind people might use reflected sound to avoid obstacles. Subjects were therefore tested with their ears blocked, or while wearing headphones, the latter emitting a hum which would prevent response to echoes (**B**). Under both of these conditions there was a dramatic change in behavior. Blind subjects who had approached a partition confidently, and had avoided it, now were hesitant. Moreover, they no longer perceived the partition before colliding with it (**C**).

Thus it became apparent that hearing and not skin sensitivity is responsible for obstacle avoidance in the blind. This was further borne out by the observation that deaf-blind subjects are unable to perceive obstacles from a distance. A later experiment demonstrated, moreover, that high-pitched sounds reflected from obstacles provide the important cues for avoidance in hearing subjects. These sounds come from footsteps, breathing, and sources in the environment. Thus a series of experiments, supplementing what naturalistic observation could indicate, disproved a widely held theory and also provided the correct answer to the question, "How do the blind perceive obstacles?" This knowledge can be used to provide better methods of training the blind. (From M. Super, M. Cotzin, and K. M. Dallenbach, " 'Facial Vision': The Perception of Obstacles by the Blind," *American Journal of Psychology*, 1944, *57*, pp. 133–183.)

over whatever is being investigated and it provides ways of measuring the factors involved.

To say that we have *control* over conditions and events means that we can produce them whenever we wish and vary them in such a way as to force answers to our questions. We observed such control in the experiments with the blind and with sticklebacks.

By saying that experimentation provides for *measurement* of the factors involved we mean that it allows us to specify the extent or magnitude of their influence. For example, we measure in inches how far the blind man was from an obstacle when he perceived its presence. Similarly we measure how many trials are necessary before some skill is mastered, how many items are recalled after being seen briefly, or how quickly (in thousandths of a second) a subject responds to certain stimuli.

We have been referring to the *stimulus*

and the *response*, or to *stimuli* and *responses*. It is with these that the psychological investigator is especially concerned, as already indicated in our historical discussion.

☐ Anything that initiates some activity of the organism is a *stimulus*, the Latin word for *spur*. This term is used very broadly in psychology, referring sometimes to a precisely specified and measured energy change (like the wavelength or intensity of light) and sometimes to a general situation (like someone yelling that the theater is on fire). But, even in the latter instance, the stimulus could, if necessary, be reduced to the physical terms used in the measurement of energy. It is always true that when objects of everyday life are called "stimuli," a careful study of them will show that they involve measurable energy able to act physiologically upon the sense organs.

The stimulus is always the antecedent event; that which initiates an activity (whether the activity is contraction of the pupil of the eye, the subject's statement that he sees red, or rushing toward the exit of the theater). Any activity that is known to be dependent upon (to always follow) the stimulus is said to be a *response* to that stimulus. Some responses are evident to any observer, hence *explicit* or *overt*. Others, like sensory experiences and feelings, are hidden from all but the person experiencing them. These are accordingly said to be *implicit* or *covert*. ☐

In the most general sense, psychologists deal with responses of organisms to stimulation. This fact is usually represented by the symbols S→O→R, where S represents stimuli; O the organism; and R the organism's response. Sometimes a formula like $R = f(O,S)$ is used, meaning that response is a joint function of the organism and stimulation.

The psychological investigator varies stimuli (as in the obstacle experiment with the blind) and he varies conditions within the organism (as when he studies the effect of different degrees of hunger on learning). Usually he is interested in measuring the effect of such variations on the organism's behavior. Sometimes, as we have seen, the investigator observes a response and asks, "What is the stimulus?" or "What stimuli are significant in eliciting this response?" He knows the organism and he observes the response, but his task now is to complete the psychological equation by filling in the value of S. The experiments with the blind, as well as those with the stickleback, were of this nature.

☐ Stimuli may be classified, in the most general terms, as *external* or *internal*. External stimuli are those in our surroundings which impinge upon the external sense organs. Light waves, sound waves, odorous substances, mechanical pressures, and temperature changes exemplify these. Aspects of the world are of course not stimuli unless they produce some effect upon the organism's experience or behavior. Some external stimuli are *social*, as when behavior is influenced by the presence

● **1.11**

A Fish Experiment. The male three-spined stickleback exhibits in the mating season a complicated behavior pattern during which he constructs a nest and then induces the female to enter it and deposit her eggs. This mating pattern, alike in all these fish, has been described in detail; but what aspect of the female is responsible for starting it? The answer was obtained by introducing models which resembled in various ways the configuration of a female about to lay eggs. In this way it was discovered that the male responds to the female's swollen abdomen. Models which look like a fish but which do not have this feature are ineffective; and a model which does not look much like a fish but which has a swelling in about the right place sets off the characteristic mating behavior. (From N. Tinbergen, *Social Behavior in Animals*, Wiley, 1953, p. 27.)

of others. Social stimuli are reducible, in the last analysis, to sounds, movements, and so forth, which can, if we wish, be measured as discussed in our statement concerning stimuli as physical energies. When behavior is influenced by what others say, we are dealing with social stimuli, but more specifically, *verbal stimuli*. *Internal stimuli* are those which originate within the organism. A lowering of blood sugar is an internal stimulus if it increases stomach contractions (which may themselves be internal stimuli), leads to feelings of depression, or induces us to eat some candy. Chemical and electrical activities associated with glandular and nervous functioning may serve as internal stimuli. Activities within the brain, to take another example, may elicit further activities, as when you think of something, then go to look for it. □

Some special methodological problems

Although psychological research is basically similar to research in other sciences, the complexities of behavior give rise to unique methodological problems. We have already suggested some of these in referring to social and verbal stimuli, with which other biological sciences are not concerned.

A very special problem in much of psychological research has to do with internal factors known as *instructional sets*. The subject in a reaction time experiment, for instance, may be told to respond when the light is red and not when it is green. These instructions produce an internal set which facilitates response to red and inhibits response to green.

□ Sometimes it is necessary to control set in other ways. We may make the subject think that he is taking a drug, say a capsule of caffeine, whereas he is in reality taking a capsule of water. Or we may cause him to think that he is performing very poorly on a test, even though his performance is average. Or we may induce him to think that one type of response is being studied while we are in reality studying another. Of course the subject is eventually told that, for experi-

mental purposes, it had been necessary to misinform him.

The reader may wonder why it is necessary to "fool" the subject. This sort of control is sometimes necessary because the subject's response can be greatly influenced by internal sets which he may himself assume. We try to obviate these by providing a uniform set as part of the experimental procedure. □

The psychological investigator, in arranging his experiments, must take cognizance of: (1) the type of organism being studied, (2) what the organism has already learned, (3) the current condition of the organism, (4) the stimuli operative in the experimental situation, and (5) the responses to be measured.

The type of organism to be investigated (whether animal or human, child or adult, male or female) is decided before the experiment begins.

What the subject has already learned (skills or information relevant to the experiment) is also considered before the experiment begins. For certain purposes it is necessary to choose subjects who have none of the specific skills and none of the information utilized in the experiment.

The current condition of the organism (hungry, fatigued) is something which the experimenter must either hold constant or vary as the needs of his experiment demand.

Stimuli, we have seen, must also be varied or held constant. Usually the stimuli to be controlled are external, but the investigator may have to control internal stimuli as well.

A psychological experiment, as schematically represented in Figure 1.12, has two classes of *variables* — independent and dependent.

Independent variables are those manipulated by the experimenter. Except where special statistical procedures are used, there is only one independent variable in a given experimental observation. The reason why this must be so is perhaps obvious. Suppose that the person investigating obstacle avoidance in the blind had stopped up the subject's ears and also covered his head and shoulders. Suppose, too, that the subject now collided with obstacles. How could the investigator know which of these two variables produced

● **1.12**

Schema of a Typical Psychological Experiment. The independent variable is that which the experimenter manipulates (e.g., adding or subtracting it from the situation, or varying its amount). Practice, alcohol, hunger, and visual stimulation are examples of such variables. The black lines at the left represent constant factors. Thus, in an experiment to assess the effects on reasoning of a certain amount of alcohol, such factors as the age, sex, intelligence, and previous indulgence of the subjects would be held constant. Likewise, the amount of alcohol, the test of reasoning, the time elapsed between drinking and testing, and methods of scoring results would need to be the same for all subjects. Still another of many factors to be held constant would be the attitude or set of the subjects. The alcohol should somehow be disguised so that subjects do not know when they are getting it and when a nonalcoholic beverage is being drunk. The R's (at the right) refer to dependent variables, in this case psychological changes produced by alcohol. R(B) refers to gross behavior variables (like muscular steadiness, speed of reaction, motor coordination, and performance on learning and reasoning tasks). R(P) represents internal physiological changes such as heart rate, secretion of adrenalin, and brain waves. By R(V) we refer to what the subject says in describing his experiences, such as having feelings of clumsiness, nervousness, or exhilaration.

the change in behavior? It is thus necessary to vary one factor at a time as described in our discussion of this experiment.

Even when an experiment is designed statistically so that more than one factor may be varied at the same time, statistical analysis eventually isolates the influence of each factor. With statistical procedures, also, the interdependent action of two or more variables, with the relative contribution of single variables may be studied. But the details of statistical experimental design are too complicated for discussion outside of books on advanced statistics.

In addition to varying certain stimuli or organic conditions (while holding other stimuli and organic conditions constant) the experimenter observes and measures his subjects' responses. These are said to be *dependent variables* because they are presumed to depend upon the factor whose isolated influence is under investigation. Sometimes the investigator studies gross behavior, like facial expressions or maze running; sometimes he focuses upon physiological processes, like heart action or blood pressure; sometimes he confines his attention to verbal reports which reveal feelings or perceptions; and sometimes he is interested in all such dependent variables. This may well be true, for example, in studies of emotion, where gross behavior, physiological changes, and feelings are aspects of the overall pattern of response.

☐ In many psychological experiments it is necessary to use a sequence of experimental and control conditions which will nullify progressive effects, like those of practice and fatigue. Take, for example, an experiment in which the investigator wants to discover the effect of a particular *set* on speed of reaction. One set, let us say, is to *attend only to the stimulus*. The reaction key is pressed as quickly as possible when the stimulus appears. The other set requires no special attention to the stimulus: the subject is told to *attend only to the act of pressing the response key*. The investigator of course uses the same stimulus with both the stimulus and response sets. He will also use the same chronoscope, the same type of reaction key, and the same general situation. That is to say, he will *hold these factors constant*. But suppose that the experimenter gave a number of tests (perhaps 100) with the *stimulus set*, followed by 100 with the *response set*. If there should be a progressive adaptation to the experimental situation (a learning to adjust to it), he would be stacking the cards in favor of better performance under the response set. An improvement in the second series of tests over the first might then be due to learning and not to the difference in set. Suppose on the other hand, that the subject becomes fatigued during the experiment. Then such a procedure as we have described would be biased in favor of the stimulus set. That is, quite apart from the influence of set, our subject might do better on the first 100 tests because he is less tired than during the last 100 tests. It is quite obvious, therefore, that experiments of this nature require a sequence of tests which equate, or rule out the effects of, or, in a word, *control* such factors as learning and fatigue. Such control may be achieved by using a counterbalanced order such as *stimulus set* (50 tests), *response set* (100 tests), and *stimulus set* (50 tests). This is often referred to as an *a b b a* sequence, since there are 50 *a*, then 50 *b*, followed by 50 *b*, then 50 *a*. Measurements obtained in the *a* series are added and averaged; similarly for the *b* series. One can

readily see that use of such a counterbalanced sequence throws the effect of progressive factors like learning and fatigue equally upon each of the two variables (response set and stimulus set). The outcome, in this instance, is then influenced only by the difference in set. ☐

A *control condition*, as we have seen, is the normal or natural one; an *experimental condition* is one introducing some modification designed to answer the question being investigated. It is sometimes necessary to use at least two groups of subjects, a control and an experimental group. This is true whenever responses to different conditions, which cannot be used with the same subject, are being compared. In certain kinds of research it is necessary to hold heredity constant (i.e., to control it) while varying other conditions. If, for example, we want to know the effect of a particular kind of training on some aspect of child development, there must be a control (untrained) and an experimental (trained) group. Unless both were alike in heredity, the results would be ambiguous — that is, an observed difference between the groups could have come from the training, but it might also represent an inherent difference. In such experiments the method of *co-twin control* may be used, where identical twins are separated into control and experimental groups. Since identical twins have the same heredity, the groups are alike in this respect. A so-called *split-litter* method is often used in obtaining groups of animals with similar inheritance. Out of twelve rats in the same litter, for example, six may be assigned to the control and six to the experimental group. If larger numbers are needed, other litters may be similarly split. It is also advantageous to have the individuals of a pure genetic strain. Where inherent differences are not of direct significance to the investigation, groups may be equated on the basis of an initial test — of learning ability, intelligence, speed of reaction, or sensitivity, depending upon the problem being investigated. Sometimes it is necessary to match groups with respect to several factors.

☐ Suppose, for example, that the effect of a particular type of psychotherapy is being evaluated with schizophrenic patients. It is not sufficient to take just any group of patients and give the therapy; some might recover spontaneously, and the recovery rate may depend upon (i.e., vary with) such things as sex, age, education, and the type and duration of the illness. It is customary, therefore, to arrange two equivalent groups by matching subjects. A female schizophrenic of a certain age, educational level, and duration of the illness will be matched with another who is similar in these, and perhaps other respects. Then one of the pair will be assigned to the experimental (therapy) and the other to the control (no therapy) group. A male schizophrenic might be matched, similarly, with another male schizophrenic and each assigned to a different group. After two sufficiently large groups, equivalent with respect to sex, and matched subject-with-subject are obtained, one group is given therapy and the other not. Should there be a significantly greater number of recoveries or improvements in the therapy group, this would then be attributed to the therapy. It could not be attributed to spontaneous recovery or to other nonexperimental conditions. □

Psychological methods developed gradually as psychology expanded its scope. New fields of investigation and new problems called for special procedures. The study of individual differences introduced statistical methods. These were found, eventually, to be essential in the analysis of experimental findings, especially those involving comparisons among groups.

Beyond finding an average (mean) to represent the performances of individuals in a group, there was the problem of deciding whether an observed difference was a chance one or one that came about as the result of experimentally introduced conditions. The question here is whether the difference is reliable statistically. We ask, more specifically, "What is the probability that a repetition of the experiment would still reveal a difference?" In deciding such issues certain assumptions must be made and then the investigator must carry out some rather involved statistical calculations which need not concern a beginner in psy-

chology. The statistical supplement to Chapter 3 does, however, provide some introductory information on how the reliability of differences may be calculated.

□ Appropriate statistical analysis may indicate that a difference in the direction found would occur by chance less than once in 1,000 times. If this were so, the experimenter would be correct 999 times in 1,000 in assuming that he had obtained a real (not merely a chance) difference between responses in the control and in the experimental conditions. This would of course indicate a very high degree of reliability. Usually a difference is regarded as statistically *insignificant* unless the level of confidence is at least 5 per cent — i.e., unless the chances are at least 95 in 100 that it has been experimentally produced. To the student this may appear to be an overly cautious attitude, but scientists must be reasonably sure that findings on which they base their conclusions are reliable. □

In the last analysis, all psychological research deals with S→O→R (stimulus-organism-response) relationships. As indicated in our earlier discussion, it focuses on responses elicited by internal and external stimuli. Often, however, an investigator is interested not so much in what stimuli produce particular responses but in *how one response is related to another response*. In one study with adolescent boys, for example, the investigator was interested in discovering a possible relationship between a boy's physical strength (as measured by a test of strength) and social prestige (as represented by measures of social acceptance among other boys). In studying responses indicative of strength on the one hand and those which make for acceptance by the peer group on the other, this investigator was looking for a possible response-response, or R-R, relationship. He did, in fact, obtain results indicative of such a relationship.[5]

The discovery of R-R relationships calls not only for measurement of the respective responses but also for a detailed statistical analysis of such measurements. The statistical procedure is that of *correlation* and the outcome is an index of the degree of relationship between the measurements. One such index is the *coefficient of correlation*. How some of these indices are calculated is demonstrated in the statistical supplement to Chapter 3.

When experiments and statistical calculations have revealed that there is a high correlation between what we will call response X and response Y, it means that we can predict X from Y or Y from X. We make such predictions whenever we select students or workers on the basis of standardized tests. In Chapter 18, some data are presented which show that, of those candidates for pilot training who made above a certain score on a battery of aptitude tests, approximately 95 per cent became pilots. The data also show that, of those who made below a certain score, only 20 per cent became pilots. On the basis of such R-R relationships, those charged with selection of pilot trainees during the second world war could, in terms of test responses alone, predict the effectiveness of responses in the training situation. They did, in fact, select a large group with the knowledge that a predictable percentage would pass the course.[6] This illustrates one of many practical outcomes of the investigation of R-R relationships. Other R-R relationships are revealed in later discussions of individual differences in intelligence, aptitude, and personality. ■

SYSTEMS OF PSYCHOLOGY

Science, as we have seen, is based on observation. A theory without verifiable evidence from unprejudiced observation or experimentation has no chance of scientific acceptance. Thus the scientist needs facts. But when sufficient facts have been uncovered, there is need for classification and organization. What is known must be integrated. Significant relationships must be sought. Provisional theories or predictions must be made. These must in turn be tested by further observations. The outcome of such observations leads to acceptance, rejection, or modification of the theories which they were designed to test. In this way scientists use knowledge already gained as a springboard for advances into new terri-

tory. As James B. Conant, a former president of Harvard University put it, "Science is an interconnected series of concepts and conceptual schemes that have developed as a result of experimentation and observation and are fruitful of further experimentation and observations . . . emphasis is on the word 'fruitful.' Science is a speculative enterprise."[7]

Until the present century, psychologists were doing little more than asking questions and collecting a sundry array of facts about limited areas like sensory experience, individual differences, animal intelligence, child development, and normal and abnormal personality. In all of this effort there was no general plan. There was not even a generally accepted definition of what psychology is. Obviously an integration of psychological knowledge was needed, not only to pull the disconnected threads into a meaningful pattern, but also to give direction to further research. This need brought forth various "psychologies" or "schools of psychology." Although none of these achieved universal acceptance among psychologists, each served as a rallying point for various groups and gave a certain degree of direction and meaning to their work.

In describing the origin and expanding scope of psychology, we have already touched upon two early schools (the structural and functional) and upon factors which influenced development of certain other schools.

Structuralists said that psychology should focus upon conscious experience as revealed by experimental introspection. They received their inspiration from Wundt. The outcome of their approach was a sort of mental chemistry. Conscious experience was analyzed and described in terms of its makeup; that is, its structural elements (sensations, images, feelings) much as matter is analyzed and described by chemists in terms of its basic structures. The structural school dealt, in a sense, with the *contents* of consciousness. One outcome, as we have seen, was a unified body of knowledge about the processes involved in knowing our world. Neurological and other physiological structures and functions which underlie these processes were also of interest to structuralists.

Functionalists emphasized the functions

rather than the contents of consciousness. As we pointed out earlier, they were more interested in what consciousness *does* than in what it is. Theirs was, in every sense, a psychology of adjustment. In this the functionalists were, as we have seen, greatly influenced by Darwin's ideas about the struggle for existence and the survival of the fittest. Introspection was used, but behavior (from the standpoint of adjustment to the environment) came into prominence. The scope of psychology thus expanded to take in adjustment as well as conscious experience.

Present-day psychology is broadly functional in the sense that it studies adjustment of organisms to their environment. Since sensory and perceptual processes are important aspects of adjustment, these find a place in the functional approach. Within this overall functional trend, however, one finds the imprint of other schools of psychology. The most influential of these is behaviorism.

Behaviorism

The leader of the behavioristic movement was John B. Watson, who, from 1908 to 1920, taught at The Johns Hopkins University. Watson's training had been in the functional tradition and he retained his broad functional orientation. But he argued for what might be called an "objective functionalism." Watson contended that psychology should give up studying conscious experience, whether in terms of its contents *or* its functions. He stressed the point that introspective data are *subjective*; that is, evident only to the experiencing individual. He could not, of course, deny that conscious experience exists. His argument was merely that since this is private, it cannot be studied scientifically. The fact that introspective reports were taken as descriptions of conscious experience did not impress him. Let us see what lay behind this attitude.

Physicists studied phenomena which any trained physicist could observe, not just privately but in common with others of similar training. Likewise, a biologist studied other organisms, or even his own organism, through observations which other biologists could make

at the same time. Observations made under such "social" circumstances are said to be *objective*. Psychologists, on the other hand, were attempting to obtain scientific data by looking inward. Watson wanted them to look outward, as the natural scientists do and, even in the case of man, to study him as an object in nature. Observations of an objective psychologist would thus be restricted to overt responses, the stimuli which arouse them, and the observable aspects of underlying physiological mechanisms, like nerves, glands, and muscles. This would then be a "stimulus-response" psychology.

In taking his stand that psychology should be a science of behavior, Watson was also influenced by several earlier developments. Some of these have already been considered. Many psychologists were, in fact, confining their attention to behavior. Investigations of memory, of individual differences, of child development, and of learning in human and animal subjects were as objective as any in physics, biology, and the other sciences. These, and many other psychological phenomena, could be investigated without introspection and without any reference to how the individuals under observation felt about what was happening to them. In the case of animals, moreover, one could have a science of behavior even though there was no hope of obtaining reports from the organisms themselves. In fact, various physiologists were carrying out experiments with animals and human beings which did not involve introspection and which were nevertheless of great interest to all psychologists. As an example of this, one may take the work of Pavlov on conditioned reflexes. One of Pavlov's experiments is illustrated in Figure 1.13.

Watson saw in the conditioned reflex a way to circumvent introspective reports and thus to obtain objective data, not on experience, but on the sensitivity of organisms to stimuli. Sensitivity in this sense implied no more about conscious experience than we mean when we speak of the sensitivity of a light meter, a galvanometer, or a photographic film.

Enough has been said about the antecedents of behaviorism to show that its roots

● **1.13**

An Experiment by Pavlov. Food was introduced into the dog's mouth mechanically from the adjoining room. The conditioning chamber itself was soundproofed. Food stimulated the secretion of saliva, which was collected via one of the tubes illustrated. A beating metronome at first produced no saliva. It was then started just before food entered the dog's mouth. This pairing of sound and food continued until conditioned salivation occurred, i.e., until the sound by itself produced salivation. Once the dog had been conditioned to salivate to a particular frequency, another frequency was introduced. Having been conditioned to salivate to one frequency, the dog also salivated to another. However, by giving food with one frequency and withholding it when the other was presented, Pavlov induced the dog to salivate for one frequency and not for the other. Then the difference between the two frequencies was reduced. This was done, for instance, by increasing the frequency of the no-food stimulus. It was increased until the difference between the two stimuli was so small that the dog salivated for both, or salivated for neither. In this way, without any reports from the dog, it was possible to discover how small a difference the animal discriminates. If one wished to do so, he could carry out psychophysical research by comparable objective procedures. (After Razran)

were in the history of psychology itself and also in biology. Some said that the new movement was not psychology at all, that it was no more than biology. There have been at least two answers to this criticism of behavioristic psychology.

(1) Psychologists are interested in adjustments of the *whole organism* to its environment, whereas biologists are preoccupied with particular biological processes such as circulation, digestion, and heredity. This distinction, while correct in general, falls down when, as often happens, biologists study overall adjustments like the nest-building of birds, and psychologists study partial reactions like reflexes. All that can be said in favor of such a distinction is that, from the standpoint of the relative emphasis given to part and whole reactions, psychologists are more concerned with the latter.

(2) Psychologists study behavioral processes to which biologists, as such, give little or

no attention. One can see this by comparing a biology and a psychology textbook. Generally speaking, the concern of biologists is primarily with unlearned (innate) processes; that of psychologists with learned (acquired) processes. Biologists, for example, give no more than passing attention to such aspects of life as memory, learning, problem-solving, and individual differences in intelligence and personality. They are not especially concerned, as psychologists are, with the development of behavior in children, behavior of human beings in groups, and psychological aspects of adjustment such as fall within the province of clinical psychology. Our point is not that the interests of biologists and psychologists are foreign to each other. Indeed, they frequently overlap. It is merely that those who regarded behavioristic psychology as *nothing but* biology were incorrect.

Watson began a trend which has culminated in the modern preoccupation of psychologists with behavior, studied by methods as objective as those used in the natural and physical sciences. It is interesting to note in this connection that modern psychology, as frankly objective as it is, leaves out very little that has been derived from other approaches. In fact, it embraces much that was formerly dealt with from the standpoint of experience. Some suggestion of this was given in the discussion of conditioned reflexes, where we pointed out that sensory processes (but not experiences) can be studied objectively. The ability of an objective psychology to encompass data which were previously considered from a so-called subjective standpoint can be further illustrated in this way: Suppose that a colored signal light is flashed. The objective investigator is not interested in your experience — for that is private, known only to you. He may be interested, however, in the fact that you respond to light and that you, like himself, distinguish one color from other colors, for example, by altering your response as the color changes. You say "red" or "green," or you press one button for red and another for green, or you step on the brake for a red light and on the accelerator for green. The investigator of behavior is satisfied to demonstrate that an organism distinguishes two lights, as above. He believes that nothing is added to our scientific understanding by saying that the lights produced different conscious experiences.

Before leaving behaviorism as a school, it is well to make a distinction between behavioristic methodology, which is what we have been discussing, and Watson's materialistic philosophy, which did much to bring criticism upon this movement. While arguing that psychologists must restrict themselves to the facts revealed in their observations and experiments, Watson went considerably beyond the observable facts himself. His theories went beyond the facts in various areas, as will become apparent in some later discussions. Especially disturbing to some, however, was his claim that behaviorism demanded a materialistic philosophy. While many psychologists accepted the concept of psychology as a natural science of behavior and, accordingly, its objective methodology, they rejected as philosophically naive the idea that because psychologists must limit their observations to such apparently material things as stimuli and nervous and muscular reactions, they are forced into a materialistic philosophy. The present-day psychologist with behavioristic leanings, who is known merely as a *psychologist*, might embrace any philosophical or religious viewpoint. This is because behavioristic psychology is for him a methodology, a means of discovering information about behavior and in no sense a concept of the nature of ultimate reality. For practical purposes in carrying on his investigations, any scientist must treat what is before him *as if* it were material, but he has no more notion than anyone else as to what, if anything, lies beyond the range of his senses, even when these are amplified by such instruments of science as microscopes, galvanometers, and electronic devices. As a scientist he can neither affirm nor deny any particular theory or doctrine of ultimate reality. Nor should he be expected to do so, any more than a physicist, a chemist, or a physiologist. Objective psychologists, like individuals in other sciences, actually vary a great deal from one to the other with respect to their philosophical or religious beliefs.

Gestalt psychology

This school developed in Germany around 1912 under the leadership of Wertheimer, Koffka, and Köhler, all of whom went to the United States and continued their work there. Wolfgang Köhler has been the chief spokesman for this group. Gestalt psychology is, in many respects, a protest against certain aspects of both structural and behavioristic psychology.

The word *"gestalt"* may be translated as "form" or "configuration." Those who follow gestalt principles are, in fact, often referred to as *configurationalists*. The term *holistic* is also applied to certain configurationally oriented studies, the reason being that these emphasize the *whole person*, or the *whole situation* in which he adjusts. Those who hold this general position disparage analytical or piecemeal investigations.

Gestalt psychologists argued that analytical (molecular) procedures such as the structuralists used were artificial and that what was revealed did not represent the true nature of conscious experience. Perception, for example, was said to be more than the sum of sensations and other elements revealed by experimental introspection. It was felt that one should begin with the complex; that wholes come first and parts have little or no meaning except when considered with respect to their place in the whole. Behaviorists were criticized for their study of isolated behavior segments, such as conditioned reflexes. Pavlov and some behaviorists had argued that habits are chains of conditioned reflexes, one reflex in the series serving as a stimulus to set off the next. To configurationalists, however, behavior is more than a "bundle of reflexes."

Gestalt psychologists demonstrated that animals and men learn certain things which defy piecemeal analysis. In doing this they introduced some new concepts to areas of psychology concerned with learning and thinking. This influence becomes evident in later discussions.

It is interesting to observe that gestalt psychologists studied animal and child behavior as well as perceptual experience. One should also note that some behavioristic psychologists, without deserting their overall functional and objective position, were led, through the influence of gestalt psychology, to study and interpret behavior in accordance with configurational principles. This school has also had a marked impact on our conception of how behavior develops and even of how the brain functions.

There were of course other schools of psychology, but an introductory text is not the place to discuss all of them. The most prominent of those we have failed to discuss, as schools, is *psychoanalysis*. Under Freud's leadership this was indeed *a* school, but psychoanalysts have separated into a variety of groups so that now there are several psychoanalytical schools. All are definitely holistic in their general approach and all are concerned with personality and with what moves us to behave as we do, but beyond that they differ markedly. As we have already pointed out, psychoanalysts differ among themselves with respect to the importance of sexual motivation. There are many other differences, not only in concepts, but also in clinical procedures.

The major scientific contribution of psychoanalysts has come from their introduction of concepts which suggested new approaches to the study of human behavior. Some of these, as later discussions of motivation and personality will show, have been susceptible to verification through experimental studies with children and adults, and even with white rats.

Each of the schools changed psychology a great deal — with respect to its scope, its methods, and its theoretical orientations. Some of them, after leaving an indelible imprint, passed out of focus. Today these schools, insofar as they may be said to exist at all, are more or less peripheral. The emphasis today is on *psychology*. Rather than allowing themselves to be classified as structuralists, functionalists, behaviorists, or configurationalists, most students of behavior prefer to be known merely as psychologists. With respect to overall methodology and fact, there is, today, little controversy among them. Their attitude is that any approach which adds to our understanding of human behavior is worthwhile. Where scientific methods are used, the facts, once verified, are of course beyond dispute. The only possible argument is about our interpretation of the facts, and this is where the so-called miniature systems of psychology come into the picture.

Miniature systems

Whereas schools of psychology attempted an overall integration of psychological knowledge, miniature systems have been much less ambitious. They have dealt with restricted areas of psychological investigation.

Most of the current miniature systems focus upon the learning process. Starting with certain well-established facts about learning, the proponent of a particular theoretical approach conceives of underlying or unifying principles which offer the possibility of explaining these facts. After formulating his theoretical explanation, the investigator sees that, if his theory is true, organisms tested under certain conditions ought to yield such and such results. He or his associates then test the theory by carrying out the projected experiment. If the outcomes are as predicted, this is of course a point in support of the theory. If results are not as predicted, then the theory must be discarded, or at least modified to take the negative findings into consideration. One such theory, to be considered when learning is discussed, has given rise to many investigations — some of which have supported it and others not — and the theory is still being modified as a result of research findings.

Through theories like this, even though they may turn out to be incorrect or inadequate, we obtain facts relevant to our understanding of behavior. We thus advance the frontiers of knowledge.

It is important to remember, in the above connection, that a scientific theory is useful only if we can test it, and that it stands or falls or undergoes modification in terms of relevant facts. There is a marked contrast between this approach and the acceptance of a theory because some great man propounded it, or because, in thinking about the theory, it seems reasonable to us.

We said that miniature systems are less ambitious than were the schools of psychology. This is true with respect to their immediate scope. However, it is possible that the final outcome will be an all-embracing theory enabling us to understand and predict every aspect of human behavior. Today, as we have said, much theoretical discussion centers around the nature of learning. The reason for this is that almost everything that man does is learned. Thus, if we understand the learning process in its many details, we will also understand, to a very large extent, why man behaves as he does.

☐ In focusing upon behavior, the science of psychology may appear to neglect some highly significant aspects of human life. However, as Carmichael[8] says, "The psychologist, instead of viewing man first of all from the standpoint of his social, esthetic, intellectual, or religious life, sees him primarily as an object in nature. This point of view does not deny or try to explain away man's highest attributes, but rather aims to describe the sort of creature that is capable of having the modern man's intellectual, social and spiritual life." ■

GENERAL PSYCHOLOGY

General psychology, the province of this textbook, cuts across various fields and systems to give a survey of scientific psychology as it exists today. Although diverse points of view receive attention from time to time, and different methods of investigation are discussed, our survey is largely factual.

There are various ways in which psychological information can be organized. In this text we have sometimes used the theme of development, tracing the evolution of behavior in different representative organisms and then its growth in the human individual from conception until old age. Psychological knowledge can also be dealt with in terms of major psychological processes, like motivation, learning, and perceiving. In some sections we have used this approach, presenting a survey of what is known about such processes. Other information has been organized around the theme of individual differences, concentrating from this standpoint upon differences in intelligence and personality. Since social interaction plays an important role in human life, two chapters are devoted to it. One of these deals with collective behavior and the other with language and communication.

Although certain applications of psychology are discussed in relation to development, sensory processes, individual differences, collective behavior, and communication, a final section of this text deals with what psychologists are doing to improve human efficiency in aspects of everyday life. ■

• SUMMARY

Beginning its scientific career as an attempt to analyze consciousness, psychology gradually broadened its scope and, in doing so, became a science of behavior.

Certain studies in physics and physiology which had obvious relevance for psychology led Wundt to start a separate science of psychology. The source of data for this new science was experimental introspection by trained observers. Investigators in Wundt's laboratory and others outside of it soon extended psychological observation to individual differences, memory, and the learning process. Animals and children began to play a part in psychological research. Psychologists also extended their investigations to abnormal people — the psychotic, the neurotic, and the feebleminded. Freud, a leader in the study of neuroses, founded the school of psychology known as psychoanalysis. By this time there was much less emphasis upon consciousness and the introspective method and more upon behavior. In the course of these developments, many general fields of psychology began to emerge. For example: findings on memory, the learning process, child behavior, individual differences, and mental testing were of obvious practical value to education, hence they became the backbone of educational psychology. The field of clinical psychology grew out of work on child development, abnormal behavior, and mental testing. Today there are many other fields — usually of multiple origins, like those mentioned. Among these are industrial psychology, vocational psychology, and social psychology.

The ultimate aim of psychologists is to discover the stimulating and organic conditions of which psychological processes are functions; that is, the S→O→R (stimulus, organism, response) functions. Investigation begins with relevant questions, either theoretical or practical, and systematic observations or experiments are designed to force an answer to these questions. Sometimes an experimental procedure is introduced into a naturalistic setting in an effort to discover the nature of stimuli which elicit certain behavior. Methods of controlling stimuli (external or internal), organic conditions, and sets (attitudes) in experimental investigations have been described. Special note has been made of procedures for holding certain conditions constant while others are varied. Among these are counterbalancing and the obtaining of comparable control and experimental groups. The importance of statistical procedures, especially in discovering the reliability of differences and the relationship between two or more variables (correlation), has also been pointed out.

As psychological information accumulated, there were efforts to pull the threads together — to integrate what was known and to plan meaningful research for the future. Thus several so-called schools or systems of psychology arose. Psychoanalysis was such a system, only it focused rather specifically upon personality and behavior problems. Another school, taking its origin from Wundt and his interest in the structure of consciousness, was known as structuralism. Functionalists envisaged their task as that of discovering how consciousness facilitates adjustment. They were influenced in this by Darwin's concept of evolution. But consciousness proved so elusive that investigators finally concentrated their attention on the learning process without reference to its conscious aspects. Behaviorism, which emphasized the objective as against the subjective approach to psychological problems, was influenced by functional studies of learning, by earlier work with animals and children, and by the conditioned-response studies of Russian investigators. Gestalt psychology, dealing with aspects of experience as well as behavior, emphasized the holistic as against the extremely analytical approach of earlier schools. Each of these systems integrated what it could and pushed into new territory. Thus each left an indelible mark upon modern

scientific psychology. The newer systems, referred to as "miniature systems" because of their relatively narrow scope, grew out of the earlier schools. These focus upon particular psychological functions; for example, the learning process.

Psychology today is best defined as the science of behavior. It emphasizes the objective approach so characteristic of the other natural sciences. However, it is to some extent a social as well as a natural science. This is because living organisms, and especially human beings, are influenced by the behavior of those around them. ■

REFERENCES AND NOTES FOR THIS CHAPTER ARE IN THE APPENDIX.

• SELECTED READINGS

Boring, E. G., *A History of Experimental Psychology* (rev. ed.). Appleton-Century-Crofts, 1950. A lucid and interesting account of how psychology became an experimental science.

Chaplin, J. P., and T. S. Krawiec, *Systems and Theories of Psychology*. Holt, Rinehart and Winston, 1960. A good book to supplement the discussion of systems.

Daniel, R. S. (Ed.), *Contemporary Readings in General Psychology* (2nd ed.). Houghton Mifflin, 1965. Parts 1 and 2 on psychology as a science.

Dennis, W. (Ed.), *Readings in the History of Psychology*. Appleton-Century-Crofts, 1948. The great psychologists, from Aristotle to contemporary systematists, speak for themselves.

Keller, F. S., *The Definition of Psychology*. Appleton-Century-Crofts, 1937. A good brief discussion of the major schools.

Murphy, G., *Historical Introduction to Modern Psychology* (rev. ed.). Harcourt, Brace, 1949. A highly stimulating excursion into history as well as contemporary trends.

O'Neil, W. M., *Introduction to Method in Psychology* (rev. ed.). Cambridge University Press, 1962. Psychological investigation demonstrated in relation to special problems.

Postman, L., *Psychology in the Making*. Knopf, 1962. History of selected research problems.

Watson, R. I., *The Great Psychologists: from Aristotle to Freud*. Lippincott, 1963. Much on the psychologists themselves as well as their contributions.

Woodworth, R. S., and M. R. Sheehan, *Contemporary Schools of Psychology* (3rd ed.). Ronald, 1964. A very readable and sound discussion of, among other things, behaviorism, gestalt psychology, and psychoanalysis.

2

The Human Organism

*P*sychological processes are functions of the organism, as first suggested by Aristotle. The structures which most directly underlie psychological processes are: (1) sense organs, referred to as *receptors* because they receive stimulation and provide information about our world; (2) muscles and glands, otherwise known as *effectors* because it is through their responses that stimuli have their ultimate effects; and (3) nervous mechanisms which interconnect receptors and effectors. What we call the *nervous system* comprises the nerves, spinal cord, and brain. Functions of the nervous system are referred to, in general, as *neural*. In discussing receptor, effector, and neural structures and functions, we are not trying to teach anatomy, physiology, or neurology. Our only aim is to show the biological anchoring of psychological processes like learning, motivation, emotion, and perception. Without some understanding of relevant biological mechanisms, the student of psychology may form inaccurate ideas about inner processes which intervene when stimuli elicit responses; or he may imagine that psychological processes exist in a disembodied state, like the Cheshire cat's grin in *Alice in Wonderland*.

It can be particularly instructive to trace what is complex from its simplest beginnings. Accordingly, we begin our discussion of the human organism by considering how the initial fertilized cell becomes an organism of many cells with mechanisms specialized for particular functions, like reception, conduction, integration, and response. Such a developmental approach introduces basic structures in their initial simplicity and places us in an advantageous position to delve into certain details of the mature organism which have special significance for psychology.

The minute cell with which each life begins is, of course, without psychological functions; but it has chemical constituents (genes) which, given the appropriate materials and conditions, will determine the eventual growth of sensory, effector, and neural mechanisms and the emergence of sensitivity and behavior. As will become evident in the next chapter, the genes are instrumental, not only in the growth of those mechanisms in which we are all alike, but also in the development of individual differences in these mechanisms. Thus, we all develop eyes, but our eyes differ in certain respects; and this applies to other structures as well, including muscles and brains. ■

LIFE BEGINS

The minute cell with which life begins, and which contains a "blueprint" for further biological development, soon divides to form two identical cells, these to form four, and so on, until a ball-like mass of cells is evident. As growth continues, a cavity appears in the mass of cells so that a hollow sphere is produced. Some of the cells within this sphere give rise to the embryo itself. Others continue their development to produce protective membranes for the developing individual, including the placenta through which it will become attached to the mother's circulatory system.

The mass of cells from which the embryo develops has two layers initially, then three. These are illustrated in Figure 2.1. The external layer, the *ectoderm*, is the chief origin of the sense organs and the nervous system. From the *mesoderm* come the skeleton, muscles, and blood vessels. Vital organs, including the glands of internal secretion, originate in the *endoderm*. Many organs develop partly from one layer and partly from another.

Within two weeks after conception the ectodermal layer has begun to form a neural groove, the origin of which is pictured in Figure 2.2. The groove finally closes to form a hollow tube from which the central nervous system develops. This tube is also illustrated in Figure 2.2.

☐ By the second week after fertilization the developing organism becomes attached to the uterus through what is eventually its umbilical

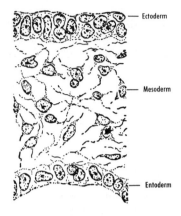

● 2.1

Section from an Early Human Embryo. This section has been enlarged 600 times. The three layers indicated here give rise to the structures of the organism indicated in the text. (From L. B. Arey, *Developmental Anatomy*, 7th ed., Saunders, 1965.)

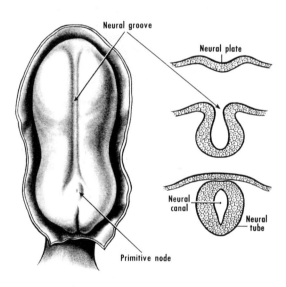

● 2.2

The Neural Tube and Its Origin. The picture at the left shows the neural groove as it appears in a nineteen-day human embryo. As illustrated at the right, a neural plate folds so as to produce a groove, which then closes to become a tube and canal. Out of this structure, a spinal cord and brain emerge.

cord. From this time until the beginning of the third month of prenatal life it is known as an *embryo*. Later, until the time of birth, the organism is referred to as a *fetus*. Nourishment is obtained and waste products are secreted through the mother's circulatory system; but the two systems are not joined. The maternal and fetal blood systems do not intermingle. Oxygen and nourishing substances pass from the maternal to the fetal blood through separating membranes. In a similar way, waste products, including carbon dioxide, pass from the fetal to the maternal circulatory system. The fetal heart, although at an elementary stage of development, begins to beat at the third week. ☐

By the sixth week of prenatal life the embryo has already begun to develop some recognizable structures which will later be basic to the sensory and motor functions of the organism. One can see the beginnings of eyes, arms, and legs. Even hands and feet are beginning to make their appearance.

The embryo of six weeks is motionless. When removed by Caesarian section,* it makes no response, even to pressure on the skin. This is because the necessary receptors and effectors, although present, have not yet become sufficiently developed and neurally interconnected. Such connections are not present until about the eighth week of prenatal life.[1] Then, as shown in Figure 2.3, stimulation may produce responses. Neural developments which precede the appearance of behavior will now be considered. ■

NEURAL DEVELOPMENT

The hollow tube out of which the nervous system develops has three bulblike vesicles at one end, as seen in Figure 2.4. Various brain structures develop from these vesicles, but the stem becomes the spinal cord.

☐ How the spinal nerves originate and develop is a complicated story. In essence, how-

---

* An operation made necessary because continuance of pregnancy would endanger the mother's health.

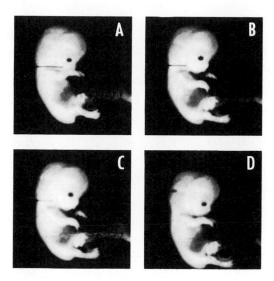

● **2.3**

Early Fetal Behavior. This fetus had a developmental age of about 8½ weeks. Similar responses have been observed in slightly younger fetuses. Note, especially, the downward movement of the arms and their return to the earlier position. There is also, as described in the text, a rotation of the trunk and a movement of the head away from the stimulus. (Copyright by Davenport Hooker)

ever, this is what happens: There are primitive nerve cells within the spinal cord and others just outside. Nerve cells within the cord develop fibers which grow outward, eventually connecting with the growing muscles. These fibers thus have motor functions. From nerve cells just outside the spinal cord, nerve fibers grow in two directions — toward the spinal cord and away from it. Those which grow toward the spinal cord terminate within it, while those which grow outward connect, eventually, with the developing receptors. These nerve cells and their projections thus have sensory functions. Some cells within the spinal cord also develop fibrous projections. Their fibers connect incoming (sensory) and outgoing (motor) impulses. Some such cells send fibers up the cord, where they eventually provide a medium for the interconnection of impulses at various levels of the spinal cord and the carrying of impulses to the brain itself.

When motor, connector, and sensory mechanisms are sufficiently developed and adequately linked, stimulation of a receptor can be followed by a response. Until these developments have taken place the organism is incapable of overt response.

Functional connections like those described first occur in the head region. That is why stimulation of an early fetus (with a developmental age of about eight weeks) must be in the head region to have an effect. Parts of the body below the head are apparently insensitive at this time. Applying a stimulus to them has no observable effect. If the receptors and muscles were sufficiently developed, the absence of response would mean that adequate neural linkages had not yet been established. Sometimes the requisite nerve network has been laid down, but the nerve fibers themselves and the places where they interconnect require further structural and chemical development before impulses can be transmitted. Some of the details relating to this are discussed later in this chapter. Up to now we have avoided much of the technical terminology of neurology in order to present the overall picture of development as simply and generally as possible. □

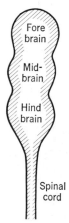

● **2.4**

Beginnings of the Spinal Cord and Brain. The brain develops from the three vesicles, which are named *forebrain, midbrain,* and *hindbrain,* because, in mammals that walk on all fours, the brain is in the forward end, rather than on top, as in man.

The earliest fetal response, as may be seen by referring again to Figure 2.3, is one involving various body parts. The head turns away from the stimulus, the arms move downward, the rump is rotated, and the body arches away from the side stimulated. Within a second or so the fetus resumes its earlier posture. This overall response occurs because motor fibers from the region stimulated are connected with upper spinal nerve fibers which activate the longitudinal back muscles of the opposite side. These fiber interconnections have been studied by neurologists and described in great detail.[2] Actually the arms and legs are involved in this early behavior only because they are moved passively with the trunk. It is some time before the limbs are capable of independent activity. Until this time tactile stimulation brings a generalized response like that described rather than a specific response of the part stimulated.

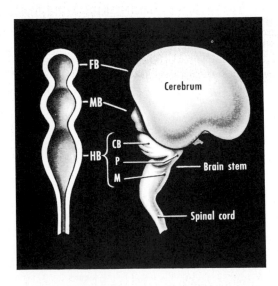

Early Development of the Brain. A neural tube is shown at the left and the brain of a twelve-week fetus at the right. The primitive forebrain (FB) becomes the cerebrum and other structures not shown. The midbrain (MB) undergoes less obvious change. The hindbrain (HB) gives rise to cerebellum (CB), pons (P), and medulla (M).

Although the earliest responses cannot be elicited except through stimulation of the head region, other parts of the body, including the extremities, gradually develop sensitivity. Moreover, fetuses removed from the mother are also observed to move without external stimulation being applied.

By the fourth month of prenatal life, typical reflexes make their first appearance. If a foot is touched, for example, it is withdrawn, then returned to its former position. This reaction is quite specific. Unlike earlier responses, it does not involve activity of other parts of the body. This specificity of response is possible because *reflex arcs* (relatively simple nerve pathways over which impulses may pass from receptors to muscles or glands) have developed within the spinal cord. When stimulated, receptors in the foot send impulses to the lower region of the spinal cord. These are switched over to motor fibers which activate the leg muscles so as to retract the foot. As fetal growth continues, comparable pathways are established throughout the body and reflexes become increasingly evident — grasping when the palm is touched, sucking an object placed in the mouth, movements suggestive of breathing, and so on.[3] By the time of birth there are many reflexes.

While reflex pathways are being established, the brain itself is growing and becoming involved in the developments already described. ■

GROWTH OF THE BRAIN

The three bulblike vesicles at the upper end of the human spinal cord continue their development until the various structures of the brain emerge. These vesicles are shown again in Figure 2.5 and with them the brain structures that have become evident by the time a human organism has been developing for twelve weeks. Note that the *cerebrum*, the largest and most evident brain structure in mammals, is already the dominant structure three months after conception.

The cerebrum continues to grow in size and complexity, but its surface, the *cerebral*

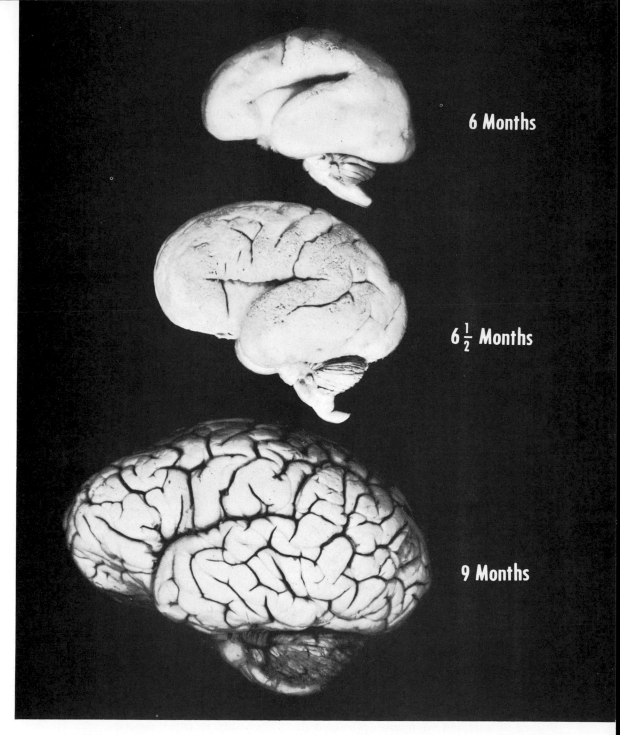

6 Months

6 ½ Months

9 Months

● 2.6
Further Growth of the Brain Until Birth. These brains are pictured in their actual sizes. Thus, the illustration gives an idea of the increasing size of the fetal brain as well as the increasing complexity of its surface structure. Note changes in the cerebellum as well as the cortex. (The Smithsonian Institution)

cortex, remains smooth until around the sixth month of prenatal life. Then, as illustrated in Figure 2.6, convolutions begin to appear. The brain continues to change until, by the time of birth, its main features are those of the adult brain. Nevertheless, the brain at birth is only one-fourth its adult size. It continues to grow in size and complexity, at first by large increments, then smaller and smaller increments, until adulthood.

All of the brain cells that an individual will ever have are present at birth. The brain's increasing size after birth therefore comes from the further growth of its cells in size and complexity and from the growth of supporting tissues and blood vessels, with which the brain is richly supplied.

Although our attention has been focused on the growth of the cerebrum, as the largest brain structure, other structures which take their origin from the primitive neural vesicles are growing in size, complexity, and importance at the same time. Some of these structures participate in fetal behavior before the cerebrum itself is sufficiently mature to do so. Indeed fetuses may develop to the time of birth without a cerebrum, yet their prenatal behavior is comparable with that of normal individuals.[4] This means that the brain structures of significance in early behavior are those below the cerebrum — those referred to in Figure 2.4 as the *cerebellum* and the *brain stem*. These structures are studied in more detail later, but note how the cerebellum grows in size between the third and ninth months of fetal life (Figures 2.5 and 2.6). This structure continues to grow and its growth is especially related to the development of crawling, walking, and other coordinated activities. The pons (Figure 2.5) is also important in this connection, since, among other things, it interconnects the two halves of the cerebellum and also the cerebellum with the cerebrum. The midbrain, also shown in Figure 2.5, is involved in head and eye reflexes. The medulla contains reflex centers essential to life, including those which control respiration.

After this preliminary survey of the developing organism we are prepared to take a closer look at the nervous system and become familiar with some of the technical terminology relating to its structures and functions. Its functions, as revealed in human experience and behavior, will be our prime concern. ■

ELEMENTARY NERVOUS MECHANISMS

We have already observed that the primary purpose of the nervous system is to conduct impulses between receptors and effectors and that such conduction is carried on via sensory, motor, and connecting fibers. The simplest example of this is seen in the reflex arc, which mediates such simple reflexes as withdrawal of the foot or hand when it is subjected to such stimulation as a pinprick.

Reflexes are highly restricted responses. They appear in all organisms that have what is known as a *synaptic nervous system*. In this system, of which our own is the most complicated form, there are relatively discrete nerve cells called *neurons*; each of these makes functional contacts with others through *synapses*.

As illustrated in Plate 1 (facing page 48), each neuron has a *cell body* and projections known as *dendrites* and *axons*. These projections are the fibers referred to in our discussion of fetal development. Dendrites carry impulses toward the cell body, axons away from it. Both may be either long or short. Some are quite long. For example, the dendrites carrying impulses from the skin on one's foot run to a point just outside the lower portion of the spinal cord, where their cell bodies are located. From the cell bodies, axons run into the cord. The longest axons run from the lower end of our spinal cord down to our toes.

When we speak of *nerve fibers*, we refer, as suggested above, to the threadlike structures which extend from the cell body of a neuron and transmit the nerve impulses. The axon is, for example, a nerve fiber. So is the dendrite. Although an isolated nerve fiber may conduct impulses in either direction, such conduction is not typical. Conduction is normally in only one direction. We will see that this is because of the way neurons are laid down in relation to receptors, to effectors, and to each other.

Neurons originating in receptors, i.e., those having sensory functions, are called *afferent*. Their function is input. Afferent dendrites convey impulses to the cell body. From there, impulses are relayed to the next synapse by the axon. Beyond the synapse, impulses pass to dendrites (and sometimes directly to the cell body) of another neuron. Plate 1 shows the second link in this chain as a motor (*efferent*) neuron. However, as we can see in Plate 2, the second link may comprise *association* or *connector* neurons.

After reaching a connector neuron, the impulse passes along it until another synapse is reached. Beyond this may be still other connecting neurons, as indicated later. In Plate 2, a connector neuron is shown linking afferent and efferent neurons. Before activating an effector (in this case a muscle), the impulse must pass along the axon of an efferent neuron connected with the latter.

The series of links that we have described — receptor, afferent neuron, association neuron, efferent neuron, and effector — comprise the already familiar reflex arc. In the intact organism, however, impulses entering the spinal cord not only travel in circuits like those described, but they also ascend the spinal cord and make connections in brain centers. Some such connections are shown schematically in Figure 2.7. Descending impulses (those coming from the brain) have access to efferent neurons as illustrated. Thus they can participate in what is happening at a particular spinal level.

Our relatively simple diagrams represent minimal connections involved when, for instance, your hand touches a hot stove and you pull it away. But thousands of impulses, traveling over many different fibers, are also participating. Some go to your brain and when they reach it, you feel pain in your hand. You look to see how much damage has been done, which means that impulses have come down from your brain, crossed over to efferent neurons connected with the arm, and produced there the movements made in turning the hand. This description ignores, of course, the neural complexities involved in looking at and observing your hand.

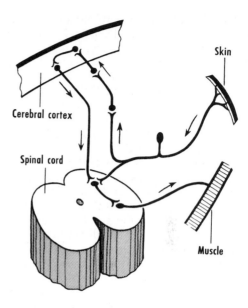

● 2.7
A Schematic Representation of Some Neural Circuits in the Brain and Spinal Cord. Connections on only one side are shown. This diagram, which is simplified to an extreme degree, shows a reflex arc, an ascending and a descending pathway, and upper connections. (After Herrick)

More about synapses

The synapse is an extremely important concept in the understanding of the nervous system. An impulse at a synapse may go no farther. It may, so to speak, be *inhibited*. On the other hand, an impulse coming to a synaptic junction may release impulses in a number of adjacent neurons. This is what is meant when we say that the impulse crosses the synapse. What happens, in reality, is that some chemical and/or electrical activity is initiated by the incoming impulse. If this is insufficient to activate adjacent dendrites, no further transmission occurs, the impulse is inhibited. In fact, many impulses converge upon synapses and, while some are inhibited, others "get across."

When an impulse finds new pathways open to it at the synapse, it may do so through the combined influence of other impulses. We

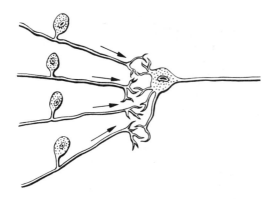

● **2.8**

A Synaptic Junction. Several afferent neurons are shown schematically as converging upon a single efferent neuron. Spatial summation may occur if two or more of the neurons "fire" together. Temporal summation may occur when only one of these incoming neurons is firing, if it is firing frequently.

say, in this instance, that *facilitation*, or *summation*, has occurred.

There are two kinds of summation, *spatial* and *temporal*. The former may be described with reference to Figure 2.8, where several axons are pictured as converging upon a synaptic junction. An impulse coming over one of these axons may not get across. But if impulses are coming into the synapse at the same time from other axons, the effects of each may combine (summate) in such a way as to start up an impulse in a dendrite (or dendrites) beyond the synapse. This kind of summation is said to be *spatial* because the summating impulses come from different neurons — from different places in space. *Temporal* summation, on the other hand, is that which occurs when impulses in the same neuron come one after the other in quick succession. There may be very few impulses per second in this neuron or there may be hundreds per second. One impulse may have insufficient effect to force a passage through the synapse, whereas many impulses coming in quick succession may, through their summated effects, start an impulse in the dendrite (or dendrites) beyond the synapse.

Actually, both spatial and temporal summation occur at the same time. A synaptic junction may be receiving impulses from many axons and, simultaneously, within particular axons, at different rates of discharge, i.e., at different *frequencies*.

Synaptic inhibition and facilitation play a very important role in behavior. Think, for example, of the fact that as you flex your biceps your triceps must relax. This is *reciprocal innervation*. It is brought about because some impulses (in this case going to the biceps) are facilitated and others (going to the triceps) are at the same time inhibited. Strychnine, a drug which facilitates synaptic transmission, destroys such inhibitory-facilitatory relationships, with serious consequences to the organism. A frog injected with strychnine and then stimulated is "torn apart" through the simultaneous contractions of opposing muscle groups.

One effect of the synapse, beyond that of inhibition of certain impulses, is to slow down transmission. We speak of this as *synaptic delay*. It is related to the time required for summation effects to occur and also to anatomical and chemical features of the synapse itself.

This is a greatly oversimplified picture of synaptic junctions. At all levels of the nervous system many afferent axons converge upon motor neurons. At the ends of these, in contact with cells of motor neurons, are knoblike structures, as illustrated in Figure 2.9. Through such knobs, a particular cortical neuron may synapse with possibly thousands of axons.[5]

The nerve impulse

It has long been known that nerve impulses are electrochemical in nature and that the function of a stimulus is to release energy already in the fiber. The general effect, so far as transmission is concerned, is like that of a fuse lit at one end. Chemical activity in one part ignites the next, and so on, until the end of the fuse has been reached. In a nerve fiber, however, the energy is restored soon after it has been used up. Thus the fiber may be activated again and again.

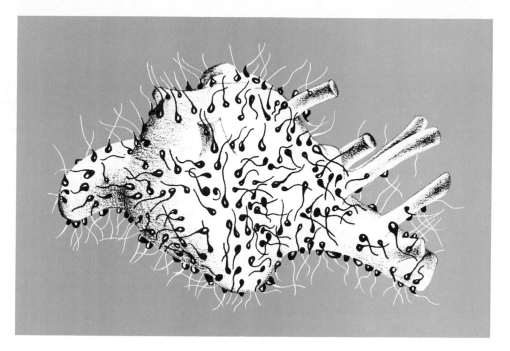

Diagram Showing Synaptic Knobs on the Cell Body and Dendrites of an Afferent Neuron.
The stumps of dendrites are shown toward the right. To the left is the stump of the cell's axon. Knobs are at the end of axons converging upon the motor neuron. These knobs are of particular interest to psychologists, because it has been suggested that their size or chemical constitution may change during the process of learning and thus provide a physical basis for retention. It is generally believed that the impulse coming into one knob, or the impulses coming into only a few of them, may be insufficient to activate the motor neuron (i.e., to set up a postsynaptic impulse). What each presynaptic impulse does, apparently, is to liberate a "specific transmittor substance." In some instances, this has an inhibitory effect, tending, that is, to retard chemical conditions within the synapse that are conducive to arousal of a postsynaptic impulse. Other knobs liberate excitor substances which facilitate transmission. Although the biochemistry of synaptic transmission is not completely known, it seems that "under a barrage of incoming impulses, a neuron must sum the opposing synaptic effects and can fire only when its net excitation exceeds the critical level." Our earlier illustration of spatial and temporal summation at the synapse is thus a highly simplified version of something very complex. (Illustration and quotation from Sir John C. Eccles' "The Physiology of Imagination," *Scientific American*, September 1958.)

The biochemistry of neural transmission is quite complicated. However, the following quotation from a popularized presentation indicates something of its general nature.[6]

□ "Much of our knowledge of the nerve cell has been obtained from the giant axon of the squid, which is nearly a millimeter in diameter. It is fairly easy to probe this useful fiber with microelectrodes and to follow the movement of radioactively labeled substances into it and out of it. The axon membrane separates two aqueous solutions that are almost equally electroconductive and that contain approximately the same number of electrically charged particles, or ions. But the chemical composition of the two solutions is quite different. In the external solution more than 90 per cent of the charged particles are sodium ions (positively charged) and chloride ions (negatively charged). Inside the cell these ions together account for less than 10 per cent of the solutes; there the principal positive ion is potassium and the negative ions are a variety of organic particles (doubtless synthesized within the cell itself) that are too large to diffuse easily through the axon membrane. Therefore the concentration of sodium is about 10 times higher *outside* the axon, and the concentration of potassium is about 30 times higher *inside* the axon. Although the permeability of the membrane to ions is low, it is not indiscriminate; potassium and chloride ions can move through the membrane much more easily than sodium and the large organic ions can. This gives rise to a voltage drop of some 60 to 90 millivolts across the membrane, with the inside of the cell being negative with respect to the outside.

"To maintain these differences in ion concentration the nerve cell contains a kind of pump that forces sodium ions 'uphill' and outward through the cell membrane as fast as they leak into the cell in the direction of the electrochemical gradient. The permeability of the resting cell surface to sodium is normally so low that the rate of leakage remains very small, and the work required of the pumping process amounts to only a fraction of the energy that is continuously being made available by the metabolism of the cell. We do not know in detail how this pump works, but it appears to trade sodium and potassium ions; that is, for each sodium ion ejected through the membrane it accepts one potassium ion. Once transported inside the axon the potassium ions move about as freely as the ions in any simple salt solution. When the cell is resting, they tend to leak 'downhill' and outward through the membrane, but at a slow rate." □

In the resting stage, as described above, a nerve fiber is polarized, with ions on the inside of its membrane being negatively charged with respect to those on the outside. Each part thus resembles a tiny battery with its positive and negative poles. The effect of stimulation is to depolarize the region stimulated — i.e., to allow the positive and negative ions to unite. This disturbance in the stimulated region depolarizes the adjacent region, and so on, as the impulse

traverses the length of the fiber. As we have already said, the polarized state is soon restored, so that further impulses may pass along the fiber. Restoration is accomplished by the so-called sodium pump.

Electrical recordings picked up from nerve fibers demonstrate that stimulation is followed by a wave of negative electrical potential which sweeps the entire length of the fiber. One method of recording this propagated disturbance, or *action potential*, is shown in Figure 2.10.

Nerve fibers differ in thickness and it is known that the speed of the nerve impulse is greater, the thicker the fiber. The maximum speed is roughly four miles a minute.

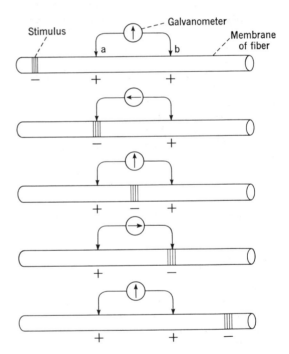

● **2.10**

One Method of Recording Action Currents in a Single Nerve Fiber. We see here a galvanometer making two contacts with a nerve fiber. The stimulus sets off a wave of negative electrical potential which passes along the membrane and deflects the galvanometer as illustrated. With suitable instruments, such deflections may be recorded on photographic film.

• *The all-or-nothing principle.* Impulses traveling along a particular nerve fiber have the same potential, regardless of the nature or intensity of the activating stimulus. The reason for this is perhaps evident in what has been said about a stimulus *releasing* energy in the fiber. It does not contribute energy. What we have here is analogous to a chain of gunpowder. The magnitude of the resulting disturbance is the same whether we ignite the powder with a spark, torch, or hammer blow. In the case of gunpowder, there is an all-or-nothing effect. We get a complete explosion or none at all. Similarly, the nerve fiber is discharged completely or not at all. Once activation occurs, a wave of electrical potential of the same magnitude at each point travels to the end of the fiber. This property which the nerve fiber has of responding completely or not at all is known as the *all-or-nothing principle.*

If part of the fiber is immersed in a narcotizing solution such as alcohol, the potential is weaker while an impulse passes through the solution. The impulse returns to normal, however, in the part of the fiber beyond the solution. This is further proof of the fact that the energy utilized is in the fiber and has nothing to do with the nature of the stimulus which starts the impulse.

• *The refractory period.* Shortly after an impulse has passed and the energy has been used up in a particular portion of the fiber, there is, as already suggested, a re-establishment of the original state, so that another impulse can be transmitted. The interval between passage of an impulse and recovery is known as the *absolute refractory period.* This interval differs from one fiber to another. Its shortest duration is about one-thousandth of a second.

During the absolute refractory period no form of stimulation, of whatever strength, will start a nerve impulse. After this brief period, however, there is a progressive increase in excitability so that stronger than normal stimulation may produce a response. This interval between the absolute refractory phase and a normal excitability level is known as the *relative refractory period.* In order to be effective, a stimulus applied early in this period

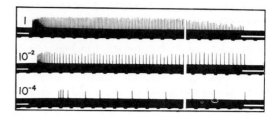

• **2.11**

Action Potentials in an Optic Nerve Fiber. These action potentials were taken from a king crab's optic nerve fiber while its retina was stimulated with steady illumination at three different intensities (represented at the left). Time markings (at the bottom of the record) are in ⅕-second intervals. Note that the relatively high intensity (top) produced many more impulses per unit of time than did the intermediate intensity. The weakest intensity produced a low frequency of impulses. (From H. K. Hartline, *Harvey Lectures*, Academic Press, Inc., 1941, *37*, p. 41.)

must have much greater than normal intensity. As excitability builds up, however, progressively weaker intensities may become effective. The more intense the stimulus, therefore, the sooner it can activate a fiber that has recently responded. This means that a stronger stimulus produces impulses more frequently than does a weaker one (Figure 2.11). The *frequency* of nerve impulses is thus seen as a function of the intensity of the stimulus.

Nerves

We have been discussing the activity of single nerve fibers. Actually, most fibers are in bundles where, like wires in a cable, they are packed tightly together and insulated one from another by a white fatty covering known as a *medullary* or *myelin* sheath. The optic nerve, for example, has an estimated 400,000 fibers. A particular intensity of light excites many of these. An increase in stimulus intensity activates still more. Hence, increasing the intensity has two immediate effects: it *increases the frequency* of discharge in each responding fiber and it *activates more fibers*.

Sensory nerves carry impulses which may

eventually reach specialized areas of the brain. When impulses reach such areas, we have corresponding sensitivity. The optic nerves, for example, send their impulses to brain areas specialized for vision. When these impulses reach such areas we see, and when there is a sufficient increase in the number of impulses pouring into these regions, what we see is seen as brighter. From the foregoing, it is apparent that some of this increase comes from a greater frequency of impulses per fiber and some of it from the fact that more fibers are involved. The same principles are involved in hearing and the other senses, as will be evident in more detail in Chapter 15, which deals with sensitivity. Similarly, motor nerves carry impulses to muscles or glands, where the number of fibers activated and the frequency of discharge in these determines the magnitude of response.

To recapitulate: each impulse triggered by a strong stimulus has the same potential as one set off by a weaker stimulus (the all-or-nothing principle), but there are more impulses per second with the stronger than with the weaker stimulus (the frequency principle). The stronger stimulus may also activate more fibers. The experienced intensity associated with stimulation is dependent upon the number of impulses reaching the relevant part of the brain. This represents a combination of the number of fibers activated and the frequency of discharge in each. Increased magnitude of muscular response has a similar explanation. ■

NEURAL ORGANIZATION

In a synaptic nervous system the impulses travel in paths which are more or less restricted, the course followed depending upon the receptors stimulated, the neural links between these and synaptic junctions, the conditions at synapses, and the circuits opening beyond the latter.

In more complex organisms, the coordination of nerve impulses becomes especially important. Appropriate environmental adjustments can be accomplished only if activities in one part of the organism are correlated with those occurring elsewhere. Activity of any effector must be subordinated to the needs of the organism as a whole.

The elementary model of our nervous system is found in backboned animals like bony fishes and frogs. All backboned organisms are referred to as vertebrates, the reason being that the backbone of each is a chain of bony segments, or vertebrae. The *spinal cord* runs through the center of the vertebral column and projects outward through *spinal nerves* to every receptor and effector below the head region. Impulses enter from the receptors. Then, following appropriate integration in the spinal cord and higher centers, the proper effectors are activated. The higher centers of vertebrate nervous systems are in the head end. We refer to them collectively, and in the most general terms, as the *brain*. Our earlier discussion of neural development referred to such brain structures as the cerebrum (and cerebral cortex), the cerebellum, and the brain stem.

The brain and spinal cord form the *central nervous system*. Nerves connecting these structures with the rest of the body, both on the inside and on the surface, are known collectively as the *peripheral nervous system*.

The spinal cord

The spinal nerves run into the cord between the vertebrae (see Figure 2.12). Each nerve has two roots, a *dorsal* (toward the back) and a *ventral* (toward the belly). The former carry afferent (sensory) and the latter efferent (motor) impulses. Thus, if the dorsal fibers were cut, one would lose sensitivity in the part of the body connected with them. However, if the ventral fibers were cut, the connected part of the body would be paralyzed. In polio, ventral cells are destroyed, hence the corresponding paralysis.

Impulses entering the spinal cord may connect directly, or via connector neurons, with efferent neurons on the same level (Plate 2), thus forming reflex arcs like those already discussed. Connections of this nature underlie reflexes such as the knee jerk (a minimum of two neural links) and withdrawal of

PLATE 1

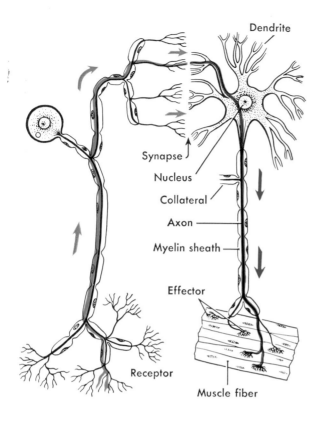

Dendrite

Synapse

Nucleus

Collateral

Axon

Myelin sheath

Effector

Receptor

Muscle fiber

Two Neurons. To the left is a sensory (afferent) neuron; to the right, a motor (efferent) neuron. Nerve impulses are represented as crossing from the end brush of the afferent axon to the dendrites of the efferent neuron. The myelin sheath, a white fatty substance, is referred to later in the text.

PLATE 2

A Spinal Cord Cross-section. The pathway shown schematically here is greatly simplified. Actually there are many incoming, connector, and outgoing fibers as well as connections with ascending and descending paths in the spinal cord. This reflex has three types of units. Some, like the knee jerk, require only two. As described in the text, sensory neurons in this case synapse directly with motor neurons.

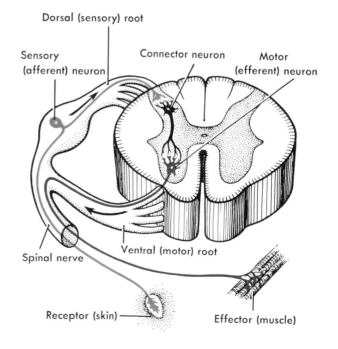

Dorsal (sensory) root

Sensory (afferent) neuron

Connector neuron

Motor (efferent) neuron

Ventral (motor) root

Spinal nerve

Receptor (skin)

Effector (muscle)

PLATE 3

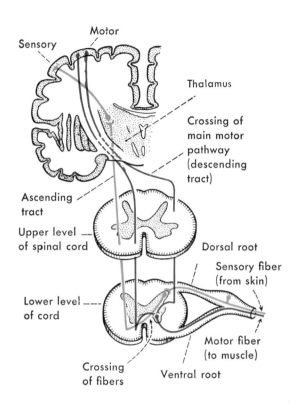

Sensory

Motor

Thalamus

Crossing of main motor pathway (descending tract)

Ascending tract

Upper level of spinal cord

Dorsal root

Sensory fiber (from skin)

Lower level of cord

Motor fiber (to muscle)

Crossing of fibers

Ventral root

Sensory and Motor Pathways. Sensory pathways are shown in blue; motor pathways in red. Impulses from skin receptors (pain and temperature) enter over sensory (afferent) fibers, via the dorsal (back) root of the spinal nerve. Some impulses cross the gray matter of the cord and go up the tract which terminates in the thalamus. From there impulses may go, via a different set of fibers, to the appropriate sensory area of the cortex. Note that these impulses (pain and temperature) cross at the level on which they enter the spinal cord. Other fibers (not shown) ascend on the side on which they enter, and cross later. All ascending fibers thus eventually cross to the opposite side from that on which they enter the cord. Impulses from the motor area of the cortex also cross to the opposite side of the body, some in the lower region of the brain and others in the cord at the level at which contact is made with the motor (efferent) fibers. Descending tracts connect with motor fibers leaving via the ventral (front) root of the spinal nerves. Observe that concentrations of cell bodies, as in the cerebral cortex and in the butterfly-shaped central region of the spinal cord, are represented as gray. These are often referred to, respectively, as the "gray matter" of the cortex and spinal cord. (After Carlson and Johnson.)

PLATE 4

Some Tracts in the Spinal Cord. Tracts shown in red are descending (motor) and those in blue ascending (sensory). Several sensory tracts are not represented. (After Carlson and Johnson.)

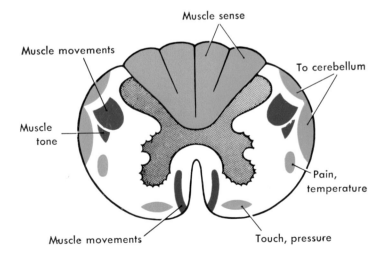

Muscle sense

Muscle movements

To cerebellum

Muscle tone

Pain, temperature

Muscle movements

Touch, pressure

PLATE 5

A Schematic Representation of the Autonomic Nervous System. Some typical relations between the visceral and other internal organs and the two major divisions of the autonomic nervous system, from various sources. Connections with the sympathetic system are represented in red; those with the parasympathetic in blue. Note that the upper (cranial) parasympathetic connections come from cranial nerves, the most important of which, from this standpoint, is nerve X (the Vagus). While most of the internal organs have dual connections with the autonomic system, an apparent exception is the adrenal gland, the only known autonomic connections of which are with the sympathetic division. This division accelerates adrenal functions. It also accelerates the functions of certain other organs, like the heart. The functions of these organs are normally held in check by the parasympathetic. On the other hand, the functions of the stomach and certain other organs are accelerated by the parasympathetic and retarded by the sympathetic.

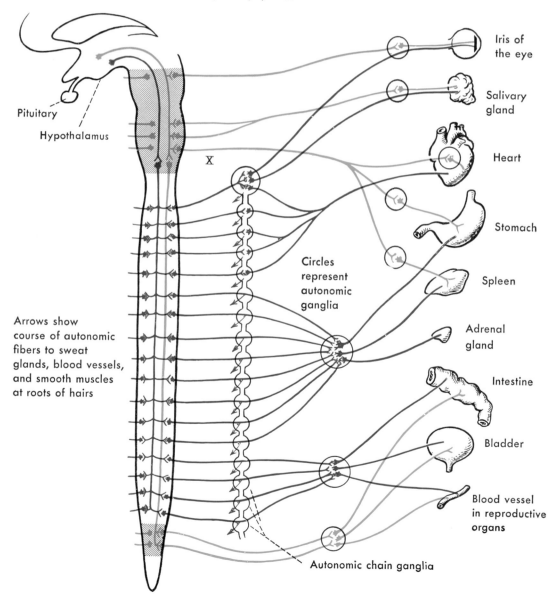

Pituitary

Hypothalamus

X

Circles represent autonomic ganglia

Arrows show course of autonomic fibers to sweat glands, blood vessels, and smooth muscles at roots of hairs

Iris of the eye

Salivary gland

Heart

Stomach

Spleen

Adrenal gland

Intestine

Bladder

Blood vessel in reproductive organs

Autonomic chain ganglia

PLATE 6

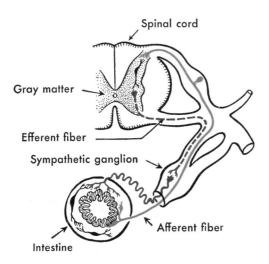

Spinal cord

Gray matter

Efferent fiber

Sympathetic ganglion

Afferent fiber

Intestine

Some Sympathetic Connections with the Spinal Cord. Afferent (sensory) connections are blue. Sympathetic connections all efferent (motor), are red. The intestine, for example, is activated by sympathetic fibers. There are two sets of efferent fibers concerned. One, represented by the broken line, comes from the spinal cord into a group of nerve cells (ganglion) in the sympathetic system. Here such fibers connect with others (wavy line) which activate the intestine. The intestine also has afferent connections with the central nervous system. Sets of fibers (blue) go from it to the dorsal gray matter of the cord, there making reflex connections on the same level, as well as sending impulses up the cord. Parasympathetic connections with the intestine are not shown. Compare this figure with Plate 5. (Modified from Turner's *General Endocrinology*, Philadelphia: Saunders, 1949, p. 214.)

PLATE 7

Some Interconnecting Circuits. Note the reverberating circuit (feedback) at A. (After Ranson and Clark.)

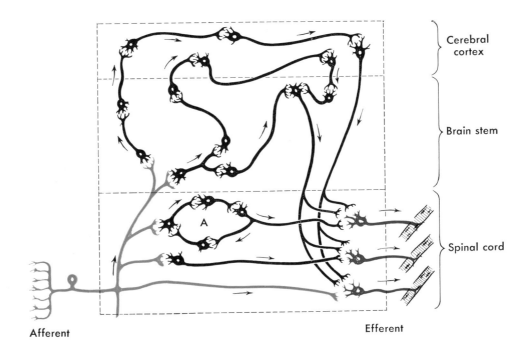

Cerebral cortex

Brain stem

Spinal cord

Afferent

Efferent

the hand from a painful stimulus (involving at least three neural links). In a frog with all neural mechanisms above its spinal cord removed, we observe relatively uncomplicated reflexes. For example, if we pinch the frog's foot, that foot is retracted but nothing else happens.

In an intact organism, however, impulses are seldom (if ever) confined to particular segments. Some ascend the spinal cord and, in the brain stem, cerebellum, or cerebrum, give rise to impulses which descend the cord to connect with efferent neurons. Plate 3 shows the general nature of such connections. Sensory impulses (ascending) are represented in blue and motor impulses (descending) in red. All ascending impulses cross to the other side, some at the level of entry and some higher up. Likewise, all impulses from the motor control regions of the cerebral cortex eventually reach effectors on the opposite side of the body.

The general position of the columns of ascending and descending fibers can be gathered from Plate 4, which represents some of them schematically. At the center of this spinal cord cross section, we see a butterfly-shaped mass of *gray matter*. This contains association neurons and cell bodies of efferent neurons. The ascending and descending columns form the *white matter* of the spinal cord. They have a whitish appearance because the fibers within are covered by a white fatty sheath.

Since nerve impulses travel up and down the spinal cord and are integrated at higher levels of the central nervous system, it is not surprising that reactions of an intact organism are much more complicated than those of a frog with its brain removed. One not only withdraws the affected hand when stuck with a splinter, but he uses his other hand to remove the offending object. Then he may do such things as suck the wound, paint it with an antiseptic, or bandage it. Even the simplest of these acts (withdrawing the splinter) requires the integration of countless nerve impulses and involves various levels of the central nervous system, including the cerebral cortex.

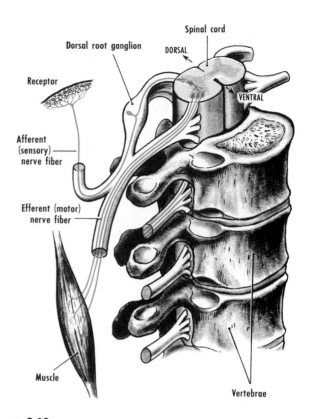

● **2.12**
The Spinal Cord. The cord runs along the center of the vertebral column, and the spinal nerves emerge between the vertebrae.

Autonomic mechanisms

The autonomic nervous system receives its name from the fact that, in structure and function, it is more or less autonomous. It carries on its functions for the most part automatically, without our intentional control and without arousing in us a very clear awareness of the activities involved. Many of its connections are with organs of the abdomen, known in general as the *viscera*.

There are two divisions. One of these, the *sympathetic nervous system*, is significantly involved in emotional behavior. It therefore receives further consideration in the chapter on emotion. This system tends to function as a unit and to have diffuse effects.

As is apparent in Plate 5, the sympathetic nervous system (red) occupies a middle position, with all of its connections to the central nervous system being made through the spinal cord. Note, too, that impulses do not go directly to the organs activated, but reach them only after crossing synapses in groups of nerve cells, the *autonomic ganglia*. The other autonomic division, known as the *parasympathetic nervous system*, is also illustrated in Plate 5. This system (blue) has an upper and lower division.

Most of the internal organs have dual connections with the autonomic nervous system, one with the sympathetic and one with the parasympathetic division. Such connections are also shown in Plate 5.

Generally speaking, the autonomic nervous system is part of what was referred to earlier as the *peripheral nervous system.*

The autonomic system is, by definition, a *motor* system. It acts upon the various organs connected with it by accelerating or slowing down their functions. The activity of some organs is accelerated by the sympathetic division and held in check by the parasympathetic division; the activity of others is checked by the sympathetic division and accelerated by the parasympathetic. For example: the heart, which beats faster in emotion, is accelerated by sympathetic fibers and maintained at a normal rate by parasympathetic fibers. Stomach activity, on the other hand, is retarded by sympathetic connections and accelerated by parasympathetic connections. The two systems thus work in opposition, with the sympathetic tending to take over in emotion-provoking situations and the parasympathetic tending to restore a normal balance. The adrenal gland, which is connected only with the sympathetic system, secretes adrenalin and other hormones. During emotion this secretion of adrenalin is accelerated, with resulting diffuse effects upon various bodily processes. More attention is given to adrenal functions when we discuss emotion and personality.

Although the autonomic nervous system is by definition a motor system, most of the organs controlled by it also have afferent connections with the spinal cord and brain stem.

Plate 6 shows afferent as well as sympathetic connections as they occur at spinal levels. Impulses reaching the brain over such afferent channels underlie whatever awareness we have of what is taking place within our internal organs. So-called butterflies in the stomach, intestinal cramps, and feelings of nausea are dependent upon these connections.

The brain stem

All nerves which do not enter the spinal cord reach the central nervous system via the brain stem (see Figure 2.13). Because they enter the head (cranium), these are designated *cranial nerves*. Afferent cranial nerves come from such sensory structures as taste receptors, the eyes, and the ears. Efferent cranial nerves run from the brain stem to muscles and glands in the head region, where they activate facial muscles and duct glands such as those involved in weeping. But some cranial nerves carry both afferent and efferent fibers. One with such mixed functions (nerve X, known as the *vagus* or "wandering" nerve) sends motor impulses (over its efferent fibers) to organs like the stomach and intestines. It conveys impulses back from these (over its afferent fibers) to the brain stem. (Look again at Plate 5.) There are twelve pairs of cranial nerves and although some are mentioned specifically in later chapters dealing with sensory, motor, and emotional functions, there is no need for the beginner in psychology to learn their names.

All impulses traveling between the spinal cord and the cerebral cortex must run through the brain stem. Many make synaptic connections at this level with (1) cranial nerves, (2) other ascending or descending fibers, and (3) important integrating centers within the brain stem itself. Some such connections are schematically represented in Plate 7. This also shows how impulses, once they enter a circuit, may continue to travel around it. Such *reverberating circuits* occur at all levels of the central nervous system, but they are especially active within the brain stem and cerebrum. Circuits involving various structures of the brain stem and cerebellum are responsible for the control of such automatic and usually unconscious acts as breathing, maintaining

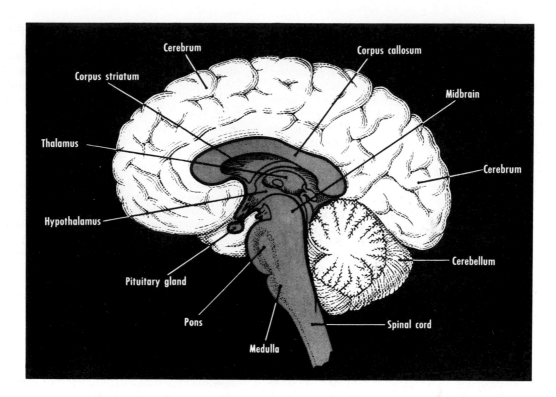

Cerebrum

Corpus callosum

Corpus striatum

Midbrain

Thalamus

Cerebrum

Hypothalamus

Cerebellum

Pituitary gland

Pons

Spinal cord

Medulla

● 2.13

The Relation of the Brain Stem to the Cerebellum and the Cerebrum. The brain stem shown in gray comprises the medulla, pons, midbrain, hypothalamus, and the thalamus, although the two latter structures, together with the corpus striatum, are sometimes regarded as part of the upper brain stem and sometimes as basal ganglia of the cerebrum, hence part of that structure. The corpus callosum is part of the cerebrum since it connects the two cerebral hemispheres. The *medulla* is concerned with reflex physiological activities like breathing. The *pons* is a bridge connecting the lobes of the cerebellum with the opposite side of the cerebrum and with each other. It is especially important in muscular coordination. The *midbrain* is involved in auditory and visual reflexes. The *hypothalamus* (which means "below the thalamus") participates in many emotional and motivational functions and will be referred to time and again in later chapters. Many automatic reflex activities are under the control of motor centers in and around the *thalamus*. This is also an elaborate switchboard mechanism for the projection onto the cerebral cortex of impulses coming from receptors — impulses from the skin are sent, via the thalamus, to one part of the cerebrum, impulses from the eyes to another, and so on. The thalamus may also mediate a simple form of learning, and we will refer to it in this connection when conditioned reflexes are discussed. The *corpus striatum*, although strictly speaking not a part of the brain stem, is included to show its anatomical relation to the brain-stem structures with which its functions are closely integrated. Its functions are also closely tied in with those of the cerebellum. Motor incoordinations such as tremors and muscular rigidity often result from injuries in the corpus striatum. Actually this is a very complicated structure, containing several basal ganglia (groupings of nerve cells) as well as pathways descending to the brain stem from the motor areas of the cerebral cortex, fibers referred to *in toto* as the *internal capsule*.

equilibrium, and walking. Take walking, for example. Each leg muscle responds to nerve impulses from the brain stem. The resulting contractions stimulate kinesthetic receptors within the muscle. Thus impulses are sent back to the central nervous system. A continual feedback of this nature keeps the brain stem informed about activities in the muscles from one moment to the next. It is this feedback which allows walking to occur as it does — coordinated, yet without our having to attend to what our muscles are doing.

The general anatomy of the brain stem is shown in Figure 2.13, the legend of which identifies and describes the functions of its major structures. Some of these, especially the *hypothalamus* and the *reticular formation*, receive further attention in later discussions dealing with emotion, wakefulness, motivation, and the coordination of various bodily activities.

The cerebellum

This structure, as we said in discussing its early development, is a major mechanism for coordination. It coordinates reflex activities in various parts of the body — activities like those involved in the flying of birds, in the swimming of fish, in walking, and even in speaking, writing, and playing tennis or football.

Adjacent to the brain stem at about the level of the pons, the cerebellum has widespread connections, not only with the pons itself but with various other parts of the brain stem, including the reticular formation (Figure 2.14, and legend). There are also connections with structures at the base of the cerebrum (especially the *corpus striatum*) and with ascending and descending pathways in the spinal cord. Impulses are fed into the cerebellum from two types of receptors, the static and the kinesthetic. Static receptors (located in the nonauditory labyrinth of the ear) respond to changes in the position of the body. Impulses entering the cerebellum from these enable the organism to compensate for changes in position, thus maintaining equilibrium. Kinesthetic receptors (in the muscles, tendons, and joints) indicate the changing activities (the contractions and relaxations) of muscles throughout the body. This information is in-

tegrated in the cerebellum and associated mechanisms. Thus impulses returning to the motor mechanisms initiate the proper reactions, and in appropriate sequences. If a bird's cerebellum is destroyed, the bird can still move

● **2.14**

The Reticular Formation. This runs through the center of the brain stem from the level of the medulla to that of the lower thalamus, as shown by the cross-hatching. It is a small network (*reticulum*) of intricately interconnected nerve cell groupings which have indirect connections with many other structures, including the cerebral cortex. The ascending nerve tracts, carrying sensory messages directly to the thalamus and via it to the cerebral cortex, give off collaterals which enter the reticular formation. This, in turn, discharges impulses which, entering the cerebral cortex indirectly and diffusely, have an activating effect upon it. Nerve pathways are shown in gold. It has been claimed, on the basis of experimental evidence discussed in the chapter on motivation, that "a background of maintained activity in this ascending activating system is . . . essential for consciousness, wakefulness, and alertness." (A. Brodal, *The Reticular Formation of the Brain Stem*, Thomas, 1956, p. 62.) But the reticular system also has inhibiting functions. Its lower part is involved in feedback circuits with the cerebral cortex which have a restraining, or inhibiting, influence over certain motor activities.

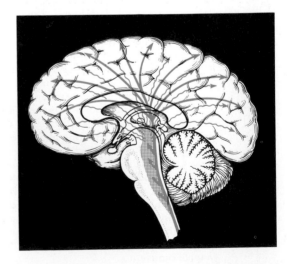

but it cannot fly. This is because the separate activities required for flying are inappropriately patterned and timed. Similarly, a man with his cerebellum seriously injured is unable to walk normally. When he walks, he does so with a jerky, incoordinated gait known as *cerebellar ataxia*.

The cerebrum

The central nervous system of a fish or frog is little more than a spinal cord, a cerebellum, and a brain stem. As indicated in Figure 2.15, the dogfish has no cerebrum. The nearest thing to it is a forebrain enlarged and specialized to serve the sense of smell. This is, in fact, referred to as a "smell brain." Since the smell brain foreshadows the cerebrum of higher forms, it is also called the "old brain." All higher vertebrates retain these primitive brain structures, but with the so-called new brain superimposed on them. Birds and lower mammals like the rat also have a large smell brain. As shown in Figure 2.15, however, they have a cerebrum too.

The cerebrum becomes larger and more elaborate as we go from rat to man. Its surface turns inward (invaginates) in many places to form a large number of convolutions, thus providing a more extensive surface within the limited space of the cranium. The significance of this is that it provides space for an increasing number of brain cells. These become concentrated in the outer surface of the cerebrum and form the *cerebral cortex*: literally, the brain's bark. It is estimated that the human cortex contains nine billion nerve cells. These are interconnected to form the most complex structure known to man. Electronic brains,

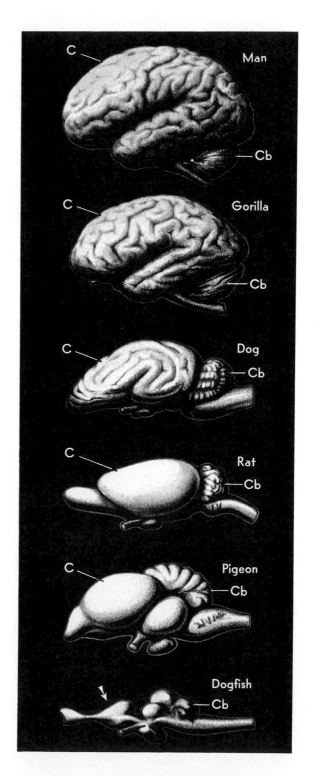

● **2.15**
The Brain from Fish to Man. These brains were drawn to the same length so that adequate details could appear in the smaller ones. The cerebrum (C) is absent in a dogfish, but an arrow indicates the location of comparable structures. Invaginations are first evident in animals like the cat and dog, the latter of which is represented here. Note that the gorilla and human brains are highly invaginated. *Cb* is the cerebellum.

which are designed to carry on certain functions of the cerebral cortex and which do this on an elementary level, are of course simple in comparison.

The cerebrum has two elaborately interconnected halves, the *cerebral hemispheres.* In each of these there are four lobes having special functions. They are considered later in this chapter.

□ From lower animals to man the brain grew larger. But man's brain is by no means the largest. It weighs about three pounds. Elephants have brains weighing up to ten pounds and whales up to fourteen pounds. The latter are of course extremely large animals and the increased size of their brains is offset by the fact that there is such a large body to control. However, the great apes, which are closest to us in size, have brains much smaller than ours. A gorilla's brain, for example, weighs less than one pound.

It has been suggested that the ratio of brain weight to body weight might provide a better physiological index of the evolution of intelligence than brain weight alone. This ratio in whales is 1/10,000. That is, for every 10,000 pounds of body weight, there is only one pound of brain tissue. Elephants fare much better, with a ratio of 1/500. Gorillas have a ratio of 1/250. Man's ratio is 1/50. However, such ratios are not dependable. For example, some monkeys also have a 1/50 ratio. On this basis alone, therefore, monkeys should be as intelligent as human beings.[7]

Of possibly greater significance than the weight of the brain in proportion to body weight is the ratio of brain weight to spinal cord weight. The spinal cord, as we have seen, is concerned with relatively simple sensorimotor integrations. Thus a brain no heavier than its spinal cord would presumably serve little more than elementary functions. A frog's brain actually weighs less than its spinal cord. In successively higher vertebrates, however, the brain becomes larger in relation to the spinal cord. In humans, the brain is more than 50 times the weight of the spinal cord. The gorilla's brain, on the other hand, is only 15 times the weight of its spinal cord.[8]

In terms of this index, therefore, we appear to be ahead of all other vertebrates. □

• *Associative functions.* The nervous system in lower forms of animal life is specialized for particular sensory and motor functions. There are few, if any, nerve cells without such duties. During the course of evolution, however, as the brain became larger and more complicated, there appeared an increasing number of brain cells without such specialized functions. These are quite evident in the *association areas* of the cerebral cortex.

Association tissues are modified by what happens to the organism, and such modifications serve to represent past experience. Because of these persisting changes, the organism may recall what it has learned and, in addition, utilize such information in adjusting to new situations.

How brain cells store information is not known. It has been suggested that the process may be analogous to the storing of information on electromagnetic tape. After a record is made we can play it back. In mechanical brains, information retained electromagnetically is combined in various ways to provide solutions to arithmetical and other problems. The human brain uses comparable information to solve even more intricate problems, including how to devise machines which simulate its own activities.

Rats have enough association tissue to solve elementary problems of adjustment by "putting two and two together" — that is, by reasoning.* Higher animals like monkeys and apes have larger association areas than do rats. Thus they have better memory than rats, they remember over a longer period of time, and they solve problems of much greater complexity. The human brain mediates such functions at a still higher level and, in addition, gives us the ability to acquire and utilize language. These and other functions of the human cerebral cortex are worthy of special attention. The following pages describe some details of cortical structure and the related functions. ■

* Reasoning in animals, as defined above, is discussed in Chapter 14.

THE HUMAN CEREBRAL CORTEX

The cerebral cortex, the convoluted surface of the cerebral hemispheres, makes its appearance about the sixth month of prenatal life, as indicated earlier and illustrated in Figure 2.6 (p. 41). At that time there are few invaginations, and the whole structure of the cerebral hemispheres is relatively simple. The cerebral cortex of a mature human brain is illustrated in Figure 2.16.

The two halves of the cerebrum, the *cerebral hemispheres*, are connected through the brain stem, but more obviously and directly through the *corpus callosum*. Large masses of nerve fibers cross from the cortex of one hemisphere to the cortex of the other through the corpus callosum. If the right and left hemispheres are pried apart along the fissure which runs the length of the cerebrum (see Figure 2.16A), one can see the upper part of the corpus callosum. If this structure were cut, the only remaining connections between the hemispheres would be through certain tracts in the brain stem, including the *optic chiasma*, which is shown in about the center of Figure 2.16B. One can see there the two stumps of the optic nerves. Each of these carries fibers to both halves of the cerebral cortex. The optic nerve on the right, for example, sends about half its fibers to the right, and half to the left. If the latter fibers were cut, all visual impulses from the right eye would be confined to the right cerebral cortex; and correspondingly for the left eye.

☐ Once taken for granted as a structure merely to hold together and interconnect the cerebral hemispheres, the corpus callosum is now receiving closer attention because of a new type of experiment involving so-called *split brain preparations*. These are animals in which the hemispheres are separated at the level of the corpus callosum by cutting through this structure.[9]

If the crossing fibers of the optic chiasma are cut, as described above, stimuli presented to the right eye send impulses only to the right cerebral cortex. Suppose, then, that we leave the corpus callosum intact for the time

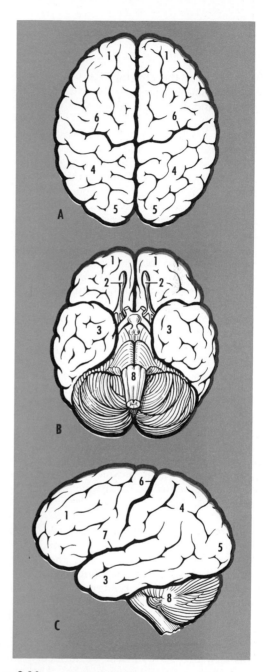

● 2.16

Three Aspects of the Human Brain. A is Dorsal; **B** is Basal; **C** is Lateral. The numbers refer to the following things: 1, frontal lobe; 2, olfactory bulb; 3, temporal lobe; 4, parietal lobe; 5, occipital lobe; 6, central fissure (fissure of Rolando); 7, lateral fissure (fissure of Sylvius); 8, brain stem and cerebellum.

being, but cut the crossing optic tracts. This has been done in monkeys. Now we cover the left eye and teach the monkey a visual discrimination habit with the right eye. After the habit has been learned, we cover the right eye, expose the left, and test to see whether the habit is retained. The findings show that such habits are retained under these circumstances. This means that although only the right cerebral cortex received visual stimulation, the information contained in such stimulation was transmitted to the left side of the brain, presumably through the corpus callosum. That this was so became evident when the same kind of experiment was performed with split-brain monkeys. In these animals, what the right eye and right half of the brain had learned was limited to that side. When the left eye was exposed and the trained eye covered, the animal acted as though confronted by a new problem to be learned. It has also been demonstrated that a split-brain animal can learn two different discrimination problems simultaneously, one with the right eye and one with the left.[10] In an animal with its corpus callosum intact, the presentation of two such problems simultaneously would lead to great confusion. The corpus callosum, then, is a mechanism that provides for one hemisphere a "carbon copy," as it were, of what the other learns. ☐

Referring again to Figure 2.16A, note that the large area from about the middle to the front of each hemisphere is the *frontal lobe*. Just behind it is the *parietal lobe*. Toward the back of the cerebrum, the parietal lobe merges with the *occipital lobe*.

A view from below the brain (Figure 2.16B) shows how the cerebral hemispheres are related to the brain stem and cerebellum. This view also shows a lobe not evident from above, namely, the *temporal lobe*. Also evident are the olfactory bulbs (relics of the old smell brain) and the already mentioned optic nerves. Other cranial nerves also enter the brain stem. It is through these that many impulses reach the thalamus and, finally, the cerebral cortex.

A side view of the left cerebral hemisphere appears in Figure 2.16C. Here we see the four lobes more clearly. The frontal and parietal lobes are separated by a long deep central fissure, the *fissure of Rolando*. The temporal and frontal lobes are separated by a long natural fissure, the *fissure of Sylvius*. Situated at the extreme back of the hemisphere, and not clearly marked off from the adjoining lobes, is the *occipital lobe*.

Inside the cerebrum

The thickness of the cerebral cortex varies, depending upon the region measured. Its greatest thickness, however, is about half an inch. We have already, in discussing the development of the cerebral cortex, and in describing its synaptic junctions, called attention to its great complexity. The complexity of cortical integration may also be illustrated by the assertion that "one incoming axon may influence up to five thousand neurons" and that each of these may have dendritic connections with four thousand nerve cells.[11]

The course of incoming fibers, those projected to the cerebral cortex from the thalamus, are schematically represented in Figure 2.17A. Also shown are paths over which descending impulses travel. These impulses terminate, eventually, in effectors connected with the brain stem and spinal cord. In addition to countless fibers entering and leaving the cerebral cortex in the manner illustrated, there are interconnecting paths within the cortex (Figure 2.17B).

Interconnections at the cortical level may result in the initiation, facilitation, or inhibition of activities in various parts of the body. Such interconnections are also responsible for intrasensory and intersensory associations. For example, certain visual stimuli arouse visual associations (intrasensory) and auditory, tactual, or olfactory associations (intersensory). Thus the sight of a word (visual stimulation) arouses meanings which involve visual and other sensory association areas. Take the word APPLE. What associations does it have for you? Some are visual — representing the apple's shape, size, and color. Some are kinesthetic — representing its weight and the shape that we feel when it is in our

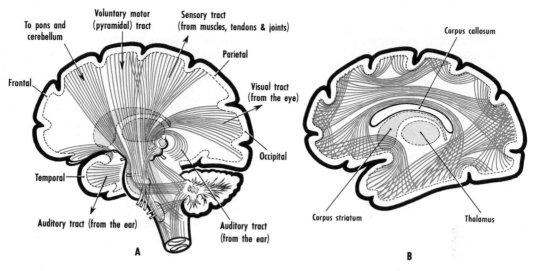

● **2.17**

Paths of the Human Brain. A. Projection paths. The sensory projections begin in the thalamus. Here impulses from the eyes are switched to the occipital, those from the ears to the temporal, and those from the muscles and skin to the somaesthetic region. Observe at the bottom of the brain stem that some motor fibers cross to the other side while some descend on the same side. **B.** Association paths. Observe how each part of the cortex is connected with other parts. These diagrams are, of course, simplified to an extreme degree. (After Starr)

hand. Some associations represent the odor and taste of apples. Thinking of apple cider or apple pie, of keeping the doctor away, and of Adam and Eve in the Garden of Eden are further associative complications. Intrasensory and intersensory associations are made possible, in the first place, by information somehow stored in the brain cells and, in the second place, by the fact that brain cells in different locations and representing certain aspects of past experience are interconnected. Without such interconnections, each stimulus situation would arouse only the activities and correlated experiences peculiar to itself.

Processes like imagining, thinking, and reasoning are especially dependent upon integration of information represented in the various areas of the cortex, hence upon such association paths as those illustrated. We say "such paths" because no picture could possibly do justice to the actual complexity of interconnecting fibers. Sir Charles Sherrington, the eminent neurologist, represented this complexity in the following verbal picture of human cerebral activity:

☐ "Imagine [he said] a scheme of lines and nodal points, gathered together at one end into a great ravelled knot, the brain, and at the other trailing off to a sort of stalk, the spinal cord. Imagine activity in this shown by little points of light. Of these some [that are] stationary flash rhythmically, faster or slower. Others are travelling points streaming in serial trains at various speeds. The rhythmic stationary lights lie at the nodes. The nodes are both goals whither converge, and junctions whence diverge, the lines of travelling lights. . . .

"Suppose we choose the hour of deep sleep. Then only in some sparse and out-of-the-way places are nodes flashing and trains of light points running. . . . The great knotted headpiece of the whole sleeping system lies for the most part dark. . . . Occasionally at places in it lighted points flash or move but soon subside. . . .

"Should we continue to watch the scheme we should observe after a time an impressive change which suddenly accrues. In the great head end which had been mostly darkness spring up myriads of twinkling stationary lights. . . . It is as though activity from one of those local places which continued restless in the darkened main-mass suddenly spread far and wide and invaded all. The great topmost sheet of the mass . . . where hardly a light had twinkled or moved, becomes now a sparkling field of rhythmic flashing points with trains of travelling sparks hurrying hither and thither. The brain is waking and with it the mind is returning. It is as if the milky way entered upon some cosmic dance. Swiftly the head mass becomes an enchanted loom where millions of flashing shuttles weave a dissolving pattern, always a meaningful pattern though never an abiding one."[12] □

Electroencephalograms

Nerve cells in the brain stem and cerebrum give off electrical discharges which, with suitable equipment involving very high amplification, may be recorded as electroencephalograms (EEG's), or what are popularly referred to as "brain waves." Although leads may be inserted into the nervous system directly, human EEG's are usually recorded from the scalp.

The various regions of the brain stem and cerebral cortex yield somewhat different rhythms. Other differences are dependent upon the kind of activity in progress and upon the influence of drugs or disease. The most commonly recorded rhythm (*alpha*) is obtained in clearest form from the occipital and parietal lobes when the individual is resting with his eyes closed. This rhythm has about ten pulsations per second. When the individual opens his eyes, the wave flattens out. As one falls asleep, his alpha rhythm is replaced by a rhythm (*delta*), less regular but of relatively high amplitude. During an epileptic attack there are marked pulsations without any perceptible rhythm. These fluctuations sometimes suggest an "electrical brainstorm."

Although many different EEG's have been identified and related to particular structures

and activities, it would divert us too much to consider them in more detail at this point.[13] ■

A CLOSER LOOK AT CORTICAL FUNCTIONS

The cerebral cortex has four basic functions: to *receive* messages from lower brain centers related to the receptors, to *send* messages to the effectors under its control, to *retain* certain effects of past activity, and to *integrate* incoming and outgoing impulses, often in terms of what has been retained from the past. The retaining and integrating functions are together referred to as *associative*. With one exception having to do with speech, all of the above functions are served equally by corresponding areas in *both* cerebral hemispheres.

Sensory functions

Specialized areas for reception of impulses originating in receptors are located in the parietal, occipital, and temporal lobes.

The *parietal* lobes receive impulses from *somaesthetic* (body-feeling) receptors in the skin and from the kinesthetic receptors in muscles, tendons, and joints. In patients whose cortex has been exposed prior to brain surgery, electrical stimulation within a parietal area is often followed immediately by such statements as, "My hand feels warm," "I have electrical feelings in my leg," or "I can feel my leg moving," even though the limbs mentioned are not stimulated.[14] Such feelings are referred to the opposite side of the body — that is, stimulation of the right parietal lobe leads to feelings in limbs on the left side of the body. This is because, as pointed out earlier, tracts ascending the spinal cord cross to the side opposite that on which they originated. It is of interest, furthermore, to note that patients suffering from epilepsy often report body feelings of various kinds prior to a seizure. This probably means that the disturbance in such instances begins in a parietal area.

The visual areas are in the *occipital lobes.* Each eye, as will be more clearly apparent when we discuss vision, sends impulses to both occipital lobes. Later we shall also observe that ability to differentiate visual details, including color differences like red and blue, depends upon the dispersion in this region of impulses originating in various structures of the eyes. Surgeons have noted that electrical stimulation within the occipital cortex leads to visual experiences, like flashing lights, whirling colors and sometimes stars or particular colors such as pink or blue. Similar experiences are sometimes reported by people with epilepsy just preceding a seizure, suggesting a cortical disturbance originating in the occipital region.

Impulses from our auditory receptors go to the *temporal lobes*. Each ear is represented in both lobes, as indicated more fully in the chapter on hearing. Direct stimulation of a temporal lobe may produce humming, buzzing, or other auditory experiences. Epileptic seizures are often preceded by such experiences, presumably because the seizure first involves the temporal cortex.

Our other senses do not have such clearly established cortical locations as is the case with somaesthesis, vision, and hearing. Even one of the somaesthetic senses, pain, has no clear cortical representation. Surgeons carrying out necessary operations have, in different patients, cut into every part of the cerebral cortex, yet without reports of pain.* It is possible that this sense is mediated at subcortical levels.

The olfactory sense utilizes what is left in us of the smell brain,† although some cortical area not yet located may also be involved. The sense of taste, which is closely related to that of smell, may involve cortical as well as subcortical mechanisms, but there is no generally accepted conclusion about this.

---

* The only pain is that experienced while the scalp is being penetrated prior to the brain operation. This pain can of course be prevented by use of a local anesthetic.

† Recent studies on the so-called limbic system, or "visceral brain," which was long considered to have olfactory functions, show that this has centers concerned in the elaboration of certain motivational states of the organism. For a further discussion, see Chapters 8 and 9.

Motor control

Our motor cortex is a relatively narrow strip of tissue running along the frontal portion of the fissure of Rolando, which was pictured in Figure 2.16 (p. 55). Within this area are many large pyramid-shaped (*pyramidal*) cells. Destruction of these is followed by loss of voluntary movement in the effectors activated by them. This is because the axons which normally carry impulses to lower levels degenerate. In post mortem examination the degeneration may be traced to levels of the brain stem or spinal cord in which synaptic connections with efferent neurons occur.

Some motor fibers cross to the opposite side of the body when they reach the level of the medulla but others do not cross until, at various levels of the spinal cord, they connect at synapses with efferent neurons. Look again at Plate 3, where the motor paths are shown in red. These are not the only paths from the motor cortex to lower levels, but they are the main ones.

Since all motor fibers eventually cross to the opposite side, injury to the motor cortex is followed by paralysis on the opposite side of the body. Paralysis may be restricted or widespread, depending upon the extent of the injury. There is often recovery from paralysis, especially when it is caused by circulatory disorders (blood clots or hemorrhages), which clear up. But even when motor cells are irreparably destroyed, there may be some recovery of voluntary control. This is particularly true when appropriate training of the affected limbs is undertaken. When it does occur, recovery is due to the taking over of lost motor functions by cells adjacent to those destroyed. The term for this is *vicarious functioning*.[15]

Electrical stimulation of the motor cortex has led to the discovery of regions which control various parts of the body (Figure 2.18). When the upper region is stimulated, for example, the limbs on the opposite side of the body, or parts of them, are forced to move. When the lower portion is stimulated, the face may twitch or the mouth open or close. But the points from which these responses

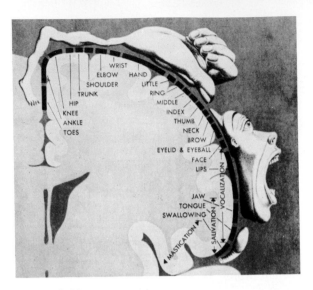

● 2.18

A Motor Homunculus. This represents the voluntary motor control area of the human cerebral cortex. It is shown for only one side here; the other side is similar. Note the large proportion of tissue given over to control of the hands and face. These structures are accordingly enlarged in the drawing. (After Penfield; courtesy, *Scientific American*.)

are aroused are not absolutely fixed.[16] We should not, in all strictness, regard control of an activity as localized at a particular point, especially since stimulation at such a point sometimes arouses a response and at other times does not.*

Associative functions

In addition to receiving sensory information and initiating muscular and glandular activities, the cerebral cortex is a high-level switchboard for connecting, relating, and integrating. These cortical functions, combined

---

* Variations are to be expected. Remember that the cortex is indescribably complex; that its function is influenced by impulses coming in from lower centers as well as those within it; that the stimulus, although applied at a point, actually activates complex circuits (which stimuli applied at other points in a circuit may also activate); and that the effects of direct stimulation applied at any point will depend upon prior activity of the circuits involved. Thus, to quote two authorities on epilepsy, "Response from an individual point in the cortex depends upon antecedent influences and coincidental influences of many types."[17]

---

with susceptibility of the cortex to modification during an organism's lifetime, provide the foundations of such higher psychological processes as learning complex verbal and motor skills, recalling past experiences, and thinking.

We have already noted that higher psychological processes depend upon association areas in the cerebral cortex and that the proportionate amount of association tissue (in relation to sensory and motor) is greater in the human brain than in the brains of infrahuman organisms.

• *Sensory association.* Some of the association areas, as shown in Figure 2.17 (p. 57), are adjacent to those specialized for sensory reception. Thus there are visual, auditory, and somaesthetic association areas. These retain relevant sensory information and relate it to incoming impulses. Red light, for example, starts visual impulses which eventually reach the visual area of the occipital cortex. But red also arouses such associations as "danger" or "stop." This is because the visual association area, retaining effects of one's former experiences with red light, is also aroused by stimulation with red light. It adds "meaning" to this stimulation. Similarly, sounds and tactual experiences are given meaning in accordance with relevant past experiences.

The significance of tactual association may be illustrated by reference to a disease known as *astereognosis* — meaning, literally, without tactual knowledge of space. If you were blindfolded and then asked to handle such objects as a small cube, a ball, or a pyramid, you would have no difficulty in naming these objects. But if you subsequently suffered serious damage to your tactual association areas, you would be unable to recognize them through touch alone. This is because the loss of association tissue would cause tactual impressions to lose the meaning they once had for you.

When associative disorders involve language functions, we speak of *aphasia*, meaning without speech. Sensory aphasia results from injury to the visual and auditory association areas (Figure 2.19). The visual impressions reaching your eyes from this print have meaning for you only because the relevant association areas retain what you have learned about the significance of the marks seen. Similarly, you understand what you hear only because your auditory association areas give meaning to what would otherwise be meaningless sounds. When the functioning of these visual or auditory association areas is seriously disturbed, therefore, the individual has an impairment of the corresponding speech functions. The disturbance may be so serious that, although he sees written words, and can even trace them, he no longer understands what they mean. This is visual aphasia, known technically as *alexia*. Similarly, a patient may be able to hear but no longer be able to understand what he hears (*auditory aphasia* or *word deafness*).

• *Motor association.* Adjacent to each of the motor areas proper are motor association areas of great importance for speaking and writing. Serious damage to one such area is followed by *motor aphasia*, an inability to produce articulate speech. The individual thus afflicted can move his vocal mechanisms but he can no longer produce meaningful sounds. Impairment of another region within this general motor association area is followed by *agraphia*, the inability to write. The patient makes motions with a pen or pencil but his difficulty is that he has lost the habits which once enabled him to produce meaningful marks.

With respect to control of motor speech, the left side of the brain usually dominates.* We often see an example of such dominance when someone has a cerebral hemorrhage. If there is paralysis on the right side of the body (controlled by the left side of the brain), speech is usually also affected. If the paralysis is on the left side of the body, however, speech is usually not affected.

• *The prefrontal cortex.* In addition to containing the motor and motor association areas,

* It has generally been thought that the left side dominates only in right-handed people. However, a new report by Wilder Penfield and Lamar Roberts (*Speech and Brain Mechanisms*, Princeton, 1959, p. 137) shows that "the left cerebral hemisphere is usually dominant for speech regardless of the handedness of the individual, with the exclusion of those who have cerebral injuries early in life."

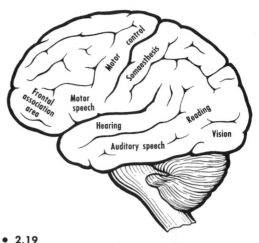

● **2.19**
The Left Cerebral Hemisphere, Showing Association and Specialized Sensory Areas. Note that each sensory association area is adjacent to the specialized reception area for the same sense. The motor speech area is in the lower motor area, the area concerned with control of motor activity in the head region.

the frontal lobes have a great expanse of relatively unspecialized association tissue. This is at the extreme front of the lobe, the *prefrontal* region. The prefrontal area is regarded by many as important for higher processes like recall memory and reasoning, processes which play such a large part in intelligence. We shall see in a later discussion, however, that the evidence is conflicting.[18] There have been cases in which both prefrontal areas were removed, but without clear evidence of lessened intelligence. Such removal is occasionally necessary because of tumors. Moreover, the prefrontal areas are sometimes severed or removed in order to relieve the individual of depression and other emotional disorders. This type of operation produces marked changes in personality. The person usually becomes less anxious about the past, present, and future, less self-conscious, and more content with his lot than before the operation. However, his intelligence, as measured by tests, is not always affected.

• *A final word on localization.* We have seen that the human cerebral cortex is an extremely complex structure, with regions that serve particular sensory, motor, or associative functions and others that have less clearly defined functions. It is important to remember, however, that all parts of the cerebral cortex and, indeed, of the entire nervous system, are closely interdependent. It is possible to "localize" certain functions (vision, hearing, touch, motor speech, and so on) in particular parts of the brain, as our discussion has shown. But, as was pointed out with respect to motor control, there is no localization in an absolute sense. It is incorrect to regard speech, for example, as localized in what we call the "motor speech area." Rather we should look upon this area as containing neural links of *crucial importance* in a network of interconnecting fibers. Without these there can be no speech. But with them, speech occurs and involves much

more. There are (1) the stimuli which produce the occasion for speech, and these may involve many areas of the cortex; (2) the interconnecting pathways, with many associative connections, which make one decide to speak or to refrain from speaking; (3) the words to be spoken, with all of the associative and motor connections which must be made if the right words are to follow each other in proper sequence; and (4) included in all of this, such things as hearing oneself speak and the kinesthetic feedback from the muscles with which we speak. Thus the motor speech area, although a crucial link in the neural communication network, is not a repository of speech. The same interpretation is relevant for every other area of the cerebral cortex, however its functions (visual, auditory, motor) are designated. ■

• SUMMARY

Psychologists are particularly interested in the receptors (which attune the organism to aspects of its environment), the effectors (organs of response), and the nervous system, which conducts impulses between receptors and effectors, integrates activities in various parts of the body, and mediates all of the higher psychological processes, like language, memory, and reasoning.

The human organism begins its existence as a single fertilized cell which, through a process of division, is transformed into a many-celled structure. Some cells combine to produce the enveloping membranes, but others give rise to the developing embryo itself. From three primitive cell layers the receptors, effectors, and the nervous structures gradually make their appearance. A neural tube develops from the outer layer of cells and becomes the spinal cord and brain. From the time of conception until about eight weeks there are no responses to external stimuli. Near this time, however, stimulation of the head region produces a widespread movement involving the neck and trunk muscles. No other part of the body is responsive to tactile

stimulation at this time. The initial response of the fetus to external stimuli waits upon the development of receptors in the skin, the development of muscular (effector) mechanisms, and connecting nerve fibers. By the fourth month of fetal life, sensitivity has spread throughout the body and many very precise responses to stimuli, like withdrawal of the foot, have become evident. These *reflexes*, mediated by receptor-connector-effector mechanisms known as *reflex arcs*, increase in number until the time of birth. Some of them, like sucking and breathing, are essential for the continuance of life after birth.

The unit of the nervous system is the neuron — a cell body with dendrites (carrying impulses toward it) and an axon (carrying impulses away from it). There are three basic neuron types — afferent (sensory), efferent (motor), and connector (association). Afferent neurons have an input function, carrying impulses from receptors to the central nervous system (brain and spinal cord). Efferent neurons carry impulses to muscles and glands. The afferent and efferent linkage is usually mediated by connector neurons. The place where an impulse passes from one neuron to another is the synapse. It is here that inhibition and facilitation (summation, temporal and spatial), may occur. Nerve fibers are the dendrites and axons of neurons. A nerve is a bundle of such fibers.

In a single nerve fiber, the impulse set off by the stimulus is a chemico-electrical disturbance which normally travels in only one direction, which may have a speed ranging up to four miles per minute, and which, once aroused, is independent of the properties of the stimulus which started it. The latter point refers to the *all-or-nothing principle*. For a short period after a fiber has discharged, no stimulus, however intense, can set it off again. This is the absolute refractory period. As the fiber regains excitability, it enters the relative refractory phase. Now a relatively intense stimulus may excite it. Because it excites a fiber during the relative refractory phase, a strong stimulus produces more frequent impulses than a weak one. It may also excite more fibers.

An increased intensity of experience is related to an increase in the intensity of stimulation. A higher intensity activates each fiber more frequently; it also activates more fibers. The mode or quality of experience (visual, auditory, and so on) is dependent upon the place in the cerebral cortex to which the impulses go.

Nerves outside the brain and spinal cord (central nervous system) comprise the peripheral nervous system. This includes the spinal and cranial nerves and the autonomic nervous system (sympathetic and parasympathetic).

The autonomic system is entirely motor, but receptors in the structures activated by it feed impulses (sensory) back into the spinal cord and brain which, reaching the latter, give rise to related visceral experiences (like "butterflies" in the stomach). The sympathetic nervous system accelerates certain functions (like those of the heart) and inhibits others (like those of the stomach). The parasympathetic nervous system likewise accelerates the activities of some structures (stomach) and

inhibits the activities of others (heart). Thus, if the sympathetic accelerates a function, the parasympathetic tends to suppress it; if the sympathetic suppresses it, the parasympathetic tends to accelerate it.

Each impulse, after entering the spinal cord, may travel over connector neurons to an efferent neuron and out again, where it activates muscles or glands. This circuit within a given spinal cord segment is the reflex arc. But impulses are not confined to reflex arcs. Some ascend the cord, making further connections in the brain stem, cerebellum, and cerebrum.

The brain stem begins in a structure known as the medulla (concerned with certain reflex activities). Other structures of the brain stem are the pons (connecting the lobes of the cerebellum, the midbrain (visual and auditory reflex functions), the hypothalamus (significant for various processes including motivation and emotion), and the thalamus (switchboard mechanism which, in addition to meditating automatic reflex activities and an elementary type of learning, is a projection center for sensory impulses on their way to various parts of the cerebrum). Running through the brain stem from the medulla to the lower thalamus is the reticular formation. Fibers ascending to the thalamus and cerebrum give off collaterals which enter the reticular formation and, by activating it, alert the cerebrum. The lower part of the reticular formation, participating in feedback circuits, has an inhibitory effect upon motor activities.

Motor impulses originating in the cerebral cortex (or in lower centers) descend the spinal cord in well-defined tracts. Some fibers cross in the medulla, but others do not cross until they reach the spinal cord segment at which they connect with efferent neurons. All motor impulses cross to the other side, either in the medulla or lower down. This is why injury to one side of the motor cortex paralyzes structures on the opposite side of the body.

Within the spinal cord and upper levels of the nervous system are reverberating (self-exciting) circuits which keep impulses going after external stimulation has stopped. These circuits are particularly complex among the nine billion neurons which make up the cerebral cortex. Some such circuits may account for the electrical brain rhythms recorded with the electroencephalograph. The most prominent of these EEG's is the alpha rhythm, with approximately ten oscillations per second. Another EEG mentioned in this chapter is the delta rhythm, a slow oscillation of high amplitude observed during sleep.

All sensory impulses originating on one side of the body and entering the spinal cord go to the opposite side of the brain. Impulses from the eye (or ear) on one side go some to the same side of the brain and some to the other side. The cerebral cortex has specialized areas upon which ascending impulses are "projected." There are sensory projection areas for vision, hearing, and somaesthesis. These are in, respectively, the occipital, temporal, and parietal lobes.

Studies with split-brain preparations have shown that the corpus callosum not only holds together and interconnects the cerebral hemispheres but that it also provides a channel for the duplication in one hemisphere of information acquired by the other.

The parietal and frontal lobes are separated by the central fissure (fissure of Rolando). In the frontal lobe just forward of this fissure, is an area concerned with voluntary motor activity. It is from the large pyramidal cells in this motor region that fibers descend, through the internal capsule of the corpus striatum, to connect with effectors at lower levels. The cortical location of motor control is, so to speak, upside down. That is, the upper part of the motor cortex controls the leg muscles while the lower part controls the facial muscles. Cortical tissue, once destroyed, cannot be replaced, but neighboring tissues sometimes take over lost motor functions (vicarious functioning).

Associative functions of the human cortex, although somewhat specialized, are less so than sensory and motor functions. Association areas in the parietal, temporal, and occipital lobes are adjacent to the specialized areas for somaesthesis, audition, and vision. Except for the strip of motor cortex along the frontal lobe at the region of the fissure of Rolando, this lobe is concerned solely with associative functions.

The modification of association tissues during an individual's lifetime is very important. It is the basis of memory, language, and higher processes, such as reasoning. When association tissues are destroyed after language activities have developed, various forms of aphasia may result, the particular kind depending upon the cortical area involved. The left cerebral hemisphere usually plays a dominant role in language activities. Thus, when the left motor association area is injured, the individual may be able to make sounds, but not intelligible ones.

Other forms of aphasia involve inability to understand written or spoken language. When the forward portions of the frontal lobes are seriously injured, an individual may undergo personality changes, such as a reduction of self-consciousness.

Although sensory, motor, and associative functions have been "localized" in the cerebral cortex, this merely means that the parts to which they have been attributed are crucially involved in their manifestation. Actually, the entire brain participates in every function.

This summary, extensive as it is, does not mention all of the structures and functions that we have discussed in this chapter. It would be well, for review purposes, if the reader checked off each neural term in the glossary, noting the definition and also the functions cited therewith. ■

REFERENCES AND NOTES FOR THIS CHAPTER ARE IN THE APPENDIX.

• SELECTED READINGS

Best, C. H., and N. B. Taylor, *The Living Body* (4th ed.). Holt, 1963. An up-to-date, interesting, well-illustrated text on human physiology.

Daniel, R. S. (Ed.), *Contemporary Readings in General Psychology* (2nd ed.). Houghton Mifflin, 1965. Selections 49–53 cover various aspects of the behaving organism.

Eccles, J. C., *The Neurophysiological Basis of the Mind.* Oxford University Press, 1958.

Gardner, E., *Fundamentals of Neurology* (4th ed.). Saunders, 1963. More detail on the topics in this chapter.

Hooker, D., *Evidence of Prenatal Function of the Central Nervous System in Man.* American Museum of Natural History, 1958. A lecture that will be of interest to the student who wants to know more about prenatal behavior.

Morgan, C. T., *Physiological Psychology* (3rd ed.), McGraw-Hill, 1965. The first three chapters provide additional information on the peripheral nervous system, the central nervous system, and the physiology of the neuron.

Munn, N. L., *The Evolution and Growth of Human Behavior* (2nd ed.). Houghton Mifflin, 1965; Chapter 6 (prenatal behavior) and various sections on the nervous system.

Ruch, T. C., H. D. Patton, J. W. Woodbury, and A. L. Towe, *Neurophysiology.* Saunders, 1961.

Sheer, D. E. (Ed.), *Electrical Stimulation of the Brain.* University of Texas Press, 1961.

Warren, J. M., and K. Akert (Eds.), *The Frontal Granular Cortex and Behavior.* McGraw-Hill, 1964. A symposium on the psychological functions of the frontal lobes; of interest to advanced students.

3

Individual Differences

A great deal of psychological interest focuses upon the individual. This stems, in part, from the early interest of Galton and Cattell in individual differences, an interest noted in our discussion of how psychology became a science. At a time when most psychologists were attempting to analyze conscious experience (not the conscious experience of different individuals, but of *man* in the abstract) these men threw the scientific spotlight on differences in mental ability. Galton was especially interested in genius and in how inheritance contributes to it. His studies also led him to develop statistical procedures for the study of individual differences, particularly to represent their distribution and the relationship between superiority in one psychological trait and superiority in others.

This chapter describes basic procedures for the measurement and statistical analysis of individual differences. It contains an elementary and purely descriptive discussion of statistical analysis, which all students should read so that they will understand later discussions. There is also a supplement which, although elementary, presents additional concepts, statistical formulas, and illustrative calculations. Readers who wish to omit the supplementary discussions may do so, unless their classwork calls for statistical calculations. Before launching into the more technical study of individual differences, however, we should give some consideration to their prevalence, magnitude, and significance.

Human beings obviously differ in many ways, physically and from the standpoint of behavior. But individual differences are also prevalent in animals. They are most evident in human beings because we know these so well and observe them so closely.

Although all ants, or fish, or rats look alike to the casual observer, any student of animal behavior soon observes that his ant, fish, or rat subjects differ markedly from each other, in behavior as well as structure. Some are active and others sluggish; some learn quickly and others slowly; some remember well and others forget. Indeed, there are gradations of activity level, learning ability, and other characteristics, sometimes over a wide range. The farmer is also aware of differences among his sheep, his cows, and his hens — although he is likely to be impressed especially with differences of practical interest to him, such as how these animals differ in wool clip, milk production, or egg output. ■

HOW HUMAN BEINGS DIFFER

Among human beings the most obvious differences are in such bodily characteristics as height, weight, color, and facial appearance. These impress the observer almost immediately. Differences in behavior are much less evident. We may observe that a person's handshake, his accent, or his general conduct is different from that of others we know; but it is not until we have had closer acquaintance with him that we appreciate in how many ways his behavior marks him off from other people. Even then, many differentiating features of behavior escape us. We observe only what is on the surface — and then perhaps only what the individual wants us to observe. Much

that is hidden, whether intentionally or otherwise, becomes evident only if we can study the individual as psychologists do, using tests and measurements designed to reveal psychological differences. This is especially true in respect to differences in ability to perform certain kinds of work, scholastic or otherwise. Many differentiating aspects of his behavior, including his abilities, may not be known even to the individual himself. Thus, he may ask to be tested or observed so that he can learn for himself how much he is alike or different from others. He may, for example, want to know whether or not he is fitted for a particular line of work. On the other hand, the individual may be asked by a prospective employer to take various tests, the aim being to observe whether he has characteristics required in a particular job.

Although individual differences have been recognized since ancient times, and it has been generally conceded that an ideal society would be one in which each person contributed in accordance with his abilities, the scientific study of individual differences is of relatively recent origin. Even the pioneer work of Galton, Cattell, and Binet which has already been noted did not make much impact until 50 years ago, when the First World War led to an upsurge of interest in the detection and utilization of individual differences — especially differences in intelligence. This was due to the need to select men with sufficient intelligence to profit from special forms of military training. Research on individual differences gathered momentum and reached another peak during the Second World War, when many specific abilities as well as intelligence were under investigation, particularly those needed in aviation and other special branches of the armed services.

Obviously there are larger individual differences in some abilities than in others. Most of us can learn such relatively simple skills as driving a nail or cutting with scissors. In acquiring such skills, we do not differ much, one from the other. But when highly complex skills are called for, the difference between the least and the most skilled is very large. Some skills are so complex that certain individuals are unable to achieve them even to a minimal degree. This is especially true in the case of skills requiring a high level of reasoning ability. The person skilled in atomic physics, for instance, has left all but a few of his fellows far behind. This being the case, it is not surprising that the United States and other countries are engaged in a vigorous search for those with talents needed in national defense. In this "talent search," psychological tests are playing an important role.

Although our discussion so far has emphasized the existence of individual differences in bodily characteristics and the less obvious differences in ability, there are other differences. Among these are differences in aspects of personality, in character, and in attitudes.

As later discussions will show, these are also of great interest to psychologists. ■

THE SCIENTIFIC STUDY OF INDIVIDUAL DIFFERENCES

It is one thing to observe individual differences in a general way and quite another to study them scientifically. The latter requires measurement of individual characteristics, or *traits*.

Measurement of individual characteristics

It has been said[1] that "Whatever exists at all exists in some amount." This is as true of psychological characteristics, including talent, as it is of the various physical aspects of our world.

The first task of the student of individual differences is to discover how much each individual has of whatever is being investigated. Only after this has been ascertained is it possible to discover the difference which exists between one individual and others. Only after this, moreover, can the study of individual differences be put to practical use.

It is not sufficient for scientific purposes to use general terms. Statements that someone has "a lot of talent," "not much talent," or " a great deal of personality" may be correct; but a scientist must know more precisely how much of each trait is present. He needs to quantify, which means that he needs to be able to use numbers rather than adjectives to represent what he observes.

• *Physical units.* Measurements of traits like height, weight, chest expansion, the shape of the skull, and strength of grip are made in physical units. Take strength of grip as measured by a dynamometer (Figure 3.1). The individual measurement is in units of weight; in this case, kilograms. Theoretically the individual could score zero (no measurable grip) or anything between this and 100 (the strongest conceivable grip). Note that not only is there a zero point, but all units of measurement are equal. The unit between 45 and 46, for example, is equivalent to that between 10 and 11. In view of the zero anchor-

and are equal one with another, are used to measure such things as how far or how high an individual jumps or how far he throws the discus. Units of time, also scaled in absolute units from zero up, give us such information as how fast an individual reacts, how long it takes him to solve a problem or how long he persists at a task before giving up.

• *Psychological units.* All of the above is fairly obvious, but it provides a background for discussing psychological measurements in which physical units such as weight, length, or duration are not applicable. This is especially true with respect to traits like intelligence, aptitude or talent, character, and sociability. How can we specify the intelligence, scientific aptitude, or honesty of an individual? We certainly cannot do it in physical units, or in absolute units of any kind. Except theoretically, there is no lower limit to intelligence, honesty, or scientific talent.[3] Nor is there a measurable upper limit to such characteristics. Moreover, at higher levels, it is increasingly difficult for one person to surpass another. At lower levels, it would be relatively easy for this to occur. In short, there is no known zero, there is no known upper limit, and increments in which individuals might be said to differ may vary along the scale. This does not, however, leave us at an impasse as far as measurement is concerned. As will be clearer when the statistical analysis of individual differences is discussed later in this chapter, we use a relative rather than an absolute scale — and this works very well for our purposes. Instead of cardinal numbers, like the one, two, three, . . . of physical scales, we use ordinal numbers; those which represent orders of magnitude, like first, second, third, and so on. Thus the scales with which we measure specific talents, aspects of character, and many other traits are *ordinal scales.*[4]

• *Ordinal scales.* As an example of ordinal measurement let us consider the two items in Figure 3.2, which were taken from a test designed to measure scientific aptitude. Each individual is given many such items, which have been especially selected to tap various qualities which underlie scientific success. In our example we have one item which gives

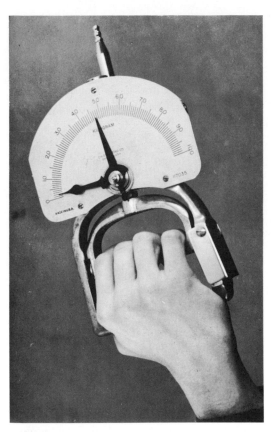

● 3.1
A Hand Dynamometer. The instrument is adjustable for hands of different size. Note that the scale is in kilograms and that it reads, in equal units, from zero to 100.

age and the equivalent units along this scale, the person who registers 50 kilograms has twice the strength of the individual who, under comparable conditions, registers only 25. Because such scales allow us to say that one person has twice (or half) the amount of something possessed by the other, they are often referred to as *ratio scales.*[2]

The existence of a zero point and equal units of measurement from zero to 100 makes it possible to measure the strength of different individuals in *absolute units.* Here the *amount* of a characteristic is measured in units of weight. Linear units, which also begin at zero

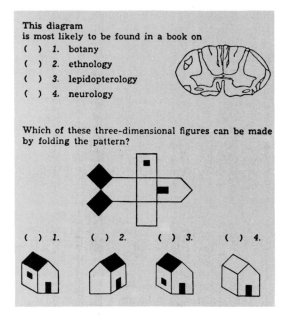

This diagram
is most likely to be found in a book on
( ) 1. botany
( ) 2. ethnology
( ) 3. lepidopterology
( ) 4. neurology

Which of these three-dimensional figures can be made
by folding the pattern?

( ) 1.   ( ) 2.   ( ) 3.   ( ) 4.

● 3.2
Items from a Science Aptitude Test. The complete test, which varies in content from year to
year, is used in the Annual Science Talent Search
to select those who will receive Westinghouse
scholarships. In case they are needed, the answers appear in the Appendix. (Courtesy,
Science Service)

Tested with others under comparable conditions, the individual obtains a score based
upon the number of items answered correctly
within the time limit. This score in itself is
interesting, but we need to know much more.
We need to know how it compares with other
scores. Where does it place this individual
with respect to the others? Is the score average? Is it above or below average? More
specifically, if the score is above or below
average, how far is it above or below? We may
consider the score in terms of rank. Is it in
the top tenth, or even the top hundredth?
Although there are more refined ways of indicating the value of a score on such tests,
it is clear that a test score in itself (unlike
kilograms on the dynamometer) is largely
meaningless. What counts is where it ranks
within the distribution of other scores. We
may say that, in such tests, the individual's
performance is rated in terms of how much it
differs from that of others.

Ordinal scales are not always tests, in the
above sense. There are, for example, a number
of social maturity scales with which individuals are rated for various social activities.
Such scales are essentially checklists. A rater
checks the items which apply to the individual and the score is the number of items
checked. This score is evaluated in terms of
how the individual's rating compares with that
of others of his own age. In some instances the
rater indicates the degree to which a particular
characteristic is present. Instead of saying that
a child is or is not sociable, for instance, the
observer rates him on a five-point scale: (1)
plays by himself, (2) merely looks on, (3) joins
group but does not play, (4) plays in group
but does not cooperate, (5) cooperates in joint
enterprises. There is no question here of zero
or maximum sociability. Nor is there any idea
that the difference between 1 and 2 is equivalent to that between 4 and 5. The numbers
are merely ordinal.

• *Interval scales.* A test of intelligence or
some other aspect of behavior can be designed,
at least theoretically, so that its scores give
equal increments even though an absolute
zero cannot be determined. The selection of
items and their weighting can be such that

some indication of achievement in a special
field — neurology. In the whole test there are
items like this from various fields of science.
The person who already knows a lot about
many scientific fields is one in whom the tester
of scientific talent is of course interested.
But our other item, representative of many in
such tests, does not depend so much upon
what the individual has already learned. Its
solution calls for keen observation, for ability
to handle spatial relations symbolically, and
perhaps other qualities. This is a very inadequate sampling of aptitude tests, which are discussed more fully in Chapter 18. What is of
particular interest to us now, however, is how
such tests indicate the *amount* or *degree* of a
person's aptitude, or whatever other trait is
being investigated.

the difference between a score of 50 and a score of 60, for example, is equal to the difference between the scores 120 and 130. When a test is constructed so that its increments are equal in this way, it is referred to as an *interval scale*. It is then somewhat analogous to the scale on a thermometer, where zero must be arbitrarily set, but where the successive units are equal.

The advantage of an interval scale, as compared with an ordinal one, is that results obtained with it lend themselves to statistical analyses which would not be justified in the case of the latter.[5]

Although it is theoretically possible to develop tests which provide an interval scale, most are scaled in ordinal units.

Reliability of measurements

The reliability of any set of measurements is judged in terms of consistency. Maximum consistency is found in measurements on a physical scale. Take measurements of height, for example. Such measurements are relatively free of error or other sources of variation from one measurement to another. Different persons may measure your height, each without reference to what the other has found, and they will get approximately the same number of feet and inches. Measuring to fractions of an inch will naturally lead to more variation, but this is insignificant for practical purposes. Where necessary, as in the manufacture of precision equipment, measuring devices are refined to give almost any desired level of reliability. But we are concerned only with measurement of human beings, where such precision is needless.

Suppose that your height and that of many others has been measured to the nearest inch. How do we determine the reliability of the measuring instrument? We may do it in various ways, but one simple illustration will suffice. This illustration involves a statistical technique known as correlation. The reader may recall that correlation was referred to in an earlier discussion (p. 28). A more detailed consideration comes later in the present chapter.

We have, then, the height of each individual in the group. Now we repeat the measurements, perhaps having a different person make them. Then we place the first set of measurements in rank order: Rank 1 to the person who is, let us say, 6 feet 9 inches tall, Rank 2 to the person who is next in height, and so on, down to the person who is shortest. The second set of measurements is similarly ranked. If all individuals maintain the same rank in both sets of measurements, we will have a positive correlation, and a perfect one, between the two sets of measurements. Application of a correlation formula to our data will in this event yield a *reliability coefficient* of 1.00, the highest possible. However, some persons may have straightened up more, and others less, during the second measurement. Moreover, the person measuring height may have misread the scale at times. Hence it is unlikely that the correlation will be 1.00, and it will not be if the above variations cause some persons to change their rank in the second series.

When used properly, physical scales yield measurements which, like those in our example, are highly reliable. We can depend upon them both in measuring individuals and in measuring the magnitude of individual differences.

Many ordinal measurements also have high reliability, although not as high as that typically found for physical measurements.

The reliability of ordinal measurements may be determined in a manner comparable with that described for measurements of height. Let us suppose a test is administered to a large group and then, perhaps after a day or so, it is repeated. The sets of measurements obtained on these two occasions are then correlated. If each individual maintains a comparable rank on the first and second testing, even though his score changes somewhat, a reliability coefficient of 1.00 will result.

Another method is to devise equivalent forms of a test, give both forms to the same individuals, and then correlate the scores obtained with each form. If each individual had the same rank order position on the two tests, we would again have a perfect correlation.

Our discussion of reliability has emphasized tests. Quite frequently, however, individuals are rated for a particular trait, as in the case of sociability, which has already been mentioned. The reliability of such measures is evaluated by correlating separate ratings. Suppose two or more persons rate each individual independently. The separate ratings are then correlated. A perfect correlation would signify that individuals were given equivalent ratings by each observer.

In reality, perfect correlations are seldom, if ever, found for different administrations or equivalent forms of the same test, or for the ranks assigned to individuals by different raters. The highest reliability coefficient obtained with an intelligence test is .98. It is not uncommon to have reliabilities around .90. Personality tests, as one might expect, have much lower reliability than this. Nevertheless some have a sufficiently high reliability to justify their use in personality assessment. This will be evident when we get to Chapter 5.

Ratings vary a great deal in reliability, depending upon the characteristics of the raters and upon what is rated. For example: three raters observed social behavior in children well known to them and rated thirty traits, each on a five-point scale. The lowest correlation between one set of ratings and another was .62; the highest was .82.[6] In another investigation, where observers merely rated children in terms of how active they were, reliability coefficients ranged from .92 to .98.[7]

Before closing this discussion it should be recognized that reliability is dependent upon much more than the nature of a measuring device. Take the dynamometer, for example. Even though it measures in physical units on a ratio scale, it may yield results which are far from reliable. Each individual must be instructed about what he is to do. Different instructions will yield different results. Moreover, one individual may "give it all he has" while another squeezes in a disinterested manner. All such variations lower the dynamometer's reliability as a measuring device. The same is true for tests of any kind. It is for this reason that psychological tests are preceded by standardized instructions and are best administered by fully trained experts. These precautions guarantee, so far as possible, that each individual works at the test in a comparable manner. With respect to scoring, there are again standard instructions. If this were not so, the performance of different individuals might be evaluated in different ways rather than on a comparable basis. ■

STATISTICAL ANALYSIS OF INDIVIDUAL DIFFERENCES

From our discussion so far it is apparent that the investigator of individual differences must know the degree to which each individual has the trait studied and that, in order to obtain such knowledge, he needs reliable measuring devices, whether these are physical instruments, tests, or rating scales. But after individual measurements have been obtained, the investigator must analyze and interpret his data. This requires statistical procedures.

Since the days of Cattell, Binet, Galton, and other pioneers in the study of individual differences, some of whom introduced statistical procedures into the life sciences, there has been a great expansion in the use of these techniques. Indeed statistical analysis has become highly specialized — so much so that investigators normally achieve competence only after years of study, usually at the graduate level. In an introductory course, therefore, one need not expect to attain anything beyond an understanding of a few basic statistical concepts.

It was necessary to introduce some statistical ideas into the discussions of scientific method and psychological measurement. In Chapter 1 we mentioned use of the *mean* (or average) to represent the central tendency of a group and also to compare groups. In that chapter we also pointed out that it is necessary to determine the reliability of differences between groups, and that this requires statistical analysis. Our discussion of R–R (response-response) laws in psychology introduced another statistical concept, *correlation*. This concept was used in the present chapter to show how the reliability of measurements may be discovered.

Now we turn more directly to the statistical analysis of differences between individual human beings and how these differences are interrelated. The discussion deals with statistical concepts largely in verbal and graphic terms. However, the student who would prefer to delve a little more deeply and to work through some elementary statistical problems will find what he needs in the supplement at the end of this chapter. If he wishes to go still further, the references should prove helpful.

THE DISTRIBUTION OF INDIVIDUAL DIFFERENCES

How do individuals differ with respect to a particular trait such as strength, speed of reaction, or intelligence? Can we divide them into the strong or weak, fast or slow, intelligent or unintelligent? Obviously we cannot. There are gradations from one extreme to the other and no application of statistical procedures is required to convince us of this point. But how are the observed variations distributed? That is a question which cannot be answered so easily.

The frequency distribution

We begin our analysis by making what is called a *frequency distribution*. The procedure is quite simple. Let us tabulate, for example, the scores made by 100 students on a test of memory span. Each score is the longest list of simple words (like tree, box, ice, etc.) which the individual recalled in correct order after hearing them once. Here the scores are arranged haphazardly as we might have recorded them.

```
4 5 5 5 4 6 6 5 7 6 5 5 5 7 6 5 4 5 4 5
6 5 6 3 7 6 7 6 6 8 7 6 7 6 7 7 6 6 6 6
7 8 6 7 5 5 7 6 6 5 6 7 6 5 7 5 6 7 6 4
8 6 6 5 7 6 5 7 7 8 5 6 5 6 5 7 7 6 6 7
7 6 7 7 6 6 6 5 4 6 5 6 5 5 5 5 7 6 9 5
```

Observe that the lowest score is 3 and the highest 9. These and the scores between them are next arranged in a vertical column as illustrated in Figure 3.3. At the side of each score a tally has been placed to represent each occurrence of this score. Adding tallies gives the *frequency* of each score. For example, a memory span of 6 words was attained by 36 of the students. Its frequency is therefore 36.

● **3.3**

A Frequency Distribution and Frequency Polygon. In all such curves, scores are represented as distances along the abscissa. The height of the curve (ordinate) above each score indicates the number of individuals making that score — that is, the score's frequency. As indicated in the text, the scores in this example are for memory span.

Score	Tallies	Frequency
3	|	1
4	ⅤⅡ |	6
5	ⅤⅡ ⅤⅡ ⅤⅡ ⅤⅡ ⅤⅡ |||	28
6	ⅤⅡ ⅤⅡ ⅤⅡ ⅤⅡ ⅤⅡ ⅤⅡ ⅤⅡ |	36
7	ⅤⅡ ⅤⅡ ⅤⅡ ⅤⅡ ||||	24
8	||||	4
9	|	1
		N = 100

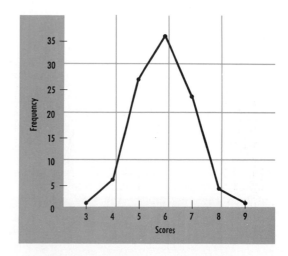

After getting the frequency of each score, we may represent the distribution graphically, again as in Figure 3.3. Distances to represent scores are laid out along the horizontal axis, known technically as the *abscissa*. Frequencies are represented on the vertical axis, or *ordinate*. Since there are 100 subjects in this particular sample, our ordinate represents not only the number making each score, but also the percentage. After marking above each score the height necessary to represent its frequency, we connect the points with straight lines, as illustrated. The result is a *frequency polygon*.

When there are many cases, and scores cover a wide range, one may group the latter into *class intervals*. Thus, if scores range from 8 to 55, we perhaps gather them into intervals as follows: 8–11, 12–15, 16–19, and so on until we get to 52–55.

In making the frequency distribution we then obtain the frequency of each interval rather than the frequency of each individual score. Likewise, when a frequency polygon is drawn, the class intervals rather than the individual scores are placed along the abscissa. The units on the ordinate are then class-interval frequencies.

● **3.4**

Normal Probability. A. If everything operated in accordance with chance, tossing 20 pennies (shaking them up in a box and tossing them out on a table) 1000 times would yield the normal probability curve shown by the solid-line curve. The number of heads from 0 to 20 appears on the abscissa, and the number of throws in which each number of heads appeared is represented on the ordinate. The broken-line curve is the result of an actual experiment. Instead of the expected average of 10 heads, the average was actually 9.98. The mode is, of course, 10 in both curves. **B.** Galton's device to demonstrate a probability distribution. Shot is released from above, pieces of shot hit the nails and each other, and finally arrange themselves in the grooves below. A device like this was used by IBM at the New York World's Fair, 1964–1965, to illustrate probability. (Courtesy, Dr. E. O. Dodson and General Biological Supply House)

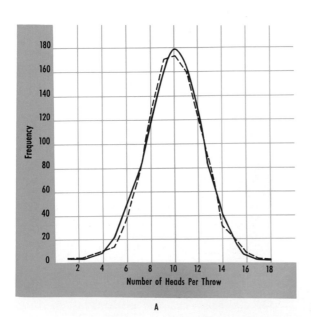

A

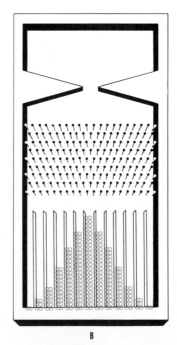

B

□ Instead of plotting a frequency polygon for grouped data we sometimes erect a *histogram* which looks very much like the succession of columns in Figure 3.4B. When we do this, the intervals are spaced out on the abscissa and a line of equal width is placed at the proper frequency level above them. Taken together, these lines look like an outline of the figure in B except that this is a normal frequency histogram and actual data may depart widely from it in shape.

Sometimes a *bar graph* is used to represent a frequency distribution. This is similar to a histogram except that the columns are separated rather than joined. Figure 3.4B is, in reality, more like a bar graph than a histogram because of the separation of its columns. The tallies in Figure 3.3, if turned with the scores at their base would constitute a simple bar graph.

We can also use bar graphs to represent grossly discontinuous data, which should not be represented by polygons or histograms. For example, in representing how many individuals pass and how many fail; how many vote Republican, Democrat, or Socialist; or how many receive each rating on some such device as the sociability scale referred to earlier, where there are five abrupt steps with no measurable gradations between them. □

The normal probability curve

When there are many unselected cases, a frequency polygon often approaches the shape of a normal probability curve. The characteristics of such a curve are produced by so many unobserved factors that it is said to result from chance. Sir Francis Galton, referred to earlier as a pioneer in the scientific study of individual differences, made a pinball machine to demonstrate that many unknown factors, acting conjointly, produce a probability distribution. His device is illustrated in Figure 3.4B. Beside it (A) is a normal probability curve obtained by students who tossed twenty pennies 1000 times and recorded the number of heads in each throw. Superimposed upon this curve is a mathematically derived probability curve. If the pennies had been tossed 10,000 times, the two curves would almost have coincided.

Observe that scores pile up in the center and that the most frequent score, referred to by statisticians as the *mode*, is represented on the abscissa as in the exact center of the normal distribution. When the population tested is very large, most psychological measurements, and such biological factors as height and weight, are distributed in approximate accordance with normal probability. The "chance" factors here are, as we shall see, related to differences in heredity and environment.

Divergences from the normal curve provide important information about the makeup of the population tested. Some such variations are illustrated in Figure 3.5 and discussed in the legend.

When two or more groups (male and female, for example) are given the same test, it is usual to find overlapping. Sometimes, of course, the overlap is complete. The distributions of intelligence for boys and girls, for example, are practically identical. A test of strength with a dynamometer, on the other hand, yields somewhat different distributions, with much overlapping, but with boys ahead of girls. In some tests, especially those involving linguistic skills, girls are ahead, but again there is considerable overlapping.

One should keep in mind that when distributions overlap, some individuals in the group with the lower mean may surpass the mean performance of the other group. Thus, some women are stronger than the man of average strength and some men have better verbal skills than the average woman.

Variability

Frequency distributions also give us information about the extent of individual differences. The overall spread from the highest to the lowest score is the *range*. But another index of variability (see the supplement at the end of this chapter) represents the degree to which scores are clustered around the central tendency (mean or mode). If scores are piled up at the center of the distribution, with very little spread in either direction, it is evident that differences in what is represented are not large. If there is a wide spread, on the other

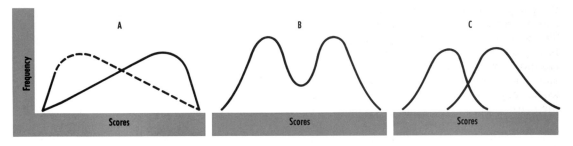

• 3.5
Variations from a Normal Distribution. The *skewed* curves in **A** show, at a glance, that more people in the group tested made high (or low) scores than made intermediate scores. Such distributions are said to be skewed to the right or left, depending upon the direction of the tail. Thus, the distribution represented by a broken line is skewed toward the right. Distribution curves are sometimes like the curve in **B**. Instead of having only one score with a relatively high frequency, there are two such scores — in our illustration, those directly below the two humps. Because there are two modes, such curves are said to be *bimodal.* Even if one of the humps were somewhat lower than the other, such a curve would still be designated as bimodal. Bimodal curves are especially evident when there are two different groups in the population tested — say, a skilled and an unskilled group; or a group with a low level of education and a group with college training. Thus, a distribution of intelligence test scores for soldiers, some with only a fourth-grade education and some with a college education, had two modes, one at around 20 points and the other at around 150. (A. Anastasi and J. P. Foley, Jr., *Differential Psychology,* Macmillan, 1949, p. 69.) When different groups making up a bimodal distribution are identified and separate curves drawn, the result is similar to that illustrated in **C**, where it can be seen that there are really two overlapping distributions. Some distributions have more than two modes. These are referred to as *multimodal.*

hand, one can see that differences within the group are relatively large. Two distributions, one with a large and the other with a relatively small spread of scores are shown in Figure 3.6. In statistical terminology we would say that there is less *variability* in the *a* than in the *b* group. Although our example shows two groups with the same mean, it usually happens that different groups differ in their mean scores and also in their variability. ■

THE STATUS OF THE INDIVIDUAL

A mean or a measure of variability does not tell us the status of a particular person. The mean grade or the variability of your college class, for example, would not tell us your standing in the class. Knowing your score and knowing the mean, however, we could

say whether your performance was higher or lower than that represented by the latter. But there are several other ways in which your standing might be indicated more specifically than in the example given. One of these is, of course, to say how far your performance deviates upward or downward from the mean, or by how much it deviates from the maximum or minimum performance. This can be done in terms of actual scores or in terms of rank standing.

One method widely used to indicate the rank standing of an individual score uses *percentiles.* Rank is then indicated in terms of the percentage of the scores above or below this score. Since there were 100 subjects in our memory span experiment, we can give a rough idea of the meaning of percentiles by indicating that the person with a memory span of 9 had a longer span than 99 per cent of the group. It was in the upper one-hundredth, and his percentile rank was therefore between 99 and 100. No more precise statement than this would be warranted in the present case. However, when there are large numbers of scores, and percentiles are calculated for the whole range of data, we can tell at a glance the percentile standing of any particular score.

Suppose we find that an individual's score is in the 90th percentile. This means that it is equaled or exceeded by 10 per cent of the scores.

Statisticians have worked out other ways to indicate the status of an individual score and some are superior to the simple observation that the score is above or below the mean or that it is equaled or exceeded by a certain percentage of the group. One of these methods, as indicated in the supplement, evaluates a score in terms of: (1) how far it deviates from the mean, and (2) the spread (i.e., variability) of the distribution in which it occurs. The score thus evaluated is known as a *standard score*. To learn how standard scores are calculated see the supplement. One will also find there a figure (3.9) which compares percentile and standard scores derived from a normal distribution. ■

CORRELATION

Individual differences in one ability are often related to individual differences in other abilities. There may, for instance, be a relation between performance on an intelligence test and performance in school such that the higher the test performance the higher the school grades. In this event, analysis of the data by suitable statistical techniques would reveal the presence of a *positive correlation* between scores on the intelligence test and school grades.

The correlations mentioned in our discussion of test reliability were all positive. Quite often, however, we correlate one set of scores with another and find that there is no relationship. There is, for example, no relation between motor dexterity and vocabulary. In this instance we would say that there is *zero correlation*.

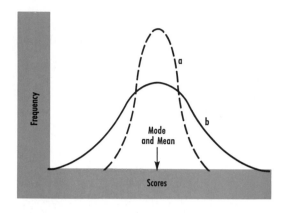

● **3.6**

Distributions Differing in Variability. Although the modes (and means) of the two distributions are identical, there is more spread (variability) in the *b* distribution.

Of course the correlation between two traits may be anywhere between zero and 1.00, as indicated in earlier discussions. Nevertheless, some traits are related in such a way that a high value in one goes with a low value in the other. There may be a relation between weight and speed of running, for example, such that the heavier the runner the slower his speed. In this event we would have a *negative correlation*. Negative correlations might range anywhere from zero to —1.00.

Note that, even though a relationship is negative, a correlation *does* exist. Here is an example. There is a correlation of .40 between measurements of a personality trait known as *extraversion* and measurements of another personality trait known as *dominance*. But suppose we evaluate the same results in terms of the opposite trait to dominance — that is, *submissiveness?* Now we may obtain a correlation of —.40. We can then say that extraverts tend to be dominant or that extraverts do not tend to be submissive. In either case there is a relationship.

Correlation techniques like those described in the supplement are used to answer questions about many aspects of individual differences, in addition to discovering the reliability of measurements and the possible relations between performance on one test and performance on another. For example: Identical twins have identical heredity and fraternal twins do not. Is there, then, a greater psychological similarity between the former than between the latter? Other things being equal, a significantly higher correlation between the traits of identical twins than between those of fraternal twins would suggest the strong influence of heredity in making people alike.

Other relevant questions are: What is the correlation between intelligence and differences in economic status, or educational opportunities, or differences in the home environment? In each instance we must measure the variables in question. In the case of home environment, for instance, different homes would have to be rated in some way — perhaps in terms of the presence of books and other enriching aspects.

The coefficient of correlation

The most commonly used measure of correlation yields a *coefficient of correlation* otherwise referred to as *r*. Calculation of *r* is demonstrated in the supplement. As a further illustration of much that we have been discussing, however, the graphs in Figure 3.7 have been drawn. These are known as *scatter diagrams*. Comparable graphs are frequently used to represent the degree of correlation between two variables. The data represented here are of course hypothetical. We assume that subjects A, B, C, D, and E were each required to solve three problems, X, Y, and Z. Their errors were, let us say, those tabulated at the top of the next page.

We see that subject A made only one error before learning problem X, 2 before

● **3.7**

Scatter Diagrams Showing Different Degrees of Correlation. In **A** is shown the scattergram for the correlation between X and Y. It is interpreted as follows: Subject A made one error on X and two errors on Y; so we represent him with a point at X one and Y two. We do this with each subject. When the scores thus arranged slope toward the right as illustrated in **A**, the correlation is positive (and in this case perfect, or +1.00, because the slope is a straight line). The diagram shows at a glance that the higher a subject's score in X, the higher his score in Y. If we reverse the figures, assuming that subject A, who made one error on X, made 6 on Y, and so on, we get the scattergram shown in **B**. This represents a negative correlation (again, in this case perfect, or −1.00). That is to say, the fewer errors made in solving one problem, the more there are in solving the other. In **C** the correlation, as one can judge from inspection, is negative, but of doubtful magnitude. We know that it is negative because three of the cases slope definitely to the left as in **B**. Calculation (see the statistical supplement at the end of this chapter) shows that the correlation in **C** is actually −.52.

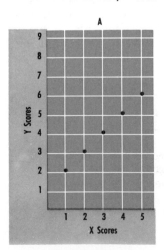
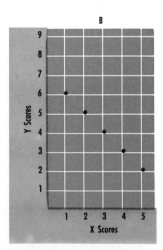
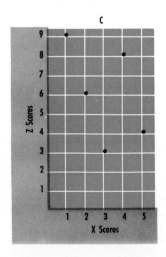

Subjects	Errors made in learning three problems		
	X	Y	Z
A	1	2	9
B	2	3	6
C	3	4	3
D	4	5	8
E	5	6	4

learning problem Y, and 9 before learning problem Z. One will note immediately that subject A made the lowest number of errors in X and also the lowest number in Y; that subject B made the next to lowest number of errors in X, and the next to lowest number of errors in Y; and so on, down to subject E, who made the greatest number of errors in both X and Y. The correlation here is of course + 1.00.

Suppose, now, that we should have the error scores for X (or Y) in reverse order — that the person who made the smallest number of errors in X made the greatest number of errors in Y, the person who made the next lowest number of errors in X made the next to highest number in Y, and so on. Such an arrangement would give us a perfect negative correlation; that is, a correlation of −1.00. Our remaining example illustrates another correlation. The exact correlation is not as evident from the scatter diagram as were those for r's of 1.00 and −1.00. Actually, as calculated in the supplement, the coefficient here is −.52.

Interpretation of r

Providing that statistical evaluation shows it to be reliable — that is, dependable or unlikely to disappear in repetitions of the experiment — r is accepted as revealing or failing to reveal a relationship between the variables correlated. The higher r is found to be, the greater the relationship (positive or negative) between the variables correlated.

But what does a reliable r of a certain magnitude indicate concerning the degree of relationship? Students frequently, and quite erroneously, think of r as indicating the per cent of relationship between two variables. Now, it is quite evident, from our simple scatter plots of perfect correlations, that here we have a 100 per cent relationship between X and Y. But this holds only for an r of plus or minus 1.00.

According to one method of calculating the dependence of X on Y, when the two are correlated, even an r of .99 would indicate only 88 per cent dependence. The per cent of dependence drops rapidly, so that an r of .50 indicates only 37 per cent dependence.[8]

From a somewhat different angle we may ask, "With what degree of accuracy does a certain r allow us to predict scores in Y from scores in X?" One can see from our first scatter diagram that, when r is 1.00, it is possible to predict Y from an individual's X score. There is no need to give him test Y. However, the predictability of one score from another decreases rapidly as r becomes smaller. In Figure 3.8, for example, is a scatter diagram representing the midterm and final grades of fifty students in an introductory course in psychology. The correlation is .90, indicating a high probability that final grades will be closely equivalent in value to midterm grades. Observe, however, the discrepancies between midterm and final grades. Suppose we had predicted that students who made a B at midterm would get a B in the course. There were 10 with midterm B's. But only seven of these made a final B. Of the remaining three, two went up to an A and one dropped to a C. Our prediction would have erred, but of course only by one grade in either direction. Generally speaking, prediction from this particular set of data would have been about 75 per cent accurate.

Does r signify a causal relationship?

The fact that variables are correlated does not mean that one is the cause of the other. They may both be dependent upon a third factor. In growing children, for instance, weight and intelligence are positively correlated. But one would not conclude that weight alone determines intelligence, or vice versa. Actually this correlation is spurious. It depends upon the fact that both weight and intelligence increase with a third variable, the child's age. This is quite evident when we correlate intelligence and weight in children of the same age. When we do this the correlation between intelligence and weight becomes negligible.

As another example we may take the correlation between intelligence test scores and college grades where *r* is often found to be as high as .60. This relationship means that factors contributing to intelligence test performance are also contributing to academic performance. Linguistic versatility is certainly involved in both kinds of performance. The ability to concentrate attention on the task at hand is also certainly involved. There are doubtless many such overlapping skills.

Absence of a higher correlation between intelligence and college grades may result from lack of sustained interest such as good scholastic performance requires, preoccupation with extracurricular activities, and possession of personality characteristics which are not measured by an intelligence test but which are also important in academic success.

Thus a coefficient of correlation is not to be taken at its face value. There are various ways of interpreting it, both from the standpoint of the actual magnitude of the relationship and from the standpoint of what it means in terms of possible causal or contributing influences. ■

● 3.8
A Scattergram of Midterm and Final Grades. Variations in the position of the fifty dots, each representing one student, are based upon points made on the tests. Our discussion is concerned only with the letter grades, and, more specifically, with prediction of final grades from B grades at midterm. (Unpublished data obtained by G. A. Kimble. From G. A. Kimble and N. Garmezy, *Principles of General Psychology,* 2nd ed., Ronald, 1963, p. 64.)

• STATISTICAL SUPPLEMENT

The reader who turns to this supplemental discussion of statistical analysis knows how to make a frequency distribution and plot a frequency distribution curve. He is also acquainted with certain characteristics of such curves and what these reveal about the distribution of individual differences. In delving a little more deeply into statistics and doing some simple calculations we again start with the memory span data that were represented in Figure 3.3.

Measures of central tendency

When we ask, "What is the typical memory span?" the *mode*, with which we are already familiar, may be given (in this case, 6.00). More commonly, however, either of two other measures of central tendency is given. Most frequently, this is the average or *mean*.

• *The mean.* Calculation of the mean is illustrated below. One may either add all scores and divide by the number, in this case 100, or he may use grouped data, as illustrated. Here each score (s) is multiplied by its frequency (f), the sum (Σ) of the products is obtained, and this is divided by the number of cases (N).

Score	f	$f \times s$
9	1	9
8	4	32
7	24	168
6	36	216
5	28	140
4	6	24
3	1	3

$$N = 100 \qquad \frac{\Sigma(f \times s)}{N} = \frac{592}{100} = 5.92$$

The mean, as calculated, is 5.92. In an experiment like ours, however, where the subject could not make a fractional score, it would be better to regard the mean as 6.00, the nearest whole number.

• *The median.* The median is, by definition, the middlemost score, the score on each side of which 50 per cent of the cases in the distribution fall. Its calculation is given below. Observe that, in our distribution, the 50th score from the top or bottom is assumed to fall within the interval 5.5 and 6.5. Starting at 5.5 we go up $50 - 35$ (or 15) cases to reach the 50th. Since the interval includes 36 cases, we add 15/36ths to 5.5, which gives the median score as 5.92. Starting from the other end of the distribution and subtracting from 6.5, we get the same result. As in the case of the mean, a median of 6.00 would be considered most representative for our data.

Score	f	
9	1 ⎫	
8	4 ⎬ 29 cases	
7	24 ⎭	
6.5		
6	36	
5.5		
5	28 ⎫	
4	6 ⎬ 35 cases	
3	1 ⎭	
	100	

$$\text{Mdn} = 5.5 + \frac{50 - 35}{36}$$

$$= 5.5 + \frac{15}{36}$$

$$= 5.5 + .4167 = 5.92$$

or

$$\text{Mdn} = 6.5 - \frac{50 - 29}{36}$$

$$= 6.5 - \frac{21}{36}$$

$$= 6.5 - .58 = 5.92$$

In a completely normal distribution the mode, median, and mean are identical. It happens very rarely, however, that actual measurements do any more than approximate a normal distribution. Hence the three measures of central tendency, although often of similar value, are seldom interchangeable.

When a distribution is skewed, the mode, mean, and median may differ considerably. Then the investigator has to decide which measure is most representative. For further statistical analysis such as we are about to describe, however, the mean is customarily used.

Variability

In our preceding discussions of variability we considered it only in graphic terms, as represented by the spread of the total distribution. This is essentially the measure of variability known as the *range*, which is the difference between the highest and the lowest score in the distribution. In statistical analysis, however, a more accurate measure of variability is desirable — one which represents not merely the spread of the distribution but the degree to which scores are clustered around the mean. This measure is known as the *standard deviation* of the distribution. It is referred to as the S.D. or merely as σ (sigma).

A standard deviation is found, as illustrated on the following page, by obtaining the deviation (D) of each score from the mean, squaring these deviations (D^2), multiplying these squared deviations by the frequency of the corresponding scores and adding the products

Score	f	D Deviation from Mean	D² Deviation Squared	fD²*
9	1	3.08	9.4864	9.4864
8	4	2.08	4.3264	17.3056
7	24	1.08	1.1664	27.9936
6	36	.08	.0064	.2304
5	28	.92	.8464	23.6992
4	6	1.92	3.6864	22.1184
3	1	2.92	8.5264	8.5264
	100			$\Sigma fD^2 = 109.3600$

$$M = 5.92$$

$$\sigma = \sqrt{\frac{\Sigma fD^2}{N}} = \sqrt{\frac{109.3600}{100}} = \sqrt{1.094}$$

$$= 1.045 \text{ (approx.)}$$

(ΣfD^2), dividing by the number of cases (N), and extracting the square root $(\sqrt{\Sigma fD^2/N})$. Our calculation shows σ for the memory span data to be approximately 1.045, or 1.05.

The standard deviation is represented graphically as a distance along the abscissa (the score dimension) of the distribution curve. It is not properly used, however, unless there are many scores distributed symmetrically. Only to the degree that our distribution of scores approximates a normal distribution are we justified in speaking of the probable location of given scores or percentages of scores within a given range. This is because, when we mark off 1σ on each side of the mean of a normal probability curve, 68 per cent of all scores fall within this range. When we mark off 2σ on each side of the mean, approximately 95 per cent of the cases fall within these limits. Plus or minus 3σ takes in over 99 per cent of the cases. It should be clear, then, that if σ is large, the scores are widely scattered from the mean. If it is very small, however, scores are piled up or concentrated closely around the mean. Thus, if we had found a significantly smaller σ for women than for men, we could have concluded that women are less

* Note that, instead of taking the deviation of each separate score, we took the deviation of one score of each magnitude and multiplied it by its frequency.

variable, with respect to memory span, than men. Comparison of their respective sigmas could also tell us such things as the per cent of men exceeding the highest score made by women.

Standard scores

When we know the σ of a distribution we can also place the individual better than by saying merely that his score is above or below average; or even better than by stating its percentile position. We can now derive what is called a *standard score*. This is obtained by dividing the individual's deviation from the mean by σ. Thus the person with a memory span of 8 has a score 2.08 points above the mean (5.92). The σ is 1.045. Thus he has a standard (Z) score of approximately + 1.9 (see Figure 3.9).

One advantage of standard scores, when raw scores are similarly distributed, is that they are comparable from one test to another.* Under these circumstances, the person whose standard score on two tests is 2.5 has comparable status on both tests.

Another advantage of standard scores is that they may be averaged for different tests to show the individual's overall standing. This is because they reduce all measurements to a common scale of units — i.e., deviation units based upon properties of the normal distribution curve. It would be nonsense to add scores on arithmetic, science, and reading in order to derive an average measure of school performance. If such diverse measures were reduced to standard scores, however, it would be quite sensible to average them. Thus a person with a Z score of 1.2 on one test, of 2.3 on another, and of 2.5 on another would have overall status indicated by a Z score of 2.0.

We have not yet considered the reliability of a mean, or of any other measure of central tendency. The meaning of this concept and

* Sometimes, in order to remove minus signs, testers multiply standard scores (Z) by 10 and add 50. T scores are thus derived. This has the effect of making each S.D. = 10 and the Mean = 50. Thus a Z-score of 1.9 becomes a T-score of 69.

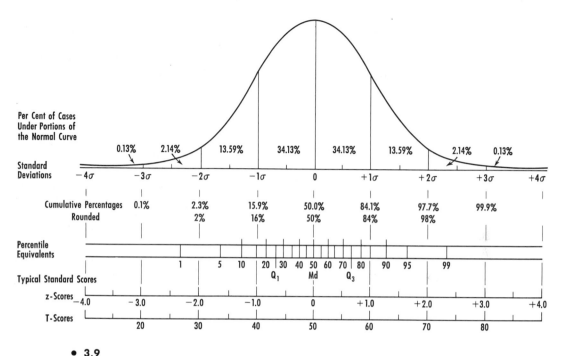

Per Cent of Cases
Under Portions of
the Normal Curve

Standard
Deviations

Cumulative Percentages
Rounded

Percentile
Equivalents

Typical Standard Scores

z-Scores

T-Scores

● **3.9**

A Normal Distribution Curve and Some Related Statistical Terms. This curve shows the per cent of cases under segments of the curve (marked off in terms of sigma units) and also percentiles and standard scores.

its significance in statistical analysis is given brief consideration in the following discussion.

The reliability of a mean

How closely did the group of students who took our memory test represent college students in general? The only way we could answer this question with assurance would be to test all college students. This would, of course, be impossible. However, if we were careful to select our subjects randomly from the larger student population, we could estimate the probable amount of error involved in using a limited sample rather than the whole population. This is because we know that chance errors of sampling tend to be distributed according to the normal curve of probability.

As we have seen, the mean memory span of our sample of subjects was 5.92. In another sample taken from the same total population, we might obtain a mean of 6.0, or of 5.8.

Were we to continue taking random samples and finding their means, we would discover that these sample means form a normal distribution. The mean of this distribution could be considered the *true mean* — that is, the mean of the larger population from which the samples were taken. The standard deviation of such a distribution of means is called the *standard error*, to distinguish it from the σ of a sample. It provides a measure representing the reliability of the mean.

The size of the standard error of the mean (SE$_M$ or σ$_M$) tells us how much variability we might expect to find in repeated samplings from the larger population. It tells us, in other words, how *reliable* our mean is. We shall see that this reliability can be estimated from our particular sample. We shall also see how (1) the size of the sample taken, and (2) the variability of the subjects in this sample, both influence the degree of confidence we can place in our mean.

The formula for σ_M takes into consideration the two chief factors, other than errors of measurement, which would affect the reliability of the mean. One of these is the *number of cases*. Obviously, the larger the group tested, the greater the probability that the obtained mean is representative of all college students. It can be shown that the square root of the number, rather than the number itself, is significant here. One hundred subjects give not 100 times the reliability obtained with one subject, but $\sqrt{100}$, or 10 times. The other factor which influences reliability is σ. It will be recalled that σ shows how closely scores cluster around the mean. One can readily see that, if the σ of our memory span results were small, which would signify that scores were closely piled up around the mean, our measure of central tendency would be more likely to be representative of students as a whole than if the scores were widely scattered — that is, if σ were large.

The σ_M of our data on memory span was found to be .1045. This was obtained by dividing σ (1.045) by the square root of the number of the subjects ($\sqrt{100}$). A σ_M of .1045, or approximately .10, allows us to say that the mean memory span is $5.92 \pm .10$. Reference to a table giving the properties of the normal probability curve shows that we are warranted in saying that the chances are 68 in 100 that the true mean (for an infinitely large sample of college students) would not be likely to fluctuate from the obtained mean more than plus or minus .10. In repeated samples, that is to say, we will be correct 68 times in 100, or 68 per cent of the time, in assuming that the population mean (the *true mean*) will fall between 5.82 and 6.02. Again referring to the characteristics of the normal probability curve, we note that the chances are over 99 in 100 that the true mean will be within the limits of 5.92 plus or minus three times σ_M, or between 5.62 and 6.22.

Precisely why σ_M makes possible such determinations will not be apparent until one has a greater knowledge of statistics than can be presented in an elementary course in psychology. At this stage it is necessary only to get some idea of the kind of information which statistical analysis provides concerning the reliability of the mean.

Reliability of a difference between means

Suppose an investigator wished to discover whether there is a difference in the learning ability of males and females, or of rats deprived of vitamin B_1 and rats fed a normal diet. He would apply a comparable test to a large number of comparable individuals from each group. His next step would be to calculate the mean for each group. Suppose that the mean of one group were 95 and that of the other 105. Is this difference of ten points a reliable one? Perhaps in a repetition of this experiment, the difference in means would disappear or even be reversed. Statistical analysis tells us the probability that the true difference is greater than zero.

The measure used here is the standard error of the difference between two means, or $\sigma_{Diff.}$ It makes use of σ_M. The reason for this is rather obvious, for the more reliable the two means, the more probable is it that the difference between them is also reliable.

Suppose we found the standard errors of the means of 95 and 105 to be respectively, .6 and .9. Then, as calculated below, $\sigma_{Diff.}$ would be 1.08.

$$\begin{aligned} \sigma\,\text{Diff.} &= \sqrt{(\sigma_{M1})^2 + (\sigma_{M2})^2} \\ &= \sqrt{(.6)^2 + (.9)^2} \\ &= \sqrt{.36 + .81} \\ &= \sqrt{1.17} \\ &= 1.08 \text{ (approx.)} \end{aligned}$$

The ratio of this to the actual difference (known as the *critical ratio* or CR) would be 10 over 1.08, or 9.26.

The CR is interpreted in relation to the properties of a normal distribution. Thus interpreted, it tells us the level of confidence we may have in making certain assumptions about the difference obtained. Psychologists commonly talk about the "1 per cent level of confidence" and the "5 per cent level of confidence." If the CR is more than 2.58, as in our example, a difference as great as that found would occur in repeated sampling less than 1 time in 100. This is another way of saying that 99 per cent of the time we would be correct in assuming that there is a real difference between the two means; the means of the sexes, or of the rats fed a normal diet and those deprived of vitamin B_1. Such an assumption would be at the 1 per cent level of confidence. A lesser level of confidence is illustrated when, for example, we get a CR of 1.96. This tells us that, if errors due to random sampling alone were present, we would be correct 95 per cent of the time in assuming the existence of a true difference. Here our assumption would be lowered to the 5 per cent level of confidence.*

This is only one of several methods for testing the significance of a difference between groups. In a particular research, the method used will depend upon such things as size of groups, and how well they are matched. Such methods are considered in courses on statistical analysis and experimental design.

Calculation of correlations

There are several methods of calculating a coefficient of correlation. All give similar re-

* Books on statistics have tables from which such evaluations of critical ratios may be made.

sults, although, under given conditions, certain of them are more conveniently used than others. The *product-moment* method is most widely used. It is preferred when one has a large number of cases (over 30).

One formula for this method is:

$$r = \frac{\Sigma xy}{N\sigma_x\sigma_y}$$

where r is the coefficient of correlation calculated by the product-moment method; x and y, the deviations of X and Y scores from their respective means; N, the number of subjects, and σ_x and σ_y the standard deviations, respectively, of the x and y series of deviations. The application of this formula to the hypothetical data of Figure 3.7 is shown in Table 3.1. As is obvious by inspection of the data, r is 1.00. By reversing the figures in either X or Y and following the same procedure, one comes out with $-10/10$ or -1.00. As calculated by this method, the r between the X and Z scores of Figure 3.7 is approximately $-.52$.

We shall illustrate the *rank-difference* method by correlating the X and Z columns. This method gives a rough estimate of r and is

---

■ **TABLE 3.1   Computing a Coefficient of Correlation (r)**

Subjects	Errors		Deviations		Calculation of σ_x and σ_y		
	X	Y	x	y	xy	x^2	y^2
A	1	2	−2	−2	4	4	4
B	2	3	−1	−1	1	1	1
C	3	4	0	0	0	0	0
D	4	5	1	1	1	1	1
E	5	6	2	2	4	4	4
	15	20			$\Sigma xy = 10$	$\Sigma x^2 = 10$	$\Sigma y^2 = 10$

$$M_X = \frac{15}{5} = 3 \qquad \sigma_x = \sqrt{\frac{10}{5}} = \sqrt{2}$$

$$M_Y = \frac{20}{5} = 4 \qquad \sigma_y = \sqrt{\frac{10}{5}} = \sqrt{2}$$

$$r = \frac{10}{5(\sqrt{2} \times \sqrt{2})} = \frac{10}{5 \times 2} = 1.00$$

easier to calculate. The formula for calculating a rank-difference coefficient, Rho (ρ), is

$$\rho = 1 - \frac{6\Sigma D^2}{N(N^2 - 1)}$$

where ΣD^2 is the sum of the squared differences between the ranks of scores in the two series and N is the number of cases. It is first necessary to determine separately the ranking of individuals in each of the performances to be correlated. The computation follows at the right.

The coefficients r and ρ are seldom identical, although they are usually similar. The difference occurs because the formula for ρ, unlike that for r, ignores the differences in actual magnitude of the scores, dealing with them merely in terms of rank. Tables have been worked out so that one can read off the value of r for a given value of ρ. The value of r for a ρ of $-.50$ is, for example, $-.518$.

The more closely r approximates plus or minus one (± 1) the higher the relationship between the variables correlated. But, as we said earlier, a coefficient of correlation does not mean per cent of relationship. Percentages

of dependence of one variable on another, or of both on some third variable, can be calculated from r, but except when r is very high, these percentages are much lower than r.

Subjects	Errors		Ranks		D	D²
	X	Z	X	Z		
A	1	9	1	5	4	16
B	2	6	2	3	1	1
C	3	3	3	1	2	4
D	4	8	4	4	0	0
E	5	4	5	2	3	9

$$\Sigma D^2 = 30$$

$$1 - \frac{6(30)}{5(25 - 1)}$$

$$1 - \frac{180}{5(24)}$$

$$1 - \frac{180}{120}$$

$$1 - 1.50$$

$$- .50$$

• SUMMARY

Before individual differences can be studied scientifically it is necessary to measure individual traits. Some of these (like height, weight, and speed of reaction) are measurable in the absolute units (inches, pounds, seconds) of a ratio scale. Scales of this nature begin with zero and increase by equal increments. They allow us to say, for example, that one individual is twice as strong as another. But many psychological traits do not lend themselves to such measurement. The individual's score on an intelligence test or a rating scale has no absolute value. One must evaluate it in terms of what others score. When such measures are used, the scores are interpreted from the standpoint of their ordinal position, or rank.

For this reason, such scales are referred to as ordinal. Interval scales are those which, as in the case of the thermometer, start from an arbitrary zero but have increments of equivalent value. Although most psychological measurements involve either a ratio or an ordinal scale, it is theoretically possible to design tests in accordance with an interval scale.

In general, the absolute measures of a ratio scale are more consistent (reliable or dependable) than the relative measures of an ordinal scale. Nevertheless, many psychological tests and rating scales are sufficiently reliable for measurement of individual differences. This is evident when we correlate two administrations of a test, or the ratings of behavior by one observer with the ratings of the same behavior by another observer.

After measurements have been made with a reliable test, the next step is to see what they reveal about individual differences. Here statistical devices are indispensable. We may begin by making a frequency distribution. From this we observe the modal (most frequent) score, the range (difference between the highest and lowest score), and how closely scores are bunched around the central tendency (mean or mode). A distribution may be represented graphically by a frequency polygon, a histogram, or a bar graph. When there are many cases, the frequency polygon may approximate a bell-shaped (normal probability) curve. In such a curve, scores pile up near the middle and have a decreasing frequency outward in both directions. Sometimes, however, scores are concentrated toward one end of the distribution. Such curves are said to be skewed. Some curves have two modes (bimodal) or several modes (multimodal). Distribution curves for different groups given the same test may overlap more or less. This is of course true when their means are similar. There may be much overlapping, however, even when the means are far apart. The average strength of males is far greater than that of females, for instance, yet some females are stronger than the average

male. There are also differences in variability. Two groups can have the same mean, yet differ in range and in other measures of variability, as shown in the statistical supplement.

An individual's status is indicated with respect to how much and in what direction his score differs from the mean, its rank, or its percentile standing. His score may, for example, be at the 75th percentile, in which case it is equaled or exceeded by 25 per cent of the scores.

Differences in one variable may be related to differences in another. This is indicated by a scatter diagram or by more refined statistical calculations, one of which yields a coefficient of correlation, or r. This coefficient may be positive or negative. It may vary on the positive side from 0 to 1.00 and on the negative side from -1.00 to 0. The higher the correlation (positive or negative) the higher the relationship between the two variables. But r is not a percentage. Nor does it necessarily indicate causality.

Readers who studied the statistical supplement became acquainted with some additional concepts, such as the median, standard deviation of a distribution, standard error of the mean, and the critical ratio. They also learned how to calculate these, as well as the coefficient of correlation (r) and the coefficient of rank-difference correlation (ρ). ■

REFERENCES AND NOTES FOR THIS CHAPTER ARE IN THE APPENDIX.

• SELECTED READINGS

Anastasi, A., *Differential Psychology* (3rd ed.). Macmillan, 1958. A particularly good source of information on every aspect of individual differences.

Blommers, P., and E. F. Lindquist, *Elementary Statistical Methods*. Houghton Mifflin, 1960. See this for more detail on statistics.

Daniel, R. S. (Ed.), *Contemporary Readings in General Psychology* (2nd ed.). Houghton Mifflin, 1965. See selections 23 and 27 for discussions of human variability and of differences and similarities between the sexes.

Hammond, K. R., and J. E. Householder, *Introduction to Statistical Method*. Knopf, 1962. Another good source for more detail on statistics.

McCulloch, C., and L. Van Atta, *Statistical Concepts*. McGraw-Hill, 1963. A program for self-instruction.

4

How Individual Differences Originate

*E*ach of us undergoes a process of development which begins with fertilization of the ovum and continues until maturity. Development may continue, in some, until senescence. New skills may be acquired and aspects of personality may change. At the beginning, every human embryo looks like every other. It is through the process of growth that we come to differ in appearance and in many aspects of our behavior. Differences are obvious even at birth. When examined even casually, newborn babies look very different in size, in the color of their hair and eyes, and in body shape. Their behavior also differs. Some are more active than others, some cry more, and some have better appetites. As the years go by, the characteristics in which individuals differ become so numerous that it is difficult to catalog them.

Since we all have such a similar beginning, it is interesting to ask what makes us so different as we grow older. One answer is that, except in the case of identical twins, we have different heredity. Our environments also differ. There is, however, a constant interplay between hereditary and environmental influences and our physical and mental characteristics are complex resultants of this interaction.

Heredity is a constant factor, established at the time of fertilization. The individual's environment, on the other hand, is continually expanding. From the relatively simple chemical environment of the newly conceived organism we get, eventually, to the highly complicated social environment of people, books, schools, and so forth. It is interesting to note, moreover, that although heredity is a constant factor, its potentialities are realized at different stages of growth and always in relation to present and past environmental conditions.

When we say that inherent potentialities are realized at different stages we are referring to facts which underlie the concept of *maturation*. Certain aspects of behavior, of which reflexes are the most obvious example, appear whether or not the individual has had any opportunity to learn them, and they appear at about the same time in all individuals of a particular species. Many activities of greater complexity than reflexes also characterize a species (like flying in birds, walking in humans), and they have their characteristic schedules of development, even under conditions of environmental restriction. We say, therefore, that their development depends primarily upon an inherent growth potential, or maturation. We say, too, that individuals mature at different rates. This is quite obviously true when we consider, for example, the developmental maturity of a young ape and the relative immaturity of a human child of the same age. That the child eventually goes on to achieve high levels of performance in intellectual spheres while the ape reaches his limit in a few years is also determined, in large measure, by differences in their inheritance. The same thing is true, on a more limited scale, when we consider two human beings. If they have the same inheritance (as in the case of identical twins), they normally develop at the same rate and remain very much alike throughout life. But if they have markedly different heredity, one may mature at a fast rate, soon outdistancing the other. As our later discussion will show, environmental differences are also always important. Included among these are various aspects of early experience, opportunities for self-initiated practice, and special training. The rate of physical and behavioral growth can be greatly accelerated or retarded by such environmental conditions. It is only when such conditions are held constant that we witness, as it were, the unadulterated influence of maturation.

The following discussions are designed to answer such questions as: What is heredity? How does it produce individual differences? What is meant by environment? What are the different kinds of environmental influence? How do heredity and environment interact to produce individual differences? How may we differentiate their respective influences? What are the respective roles of maturation and exercise? ∎

HEREDITY

Each of us begins life as a single fertilized cell smaller than the head of a pin. This fertilized egg (ovum) has a nucleus surrounded by cytoplasm, as shown in Figure 4.1. The determiners of heredity are complex organizations of chemical materials within the nucleus. More specifically, they are contained in nuclear structures which, because they show up when stained, are known as *chromosomes*, or colored bodies.

Microscopic studies of human body cells show that chromosomes come in pairs. Females have twenty-three pairs. Males have twenty-two pairs, plus two singles.* One of these, identified in Figure 4.2, is the Y chromosome found only in males. Females have a pair of X chromosomes while males have only one. The X and Y are called sex chromosomes because our sex depends upon whether we get the XX or XY combination.

Sets of chromosomes from different persons of the same sex look very much alike. Since they are the chromosomes which characterize the human race, we would expect this. But, except in the case of identical twins, the similar-looking chromosomes of different persons actually differ internally. These differences are most pronounced in unrelated individuals.

Genes

All of our innumerable inherited characteristics are represented in the forty-six chromosomes. Thus each chromosome must carry many determiners. From this fact, and the way in which inherited characteristics, singly and in diverse combinations, are transmitted from one generation to another, geneticists long ago inferred that the chromosomes must be differentiated internally. It was assumed, in other words, that different regions of a chromosome determine different characteristics, such as eye color and skin texture. Some of these regions were located and represented on chromosome maps.

* Human beings were long thought to have forty-eight chromosomes but recent observations show that the correct number is forty-six.

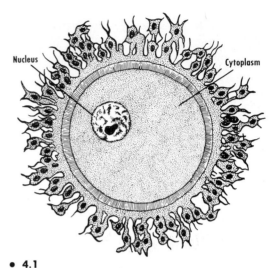

● 4.1
A Human Ovum. The ovum comprises the nucleus, cytoplasm, and surrounding membranes. Cells shown on the outside belong to the mother, not to the ovum. (After Arey)

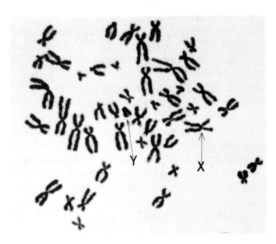

● 4.2
The Human Chromosomes. In this photomicrograph we can see not only that there are forty-six chromosomes in all, but also that the cell is from a male. The latter is made evident by the existence of an X and a Y chromosome. If it had been a female cell there would have been two X chromosomes. The doubled appearance of the chromosomes shows that, when the photo was taken, they were in the process of duplication, known as mitosis. This process is discussed a little later. (Photo from Dr. J. H. Tjio)

The hereditary factors hidden within the chromosomes were called *genes* (which means determiners). They were assumed to be "packets of chemicals" strung along the chromosome like beads on a thread or peas in a pod. But nobody had yet seen anything that might be identified as a gene.

Then geneticists discovered that the salivary gland of the fruit fly contains exceptionally large chromosomes which, when viewed microscopically, have dark and light bands throughout their length (Figure 4.3A). The genes were thought to be in these bands. Now the electron microscope reveals the sort of detail shown in Figure 4.3B, which represents a piece of salivary gland chromosome magnified 26,000 times. Observers of this, and even higher magnifications, believe that "the discrete particles" they have seen are genes.

☐ The chemical makeup of genes is now under intensive investigation, but it has been apparent for some years that the most important constituent is deoxyribonucleic acid, or DNA. DNA is found in all chromosomes and some of its properties are those which genes must have, including variations in its forms and ability to duplicate itself. The Watson-Crick model of the structure of DNA molecules, which shows how they may maintain their constancy from generation to generation and also how duplication may occur, won its authors the 1962 Nobel Prize, which they shared with Wilkins, whose X-ray diffraction studies of DNA provided a basis for their work.[1] The structure of DNA is believed to contain genetic information in coded form. At appropriate times in the development of cells, this information is communicated, in some as yet unknown way, to determine the course of their further development. ☐

Action of the genes on cytoplasm changes the shape and other characteristics of cells. Genes, together with internal environmental conditions, change cells from their original shape to form the great variety (muscle, bone, nerve, and so on) which make up the response mechanisms. Each gene combines with other genes to produce a variety of characteristics.

A

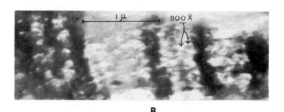

B

● **4.3**

A Portion of a Salivary Gland Chromosome. This is one of the giant chromosomes of the fruit fly's salivary gland. **A** shows such a chromosome under a high-powered microscope. **B** is not a photograph, but an electron micrograph of a very small portion of a salivary gland chromosome. The differentiations, enlarged here 26,000 times, are believed to be, or to contain, genes. (From D. C. Pease and R. F. Baker, "Chromosomes, Genes, and the Electron Microscope," *Science, 1949, 109,* p. 9.)

Multiplication of cells

When a fertilized ovum is about to divide, its chromosomes (and genes) are duplicated. A complete set is subsequently passed on to each resulting cell. Through this process of chromosome duplication and cell division, all except reproductive cells (to be discussed in detail later) receive an identical inheritance.

Sometimes, instead of remaining together as parts of a single organism, the first two cells separate and form two identical organisms. This is how identical twins originate. Siamese twins come from an incomplete separation of identical cells. Identical quadruplets come from separation at the four-celled stage.

In all subsequent divisions, up to the time of puberty, when reproductive cells develop, the chromosomes are duplicated as already described.

Maturation of reproduction cells

At the time of puberty, cells set aside for reproductive purposes undergo a kind of division different from that described. Instead of the chromosomes being split and duplicated just prior to cell division, one member of a pair goes to each new cell. Thus, each cell has only one-half of the chromosomes, twenty-three instead of forty-six. The ovum gets only one-half of the mother's chromosomes and the sperm gets only one-half of the father's. Different ova (or sperms) produced by the same individual receive different combinations of chromosomes. Which one of each pair of chromosomes shall go to a particular ovum or sperm is determined by "chance." Thus two persons receiving twenty-three chromosomes from their father will not (unless they are identical twins) get the same twenty-three; similarly, of course, for the mother's chromosomes.

Fertilization re-establishes the full complement of chromosomes. Which sperm (which set of twenty-three chromosomes from the male) will unite with which ovum (which set of twenty-three chromosomes from the female) to produce the new individual is again a matter of "chance." The laws of inheritance are laws relating to (1) the "chance" assortment

● **4.4**

How Our Grandparents Contribute to Our Inheritance. Here we have assumed, for purposes of simplicity, that only six instead of forty-six chromosomes are involved. Observe that the four grandparents may contribute different numbers and kinds of chromosomes to their grandchildren. Only two of many possible combinations are illustrated. At the time when sperm are developed, the set of chromosomes coming from the potential father's parents is a "chance" affair. Theoretically, they may be all from his mother or all from his father. Likewise, the contributions of each parent of the potential mother are determined by "chance." One-half of the chromosomes must come from the mother's parents and one-half from the father's, as indicated, but how much each grandparent has actually contributed cannot, of course, be known.

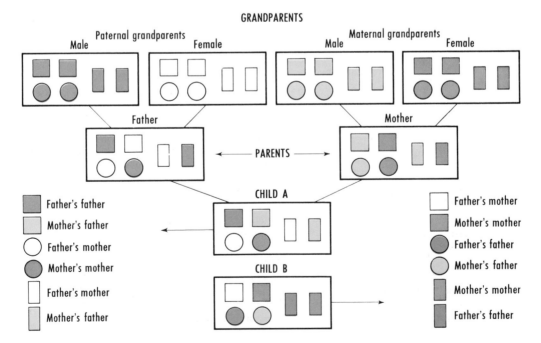

of chromosomes within ova and sperm, and (2) the "chance" association of particular sperms and ova at fertilization.

During the production of sperms and ova and the process of fertilization, the contribution of each grandparent is also determined in a "chance" fashion. This contribution is illustrated in Figure 4.4 and discussed in the legend. ■

ENVIRONMENT

The most obvious environmental influences are those which act upon the organism from without, and especially those which operate after birth. There exists, however, an internal environment, which, at the earlier stages of development, is more influential than the external environment.

The internal environment

The nucleus, with its chromosomes and their genes, is surrounded by a jelly-like substance known as cytoplasm. This substance was illustrated in the picture of a human ovum with which our discussion of heredity began.

The cytoplasm is often referred to as an *intracellular environment* because the genes surrounded by it are influenced by, and in turn influence, its characteristics. In fact what the organism becomes is determined by its cytoplasm as well as its heredity. In lower organisms one can sometimes change the cytoplasm without altering the nucleus. This produces a markedly abnormal organism.[2]

After the interaction of genes and cytoplasm has produced several cells (each with identical heredity) a new internal environment comes into existence. The cells press one upon the other. Some influence their neighbors chemically and electrically. We thus have the sort of *intercellular environment* represented by Figure 4.5.

Experimental embryologists have changed the position of certain cells in relation to others, and these have developed characteristics appropriate to their new location. This

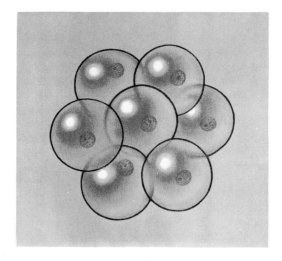

● **4.5**

The Early Intercellular Environment of a Cell. When several cells have developed, those which surround a given cell (center) constitute its intercellular environment.

ability of certain cells to substitute for others is attributable to the possession of the same hereditary factors by all cells. The actual structure of a cell depends, however, upon its relation to other cells.[3] Developing in one location, the cellular substance becomes brain tissue; developing in another location, the same substance becomes part of the visual mechanism.

Later, when the endocrine glands develop and pour their hormones into the blood stream, still another intercellular influence is produced.

Hormones are important for further development of the entire organism. Indeed many deformities evident at birth are the result of overactive or underactive endocrine functioning. Other chemical characteristics of the blood are also important in development.

We have discussed the internal environment only as it influences early growth and produces individual differences. However, one should not overlook the continuing importance of the internal environment of blood (with its hormones and other substances). It continues to be a major influence throughout life.

External environments

As the cells multiply and become transformed to serve their respective functions, the embryo itself emerges and becomes increasingly complex. Then the growing organism is surrounded by amniotic fluid and attached to the mother by what becomes its umbilical cord. Through the latter, nourishment is obtained and waste products are excreted. This *prenatal external environment* is extremely important, for normal development can proceed only if the liquid which surrounds the organism has the proper thermal and chemical properties. Moreover, nourishment coming from the mother's bloodstream must have properties that are conducive to proper growth.[4]

After birth there is the broader external environment with its immense variety of physical and social contacts. This is what we customarily think of as the environment. One part of it, our social environment, includes language, customs, and many other aspects of culture. Together, these comprise our *social heritage*.

From the time of conception on, there is a constant interplay of hereditary and environmental influences. It is this interplay that we shall now consider. ■

HEREDITY AND ENVIRONMENT

Some babies are born with physical and psychological abnormalities which depend almost entirely on defective heredity. Others are born with similar abnormalities, but which in their case are determined almost exclusively by a defective prenatal environment. A study of such cases suggests the respective parts played in prenatal development by hereditary factors and environmental conditions.

Hereditary abnormalities

These seldom occur in isolation. They crop up here and there among related individuals. These anomalies occur, too, in related persons with different mothers, which would mean different prenatal environments. Some examples of rather obvious hereditary defects are the "lobster claw," which appeared in a man and both of his children; the absence of hands and feet, which happened in a father and six out of twelve of his children; and polydactyly (see Figure 4.6), which runs in families. Such bodily changes, appearing suddenly and thereafter inheritable, are known as *mutations*. They are due to alterations in chromosomes or genes. Many mutations occur spontaneously. However, the mutation rate is greatly accelerated by artificial radiation, which also produces mutations not otherwise found.

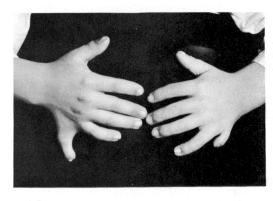

● **4.6**
Polydactyly. The inheritance of six fingers and six toes runs in certain families. Sometimes the extra finger is removed surgically. (Photo, courtesy of C. Nash Herndon)

In addition to inherited bodily abnormalities directly attributable to mutations, there are numerous behavior disorders which appear repeatedly through generation after generation of certain families. Among these are a nervous affliction known as Huntington's chorea and certain kinds of feeblemindedness.

Human beings sometimes inherit more than the usual number of chromosomes, with resulting abnormalities of development. In a form of feeblemindedness called *mongolism*, for example, the chromosome known to geneticists as number 21 is present in triplicate instead of duplicate. Thus the individual has 47 instead of the usual 46 chromosomes.[5] The psychological defects present in mongolism are discussed in the next chapter.

Environmentally produced abnormalities

Many abnormalities result from defective prenatal environments. These are isolated occurrences. They appear in related individuals no more often than in those who are unrelated. In many instances, the environmental defect is apparent. Here, for example, is a boy whose arm is withered because the umbilical cord twisted around it during the fetal period. Here is a physically deformed organism whose prenatal quarters were too cramped, or who maintained during the fetal period a position not conducive to normal growth of certain structures.

If the mother's bloodstream does not supply enough calcium, abnormalities of the skeleton appear. If her blood sugar is too high as a result of diabetes, the pancreas of her fetus may work excessively. This excessive functioning may continue at birth, reducing the blood sugar of the infant so much that, unless special treatment is given, it dies from insufficiency of glycogen (i.e., from hypoglycemia). Foreign substances in the mother's blood may also influence the development of the embryo. We see a tragic example of this in the case of so-called thalidomide babies, whose mothers took a sleeping tablet containing the drug thalidomide at a time when the limbs of the embryo were forming. This often resulted in shortened and otherwise deformed limbs. In many infants the hands or feet failed to develop.

Many cases of abnormal head and brain development are believed to result from improper prenatal conditions — perhaps chemical inadequacies of the mother's blood. Head injuries at birth, either through prolonged pressure on the head during a difficult labor or from instrumental delivery, often result in spastic paralysis, feeblemindedness, epilepsy, and other defects. All defects produced in these ways are, of course, environmental. Heredity has nothing whatsoever to do with them.

Significance of the postnatal environment

The external environment after birth is extremely variable, and unrelated to the sort of genes which the individual has. No two human beings, even living in the same home and going to the same school, have the same environment. Geographically and socially their environment may seem the same. From the standpoint of its effect on their development, however, it may be quite different. Different individuals within the same environment meet different people and are influenced differently by the same people. They develop different interests and attitudes, and they identify themselves with different groups — religious, political, and recreational.

The fact that the postnatal environment is so variable, and its effects so unpredictable, makes it difficult for us to discover the relative influence of heredity and environment on psychological development after birth.

Every one of us, as we have said before, is a product of both heredity and environment. We could not develop without genes, and the genes could have no effect without normal surrounding tissues. But is the difference between Mary Brown and Jane Smith due to a difference in their heredity, or in their environment? Unless they are identical twins with different names, as in some cases to be mentioned shortly, they differ in heredity; some of the observable difference between them is attributable to this. They certainly have a somewhat different environment, even if living in the same home. And part of the difference, especially in psychological characteristics, is attributable to this. The difference, therefore, between two or more individuals is normally attributable to both heredity and environment.

Which is more important in producing these differences — heredity or environment? The answer depends upon the traits under examination. Any difference in the appearance and other physical characteristics of Mary Brown and Jane Smith at birth is due primarily to their different genes, for it is probable that their environments before birth were similar. Even after birth, the difference in their environments would produce only superficial differences in physique. But how about traits like intelligence? One may be much brighter than the other. Again, the difference in genes may be important, but we cannot be as sure as in the case of physical traits.

The only scientific procedure that can be used in studying the relative influence of hereditary factors and environment on physique, intelligence, personality, or other characteristics is to hold either heredity or environment constant while the other is varied. The possibility of carrying out such experiments with human beings is limited. We cannot mate persons of known heredity so as to control the inheritance of their offspring as, for example, we can mate mice or rats. Nor can we subject human beings to a constant environment, because what appears to be the same environment is not psychologically the same. ■

EXPERIMENTAL INVESTIGATIONS

Here we consider two kinds of investigation. In one of these heredity is held constant and environment is varied. The constant heredity is provided by nature, in the production of identical twins. The varied environment comes, not from experimental intervention, but from social conditions dictating that the twins be separated at or soon after birth. In effect, then, we have an experimental situation already arranged and the role of the investigator is only to observe the results and interpret them. In the second kind of investigation considered here we use animals because we can hold their environment nearly constant, and, through selective breeding, produce desired variations in heredity.

Heredity constant

Identical twins are normally reared in the same home and, while their environment is not psychologically the same, it is more similar than in the case of individuals not so intimately related. Generally speaking, identical twins have very similar educational opportunities. In view of this and their identical heredity, it is not surprising that the average difference in their I.Q.'s (intelligence quotients) is only around six points and that the correlation between their I.Q.'s is .87. Fraternal twins differ in heredity but usually have somewhat comparable educational opportunities.

The average difference in their I.Q.'s is around ten points. The correlation between these is .53.[6]

Is the closer physical and psychological similarity of identical twins due to their identical heredity, their similar environments, or both?

When identical twins are adopted into different homes, we have a basis for answering this question. Data have now been reported for 107 pairs of separated identical twins.[7] In appearance and in other purely physical characteristics the twins, when brought together again, are found to be very much alike. Those in Figure 4.7, for example, were separated at two months. Paul C, the twin on the left, lived in a small town until he was thirteen, in a larger town for two years, and finally in a medium-sized city. He completed high school at eighteen, after which he took some business courses while working. His brother, Paul O, lived for the most part in rural environments, shifting from place to place a great deal, because his foster father, a telegraph operator, moved from one job to another. This twin completed high school at the same age as his brother. After less than one year in college, where mathematics proved a stumbling block, Paul O became an assistant postmaster.

When these twins were brought together and tested at twenty-three, the I.Q. difference was only two points. It should be noted, however, that they had a somewhat comparable schooling. Among other twins, some of whom differed more widely in educational opportunity, the differences in I.Q. ranged up to twenty-four points. It is interesting to observe, moreover, that there was a fairly high and significant correlation (r of .79) between educational opportunities (as estimated from schooling and other data) and the magnitude of the difference in I.Q.[8] This correlation suggests that, even in persons of the same heredity, differences in educational opportunity produce significant differences in the abilities measured by intelligence tests.

The average difference in I.Q. for identical twins reared apart is around eight points. This is about two points more than in those reared together. The correlation between I.Q.'s is

.87 for those reared together and .75 for those reared apart.[9] In personality traits the separated twins were sometimes very similar and sometimes very different. By and large, however, there were larger differences in personality than in I.Q.

We see, then, that identical heredity makes individuals very much alike in physique, somewhat less alike in I.Q., and still less alike in personality. With respect to I.Q. and personality the effect of environmental differences is relatively large.

Environment constant

It is impossible to hold the environment of two human beings strictly constant. We might hold the environment constant geographically and in almost every physical sense, even to the extent of having the same parents, the same home, the same school, and the same teachers. But its effective constancy could still not be guaranteed. Psychologically the environment might still be very different for one individual than for another. This is because human beings react selectively to the varied details of their surroundings. In the case of animals like mice and rats, on the other hand, we can approximate environmental constancy by rearing them in the same cages, in the same general surroundings, and with the same food and care. In view of the simplicity of such environments and the simplicity of the observational processes of these animals, it is unlikely that uncontrolled differences in the psychological environment are involved. Therefore, we can conduct experiments on heredity with assurance that hereditary factors rather than environmental variations are responsible for the resulting differences in behavior.

There have been many experiments on the hereditary determination of behavior but we will restrict our discussion to three examples — a form of waltzing locomotion in mice, a tendency toward audiogenic seizures in mice, and maze-learning ability in rats.

• *Locomotion.* Some mice have an inherent defect which produces a whirling or waltzing type of locomotion.[10] Let us take a female

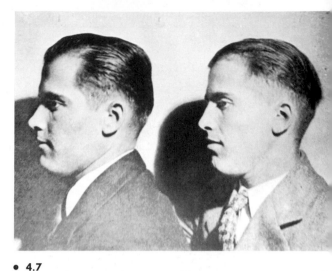

• 4.7

Identical Twins Reared Apart. These twins, as described in the text, were reared apart for twenty-three years, one in a rural and the other in an urban environment. When tested at 23 years, the difference in their I.Q.'s was two points. (From H. H. Newman. Reprinted by special permission of *The Journal of Heredity.*)

thus afflicted and mate her with a mouse which runs normally. We will need to suppose that both the female waltzer and the male runner come from stock that is pure with respect to the traits under consideration.

It will be recalled that genes come in pairs. Purebred runners have genes which we will refer to as *RR*. Capitals are used because the gene for running is *dominant*. That is, if it appears with a gene for waltzing, the possessor of this combination will run rather than waltz. The ineffective gene is said to be *recessive* and it is customarily referred to by use of a lower case letter, in this instance *r*. Our female waltzers, then, must have the gene combination *rr*.

Every sperm of normal purebred males has an *R* gene and every ovum of purebred waltzing females an *r* gene. The combination in all of their offspring must therefore be *Rr*. For this reason we would predict that all offspring will be runners, and this is what is found. But suppose we now mate *Rr* with *Rr* mice? Can the outcome again be predicted? It can, for there are, as shown in Figure 4.8, only two kinds of sperm (*R*, *r*) and two kinds of ova (*R*, *r*). Chance combinations of

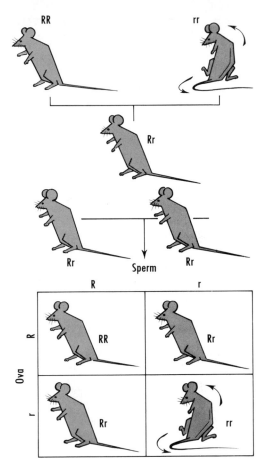

• **4.8**

Inheritance of Waltzing Locomotion in Mice. This is inheritance involving dominance of one trait, viz., normal locomotion. Observe that both waltzers have two recessive genes for this trait. (Modified from Sinnott and Dunn.)

these at fertilization will result in one-fourth of the offspring having *RR*, one-half *Rr*, and one-fourth *rr* genes. Moreover, because running is dominant, we can predict that three-fourths of the offspring will be runners and one-fourth waltzers, and our prediction is confirmed. This supposes, of course, that large numbers of individuals are involved. If only one litter of four mice were concerned, one might or might not obtain three runners and one waltzer.

If dominance were not present, we would find one-fourth runners, one-fourth waltzers, and one-half with some sort of compromise between waltzing and running. Many inherited traits, including skin color in human beings, are dependent upon the combined effects of genes which are neither dominant nor recessive. Also, and this is true of skin color, many traits are dependent upon more than one gene pair. The waltzing example, therefore, is a comparatively simple one.

• *Audiogenic seizures.* These seizures are so named because they are initiated by auditory stimulation. When stimulated with an intense, high-pitched sound, some mice react much as if they were having epileptic seizures. After running widely in a circular path they fall to the floor (Figure 4.9) and go into convulsions.[11] In one species of mouse, such a seizure is frequently followed by death.[12]

The fact that some mice react to high-pitched sounds by having a seizure and others do not suggests that susceptibility may be inherited. Efforts to discover hereditary factors have led to various results, depending upon the strain of animals involved. In the common house mouse, however, there is apparently a dominant gene for susceptibility to audiogenic seizure.[13] The dominant gene is here referred to as *As*, the recessive gene as *as*. If susceptibility were determined by *As*, one would predict that a cross between purebred reactors and nonreactors would produce 100 per cent reactors. Actually the percentage of reactors in a group of 81 offspring of such a cross was 90. From a cross between these hybrid reactors (with a hypothetical *As*, *as* gene combination), one would expect 75 per cent reactors and 25 per cent nonreactors. The respective percentages actually found were 77 and 23; close enough to those predicted to lend support to the hypothesis that a single dominant gene is largely responsible for susceptibility. However, the discrepancies between predicted and actual percentages, as well as other considerations which need not concern us here, suggest that the *As* gene is supplemented by other genes in producing the above effects.

• *Maze-learning ability.* One hundred forty-two white rats were each given nineteen trials

● 4.9

Mice of Sensitive Strain in Audiogenic Convulsions. Upon hearing a loud doorbell, they go into convulsions. (Courtesy of B. E. Ginsburg and D. S. Miller, whose research it illustrates. See B. E. Ginsburg and D. S. Miller, in D. Hooker and C. Hare, Eds., *Genetics and the Inheritance of Integrated Neurological and Psychiatric Patterns,* Williams and Wilkins, 1954. Photo by Wallace Kirkland, *Life,* © Time, Inc.)

in a maze.[14] The number of entrances into blind alleys (errors) for each rat was recorded. The smallest number of errors was 7, and the greatest 214. Rats making very few errors were designated *bright,* and those making many errors were designated *dull.*

Keeping the environment (food, lighting, caging, temperature, and so on) constant, the experimenter bred the brightest rats in each generation with each other. Likewise, he bred the dullest with the dullest. After following this procedure for seven generations, two races of rats — a bright and a dull — were developed. The error distributions at the beginning and after seven generations of selective breeding are illustrated in Figure 4.10.

At the beginning, the rats were distributed so that most of them made scores in about the middle of the two extremes. After seven generations, however, there was a bimodal distribution — a distribution in which many rats (the bright) made low error scores, and many other rats (the dull) made very high error scores. Few animals had ability in the middle of the range. Selective mating was continued through the eighteenth generation, but without producing any greater difference than that indicated.

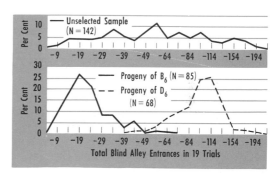

● 4.10

Inheritance of Maze-Learning Ability in Rats. In the parent generation (142 rats), the number of errors made in nineteen trials ranged from 5 to 214. The intermediate number of errors was made by around 12 per cent. Smaller percentages of rats made the successively lower and successively higher numbers of errors. The lower figure represents the seventh generation, in which the dull (large number of errors) were mated with the dull, and the bright (small number of errors) were mated with the bright. It shows two races, a bright and a dull, with slight overlapping near the center of the error range. (From R. C. Tryon, "Genetic Differences in Maze-Learning Ability in Rats," *39th Yearbook, Nat. Soc. Study Educ.,* Part I, 1940, pp. 111–119.)

99

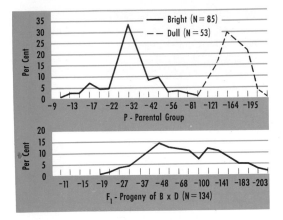

● 4.11

The Effect of Mating Bright and Dull Rats. Observe that the bright rats had error scores ranging from 9 to around 80, while the dull rats had error scores ranging from around 80 to around 200. Very few rats had scores in the range from 40 to 100. In a cross of bright and dull rats, however, most of the rats had scores in this intermediate range. (From R. C. Tryon, "Genetic Differences in Maze-Learning Ability in Rats," *39th Yearbook, Nat. Soc. Study Educ.*, Part I, 1940, pp. 115.)

Bright and dull rats were then mated, with the result illustrated in Figure 4.11. One can see that mating bright and dull rats produced a distribution much like that with which the experiment began. There were now few bright and few dull rats. Rats of intermediate ability predominated.

Subsequent research has shown that bright rats developed as described above are not generally brighter than other rats. They are merely "maze bright." On problems not involving mazes they are not necessarily brighter than "maze dull" or unselected rats.

In a more recent investigation,[15] rats were selectively bred in terms of their performance on an intelligence test designed for rats. This device, the Hebb-Williams test,[16] requires ability to circumvent different detours from time to time in order to get from the entrance to the food box of a maze. Again, the score was in terms of errors: animals making relatively few errors being designated "bright" and those making a relatively large number of errors

being designated "dull." The outcome of selective breeding on this basis is seen in Figure 4.12. Observe that, beginning with the second generation, the mean error scores of the two groups became increasingly divergent. Again we have clear evidence of differences produced, in a comparable environment, by variations in inheritance.[17]

Complex traits, like maze-learning ability, and facility in fitting behavior to changing circumstances — a mark of intelligence — are doubtless influenced by many genes. It has been posited, in fact, that multiple genes

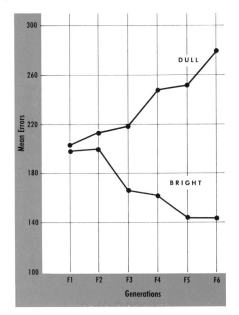

● 4.12

The Effect of Selective Breeding for Brightness and Dullness Shown on an Intelligence Test for Rats. The "intelligence" test is carried out in the Hebb-Williams maze. After a rat has been familiarized with the entrance and the exit, where food is received, and also with certain sample detours, it is given a series of tests, spread over several days, in which detours of various kinds are introduced. Its score is based upon its ability to take the most direct route in each setting. Errors are divergences from this. (From W. R. Thompson, "The Inheritance and Development of Intelligence," *Proc. Assoc. Res. Nerv. Ment. Dis.*, 1954, *33*, p. 217).

(polygenes), are responsible for inherent maze-learning ability in rats.[18]

☐ In polygenic inheritance, each gene is assumed to have two degrees of expression. One gene, for example, may have the degrees of expression *A* and *a*, another the degrees of expression *B* and *b*, still another *C* and *c* — and so on for many relevant genes. It is assumed that a rat with the *AA* gene combination is, to this extent, brighter than the rat with the *aa* combination. A rat with the *Aa* pair of genes would then lie between the extremes. No dominance is assumed to exist.

If we assume that many genes determine maze-learning ability, and that each pair functions as above, the relevant genes possessed by the brightest possible rat would be *AABBCC-DDEE*. . . . The dullest rat would have the genes *aabbccddee*. . . . A cross between such rats would, in terms of probability, produce many combinations. Such combinations as *AaBbCcDdEe* . . . would occur with the highest frequency and there would be gradations toward the extremes of the distribution. If inheritance of maze-learning ability were determined in this way, we would expect that crossings of bright with dull rats would yield a normal distribution rather than the separate classes of animals obtained when, for example, single pairs of genes are involved. That is, instead of having bright rats, dull rats, and average rats (as we had runners and waltzers), we would have a distribution without breaks. This is, in fact, what was found in the above maze study, the results of which were illustrated in Figures 4.10 and 4.11. The frequency polygon representing errors, while it deviated from a normal frequency curve in some respects, was at least continuous, with the highest frequencies in an intermediate position. ☐

It is a far cry from rats in a maze to human beings with their complex behavior mechanisms and highly complex environment. Nevertheless there is every reason to believe that heredity operates in men as it does in rats. The number of chromosomes and genes is different, to be sure, but there are dominant and recessive genes, and their random assort-ment is like that described in our first example. There are also genes whose effects blend, as in the determination of skin color and perhaps many structures which underlie differences in behavior. Human intelligence is also influenced by heredity, for we inherit our brain structures and these play a key role in learning and retention. The hereditary contribution to individual differences in human intelligence is no doubt determined by multiple genes complexly assorted. Integrated with hereditary complexity in this instance is environmental complexity. ■

MATURATION AND EXERCISE

Related to the hereditary conditions that we have been considering, and also to environmental variations, are the interdependent processes of maturation and exercise. As suggested earlier, *maturation* is the growth process which, even in the absence of opportunities to learn, provides organisms with structures and modes of adaptation characteristic of their species. It represents an influence that is primarily due to an organism's inheritance — the genes that are typical of its race and those which comprise its particular sample. Contrasted with this, but related to it, is the influence of what we shall refer to, in general terms, as *exercise*. This represents an influence that is basically environmental, although it is limited by the organism's level of maturity and its previous experience.

Experiments on maturation

Experimental studies of maturation can be carried out most easily with animals. We begin by asking such questions as: "If an activity typical of the species is prevented until after the normal time of its appearance, will the response mechanisms continue to develop so that this activity occurs upon the first opportunity for its arousal?"

☐ Take, for example, the swimming of salamander tadpoles. Eggs were separated into two comparable groups. After head and tail buds appeared, but before any movement was evident, one group was placed in tap water and the other in a solution of chloretone, a drug which, while it does not interfere with growth, prevents all movement. Frequent observation showed that tadpoles in tap water went through the usual sequence of development, culminating in typical swimming reactions. Meanwhile, the drugged tadpoles, although growing at the usual rate, were motionless. Subsequently, however, they were placed in tap water. Within thirty minutes all of these previously motionless animals were swimming in the usual way. Several days are normally required before a tadpole progresses from its earliest movements to the swimming response itself. But these previously inactive animals were beginning to swim in thirty minutes or less. Why didn't they swim immediately after being placed in tap water? The answer, obtained in a control experiment, was that it requires thirty minutes for the effects of chloretone to wear off. Even the normally reared and freely swimming tadpoles needed this long to resume swimming after they had been placed in chloretone and then back into tap water. This experiment demonstrates quite clearly that the swimming response in tadpoles develops even when there are no opportunities to learn it, and even when the animal cannot move during the period of development.[19] □

Swimming in tadpoles is by no means an isolated example of behavioral maturation. The instinctive responses of insects, fishes, birds, and rats provide us with endless examples. Spiders do not learn to spin the web characteristic of their species, fishes do not learn to take care of their offspring, and rats do not learn to mate. These forms of behavior are, as it were, built into the organism. Given an environment in which the animal can live and grow, the structural developments which culminate in these forms of behavior unfold in their characteristic way.

Human maturation

The maturation process is not confined to infrahuman organisms. One of the clearest examples of this process at the human level is found in neural development. The nervous system grows during the prenatal period and

reflexes finally emerge as a result of its growth. The brain itself enlarges and approximates human shape long before the organism is capable of movement. When movement does occur, moreover, it is similar in all fetuses. Fetal development follows this course because the fetus has a human heredity and because it lives in a human prenatal environment — the amnionic fluid, oxygen, and other nutriments obtained from the mother's circulatory system; a limited space in which to move; limited sensory stimulation; and so on. With the heredity of a chimpanzee on the other hand, the fetus would have become a chimpanzee rather than a human being, and its structures, reflexes, and other characteristics — including its rate of development — would have been typical of chimpanzees rather than of human beings. Subjected to an unusual prenatal environment, the fetus would either stop growing or develop atypical structures, like extra appendages or a defective cerebrum.[20]

Early postnatal growth is also to a large extent due to maturation, but after birth there are increased opportunities for environmental stimulation and for the use of structures already developed. Moreover, the stimulation received and the opportunities to use structures and functions already present are not so typical of all human beings as before. That is to say, with increasing age there are greater differences from one individual to another. One may receive stimulation of various kinds which another does not receive. And one may engage in a variety of activities not engaged in by another. For these reasons, it is more difficult in postnatal life to distinguish between maturational development and growth resulting from the use, or *exercise*, of behavior mechanisms.

In spite of the difficulties experienced when we try to differentiate maturation and exercise in human postnatal development, many investigations have attempted to make such a differentiation, some of them with a degree of success.

Maturation in child development

As we said in the chapter on scientific method, identical twins are often useful in experiments requiring control of maturational development. Since the rate of maturation is largely under hereditary control, and since they have the same heredity, identical twins mature at the same rate. We referred to this experimental use of identical twins as *co-twin control.*

Suppose that one wants to know the influence of early training upon the rapidity with which children learn to urinate in the toilet. Some children are given special toilet training while others are left to their own resources. But since some children naturally develop faster than others, a particular child's ability to withhold urination until he is on the toilet might develop without training. Even with training, the habit might develop faster in some children than in others. It is apparent, then, that we must use two groups and equate them for the maturation, or growth factor. Since the latter is dependent upon heredity, the only adequate procedure is to use identical twins. An experiment conducted along these lines revealed that toilet training before a certain level of maturity had been attained was useless. Until attainment of this level, which differs from one child to another, the "toilet-trained" children had no better toilet performance than their identical-twin controls.[21] This experiment therefore demonstrated that control of urination develops whether or not special training is instituted. One cannot, of course, rule out the possibility that a certain amount of relevant learning occurred outside the toilet situation. On their own, children may learn to avoid the discomfort of wetting themselves by retaining urine as long as possible. Improvement on this basis is not properly attributed to maturation, even though it is initiated by the individual himself, rather than being the result of formal training. Development due to learning, but on an untaught basis, is said to be *autogenous* — that is, self-initiated.[22] In the present instance we may conclude that toilet training is ineffective until a certain degree of urinary control has already developed. This control may result from maturation, or from autogenous learning, or both.

Another co-twin experiment dealt with

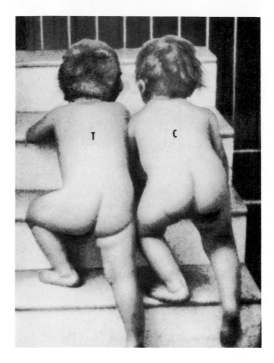

● **4.13**

Stairclimbing in Identical Female Twins. The trained twin (at left) and the control twin (untrained) are shown at the age of seventy-nine weeks. Note the similar postures. (Courtesy, Dr. Arnold Gesell)

stair-climbing. One twin (T in Figure 4.13) was given relevant training from the age of 46 weeks. When tested at this age, however, she was passive and had to be helped up each of the steps. After four more weeks T was climbing without assistance. At the age of 52 weeks, she climbed the stairs in 26 seconds. The control twin (C) had no chance to climb stairs until she was 53 weeks old. But then she climbed them unaided. The time required was 45 seconds, nearly twice the time required by T at 52 weeks. But after two weeks of practice, C was climbing in 10 seconds. She was thus superior to T, who had received three times as much practice, but at an earlier age.[23]

Was C's greater susceptibility to training at the later age level due to maturation alone? Perhaps not. As in the other twin experiment, autogenous learning may have contributed to this greater readiness to learn. Although C was not climbing stairs, she was doing other things which, combined with maturation itself, may have contributed to her stair-climbing performance when formal training began. ■

SOME ASPECTS OF MOTOR DEVELOPMENT

Because they tend to develop sequentially, which suggests maturation, and because they are so important in the development of independence in children, prehension and locomotion have been extensively investigated. We will consider the prehensile and locomotor sequences briefly and also examine their dependence upon maturation and exercise.

Prehension

This involves reaching and voluntary grasping. The latter is in contrast to the reflex grasping of the neonate which occurs only when something is already in contact with the hand. Several months elapse before the

● 4.14
Testing the Development of Prehensile Activity. Here the infant is reaching for a small pellet which the experimenter has placed on the table. (Courtesy, Dr. Arnold Gesell)

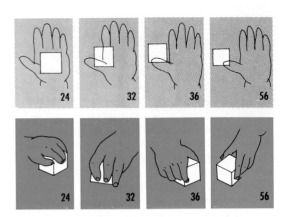

● 4.15
Development of Prehensile Grasping. The numbers refer to age in weeks. In the upper series the relation of the cube to the palm is shown. The lower series shows the position of the fingers and thumb in grasping. (After Halverson)

infant reaches toward objects and tries to pick them up.

If a baby of about twenty weeks is placed at a tabletop, as in Figure 4.14, and a small object is put on the table before his eyes, he may look at it and make random arm movements. He does not reach. By the age of thirty weeks, however, reaching is likely to occur. The hand may go out, withdraw, and perhaps go out again while the infant looks at the object. Somewhat later it is common for him to look at the object and then reach without continued fixation.[24] During the first six months there is usually no hand preference. Both hands may reach, or the right or left hand alternately. Finally one hand, usually the right, is used. By this time reaching is more direct and it is more likely to bring the hand in contact with the object. There is at first a great deal of excess activity. This is finally reduced to a minimum.[25]

Prehensile grasping also develops gradually. Some aspects of this development are illustrated in Figure 4.15. Observe that the palming response, which involves indiscriminate use of the hand as a whole, is evident at about six months. Gradually the fingers are opposed to the thumb. Finally, at about twelve months, forefinger-thumb opposition appears.

Then the child can pick up with precision, using thumb and forefinger, objects as small as beads and even pieces of thread. This is a form of manipulatory skill present to a high degree only in human beings.

Locomotion

It is convenient to consider three aspects of locomotion separately, even though their development shows much overlapping. These are: prone progression, assumption of an upright posture, and walking.

In prone progression, as in other aspects of locomotor development, there are several phases, each shading more or less imperceptibly into the other. When a newborn baby is placed on a surface face downward (Figure 4.16A), it usually cannot lift its head, and although its legs are often active, there is no progression. At about the age of five months, however, the posture shown in Figure 4.16B is frequent. There is sustained raising of the head and chest and generalized activity of the hands and feet (patting the floor and kicking the feet), but still no progression. According to McGraw,[26] whose observations we are reporting, the typical infant at this age has no evident urge to move its body forward. About two months later, as illustrated in Figure 4.16C, there develops an impulse to progress. The infant arches its feet as if to gain a leverage and it moves its hands forward. The body may pivot at this stage, but forward progression is still not present. This is true even when the infant, as in Figure 4.16D, assumes a creeping posture. Various other phases are evident (and with a wide age range) until well organized progression such as that represented in Figure 4.16E is present. Some infants reach this stage by their seventh month, others not until months later. McGraw points out that growth of the organized movement which culminates in prone progression reflects an increasing control of body movements by the developing cerebral cortex. No doubt cerebellar growth, of great importance for body coordination, is a contributing factor.

Infants of course sit before they can stand and they often pull themselves to an erect position by holding onto something long before

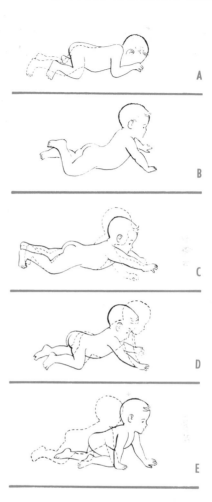

● **4.16**

The Development of Prone Progression. This progression from ineffective motions to crawling represents gradual assumption of control by the maturing cerebral cortex. For description of the phases involved, see text. (Redrawn from M. B. McGraw, *The Neuromuscular Maturation of the Human Infant*, Columbia University Press, 1943, p. 51.)

they can stand without help. Although there is a wide age range in achievement of the latter, it is usually evident early in the second year.[27] The ability to roll from a supine to a prone position and to assume a sitting position on the floor are necessary antecedents. Standing alone, after being pulled to an upright

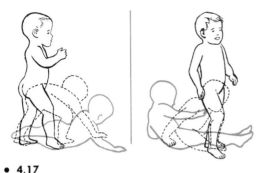

● **4.17**
Two Ways of Assuming an Upright Posture. At earlier stages than those illustrated, the upright position is achieved only by holding onto furniture or other objects, or by being helped by others. (From M. B. McGraw, *The Neuromuscular Maturation of the Human Infant,* Columbia University Press, 1943, p. 87.)

delay in unaided walking is no cause for alarm.

When they begin to walk, children usually spread the feet far apart, flex their knees a great deal, hold their arms apart for balance, and make many movements not found in mature walking. Sometimes the feet are lifted very little and at other times they are lifted much higher than they need to be. Moreover, walking is at first flat-footed. The mature heel-and-toe progression develops slowly. In short, a child walking alone for the first time exhibits a great deal of excess activity. Further development is characterized by reduced movement, increased distance traveled, and increased speed. Within a few months after taking its first steps, the child walks, and may even run, in a seemingly effortless fashion.

While these locomotor accomplishments are taking place, the cerebral cortex is not only growing rapidly but also becoming more involved in the control of behavior.[29] This involvement is evidenced by the urge that the infant now has to move toward objects, to stand up, and to walk as those around him are doing. Increasing ability to maintain equilibrium in an upright position and to make the complex coordinations required for walking is related more specifically to growth of the cerebellum, which increases its weight by 300 per cent within the first year.[30] ■

position or after having achieved this position by holding onto furniture, is of course simpler than standing unaided. Two ways of accomplishing the latter are represented in Figure 4.17. However, maintenance of the upright posture is far from easy. Most infants do not maintain it for very long before falling down. When the infant stands up, his biggest problem is a mechanical one. He now has only two small points of contact with the surface, the center of gravity is high, and the weight of his body is relatively slight. All these factors are conducive to unstable equilibrium. Such handicaps are partially overcome by spreading the feet. Eventually the child counteracts imbalance through the use of appropriate muscular coordinations.

When newborn babies are supported with their feet just touching a surface they often make reflex stepping movements. These are replaced, eventually, by jumping-up-and-down movements of the feet and new stepping motions. Deliberate stepping while supported is usually present at around the end of the first year. Some infants are of course walking alone by then. The average age for walking alone, however, is around fifteen months.[28] But, as any observer of children knows, some begin to walk earlier than fifteen months and some much later. Thus it goes without saying that

EFFECTS OF RESTRICTED ACTIVITY

Tadpoles develop their characteristic swimming response even when they are rendered completely inactive. What would happen if children were likewise immobilized? This we cannot say. It is of course impossible to prevent all activity in children. The best that one can do is limit activity and see whether this influences the growth of behavior.

In one such study, the activity of a pair of fraternal twins was restricted between the ages of one and nine months.[31] Their behavior was then compared with that of children reared under normal conditions. Restriction consisted in keeping a child on its back, having the bedclothes tucked in so tightly as to prevent withdrawal of the hands, and withholding any social stimulation which might encourage reaching, sitting, or standing.

None of the latter responses appeared at the normal age. Reaching toward a dangling ring normally occurs by the 200th day. A ring was first presented on the 245th day, but neither child reached for it. Sitting alone normally appears before the 245th day. The twins were given their first opportunity to sit when they were 262 days old. Neither of them sat at this time. Standing with help is normally evident by the 270th day, but the twins failed to stand when given their first opportunity to do so at the age of 364 days. With continued opportunity to acquire these responses, however, the infants soon reached, sat, and stood. Standing with help developed only three days after the twins were given their first opportunity to stand.

Even after restrictions were removed and the children were given an opportunity to develop the respective responses, no training was undertaken. Thus the activity which preceded reaching, sitting, and standing was autogenous.

Although reaching, sitting, and standing did not occur as soon as restrictions were removed, there was still evidence for maturation. These responses appeared without the months of activity normally present before such responses occur. Despite relative inactivity, muscular and neural mechanisms were maturing and providing the twins with equipment for reaching, sitting, and standing. On the other hand, there was undoubtedly some self-initiated use of relevant mechanisms, for restrictions were not sufficiently rigid to prevent this.

A study of Hopi children provides further evidence that restricted activity in early childhood does not prevent motor development.[32] Hopi infants are from the time of birth usually bundled up and bound to a stiff board (Figure 4.18). This treatment prevents such responses as flexing the legs, bringing the hands to the mouth, and turning the body. Until the third month, when more freedom is given, the Hopi child is confined to its board except for about one hour daily, which is necessary for cleaning and bathing. General observation shows that

Hopi infants thus restricted develop the usual infant activities, and without retardation.

Some Hopis, influenced by white people, have given up use of the baby board, thus providing conditions for controlled observations on the effect of binding upon the appearance of such activities as walking. These observations have shown that there is no differential effect of binding. For example, both bound and unbound Hopis walk alone at an average age of approximately 15 months.[33]

Observations made in two foundling homes, one in Lebanon[34] and the other in

● 4.18

A Baby Bundle. Babies bundled up in this fashion so that they are unable to reach, sit up, creep, or walk, show no handicap in motor development. For example, they walk at the same age as children who have not been subjected to such restriction. (Courtesy, American Museum of Natural History, New York; copyright Mischler and Walker.)

Iran,[35] revealed greater and more prolonged restriction than was involved in the two preceding studies, and this resulted in marked retardation of motor development. The children entered these institutions soon after birth. Because of inadequate staffing, there was no effort to do any more than was necessary to keep them alive and clean. A baby was given no attention other than that involved in feeding, changing, and cleaning it, and it was fed with the bottle propped on its pillow. It was always placed on its back, whereas children are usually turned on their stomachs from time to time and also placed in a sitting position. In another institution in Iran there were no such restrictions.[36] Indeed it was set up to show what institutional care of babies should be. Since the babies in both institutions were taken in on a comparable basis, one may compare the effects of these different treatments on motor development.

In the age group 1–1.9 years, only 42 per cent of the restricted children sat alone, as compared with 90 per cent of the non-restricted. Creeping was present in 14 per cent of the restricted and 75 per cent of the non-restricted group. Only 4 per cent of the restricted children stood while holding onto something, whereas 70 per cent of the non-restricted did so. Walking while holding onto something was evident in only 2 per cent of the restricted as compared with 60 per cent of the non-restricted children. None of the restricted children walked unaided, while 15 per cent of the others did so.[37] Retardation was attributed by the investigators to limitation of learning opportunities. From the fourth year on, in these institutions, there was no further evidence of motor retardation. The effect of restriction is thus to slow up but not prevent development of locomotor skills. Limitations such as we have cited may have a more permanent effect on intelligence, but this question is considered in the following chapter.

Even though locomotor and prehensile activities are part of our racial heritage, it is evident that certain kinds of restriction can retard their development. But the question of how much they depend upon maturation *per se* and how much upon observing others, autogenous activity, and encouragement from parents, is still unanswered because we cannot, as in the tadpole experiment, restrict children completely. ■

MATURATION AND LEARNING

The specific effects of maturation are maximal during early development and they are more evident in some activities than in others. The activities especially influenced by maturation are those found in all normal children — viz., reflexes, creeping, standing, and walking. Since these are characteristic of the human race, they are called *racial*. Maturation has a less specific influence upon activities which the human being may or may not develop; that is to say, *individual activities*. Among such are skating, bicycling, painting, playing golf, and so on; all are quite evidently learned.

☐ The different role of maturation in development of racial and individual responses is interestingly illustrated by an experiment on a pair of fraternal twins, Johnny and Jimmy.[38]

Beginning at the age of twenty days, one twin (Johnny) was given extensive practice in a wide variety of activities — some racial (like crawling and standing) and the others individual (like swimming and skating). During the same period Jimmy was simply lying in his crib behind a screen. He received no training or encouragement, hence any activity engaged in by him was self-initiated. Johnny and Jimmy were given comparable tests from time to time to see whether or not the special training of the former was having differential effects. Later in the experiment Jimmy played alone with toys while Johnny was learning to swim, climb, and skate. Altogether the experiment lasted three years and there was a follow-up at later ages.

The general outcome of this study was quite clear. In racial activities there was no significant difference. The trained and untrained twin developed at about the same rate. Quite obviously, however, Johnny was far in advance of Jimmy in the individualistic activities. He could swim, skate, and climb while

Jimmy could not. When he was finally trained in such activities, however, Jimmy learned them faster than Johnny had done at an earlier age. This is a result similar to those found in the studies already mentioned, where learning proceeded at a faster rate in older children. □

A further example of greater maturity resulting in faster learning comes from comparing the development of a chimpanzee and a child (Figure 4.19) reared in a home environment.[39]

□ Gua, the female infant chimpanzee, was treated like the investigators' infant son Donald, even with respect to dress, kissing, and other endearments. One aim was to see how much Gua would be humanized by this treatment. Interestingly enough, she was ahead of the child in such acquisitions as skipping, cooperating, obeying requests, opening doors, anticipating bowel and bladder needs, eating with a spoon, drinking from a glass, understanding the significance of certain words, shaking hands, and kissing to "make up." Although she was two months younger than Donald, Gua was ahead of him in all of these accomplishments. This resulted from the fact that chimpanzees mature relatively fast. It is part of their inherent makeup. However, chimpanzees reach their upper limit early and human beings continue to mature, even up to the age of fifteen months, in fact, Donald had largely caught up with Gua. He was then ahead in everything but strength. Partly for the latter reason, the experiment was terminated when Gua was sixteen and one-half months old and Donald nineteen months.

Thus Gua, although of an inferior race, was superior in certain respects to Donald — superior because of greater maturity and resulting facilitation of the learning process. Another outcome of especial interest is that Donald did certain things eventually which the chimpanzee could not do. Gua could not oppose the forefinger and thumb as human children do. She could not walk upright in an easy manner without balancing by holding her arms out. Nor could she speak. At

● 4.19
Human and Chimpanzee Infants Reared Alike Experimentally. This form of locomotion, which occurred even without Gua's hand being held, is not normal in chimpanzees. It is one activity which Gua learned as a result of her close association with human beings. Both infants were dressed alike, ate alike, slept in similar beds, played with the same things, and were treated alike in all important respects. (From W. N. Kellogg and L. A. Kellogg, *The Ape and the Child*, McGraw-Hill, 1933, p. 275.)

least two apes have, in fact, been taught to make a few vocalizations approximating words, but only after months of special training.[40] Donald learned to speak without such training. Under the same conditions, Gua's only vocalizations were emotional cries. □

We have seen that maturation is especially important in early development, and in relation to the emergence of responses normally found in all human beings. We have also seen that maturation is important for early development in that it influences the learning process. The more mature an individual, the more readily he can modify responses already present and the more readily he can acquire new and more complex responses.

Although especially important at earlier age levels, maturation is not confined to early childhood. It continues, although at a slower

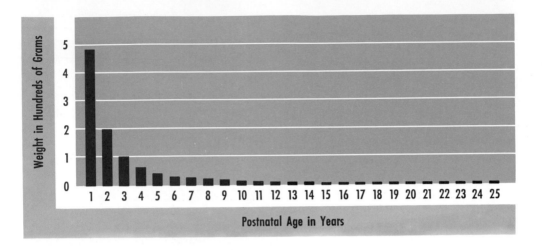

● 4.20

Growth of the Brain. The increments represent grams added per year to the brain weight at birth. Observe that the largest increments are added in the early years, although small increments still occur into the twenties. (Adapted from A. M. Lassek, *The Human Brain*, Thomas, 1957, p. 28.)

rate, until maturity is attained. We see this most clearly in the case of gross bodily changes like height and weight. It also occurs in muscular strength which, especially in boys, grows rapidly during the early adolescent period.[41]

The brain offers another instance of prolonged maturation. As already noted, the total number of brain cells does not increase after birth, but their size increases and their functional interrelationships develop. The insulat-

ing myelin sheaths of the neurons also undergo considerable growth. Indeed it may be said that the growth of the brain continues into early adulthood, although the greatest increments are evident in childhood (Figure 4.20).

Another example of later maturation is provided by sexual growth. The gonads and secondary sex characteristics grow toward maturity during adolescence, and this happens whether or not the individual has been sexually active. ■

• SUMMARY

The origins of individual differences are found in heredity and environment. Biological inheritance is determined by the chromosomes — more specifically by the genes (chemical determiners) within them.

Genes differ in certain respects from one person to another and this variation is the hereditary basis of individual differences. The genes interact with their most immediate environment, the cytoplasm of the cell (intracellular environment). As cells multiply, there is an influence of cell on cell (intercellular environment). Endocrine glands, for example, secrete hormones which influence the growth of other cells. The entire developing organism

is surrounded by amnionic fluid, receives nourishment from the mother's circulatory system, and is subjected to various restrictions. These are features of the prenatal external environment. Birth brings the individual into contact with new stimulation, including the social. It is through his social environment that he comes into contact with the social heritage — what has been transmitted culturally from former generations. Every trait is derived from an interplay of heredity and environment, but differences between individuals may be hereditary, environmental, or both. Thus, differences in eye color are hereditary, differences in social attitudes are environmental, and differences in intelligence are both hereditary and environmental — except between identical twins, where they are purely environmental.

It is only in animals that we can introduce hereditary variations while holding the environment constant. It has been shown, for example, that a certain form of abnormal locomotion, a susceptibility to audiogenic seizures, and maze-learning ability (brightness and dullness) are inherited. Maze-learning ability appears to depend upon the interaction of multiple pairs of genes, otherwise referred to as *polygenes*. Human intelligence is also believed to be determined in large measure by polygenes, but environment is also of great significance, as will be indicated in the following chapter.

Much of the individual's early development is due to the growth of response mechanisms, a process referred to as *maturation*. This is especially important in the development of activities which typify the race — human reflexes, mode of locomotion, finger-thumb opposition, and so on. Individuals appear to have an inherent growth potential which makes them develop at different rates, some being more mature than others at a particular age level. We see this clearly indicated in development of prehensile and locomotor activities. The potential for prehension culminates in ability to oppose the finger and thumb, as in picking up small objects like a pea or a thread. Most children achieve this by the end of the first year. The various sequential stages in locomotion lead up to walking unaided. Some children walk alone before their first birthday, but the average age for unaided walking is fifteen months. Severe restriction of opportunities to be active and to be stimulated by others tends to retard motor development, thus suggesting the influence of learning. However, children do not need training in order to develop the prehensile and locomotor activities characteristic of their race; they engage in a great deal of autogenous learning — learning based upon self-initiated activity.

While all human activities are limited by maturation, in the sense that one must be sufficiently mature before he can acquire certain skills, individualistic activities like skating, doing the Australian crawl, and riding a bike do not develop without special training. In this sense they differ from activities which typify the human race.

The various studies on maturation and exercise show that maturation and activity are jointly involved in human development, hence in the production of individual differences. Thus we see again the interaction of hereditary and environmental conditions. ■

REFERENCES AND NOTES FOR THIS CHAPTER ARE IN THE APPENDIX.

• SELECTED READINGS

Bonner, D. M., *Heredity*. Prentice-Hall, 1961.

Carmichael, L. (Ed.), *Manual of Child Psychology* (2nd ed.). Wiley, 1954, Chapters 5 and 6.

Dennis, W., *Readings in Child Psychology* (2nd ed.). Prentice-Hall, 1963.

Fuller, J. L., and W. R. Thompson, *Behavior Genetics*. Wiley, 1960. A comprehensive treatise on hereditary bases of behavior.

McCandless, B. R., *Children and Adolescents*. Holt, Rinehart and Winston, 1961, Chapter 9.

McGraw, M. B., *The Neuromuscular Maturation of the Human Infant*. Columbia University Press, 1943 (reissued by Hafner, 1963).

Munn, N. L., *The Evolution and Growth of Human Behavior* (2nd ed.). Houghton Mifflin, 1965, Chapters 7 and 10.

Palermo, D. S., and L. P. Lipsitt (Eds.), *Research Readings in Child Psychology*. Holt, Rinehart and Winston, 1963; especially the readings from Harris, Anastasi, and Shirley.

Stern, C., *Principles of Human Genetics*. Freeman, 1960.

Winchester, A. M., *Genetics* (2nd ed.). Houghton Mifflin, 1958. Clear and well illustrated.

5

Intelligence

When we say that one organism is more intelligent than another, what do we mean? Why, for example, do we regard chimpanzees as less intelligent than men and more intelligent than rats? Why do we say that adults are more intelligent than children? And why do we look upon men like Einstein as more intelligent than most other men? The answers to such questions are given in this chapter.

In the last analysis, intelligence derives from ability to learn and to utilize what has been learned in adjusting to new situations and solving new problems. The concept of intelligence owes much to early studies of animal learning. About a century ago, following publication of Darwin's *Origin of Species*, there was a flurry of interest in the evolution of intelligence and many tests (tests of learning ability) were devised to measure intelligence in animals ranging from ants to chimpanzees. The general procedure was to block a customary access to food (requiring the animal to learn an alternate route) or to introduce a disturbing element from which escape was possible.

Mazes of various kinds are sometimes used to test animal intelligence. These range in complexity from a single T unit (with one blind alley) to complex patterns of units, sometimes with a dozen or more blind alleys. In these maze tests the animal's intelligence is rated in terms of how quickly and with how few errors it is able to get from the entrance to the exit, usually for a bite of food. A single T unit is sufficiently complex to test a worm's intelligence, for worms, even in a maze this simple, differ considerably in the number of trials required before they can make the proper turn, and thus avoid an electric shock. On the basis of such findings, worms are said to differ from one another in intelligence.

A T-maze like that used with worms is too easy for rats. It fails to differentiate them sufficiently. When we wish to test the intelligence of lower mammals, like white rats, it is necessary to use mazes of greater complexity than those suitable for measuring worm intelligence. In the preceding chapter we discussed the inheritance of brightness and dullness in rats. Bright rats were so designated because they made few errors, and dull rats because they made many errors, in maze learning. In one study a multiple T-maze with 14 units was used. The other study used the Hebb-Williams intelligence test for rats, which requires the animal to circumvent various detours, which differ from trial to trial, in getting from the entrance to the food box. Such complications are valuable in measuring rat intelligence. In fact, intelligence is not simply a matter of how fast an organism can learn, nor of how accurately it can learn, but also of the *complexity of what it can learn*. Rats can learn more complex things than worms, so we need intelligence tests which make use of such advanced abilities.

It is interesting to observe that maze tests such as we use with rats are poor tests of human intelligence. They do not sufficiently differentiate human beings and, as a matter of fact, human beings do no better on such tests than rats.[1] Even college students, walking through enlarged versions of rat mazes or tracing through grooved paths of the same pattern while blindfolded, learn no faster than rats, and they make as many errors. Why is this so? The reason is that problems of this nature require only the elementary learning processes which human beings share with rats. Using ordinary mazes to test human intelligence is comparable, in a way, with using worm mazes to test rat intelligence. Human beings have acquired higher learning processes (often referred to as *symbolic* processes) which the maze does not allow them to utilize effectively. Much better than rats, they can recall past happenings, put two-and-two together, and apply what they have learned in other situations. But more than this, they can use words to represent situations and events; i.e., they can *verbalize*. Such processes are of no help in learning a typical maze. One can do about as well by proceeding in a blind hit-or-miss fashion. In view of these facts, any maze that is used to test human intelligence must be so designed as to allow free play to man's higher learning processes. One such maze is pictured in Figure 5.1. The reader should try to find his way through it, mentally. Here one can look ahead and figure out the path to be followed. Errors can be avoided by anticipating the consequences of actions not yet taken — actions perhaps represented by such words as, "If I do that, I'll be blocked over there." Mazes like this are often used to test human intelligence. The Porteus Maze Test is an example.[2] Such tests are especially useful when the subjects to be tested are illiterate or are for other reasons unable to follow complicated verbal instructions.

We shall see in the present chapter that intelligence tests for human beings who are literate place a great deal of emphasis on language, both in their administration (which requires an understanding of instructions) and in the responses called for (which are usually verbalizations). These are referred to, in general, as *verbal* tests. Maze tests such as we have been describing are, by contrast, *performance* tests. They are scored in terms of what the individual does rather than in terms of what he says.

The concept of intelligence, as we said earlier, is closely tied to learning ability. Tests of animal intelligence and mazes like those adapted for use with human subjects measure *learning in process*. The measure of intelligence is then the rapidity or accuracy of learning. The more widely used tests of human intelligence also place a premium on learning ability, but for the most part they measure *learning accomplished before the test is taken*. The basic idea is that, when individuals have been given comparable opportunities to learn, those who know most and can apply their knowledge best in answering the test items, are the most intelligent. We will observe, in this connection, that the items involved in intelligence tests utilize knowledge and skills which, presumably, everybody tested has at least had an opportunity to learn. ■

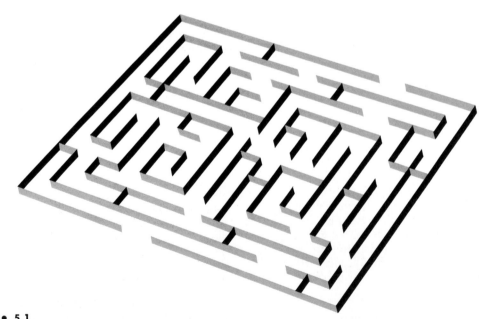

● 5.1

A Maze Problem. Attempt to trace through this maze from one opening to the other without entering a blind alley. Trace with a hairpin or something else which leaves no mark. (Courtesy, International Telephone and Telegraph Company)

THE MEANING OF INTELLIGENCE

Intelligence may be defined in various ways. The most general definition stresses versatility (or flexibility) of adjustment.[3] This definition has the virtue of being applicable at all levels of evolution. Versatility at lower levels is evidenced mainly by the speed with which learning occurs. At somewhat higher levels, versatility involves much more than speed of learning, for problems of greater complexity can be learned. Higher still we find symbolic versatility. Organisms may learn by looking over a situation, even by observing what others do. Moreover, they have the ability to recall and to reason. These processes are most evident in human beings, hence the tests which most clearly measure differences in the versatility of human adjustment involve such complex symbolic processes as recall, reasoning, understanding of concepts, and linguistic skills. These processes are of major significance in human adjustment and tests built around them provide our best measures of human intelligence. We may say, therefore, that so far as human beings are concerned, intelligence is versatility in the use of symbolic processes.

Some psychologists define intelligence as ability to carry on abstract thinking. This is all right if we are considering only the human level, but it implies that most animals have no intelligence and it ignores the differences in performance from one level of animal life to another that have been revealed by animal experiments.

Some define intelligence as whatever it is that the intelligence tests measure. This is true, presumably, but not very revealing. The reader may ask — "Well, *what* is it that they measure?" We could answer this by saying that, in the most general sense, they measure differences in versatility of adjustment; differences which, at the human level, are most evident in the acquisition and use of symbolic processes.

One should recognize that the tests measure *differences in performance* rather than intelligence directly. There is no way to measure intelligence as we measure strength. This point is raised because many students, when asked to define intelligence, think of it as some sort of power possessed by the individual. What we are dealing with — what we are measuring with intelligence tests — is a function which, to recall an earlier discussion, can usually be represented only in ordinal terms. In fact it is more correct to speak of one person as being more intelligent than another than it is to say that either has a given amount of intelligence. This will become increasingly apparent as the tests themselves are discussed.

Intelligence and the organism

It is well to think of intelligence, or versatility, as a function of living organisms in much the same sense that maneuverability is a function of airplanes. One plane is more maneuverable than another because it has structures concerned with maneuverability which are superior to those of the other. Intelligence is likewise based upon structures, particularly those of the central nervous system; but it also depends upon what happens to these structures as the organism grows and interacts with its environment.

The structure of greatest importance is the brain, for the brain that one is born with has much to do with how intelligent he can become. Human adjustment is at a high symbolic level because man has a brain sufficiently complex to acquire and use symbols.

The brain is relatively small at birth and its size increases fourfold before maturity is attained. As we said in Chapter 4, no new cells are added. However, as represented in Figure 4.20 (p. 110), the growth of cells already present continues and their interconnections become increasingly complex. The growth of intelligence from birth to maturity is doubtless related to these developments. The growth of some brains is arrested in early life and feeblemindedness results.

The importance of stimulation

Another factor of importance for intelligent behavior is what happens to the individual, or how his brain is used. One could inherit a brain with high capacity for acquiring and retaining symbolic and other skills, yet live in a relatively nonstimulating, or impoverished environment. The brain would continue to grow, but the information fed into it would be relatively meager and, as a result, versatility would be at a much lower level than it might otherwise have been.

The blind, the deaf, and especially the deaf-blind often grow up to be feebleminded unless steps are taken to circumvent their handicap and bring information to their brains. The deaf-blind Helen Keller would doubtless have had a low order of intelligence were it not for the fact that she was painstakingly taught, through her sense of touch, to know a great deal about the world, as well as to acquire symbols with which she could communicate with others.

The point that we have been making — that intelligence is dependent upon learning ability and that it cannot develop in an environmental vacuum — may be further illustrated by a hypothetical experiment.

A hypothetical experiment

Suppose that we separate identical twins at birth and bring them up in environments more widely different than was the case with the identical twins reared apart that we have already discussed (pp. 96–97). One is reared, let us say, by foster parents of very low intelligence and in some isolated community with extremely poor educational opportunities and a general intellectual impoverishment. The other is reared in the home of well-educated foster parents, where he is read to, sent to good schools, and given every opportunity to be stimulated intellectually and to acquire knowledge.[4] Being identical, these twins have identical brains, to begin with, and the inherent growth processes are the same in each.

We shall assume that, given average opportunities to learn, the intelligence of these twins would be average, i.e., that they began life with average brains. The only difference between them would be the environmental one already posited. Suppose now, that this environmental difference continued until the early teens and also that the intelligence of the twins was then measured by tests like those to be considered in this chapter.

There is no doubt whatever about the general outcome of such an experiment. The twin brought up in an impoverished intellectual environment would be below the other in his test performance, and below the level he might have attained if reared under average conditions. And the twin given superior opportunities would doubtless have a higher level of performance than he would have attained if reared under average conditions.

What might happen if the twins were now brought together and given good opportunities in a comparable environment? Would the one who was handicapped earlier now catch up with the other? That is a question which we cannot answer with any degree of assurance. The level of intelligence of this twin would probably improve, but would it improve as much as it might have improved without the earlier environmental handicap? There is a good possibility that it would not. Early in life we *learn how to learn*, and each accomplishment prepares the way for others. There is a "snowball effect." Early educational handicaps are not easily overcome.

For our example we took two individuals whose intelligence would normally have been average. If we had taken children whose brains were initially below average, the diversity produced by the difference in environments would not have been as great as that suggested. This is because the child given exceptionally good opportunities could not have responded normally to them. If, on the other hand, we had taken twins with far better than average brains, the difference between them might have been far greater than that suggested. The twin in the intellectually impoverished environment might have broken through the environmental barriers to some extent. But his brother would most likely have made such excellent use of his intellectually enriched environment as to have greatly increased the difference in their intelligence, especially as compared with the difference which would have existed had they been potentially average. If our examples were far above average, moreover, the early handicap of the environmentally impoverished twin might have been overcome to a greater extent when better opportunities occurred. The difference between the twins, if not eliminated, would in this event at least have been narrowed more than if they had possessed no better than average brains.

This discussion has served to point up the fact that one's intelligence is a function of the brain he is born with, its growth to maturity, and how it is modified by what happens to him. Thus intelligence is not something he is born with. It develops and, at every stage of development, reflects the individual's interaction with his environment. At birth he may have a *capacity*, a *potentiality* for intellectual growth, but this cannot be realized except through learning.

One of our leading child psychologists has said that the growth of human intelligence "depends pre-eminently upon the acquisition of the verbal tools of problem solving."[5] It is indeed true that differences in the versatility of human beings are most evident with respect to such tools. They are of major significance in human adjustment and we shall now see that tests built around them provide our best measures of human intelligence. ∎

BEGINNING OF INTELLIGENCE TESTS

In 1896 a French psychologist named Binet, who had been studying psychological processes in school children, suggested the creation of special classes for those children who, because of low intelligence, were unable to progress as fast as others. Eight years later, Binet was asked to serve on a commission formed for the express purpose of discovering which children in the public schools had insufficient intelligence to profit from the usual instruction. Obviously it would be impossible, without doing an injustice to many children, to segregate them on the basis of teachers' judgments. Teachers would almost certainly have prejudices and be subjected to various influences from parents and others. They could not be relied upon to make objective judgments. What was needed was a set of objective tests, tests which would measure the intelligence of all children on a strictly comparable basis. Binet felt that a graded series of psycho-

logical tests could be devised which would indicate the level or degree of each child's intelligence.

Development of the first "scale"

By experimenting with children who were making average progress in school, Binet and a collaborator named Simon discovered which of many attention, memory, discrimination, and other tests could be performed by average individuals. They devised a scale comprising thirty tests arranged from the simplest to the most complex. By applying the scale to individuals known to be feebleminded, Binet and Simon were able to obtain norms for them. They found out, for example, how many tests in the average scale could be done by idiots and other individuals classified as feebleminded.

By applying their intelligence test to school children, Binet and Simon attempted to discover each child's mental development. If a child of five did only the first nine tests in the scale, the tests performed by a normal three-year-old, it was obviously retarded about two years. If a school child failed to go beyond the first six tests, those passed by idiots, he was designated an idiot. As Binet and Simon put it, they wished "simply to show that it is possible to determine in a precise and truly scientific way the mental level of an intelligence, to compare the level with a normal level, and consequently to determine by how many years a child is retarded."[6]

The revised Binet-Simon tests

It became evident that there were many defects in their original scale, so Binet and Simon eventually devised improved scales in which an attempt was made to eliminate all items which would require special schooling for their performance. Binet realized that, if the test were to measure *ability to acquire*, and not merely information, it must use items which any normal child, regardless of whether or not he had received training in special fields of knowledge, could be expected to perform. Moreover, the items of the new scale were arranged into age groupings.

The test items to be used at a particular age level were not decided upon in an arbitrary fashion. They were tried out at different age levels. For illustrative purposes, let us consider the items at age five: weight discrimination, copying a square, repeating a sentence of ten syllables, counting four pennies, and fitting together the halves of a divided triangle. Each of these items was included at this age level because the average five-year-old could do it.

More specifically, Binet and Simon proceeded somewhat as follows: An item was regarded as adequate for testing five-year-old intelligence if from about 60 to 75 per cent of children at this age were able to perform it accurately, if less than about 60 per cent of four-year-olds could do it correctly, and if it was mastered by more than 75 per cent of six-year-olds. Thus the item had to be too difficult for the age level below and too easy for the age level above, in order to be included at the intermediate level.

The concept of mental age

In line with their arrangement of the scale into age groupings, Binet and Simon developed the concept of *mental age,* or M.A. The child who could do the five-year tests, but who could not go on to the six-year level, was credited with a mental age of five years. The child of chronological age (C.A.) five who achieved an M.A. of five was, of course, regarded as having average or normal intelligence. However, the child with an M.A. of five might actually be ten years old (C.A., ten years). He would, of course, be extremely dull for his age. On the other hand, a child with an M.A. of five and a C.A. of three would be extremely bright. The concept of M.A., therefore, indicated the level of intelligence achieved, but it gave no indication of the brightness or dullness of the individual concerned. A person is not regarded as bright unless we know that his level of performance is better than the level achieved by others of his own age. He is not thought to be dull unless his performance is below that of others of his own age.

The intelligence quotient

It was later suggested that an intelligence quotient (I.Q.), derived by dividing C.A. into M.A. and multiplying by 100 (to remove decimal places), would be much more meaningful than M.A. alone.[7] Such a quotient would show the rate with which M.A. was increasing in relation to C.A. In a child of average intelligence, whose M.A. equaled his C.A., the I.Q. would be 100, regardless of the actual age. A child of ten years whose M.A. was found to be 10 would have an I.Q. of $10/10 \times 100$, or 100. A child of ten years whose M.A. was 5 would have an I.Q. of $5/10 \times 100$, or 50. This child would be fifty I.Q. points below average. However, a child of ten years with an M.A. of 14 would have an I.Q. of 140 ($14/10 \times 100$) and this would place him forty points above the average child of his own age.

Infant tests

The Binet-Simon tests extended down to the three-year level, as we have seen. A widely used American modification, to be discussed presently, goes down to two years. But there has been an insistent demand, especially from adoption agencies, for tests extending to the first few months of life. The desire to test intelligence at early age levels produced several baby tests beginning with one developed at Yale in the early nineteen-twenties by Arnold Gesell. This and all later infant tests are alike in emphasizing sensory and motor development.[8]

We must report, however, that infant tests have failed to fulfill the hopes of those who would like to predict later intelligence while the individual is very young. One study after another has shown that infant performance is insignificantly correlated with that of later childhood.[9] What appears to be a bright baby may turn out to be average or even dull when tested years later.

Why have infant tests failed to predict later intelligence? There are several possible reasons, but two are especially important. One reason is that infants are not very versatile anyway, so there is not much to test. That is why all of the baby tests are alike, why they are all concerned predominantly with the same sensory and motor activities. The second reason for the failure of infant tests to predict later intelligence is that this differs significantly from infant intelligence. This point is emphasized by Dr. Nancy Bayley whose Berkeley Growth Study has involved repeated testing of the same individuals from the age of two months into adulthood. She says that "It may be a mistake to try to call any infant behavior before 6 months more characteristically 'mental' than motor."[10] Another psychologist, who analyzed the Berkeley data statistically, found evidence that three different functions were measured at different age levels. Although the three showed much overlapping, "sensory motor alertness" predominated during the first two years, "persistence" from the second to the fourth year, and "manipulation of symbols" thereafter.[11] The two reasons that we have given are of course related. The only infant test that could be expected to predict later performance would be one with a great deal of symbolic content, but babies are not functioning at a symbolic level, at least not sufficiently to permit items which differentiate between them at this level.

The tests which we are about to describe begin at the earlier age levels, with several items that are predominantly sensory and motor. Then, at successively higher age levels, they increasingly use symbolic material. ▪

THE STANFORD-BINET TESTS

These tests, so named because they were devised by psychologists at Stanford University following lines laid down by Binet, have appeared in three editions. The first Stanford-Binet Intelligence Scale was devised in 1916 by Professor Lewis M. Terman. A more extensive scale, with two forms, was later developed with the collaboration of Professor Maud Merrill. This scale, which appeared in 1937, became the most extensively used device for testing the intelligence of children individually. It was translated into many languages and adapted in other ways for use throughout the civilized world. Most of the I.Q.'s discussed in this chapter were derived by using either the L or M form of the 1937 revision. In 1960 another revision appeared.[12]

The 1960 Stanford-Binet Scale

This revision incorporates the best items from the L and M forms of the earlier test and is thus designated the L-M form. By "best" items is meant those which have current value in differentiating various age groups (i.e., mental age). This was determined by analyzing the results obtained in administering the L and M forms to 4498 subjects ranging in age from 2½ to 18 years. One of the major bases for selection of any item was an increase in the per cent passing it as age (or mental age) increased.

Some typical materials for the L-M form are pictured in Figure 5.2. As was the case

● **5.2**
Some of the Stanford-Binet Test Materials. The subject being tested is to name some of these items. Some are used in more complex tests, as when one is covered and the child is asked to recall what it is. The strictly verbal material used at higher age levels, including the vocabulary list, is of course not evident here. (Photo by A. M. Love, Jr.)

with earlier forms of this test, the items are used in accordance with a carefully standardized procedure. Very little is left to the tester's judgment. This is also true with respect to scoring.

In the L-M form, there are both yearly and half-yearly tests for ages two to five, with six items at each level. Passing an item adds one month of mental age to the child's score. For years 5 to 14, however, there are six items at each yearly level, with each item carrying an M.A. weight of two months. There are also four adult tests, ranging from average to very superior. Here again, passing an item adds a specified number of months to the individual's M.A. score.

Although the exact details of mental tests must be reserved for those qualified to administer them, an idea of the nature of items at widely different age levels of the Stanford-Binet Intelligence Scale may be gained by examining the selection given.

Items Illustrating the 1960 Revision (L-M Form) of the Stanford Binet Intelligence Scale

Year II
1. Three-hole form board. (Places forms in holes.)
2. Delayed response. (Finds toy animal after it has been hidden.)
3. Identifying parts of the body. (Indicates named parts on doll.)
4. Block-building: Tower. (Builds tower from model after demonstration.)
5. Picture vocabulary. (Names common objects while looking at pictures of them.)
6. Word combinations. (Spontaneous word combinations made by child during the session are noted.)

Year XI
1. Memory for designs. (Draws certain designs from memory.)
2. Verbal absurdities. (Tells what is foolish about given statements.)
3. Abstract words. (Tells what we mean by given words.)
4. Memory for sentences. (Repeats what has been read.)

5. Problem situation. (Tells why people acted as they did in a story situation presented by the tester.)
6. Similarities. (Says in what way certain groups of objects are alike.)

Average adult
1. Vocabulary. (Defines a specified number of words from a standard list.)
2. Ingenuity. (Solves a reasoning test.)
3. Differences between abstract words. (Pairs of words are given and the subject tells how they differ in meaning.)
4. Arithmetical reasoning. (Standard arithmetical problems are solved.)
5. Proverbs. (Tells the meaning of given proverbs.)
6. Orientation: Direction. (The subject tells in what direction he would be going after specified turns.)

The reader should note, in passing, that this test utilizes language to a high degree. There are vocabulary tests at various levels in addition to that of the average adult; and, at every level, there are items involving the subject's understanding and use of words. It is not surprising, therefore, that this is designated a "verbal" test.

How a child is tested and scored

Those who administer the Stanford-Binet Intelligence Scale are instructed to win the child's confidence and attempt to overcome any evident nervousness and timidity. One way in which this may be accomplished with young children is to suggest that the tester and the child are playing a game. The tester also encourages the child by praising his performance. Such encouragement is given whether the response is correct or incorrect. The child is never told, "That is wrong." He is encouraged by such comments as, "That's very good, now we'll try the next one."

After the child is at his ease, the test is administered in accordance with established procedure. If the child is judged to be below normal (that is, mentally below others of his age) the test begins with items well below those designed for his actual C.A. level. Should the child appear average, however, the first items administered are those for children one year below his C.A. Take a child of nine years and two months, for example. If he appears to be approximately normal, he is given the items for year VIII. If he passes the six items at this level, he is next given those for year IX. Should he pass all of these, the child is next given the items for year X. Here, perhaps, he passes only four of the six tests. At the next level, year XI, he succeeds, shall we say, in doing two tests. Let us suppose, furthermore, that he does one test at the XII-year level and fails all at the XIII-year level. The test terminates at this point. The child's M.A. is then calculated as follows:

Year IX	All tests passed	108	(basal age)
Year X	Four tests passed	8	
Year XI	Two tests passed	4	
Year XII	One test passed	2	
Year XIII	All tests failed	0	
		122	months

His M.A. is thus 10 years and 2 months (or 10-2). Observe that the child is credited

with all the months of mental age prior to the highest level at which he passes all items. This is called the basal age. In the present example, it is nine years, or 108 months. The child is then credited with an additional two months for each item passed between the basal age and the age level on which he fails all items.

If this child's I.Q. were determined by the conventional method (i.e., using the formula M.A./C.A. $\times$ 100), it would approximate 111. With the 1960 revision, however, the conventional I.Q. is replaced by a *deviation* I.Q. In the present instance, this would have been 108.

Deviation I.Q.'s are standard scores. The reader is already to some degree familiar with such scores. We discussed them in Chapter 3 while evaluating the status of an individual score in a distribution of scores. The standard score, it may be recalled, takes into consideration both the *deviation of the individual score from the mean* of the distribution and the *standard deviation of the distribution*, sigma. A graphic presentation of the meaning of deviation I.Q.'s is given in Figure 5.3.

On the basis of standardization, the mean I.Q. for the 1960 revision of the Stanford-Binet Intelligence Scale is 100 at each age

● **5.3**

A Normal Distribution Curve and Deviation I.Q.'s for the 1960 Stanford-Binet Intelligence Scale. Note that the mean I.Q. is 100 and that a score one sigma above this is evaluated as an I.Q. of 116; a score one sigma below, as an I.Q. of 84. Observe, also, the percentage of the population which might be expected to have a particular I.Q. For example, an I.Q. of 140 (at the very superior, or "potential genius" level) could be expected in only about 2 per cent of the population.

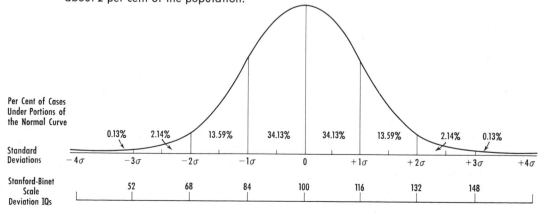

level. The sigma is 16. On this basis, tables are provided from which, given a child's M.A. score and his C.A., one can read off his I. Q.

We read from this table that the above child, with a C.A. of nine years and two months and an M.A. of 10-2, would be credited with a deviation I.Q. of 108. In most instances, the difference between conventional and deviation I.Q.'s is smaller than in our example. However, deviation I.Q.'s are preferred, because, like other standard scores, they facilitate the statistical interpretation of test data.

The Stanford-Binet Scales are referred to as *individual* tests because they must be administered to one person at a time. In this respect they differ from *group* tests, to be considered later in this chapter. For reasons already cited, these tests are also designated as *verbal.* Exceptions to their predominantly verbal nature are items calling for such performances as placing forms in a form board and stringing beads. But these are used only at the early age levels. Scales which use such nonverbal items exclusively are known as *performance* tests.

The interpretation of Stanford-Binet I.Q.'s

Calculation of an I.Q. is not enough. The tester needs to examine the test record closely, making an inventory of the child's strong and weak functions. For diagnostic purposes, this analysis is often much more useful than the mere determination of an I.Q. In fact two individuals may have the same I.Q. and yet differ a great deal in their intellectual abilities.

An I.Q., however it is measured or scored, is not, and should not be construed as, an index of native ability, or what has often been referred to in popular parlance as "raw intelligence." It is, as we said earlier, a comparative index, showing how a particular child performs as compared with others of the same chronological age. An I.Q. of 100 means only that the child achieves the mean performance of his age group. An I.Q. significantly lower than 100 signifies that the child's performance is correspondingly poorer than

■ **TABLE 5.1   Levels of Intelligence in Terms of Stanford-Binet I.Q. Ranges**

	I.Q. Range
Idiot	Below 25
Imbecile	25–50
Moron	50–70
Borderline defective	70–80
Low normal	80–90
Normal or average	90–110
High average	110–120
Superior	120–140
Very superior	Above 140

that of his age group; an I.Q. significantly above 100, that his performance is correspondingly better than that of his age group. This presupposes, of course, that the children compared have had basically similar opportunities to develop their intellectual abilities. More will be said about the comparative nature of I.Q.'s when we discuss group differences and also the question of whether these differences indicate anything about native capacity.

It is customary to refer to levels of intelligence in terms of I.Q. ranges, as indicated in Table 5.1. But this is only a rough frame of reference, for other things besides I.Q. enter into such designations as "idiot," "imbecile," and the like. The terms "gifted" and "genius" are often used to categorize upper levels of test performance. Terman spoke of individuals with I.Q.'s higher than 130 as gifted. It is sometimes said that those of 140 I.Q. and above are at the "potential genius" level of intelligence. But, here again, factors other than I.Q. usually enter such considerations. This will be evident when we discuss the mentally gifted.

There are many individual tests, both verbal and performance, but the tests that we shall now consider are of particular interest to us here as illustrating the use of percentiles instead of M.A.'s and I.Q.'s. Moreover, one of these tests, like the 1960 Stanford-Binet, also uses a deviation I.Q. ■

THE WECHSLER TESTS

These tests, developed and standardized under the direction of Dr. David Wechsler of Bellevue Psychiatric Hospital, began with a scale designed to test the intelligence of adults. This, the Wechsler-Bellevue intelligence scale, was superseded by an improved test, the Wechsler Adult Intelligence Scale (WAIS).[13] A separately standardized test known as the Wechsler Intelligence Scale for Children (WISC) is similar to the adult tests in that it has both verbal and performance items and yields separate scores for these.[14] This test is also similar to the adult scales in that the items are arranged in order of difficulty without reference to age. Thus, although the scale covers the years from five to fifteen, there are no five-year tests, six-year tests, and so on. The child starts on the simpler items of a series and goes to items of increasing difficulty until his limit for that series is reached. He then goes to other series. His accomplishment is evaluated, not in units of mental age, but in terms of how it compares with that of others his own age. One such evaluation, as suggested above, uses the percentile standing of the individual with respect to his age group. Another way in which the individual score is evaluated is to note by how many standard deviation units it exceeds or falls below the average. The normal distribution curve in Figure 3.9 (p. 121) shows how percentile and standard scores are related.

Performance on adult intelligence tests is seldom evaluated in terms of I.Q. Percentiles or standard scores are most frequently used. The WISC uses the same method of interpretation with children as with adults. Nevertheless it is possible to calculate deviation I.Q.'s such as those used in the 1960 Revision of the Stanford-Binet Intelligence Scale. These I.Q.'s differ very little in value from those obtained with the Stanford-Binet. Whereas the latter uses 16 as the value of a standard deviation, the WISC uses 15. Since both scales take the mean to be 100 (see Figure 5.3), a WISC score one sigma above the mean yields an I.Q. of 115, as compared with 116 for the Stanford-Binet Scale.

The verbal items in the Wechsler scales test general information, comprehension, arithmetic, memory, and vocabulary. Most of them are similar, in essential respects, to the verbal items in other tests, including the Stanford-Binet. The performance items include such relatively complex tasks as arranging blocks to match a sample design (Figure 5.4) and placing pictures into a meaningful sequence (Figure 5.5). These complex performance items require a high level of perceptual and reasoning ability and they provide a link between tests that are predominantly verbal and those that are predominantly motor, like certain simpler performance tests considered later in this chapter.

● **5.4**

The Kohs Block Design Test Used in the Wechsler Scales. The subject is required to arrange the blocks to match sample patterns, of which the one illustrated is the most complex.

● 5.5
A Picture Arrangement Test. This is not one of the Wechsler-Bellevue items, but it is similar to those in the picture arrangement section of that test. The subject is required to arrange the items in the proper sequence. The correct sequence for these pictures is given in the Appendix. (Drawing by Alain, reproduced by permission. Copyright 1943 *The New Yorker Magazine*, Inc.)

It is interesting to note that, when groups of children are given both the WISC and the Stanford-Binet, the correlations between scores on the two tests range from .60 to .90. The verbal scale of WISC correlates more highly with Stanford-Binet scores than does the performance scale. This is not surprising, since the latter test places so much emphasis upon verbal skills.[15] ■

PERFORMANCE TESTS

Strictly speaking, of course, all intelligence tests are measures of performance. Nevertheless, as previously noted, the term *performance* is customarily applied to tests which require a minimal understanding and use of language. They are *nonverbal* in contrast with predominantly *verbal* tests like the Stanford-Binet. An early performance test (Seguin's) was pictured in Figure 1.9 (p. 20).

Our discussion of infant tests revealed that these are wholly of a performance nature. One will recall that the Stanford-Binet test at lower age levels includes performance items and that 50 per cent of the items on the Wechsler scales (WAIS and WISC) are likewise nonverbal. There are, however, many single performance tests for which age-norms are available. Some of these are illustrated in Figure 5.6. Batteries of such tests are sometimes incorporated into broader tests (like the WAIS and WISC) and standardized as a battery.

Performance tests may provide a measure of fundamental psychological processes, like reasoning and perceiving relationships, yet without depending upon particular cultural or educational opportunities. They enable us to estimate the intelligence of individuals: (1) who are too young to have used a language, as in the case of infant tests; (2) who are illiterate through lack of educational opportunity or feeblemindedness; and (3) who speak only a foreign tongue. They have been used in numerous situations in which tests of the Stanford-Binet variety would be useless.

The correlation of performance test scores with scores on verbal tests like the Stanford-Binet is, as one might expect, not as high as the correlation between other verbal tests and the Stanford-Binet. For example, the performance scale of the WISC correlates about

● **5.6**

Some Typical Performance Tests. These are used in the *Arthur Point Scale of Performance.* A similar manikin test (left) and profile test (right) are also used in the performance scales of the WAIS and WISC. In these tests the parts are presented in a scattered array and the individual puts them together. The sections of the formboards, the mare and foal picture, and the picture completion test (lower left) are removed before the test begins and the child is required to place them in their proper positions. Blocks are arranged into patterns like those on the cards, as illustrated. Four of the cubes are tapped in a certain order and the child is asked to imitate this. (Courtesy, C. H. Stoelting Co.)

.60 with the Stanford-Binet, whereas the verbal scale correlates about .90. Generally speaking, psychologists prefer to use verbal tests when these are applicable, but performance tests are useful when, for the reasons given above, one encounters linguistic handicaps. ■

GROUP TESTS

All of the tests which we have so far described are referred to as *individual tests* because they involve the testing of one person at a time. But the administration and scoring of individual tests is laborious and time-consuming. Administration of the Stanford-Binet test is a case in point. It requires a highly trained tester to spend one hour or more with each individual. Added to this is the time required for evaluating each response, in relation to carefully standardized and specified norms, calculating the M.A., and finding the I.Q. In many practical situations it is necessary to test large numbers of individuals quickly and without such highly specialized personnel as most individual tests require for their administration and scoring. At such times group tests are indispensable.

□ The need for group tests of intelligence was especially pressing in 1917–1918 when 1,750,000 draftees were tested, and even more so in the years from 1941–1945, when over 10,000,000 were tested.

Psychologists had begun to devise group tests of intelligence before 1917, but these had not been published. When psychologists were asked to investigate the intelligence of draftees, they formed a committee which considered all earlier intelligence tests and finally developed two, a verbal and a nonverbal, which could be very quickly administered to large groups, and just as readily scored. These were known, respectively, as the *Army Alpha* and *Army Beta* tests.[16] Principles underlying selection of items for the tests were similar to those followed in the development of the Stanford-Binet Test. That is to say, the items were such as to measure those psychological processes regarded as important aspects of intelligence, the tests were intrinsically interesting, and their performance did not require special schooling. Administration and scoring of the tests was quickly mastered, hence a long period of training and practical experience such as that required for administration and scoring of tests like the Stanford-Binet was not required. During the last war, as a matter of fact, the somewhat comparable Army General Classification Tests (AGCT) were machine scored. A similar test, known as the Armed Forces Qualification Test (AFQT), has been used more recently to screen recruits for the Armed Services.[17]

The value of group intelligence tests became so apparent, as a result of the army experience, that many other group tests, designed for school and college use, soon appeared. ☐

One of the recently developed group tests was standardized on 136,000 school children from kindergarten through high school. This is the *Lorge-Thorndike Test*.[18] The standardization group was selected to provide proportional representation of the various socioeconomic levels in the United States. A few items similar to those in this test are shown in Figure 5.7. It includes verbal and nonverbal items. Scoring provides such information as the individual's deviation I.Q. and his percentile rank.

Disadvantages of group tests

The chief disadvantage of group tests as compared with individual tests is that those who administer the former cannot be sure that each individual is at his ease, that he is in a fit condition to be taking the test at that time, that he is trying to do his best, or that he is following instructions properly. With respect to the last point, consider the following example: A child with a Stanford-Binet I.Q. of over 130 took a group test and his I.Q. on this was 108. I.Q.'s determined with different tests often differ, but this was not the chief reason for the discrepancy in this case. The teacher giving the test had emphasized that the children must be *sure* to blacken the space between the lines which indicate the correct answers, as in Figure 5.7. This child, an especially conscientious one, was observed to spend a lot of

time blackening the spaces, and even going back to make sure that he had done a good job. The result was wasted time, fewer items marked than should have been marked in the time limit, and an I.Q. which did not represent the level of the child's intelligence. When obvious instances of improper following of instructions are observed, as in this case, the I.Q. can be discounted. However, when hundreds take a test at the same time, there are bound to be some such uncontrolled aspects as we have indicated. In short, while they are indispensable in many practical situations, group tests cannot be as well controlled as individual tests.

Group tests in education

When group intelligence tests are used in school and college, they serve two main purposes. In the first place, they may be used to select those who will be admitted. The correlation of about .60 between scores on such tests and college marks suggests their predictive value. In the second place, they may be used for guidance purposes. Most students take such a test when they enter college, and their scores are filed away in the registrar's office or the office of the dean. If a student makes a very low score on the test, he may be asked to take an individual test, perhaps the Wechsler Adult Intelligence Scale, as a check on his group test performance. In any event, if he gets into scholastic difficulties, and a record of test performance is available, it may be used in counseling him concerning his special difficulties. If the record shows low intelligence, the student may be asked to leave school or to change his course to one more in keeping with his specific aptitudes. If the record shows a high score on the intelligence test, however, the registrar or dean may investigate the student's motives for being in college, look into his study habits, or perhaps consult with him concerning personal problems which might interfere with his school work. ■

THE SEARCH FOR FACTORS IN INTELLIGENCE

Versatility in intelligence-test performance is obviously not a unitary process. We have

VERBAL BATTERY

VOCABULARY — Choose the word that has the same meaning or most nearly the same meaning as the word in dark type at the beginning of the line.

benevolent **A** lordly **B** stingy **C** kindly **D** poor **E** evil

hyperbola **A** stupidity **B** horizon **C** criticism **D** position **E** curve

SENTENCE COMPLETION — Choose the word that will make the best, the truest, and the most sensible complete sentence.

Adversity makes a man . . . , not rich.
  A wealthy **B** joyous **C** holy **D** wicked **E** wise

Men are more apt to be mistaken in their generalizations than in their particular . . .
  A retractions **B** observations **C** intuitions **D** inferences **E** presumptions

ANALOGIES — Find the word that goes with the third word in the same way as the second word goes with the first word

harmony ⟶ **discord** **: :** **agreement** ⟶
  A dissonance **B** incongruity **C** antagonism **D** dissension **E** divergence

irrelevant ⟶ **extraneous** **: :** **pertinent** ⟶
  A congruous **B** constitutional **C** prerequisite **D** intrinsic **E** comprehensive

NON-VERBAL BATTERY

NUMBER SERIES — The numbers at the left are in a certain order. Find the number at right that should come next.

159 53 51 17 15 5 **A** 3 **B** 6 **C** 9 **D** 12 **E** 18

64 16 48 12 36 9 **A** $2\frac{1}{4}$ **B** $6\frac{3}{4}$ **C** $9\frac{1}{4}$ **D** 27 **E** 81

FIGURE ANALOGIES — The first two drawings go together in a certain way. Find the drawing at the right that goes with the third drawing in the same way that the second goes with the first.

● 5.7
Items Illustrative of Those in the Lorge-Thorndike Intelligence Tests. These items are not in the actual test but are used to illustrate its nature. The proper space at the right is to be filled in. (Courtesy, Irving Lorge and Robert Thorndike, and Houghton Mifflin Company)

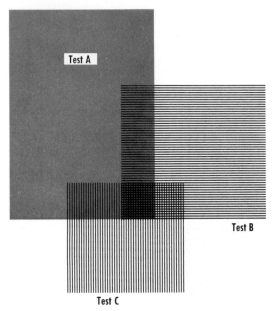

• 5.8

Graphic Illustration of a Common Factor Measured by Three Tests. Assume that A, B, and C are abilities measured by correspondingly designated tests. A and B have more in common (are more highly correlated) than either A or B with C. The common ability (factor) is represented by the square produced by the overlapping of A, B, and C. (From L. E. Tyler, *Tests and Measurements*, Prentice-Hall, 1963, p. 61.)

already suggested that intelligence tests measure memory, reasoning, and other processes. But how many really different abilities are measured? What, in other words, are the primary abilities? Statistical analysis of test performances offers a means of answering this question.

When different psychological tests are given to the same individuals we usually find that the scores are positively correlated, with some pairs of tests having higher correlations than others, as illustrated graphically in Figure 5.8. Factor analysts usually assume that the higher the positive correlation between two tests, the more likely it is that they are measuring similar functions.

Spearman, an eminent English psychologist of the last generation, claimed that dif-

ferent tests yielding positive intercorrelations are measuring some common factor, which he called *general intelligence*, or *g*.[19] Spearman claimed that many different skills "dip into" this common pool of ability. Mechanical ability, musical ability, mathematical ability, spelling ability, and many other abilities which show even a slight positive correlation with each other, do so, Spearman said, because they all require a certain amount of the common ability, *g*. He claimed that each skill involves special abilities in addition to *g*. These he referred to as *s*'s. Thus, besides a certain large amount of *g*, facility in mathematics would require specific mathematical skills (or abilities). These might be facility with numbers, ability to factor, ability to multiply, and so on. Such would be referred to as the *s*'s of mathematical performance. Certain other skills would require relatively little *g*. Mechanical skill, according to this view, would require special *s*'s but less *g* than mathematics.

Some other psychologists have taken exception to the claim that there is a general intelligence factor such as Spearman posited. They claim that what he called *g* is itself analyzable into a number of subsidiary abilities or factors.

Thurstone, for example, gave large batteries of tests, verbal and performance, to high-school and college students. All the students did all the tests. The scores on each test were then correlated with the scores on every other test and a table of intercorrelations arranged.

Although most tests correlated somewhat with each other, some tests correlated among themselves much more than others. It was assumed that any tests which correlated highly with each other were to a high degree measuring the same ability.

Following this line of reasoning, but using statistical and other devices too complicated for presentation here, Thurstone defined seven primary abilities, or factors, involved in the performance of a battery of sixty group tests, both verbal and nonverbal.[20] These factors were *number ability* (N), *word fluency* (W), *verbal meaning* (V), *memory* (M), *reasoning* (R), *spatial relations* (S), and *perceptual speed* (P). Figure 5.9 illustrates the nature of the tests designed to measure Thurstone's seven factors. There are twenty-one different tests in the battery, three for each of the factors. Each of these tests has a large number of items, most of them more difficult than those given here.

Thurstone's multiple-factor theory, based on the application of these test batteries, is illustrated in Figure 5.10, which shows, among other things, that even tests designed to measure particular factors still correlate positively with each other as well as with tests designed to measure "general intelligence."

The seven primary abilities that we have been discussing are not the only factors involved in intelligence-test performance, but Thurstone concluded that they are the ones most clearly identifiable in the batteries of tests analyzed by him over a period of several years. Speed, learning ability, and several other functions which one might expect to be involved in intelligent behavior are not identified, but this is perhaps because the tests have not been designed to measure these functions. More recently investigators have identified several additional factors. Some of these represent a further breakdown of Thurstone's *reasoning* factor.[21]

The value of measuring primary abilities instead of a heterogeneous integration of such abilities as in most intelligence tests is probably obvious. There are certain skills, like mechanical skill, which have a low correlation with scores on tests of general intelligence," yet which might correlate highly with a particular primary factor (or group of primary factors). A test of this factor (or group of factors) might then be useful in selecting those with mechanical skill. It

● **5.9**

Sample Items from Thurstone's Tests. Each of the tests from which these samples have been taken was designed to measure one primary ability and little else. (The items are from two sources: L. L. Thurstone and T. G. Thurstone, "Factorial Studies of Intelligence," *Psychometric Monographs,* 1941, No. 2; T. G. Thurstone and K. M. Byrne, *Mental Abilities of Children,* courtesy, Science Research Associates.)

Number Ability (N)

In the row below mark every number that is exactly three more than the number just before it. Work as fast as you can.
15 19 21 26 29 22 25 5 8 7 11 4

Word Fluency (W)

Write as many words as you can which end with *tion*.

Verbal Meaning (V)

Underline the word in each line which means the same as the first word in that line. FETID amusing feverish putrid contagious

Memory (M)

In each row is written a name. You are to learn the names so well that when the last name is given you can write the first name.

Reasoning (R)

Three of the groups of letters are alike in some way. Which are alike?
XURM ABCD MNOP EFGH

Spatial Relations (S)

In each row mark the figure which will make a complete square of the first figure.

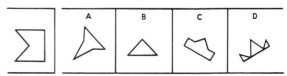

Perceptual Speed (P)

See how quickly you can recognize likenesses and differences. In each set of four pictures, mark the two which are exactly alike.

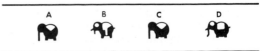

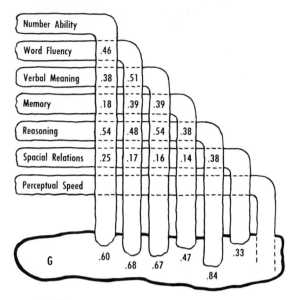

Number Ability

Word Fluency — .46

Verbal Meaning — .38 .51

Memory — .18 .39 .39

Reasoning — .54 .48 .54 .38

Spacial Relations — .25 .17 .16 .14 .38

Perceptual Speed

G — .60 .68 .67 .47 .33 .84

● **5.10**

Thurstone's Multiple-Factor Theory. Thurstone's seven factors, as discussed in the text, are shown at the left. The numbers are coefficients of correlation. For example, number ability and word fluency are correlated to the extent of .46. Such positive correlations show that, despite an effort to obtain "pure" tests of these factors, there is much overlapping. The largest overlap is between reasoning and number ability (r of .54), and between reasoning and verbal meaning (r of .54). There is least overlap between spatial relations and memory (r of .14). This diagram presents the idea that, whether or not there is some unique g factor, as posited by Spearman, there is evidence that any test of *general intelligence* (G) will implicate the separate factors to varying degrees. Observe, for instance, that there is a correlation of .84 between Thurstone's reasoning test and a test of general intelligence. No correlations are given for perceptual speed because none have been reported. (From L. J. Bischof, *Intelligence: Statistical Concepts of its Nature*, Random House, 1954.)

might serve, that is, as part of a battery of tests, some of which measure more specific mechanical skills. Some such tests are discussed in Chapter 18. ■

THE GIFTED CHILD

Gifted children were recognizable long before we had intelligence tests. Some of the geniuses of history bear witness to this fact. Let us review the childhood accomplishments of a few of them.

☐ John Stuart Mill, the great English philosopher, logician, and economist, began to study Greek at three, read Plato at seven, studied Latin, geometry, and algebra at eight, and at twelve was studying philosophy. At the age of six years he began a history of Rome.[22]

Charles Dickens, before the age of seven, was reading such books as *The Vicar of Wakefield, Don Quixote,* and *Robinson Crusoe.* He also wrote a tragedy before he was seven.[23]

At the age of eight, Goethe was preparing for the university. During his tenth year he wrote what are said to be "clever Latin essays." At sixteen he not only read five languages in addition to German, but he was reading the classics in them. He studied law, philosophy, and literature. At twenty-three he published his first important work. In adult life he excelled in the writing of literature, but he was also a scientist and statesman.[24] Similar feats could be cited for most of the three hundred geniuses of historical importance whose careers have been studied by psychologists.

Many of our great present-day scientists and writers also demonstrated their brightness at an early age. Others failed to exhibit any great childhood precocity. Even Einstein was no infant prodigy. At nine, according to a biographer, Albert was an "amiable dreamer," and everything he said was expressed only after careful consideration.[25] The potential genius of Einstein may have been veiled at that time by his reticence. It is quite likely, on the other hand, that intelligence tests, had they been available in his childhood, would have revealed then Einstein's very high level of intelligence. ☐

Table 5.2 lists the estimated I.Q.'s of some famous persons. Estimations were based upon various criteria, including comparison of their childhood accomplishments with those of children of known I.Q. These individuals undoubtedly inherited superior brains, but they also enjoyed unusual opportunities to learn.

We will now see how intelligence tests

■ **TABLE 5.2 Estimated I.Q.'s of Some Famous People**

Sir Francis Galton	200
John Stuart Mill	190
Johann W. von Goethe	185
Samuel Taylor Coleridge	175
Voltaire	170
Alexander Pope	160
William Pitt	160
Lord Tennyson	155
Sir Walter Scott	150
Mozart	150
Longfellow	150
Victor Hugo	150
Lord Byron	150
Thomas Jefferson	145
John Milton	145
Benjamin Franklin	145
Disraeli	145
Francis Bacon	145
James Watt	140
Rubens	140
Alexander Dumas	140
Napoleon Bonaparte	135
Charles Darwin	135
John Calvin	135
Edmund Burke	135

These were selected, and reprinted with permission of the publisher, from *The Early Mental Traits of Three Hundred Geniuses,* Vol. II, *Genetic Studies of Genius,* by Catharine Morris Cox (Stanford: Stanford University Press, 1926). The childhood of some has been reported in considerable detail by McCurdy, who shows that each had an unusually high degree of attention focused upon him as a child. This attention, upon a "groundwork of inherited ability," undoubtedly contributed to his genius. (See H. S. McCurdy, "The Childhood Pattern of Genius," *J. Elisha Mitchell Scientific Society,* 1957, 73, No. 2, pp. 448–462.)

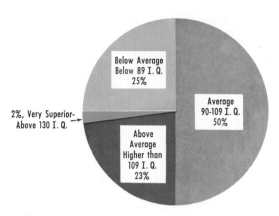

● **5.11**

The Gifted Are Relatively Few. This graph based upon Wechsler I.Q.'s shows that only about 2 per cent of the population are in the gifted class. (Data from D. Wechsler, *The Appraisal of Adult Intelligence,* 4th ed., Williams and Wilkins, 1958, p. 42.)

can be used to *discover* potential geniuses and how children so discovered can be encouraged to fulfill their evident promise of future accomplishment.

Terman's gifted children

In 1921 Terman began a study of gifted children that is still in progress. Over 1000 children with I.Q.'s ranging from 130 to 200 were located. We have already noted, with reference to Figure 5.3 (p. 121) that an I.Q. this high is found in only 2 per cent of the population. Figure 5.11 provides comparative percentages on this and other I.Q. levels. The average I.Q. in Terman's group was 150. Eighty of the children had I.Q.'s of 170 or higher. Most of these gifted individuals, including some added later, have been interviewed at intervals over the years.* Their careers are also being studied to see whether the promise of youth is being fulfilled. The most recent survey of the group was reported in 1959.[26]

It is of interest to note, in the first place, that the early level of intelligence was retained, thus indicating the predictive value of the initial I.Q.'s. When tested again at an average age of 30 years, for example, the group's performance was such as to place it in the upper 2 per cent of the population in intelligence. In 1951–52 an especially difficult Concept Mastery Test, designed to reach into "the stratosphere of adult intelligence," was given to over 1,000 of the original group. This indicated that the intelligence of the gifted group at that time was as much above the general

* They are often referred to as "Termites"!

adult level as it had been above the general child level initially.

☐ With respect to educational performance the following facts are of particular interest: 70 per cent of the group graduated from college. Of these, about one-third received honors. About two-thirds of the college group went to graduate school. Dr. Terman points out that the educational record would have been better but for the fact that many reached college age during the depression. It is interesting to observe that 40 per cent of the men and 20 per cent of the women earned half or more of their undergraduate expenses. Among 800 gifted males, there were 78 Ph.D. or equivalent degrees, 48 medical degrees, and 85 law degrees. There were 74 college teachers, 51 of them engaged in research in the basic sciences or engineering. Over 100 were engineers, some of whom did applied research. Attention is called to the fact that "Nearly all of these numbers are from 10 to 20 or 30 times as large as would be found for 800 men of corresponding age picked at random in the general population, and are sufficient answer to those who belittle the significance of I.Q. differences."[27]

In general, this group had more than eight times its proportional share of positions in professional fields. Moreover, a large proportion of the men had distinguished war records. One became director of a major laboratory devoted to applications of atomic energy. Another headed a major project for the Office of Strategic Services (OSS). Still another was co-director, during the war, of a large-scale investigation of the physiological, biochemical, and psychological effects of semi-starvation.

The number of books and articles written so far by the men of Terman's group has been prodigious. According to a 1954 report, these men, at an average age of 40, had published 67 books (21 fiction), 1,400 scientific, technical, and professional articles, over 200 short stories, novelettes, and plays; and 236 miscellaneous articles. In addition, journalists of the group authored hundreds of news stories, columns, and editorials. The group also wrote in-numerable radio and television scripts and received 150 patents for their inventions.

Although most of the gifted women became housewives or entered nonprofessional fields, some achieved notable public distinction. For example, one became a talented actress and playwright, another a composer and concert pianist.

It is to be expected that such a large group would include some failures. Quite a few did well through high school, but were not interested in going to college. Some could not afford to go. Others went to college but lost interest. One girl purposely "flunked out" so that she could do something more to her liking.

The average physical and mental health, character, personality, and marriage adjustment of Terman's gifted group has remained at or above the average of the general population. There is thus no basis for the commonly held view that brightness is offset by poor health and poor personal adjustment.

A large number of children with amazing erudition have been paraded before radio and television audiences as "quiz kids." Many people have doubtless wondered what becomes of these children: whether they "fizzle out" when they grow up or whether they retain their superior mental status. A follow-up study of such children has shown that they tend to become outstanding adults.[28] They are usually healthy, and they enjoy life. One former radio "quiz kid," J. D. Watson, shared the Nobel Prize in Medicine and Physiology with F. H. C. Crick and M. H. F. Wilkins in 1962 for a contribution made when he was 25. These men, working as a team, developed a "model" of the DNA molecule, a model which promises (see p. 91) to reveal, among other things, how the genes retain their characteristics from one generation to another and how they duplicate themselves. ☐

Education of the gifted

Children with exceptionally high intelligence are often a problem to their parents, to their teachers, and to their other associates, unless sorted out and given opportunities to

Gifted Grade School Children Do High School Work. These youngsters, whose I.Q.s' average 166, are reading in the library of a college, where they are enrolled in a special advanced program in high-school English, mathematics, and science. They do most of their mature work in private study. (Photo by Cravens, *Life*, © Time, Inc.)

use their abilities, as are the gifted children shown in Figure 5.12.

Teachers without special training are not always good at recognizing superior intelligence. Here is a case in point. A Negro girl with an I.Q. of 200 was rated by her teacher as lower in intelligence than a child whose I.Q. turned out to be 100.[29]

Inability of the teacher to recognize genius in her pupils sometimes leads her to report as "trouble-making" what, for the child far more advanced than she is in intelligence, is only natural. According to the late Dr. Leta Hollingworth, herself mentally gifted and a leader in education for the gifted, "Too many children of I.Q. 170 are being taught by teachers of I.Q. 120." She illustrates some of the difficulties by citing a conversation with a 10-year-old boy of I.Q. 165 — a boy referred to her as a school problem: without interest in school, impudent, and a liar.

☐ What seems to be your main problem in school?

Several of them.

Name one.

Well, I will name the teachers. Oh, boy! It is bad enough when the pupils make mistakes, but when the teachers make mistakes, oh, boy!

Mention a few mistakes the teachers made.

For instance, I was sitting in 5A and the teacher was teaching 5B. She was telling those children that the Germans discovered printing, that Gutenberg was the first discoverer of it, mind you. After a few minutes I couldn't stand it. I am not supposed to recite in the class, you see, but I got up. I said, "No; the Chinese invented, not discovered printing, before the time of Gutenberg — while the Germans were still barbarians."

Then the teacher said, "Sit down. You are entirely too fresh." Later on, she gave me a raking-over before the whole class. Oh, boy! What teaching. . . .

"Ned, that teacher is foolish, but one of the very first things to learn in the world is to suffer fools gladly." The child was so filled with resentment that he heard only the word "suffer."

Yes, that's it. That's what I say! Make 'em suffer. Roll a rock on 'em.

Before we finished the conversation, Ned was straightened out on the subject of who was to do the suffering. He agreed to do it himself.[30] ☐

In a language arts class, this was the experience of a gifted ten-year-old, Paula:[31]

☐ Miss Jones was showing a colored picture. . . .

"What do you see?" she asked.

Some answered, "An Arab."

"Why do you think he is an Arab?"

"Because of his clothes."

"What about his skin and complexion?"

"It's dark," several children said.

"Yes, you can recognize an Arab by his dark skin." Paula's hand went up but she received no recognition.

"But Miss Jones, I saw an —— "

Miss Jones, ignoring Paula's attempt to comment, went on. "You can also tell he's an Arab by his dirty clothes."

"But," Paula persisted, "all Arabs are not dirty . . . I saw. . . ."

"Paula, will you speak when you are spoken to. Now class, another way you can recognize an Arab is by his straight black hair. He. . . ."

"But, Miss Jones," Paula interrupted, "I saw blond Arabs when I was travelling in Syria and the near East. They. . . ."

"I told you to speak when you are spoken to. You have interrupted me three times. This time I am going to send you to the office." ☐

One can readily see that children like this might give up the struggle or get into many difficulties, perhaps drift into delinquency, unless treated by parents, teachers, and others with due regard to their intelligence. ■

MENTAL RETARDATION

Let us now turn to individuals at the lower end of the distribution, those referred to as retarded or feebleminded. Many of these start their lives with a defective brain. They can therefore get relatively little from even the best of environments. In Figure 5.13, for example, are four such extreme types of feeblemindedness.

The forms of feeblemindedness represented in Figure 5.13 have clear-cut physical stigmata, but there are other kinds in which the afflicted individuals look like normal people, although they do not behave normally. *Phenylpyruvic feeblemindedness* is an example of this. Moreover, it has a known cause and something can be done about it. In this respect it resembles cretinism. Its cause, however, is quite different, for it results from defective protein metabolism. Most proteins contain an amino acid known as *phenylalanine*. The normal liver provides an enzyme which changes phenylalanine to another substance used by the body for energy. In cases of phenylpyruvic feeblemindedness, however, this important liver enzyme is missing or ineffective. Consequently phenylpyruvic acid accumulates in the body and, among other things, interferes with brain functioning. One outstanding symptom is mental sluggishness. This disorder, estimated to afflict more than 6,000 of our feebleminded, is diagnosed by testing urine for the presence of phenylpyruvic acid. Some success in correcting it is being achieved by removing phenylalanine from the diet. This therapy, which is very difficult to accomplish, has led to marked gains in alertness and in mental-test performance, especially when started at an early age.[32]

In most cases of feeblemindedness there is no known cause and there are no general physical abnormalities like those found in cretinism and other clinical types of feeblemindedness. These cases, however, tend to run in families and it is not uncommon to have parents, children, and even grandchildren in the same institution. Where this occurs, the feeblemindedness is clearly inherited. What is inherited in such cases is a defective brain or some biochemical defect which interferes with normal brain functions. Most of these individuals are morons (I.Q. 50–70). The following example is more or less typical of moron intelligence. It also illustrates what may be accomplished with appropriate educational procedures.[33]

☐ Donald Noname . . . was a young man of twenty in an institution for the feeble-minded, the Training School at Vineland, New Jersey. Here Donald was being educated along the lines in which he could most easily advance. He was a handsome chap with a pleasant face, an alert manner, and but little awkwardness. He was an excellent farm hand

● **5.13**
Some Clinical Types of Feeblemindedness. *Microcephalics* (**A**) have a small brain with incompletely developed cerebrum and they are usually idiots (I.Q. below 25). *Hydrocephalics* (**B**) have excessively large heads resembling an inverted pear, the result of excess cerebrospinal fluid, which expands the initially plastic skull and also, from intracranial pressure, damages brain cells. Intelligence may range from the idiot to the moron level, i.e., up to 70 I.Q. Draining or otherwise diverting the excess fluid sometimes succeeds in reducing brain damage and the resulting mental retardation. The features of *mongoloids* (**C**) bear a superficial resemblance to those of the Mongolian race, hence the name. Metabolic, glandular, and neural defects are associated with this condition, but the basic disorder apparently stems from possession of an extra chromosome. The chromosome referred to by geneticists as #21 is present in triplicate, because, during development of reproductive cells (see page 92), a pair kept together instead of going to different cells. Fertilization produced an ovum with three instead of two #21 chromosomes. Another complicating factor is an increase in the incidence of mongolism as mothers become older, i.e., as they approach the menopause. Most mongoloids are imbeciles (I.Q. 25–50), but some are morons. *Cretinism* (**D**) comes from insufficient thyroid secretion during early development. Cretins are usually dwarfed, pot-bellied, and overweight in appearance. They are markedly lethargic, with intelligence generally at the imbecile level. Early diagnosis and regular administration of thyroxin is followed by normal development, physical and mental. (Illustrations after, respectively, Tredgold, Wallin, Tredgold, and Wolf.)

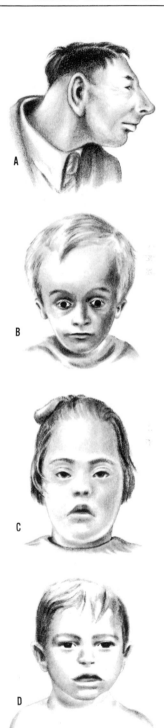

and especially apt in handling farm machinery. One of his teachers called him "the finest industrial worker in the school." He had learned to play the bass horn well in the school band. His education in public school had progressed to the level of the first grade but there he stuck for four years. After five years of good instruction at Vineland with more personal attention than he would ever have got in public school, he was still at the first-grade level. At the age of fifteen he did not do quite so well on intelligence tests as the average ten-year-old, and, curiously enough, in school work he was still back below the seven-year level. He could not put the words, *girl, river* and *ball* together into a single unitary sentence. He could not define words like *charity* or *justice*. Given money he could not make correct change. Conversation with Donald soon broke down the first impression of his intellectual competence. He had a poverty of ideas, a lack of originality, a very limited stock of general information, only a vague comprehension of abstract relationships.

At last report, Donald was working for a family which took care of him, but expected no intellectual brilliance from him. ☐

If a child's I.Q. is lower than that of the least successful children in the school system, we can keep him from going through the regular educational channels, where he will fall farther and farther behind his schoolmates. Many school systems provide so-called "opportunity classes" where special attention is given the mentally backward child. He can go farther this way than in the regular classes — without being made to feel inferior and without detracting from the attention other children should receive from the teacher. Moreover, there can be an increasing emphasis, as the child gets older, on practical things that he can learn to do instead of increasing emphasis on symbolic activities that are beyond him.

Those children who have insufficient intelligence to profit from any regular schooling are usually placed in institutions where, with others of their kind, they can be reasonably well adjusted.[34]

Some of the higher-grade feebleminded,

like Donald Noname, make useful citizens if properly trained. Most institutions for the feebleminded train their higher-grade inmates to do useful work around the institution and, in some instances, to work on farms or do housework in homes where they are placed and supervised. ■

INDIVIDUAL DIFFERENCES IN MENTAL GROWTH

Generally speaking, children who are very bright continue to be bright and children who are very dull continue to be dull. But what about the children in between these extremes? Does their I.Q. remain constant? On two tests given within a year or so of each other, the I.Q. usually changes very little if at all. That is to say, a child who has an M.A. of 6 at six years usually has an M.A. of 7 at seven years, which gives him an I.Q. of 100 at six and an I.Q. of 100 at seven. But as the years between tests increase, the I.Q. may undergo more or less change. In some children the I.Q. fluctuates without any evident upward or downward trend while in others it gets larger or smaller with increasing age. The cases in Figure 5.14 illustrate this fact.

When changes in I.Q. do occur, we may well ask what causes them. Some improvements may be due to repeated tests, making a child "test wise." Some fluctuations may result from the use of different tests at different age levels. Some may be due to administration of a test by different testers at different age levels. These may be factors when the same children are tested repeatedly from infancy until later childhood or adolescence. However, they do not account for all the changes which occur. Two major *longitudinal** studies of mental growth are in progress, one at the University of California at Berkeley[35] and the other at Antioch College in Ohio.[36] The first, known as the *Berkeley Growth Study*, has followed the development

* This general procedure is contrasted with *cross-sectional* studies which, instead of following the same individuals from one age level to another, test different groups at each age level.

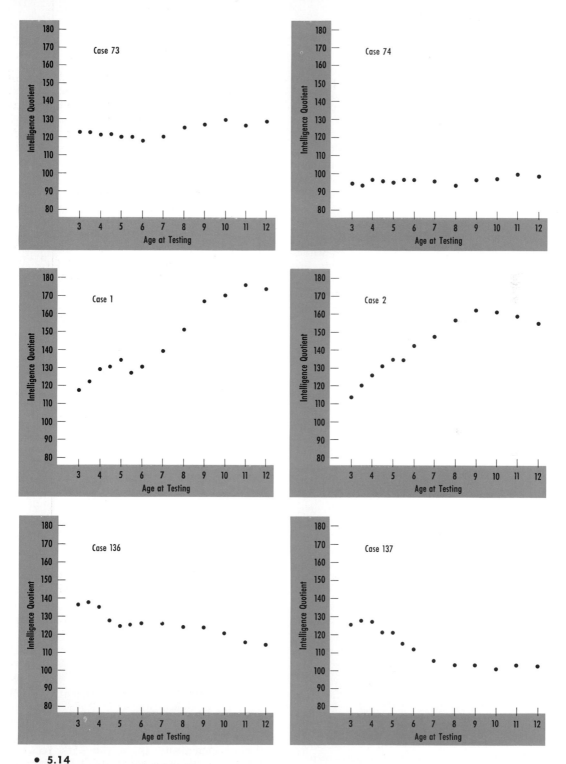

● 5.14

I.Q. Changes Observed in Tests Given at Yearly Intervals. The curves are smoothed to indicate trends. These six cases were selected from 140 in the Fels research. (L. W. Sontag, C. T. Baker, and V. L. Nelson, "Mental Growth and Personality Development: A Longitudinal Study," *Monogr. Soc. Res. Child Develpm.*, 1958, 23, No. 2.)

of the same sixty-one individuals from the age of two months on into adulthood. At last report the subjects of the study were 25 years old. The other longitudinal study, carried on at the Fels Institute for the Study of Human Development at Antioch College, has reported developmental information on 200 individuals studied from the time of birth until their twelfth year. The cases in Figure 5.14 were from this study.

The findings of the Berkeley and Fels studies are in substantial agreement. Some children develop at a constant rate while others either fluctuate inconsistently or increase or decrease their rate of mental growth. They show, also, that most children eventually reach a more or less constant rate of growth. This means, of course, that their I.Q. becomes relatively constant. Note, for example, the leveling off of growth rates in Figure 5.14. Dr. Nancy Bayley, director of the Berkeley study, finds "a strong underlying consistency or constancy. Some children forge ahead and maintain relatively advanced positions after five or six years of age. Others grow slowly and lag behind. There is some shifting of position, but the changes are gradual over rather long intervals of time. Within such intervals we can expect to obtain fairly constant standard scores (I.Q.'s)."[37] With respect to observed changes, she says, "Slight irregularities may reflect temporary conditions of motivation, health, or emotional factors. The more constant shifts require other explanations. Though they may result from prolonged emotional or environmental influences, they may also express inherent tendencies to develop at given rates. I suspect that each child is a law unto himself: in some instances certain factors are more important, while in others, different factors play the determining role."[38] With respect to the suggestion that each child is a law unto himself, it is interesting to note that the Fels investigators also stress the "highly idiosyncratic nature"* of I.Q. changes. This they attribute to "complex environmental causes."[39]

* They mean by this that the changes observed are peculiar to the given individual under study and not characteristic of most individuals.

It is quite evident, then, that we should not take a specific I.Q. too literally, especially when it is based upon a single test and, even more so, when this test is given in early childhood. ■

LIMITS OF MENTAL GROWTH

Mental growth continues until, and even beyond the time of physical maturity. But when does it reach its upper limit? When does the individual reach the point where he is as versatile as he ever will be in acquiring further skills and information? Does he ever reach a stage where he cannot learn new things as well as he once could? In other words, does versatility undergo a decline? If it does, at what age level does this occur? It is with these and related questions that we now concern ourselves.

The upper limit of mental growth varies between individuals and is related to their general level of intelligence. Generally speaking, those with low intelligence reach their upper limit quite early and those with high intelligence reach theirs at a relatively advanced age.

The general trend of mental growth, as indicated in the Berkeley study, is represented by the curve in Figure 5.15. This curve is based upon group averages, hence is much smoother than any individual growth curve could be. Individuals, as we have already pointed out, may show a great deal of fluctuation. Note that the slope of the curve is fairly constant between about the third year and the early teens. This means that, on the average, mental growth increases by steady yearly increments as chronological age increases. In the teens, however, the average yearly increments of mental growth become relatively small. By 21, the last age represented, these increments become so small that the curve tends to flatten out. The fact that it does not quite do so shows that mental growth is continuing, although at a very slow pace. A more recent report for the same group showed further increments up to the 25th year. A point of particular interest about this curve is that it is based upon a group of individuals

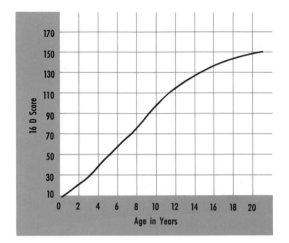

● 5.15

Growth of Intelligence from Birth to Twenty-One Years. This curve is based upon the Berkeley Growth Study. The scores indicated are not raw scores nor are they based upon a single test. They are derived from several tests in terms of standard deviation units, with age 16 as the basis of comparison. Dr. Bayley regards this curve as "not too far from probable trends of growth in intelligence." (From N. Bayley, "On the Growth of Intelligence," *American Psychologist,* 1955, 10, p. 811.)

with higher than average intelligence. Their mean 17-year Stanford-Binet I.Q. was 129. A mental growth curve for a group of below-average intelligence would have flattened out sooner.

Cross-sectional investigations have sampled intelligence at age levels far beyond those yet reached by the above study. One of the most extensive of these, which covered the span from 20 to 70 years, yielded the results represented in Figure 5.16. Note that average performance in all categories declined markedly at the upper age levels. In general, this investigation verifies the results of several earlier studies using various intelligence tests.[40]

The decline in test performance at the upper age levels is more evident for some functions than for others. Note, for example, that number ability continues to improve until middle life, a time when other functions have greatly declined. Other studies show that

vocabulary remains at a high level throughout the life span while new learning and reasoning both undergo a rapid decline.[41] Observe in the reasoning curve of our illustration that this ability begins to decline even in the twenties.

What we have said about the changes in test performance as old age approaches applies, of course, to groups. It sometimes happens that older persons demonstrate a high degree of test ability. Such persons are rare. What the experiments show is *not* that the older person knows less as he reaches the higher age levels, but that the readiness with which he acquires further knowledge decreases. When the older adult competes with younger ones and, as is often the case, reaches a similar level of achievement, he usually does so by putting forth a disproportionate amount of effort. It takes him longer to acquire further knowledge, and he tends to be more handicapped than the younger person in retaining and applying it. ■

THE INFLUENCE OF UNUSUAL ENVIRONMENTS

Environmental conditions influence the growth of intelligence in many ways, as previous discussions have indicated, including those dealing with identical twins reared apart. Here we examine some outcomes of research on adverse and superior environmental conditions.

Adverse environmental conditions

Information on the effects of adverse environmental conditions comes from various sources and, as we will see, is subject to different interpretations depending upon one's disposition to favor an hereditarian or environmental explanation. Interpretations differ because the individuals involved differed both in heredity and in environment.

Take, for example, the average I.Q. of children isolated from normal educational opportunities. Among these are children reared in isolated mountain communities, children of gypsies, and children reared on houseboats

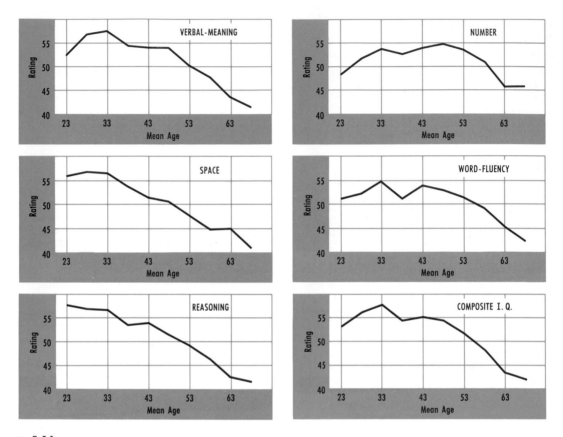

● 5.16

Age Changes in the Primary Mental Abilities. The mental abilities here represented are those so designated by Thurstone and described earlier in this chapter. (From K. W. Schaie, "Rigidity-Flexibility and Intelligence: A Cross-Sectional Study of the Adult Life Span from 20–70," *Psychological Monographs*, 1958, 72, No. 9, p. 18.)

along the River Thames in England. The average I.Q. of such children is usually far below the national average. One interpretation is that people who live in such conditions have poor inherent capacity to begin with and that their children accordingly inherit a low capacity. This argument may be countered with the fact that the I.Q. of such isolated children is not only low, but that it declines with age. This suggests that, whatever the hereditary background may be, continued residence in an educationally impoverished environment increases the child's handicap in doing mental tests and that the handicap becomes greater the older he gets. A poor en-

vironment does not handicap very much at lower age levels, where test items are relatively simple and not especially dependent upon a formal education. At higher age levels, where the tests are more complex and more dependent upon what children usually learn in classrooms, from books, and from intelligent conversation, there is a relatively greater handicap. Thus the older child living in educationally impoverished surroundings falls farther and farther behind the group on which the tests were standardized and with which his performance is compared in determining his I.Q. Thus his I.Q. declines the longer he suffers such an educational handicap. It is interesting to observe, in this connection, that improved schooling in an isolated mountain region raised the average I.Q. 10 points over a period of 10 years.[42]

In line with what we have just said about relatively isolated children, it is interesting to observe that the average I. Q. of rural children is usually below the average I.Q. of city children, the difference averaging between 5 and 10 points.[43] This is sometimes interpreted to mean that people who live in rural communities are somewhat lower in inherent ability than those who live in cities, the same argument as used in the case of children living in isolated communities. On the other hand, it can be shown that, in general, the educational opportunities of rural children are usually somewhat inferior to those of city children. This could well account for the small difference between rural and urban I.Q.'s. In any event, one should recognize that these studies are concerned with averages. Some of our brightest college students come from rural schools and some of our dullest from the most advanced city schools.

Superior environmental conditions

That superior environmental conditions favorably influence the I.Q. is evident from identical twin studies. It is also suggested by other studies in which heredity was not controlled. The latter are, of course, subject to hereditary as well as environmental interpretations.

Our first illustration is based upon research which shows that a child's I.Q. tends to be higher the higher the socio-economic status of his parents. The average I.Q. of children whose fathers are unskilled laborers is 95 as contrasted with an average I.Q. of 125 for children whose fathers are in the professions.[44] What is the explanation? Is it that people who enter the professions are inherently more capable and thus endow their children with a better inherent capacity than is received by the children of unskilled laborers? This is a possible explanation and it doubtless, in the long run, does account for at least some of the difference in I.Q. But it is by no means the whole explanation, for people with supe-

rior socio-economic status usually also have a superior education and more money than those lower in the scale. By and large, therefore, such parents provide their children with a more intellectually stimulating environment than is common at the level of unskilled labor. Compare, for example, the home environments pictured in Figure 5.17. Homes at higher socio-economic levels are likely to have more books, periodicals, newspapers, music, and intelligent conversation than those at lower levels. Moreover, many children at higher socio-economic levels go to better schools than those at lower levels.

It is well to note, however, that there is much hidden capacity among the lower socio-economic groups. This is proved by the fact that many children rise far above the level of their parents. Such capacity can of course best come to light in a society where educational and socio-economic opportunities depend upon capability rather than upon wealth or social prestige.

Other information on how environmental conditions may influence the I.Q. comes from studies of foster children.[45] These are children who, because their mothers are unmarried or because their parents have died or cannot keep them, are placed with foster parents. There are many related problems, but we shall deal with only one of them. This has to do with the effect on the child's I.Q. of the foster home in which he is reared. One study demonstrated that children in foster homes rated as poor, average, and good had average I.Q.'s, respectively, of 91, 103, and 111.[46] But were these I.Q. differences produced by the environmental differences? There may be such a relation, but this is not the sole explanation. Agencies usually try to place the child in a home which corresponds to, or is better than, the home he might have had with his true mother. Thus there is possibly an hereditary bias at the outset. That is to say, children placed in better homes may have better hereditary backgrounds to begin with. In fact it has been shown in several studies where the intelligence of the true parents was known that the foster child's I.Q. is more closely related to the I.Q. of the

● 5.17

A Comparison of Two Home Environments. Consider the different intellectual stimulation provided by each of these homes. (Courtesy, John Hancock Mutual Life Insurance Co.; *St. Louis Post-Dispatch*, from Black Star.)

true parents than to the I.Q. of the foster parents.[47] It is therefore evident that both hereditary and environmental factors must be considered in accounting for the results of studies relating intelligence and foster-home experience.

Except in the cases of identical twins reared in different environments, there is al-

ways the possibility that inherent differences rather than, or in combination with, different environmental conditions, are responsible for observed I.Q. differences. The fact that identical twins subjected to markedly different educational opportunities differ in I.Q. (pp. 96–97) demonstrates that inferior and superior environments may, in themselves, influence the level of intelligence. ■

ARE THERE RACIAL DIFFERENCES IN INTELLIGENCE?

Many investigations involving comparisons of Negro-white and Indian-white test performance have revealed differences in favor of whites. Do such differences reflect inborn differences in ability between the races? That is a question to which we can give no definite answer, for reasons which will soon be apparent.

Negro-white comparisons

The average I.Q. of northern Negroes* is about 90; of southern Negroes, about 80.[48] The median Negro I.Q. in twenty-seven studies was 86.[49] The average white I.Q., as the reader knows, is approximately 100. Somewhat comparable differences are found for the Stanford-Binet Scale and other tests. On the AGCT, for example, the average score (not I.Q.) for Negroes is about 69 as compared with 95 for whites.[50]

A recent large-scale sampling of intelligence in terms of a standardized vocabulary also yielded a lower average score for Negroes than for whites, the respective scores being approximately 8 and 11.[51]

Comparisons are less favorable to Negroes when tests are largely verbal. At the preschool age, where measurement is primarily with nonverbal tests, the average Negro score may equal the average score for whites. Here

* A seemingly inescapable difficulty in all these comparisons is the definition of "Negro." From a genetic standpoint, a Negro is a person all of whose chromosomes are from Negro ancestors, yet many of the "Negroes" of these comparisons may also have chromosomes from white ancestors.

is an example based upon the Goodenough Draw-a-Man Test. The child is asked to draw a man and he can score as many as 51 points, depending on the number of details included. Since there are age norms, I.Q.'s may be derived. The average white draw-a-man I.Q. is 100. In an investigation in which this test was given to Negro school children, the I.Q. of southern Negroes averaged 79; that of California Negroes 86.[52] But a comparison of Negro and white *preschool children* in New York City yielded no difference between Negro and white I.Q.'s.[53] A study of linguistic development in the same children favored the whites, something about which we will have more to say presently.

Although most studies of Negro-white intelligence favor whites, a few additional facts are worthy of attention. We mentioned earlier (p. 133) the Negro girl with a Stanford-Binet I.Q. of 200. A survey on upper limits of Negro intelligence has revealed other potential geniuses — 18 cases with I.Q.'s above 160, four of them over 180 and one over 200. This indicates that some Negro children are as bright as any white children. As one investigator has said, "Such high I.Q.'s could not be obtained if native potential, environmental stimulus potential, or motivation were at a low level."[54]

Consider, now, the fact that there are regional differences in I.Q. We mentioned in an earlier discussion that white I.Q.'s tend to be lower in rural than in urban communities, where educational opportunities are generally better. Part of the difference in I.Q. between southern and northern Negroes may be due to the fact that most of the latter live in cities. However, there are other possible reasons and these are worth considering for the light they throw on the general problem of trying to discover native differences in intelligence. One suggestion is that the Negroes who migrate are, on the whole, the brighter ones. If such a selective factor were present it could very well account for the better test performance of northern Negroes. There is evidence that selective migration has not occurred. However, there is another possible explanation. This is the better economic position and educational opportunity available

to northern Negroes. In support of this environmental interpretation is the fact that the Negro I.Q. increases with the duration of northern residence. In one investigation the same children were studied from the time they left the South until they had lived for several years in Philadelphia. Their average I.Q. continued to rise throughout the period of observation.[55] This suggests that, whether or not migrants to the North have higher native ability than those who stay in the South, the educational and other advantages to be gained by Negroes from residence in a northern city are definitely influential in raising the I.Q.

Why does residence in the North increase the level of the Negro I.Q.? One should keep in mind that the Stanford-Binet, the Wechsler Scales, and other tests involved in Negro-white comparisons were standardized mainly on white children given average or above-average educational opportunities. They are therefore biased in favor of white children with such opportunities. But the longer a Negro child resides in the North and has improved educational opportunities, the more closely his background corresponds to that of the white children on whom the tests were standardized.

The relative disadvantage of Negroes on tests of verbal skill is worthy of closer attention. We pointed out, in discussing the Draw-a-Man results, that Negro and white preschool children did equally well on this test, but that the white children were more advanced in linguistic development. This comparison was based on the length of sentences used by the Negro and white children. Why should Negro preschool children be behind white children of the same age in this respect? Is there a difference in intelligence that is reflected in length of sentences and not in the performance test? These questions cannot be answered with any degree of certainty, but presumptive evidence favors an environmental explanation. The investigators call attention to the fact that Negro families tend to be large, that one usually finds both parents working, and that, as a result of this situation, relatively little time is spent in playing and conversing with the children in such a fashion as to further their linguistic development. Moreover, the Negro parent may himself provide an inferior linguistic model for the child, owing to his own educational deficiencies. Since language plays such a basic role in most of our thought processes, the linguistic retardation of the Negro child could in turn interfere with his overall intellectual development.[56]

In comparing Negro and white performances on intelligence tests we have referred to only a few of the many studies in this area. These are representative, however, and they show the difficulties involved in attempting to reveal the presence or absence of inherent differences. The following quotation from a recent comprehensive study in this area accents the points already made and adds others.

☐ "None of these studies tell us anything about racial differences in native potential. . . . intelligence tests do not in any sense tap native, inherent capacities. In spite of a good deal of research and a rather large body of literature, we know no more today than we did forty years ago. In order to determine whether or not such differences exist, it would be necessary to equate Negro and white groups on all aspects of environmental stimulus potential that might be related to performance on the measuring instrument. In addition, and this is perhaps the crucial factor, motivation to develop learning sets would have to be controlled. The children, white and Negro, would have to attend the same schools for the same number of days a year and come from the same or practically identical homes. The teachers and parents not only would have to assure an equally rich environment for the white and Negro children but also would have to instill the same degree of motivation to make use of this environmental stimulus potential. None of the studies reviewed achieved anything like this kind of control. The factor that is most difficult to deal with is probably that of motivation. Negroes do not have the same expectations of achievement as whites have, not even at the same socio-economic level. They expect to be restricted to certain occupations and to be deprived of many cultural advantages that are open to whites. It seems highly probable that Negroes, therefore, are not even motivated to make full use of such environmental opportunities as are offered. Learning sets may not be developed because they are presumed to have no real value for the individual. Obviously, setting up an experiment to control for motivational differences that are a function of caste values would be a prodigious undertaking."[57] ☐

Indian-white comparisons

In various studies comparing whites and American Indians, the average Indian I.Q. has been around 80 as compared with 100 for whites.[58] This difference is not at all surprising in view of the socio-economic and cultural differences which exist between typical reservation Indians and whites. Indeed, everything in the above quotation about the inadequacy of our tests to measure potential ability in Negroes as compared with whites applies equally well to Indians.

There has been much less research on Indian than on Negro test performance. Nevertheless we know that here, as in the case of Negroes, improvements in socio-economic and educational status raise the I.Q. For example, the average I.Q. of Indian children placed in good white foster homes was shown in one study to be 102.[59] Moreover, the oil-rich Osage Indians, with a superior socio-economic and educational status, have an average I.Q. which equals that of whites.[60] However, such results are not clear-cut. There may have been placement of brighter Indian children in white foster homes. It may be argued, moreover, that the Osage Indians with high socio-economic status failed to do as well on the tests as white people of comparable socio-economic status, whose I.Q.'s, as we have seen, are generally above average.

Part of the Indian-white difference in I.Q. may result from the fact that Indians, with their different cultural background, place less value on education and other aspects of our culture. Motivational differences are also revealed in test administration. Indians tend to "take their time" while whites hurry to achieve as much as possible within a time limit.

The use of intelligence tests in racial comparisons has not been completely useless, despite the inadequacies of the tests and our consequent failure to reveal the presence or absence of inborn differences. These studies have revealed the wide range of individual differences in all of the groups tested. They have shown, in the case of Negro children, that there is much more ability than was hitherto expected and that, instead of depreciating the mentality of a race, as such, we should respect and utilize ability wherever we find it. Finally, these racial comparisons supplement other data which show that performance on intelligence tests is correlated with various aspects of the individual's social environment.

With the background provided by our discussions of environmental conditions and racial differences, we are now ready to look again at the respective roles of heredity and environment in the development of individual intelligence. ■

THE RELATIVE INFLUENCE OF HEREDITY AND ENVIRONMENT

The individual's intelligence is a function of both heredity and environment. He inherits his organism, with sense organs, brain, and other structures that are important in acquiring intelligence. To the degree that these are defective his intelligence will also be defective, no matter how potentially stimulating his environment may be. But even a normal or superior organism does not guarantee any given level of intelligence. This depends upon the sort of environmental stimulation the individual has had and upon how he has used his opportunities. Thus, for a particular individual, both heredity and environment are important and it would be difficult, if not impossible, to say how much each has contributed to his intelligence. All that we know directly is the level of his test performance and, since this obviously utilizes what he has learned (what has come from his environment) there is no way to disentangle the environmental and the hereditary contributions. In this connection, Figure 5.18

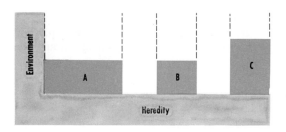

● **5.18**
Heredity and Environment. A and B are represented as having the same environmental opportunities but as differing in heredity. B and C, on the other hand, are shown as having the same heredity but differing in environmental opportunities. (After Woodworth and Marquis)

is of interest. It represents test performance (or intelligence) as a function of heredity and environment.

Differences between individuals may result from heredity, or environment, or both. Take identical twins, for instance. The intelligence of either is due to heredity *and* environment. But one twin may, as we have seen, differ from the other in intelligence, especially when there are large environmental differences. Since they have the same heredity, this difference must be purely environmental. If we could hold the environment constant, as we can with rats, and produce variations in intelligence by selective breeding, these differences would be purely hereditary. In most instances where we study individual differences, both heredity and environment differ and one cannot disentangle their separate influences. We were made well aware of this fact in discussing differences related to cultural isolation, socioeconomic status, foster homes, and different races. In each of these instances, although a strong influence of environmental opportunities was indicated, the results were confounded by the fact that heredity was not controlled and, in fact, could not be controlled.

Perhaps a few words should be said, in this connection, about I.Q. differences among children who have had "equal opportunities to learn." Under these circumstances it is sometimes assumed that the difference in I.Q., if it is significantly large, reflects a difference in inherent capacity. But "equal opportunities" are impossible to specify. Even two children in the same school, and perhaps from the same home, may differ in opportunity. They may have had a different health history. Their motivation may differ. That is, one may like school and the other not; one may take school seriously and the other regard it with disdain. The teacher may treat one child kindly and the other harshly. The parents may help and encourage one child more than the other. How much difference in I.Q. such variations might produce is not known, but that they would produce some difference is almost certain. One cannot, therefore, assume that differences in I.Q., even under seemingly similar circumstances, are due to differences in heredity and to these alone.

Although it is evident that an individual's intelligence is due to both heredity and environment, and that differences in intelligence between one individual and another, except in the case of identical twins, are also due to both heredity and environment, one may well ask "Which produces larger differences in intelligence — heredity or environment?" We must answer that, in the most general terms, larger differences are produced by variations in heredity than by variations in environment.

There are no experimental data on human beings to support this view — because we cannot hold environment strictly constant for them — but the results of animal experiments and inferences which may be drawn from the evolution of intelligent behavior unqualifiedly support it. An old saying, which is quite to the point, is that "you can't make a silk purse out of a sow's ear." What you have to

begin with (heredity) always places very large limitations on what you can develop from it by the means at your disposal (environment). A rat in a human environment responds only to the grosser aspects of it. A monkey is more responsive than a rat to what a human environment has to offer. A chimpanzee is still more responsive. But the most favorable human environment could never make a genius out of a chimpanzee any more than it could out of a monkey or a rat. The differences in intelligence from one of these levels to another are obviously attributable to the inherited makeup of the organisms involved.

Likewise, a congenital idiot, whose idiocy results from a defective inheritance, a defective prenatal environment, or defective biochemistry (pp. 134–135), will also make relatively little of the opportunities for development offered by a human environment — even the finest that one might provide. His mental growth may be no more influenced by the educational opportunities available than would that of a chimpanzee. On the other hand, a child with superior endowment may make the fullest use of the opportunities provided by his environment. He may even escape from a nonstimulating educational environment, whereas the idiot could not if he wanted to.

We say that the initially superior individual *may* make the fullest use of his opportunities. This is because there are many instances, especially at the upper school ages and in college, where those of superior endowment do not do this. Those of low initial ability could not, even if they would, respond to these opportunities in an effective way. Those of high ability, on the other hand, can make good use of them if they are so inclined. ■

• SUMMARY

Intelligence is a function which may be defined as versatility of adjustment. Its beginnings are found in the learning ability of lower animals. To be modified by what happens and to retain the modifications are important features of intelligence at all levels.

Intelligence reaches its ultimate development in the symbolic processes and verbal skills of human adults.

Intelligence is based upon the kind of brain one is born with, its growth to maturity, and the way it has been modified as a result of interaction with the environment. Individuals with identical brains at birth would attain different levels of intelligence if they were subjected to widely different educational environments; that is, if one were reared in an enriched intellectual climate and the other in an impoverished one.

The first "scale" of intelligence was devised by Binet and Simon. This had various revisions, culminating in the widely used Stanford-Binet Intelligence Scales. These have themselves undergone three revisions. The latest, an L-M form adapted from the L and M forms of the 1937 revision and newly evaluated, appeared in 1960. In place of the conventional I.Q., derived by dividing the M.A. by the C.A. and multiplying by 100, this uses a deviation I.Q. The deviation I.Q. is a standard score. It is based upon the deviation of the child's score from the mean score of his age group. The test is so devised that the mean I.Q. is 100. A lower than average performance results in an I.Q. lower than 100; a higher than average performance, in an I.Q. higher than 100. The meaning of an I.Q., whether conventional or deviation, is always relative to the standardization group on which the test was developed — that is, an I.Q. indicates how well a child does in comparison with others.

Infant tests are of little value in predicting the ultimate level of intelligence. This is because they do not (and cannot at this age level) provide a measure of symbolic functions.

The Wechsler Adult Intelligence Scale and the Wechsler Intelligence Scale for Children include motor and verbal tests. They differ from the Stanford-Binet Test in that items are arranged in order of difficulty without reference to age.

Performance tests are especially useful when the individual suffers from linguistic or other handicaps which make verbal tests inapplicable. Group tests (verbal or performance) can be given and scored by individuals with little training, and they may be administered to large numbers at a time. While not as reliable as individual tests, these are especially useful when conditions preclude giving the more reliable, but time-consuming, individual tests.

Factor analysis is used to discover how many primary abilities are involved in intelligence-test performance. Spearman believed that there is a general intelligence factor (g) involved in all intelligence-test performances, and in many other skills. According to this view, there are also specific factors, or s's. A widely accepted view today is that "general intelligence" comprises several primary functions (or factors). Among those already identified are: number ability, word fluency, verbal meaning, memory, reasoning, spatial relations, and perceptual speed.

The mentally gifted (I.Q.'s above 130) comprise about 2 per cent of the population. Intelligence tests can reveal gifted children and our educational procedures can be adapted to their special needs. With few exceptions, these children become outstanding adults and make important contributions to civilization.

Mental retardation has various origins, environmental and organic. In some instances (isolated mountain children, canal boat children) it may be due, in part at least, to inadequate educational opportunities. Blindness and deafness, unless circumvented by education through touch, can contribute to mental retardation by restricting the environmental input. Many of the feebleminded (I.Q. 70 or below) are born with organic defects which are more or less obvious in that they involve bodily stigmata. The microcephalics have a small head, the hydrocephalics a peculiarly-shaped large head, the cretins a somewhat grotesque facial, trunk, and leg structure, and so on. It is definitely established that cretins suffer from an inadequate thyroid secretion and that the condition may be successfully treated by administration of thyroxin, if this is started sufficiently early in life. Another condition with obvious signs is mongolism, in which the features have a superficial resemblance to those of the Mongolian race. It has been discovered recently that mongoloids possess 47 chromosomes instead of the normal 46; but how this is related to the metabolic, glandular, and neural defects which go with this condition has not yet been worked out. The incidence of mongolism is greater in children born late in the mother's reproductive period, i.e., when she is nearing the menopause. Phenylpyruvic feeblemindedness is the side effect, as it were, of defective metabolism which allows phenylpyruvic acid to accumulate and interfere with brain functions. Most of the feebleminded are at the moron level (50–70 I.Q.) and have no obvious abnormalities other than defective intelligence. Many of these can be educated to perform the relatively simple tasks of everyday life.

The mentally gifted and retarded tend to maintain their relative mental status throughout the growth period and at the adult level, but many individuals nearer the middle of the distribution show considerable change in I.Q. Some I.Q.'s increase with age, some decline, some go up and down, and some remain constant. Most individuals finally reach a relatively constant rate of mental growth, their M.A. keeping pace with their C.A. so as to produce a fairly constant I.Q. A mental growth curve plotted from group averages suggests that intelligence (mental age) increases at a rather constant rate until the teens, then increases more slowly. The upper limit of mental growth (the level at which the individual is as mentally versatile as he will ever be) is dependent upon the individual, and particularly on the general level of his intelligence. The upper limit of mental growth in the feebleminded is reached relatively early. In the gifted it is reached relatively late. Eventually there is a decline in mental ability, but this comes earlier for some than for others. It also comes earlier for some aspects of intelligence (new learning, reasoning) than for others (numerical and verbal ability).

The I.Q. is greatly influenced by environmental conditions, both adverse and superior. An adverse environment does not depress it in early as much as in later years, when the child gets increasingly out of step with children who attend good schools and have intellectually stimulating homes. Studies showing that the I.Q. rises with the socio-economic status of parents are subject to different interpretations — those at higher levels may be inherently brighter, or they may give their children an environment that is intellectually more stimulating. Perhaps both of these factors are involved. Foster-home studies show that children placed in homes rated as superior have higher I.Q.'s. But there may be an hereditary bias — children of superior parents being placed in superior homes. Moreover, the child's intelligence correlates more highly with that of his real parents than with that of his foster parents. There is no doubt that superior educational opportunities are effective in raising the I.Q., but there is always the possibility (when heredity and environment are both varied) that some of the improvement depends specifically upon heredity.

Differences in the average I.Q.'s of Negroes and whites, and of American Indians and whites, as commonly tested, are almost universally in favor of the white average. There is much overlapping, however, with many Negroes, for example, having higher I.Q.'s than average whites — I.Q.'s even at the gifted level. But we have seen that racial groups differ widely in educational and other opportunities. To the degree that these differences are narrowed, differences in I.Q. become smaller. The intelligence tests involved in racial comparisons were standardized on white children in average schools and with wide-open opportunities to advance to any position in our society. No group that had been denied such educational and social opportunities (Negro, Indian, or white) could reasonably be expected to have as high an average I.Q. as typical whites. Thus there is no basis for concluding that the observed differences in test performance come from inherent differences in intelligence between the races compared. ■

REFERENCES AND NOTES FOR THIS CHAPTER ARE IN THE APPENDIX.

• SELECTED READINGS

Anastasi, A., *Psychological Testing* (2nd ed.). Macmillan, 1961.

Bischof, L. J., *Intelligence: Statistical Concepts of its Nature.* Random House, 1954.

Cronbach, L. J., *Essentials of Psychological Testing* (2nd ed.). Harper, 1960.

Daniel, R. S. (Ed.), *Contemporary Readings in General Psychology* (2nd ed.). Houghton Mifflin, 1965. See especially Readings 26 (race and intelligence, by Tead), 28 (facts about mental deficiency, by Yepsen), and 29 (nature and nurture of genius, by Pressey).

Dulany, D. E., Jr., R. L. DeValois, D. C. Beardslee, and M. R. Winterbottom, *Contributions to Modern Psychology* (2nd ed.). Oxford University Press, 1963. Readings 6, 7, and 8 on, respectively, testing intelligence, parental occupations and intelligence, and exceptional talent.

Hunt, J. McV., *Intelligence and Experience.* Ronald, 1961. A marshaling of evidence in support of the view that early learning plays an important role in determination of intelligence. Includes a good resumé of Piaget's views on development of intelligence.

Jordan, T. E., *The Exceptional Child.* Merrill Books, 1962. Problems of retarded, gifted, brain-injured, and handicapped children.

Kuhlen, R. G., and G. G. Thompson, *Psychological Studies of Human Development* (2nd ed.). Appleton-Century-Crofts, 1963, Chapters VII and VIII. An excellent series of readings on patterns of intellectual growth and intelligence and adjustment.

Masland, R. L., S. B. Sarason, and T. Gladwin, *Mental Subnormality.* Basic Books, 1958. A survey of biological, psychological, and cultural factors in mental deficiency.

Terman, L. M., and M. H. Oden, *The Gifted Group at Mid-Life.* Stanford University Press, 1959. The latest report on the gifted group studied by Terman and his associates. There is a recapitulation of earlier reports.

6

Motivation

*T*his chapter is concerned with what is sometimes referred to as "the dynamics of behavior." Dynamics, a term taken over from the physical sciences, refers to the energies or forces which produce motion in physical bodies. The appropriateness of this term, as applied to the motivation of behavior, can be seen from the fact that our concern here is with what moves the organism to do what it does. We are concerned not so much with what the organism does, nor with how it accomplishes what it does, as we are with *why* it acts as it does. This interest, as will soon be apparent, leads us to infer the presence of internal energizers or driving forces which activate the organism and influence its responsiveness to external stimuli.

In terms of its derivation, the word *motivate* means to move, to activate. In this general sense, anything that initiates activity, whether external or internal, is motivating. In psychology, however, the terms *motivation* and *motive* refer to activation from within the organism. Thus motivated behavior is internally activated, or at least modified by, internal conditions. A motive, therefore, is some internal activator or modifier.

The general meaning of the concept of motivation can be made plain by reference to the activity of a puppet. The puppet is a static mechanism, incapable of initiating its own activity. It moves only when its strings are manipulated. Its movements are forced upon it. It is completely under external control. Moreover, every movement is predictable from a knowledge of how the puppet is constructed and of the forces applied to it. In view of these facts we say that the puppet is without motivation. We attribute no motives to it.

Contrast with this the behavior of living organisms. The simpler organisms act in many respects like puppets. They exhibit forced movements, known as *tropisms*, in which the whole body is turned toward or away from certain stimulating situations. Thus the cockroach runs from the light and a moth is attracted to it. Moreover, all organisms with a nervous system exhibit partial reactions — *reflexes* — which are equally puppet-like. In humans, for example, there is a reflex pupillary response to changes in illumination, a reflex kick of the foot (knee jerk) when the patellar tendon is struck, and a reflex gagging when the doctor applies a spatula to the back of our tongue. We have, in fact, many such reflexes.

Because they are puppet-like, neither tropisms nor reflexes are said to be motivated. In other respects, however, all animals have a certain degree of autonomy. That is to say, they are self-regulating. This is so for a number of reasons, as we will now see.

All animals undergo internal physiological changes related to the necessities of life — changes associated with such needs as for liquid, nourishment, and elimination. Through their effects on the nervous system, these physiological changes initiate relevant activities such as drinking, eating, and eliminating. They also influence receptivity to certain kinds of stimulation. The odor of food, for example, is especially evident to the hungry organism.

It is customary to refer to the necessities of life as *physiological needs* and to the related conditions which motivate behavior as *physiological drives*. There are, however, some inborn drives which have no direct relation to the maintenance of life. The sexual urge, for example, need not be satisfied in order that the individual may survive. It does, of course, have significance from the standpoint of perpetuating the race. There are some other drives which, although important for survival, and perhaps more or less instrumental in satisfying physiological needs (like the need for food), are of a quite different order from hunger itself. Organisms are so constituted, for example, that they are especially responsive to changes in their environment. Instead of responding passively, they actively explore and examine their surroundings.

Other inborn drives which have no direct relation to physiological needs, are those involved in emotional motivation. A frightened organism may run away or, if cornered, attack an aggressor. The organism that has experienced painful stimulation may become anxious and, as a result, avoid certain situations when avoidance is possible. Fear, anxiety, and other emotions have much to do with our responses to the world about us.

Still another reason why organisms are different from puppets is the fact that they learn. Their nervous system is modified by what happens to them. They learn where and how to satisfy their needs and they act accordingly. They do not merely wait for something to happen. Human beings also develop attitudes, interests, aspirations, and life goals. They pursue their long-range goals despite environmental distractions and frustrations. Indeed, persistence in a given direction is one of the clearest signs of motivated behavior. The man of Henley's *Invictus* who says, "I am the master of my fate: / I am the captain of my soul. . . ." is a "self-starter" and shows persistence of a high order. The fact that he thinks himself master of his own fate, whether or not this is ultimately so, is itself motivating and may have a significant influence upon his conduct.

At birth and for some time thereafter we are completely dominated by physiological motives. We sleep most of the time, but wake and take in nourishment when hungry, protest noisily against irritating or painful stimuli, and eliminate waste products as they accumulate. These primitive motives, which we share with other animals, are represented in Freudian terminology by the general term *id*. According to Freud, the id is "the oldest of mental provinces," which "contains everything that is inherited, that is present at birth, that is fixed in the constitution," including the drives "which originate in the somatic organization."[1]

Animals and human infants are almost completely dominated by their physiological motives. Although we retain such motives, their expression undergoes considerable change as we grow older. Animals living in a wild state satisfy them directly, as soon as they arise. When hungry they seek food where they have learned to find it and they usually rend, and tear, and guzzle without reference to the needs of others or to rules of conduct. At appropriate times and seasons they seek mates, and again they are dominated completely by the exigencies of the moment. As excretory needs arise, they satisfy them immediately, wherever they happen to be. When animals are frustrated by others, they often fight and kill.

Human beings, on the other hand, learn to behave in ways decreed only in part by their biological heritage and the immediate situation. Beginning soon after birth, they engage in reality-testing and, as a result, develop a self, an *ego*. Some animals below man perhaps also develop an ego on this basis, but the id retains a major place in their motivation. Human beings also take on the ways of others, even to the extent of acquiring moral principles, in short, a conscience or *superego*. They are increasingly modified by customs, traditions, and man-made laws. Consequently, even though human beings have the same physiological needs as other animals, they come to behave more like men and women than like animals. In Freudian terms, the ego and superego assume dominance over the id.

In this transformation of animal into human behavior, a significant role is played by social influences, and especially those dependent upon one's culture. The life of all human societies is organized around the problem of satisfying physiological needs. All agricultural activities are in one way or another linked with the need for food. Many of the most rigid social customs have to do with regulation of sexual activities. There are definite customs for the control of excretory needs. Various measures to protect the individual from injury have been instituted. There are prescribed ways of settling disputes so that angry men are restrained from attacking their fellows. ■

NEEDS AND DRIVES

Some physiological needs give rise to inner conditions which impel an organism to engage in activities that are more or less relevant to these needs, like seeking food when hungry, or water when thirsty. The observer of such activity gets the impression that the organism is *driven* from within. This is why we speak of *physiological drives*. When it is impelled by such conditions, the organism continues its activity until the need is satisfied, or until weakness or death makes it inactive. Thus a rat deprived of food for 24 hours or so becomes excessively active. If food is accessible, it eats until satiated. If food is not available, and the animal is admitted to a revolving drum, or some other activity-measuring device, it maintains excessive activity for long periods before weakness sets in.

When white rats on reduced rations of food and water were given access, for one hour daily, to the revolving drum pictured in Figure 6.1, the resulting activity level increased as the normal body weight was reduced.[2] The correlation between activity level and the per cent of normal body weight remaining was −.99. This is an extremely high correlation. It indicates that as the normal body weight went down the level of activity went up. Another investigation used the same method, but gradually restored body weight.[3] As one would predict from the above results, activity decreased as a function of the degree to which normal body weight was restored.

These changes in activity level occurred in an environment that was constant with respect to light, temperature, and other controllable features. It appears, therefore, that they were controlled by internal conditions, i.e., internal (physiological) drives. When the internal conditions are produced by food deprivation we speak of a *hunger drive*; when they are produced by water deprivation, we speak of a *thirst drive*. In the above-mentioned experiment, since body weight was lowered (or raised) by manipulation of both food and water, a combination of hunger and thirst may have been involved.

Here are some further examples. A rat in

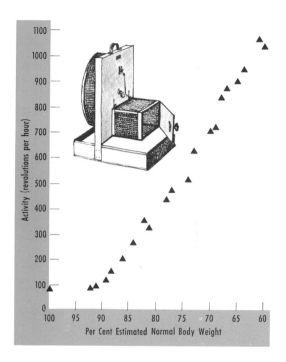

● **6.1**

Activity as a Function of Weight Reduction. Activity was measured with the revolving drum. As the rat ran in, and thus turned the activity wheel, revolutions in either direction were recorded on a counter. Observe that the activity level (in revolutions per hour) increased as body weight was reduced. The maximum activity level (over 1000 revolutions per hour) was exhibited by rats that had been reduced to 60 per cent of their estimated normal body weight. (Data from M. J. Moskowitz, "Running-Wheel Activity in the White Rat as a Function of Combined Food and Water Deprivation," *J. Comp. Physiol. Psychol.*, 1959, 52, pp. 621–625.)

heat is very active. In a revolving drum, it may run the equivalent of fifteen or more miles in a day. On days when the rat is not in heat, even though external conditions are the same, it runs very little.[4] We say, in this case, that a *sex drive* is responsible for the excessive activity.

Now let us examine a quite different activity, nest-building. If strips of paper are available, and the temperature falls, the rat actively engages in nest-building, and the intensity of such activity (as determined by the pieces of material used) increases as a function of the drop in temperature. As the temperature rises, however, nest-building declines and, when the temperature reaches an optimal level, stops altogether.[5] Here is an externally stimulated drive, but one which depends upon the need to maintain a normal body temperature. This is commonly called a *nest-building drive*, although one might just as appropriately call it a *temperature drive*.

The temperature drive was mentioned chiefly to set the stage for discussing another condition in which, regardless of the external temperature, the rat becomes excessively active in building nests. This behavior is shown by a rat that has just recently given birth to a litter. Some condition associated with having given birth drives her to build nests, in which she puts the young, even though, under other conditions, she would build no nests at all.[6] The fact that she persists in this activity even when the temperature is very high, is evidence enough of some inner condition which has the characteristic of a drive. We speak, in this case, of the *maternal drive*.

The concept of drive is a useful one for purposes of discourse, but the actual condition which impels the organism — what is sometimes referred to as the *drive state* — is often difficult or impossible to specify. A large amount of research on motivation is aimed at discovering what hunger is, physiologically. Similar research is focused upon thirst, sex, and other inborn drives. Interestingly enough, however, when we are able to specify the precise biochemical and neural basis of hunger, thirst, and other drives, we will have no further need for the general term, *drive*. The specified condition will be cited to account for food-seeking, drinking, mating, and so forth. Progress in this direction is being made, and some of the details will be considered presently. But much is still to be discovered and the concept of drive remains a useful one.

As we have seen, a physiological drive is named in terms of (1) the sort of deprivation which gives rise to it, (2) the physiological processes involved, insofar as these are known, and (3) the culminating activity, i.e., that which alleviates the need or which is relevant to such alleviation. In the case of hunger, for instance, the drive is aroused by depriving the animal of food, or at least cutting down on its rations. One of the conditions which is known to underlie hunger is the presence of stomach contractions. The appropriate culminating activity — that which satisfies the organism's need — is eating.

☐ We do not mean to imply that every physiological need has a corresponding drive. Indeed, some needs are so completely satisfied under normal conditions that we are not aware of them. How we are supplied with oxygen makes an interesting example. We live in an ocean of air which is one-fifth oxygen. If deprived of it for even a few minutes we would die. Here certainly is evidence of physiological *need*, yet, curious as it may seem, this need is not the basis of any strong physiological drive. The reason that man can continue to exist without such a drive is that under normal circumstances the need for oxygen is completely satisfied as a consequence of the satisfaction of a different need — the need to eliminate carbon dioxide. This function, with which a very strong drive is associated, is carried on by the lungs simultaneously with oxygenation of the blood. If a man is prevented from breathing, he soon gasps and struggles. He "wants air" — but he "wants" it only to flush out the accumulating carbon dioxide. Deoxygenated air, or pure nitrogen, relieves him as adequately as normal air would; and when the carbon dioxide concentration is normal he will relax contentedly in a deoxygenated atmosphere, there to succumb to asphyxiation, while feeling neither want nor discomfort.[7] Men who ascend to great heights in balloons or airplanes reach, at ten to twenty thousand feet, a region where, because of the thinness of the air, the amount of breathing which is adequate to eliminate wastes from the lungs does not supply sufficient oxygen. Here the airman takes additional oxygen, not because of any felt need for it but because he has been convinced by persuasion that it is necessary — much as he has been convinced of the value of vaccination against smallpox. ■

HOMEOSTASIS

It is possible to regard the physiologically driven organism as in a state of physiological disequilibrium. Then the culminating act, such as getting food, is thought of as compensatory — as restoring equilibrium.

The tendency of motivated behavior to maintain a balanced condition within the organism is called *homeostasis*. As one physiologist put it, "The living being is an agency of such sort that each disturbing influence induces by itself the calling forth of compensatory activity to neutralize or repair the disturbance."[8] He had in mind such compensatory activities as the following: restoration of injured tissues involving action of white blood cells, maintenance of normal body temperature during fluctuations in the external temperature, and preservation of normal carbon-dioxide level in the blood when the air is deficient in oxygen. When the external temperature is low we tend to become more active, to seek shelter, or to put on heavier clothing. A rat given the opportunity to supply itself with warmth does so, as pictured and described in Figure 6.2. When the external temperature is too high we sweat more, slow down, or seek the shade. The maintenance of a normal carbon-dioxide level is accomplished by faster or deeper breathing. It has been reported that Indians living in the Peruvian Andes at a height of 10,000 to 11,000 feet "have tremendous chests that allow them to take in enough oxygen for the heavy work they do."[9]

The concept of homeostasis is relevant to certain physiological drives, but not to others. The tension built up when one wants to relieve his bladder is dissipated quickly when urination occurs. The drowning person's struggles cease when he is rescued and can breathe again. Similarly, rest and sleep revive the fatigued organism. In certain other instances there are difficulties with a homeostatic interpretation, especially if considered

● 6.2
Thermoregulatory Behavior. This is a Plexiglas cylinder with a red-bulb infrared heat lamp above it. The rat's fur is clipped and the animal is put into the cylinder in a room so cold that body temperature cannot be maintained unless the lamp goes on at intervals. It can be controlled so as to maintain normal body temperature if the rat periodically presses the lever, as illustrated. When initially placed in the cylinder, a rat explores. During this exploratory activity it happens to press the lever and heat comes on for a few seconds. Then the typical response is to huddle and shiver for several hours. Finally, after body temperature has reached a critical level, the animal begins to press the lever. From then on it presses at a rate sufficient to maintain normal body temperature. This behavior, so "exquisitely attuned to the regulation of body temperature," is a good example of homeostasis. (From B. Weiss and V. G. Laties, "Behavioral Thermoregulation," *Science*, 1961, *133*, p. 1339.)

from a purely physiological standpoint. As the following statement by an outstanding investigator of sex behavior indicates, it is difficult to see how copulation could be considered an example of homeostatic response.

☐ "The individual deprived of sexual outlet does not perish, regardless of the length of time involved. No genuine tissue or biological needs are generated by sexual abstinence. It used to be believed that prolonged sexual inactivity in adulthood resulted in progressive accumulation of secretions within the accessory sex glands, and that nerve impulses from these distended receptacles gave rise to sexual urges. Modern evidence negates this hypothesis. Work in my own laboratory has shown that male animals which have been surgically deprived of the glands in question continue to display unmistakable signs of sexual arousal and potency. Furthermore, homologous structures in the female are undeveloped, and yet, if we are to believe Professor Kinsey and other experts, sexual motivation is not exclusively a masculine prerogative."[10] ☐

Since the concept of homeostasis was first propounded, however, some psychologists have come to use it as synonymous with compensatory behavior of any kind.[11] It might then be said that the *psychological tension* associated with sexual desire (even on a purely symbolic level, as in the person preoccupied with thoughts of sex), is relieved by sexual activity. In the following chapter we will observe further use of the homeostatic concept in relation to the maintenance of self-esteem by so-called "ego-defensive" or "ego-compensatory" activities. This use of the term *homeostasis* divorces it almost completely from its original physiological meaning, as described above. ■

HOW DO DRIVES OPERATE?

There is much controversy as to how physiological drives activate the organism. Are they sources of energy? If so, does each drive have specific energizing effects? Does the sex drive, for instance, energize only those reactions involved in sexual behavior? Or, on the other hand, do the energizing effects of different drives summate? Is the organism that is "driven" by hunger, let us say, more "driven" to acquire food-getting habits if it is at the same time thirsty and sexually deprived?

Questions like the above are raised with respect to the concept of drives as sources of energy — as *energizers* of behavior. But there are some who have a very different conception of how drives work. They think in terms, not of energy, but of neuromuscular and receptor mechanisms. They ask questions like these. Could it be that drive-states activate the organism by lowering the excitability of certain relevant neuromuscular mechanisms? In the case of sex, let us say, do sex hormones have a differential influence upon the passage of nerve impulses over certain pathways — inhibiting here and facilitating there? Or, on the other hand, could it be that a drive-state makes the organism more sensitive to certain aspects of its environment, the sexually deprived male organism, let us say, being thereby made more sensitive to the sight or odor of females? Does the drive, through such sensitizing effects, give an organism cues as to how needs may be satisfied, perhaps guiding it toward relevant objects and situations?

Drives as energizers

Those who hold that drive-states energize behavior often speak of them as the "mainsprings of behavior," the "inner dynamic forces" without which the organism would be "as inert as an engine without fuel." The *libido* which Freud stressed so much was assumed to be dammed-up sexual energy. Freudian psychoanalysts think of this as demanding expression and, when denied a direct outlet, as manifesting itself in devious ways, for instance, in dreams and in artistic creation.[12] Play in children has been regarded by some as an expression of excess energy. There is also an energy concept in the idea that emotionally aroused people feel better if they "let off steam."

☐ There is actually no known reservoir of energy in the body. The primary source of

energy is food. This is composed of carbohydrates (sugars), proteins, fats, vitamins,
minerals, and other substances. Digestion
changes food into soluble products which,
when they enter the bloodstream, are carried
to nerve cells, muscles, and other structures,
thus providing the energy necessary to their
functioning.

For illustrative purposes, let us consider
the energizing effect of carbohydrate and how
this is implicated in the concept of drives as
energizers. When the blood sugar falls below
a certain level, an individual becomes extremely weak, suffers muscular incoordination,
has extremely low morale, and, if the blood
sugar continues to fall, goes into a coma
and dies. Dextrose or some other form of
sugar reverses this trend. With respect to the
morale aspect, a famous chemist remarked that
"the difference between a coward and a hero
may be a lollipop." Sugar has this energy-
building and morale-raising effect because it is
needed by nerve cells; indeed it seems to be
their only source of energy. Without sufficient
carbohydrate, they stop functioning. □

Hormones (secreted by the endocrine
glands) contribute to the energizing of behavior by bringing about changes in blood
chemistry which, in turn, influence neural and
muscular functions. How this energizing occurs is not known in any detail, but Clark L.
Hull, who believed that drives have effects
which are both specific and general, had this to
say: "The action of these endocrine substances,
while apparently lowering the reaction threshold of certain restricted effectors, seems also to
have a generalized but possibly weaker tendency to facilitate action of *all* effectors, giving
rise to a degree of undifferentiated motivation
analogous to the Freudian libido. Thus a sex
hormone would tend to motivate action based
on any habit, however remote the action from
that involved in actual copulation."[13]

The question of generalized drive-states

The concept of a generalized drive-state
like that suggested in the above quotation is
difficult to investigate in such a way as to yield

clear-cut results. Of the many experiments designed to test it, some have confirmed and
others have failed to support the idea.

The strength of a drive is often inferred
from the speed with which the animal runs
toward an *incentive*, like food, water, or an
animal of the other sex. In the case of avoidance behavior, the strength of the drive may
be inferred from how fast the animal runs
to escape from painful stimulation, like electric shock. The experiment that we are about
to describe used the runway diagrammed in
Figure 6.3.

The experiment began with the floor electrified and with escape possible by running
into the goal box. These conditions produced
an acquired "drive of anxiety" which led the
rats to run into the goal box even though the
electric current was turned off. The question
which now arose was this: would the addition
of a hunger drive, which was not satisfied
during the runs, lead to faster running? In
other words, would the anxiety drive (need
to avoid pain) combine with the hunger drive
so as to increase the speed of running. There
was clear evidence that the overall drive
strength did increase under these conditions.

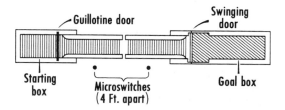

● 6.3
A Runway for Measuring Drive Strength. The
rat is placed in the starting box and a guillotine
door admits it to the runway. A swinging door
gives entrance to the goal box. Microswitches
are located at the points indicated. The first
switch, when the rat runs over it, starts a timer.
When the animal reaches the second switch, the
timer is stopped. In this way the speed of
running is indicated. Vertical lines represent
electric grids. (From A. Amsel, "A Combination
of Primary Appetitional Need with Primary and
Secondary Emotionally Derived Needs," *J. Exper.
Psychol.* 1950, 40, pp. 1–14.)

Of rats with the same anxiety level (in terms of amount of original shock) those that were also hungry ran faster than those that had eaten before the run.[14]

In the study just described, anxiety and an appetitive drive apparently combined in some way to produce a drive strength greater than that of anxiety alone. But what would happen if two appetitive drives, such as hunger and thirst, were involved? The answer is in doubt, because the researches designed to find an answer to this question have run into insurmountable complications, such as the fact that depriving an animal of water reduces its hunger (its eating) — and giving the thirsty animal water makes it hungrier.[15]

We see, therefore, that no broad generalization can be made about summation of drives. Whereas anxiety and hunger appear to summate, it is not yet known whether this applies to other drives.

Drives as sensitizers

Apart from their energizing effects, whether specific or general, drives may be said to sensitize the organism so that certain types of response appear more readily when particular drive states are present than when they are absent.

Hormones probably sensitize by making nerve pathways more excitable. It is said of the testicular hormone *androgen*, for example, that it "acts in some way to lower the resistance of definite reflex pathways so as to integrate or make excitable the reflex mechanisms of the sexual reactions, and the effect seems to be specific upon these, leaving other reaction systems unaffected."[16] The emphasis here is on the activation of *motor mechanisms*, but receptor processes may also be affected by drive states. We are referring, of course, to the previously mentioned *cueing* or *guiding* function of drives.

In the sexually deprived organism, for example, not only may motor centers be rendered more excitable by the presence of sex hormones, but the animal may also be more attentive to sexually relevant stimuli, like the color, odor, or movements of the opposite sex.

The sexually motivated male rat is especially responsive to certain forms of stimulation provided by the receptive female, in particular her so-called "courting run," wherein she "darts swiftly away from the male for a relatively short distance and then comes to an abrupt halt, posing with the head pointed slightly upward and the hind feet planted somewhat farther apart than usual."[17] The male, if sexually motivated at the time, goes in pursuit, examines the female's anogenital region, and sometimes even her ears and her head, then copulates. But if the male is sexually satiated, it does not respond to these signs of sexual receptivity. Then the female will usually go back and examine various parts of his body. On days when she is not sexually aroused, the female pays no such attention to the male.

Some investigators have held the view that physiological drives merely provide a "push from within," and that the organism must learn, through a process of trial and error, how to satisfy them. However, to the extent that drives make animals especially responsive to relevant cues, they also have a guiding function. Where learning is necessary, an organism's responsiveness to relevant cues may be said to facilitate it.

Many animals are born with drives which not only energize but which appear to have rather definite guiding functions. Consider, for example, this description of the food-getting behavior of a newborn giraffe.

☐ For a few minutes after birth this animal lay inert upon the floor. It then struggled to its feet, after falling several times. But in less than twenty minutes after first coming into the external world, it stood upon its still trembling legs and without guidance from its mother and almost with no observable random activity it moved directly to one maternal nipple and began to suck milk. When the first nipple seemed to be exhausted, once more without random activity, it moved directly to another nipple and continued sucking. Here a drive-state seemed to set in action adaptive responses that led to satiating without previous trial-and-error learning.[18] ☐

One cannot always tell what the guiding factor, or factors, are in such instances. It may be that a state of hunger makes the animal more responsive than it would otherwise be to the odor of milk, and that, with this odor as a cue, it is guided to the nipple. This is like saying that it "follows its nose."

Perhaps the visual impression of a relevant object is such that this "stands out" from the surroundings. An ingenious photographer pictured the perceptual world of a hungry baby as though its bottle were the only clear object in an otherwise out-of-focus environment.

Investigators of instinctive behavior have observed that physiologically driven organisms are especially responsive to certain aspects of others of their kind, aspects which perhaps "stand out" in some such manner as that suggested above. Thus, to a hungry Herring Gull chick, the red spot on the mother's bill is especially provoking. The chick responds to this spot by pecking at the tip of the bill, thereby inducing the mother to regurgitate food and to feed it. How can one tell that the red spot is so important? Its importance is inferred from the fact that a dummy head with the spot is much more effective in eliciting the chick's "begging" reaction than a comparable dummy head from which the spot is absent. This is but one of many illustrations that we could give of the cueing or directional effects which certain forms of stimulation have for the organism activated by a drive-state.[19]

In human beings, for reasons to be discussed later in this chapter, drives do little more than energize. Except in a few instances they fail to provide us with an inborn behavior pattern to alleviate our drives. It is true that we do not have to learn to breathe, to defecate, or to urinate. In these instances, the drive-state elicits more or less directly the appropriate culminating behavior. But with respect to hunger, thirst, and sex this is not the case. A certain degree of learning intervenes between the initial appearance of the drive-state and the means of satisfying it. There may be, of course, some degree of cueing associated with the drive-state itself, and this may facilitate the learning of appropriate behavior. ∎

THE ROLE OF NEURAL MECHANISMS

Recent years have seen great advances in the detailed study of neural mechanisms. It has been shown, among other things, that the reticular formation of the brain stem may hold the key to how glandular and other changes associated with physiological needs are able to energize and provide cues for the behavior which satisfies these needs.

The reticular arousal system

We have already (Figure 2.14) given a brief description of the reticular system. It is a core of cells running through the brain stem from its lower to its upper end. This system, generally regarded as more or less nonspecific in its effects, may be contrasted with the ascending afferent projection system, which (as illustrated in Figure 6.4) feeds impulses into the reticular formation through numerous collaterals, but which is itself concerned rather specifically with transmission of sensory impulses to their appropriate locations in the cerebral cortex. In addition to impulses received through these collaterals, the reticular formation also receives impulses from the cerebral cortex. It is intricately connected, moreover, with such brain-stem structures as the thalamus and hypothalamus. Thus impulses enter the system from various directions. Its resulting activities likewise spread their influence in many directions. Impulses go to the cerebral cortex, where they spread out to activate many structures in an apparently indiscriminate way.

☐ Impulses from the lower part of the reticular formation have inhibiting effects upon various motor activities. Within the context of motivation, however, we are more interested in those impulses which have an activating effect on the cerebral cortex — those which arouse, or alert it — thus facilitating perceptual and motor processes.

Electrical stimulation of the reticular formation in a sleeping animal immediately activates the cerebral cortex. This is revealed by resulting changes in electroencephalograms. The change is from a pattern normally associated with sleep to one characteristically

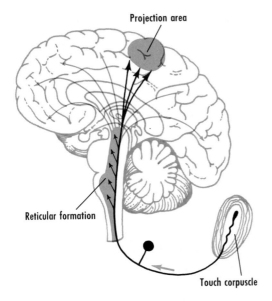

Projection area

Reticular formation

Touch corpuscle

• **6.4**

The Reticular Arousal System. A sense organ (tactual) is seen feeding impulses into an ascending (afferent) pathway that sends collaterals into the reticular formation as it passes through the brain stem on its way to the sensory projection area (somaesthetic) in the cerebral cortex. Other senses and their projection areas could be similarly represented. When stimulated by such collaterals, and/or impulses descending from the cerebral cortex (not shown), the reticular formation discharges diffusely to the cortex, thus arousing, or alerting it. The finer arrows are put in to represent such a reticular influence on the cortex. Only the arousal part of the reticular formation is represented. (From various sources)

found in wakefulness. The animal wakes up, in fact, and becomes alert and attentive to aspects of its environment.

On the other hand, if we destroy the corresponding area of the reticular formation, the animal is permanently reduced to a state resembling deep sleep or coma. Its electroencephalograms are those typically present during coma.

Suppose, now, that the cerebral cortex of a normal cat or monkey is electrically stimulated. In this case, concomitant electrical impulses can be picked up from the reticular formation itself. This shows that the cortex is not only aroused by impulses coming from the reticular formation, but that it, in turn, activates this structure. ☐

Our interest in the reticular formation in relation to physiological drives comes from the possibility that drive-states may have an energizing influence on behavior by arousing the reticular system and, through it, activating or alerting the cerebral cortex. What the organism has learned, which is probably in large part represented by cortical modifications, may also influence the reticular formation through impulses feeding into this system from above. There is probably a constant interplay, or feedback, between the cerebral cortex and the reticular formation, with involvement of other regions in the cerebrum and brain stem.[20]

Pleasure and pain areas

Activities in which an organism engages repeatedly are inferred to be pleasurable, while those which he attempts to avoid are inferred to be painful, or at least unpleasant. Considerable interest was therefore aroused when psychologists were able to locate apparent pleasure and pain areas in the brain. This was first accomplished with rats, but similar experiments, yielding essentially the same results, have now been carried out with a wide variety of organisms, including porpoises, monkeys, and human beings.[21] The regions of the brain involved in these experiments lie around the upper end of the brain stem and the base of the cerebrum, and they are referred to *in toto* as the *limbic system*. This system is pictured in Figure 6.5, the legend of which provides some details relevant to the research on pain and pleasure areas. The research with rats provides a good illustration of basic procedures.[22]

☐ Utilizing a painless technique, a small hole was made in the rat's skull and a thin bipolar electrode was inserted into the brain tissue and so directed that its tip made contact with a specific region. The electrode was insulated so that stimulation could occur only at its tip.

At its upper end, it was screwed to the skull via a small permanent socket. Thus an electrical cord from the stimulator could be plugged in whenever the experimenter desired. This cord was long and flexible so as to allow the rat considerable freedom of movement. The stimulating equipment was arranged so that, by pressing a bar, the rat could stimulate its brain with a weak electrical current. If the bar was not released, the current automatically shut off. Thus, in order to continue stimulation, it was necessary for the rat to press the bar repeatedly.

Although only a single electrode per animal is mentioned in the above description of this technique, it is possible to have several (differently directed) electrodes chronically implanted in the same animal.[23] Then the investigator plugs into the particular socket which provides contact with the part of the brain that he wishes to stimulate. This is the usual arrangement in the case of animals larger than the rat. □

The general situation involved in self-stimulation experiments with rats is illustrated in Figure 6.6.

When placed in the situation illustrated,

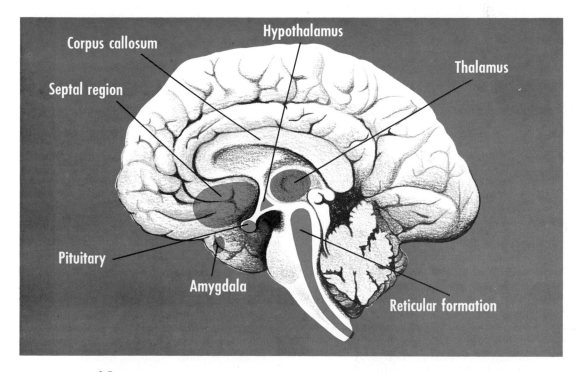

● 6.5
Sketch of the Limbic System in Man. In this highly diagrammatic sketch, the main components of the limbic system are shown in their approximate positions with respect to the left cerebral hemisphere. Only a tridimensional representation could show their actual locations. Considered as a whole, the limbic system (*limbic* means border) encircles the upper end of the brain stem. This system of structures was once thought to be concerned with smell, but we now know that only a small portion of it has olfactory functions. The rest is primarily involved in aspects of motivation and emotion. In the present context the septal region and the hypothalamus concern us most; but when we get to the topic of emotion, the amygdala will claim our attention as well. (From various sources)

● **6.6**

A Rat Electrically Stimulating Its Brain. Whenever the rat presses the bar, as illustrated, a contact is made which sends a weak electrical current along the implanted electrode into a particular region of its brain. (From J. Olds, "Pleasure Centers in the Brain," *Scientific American,* October 1956, p. 108.)

a rat explores its surroundings, even though it has not been deprived of food, water, or other necessities. During this exploratory activity, the bar is usually pressed, and the brain is electrically stimulated. What happens from then on depends upon the part of the brain that the animal has stimulated.

Rats with electrodes implanted in the septal region or in some other areas of the limbic system continue pressing the bar, with the rate of response depending upon the particular area stimulated. Parts of the lateral hypothalamus as well as the septal region produce especially high rates of response, sometimes as high as 1000 bar presses per hour. When the current is switched off, responding soon stops. However, when the experimenter gives one stimulation to show that the current is on again, the rat resumes its bar-pressing.

The regions which produce high rates of response are those which the investigators have called "pleasure areas." It is quite evident that electrical stimulation of such regions has a rewarding effect, much as if the animal were hungry and bar-pressing brought food, or thirsty and its response brought water. One difference, of course, is that an animal in either of the latter situations would have been satiated, with a consequent slowing down, or extinction, of bar-pressing. The electrical

"reward," however, did not satiate. Stimulation of the so-called "pleasure area" was also effective as a reward in maze learning and discrimination learning.[24]

Rats with electrodes implanted in certain other regions acted, when they pressed the bar, as though they had received painful stimulation. If they responded more than once, they did so only after long intervals.

Stimulation of the limbic system is not always rewarding or punishing, for stimulation of some areas is followed by neither approach nor avoidance responses to the bar. Typical behavior in such cases is to press the bar a few times, then go elsewhere, or sleep.[25]

The results with other animals, including porpoises and monkeys, have been similar to those described. Both "pleasure" and "pain" areas have been found in parts of the brain which correspond to those stimulated in the rat. It is interesting to note, moreover, that electrical stimulation of the septal area in mental patients has produced marked changes in responsiveness to people and things around them. While being stimulated through electrodes implanted in the septal region, some patients reported "pleasurable" reactions, some became more alert and recognized people and things previously ignored, some became less tense and fearful, some who had been mute were induced to speak. A few either showed no effects of such stimulation or experienced fright. Some reported "anxiety," "a glowing feeling," "faintness," or "a queer feeling." In most cases the results were to some degree favorable. Some retained the benefits after stimulation was over and were therefore more receptive to psychotherapy. Several were able to leave the hospital.[26]

This research is in its infancy and one cannot, at present, predict what its significance will be. Some regard it as an important "breakthrough" in efforts to understand the "energizing" of behavior. But many details are yet to be filled out, including the relation between pleasure areas and the arousal and satisfaction of such appetites as hunger and thirst. Recent research has disclosed, for example, that the same areas of the hypothalamus which produce high rates of bar-pressing when stimulated also have some relationship to the hunger drive, for electrically stimulating these areas while food is present will elicit eating in animals whose need for food has been satiated.[27] There is some evidence, too, that "pain areas" are the same ones which, when electrically stimulated, stop hungry animals from eating.[28] ■

HUNGER

When deprived of food for a long time, human beings report aching or gnawing experiences known as *hunger pangs*. These are correlated with muscular spasms of the stomach walls. This may be shown by using subjects who have been trained to swallow a small balloon with rubber tubing attached. The balloon is inflated in the stomach and the rubber tube then connected to a kymograph recording mechanism (Figure 6.7) so that each spasm of the stomach muscles causes a mark to be made on the smoked drum. In addition, the subject is told to press on a key whenever he feels hunger pangs. A mark is thereby made on the drum just below the record of stomach activity. The subject's abdominal breathing is also recorded, so that the investigator may decide whether the spasms represented in the record are due to stomach or to abdominal movements. The results show that hunger pangs coincide with stomach contractions, but are unrelated to movements of the abdominal muscles.

Hunger and blood chemistry

Various lines of evidence suggest that hunger pangs and stomach contractions both depend upon blood chemistry. In the first place, the stomach may be removed, or nerves between it and the brain severed, without destroying the hunger drive.[29] In the second place, if the blood sugar level is lowered by injections of insulin (the hormone given diabetics to control carbohydrate metabolism), stomach contractions and hunger pangs are

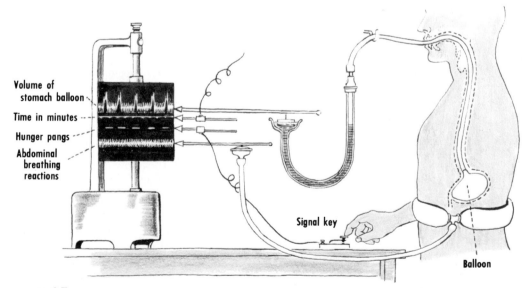

Volume of
stomach balloon

Time in minutes

Hunger pangs

Abdominal
breathing
reactions

Signal key

Balloon

● 6.7
The Relation Between Hunger Pangs and Stomach Contractions. Observe that the peaks in the upper record are quite independent of abdominal breathing. They are produced by spasms of the stomach itself, and are correlated with signals given by the subject when he experiences hunger pangs. (After Cannon)

induced. When dextrose, which raises the blood sugar level, is given, these contractions and hunger pangs cease.[30] In the third place, if blood from a starved dog is injected into a normal dog, the stomach of the injected animal shows the kind of contractions found in hunger. Injection of blood from a well-fed animal, on the other hand, stops the stomach contractions.[31]

The fact that injection of blood from a starving dog into a normal one elicits stomach contractions suggests that lowering of nutrient reserves releases specific chemical activators (hormones) into the bloodstream and that these, through their effect upon the nervous system, are responsible for both the stomach contractions and the hunger pangs.[32]

Hunger and the hypothalamus

Destroying a certain area of the hypothalamus (large loop in Figure 6.8) is followed by eating which goes far beyond the need for food.[33] Consequently, the animal becomes extremely fat.

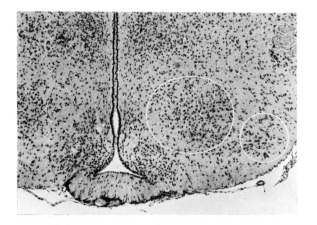

● **6.8**
Photomicrograph of a Section Through a Mouse Brain. The lower portion is the hypothalamus. Within the larger loop are so-called satiety cells. The smaller loop marks the position of "feeding centers." As described in the text, bilateral destruction of "satiety cells" is followed by overeating. (From J. Mayer, "Appetite and Obesity," *Scientific American*, November 1956, p. 116.)

Why is destruction of these brain cells followed by excessive eating? One possibility is that it produces extreme hunger. But there is much evidence that this is not so.

☐ In situations designed to measure the strength of the hunger drive, the operated animals do not act as though they were hungry.[34] A bar-pressing apparatus like those already illustrated in Figures 6.2 and 6.6, but arranged to deliver pellets of food, has been used. Hungry rats press the bar repeatedly and eat the pellets as delivered, but operated animals show a much lower rate of bar-pressing. In a runway like that of Figure 6.3 (p. 157), but with food at the end, and an electric grid to be crossed in order to get it, operated animals are stopped by shocks weaker than those which stop intensely hungry rats. These and other tests make it appear that the operated rats keep nibbling at food even though they are not very hungry.[35] The cells destroyed in the operation apparently influence eating, but not hunger. It appears that they normally inhibit eating when the organism has had enough. With this "brake" removed, eating continues even though there is little or no hunger. The animal therefore gets much more than it needs, or is good for it. One investigator has called these "satiety cells" on the grounds that they appear to tell the organism when it has eaten enough. As suggested earlier, the intact satiety area, when stimulated electrically, also seems to put a "brake" on eating. Moreover, there is some evidence that satiety areas and "pain areas" are one and the same.[36] ☐

Another region of the hypothalamus (small circle in Figure 6.8) has been stimulated with implanted electrodes in such a way as to activate eating. A rat that has eaten to satiety and is no longer eating resumes eating when the current is turned on. Likewise, the rat that has been satiated in a bar-pressing situation starts pressing again if its hypothalamus is electrically stimulated. This stimulation seems to arouse hunger in a rat whose hunger drive has otherwise been satisfied. We have already called attention to a possibly significant further fact: rats which electrically stimulate their "pleasure areas" at a high rate are also induced to begin eating when the experimenter stimulates the same areas, even though these animals are satiated.[37]

These experiments have demonstrated that parts of the hypothalamus are somehow involved in the hunger drive, or in activities associated with it, but much is yet to be learned about the details of this involvement.

Other physiological aspects of hunger

Food may be passed through a long tube, called a *fistula*, directly into the stomach. When milk (20 milliliters) is injected in this way, the hungry rat acts as if its hunger is reduced.[38] Its rate of responding in a bar-pressing test drops significantly. If a stomach balloon like that of Figure 6.7 (p. 163) is inflated with an equal amount of liquid, the rate of responding is also reduced, but not as much as when milk enters the stomach. Thus milk in the stomach and stomach distension both reduce the hunger drive, but milk is more effective.

Is the rat "fooled" by stomach inflation? Apparently not, for this is ineffective as a "reward" in learning situations. Rats were trained in a T-shaped maze to turn in one direction or the other at the upper end of the T. If they turned in the proper direction, 14 cc of milk was injected into the stomach as they entered the goal box. They learned this habit. By contrast, a comparable group of rats subjected to a 14 cc inflation of a stomach balloon learned to *avoid* the side which produced such distension of the stomach. Distension of the stomach was therefore a deterrent rather than an incentive.[39]

Why did food and stomach distension have such diametrically opposed effects? The answer may be that inflating a balloon in the stomach produces nausea, which would reduce hunger, and hence the rate of response in the bar-pressing situation, and also act as a deterrent in a situation where it could be avoided.[40]

Other investigations have compared the relative effectiveness of milk taken by mouth and milk injected into the stomach via a fistula. One comparison used bar-pressing; the other used learning to make the appropriate turn in a T-maze.

Under certain conditions, the details of which need not concern us here, a hungry rat's rate of responding in a bar-pressing situation remains relatively constant. Since an increase in the amount of food received decreases the rate of response, the latter is taken as an indication that the drive has been reduced. In the comparison of interest to us here, a given amount of salt solution was injected into the stomach as a control and the effect of this was compared with that of an equal amount of milk injected into the stomach. With salt solution, the rate of response dropped to about 12 per minute, with milk to about 7 per minute. Thus milk reduced the hunger drive more than salt solution did. Milk in the mouth, however, was even more effective. It reduced the rate of responding to about 5 per minute.[41]

The finding that milk given by mouth has a greater effect than milk placed directly into the stomach is supported by results with the T-maze, for the milk-by-mouth subjects learned the habit much faster than those given stomach injections of an equal amount of milk.[42]

The preceding results are of considerable interest. On a long-time basis, of course, the *need* for food can be satisfied only by food. But it takes time for food to be digested, to change the constitution of the blood, and to alleviate the need, i.e., restore equilibrium. If all of this were necessary in order to reduce the hunger drive and to stop the rat's eating, the effects would be too long delayed, and the animal would over-eat. Moreover, as we will see in Chapter 11, hunger reduction on such a homeostatic basis would come too late to serve as a reward in learning, as when the rat in the T-maze learned to go in the direction where milk was obtained. What is of special interest, therefore, is the fact that milk in the mouth and milk in the stomach reduced the hunger drive almost immediately. Apparently there is something about the taste, smell, or feel of food which itself rewards a hungry animal.[43] Even injection of milk into the stomach via a fistula appears to reduce the hunger drive almost immediately rather than after a long enough period for the physiological need to be alleviated.

Specific hungers

Organisms need proteins, fats, and carbohydrates. They also need various minerals and vitamins. Lack of one of these substances often creates an appetite for it.

Cravings for special foods are well known under conditions of everyday life. Children whose diet is inadequate often develop a craving for salt, chalk, and other substances. Pregnant rats, given a free selection of food, eat about three times the usual amount of salt.[44] Certain glandular disturbances produce intense appetite for such substances as calcium and salt.[45]

Animals living in a state of nature select food in accordance with bodily needs. This has suggested that the organism does not need scientists to tell it what to eat. Several laboratory experiments with pigs, cows, rats, chickens, and human infants have supported this suggestion.[46] Such studies are often referred to as *cafeteria-feeding* experiments because, as in a cafeteria, the organism is confronted with a wide variety of foods from which it may select freely.

A somewhat comparable cafeteria-feeding experiment with fifteen human infants, who selected their own food over periods ranging from six months to four and a half years, yielded results similar to those found in animal experiments.[47]

That organisms have definite food preferences is shown by their selection of certain foodstuffs much more often than others which are equally accessible. Several experiments have shown, moreover, that these preferences change with bodily need. Thus rats which ordinarily prefer sugar to fat will select fat rather than sugar if they have been fat-starved. Likewise, rats deprived of vitamin B_1 soon exhibit a marked preference for foods rich in vitamin B_1.[48]

How do organisms come to select the proper diet? One possible basis of selection is trial and error. That is to say, the organism selects at random to begin with, but learns that certain substances (recognized by visual appearance, feel, taste, or smell) alleviate its needs while others do not. It then seeks these substances.

Actual changes in blood chemistry after one has eaten are perhaps too-long delayed for a connection to be established; but food itself tastes good to the hungry, and that effect is immediate. Experiments with rats have shown, in fact, that they have a "sweet tooth," and will work and learn for a taste of saccharine, which has no nutritional value. Moreover, the fistula experiments discussed earlier indicated that food in the stomach, even before it begins to change blood chemistry, is rewarding to rats. As one investigator has said, there are normally "at least two means of producing immediate reductions in hunger, one involving the mouth and throat and the other the stomach."[49]

Hunger in everyday life

It has been estimated that a billion and a half human beings live in a permanent state of hunger. Sometimes a whole society (Figure 6.9) is dominated by the hunger drive. Australian aborigines living in a state of nature in the interior of the continent search continually for edible plants and animals. Even ants, grubs, and worms are relished. The Siriono Indians of Eastern Bolivia are also continually searching for food and their fantasies and dreams are largely concerned with it. Married men of these tribes often have sexual relations with women other than their wives and pay for these services with food. Interestingly enough, the wives get angry about this only because their husbands are squandering food that the family needs. The aged and infirm are abandoned and killed when they no longer contribute to the search for food. Successful hunters have high prestige in this hunger-driven society. Other societies are similarly situated, and many of the less fortunate in so-called civilized societies are preoccupied with hunger and its satisfaction. For the more fortunate of us, severe hunger is seldom experienced and the experienced need

• 6.9

Some Hunger-Dominated Peoples. The Australian aboriginal woman, completely naked, as are all of her people in a natural state, is digging for yams. There is no agriculture. Food is very scarce and the tribe wanders from place to place in search of it. (Courtesy, C. P. Mountford, whose Adelaide University film, *Walkabout*, portrays the life of these people. It can be rented from the Australian News and Information Bureau, 636 Fifth Avenue, New York.) The Siriono, in the photograph at the right, are about to eat a monkey that they are cutting up. (Courtesy, A. R. Holmberg, from his monograph, *Nomads of the Longbow*, Smithsonian Institution.)

for food is on a par with, or secondary to, other needs. Man "lives by bread alone" only when the search for bread occupies all his efforts.

☐ An excellent opportunity for scientific research on hunger occurred during the Second World War when thirty-two conscientious objectors volunteered to serve as subjects in experiments involving semistarvation. Scientists at the University of Minnesota.[50] studied these men for three months under normal conditions. Each man was then systematically dieted for a period of six months, during which his weight was reduced by approximately 25 per cent. A three-month period of rehabilitation was then instituted.

The experimenters investigated many aspects of health, general physiology, and behavior. Large individual differences appeared. Among the outstanding psychological effects were feelings of weakness, hunger pangs, irritability, loss of interest in sex, and unusual interest in cook books and food illustrations. The hunger drive became all-important. While

there was no reduction in general intelligence as measured by tests, the general intellectual life of the subjects was channelized by their need for food. It is reported, for example, that "The intensive preoccupation with food made it difficult for the men to concentrate upon the tasks they had intellectually decided they would work on. If a man tried to study, he soon found himself daydreaming about food. He would think about food he had eaten in the past; he would muse about opportunities he had missed to eat a certain food when he was at this or that place. Often he would daydream by the hour about the next meal, which was not very far away.[51] The men wrote notes to themselves as reminders of things to be done. There was general apathy. Poor manners appeared in some men. Others showed a deterioration of ethical control; as, for example, by buying food or, in one case, stealing it. "Most of them felt that the starvation had coarsened rather than refined them, and they marvelled at how thin their moral and social veneers seemed to be."[52]

167

Thus we see how hunger tensions may subvert an individual's higher motives and intellectual activities. The outcomes of this research are of practical as well as theoretical value, for they give understanding and provide guidance for those who have the task of rehabilitating the world's semistarved populations. ■

THIRST

When deprived of water over a period of hours, an organism becomes excessively active. This is true even when all other needs are satisfied. If water becomes available, drinking terminates the activity.

What provides the drive behind water consumption? According to a well-known theory, the drive comes from dryness of the mucous lining of the mouth and throat.[53] When the organism is deprived of water over a period of several hours, the mouth and throat indeed become dry, reflecting dehydration of body tissues in general.

When water is placed in the stomach directly via fistula, a period of several minutes must elapse before the thirst experience ceases. This suggests that the water, in order to be effective in removing thirst, must get into the tissues sufficiently to remove the dryness of mouth and throat. On the other hand, merely wetting the mouth temporarily removes the thirst experience.

Dogs subjected to different degrees of water deficit drink an amount of water directly proportional to the known deficit.[54] But such an accurate "estimation" by the dog of its need for water is hard to explain in terms of dryness of the mouth and throat alone. The first mouthful would wet the mouth and throat, removing the condition which might otherwise provide a dog with a guide to the amount needed.

As in the case of hunger, some unknown condition or conditions, aroused by a state of deficit, must regulate both thirst and water consumption. The most important single condition appears to be cellular dehydration.

As dehydration proceeds, blood cells lose water. Consequently there is a rise in the osmotic pressure of the blood. It is believed that certain tissues adjacent to the main arteries which come together at the base of the brain are especially sensitive to such a change. These are often referred to as "osmoreceptors." What they do, presumably, is send a signal to the pituitary gland or the hypothalamus, or both, indicating the need for water.[55]

It has been known for a long time that the pituitary gland (see Figure 6.10) is implicated in control of water consumption. This is because a disease which involves the posterior lobe of the pituitary produces excessive urination, which is compensated for by consumption of large amounts of water. Some investigators think that signals from "osmoreceptors" cause the posterior lobe to secrete a thirst-regulating hormone. Others believe that this hormone is manufactured by certain cells of the hypothalamus and then passed down to the posterior lobe of the pituitary gland.[56] Be this as it may, there is direct evidence of the involvement of the hypothalamus in control of water consumption.

□ Several related experiments were carried out on goats, dogs, and cats. In one of these, very small amounts of salt solution were injected into the goat's hypothalamus.[57] Salt solution, incidentally, leads to a rise in osmotic pressure. The effects of these injections depended upon the region involved. In certain regions, however, the injection was followed, within one minute or less, by drinking, which lasted from two to five minutes. Similar results with cats were found by other investigators.[58] They also found that injecting water instead of salt solution decreased the subject's water consumption. Moreover, the cat's rate of responding to get water (in an experiment somewhat comparable with those on bar-pressing that we have already described) rose with hypothalamic salt injections and fell with corresponding injections of water.[59]

Electrical stimulation within certain restricted regions of the hypothalamus induces goats to drink. Repeated stimulation leads to consumption of abnormal amounts of water.[60] When the corresponding region of the hypo-

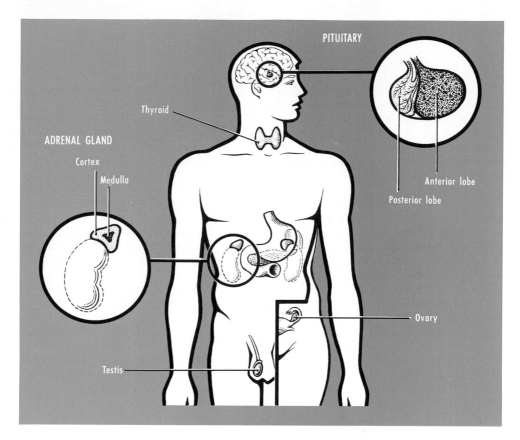

● 6.10

Some Endocrine Glands of Special Importance in Motivation. The *pituitary gland,* at the base of the brain (see Plate 5), has an anterior lobe and a posterior lobe. Its anterior lobe secretes several hormones, of which ACTH and prolactin enter our discussion of motivation. The posterior lobe has a role in thirst and water consumption and excretion. Note that the *adrenal gland* (above the kidney) has an inner structure (medulla) and an outer layer (cortex). Its medulla secretes adrenalin, a hormone of great significance in the energizing of emotional reactions. The adrenal cortex, under control of the anterior pituitary gland, is important for general energy maintenance and for maintenance of sexual motivation as described in the text. Pituitary control comes in the form of ACTH, meaning the hormone which activates the adrenal cortex (adrenocorticotropic hormone). The *thyroid gland* does not specifically enter our discussion of motivation; but, as is well known, it plays an important part in energizing the organism. The testes and ovaries are known, in general, as the *gonads.* Androgenic hormones (from the testes) and estrogenic hormones (from the ovaries) are discussed in the context of sexual motivation.

thalamus is destroyed in dogs by electrically causing the hypothalamic cells to coagulate, the animals drink insufficient water and extreme dehydration results.[61] Apparently, then, there is a "drinking center" in the hypothalamus, but how this is related to the nearby posterior pituitary and its involvement in thirst is not yet evident. ■

THE SEX DRIVE AND MATING

The physiological bases of sexual motivation are well known, largely through research on animals. This has shown that there are certain basic similarities in the sexual motivation of human beings and other organisms; but it has also revealed important differences.

The sex drive

Hormones secreted by the *gonads*, that is, the testes in males and the ovaries in females, are responsible for sexual motivation. The male sex hormones (*androgens*) come from the testes. Castration cuts these off at their source. When this occurs prior to puberty there is no sex drive.

The ovarian hormones are known as *estrogens*. When the ovaries are removed prior to puberty the typical female characteristics, including periodic heat, fail to appear.

If mature female rats are placed in cages with revolving drums attached, as already illustrated in Figure 6.1, they spend a great deal of time running. Every fourth or fifth day, activity reaches a peak and it is not unusual for the animal to run the equivalent of fifteen or more miles.

This periodic activity begins at around the time of puberty and ceases at the menopause. It is on the day of greatest activity that the female is especially receptive to mating. Its own activities at this time are such as to excite sexual activity in the male. If the ovaries are removed before the time of puberty, however, such behavior never develops. Activity is greatly reduced, there is no cycle, and mating fails to occur.[62]

When a mature female rat is spayed, her activity drops to a low level. The activity cycle is obliterated, and sexual behavior ceases. This situation may be remedied by ovarian grafts or by periodic injections of ovarian hormones.[63]

It is thus apparent that estrogenic hormones activate the female rat and provide a high level of sexual motivation. In human females the same hormones are present, and their production becomes greatly accelerated at puberty. They account in large measure for the development of breasts and other aspects of the typically female physique, but their effect on sexual motivation is problematical. They may affect feminine interests in subtle ways, and make them more susceptible to male advances. There is, however, no obvious emergence of sexual motivation such as animals characteristically exhibit.

One possible explanation of this difference between animal and human motivation is that purely physiological motivation has been suppressed in the latter by cultural influences, which of course play no part in animal behavior. Fears of pregnancy, of disease, and of breaking the taboos are prominent among such restraining influences.

Research with animals, as well as clinical observations on human beings, have demonstrated that sexual motivation, while most intimately related to functions of the gonads, is also influenced by other endocrine glands. The pituitary and adrenal glands are implicated. The pituitary gland plays a key role. Inadequate functioning of its anterior lobe disturbs the functioning of the gonads and other glands. One hormone from the anterior pituitary (ACTH) stimulates the adrenal cortex, which produces cortisone. Sometimes the adrenal cortex is itself defective. It puts out no cortisone, or insufficient amounts of it. When there is inadequate cortisone, for whatever reason, one of the effects is loss of sexual desire. This may, however, be but a reflection of the general disturbance of body metabolism in individuals thus affected. General vigor, as well as sexual desire, may be restored by administration of ACTH, or cortisone.[64]

When removal of either male or female gonads occurs in mature human beings, there may be little influence upon further sexual activity. Continuance of sexual motivation under these conditions is probably due to retention of interests and habits which, while they originally developed under the influence of the gonads, are no longer dependent upon secretions from these glands. It is interesting to observe, in this connection, that men and women whose gonads have degenerated during middle or late life (the menopause in women) usually continue to participate in sexual activities. Kinsey reports that women who have gone through the menopause often increase their sexual activity, perhaps because they no longer fear pregnancy.[65] In those cases where a decline in a sexual vigor does occur, it can now be revived through injection of hormones, estrogenic for women, and androgenic for men.[66]

☐ The human sex drive varies considerably both in its intensity from one individual to another and in the ways in which satisfaction may occur. Repressive influences (such as ideas that sex is evil or dirty) sometimes lead to absence of sex interests or inability to engage in sexual activity, despite the fact that the individual is structurally normal. Frigidity (in women) and impotence (in men) represent this low tide in sexual drive. At the other extremes are nymphomania (in women) and satyriasis (in men). Individuals thus affected, because of excessive glandular secretions or excessive social stimulation involving sex, have an unusually strong sex drive.[67] Kinsey's studies, based upon questionnaire data, suggest that there is a very large variation in frequency of male sexual outlet. His tables indicate a variation of from 0 to 29 or more outlets per week.[68]

Variations in the form taken by the sex drive often begin to develop in childhood. Just as hungry organisms continue to seek out that which satisfies their hunger, so do they seek a repetition of those acts which have in the past resulted in a sexual satisfaction. It often happens that a child whose sex urge has already made its appearance stimulates himself sexually, is stimulated sexually by another member of the same sex, or receives sexual stimulation from some object or situation. The satisfaction obtained from such stimulation may lead the individual to seek a repetition of it. Continued into adulthood, unusual forms of sexual satisfaction may prevent the kinds of sexual release sanctioned by society. The individual is then regarded by the group (and often by himself) as abnormal or perverted. Similar "perversions" often occur in animals (especially in the higher ones), but they are more frequent and more varied in man.[69] ☐

Mating

The physiological needs of many organisms are satisfied in ways characteristic of the species, ways which individuals do not have to learn. Thus one male rat mates in approximately the same manner as any other, but in a different manner from dogs, cats, or monkeys. Moreover, it mates in the same stereotyped way — that is, in the same position and with the same sequence and pattern of movements — whether it has observed other rats mate or has been reared entirely by itself. The female rat also has a stereotyped, unlearned mating pattern.[70]

Such complicated patterns of behavior, which are universal in the species and which do not have to be learned, are called *instincts*. Both male and female rats may thus be said to have a mating instinct.

Mating in monkeys is less stereotyped than in lower mammals like the rat, dog, and cat. When the level of the higher apes is reached, it is doubtful whether a mating instinct, as defined above, any longer exists. The chimpanzee, like the rat, has a strong *sex drive*, and it of course has reflexes, like erection and ejaculation, which play a part in the act of mating and which are unlearned. But a universal, stereotyped mating pattern is absent. The pattern which finally emerges must be learned by the individual animal. It is thus a *habit* rather than an instinct.

☐ Studies carried out with chimpanzees observed from an early age until adulthood, show that mating develops in an exploratory, trial-and-error manner out of play behavior. In one study, five sexually naïve adolescent females were paired with an equal number of sexually naïve adolescent males.[71] The chimpanzees lived together as youngsters, but prior to puberty they were segregated by sexes. Then they were brought together again, in all possible pairings. This occurred at least one year after the females had menstruated, and during a period of greatest sexual receptivity. There were over 100 observations of such pairings. Normally there would have been at least 200 matings. Among these inexperienced chimpanzees, however, there were no copulations at all. Nevertheless, a great deal of activity occurred. This included individual and mutual grooming (picking at their own and each other's skin), aggressive acts, play-fighting, wrestling, playful slapping, and playing tag. Although no mating occurred, "there was a great deal of social behavior, including most of the constituent acts which enter into the mating pattern." These observations are in complete agreement with others made on chimpanzees. The pattern of behavior which finally develops, including the position used, differs from one animal to another, and even in the same animal from time to time. ☐

Human beings also learn to mate. Such learning is based on hearsay, observation, and trial and error, as well as direct instruction. The varieties of human sexual behavior found in different cultures have been described by anthropologists.[72] In many respects, the pattern most commonly adopted is culturally rather than biologically determined. Volumes have been written on the varieties of sexual behavior in our own society, as revealed by interviews and clinical reports. Books have been written for the sexual education of newlyweds. If we possessed a mating instinct there would be little or no variety to mating behavior and we would not need books or other sources of information on how to mate.

It is apparent that man has an unlearned sex drive and various sexual reflexes, but we may question whether he has a mating instinct in any strict sense of the term. ■

MATERNAL MOTIVATION

Lower mammals such as rats, cats, dogs, pigs, and sheep exhibit patterns of maternal behavior that are typical of their kind, and there is relatively little variation from one mother to another.[73] These maternal behavior patterns have been studied in considerable detail; so, also, have the conditions of their arousal. It is known that prolactin, a secretion from the anterior pituitary gland, plays a role in maternal motivation. It is known, too, that mothers at this level of animal life do not have to learn to take care of their young. There are thus good reasons for regarding their maternal behavior as inborn, or instinctive. As the primate level is approached, however, maternal behavior becomes increasingly variable. In human beings, neither the maternal drive nor maternal behavior itself

is clearly inborn. Prolactin is secreted by the anterior pituitary as in other mammals, and the physiological conditions surrounding the birth process are also similar to that of other mammals; but the outcomes are not as predictable and one may question the claim that women have a maternal instinct.

Maternal motivation is by no means universal in women. Many say that they do not want children. There is the possibility, of course, that something has happened to suppress a "natural urge." What is more evident, however, is that human beings, unlike the lower mammals, show marked variation in their maternal activities. There is no universal pattern of mothering unless it be that of feeding the child at the breast when this is possible. How infants are handled varies from one culture to another. In our own society, mothers are often so ignorant of how a child should be cared for that they must receive instruction from books or from attendance at clinics. These are some of the reasons we give for saying that human beings lack a maternal instinct.

In this chapter we have mentioned a number of inborn physiological needs, some clearly homeostatic, and all directly or indirectly involved in survival of the individual or his race. Among these are the need for food, water, elimination of waste products, sleep, warmth, activity, and, of particular racial significance, the need for reproductive and maternal activity. In addition to such obviously physiological needs there appear to be others which, while also inborn, have less urgency for the individual or the race and lack any clearly discernible drive-states. These needs, or more particularly the drives assumed to be associated with them, are often referred to as *nonhomeostatic*, which is hardly a good designation because some of the other drives are also nonhomeostatic, in a physiological sense. For want of a better term, we will call these *stimulation drives*. ■

SOME STIMULATION DRIVES

As examples of what we have elected to call "stimulation drives," we shall consider an alleged "need for affection," a "need for stimulation," and a "need to explore and manipulate." All of these imply a reaching out for various kinds of external stimulation.

Is there a need for affection?

It has been claimed that infants have a need which is satisfied by feeling the warmth of the mother's body and being cuddled, fondled, and petted, and that failure to satisfy this need has dire consequences both for physical and for psychological development.[74] Influenced by this viewpoint, a prominent anthropologist declared in a public lecture that babies should remain in bed with the mother after birth instead of being removed to a nursery, because the latter procedure prevents them from satisfying the need to feel the mother's warmth and to be hugged and fondled by her.[75] It has been claimed, in fact, that when the infant's own mother is not available, a substitute mother should be provided to cuddle it. Some institutions use volunteers to "mother" children in this way for given periods daily.[76]

It is a well-known fact that institutional children who receive only perfunctory attention are often retarded physically and emotionally. Moreover, to those with our cultural background, it seems only humane that babies should received loving attention from those charged with their care, and receive such attention whether or not there is an inborn need for it. The existence of such a need, however, has been questioned.

Infants who fail to receive affectionate attention are also usually denied a great deal of general stimulation as well as opportunities to explore and interact with aspects of their environment. The babies most affected in one institutional study "experienced not only relative social isolation but virtual stimulus starvation in their toyless, walled-in cubicles."[77] The writers from whom this quotation is taken point to the fact that even adults are seriously disturbed by stimulus deprivation. We will consider such deprivation later in this chapter.

Another criticism of the conclusion that infants need mothering of the kind described comes from those who have studied infant care in societies other than our own. In some societies caring for infant needs is quite routine and the fondling and other endearments that our babies normally receive are almost completely absent; yet there are no evident bad effects upon physical development and personality.[78]

One may well ask whether an infant perceives the warmth of its mother's body, the fondling, the rocking, and other aspects of motherly attention. What is more to the point, of course, is the question as to whether it perceives the lack of such — whether it has a *drive to seek it.* Since the infant cannot communicate, such questions must remain unanswered. Somewhat relevant to the first question, however, are certain experiments with infant monkeys given a "mother machine" to love.[79] These infants gave the usual infant-to-mother reactions even though the mothers of the experiment were synthetic (Figure 6.11). The most acceptable mother substitute was a block of wood surrounded by sponge rubber, sheathed in terry cloth, and with an electric bulb inside to provide warmth. This was more effective than a wire-mesh substitute which, even though it provided milk and warmth, lacked softness and cuddliness. In times of stress, the baby monkeys ran and clung to their substitute mothers much as monkeys normally do to their real mothers. Does this mean that infant monkeys, and perhaps human infants as well, need soft cuddly contacts? One cannot say. It is one thing to *need* these and quite another to prefer them to other contacts that are available.

From the foregoing it should be apparent that the question of a need for affection (or related stimulation) cannot be answered on the basis of evidence at present available. One would have to do an experiment in which comparable groups were reared, one with mother love (real or synthetic) and the other without it, but with both groups receiving normal stimulation in other respects. It is doubtful, because of humane considerations, whether any experiment of this nature would be undertaken with human infants.

A Mother Machine. As described in the text, this sponge-rubber and terry-cloth figure is warmed with an electric bulb. The infant monkey (of course more mature than human infants) clings to the figure as though it were alive. Now that these motherless monkeys have grown up, it is evident that they are defective in two important respects. Normal mating behavior is rare; and the females, when they do have young, treat them in a callous fashion, as though lacking in maternal feeling. (From H. F. Harlow, "The Nature of Love," *American Psychologist,* 1958, 13, p. 679. On the monkeys now grown up, see Harlow's "The Heterosexual Affectional System in Monkeys," *American Psychologist,* 1962, 17, pp. 1–9.)

The need for stimulation

The above discussion made passing reference to an apparent need for stimulation, saying that deprivation of this, rather than lack of affection as such, might be responsible for the retardation sometimes found in institutionally reared children. Some experimental evidence for such a need comes from a study in which college students lived in an environment as devoid of variable external stimulation as the investigator could make it. The details of the experimental environment are pictured in Figure 6.12 and described in the legend. What was especially lacking was *change* in external stimulation. Since variation in external stimulation is an important basis of general alertness, probably because it activates an alerting mechanism in the brain, the subjects at first slept a great deal of the time. Later, to quote the investigators,

□ "they slept less, became bored, and appeared eager for stimulation. They would sing, whistle, talk to themselves, tap the cuffs together, or explore the cubicle with them. This boredom seemed to be partly due to deterioration of the capacity to think systematically and productively. . . . The subjects also became very restless, displaying constant random movement, and they described the restlessness as unpleasant. Hence it was difficult to keep the subjects for more than two or three days, despite the fact that the pay ($20 for a 24-hour day) was more than double what they could normally earn. . . .

"The subjects reported that they were unable to concentrate on any topic for long while in the cubicle. Those who tried to review their studies or solve self-initiated intellectual problems found it difficult to do so. As a result they lapsed into day-dreaming, abandoned attempts at organized thinking, and let their thoughts wander. There were also reports of 'blank' periods, during which they seemed unable to think of anything at all."[80] □

The subjects had hallucinations and dream-like experiences and their performance on items from intelligence tests was inferior to that under control conditions. It is claimed that "both the changes in intelligence-test performance and the hallucinatory activity, induced merely by limiting the variability of sensory input, provide direct evidence of a kind of dependence on the environment that has not been previously recognized."[81]

Investigators at the National Bureau of Mental Health have also been studying the effects of isolation, but with a situation somewhat different from that described. They immersed naked subjects in a tank of slowly flowing water, the temperature of which was kept at a point where it felt neither hot nor cold. Only the top of the head was above water level. The subjects wore a lightproof helmet which enabled them to breathe through a tube. In addition to being in darkness, in a medium of constant temperature, and in a suspended position, the individuals were also subjected to reduced stimulation in other respects. The sound level was low. A subject could hear only his own breathing, the lapping of the water, and some faint water sounds from the piping. Subjects reported the environment to be the most even and monotonous that they had ever experienced. It is reported that after an hour or two in the tank, "a tension develops which can best be called a 'stimulus-action' hunger; hidden methods of self-stimulation develop; twitching muscles, slow swimming movements (which cause sensations as the water flows by the skin), stroking one finger with another, etc." Continued subjection to this environment eventually brought such effects as intense concentration on some aspect of the situation (such as the mask), reveries and fantasies, and visual hallucinations.[82]

Exploration and manipulation

The exploratory and manipulatory behavior so evident in many organisms is perhaps comparable with what Freud has called *reality testing*. It is undoubtedly related to the "need for stimulation." The term "stimulus starvation" has been used in this connection. One investigator speaks of "perceptual curiosity,"[83] another of "motivation to know one's environment."[84] Most of the relevant research has been done on rats, monkeys, and chimpanzees.

In experiments on "perceptual curiosity" in rats, the investigator gave his subjects an opportunity to approach and explore such objects as painted and unpainted cubes.[85] Two of the findings are of special interest. One is that an increase in the number and complexity of the stimulus objects increases the amount of exploratory behavior. The other finding is that exploratory behavior declines as the period of exposure to the objects increases. The rats begin to "lose interest" after about one minute. It is as though their exploratory drive is being satiated. Other investigators, studying exploratory and manipulatory behavior in different situations, have also observed a satiation effect.

That the exploratory drive can motivate learning is shown by an experiment in which rats learned to choose the white rather than the black arm (others the black rather than the white arm) of a T maze even though

● 6.12

Environmental Restriction. The subject is lying on a foam-rubber bed and wears translucent goggles which prevent seeing of any details. He has on gloves which permit free movement of joints but limit tactual perception, and has his head in a foam-rubber pillow containing earphones. This pillow is not shown here, it having been removed so that the EEG's could be recorded from the device pictured. A constant hum from fans, an air-conditioner, and an amplifier leading to the earphones masks all other sounds. A microphone near the subject's mouth (removed for the picture) is used in reporting experiences. Subjects leave the booth only to eat and go to the toilet. (From the Bell System Science Series Film, "Gateways to the Mind.")

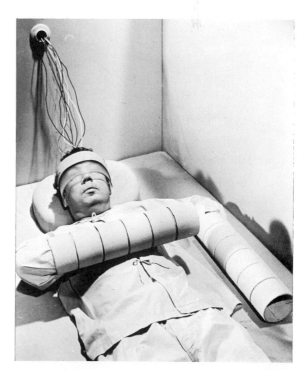

their choice brought nothing beyond the opportunity to explore some additional maze pathways.[86] In other experiments mice learned to press the bar of a box, their only reward being the onset of a dim light.[87] Rats learned to step on a small platform which "rewarded" them with such forms of stimulation as its movement and a clicking sound.[88]

Monkeys are notorious for their curiosity; hence it should not surprise us to learn that several studies have focused upon their exploratory and manipulatory behavior. Monkeys have learned to discriminate between pairs of colors with no reward other than an opportunity to look out of a small window (Figure 6.13) and visually explore the environment.[89] When the monkey pushes against a panel of the "correct" color, the window opens and he may look through it for thirty seconds before a screen drops. The "correct" color is of course sometimes on the right and sometimes on the left, so that a different panel has to be pressed from time to time, in a chance sequence. When the "incorrect" panel is pressed, the window fails to open.

In another experiment, monkeys learned a similar discrimination with no reward other than the sound of other monkeys heard through a loudspeaker. A correct response brought this sound and an incorrect one failed to bring it. Monkeys have also solved mechanical puzzles with no reward beyond satisfaction of their manipulatory drive.[90]

Chimpanzees engage in a large amount of exploratory and manipulative behavior. Grooming (picking each other's hair and skin), is illustrative of this. In a situation in which various objects are presented, "The initial approach of the animal to the new object is usually tentative — it gives a quick poke and then quickly withdraws. After the chimp has satisfied itself that the object is not dangerous, it begins to explore and investigate it more thoroughly. The more heterogeneous or variegated the object, the more attention it gets." The results obtained by presenting various objects to the animal indicate that "An object that moves, or one that produces an effect when touched, such as ringing a bell, elicits longer and more detailed manipulations than one which does not move or produce an effect."[91] Interest in a particular object is soon satiated, but the introduction of new objects induces the animal to engage in further exploratory activity.[92]

The exploratory and manipulatory behavior observed in monkeys and chimpanzees is even more evident in human beings. It obviously plays an important role in the learning process, and in what we have already referred to as "reality testing." As one investigator[93] has said,

☐ "The human organism expends considerable energy just finding out about the world in which he lives. He explores, he tries things out, or is just curious about things. This kind of behavior is, of course, especially noticeable in children, but it is equally marked in adults who find themselves in a new situation. It would almost seem as though there is a positive motivation to know one's environment.

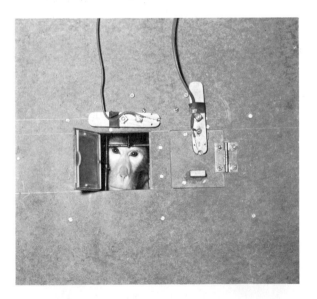

● 6.13

Visual Exploration. Each time the monkey made a correct discrimination (pressing a panel of the proper color rather than the one paired with it), the door opened and he could explore with his eyes for thirty seconds. (From R. A. Butler and H. F. Harlow, "Persistence of Visual Exploration in Monkeys," *J. Comp. Physiol. Psychol.,* 1954, *47,* p. 259.)

"Persons usually try to find out what they can and cannot do in the environment in which they live. This represents a kind of exploration of themselves which is essentially similar to the exploration of the environment. Taken together we can say that the human being attempts to know what exists in the world around him and to know what his possibilities of action are in that world." □

Although men and animals have the same basic drives, there is an important biological difference between them in the nature of the behavior that is instrumental in alleviating these drives. Most animals do not need to acquire appropriate habits — the necessary behavior patterns are built into them, in the form of instincts. Human beings, on the other hand, begin their lives as helpless creatures completely dependent upon others. Independence comes to them only as they learn from others how to take care of themselves. ■

PERSONAL-SOCIAL MOTIVES

We have dealt so far with motives which, to some degree at least, are part of man's biological heritage, hence inborn and universal. Their existence is determined primarily by our animal ancestry and not by anything that has happened to us as individuals. Infants express these motives directly, without reference to social niceties. Adults, on the other hand, are constrained to some degree by personal experience and by what is said to be "proper." In this way, personal experience, although not the origin of physiological motives, comes in humans to play a role in their expression.

We turn our attention now to motives which most of us acquire during our lifetimes, largely through individual experience involving other people. It is because of this personal and social origin that acquired motives are often referred to as *personal-social*.

Some personal-social motives are universal, or nearly so. Take, for example, the motive called *gregariousness* or *need for affiliation*.[94] This is the motive to maintain social contacts. It is manifested in an extreme form when people who have been isolated crave association with others. Although some have called this an instinct, it is much more likely that it is learned, and that it is learned by practically all human beings, because everybody goes through a period of helplessness and dependence upon others during childhood. Indeed, a term has been coined to represent these "common modes of learned response that are the products of original nature and commonly shared environment." The term is *coenotrope*, from two Greek words meaning "common habit."[95]

There would be no point in attempting to list all of the human coenotropes.[96] In addition to gregariousness, two good candidates for such a list would be: (1) the tendency to imitate, which most human beings learn because they find it to their advantage to do so, and (2) the tendency to appeal to individuals stronger than ourselves or to superhuman agencies when our own resources fail. These motives also have their beginnings in human helplessness and in the necessity in early years of being cared for by others.

Common social motives are of course fostered by literature as well as by face-to-face contacts of many kinds.

Many motives, rather than being universal, are limited to our more restricted cultural group. In our society, for example, most of us develop a very strong urge to assert ourselves, to achieve, or to get recognition in some shape or form. This has been called the *achievement*, *self-assertive*, or *mastery* motive. It is expressed in leadership, in self-display, and in a wide range of competitive activities. Moreover, this motive may derive, in part, from the sort of independence-training to which children in our culture are subjected.[97] It is interesting to observe, on the other hand, that the motive to achieve, or to assert oneself, is absent in certain societies. Among the Arapesh of New Guinea, self-assertion is so rare as to be regarded as abnormal.[98]

Self-assertiveness is rare among the Arapesh and certain other groups because it is frowned upon by the adults and discouraged. In our own society self-assertiveness is a strong motive because from very early childhood it is encouraged. We want our children to excel and we set an example of self-assertiveness which they cannot fail to observe or to find advantages in copying.

Another motive that is prevalent in many societies, including our own, but which is extremely rare in some others, is *aggressiveness*. The motive is most typically aroused by frustration, or by hindering the satisfaction of needs, physiological or acquired; but it is suppressed or fostered, depending upon the group norms.

☐ The Arapesh of New Guinea are a peaceful people who discourage displays of anger and aggression. The Mundugumor, on the other hand, foster aggressiveness, even from the time of infancy. Take the feeding situation, for example. It is one where the child must keep sucking or forego his meal. In this situation, "Children . . . develop a very definite purposive fighting attitude, holding on firmly to the nipple and sucking milk as rapidly and vigorously as possible. They frequently choke from swallowing too fast; the choking angers the mother and infuriates the child, thus further turning the suckling situation into one characterized by anger and struggle rather than by affection and reassurance."[99]

As he becomes older, the Mundugumor male is trained in a manner calculated to fit him for survival in battle. In this training, modes of fighting have a large place. We see the same sort of parallel between the Zuñi and Comanche Indians. The Zuñi, a pastoral people, expressed their peacefulness even in their long flowing robes. The Comanches, on the other hand, were noted for their pugnacity. Comanche males were taught to be fighters and they dressed and equipped themselves in a manner suggesting aggressiveness. ☐

Aggressiveness was once thought to be universal, inborn, and ineradicable. Its alleged innateness was often offered as evidence in support of the proposition that war is inevitable. Today we realize that man is by nature neither warlike nor peaceful. It is true that he has certain physiological needs which demand satisfaction. But if he can satisfy these without hindrance, and if he has not been conditioned toward pugnacity by his group, his behavior is characterized by peacefulness. On the other hand, actual or anticipated frustration of basic needs arouses anger and, quite frequently, aggression directed toward the persons or situations responsible. We must not overlook the additional fact that each of us is born into a situation in which certain culture patterns, including traditional antipathies, already exist. These may mold us into aggressive or peaceful individuals, regardless of whether satisfaction of our needs is thwarted or threatened with frustration.

Many motives are much more personal than those already mentioned. They are, so to speak, variations on the universal or cultural theme. Thus, while all normal men are gregarious, their gregariousness is expressed in individual ways. Some are satisfied to limit their contacts to family and neighborhood, while others crave attendance at clubs or participation in larger social groups. Some are passive in group situations and others active. Some lead and others follow. By the same token, the self-assertive members of our civilization assert themselves in a variety of ways, some in bodily contacts and some through the spoken or written word. Most men seek recognition in limited ways, but some are satisfied only with national or world-wide recognition.

Specific goals also differ. Whether their basic aim is to achieve recognition or merely to achieve security, some men want to be doctors, others lawyers or engineers. Still more individualistic are such motives as the desire to collect stamps, coins, or antiques. More individualistic still is the desire to marry a particular person or fill a particular position.

Although such personal motives may at times be traced back to physiological drives and cultural influences, the roots are usually devious and widespread. It often happens that two or more competent psychologists start from the same point and arrive at quite different conclusions concerning the motivation underlying particular cravings, desires, or ambitions.

The problem of what motivates people to act as they do is also complicated by the fact that motives are strengthened or weakened by outcomes. Quite often we get what we want only to find that it is no longer as appealing as it once was. Sometimes we work toward a limited goal and, after reaching it, acquire many wants that were not present before and which require additional efforts. Sometimes, too, motives undergo radical changes — we are converted to new ideals and change our goals accordingly.

When we consider motives like the desire to become a doctor, a sailor, a lawyer, a banker, a merchant, or a teacher, the roots spread in so many directions that it is all but impossible to follow them. Every individual's life goal, even when it is shared by others, has somewhat different origins. One may wish to be a doctor because he sees it as a good way to make a living; because his childhood curiosity about bodily functions was never satisfied; because, in his play activities as a boy, he obtained satisfaction out of doctoring other children with the aid of the toy doctor's kit which somebody gave him; because religious teachings have imbued him with the idea of serving his fellow men and he sees the doctor as a servant of mankind; because his pals are going to be doctors; or perhaps for any one of a hundred other reasons. Sometimes a combination of influences like these underlies one's selection of a life goal.

It is often apparent, when we investigate a person's life history, that his many different activities have a common theme — are similarly motivated. Sometimes the motive is a desire for recognition, and sometimes it is a desire merely to become self-dependent. The so-called "will to power" is often suggested as the connecting thread.

While personal histories differ in details, most of them suggest that a predominant motive is established in childhood, largely through the influence of social contacts. As the individual gets older, one activity after another may be taken up, while others, which no longer contribute to satisfaction of the predominant motive, or which contribute less than the new activity, are dropped.

It quite frequently happens that frustration early in childhood creates a strong desire for recognition, for mastery, or for self-assertion. The aggression of men like Hitler has been attributed to early frustration. Adler has claimed that the frustrations of childhood create in most of us a "will to power." At least it is clear that, if an individual has some predominant motive, like a desire for recognition, it is a "thread" which runs through many different activities. ■

LEVELS OF ASPIRATION

In choosing life goals and in undertaking everyday activities, individuals differ widely in their levels of aspiration — that is to say, in their expectations of accomplishment or in the demands which they make upon themselves. One individual, let us say, aspires to become a cab driver; another a doctor. Some expect to attain a salary of twenty thousand dollars per year while others expect to attain only five thousand dollars. Likewise, if you ask individuals how accurately or how quickly they can perform a particular task, some will set for themselves a high level of accomplishment and others a much lower level.

General observation shows that one's level of aspiration is usually modified from time to time in terms of his success or failure in attaining his goals. Students who aspire to be physicians, but find the premedical requirements beyond them, eventually lower their level of aspiration. Some then aspire to be salesmen for pharmaceutical manufacturers. One student, known to the writer, aspired successively to becoming a physician, a dentist, and a mortician. The latter occupations are, of course, worthwhile and necessary; but for one who first aspires to become a physician, they represent a lowered level of aspiration.

Laboratory investigations on levels of aspiration deal with this concept in a more limited sense than that already described. Subjects are asked to indicate what level of performance they will undertake to achieve on some such task as solving puzzles, placing pegs in holes, tracing through mazes, or shooting a steel ball along a groove as illustrated and described in Figure 6.14. They then perform the task one or more times. After this, they are told their actual performance and asked to state their level of aspiration for a further per-

● 6.14
A Level of Aspiration Board. The subject tells the investigator what score he expects to make as he projects the ball up the groove. By repeating the procedures for a series of trials, the experimenter is able to study how success or failure influences the verbalized expectancies (or aspirations) of the subject concerning his future performances. (From J. B. Rotter, *Social Learning and Clinical Psychology*, Prentice-Hall, 1954, p. 129).

formance of the task. This is continued for a number of trials. Sometimes an individual is not told his actual accomplishment, but is given a fictitious score which he believes to be his own. Sometimes he is told that others have accomplished a particular score on the task. This is to test the significance of social influences. Finally, the differences between levels of aspiration and levels of actual achievement are determined. The experimenter then calculates how success or failure in meeting the designated level influences the level of aspiration.

The results of these investigations are not easily summarized. In general, the level of aspiration stays pretty close to actual performance, but there is a tendency for it to remain above rather than below actual performance. There is a greater tendency, too, for the individual to raise his goal after success than to lower it after failure. The influence of social factors is suggested by the observation that individuals tend to raise their level of aspiration when told that average performance, especially of a group regarded as inferior, is above their own.[100]

Such findings as these are often closely duplicated in everyday life. This has been revealed by a study in which college students reported on incidents in their own lives. Each student wrote a description of three well-remembered incidents in his life — one involving frustration which prevented him from reaching a goal, one involving achievement of a goal following frustration, and one involving attainment of a goal without appreciable frustration. In each instance involving frustration, this was to have been brought about by another person, and the goal achieved was to have involved other persons. After the frustrating incidents had been reported, the students were asked to tell the effect of the incident on their level of aspiration. The chief results are summarized in Table 6.1. It is clearly evident that complete frustration led about twice as many students to lower as to raise their levels of aspiration.[101] Success in goal attainment led a very large proportion to raise their level of aspiration.

Levels of aspiration are influenced by the person's attitudes toward himself and by his estimate of his group status. He gains or loses self-esteem as he succeeds or fails to reach his goals; and, if the group is directly involved, so as to be a "witness" to his achievements, he feels that he has gained or lost status, or "face." Such self-attitudes have been called *ego-involvements*. A concept of self, with related ego-involvement, probably precedes the

■ **TABLE 6.1 Summary of Frequency of Reported Shifts in Level of Aspiration Produced by Each of Three Types of Incidents**

Type of incident	Frequency of each shift in level of aspiration		
	Lowering	None	Rise
Complete frustration	66	36	33
Frustration followed by goal-attainment	15	15	95
Simple goal-attainment	3	17	121

From I. L. Child and J. W. M. Whiting, "Determinants of Level of Aspiration: Evidence from Everyday Life," *J. Abnormal & Soc. Psychol.*, 1949, 44, 308.

setting of a level of aspiration. "The level of aspiration does not seem to appear clearly until the child has formed some conception of his 'self' — until he has developed a sense of 'pride' which he feels must be maintained."[102] ■

INCENTIVES, INTERESTS, AND ATTITUDES

Incentives, interests, and attitudes are aspects of motivation in that they determine the goals of behavior and the attracting or repelling aspects of objects and situations in the organism's environment.

Incentives are the objects or goals toward which motivated behavior is directed. In a sense we may regard them as inducements to act. In experiments on animal learning, we offer the animal food, sex, water, a means of escape from punishment, a means of returning to familiar surroundings, or perhaps an opportunity to return to the young. Food, sex, water, and opportunities to return to a more desirable situation are inducements to effort — in other words, incentives. It is perhaps obvious that these are incentives only if the animal is suitably motivated. For instance, to an animal whose stomach is full, food is often no incentive at all.

Incentives such as we have mentioned are also effective, under suitable physiological and external circumstances, in arousing human action. In the home, classroom, and industry, however, the incentives used are indirectly, if at all, related to basic physiological drives.

Money may satisfy the hunger drive by making possible the purchase of food. Its incentive value then rests upon satisfaction of hunger. On the other hand, people who are not hungry, and who do not need additional money in order to satisfy hunger, are still induced by money to put forth much effort in the performance of various tasks. In some instances they are motivated, not by hunger, but by the knowledge that money will buy clothes which enhance their attractiveness to the opposite sex. In other instances money has incentive value because it provides a means of gaining prestige, and thus of satisfying social

motives such as self-assertion and the desire for recognition. This by no means exhausts the motives — physiological, social, or personal — which money may tap.

Objects or situations which repel the organism, like an electric shock that it is trying to escape, are referred to as *deterrents*, in contrast to incentives. One could say in the present instance, however, that the animal's incentive is to escape. Stimuli which have a deterrent effect are also referred to as *aversive*, since the organism may be said to have an aversion for them; that is, tendency to dislike, or avoid, them.

Interests are closely related to incentives. They tend to direct behavior toward incentives, as when a person is interested in money, sex, prestige, or some other incentive. We can also regard interests as attitudes favorably disposing one toward some object, situation, or idea.

Many interests are acquired in early childhood. They are usually developed in relation to, and remain allied to, more basic motives. In satisfying his need for activity, or his curiosity, or both, a child may, for example, play with toy trains, go to the railroad station to watch the trains coming and going, read about trains, and so on. This interest in trains, perhaps beginning with a train trip, receiving a toy train, or the like, may be retained through the years until, in adulthood, the individual finds his career in some aspect of railroading. On the other hand, through fortuitous circumstances, such as receiving a gift of something more enticing than toy trains, moving to a new locality, or being preoccupied with school, the boy's interest in trains may become secondary, or even disappear. He may turn his attention elsewhere.

Whereas interests are always positive in direction, attitudes may be positive or negative. Our attitude toward a political party, a person, a race, a nation, a book, or a movie may, if we have any attitude at all, be favorable or unfavorable. Interests are directed toward specific objects and persons, while attitudes tend to be broader in scope, being directed toward such targets as races, nations, institutions, groups, and general ideas and issues. Moreover, attitudes are more passive than interests. We are more likely to have attitudes and do nothing about them than we are to have interests and do nothing about them. Nevertheless, when we are called upon to make decisions, to act, and to express opinions, our attitudes determine the outcome just as strongly as do our interests. As a matter of fact, attitudes are usually defined as *determining tendencies*.

Attitudes toward races, nations, ideas, institutions, and the like, are sometimes referred to as *prejudices*, because such attitudes lead us to prejudge an issue. Thus, if we are prejudiced against a person who is accused of a crime, we are likely to regard him as guilty, regardless of the evidence; or, if we examine the evidence, we will probably do so with partiality, giving more weight to the damaging than to the exonerating evidence. We can also be prejudiced in favor of some individual or thing. Thus, our country can do no wrong, our children are the most beautiful and best-behaved, and our school is beyond criticism, at least from an outsider. When the word "prejudice" is used without qualification, however, it customarily refers to a negative attitude.

Like many attitudes, prejudices begin in childhood. They are usually taken over from parents and others through verbal contacts rather than from personal experience. Some may be purely verbal, at least initially. A case in point is the small boy whose mother told the psychologist that he hated colored people. When interviewed, the child made it evident that his mother had warned him about colored people. He said: "I don't like colored people. I just like people who are black and white." There have been studies comparing the thought processes of highly prejudiced children and adults with the thought processes of the relatively unprejudiced. Among other things, these studies have shown that racial, religious, and other forms of prejudice are related to mental "rigidity" as opposed to "flexibility." By rigidity is meant a tendency to hold to one's views regardless of the evidence.[103] This was exemplified by a person who told the writer, "I don't care what the research shows, I have a feeling in the pit of my stomach that this race is innately inferior to our own."

Various devices have been developed for measuring the degree to which individuals and groups possess certain attitudes, or prejudices.[104] These so-called "attitude scales" have a number of statements and the individual indicates his agreement, disagreement, or indecision with respect to each. In an attitude scale dealing with war, for example, there are statements like: "He who refuses to fight is a true hero," and "The benefits of war outweigh its attendant evils." The scale value of each item is determined by procedures which need not concern us here. After statements that the individual endorses have been scored, a composite score is calculated and this serves as an index of the strength of the attitude.[105]

A projective study of attitudes

One type of personality test requires subjects to complete partial statements such as "My chief aim in life is. . . ." In the investigation to be described here[106] there were two types of such statements. One said, for example, "If a Negro moved onto my street I would. . . ." This is of course a direct statement which puts the individual who completes it on record as having a particular attitude. In the study under consideration, statements of this type were regarded as *direct* rather than projective. A parallel statement, on a projective basis, would be: "If a Negro moved onto his street, Bill would. . . ." The latter statement did not so evidently implicate the person who completed it. His own involvement was even less evident when he filled out such a series of statements as quickly as possible in the belief that he was taking a speed test of Verbal Intelligence. The assumption here was this: Since the subject does not have to state what *he* would do, and since his attention is diverted from the true purpose of the test through the instruction to *complete these tests of Verbal Intelligence as quickly as possible*, he will seek the readiest possible completion and this will represent his personal attitude on the issue involved. The real purpose of the test was further disguised by mixing in many items on noncontroversial things, such as, "When he has an opportunity to do so, John likes to. . . ." or "John often feels that he should. . . ."

A group comprising forty-eight freshmen and sophomores in a New England women's college filled out as quickly as possible a "Verbal Intelligence Test" containing fifty-nine projective items such as we have described. These dealt with attitudes toward mother, father, religion, racial groups, and noncontroversial and impersonal issues. Ten items relating to Negroes were included and subjected to special study because, "In a New England liberal arts college community there are normative standards as to the proper attitudes to express regarding . . . 'Negroes moving in next door' or 'Having a Negro doctor.' "[107] The investigators felt that, although absence of prejudice toward Negroes is expected and expressed in such a community, there is the possibility that "covert feelings to the contrary" might exist.

Sixteen days after doing the "Verbal Intelligence Test" the same students were asked to fill in a "Personal and Social Attitudes Record," which they were led to assume would be filed in the office along with their other records. The items in this questionnaire were comparable to those of the other test but each was framed directly. That is, the student said, in each case, what *she* would do under the stated circumstances. There was no time limit.

One interesting outcome of this study is illustrated in Figure 6.15. The upper histogram represents the frequency of completions on the ten projective Negro items which, in the opinion of judges, were negative or prejudicial to Negroes. Observe that there is a wide distribution of negative attitudes — one of the group gave no negative reactions, three gave one negative reaction, and so on. At the other extreme were three who reacted negatively to all ten items. We see, then, that the private attitudes of this group differed widely. But how about the attitudes which were to go on record and be identified with the person who expressed them? The outcome here was very different from the above. Instead of a wide distribution, suggesting a normal curve, there was a markedly skewed distribution. Most

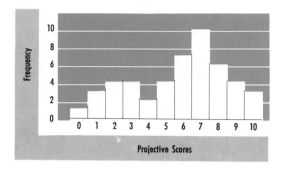

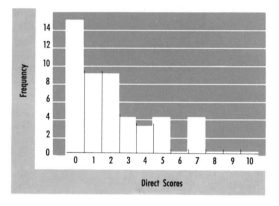

● 6.15

Comparison of Projective and Direct Attitude Scores. Each column represents the frequency of the indicated number of negative (i.e., prejudiced) responses. Note the reversed J shape of the lower curve. (From J. W. Getzels and J. J. Walsh, "The Method of Paired Direct and Projective Questionnaires in the Study of Attitude Structure and Socialization," *Psychological Monographs*, 1958, 72, No. 1, p. 15.)

reactions were in a direction favorable to Negroes. Fifteen students, for example, gave no negative reactions, nine gave only one negative reaction, and so on. No subjects expressed prejudice to the extent that they gave negative completions for all ten items. On noncontroversial items the distribution was similar regardless of whether the projective or direct form of the test was used.

A skewed distribution like that obtained for the Negro items is commonly found when individuals react openly to controversial issues.

Because of its shape (a reversed **J**) this is customarily referred to as a *J-curve*. It represents a trend toward conformity.

Children's attitudes

The investigators who studied attitudes in college students as described above subsequently made an extensive survey of children's attitudes.[108] More than 900 children ranging in age from 8 to 13 years were tested. The method was similar to that described except that the items were simpler and the instructions were modified to adapt them to children. In the *direct* type of test, the children were asked to say how they would behave if certain things happened to them. Corresponding projective items were given as part of a test "to see how fast you can make sentences." In each projective item, however, the behavior was attributed to Jane, Mary, or some other person named in the item. The items had reference to such issues as cheating, religion, race, belief in God, honesty, and helping others.

In this investigation an index of differentiation (ID) was derived from the direct and projective responses. It represented the discrepancy between the personal attitude (as revealed by projective responses) and the overtly expressed attitude (as revealed by direct responses). It was predicted, on the basis of what is known about the socialization of children, that the ID would increase with age. This is what did happen, as illustrated graphically in the bar graph of Figure 6.16. This increase in the ID with age came about because the children's personal attitudes underwent greater suppression as they grew older. Their personal attitudes, as indicated by the projective reactions, did not change appreciably. At successive yearly age levels from 8 to 13, for example, the mean projective scores were 18.04, 17.33, 18.62, 18.73, 18.83, and 18.73 — a difference between the lower and upper age levels of only .69 points. The direct scores, however, decreased between the eighth and thirteenth years as follows: 13.23, 12.40, 11.71, 11.12, 10.99, and 10.83.

It is interesting to note that the tendency to suppress overt expressions of personal attitudes was significantly more marked in girls than in boys, in only children than in those with siblings, and in children from homes of high socio-economic status than in those from homes of low socio-economic status. These outcomes had been predicted on the basis of other information concerning the relative degree of socialization in these groups. ∎

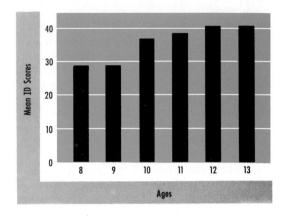

● 6.16

Mean ID Scores for Children from Eight to Thirteen Years of Age. The figures at the left are mean ID scores (see text) to the nearest whole number. These were obtained from 133 to 174 children in each age group. (Data from J. W. Getzels and J. J. Walsh, "The Method of Paired Direct and Projective Questionnaires in the Study of Attitude Structure and Socialization," *Psychological Monographs*, 1958, 72, No. 1, p. 15.)

INTERACTION OF PERSONAL-SOCIAL AND PHYSIOLOGICAL MOTIVATION

We have now surveyed a wide variety of motives ranging from obviously physiological (hunger, thirst, sex, etc.) to the clearly personal-social (gregariousness, achievement, and particular aspirations, interests, attitudes, and prejudices). A question which now naturally arises is whether the latter are related to the former and, if so, in what ways.

It is well to remember, first of all, that personal-social motives are learned and that the original motivation for learning them is often physiological. It may well be, as some have said, that the organism without physiological motivation would be inert, like a clock minus its mainspring. But even apart from the energizing that comes from such motivation, we know that many personal-social motives have their origin in the need to satisfy physiological needs. The desire for money is not a physiological motive, but it is nevertheless related to physiological needs when the motivation to obtain it is the desire to satisfy these in the future. Some investigators speak of physiological needs as *primary* and of those related to securing their satisfaction as *secondary*. Thus, while hunger is a primary drive, the hoarding of food or money to buy food is a secondary drive. Even prejudices sometimes have their roots in physiological motivation, as when economic competition from other peoples is believed to endanger one's own security. Thus certain races may be excluded from a region because they "live on the smell of an oily rag" and "lower the standard of living."

It is quite evident, then, that personal-social motives may be linked to physiological needs and that those which are indirectly linked are secondary in the above-mentioned sense. We do not mean, however, that all human motivation is, in this sense, physiologically grounded. Some personal-social motives appear to have no current physiological ties, except the neurological basis that is common to all learned activities. This is true in spite of the fact that these motives may have had some connection with physiological need-states in early childhood. Allport looks upon:

□ " . . . adult motives as infinitely varied, and as self-sustaining, *contemporary* systems, growing out of antecedent systems, but functionally independent of them. Just as a child gradually repudiates his dependence on his parents, develops a will of his own, becomes self-active and self-determining, and outlives his parents, so it is with motives. Each motive has a definite point of origin which may possibly lie in the organic tensions of infancy. Chronologically speaking, all adult purposes can be traced back to these seedforms in infancy, but

as the individual matures the tie is broken. Whatever bond remains is historical, not functional."[109] □

The idea that many adult motives may have broken their physiological ties is known as the concept of *functional autonomy*. This concept has been applied by Allport and others to the persistence of habits even when the motives (physiological or personal-social) which led to their acquisition are no longer operative. It does appear, at times, as if habits have themselves acquired the status of drives. Some possible examples of functional autonomy are persistence of sexual behavior after the menopause, when estrogens are no longer present; persistence of a vocational activity after the individual has made his fortune and achieved distinction; and living to eat instead of merely eating to live.

In most instances of apparent functional autonomy there is a possibility that new motives have supplanted the original ones and that the habit in question is not, in reality, operating without extraneous motivation. Even the man who has made his fortune and achieved the utmost recognition may feel that he must keep working so as not to be considered "a has been," "a quitter," or one of the "idle rich." In such instances habits are autonomous from the standpoint of the original motives, but they are not altogether without extraneous motivation.

Perhaps a good example of functional autonomy is to be found in the case of some gifted people who are alleged to "demand the exercise of their talents, even when no other reward lies ahead."[110] ■

FORCE OF HABIT

In cases of functional autonomy, as we have seen, the habit is freed from at least its original motivation. Force of habit, on the other hand, is persistence of a particular way of satisfying a given motive. For example, if one has regularly satisfied the hunger drive by eating foods prepared in a certain way, there is often resistance to eating foods prepared in some other way. Likewise, if an older person's need for rest and recreation is customarily satisfied by sitting quietly at home, perhaps reading, he may resist the suggestion that he go to a movie or to a bridge party. In other words, habit forces us "into a rut." This phenomenon is often referred to as "force of habit," as though habits once formed act somewhat as drives, impelling us to continue the accustomed ways instead of taking up new ways of satisfying our motives. The social significance of this tendency for habits once formed to persist is indicated in the following quotation from William James, one of the greatest American psychologists.[111]

□ "Habit is the enormous fly-wheel of society, its most precious conservative agent. It alone keeps us all within the bounds of ordinance, and saves the children of fortune from the envious uprisings of the poor. It alone prevents the hardest and most repulsive walks of life from being deserted by those brought up to tread therein. It keeps the fisherman and the deck hand at sea through the winter; it holds the miner in his darkness, and nails the countryman to his log cabin and his lonely farm through all the months of snow; it protects us from invasion by the natives of the desert and the frozen zone. It dooms us to fight out the battle of life upon the lines of our nurture or our early choice, and to make the best of a pursuit that disagrees, because there is no other for which we are fitted, and it is too late to begin again. It keeps different social strata from mixing. Already at the age of twenty-five, you see the professional mannerism settling down on the young commercial traveler, on the young doctor, on the young minister, on the young counselor-at-law. You see the little lines of cleavage running through the character, the tricks of thought, the prejudices, the ways of the 'shop,' in a word, from which the man can by and by no more escape than his coat-sleeve can suddenly fall into a new set of folds." □

James may have exaggerated somewhat the permanency of our habitual modes of behavior, for people often do change their prejudices and, during war or other emergencies, their ways of living. However, there is usually a very strong resistance to change. Anyone who wishes to change the behavior of an adult must take into consideration this tendency to persist in well-formed habits, even when these have become outmoded or dangerous. ■

• SUMMARY

All organisms have physiological needs — need for food, liquid, elimination, and so on. When such needs are not readily satisfied, the organism is driven to activity. This is the basis for speaking of physiological drives — such as the hunger drive, thirst drive, or excretory drive. Compensatory activity which alleviates needs is referred to as homeostatic since its function is to maintain a constant state.

Drives may be regarded as energizers. Whether each drive contributes generally or only in a specific way to the energizing of the organism is a controversial question. Research has demonstrated drive-summation effects in the case of anxiety and hunger; but whether two or more appetitive drives (like hunger and thirst) will show energy summation is still an open question. The presence of a drive may sensitize an organism to relevant aspects of its environment (such as odor of food, behavior of a sexual partner). This is a "cueing" function. Stimuli to which a drive has sensitized the organism may guide it to the incentive (Herring gull to the red spot, newborn giraffe to the nipple). In addition to their possible energizing and cueing or guiding effects, drives lower the threshold of certain motor pathways, thus giving relevant responses (sucking, sexual reflexes) precedence over other responses.

Hormones and neural mechanisms both contribute in important ways to motivation. The influence of hormones is clearly established in the case of sexual and maternal behavior, but there is evidence that hormones are also involved in hunger and thirst. Among the neural mechanisms, the reticular formation, the septal region, and the hypothalamus have received special attention. The importance of these structures for motivation has been revealed by studies involving electrical stimulation, destruction of nerve cells, and injection of various substances.

Nerve impulses stream into the reticular formation and, through its activation, have an alerting function. Impulses reach it through collaterals from the projection paths (those which carry sensory impulses to specialized areas of the cerebral cortex) and also from the cortex itself.

At the base of the cerebrum, encircling the upper end of the brain stem, is an aggregation of nerve centers known, in general, as the limbic system. Two of these centers to which we have specifically referred are the septal region and the hypothalamus. Within these structures are the so-called pleasure areas. Their existence is inferred from the fact that, when an animal can electrically stimulate certain areas by pressing on a bar, it does so repeatedly, as though it were being rewarded for its activity. This effect has been observed in various organisms, including human beings.

The hunger drive seems to depend not only on the easily observed stomach contractions, but also on blood chemistry. The hypothalamus is also implicated. Destruction of nerve cells in a particular region of the hypothalamus is followed, in rats and mice, by excessive eating, which seems to be motivated not so much by hunger as by a loss of the sense of having eaten enough (satiety). Electrical stimulation of a nearby hypothalamic region leads animals to eat even though they have been satiated. The hunger drive may be reduced by food in the mouth or in the stomach, even before there has been time for a change in blood chemistry. Thus, reduction of hunger drive is not necessarily the same as need reduction, or the restoration of normal blood chemistry. Studies of semistarvation have shown that hunger may subvert man's cultural ideals.

Thirst is a drive initiated by cellular dehydration. It is often experienced as a dryness of the mouth and throat. Experiments have revealed that thirst and the related intake of liquid are regulated by a center in the hypothalamus. The posterior pituitary gland is also involved.

The sex drive is primarily related to secretions from the gonads (ovaries and testes), although it is also disturbed by injury to the anterior pituitary gland or to the cortex of the adrenal glands.

In females the sex drive is dependent, initially at least, upon estrogens (from the ovaries). In males, the corresponding secretions are androgens (from the testes). Although the human sex drive has the same physiological motivation as that of other animals, it shows much wider variation both in intensity and in mode of satisfaction. Social influences are largely responsible for such variation.

Maternal motivation and the pattern of infant care are unlearned in lower organisms like the rat; but as the human level is approached there is great variation and every indication that both the motivation and the pattern of maternal behavior are, in large measure, acquired through individual experience and social contacts.

Whether infants have a "need" for affection, as some have claimed, is in doubt, because the evidence is from infants also denied normal stimulation. Human adults denied such stimulation show adverse effects. Associated with this apparent "need for stimulation" or "to know the environment," there are exploratory and manipulatory drives. These have been demonstrated in rats, monkeys, chimpanzees, and human subjects.

Many human motives are acquired in social situations as the outcome of personal experience, hence the term personal-social. Some of these motives have no obvious relation to physiological drives although they do have a basis in anticipation of physiological emergencies.

Personal-social motives are in some instances acquired universally. This is because, despite cultural diversities, all human beings are exposed to certain environmental influences. All are, initially, helpless; all depend upon social contacts for survival; all are positively conditioned to persons instrumental in satisfying their early needs; all learn to appeal to others for help; and all learn the advantages of copying certain aspects of the behavior of those around them. These similarities give rise to such coenotropes as gregariousness and appealing to others when in need.

Some motives are characteristic of a particular culture. Thus the typical American is self-assertive, with a strong achievement motive, while the Arapesh is submissive. The individual origins of such motives go back to childhood training.

Motives also vary from one person to another. Thus the self-assertiveness found so predominantly in our own culture has various individual manifestations. In addition to personal variations in universal and common forms of motivation, there are motives which, of their nature, vary from one individual to another. These personal motives include such things as the desire of one to be a doctor, of another to be an engineer; of one to gain world-wide recognition and of another to avoid publicity, and so on.

Personal aspirations depend upon experiences of success or failure, sometimes going back to early childhood. Experimental studies on levels of aspiration have shown that success tends to raise the level and failure to lower it. Interests and attitudes predispose us to react in different ways to the same external situations. Interests are positively directed, are directed toward specific goals, and are active, or dynamic. Attitudes may be positive or negative. Negative attitudes are what we customarily refer to as prejudices.

Projective and direct studies of attitudes toward controversial issues show that overt attitudes (direct expressions) tend to conform to the prevailing social climate and yield a J-curve. Private attitudes (projectively revealed) approximate a normal curve. In children, the discrepancy between private and public attitudes (differentiation index) increases with age. This is not because private attitudes change a great deal in the age-range studied (8 to 13) but because public expression of them is suppressed to an increasing degree as the child grows older.

Some habits seem to acquire the status of drives, i.e., to become independent of their original motivation. This is referred to as functional autonomy. Persistence of particular ways of satisfying a motive is distinguished from functional autonomy because the motive as well as the habit persists. This is known as force of habit. ■

REFERENCES AND NOTES FOR THIS CHAPTER ARE IN THE APPENDIX.

• SELECTED READINGS

Berlyne, D. E., *Conflict, Arousal, and Curiosity.* McGraw-Hill, 1960. Emphasis on exploratory behavior in animals and human beings.

Bindra, D., *Motivation.* Ronald, 1959. A systematic review of the literature on animal motivation, with some human material.

Birney, R. C., and R. C. Teevan, *Instinct,* Van Nostrand, 1961; and, by the same authors, *Measuring Human Motivation,* Van Nostrand, 1962. Reprints of outstanding papers in these areas.

Cofer, C. N., and M. H. Appley, *Motivation: Theory and Research.* Wiley, 1964. A very comprehensive treatment of both animal and human motivation.

Hall, J. F., *Psychology of Motivation.* Lippincott, 1961. A survey of constructs, theories, and research.

Munn, N. L., *The Evolution and Growth of Human Behavior* (2nd ed.). Houghton Mifflin, 1965. See Chapter 3 for a discussion of unlearned behavior, including instincts.

Rethlingshafer, D., *Motivation as Related to Personality* McGraw-Hill, 1963.

Rheingold, H. L. (Ed.), *Maternal Behavior in Mammals.* Wiley, 1963. Original studies.

7

Feeling and Emotion

*F*eeling and emotion are inextricably related. When emotionally aroused we have such experiences as pleasantness, excitement, happiness, sadness, fear, anxiety, and so on. These "affective experiences," as they are called, can be known to us only through our own experience or what others tell us of theirs. When such terms are used in connection with animal behavior — as when we speak of "pleasure centers" in the brain or "anxiety" following punishment — it is not necessarily implied that the animal *feels* pleasure or anxiety. The only evidence for pleasure in this case is repeated performance of an act, and the only evidence for anxiety is running away, trembling, or some other aspect of behavior. One can say, if he wishes to, that the animal acts *as if* it were receiving pleasure, or *as if* it were anxious. This is the only justification, in fact, for using such subjectively derived terms to categorize aspects of animal behavior.

The terms *emotion* and *motivation* have a common derivation. The Latin word *emovere* means to stir up, agitate, excite, or move. To be *moved* in an emotional sense means to be "stirred up." In a motivational sense it means to "bestir oneself" or to "be pushed." Sometimes emotion not only stirs us up but also causes us to bestir ourselves. Moreover, it may impel us to say and do things which we would not normally say and do.

When emotion is intense there are widespread changes which embrace every aspect of our body and its activity. Physiological and neural processes are altered. Thoughts and actions are affected. Marked disorganization may occur. What we were doing may be dropped, or even forgotten. Overall adjustment may be disturbed. In an emotion-provoking emergency we may exhibit unusual energy; or, we may be "rooted to the spot" or "lose our heads."

But emotional life is infinitely varied and it has integrating as well as disintegrating aspects. Variation can be seen not only in the intensity of emotional activation but also in emotional experience and in external expressions of emotion — in emotional feeling as observed in oneself and as reported by others, in facial expressions, in gestures, and in overall behavior patterns.

Looked at from the *intensive* angle, emotion is merely a sort of physiological, neural, and experiential activation. Thus it may be said[1] that "the angry man overreacts to stimulation"; that "Strong emotion . . . represents one end of a continuum of activation"; and that "The opposite end, the condition of minimal activation, is found in the sleeping man, who does not react to stimulation." Emotion is not essentially different, in this respect, from tensions associated with physiological drives. Indeed one psychologist[2] calls emotion a form of "energy mobilization" and attempts to identify it with other motivational phenomena.

When we consider emotion from the standpoint of activation or energy mobilization, disrupting emotion is of course nothing more than exceptionally strong emotion. But intensity of activation is not the most characteristic aspect of emotion. The emotionally aroused person will tell you not only that he is slightly or strongly excited but also that he has such and such an *emotion*. He will say that he is afraid, angry, jealous, or in love.

There are many emotional experiences and many forms of overt emotional behavior over and above the intensity variations. Any dictionary contains many terms to represent these different emotions. A checklist used in research has over one hundred adjectives — amused, annoyed, cheerful . . . tense, unhappy, worried — to indicate how emotionally aroused people feel.[3] There are also many adjectives to describe overt emotional behavior — affectionate, aggressive, belligerent, entreating, and so on.

How do we know, for example, that a person is not only aroused intensely but that

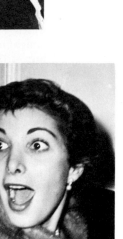

● **7.1**

Some Unposed Emotional Expressions. What emotions are expressed? What kind of situation precipitated each? After answering these questions, refer to the Appendix. (Press Herald Evening Express; *Life,* © Time, Inc.; Rosen Studios; Sydney Morning Herald; Herb Gehr, from Black Star.)

he is afraid, or angry, or in love? The answer is that the subject says in one instance that he is afraid and in the other that he is angry. We may observe, too, that different stimuli are present in each case, that the general situation is somewhat different, and that different overt behavior occurs. To make him afraid we may fire a revolver behind his head, put a snake or a rat in his hands, or make his chair collapse suddenly. But to make him angry we tell him that we are not going to pay him what we owe him, that we are going to fail him in the course, or that somebody has made derogatory remarks about his honesty. When the stimuli are fear-provoking, the subject jumps back, tries to get away, or screams. When they are anger-provoking, on the other hand, he argues, makes threats, or strikes the offender. Even when no such actions are elicited, the situation may bring out different facial expressions which we have learned to interpret as representing particular emotions. The reader might attempt to name the emotions represented in Figure 7.1 and also describe the sort of situation that he thinks may have precipitated them.

We do not wish to imply that one can find experiential and behavioral differences to verify every emotional term in the language. As in the case of intensity, there are almost imperceptible gradients between the so-called *emotions*, or what might better be referred to as the *ways of behaving emotionally*. The well-recognized emotions are those which stand out, like mountain peaks, from the general emotional terrain. They stand out because they are quite often intense and because they have clearly recognized experiential and behavioral aspects. These are the emotions most easily recognized in ourselves, most easily expressed in our language, and most easily identified when we see them represented in pictures or on the stage. They are also most readily predicted in terms of the situations which arouse them. We can predict, for example, that fearful behavior will probably be elicited by a gun poked into one's ribs and that anger will most likely occur if strong motives are frustrated.[4] It is in terms of such emotions, moreover, that emotion has often been defined as disturbing and disorganizing in its effects.

The emotions most obvious to the poet, the novelist, the dramatist, and the casual observer of himself and others are, however, no more truly representative of emotion in general than the mountain peaks in a terrain are truly representative of its geography. Most of our everyday emotional life is no more obvious than the physiological drives and other motives already considered. We may go for days, or even weeks, without any obvious expressions of emotion yet never be free from emotional undercurrents which influence our perceptions, our interests, our attitudes, our prejudices, our thoughts, our learning, and all of our actions. ■

AFFECTIVE ASPECTS OF EMOTION

To the emotionally aroused individual himself the most obvious aspect of emotion is feeling. He experiences "butterflies" in his stomach. His "heart sinks" within him. He has "his heart in his mouth." He feels hot or cold, excited or calm, tense or relaxed, happy or sad. What he hears and reads supports his belief that such feelings, rather than being peculiar to his own experience, are universal aspects of emotion.

The subjective nature of feelings, or of "affects," as they are called technically, is a major obstacle to scientific investigation. Nevertheless a great deal is known about affective experience. We know, for example, that some emotions, like fear and anger, are unpleasant, while others, like happiness and love (except when frustrated), are pleasant.

When subjects are emotionally aroused, as in Figure 7.2, their descriptions of experiences are extremely meager. About all they do is name their emotions. Thus girls who

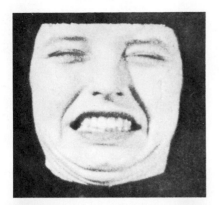
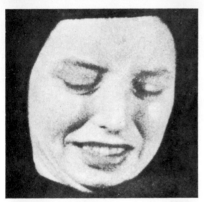

● **7.2**
Emotional Expressions Aroused Experimentally.
These expressions were aroused (top to bottom, respectively) by electric shock, crushing a snail, and the proximity of a snake. (From J. C. Coleman, "Facial Expressions of Emotion," *Psychological Monographs*, 1949, No. 296, pp. 10–11.)

were forced to crush a snail between their fingers said merely that the act was repulsive, distasteful, disgusting, or unpleasant.

More information is obtained when, instead of depending upon their own vocabulary, subjects use a checklist of such affective items as pleasant, unpleasant, exciting, tension-producing, and so forth. What one learns from such studies, if he doesn't know it already, is that *fear* is unpleasant and exciting, with tension and strain involved; that *joy* is pleasant and bright; and that *sorrow* is unpleasant, depressing, and dull. The feelings cited most frequently, and with greatest uniformity from one subject to another, are pleasantness and unpleasantness. Indeed it is relatively easy for them to classify their emotions into the predominantly pleasant and the predominantly unpleasant.[5]

In studies of facial expression in emotion, where subjects are asked to name the emotion expressed, the terms applied to a particular expression may differ considerably. Nevertheless, there is seldom any doubt as to the pleasantness or unpleasantness of the experience behind it. Observe, for example, the posed facial expressions, in Figure 7.3. It is not at all difficult to discern a gradual transition in pleasantness, as the reader will find if he does the exercises described.[6] ■

EMOTIONS AND MOTIVES

In some respects, the emotional undercurrents of life, together with the more obvious emotions, are comparable with physiological motives. They may actually have evolved from such motives, thus facilitating adjustment.

□ Darwin[7] and later writers on evolution stressed the value of emotion for survival and they presented evidence that human emotions have animal origins. But at what level of animal life did emotions emerge, and from what earlier behavior did they take their departure? The answer is that nobody knows. We have no way of communicating with animals to learn whether they have emotional experiences and we cannot, with any degree of assurance, infer emotions from their behavior.

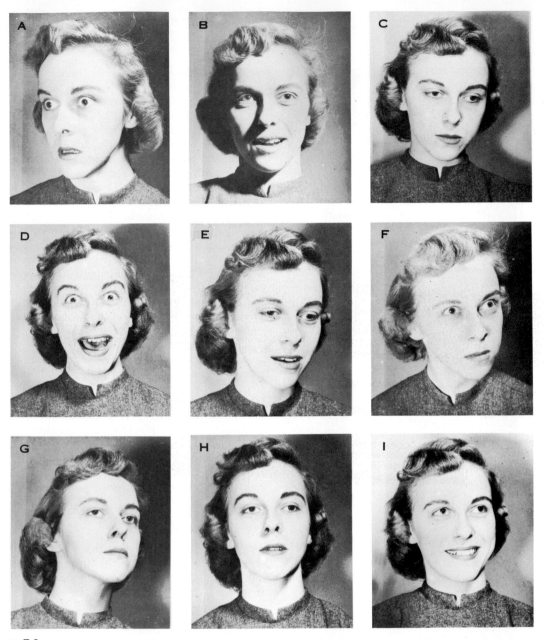

● 7.3

Some Posed Emotional Expressions. Arrange these into a sequence, from unpleasant to pleasant; then check with the Appendix. (Courtesy, Harold Schlosberg)

We may infer that apes, monkeys, and dogs have emotions somewhat like ours because we see resemblances between their behavior and our own under comparable circumstances. As we go down the scale toward lower organisms, however, such inferences as these become in-

creasingly difficult and more highly speculative.

Nevertheless it has been claimed that emotions, at whatever level they emerged, took their departure from physiological motives. The proponent of this theory[8] suggests that a clam is motivated, but presumably without emotion. Somewhere above this level, he says, "Animals became more complex in their receptor equipment, motor equipment, and capacity for learning. As such complex creatures developed, those that were motivated merely by the long-established physiological motives were not so well equipped for survival. The animal that did not make avoiding responses until it was grabbed by an enemy was less likely to survive than an animal capable of reactions of fear that would be set off by relatively slight stimuli. The animal that had an interest in its offspring — even in the case of the male and in the case of the female even beyond the period of nursing the young — was more likely to reproduce its kind." □

Whether emotions evolved from physiological motives or originated in some other way, it is clear that they have motivational significance and, under certain circumstances, survival value also. Like physiological motives, they impel us to activity. They also engender goal-oriented activities, like the lover's affectionate behavior toward the loved one and the angry man's aggression toward the object of his anger. Some arouse the escape motive. Fear exemplifies this fact. Annoyance, also, may motivate escape from the thing or person that annoys. Sometimes emotions "move" us to tears, or to the performance of sympathetic or charitable acts.

Emotion as a source of energy

The energizing function of emotion, which is probably always present to some degree, is quite obvious in certain emergencies.[9] It is then that emotional activation most clearly has survival value. Take for example, fear aroused in situations requiring struggle or escape. The physiological conditions associated with this emotion may provide "superhuman" energy or "lend wings" to our feet. This is because the medulla of the adrenal gland (Figure 6.10, p. 169) gives forth an excessive supply of adrenalin which, among its other effects, causes the liver to release stored up glycogen (a form of sugar).[10] If emotional

activation is too intense, however, fear may paralyze action; "rooting" us to the spot, "freezing" us in our tracks, or making us "leaden footed." Indeed some animals are literally paralyzed by sudden, threatening stimuli. We speak, then, of "tonic immobility" or "animal hypnosis."[11] Paralysis under these conditions may actually have survival value. Many animals, although they have poor vision for certain aspect of their environment, are quick to sense the slightest movement. Thus the motionless prey is relatively safe. But we could hardly claim such an emergency value for comparable conditions in man, except in the jungle.

Although the physiological correlates of emotion may energize in the sense that physiological drives energize, they do not appear periodically, as do the conditions underlying hunger and thirst. This is because they are not dependent upon recurring physiological needs. The most obvious emotional episodes are, as we have seen, usually *acute*. They are isolated occurrences which do not depend for their arousal upon changes within the body. Rather, they are dependent upon circumstances — a feared object appears, somebody says or does something which angers us, what we observe makes us envious or jealous, the time nears for an important event and, with fear or joy, we anticipate its arrival.

In addition to acute emotional episodes contingent upon occurrences such as we have mentioned, there are also *chronic* emotional states. There may be prolonged anxiety, depression, or elation. Sometimes an emotion-provoking situation is itself prolonged; as on the battlefield, or in a home where there are continued frustrations. Quite often, however, such prolongation of emotional states has symbolic support. That is to say, one *remembers* and dwells upon past provocations, he *imagines* that his wife is unfaithful, or *anticipates* failure. This tendency of man to live in the past and to project himself into the future is attributable in great measure to his possession of words to represent the past and the future. Man fears many things which never happen. He also fears fear itself, as Thoreau suggested by saying in his *Journal*,

"Nothing is so much to be feared as fear itself."*

Emotion infiltrates many aspects of human life. It is an important aspect of frustration and conflict, to be considered in the following chapter. Some chronic emotional states, like prolonged anxiety, may be regarded as personality traits. Susceptibility to emotional provocation also differs greatly from one person to another and is an aspect of temperament. These involvements of emotion in personality are considered in Chapter 9. In the chapters on learning we shall have occasion to consider how emotional motivation contributes to this process. Our discussions of thinking, attending, and perceiving will give further emphasis to the motivating role of emotion.

Emotion in politics

The motivational function of feeling and emotion has long been recognized in politics.[12] An astute politician plays on the feelings of his audience. He does not depend too heavily upon a purely rational appeal. Rather, he capitalizes upon fears, hatreds, and hopes. Those who agree with his listeners are their friends; those who do not agree, their enemies. Quite often a crowd, and sometimes the whole community or even a nation, is so stirred emotionally that it does things which, in its "right mind," it would not do. Of course the "right" emotions may be appealed to, in which case desirable actions may result. Television audiences, when their sympathies are aroused by an emotional appeal, often contribute large sums to worthy causes. It is doubtful if a more rational appeal would have as much impact.

The pleasure principle

Many philosophers of human nature have maintained that pleasure is the ultimate goal of life, that all activities are motivated by the pursuit of pleasure and the avoidance of pain.

Freud made the *pleasure principle* a basic postulate in his theory of human motivation. According to this principle, our physiological

* This is perhaps the inspiration behind President Franklin D. Roosevelt's famous statement in 1933, following the financial collapse, that "The only thing we have to fear is fear itself."

drives (id) come, in the course of time, to be controlled by the self (ego). This has developed to act "as an intermediary between the id and the external world." The ego's activities "are governed by consideration of the tensions produced by stimuli present within or introduced into it. The raising of these tensions is in general felt as *unpleasure* and their lowering as *pleasure*. It is probable, however, that what is felt as pleasure or unpleasure is not the *absolute* degree of the tensions but something in the rhythm of their changes. The ego pursues pleasure and seeks to avoid unpleasure. An increase in unpleasure which is expected and foreseen is met by a *signal of anxiety;* the occasion of this increase, whether it threatens from without or within, is called a *danger*."[13]

Many who are not Freudians also emphasize the motivating function of pleasure and pain. We find aspects of the pleasure principle involved in theories of learning (see Chapter 11) and also in a recent theory of motivation[14] where a motive is defined as "*a strong affective association, characterized by an anticipatory goal reaction and based on past association of certain cues with pleasure or pain*."[15] This implies that when our acts produce pleasurable results, there develops a tendency to repeat these or comparable acts, the aim being to gain a repetition of the pleasure associated with them. What motivates us, under such circumstances, is *anticipation* of the results of such activities. Anticipation is of course learned. Take happiness or pleasure, for example. "When the person is experiencing it we call it an emotion, but if it or the conditions producing it give rise simultaneously to anticipations of a change in affective state (either an increase or decrease in pleasure, or increase or decrease in pain), then a motive may be said to be involved. In short, it is the anticipatory goal response or redintegrated [remembered] change in affective state which gives the motive its *directing* power as compared with an emotion which is an affective arousal *now* with no associated reference to another affective state."[16]

The deterrent function of unpleasant affective states may be given a comparable interpretation. Experiments on the startle reaction in human beings may be used to illustrate this. In these experiments, ultra-rapid movies pictured the changes in facial and postural expressions following an unexpected revolver shot. The initial reaction (see Figure 7.4) was uniform from one subject to another. It was followed, however, by reactions which differed from person to person — such reactions as blinking the eyes, turning, and moving away. In interpreting these outcomes in accordance with the theory under discussion, its author points out that the relatively slow and varied reactions which follow the initial

● **7.4**

The Startle Pattern. This expression, which is remarkably uniform from one person to another, has been photographed with cameras running from 64 to 2200 exposures per second. The stimulus was a revolver shot. "The first and most notable feature of the facial pattern is the immediate closing of the eyes. Then there is a widening of the mouth as though in a grin, although this only occasionally leads to a real baring of the teeth. The head and neck are brought forward. Sometimes, as the head comes forward and down, the chin is tilted up so that the features are still directed straight ahead despite the movement. The muscles in the neck stand out. . . . It is even possible in rare instances, to notice a twitching movement in the scalp and ears." Although certain aspects of this pattern may be absent on some occasions, the eye-blink is always present. (After Landis and Hunt)

response to a loud noise are expressions of an *avoidance motive.* They are slow and varied because they depend upon learned modifications at levels of the brain higher than those which mediate purely reflex responses. He points out, however, that certain other strong stimuli, like those which produce pain, become associated so frequently and early in life with painful consequences that they cue off motivational associations with great dependability; i.e., responses which resemble the quick and stereotyped reflex response to a loud noise.[17]

We see, therefore, that affective processes may have motivational significance. Some, like sudden noises, injuries, and foul odors, are inherently unpleasant; others, like bodily warmth, are perhaps inherently pleasant. Drive reduction is pleasant, drive frustration unpleasant. The objects, persons, and situations associated with these consequences acquire relevant affective value. We react to them positively or negatively depending upon their respective pleasant or unpleasant associations, and our anticipation of such affective outcomes. Objects, persons, and situations without affective associations arouse neutral reactions.

A knowledge of what commonly pleases people is of great practical value to advertisers and others who wish to influence our behavior. Some of the relevant research has dealt with the affective values of colors, tones, and odors.[18] Investigators have also studied various aspects of aesthetic appreciation, especially as it relates to literary, pictorial, and musical arts.[19] Even the things which commonly annoy people have been subjected to intensive study. One outcome has been the discovery that people are annoyed more frequently by what others do and say than by nonhuman objects and events.[20] ■

PHYSIOLOGICAL ASPECTS OF FEELING AND EMOTION

Some of the physiological concomitants of emotion are evident in everyday experience. Palpitation of the heart, accelerated breathing, a sinking feeling in the stomach, sweating, trembling, and many other organic phenomena are commonly reported aspects of emotion. Thousands of men in the armed services have reported organic symptoms of fear aroused in combat situations. The most commonly mentioned symptom is a pounding heart; but muscular tenseness, irritability, dryness of mouth and throat, cold sweat, and "butterflies in the stomach" are all reported with a high frequency (70 per cent or more of those reporting). There are also such delayed effects as tiredness, restlessness, depressed feeling, and jumpiness.[21] In another investigation, soldiers that had recently been in combat were given a checklist of symptoms and asked to indicate whether each symptom was experienced, whether often or only sometimes, and also its severity. A scale was then developed with nine items arranged (from least frequent to most frequent) as follows: urinating in pants, losing control of bowels, vomiting, feeling faint or weak, feeling stiff, feeling sick at the stomach, shaking or trembling all over, sinking feeling in stomach, and violent pounding of the heart. The first of these was rated most severe; the last, least severe. What is of special interest, however, is the fact that symptoms were grouped. If a man felt sick at his stomach, for instance, he usually also shook, had a sinking feeling, and experienced a pounding heart.[22]

Many organic concomitants of feeling and emotion have been investigated with such instruments as those illustrated in Figure 7.5 and discussed in the legend. Some of these are referred to in the following discussions.

☐ The so-called *lie-detector* is an adaptation of three of the devices illustrated in Figure 7.5. What it detects, actually, is physiological reactions in emotion. It contains instruments to record changes in heart action, in respiration, and in electrical conductivity of the skin — the galvanic skin reflex, or GSR. This conductivity is a function of sweat gland activity.[23] The various physiological reactions are recorded on a moving polygraph tape, as illustrated. The person taking a lie-detector test is required to answer questions, some of which are relevant and others irrelevant with respect to a crime.

It is assumed that the criminal will be more emotionally aroused by the relevant than by the irrelevant questions, hence "give himself away." The innocent person, on the other hand, will not "see the point" of the relevant questions (unless he knows the details of the crime) and he will thus react no more emotionally to them than to the irrelevant ones. The lie-detector is not foolproof, however, and its results are not readily admitted as legal evidence of guilt or innocence. Nevertheless, it has been quite useful in narrowing the field of suspects and in persuading many criminals to confess.[24] ☐

Devices like those illustrated have been used in attempts (1) to differentiate emotional from nonemotional states, (2) to discover the degree of emotional activation, and (3) to discern physiological differences between emotions like fear and anger.

Emotion versus nonemotion

In one attempt to differentiate emotional from nonemotional states in terms of their physiology, emotion-provoking stimulation was provided by collapse of a chair.[25] Eighteen college students volunteered to serve as subjects in what was ostensibly a study of heart action. One at a time, they sat in the dark with devices attached to them which recorded heart activity, respiration, and the GSR. In control sessions, the chair did not collapse. Thus records of normal functions were obtained. Then, under conditions which were otherwise similar to those already experienced, the chair suddenly fell backwards, its fall being absorbed by a door stop. All subjects reported fear and most of them yelled, called for help, or tried to escape. The subjects used in later sessions were sometimes told when the chair was going to collapse, and sometimes not. When they knew that collapse was imminent, there was no fear. Fear was thus reported only whenever the chair collapsed without warning. Physiological changes occurred under both conditions. Sometimes, as in the case of the GSR, the same responses occurred whether or not fear was present. Some other indices did, however, reveal consistent differences. The initial ac-

● **7.5**

Measuring Some Physiological Concomitants of Emotion. The polygraph is registering the onset of the stimulus and seven aspects of physiological reaction. Electroencephalograms (brain waves) are being picked up from the instrument on the subject's head. The pneumographs around her chest and abdomen provide records of thoracic and abdominal breathing. Below one knee is a sphygmomanometer, which picks up changes in pulse rate as well as blood pressure. Changes in the electrical resistance of the skin are picked up from electrodes on the hand and sent into a psychogalvanometer connected with the recording polygraph. Changes in skin temperature are also recorded. An instrument for picking up tremors in the fingers may also be used. A wire recorder is shown at the extreme right. (From the Harvard University Department of Social Relations. Photo, courtesy of *Look* Magazine.)

celeration of the heart, for example, averaged 16 per cent with fear and 10 per cent without; the average duration of the change in respiration was three minutes under the first condition and only one minute under the second.

In experiments like this the psychologist knows whether or not there is an emotion, irrespective of the physiological records. He knows because the subject tells him so, or because he can predict that the stimuli used will produce an emotional response. But suppose we should give the psychologist no other information than that provided by the physiological records alone? Could he tell whether or not an emotion had occurred? The chances are that he could not. This is because similar changes are also elicited by

mental and physical work. Thus, although one could observe that physiological changes had occurred, he could not tell whether they resulted from emotion or from work.

Observations of electroencephalograms (p. 58) offer a further approach to the physiology and neurology of emotional as compared with nonemotional states. It has been shown (Figure 7.6) that there is a marked difference between the electroencephalograms (EEG's) obtained from the same subject under conditions of apprehension and relaxation.[26] When the subject is brought in and preparations for taking EEG's are in progress, he is usually "tense, worried, and generally apprehensive about the procedure." The initial records show poorly developed rhythms.

"After a few minutes of recording, the subject usually quiets down and assumes a relaxed state, with the result that . . . the alpha waves are well developed and of considerably greater magnitude than in the initial record." It is pointed out, however, that a blocking of the rhythms similar to that associated with apprehension may be produced by "discrete sensory stimuli." Thus one could not, from these effects alone, tell whether emotional activation was responsible.

☐ Can emotional and nonemotional states be differentiated biochemically? It seems evident that they can be. The role of adrenalin in energizing fear has already been cited (p. 195) and we shall presently indicate the involvement of adrenalin (and noradrenalin) in anxiety and anger. It is also known that conditions of emotional stress produce increased

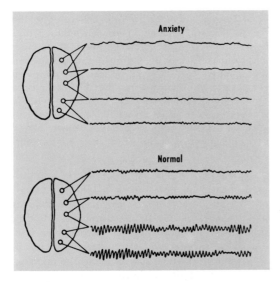

● 7.6

EEG's of Normal and Anxious Subjects. Only a portion of each record is shown. The separate waves are picked up from different areas of the brain. Normal and anxious states are not always so clearly differentiated as in this instance; but the effect of anxiety, if apparent, is to flatten the waves as illustrated. (From D. B. Lindsley, "Emotion," in S. S. Stevens, Ed., *Handbook of Experimental Psychology*, Wiley, 1951, p. 499.)

secretion of ACTH and cortisone (pp. 169–170).

Recent research has focused on the white blood cells (leucocytes), one type of which tends to change in number immediately following the individual's involvement in a stress-provoking situation.[27] These (granular) leucocytes, which stain with the red dye eosin, normally make up from 2 to 3 per cent of the circulating leucocytes. A marked reduction in the eosinophil count is known as *eosinopenia*; a marked increase, as *eosinophilia*. Students of emotional behavior became interested in the circulating eosinophils after it was discovered that administration of ACTH or cortisone is followed immediately by eosinopenia. It has subsequently been demonstrated that paratroopers in training have a lower than normal eosinophil count after their first jump. A low count is found even in those who refuse to jump.[28] Eosinopenia has also been found immediately following experimentally contrived conditions like being on a plane that is ostensibly about to be ditched, making an electrical wiring "mistake" that causes TNT to explode and "seriously injure personnel," and apparent subjection to dangerous fallout from an "accident" with radioactive material.[29]

Since excessive physical exercise also produces a change in the eosinophil count, a question naturally arises as to whether the eosinophils can be used to differentiate emotional from nonemotional states. However, a recent investigation involving exercise to near-exhaustion has shown that the initial reaction is eosinophilia, with eosinopenia following from two to four hours later. This leads to the conclusion that the emotion-provoked condition is immediate, while that produced by exercise is delayed.[30]

Another widely used biochemical test of emotional activation involves measurement of the hourly secretion of steroids in the urine. This represents "an accumulation of waste products of adrenal cortical metabolism, widely regarded as indicating the extent of mobilization of body resources to cope with all forms of stress."[31]

It is clear that all of the biochemical indicators used in efforts to differentiate emotional from nonemotional states are directly or indirectly related to the functions of three glands — the adrenal medulla, the adrenal cortex, and the anterior pituitary. These are sources of, respectively, adrenalin and noradrenalin, cortisone, and ACTH. □

Intensity of emotional activation

We all know that our emotional experiences differ in intensity. A situation may be mildly annoying or it may produce paroxyms of anger or rage. We may be mildly fearful or literally paralyzed with fear. And so it is with the other emotions. These facts are revealed by our own introspections. They are also evident from verbal reports given to us by others. But it is impossible to quantify such reports. If one wishes to compare individuals in terms of their degree of emotionality in particular situations, or to compare situations for their emotion-provoking effectiveness, a quantitative measure of emotional response is required. One possibility, of course, is a biochemical index like those described, but this tells us nothing about the intensity of the person's experience, of how strongly he feels the emotion. The best approach to date is a rating scale which individuals check. One such scale, developed in U.S. Army research on leadership, is reproduced in Table 7.1. This so-called *Subjective Stress* (or *SS*) *Scale* consists of items arranged in order of intensity; each item is given a scale value determined by experimental procedures similar to those involved in development of attitude scales.

After being subjected to an emotion-provoking situation, the individual indicates the intensity of his feeling by placing a check against the item which best describes how he feels. His reaction is scored accordingly. The mean stressfulness of a standardized situation may be gauged by the mean SS score obtained from the individuals subjected to it. We mentioned earlier a situation in which soldiers thought that their plane had to be ditched. The mean SS score for this situation was 60. Another situation already referred to was one in which a soldier's "mistake" in connecting some wires produced an explosion of TNT,

■ **TABLE 7.1   The Subjective Stress Scale**

Item	Scale value or score
Wonderful	00
Fine	09
Comfortable	17
Steady	27
Didn't bother me	40
Indifferent	48
Timid	57
Unsteady	64
Nervous	69
Worried	74
Unsafe	76
Frightened	83
Terrible	87
In agony	92
Scared stiff	94

The subject is given this scale with the words in scrambled order and without intensity designations. He merely picks the word or phrase which best represents how he feels (or felt) during an emotion-provoking experience. The scale was originally developed by R. Kerle. (From M. M. Berkun, H. M. Bialek, R. P. Kern, and K. Yagi, "Experimental Studies of Psychological Stress in Man," *Psychol. Monogr.*, 1962, 76, No. 15, p. 4.)

with ostensible injury to another soldier. The SS score for this situation was 75, the highest obtained for several situations involved in the research. It was thus rated the most stressful of all.[32]

The intensity of stimulation — such as the severity of an electric shock — may also be used to gauge the degree of arousal, since the more intense the shock the more unpleasant it is rated; but this is an artificial procedure as compared with those already cited.

The magnitude of the galvanic skin reflex has been shown to increase with the reported pleasantness (as well as unpleasantness) of experience.[33] Those stimuli which the individual rates as pleasant (or unpleasant) usually arouse a more pronounced GSR than those rated as neutral in affective value.[34] Moreover, a high intensity of emotion, as indicated by verbal reports, is associated with a more marked GSR than is a weak intensity of emotion.[35]

Differentiating emotions

Do the physiological concomitants of different emotions, like fear and anger, also differ in any measurable way? There is some evidence suggesting the possibility of certain physiological differences, but these are not, as yet, clearly established.

Differences in stomach activity associated with fear, on the one hand, and with anger or resentment, on the other, were observed in a clinical case.[36] This subject and one of the doctors who carried out the investigation described here are shown in Figure 7.7; a record of stomach contractions in serenity and anger is also shown. The subject's esophagus had been closed off following an accidental injury and it was thus necessary for him to take food through an opening in his stomach. This

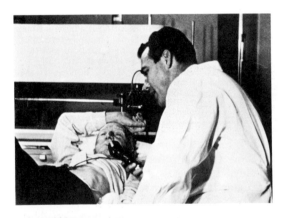

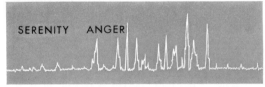

SERENITY　ANGER

● 7.7

The Stomach and Emotion. As described in the text, the wall and contents of this man's stomach became accessible to direct observation. The curve below shows changes in muscular activity of the stomach when something was said which made the subject angry. (From Sturgis Grant Productions, Inc.; courtesy, Smith, Kline & French Labs. and Cornell University.)

made it possible to observe circulatory changes in the stomach and also to collect samples of its contents. Under a fear-producing condition, a "decided pallor" occurred in the subject's gastric mucosa, and there was also "a fall in the rate of acid production." When he was subjected to reproof which produced hostile reactions or resentment, the subject's stomach "became red and engorged and soon the folds were thick and turgid. Acid production accelerated sharply and vigorous contractions began." Although this is an unusual case, it suggests the possibility of a difference in stomach reactions associated with different emotions.

In another attempt to differentiate emotions physiologically, the subjects were connected to a wide variety of instruments like those already illustrated in Figure 7.5 (p. 199).[37] Fear was produced by electric shocks and by certain activities of the experimenter which were calculated to produce alarm. Anger was provoked by derogatory comments made at the subjects' expense.

Under fear-provoking circumstances the pulse rate was higher and there was more sweating than under conditions which produced anger. There were also certain differences in blood pressure, the details of which need not concern us here.

A laboratory experiment in which medical students were subjected to intense frustration yielded results which enabled the investigators to differentiate between anger directed toward the experimenter or situation, anger directed toward the self, and anxiety. Most of the data came from two stress-inducing situations. In one of these the subject was given various mental problems to do. The problems became progressively more difficult and as the subject began to miss the correct answers, he was the target of sarcastic remarks. The other stress-inducing situation involved a sonic-confuser. This is an instrument with earphones through which the person, while talking, heard his voice with a slight time delay. The delayed feedback was extremely frustrating and, among other things, produced marked stammering. Under these conditions the subject was given a story to read. He was then asked to read faster and at the same time to maintain accuracy. Whenever reading became slower, a slight electric shock was administered to indicate that the subject must speed up.

Before, during, and after the above forms of stress the investigators took tracings of heart activity and also the pulse rate and blood pressure. After a session was completed, the subject was interviewed to obtain his verbal reactions. It was from these that the *anger out*, *anger in*, and *anxiety* designations were derived. Most of the verbal reactions could be placed in one or another of these categories. Subsequent analysis of physiological data lent support to the view that experimental reports were correlated with physiological differences. Typical records are reproduced in Figure 7.8.

From the physiological reactions and the known effects of adrenalin and noradrenalin (p. 195), it was possible to infer that *anger out* (with a low intensity of physiological response) is associated with the presence of noradrenalin in excessive amounts, and that *anger in* and *anxiety* (with a high intensity of physiological response) are associated with the presence of excessive amounts of adrenalin. The few subjects who reported no anger had physiological reactions of low intensity like the anger-out group. Evidence from animal experiments is cited which suggests that noradrenalin is the resting secretion of the adrenal medulla and that adrenalin is secreted only when an emergency reaction is elicited. It appears, therefore, that the subjects who were angry at the external situation did not react in an emergency manner whereas those who became angry with themselves, and those who became anxious, did react as if they were in an emergency.[38]

In the above experiments, as in efforts to differentiate emotion from nonemotion, the physiological records alone did not tell the whole story. These had to be interpreted in terms of the situations which produced them and also the verbal reports of the subjects.

Injection of a sufficient amount of adrenalin produces such physiological aspects of strong emotion as trembling and accelerated heart action, yet without arousing any one

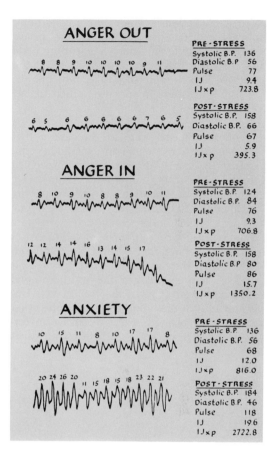

● **7.8**

Differentiation of Anxiety and Two Directions of Anger. These are ballistocardiograph tracings typical of those which differentiate anger directed outward, anger directed inward, and anxiety. The ballistocardiograph records heart activity indirectly, through movements of the body while the subject is delicately balanced on a stabilimeter-like table. The propulsive flow of the blood produces the recorded movements. The systolic and diastolic blood-pressure readings were taken with a sphygmomanometer (see Figure 7.5). IJ refers to the mean height of a tracing (observe the numbers next to the tracings). P refers to the pulse. Note especially, the higher systolic blood pressure associated with post-stress conditions. This indicator was highest (184) for anxiety. (From D. H. Funkenstein, S. H. King, and M. E. Drolette, *Mastery of Stress,* Harvard University Press, 1957, p. 40.)

particular emotion.[39] Under these conditions, however, one emotion or another may be experienced by different people, depending upon how internal processes and external events are perceived and interpreted. Take, for example, the following study, represented schematically in Figure 7.9.

☐ College students were led to believe that they were participating in an experiment concerning the effects on vision of an unspecified substance (in reality, adrenalin). Some were given correct information on general physiological effects to be expected, such as trembling and accelerated heart action. Others were given incorrect information, being led to expect numbness, itching, and possibly a slight headache. After the injection, each student was asked to join another in the waiting room, where both were to await the visual tests. Unbeknown to the real subject, however, the other student was "planted" there to engage in certain well-rehearsed antics, like throwing paper airplanes and doing a hula dance with a piece of equipment in the room. The room was under observation through a one-way-vision screen.

In this situation, subjects with the same adrenalin-produced changes going on within them reacted differently, depending upon what they had been told. Those with correct information were experiencing a faster than normal heart beat, trembling, and so on, as expected, and they were not amused at what was going on. But those with incorrect information, even though they were also experiencing the faster heart beat and the other physiological effects of adrenalin, reacted quite differently. They tended to develop a happy mood and to join in the tomfoolery. In another experiment the "plant" acted aggressively and angrily toward the subject. This did not greatly disturb the informed subjects. There were no misinformed subjects in this experiment; but a placebo group (given an ineffective injection of salt water) and an ignorant group

● **7.9**

An Experiment with Adrenalin. As described in the text, similar adrenalin-aroused physiological reactions led to different emotional effects, depending upon expectations and situational factors. The visceral reactions referred to are those of the internal organs. (From G. Mandler, "Emotion," in Roger Brown et al., *New Directions in Psychology*, Holt, Rinehart and Winston, 1962, p. 287.)

(given no information about what to expect from the injection) were used. These were irritated by the other student's actions, the placebo group somewhat more so than the ignorant group. The reactions described were indicated by responses to a questionnaire given after the waiting-room session. Finally the subjects were told that this was not an experiment on vision after all, and its real nature was explained to them before they departed.[40] □

It remains to be seen whether physiological (including biochemical) aspects of emotion will come to have diagnostic value in themselves. At present, verbal reports, overt behavior, and information about the stimulating circumstances tell us more about different emotions than the physiological and biochemical concomitants tell us. ■

EMOTION AS A FUNCTION OF THE WHOLE ORGANISM

The emotionally aroused organism is aroused all over. There is an overall interaction of receptors, muscles, internal organs, and nervous mechanisms, with resulting changes in blood chemistry, in brain waves, and in the physiological reactions already considered.

It had long been held that one has an emotional experience and that this in turn produces the bodily changes associated with it. The James-Lange theory of emotion[41] claimed that exactly the reverse is true. It argued that one first has the bodily changes and that emotional experience is *the feeling of these changes* as they occur. This theory was followed by another (the Bard-Cannon theory) which claimed that *both* the experiences *and* bodily changes are set off simultaneously through activation of the *hypothalamus* (p. 51).[42] These theories stimulated research on various aspects of emotion, and although this research has not yet settled all of the issues involved, it has greatly extended our knowledge of underlying physiological mechanisms, some of which are represented in Figure 7.10.

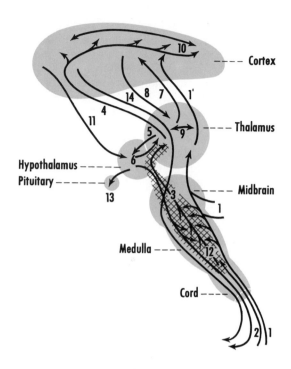

● 7.10

Schematic Representation of Principal Central Nervous Structures and Probable Pathways Involved in Emotional Behavior. This diagram does not include the septal region, or the amygdala, both of which would have to be pictured as in the vicinity of the hypothalamus and interconnected with it. However, the following parts are indicated by numbers: (1) somatic and cranial afferent neurons, (2) visceral afferent pathways, (3) projections of the reticular formation, (4) diffuse cortical projections originating in the thalamus, (5) and (6) interconnections between hypothalamus and thalamus, (7) and (8) interconnections between thalamus and cortex, (9) connections between different regions within the thalamus, (10) connections between regions of the cerebral cortex, (11) pathways from cortex to hypothalamus, (12) visceral efferent pathways, (13) connections between hypothalamus and pituitary gland, (14) pathways from cortex to spinal cord. The cross-hatched area is the reticular formation. (From D. B. Lindsley, "Emotion," in S. S. Stevens, Ed., *Handbook of Experimental Psychology,* Wiley, 1951, p. 507.)

The receptors

First of all, consider the receptors. External receptors in the eyes, in the ears, and in our skin are necessarily involved in making us aware of our surroundings. Any emotion-provoking situation first activates such receptors. Receptors in our muscles are activated whenever we move. Thus running, struggling, trembling, and other overt responses associated with emotion activate these receptors. There are also receptors in our internal organs. In the abdominal region are organs known as the *viscera.* These include the stomach and intestines. The feeling of "butterflies in the stomach," of nausea, and so forth, depend upon impulses originating in the receptors of such visceral structures. How visceral impulses enter the spinal cord was illustrated in Plate 6.

The limbic system and the cerebral cortex

Impulses from all receptors travel into the central nervous system. Some enter the spinal cord and ascend it until they reach the brain stem and higher structures. Others enter the brain stem directly. Before they get to upper levels of the cerebrum, however, impulses must pass through the thalamus. Some, as we have seen in earlier discussions (pp. 160–161), enter the reticular formation; through it they have an activating effect on the cerebral cortex. Other impulses enter such limbic structures as the hypothalamus, septal region, and amygdala (see Figure 6.5, p. 161). We have already (pp. 160–163) referred to the so-called *pleasure* and *pain* regions of the limbic system, revealed by self-stimulation studies involving implanted electrodes. These regions no doubt play a part in emotion, but the involvement of the hypothalamus and amygdala has been highlighted in recent research.

• *The hypothalamus.* It was first suspected that the hypothalamus was relevant to emotion when neurologists observed that injuring it, accidentally in human beings and experimentally in animals, was followed by loss of emotionality — or what is usually called *apathy.*

Impulses from the receptors pass through or close to the hypothalamus on their way to the cerebral cortex. This is true of impulses from the muscles and viscera as well as those from external sense organs. Impulses also come into the hypothalamus from the cerebral cortex above. These may be initiated when, for example, we have some emotion-provoking memory or thought. The hypothalamus sends impulses to the viscera and muscles. These are motor impulses. They therefore activate the structures with which they connect. The adrenal gland, for example, is stimulated to secrete adrenalin. Receptors in many of the reacting structures are stimulated in turn, and sensory impulses are fed back into the brain.

We have seen that one theory gives a key position to the hypothalamus. It assumes that when stimuli are emotion-provoking, the hypothalamus is activated by the incoming impulses. This in turn relays such impulses to the cerebral cortex. These, according to the theory, arouse feelings. Simultaneously the hypothalamus sends impulses to our viscera (giving us, for example, "butterflies" or nausea) and to our skeletal muscles (making us do such things as tremble, run, or go through facial expressions of emotion).

Nobody has yet shown that the hypothalamus activates full emotional experience or behavior.[43] There is, however, clear evidence that it contains a group of nerve cells which activate overt expressions resembling those which occur in emotion. When these cells are electrically stimulated in a cat, for example, the animal retracts its ears, crouches, growls, raises its back, lashes its tail, and shows other reactions resembling those which occur in emotion. One investigator has found such reactions "stereotyped" and "stimulus-bound," and therefore suggestive more of reflexes than of true emotional behavior. He thus designates them as "pseudo-affective," or "sham emotions."[44] Another investigator finds reactions which do resemble true emotion. His subjects, one of which is shown in Figure 7.11, exhibited expressions of rage, and also attacked him.[45]

• *The amygdala.* Numerous investigations involving electrical stimulation of the amygdala have shown that this structure (illustrated in Figure 6.5, p. 161) plays an important part in

• 7.11
Electrically Stimulated Emotional Expression.
Note the permanently implanted electrodes in
the head. The cat not only exhibited expressions
simulating rage, but it also attacked the investigator. This sort of reaction occurred only
when the electrodes entered a restricted region
of the hypothalamus. (Courtesy, Dr. W. R. Hess,
Hypothalmus und Thalmus, Georg Thieme Verlag,
Stuttgart, 1956.)

such emotions as anger, rage, and the resulting
aggressiveness. Stimulation of the amygdala
has sometimes elicited rage and has sometimes had a calming effect upon an enraged
animal. However, "oppositely acting structures
lie side by side or intermingled in the amygdala" and electrodes separated by only a millimeter or two have produced different effects.[46]
Research is also complicated by the fact that
different intensities of electrical stimulation
vary in their effectiveness. Another complication comes from the wide interconnections of
the amygdala with other limbic structures, including the hypothalamus and the septal
nuclei. These complexities notwithstanding,
it now appears that the amygdala "modulates
the emotional activity of the hypothalamus."[47]
Another way of saying this is that the amygdala
acts "as a 'funnel' through which inhibitory
impulses originating in the transitional cortex
and the neocortex [the old brain and the new
brain] exert an inhibitory influence on the
posterior hypothalamus, which subserves the
rage response."[48]

□ Electrodes were placed in the hypothalamus
and amygdala of ten cats which did not
normally attack rats placed in their cages. The
hypothalamic electrodes were "aimed at a region known to produce directed attack." That
they were effectively placed is evidenced by
the fact that nine of these animals "savagely
attacked" rats placed in their cages as soon as
the current was turned on. When it was
turned off, attack ceased. Normally, the
stimulation was terminated as soon as "the
attacking cat touched the rat with tooth or
claw." When stimulation was prolonged beyond this point, the rat was often killed
before it ceased. The other electrode was
aimed at the amygdala and subsequent histo-
logical examination of brain sections showed
that, in five cats, it was located in the lateral
nucleus. In these animals, simultaneous stimulation of the hypothalamus and the amygdala
suppressed such rage-like and aggressive behavior as stimulation of the hypothalamus alone
produced. Sometimes it delayed such behavior; at other times it eliminated it. In three
of the other cats aroused by hypothalamic
stimulation, the electrodes were subsequently
found to be outside of the amygdala. The remaining cat died before completion of the
experiment.[49] □

• *The cerebral cortex.* While the limbic system is part of the old brain, once believed to
have significance only for smell, it is intricately interconnected with structures of the
new brain, particularly the cerebral cortex.
Indeed, the cerebral cortex may be more important for emotion, at times, than the hypothalamus, the amygdala, and other related
limbic structures. In this connection consider
these facts. Naturally-aroused emotional behavior is not turned on or off like the reactions
produced by electrical stimulation. The organism shows persistent motivated behavior. It
does something about the situation in which
it finds itself. A human being, for example,
may do any of a number of things when emotionally aroused — he may swear, plead, pray,
hide, run away, attack, or bluff his way out of
a situation. Even after the emergency has
ended, he may continue to be emotionally
aroused. He may have prolonged anxiety, he
may brood, and, if he suspects that certain

persons are responsible for his predicament, he may plan a campaign of retaliation. These are higher-level activities, neurologically speaking, and they show that the cerebral cortex plays a very important role in human emotion over and beyond that played by the limbic system.

The autonomic nervous system

Physiological changes in emotion — sweating, more rapid heart beat, and so on — are controlled through the *autonomic nervous system*. This is so whether the initiating impulses come from the cerebral cortex, the hypothalamus, or other structures of the brain stem. Those initiated at the cortical level, as when we think of something that makes us angry or afraid, are transmitted to the hypothalamus and through it to the autonomic nervous system.

The autonomic system has a purely motor function. As we observed in Chapter 2, there are two main branches, the *sympathetic* and the *parasympathetic*. These systems work in opposition. If one activates (accelerates) an organ the other checks (inhibits) it. Although both branches are involved in emotion, the sympathetic plays the predominant role. It accelerates the functions of some organs and inhibits the functions of others. For example, the sympathetic connection with the heart accelerates its activity; the parasympathetic connection checks it. The activities of the stomach, on the other hand, are checked by the sympathetic system and accelerated by the parasympathetic. Secretions of the adrenal gland are accelerated by the sympathetic and are under no known parasympathetic control. An emotionally aroused individual's heart pounds, his stomach contractions and gastric secretions are checked, and his secretion of adrenalin is accelerated — all because his sympathetic nervous system has assumed control.

With this survey of the various mechanisms involved in emotional activation, we can perhaps appreciate why emotion is as complex as it is. We can perhaps also appreciate why it is difficult to differentiate between emotional and nonemotional states, why one emotion cannot be distinguished from another in terms of physiological changes alone, and why psychologists do not as yet have a satisfactory theory relating bodily changes and affective experiences.

The mechanisms involved in emotion are functioning continually and the change from nonemotional to emotional states is often represented, physiologically, by no more than a shift in relative levels of activation. This fact is well illustrated by the following quotation, which begins with reference to a sleeping man:

☐ "His cerebral cortex is relatively inactive, showing only slight bursts of electrical activity on an electroencephalograph. The muscles are relaxed and send few return impulses to the central nervous system. The sympathetic or emergency division of the autonomic nervous system is inactive. . . . Now let the alarm clock ring. . . . Gross muscular responses occur and feed impulses back into the central nervous system. There is also autonomic discharge and some secretion of adrenalin, a 'stimulant.' The resulting changes in smooth muscle also feed back impulses. . . . A very important terminus is the hypothalamus, which amplifies these return impulses and activates the cortex. The electroencephalograph shows that the cerebral cortex is functioning at a higher level. [A] state of alert attention [exists] in which there is excellent discrimination among stimuli and appropriate responses. . . . But the level of activation is still far from its upper limit. Suppose that someone has taken a book our subject needs in his work. He becomes a bit angry, i.e., the level of muscular activity goes higher, there is more autonomic activity, and his hypothalamus feeds more impulses into the cortex. [Upon further provocation] he may go into a strong rage. Here the activation is very high, with resulting violent behavior. But the behavior is no longer nicely adjusted to stimuli; it is 'blind' and uncoordinated. The increased feedback and chemical changes have so stimulated the hypothalamus that it largely breaks loose from cortical control. He responds almost as if he had no cerebral cortex, no previous learning about office routine or polite behavior."[50] ∎

EMOTIONAL DEVELOPMENT

Although it is possible to recognize various emotions in older children and adults, these emotions are not evident at birth. Initially, as far as one can tell, there is merely excitement. Emotions develop gradually. It will soon become apparent that certain aspects of this emotional development depend upon the maturation of neuromuscular mechanisms. Other aspects are clearly learned.

Much of an infant's emotional activation is related to physiological needs, like the need for nourishment, to avoid injury, to keep warm, and to be active. Indeed, the infant's emotional reactions signal the presence of such needs. When its needs are satisfied, it is quiescent.

As discernable emotions appear, these supplement the motivation already present. The newly emerged emotional expressions are used to control others. Some emotions, like fear, anger, and affection, motivate the individual himself.

An early investigation of emotional behavior in infants suggested that three emotions are present at birth; namely, *fear, rage,* and *love*.[51] More recent investigations, however, have failed to verify this suggestion. They have shown that,

☐ "any form of sudden stimulation such as dropping, loud noises, restraint, pain, or a rush of air on the face, produces in the young infant aimless activity of most of the musculature, accompanied by crying. The stimuli must be sufficiently strong, however, to produce a reaction. When an infant below four or five days of age is dropped one or two feet, it frequently shows no perceptible response, except for vague movements of the arms and legs. The younger the infant the stronger must be the stimulus. This is also true for so-called 'pleasurable' stimuli, such as stroking or petting, to which many newborn infants show no reaction."[52] ☐

One investigator found only "mass activity."[53] Another found that any of four stimulating conditions produced "any and all responses."[54] Still another found only "excitement."[55]

The original investigators were apparently labeling the behavior fear, rage, and love in terms of how *they* would react if stimulated as the babies were stimulated. Knowing that sudden loss of support would produce fear in themselves, they designated as fear the behavior elicited by loss of support. Moreover, they failed to observe or take into consideration such differences in reaction as were apparent to later observers.

☐ Psychologists must always be on guard against "reading into" behavior something that is not there. In an experiment to determine how much graduate students in psychology, nurses, and medical students agree concerning emotional reactions of newborn infants, it was found that significant agreement was present only when the stimulating circumstances were known to the observers, and they were thus able to "read" their own reactions into the situation.

In the experiment here referred to, the emotional reactions elicited by hunger, dropping, a loud noise, a pin-prick, and several other stimuli were presented in some instances on a motion-picture screen and in other instances directly, by having the judges look at the baby after a screen had been removed. In the first series of observations, the stimulating circumstances were not known to the observers. Here there was little or no agreement concerning the emotion exhibited. For example, forty-two medical students who observed the reactions to dropping directly, but without knowing that the baby had been dropped, gave eight different designations, with *awakened* (11), *colic* (11), and *anger* (7) the most frequent. Only two said that the behavior was *fear*. Thirty-two graduate students in psychology who saw films of reactions aroused by dropping, but did not know that dropping had occurred, also gave widely scattered designations. The most frequent in this instance were *anger* (14), *hunger* (6), and *fear* (5). There was similar lack of agreement concerning behavior aroused by other stimuli. It is apparent that an individual is not likely to label the behavior as others label it when he does not know the stimulus which

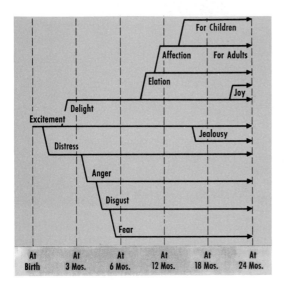

the investigator could discern only *general excitement*. But in the three-month-old child *distress* and *delight*, as well as general excitement, could be distinguished. Within the next three months, distress was differentiated so that *fear*, *disgust*, and *anger* were also apparent. At about twelve months, delight had differentiated so that *elation* and *affection* were added to the repertoire of emotions. *Jealousy* and *affection for children*, distinguished from *affection for adults*, appeared between the twelfth and eighteenth months. Between the eighteenth and twenty-fourth months, delight was differentiated so that *joy* was also evident.

We should not, of course, accept as gospel the particular labels and age levels indicated in the diagram. We should look upon it rather as one psychologist's attempt to represent emotional development in children. The above discussion of early investigations of infant emotion should warn us that even an experienced psychologist may "read into" the behavior of infants more than is actually present, and that different observers may assign different labels to the same reactions. The classification is presented here merely to illustrate the fact that one who perceives only general excitement in the newborn discerns an increasing variety of emotions as the child grows.

The possibility of differentiating between emotions at advancing age levels is further illustrated in Figure 7.13. Nobody would judge the baby at the left to be happy, but what emotion is he expressing? Without a knowledge of the cause, one cannot say. The two-year-old at the right exhibits a clearer pattern of emotion. Anger, resentment, or disappointment appears to be present.

Maturation and learning in emotional development

Both maturation and learning play important roles in emotional development. In some instances it is possible to recognize their respective influences, but in others they are inextricably related.

• *Maturation.* As the infant grows, even when no opportunity has been presented for learning them, such emotional responses as

• 7.12
Approximate Ages of Differentiation of Emotions in Early Childhood. (Adapted by Dashiell from K. M. B. Bridges, "A Genetic Theory of Emotions," *J. Genet. Psychol.*, 1930, 37, 514–527.)

caused it. When the same graduate and medical students saw the stimulus as well as the behavior, they were in much closer agreement than when they witnessed the behavior alone. For example, 27 out of 41 said that dropping produced fear and 24 out of 39 that restraint produced rage.[56] ☐

Growth of emotional behavior in children

Although the newborn child shows only general excitement when stimulated by situations which arouse emotion in older children and adults, other emotional reactions are soon apparent. Psychologists do not agree on the labels to be attached to manifestations of emotion at particular age levels, but they agree that, as the child grows older, an increasing number of emotions become apparent.

The diagram shown in Figure 7.12 illustrates one of the several classifications of emotional behavior in early childhood. It is based upon observations of a large number of babies in a foundling home, who ranged in age from newborn to two years.[57] In newborn infants,

Differentiation of Emotion at Different Age Levels. One might have difficulty in judging the emotion expressed by the baby at the left, but the older child almost certainly is expressing anger, resentment, or disappointment. (Photos by Roy Goin and Spenser, from Black Star)

crying, weeping (crying with tears), smiling, and laughing begin to appear. These emotional reactions appear at about the same age in all children, regardless of variations in stimulation provided by adults. They also occur where all opportunities to witness them in others have been removed.

Further evidence that maturation plays a large role in emotional development comes from observations of facial expressions in the deaf-blind (Figure 7.14). Those born both deaf and blind would have very little, if any, opportunity to acquire emotional behavior by imitating others. They certainly could not hear the sound of laughter and observe how it is produced, they could not see individuals clench their fists in rage, and they could not see the various facial expressions of emotion. The only way in which such expressions could have become known to them would have been through touch. But even when they have been given no tactual training, they exhibit emotional reactions which have much in common with those of normal people. Take, for example, these observations of emotional behavior in a ten-year-old-girl who was blind and deaf from

● 7.14
Emotional Expression in a Deaf-Blind Child. The facial and vocal expressions of emotion in the deaf-blind have much in common with those of hearing and seeing children. This is true even when a child has been both deaf and blind since birth, thus prevented from ever hearing or seeing the expressions of others. (Photo, courtesy of Perkins Institution for the Blind)

birth, who had not been able to learn to speak or to care for herself, and who had received no training in emotional expression.

□ "A small doll was dropped down the child's dress, whereupon neck and shoulders tensed and the mouth half-opened. The sightless eyes opened to the fullest extent and the eyebrows were raised. The left hand at once began to grope for the toy. But the posture and the facial expression were suggestive of what we should ordinarily interpret as startled attention. After several minutes of unsuccesful efforts to get the doll, which caught in the folds of her dress, she did not cry, but made slight whimpering sounds. . . . Suddenly, as if struck by a new idea, she renewed the attack, this time from a different angle. Her behavior took on the appearance of a struggle, determined in part by exasperation and mild rage. Her body writhed and twisted; the right hand impatiently beat the arm of the chair. . . . At the instant of success in extricating the doll, she threw herself back into the chair with feet drawn up under her. Both the hand containing the doll and the empty hand were raised in an attitude of delight, which was

● **7.15**
Many Fears Are Learned. Children do not fear mice, rats, and other animals unless they are negatively conditioned to them. (Esther Bubley)

further attested by peals of laughter. . . . The exultant laughter faded to a smile of pleased satisfaction."[58] □

• *Learning.* The role of learning in emotional development is clearly evident when we consider the stereotyped gestural and facial expressions which are not common to all men, but which characterize a particular culture. An interesting comparison is provided by our own and Chinese expressions of the same emotions, or what are presumed to be the same emotions. Some emotional expressions are similar in us and in the Chinese, but others are very different. Surprise in us is made evident by raising the eyebrows and opening the eyes wide, but the Chinese usually express surprise by sticking out their tongues. Scratching ears and cheeks is a sign of embarrassment in us, but to the Chinese it means happiness. Clapping the hands is a sign of happiness in us, but of worry or disappointment in the Chinese.[59] These emotional expressions are superimposed upon inborn expressions like those of the deaf-blind child. They are acquired by observing similar expressions in others.

The role of learning is also evident when we consider how particular emotions are aroused by different objects and situations as we get older. Infants are usually not afraid of snakes, white rats, or mice (Figure 7.15). Fear of snakes, for example, usually begins to develop at about two or three years of age.[60] Maturation, in the sense of giving the older child a keener perception of the peculiarity of the snake's movements, may be involved. But fear of snakes as particular objects comes from hearing stories about snakes, observing how older children and adults react to snakes, and perhaps by transfer to snakes of a fear of the strange or the unusual, acquired in other circumstances. Some older children and adults never develop a fear of snakes, of white rats, of mice, or of other animals and objects which arouse fear in others.

Studies of children's fears and those of their parents have shown that if the parent is afraid of the dark, of lightning, of snakes, or of particular individuals, the child will be very likely to have the same fears.[61]

A classical experimental study of the acquisition of fear in a child is the case of Albert.

☐ Albert, a normal child of nine months, exhibited fear reactions to a loud noise unexpectedly presented, but had no fear of white rats. Fear of rats was acquired under the following circumstances: When the rat was first placed before him, Albert reached for it, showing no signs of fear. Just then a loud noise was made behind his head by striking an iron bar. Albert started and fell forward on his face. . . . The rat and the noise were again presented, the noise just after the rat. This time Albert responded as before except that a whimper was added. After five further presentations of the rat and noise, separated from the other two trials by a week, Albert was afraid of the rat alone. Not only this, but he was now afraid of objects closely resembling the rat in certain respects. For example, the same fear reactions (Figure 7.16) was aroused by a rabbit and a white beard. Wooden blocks and other objects bearing no similarity to the rat did not produce the response. The fear reaction to a rat, rabbit, dog, coat, and cotton was evident a month later, but it had decreased in intensity.[62] ☐

It is evident that, by associating some stimulus which produces emotion with a stimulus which does not produce it, we may give emotion-provoking potency to the previously neutral stimulus and to stimuli similar to it. The technique here is that of conditioning, discussed more fully in Chapter 10.

When a newborn infant is emotionally aroused, he can do little more than cry and thrash his limbs about. As he grows older, however, his emotional behavior shows a much wider range, some of it attributable to maturation and some to learning. Thus, the emotionally aroused one-year-old can stiffen his body, hold out his arms, throw things, call out, and cling to an object or person, as well as cry and thrash his limbs about. As he gets older, language responses play an increasing role in his emotional behavior. He makes demands, scolds, pleads, swears, talks about others, and makes his feelings known in many other ways.[63] Most of these acquisitions are not emotional

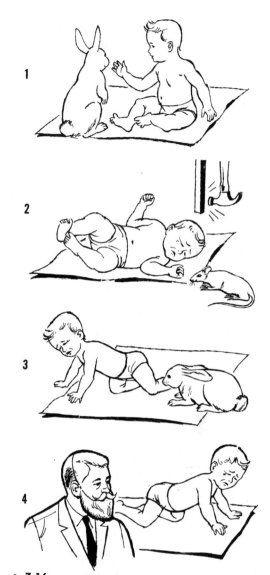

● **7.16**
Conditioning Fear in an Infant. Before conditioning (1), the child makes positive (approach) reactions to the rabbit. A loud noise produces startle and apparently fear (2). Paired association of a white rat and noise produces an avoidance response not only to the rat but also to the rabbit (3). Finally, furry objects of various kinds, which were ineffective earlier, also elicit avoidance reactions (4). (After Watson, from G. G. Thompson, *Child Psychology*, 2nd ed., Houghton Mifflin, 1962, p. 165.)

in themselves. They are utilized in emotional situations as well as nonemotional ones.

Other acquisitions give the child a greater ability to cope with his environment, thus reducing frustration and other emotion-provoking situations. He learns to help himself by getting out of bed alone, to satisfy his hunger by going to the pantry shelf, and to protect himself by fighting the neighborhood bully. ■

SITUATIONAL ASPECTS OF EMOTIONAL DEVELOPMENT

At birth, relatively few situations arouse emotional behavior, or the generalized excitement we can observe to be present. Such stimuli as a loud noise, a sudden loss of support, and stroking of the erogenous zones are often emotion-provoking to the newborn, but they do not, as we have seen, arouse differentiable reaction patterns. Marked restriction of activity, as by holding the head between the hands, is also prone to arouse excited behavior.

Emotional reactions are frequently elicited by hunger, colic, having the nose cleaned, and other bodily discomforts. Crying is the most specific response to such discomforts, but it is usually accompanied by thrashing about of legs and arms. Any abrupt change in the situation, such as the turning on of a light, a sudden noise, or the appearance of a person, will usually produce a startle reaction.

During early development, maturation and learning give potency to many stimuli which failed to elicit emotional reactions at birth. Following the conditioning principles already mentioned, fears of particular objects, persons, and situations are likely to develop. Grotesque masks do not frighten an infant in its first months, but they do frighten an older infant, until he becomes accustomed to them.[64] Scolding and frowning at a baby of three months is likely to elicit laughter, if anything at all, but frowning at or scolding a child of six or seven months is more than likely to arouse behavior suggesting anxiety or astonishment.[65] ■

● 7.17

Per Cent of Children in Each Group That Were Fearful in Four Emotion-Producing Situations.
(Drawn from data in A. T. Jersild, F. V. Markey, and C. L. Jersild, "Children's Fears, Dreams, Wishes, Daydreams, Dislikes, Pleasant and Unpleasant Memories," *Child Develpm. Monogr.*, 1933, No. 12.

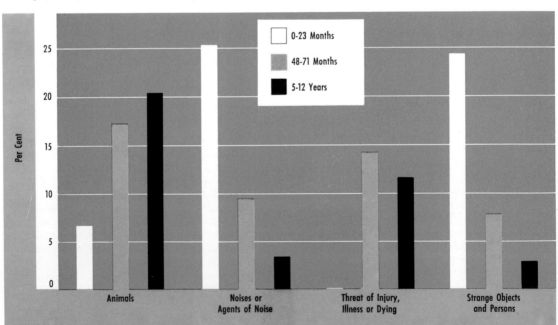

FEAR AND ANXIETY

These emotions are closely related. One usually has had experiences of fear before he experiences anxiety. This will be evident from experiments to be described shortly. We have seen, too, that some subjects respond to a stressful situation with fear (directed outwardly or inwardly) while others respond to the same situation with anxiety (p. 203).

Fear

In one investigation of the situations which arouse fear in children of various age levels, observations by parents were supplemented by interviews with children. The parents were especially trained to make and record their observations. An idea of the nature of the findings from this study may be gathered from Figure 7.17, even though only four of the ten classifications of fear-provoking situations are included. It is quite apparent that animals increase and that noises and strange things decrease in emotional significance as the child grows older. Threats to life and limb, on the other hand, are completely ineffective as instigators of fear during the first two years. They increase, then decrease in potency as the child grows older.[66]

As the individual grows beyond childhood, real fear, at least in our society, is a relatively infrequent occurrence, the reason being that we can cope with most situations that arise. Fear-provoking incidents — such as being accosted by a stranger in a dark alley, having (or narrowly escaping) an automobile accident, being on a plane with its engine on fire or with landing gear that fails to function, going into action under fire — are seldom if ever experienced by most people. But this does not mean that fear is absent from their lives. As we said earlier, human beings have the capacity to anticipate all sorts of dangers and to worry about them. We then speak of *anxiety* rather than fear, although anxiety takes its origin from fear.

Anxiety

Psychologists and psychiatrists use the concept of *anxiety* a great deal. Synonymous terms are *worry, apprehension, dread,* and *uneasiness*. Although all anxiety is related to fear, its meaning differs somewhat depending upon the context in which the concept is used. An animal psychologist who wants to make a subject "anxious" gives it strong electric shocks. It attempts to escape, squeals, defecates, urinates and in other ways justifies the inference that it is afraid. When placed in the same situation later, without electric shock, the animal again appears to be afraid. Now, since it is no longer being shocked, it is said to show "anxiety." If it persists in attempting to escape, the investigator says that it has acquired "an anxiety drive."[67] Anxiety in this sense was discussed earlier (p. 157) as an energizing factor in behavior.

Many people who have never suffered pain or threat in the situation in which they are anxious are said to be neurotic. Anxiety neuroses and abnormal fears are considered in our discussion of personality (Chapter 9).

Albert's fear of a rabbit after fear-provoking experiences with a white rat (p. 213) could be regarded as anxiety. In a somewhat comparable manner, the child who has been inoculated becomes anxious when he sees the preparations for another shot, or even when he sees or hears the doctor approaching. The child who has had painful experiences in the dentist's chair likewise becomes anxious, even at any mention of going to the dentist.

All such uses of the term *anxiety* have some reference to fear. What the individual is anxious about is something that has happened which he fears may happen again.

But human beings also worry about things that have never happened to them. As we said earlier, they anticipate what *could* happen — like losing their loved ones, being without a job, becoming ill, and so on. The superego is also a source of worry, for many have guilt feelings about things they have done. They often fear too that they *may* do something reprehensible.

Psychologists have used various tests and rating scales to reveal the nature and extent of children's anxieties, which often concern such things as losing affection and security. The child may worry about being abandoned, the possible death of his mother or father, and, at later age levels, of losing friends, having a bad report card, and many other things. Some of the earlier anxieties are tempered where the child makes friends outside of the home. The following anecdote[68] illustrates this.

□ "A grandmother was recently reminded of the significance of child friends when her daughter and son-in-law stopped by her house to leave their three drowsy and half-awake children while their mother went to the hospital to have her fourth child. Though the arrangements had been explained to the children in advance and although their grandmother and grandfather were loved figures, the middle-of-the-night change in the children's circumstances apparently called for some reappraisal of the sources of their security. As the grandmother tucked in the six-year-old, the child said thoughtfully, 'Well, I have a friend now in the first grade,' and with that consoling reflection, fell asleep." □

Psychologists have devised "worry inventories" and "anxiety scales" for use with adults. One of the most widely used of these is the *Taylor Scale of Manifest Anxiety*, made up of a series of statements which the subject answers *True*, *False*, or *Cannot say*. The following items are typical:

I am unusually self-conscious
I am happy most of the time
I am entirely self-confident
It makes me nervous to have to wait
I am often afraid that I am going to blush

There are fifty such items scored in terms of the number answered in the anxiety direction — for instance, *true* to the first and the last two of the above examples and *false* to the others. In a group of nearly 2000 college students, the range of anxiety scores was from 1 to 46, with the median at around 13. Among 103 psychiatric patients the range was similar, but the median was approximately 34.[69] This scale has been used in several investigations to select groups of subjects with high and with low anxiety.[70] The aim has been to see how anxiety influences learning and other processes.

In another type of investigation, students kept a diary for one week and, from this, noted the things conducive to anxiety. Among a group of college girls, anxiety centered mainly around school work (40 per cent of all instances), anticipated loss of prestige (30 per cent), and illness and physical danger (17 per cent).[71]

A recently developed inventory of anxiety administered to college students is designed to reveal self-reported anxiety, physiological anxiety, and anxiety defense.[72] Verbal and physiological indices of anxiety, regarded as response to threat, have shown promise of differentiating between general anxiety and anxiety in response to particular kinds of stimuli.[73] ■

ANGER AND AGGRESSION

We have already discussed the eliciting of rage and aggression in animals through stimulation of cells in the hypothalamus, and the inhibition of such behavior through amygdaloid stimulation. It has also been found that removal of a cat's cerebral cortex produces behavior resembling rage, as if a checking influence had been removed.[74] In the normal animal there appears to be "a balance between regions which excite anger and those which inhibit or repress it."[75] In instances of "blind rage" in human beings, where they seem to "take leave of their reason" and commit unwarranted aggressions against others, there must be some slip-up in cerebral control. The writer knew a man who became so angry when his car failed to start that he cursed it and kicked it again and again. Such unreasonable behavior in an otherwise intelligent person could be produced chemically, as when alcohol makes an individual less inhibited by inactivating cells in his cerebral cortex, or it could have some other basis. It has been claimed, for example, that a temporary shutting off or reduction of the blood supply to certain areas of the cortex might be responsible for the tendency of many old people to show "irrational changes in behavior, sometimes becoming more fearful and sometimes unreasonably belligerent."[76]

Although much is yet to be learned about the physiological bases of anger, and why it may lead people to act in such an unreasonable manner as it often does, we do know that the precipitating factor is usually frustration or anticipated frustration. Restriction of activity is a form of frustration which often arouses anger in human beings.

Anger in children is most often aroused by such frustrating situations as having something taken away, being pushed around by another child, or having ongoing activities interrupted, perhaps as in Figure 7.18. Even in college students frustrations of everyday life which arouse anger are common. In the group mentioned earlier, anger was most frequently aroused by interference with their plans (52 per cent of all instances).[77] In another study, involving college men and women, thwarting of self-assertion (that is to say, the opposition of others to their plans) accounted for most of the outbursts of anger which occurred during one week of self-observation.[78] What other people do and say is, as we said earlier, an important basis of annoyance, which can be considered a mild form of anger.

☐ Anger and aggression threaten world peace, hence it is not surprising that psychoanalysts and psychologists have had conferences on what to do about human violence, or that research is being focused on conditions which underlie anger-provoked aggressiveness.[79] Everybody knows, of course, that anger does not necessarily end in violence. The individual may "stew" inwardly or he may use purely verbal means of venting his wrath. On the other hand there are, in the home and in society, certain influences which tend to foster overt violence. Children often copy the model provided by their parents who, when angry, slap them. In television programs and in motion pictures (not to mention comic strips and books) there are also models of aggression. Sometimes children copy these outright in dealing with their peers.

Experiments with adults have shown that violence in films does more than provide models of aggression. It also increases the viewer's readiness to punish others, his *punitiveness*. In one experiment a group of hospital

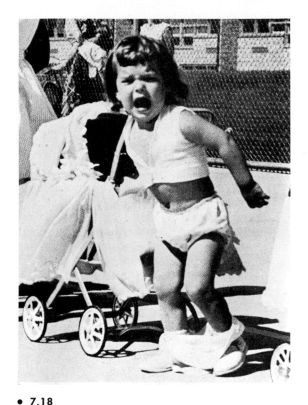

● 7.18
Frustration and Anger. This child, twenty months old, was in a doll parade when her on-going activity was restricted as illustrated. (Courtesy, United Press International)

attendants, who believed that they were aiding in an experiment on conditioning, were required to administer electric shocks to the "subjects." In the course of this experiment, some attendants (experimental group) viewed the knife-fight sequence from *Rebel Without a Cause*, while others (control group) witnessed a scene of equal length on *Picture-Making by Teenagers*. Following this exposure to violence (or nonviolence), the "conditioning experiment" began. In this it was found that the experimental group used a significantly higher intensity of punishing shock than did the control group.[80] In another, somewhat similar investigation, those who administered shock were to do so in terms of their evaluation of a creative floor-plan devised by the recipient of the shocks. One shock was to be given for a satisfactory plan and more for one that appeared unsatisfactory; the poorer the plan the more shocks. Actually, the recipient of the shocks was a "stooge" and all of the plans

217

were alike. All subjects saw the fight scene in the *Champion* where Kirk Douglas takes a terrific beating; some after a synopsis which represented Douglas as deserving of his punishment and others after a synopsis that aroused their sympathy toward him. Another aspect of this experiment involved the annoyingness of the recipient's behavior. Following a procedure rehearsed beforehand, the recipient sometimes angered a subject by making insulting remarks. Thus a particular subject had either a neutral or an angry (or annoyed) attitude toward the person he was to shock and had also been subjected to filmed violence that was or was not, in his opinion, deserved. The results showed that the person who lacked sympathy for Douglas and who was shocking someone who annoyed him gave more shocks, and shocks of longer duration, than the person who sympathized with Douglas and had a neutral co-worker.[81] ■

SMILING, LAUGHTER, AND HUMOR

Smiling in response to a smile does not usually occur before the child is about two months old. Laughter appears about a month later.[82] Such situations as peek-a-boo games, tickling, and word play are common laughter-provokers in young children. Later there is ability to appreciate things that older persons might regard as humorous — like seeing someone fall, become the victim of a practical joke, or act in an incongruous manner. Appreciation of cartoons, verbal jokes, and the humorous aspects of such stories as *Penrod* and *Tom Sawyer* develop during the early school years.

□ The essential conditions for laughter, or humor, have intrigued philosophers for centuries. There are various theories as to what constitutes the humorous, none of which seems likely to receive general acceptance, but each of which may have an element of truth. Some of these alleged causes of humor are: "An error or deformity which is not painful or destructive" (Aristotle), "a strained expression suddenly being reduced to nothing" (Kant), "an expression of incongruity" (Schopenhauer), a feeling of "sudden glory"

(Hobbes).[83] Freud also had a theory which, simply stated, says that "humor gives pleasure by permitting the momentary gratification of some hidden and forbidden wish and at the same time reducing the anxiety that normally inhibits the fulfillment of the wish. By making light of the forbidden impulse, treating it as trivial or universal, a joke or cartoon releases inner tension. The sudden release of tension [cf. Kant, above] comes as a pleasant surprise, while the unconscious source of the individual's tension is so disguised in the joke that it is usually not disturbing."[84] □

Psychologists have developed various tests designed to rate people for "sense of humor." One of these, part of a test of "social intelligence," describes various situations, each with four possible outcomes, and the subject indicates the most humorous of the four.[85] Thus:

"Johnny, if you eat more cake you'll burst." (1) "Why, I've eaten this much before." (2) "No, I have a tough stomach." (3) "Then, I'll be able to take still more." (4) "Well, pass me some and get out of the way."

There are a large number of items, some more subtle than this, with one possibility in each rated as the most humorous.

Another device, known as the *Mirth Response Test*, utilizes twenty cartoons selected from the *New Yorker* and the *Saturday Evening Post*. A subject is shown the cartoons one at a time and his reactions are recorded. He is then asked to sort the cartoons into three piles — those he likes, those he is indifferent to, and those he dislikes. An interesting outcome of this research is not only that it reveals marked individual differences in mirth, but that it also, through the subject's remarks, tells a great deal about *why* he likes, dislikes, or is indifferent to what is supposed to be a humorous situation. One cartoon shows a man who, "while watering his lawn with a garden hose turns to look at a pretty girl in shorts walking by and in doing so sprays his wife, who is sitting on the porch. Most men will laugh at this 'accident' because it dramatizes in innocent form a common secret dissatisfaction and desire to philander. Women, understandably, tend to see nothing funny in this type of cartoon; too often they find themselves close to the role of the sprayed wife."[86] Such an interpretation is in keeping with the Freudian concept of humor. ■

HAPPINESS AND AFFECTION

Happiness in childhood is associated primarily with parental endearments and such things as playing and being read to. Later it is also associated with reading, hobbies, and engaging in various social activities, including games. A continuously happy or unhappy child is rarely observed. It is also unusual to observe a continuously happy or unhappy adult. In a study of happiness in college students, 33 of a group of 112 students reported that they were almost always happy and only three said that they were almost always unhappy. Forty-eight were more often happy than unhappy. Of particular interest to us here, however, are the situational bases of happiness. The bases of happiness which rated highest were, in order of frequency, good health, joy of work, love, and a clear conscience.[87] In another study, graduate students in education rated joy in work as the major factor in happiness.[88] In still another study, students who were rated by themselves and associates as above average in happiness were also rated above average in competence and efficiency.[89]

The most primitive basis of affection is doubtless pleasure associated with stimulation of the erogenous zones, warmth of the mother's body, suckling at the breast, and being fondled and cuddled.

The stimuli for affection in older infants are many. One of the writer's boys had a toy rabbit, soft and woolly, which he took to bed with him for years, and hugged and kissed as if it were a person, even when it grew decrepit beyond description. This sort of thing happens in almost every family. The basis of such affection for objects and persons is not very readily traced. There is reason to suppose, however, that the original stimuli are such as the

parents provide and that other objects and persons become substitute stimuli for affection. As the child grows older, however, the stimuli which will arouse affection are limited by cultural influences. Sexual attraction of course becomes a potent factor when members of the opposite sex, and sometimes of the same sex, are concerned. Sexual factors probably play a minor role in maternal and paternal affection and in normal affection for members of the same sex.

Even in heterosexual love, as between normally adjusted husbands and wives, sex is no more than a contributing factor, although an important one. Under normal conditions of marriage in our society, sex, like eating, becomes subsidiary to other aspects. Human love, in addition to its sexual aspects, satisfies a number of motives, and perhaps somewhat different motives in different individuals. Some men want to be "mothered" by their wives, some women want husbands who will take a paternal attitude toward them — perhaps men who are like "Daddy." Some feel pride in possession — in having made a "good catch." Affection between partners, even beyond the sexual attraction, may become very important. In any event, there is a great deal of "ego-identification," as suggested by the following quotation: "Since the lover is very concerned with the happiness and growth of the [loved one] he will himself *feel* the pleasures and pains, the dangers to and happiness of his [loved one] *as if they were his own*. It is as if he had extended the "contact-surface" of his mechanisms for feeling and experiencing. He reacts emotionally to the events which affect his [loved one] as well as to the events which affect him personally."[90] ■

JEALOUSY

Jealousy, as we saw earlier (p. 210), is a late-appearing emotion. It can only occur in social situations, hence it does not appear until a certain degree of social perception and participation has developed.

The most frequent cause of jealousy in young children is the arrival of a new child in the household. Parental attention to the newcomer, especially when it deprives the older child of accustomed attention and affection, often produces jealousy. Sometimes the younger child is attacked, even seriously injured. Jealousy may also be expressed by ignoring the other child, denying that it exists, refusing to eat, bed-wetting, and various ways of getting attention.

Jealousy like the above may often be prevented. It is motivated by anxiety. The older child feels "dethroned" by the newcomer and rejected by those who have formerly loved him. One way in which such anxiety may be avoided is to prepare the child for the coming of a brother or sister. This preparation should be informative, and also such as to make the child feel that the newcomer will be an asset — someone to be proud of, to care for, and later to play with. When the baby arrives, the child can be allowed to help — in bathing it, powdering it, and so forth. Moreover, the parents can refrain from giving it all of their attention and affection. Under these circumstances, the older child will not feel that he is "left out" and there is less likelihood that jealousy will develop.

Jealousy also appears in many other situations where a threat to accustomed pleasures, to prestige, and to other forms of ego-involvement are present. Children become jealous when a friend forms new attachments. The child may become jealous of one parent's relations with the other. Freudian psychoanalysts[91] have stressed the so-called *Oedipus complex* (in which the boy becomes jealous of his father's relations with his mother) and the reverse of this, the *Electra complex* (wherein the girl becomes jealous of her mother's relations with her father).* These complexes are prevalent in our society, but by no means universal. There are often sexual implications in these and other forms of jealousy, as when a person is anxious for fear someone else will deprive him of his loved one.

In older children and adults, jealous behavior has many facets, although sulking and

* Freud took these terms over from Greek mythology. Oedipus killed his father and married his mother. Electra helped kill her mother to avenge the death of her father.

direct or verbal attacks are rather prevalent at all ages. ■

SYMPATHY

The most common stimulus for sympathy is seeing, hearing, or learning of someone else in distress. Identification is involved. This is "feeling oneself into" the other person. Why we feel sympathy for others has received considerable discussion. Some have regarded it as an essential aspect of gregariousness and as inborn. According to McDougall,[92]

□ ". . . sympathetic induction of emotion and feeling may be observed in children at an age at which they cannot be credited with understanding of the significance of the expressions that provoke their reactions. Perhaps the expression to which they respond earliest is the sound of the wailing of other children. A little later the sight of a smiling face, the expression of pleasure, provokes a smile. Later still fear, curiosity, and, I think, anger are communicated readily in this direct fashion from one child to another. Laughter is notoriously infectious all through life, and this, though not a truly instinctive expression, affords the most familiar example of sympathetic induction of an affective state. This immediate and unrestrained responsiveness to the emotional expressions of others is one of the great charms of childhood." □

This statement implies that there is a more or less automatic response, as well as considerable ability to respond differentially, to variations in another's emotional expressions. It should be noted here, however, that the person in whom sympathetic response is aroused may be responding to the emotion-provoking situation rather than, or in addition to, the emotional expressions of another. One theory supposes that a person's sympathy is based upon how *he* has responded (or felt) in comparable situations. According to this theory, "the emotion aroused in the sympathizer is a part of his own system of emotional habits from past experience, evoked as a conditioned response to some element common to the original and the present situations."[93] This is to say that a child who cries or feels sad when he sees another child in trouble is exhibiting the response which he has himself previously exhibited in comparable situations. This is a plausible explanation of many instances of sympathetic behavior, but it needs much amplification if it is to account for all of them. This seems but a first step. It is one thing to laugh or weep because others are doing it (sympathetic imitation), or to act as others do because of common conditioning in comparable situations, but something beyond this type of behavior is involved when we feel for and comfort someone in distress. Various aspects of sympathetic behavior are already evident at the preschool level.

□ "Some children seem to be much more sympathetic than others — that is, they are moved or affected by another's distress. As a rule children make no attempt to express such sympathy at first, they only stare or perhaps cry in sympathetic imitation. Later, when they are more socially adjusted, they express their feelings by trying to comfort the child in trouble. This may take the form of an affectionate embrace or an arm put gently around the distressed child. It may take the form of comforting words such as 'Don't cry, I'll ask my Mummy to get one for you,' or of simply asking 'What are you crying for?' or 'Does it hurt?' in gentle, kindly tones."[94] □

There seems little doubt but that, whatever the basis of sympathy, as an emotion, the sympathetic responses described above, and they are perhaps typical, are acquired from the social milieu. The child does what his parents and others have done for him and what he has observed people do for others in times of distress. ■

• SUMMARY

The term *emotion* covers a wide range of behavior — behavior that is agitated and without definite orientation, as well as behavior that is highly motivated and goal-directed. Milder forms and intensities of emotion provide a motivational background to much that we do. In emergency situations, largely through adrenal secretions, we have energy in excess of that normally present. The feeling aspect of emotion is sometimes definitely related to physiological activities (butterflies in the stomach, pounding heart). Feelings (affective processes) such as pleasantness and unpleasantness (and related facial and other bodily expressions) have been studied. Freud stressed the "pleasure principle" as an aspect of motivation. However, such subjective aspects of emotion are difficult to investigate scientifically.

Laboratory research on emotion has dealt primarily with physiological concomitants of emotion-provoking situations and reported experiences. Such facts as the following have been revealed: Emotional activation is widespread rather than restricted to any particular parts of the body. Efforts to differentiate emotion from nonemotion have achieved a certain degree of success with respect to the identification of biochemical components, including eosinophils in the blood and glandular byproducts of the body's emergency functioning. Some emotions can be differentiated from others in terms of stomach activity, electroencephalograms, heart activity, and blood pressure. Stronger emotional feeling produces more intense physiological reaction, including psychogalvanic response, than weaker emotional feeling. Anger directed outward can, on various physiological bases, be differentiated from anger directed inward and from anxiety. In general, however, overt behavior and verbal reports, supplemented by knowledge of the stimulating circumstances, give us a surer differentiation of emotion than that provided by records of physiological activity alone.

Adrenalin plays an important role in energizing emotional behavior and in producing a variety of physiological components, yet injecting it does not produce definite emotions. An experiment was described in which subjects injected with adrenalin experienced different emotions in relation to their expectations of the adrenalin's effects and reacted differently to a social situation with which they were confronted.

Structures known to be of especial importance in emotion are the receptors (without which we could not perceive a situation); various structures of the limbic system, especially the hypothalamus and amygdala; the autonomic nervous system (the sympathetic division of which, under control of the hypothalamus, is most directly involved in producing the physiological changes associated with emotional activation); and the cerebral cortex (activities of which can set off emotional reactions, prolong and direct their expressions, and give rise to emotional experiences). All of these structures are integrally related in emotional behavior and experience. The reticular formation and septal region have also been considered to play a role in emotion — the former through its alerting function and the latter because it has been regarded as a "pleasure area." Two theories of emotion (James-Lange, Bard-Cannon) relate bodily and neural changes in emotion with emotional experiences, but neither has received general acceptance. It is probable that a completely adequate theory would have to include features of both theories.

The development of emotion in children has been studied intensively. At birth there is apparently only one emotional response, namely, general excitement. As an infant grows, its repertoire of emotions and specific emotional reactions becomes increasingly varied. During the first two years of life, one may discern the emergence of several new emotional expressions.

Occasions for emotional upset tend to decrease as the child learns to master his environment. Nevertheless, objects which previously aroused no emotional reactions often come to do so. Thus fear of snakes, of the dark, and of particular persons may develop. The facial and postural aspects of emotion

soon conform, more or less closely, to the expressions which characterize members of the child's own group. Some aspects of emotional expression are undoubtedly due to maturation. This is especially true of weeping, laughing, and certain other relatively simple reflexes. These responses appear even when there have been no opportunities to learn them, as in the case of the congenitally blind and deaf.

Fear and anxiety are closely related and the latter is often the aftermath of fear-provoking experiences. Studies of college students, as well as children, show that anxiety is a very common experience in our society and that it centers around a wide variety of possible events — like loss of loved ones, loss of status, and illness.

Anger and aggression are induced by frustrating situations. Electrical stimulation of the hypothalamus, when electrodes are appropriately placed, produces rage-like behavior and aggression in animals. Stimulation of the amygdala appears to modulate or inhibit such reactions. Investigations with human beings have shown that punitiveness is increased when the subjects are angered, and even more so when they have recently witnessed films involving violence.

Smiling first appears at the age of about two months, and laughter about a month later. There are several theories which purport to explain why certain situations provoke humor.

Happiness and affection begin in parent-child relations. Mature heterosexual love has many aspects besides the sexual one.

Jealousy is by its very nature a socially instigated emotion. It is in relation to this emotion that the Freudian Oedipus and Electra complexes are discussed. Sympathy is also a socially instigated emotion and it appears to involve identification with others in distress.

Further aspects of emotional adjustment are considered in the following chapter, in which we discuss compensatory and other reactions aroused by frustrating situations. ■

REFERENCES AND NOTES FOR THIS CHAPTER ARE IN THE APPENDIX.

• SELECTED READINGS

Arnold, M. B., *Emotion and Personality*. Columbia University Press, 1960. Vol. I, *Psychological Aspects,* is on feeling and the various theories concerning it. Vol. II, *Neurological and Physiological Aspects,* discusses emotion and the brain, and various physiological and biochemical components.

Candland, D. K. (Ed.), *Emotion: Bodily Change.* Van Nostrand, 1962. A book of readings, chiefly reprints of research on physiological aspects.

Carmichael, L., *Basic Psychology.* Random House, 1957. Chapter 9 (Emotion) is an elementary discussion, but with consideration of some facets not dealt with in this chapter.

Darwin, C., *The Expression of the Emotions in Man and Animals.* University of Chicago Press, 1965. A reprint of this classic (published in 1872) with a new introduction by Konrad Lorenz.

Davitz, J. R. (Ed.), *The Communication of Emotional Meaning.* McGraw-Hill, 1964. A series of researches on facial and vocal expressions of emotion.

Dulany, D. E., R. L. DeValois, D. C. Beardslee, and M. R. Winterbottom (Eds.), *Contributions to Modern Psychology* (2nd ed.). Oxford University Press, 1963, Chapter 6. Readings 29–33 are especially relevant to this chapter.

King, R. A., *Readings for an Introduction to Psychology.* McGraw-Hill, 1961. Readings 15 (James) and 16 (Cannon).

Mandler, G., "Emotion," in *New Directions in Psychology.* Holt, Rinehart and Winston, 1962.

Morgan, C. T., *Physiological Psychology* (3rd ed.). McGraw-Hill, 1965. Chapter 11 provides more detail on physiological aspects.

Plutchik, R., *The Emotions: Facts, Theories, and a New Model.* Random House, 1962.

Woodworth, R. S., and H. Schlosberg, *Experimental Psychology* (rev. ed.). Holt, 1954. See Chapters 5–7 for a survey of experimental research on emotion.

Young, P. T., *Motivation and Emotion.* Wiley, 1961. Chapters 9 and 10 deal with bodily mechanisms and development.

8

Conflict and Adjustment

When we are hungry and dinner is long delayed, we experience displeasure. There is internal tension, irritability, and perhaps annoyance or anger directed toward the situation or persons responsible. When the dinner appears, our emotional tensions subside.

Such temporary delays are experienced by all of us and they are of little or no consequence. But some motives cannot be so easily satisfied. It takes years of study before one can graduate. It may take longer still to save enough money to build one's own home. We may have to mark time, as it were, by serving in the armed services — perhaps by going to war. But even these barriers, which are disturbing to many, are eventually overcome.

Suppose, however, that strong motives are blocked by impassable barriers, or by barriers which we cannot circumvent. It is then that such terms as *frustration, stress,* and *conflict* are most appropriately applied. All such terms mean about the same thing. We may speak of a *frustrating situation*, which is comparable with a *barrier* or *obstacle*, and we may speak of the *frustrating experience*. This is comparable with what is otherwise designated as psychological stress (*distress*) or *mental conflict*.

Frustrating situations (barriers) may be nonsocial or social. Nonsocial barriers are exemplified by transportation breakdowns, floods, storms, and power failures. Social barriers are placed in our way by other people. These barriers play an important part in our socialization, in the development of the ego and superego. They are operative when parents force a child to sit on the toilet, when they enforce cleanliness, and when they make him refrain from sex play. Social barriers are also present when a parent makes a child stay in his room or forces him to study instead of watching television. They are present, too, when the instructor sets an exam for the day on which a student expects to take a trip. Moreover, the prejudices of his society may restrict a person's companions to those of a particular racial or socio-economic group. They may prevent him from getting the education he desires, or from entering a particular occupation.

Psychologically speaking, such factors as we have mentioned are barriers only when the individual has goals which are blocked by them, and when he is aware of the fact that they impede progress toward these goals.

In addition to external barriers (social and nonsocial) there are internal, or personal barriers. Personal defects are of this nature, especially when they thwart our aspirations. Weakness, unattractiveness, lack of skill, or low intelligence may stand in the way of achievement. Deformities may prevent us from engaging in athletics, from following certain occupations, and even from marrying. Barriers like these are often much more lasting than those imposed from without. Here again, however, we must emphasize the fact that there is no psychological significance to barriers which the individual himself fails to recognize. Feeblemindedness, for example, makes a college career impossible. In this sense, it may be considered an impassable barrier. But it is not frustrating to the feebleminded individual himself. He knows little or nothing of colleges. They are beyond his comprehension. Nor does he have insight into his defect, his inability to do what college students do. But to his parents, who know the circumstances, and who may at one time have had aspirations for their child, his feeblemindedness may be frustrating indeed.

Even when we are not frustrated by personal defects there may be internal conflict — a conflict between different motives, or their expression. Inability to "make up one's mind" on some issue demanding decision exemplifies such conflict. The presence of conflicting possibilities of action may be even more frustrating than any of the barriers already mentioned.

People differ a great deal in the way they cope with frustration. In apparently similar circumstances, some give up, some persist in their endeavors, and others break under the stress. Those who can stand a great deal of serious frustration without breaking down are said to have a high *frustration tolerance*, which is defined by Rosenzweig as "capacity to withstand frustration . . . without resorting to inadequate modes of response."[1]

Objects or circumstances which serve as incentives are sometimes said to have *positive valence*. This means that they "attract" the person or that he will strive for their achievement. Objects which repel, or circumstances which the individual will work to prevent or eliminate, have *negative valence*. A barrier, standing as it does in the way of goal achievement, may readily acquire a negative valence, even though it was not previously regarded as repellent. If the barrier is unassailable, or if all routes to the goal necessitate approach to, or acceptance of, negative valences which are more potent than the positive valence of the goal, then the goal may be relinquished, or the person may withdraw from the situation, either by running away, or by indulging in the fantasy that the barrier does not exist or that it has been circumvented. This general approach to the study of conflict characterizes Lewin's so-called *vector psychology*.[2] Lewin regarded behavior as the resultant (vector) of the attracting (+) and repelling (−) aspects of a situation, *as this is experienced by the behaving individual*. It is perhaps obvious that what attracts one individual may repel another, and that an attracting (or repelling) situation may vary in the magnitude of its valence for different persons. Hence the attracting or repelling "forces" with which we are concerned in discussing conflict do not reside in the physical environment itself but in the environment *as the individual perceives it*. ■

CONFLICT

We have said that indecision acts as a barrier, in that it delays or prevents action. This occurs in situations where the individual must choose between alternatives, and also in those where what he wants to do has undesirable as well as desirable consequences.

Let us first look at situations involving alternatives. Basically, such situations involve either an *approach-approach* or an *avoidance-avoidance* conflict.[3]

Approach-approach

In an approach-approach conflict the person (P) is between two alternatives with equally positive valences. This may be represented as follows:

If the alternatives were not equally attractive there would be no conflict. The greater attractiveness of one alternative would, so to speak, "pull" the individual in its direction.

Suppose, for instance, that a student who is poor at mathematics and who does not like this subject, is trying to decide between equally attractive colleges. There would be considerable conflict until he learned that one required mathematics for graduation and the other did not. In many situations of everyday life we are "pulled" in various directions and, as a result, we hesitate, vacillate, or perhaps find ourselves temporarily unable to act (Figure 8.1). We say "temporarily" because conflicts of this kind are usually soon resolved. The legendary ass, flanked by equally enticing and equidistant bales of hay, is said to have starved in the midst of plenty. But there is no doubt that, in the course of his vacillation, his head got closer to one bale. Its closeness would give it an advantage over the other if for no other reason than that its attractive odor became more intense. The man who cannot decide whether he will propose to Jane or Mary may delay action, and even lose some sleep, but when he is with Jane, Mary's attraction weakens or becomes stronger, depending upon the circumstances. After a certain amount of

● 8.1

Conflict. (Reprinted by special permission of *The Saturday Evening Post.* Copyright 1949 by the Curtis Publishing Company.)

further experience with each, he finds that one is more desirable than the other and his conflict is resolved.

Avoidance-avoidance

In avoidance-avoidance conflict the alternatives are equally unattractive, or repulsive, and the situation in which the person finds himself may be represented as follows:

A student for whom study is distasteful finds that he must study or suffer the equally distasteful consequences of failing the course. A youth does not want to "drag race," because he is afraid for his life and knows that he is breaking the law, but he also does not wish to be regarded by his buddies as "chicken." The man who has had too much to drink with "the boys" knows that he will "catch hell" if

he doesn't go home, and also if he does go home. In such situations one is caught "between the devil and the deep blue sea." It is common, under such circumstances, to "leave the field." The student perhaps daydreams about things more pleasant than studying, examinations, and flunking out of college; the youth perhaps finds that his car isn't functioning just right, or remembers an important date elsewhere; and the inebriate perhaps has another drink so that he is too far gone to suffer the unhappy consequences of his drinking, at least for the time being.

Approach-avoidance

There are many situations which have both positive and negative valences, as follows:

The would-be swimmer runs toward the icy water, but slows down as he gets nearer and perhaps comes to a dead stop before diving in, as represented by Figure 8.2.[4] The child starts to pat a dog, but is afraid to do so and pulls back its hand. A boy starts to climb a tree, but as he gets higher, he feels that he may fall. If such positive and negative valences are equally strong, the individual suspends action or vacillates. The swimmer goes toward the water and then away from it repeatedly until he "gets his courage up" or until others arrive on the scene and perhaps exert social pressure. The child hesitates to pat the dog, and he may not do so, unless he sees that someone else is patting it and not getting hurt. The climber may continue to climb because he sees an intriguing bird's nest.

Somewhat comparable conflicts at the adult level are one's inability to make up his mind about an attractive job offer because he fears that he may fail; or hesitating to propose to a girl because he has doubts about his ability to make her happy. In such instances, the person may provide himself with some safeguard, thus reducing the negative valence. The first man may find that he can take special training to equip himself for the job; the second may seek advice from a counselor and perhaps prepare himself for marriage.

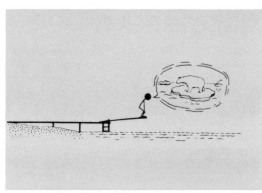

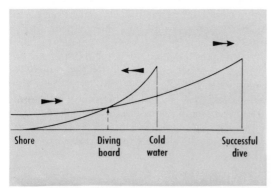

Shore   Diving   Cold   Successful
board   water   dive

A disturbing form of conflict resembling approach-avoidance is that in which the individual has both positive and negative attitudes toward the same person. A girl may have a great deal of affection for her mother, yet also hate her intensely for some particular reason — because she thinks that her mother fails to appreciate the good qualities of her father, or because the mother interferes too much in her personal affairs. Parents love their children yet are so angry with them at times that they inflict cruel punishment, and may even have an inclination to kill them. This kind of mental conflict, known more specifically as *ambivalence*, is often accompanied by great mental stress. The individual fully appreciates that one is supposed to love his parents or his children, hence he becomes extremely worried when such conflicting impulses arise.

In many situations of everyday life we are confronted with various possibilities of action and each of these may have both desirable and undesirable aspects. Shall we go to the movie or watch television? The movie is one we don't want to miss, and this is its only showing. But we are also short of cash. The television program perhaps cannot be seen again. But we can't see it and also the movie.

● **8.2**

Approach-Avoidance Conflict. Our diver has a strong approach tendency, for he runs rapidly toward the diving board. The long curve represents this positive motivation, which, if the water were warm, would increase in strength as the goal (a successful dive) came nearer. But the water is cold; and, in the diver's imagination, its coldness becomes increasingly evident as he nears the end of the diving board. He slows down and finally stops, or at least hesitates before taking the plunge. This increasingly strong negative aspect of the situation as the moment for the dive approaches is represented by the shorter curve. In our example the would-be diver is pictured as coming to a standstill where his approach and avoidance tendencies are of equal strength, i.e., at the diving board. (Drawings by E. Parker Johnson, from N. L. Munn and E. P. Johnson, *Student's Manual to Accompany Psychology*, Houghton Mifflin, 1956.)

If we watch it, though, we will save our money. The situation is something like this:

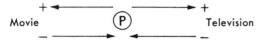

What we do under such circumstances depends upon the relative strengths of the positive and negative valences — unless visitors come, in which case we either watch the television program with them or give up this and the movie too. Such conflicts are often referred to as *double approach-avoidance*.

As we continue our discussion of conflict it will become apparent that many situations involve a variety of attracting and repelling features and thus do not readily yield to the sort of analysis that we have described. The case to be discussed presently is a good illustration of such motivational complexity. ■

SEVERE FRUSTRATION

There are many situations in adult life in which no escape from external or personal barriers, or from conflict situations, seems possible. Sometimes, in such circumstances, the pressures are so intense that a person feels trapped.

One example from many that we might choose is the case of a man who once came to the writer for aid. Whenever this man became interested in a girl, his widowed and wealthy mother, who had encouraged his financial dependence upon her, and who had a heart condition, threatened to withdraw financial support. Without such support, marriage seemed impossible. Since the mother also had an aggravation of her heart condition at such times, the son felt that going ahead with marriage plans would perhaps kill her. He was in his forties. Crises of the nature described had been recurring for years, in each instance causing him to reject marriage. His desire to marry persisted, but so, also, did the seemingly insurmountable barrier. The mother continued to use her illness as a device to keep her son nearby and as a weapon to prevent him from getting lucrative employment. The son said he was trapped. Despite intense hatred for his

mother, he could not bring himself to leave her, to thwart her wishes, or to do anything which might, as he said, make him feel for the rest of his life that he had been the cause of her death. This problem could be solved, apparently, only by the death of the man's mother or by her re-education. The latter seemed, at the time, hopeless. The man was advised to get married despite his mother. The suggestion that she would probably survive, and that she would eventually become reconciled to his marriage did not seem convincing to him. His mother could not, so he said, do without his aid and companionship. He could not be near her and married too. Moreover, she had arranged to disinherit him if he married against her wishes. Her death as a result of his marriage would thus leave him penniless.

One will recognize that the barrier here was not the mother alone. It included the attitudes that she had implanted in her son.

If the son had become so involved with a girl that he was obligated to marry her, or impelled by the pressure of public opinion to do so, and the maternal barrier had remained, he would then have been in the plight represented in Figure 8.3. He would have had to choose between the conflicting alternatives. These could of course also be represented as in the double approach-avoidance paradigm above, with the alternatives being the mother and the wife or bachelorhood and marriage. However, there would be several positive and several negative valences associated with each alternative.

In frustrating circumstances like these, the term *mental conflict* is clearly applicable. The individual is indeed "between the devil and the deep blue sea." His distress is often acute.

Frustration and goal orientation

When frustrated, most people retain their goal orientation, attempting to discover a way out of their predicament or some means to diminish their distress. Even extreme frustration, like that suffered by the man whose case we have just considered, often fails to disrupt goal orientation. In many instances, how-

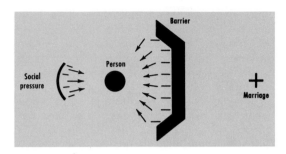

● 8.3

Situation Involving Extreme Conflict. The barrier (in this case a man's mother and his attitudes) remains fixed and insurmountable. The goal (marriage) also remains. Without social pressure the son might evade the issue, going along with his mother's wishes. But with this pressure he is forced to do something — either marry, resulting in loss of his source of income and possibly loss of his mother; or not marry, resulting in loss of standing in the community and of self-respect. The social pressure is also negative in valence, because it forces him in the direction of unpleasant alternatives. (Adapted from N. R. F. Maier, *Frustration*, McGraw-Hill, 1949.)

ever, the individual becomes panic-stricken and his acts defeat rather than further his aims.[5] Then he may "vent his spleen" on innocent people. He may even commit suicide.

Acts of aggression, of which lynchings and wartime atrocities are extreme examples, often stem from frustration and the resulting anger.[6] Whether or not they serve any purpose, from the standpoint of the aggressor, is controversial. Aggression against innocent persons certainly solves no problems; but it may, of course, serve to release pent-up tensions in the aggressor. Even when this is so, aggression is hardly justified. The man who turns upon his child or his subordinates when frustrated by his wife, against whom he dare not aggress, may feel better, at least temporarily, but he has done nothing to solve his problem. Nor has the perpetrator of atrocities against individuals or groups. If anything, he has erected new barriers, the enmity of his victims and of those who sympathize with them.

Whether frustrations are mild or of great intensity, a realistic goal-seeking approach is

alone commendable. One should recognize that he is confronted with a problem to be solved and he should use all of the resources at his disposal or seek competent advice in an effort to overcome the obstacles.

Unconscious conflict

The advice to resolve conflict through a realistic goal-seeking approach is good as far as it goes, but what if the person does not know what is really bothering him? He feels nervous, has headaches, or is the victim of unreasonable fears without knowing that some sort of conflict is at the root of them. Indeed, it often happens that individuals *repress*; that is, refuse to recognize, or "put out of mind," the real sources of their difficulties. The fact that individuals are not always aware of their motives and related conflicts, or of why they do what they do, has been given prominence in Freudian psychoanalysis. One aim of psychoanalytic procedures is to delve into the unconscious (see Figure 8.4) and bring such conflicts into the light of conscious scrutiny, where they can be dealt with realistically.

Phobias are abnormal fears of particular objects and situations. Such objects and situations arouse a strong avoidance motive, yet the individual does not know why. A woman had a fear of elevators which led her to climb long flights of stairs rather than enter one. A student in one of the writer's classes scrupulously avoided walking over gratings (in the street or in buildings) and became panic-stricken when crossing them seemed unavoidable. Sometimes such conflicts seriously interfere with everyday adjustment.

□ A Midwestern English professor had experienced, for as long as he could remember, an intense fear of going more than a few blocks from his home. This fear was so strong that he had always lived in the same house and moved only within a narrowly circumscribed area. He did not know the basis for his fear. During the course of psychoanalysis he recalled that, as a child of three, he had wandered from his mother over to the railroad tracks. A train coming into the station rushed by and he was scalded by the steam. Although he failed to remember the incident until adulthood, the fear aroused by it had motivated him to stay near his home The professor's book, entitled *The Locomotive God*, gives an account of the effect of this incident on his subsequent conduct.[7]

A girl had a fear of running water which was so strong that it required the combined efforts of several members of her household

● **8.4**

Schematic Representation of Freud's Concept of the Unconscious. This shows Freud's concept of the relation of the id, ego, and superego, and illustrates his conception of the id as completely unconscious, and the ego and superego as partially so. The gold portion (unconscious) represents everything in one's mental makeup of which he is never aware — i.e., what can never be verbalized. Anything represented by the gray area (preconscious) may come into awareness — i.e., may be recalled. The white region represents everything of which one is aware at any given time. The student should not take this as a representation of any physical structure, like the brain. Rather, it deals with functional relationships, and then only in terms of analogy. The basic model is an iceberg, with most of its mass always below the surface. Discussion of the id, the ego, and the superego appeared in the introduction to Chapter 6. (After Healy, Bronner, and Bowers)

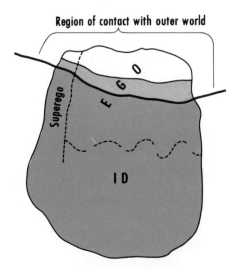

Region of contact with outer world

to bathe her. Even when she went to school, the sound of a drinking fountain frightened her. While riding on a train, she lowered the curtain so that she would not see streams over which the train passed. The girl, even at the age of twenty, did not know why she acted in this way. However, when she was twenty an aunt whom she had not seen for thirteen years came to visit the girl. The aunt's first words on again meeting her were, "I have never told." This led the girl to recall an accident which she experienced at the age of seven years while walking in the woods with her aunt. The child had promised her mother, when she left, that she would be strictly obedient. However, she ran off from the aunt and, when found, was wedged among the rocks of a small stream into which she had fallen. A small waterfall was pouring down on her head and she was screaming with terror. Her aunt dried the child's clothes and promised that she would never tell the mother of her disobedience.[8] □

Unconscious conflicts may be produced experimentally under hypnosis. After he has gone into an hypnotic trance, the subject may be told, for example, that he will dislike cigarettes. When he comes out of the trance there is no awareness of what has been said to him, yet the offer of a cigarette elicits quite evident conflict. He may take it, if sufficiently urged, but then use every possible excuse for failing to light it. If another offers to light the cigarette for him he accidentally blows out the match, fails to draw on the cigarette, or drops it. The suggested effects are experienced for various periods, depending upon the individual and the effectiveness of suggestions.[9]

Frequently an act suggested under hypnosis is carried out without the subject knowing why.

□ A girl (S) in a psychology class was hypnotized. Tests demonstrated that she was in a deep trance. Then the hypnotist (H) said, "After I have counted to ten, you will wake up. You will return to your seat and be wide awake. When I scratch my head during the course of the lecture, you will get up from your seat and go to my office, where you will find a laboratory coat hanging behind the door. You will bring the coat here, into the classroom, and put it on me. I may not want to put it on, but you must get it on me." H then said, "One-two-three — you are waking up — four-five — you are becoming wider awake — six-seven-eight — you are getting wide awake — nine — you are almost awake — ten — you are awake." S opened her eyes, looked a little embarrassed, and returned to her seat. When asked, she said that she remembered nothing that had happened from the time she felt her eyes getting tired until she woke up. H continued with the lecture and, several minutes later, scratched his head. The subject sat still, but looked a little uneasy. However, the lecture was continued. A minute or so later, S, with a great deal of hesitation, left the room. Shortly she returned with the laboratory coat. She said to H, "You had better put this on." H said that he didn't need it. S insisted, saying, "It is rather cold in here and this will keep you warm." H insisted that he did not need it; that the room wasn't cold enough to put it on. S now became very insistent. She tried to get H's arm in the sleeve, insisting, now, that chalk might get on his clothes if he didn't put on his coat. After a few minutes, S began to plead with H to put on the coat. This he finally did. S then seemed greatly relieved and returned to her seat.

When asked why she had done what she did, S said that she didn't know. She said that the idea occurred to her when the instructor scratched his head, but, realizing how silly it was, she decided not to do it. Finally, she could not resist. S said she knew she would feel better if the impulse were followed. ■

REACTING REALISTICALLY TO FRUSTRATION

The most direct reaction to frustrating external conditions is to try to remove or get around them. It involves trying out various procedures which might occur to us until one of them succeeds or until we are forced to give in. This may be an overt trial-and-error process or it may involve insight and reasoning.

Frustration resulting from personal defects may be dealt with in a similar fashion, especially where the defects are remediable. One could not change his intelligence nor repair the ravages of polio by a problem-solving approach, but he might, if he knew it to be the source of his frustration, change some aspect of his appearance or behavior. Many girls make themselves more attractive to the opposite sex by experimenting with this and that cosmetic, this and that coiffure, or this and that type of dress. Some colleges, through courses or other means, try to help the less attractive girls overcome their deficiencies.

The chief difficulty is that many individuals thwarted by personal defects do not realize the source of their trouble and quite often their friends hesitate to make any suggestions. As we shall point out in more detail shortly, those with personal defects are often ready to attribute their difficulties to almost anything except the defects themselves.

When conflict comes from incompatible motives, a direct problem-solving attack may be helpful. If one does not know whether he should prepare himself to be a teacher or a salesman, or whether to do his major college work in sociology or in psychology, he can at least gain as much relevant information as possible about these alternatives and perhaps also try his hand in each field.

Then, too, he may list the pros and cons and see where these seem to lead. Benjamin Franklin recommended this method in the following letter to Joseph Priestley:[10]

☐ "In the affair of so much importance to you, wherein you ask my advice, I cannot, for want of sufficient premises, advise you *what* to determine, but, if you please, I will tell you *how*. When those difficult cases occur, they are difficult, chiefly because, while we have them under consideration, all the reasons *pro* and *con* are not present to the mind at the same time; but sometimes one set present themselves, and at other times another, the first being out of sight. Hence the various purposes or inclinations that alternatively prevail, and the uncertainty that perplexes us.

"To get over this, my way is, to divide half a sheet of paper by a line into two columns; writing over the one *Pro* and over the other *Con*. Then during three or four days' consideration, I put down under the different heads short hints of the different motives, that at different times occur to me, *for* or *against* the measure. When I have thus got them altogether in one view, I endeavor to estimate their respective weights; and where I find two, one on each side, that seem equal, I strike them both out. If I find a reason *pro* equal to *two* reasons *con*, I strike out *three*. If I judge some two reasons *con* equal to some *three* reasons *pro*, I strike out five; and thus proceeding, I find where the balance lies; and if after a day or two of further consideration, nothing new that is of importance occurs on either side, I come to a determination accordingly. And tho' the weight of reasons cannot be taken with precision of algebraic quantities, yet, when each is thus considered separately and comparatively, and the whole lies before me, I think I can judge better, and am less liable to make a rash step; and in fact I have found great advantage from this kind of equation, in what may be called *moral* or *prudential* algebra." □

This method works very well providing the pros and cons do not balance. If they do balance, then the individual is back where he started. ■

CONSEQUENCES OF UNRESOLVED CONFLICT

When frustration is prolonged and no resolution occurs, there is usually a condition of chronic emotional tension, referred to in our discussion of emotion as *stress*. The latter is defined by Dr. Hans Selye in his book *The Stress of Life* as "the bodily changes produced, whether a person is exposed to nervous tension, physical injury, infection, cold, heat, x-rays or anything else. . . ."[11] One reason for lumping all of these unusual conditions together as "stressors" is that all of them tend to produce a homeostatic change in the body which has been referred to by Selye as the *general adaptation syndrome*, abbreviated *G.A.S.* A *syndrome* is a particular pattern or grouping of symptoms. The appearance of such symptoms is first evident in what has been called the *alarm reaction*, a "generalized call to arms of the defensive forces in the organism."[12] Among these defensive forces are increased secretions from the pituitary (ACTH) and the adrenal glands (cortisone) (see Figure 6.10, p. 169). Continued stress enlarges the adrenals and certain other organs. Moreover, when the adrenal glands are removed, the organism's ability to withstand stress is greatly impaired. Increased secretion of cortisone, stimulated by ACTH as previously described (p. 170), as well as various other stress-reducing changes, make it possible for the organism to enter a second stage of the G.A.S. This is an "emergency" reaction referred to by Selye as *resistance*. But stress may continue, the individual's psychological and physiological resources being insufficient to overcome it. In this event, a third and final stage of the G.A.S. is reached. Selye refers to it as *exhaustion*. With respect to the function of the adrenal cortex, for example, the course of the G.A.S. is described as follows: "the adrenal cortex first discharges all its microscopic fat granules which contain the cortical hormones (alarm reaction), then it becomes laden with an unusually large number of fat-droplets (stage of resistance) and finally it loses them again (stage of exhaustion). As far as we can see, the same triphasic course is followed by most, if not all, of the manifestations of the G.A.S."[13]

Emotional stress and ulcers

One frequent outcome of prolonged stress, emotional or otherwise, is the production of gastric ulcers. According to Selye, this is due in part to the overactivity of the adrenal cortex.[14]

The first clear evidence that ulcers could be produced by emotional stress came from observations of a man whose stomach was exposed and whose gastric activities were thus observable. The accident giving rise to exposure of the stomach was described earlier (p. 202). During two weeks of prolonged anxiety, the subject developed small hemorrhages in the lining of his stomach and also a heightened gastric acidity. Something resembling a small ulcer finally developed and the investigators were impressed with the possibility that "the chain of events which begins with anxiety and conflict and associated overactivity of the stomach and ends with hemorrhage or perforation is that which is involved in the natural history of peptic ulcer in human beings."[15]

Since the above observations were made, there has been additional direct evidence that psychological stress produces ulcers. In one experiment, nine hungry and thirsty rats were kept in a situation involving marked approach-avoidance conflict. They lived in a rectangular box with food at one end and water at the other. Both ends were electrified. When a rat approached either the food or water, it received a strong electric shock. The shock was on continuously for forty-seven hours, then turned off for one hour. This sequence was repeated for a period of thirty days. Rats of a control group lived in similar boxes, but without shock. Of the nine experimental animals, six developed gastric ulcers. Two of these died from hemorrhages toward the end of the experimental period. None of the controls developed ulcers. The three experimental rats which failed to develop ulcers received a respite on the twentieth day, and for three

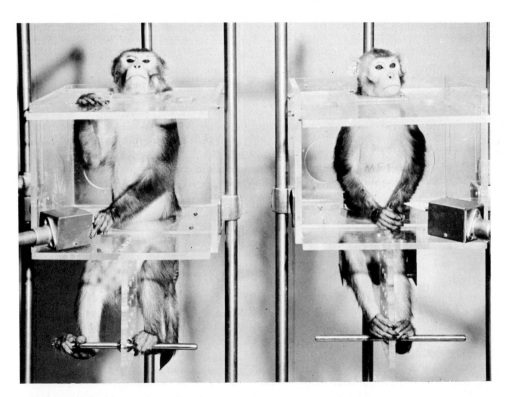

● 8.5

An Avoidance Situation Which Produced Ulcers. When the monkey at the left pressed a lever at proper intervals, it postponed an electric shock for both itself and its partner (right). This "executive" monkey developed ulcers. The partner's lever had no function and was soon ignored. This animal, with no avoidance behavior, failed to develop ulcers. (Courtesy of the investigator, Dr. J. V. Brady, and the Walter Reed Army Institute of Research, Washington, D.C.)

days thereafter. This was because the shocking apparatus connected to their boxes broke down. Perhaps this respite reduced their "anxiety level" and thus saved them from ulcers.[16]

An experiment somewhat comparable with the above has been done on monkeys. The monkey on the left in Figure 8.5 could escape electric shocks which came at twenty-second intervals if he pressed the lever at appropriate times. He was therefore designated an "executive" monkey. The animal shown with him received the same shocks, when the "executive" reacted inappropriately, but itself had nothing relevant to do. This monkey had the same kind of lever as the "executive," but this was not connected with the current and it was finally ignored. The investigators report that the "executive" monkeys developed ulcers while the others, even though punished for the "executive's" mistakes, did not.[17]

Although there is no indication that ulcers in human beings are always produced by emotional stress, there is no doubt that they occur more frequently in people undergoing prolonged anxiety than in those who are more serene. One clinical study showed that, of seventy-five persons suffering from critical stages of ulcer, sixty-three had been subjected to unusual anxiety. This involved financial difficulties in some instances, but in others there had been family conflicts and worry over real or imaginary illnesses.[18]

□ A relatively new field of investigation and clinical service known as *psychosomatic medicine* has called particular attention to the bodily harm that protracted emotional stress can cause.[19] Development of ulcers is only one of these harmful effects. Among others that have been attributed wholly or in part to emotional stress are sinus disorders, asthma, high blood pressure, and certain skin disorders.

In one published account a well-known woman journalist tells how a resolution of conflicts improved her sinus trouble and also her social adjustment.[20] Another account by a research chemist reports how conflicts which aggravated an ulcer were alleviated, with a subsequent improvement in physical and mental well-being.[21] In this case, as in the other, psychoanalysis had revealed unconscious sources of conflict. Many other cases are reported in books on psychosomatic medicine and in a journal with that title.[22] Although only psychoanalysis has been mentioned, other psychotherapies are also helpful. Some of these are described in the next chapter. □

Escape from conflict

Studies of emotional stress have demonstrated that continued conflict, in addition to being unpleasant, is also deleterious to physical health, but a certain amount of conflict is perhaps inevitable and there may be some conflicts from which we cannot escape through any effort of our own. The man "trapped" by his mother in the case already described was in a dilemma from which he saw no way of escape. It is quite evident, however, that many conflicts may be resolved if the individual assumes a problem-solving attitude toward them. Students often worry about such relatively simple problems as getting assignments done on time. Obviously the best way to remove such conflicts is to stop procrastinating and go to work on the assignments, thus getting them out of the way. The best corrective to worry over a difficult decision is to make the decision as soon as possible — perhaps utilizing Benjamin Franklin's method of balancing the pros and cons. When conflicts are more serious and we cannot solve them on our own, it is always well to seek professional guidance, thus alleviating the stress and preventing its inroads on mental and bodily health.

When conflicts are not resolved in the direct ways already suggested, various indirect reactions or subterfuges are often utilized. These are goal-directed, in that they *seem* to alleviate or to solve the problem. Some have been called *ego-defensive* or *compensatory*, since they defend the person's self-esteem (his ego) in situations where, without such defenses, he would be forced to admit ignominious failure.

Ego-defensive behavior is somewhat comparable with the compensatory (homeostatic) mechanisms which, as we have seen, underlie certain physiological drives. Psychologists have adopted the term *homeostasis* to represent, also, the compensatory reactions aroused when self-respect is threatened. One psychologist prefers the term "autocorrectivism," which has a very similar meaning.[23] Human beings compensate in many ways, as we shall now see. ■

COMPENSATORY REACTIONS

The term *compensation* is most often used in psychology to refer to: (1) emphasis on one motive when expression of another is blocked or (2) the substitution of one means of expressing a motive when another more direct means of expression is not possible. In both instances we have substitution — either of another motive or of a new form of expression of the same motive.

As examples of the first type of compensation we may take the man who, because his sex motive is thwarted, emphasizes strenuous athletics, and the unattractive girl who emphasizes scholarship.

Examples of the second form of compensation are found in the woman who desires children, but is unable to have any of her own, hence enters kindergarten work; the business man who, after having a morning scrap with his wife in which he couldn't answer back, takes it out on his employees; the individual whose desire for new experience is thwarted except when he reads a novel, or, better still, goes to the movies — where he can, vicariously at least, go on a safari through the jungles of Africa, man a machine gun on the deck of a plunging battleship undergoing air attack, or carry on a flirtation with Brigitte Bardot; the parent who, unable to have a college education himself, makes sacrifices so that his son can have one, and then experiences vicariously all of his son's failures and successes; and the man who, in a gabby world, finds joy in belonging to a secret society, or, in a humdrum world, can join a lodge and be a Thrice Exalted Knight of the Enchanted Realm. All of these are examples where one expression of a motive is blocked, but another expression serves, in some degree, the same purpose.

The man who satisfies his desire for new experience by following the hero of a novel or movie, and the parent who experiences the successes and failures of his child as though they were his own, are *identifying*. We say that the individual identifies himself with the character in question. People often have palpitations of the heart, weep, grimace, and even cry out when identifying with characters in movies or on the stage. Sometimes identification is with an institution rather than with an individual. Thus a certain low-paid and academically frustrated instructor in a very large university got compensation out of the fact that he was connected with a university having many thousands of students. The bigness of the institution in which he taught was, for him, the only consoling aspect of his predicament. It bolstered his ego where his academic rank and his salary did not. Membership in a certain fraternity, lodge, or other organization having great prestige often serves a similar function. The member feels himself a better, more successful person, because of his affiliation. ■

FANTASY

Fantasy too may be compensatory. This is a form of dreaming (day or night) where we go through certain acts in imagination. It plays an important role in human life, and especially as an outlet for the frustrating circumstances of everyday experience.

When hostility resulting from frustration is not expressed in hostile acts, it is often represented in fantasy. Such "fantasy aggression" is a common human experience. It occurs in covert verbalizations like, "Who does he think he is? I'll get even if it's the last thing I do!" Fantasy aggression is sometimes evident in children's drawings. The "angry boy" of a documentary film* hated his mother, his teachers, and other children. His spontaneous drawings were of maimed and bandaged people and of houses and cities being destroyed by bombers. One evidence of the effectiveness of

* This film is *Angry Boy*, sponsored by the Michigan Department of Mental Health and distributed by the International Film Bureau, Inc.

psychotherapy was the fact that this boy began to draw pictures of children happily at play.

Children's fantasies are often revealed in their play, and especially in that involving make-believe persons and objects of everyday life. Doll play, for example, can reveal the frustrations and conflicts as well as the happier aspects of child life. Figure 8.6 illustrates fantasy aggression in doll play.[24] The child has been given a stylized doll's house representing the layout of its own preschool. There are school fixtures, two teacher dolls, and six preschool children dolls. The child tells a story and arranges the items to conform with its theme. What is implied by the arrangement illustrated is that this child is hostile toward teachers and boys, probably because these have in some way frustrated her and made her angry.

Psychologists have made wide use of the so-called *Thematic Apperception Test*, involving a series of pictures about which the subject tells a story and, in doing so, reveals his "innermost fantasies." Quite often a particular theme runs through each of these stories. Thus a person named "Karl" had an unusual number of death themes.[25] The way in which the people died in these stories was unusual in that, instead of being killed by persons, they died from impersonal agents or unknown causes. Moreover, the kind of person who died was usually a parent or relative. The unusual number of deaths is taken by the psychologist who studied Karl to suggest aggression fantasy and an underlying insecurity or anxiety. The way in which people died in Karl's stories suggests to the psychologist "(a) that Karl has acute anxiety over his aggressive impulses; (b) that he was severely punished for aggression in childhood; and (c) that his high punishment was probably associated with high nurturance." Nurturance refers, of course, to parental attention or control. The fact that it was a parent or relative who died is taken to mean that Karl has had since childhood a basic fear of being orphaned, or rejected, and at the same time has had such hostility toward his parents that, symbolically in his stories, he gets rid of them by having them killed off.

● **8.6**
An Example of Projective Doll Play. This is an instance of what Bach characterizes as "hostile fantasy aggression." One teacher is "burning" on the stove, another's head is pushed into the toilet, and a boy is squeezed under a washbasin. (From G. R. Bach, "Young Children's Play Fantasies," *Psychological Monographs*, 1945, 59, No. 2.)

One of a series of pictures used to study adolescent fantasies is shown in Figure 8.7. The themes of love and aggression were prominent in the stories told, one of the more detailed of which is reproduced in the legend.

The doll-play and picture-story tests that we have been describing are said to be "projective" because they induce the individual to identify himself with the situations and thus, without being conscious of it, reveal (project outward) his own conflicts and attitudes. Tests of this nature are given more detailed consideration in the following chapter where their use in assessing personality is discussed. Projecting as a compensatory mechanism will occupy our attention shortly.

Dreams

Dreaming is a form of fantasy which, like daydreaming, often gets its impetus from personal problems. Freud[26] regards the dream as a wish-fulfilling device, and also as a guardian

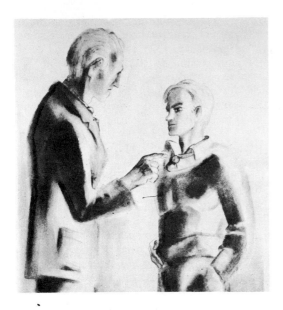

of sleep. For him, "every dream is an *attempt* to put aside a disturbance of sleep by means of a wish-fulfillment." Our biological urges (represented in Freudian theory by the id) demand satisfaction. This demand is made upon the sleeping ego. Sometimes it stems from doubts, conflicts, or inability to reach decisions. "The sleeping ego," according to Freud, "is focused upon the wish to maintain sleep; it regards this demand as a disturbance and seeks to get rid of the disturbance. The ego achieves this by what appears to be an act of compliance: it meets the demand with what is in the circumstances the innocent fulfillment of a wish and thus disposes of the demand. This replacement of a demand by the fulfillment of a wish remains the essential function of dream-work." Examples of dreams having this function would be found when a person who is hungry dreams of going to the refrigerator and having a meal; when the time to wake up and go to work has come but the worker merely dreams that he is up and on his way; and when the person who is sexually aroused dreams that sexual desires are being satisfied. In each instance, satisfying the demands of such situations directly would mean waking up. By satisfying them symbolically, as in the dream, the person's sleep is safeguarded.

● 8.7

One of the Pictures Used to Study Adolescent Fantasy. In response to this picture, one adolescent told the following story: "The boy looks like a roughneck. He is young and looking for adventure. He acts wise to the whole world. His environment is not the best thing for his character. He gets mixed in with crooks, and they start training him. An old hand at crookery gives him advice on the best way to do things; to steal. He plans for the boy to help in pulling jobs. First the boy is to be a lookout. They finish the job with a good haul and congratulate the boy. The next job they let him come inside and teach him how to do it. On another job they let him do it alone. Then they go to the hideout after each job. The boy sees them attacked one night by the police. During the raid he sees the true character of the men — how they sacrifice each other for themselves. They make one man run out. They are all for themselves. He tries to break away. They won't let him, as he is involved too deeply. He doesn't know what to do. He wants to tell the police, but he has learned the code of the criminal never to squeal. Finally he decides it would be right, for they are doing wrong and hurting men. He tells, and the men are captured. He is acquitted for turning state's evidence. He thinks now that he can go straight. But it's not that way. People won't hire him. They thought he was criminally inclined. He tries to get back to the mob, but they don't want him. They didn't want a squealer. Besides, his life is in danger. He goes on, an outcast. He is most likely an outcast even after he dies. He has done wrong, has repented, and now will probably have to spend the rest of his time in Erebus between Heaven and Hell." (From P. M. Symonds, *Adolescent Fantasy*, Columbia University Press, 1949, p. 285.)

There is no doubt that many dreams can be given this interpretation. It is not surprising, therefore, that psychoanalysts use dream analysis in seeking to discover the desires, frustrations, conflicts, and anxieties of their patients. We saw earlier (p. 18) that dream analysis is used both to diagnose and to treat certain personality disorders. It was involved in the diagnosis and therapy of the psychosomatic disorders mentioned a few pages back.

☐ There is an extensive theoretical and experimental literature on dreams, quite apart from that dealing with dream analysis and personality. Dreams are often aroused experimentally, by stimulation of the sleeping subject. They may also be induced hypnotically. Some studies deal with aspects of dream imagery (for example, with its color or lack of color). Others concern the duration of dreams. Still others deal with the relation between dream content and stimulating circumstances. Evidence that a person is dreaming comes from observing eye movements under the closed lids, or through electrical recording of such movements.[27] These eye movements make it appear as if the individual is watching his dream, as though it were projected before him. Electroencephalograms reveal the depth of sleep and also give some indication that dreams are occurring.[28]

All of this is of course peripheral to our main interest in this chapter, but the reader who wants further information may obtain it from the references cited. ☐

Fantasy may be expressed in fiction and other products of creative imagination. Psychiatrists and psychologists have analyzed such products in an effort to discover the basic motivation of their creators.[29] Many artistic creations may be regarded as compensatory. Some are indirect, socially acceptable expressions of frustrated love, homosexuality, aggressiveness, and other hidden motives. Freud coined the term *sublimation* to represent the various indirect, socially acceptable expressions of frustrated motives. While sublimation may occur in fantasy, it sometimes appears in overt behavior, as when a sadist becomes a boxer, a dentist, or even a surgeon.

Experimental investigations of fantasy

Many investigations of fantasy have asked subjects to make up stories about pictures. In such investigations, special interest has been attached to the possibility that fantasies might be manipulated in predictable ways by altering a person's motivation. It has been found, in fact, that subjects deprived of food for periods up to sixteen hours use more food fantasy than under normal conditions.[30] This is reminiscent of the finding (p. 167) that semistarved men become preoccupied with thoughts of food and things associated with it. It is also in line with the commonplace observation that the conversation of hungry people often turns to food. One is reminded, too, of the pin-up girls favored by frustrated males, and of such songs as *South Pacific's* "There Is Nothing Like a Dame."

Our society places a great deal of emphasis upon getting ahead, making something of oneself, or obtaining recognition; thus instilling an *achievement motive*. Laboratory investigations have shown that this motive may be manipulated in such a way as to change the subject's fantasies. Pictures like that illustrated in Figure 8.8 were used. Male college students looked at such pictures and then answered the following questions: What is happening? Who is the person? What has led up to this situation? That is, what has happened in the past? What is being thought? What is wanted? By whom? What will happen? What will be done?

The subjects were told that they were being tested for creative imagination. There were thirty-nine students in each of three conditions (relaxed, neutral, and ego-involved). Each subject made up a story about each of four pictures.

Subjects tested under the *relaxed* condition were told that the investigator was a graduate student trying out various tests in the developmental stage. The investigator joked, showed no concern for the outcome of the tests, and did not ask the subjects to sign their names. The picture tests were given along with an assortment of others (anagrams, scrambled words) which actually had no significance in the experiment.

The *neutral* condition was designed to produce normal motivation such as usually exists in the classroom. Thus the investigator was presented as a graduate student gathering data for his Master's thesis. He said that he wanted to establish norms, and asked for serious cooperation. Again the unrelated tests were given with those on "creative imagination."

● **8.8**

A Picture Used to Elicit Stories Which Could Be Scored for Achievement Imagery. Stories created by different subjects in response to such pictures are given in the text. (Photo, courtesy of Dr. D. C. McClelland.)

Under the *achievement-oriented* condition, every effort was made to get the subjects ego-involved. The investigator ostensibly came from another university. The subjects were told that the tests were for the purpose of measuring their intelligence and that these were being given under the auspices of the Office of Naval Research with a view of discovering men with leadership qualities. These and similar remarks were calculated to arouse the achievement motive. The pictures and associated tests were identical with those used in the other groups.

That the latter condition aroused more achievement fantasy than the other conditions, and considerably more than the relaxed condition, is shown by the results summarized in Figure 8.9. Some stories scored as having achievement imagery are as follows:

The boy is a college student. He is trying to recall a pertinent fact. He did not study this particular point enough for an examination he has to take. He is trying to recall that point. He can almost get it but not quite. It's almost on the tip of his tongue. Either he will recall it or he won't. If he recalls it, he will write it down. *If he doesn't he will be mad.*

The italicized words suggest competition with a standard, which is of course achievement motivation. In the following example, the italicized words suggest "unique achievement."

The boy is a student and doing a boring clean-up job. His mind is going off on a tangent, and he is daydreaming. He has just come from a class in medieval history, and the instructor's reference to the knights of old has made the lad project himself into such a battle arrayed with armor and riding a white stallion. The boy is thinking of riding out of the castle, waving goodbye to his lady fair, and *going into battle and accomplishing many heroic deeds.* The boy will snap out of it when he sees his boss coming along and will become frantic, realizing he had not been paying attention to his work.

Achievement imagery with "long-term involvement" is illustrated in the following excerpts from stories:

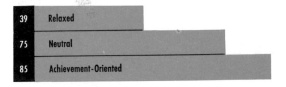

39	Relaxed
75	Neutral
85	Achievement-Oriented

● **8.9**

Effect of Motivation on Fantasy. Each bar represents the frequency of achievement imagery elicited under each of the three conditions. The highest possible frequency would be 156 (because there were thirty-nine subjects and each reacted to four different pictures). Observe that the achievement-oriented condition aroused 85 instances of achievement imagery out of the possible 156. (After D. C. McClelland *et al., The Achievement Motive,* Appleton-Century-Crofts, 1953, p. 141.)

The boy is thinking about a career as a doctor. He sees himself as a great surgeon performing an operation. . . .

A boy is *to take an examination for entrance into the Army Air Corps.* He has studied very hard in high school *hoping all along that he will someday be a fighter pilot. . . .*

The boy is a thinker. . . . He has faith in his capabilities and *wants to get started on the job he has lined up, dreaming of advancements. . . .*[31]

Stories like these may tell the investigator a great deal about the motives, values, and ideals of the person who creates them.

Fantasy becomes dangerous, from the standpoint of mental health, when it loses contact with reality by dealing with desires impossible of fulfillment; when it involves impractical solutions; and when it is continually substituted for the real thing, thus preventing an actual adjustment. ■

BELITTLING AND BLAMING OTHERS

These reactions are also compensatory. They are ways of maintaining self-respect in the face of failure. The person whose ego is badly deflated often inflates it, so to speak, by thinking of or pointing out the faults of those who have succeeded where he has failed. Thus, the girl who fails to get into a sorority may point out that those who do so are a lot of handshakers, that they think more of politics than of scholarship, or that they are too cliquey a bunch anyhow. This makes her feel a little more happy with her lot. It may go to such an extreme that she is "glad" she didn't get in with such a bunch.

Students who fail courses, for example, often say that they had a "punk" teacher, that the text was beyond comprehension, or that their class came at a bad hour. Sometimes they are right. In the majority of instances, however, such students are attempting to maintain self-respect at a high level by refusing to recognize their own faults. A student once said that the writer's chief weakness was an inability to make up exams that students like her could pass.

Mental hospitals contain many people who place responsibility for their troubles upon others. They accuse others of putting ground glass in their food, of poisoning them, of throwing radio waves on them, and of perpetrating other criminal acts. ■

OVERCOMPENSATION

Another important compensatory reaction is *overcompensation.* Like other compensatory phenomena, this is associated with efforts to overcome threatened inferiority or threatened loss of self-respect. It is associated especially with conflict due to personal defects. As the name implies, overcompensation is a tendency to do more than remove the defect. The former weakling who does not stop when he has developed a normal body, but strives to become the "World's Strongest Man," is overcompensating for his original defect. Theodore Roosevelt and Helen Keller exemplify people who more than overcame their physical defects. Louise Baker's *Out on a Limb*[32] is an interesting account of how one girl, who lost a leg in childhood, made herself a one-legged celebrity. At the end of this biographical account of her life, the author implies that if she had possessed two legs, she would have had nothing interesting to write about. Many "ugly ducklings" have become great actresses, and many people of small stature (Franco, Mussolini, Napoleon — to mention but a few) have become dictators or great military leaders. Many of the radicals in politics are obviously overcompensating for feelings of inferiority. A book dealing with psychology in politics traces the radical tendencies of several such individuals to childhood frustrations.*

A form of overcompensation, but in reverse, is *self-repudiation,* or *self-depreciation.*

* Lasswell, H. W., *Psychopathology and Politics.* University of Chicago Press, 1930; also see H. Cantril, *The Psychology of Social Movements.* Princeton University Press, 1941, and G. M. Gilbert, *The Psychology of Dictatorship.* Ronald, 1950.

The individual says, "Oh, I'm terribly dumb," "You know, I'm awfully homely," or, "I'm just not good for anything." The answer they desire is, "Of course you're not dumb," "I think you're beautiful," or "You may not be able to cook, but you're a sweet little woman just the same." In many such instances the individual does not really feel inferior, but is merely "fishing" for compliments. He is rudely disappointed if the other person says, "That's right, you *are* dumb."

An extreme degree of self-depreciation often appears in neurotic depression, in which the patient may claim that he has committed serious sins, that he is good for nothing, or that he is a burden to others. The writer of a recent book on psychopathology[33] says that such statements are "the irrational products of deep unconscious conflicts, of ego defense and ego adaptation, of superego pressure and appeals for outside aid. The original sources of depressive self-depreciation, the sources that defeat all attempts by other persons to reassure and to reason, lie in a state of ego-superego tension which we call *unconscious guilt*." In this condition, "the patient rejects, despises, looks down upon himself, in much the same way that he felt his parents rejecting, despising and looking down upon him when he was a disobedient, disappointing, unwanted or 'bad' child."[34]

PROJECTING

Projecting is somewhat like the reactions already considered, in that it often has a compensatory function. We project whenever we attribute our thoughts or desires to others. Projection is also involved when otherwise meaningless situations are given meaning in terms of our own motives. It is for this reason that picture tests like those already discussed are said to be projective.

Projection is very often an indirect wish-fulfillment. Thus, the girl whose desire for response from men is frustrated may imagine that men have designs upon her. A college girl once known to the writer accused men of chasing her while she went home through a

park. Upon investigation, however, it became apparent that she had not been chased. As the psychiatrist put it, "She wished that men would chase her, the wish was father to the thought, and her imagination got the better of her."

Projection sometimes comes from feelings of guilt. If one has done something of which he is ashamed, he may imagine that people have found it out, and he may see relevant significance in their actions. A person who "felt like spitting on himself" got the idea that men whom he passed on the street wanted to spit on him.

A girl who was told, under hypnosis, that she had stolen some money was very depressed when awakened. She did not know why. When shown and asked to comment about two men in a picture (Figure 8.10) she saw one as sad and the other as reprimanding him. Later she said that the boy sitting next to her stole

● **8.10**

An Example of Projection. In the book that these subjects are looking at is a picture of a man sitting and another standing. The girl says that the man sitting is sad because the man who is standing is accusing him of some wrong that he has done. Different people give different interpretations of this picture. The girl's interpretation is based upon a "guilt complex," as described in the text. (From the sound film "Unconscious Motivation," prepared by Lester F. Beck, and distributed by Association Films, Inc.)

the money. She was obviously projecting her own depression and her own guilt.

In an experimental study of projection, fraternity brothers rated themselves and each other. Such traits as stinginess-generosity and bashfulness-forwardness were rated. Subjects who failed to see themselves as others see them — those who were relatively lacking in social insight — showed a marked tendency to rate others as they rated themselves. If one of these rated himself high on stinginess, for example, he rated others high on this trait; if he thought himself generous, he attributed generosity to others.[35]

Indeed, a person who feels guilty often lessens this feeling by imagining that others are guilty too. For example, the married woman who carries on a flirtation may accuse her husband of unfaithfulness, and the college student who cheats may say that his fellow students cheat when they get a chance to do so.

Like some other reactions already mentioned, projecting is often found to an extreme degree in the mentally ill. Many inmates of mental hospitals attribute their desires, their thoughts, and even their acts to others. One man said that his every act (even crime) was the "will of God." Another had shot at a girl whose impending marriage was just announced. He did this because, for the year or so that they had been passengers on the same streetcar, she "had deceitfully led him on by her actions." The girl hardly knew of the man's existence and had never given him any reason for his accusations, but her acts had been interpreted as having amorous reference to himself. Later, discussing delusions and direction in thinking (Chapter 13), we shall cite further instances of such projecting. ■

RATIONALIZING

Rationalizing is faulty, defensive thinking, motivated by the desire to retain self-respect. It serves this purpose, at least temporarily, by enabling us to avoid facing issues and to excuse our failures. Rationalizing often takes the form of "kidding oneself" as to the real motives for his conduct.

Perhaps the most common kind of rationalizing is the attempt to justify decisions or actions by finding "good" reasons for them. A student knows that he should study, but wants to go to the movies. He resolves the conflict by telling himself that too much study will ruin his eyes, that he needs a rest anyhow, or that he'll be able to study even better the next day. Likewise, a married man who carries on affairs with women other than his wife saves his self-respect by concluding that "man is by nature polygamous" or that his wife doesn't really appreciate him anyway. Why doesn't he tell his wife about his unfaithfulness? If he did so, "she would feel unhappy" and "what she doesn't know won't hurt her." The girl who says, "Oh, I didn't want that man anyway — he'd perhaps have turned out no good," or, "Who'd want to join *that* sorority?" is belittling others, but she is also rationalizing. This form of rationalization is very appropriately designated a *sour-grapes* reaction. It is obviously compensatory, since it eases the sting of defeat.

Rationalizing often begins at an early age. A three-year-old who did not want a neighborhood child of five to visit him because this child monopolized his "fire engine" was told that he must invite the other child to come over and have a ride. He said that the other boy might be having his nap. When told that the other boy was up, he said the sky looked as if it might rain. When he was told that it would not rain, he said that the boy's mother might not want him to come. He made one excuse after another, and never did get around to giving the child an invitation.

A child confronted by the alternatives of taking his teddy bear to school and being thought a "big boy" did not take the bear, but his excuse was that the bear might get a cold.

It is probable that children acquire this tendency to rationalize by copying patterns of rationalization set by adults. The "sour-grapes" pattern is obviously copied, for parents frequently tell a child, when they do not wish him to have something, that it is "no good," that it will "make him sick," or that boys who play with such things are "sissies."

It seems only natural that, when frustrated under similar circumstances, he should tell himself things like those his parents have told him.

Rationalization is so prevalent a reaction to situations involving conflict that it cannot be regarded as abnormal. It is sometimes excused on the ground that it reduces the qualms of conscience or misgivings from which all of us suffer from time to time. Some assert that "if we did not rationalize, we'd go crazy." There is at least a grain of truth in such assertions, but they are themselves largely rationalizations. There is no good substitute for facing life squarely and meeting difficulties realistically. ∎

REGRESSION

Whenever an individual confronted by difficulties "gives up" and reverts to such reactions as weeping, kicking objects around, stamping his feet, and even "cussing," he is regressing to an earlier, less adequate mode of reaction. These reactions may release tension — help us "let off steam" — but they seldom solve our problems. We say "seldom" rather than "never" because many a child learns that temper tantrums or sulking get him the things he desires. He may, in fact, continue to use these long after adequate modes of adjustment are possible. Men and women often revert to these earlier responses when frustrated. Wives sometimes dominate their husbands, and husbands their wives, by fits of sulking, weeping, and threats that they will "do away with themselves" or "go home to mother" if they do not get their own way.

Psychologists have carried out several experimental investigations of regression in animal and human subjects. Emotion-provoking stimuli like electric shock, a cold shower, or a sudden loud noise presented just before the moment of response lead many subjects to revert to earlier, less adequate forms of adjustment.[36] An experimental production of regression in rats is illustrated and described in Figure 8.11.[37] Children who have been toilet-trained sometimes revert to soiling and wetting when frustrated by the arrival of a baby who gets some of the attention that they previously enjoyed. They may also become more dependent in other ways, such as again wanting to be picked up a great deal and wanting help where it is not needed. Regressive behavior is also exhibited in play activities. As they approach school age, children become increasingly constructive in their play. Instead of merely moving things around, pulling them apart, or knocking them down, a child *uses* them in various ways. He uses one to manipulate another, he joins things, and he builds. When frustrated, however, children often become less constructive than formerly. This has been demonstrated experimentally.[38]

□ The play activity of thirty preschool children was rated for constructiveness. A frustrating situation was introduced and play activity was again rated. The children were observed individually in a specially designed playroom consisting of two areas separated by a partition. After playing with various toys for a specified period and having its activities rated for constructiveness, a child was introduced to the other area, previously hidden by an opaque partition. Here it was allowed to play for fifteen minutes with some very enticing objects, including a doll's house with accessories, a truck and trailer, and other toys. The child was then returned to the other play area and a wire screen was lowered and padlocked. The more enticing toys could now be seen, but not reached. Some children attacked the barrier and others appealed to have it raised. Such attacks or appeals being of no avail, the child began to play with the toys originally available. Again its constructiveness was rated. Under free-play conditions before frustration, the average constructiveness score was 4.99. During frustrated play it dropped to 3.94, a change of 1.05 points (equivalent to an 18-month regression). That is to say, the children's constructiveness was, on the average, like that of children 18 months younger. Of the thirty children, twenty-two showed varying degrees of regression, three showed insignificant decreases in constructiveness, and five actually became more constructive. ∎

● 8.11

A Regression Experiment with Rats. The floor of the apparatus carried an electric charge, the effect of which could be diminished by sitting on the hindlegs, as illustrated at the left. When a lever was later inserted, as at the right, the shock could be eliminated entirely by pressing it. The experimental rats were placed in the apparatus (without the lever) one at a time and given a continuous shock through the floor. They soon learned that they would receive comparatively little shock if they sat quietly on their hindlegs and held their forepaws off the floor. Eventually all of the experimental animals held this position (with occasional random activity) until the shock went off. The duration of the shock was fifteen minutes. The posture eventually adopted by this group may be designated Habit One. Rats in the control group were not given an opportunity to acquire this habit. After a member of the experimental group had learned Habit One, it was placed in the same box, now containing the lever illustrated. These rats soon learned to give up Habit One in favor of terminating the shock altogether by pressing the lever. This is designated Habit Two. The control group also learned to terminate shock by pressing the lever. Both the experimental and control groups were, in fact, trained until they had acquired equal facility in escaping shock by this means. The crucial part of the experiment was then introduced. This involved electrifying the lever itself so that, as the rat touched it, but before pressing, he received a shock on the forepaws. Under these conditions, four out of five experimental rats reverted to Habit One (i.e., regressed). They merely crouched on the floor. All of the control rats, on the other hand, continued to press the lever. (After O. H. Mowrer, "An Experimental Analogue of 'Regression' with Incidental Observations on 'Reaction Formation,'" *J. Abn. Soc. Psychol.*, 1940, 35, 56–87.)

REPRESSION

Some people react to conflict situations by refusing to admit the existence of difficulties, of defects, or of particular motives. These people are said to be repressing. A jealous child who refuses to admit the existence of his baby sister is repressing. So also is the person who has conveniently forgotten some unpleasant obligation.

Repressing is not merely inhibiting, although one may, in repressing, inhibit an unpleasant thought. A clear case of inhibiting occurs when you decide to study instead of going to a movie. We may say that you inhibit movie-going activity, but it would not be correct to say that you have repressed such activity. Repressing would clearly be present, however, if you refused to admit the existence of the movie or of your desire to see it. In repressing, therefore, you close your eyes to reality.

What we put out of mind or try not to think about is usually the unpleasant. Sometimes we repress by dropping off to sleep. An old gentleman known to the writer always dozed off when he began to read something which seriously assaulted certain ideas to which he firmly held. Charles Darwin was so cognizant of this tendency to avoid or forget the unpleasant, and so intellectually honest, that he made a point of jotting down immediately any observation which failed to support his views. Confirming observations were also noted, but not with the same urgency.

☐ Ego-defensive repression is interestingly demonstrated in an experiment involving failure to solve a series of jigsaw puzzles. College students were divided into two groups, members of each group being given a different "set" concerning the reason for giving them the task to be performed.[39] Members of one group were told that the experimenter wanted to classify the puzzles for further use and that their reactions would assist him. In this group, "interest was mainly centered on the task so that incompletion could mean very little beyond residual tension related to the problem in hand." Members of the other group were given the puzzles as an intelligence test. Thus they might be expected to assume an ego-defensive "set." The investigator says that under these conditions "incompletion would almost inevitably be experienced as failure." Members of both groups were permitted to finish half of the series, but were stopped midway in each of the remaining tasks. Later, each student was asked to name the puzzles attempted.

Earlier research on completed and incompleted tasks had shown that unfinished tasks are recalled more readily than finished tasks.[40] The hypothesis to be tested by this experiment was that the "intelligence-test" group, experiencing personal failure when prevented from completing tasks, would recall fewer unfinished tasks than the other group. The experimental outcome supported this hypothesis. Only eight out of thirty students given the puzzles as an "intelligence test" recalled a preponderance of unfinished tasks. This number is to be compared with nineteen out of thirty for the control group. The group subjected to greater stress actually recalled more finished than unfinished tasks, as one might expect. Two more recent experiments,[41] with different materials and somewhat different methods of producing a "threat to self-esteem," also demonstrated poorer recall of unfinished tasks by those subjected to threat. In these experiments, however, the threatened group did not recall more finished than unfinished tasks. ■

REACTIONS TO EXPERIMENTALLY PRODUCED CONFLICT

If a dog is trained to respond to a circle and not to an ellipse, and the ellipse is then gradually made more and more like the circle, a point is eventually reached where the animal does not "know" whether or not to respond. That is to say, it is unable to differentiate between the two stimuli. When this point is reached, many of the animals suffer a "nervous breakdown." They may whine, struggle when restrained, refuse to eat, and show, in general, what might be characterized as "nervousness." Pavlov, in whose laboratory this type of reaction was first studied experimentally, thought that the breakdown resulted from a conflict between the tendency to make and the tendency not to make a response to the situation.[42] Many later writers have stressed the "conflict" basis of neurotic behavior in human beings.

Reactions suggestive of neurotic behavior have been observed in rats,[43] cats,[44] dogs,[45] pigs,[46] and monkeys[47] subjected to approach-avoidance conflict situations. The animals are hungry and approach is elicited by food. Most often, in such studies, shock is the aversive stimulus. In order to satisfy its hunger the animal must cross an electric grid, or receive a shock as it presses on a pedal that opens the food box. Indeed the grid-crossing situation has been used to measure the relative intensities of drives, the idea being that the stronger the drive the more often an animal will take shock in order to satisfy it.[48]* When the shock is sufficiently strong, however, the approach tendency is counterbalanced by the avoidance motive and an intense conflict is elicited. The reactions of animals to such a conflict vary, but fear or panic, resembling fear and panic in human beings, is the most frequent outcome.[49] Vacillation is also a common response. The subject approaches the food, retreats, approaches, and retreats, again and again. Finally it either eats or gives up. Similar results are obtained when the aversive stimulus is a blast of air (used with cats) or a feared object (a toy snake, used with monkeys).

Conflict situations more closely resembling the type used by Pavlov have produced abnormal reactions in rats and pigs. In one experiment, rats were trained to flex a leg whenever a bright light went on, and to refrain from flexing it whenever the light was dim. The difference in brightness was then reduced until the rat could no longer clearly discriminate a difference. Then it didn't know whether to flex its leg or refrain from flexing it. Under these conditions, one rat seemed unable to inhibit leg flexion. It squealed and tried to avoid the experimenter's hand. Another seemed unable to flex its leg.[50] Somewhat similar conditions in a different experiment produced a rigid posture, in which the rat's whiskers were motionless. When removed from the apparatus, the animal maintained positions in which the experimenter placed it. Excessive urination and defecation, suggesting emotional upset, also occurred in such situations.[51] Conflict

* The general outcome of such experiments has been that maternal behavior in rats (mother running to her pups and taking shock to do so) is strongest of all. Thirst comes next, with hunger a close third. The sex drive in both males and females (in heat) is much weaker than thirst and hunger. The exploratory drive (with a chance to explore materials placed beyond the electric grid) is weaker still.

situations similar in nature to that described have also produced convulsions in rats.[52] A pig learned that cessation of one tone was to be followed by a shock to the foot and that cessation of another signaled the dropping of an apple into the food box. The animal either lifted its foot to avoid the shock, or opened the box to get the apple. After this had been learned, more stringent conditions were introduced which resulted in more shocks. Now the pig became greatly disturbed. It showed a marked tendency, first of all, to lift the lid of the food box and its foot at the same time, as if "torn apart." Finally, the animal became "sulky," went into a sleep-like trance, and exhibited other apparently "neurotic" reactions.[53]

The studies that we have been describing were carried out to test the hypothesis that conflict — of motives or of response tendencies — is a basic factor in the origin of neurotic behavior. Animals are useful here because it would be unethical to attempt to make human beings neurotic. On the other hand, many case histories reported by psychiatrists, including psychoanalysts, show that conflict contributed to the neuroses of their patients.[54] ∎

CONFLICT, "WILL POWER," AND INITIATION OF ACTION

While they have wide popular usage, the terms *will* and *will power* are seldom used by psychologists, because they really explain nothing. To say that one "wills" to do something, or that he exerts "will power," tells us that he decides or intends to do what he does — that he is not doing it automatically or unthinkingly — but it does not tell us how his decisions are reached or how they are carried over into action. These are the crucial problems. We know much more about the basis of making decisions than we do about the carrying over of decisions into action.

The concept of will power

You are, let us say, confronted by a very difficult decision and, after much deliberation, you assert, "I will do so and so!" Or you are confronted by a very difficult task which will take years to complete. There are many temptations to quit or to put it aside, but you persist until the task has been completed. Or, to take one more of many possible examples, you are listening to an uninteresting lecture, but with great effort keep your attention on what the lecturer is saying. In each of these instances you have, it is claimed, used "will power." Will power is thus usually inferred when your decisions are difficult to make, or when you persist in your endeavors, despite distracting influences. It is never inferred when decisions are easily made or when behavior is lacking in persistence. Nor is it assumed to exist in animals below man. The mother rat may persist in gathering her young, despite the electric grid that she must cross in doing so, but we would not infer that she was using will power. Rather obviously, her behavior persists because the motive to get to her young is stronger than the motive to escape an electric shock.

Psychologists have come to regard the varieties of behavior attributed to "will power" as expressions of the relative strength of motives. If we think in terms of vector psychology, the decision stems from the incentives having the strongest positive valence. In other words, those alternatives which, in terms of innate drives and past experience, promise the greatest ultimate satisfaction of motives determine the direction of choice. To say that "will power" swings the balance is to say no more than that the decision was difficult, but that the motivation to perform one act was stronger than the motivation to perform the other. The Japanese soldier confronted by the imminence of capture had two alternatives. One of these was to save his life by surrendering. But this, in terms of his training from childhood, meant that he would lose self-respect and also the respect of his ancestors and associates. The other alternative was to kill himself. This, in terms of his training, meant that he would have everlasting glory and honor in the supernatural life that had been promised him. So the soldier killed himself. Because our training does not put life and

death in the same light, it seems to us either that such people are "barbaric" or that they have exceptional "will power."

A similar interplay of motives is involved whenever behavior persists in the midst of temptations to give it up. If you persist in your efforts to get a college education, and put aside temptations to get married and quit, to take a job which offers immediate financial rewards, or to enjoy yourself at the expense of studying, it is probably because, as you think of the various alternatives, getting a college education exerts more "pull." You may be motivated by the desire to gain prestige, to prepare for further professional training, to avoid disappointing your parents, to finish what you have started, or by a combination of these or other motives.

Some of us find that persistence is made easier if we publicly state what we intend to do. Then, whenever associates ask, "How is that project going?" it acts as a spur to continued effort. By following this procedure, we put ourselves "on the spot." Most of us hesitate to admit that something we have started has to be given up because of our own lack of persistence. If we do give up under such circumstances, we usually find "good" excuses for it — like ill health or interference of other work.

The person who does not persist in his endeavors, who seems to have little "will power," may be one who does not weigh the pros and cons, who does not have any long-range goals, or for whom such goals have only a weak attraction.

Initiation of action

Under such conditions as extreme fatigue, alcoholism, low oxygen tension, low blood sugar, hypnosis, and brain injury, we may make decisions, yet be unable to carry them out.

An individual had several drinks and then felt that he should go home. He arrived there all right, but sat down in a chair and read for a while. He then said to himself, "I guess I'll go to bed now." But he did not go to bed. Two hours later he was still sitting and thinking about going to bed. The alcohol had temporarily robbed him of the ability to act in accordance with his intentions.

Investigators of high-altitude flight have found that insufficient oxygen often produces a state like the above. Individuals who wait too long to take oxygen are unable to do so, even when they are conscious and know what to do.

An inspector sat in a mine writing a last letter to his wife while he slowly approached asphyxiation from monoxide gas.[55] His letter did not make sense. It was incoherent and repetitive. But the important point for our purposes is that he knew perfectly well that, by walking twenty yards, he could avoid death. He had lost the power to initiate appropriate movements.

Related to the problem of "will power," therefore, is the problem of how, once we have chosen a course of action, we initiate the appropriate responses.

Reactions are customarily classified as *voluntary* (literally under the control of will) and *involuntary* (literally not under the control of will). Opening and closing my hand are called voluntary acts because I can control them myself. The contraction of my pupil, however, is involuntary. I have no control over it. It must be aroused by a stimulus which I myself cannot provide by thinking of, imagining, or intending its contraction.

The nervous pathways most directly involved in voluntary activity begin in the motor area of the cerebral cortex and terminate in the skeletal muscles (as discussed and illustrated in Chapter 2). It is therefore apparent that the neural events which initiate the voluntary movement must activate the cerebral end of these fibers. It is also apparent (from what we know about activities in the association neurons of the cortex) that these activities provide stimulation of the voluntary motor fibers. But what kind of associational activity necessarily precedes voluntary movement? This we do not know in any detail.

Introspective reports indicate that thinking or having an "idea" of a movement precedes voluntary arousal of the movement. We know that thinking of a movement, such as clenching the fist, automatically elicits slight movements of the muscles involved and that these movements produce action currents which may be measured with a galvanometer.[56] The activities of association neurons which underlie thinking of the movement apparently serve to activate the cortical end of the motor pathways. Introspection also reveals that merely thinking of the movement does not produce it — all that occurs is a very slight, or an incipient, movement. If I want actually to clench my fist, I must *intend* to clench it. Here again, although we do not know the details, whatever cortical activities underlie intention apparently stimulate the motor paths which end in the appropriate muscles, and stimulate them in a somewhat different manner from that involved when we merely think of the movement.

We have already pointed out the important role which language, especially in the form of implicitly talking to ourselves, plays in motivational activities. Language is especially important in the voluntary control of behavior. This conclusion is supported by general observations and experiments on the development of voluntary control. Individuals have learned to move their ears.[57] They have learned to move in isolation muscles of the body that are not usually subject to such control.[58] They have even learned to make isolated motor units within a muscle twitch while the rest of the muscle is relaxed (Figure 8.12).[59] They have learned to make hairs on the forearm rise "at will."[60] They have learned to contract the small blood vessels in the arm by thinking of a visual pattern or saying a word repeatedly associated with placing of the hand in icewater and thus, with automatic constriction of blood vessels.[61] Not all the above obviously involved language, but they all involved either thinking or language responses. Thinking in man is partly a subvocal or implicit form of speech, as will be brought out in Chapter 13.

Suppose, for example, that I intentionally contract my biceps. While intending to contract the muscle, I must have some representation of it in mind. I may look at the muscle; but, if it is covered, an image of it, or only its name, may suffice. Beyond this there is some-

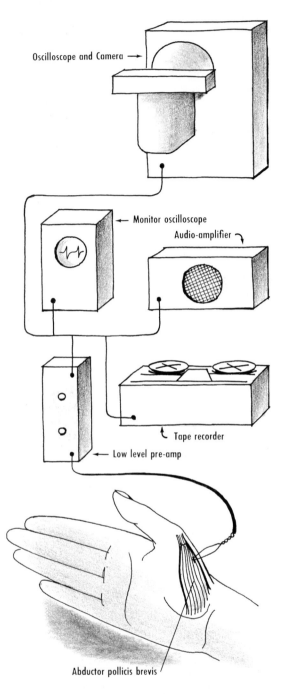

Oscilloscope and Camera →

← Monitor oscilloscope

Audio-amplifier

← Low level pre-amp

Tape recorder

Abductor pollicis brevis

Voluntary Control of Individual Motor Units. With electrodes placed in a muscle, contraction brings action potentials which may be seen on an oscilloscope (and recorded on film) and which may also be heard through an audio-amplifier (and recorded on tape). Thus a person contracting a muscle may have visual and auditory feedback in addition to that normally present through the kinesthetic sense. With an appropriate placement of indwelling electrodes, moreover, it is possible to identify individual motor units, each of which has its characteristic visual and auditory action pattern. The motor units involved in this research each comprised a motor cell in the ventral root of the spinal cord (see Plate 2, facing page 48), its axon, and all of the muscle fibers activated by the terminals of this axon. The outcome of stimulation via these channels was a twitch. Subjects with indwelling electrodes in the *abductor pollicis brevis*, as illustrated, could at first only voluntarily move the whole muscle. That is to say, when they intended to move only the unit in which the electrodes were placed, they moved the whole muscle. But with practice, aided by visual and auditory feedback from the motor unit, they gained voluntary control of this unit while the rest of the muscle was relaxed. Some subjects retained their ability to control this unit after external feedback had been withdrawn. In the investigator's words, "subjects can recall into activity different single motor units by an effort of will while inhibiting the activity of neighbors. Some learn such exquisite control that they soon can produce rhythms of contraction in one unit, imitating drum rolls, etc." (From J. V. Basmajian, "Control and Training of Individual Motor Units," *Science*, 1963, *141*, pp. 440–441.)

involved in the control of voluntary movement are those generated by the behavior of the organism itself. The kinesthetic, tactual, and auditory stimuli involved in language are the most important self-induced stimuli in man. By the aid of such receptor processes the organism becomes relatively independent of its external environment and can regulate its own behavior to an extent impossible in the infrahuman animals. Behavior controlled by the organism's own language responses is voluntary in the highest degree." ∎

thing equivalent to saying "contract," as if this command were directed at the muscle. The importance of such linguistic activity in voluntary behavior is stressed in the following statement.[62]

"The particular stimuli most significantly

• SUMMARY

Frustration, and associated psychological stress, have various sources — environmental obstacles, including other people who thwart us, our personal defects, and conflict situations. Among the latter, several basic types have been outlined. These are approach-approach, avoidance-avoidance, approach-avoidance, and double approach-avoidance. Ambivalence is a form of approach-avoidance in which a person may be both loved and hated.

People differ in their ability to retain normal reactions when frustrated. Those who do not "go to pieces," those who can "take it," are said to have a high frustration tolerance. Many people whose frustration tolerance is low lose their goal-orientation in times of stress. They do and say things which defeat rather than advance their aims. Aggressive behavior is often instigated by frustration.

The causes of particular conflicts are often hidden from the troubled person. He may, for example, know only that he has conflicts, like unreasonable fears (phobias) or the compulsion to carry out some act. We say, then, that the relevant motives (or motivational conflicts) are "unconscious." One function of psychoanalytic procedure is to bring such conflicts into consciousness, where they can be examined and possibly dealt with. When he knows the basis for his frustrations, a person may assume a problem-solving attitude, using all his resources to reach a goal, or to force a resolution of conflicting alternatives. He should attempt this in the interest of his health as well as his happiness. Reference has been made in this connection to the general adaptation syndrome (alarm reaction, resistance, exhaustion) associated with various forms of stress, including the psychological. The adrenal cortex seems to play a critical role in this "emergency reaction." It has been established that prolonged emotional conflict can produce ulcers and other psychosomatic disorders.

Associated with frustration are various compensatory or subterfuge reactions. Some of these resemble the physiological compensatory activity known as maintenance of homeostasis. This is because their prime function is not so much to solve one's problems as to cushion the ego (feeling of self-esteem) against threatened deflation. Among such ego-defensive reactions are *fantasy* (including wish-fulfilling dreams and daydreams), *projecting* (imputing one's thoughts and desires to others), *rationalizing* (finding "good" reasons for our actions or assuming a "sour-grapes" attitude), *repressing* (trying to ignore or forget the things that bother us), *regressing* (a reversion to childish ways), *identifying* (becoming ego-involved with other persons and situations), *blaming others* (excusing ourselves on the ground that others are responsible for our failures), *overcompensating* (doing more than is necessary to overcome defects, perhaps capitalizing on them), and *sublimating* (getting indirect but socially acceptable satisfactions).

This does not exhaust the list of compensatory mechanisms, nor does it imply that those mentioned are non-overlapping. Blaming others, for example, may be considered a form of rationalization under certain circumstances, and it may represent a reversion to modes of reaction adopted in childhood (hence regression).

Abnormal reactions may be produced in animals by placing them in critical approach-avoidance situations (like having to take an intense electric shock in order to eat) and by requiring them to make especially difficult discriminations (where it is difficult to decide whether to make or not make a particular response). Extreme excitement resembling panic is a common outcome; but animals may also show such "neurotic" behavior as regression, extreme passivity, and a sleeplike trance.

"Will" and "will power" are inferred from behavior in conflict situations, especially the making of difficult decisions and the persistence of activity in a given direction despite obstructions and temptations to give up. Decisions made under such circumstances may be interpreted as a resolution of conflicting alternatives. When decision is difficult to make, pros and cons are closely balanced. The effort involved in making the decision may be that of "weighing" the alternatives. Persistence can be interpreted similarly. The individual who persists in pursuing a long-range goal is perhaps one for whom this goal, in terms of his past experience, has a greater attraction than more immediate goals.

Language appears to play an important part in the initiating of action, once decisions to act have been reached. The cortical activities which mediate linguistic processes may initiate the impulses which, running from the motor cortex to the muscles, produce voluntary movement. Activities that are normally involuntary may come under voluntary control through special training. With auditory and visual feedback supplementing that from kinesthesis, it has even been possible to gain control of individual motor units. ■

REFERENCES AND NOTES FOR THIS CHAPTER ARE IN THE APPENDIX.

• SELECTED READINGS

Atkinson, J. W. (Ed.), *Motives in Fantasy, Action, and Society.* Van Nostrand, 1958. The assessment of motives and frustrations through the general thematic apperception approach. A compendium of 46 studies.

Cameron, N., *Personality Development and Psychopathology: A Dynamic Approach.* Houghton Mifflin, 1963. Chapters 5 and 6 are especially relevant to the present chapter.

Cofer, C. N., and M. H. Appley, *Motivation: Theory and Research.* Wiley, 1964, Chapter 9, on frustration, conflict, and stress.

Daniel, R. S. (Ed.), *Contemporary Readings in General Psychology* (2nd ed.). Houghton Mifflin, 1965, readings 41 (dreams), and 44 and 45 (psychoanalysis).

Freud, S., *An Outline of Psychoanalysis.* Norton, 1949. This is a translation of a study first published in German in 1940. It was an attempt by Freud to state his views in concise terms. The book is 127 pages long.

Hall, C. S., *The Meaning of Dreams.* Harper, 1953. A comprehensive study of dreams and their meaning, with much of the data gathered from college students.

Hall, C. S., *A Primer of Freudian Psychology.* New American Library (Mentor Book), 1955. A good brief review of Freudian concepts of human adjustment.

Miller, G. A., E. Galanter, and K. H. Pribram, *Plans and the Structure of Behavior.* Holt-Dryden, 1960. The literature dealing with the influence of plans on behavior is organized in accordance with a model devised by the authors.

Miller, N. E., "Liberalization of Basic S-R Concepts," in S. Koch (Ed.), *Psychology: A Study of a Science.* McGraw-Hill, 1959. Includes a discussion of conflict.

Selye, H., *The Stress of Life.* McGraw-Hill, 1956. A general survey of stress, with the author's revolutionary views on its role in disease.

Young, P. T., *Motivation and Emotion.* Wiley, 1961, Chapter 12. This is a general discussion of the dynamics of frustration and adjustment.

9

Personality

The term *personality* refers to the whole person — to the characteristic and overall integration of his various motives, abilities, reaction tendencies, and other aspects. With respect to this, each of us is unique, for no two persons can be said to have the same personality.

A personality is exceedingly complex and has many aspects, depending upon how we view it and the situations in which it finds expression. We might say that it has many facets, components, or dimensions. Psychologists refer to these as *personality traits*. Some traits are quite evident — like a person's sociability. These are so-called *surface traits* and we attempt to measure them with rating scales and question-and-answer tests of various kinds. But there are other traits which such tests fail to reveal. Our sociable person has "depths" to his personality. Below the surface are motives, aspirations, perhaps anxieties. These so-called depth factors are often not evident even to the person himself. We say, then, that they are *unconscious*. When this is so, special techniques must be used to reveal them. Our earlier discussions of the unconscious, unconscious motivation, and psychoanalysis may be recalled in this connection. Probing the depths of personality by the methods of free association and analysis of dreams has already been discussed. Projective tests also probe the unconscious and we have mentioned some of these in discussing fantasy. More will be said about such methods in this chapter.

Nobody knows how many really different personality traits there are. A study of standard dictionaries shows that the English language includes eighteen thousand terms representing aspects of personality.[1] However, many of these mean the same thing, or nearly so. Take, for instance, the terms: *anxious, fearful, apprehensive, troubled,* and *worried.* Perhaps one word, like *anxious,* would serve for all of these, and many more. This sort of reduction leaves us with the key term *anxious.* After selecting such provisional trait designations, psychologists have developed tests designed to measure the corresponding aspects of personality. These tests have then been given to large groups, the scores have been analyzed statistically, and efforts have been made to discover traits which are essentially different. Suppose, for example, that tests designed to measure anxiety were found to be highly correlated with tests designed to measure submissiveness. The question would then arise as to whether these tests were not measuring the same trait. Suppose, on the other hand, that scores on the two tests were not correlated, or that the correlation between them were negligible. It would then appear that two different traits were being measured. The general technique used in such studies is factor analysis and the problem resembles that involved in trying to discover the primary intellectual functions, as described in the chapter on intelligence. Although much research along these lines has already been done, there is no clear indication of how many essentially different personality traits there are. One comprehensive investigation suggests that there are twelve such traits,[2] another suggests only seven.[3] It is interesting to note that only a few "traits" in the two lists are comparable. *Intelligence* appears in one list as a personality trait, but not in the other. The same is true of *sociability.* On the other hand, one lists *emotional stability* and the other lists both *emotional maturity* and *sensitive anxious emotionality.*

Our everyday judgments about the personalities of others tend to emphasize social aspects. We are impressed by manners, mode of speech, taste in dress, and how, in general, the person pleases us, annoys us, or, as the saying goes, "leaves us cold." If we know the person fairly well, we are also likely to judge him in terms of such things as his honesty, sexual morality, and consideration for the welfare of others. Such ethical and moral aspects of the individual's behavior are the basis for speaking of his *character*. Honesty, for example, may be regarded as a personality trait, but it is more specifically a *character trait*. Emotionality, on the other hand, has no particular ethical or moral implication, hence would be designated only as a *personality trait*.

Personality is, to most people, the social self of the individual, as revealed in his relations with others. There is evidence, in fact, that the term *personality* was derived in ancient times from the mask (*persona*) that an actor wore to show the audience whether he played the hero's or the villain's role.

Each of us began life looking different from other babies (unless we had an identical twin) and differing from them in such aspects of behavior as activity level and general excitability. If it could be said that we had any personality traits, they would be just two — *motility* and *excitability*. Other traits, including character traits and a social self, would come in time, depending upon the growth of our glandular and nervous systems and our interaction with the environment, especially in its social aspects. The most important of the latter would involve parents and other members of the family circle. It may be said, in general, that we begin as little animals, reacting so as to satisfy our biological needs; we have parents or others who place restraints on animal-like behavior; through our parents and others, we are molded to fit culturally accepted patterns of conduct; and even the nonsocial environment, as we interact with it, imposes limitations. We are attracted to those aspects which bring rewards and other desirable consequences and repelled by those which have punishing aspects. Moreover, we experience frustrations and, in accordance with how we cope with these, our further life adjustment is weakened or strengthened. The unique outcome of such developmental influences is what we call *a personality*.

We begin by considering the development of personality in more detail. Then the question of personality types will be dealt with, especially in relation to physique and temperament. Glandular contributions to personality are also relevant in this context. In discussing the assessment of personality we describe some typical procedures and their outcomes. Our chapter ends with a discussion of normal and abnormal personalities and certain aspects of psychotherapy. ■

DEVELOPMENT OF PERSONALITY

The development of personality is greatly dependent upon social perception and social interaction, neither of which is present to a significant extent for some months after birth. It is two months, for example, before infants begin to differentiate between the human and nonhuman aspects of their environment — to respond differently, let us say, to a human voice and the sound made by a quacking toy duck.[4] A further three or four months must elapse before infants distinguish between a scowling and a smiling face, or kind and scolding tones.[5] Perhaps the earliest evidence of social interaction is crying to be picked up, which begins at approximately two months. Smiling back at another person is also present at around this age.[6] Such evidences of social perception and interaction develop gradually. By the first

birthday, however, most babies are pulling at a grownup's clothes, imitating grownup activities, saying a few words learned from grownups, and using grownup expressions, like looking "amazed" at a strange happening.[7] Interaction with older children has similar aspects, but interaction with babies of the same age does not begin until the eighth or ninth month.[8] During the processes just described, the child is acquiring personality traits, like sociability and dominance or submission, and he is also acquiring that inner aspect of personality referred to as the self.

Emergence of the self

Along with his social perceiving and interacting with others, the child learns to differentiate his own body from inanimate objects and the bodies of others. He explores his body, visually and tactually, and becomes aware of the fact that it is *his*. He comes to notice the difference between tactual stimulation incidental to his own activities and that produced by others, to distinguish between self-produced and other-produced visual stimulation, and to notice the difference between speaking and being spoken to.[9] When the infant grasps his own foot, for instance, there is a double stimulation. His hand stimulates his foot and is stimulated in return. When someone else touches his foot, there is, by contrast, no more than stimulation of the foot. Visual stimulation produced by his own activity, as when he puts his hand in front of his face, is under the infant's own control. He can make the stimulus appear or disappear at will. This is not so when such stimulation comes from others. Likewise, when the infant vocalizes, he may, as pointed out earlier, hear the sound and also feel himself making it. When others vocalize there is no such feedback. He hears *them* and that is all. Gradually the perception of *self* as distinguished from other selves is developed. This is embodied, eventually, in such verbal terms as the pronoun *I* and derivatives like *my*, *mine*, and *me*. Concomitantly, the child comes to use such terms as *you*, *he*, *it*, and *they*.[10]

The *self* is essentially what Freud called the *ego*, with which we are familiar from earlier discussions. It is pictured schematically in Figure 8.4 (p. 231) as partially unconscious and an outgrowth of the more primitive and completely unconscious *id*. What Freud emphasized in his discussions of the ego was not so much the self-knowledge and identification of *I* and *mine* with the body and its processes and possessions, as considered above, but the dynamic properties of the ego in adjustment. One will recall that Freud looked upon the ego as an "intermediary between the id and the external world," an almost personified force. The child's reaching out toward his surroundings and being hurt or gaining pleasure in the process — in short, his *reality testing* — was considered by Freud to be the process which shaped his ego. One will recall, too, that the *superego* was regarded by Freud as a modification of the ego. In his reality testing, the child normally gains an awareness

of right and wrong and develops what is commonly called a *conscience* or, as Freud would say, a *superego*. This is to a large extent dependent upon parental influences. As Freud says, "The long period of childhood, during which the growing human being lives in dependence upon his parents, leaves behind it a precipitate, which forms within his ego a special agency in which this parental influence is prolonged." As the superego develops, the ego is called upon to satisfy simultaneously, "the demands of the id, of the superego and of reality. . . ." The ego's action is as it should be "if it is able to reconcile their demands with one another."[11]

Infant care

Some investigators have claimed that the sort of "mothering" a child receives during infancy does much to shape his personality. They have claimed that the inadequate mothering sometimes experienced by institutionalized babies tends to make them apathetic, depressed, and withdrawn.[12] Others have failed to observe such dire effects.[13] In one study, a group of babies given only the usual institutional care was compared with a matched group given special mothering. The only significant difference in outcome was greater social responsiveness in the mothered infants.[14] This, of course, raises the problem discussed earlier (pp. 173–174), when we considered an alleged "need for affection." It was pointed out in that discussion that institutionalized children usually have a restricted environment — one that lacks the varied stimulation, social and otherwise, that is normally experienced in the family situation. This, quite apart from inadequate mothering as such, could account for any observed personality defects. One should not overlook the fact that many infants, even in their own homes, are inadequately mothered. Some are given only minimal care. Their mothers cannot be bothered with them. What effect this has on personality is not known. One writer believes that "rejected" children, institutionalized or in their own homes, may lack the opportunity to develop a feeling of trust in others. He says, "The problem of the first year of life is to establish dependency on firm and natural foundations." Unless this occurs, "the whole life may manifest greediness, possessiveness, and similar efforts to obtain the condition of loving dependence that the individual was at first denied. In place of trust, the life is built on mistrust."[15]

Harlow's experiments with monkeys deprived of normal mothering (Figure 6.11, p. 174) may have some relevance in the present context. The animals reared with inanimate mothers had defective "personalities," as indicated by their later sexual inadequacy and callous treatment of their offspring — when they had any.[16] One could not, however, claim that inadequately mothered human infants show such defects in adulthood. For one thing, no human infant has, to the writer's knowledge, ever been as deprived as Harlow's monkeys were. Also, human children have more opportunities than monkeys do to compensate for what may have been lacking in their experience as infants. Failing to find security at home, they may form attachments outside the home which, in some measure, at least, give them what they have not hitherto experienced.

Particular forms of mothering may be very important in shaping personality, but no general conclusion about their effects is possible at the present time. Studies of child-rearing practices have shown that the outcomes of any particular practice, such as breast-feeding, early toilet-training, and early or late weaning, depend a great deal upon "the whole personal situation in which they find their expression, including the attitudes and behavior of the mother."[17] As other investigators have pointed out, there are "styles of mothering" and whether early toilet-training has any specified effect on personality may not depend so much upon toilet-training itself as upon how the mother goes about it. The same may be said for other aspects of infant care. Failure to obtain predictable outcomes also depends upon the child himself. The same mother could train two of her offspring with the same technique, yet differences in the inherent makeup of the children could lead to different outcomes. In addition, the later experiences of

the child, as suggested earlier, could alter trends established in infancy. Thus it does not seem that any general conclusion about the effects of mothering or of any particular infant training practices can be made at this time.[18]

The role of the parents

From the time of birth there is a more or less constant conflict between what the child wants to do and what his parents and others want him to do. When he sucks his fingers, his parent says, "mustn't," "dirty," "only babies do that." There is much "hush, hush" concerning sex. He must forego the pleasure of playing with his sex organs. He must not go around naked. He must not ask questions about sex or look at the sex organs of other little boys and girls. He must not scratch. He must not say certain words. There are literally thousands of "must nots" drummed into the child's ear. Whenever he refuses to obey these parental inhibitions, he is punished, perhaps by a harsh word, perhaps by being made to feel ashamed of his babyishness, perhaps by seeing the displeasure of his parents, perhaps by having various pleasures withdrawn, or perhaps by application of a switch or strap. In any case, he eventually comes to control his own behavior as the parents would control it; often repeating as if they were his own the parental words of admonition. The parent said, "You are filthy," and he now says or thinks, "I am filthy"; the parent said, "You should be ashamed of yourself," and he now says, "I ought to be ashamed of myself," or "I am ashamed of myself."

The superego represents this "internalization" of parental prohibitions and reproofs. Since these are framed in verbal terms, their acquisition in such terms is to be expected.

The parents of course reflect the cultural patterns and values of their own society, as these were impressed upon them by their own parents, teachers, and others. Their influence is, however, not merely negative. They set a pattern, an example which, whether the child follows it or not, does much to influence his own conduct and his attitudes toward himself and others.

In the course of such developmental organization as we have sketched, the child obtains his values, his ideals, his social attitudes, and a concept of his own role in the scheme of things. The parents are especially important because they get at him in his earliest, most dependent, and most formative years and because he is so long under their control.

☐ Most of us develop a superego which adjusts us reasonably well to our society. We learn not to be destructive, to be honest, to tell the truth, to refrain from hurting those around us, to be conscientious with respect to the responsibilities thrust upon us and, in general, to be "good citizens," to have "a good character." But, in some people the superego, if they can be said to have one, is defective. Although such persons differ a great deal among themselves, they are sufficiently alike in certain respects to be designated, in general, as *psychopathic personalities*. Most are bright enough to have learned the lessons that others learn and they are not mentally ill, at least not in the same sense as the psychoneurotic and the psychotic people considered toward the end of this chapter.

Psychopaths are characterized, in general, by irresponsibility and disregard for the feelings of other people. They have markedly defective characters. They lack moral values. Although each psychopath has his own particular kinds of misconduct, the following are commonly found, singly or in combination: lying without restraint, stealing for no apparent purpose, assuming responsibilities with no intention of carrying them out, and commiting sexual and other crimes with complete disregard for the rights and welfare of others.

Psychopaths tend to act on impulse, as if dominated by their id, or at least by their id and a very immature ego. How they failed to acquire the normal restraints is not known. Some of them come from homes of high, or relatively high, socio-economic status. Thus poverty is not a factor, as it frequently is in ordinary crime and delinquency.

The major source of psychopathic personality is some defect in interpersonal relations within the home. The individual may, to all outward appearances, have a very good home, with excellent parents. But his parents may lack affection for him, shower too much affection upon him, or use inadequate disciplinary measures. Indeed, extensive investigation of patterns of child rearing leads the investigators to conclude that a highly developed conscience comes largely through the mother's influence.[19] They say that "mothers who love and accept their children, and who use love-oriented techniques of discipline rather than material or physical techniques, produce relatively more children with high conscience." By love-oriented techniques they mean temporary withdrawal of affection, such as withholding the usual endearments. This is often quite influential if there is already a warm relationship between mother and child. Material and physical techniques involve material rewards, physical punishments, and withdrawal of privileges. ☐

We have said very little about the broader cultural and other situational backgrounds of personality. Cultural influences are, as it were, focused upon the developing child in the home, in school, and in the neighborhood. In addition to influences which stem from the culture itself, there are others — like having or not having brothers and sisters.

Cultural influences

Our personalities would be very different if we had been brought up by the Eskimos, the Sioux, the Balinese, or by some other cultural group (Figure 9.1). Not only would we dress differently, live in a different kind of dwelling, eat different food, use different implements and weapons, and have different social customs, but we would also have a very different conception of the world and of our own place within it. Our egos and superegos would differ greatly from what they are.

Cultural anthropologists have rightly placed much emphasis upon the "socio-cultural matrix" in which personalities develop.[20] Children reared in the United States acquire a way of life, and with it a personality, which an outside observer might well characterize as "typically American." But, even within this cultural matrix, aspects of personality may

● 9.1

Cultural Backgrounds of Personality. Personality traits and overall patterns of personality are greatly dependent upon the cultural matrix in which the child develops. The illustrations show the family situations of (1) Chinese; (2) Karba and his father and mother, Bali; and (3) Australian aborigines. (From: 1, Hil Pabel from Black Starr; 2, photographed by Gregory Bateson, 1936; 3, Australian News and Information Bureau.)

differ depending upon whether a child is reared in the North or the South, the East or the West; whether he is reared in the country, in a city, or a town; whether he grows up in the slums or in the best residential section; whether his early life is spent in a house or an apartment; whether his parents are rich or poor, together or separated, cultured or uncultured, religious or irreligious; whether he goes to a standard, substandard, or superior school; whether he has, or does not have, close friends; whether they conform, or fail to conform, to the mores of our culture; and so on.

Such socio-cultural influences are focused upon a child from the moment of birth and they continue to influence him all the days of his life. Some are especially influential in the early years and some not until the upper levels of maturity are reached.

Home influences

The most important early contacts are of course those between a child and its parents or guardians. These, as we have already suggested, provide a focal point for the culture. Parental behavior — whether stern or affectionate, permissive or prohibitive — is often culturally patterned. Within our own culture, however, child care and training, although culturally patterned in many respects, leave much to the discretion of the parents. If a child's parents are repressive and show no affection this often leads to *introvert* tendencies, the child withdrawing into a world of fantasy where, perhaps, he does what his parents will not allow him to do and finds the affection denied him in real life. This is not the inevitable reaction to suppression and lack of affection, however, for the child's temperament, which is doubtless partly inborn, plays a role. The same objective situation, although fraught with the possibilities suggested, may actually lead to resistance and a show of defiance. "The same fire that melts the butter hardens the egg."[21]

On the other hand, the parents may be overindulgent or overaffectionate, and they may encourage the child to "show off" in the presence of others, making him more *extraverted* than he might otherwise be. Then, too, they may encourage him to look to them for important decisions, creating a dependence that, with continued encouragement, may carry over into adult life. One mother may ask a child what kind of cereal he would like for breakfast, what book he would like to have read to him, which suit he would like to wear, and so on, requiring him to make his own decisions early. Another mother might give him what she thought he ought to have, and herself decide what he ought to wear and what he ought to have read to him. The second mother, wittingly or unwittingly, is encouraging dependence rather than independence.

How the parents react to curiosity about sex, what they say about relatives, about neighbors, and so on, all have possible effects.

Some parents continually go bull-headedly into conflict situations within the home, while others get around them in a manner conducive to eventual harmony and a minimal display of emotion. The following is an illustration of how children may be diverted from a certain course of action, yet without causing emotional disturbance.

□ A child came home from school with plans to go to an amusement park with several of her friends. Her parents felt that the park was not a fit place for young children to go unaccompanied. However, the children had made their plans. The next day, a school holiday, they were going early in the morning and were to stay all day. Many a mother would say, "You can't go!" — perhaps giving the reasons for her objections — and arouse antagonism. The mother in question solved the problem without eliciting the display of emotion which such parental frustration might arouse. She agreed to let the child go, then dropped the matter for a time. At the supper table, however, she said, "Mary, since you are going to _____ park tomorrow and will be out all day, I think I'll go into town in the morning, do some shopping I've been wanting to do for some time, eat my lunch downtown, and go to see a movie. I'll be home in plenty of time to get your supper." The mother knew well enough the attractiveness of the respective alternatives. After a moment or two of hesitation, the child said, "Mother, do you suppose that I could go with you if I don't go to _____ park?" The mother said, "Why, if you'd rather do that, we can go downtown together." □

There is literally no end to the examples of home influence that one might give. The above illustrations serve to point out that it is very important in the development of personality.

The same home situation does not, of course, always have the same effect. The child may become like the parent or just the opposite; he may conform or not, depending upon earlier modes of reaction, and perhaps upon the sort of individual he is constitutionally. Influences outside the home may also have their effect upon what the home itself does. One child feels trapped and does nothing about it, while another stays away as much as possible in the homes of friends.

The only child and birth order

Do only children differ in personality from children who have siblings? There is a widespread impression that the only child is "spoiled" and that he (or she) has personality traits not found in children with brothers or sisters. However, it is apparent from the extensive research on only children as compared with others that no general conclusion of this nature is justified. As one might expect, only children tend to be more restricted in their activities because of what has been called the mother's "controlling overprotection." They usually get more attention than other children, except perhaps the oldest child, who may be an "only child" for a year or more. Research on child-rearing practices in the United States has shown, moreover, that only boys are usually disciplined by their fathers; only girls, by their mothers. There is some evidence that only children, and first-born children, are more aggressive toward their parents and have a "more strongly developed conscience" than children in other family positions. In most respects, however, only children do not differ in any consistent way from children with siblings.[22] In one carefully controlled investigation on this problem, only and not-only children were matched for age, sex, socio-economic status, family organization, and I.Q. Personality tests were then given to the two matched groups, which consisted of thirty children each. Teachers also rated the children for various traits. There were small differences, sometimes in favor of the only children, sometimes in favor of the not-only children. The chief difference was that the only children had a few more "sissies" and "tomboys" among them than did the not-only children.[23]

Onliness has possibilities fraught with danger to normal development, but these are only possibilities. What is more important than onliness as such is how the parents handle the situation. If the child has other children to play with — at home, in the neighborhood, or in a nursery school — and if his parents do not center too much attention upon him, there is no reason why he should be handicapped by his onliness.

Much attention has also been focused on possible effects on personality of ordinal position in the family.[24] There is no clear evidence, however, that order of birth is related in any specific way to the child's personality. In individual cases, of course, the fact of being the oldest, middle, or youngest child may be im-

portant in determining the personality. As in the case of onliness, the most important consideration is how the parents treat a child in a particular ordinal position. Since parents differ so much in this respect, no special significance attaches to birth order as such.

Other social situations

In addition to the family situation there are, of course, the influences of the neighborhood, community, Sunday school, preschool, school, church, peer group (age-mates), and so on. Each such situation may leave its mark upon personality. Comradeships within any of these situations have, of course, possibilities for good or ill. The situations themselves, like the home situation, may have unpredictable effects on personality. School makes scholars out of some children, while it makes other children haters of school and anything relating to it.

In high school, college, and business or professional life, the situations that we meet may have an influence on certain of our personality traits. But personality is altered less at these levels than earlier, because once most habits and attitudes are acquired, they are somewhat resistant to change. Even though many individuals could change their personality in some respects, especially by reacting differently to social situations, they seldom do so. One reason is that they are often pretty well satisfied with themselves as they are. This prevents them from recognizing that they may have traits which could be improved.

Sometimes, however, the situation forces a new type of adjustment, or, if it doesn't force a change, at least becomes conducive to change. One of the most interesting examples of this is illustrated by the following experiment:

☐ A small group of college men agreed to cooperate in establishing a shy and inept girl as a social favorite. They saw to it . . . that she was invited to college affairs that were considered important and that she always had dancing partners. They treated her by agreement as though she were the reigning college favorite. Before the year was over she developed an easy manner and the confidence of knowing she was popular. These habits continued her social success after the experiment was completed and the men involved had ceased to make efforts in her behalf. They themselves had accepted her as a success. What her college career would have been if the experiment had not been made is impossible to say, of course, but it is fairly certain that she would have resigned all social ambitions and would have found interests compatible with her social ineptitude.[25] ∎

THE QUESTION OF PERSONALITY TYPES

It has been a favorite practice of human beings, including certain psychologists, to type their fellow men. In ancient times, as suggested by our discussion of actors' masks (their *personae*), there were heroes and villains. In comics, movies, and television there are likewise "good guys" and "bad guys."

When psychologists type their fellow men, they usually seek statistical justification (see p. 76) and they use a technical terminology.

Introversion-extraversion

One of the most widely used psychological typologies, that of the psychiatrist Carl Jung, refers to individuals as *introverts* or *extraverts*.[26] The introvert is pictured as reacting

negatively to situations or tending to withdraw from them. He is also characterized as inwardly reflective. The extravert, on the other hand, reacts positively. He is outwardly expressive, tending to be talkative and active in making social contacts.

We have many tests designed to measure introversion-extraversion. Some are behavior tests. One such test involves taking children into a museum and seeing how each reacts.[27] The path followed in going from one exhibit to another is traced and the time spent at each exhibit is recorded. Note, for example, the two patterns in Figure 9.2. The child rated as an introvert moved slowly, kept at the side of the adult most of the time, and did not return to any of the exhibits. But the child rated as an extravert showed a great deal of spontaneous interest in the exhibits, moved rapidly from one to another, went back to look again, and covered much more territory.

Most introversion-extraversion tests are for adults. These are verbal in nature. In taking one such test, the examinee checks, or leaves unchecked, statements like: *I daydream a lot*, *I would rather read than play games*, and *I like to speak in public*. Endorsement of the first two statements is rated as introvert: of the last, as extravert.

Another type of verbal test requires the subject to check one out of each set of items like the following:[28]

● **9.2**

Different Behavior of an Introverted and an Extraverted Child in a Museum Situation. A. The path of an extremely introverted child. The child refused to move without the experimenter, whose path is represented by the broken line. Black dots indicate stops. Gray areas represent exhibits. The figures show the subject's position at the end of each minute. **B.** The path taken through the museum by an extremely extraverted child. The long distances traveled and the frequent stops are characteristic of the extravert. (From Marston)

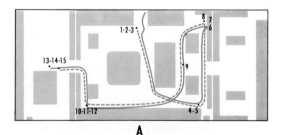

A

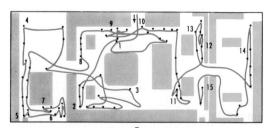

B

How do you prefer spending your odd moments?

_____ Always spend odd moments reading and planning

_____ Prefer to spend odd moments reading and planning

_____ Time equally divided between reading and physical activity

_____ Prefer to spend odd moments in physical activity

_____ Practically all odd moments spent in games and sports

Here the first statement is most introverted and the last most extraverted, with gradations between. This suggests, quite properly, that introversion-extraversion is a continuum and not a dichotomy.

What do such tests tell us about types? In an unselected group of people and even in a group of college students, we generally find something approximating a normal distribution. Most individuals, as shown in Figure 9.3, are in the middle.[29] This is because their introvert answers are balanced by extravert answers. We call these individuals *ambiverts*.

Although the data summarized in our figure show that schizophrenics tend to be introverted and manic-depressives extraverted, one should not conclude that introverts are inclined to be schizophrenic and extraverts manic-depressive. Look again at the figure and note that some normal people are as introverted as schizophrenics — and some as extraverted as manic-depressives. Some of our greatest thinkers and research scientists are decidedly introverted while some of our outstanding politicians are just as decidedly extraverted. However, the usual and most desirable tendency is ambiversion.

Physique and temperament

There is a widely held belief that human beings can be classified into physical types. Related to this is also the idea that somehow one's physique determines his *temperament*, a general term used to represent such emotionally toned aspects of personality as

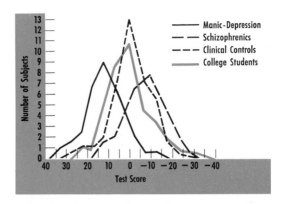

● **9.3**

Distributions Based on an Introversion-Extraversion Test. On this test, 35 manic-depressives, 35 schizophrenics, 44 mentally normal clinic patients, and 44 college premedical students were distributed as shown. The positive scores are in the extravert direction. Note that manic-depressives were more extraverted, as a group, than schizophrenics, but that many in each group fell into the ambivert range. Normal subjects, however, had predominantly ambivert scores. Thus there is no justification for saying that everyone is either an introvert or an extravert. In psychology we use these terms only to represent persons at the extremes of the distribution. This figure shows, on the other hand, that it is possible to select groups which will give predominantly introvert or extravert reactions. Manic-depressive psychoses and schizophrenia are discussed later in this chapter (pages 277–290). (From C. A. Neymann and G. K. Yacorzynski, "Studies of Introversion-Extraversion and Conflict of Motives in the Psychoses," *J. Gen. Psychol.*, 1942, 27, 241–255.)

joviality, moodiness, tenseness, and activity level. Shakespeare expressed a belief in the correlation between personality and body build when he had Caesar say,

Let me have men about me that are fat;
Sleek-headed men, and such as sleep o'nights.
Yon Cassius has a lean and hungry look;
He thinks too much: such men are dangerous.
Julius Caesar, Act 1, scene 2

● *Physique.* Differences in physique are obvious. Everybody knows a very fat person, a person who is bulging with muscle, and a person who is extremely thin. But he also knows many people who cannot be fitted into these categories. Such nondescript physiques provide the main stumbling block for those who attempt to type human beings in terms of body build.

Proving that people can be typed with respect to physique is one problem. Still another problem is to show that personality, unique in each individual, can be typed. If body types and personality types are found, one may then investigate the possibility that variations in body type and in personality type are actually correlated.

Kretschmer, in his *Physique and Character*, claimed that there are three main types: the *pyknic* (short and fat); the *athletic* (muscular); and the *asthenic* or *leptosome* (tall and thin). The pyknic type was credited with such personality traits as extraversion; the athletic with energy and aggressiveness; and the asthenic with a tendency toward introversion. It soon became apparent, however, that people do not, by and large, fit neatly into these categories. Moreover, even those who do fit the stereotype of a pyknic do not necessarily fit the personality type alleged to go with this physique. In one study, for example, 50 per cent of the pyknics were rated as extraverts while 30 per cent were rated as introverts.[30]

The most ambitious attempt to discover a possible relation between physique and personality is that of Sheldon, which substitutes quantitative ratings of both the bodily and psychological characteristics for the general impressions used by earlier writers.[31]

Hundreds of Harvard students were photographed from three different positions while naked. The thousands of photographs thus obtained were then arranged and rearranged in various series to see whether any types could be discerned. No clear-cut types were evident, but there were characteristics possessed *in varying degrees* by all individuals. Some had a very prominent abdominal region, some no prominence of this region at all, and others some degree of abdominal prominence between these extremes. This *dimension* of physique was designated *endo-morphy*, the name being suggested by the fact that our digestive viscera develop largely from the endoderm of the embryo (see Figure 2.1, p. 38). Individuals could also be arranged in a series with respect to muscle, some being extremely muscular and others less so. Since muscle comes primarily from the mesoderm of the embryo, this dimension was referred to as *mesomorphy*. One other dimension was evident, that having to do with thinness of body or with relative prominence of skin and neural structure. This was called *ectomorphy*, suggested by the ectodermal origin of skin and nervous system. As shown in Figure 9.4, each dimension is rated on a seven-point scale. It is interesting to note that a British investigator[32] refers to these three dimensions simply as *fat, muscular,* and *linear*.

It has doubtless already become apparent to the reader that those people with a predominance of endomorphy are the pyknics; those with a predominance of mesomorphy, the athletics; and those with a predominance of ectomorphy, the asthenics of the earlier classification.

• *Temperament.* The next step in this research was to devise a method of rating the subjects for temperament. Hundreds of terms describing aspects of temperament were selected and finally reduced to fifty. A group of college students was then rated for each of the traits represented — traits like relaxation in posture and movement, love of physical exertion, directness of manner, and so forth. Statistical analysis suggested that the apparently separate traits fell into three groupings, with the items within each group being closely related. One of these groupings, or "dimensions" of temperament, was designated *viscerotonia* because the many related items had some reference to visceral comforts, such as joy of eating, joviality, and relaxation. Another dimension was given the name *somatotonia* because the relevant items involved bodily (somatic) activity, as in competitiveness, energetic movement, and aggressiveness. The other dimension, *cerebrotonia*, was so named because the various related traits suggested a dominance of cerebral processes, as in apprehensiveness, restraint, shyness, and hypersensitivity.

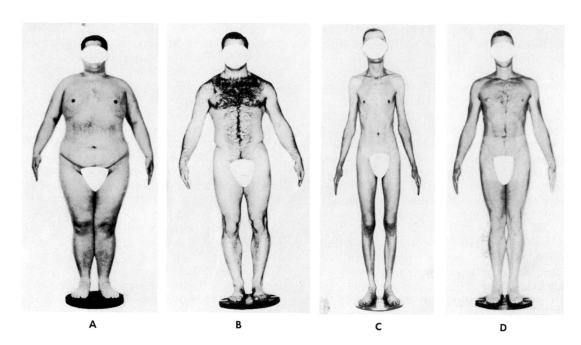

A   B   C   D

● **9.4**
Predominant Endomorphy, Mesomorphy, and Ectomorphy Compared with an Average Physique. The somatotype is given in terms of degree of endomorphy, mesomorphy, and ectomorphy, each number representing the respective degree of each. The predominant endomorph represented in **A** is somatotyped 7-3-1, meaning a maximum degree of endomorphy, a lower than average degree of mesomorphy, and a minimal degree of ectomorphy. The predominant mesomorph in **B** has the somatotype 1½-7-1; the predominant ectomorph in **C** the somatotype 1-1-7; and the average individual in **D** the somatotype 4-4-4. (From W. H. Sheldon and S. S. Stevens, *The Varieties of Temperament,* Harper, 1942.)

The investigators found that it was feasible to represent the dimensions of temperament, as in the case of physique, on a seven-point rating scale. Thus a person with extreme viscerotonia might be rated 7–1–1; one with extreme somatotonia, 1–7–1; and one with extreme cerebrotonia, 1–1–7. Case studies filled out the impressions gained from ratings. A student rated 6–3–2 for temperament had, among many other aspects, "a *persona* of joviality." Another rated 2–7–1 could be characterized as "boiling over with energy." Still another, rated 1–3–7, was characteristically "tense and apprehensive." There were of course individuals rated as intermediate in all three dimensions.

• *Correlation between physique and temperament.* Separate ratings of 200 male college students for physique and temperament yielded *r*'s in the neighborhood of .80. This high correlation is not surprising in view of the fact that (1) the same investigators did both ratings, (2) there was a tripartite classification of both physique and temperament, and (3) both sets of ratings were on a seven-point scale. Indeed the investigators admit a possible bias, but feel that this is not responsible for the correlations obtained.

Critics of the view that this research has revealed a significant correlation between physique and temperament emphasize the bias inevitably involved. What is needed is independent somatotyping and temperament typing; the latter with tests devised by others than those who do the somatotyping. The same persons should not do both the rating of physique and the rating of temperament. Until bias is eliminated in some such fashion, there are grounds for skepticism.

Sheldon's research is an interesting attempt to obtain quantitative evidence relative to the age-old belief that there is an important correlation between physique and temperament, but much additional work must be done before his conclusions can be accepted or rejected. Since his findings were published, several other investigators have attempted to substantiate them. Some studies offer support for the alleged somatotype-temperament relationship, while others fail to support it.

□ A study carried out with college students showed that, out of fifty predominantly ectomorphic students, forty-two were rated predominantly cerebrotonic, one somatotonic, one viscerotonic, and six without dominance of any of the three posited dimensions of temperament.[33] Only in the extreme of a dimension, however, could one expect such a relationship to show up so clearly. Another investigation, at a boys' academy, failed to show a correlation between the Sheldon somatotypes and various measures of personality.[34]

Sheldon's subjects were well-fed American college students. But what of people not so well fed? All subjects of an experiment on semistarvation eventually approached or attained an ectomorphic physique and the investigators concluded that "the technique of somatotyping would appear to be more useful for determining the state of nutrition than for determining the inherent constitution."[35] Another doubt comes from England, where Oxford University students were somatotyped. Unlike Sheldon's Harvard group, most of the Oxford students had average physiques. Extreme mesomorphs — men with "proportionately large bone and muscle development" — were absent, as were men with "a high proportion of fat and comparatively little musculature." The predominant tendency was toward "central somatotypes with more evenly balanced physiques."[36] People outside of universities, and especially people in middle or late life, might well differ from those who have been most commonly somatotyped. □

Should a significant relationship between physique and temperament be established beyond question, one might then ask why there is such a correlation. We should not, on the basis of this correlation, be justified in concluding that physique determines temperament, or vice versa. Both might depend to a large degree upon glandular functioning. It is possible, too, that temperament is influenced by how other people react to one's physical characteristics. If they avoid a person, or cause him to suffer indignities because of his physique, he may respond by becoming aggressive, or, on the contrary, by "crawling into his shell." If they lionize him because of his fine physique or his handsome appearance, he may act like the "cock of the walk." He may become conceited, domineering, or merely patronizing. Thus the significance of one's physical makeup, from the standpoint of personality, cannot be considered apart from its social impact and how the person himself reacts to this. A person's physique is to him the "image of himself."[37] Thus the predominant endomorph may learn that he is expected to be jovial and he may look upon himself as a jovial person. ■

PERSONALITY AND THE ENDOCRINES

We have said that endocrine secretions could account for the alleged correlation between physique and temperament, for it is well established that certain aspects of body structure are dependent upon hormones from the pituitary gland and that such aspects of temperament as sexual motivation and general energy level are influenced by pituitary, sex, and thyroid hormones. The endocrine glands were described in Figure 6.10 (p. 169) and some of their functions were discussed, particularly in relation to certain physiological drives.

One should keep in mind that endocrine secretions are essential for life. Unless they are available to the organism, directly from the glands themselves or from artificial administration, the whole body economy is thrown out of balance. Even a slight insufficiency in the amount secreted may lead to marked changes in appearance, physique, temperament, or intelligence, depending upon the gland involved. One may recall, in this connection, our discussion of cretinism (p. 135), a form of physical and mental retardation brought on by thyroid insufficiency during early growth. Changes produced by glandular deficiencies may have unfortunate social effects leading us to repel rather than attract others, or to be objects of amusement or curiosity, like the dwarf, giant, and bearded lady of the circus. In view of these facts one can see the aptness of an endocrinologist's claim that we are "terribly at the mercy of our endocrine glands."[38]

The endocrine glands comprise what is, in effect, an interlocking system. Disturbing the function of one gland may, so to speak, start a chain reaction which leads to malfunctioning of other glands. A gland of very special importance from this standpoint is the anterior pituitary, which secretes several hormones, each controlling the function of some other gland. One such hormone, familiar to us from an earlier discussion (p. 170), is ACTH, the hormone which stimulates the adrenal cortex. When activated by ACTH, the adrenal cortex secretes cortisone, a hormone necessary for life. If the pituitary is defective and fails to produce ACTH, the latter can be given by injection. Sometimes ACTH is secreted, but the adrenal cortex itself is defective. In this event, the condition may be corrected, and the person's life saved, by administering cortone, a synthesized cortisone. When there is inadequate cortisone, for whatever reason, the individual undergoes a marked change in personality; he becomes weak and lethargic, loses his sexual desire and appetite for food, and suffers a widespread breakdown of physiological functions, including salt metabolism. During regular administration of cortone, however, there is a restoration of general vigor and of other functions.

A growth hormone, already referred to as coming from the pituitary, also originates in its anterior lobe. The dwarf had an insufficiency of this hormone during early growth; the giant, an overabundance of it.

Sexual development and sexual functioning are likewise influenced by secretions from the anterior lobe of the pituitary gland. Several different hormones are important in this connection, including ACTH, as described in our discussion of sexual motivation. An undersexed male may have an underactive anterior pituitary, the underactivity being represented by insufficiency of the gonad-stimulating hormone.

Overactivity of the adrenal cortex in early life may produce puberty praecox, illustrated in Figure 9.5. There are several such cases on record, including some of little girls with the secondary sex characteristics of mature women.[39] Excess secretion of the adrenal cortex

● 9.5

A Boy with Puberty Praecox. The child's chronological age is six years, one month, and his mental age six years. Sexual development is equivalent to that of an adolescent. (Photo by Norman C. Havger.)

can also produce extremely masculine characteristics in women, such as those represented by the bearded lady.

A person's general vigor is influenced not only by ACTH and cortisone, to which reference has already been made, but also by the thyroid hormone, thyroxin. When thyroxin is insufficient, lethargy results. The condition is corrected by administering thyroxin. When thyroxin is secreted in excess, there is a condition referred to in general terms as "nervous tension." Treatment of this condition is designed to reduce the amount of thyroxin secreted. This usually involves surgery or irradiation of the thyroid gland.

In addition to the endocrine glands considered as having an influence on personality, there are others whose secretions, while important for life itself and various supporting processes, have no particular relevance in the present context. Some of these have been mentioned elsewhere; for example, the adrenal medulla and how adrenalin is involved in energy mobilization during emotion, and the posterior pituitary, some of whose secretions are related to thirst.

Perhaps a word of caution about endocrine functions is in order. Although an underactive thyroid tends to produce lethargy, one must not jump to the conclusion that every lethargic person has an underactive thyroid. Nor should we conclude that any obviously nervous individual has an overactive thyroid. Likewise, even the most sexually frigid person as well as the most sexually driven may have normal gonads. In other words, while specific glandular malfunction may produce certain changes in personality, similar changes are often produced by other conditions — disturbance of other glands, malnutrition, and attitudes and habits acquired in the course of development. Diagnosis of glandular malfunctions must come from the clinical tests of the medical laboratory. ■

THE ASSESSMENT OF PERSONALITY

Many situations in everyday life require personality assessment. In business and industry it is often very important to know certain things about the personality of a prospective employee. The armed services select men for important positions in terms of their personality. During the second world war the Office of Strategic Services (OSS) carried out an elaborate assessment program. It was designed to select personnel for such strategic services as gathering information behind enemy lines, organizing and training resistance groups, and disintegrating the morale of enemy troops. Educational institutions sometimes screen candidates for scholarships from the standpoint of personality as well as scholastic ability. The maladjusted child or adult is given personality tests designed to diagnose the nature of his difficulties. In mental hospitals and psychiatric clinics such tests are used not only to diagnose personality disorders but also to measure improvements resulting from psychotherapy.

Personality tests are also used in research, to aid in answering such questions as: How does personality change with age? Do *only* children have personality traits which distinguish them from other children? Do identical twins differ in personality? How are personality traits related to socio-economic status? What is the effect upon personality of growing up in a fatherless home? In order to answer such questions, the investigator must have at his disposal procedures for measuring personality.

The person who undertakes to assess personality, either for practical or for scientific ends, has a difficult task before him. He comes to the task with no knowledge of what we are and how we got to be what we are. Like the detective attempting to unravel a mystery, he comes in at the end. As he observes us, he finds that he can describe various aspects of our personality but that other aspects, including our motives, are obscure. To reveal these aspects he needs more than general impressions.

Sometimes the clinical psychologist obtains a case history, a reconstruction of the individual's life history as told by himself and those associated with him. In addition to revealing the person's developmental history, a case history at its best also reveals adjustment problems and the involvement of other people in these problems. An interview with the person provides additional information. But a case history and an interview are often insufficient. The individual must be observed in various situations and it may be necessary to have his behavior rated by others as well as by the investigator himself. In many instances it is also necessary to use questionnaires and a variety of standardized personality tests.

There are three general approaches to personality assessment. One of these might be called a *holistic*, or overall approach. Emphasis is placed upon evaluating the person as a whole. An answer is sought to the question: What sort of *person* is this? The holistic approach was first used by German military psychologists, then by British army psychologists, before it was adopted by the Office of Strategic Services (OSS) in the United States to select undercover agents and other strategic personnel. A second approach, which also aims to assess the whole person, but which does it less directly and with more restricted testing situations than the one already mentioned, is the *projective test* approach. The third approach is somewhat piecemeal by comparison with the other two. It goes upon the assumption that personality is a constellation of traits and also that the traits may be measured separately. This might well be called the *trait* approach.

As we pointed out at the beginning of this chapter, the trait approach has given rise to many tests designed to measure various aspects of personality, like introversion-extraversion. It is also behind the search for so-called "primary factors" in personality.

These three approaches are of course not mutually exclusive. Even the assessment staff of the OSS made some use of projective tests and also of tests designed to measure traits. The following discussion is arranged to indicate the nature of these three approaches and the sort of information revealed by each. ■

HOLISTIC ASSESSMENT

There is no one holistic procedure. Although they were aiming at overall assessment, the German, British, and American examiners used somewhat different procedures. For pur-

poses of illustration we have taken the procedure used by the assessment staff of the OSS.[40]

The staff of the OSS included psychiatrists, psychologists, and army administrators. Candidates lived with the staff in a single establishment designated as S. They arrived in groups and stayed for three days. Before arrival, each candidate was deprived of all means by which his test-mates might identify his civilian or service origins or status. He was given a fictitious name and told to create a cover story which would effectively hide his identity. Later, in a stress interview, he was grilled in an effort to make him break down and reveal his true identity.

Members of the staff began their appraisal as soon as a candidate stepped off the truck which brought him to S. How he greeted the staff, the position he took with respect to his fellows (whether he followed or led) and how he reacted to the strange situation, were all noted. Even his conversation was observed, to discover what it revealed about his attitudes, prejudices, ideology, faith, and purposes. After dinner, some stood aside while others engaged in conversation. This, too, was noted.

All were eventually given written tests and questionnaires. These were designed to reveal aspects of personality, as well as biographical information of possible value in interviews to follow.

The assessment program involved several *behavior tests*, of which the "brook test" is representative. This was designed to test group participation in problem solving and to reveal "natural leaders." In groups of from four to seven the men were taken to a brook which was to be regarded as a raging torrent, so fast and so deep that nothing could be rested on the bottom. Their job was to transport certain camouflaged equipment to the other side and to return with other camouflaged material. There were conditions which made this a difficult problem. In order to solve it, the men would need to cooperate effectively in building a bridge, an overhead cable, and other devices with the materials made available. No leader was designated. In this situation the observers looked for possible emergence of a leader, for shifting of leadership, and for such characteristics in the men as energy, initiative, relevant ideas, willingness to work with others, good nature when ineffective ideas were rejected, and so forth.

An important role in assessment was played by *interviews.* The investigators say that "No procedure yet devised by psychologists for the study of personality can take the place of the clinical interview. . . . it contributed more heavily than any other procedure to the final rating of all personality variables. It provided the frame of reference in which all other observations were evaluated. From it came a large measure of the understanding of the person. . . ."[41] The interviewers had at their disposal all of the biographical and other data concerning the candidate, and they guided the interview in terms of the kind of information needed.

The *stress interview,* to which we have already referred, was designed to discover the candidate's "capacity to tolerate severe emotional and intellectual strain." After his cover story was invented he was taken before a panel of interviewers (Figure 9.6). Here he was

• **9.6**

The Stress Interview. This candidate for OSS is being subjected to rapid-fire verbal interrogation with a view to testing his emotional stability under mental strain. The light is used to make him uncomfortable. He was not allowed to shade his eyes or turn aside. (From OSS Assessment Staff, *The Assessment of Men,* Rinehart, 1948.)

subjected to "strain created by rapid and merciless cross-questioning under disagreeable conditions." The ostensible aim was to detect flaws in his cover story. Questions were at first asked in a quiet conciliatory manner. Then, as some flaw was detected, an examiner yelled, "You're a liar." He would try to turn the candidate's story in such a way as to get him to admit a lie; then he would yell, "Now we have the truth, you admit that you lied." Tension was built up throughout the interview, so that at the end the questions were hurled at the candidate in rapid-fire staccato succession. The subject was not at any time allowed to relax. He sat straight up. If he crossed his legs he was told to uncross them. If he lowered his head to avoid the light, he was told to look up. After ten minutes of stress, the individual was told, "We have abundant evidence that you have not been telling the truth. That is all."[42]

During the interview the candidates were rated for degree of emotional control. They were observed closely to detect signs of sweating, flushing, swallowing, moistening the lips, stuttering, and so forth. Sometimes a candidate exploded with anger. Sometimes he wept. Sometimes he protested. Immediately after this stress interview, each candidate was given another interview under relaxed conditions. Here further efforts were made to get him to relax his guard and reveal secret information. The various responses of the candidates under these circumstances "gave excellent insight into their security consciousness as well as into their intellectual resourcefulness and emotional stability."[43]

Near the end of the assessment period, after many written and behavior tests had been given, many questionnaires filled out, and several interviews conducted, the men were given a *sociometric questionnnaire.* This was to discover how a particular man was *accepted* by others of the group, to reveal the men whom others *rejected,* to indicate how the person filling out the questionnaire *reacted to others,* and, in general, to reveal *leadership,* or the lack of it. The questionnaire included items like these: "With whom would you enjoy continuing your acquaintance?" "Which men seemed to antagonize other members of the group?" and "Whom would you recommend as supervisor of a group dealing with problems of planning and organization?"

The overall assessment pooled all available information and represented the combined estimate of various interviewers and other assessors. A good idea of the kind of assessment which came out of this holistic program may be gathered from the following personality sketch, which is abridged:[44]

☐ This competent, energetic, self-confident Sergeant is very well qualified for his assignment by his ability, personality, and background. He is a determined, clear-thinking person who has well-defined values and goals which he pursues with unswerving persistence, fully utilizing his capacity for hard work. In spite of his pronounced tendency toward self-reliance and independence which, combined with his rejection of indiscriminate gregariousness, often leads to bluntness in social relations, he is essentially a person of good will, is frank, sympathetic, sincere, and a good mixer. While his brusqueness and independence may alienate people upon first contact over a long period of time the student is likely to win and hold both the respect and affection of his colleagues. These traits, together with his readiness to take responsibilities for others, to solve problems, and to make decisions, qualify the candidate for a position of leadership higher than one which would be compatible with his rank.

Various relevant biographical data are given, then there is reference to the candidate's reactions in the OSS assessment situations.

Although the candidate's strong desire to do well makes him nervous and tense in test situations, or in beginning a new type of work, increasing familiarity with the situation quickly dissolves these tensions; the student is well integrated emotionally and has no disturbing conflicts or fears; while he does not seek danger he is willing to take any risks that the assignment might involve.

This candidate was very highly motivated for all of the situations at S. He entered into the assignments enthusiastically and exerted himself to the utmost in order to achieve a successful solution of his group's problems. Possessing a good measure of forcefulness and self-assertiveness, he was usually the first to make any bid for leadership. . . . He is adaptable and flexible. . . . He should wear well with any group with which he is associated over a long period of time. ☐

Holistic assessment obviously reveals a great deal about a person. But it is still in its infancy and psychologists have yet to prove that it is sufficiently superior to other methods to justify the large personnel, expense, and time involved. It was impossible, even for the OSS Staff, to discover the correlation between their estimates and actual performances in the theaters of war. This was in part due to the uniqueness of the OSS assignments themselves and to the unpredictability of conditions under which each agent worked. The many psychiatrists and psychologists who collaborated on this project concluded, however, that their type of approach can be developed into "an extraordinary instrument for accomplishing three important purposes simultaneously: (1) the selection of the most suitable persons for important jobs; (2) the advancement of our understanding of personality; and (3) the adequate training of clinical psychologists and psychiatrists."[45]

A somewhat comparable approach to personality assessment was used with Veterans Administration trainees in Clinical Psychology.[46] Here again difficulty was experienced in evaluating test results with respect to later accomplishments.[47] ■

PROJECTIVE TESTS

Projection, as pointed out in Chapter 8 (pp. 242–243), is evident whenever we attribute our own motives to others, or even to inanimate objects. Projective tests are so named because they induce the individual to project — to put himself into the test situation, or to identify with the persons therein and, by telling about them, to reveal his own motives, attitudes, apprehensions, and aspirations. The use of projective methods to assess attitudes was discussed in Chapter 6 (pp. 182–184).

There are many projective tests — sentence completion, doll play, perception of inkblots, interpretation of pictures, and so forth. Despite their apparent differences, all such tests have two features in common.

In the first place, they present the person with a relatively *nonstructured situation*. That is to say, they involve a situation, which, instead of calling for a reaction that is quite stereotyped and predictable from one person to another, may elicit many different reactions, depending upon the individual being tested. Take, for example, the incomplete sentence "All men are born free and . . . ." This is structured. It brings forth but one completion from most, the word "equal." This tells us nothing about the individual except that he has been indoctrinated in a certain way. But take the sentence, "The main driving force in life is . . . ." One person may complete the sentence with "to achieve security," another with "to achieve happiness," and still another with "sex." The item may be completed in many different ways.

In the second place, projective tests all have in common the fact that they *catch the subject off guard*. They are designed to "entice the subject into revealing himself without his being aware of the fact that he is doing so."[48] This is especially evident when, instead of telling about themselves, their home life, and their reactions to their parents, children are induced to play-act with dolls dressed like grownups and children. At first the child arranges the furniture and people in more or less stereotyped ways, "but suddenly the observer realizes there has been a change, not a quick or easily detectable one, but one that has taken several minutes and has just now reached the observer's threshold. The child is more intent on the dolls, less reactive to the observer, and he is living strangely in this new fantasy world. He begins to tell stories that have no immediate parallel in his real life; he makes the family people behave as family people virtually never do. There are fantastic punishments and cat-

astrophic accidents, social roles are reversed, and a few routines like toileting may exclude all the rest of ordinary everyday activity . . . and then the observer has a feeling that blinds have gone up, and he is seeing the inner person of this child. It is as if the child were making him see this family world as the child himself sees it — or, perhaps as he would like to see it."[49] The same sort of naivete is present, although less obviously, when adults interpret inkblots or tell stories based upon nonstructured picture situations.

The most widely used projective tests at the adult level are the Rorschach inkblots and sets of pictures for which the subject is to invent themes. These tests, or variations of them, are also widely used to study personality in children. The Rorschach test has, in addition, been used to study changes in personality associated with old age. It has also been used by anthropologists in studying primitive peoples.

The Rorschach Inkblot Test

This test utilizes ten standard inkblots. An inkblot made in the same manner as those in the Rorschach Test is reproduced in Figure 9.7. Some of the Rorschach inkblots are, however, colored. The subject is shown the ten inkblots, one at a time, in a standardized order and position. He is asked, "What could that be?" or "What do you see?" The subject is allowed to turn the blot and look at it from different positions. Different people, of course, "see" different things. Responses are scored in terms of the total number of items seen, whether the items involve the whole inkblot or only parts, qualities perceived (color, form, movement), and the kinds of things reported (like anatomical parts, animals, plants, and people). Some aspects of personality allegedly revealed by the response to the inkblots are suggested by these excerpts from the report of an expert Rorschach tester: "rich mentality," "illogical procedure and peculiarity of thinking," "ability to grasp relationships," "creative capacity," "breadth of interests," "relatively few emotional experiences that come to expression," "expresses special fantasies peculiar to his own need,"

● 9.7
An Inkblot and What Was Seen in It by Four Subjects.

"It is two cat-like creatures sticking out their tongues at each other. They appear to be joined together like Siamese twins. The small objects are apparently kidneys. The elongated object at the bottom could be a table leg."

"It is a flower opening up, or two heads facing each other."

"There are two old ladies up a tree and facing each other. Perhaps it is a diving mosquito."

"It is the spine surrounded by internal organs, with the lungs shown in white at the top. The two objects at the side are kidneys."

"large amount of self-will," "resistiveness," "introversive personality."[50]

Scoring of Rorschach data is becoming fairly well standardized, but the interpretation of the scores is far from standard. Most Rorschach testers maintain that interpretation is necessarily subjective — that it calls for experience, ingenuity, insight, and common sense. According to an expert Rorschach tester, "prolonged and extensive experience is necessary, not only with human personality but with all kinds of clinical problems. This last step, by definition, therefore, is personal to the examiner and subjective in him. It permits no norms, and it eludes all standardization."[51]

Rorschach testers have reported considerable success in differentiating between normal and psychotic individuals, and in distinguishing between different kinds of psychotics, in terms of Rorschach findings alone.[52] Nevertheless, many psychologists are not fully convinced of the scientific validity of some of the assertions made by Rorschach testers. They want more experimental evidence in support of such claims.[53]

Thematic apperception

Apperception is evident when we respond to a situation in terms of past experience instead of responding merely to what is before us.* Since our past experiences differ, we get different meanings from what is, photographically, the same for all of us. Indeed the assumption underlying the *Thematic Apperception Test* (T.A.T.) and others like it is that the meaning we get out of, or the meaning that we inject into, a pictured situation reveals something of our past experience and the motives derived from it. Recall, in this connection, our earlier discussions of picture tests resembling the T.A.T. There was the case of Karl (p. 237), whose fantasies involved death themes. Adolescents responded with themes of love and aggression (Figure 8.7, p. 238). Pictures were used to study achievement motivation in college students. The reader will remember that students who had been given information designed to arouse achievement motivation did, in fact, produce fantasies of achievement when asked to tell stories in response to pictures (Figure 8.8, p. 240).

In administering the T.A.T. one shows the subject a standard series of pictures (Figure 9.8) in a definite sequence and asks for a story in which each picture may serve as an illustration. The tester says, "Tell me what events have led up to the present occurrence, what the character (or characters) in the picture is (are) thinking and feeling, and what the outcome will be."[54] After the subject has told a story for each picture, his themes are analyzed in an effort to discover his "motivational structure." The themes are assumed to be projections of the subject's innermost fantasies. It is not unusual for one

* This is the meaning of *apperception* in the present context, but the term has had more technical meanings in psychological history. See, for example, the meanings given in H. B. English and A. C. English, *A Comprehensive Dictionary of Psychological and Psychoanalytical Terms*, David McKay, 1958.

● 9.8

Administering the T.A.T. The subject is telling a story to go with one of the pictures of the T.A.T. series. (Photo by Howard Modavis, *Life*, © Time, Inc.)

theme to recur again and again as the individual goes from one picture to another. The recurrent theme may, as we have seen, be one of death, love, aggression, or achievement. Another common theme is the need for mother love.

The criticisms of the T.A.T. are basically those already mentioned in connection with the Rorschach test. Although themes are easily identified, their interpretation has not yet been put on the quantitative basis which scientific procedure demands. Even so, the test has had value in suggesting hypotheses about individual motivation. These hypotheses, as suggested above, may be evaluated in terms of other test results and biographical information. Indeed it is customary in clinical work to use several tests and to pool all available information before reaching a final conclusion about the personality struc-

ture of an individual, or the nature of his adjustment problems. ■

MEASURING PERSONALITY TRAITS

If we want to describe an individual's personality we look at his behavior in different ways, from different angles, or in different social settings. As we said earlier (p. 254), the different facets or segments revealed in this way are called *personality traits*. We also pointed out that traits are often referred to as *surface* aspects in contrast with motivational or *depth* dimensions. Whether or not a thorough description of traits would also embrace the depth aspects is a moot question. It may be argued for instance, that traits are expressions of underlying motives.

The holistic approach used by the OSS included a certain degree of trait analysis, since the investigators looked for evidence of effective intelligence, emotional stability, initiative, and effectiveness in social relations. Likewise, projective tests are often used to discern such traits as introversion-extraversion, emotional stability, ego-involvement, and so forth. Thus there is no clear line which separates trait analysis from methods already considered. The approach which we are about to describe is nevertheless more obviously analytic or piecemeal than the holistic or projective approaches. Each trait test is designed to measure either one or a small cluster of traits — not the personality as a whole.

There are many tests purporting to measure this or that trait, but only a few can be described here. Most are of the pencil-and-paper variety. The subject writes his reactions to various questions, statements, or propositions and the test is scored quantitatively. Weights based upon earlier research are attached to each kind of reaction and the scores thus obtained are averaged and evaluated in terms of percentiles or other statistical norms.

Although some tests are designed to measure a particular trait, such as emotional maturity, our examples are drawn from pencil-and-paper tests scored to reveal several traits at the same time. One of these is Guilford's

274

Inventory of Factors STDCR.[55] The factors (traits) represented by these five letters are *social introversion, thinking introversion, depression, cycloid tendencies* (ups and downs of mood), and *rhathymia* (a happy-go-lucky disposition). Guilford says that these factors, "taken together, probably cover the area of personality generally encompassed by the concept of introversion-extraversion." It is pointed out, further, that "Each factor actually represents a dimension of personality with two opposite poles." The same answers are scored in five different ways to disclose the degree to which the five different factors are present. The following examples are typical of the 175 items in this inventory. (Each item is to be responded to by circling one of the three alternatives.)

Do you express yourself more easily in speech than in writing? .... Yes ? No
Do you have frequent ups and downs in mood, either with or without apparent cause? .... Yes ? No
Are you sometimes so blue that life hardly seems worth living? ...... Yes ? No
Do you like to play pranks upon others? .... Yes ? No
Are you frequently "lost in thought?" .... Yes ? No

As our second example, we have chosen a widely used test which has two forms, individual and group, and certain features not present in the test already discussed. This test, developed at the University of Minnesota, is known as the *Minnesota Multiphasic Personality Inventory* (or MMPI). It has 550 items.[56] The slant is decidedly psychiatric and scores are classified largely in terms of psychiatric categories. Thus are ascertained the person's leanings toward hysteria, mania, schizophrenia, and so on. When taking the individual form of the test, illustrated in Figure 9.9, a person is given 550 cards, each bearing a question. At the back of the box are three cards marked, respectively, TRUE, FALSE, or CANNOT SAY. The subject is asked to read the statement and decide whether or not it applies to him. If it is true, or mostly true,

● **9.9**
The Minnesota Multiphasic Personality Inventory. Observe that there are three classification cards. These are marked, respectively, TRUE, FALSE, and CANNOT SAY. Each of the other 550 cards has printed on it a statement relating to some aspect of personality. The subject is trying to decide whether the card with the statement "I am entirely self-confident" should be placed behind the TRUE, FALSE, or CANNOT SAY card.

he places it behind the TRUE card. If it is not usually true or not at all true as applied to him, he puts it behind the FALSE card. If the statement does not apply, or if it is something he does not know about, the subject puts it behind the CANNOT SAY card. Most of the items are very similar to those already cited. They deal with what a person characteristically does in certain situations, with bodily complaints, with fears, with feelings, and so on. Of particular interest, however, is the fact that this test includes a number of "traps" for those who, instead of answering honestly, try to make a good impression. Suppose, for example, that a statement reads: "I sometimes put off until tomorrow what I should do today." The person who is trying to make a good impression will place this, and others comparable with it, in the false group. But the person who is reacting honestly will almost certainly say that this is true — for it is true of almost everybody. If the score for all such items is above a certain level, the rest of the test is discounted as yielding more favorable scores than it should. Highly favorable scores on a set of such items do, of course, reveal something about a person's desire to make a favorable impression. The number of CANNOT SAY items provides a check on carelessness in answering or inability to understand the items. These and other checks are used to determine the validity of this inventory as applied to a particular person; that is, to test whether it is actually revealing in a particular person the traits that it is designed to reveal.

The *Allport-Vernon-Lindzey Study of Values*[57] is designed to reveal somewhat different aspects of personality from those measured by the two tests already described. It was devised to discover the weight given by a person to things theoretical, economic, esthetic, social, political, and religious. The person who gives a very high place to social things and a relatively low place to others is sometimes referred to as the "social man." According to the psychologist on whose work this study is based, there are six "types" of men, each of whom gives the highest value to one of the spheres of life indicated above. A mixed type in which the values are balanced is also recognized.

The test has two parts. The first of these has thirty statements like the first one illustrated in Figure 9.10, involving two alternatives. One indicates his preference for alternative *a* or *b*. It is perhaps evident that preferring *a* indicates a political interest and preferring *b* a religious interest. The test is designed so that statements representing each of the six value areas are paired with those representing each of the remaining five. Part II is a multiple-choice test with four possibilities for each situation, as illustrated by the second item. Preferences are ranked from 4 (most preferred) to 1 (least preferred). The various possible reactions are assigned different weights in terms of their relevance to particular values. In scoring and evaluating a subject's choices, a different score is derived for each value. A significantly higher score for one value than for the others is then taken as an indication of the individual's predominant value. Suppose, by way of illustration, that the following scores have been obtained: theoretical, 30; economic, 40; esthetic, 20; social, 32; political, 55; and religious, 25. Then it would be said

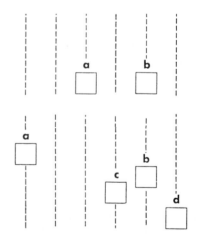

Would you prefer to hear a series of lectures on: (a) the comparative merits of the forms of government in Britain and in the United States; (b) the comparative development of the great religious faiths?

If you had sufficient leisure and money, would you prefer to —
a. make a collection of fine sculptures or paintings
b. establish a center for the care and training of the feeble-minded
c. aim at a senatorship, or a seat in the Cabinet
d. establish a business or financial enterprise of your own

● 9.10

Sample Items from the Allport-Vernon-Lindzey Study of Values. In doing Part I (for example, the first item), the subject indicates his first preference by placing a 2 in the appropriate square and a 1 in the other square. Or he may express an absolute choice by using a 3 for his preference and a 0 for the alternative. Part II (illustrated by the second item) is answered by placing a 4 in the appropriate square for the top preference, a 3 for the next preference, a 2 for the next, and a 1 for the least preferred possibility. (Houghton Mifflin, 1960.)

that the person tested is predominantly a politically-minded individual, or that his highest values are political.

When the scores based upon a variety of personality tests are put on a comparable basis — perhaps by translation into percentiles — a personality profile which represents all of the measured traits may be drawn. This tells us at a glance the person's relative standing with respect to each trait. Some individuals are consistently close to the central tendency, some are consistently above, and some consistently below. ■

THE NORMAL PERSONALITY

What is a normal personality? What is an abnormal personality? As we said earlier, the answer to these questions is not easy to find. The words "normal" and "abnormal" have different meanings for different people. From the so-called normative view, anybody who is different from the one making the judgment is abnormal. In terms of the statistical view, however, anybody is abnormal who diverges very much from the average. The average person, according to this view, is the most normal one. From the purely social viewpoint, the normal person is the one who is adjusted to his environment to such an extent that he finds life enjoyable, and the abnormal one is the unadjusted — the one, in extreme cases, who would like to escape from reality. To complicate the matter further, each of us may toe the normative, statistical, or social line with respect to some traits and not with respect to others. Moreover, we may be adjusted most of the time but not in an emergency or disaster. Generally speaking, however, the individual is regarded as normal if he has some socially acceptable goal around which his activities are integrated, if he finds the pursuit of his goal worthwhile, and if, in general, he gets pleasure out of living. The person who has no socially acceptable goal, who is at cross-purposes within himself and with his group, and who does not enjoy life as it is, but tries to shut himself off from it, is, generally speaking, regarded as having an abnormal personality. ■

PSYCHONEUROTIC PERSONALITIES

Psychoneuroses (or neuroses) are relatively mild mental disorders. They include such symptoms as excessive fatigue and bodily complaints (neurasthenia), loss of memory or of sensory or motor functions (dissociation), and abnormal anxiety (anxiety neurosis). Although such disorders may cause great distress to the person afflicted with them, and may be a nuisance to those who have to associate with him, they are usually neither incapacitating nor dangerous. Institutionalization is rarely necessary.

All personality disorders which fall within the psychoneurotic classification are generally assumed to be functional in origin. That is to say, they grow out of habits and attitudes acquired while the individual is attempting to adjust to his environment. They are varieties of *maladjustment*. A large proportion of the complaints with which general medical practitioners must deal are psychoneurotic, although thought by the patient to be organic.

Neurasthenia

Many people have symptoms which, taken together, are called *neurasthenic*. The term itself implies a "nerve weakness," although, as we have said, there is no known organic basis. Here is an illustrative case from the files of a psychiatrist:

☐ Ever since I have been married I've been nervous. If I didn't have the finest husband in the world and one who takes wonderful care of me and puts up with all of my complaining and all my sickness, I'd be a grass widow. . . . I haven't been a wife to him at all. I've been too sick. First there was that awful headache. Oh, I can't tell you how terrible it was. It just knocked me down, and I thought the end of the world had come. . . . But there's been a lot of other things. There's a sort of internal trembling, you know, a kind of inward nervousness, and I feel as though all my organs were quivering. One doctor told me my nerves were tied in knots.

I don't know why it is, but I can't stand anything. I haven't strength enough to walk from here to the streetcar and back. I may get up in the morning feeling pretty good, but by the time I get breakfast for my husband and have started on my morning's work, I'm nearly exhausted, and by noon I'm just completely played out. . . .

I guess I told you about my sweating and getting so hot and then so cold. Did I tell you about that funny twisting feeling? It runs right through my right side down into my leg. I think it's a nerve loose or something like that. None of the doctors know what to make of my case. I've been to dozens of them. Yes, and I've tried osteopaths and chiropractors. I even went to the new psychology school and I don't know what all else. Some say I ought to try Christian Science, but you can't tell me these things are imaginary, and they are not in my mind either. I'll admit I'm nervous, but there's a cause for these things somewhere. I know I never had 'em before I was married.[58] □

What is often lacking in such persons is a goal toward which they can direct their thinking instead of focusing upon bodily feelings. They often "hang onto" their ailments with grim earnestness like the shipwrecked sailor hangs onto a raft. Sometimes their ailments are "all they have." In many instances these provide a "good" excuse for failing to meet obligations or failing in marriage, the business world, or elsewhere. Like anybody else, these unfortunates are trying to adjust to the situations of life. But instead of facing their problems in a realistic manner, they find escape through sickness. They do not do this intentionally, but they perhaps learned early in life that sickness excuses one from many things, and even brings sympathy. They drifted gradually, and unthinkingly, into these mental disorders. Sometimes they are merely following a pattern set in the home.

Indecision and doubt

The following case typifies a variety of psychoneurosis characterized by indecision and doubt.

□ A boy in high school was supplied with some second-hand books. He began to doubt the accuracy of them, for, as they were not new, he thought they might be out of date and what he read might not be the truth. Before long he would not read a book unless he could satisfy himself that it was new and the writer of it an authority. Even then he was assailed with doubts. For he felt uncertain as to whether he understood what he read. If, for example, he came across a word of which he was not sure of the exact meaning, he could not go on until he had looked up the word in a dictionary. But likely as not in the definition of the word there would be another word with which he was not entirely familiar and he would have to look that up, so that at times half an hour or more would be taken up in reading a single page, and even then he would feel doubtful as to whether he had got the exact truth.[59] □

Dissociation

A large variety of psychoneurotic disorders are characterized by what has been called "dissociation." This may be defined as a state in which certain activities are no longer integrated with the personality as a whole. These activities are like bits of behavior "split off" from, yet coexisting with the rest. Many such conditions may be simulated in a hypnotic trance. The term *hysteria* is often used to designate this class of disorders. Some of the symptoms of hysteria are sensory, such as functional blindness, deafness, and anesthesia (loss of cutaneous sensitivity). There are functional motor disorders, like twitching of muscles, paralysis of facial muscles or of limbs, and muscular spasms which may involve the whole body. There are memory disorders, like amnesia and fugue. *Amnesia* is loss of memory such as one often reads about in the newspapers. A person thus afflicted may wander off, forgetting his name and where he came from. A *fugue* is a confused state in which an individual may commit some deed, perhaps murder, but later have no recollection of it. *Dual personality* such as that represented fictionally in *Dr. Jekyll and Mr. Hyde* also falls within this general classification. Sometimes several alternating personalities are apparent in the same individual and we speak

● 9.11

A Multiple Personality. "Eve White" of the *Three Faces of Eve* is shown taking a Rorschach test. She was, at various times, "a dull, unhappy housewife," "a hell-raising hoyden," or "a dignified, cultured woman." Subsequently a fourth personality, a more mature one, emerged. A 35-minute movie about this patient, "A Case Study of Multiple Personality," is available through The Psychological Cinema Register, Pennsylvania State University. (Photo by Jack Woods, courtesy of Dr. C. H. Thigpen and *The Saturday Evening Post*.)

of *multiple personality*. The highly publicized book *Three Faces of Eve*, which was also the basis of a movie of the same name, deals with a multiple personality.[60] In Figure 9.11, "Eve White," one of these personalities, is pictured while responding to a Rorschach inkblot.

Dissociative disorders are rather generally regarded as outcomes of the kinds of conflict considered in the preceding chapter. Freudians tend to stress conflict between the ego and the superego. Some psychologists give emphasis to approach-avoidance conflicts. In some cases the disorder springs from avoidance-avoidance conflicts, where the individual, so to speak, feels himself torn between "the devil and the deep blue sea." Sometimes such disorders leave spontaneously when the underlying conflicts are resolved. Take, for example, the case of a man who was engaged and otherwise obligated to a girl with whom he was no longer in love.

This man disappeared and was found wandering around in the Midwest, having forgotten his name, the girl, and everything which would identify his past. The girl finally jilted him and he gradually recovered his memory. This and many similar cases may look very much like malingering, but there is ample evidence that assumption of such states is beyond the individual's control. He drifts into them gradually, perhaps wishing that he were not the person he is with the obligations he has. One interpretation is that he suggests or even "hypnotizes" himself into the state in question.

Anxiety neuroses

Many psychoneurotics experience anxiety without sufficient cause. Abnormal fears (phobias), like fear of enclosed spaces, are anxiety neuroses. Some examples of phobias

279

were given in our discussion of unconscious conflict (pp. 230–231). Sometimes the anxiety neurosis involves panic. The person becomes panicky for fear he is about to die or that he will commit some misdeed. He may actually go berserk. There is also a "free-floating" anxiety in which the person is anxious, but without knowing why he is anxious or about what. All he knows is that *something* dreadful is about to happen. The woman portrayed in Figure 9.12 says, "Doctor, I'm worried, but I don't know why. I'm just worried. I have no reason to be, but I am." The tense attitude pictured here is typical.

Anxiety neuroses appear to grow out of a conflict between (1) the individual's biological urges (as represented by the id), (2) the demands of reality (as represented by the ego), and (3) the dictates of parents and others (as represented by the superego). Freudians stress the threatening nature of this conflict. In

• 9.12

Acute Anxiety Neurosis. The artist has pictured a typical anxiety neurotic — tense and anxious about nothing in particular. She is worried but does not know why. (After Dr. F. Netter, courtesy of Ciba.)

essence, it involves the threat that his biological urges will overpower the individual, making him do what he knows he should not, or must not, do. He is anxious lest his repressed motives break through the "cultural veneer" and cause him to lose self respect, or the affection or respect of others.

When neurotic anxiety has a focus (as in phobias, p. 230) or when it concerns some organ (say the heart), it is said to be *displaced*. The focal situation, object, or symptom is a substitute for (or hides from the individual) the inner conflict which is the real source of his anxiety. Thus a man with homosexual tendencies may develop palpitation and an intense anxiety about his heart whenever he is alone with another man. His real difficulty resides in his homosexual impulses and the threat that he may try to satisfy them, hence bring disgrace upon himself. In cases like this, anxiety is not merely displaced; it also diverts attention from the "disgraceful" urges and, for the time at least, removes the threat. ■

PSYCHOTHERAPY OF THE NEUROSES

There are many psychological procedures designed to alleviate psychoneurotic behavior. Most of these can claim a certain measure of success. Even talking with a person who will listen sympathetically sometimes relieves the psychoneurotic's tension. Quite often the only therapy involved is a series of interviews with a psychiatrist or clinical psychologist who can listen, question, and give what appears to be appropriate advice.

As our historical introduction indicated (pp. 17–19), hypnotic suggestion may relieve certain symptoms of hysteria. Freud used hypnosis before he hit upon the psychoanalytic procedures of free association and dream analysis. Psychoanalysis, he felt, gets at the root of the difficulty — at depth factors — hence is more effective than mere removal of symptoms.

Psychoanalysis

Psychoanalysis is today a widely used form of therapy. But different "schools" of psychoanalysis differ somewhat in their procedures and also in their interpretations of what these reveal.[61]

In typical psychoanalytic procedure the patient reclines on a comfortable couch (Figure 9.13) and is encouraged to say everything that comes to mind, the analyst occasionally directing association by asking questions. The patient may reach a point where blocking occurs or where ideas seem too ridiculous, or too filthy, or too horrible for expression. Here the analyst urges the patient to express the ideas in question. Many such séances may eventually lay bare the significant aspects of the individual's life history. Sometimes, in the course of these séances, the individual breaks down emotionally — weeping, cursing, and so on. This emotional flareup is often found to have therapeutic value. In dream analysis the patient relates his dreams and

these are analyzed for what they may reveal about his motives and about other "depth" aspects of his personality.

The analyst usually interprets the findings, tells the subject what is wrong with him, and suggests what might be done about it. These interpretations and the advice given are usually colored by psychoanalytic theories.

Client-centered therapy

A form of interview used for therapeutic purposes and regarded by many as a substitute for psychoanalysis has been developed by Rogers[62] and his followers. It is known as "client-centered" therapy. This usually requires much less time than psychoanalysis. It also differs from psychoanalysis in another, more important respect: the counselor refrains from telling an individual the nature of his problem

● **9.13**

A Typical Psychoanalytic Interview. The patient reclines on a couch, free associates, describes dreams, and answers the analyst's questions. (Photo by Walter Sanders, *Life,* © Time, Inc.)

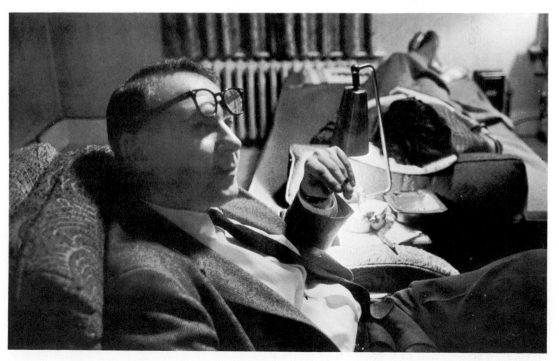

and what he should do about it. A psycho-analyst, as we have seen, injects guidance based upon dream analysis and the patient's reverie. Since these features are absent from Rogers' procedure, it is sometimes called "non-directive." The "client-centered" designation suggests that with this procedure the client rather than the counselor plays the central role in achieving a solution.

☐ The following excerpts from transcribed interviews illustrate the general nature of client-centered therapy and also why it is so designated. Observe that the counselor says very little. Note, also that the client himself here develops insight into what his problem is and what he should do about it. The counselor's aim is to facilitate the gaining of such insights. When achieved, they are recognized by the client as his own rather than the counselor's. He is thus likely to accept and to act upon them.

Excerpt from first interview[63]

S (subject). Well, it's just reached the point where it becomes unbearable. I'd rather be dead than live as I am now.

C (counselor). You'd rather be dead than live as you are now? Can you tell me a little more about that?

S. Well, I hope. Of course we always live on hope.

C. Yes.

S. But — No, I don't have any conscious suicidal urge or anything like that. It's just that — looking at it rationally, I feel that I'm — that I'm in the red now and I wouldn't want to keep on living in the red. (Pause)

C. Well, can you tell me in any more detailed way what — in what way it blocks you so much that you really feel sometimes that you'd be better off dead?

S. Well, I don't know if I can any more accurately describe the sensation. It's just a — a very impressive and painful weight as if an axe were pressing on the whole abdomen, pressing down, I can almost — I can almost sense the position and I feel that it is oppressing me very radically, that is, that it goes right down to the roots of my dynamic energy, so that no matter in what field I assay any sort of effort, I find the blocking.

Excerpt from eighth and final interview

S. Well, I've been noticing something decidedly new. Rather than having fluctuations, I've been noticing a very gradual steady improvement. It's just as if I had become more stabilized and my growth had been one of the hard way and the sure way rather than the wavering and fluctuating way.

C. M-hm.

S. I go into situations, and even though it's an effort, why I go ahead and make my progress, and I find that when you sort of seize the bull by the horns, as it were, why it isn't so bad as if you sort of deliberate and perhaps — well, think too long about it like I used to. I sort of say to myself, "Well, I know absolutely that avoiding the situation will leave me in the same old rut I've been taking," and I realize that I don't want to be in the same old rut, so I go ahead and go into the situation, and even when I have disappointments in the situation, I find that they don't bring me down as much as they used to.

C. That sounds like real progress.

S. And what pleases me is that my feelings are on an even keel, steadily improving, which gives me much more of a feeling of security than if I had fluctuations. You see, fluctuations lead you from the peaks to the valleys, and you can't get as much self-confidence as when you're having gradual improvement.

C. M-hm.

Psychoanalysts have claimed that this technique insufficiently probes the "depths" of personality. Whether or not it is necessary to go so "deep" cannot be decided until adequate comparative studies on the relative effectiveness of these two therapeutic procedures have been carried out. It may well be that some psychoneurotic conditions yield better to one approach than to the other.[64]

Group therapy

Group therapy is another procedure devised to alleviate psychoneurotic and other difficulties.[65] This may involve aspects of the therapies already mentioned, but it gets its name from its application to more than one individual simultaneously. Two or more persons with somewhat similar problems meet to talk about them under the guidance of a counselor, usually a psychiatrist or a clinical psychologist. It often helps a person to learn that others have similar problems. In the group situation, moreover, individuals may support each other in efforts to solve mutual problems. Alcoholics Anonymous works on this principle. When problem situations are acted out by the persons concerned, we have a form of group psychotherapy known as *psychodrama*.[66]

Many psychoneurotics get better spontaneously after conflicts have resolved themselves. It is with the psychoneuroses, moreover, that various cults and forms of faith healing have had their major successes. Mild tranquilizers* are also widely used to reduce neurotic tensions and anxiety. ▪

PSYCHOTIC PERSONALITIES

Psychoses are much more serious than psychoneuroses. There is usually a marked psychological deterioration. The individual is often out of contact with reality. He may have hallucinations (false perceptions). He may for example, see visions and hear voices without any objective basis. He may even "taste" ground glass or poison in his food. He may also have delusions. Thus he may have the delusion that he is God, that he is the head of the institution in which he is a patient, or that a sucking machine operating from some distant place is drawing his vital energy from him.[67]

The absurdity of such delusions shows how lacking in insight psychotic people may

be. It is not uncommon for a psychoneurotic to call himself "neurotic" and even to laugh at himself. But the psychotic is usually sure that he is all right and the world all wrong. Psychotherapy may help some such patients, but with others it is quite ineffective, largely because of communication difficulties.

Psychotics are often dangerous to themselves and to those around them; hence one must usually place them in hospitals where they can be treated and looked after. Many get well, but others must be institutionalized for long periods.

There are, as we have seen, two broad classifications of psychoses. Those with a known organic basis, like syphilis and alcoholism, are said to be *organic*. Those without any associated gross organic pathology are known as *functional*. Should it be found, however, that a psychosis now classified in the latter group is due to some structural or biochemical defect not yet evident, the psychosis would then be designated as organic. Actually, the differentiation that is customarily used, and which we adopt here for convenience in discussion may, in the long run, turn out to have been an artifact.*

With respect to schizophrenia, a "functional psychosis" to be discussed presently, there is already much controversy about proper classification. One statistical study shows that schizophrenia tends to run in families. Moreover, if one identical twin becomes schizophrenic, the other will, in 86 out of 100 cases, also develop schizophrenia.[68] Some have questioned the accuracy of these statistics.[69] But, even if they should be substantiated, there are at least two possible interpretations. One is

* There are two general groups of so-called tranquilizers. Both tend to have a quietening effect upon the organism, both animal and human. The milder group (derived from meprobamate) go under a variety of trade names and are sometimes prescribed by physicians to calm their anxious, tense patients. More powerful tranquilizers (including chlorpromazine) are used especially with schizophrenics, and are known to have rather specific effects upon the reticular formation of the brain stem (pp. 159–160). See especially C. L. Cazzullo, "Biological Aspects of Pharmacodynamics in Psychoses," pp. 331–340 in M. Rinkel, and H. C. B. Dember (Eds.), *Chemical Concepts of Psychosis.* McDowell, Obolensky, 1958. One of the most recent reports is that of R. W. Russell, "Psychopharmacology," in *Annual Review of Psychology,* 1964, pp. 87–114.

* The problem of differentiating between so-called functional and organic psychoses has been discussed by Stanley Cobb, the eminent psychiatrist. As he says, in his *Foundations of Neuropsychiatry,* 6th ed. (Williams & Wilkins, 1958, p. 127): "It may seem pedantic to expatiate upon the impossibility of drawing a line between 'organic' and 'functional,' but experience shows that it is necessary to emphasize that no such line can logically be drawn. If it be drawn arbitrarily, its position is ordained by the point to which technology has advanced in that year. It depends on what kind of a 'scope,' 'graph,' or 'meter' is used by the observer. In other words, the line between organic and functional (and between physical and mental) is an artifact."

that a susceptibility to schizophrenia is inherited, hence that the disease has an organic basis. Another is that individuals who are related, and especially those who live under the same conditions, may acquire their attitudes or modes of thinking from those around them. This would be a functional interpretation. There is even the possibility that both an inherited disposition and an acquired one are interlinked. It is possible, for instance, that there is an inherited tendency to break down under stress *if* the individual is subjected to unusual stress, but even then, only if he has acquired inadequate ways of facing problems.

The question as to how schizophrenia should be classified is also complicated by medical research. Investigators have reported from time to time that schizophrenics suffer from glandular defects, disturbed body metabolism, and chemical malfunctions of various kinds.[70] So far, no such claims have been sufficiently substantiated to warrant general acceptance. But even though a biochemical defect should be found to accompany schizophrenia, it would still be necessary to prove that this was the cause of the disease rather than a bodily disturbance which developed subsequently. We observed in discussing emotion and psychosomatic disorders (p. 233) that psychological stress often disturbs a person's biochemical equilibrium.

Should an organic basis for schizophrenia be found (hereditary or otherwise), one would still be confronted with the fact that different people classified as schizophrenic exhibit very diverse combinations of symptoms. This being so, it is evident that their ways of behaving and thinking must have been acquired through individual experience. Thus, if an organic basis were found, it would indicate only a *predisposition* toward a particular pattern of mental illness. It would not account for the actual breakdown nor for the combination of symptoms found in a particular case.

In view of the above, we will regard the so-called functional psychoses, tentatively at least, as maladjustments arising out of peculiar attitudes which the individual has developed toward his world, including his relations with other people.

Organic psychoses

The organic psychoses most clearly recognized are general paresis of the insane, senile psychosis, and alcoholic psychosis.

• *General paresis.* This is due to syphilis of the brain (Figure 9.14). But only a small proportion of people who contract syphilis become paretic. If syphilis is treated and cured early, as it now can be with penicillin, general paresis will never occur. It usually comes several years after all evidences of untreated syphilis have disappeared.

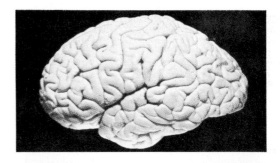

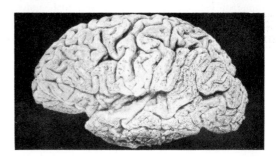

● **9.14**
A Normal and a Paretic Brain. When a normal brain (top) is compared with a paretic brain (bottom), the cortical destruction in advanced paresis can be clearly seen. Not every paretic brain shows such widespread deterioration. Indeed, as indicated in the text, paresis is today usually cured in its early stages. (Top photo from E. Gardner, *Fundamentals of Neurology*, 3rd ed., Saunders, 1958, p. 11. Bottom photo from S. E. Jelliffe and W. A. White, *Diseases of the Nervous System*, 6th ed., Lea and Febiger, 1935, p. 821.)

☐ Here is the case of a person who contracted syphilis and was not cured, although all physical symptoms eventually disappeared. His paresis came on about thirteen years after he thought he was cured of syphilis. Brought before a class in abnormal psychology, he showed absence of certain reflexes and exaggeration of others, his speech was thick and he could not distinctly say such things as "black bug's blood." Moreover, he swayed slightly when his eyes were open, a great deal when his eyes were closed.

"Mr. _____, how are you feeling today?" "Fine, never felt better in my life!" "How are you off financially?" "Oh, I'm doing quite well. I have one billion dollars in the _____ bank and another billion in the _____ bank." "Have you any children?" "No. We had one, but it died at birth. I'm going to pick up a half dozen at _____ hospital on my way back to _____. I'm going to get four girls and two boys." "What are you going to name them?" "Well, I guess I'll name the four girls after the Dionne quintuplets." "Which ones?" "All of them." "But aren't there five quintuplets?" "Five! Well, what the hell!"

Before this patient came into the hospital he was threatening to kill people who "had done him some wrong." He said he was not now mad at anyone. He was being given malarial and drug therapy and had shown considerable improvement since entering the institution. This is not necessarily a typical case, for every case is different in many respects. But delusions of grandeur (billions in the bank, picking up six children on the way home, and the like) are often found in such cases. ☐

• *Senile psychoses.* These psychoses present a variety of patterns. Quite often there are delusions of one sort or another. One old man asked the doctor to bore a hole and let out some of the air that was pressing down on his brain, talked of people trying to poison him, and so on. Such delusions are common in senile cases. There are also defects of memory. The patient may forget recent events. False memories may occur, as when the senile per-

son tells you he did something a few moments ago that he could not have done because he was sitting before you in the room. Quite often there is disorientation, the patient not knowing where he is, what year it is, how long he has been in the institution, and so on.

• *Alcoholic psychoses.* Psychoses brought on by excessive use of alcohol take many forms, including the well-known delirium tremens, in which the victim has terrifying hallucinations. Sometimes the disordered behavior is similar to that found in senile psychosis. It may also simulate certain aspects of paranoid schizophrenia, a functional psychosis to be considered shortly.

Functional psychoses

The most frequent of these are manic-depressive psychosis and the various forms of schizophrenia.

• *Manic-depressive psychosis.* This disorder is characterized by extreme ups and downs of mood. In the manic state the individual may be extremely happy, singing at the top of his voice, dancing around, working on inventions that will "shake the world to its foundations." He may also be so obstreperous that he must be kept under restraint of some kind. Delusions and hallucinations are often present. In both men and women, vile language, curses, sexual allusions, and sexual displays are common. Sometimes there is a "flight of ideas," the individual going off on one tangent after another as each idea occurs to him.

In the depressive state, these people present an even more pitiful picture. Many of them cry continually, accuse themselves of all kinds of sins, refuse to eat or drink because "it would be a sin to keep this evil body alive," and try to commit suicide. Such patients are, of course, tube-fed and watched closely to see that they do themselves no harm. The manic and depressive states alternate in a variety of ways. Some patients go into only one state, with periods of normalcy in between. Others have a period of depression followed by normalcy, and then by mania.

Many people with a manic-depressive psychosis get well. Some, of whom Clifford Beers

Clifford Beers. Beers developed manic-depressive psychosis as a young man and spent several years in mental hospitals. His book, *The Mind That Found Itself*, which tells of his illness, his experiences in mental hospitals, and his eventual recovery, became a classic in the literature of mental illness. It also did much to improve conditions in mental hospitals. (Brown Brothers)

(Figure 9.15) is the best known, have written books about their experiences as patients in mental hospitals. Through his book, *A Mind That Found Itself*, and the mental hygiene movement which he was instrumental in starting, Beers did much to improve conditions in mental hospitals and to further public understanding of the nature of mental illness and how it may be prevented. We will have more to say about this shortly.

The extreme mania and depression that Beers experienced is now seldom seen in mental hospitals, the reason being that tranquilizers are being widely used to reduce tension and excitement.[71] When these are ineffective in controlling depressive states, electric shock therapy (electroconvulsive therapy, or E.C.T.) is often used. This involves passing a weak electric current through the brain, from electrodes placed on the skull. The patient is thrown into a mild convulsion followed by a brief period of unconsciousness. A series of such treatments, days or weeks apart, often leads to recovery. Why electric shock treatments are effective in relieving depressive states is not known. There are several theories, but we will not discuss them here.[72] The gains achieved by electric shock treatments are often maintained with the help of tranquilizers.

• *Schizophrenia.* This, literally, is a "splitting of the mind." The designation *schizophrenia* is now more widely used than the earlier term, *dementia praecox*, which means "youthful insanity." While this disease does usually make its appearance in youth, it often occurs in individuals ranging in age up to the middle years of life.

A general characteristic frequently observed in schizophrenics is withdrawal from normal contacts with other people. This is an extreme form of introversion. The patients shown in Figure 9.16 are schizophrenics who illustrate withdrawal as well as other symptoms.

There are actually many symptoms embraced by the term *schizophrenia* and each individual so classified has his own combination. Nevertheless there is enough similarity amid this diversity to warrant the use of certain class names. Four categories of schizophrenia are widely recognized. These are *simple schizophrenia, hebephrenic schizophrenia, catatonic schizophrenia* and *paranoid schizophrenia.* Some distinguishing characteristics of each are considered shortly. However, the classification of a particular disorder is often far from simple. Psychiatrists occasionally even disagree as to whether the disorder is schizophrenic or manic-depressive and, if schizophrenic, as to how it should be further classified. It is not uncommon, in fact, for a patient to remain unclassified, or to be referred to as a "mixed type."

From the following descriptions of the four major schizophrenias one will see that the care, treatment, and outcome of a disorder differ somewhat depending upon its classification.

Simple schizophrenia is characterized by a general mental retardation, and "emotional

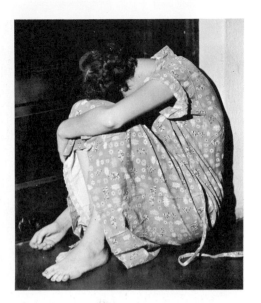

● **9.16**

Schizophrenic Withdrawal. Such attitudes, combined with disarray and lack of interest in surroundings, are typical. (Photo at left by Larry Keighley and courtesy of J. B. Martin and *The Saturday Evening Post.* Photo at right, courtesy of Saint Elizabeth's Hospital.)

blunting." The patient sits and stares into space, has no ambition, would just as soon be riding freight cars, walking the street, or living in the institution as doing anything else. These schizophrenics give the appearance of being extremely introverted, living within themselves, and taking no interest in what goes on around them. It is seldom that anything can be done for them. Sometimes they stay in the institution vegetating until they die, even at an advanced age; but in recent years real progress has been made in training such schizophrenics and returning them to their homes and the community.

Hebephrenic schizophrenia is notable for silliness and general incongruity of actions. A woman so classified was found in the men's room at the bus station with all of her clothes off, washing them, in fact, in the washbowls. She was laughing and generally silly about it. She even treated it as a big joke when it was discussed with her before a class. During the course of the session, she grimaced, made peculiar silly gestures, and failed to respond in a reasonable way to the questions asked her. She would probably giggle if told that her mother had died. One hebephrenic patient etched her name on her leg with a hairpin.

Many hebephrenics use bizzare words and expressions which they appear to invent and which have no meaning to others. One patient responded to all questions with the statement "16–21 telephone pole." But, after being treated with a tranquilizer, she said that "she was born in a small village, consisting of six homes, and that her home was situated near a telephone pole numbered 16–21."[73] Hebephrenics may also recover their sanity.

Catatonic schizophrenia often involves peculiar postures and actions. These differ from one patient to another and in the same patient from time to time. A catatonic is shown in Figure 9.17. Postures like this may be held for many hours. If the posture is changed by anyone else, the patient may resist the change, and when released, resume the former position. Sometimes he may be molded. His arm is put in a certain position by the doctor and he holds it in that position for a long while. This susceptibility to molding is often referred to as "waxy flexibility."

The patient may not have talked for years. The negativism which underlies this is illustrated by the following example: A psychiatrist who was giving a clinic could not get the patient to speak. He had actually not spoken

● 9.17

Catatonic Posture. The patient says he is "reaching for my nerves." Catatonics hold such postures for hours. If the doctor interrupts the posture, they return to it. Some without postures of their own are "plastic," in that, when placed in a posture, they hold it for a time. (Photo by Larry Keighley and courtesy of J. B. Martin and *The Saturday Evening Post*.)

for ten years. The doctor turned to the class saying, "This patient has not spoken for ten years," whereupon the patient said, "What do you want me to say?"

These patients often have to be tube-fed and also carried around when they refuse to eat or walk. Sometimes, while sitting like a statue, they smile to themselves as if amused at something running through their heads. They are the most extreme examples of introversion that one could see. "Withdrawn," "shut-in," "encapsulated," "insulated," are terms which aptly describe them. Catatonics sometimes become highly excited, in which case they can now be calmed with certain tranquilizers.*

* A catatonic who recovered and devoted himself, as a Chaplain, to helping others in similar predicaments has written his story and given his interpretation of schizophrenia. See A. T. Boisen, *The Exploration of the Inner World*. Willett, Clark, 1936. Reissued in 1962 in Harper's paperback series.

Paranoid schizophrenia. This is in many ways the most spectacular form of schizophrenia. The silly gestures and bizarre verbal expressions of the hebephrenic are absent. A paranoid schizophrenic speaks quite lucidly, and often quite convincingly, about an unreal world. Indeed, this disorder gets its name from the fact that paranoid delusions are often present. That is, delusions in which the individual sees reference to himself in what he assumes is taking place. Thus he has the idea that people are poisoning him, that ground glass is being put in his food, that his organs are all made of rubber, that he has no blood, that people are spying on him, and so on. Many cases thus classified have delusions of grandeur rather than, or in addition to, those of reference. Quite often there is a wide variety of symptoms.

☐ Mrs. _____ was a successful nurse, but began to get the idea that she was being spied upon by her neighbors, that men were hiding in her attic at night with a view of seducing her, "an honorable woman." She is a great inventress, having invented a powderless, trigger-less, shell-less, report-less, barrel-less gun — in fact a peace gun. She has sold it to the government, but spies are everywhere in the institution and the superintendent is in league with them. She has the idea that there may be some spies in the class, so she asks everyone to raise his right hand and say, "God Save America." Then she is satisfied and continues with her harangue, hinting that even greater inventions are coursing through her mind. She switches to religion, telling what a pure righteous woman she is. She was "monkied" with ten years ago and is to give birth to five monkeys. She says her term is a long one because hers is a Caesarian case. When the doctor says, "All right, Mrs. _____, you may go back now," she becomes quarrelsome, accusing him of not wanting these boys and girls to know that he is keeping her, a perfectly sane woman, in this place. She is edged out of the room, but slips a piece of paper to a girl sitting near the door. It says, "This is a house of ill repute, you had better get out of it while you have the chance."

Another patient has the delusion that he is

dead. Asked, "Do dead people bleed," he replies, "No, of course not." His finger is then pricked and a drop of blood oozes out. "There, now," he is told, "you bleed, so you can't be dead." He replies, "Well, all that shows is that dead people *do* bleed." ☐

Some tranquilizers serve to quieten paranoid schizophrenics while others often lead them to give up their delusions.[74]

• *Therapy in schizophrenia.* When a schizophrenic can be induced to "come out of his shell" to the extent that communication is possible, much can be done to help him develop insight and assume a realistic approach to his problems. When tranquilizers bring schizophrenics "back to reality," various forms of psychotherapy are available. It is possible to discuss the patient's problems with him and to help him meet them realistically.

Tranquilizers and psychotherapy are to a considerable extent replacing shock therapy. We have already discussed the use of electric shock therapy with depressed cases. The treatment used most often with schizophrenics, however, is insulin shock. Large injections of insulin lower the patient's blood sugar to the level where a coma is produced. Then carbohydrate is injected in sufficient quantity to return the blood sugar to normal, and the patient to consciousness. This procedure may be repeated at intervals of days or weeks. Many patients so treated regain their sanity, but why the treatment has this effect is not known.

Some schizophrenics get well spontaneously — that is to say, without special treatments. Thus a question which naturally arises is whether those who get well after shock treatments would not have regained their sanity anyway. However, the statistics on recovery with and without insulin shock show that more get well with these treatments than recover spontaneously.

Some patients who get well have relapses. This may be due to the fact that they must leave the sheltered life of the hospital to return to intolerable conditions which contributed to their illness in the first place. No doubt the tranquilizers, which patients often continue to take after returning home, help many to avoid a relapse. Some mental hospitals also facilitate adjustment outside by having their psychiatric social workers improve the patient's home, neighborhood, and work situations before he returns. This requires re-education of those with whom the patient will be intimately associated.

Brain operations known collectively as *psychosurgery*[75] have been used in certain cases of schizophrenia and manic-depressive psychosis which did not respond to other treatments. Psychosurgery involves either the cutting of nerve fibers or the removal of brain tissue in the frontal lobes of the brain (see p. 61). This "operation of last resort" is seldom performed now, since shock treatments and tranquilizers usually make it unnecessary.

Psychosurgery produces a radical change in the individual's "self-structure." It does not greatly impair his general intelligence as measured by the usual tests, but it makes him, in many respects, a "different person." He is rendered less anxious, less concerned with what others do or say or think, and less concerned with the past and the future. The life which had seemed intolerable to him is now tolerable. He is serene and contented with his lot. But he gains serenity at the expense of personal drive and initiative.[76] ■

PREVENTING PERSONALITY DISORDERS

We have said a great deal about the nature of personality disorders and also about methods designed to make the mentally ill person well again. But how about the much more important goal of preventing such disorders? This, as indicated earlier, is the aim of mental hygiene.

Education of the general public with regard to mental illness is one important function of mental hygiene. The reader has learned that personality disorders originate in organic disease or in maladjusted modes of thought and action. He knows that they have a natural and not a supernatural origin. This fact should be widely publicized so that the mentally ill will be regarded as sick rather than "possessed." It should also be more generally recognized that mental illness can be prevented and that the mentally ill can be cured and rehabilitated.

Parent education is important in preventing mental illness. There is no "pat" formula to be applied in raising a mentally healthy child, for every child is different and what works with one may not work with another. Moreover, a certain procedure is sometimes applied effectively by one parent and not by another. But there are certain general principles of which parents should be cognizant. For example, they should recognize that children need affection, security, and worthwhile interpersonal relations. They should learn to refrain from pushing a child beyond the limits of his intellectual and other capacities. They should realize the need to develop independence rather than overdependence. In short, they should be informed rather than ignorant about the psychological aspects of child development.

Clinics for the treatment of behavior disorders in children are also important. A child guidance clinic (usually staffed by psychiatrists, psychologists, and social workers) can do much to correct personality disorders at their inception. Such a clinic usually works with the child, his parents, and his teachers to locate the source of his difficulties and to seek ways of correcting them.

Another aspect of mental hygiene focuses upon adolescents and adults, the aim being to increase their self-understanding and thus help them solve personal problems. A course in general psychology may contribute to these ends. Moreover, many colleges and centers for adult education offer special courses dealing with various aspects of psychological adjustment.

A widely used textbook[77] on the psychology of adjustment cites the following as principles conducive to mental health: good physical health, accepting yourself, accepting other people, maintaining a confidential relationship with someone with whom you can discuss your problems, assuming an active attitude toward difficulties which is aimed at overcoming them, participating in social activities, finding a satisfying line of work, finding enjoyment in creative undertakings, and using the scientific approach to solution of personal problems. The authors point out, in elaborating upon these, that the principles are not easily applied and that many individuals need professional help.* ■

---

* Professional help is sometimes available in a college or university. Many communities also have mental health clinics. The National Association for Mental Health, 1790 Broadway, New York 19, New York, publishes a *Directory of Outpatient Psychiatric Clinics*. A *Directory of American Psychological Services* is published by the American Board of Psychological Services, 9827 Clayton Road, St. Louis 17, Missouri. It contains a listing by state and community of qualified clinics and individuals offering psychological services. Qualified psychologists may also be identified through state boards of examiners in psychology (which function in states with certification laws) and through the *Directory of Diplomates in Professional Psychology*, published by The American Board of Examiners in Professional Psychology and available from the Secretary-Treasurer of the Board, Dr. Noble H. Kelley, Southern Illinois University, Carbondale, Illinois.

• SUMMARY

Every person has much in common with others, but his particular integration of motives, abilities, and behavior patterns makes him different from everyone else. This unique integration is what we refer to as his *personality*. In assessing personality we usually give considerable weight to how the individual functions in relation to others. The moral or ethical aspects of personality, like honesty and consideration for the welfare of others, are referred to in general as the person's *character*. The various components of personality (the aspects whose integration has been referred to) are called *personality traits*. In a very crude sense, we can think of traits as parts of a jigsaw puzzle. How many essentially different traits are involved is not known. It is customary, however, to make a distinction between so-called *surface traits* (those known to the individual and revealed through his reactions to question-and-answer tests) and *depth traits* (or depth factors). Basic desires, anxieties, conflicts, and aspirations come under the latter heading. When these are not recognized by the individual himself (when he is unconscious of them) they may often be revealed through psychoanalysis, projective tests, and other methods designed to "probe the unconscious."

Looked at from one standpoint, personality is the person's *self*, the *I*. This develops as the child learns to distinguish himself from others and to differentiate self-initiated acts from those initiated by others. The development of a vocabulary of words with self-reference is also important. From being a little animal, with few if any personality traits and no concept of self, the child gradually becomes humanized in his behavior. He develops an increasing number of traits, and he becomes aware of himself as an increasingly independent member of the community. Biological and situational (including cultural) influences are both important for this process of developing a personality. One biological influence is represented by the id (physiological needs). By a process referred to as reality testing, the ego (self) and superego (conscience) develop. The parents (especially the mother) play an important role in molding personality. When an inadequate superego develops (as in psychopathic personality) the home situation is probably responsible. Again, the mother's influence appears crucial. Being an only child does not have deleterious effects on personality so long as contacts with other children are provided and the child is not the focus of too much parental attention. Ordinal position in the family does not appear to have any specific effect on personality.

Investigators have often attempted to discover personality types, such as introverts and extraverts. Introversion-extraversion tests reveal a normal rather than a bimodal distribution, hence no evidence that people are, in general, either introverts or extraverts. Most fall toward the center of the distribution and are classified as ambiverts. Whether persons may be typed with respect to physique and temperament and whether there is any valid correlation between the two is still undecided. One investigation has presented evidence for three dimensions of physique (endomorphy, mesomorphy, and ectomorphy) and three related dimensions of temperament (viscerotonia, somatotonia, and cerebrotonia). Subsequent research has in some instances supported and in others refuted the finding that these physique and temperament dimensions are significantly correlated.

The glands which most directly influence personality are the anterior lobe of the pituitary, the adrenal cortex, the thyroid, and the gonads. There is a close interrelation of glandular functions. Through its secretion of ACTH, and growth- and gonad-stimulating hormones, the anterior pituitary plays a key role. Glandular secretions have much to do with such aspects of personality as physique, general energy level, and sexual functions and interests.

Personality assessment may be holistic (observation of behavior as a whole in a broad social setting), or projective (using tests like the Rorschach and T.A.T.), or may involve tests of relatively restricted traits (introversion, neuroticism, and so on). The trait approach may utilize behavior situations or pencil-and-paper checklists. It is not unusual for holistic, projective, and trait approaches to be used in combination.

The normal person has some socially acceptable goal around which his activities are integrated, he finds pursuit of his goal worthwhile, and, in general, enjoys living.

Clinical types of abnormal personality are classified as: (1) organic or functional, and (2) psychoneuroses (neuroses) or psychoses (insanities). All of the psychoneuroses are believed to be functional. Some psychoses are classified as "functional" and some as "organic." Functional disorders are, in the present state of our knowledge, attributed primarily to the mode of living and thinking acquired by the individual. The personality disorders said to be "organic" involve recognizable damage within the nervous system, especially within the brain.

Examples of psychoneurotic disorders are: bodily complaints, indecision and doubts, some symptoms of dissociation (including multiple personality), and anxiety states. Psychoanalysis, client-centered therapy, and group therapy are often used to alleviate psychoneurotic disorders. Tranquilizers are also used.

Examples of psychoses with known organic damage are: general paresis, senile psychosis, and alcoholic psychosis. The so-called "functional psychoses" are manic-depressive psychosis and schizophrenia, or dementia praecox. There is still much discussion as to whether schizophrenia has organic bases. Four types (simple, hebephrenic, catatonic, and paranoid) are included in most classifications. Mixed types are also recognized.

Although our survey of psychoses was primarily to show the kinds of personality disorders that occur, we mentioned briefly some of the possible origins and some forms of therapy, including group therapy, shock therapy (electric and insulin), tranquilizers, and psychosurgery.

Mental hygiene is concerned with the prevention of all forms of mental illness. It works through such channels as parent education and the establishment of clinics for the treatment of personality disorders before they become so serious as to require hospitalization. ∎

REFERENCES AND NOTES FOR THIS CHAPTER ARE IN THE APPENDIX.

• SELECTED READINGS

Allport, G. W., *Pattern and Growth in Personality.* Holt, Rinehart and Winston, 1961. A revision and extension of Allport's well-known *Personality* (1937).

Anastasi, A., *Fields of Applied Psychology.* McGraw-Hill, 1964. Part V is a brief and interestingly presented review of the diagnosis, therapy, and investigation of disorders which bring individuals to the clinical psychologist.

Axline, V. M., *Dibs: In Seach of Self.* Houghton Mifflin, 1964. A case study of personality development through play therapy.

Cameron, N., *Personality Development and Psychopathology.* Houghton Mifflin, 1963. This highly original treatment, influenced by psychoanalysis, emphasizes the dynamics of behavior disorders.

Cronbach, L. J., *Essentials of Psychological Testing* (2nd ed.). Harper, 1960. Chapters 15–19 review the major methods of assessing personality.

Daniel, R. S. (Ed.), *Contemporary Readings in General Psychology* (2nd ed.). Houghton Mifflin, 1965. Readings 46, 73, 74, and 75, on aspects of mental health.

Dulany, D. E., R. L. DeValois, D. C. Beardslee, and M. R. Winterbottom, *Contributions to Modern Psychology* (2nd ed.). Oxford, 1963. Chapters VII (Personality) and VIII (Personality Disorders) contain papers by outstanding contributors in these areas.

Hall, C. S., and G. Lindzey, *Theories of Personality.* Wiley, 1957. A comprehensive review of major theories.

Koch, S. (Ed.), *Psychology: A Study of a Science,* Vol. 5. McGraw-Hill, 1963. Included are several original papers on personality and related topics. See especially the contributions by R. W. Leeper, N. Sanford, I. L. Child, D. R. Miller, E. H. Rodnick, and J B. Rotter.

Lundin, R. W., *Personality: An Experimental Approach.* Macmillan, 1961. This emphasizes operant conditioning as a technique for the experimental study of personality.

White, R. W., *The Abnormal Personality* (3rd ed.). Ronald, 1964. A good place to find further information on personality disorders.

10

The Learning Process

*L*earning is without a doubt the most important psychological process, for it is the basis of almost everything that makes us psychologically different from other animals and from other human beings. We may define learning as *the process of being modified, more or less permanently, by what happens in the world around us, by what we do, or by what we observe.* We say "more or less permanently" because some modifications are not retained, hence fail to qualify as examples of learning. When one enters a dark theater, for instance, he gradually becomes accustomed to the low illumination so that, presently, he can see better than before. This sort of temporary modification may be contrasted with that which occurs when a child is jumped upon by a loudly barking dog and thereafter is afraid of dogs, or is at least anxious in their presence; when speaking and writing develop; and when an individual plays a violin, typewrites, rides a bicycle, or accomplishes some intricate skating pattern. We would not say that a person learns to see in the dark, but we would say that he learns to be afraid, learns to speak, learns to write, and so on.

Some modifications of the organism come about through natural growth processes and we say that they result from *maturation.* Instincts, tropisms, and reflexes fall into this category. Their characteristics and their development are determined primarily by the organism's biological inheritance. Such responses are said to be *unlearned.* But any response or modification that is dependent primarily upon external stimulation and activity of the organism is said to be *learned* or *acquired.* Instincts, tropisms, and reflexes may be modified by stimulation and activity. We then say that these modifications are learned. Another term that is relevant in this context is *habit.* Learning is sometimes referred to as *habit formation.* We speak of learned activities as *habits.* Linguistic skills are called *verbal habits* and riding a bicycle, skating, and operating a lathe are said to be *motor habits.*

The main point of what we have said so far is that learning is distinguished from sensory adaptation by being relatively permanent and from maturational development by depending upon the stimulation and activity of the organism rather than upon its biological inheritance. This is not to deny, of course, that biological inheritance is influential in learning, for there are inherited differences in the capacity to learn. We observe this in comparing the learning capacity of animals at different levels of evolution and also in studying individual differences at a particular level.

Learning of the simplest kind can probably be demonstrated in all animals. There is some evidence that it exists even in the one-celled paramecium. We know for certain that it is present in such animals as worms and snails.[1] As we ascend the evolutionary scale, however, something beyond sheer modifiability becomes increasingly evident. There is faster learning and habits are retained longer as the human level is approached; but more important still is the fact that habits of increasing complexity can be acquired. The worm learns to avoid shock by turning to the right in a T-shaped alley; the rat learns to find its way through a complicated labyrinth with food at the end; the monkey learns to select the odd figure in a group of three in which two are alike; and the human being learns to speak, to find his mouth with a spoon, to dress himself, and perhaps in time to calculate the trajectory of a missile, or do something even more complicated. The lowest organisms adjust to their environments chiefly through their tropisms and instincts. As the brain becomes increasingly complex, unlearned behavior gives way gradually to learned behavior and when the human level is reached, practically everything beyond basic physiological processes and reflexes is learned. Human nature itself is thus to a large extent acquired. ■

LEARNING AND HUMAN BEHAVIOR

We are born with a number of reflexes, including such essential ones as breathing and sucking, but our immaturity and the absence of habits makes us almost completely helpless. In these respects we are all alike at the beginning. We differ, of course, in our inherited capacity to learn, but this difference can become apparent only through what we learn and how.

□ The importance of learning in human life becomes clearly apparent when we consider how a person would act if deprived of everything he had learned. Suppose that some drug were discovered which, without injuring your response mechanisms, wiped out all traces of what you had learned. You would retain your physiological maturity, but psychologically you would revert immediately to the level of a baby.

You would have all the normal reflexes and you might even creep or walk. You would have the same physiological needs, like hunger and thirst, that you now possess. But you would not know where to find the means of satisfying your needs. There would be no way of knowing, except possibly through taste and smell, which things were edible and which not. You would wear no clothes and, even if they were given you, you would have no idea, except by observing others, what they were for. If you tried to put them on, you could not button or otherwise fix them. All of the habits of buttoning, zipping, and tying that you learned so laboriously in childhood would have disappeared. If food and utensils were placed before you, you could not feed yourself with the latter. You would not even use your fingers, except, possibly, after finding other means inadequate. You would have no attitudes of cleanliness and, if you did, you could not perform the acts required to keep clean. You would have no knowledge of right and wrong; no conscience, or superego. Your surroundings would be meaningless, your parents and friends simply strange creatures somewhat like yourself. You would seem strange even to yourself, for the ego is acquired. If you had anything to communicate to others, which is doubtful, since all ideas are almost certainly learned, you could not communicate. Your vocalizations would be cries and strange sounds, not words. Your gestures would be of no avail because they would be mere reflexes; not the conventionalized motions which people understand. In other things, also, you would lack even the skill and knowledge of an infant. Only after many years of learning could you regain the attitudes, the skills, the knowledge and, in short, the intelligence, that you now possess.

The learning of our human ancestors also contributes to our own learning. Through language we learn in the comfort of our homes, our schools, and our libraries what they learned through actual struggle with their environments over a period estimated to be at least 35,000 years.[2] What has been called our "social heritage" represents the fruits of what our ancestors learned concerning themselves and the world about them. If we were dependent upon our own untutored learning — that is to say, if we were deprived of our social heritage — we would be no better off than savages — if we could survive at all, which is extremely doubtful.[3] □

In the preceding chapters and in the above statement we have referred to many things that human beings learn. Examples of human learning are actually innumerable. For convenience in discussion, however, it is possible to group them into a few classes.

One of the first things that any human being learns is *not* to react to inconsequential (or irrelevant) stimuli. A baby comes to tolerate sights and sounds which at first disturbed it, perhaps producing startle responses. It learns not to cry when its face is washed, or its hair cut. This process of becoming accustomed to what was at first attention-producing, if not disturbing, is known as *habituation*.[4] We will have little more to say about this process, although it does enter a later discussion concerned with eliminating conditioned fear responses.

We learn to make relatively simple responses to the immediately relevant aspects of our environment — like finding and sucking the nipple when hungry, crying in order to be picked up, and withdrawing from painful stimuli before they reach us. This elementary learning involves the modification of inborn reflexes and it is known as *conditioned-response learning*. We also learn, at times, to give up earlier acquisitions. This learning not to do as we have been doing is referred to later in this chapter as *experimental extinction*. Except that it involves the relinquishing of learned instead of unlearned responses, it resembles habituation.

In early childhood we also learn many *motor skills*, like reaching for and grasping objects, standing up unaided, putting on our clothes, and buttoning or zipping them up. With this sort of acquisition underway, and motor skills of increasing complexity being added to our repertoire, we begin to acquire *verbal skills*. At first there is no more than a limited understanding of what certain words and gestures mean. Then we develop such verbal skills as saying words, combining them to form sentences, and writing them.

While acquiring motor and verbal skills, we are also gaining facility in *problem-solving*. We solve simple problems at first, like finding our way around, extricating ourselves from frustrating situations, and getting others to cooperate with us. Gradually we learn to solve problems that are more complex, including those which involve a high degree of verbalization.

We also acquire *information* about ourselves and the world around us. This facilitates the acquisition of skills and the solution of problems. Sometimes the solution to a problem requires that we pool relevant information — that we "put two and two together."

Thus there is a gradual transition from simpler forms of learning to the level of problem-solving which takes us into the realm of the thought processes, discussed in Chapter 13.

While we are adding to our repertoire of skills, acquiring useful information, and solving problems of various kinds, we are also *learning how to learn*. Further acquisitions are accordingly facilitated.

The various forms of learning occur concurrently and they are inextricably interwoven and interdependent. Whether there are really different kinds of learning or whether all are reducible to a common principle, such as conditioning, remains to be seen. ∎

CONDITIONING

The term *conditioning* is often used to represent all learning, even that involved when, in the process known as "brain-washing," a person comes to accept a new concept of his country, or its enemies, or their policies. We deal with conditioning in a much more limited sense. It means for us the acquisition of conditioned responses. Thus the term is used to represent a relatively simple aspect of the learning process. This restricted use does not imply, however, that the principles involved are without wider application. Pavlov himself claimed that "different kinds of habits based on training, education, and discipline of any sort are nothing but a long chain of conditioned reflexes."[5] We know today that the evidence fails to justify such a sweeping generalization; nevertheless, many psychologists feel that principles involved in the acquisition of conditioned responses play a role in all learning.

No one yet knows, in neural and physiological terms, how learning occurs. This is because both the learning process and the nervous system which mediates it are so complex. Nevertheless the study of conditioned responses, since they represent learning in perhaps its simplest form, may provide the breakthrough that we need. In fact a conference on the central nervous system and behavior was concerned entirely with conditioned responses.[6] Investigators look upon the conditioned response as a "tool" for the study of electrical, chemical, and other aspects of neural functioning. Anything that it can teach us about these will add to our understanding of what happens in the organism when learning occurs.

The response to be conditioned is already in the organism's repertoire. In one type of conditioning procedure, what we do is to associate this response with a stimulus which previously failed to arouse it. Thus, in the experiments of Pavlov, discussed earlier from the standpoint of their influence on behaviorism, the dog which had not previously salivated to a sound came to do so (Figure 1.13, p. 30). Although we somewhat oversimplify the situation to say so, conditioning in such instances involves the substitution of a new stimulus — a previously indifferent one — for the stimulus which originally elicited the response. We could also say that the animal learns to make an old response to a new stimulus. Such statements are oversimplified, however, for we will see that the response itself may be modified during the conditioning process.

There are also occasions when the conditioned stimulus leads to the *suppression* of a former response. An interesting fictional account of such conditioning was written by a Spanish dramatist almost 350 years ago.[7] This is a free translation, in modern idiom, of what he said:

☐"Saint Ildefonso used to scold me and punish me lots of times. He would sit me on the bare floor and make me eat with the cats of the monastery. These cats were such rascals that they took advantage of my penitence. They drove me mad stealing my choicest morsels. It did no good to chase them away. But I found a way of coping with the beasts in order to enjoy my meals.

I put them all in a sack, and on a pitch black night took them out under an arch. First I would cough, and then immediately whale the daylights out of the cats. They whined and shrieked like an infernal pipe organ. I would pause for a while and repeat the operation — first a cough, and then a thrashing. I finally noticed that even without beating them, the beasts moaned and yelped like the very devil whenever I coughed. I then let them loose. Thereafter, whenever I had to eat off the floor, I would cast a look around. If an animal approached my food, all I had to do was to cough, and how that cat did scat!" ☐

We see many comparable examples in everyday life. The child reaches for the cookie jar and his mother scowls or tells him not to touch. He continues to reach and gets a spanking. After he has "learned his lesson" the scowl or verbal command is enough to stop him.

Sometimes an investigator does not know what stimuli arouse a particular response, as

Pavlov knew that food would produce salivary secretions. Nevertheless, once a response has appeared, its subsequent occurrence may be modified by conditioning procedures. The reader will recall, in this connection, how rats that pressed the lever in a box (pp. 162–163) came to press more or less often, depending upon the consequences of what they had done. This is the type of conditioning to which we are now referring. There is a more detailed discussion of it in the present chapter. All of us have seen instances of such conditioning. The infant happens to put his thumb in his mouth. Sucking it has satisfying results. Before long he has a thumb-sucking habit. And, from the negative standpoint, suppose a child happens to touch the hot stove. The painful consequences of this behavior are such that this response may never recur.

PAVLOV AND THE SALIVARY RESPONSE

Pavlov's interest in salivary conditioning arose from his earlier studies of gastric secretions, for which he received the Nobel Prize. In the course of the earlier research, he had observed that saliva and gastric juices are secreted at the sight of food, or even at the sound of the keeper's footsteps. Pavlov at first called these "psychic secretions" to distinguish them from the original ones, which were elicited only when food entered the mouth. This observation was not in itself of great significance, for it had long been known that one's mouth waters at the sound of the dinner bell, or some other indication of approaching food. But Pavlov saw in this reaction a way to investigate the functioning of the brain *in a whole organism*. Before this time it had been customary for neurologists to remove parts of the nervous system and to study the effects of their removal.

Pavlov believed that when a "psychic secretion" occurred, new pathways in the brain had been opened. As illustrated in Figure 10.1, he supposed that when the dog salivated in response to a bell, the auditory area of its brain had developed new connections with the motor area controlling salivary secretion. He wanted to study these connections without

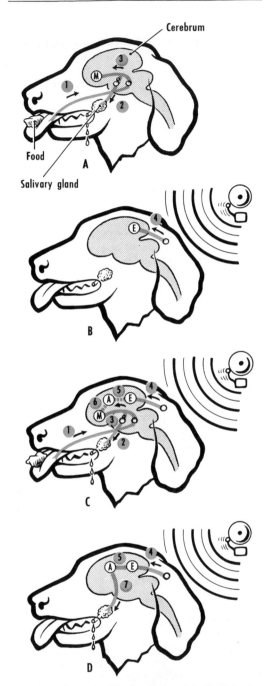

Cerebrum

Food

Salivary gland

A

B

C

D

● 10.1

Pavlov's Concept of the Neural Basis of a Conditioned reflex. In **A** is represented the fact that when food is placed in the mouth, there must be some sort of neural connection between receptors in the mouth and centers in the brain stem which activate a salivary response. The essential connection is between fibers 1 and 2; but other connections, represented by 3, mediate taste sensitivity. M represents the area of the cortex thus involved. When the bell is rung, as shown in **B**, the part of the cortex most affected is the auditory area at E. Note that there is no connection between this area and centers influencing salivation. When the bell is rung and food is placed in the mouth, as represented in **C**, there are cortical activities at both M and E, and pathways 1, 2, 3, and 4 are active. Association neurons between E and M are also involved. Thus pathways 5 and 6 in the association area (A), between the regions primarily activated, may link these regions. After the bell-food stimulation has occurred a number of times, this link is established. Then, as diagramed in **D**, ringing the bell can itself trigger salivation via neurons (path 7) connecting the association area A with the salivary glands. Although something like this, in barest outline, does occur in salivary conditioning, the details are still being worked out. There is no doubt that thousands of neurons are implicated and that any such diagram will greatly oversimplify what happens. (Adapted from G. G. Simpson, C. S. Pittendrigh, and L. H. Tiffany, *Life: An Introduction to Biology*, Harcourt, Brace, 1957, p. 244. Courtesy of Harcourt, Brace, and Routledge and Kegan Paul, Ltd.)

tion of the physiological activity of the cerebral cortex."* It was only after he had done much work on conditioned salivation that Pavlov saw the wider implications already referred to in the statement that all learning is conditioning.

Our basic vocabulary in this area of science originated with Pavlov. Salivation in response to food placed in the mouth is a natural,

injuring the animal's brain, and believed that he could do so, at least inferentially, by studying conditioned salivary responses and the conditions of their arousal. His book, *Conditioned Reflexes*, was in fact subtitled, "An investiga-

* We know now that, while conditioning of an intact animal involves the cerebral cortex, conditioning occurs in animals without a cortex and also in mammals deprived of their cortex. In the latter instance, brain-stem mechanisms must mediate the new "connections."[8]

unlearned response — in short, a reflex. This was called the *unconditioned reflex*. Food was called the *unconditioned stimulus*. When Pavlov's repeated presentation of a bell followed by food led the dog to salivate in response to the bell, he referred to the bell (or any other previously indifferent stimulus) as the *conditional stimulus*. Salivation in response to this was designated a *conditional reflex*. Use of the term *conditional* emphasized the fact that arousal of the reflex was now dependent upon stimuli other than the natural one. In translation, however, the Russian word *ouslovny* became condition*ed* rather than condition*al*, hence the widespread adoption of the adjective *conditioned*. Also, it became apparent in later research that many conditioned responses are, strictly speaking, not reflexes. When responses other than salivation are considered, what begins as a reflex may itself change as it becomes conditioned. For this and other reason's the term conditioned *response* has come into general use.

The conditioning process may be illustrated diagrammatically by showing the S–R relationships. Thus, before the salivary response is conditioned to a bell, we have the following situation:

Unconditioned stimulus   Unconditioned response
    (food) ——————————→ (salivation)

Stimulus to be conditioned   Response
    (bell) ——————————→ (pricking up ears, etc., but not salivation)

After the stimulus to be conditioned has been paired with the unconditioned stimulus a number of times, and salivation in response to it (now the conditioned stimulus) has developed, the situation is as follows:

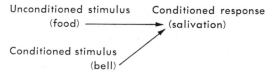

Unconditioned stimulus   Conditioned response
    (food) ——————————→ (salivation)

Conditioned stimulus
    (bell)

The previously neutral or ineffective stimulus, as well as the unconditioned one, now elicits salivation, so we say that salivation elicited by the bell alone is a *conditioned* response.

■ **TABLE 10.1   Development of a Conditioned Salivary Response to a Tone**

Presentations of sound and feeding	Drops of saliva in 30 seconds
1	0
9	18
15	30
31	65
41	64
51	69

No drops of saliva were secreted when the tone was first presented. A test with the tone, but no food, after 9 presentations of tone and food elicited 18 drops. A similar test after 15 presentations yielded 30 drops. After 31 presentations, 65 drops were elicited by the sound alone. After ten further presentations, the test with sound alone yielded 64 drops. A further ten presentations brought another increase in the number of drops. (After Anrep)

Pavlov introduced many other terms. One of these — *reinforcement* — is widely used to day, although often with a somewhat different meaning than when Pavlov used it. For him, this term referred to the following of the conditioned by the unconditioned stimulus, as when food followed the ringing of the bell. The term *reinforcement* is now also used when reward or punishment follows a particular response; for instance, lever-pressing. We use the term *positive reinforcement* for rewarding and *negative reinforcement* for punishing conditions.

Another feature of Pavlov's work is worthy of particular attention — his attempt to obtain quantitative information. He saw that it is not sufficient to observe that salivation occurs when a conditioned stimulus is presented. One needs some way of measuring this response so that variations in it can be related to conditions of arousal; for example, variations based upon the time between presentation of the bell and reinforcement. Accordingly, Pavlov made an opening in one of the dog's cheeks so that saliva would run out. The amount secreted was estimated in terms either of its volume or of the number of drops. Development of a conditioned salivary response to tone is illustrated in Table 10.1.

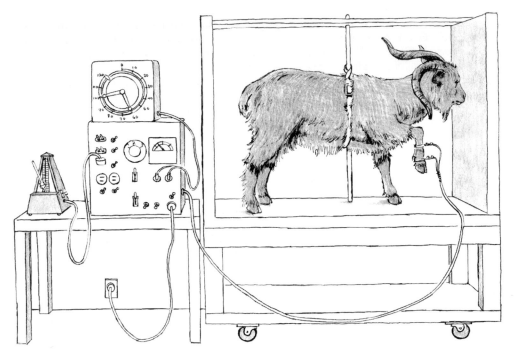

● **10.2**

Bechterev's Method of Conditioning. This is the arrangement used in research on conditioning at the laboratory of the Cornell University Behavior Farm. A mild electric shock is followed by withdrawal of the goat's right foreleg. The clicking of the metronome does not at first produce this reaction. When the metronome and the shock are presented in close association, and the animal has thus been conditioned, it raises its leg as soon as the metronome sounds. The devices shown present stimuli and record responses. (From H. S. Liddell, "Conditioning and Emotions," *Scientific American*, January, 1954, 49.)

Following the general procedure already described, Pavlov and his associates conditioned the salivary response of dogs to a wide variety of stimuli — visual, auditory, olfactory, and cutaneous.

Pavlov's procedures were soon modified to fit them for use with human subjects, both child and adult. A suction cup placed in the mouth over the salivary gland allowed investigators to collect saliva without the operation required when dogs are used. Some experiments later did away with the suction cup, using standard cotton pads instead. A cylindrical cotton pad like that used by dentists was placed in the cheek before presentation of the stimulus and was weighed after presentation. Its increased weight provided a mea-

sure of the amount of saliva secreted. Research on conditioned salivary responses in children, and to some extent in adults, has verified the phenomena observed by Pavlov in dogs.[9]

BECHTEREV'S CONTRIBUTION

Pavlov confined his attention to dogs and, in these, to the salivary response. Bechterev, his Russian contemporary, who had worked in Wundt's laboratory at Leipzig, extended the conditioned-response technique to human beings.[10] In his work with dogs and human subjects, Bechterev used an electric shock as the unconditioned stimulus and reflex withdrawal of the shocked limb as the unconditioned response. Many different kinds of conditioned stimuli were used, including the beating of a metronome, as in Figure 10.2, which shows Bechterev's method applied to a goat.

Observe that the subject conditioned with this method gets the shock whether or not it responds to the conditioned stimulus. Bechterev called the response to the new stimulus an "associative reflex," but later workers with this and related methods have adopted Pavlov's terminology.

When Bechterev's method is used the response is usually recorded graphically. Attached to the stimulated limb is a string or other device which transmits motions to a writing level. This records them on a moving tape. A record obtained in this way is reproduced in Figure 10.3. Here, using Bechterev's method, the investigators conditioned a child to withdraw its foot at the sound of a metronome. We see that the metronome, at the tenth trial, did not elicit withdrawal. But the child did withdraw its foot when the shock came. On the eleventh trial, however, the foot was withdrawn soon after the metronome went on. By the twelfth trial there was as large a response to the metronome as there was to the shock. It is as though the subject was

expecting the shock. Such *anticipatory responses* are commonly found when the conditioned stimulus precedes the unconditioned stimulus.

The general procedures used by Pavlov and Bechterev have been extended to other responses than those conditioned by them, and also to a wide range of organisms. Much of the research on adult human subjects has used the eyelid reflex to a puff of air. An air puff directed at the eye (unconditioned stimulus) produces a blink (unconditioned response). This response may be recorded as diagramed in Figure 10.4. The conditioning stimulus may be a weak light, as illustrated, or any other stimulus which does not itself produce the eyelid reflex. Some typical records and an acquisition curve are also shown in the illustration and discussed in the legend.

In all of the procedures that we have described, a stimulus is used to elicit a reflex (salivation, withdrawal, eye-blink) which, in the course of conditioning, is eventually elicited by a previously neutral stimulus. No reward element is involved. The dog gets food whether or not it salivates, it gets a shock whether or not its limb is withdrawn, and the puff of air is repeated whether of not the conditioned

• 10.3

Development of a Conditioned Withdrawal Response in an Infant of Twenty-six Months. The lowest line indicates time in seconds. Above this is a line which shows the onset and duration of the electric current. The next line indicates the onset and duration of the metronome. The infant's withdrawal of its foot is represented in the uppermost line. Note that the metronome began to sound approximately fifty seconds before the onset of the shock and that it continued to sound until the shock was given. Until the eleventh presentation of the metronome there was no foot withdrawal. At the eleventh presentation, however, there was an anticipatory reaction — a partial reaction as though in anticipation of the shock to follow. A response similar to that which had previously appeared only to the shock was elicited by the metronome on the twelfth presentation. (After F. Marinesco and A. Kreindler)

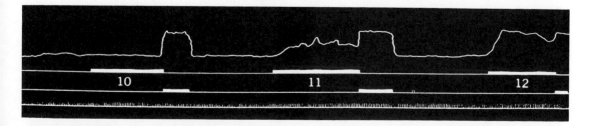

A

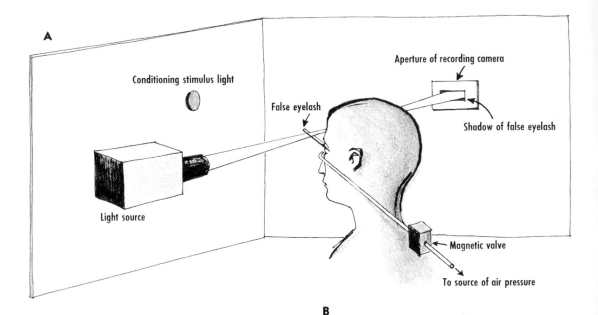

Conditioning stimulus light

Aperture of recording camera

False eyelash

Shadow of false eyelash

Light source

Magnetic valve

To source of air pressure

B

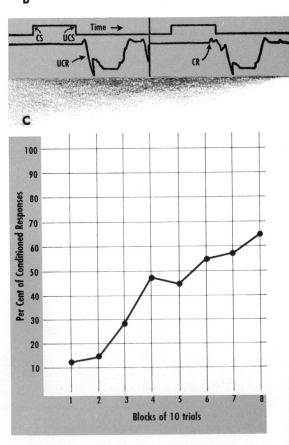

• 10.4

Eyelid Conditioning. Illustration **A** shows how movements of the eyelid are elicited and recorded. A paper extension of the eyelash throws a shadow on the moving film, which also records the onset of the conditioning stimulus, in this case a light. Tracings of actual records made in this way are shown in **B**. We see that the conditioned response comes after the onset of the light and before the puff of air. It is thus an anticipatory response. **C** shows an acquisition curve. It shows that the number of anticipatory blinks increases as a function of the number of times that the light and air puff (and unconditioned blink) are presented in close association. (Diagram redrawn from G. A. Kimble and N. Garmezy, *Principles of General Psychology,* 1963, p. 137, with permission from Ronald Press. Records from *Hilgard and Marquis' Conditioning and Learning,* 2nd ed., p. 55. Revised by Gregory A. Kimble. Copyright © 1961 by Appleton-Century-Crofts, Inc. Reproduced by permission of Appleton-Century-Crofts. The acquisition curve is the one for young adults in H. W. Braun and R. Geiselhart, "Age Differences in the Acquisition and Extinction of the Eyelid Response," *J. Exper. Psychol.,* 1959, *57,* p. 386.)

C

stimulus evokes the eyelid reflex. Use of the same sequence of conditioned and unconditioned stimuli, whether or not a conditioned response occurs, is referred to as conditioning by the classical method, or merely as *classical conditioning*. This is partly in deference to the pioneer Russian investigators and partly to distinguish the method described from another which introduces a reward element. The latter procedure makes reward contingent upon appearance of the conditioned response. Thus the subject escapes shock if it makes an anticipatory response, or it gets a pellet of food if it presses a lever. These procedures are generally referred to as *instrumental*, because the subject's response is instrumental in allowing it to escape pain or to obtain a reward.[11] When an instrumental response is initially a spontaneous one rather than being elicited by an unconditioned stimulus it is said to be an *operant* response; this type of instrumental conditioning is then referred to more specifically as *operant conditioning*, as detailed later in this chapter.

It is of no particular significance that an organism can learn to salivate, lift its foot, or blink in response to a stimulus that formerly did not arouse such responses. As additions to the animal's repertoire of adjustive responses, such things are inconsequential. Why, then, do psychologists study such simple learning? Instrumentally conditioned responses are more meaningful from this standpoint. Any response which satisfies hunger, thirst, or the need to escape from painful stimulation is a worthwhile acquisition. But even these conditioned responses are relatively simple as compared with the complex skills which animals can learn. So again we may ask, "Why do psychologists study them?" The chief reason is that such simple forms of learning lend themselves to the intensive investigation that is extremely difficult to carry out with complex habits. Intensive investigation seems worthwhile because of the neurological implications stressed by Pavlov, and also his claim that conditioning is the primitive basis of all learning.

Although conditioned responses may be viewed as simple acquisitions, the conditioning process itself is far from simple. Research has revealed its intricacies and also some important principles which apply to habit formation at various levels of complexity. ■

SOME ASPECTS OF CONDITIONING

The various phenomena which now receive our attention were revealed in experiments on classical conditioning. Many were first discovered by Pavlov and Bechterev, then verified in comparable experiments utilizing a wide variety of responses in various types of animal subjects and in human beings. Later we will observe that some of the principles worked out with classical procedures also apply to instrumental conditioning.

Sequence and time relations

In research with classical procedures, the conditioned stimulus has usually preceded the onset of the unconditioned stimulus, or it has been presented at the same time as the latter. The reverse order — unconditioned stimulus first — sometimes produces conditioning, but this is very difficult to obtain. When it occurs, we call it *backward conditioning*.

The most effective procedure is to present the conditioned stimulus first. But how much earlier should it occur? This is perhaps a question which cannot be answered for every organism or for every possible conditioning situation. Nevertheless, several experiments have suggested that the optimum interval may be somewhere around one-half second.[12]

Changes in the response conditioned

Upon superficial observation, as we said earlier, it appears that conditioning is merely the arousal of an old response by a new stimulus. This seems to be so in salivary conditioning. However, some differences between the conditioned and the unconditioned response are much more evident in withdrawal than in salivation.

The dog given a shock on the foot at first barks, struggles, and withdraws its foot. No doubt the pulse, respiration, blood pressure, and other physiological reactions are affected. If we were looking for it, we would find conditioning of any of these.[13] But our attention is focused on overt behavior, especially that associated with foot withdrawal. The responses described are at first aroused only by shock. After a bell, say, has preceded the shock a number of times, there are quite evident alterations in behavior. We observe that the dog becomes agitated even before being shocked. It acts as if it were expecting the shock. It struggles and withdraws one foot after another. These are *anticipatory responses* comparable with those referred to when we described conditioning of a child by Bechterev's method and conditioning of the eyelid reflex. But, as conditioning proceeds, we observe further changes. Much of the initial excitement disappears. That is to say, the dog becomes adapted to the situation. Finally, as the bell goes on, the animal may, with seeming nonchalance, lift its foot and do nothing else. What was at first a generalized reaction, involving the whole organism in an obvious way, is narrowed so that only the foot withdrawal occurs.[14] Similarly, when respiration is being conditioned to a tone, the tone may come to produce a slight (anticipatory) change in respiration. This is followed, when the shock comes on, by a respiratory change of greater magnitude.

Thus the conditioning procedure may have several effects. It may produce conditioned adaptation to the situation, it may produce an attitude of expectancy, it may produce an overt anticipatory response which is sometimes an abbreviated form of the response we are conditioning, and, finally, it may produce a more restricted response to the conditioned stimulus than the one originally elicited. For these reasons, it is an oversimplification to say that the conditioned response is merely an old response to a new stimulus or that conditioning is no more than substituting a new stimulus for the natural one.

Stimulus generalization

In the chapter on emotion we discussed a child who, when conditioned to fear a white rat, became afraid, also, of such previously neutral objects as a rabbit and a white beard. Fear was generalized from the original stimulus to other stimuli which resembled it. In the same way a child who is frightened by one dog may show fear of other dogs.

Generalization is prevalent in conditioning. It can be demonstrated not only for different objects, but also for spatial variations in the same sort of stimulation. An illustration of this is provided by an experiment with college students (see Figure 10.5).

☐ As an unconditioned stimulus, the investigator used electric shock applied to the right hand. This produced a reduction in electrical skin resistance which we have elsewhere referred to as the galvanic skin response (GSR).

The GSR was picked up from the left hand. On four different regions of the body there were small tactile vibrators. The vibration of one of these served as the conditioned stimulus.

When conditioning to vibration on the shoulder had been obtained, so that changes in the GSR previously associated with shock were now made to tactile vibration alone, the other points indicated in the figure were stimulated for the first time. Vibration on the middle of the back yielded a GSR, but smaller than that on the shoulder. Stimulation of the thigh likewise elicited a GSR, but one smaller than that on the middle of the back. A still smaller response was elicited by stimulation of the calf. Conditioning of points other than the shoulder region also demonstrated generalization.[15] ☐

Pavlov attributed stimulus generalization to a spread of effects from the region stimulated to other parts of the organism, especially to other parts of the brain than those primarily excited. He referred to the phenomenon as *irradiation of excitation*.

Differential conditioning

The above experiment may also be used to illustrate this phenomenon. After conditioning of one point, as we have seen, other (nonreinforced) points also yielded a conditioned response. How to prevent this is the problem now before us. We wish to condition the organism so that it responds to the reinforced stimulation alone. This is accomplished by stimulating each point instead of only one, but reinforcing only a particular point. Stimulation of the point on the shoulder, say, is always followed by shock. Stimulation of the

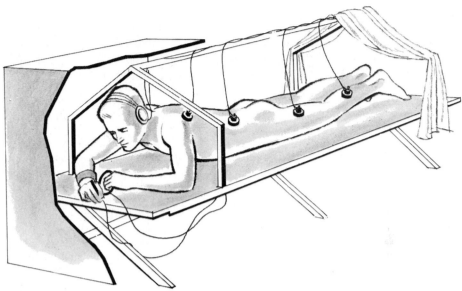

● 10.5

Arrangement for Conditioning the Galvanic Skin Reflex to Vibration of the Skin. The subject lay in a box-like compartment which separated him from the rest of the environment. Headphones in which there was a constant buzz prevented him from hearing outside noises. The unconditioned stimulus (an electric shock) was administered to the right hand. The unconditioned response was sweating, indicated by changes in electrical resistance of the skin of the left hand (galvanic skin reflex). Changes in electrical resistance were recorded by using electrodes and a sensitive galvanometer. Vibration of the skin at one of the spots where the electrically activated vibrators appear was the conditioned stimulus. The conditioning sequence was vibration of the skin followed by shock. (After M. J. Bass and C. L. Hull, "The Irradiation of a Tactile Conditioned Reflex in Man," *J. Comp. Psychol.*, 1934, *14*, p. 48.)

other points occurs randomly, and without being followed by shock. Gradually a discrimination between the reinforced and nonreinforced stimulation occurs, so that a GSR is elicited only by the former.

The same principle applies to all forms of stimulation. An organism conditioned to respond to a light, a tone, or an odor usually also responds to other visual, auditory, and olfactory stimuli. Stimulus generalization occurs. But the response will eventually be made to only one stimulus if this is repeatedly reinforced and the others receive no reinforcement.

Experimental extinction and recovery

Once a conditioned response has been formed, how may it be eliminated? Sometimes incompatible responses are learned. Thus the child who withdraws from a feared white rat may learn to overcome its fear by feeding the rat. The method most widely used to extinguish a conditioned response is, however, to present the conditioned stimulus repeatedly without reinforcing it — without following it with the unconditioned stimulus. Thus, if the bell that has been eliciting a salivary response is rung without presentation of food, the amount of saliva decreases gradually. Finally, there is no salivation in response to the conditioned stimulus.

The shoulder region of the subject in Figure 10.5 was conditioned, as we have seen, so that it yielded a GSR. Vibration of this region was then repeated without presentation of shock. The result was a gradual diminution of the GSR and, finally, complete elimination of this response.

An experimentally extinguished response usually returns after a break in the series of conditioning sessions, a phenomenon known as *spontaneous recovery*. Thus, the GSR was extinguished, but it reappeared later. Continually extinguishing a conditioned response, however, produces a gradually decreasing spontaneous recovery. Finally the response fails to return.

These aspects of classical conditioning apply to many more responses than we have used to illustrate them. We have referred to salivation, withdrawal, and the GSR, but the eyelid reflex,[16] the knee jerk,[17] the electroencephalogram,[18] the heart rate,[19] and pupillary dilation[20] have all been conditioned in human beings. In each instance the conditioning process has been essentially as described. Indeed, research with classical conditioning procedures has shown that almost any response that can be elicited can be conditioned. One first finds a stimulus that elicits the response he wishes to condition. Next, he selects a neutral (unconditioned) stimulus. He has a wide range of stimuli to select from, for almost anything to which the organism is sensitive will do. After finding an unconditioned stimulus and selecting a neutral one, the investigator's next step is to present these stimuli in close temporal proximity. Given the proper sequence of stimulation and adequate timing, the previously neutral stimulus becomes effective. It elicits the response, or modifies it in some way, as previously described. ∎

INSTRUMENTAL CONDITIONING

Instrumental conditioning is similar to classical conditioning in certain respects and different from it in others. Some investigators regard the two as essentially alike and others as essentially different.

One major point of similarity is that, in both instances, the animal is customarily isolated from the environment at large. It is placed in a soundproofed room or box so that what one investigator calls the "background racket," or "background noise of stimulation" is reduced to a minimum. Another similarity is that some particular response is, as it were, isolated for study.

The main points of difference are three. (1) Whereas classical procedures use an unconditioned stimulus (food, shock, a puff of air) to elicit a response to be conditioned, the instrumental procedure does not necessarily do this. The response conditioned, especially in a variation of the instrumental procedure known as *operant conditioning*, is not a response to experimentally controlled stimulation but rather an apparently spontaneous one. This response, lever-pressing for example, is *emitted* by the animal rather than elicited by the experimenter. (2) In the instrumental procedure, as its name implies, the animal's response is instrumental in achieving some result, whether this be access to food or water, or, on the other hand, escape from punishment or confinement. (3) In the operant type of instrumental conditioning, the animal is given more freedom than when classical procedures are used. Rather than being strapped in a conditioning frame, it is free to move around in a box or other enclosure.

What has been called *avoidance conditioning* involves a combination of the features of classical and instrumental conditioning. It is like Bechterev's method in that electric shock is used to elicit a certain class of reactions, such as avoidance or fear. There is also a conditioned stimulus which signals the coming of the shock. This may be any sort of stimulus that the animal can sense — light, metronome, or tone. The instrumental feature is introduced by arranging the situation so that, instead of getting the shock regardless of what it does, the subject can react in such a way as to avoid being shocked. Avoidance is possible if it responds to the conditioned stimulus in time — i.e., makes an anticipatory response. If the goat in Figure 10.2 were being conditioned by an instrumental procedure, one electrode would be under its foot so that, when anticipatory withdrawal occurred, this would break the circuit.

Sometimes the animal subjected to avoidance training has much more freedom than Bechterev's subjects. Dogs and other animals have been placed in an enclosure, the floor of which can be electrified. A light, let us say, signals that a shock is to come. The situation may be arranged so that, if the animal does anything at all when the light comes on, the shock is turned off. Sometimes the subject is required to do some specific thing as the conditioned stimulus comes on — for example, turn a revolving drum, or jump over a barrier to the nonelectrified side of an enclosure.[21]

Experiments like those described have been used to compare the relative effectiveness of classical and instrumental procedures. Of two comparable groups, one gets the shock regardless of what it does (classical) and the other avoids the shock if it makes an anticipatory response (instrumental). Conditioning is obtained with either. But, surprising as it may seem, the instrumental procedure is not always more efficient than the classical. One reason for this may be that, after the animal avoids the shock a few times, there is a tendency for experimental extinction to occur.[22] ■

OPERANT CONDITIONING

This gets its name from the fact that in order to get a reward the organism does something to its environment. To quote Skinner, who coined the term *operant*, it "emphasizes the fact that the behavior *operates* upon the environment to generate consequences."[23] These consequences are the delivery of food, water, or some other reward. The response which operates upon the environment as described is called an *operant*. A term commonly used to represent the reward in operant conditioning is *reinforcement*. This term, as we said earlier, was taken over from Pavlov who, however, used it in a more restricted sense. Again we quote Skinner: "Pavlov himself called all events which strengthened behavior 'reinforcement' and all the resulting changes 'conditioning.' In the Pavlovian experiment, however, a reinforcer is paired with a *stimulus*; whereas in operant behavior it is contingent upon a *response*."[24] This response is *emitted* by the animal.

The investigator usually decides beforehand which of many responses that may be emitted will be reinforced. For example, one investigator decided that he would let a cat escape from a box whenever it scratched its ear.[25] Eventually it scratched, the door opened, and it got out. In subsequent trials, ear-scratching was not so long in coming. Finally, as soon as it was placed in the box, the cat scratched its ear. In another cat, licking was reinforced. A chicken was similarly conditioned. When it pecked its feathers, the door opened. Finally, he would "whirl his head around and poke into his feathers as soon as dropped into the box."

☐ What Skinner calls "superstitious behavior" was developed on a comparable basis in pigeons.[26] A pigeon was confined in an experimental cage where, at regular intervals, a food container came into position, stayed for five seconds, then went out of reach. In this situation the experimenter did not determine ahead of time which response would be reinforced. One bird happened to be turning in a counterclockwise direction as the food appeared. It repeated this response and again was reinforced. Sometimes it was turning and sometimes not as the food came. Gradually, however, the response of turning counterclockwise gained in frequency. Another pigeon happened to be making a certain kind of head movement just prior to the appearance of food, so that this response was reinforced. The head movement was repeated, and reinforced sufficiently often to become the dominant one. In some pigeons, such a fortuitous association of a movement and reinforcement failed to occur often enough to produce "superstitious" behavior. Skinner points out that superstitious behavior in human beings may have a similar origin. He says,

"The bird behaves as if there were a causal relation between its behavior and the presentation of food, although such a relation is lacking. There are many analogies in human behavior. Rituals for changing one's luck at cards are a good example. A few accidental connections between a ritual and favorable consequences suffice to set up and maintain

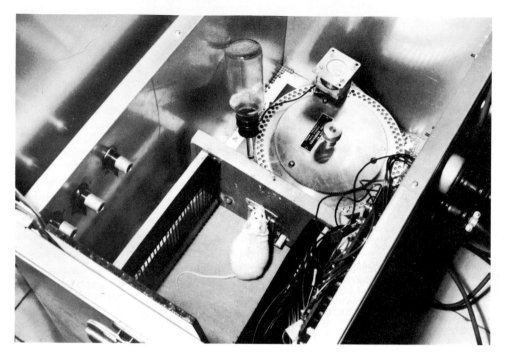

● **10.6**

Operant Conditioning Box for Mice. By pressing the lever, as illustrated, the animal gets a small pellet of food that becomes accessible in the food tray below. Water is obtainable at any time from a tube seen below the bottle at the left. The circular apparatus in the adjoining compartment can be adjusted to yield pellets in accordance with a particular schedule of reinforcement. Some such schedules are described in the text. Responses are recorded on a moving tape (see Figure 10.7) and thus a cumulative record of the conditioning process is made by the animal itself. (From J. Anliker and J. Mayer, "An Operant Conditioning Technique for Studying Feeding-Fasting Patterns in Normal and Obese Mice," *J. Appl. Physiol.*, 1956, 8, No. 6.)

the behavior in spite of many unreinforced instances. The bowler who has released a ball down the alley but continues to behave as if he were controlling it by twisting and turning his arm and shoulder is another case in point. These behaviors have, of course, no effect upon one's luck or upon a ball halfway down an alley, just as in the present case the food would appear as often if the pigeon did nothing — or, more strictly speaking, did something else."[27] ☐

As techniques of operant conditioning are discussed, it will become very evident that the psychologist has here a powerful means of controlling behavior. By using these techniques, he can increase the frequency of one response and reduce that of others, as seen in our examples of "superstitious" behavior. He can also shape behavior in other ways. Want-

ing the organism to respond in a certain manner he can arrange to reinforce one response and not others so that behavior increasingly approximates the desired form. This is what we mean by "shaping" an organism's behavior. Its significance will be clearer as we proceed. We will also observe its application to human beings.

Operant conditioning techniques

The above experiments show what is meant by reinforcing an operant but they hardly do justice to the techniques of operant conditioning as these are typically used.

In the typical research situation an apparatus like that of Figure 10.6 is used for rats, mice, hamsters, and other animals for which lever-pressing is an easily acquired response.[28] Essentially the same technique has been adapted for use with monkeys, chimpanzees, and children. One such adaptation was shown (p. 234) when we discussed ulcer formation in "executive" monkeys. Much of the recent research has used pigeons. These peck a disc (Figure 10.7) instead of pressing a lever.[29]

The lever-pressing and disc-pecking situations provide an interesting contrast with classical conditioning. As we have already indicated, the latter arouses the response to be conditioned by using an unconditioned stimulus. In operant conditioning, on the other hand, nobody can identify the stimulation responsible for the response to be conditioned. This is evident from what has already been said about this response being *emitted* by the animal. Nevertheless, if the situation contains a lever to be pressed, and lever-pressing is the only response reinforced, it is evident that the subject will eventually be lever-pressing rather than doing something else. But, one may ask, "If an investigator knows enough to arrange a situation in which a particular

• 10.7

Operant Conditioning. The operant here is pecking (**A**). Reinforcement comes from a piece of food made available in the lower aperture. The type of record obtained as the organism responds is shown as recorded (**B**) and turned around (**C**). A roller activated by electric clockwork moves the recording paper continuously and at a constant rate of speed. Each response moves the recording pen to a new position, as illustrated, thus providing a cumulative record of the conditioning process. When the record is turned around, so that the curve rises toward the right, we have an acquisition curve resembling those illustrated. The slope of such curves indicates the rate of conditioning. Note that the animal whose performance is represented by the lower curve failed to respond for a time. Then it responded and the recording pen moved to a new level. Another response shortly thereafter made a further increment in the record, and so on. Flat places in all three records of course mean absence of response. A continued flat record would mean that extinction had occurred. (Adapted from C. B. Ferster and B. F. Skinner, *Schedules of Reinforcement*, Appleton-Century-Crofts, 1957.)

A

Each response moves pen one unit in this direction

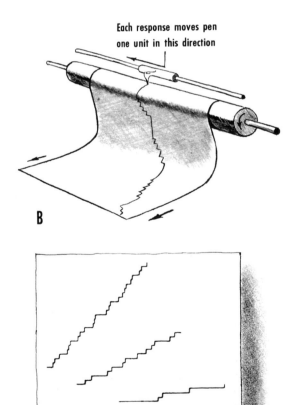

B

C

response like lever-pressing or disc-pecking will occur, and he verifies his prediction, what more is there to know — where does one go from there?" The answer is that the establishment of a predictable response is only a first step. Once this response has been established, the investigator uses it as a "tool" with which to investigate the effect of various conditions upon the organism — variations in reinforcement, changing internal physiological conditions, brain disturbances, and so forth.

The most important feature of operant conditioning, once the response has been acquired, is *rate of responding*, the number of responses per minute. Investigations like those mentioned are focused upon conditions which influence response rate.

In typical research on operant conditioning, reinforcement is provided by a small piece of food. This is an instance of *reward training*. In some studies, however, the floor of the apparatus is electrified and the subject's response turns off the shock. In this event we refer to *escape training*.

Schedules of reinforcement

In everyday life reinforcement is more often intermittent than continuous. Considerable interest therefore attaches to the study of what can be accomplished with different schedules of reinforcement.

The device which dispenses food can be set so that reinforcement occurs after every response or so that it occurs intermittently. In the latter event, there may be reinforcement at *fixed intervals* (let us say, every ten minutes), at *fixed ratios* (as when one reinforcement comes after every tenth response), or at *variable intervals* or *variable ratios*. The rate of responding varies in predictable ways as the schedule of reinforcement is varied. A large volume containing almost 1000 curves obtained with pigeons deals in detail with such relationships.[30]

In general, each reinforcement after a fixed interval is followed by a slow rate of responding. But the rate picks up as the time for the next reinforcement approaches. An animal's reactions show, in fact, that it discriminates time intervals between reinforcements.

With fixed-ratio reinforcement, the subject gets so much per unit of work. This is like piecework in industry. With this type of schedule, there is an extremely high rate of responding just so long as the animal need not work too long for each reinforcement. With a ratio of reinforcement that is conducive to a high overall rate of responding, there is, as in the case of fixed-interval reinforcement, a lag just after each payoff. The rate falls, then picks up.

☐ With both interval and ratio reinforcement it is possible to maintain a consistently high response rate by varying the interval or ratio around some middle value. Under these circumstances the animal cannot learn exactly when the reinforcement will come, and it therefore cannot adjust to any fixed interval or make any particular series of responses with expectancy of a reward. Several responses in succession may be reinforced, then there may be no further reinforcement for ten responses. The next response may be reinforced, then not another until five have occurred, and so it continues. When subjected to such a schedule, pigeons have responded for many hours at as fast a rate as five pecks per second. Skinner points out that, "The efficacy of such schedules in generating high rates has long been known to the proprietors of gambling establishments. Slot machines, roulette wheels, dice cages, horse races, and so on, pay off on a schedule of variable-ratio reinforcement. Each device has its own auxiliary reinforcements, but the schedule is the important characteristic. Winning depends upon placing a bet and in the long run upon the number of bets placed, but no particular payoff can be predicted. The ratio is varied by any one of several "random" systems. The pathological gambler exemplifies the result. Like the pigeon with its five responses per second for many hours, he is the victim of an unpredictable contingency of reinforcement."[31] ☐

Extinction

In classical conditioning, the response weakens and disappears when the unconditioned stimulus does not reinforce it. Something comparable occurs in operant reward-training. While reinforcement does not need to follow each response, the rate of responding drops whenever reinforcement is consistently absent. Extinction rates vary with motivational and other conditions, but complete absence of reinforcement is followed, eventually, by extinction of the response. As in the case of classical conditioning, however, there may be spontaneous recovery when, after an interval, the animal is returned to the situation in which it was conditioned.

Secondary reinforcement

Material rewards, such as food for the hungry animal provide *primary reinforcement.* However, reinforcement also comes from things which do not reduce a drive directly (as food reduces hunger). The sight of food precedes food in the mouth, hence *seeing* food may come to have a certain degree of rewarding value in its own right. We then say that it is a secondary reinforcer, or that it provides *secondary reinforcement.*

Many stimuli, through their association with primary reinforcers, acquire their own reward value. Pavlov observed this fact and called it "higher-order" conditioning. He found that a bell which was used in conditioning the salivary response could later be used, in place of food, to condition a response to some other stimulus, such as a light. All that was necessary was to present the light, followed by the bell, a sufficient number of times. The same principle holds for operant reward-training. The mechanism that delivers food pellets may be designed so that a click occurs every time a pellet is dispensed. After this has occurred a number of times, the click itself may reinforce lever-pressing. Evidence comes from observations like the following: The response is conditioned with click and food pellet until it is occurring at a fast rate. If both the food and the click are withheld, a typical extinction curve is obtained. But if food alone is withdrawn, extinction either fails to occur or it is much slower than under conditions when no click is used.[32]

Another illustration of secondary reinforcement comes from chimpanzees. These animals learned to operate a "work machine" which, after so much work, produced a grape and an associated poker chip. Later in the experiment, they worked for poker chips (token-rewards) alone.[33]

Secondary reinforcers are themselves subject to experimental extinction. That is to say, unless primary reinforcement is occasionally associated with them, they gradually lose their effectiveness. Thus food must be eaten as well as seen, clicks must sometimes again be associated with food, and poker chips must purchase grapes, as in the "chimp-o-mat" of Figure 10.8.

● **10.8**
Using a Poker Chip to "Purchase" a Grape at the Chimp-o-mat. The chimpanzees earned their chips by hard work at the work machine — which required that they repeatedly lift a heavy lever. At first they received a grape. Then poker chips served as secondary reinforcement. Sometimes there was a day's delay before the chips could be spent, yet the animals accumulated a large number of chips. Some animals also learned to differentiate between chips of different value — white, one grape; blue, two grapes; red, a drink of water; and yellow, return to the home cage. (J. B. Wolfe, "Effectiveness of Token-Rewards for Chimpanzees," *Comp. Psychol. Monogr.,* 1936, 12, No. 5.)

Many other examples of the effectiveness of secondary reinforcement could be given, but the following are representative. A clicking sound associated with food was later used by itself to develop discriminatory responses in pigeons and other animals.[34] When the pigeon pecked at a playing card with diamonds, the click sounded. When it pecked at a card with clubs, there was no click. On this basis it came to peck at one card and not the other. The investigator points out, in fact, that such a secondary reinforcer may be more effective than food because it "rewards" the animal immediately after the correct response occurs. A food reward would involve more delay, hence slower learning. The poker chips already referred to were also used, by themselves, to reinforce responses learned by chimpanzees.[35]

☐ Secondary reinforcers are extremely potent in the control of human learning. Money, which corresponds in a way to the token rewards used with chimpanzees, is a form of secondary reinforcement. But gestures and words are also reinforcing. A smile, a pat on the back, the words "good girl" or "big boy," the statement "correct" or the mark "A plus" are all positive reinforcers when used appropriately.

Even the expression "Mm-hmm" made after a verbal response may reinforce that response. For example, fifteen students, worked with individually, were asked to say as many words as possible until stopped by the investigator. Whenever they said a plural noun the experimenter said "Mm-hmm." A matched control group spoke without any word

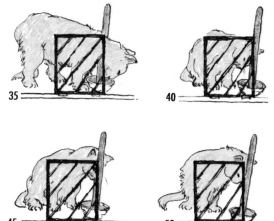

• **10.9**

A Puzzle Box and Its Solution. The hungry cat was placed in the box and rewarded with fish every time the door opened and it escaped. When the animal pressed against the pole, the glass door (striped for visibility) opened, and the cat made its exit. Moving the pole not only caused the door to open, it also activated a camera which photographed the cat, so that exact escape movements were recorded for each trial. The pattern of squares at the side of the entrance door facilitated study of the cat's position as it pushed the pole. Some cats moved the pole by leaning against it, others by a movement of the paw, and still others with the head, as shown. Usually the animal first explored the cage and accidentally bumped against the pole. After bumping the pole several times, apparently by accident, the cat would repeat one of the successful movements. Sometimes this movement would be used repeatedly (fixated) throughout the experiment and sometimes, as in trial 35, there would be some variation. (After E. R. Guthrie and G. P. Horton, *Cats in a Puzzle Box*, Rinehart, 1946.)

being reinforced. Initially, both groups gave an equal number of plural words. But by the end of twenty-five minutes, the verbally reinforced group had given almost twice as many plural words as the control group. Reinforcement was then withdrawn. Gradually thereafter the number of plural words in the previously reinforced group approached the number being given by the control group. Only one subject realized that the experimenter was attempting to shape his behavior. The results for this subject were of course discarded.[36] □

Escape training

Escape training differs from avoidance training (p. 306) in certain respects. The latter utilizes a stimulus to signal the onset of punishment. As the subject learns the significance of this signal, it makes anticipatory responses which enable it to avoid punishment. In escape training, on the other hand, the floor of the cage may be electrified so that the animal is continually punished until it finds a way to turn off the current. This it may do by pressing a lever (Figure 8.11, p. 245), by turning a wheel, or by some other action decided upon beforehand by the investigator. Under these circumstances, the subject usually exhibits a lot of seemingly random behavior during the course of which it makes the proper response. Subsequently, this response occurs with decreasing delay. Finally, as soon as the shock comes, the animal turns it off.[37]

A somewhat comparable learning is involved when the animal is confined, as in Figure 10.9. In order to escape, it must learn which of many possible responses is the correct one. Since pushing the pole is always followed by escape, and a morsel of food when it gets out, the cat soon narrows its activity to the pole.[38] One difference between this and other operant conditioning situations is the fact that someone must return the animal to the experimental box after each escape.

Successive approximations

Reinforcement of responses which successively approximate desired performance is worthy of special attention because, through it, the experimenter can shape the animal's behavior. We have learned that any response which precedes reinforcement sufficiently often will tend to increase in frequency. Suppose, now, that we want a pigeon to peck a disc. It will perhaps do this after pecking one part of the experimental box after another. But suppose that we wish to shorten the process. As the pigeon moves closer to the disc, we reinforce it (with food or a secondary reinforcer such as a click). No further reinforcement occurs until the pigeon gets closer still. Gradually, in this way, the bird is brought to the wall with the disc. Now it receives no further reinforcement until it pecks the wall. Next it must peck closer to the disc before it is reinforced. Finally, the bird's behavior is shaped so that it is pecking the disc. Thereafter, every peck is rewarded and disc-pecking grows in frequency.[39]

Reinforcing successive approximations to a desired act may produce novel acts (like pecking at a disc) and it may also develop complex sequences of activities, one activity providing the stimulus for the next activity in the chain until the final act is accomplished, and reinforced with food or some other primary reinforcer.

□ Skinner[40] demonstrated this as follows: He taught a rat to pull a string to obtain a marble from a rack, to pick up the marble with its forepaws and carry it to a tube projecting above the floor, to lift it to the top of the tube and drop it in, then to obtain food that the marble released into a tray. He said, "Every step in the process had to be worked out through a series of successive approximations, since the component responses were not in the original repertoire of the rat."[41] More recently, two other investigators have developed an even more complicated chain. Their rat first pressed a bar which sounded a bell and provided food pellets. Next it climbed a circular stairway to a platform, crossed this platform to another by operating a bridge between them. This brought the animal to a ladder, which it climbed to reach a car. Hand-over-hand pulling of an attached chain carried the rat via car to a tunnel. This was traversed by operating a pedal on the car. Then the rat climbed another flight of stairs and, upon reaching a little elevator, pulled a string that caused it to descend. Reaching the bottom, he pressed a lever and was rewarded with food pellets.[42]

By using similar operant reward-training procedures, entertainers have taught a variety of animals to perform remarkable tricks. Some of these trained animals have been exhibited at fairs and on television. How such acts are produced has been described by two people who give credit to Skinner and operant conditioning for their successful careers as animal trainers.[43] □

It is a long way from shaping the behavior of rats to teaching school subjects to children; yet this step has been taken by the teaching machines and learning programs so much in vogue today. Arithmetic, spelling, and various other subjects, including psychology, are being taught by application of the principle of reinforcing successive approximations. One of Skinner's teaching machines that has been designed to teach psychology to college students is illustrated in Figure 10.10. Carefully prepared sets of frames are presented serially. The learner makes a response to the first frame and is positively or negatively reinforced. Positive reinforcement comes from finding that his response is correct. He does not make the next step unless it is. We cannot describe these teaching techniques in detail, nor argue their pros and cons, but it is fitting that we quote Skinner on what his machines are designed to do, and how they accomplish it.

□ "Like a good tutor the machine presents just that material for which the student is ready. It asks him to take only that step which he is at the moment best equipped and likely to take. Like a skillful tutor the machine helps the student to come up with the right answer. It does this in part through the orderly construction of the program and in part with techniques of hinting, prompting, suggesting, and so on, derived from the analysis of verbal behavior.* Lastly, of course, the machine, like the private tutor, reinforces the student for every correct response, using this immediate

* Skinner, B. F., *Verbal Behavior*. Appleton-Century-Crofts, 1957.

● **10.10**
Student at Work on a Teaching Machine. "One frame of material is partly visible in the left-hand window. The student writes his response on a strip of paper exposed at the right. He then lifts a lever with his left hand, advancing his written response under a transparent cover and uncovering the correct response in the upper corner of the frame. If he is right, he moves the lever to the right, punching a hole alongside the response he has called right and altering the machine so that that frame will not appear again when he goes through the series a second time. A new frame appears when the lever is returned to its starting position." This is only one of a large variety of teaching machines. Some examples of programmed material on psychology appear in the student's manual, *Psychology in Review*, which accompanies this text. (Photo courtesy, Dr. B. F. Skinner)

feedback not only to shape his behavior most efficiently but to maintain its strength in a manner which the layman would describe as 'holding the student's interest.' "[44] □

A great deal is being written about the possibility of shaping human behavior; Skinner's novel, *Walden Two*, is concerned with this.[45] The shaping of human behavior occurs, more or less haphazardly, in every home and every schoolroom. But the idea that experts in conditioning techniques may set out deliberately to shape behavior in a particular pattern is repugnant to many and carries such derogatory labels as "mind-bending" and "brainwashing." This is of course a highly controversial area, and Skinner, among others, has discussed at length the ethical and other ramifications of scientifically controlling human behavior.[46]

We have dealt with conditioning as a simple form of learning and with conditioning techniques as "tools" with which to probe the workings of the brain and shape behavior. But our discussion would lack something of importance if it failed to consider the role that conditioning can play in eliminating, or correcting, undesirable forms of behavior. ■

ELIMINATING UNDESIRABLE BEHAVIOR

Many forms of undesirable behavior have been eliminated by application of conditioning procedures. These include nail-biting, phobias, and enuresis (bed-wetting).

Psychologists have cured students of nail-biting and other undesirable habits by a process resembling extinction.[47] Subjects are required to bite their nails on schedule. Since they now bite many times when the usual tension or nervousness is absent, there develops what amounts to a dissociation of tension and nail-biting.

Persons who are afraid of enclosed places, elevators, cats, and so on, normally avoid the feared situations, and experimental extinction cannot occur. These people are sometimes cured by repeatedly forcing the feared situations upon them.[48] Thus, a man who had avoided elevators for years was cured by forcing him to ride up and down in one. This method must be used with great care, however, for some individuals become even more fearful as a result of such treatment. With children, a more direct conditioning procedure has been successful in eliminating fear of particular objects or situations. Just as one may attach fear to a previously neutral object by presenting it with a fear-provoking one (see Figure

7.16, p. 213), the fear may be detached, as it were, by presenting the fear-provoking object with one which characteristically elicits favorable reactions. Thus a child who feared rabbits lost his fear when a rabbit was associated with feeding.[49] The psychologist first presented the rabbit at a distance. Then, in successive feeding periods, it was gradually moved closer to the child. This method, also, must be used with great care. The feeding behavior, for example, might itself become disturbed if the child were suddenly confronted with the rabbit.

What we have been describing was referred to earlier as *habituation* — an elementary form of learning found in most, if not all, animals. We see it every time that some new situation, perhaps disturbing at first, comes to be ignored. A loud noise, for example, produces a startle reaction. But if it is repeated sufficiently often, and nothing hurtful results, the startle reaction disappears.

Much has been written on the use of conditioning techniques to cure enuresis and a recent book entitled *Conditioning and Enuresis*[50] deals in detail with the various methods and the interpretations of their outcomes. One viewpoint is that a child who wets the bed beyond the age when children normally have control over urination does so because, while he is asleep, the stimuli provided by bladder tensions are not sufficiently strong to wake him before he wets. Putting it another way, the child is not sufficiently sensitive to the signals coming from his bladder. He has not been conditioned to respond to these stimuli. But they can be made effective through conditioning. One widely used technique requires that the child sleep on a mat with fine wires inside. Wetting short-circuits the wires and this causes a bell to ring or a buzzer to sound. The child is instructed to go to the bathroom whenever he is awakened by the sound, whether or not he needs to urinate further. Before going to the bathroom, he breaks the circuit by opening a switch. After several nights, the bladder tensions wake the child before he wets. Weak as his bladder tensions may be, waking and getting up have been conditioned to them. In terms of classical conditioning, we might conclude that what happens is as follows: The sound (unconditioned stimulus) wakes the child (unconditioned response). Bladder tension (which we may consider a stimulus to be conditioned) does not wake him. But by associating bladder tension and sound, in that order, bladder tension finally becomes effective in arousing the child. This is one interpretation, but there are others, including one which looks upon this as an instance of instrumental avoidance conditioning comparable, in a sense, with an animal's avoidance of a noxious stimulus (like shock or an unpleasant noise) by making an appropriate anticipatory response.[51] The correct interpretation is secondary, however, to the fact that this and somewhat comparable conditioning procedures are successful, in a high percentage of cases, in eliminating enuresis. ■

ACQUIRING SKILLS

Skill is proficiency in the performance of some task. The task might be speaking, typing, playing a musical instrument, driving a car, flying a plane, hitting a moving target, sending and receiving coded messages, reciting a poem, playing bridge, or using the procedures of some art or science.

Some skills are called sensorimotor (or perceptual-motor) because the activities involved are quite obviously dependent upon information provided by sense organs. The batter, for example, swings as he sees the ball reach a certain position, and the hunter's aim varies as his target moves. In skills there is, in fact, a constant feedback of information, not only from the external receptors but also from others within the body.

Verbal skills are those in which language activities predominate. One of the purest examples is reciting a poem or a lesson. Although we say that these are "verbal" skills they obviously include sensorimotor functions. One speaks with his vocal musculature and, as we shall see later, perhaps to some extent thinks with it. Verbalization as a "motor" skill is given brief consideration in this chapter.

While it is observing and otherwise responding to its environment, an organism may acquire potentially useful information. But whether or not this results in skilled performance depends upon motivating conditions. Thus, hungry rats allowed to explore a maze, but finding no food in it, perform very inefficiently. There is little or no evidence that they have learned anything. Yet, when a food reward is introduced, their performance sometimes shows an unusually rapid improvement — a much more rapid improvement than occurs in the performance of rewarded rats which are new to the situation. We therefore infer that, during their exploration, the animals were learning something, more or less incidentally, which their earlier performance failed to indicate. This sort of acquisition is referred to as *latent learning*.[52]

The chief reason for acquiring any skill is to correct some inadequacy of adjustment. As long as the situation is optimal — as long as it provides ready satisfaction of every need — the organism tends to stay in a rut. Thus, if we want the rat to acquire a skill, we make it hungry and give food as a reward for achievement. In the case of a child, we let him know that there is candy, or money, or praise for accomplishment.

In research on animal learning the subject's method of satisfying a drive is ordinarily disrupted in some way. For example, it can no longer get food in the accustomed place. By using suitable rewards or punishments, we then induce it to acquire the skills necessary for readjustment.

Mazes have often been used to study animal learning, as we have seen. The maze first used for this purpose was illustrated in Figure 1.6 (p. 14). Today it is customary to use multiple-unit mazes where, at each new alley, the animal is confronted by the need for either a right or a left turn. A multiple-Y maze is illustrated in Figure 10.11; the legend tells how a rat is trained.

Human learning has also been studied often with mazes. These are sometimes large replicas of rat mazes through which the subject finds his way to the exit, perhaps with his sense of accomplishment as a reward, but sometimes with such supplementary reinforcement as candy or money. Some investigators have used a foot maze (Figure 10.12) through which the subject walks while blindfolded.

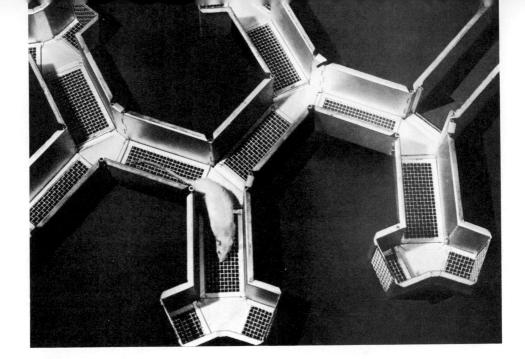

● 10.11

A Multiple-Y Rat Maze. When a rat first enters such a maze, there may be many apparently random or "trial-and-error" activities. The new environment may be explored more or less thoroughly. Blind alleys as well as units leading more directly to the food may be entered and re-entered. But when food is reached, the trial ends. A record is kept of the number of errors made, the time taken to get from entrance to food box, and, if the rat's route has been traced, the excess distance traveled. After the subject eats, it is returned to its cage, where the rest of its daily food allowance is available. This is usually a small amount which is quickly consumed. The next day, at the same time and under the same motivational and external conditions, another trial is given. Errors, time, and distance traveled are recorded as before. This procedure continues until the maze is run from entrance to food box without error. Usually we say that the habit has been learned when there are no errors on three successive days. The "criterion of learning" here is three errorless runs. Food is not always the incentive. A rat may be thirsty and get water as a reward. Sometimes a maze filled with water is used. Then the motive is escape, achieved by reaching a ramp at the end of the goal unit. In the maze illustrated, the entrance is at the left. The goal box can be seen at the right. Note that the rat has just made an error, a blind-alley entrance. (This is the Warden Y-maze. Photo by Lilo Hess, Three Lions, Inc.)

Two other human mazes are also shown in Figure 10.12, a stylus and a finger maze. A subject traces through the former with a pencil or other form of stylus, or through the latter by running his forefinger along the raised pathway. Either he is blindfolded or the maze is screened from view. The reader has perhaps already threaded his way through the pencil-and-paper maze of Figure 5.1 (p. 114). Printed mazes like this are so complicated that, even though one can see the whole layout, he finds it a difficult task to follow the correct path without error. Learning of such mazes is likely to be observational rather than merely manual. The subject looks the situation over and, with his eyes, follows one possible lead after another. When the correct path is evident, he then takes pencil in hand and traces it. Thus the learning activity with this type of maze is likely to be more implicit than overt. It is as if the subject *thinks* his way through. In learning mazes where he cannot see the way ahead, at least beyond a unit or two, the human subject, like the rat, is forced to use what

A

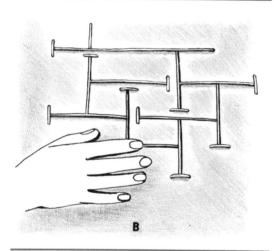

B

C

● **10.12**

Three Human Mazes. The foot (or trough) maze (**A**) may be arranged into various patterns by use of the removable stops. Since the subject is blindfolded, the feet "feel their way," so to speak, from entrance to exit. This is Warner Brown's maze, as pictured in Geldard's *Fundamentals of Psychology* (Wiley, 1962). Note that the finger relief maze (**B**) is a multiple-T pattern made of wires. Finger relief mazes are sometimes made of multiple Y's, like the animal maze in Figure 10.11. The experimenter blindfolds his subject and then places his finger at the entrance. When the exit is reached, the finger is taken from the maze until the next trial begins. The third maze (**C**) has a grooved pathway to be traced from entrance to exit with a wooden stylus, or a pencil. Sometimes a sheet of paper is placed under the maze and the pencil provides a copy of the path followed. In using miniature mazes that the subject is to traverse with his hand, the blindfold may be omitted and the maze placed behind a screen, with the subject's hand put through an opening. The maze can also be placed on the lap, with a table-top screening it from view. The stylus maze illustrated here is the one designed by Foster and Tinker.

has been called a *trial-and-error* approach. He goes at the task more or less haphazardly and, if there is no plan that can be reasoned out, he does no better than rats and other mammals do in comparable circumstances.[53] Thus the usual maze-learning habit, while more complex than a conditioned response, is a relatively simple form of learning. This is one reason why it has been studied so intensively by psychologists in their search for the fundamental principles of learning. ■

THE LEARNING CURVE

Acquisition of any habit may be represented by a *learning curve*. This shows, at a glance, the general trend of performance. Practice periods (or *trials*) are represented along the baseline (abscissa); measures of performance, at the left side (ordinate) of the graph. In the case of maze learning, these measures may be errors, the time taken, or the distance traveled per trial in getting from the entrance to the exit. A maze-learning curve which represents the average performance of twenty-five rats is shown in Figure 10.13.[54] This is an error curve. Note that the curve falls more or less gradually toward the abscissa in successive trials. Comparable curves for individual rats would, of course, show much more fluctuation. Curves based upon correct responses rise toward an upper limit set by the number of possible correct responses. Memorizing a list of words would yield a curve of this nature, with the upper limit being the number of words in the list. When learning curves approach a limit beyond which there can be no further improvement, it is customary to say that they are nearing the *physiological limit*. A rat that runs through the maze as fast as his legs will carry him has reached the physiological limit for time. He has reached the limit for errors when the error curve drops to zero.

In some learning curves we see progress up to a point, no further progress for several trials, then further improvement. In this event, the flat place in the curve is referred to as a *plateau*. What seems to be the physiological limit for a particular subject is, in reality, often a plateau, but we cannot be sure unless there is subsequent improvement. This might come about because of increased motivation. It might appear, for instance, that a rat is running the maze as fast as possible — the time curve has flattened out at a certain level. But if we make him more hungry, or give him a shock when he slows down, he may increase his speed. ■

SOME SKILLS THAT ARE TYPICALLY HUMAN

While mazes are very useful in research on the fundamentals of learning, it is not surprising that many investigators, and especially those with practical rather than theoretical interests, have turned their attention to activities of practical importance in business, industry, and the armed services. At the turn of the century, some were already studying

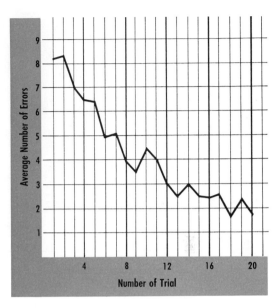

● **10.13**
A Learning Curve. This is an error curve based upon the mean performance of twenty-five rats in learning a fourteen-unit, multiple-T alley maze with food as a reward. Individual rats would have a more variable curve than this. Smoothing the curve by averaging gives us a better indication of the trend of learning. Error curves for human subjects learning comparable maze patterns in stylus form are similar to the one illustrated. Like rats, human beings make many errors to begin with, then gradually reduce these as a function of practice. When time per trial is plotted, we again get a falling curve. Curves based upon the amount of effort expended and the distance traveled in getting from entrance to exit also show such a trend. When correct responses are measured, as in many human skills, the curve *rises* as a function of practice. (This curve is derived from data reported by E. C. Tolman and D. B. Nyswander, "The Reliability and Validity of Maze Measures for Rats," *J. Comp. Psychol.*, 1927, 7.)

how individuals learn to receive and send telegraph messages and how they learn to type. Later there were studies of how novices learn various industrial operations. Today psychologists are employed in industry to improve the efficiency with which workers acquire necessary

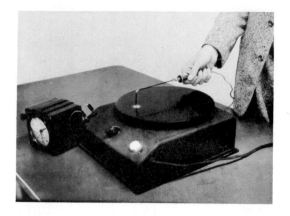

● 10.14

Pursuitmeter and Curve Showing Progress in the Acquisition of a Skill. The subject's task is to keep the tip of the stylus on a small metal disc as it revolves at the rate of one revolution per second. The length of time that contact is maintained during each ten-second test is recorded on a chronoscope, as illustrated. In the learning curve one sees that contact was first maintained for an average of only 1.4 seconds per ten-second trial. After fifty trials, the average time of contact was 6.3 seconds. (The pursuitmeter is from W. W. Grings, *Laboratory Instrumentation in Psychology*, National Press, 1954, p. 200. The learning curve is from Buxton and Spence.)

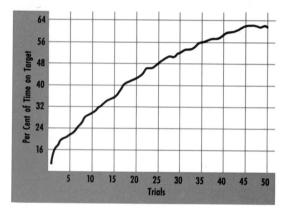

skills. With military skills in mind, many psychologists are now studying how complex eye-hand coordinations are acquired. Coordinations of this kind are involved in tracking, of which there are two widely studied varieties — *compensatory* and *pursuit*. These will serve to illustrate acquisition of typically human motor skills. Verbal skills will be discussed later.

• *Compensatory tracking* is exemplified when we keep our speedometer at, say, 45 miles per hour, or when a pilot, through his own reactions, keeps his plane on a straight and level course. The progress of learning, in the latter instance, is plotted in terms of the per cent of time that the plane (or a model which substitutes for it) stays on course. This usually starts at a low level. It rises, rapidly at first and then gradually, as a function of the number of hours of practice. In one such study, the

proportion of time on course began at 25 per cent. After one hour of practice this had doubled. Then the hourly increments grew progressively smaller. The upper level of proficiency attained in this experiment was 80 per cent of the time spent on course. This level had been reached when the experiment was terminated after eight hours of practice.[55]

• *Pursuit tracking*, as this designation implies, is a skill requiring the individual to follow a moving target. A relatively simple illustration of it is involved in rotary pursuit of a disc, as shown in Figure 10.14. This type of *pursuitmeter* is used in many laboratories. A more complicated test of pursuit tracking is illustrated in Figure 10.15. The task studied with this device simulates that of a gunner who must keep his sight on a moving target.[56] The coordinations required in order to keep the spot of light on target are described in the legend. This resembles many skills required today in military activities. A person highly proficient in such skills can keep on the target most of the time.

Verbal skills

We acquire some motor skills partly through memorizing. That is to say, we intend to remember which acts lead to the best results, what we have observed in a skilled performance, and what we have been told by an instructor. Most verbal skills acquired by

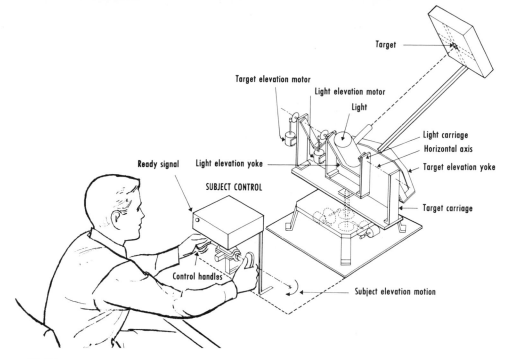

● **10.15**

Pursuit Tracking. The subject tries to keep the spot of light on the moving target. His task has been described as follows: "To move the light to the right or left, the handles and the movable structure to which they are attached are turned through a small angle by pushing one handle away while pulling the other toward the body. This is the steering response. To make the light go up, the bottoms of the handles are pushed a short distance away from the subject in a kind of twisting action, and to make it go down, the handles are pulled toward the subject. . . . The speed with which the light moves in any direction depends on how far the handles are turned from the neutral position." The measure of efficiency is time on the target, in seconds. In one study with this device, the mean score for a group of teenagers began at two seconds per thirty-second trial and, after ten trials, reached more than seven seconds. (From G. H. Miles and D. Lewis, "Age and Handedness as Factors in the Performance of a Complex Pursuit Task," *Proc. Iowa Acad. Sci.*, 1956, 63, pp. 569, 571.)

older children and adults are clearly learned by memorizing. One repeats the material with the intention to recall or recognize it later.

Speaking is a complex motor skill, as well as a symbolic or verbal one. It is acquired partly on the basis of reflex vocalizations which appear during early infancy, but also through imitation (that is, attempting to copy the vocalizations of others) and trial-and-error activity.

☐ Ability to make combinations of sounds which closely approximate those of adults (namely, "doll" instead of "da," the original vocalization) develops gradually. There is no doubt that maturational factors are involved in this development. Vocalizations produced by adults cannot be copied by the child until auditory-vocal mechanisms, including their cerebral connections, have sufficiently developed. Nevertheless, it is obvious that children learn to speak, just as they learn their manipulative habits. Saying the word "doll," for example, calls for a complex integration of lung, throat, mouth, and tongue movements in properly timed succession. The sound *d* is produced when the tip of the tongue is placed between the slightly open teeth in a certain way, and air is expelled from the lungs. Saying *o* calls for an appropriate coordination of lungs, vocal cords, tongue, and mouth, as well as of resonance cavities within the throat and mouth. The *l* sound requires movement of lungs, vocal cords, tongue, and mouth. Saying "doll" in the adult way calls for a rather definite temporal patterning of these movements. Such patterns are gradually acquired. Adequately stimulated by his fond parents, and later by formal teachers, the child vocalizes in a trial-and-error fashion, until he achieves the acceptable patterns. Thus he learns to say "doll" instead of "da," "stomach" instead of "tummy," "sugar" instead of "fugar," "light" instead of "yite," "elephant" instead of "efant," and so on. □

Verbal skills frequently involved in laboratory studies of learning include recitation of poems or narratives; recitation of lists of words, digits, syllables, or other symbols; and substitution of one kind of verbal material for another, for instance, substituting digits for words or forms. Very little need be said about such materials at this point; they will be dealt with in more detail in the chapter on remembering, which concerns not the process of memorizing as such, but what is retained after such a process.

Laboratory research on memorizing usually makes use of a device for exposing one item at a time at controlled intervals. An early version of such an apparatus was illustrated in Figure 1.3 (p. 10). Current versions use a drum bearing a list of items. This is rotated electrically in a horizontal position behind a small slit. Thus each item appears for a brief period behind the slit. An apparatus of this kind is shown in the chapter on memory, Figure 12.4 (p. 378).

□ The materials to be memorized under the conditions described may be words, figures, colors, groups of digits, or so-called *nonsense syllables* such as Ebbinghaus (p. 10) used in his pioneer research on memory. These were used by Ebbinghaus because of their apparently low meaning value. He thought that, in memorizing them, every subject would, as it were, have to start from scratch. We now know that these syllables vary a great deal in meaning value. Some, like *luc*, produce many associations, including the word *luck*. On the other hand, a syllable such as *lij* has very little meaning. It arouses few if any associations. Since "nonsense syllable" is a misnomer, the term *trigram* is used today. When a vowel appears between two consonants, as in *luc*, the item is referred to as a *CVC trigram*. Much research has been done to discover the meaning of many possible letter combinations and there are now tables from which one may select trigrams with the desired meaning value.[57] Some have so little meaning that they approximate nonsense. □

In typical experiments on memorizing the subject learns to repeat a list of items in proper sequence. This is the simple recall method of learning. Sometimes, however, he learns to repeat one of a pair of syllables when its partner is presented alone. This learning of paired associates is like learning vocabulary lists, where the foreign word is presented and one gives its English equivalent, or vice versa. ■

PROBLEM-SOLVING

The acquisition of all kinds of skills, both motor and verbal, may involve problem-solving. There are, however, many situations in which what we learn is not so much a skill as it is an *understanding* of what must be done. Once we understand, the rest is relatively simple. This is well illustrated by experiments utilizing problem boxes, detour situations, and instruments such as sticks.

Problem boxes

Problem boxes, like mazes, were first used by psychologists to investigate animal learning. The simplest of these allowed the animal to get a reward, or escape (or both) by performing one simple act. The operant conditioning devices described earlier in this chapter are essentially of this nature. So, also, is the cat problem box shown in Figure 10.9 (p. 312). A more complicated problem box is illustrated in Figure 10.16. This requires a combination of acts. Sometimes these must be made in

● **10.16**

A Problem Box Used by Thorndike. In order to get to the food seen outside the box, an animal must remove the obstructions and open the door. One motive here is escape; the other, a food reward. Sometimes the food is inside a problem box and certain devices must be manipulated in order to reach it. Higher animals, like monkeys, sometimes solve such problems with no other motive than satisfaction of a manipulatory drive. (After E. L. Thorndike, "Animal Intelligence," *Psychological Monographs*, 1898.)

serial order, as when a latch cannot be lifted until a bolt is pushed back.

Problem devices are often learned in a trial-and-error fashion. Various parts of the apparatus are manipulated until, more or less by accident, the subject hits upon the correct responses. After a number of trials, the subject manipulates the correct bolts, latches, or strings without error and in the shortest possible time.

Problem boxes suitable for animals are usually solved at a single glance by human subjects. Thus those designed for human use must be much more complicated.

Part of man's ability to solve problems more complicated than those solved by animals comes from his greater manual dexterity. More important, however, is his better ability to learn by observation, to see relationships, and

to reason. Human problem-solving typically involves reasoning. It is considered from this angle in Chapter 13.

In problem-solving the organism sometimes achieves a sudden solution, often after a great deal of trial-and-error activity that seems to get nowhere. When solutions occur suddenly, as if the individual got the right idea, we say that *insight* has occurred. Much of the sudden learning from which insight is inferred could of course be the outcome of implicit trial and error — thinking of one possibility, then another, until the correct one became apparent.

Detour problems

A well-motivated animal will go as directly as possible toward an observable and meaningful goal object, but we may change the situation so that what was a direct means of approach is now blocked, yet with the goal-object still in sight (Figure 10.17). When we do this, the animal can reach the goal only by taking an indirect (roundabout) route. Most animals persist in the direct approach. In higher organisms like monkeys and chimpanzees, however, a direct trial-and-error approach may be replaced, more or less suddenly, by a circumvention of the barrier. It is as if the animal suddenly perceived significant aspects of the situation. We may infer that it learned the problem when it *observed* the inadequacy of the direct, or the adequacy of the indirect approach. This is another instance of what is commonly called insight. While this is prevalent in human learning, it has to develop with maturation and experience. The infant in Figure 10.18 is not acting in an insightful manner.

Instrumentation

Learning in monkeys, apes, and children is often studied by confronting them with problems calling for the use of such "tools" as sticks. The animal in his cage, or the child in his playpen, is shown some desirable object which is out of reach. He can obtain it only by utilizing the nearby instruments. Thus the

● **10.17**
A Simple Detour Problem. The hen does not react with insight. Its behavior is either direct (attempting to get the food through the fence) or random. A chimpanzee, on the other hand, makes the detour almost immediately. He may even climb over the wire. (From N. L. Munn, "The Evolution of Mind," *Scientific American*, 1957, 196, 144.)

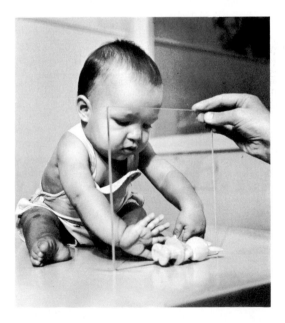

● **10.18**
A Simple Detour Problem. The baby has not yet advanced to the stage where it can discern the need for an indirect approach. (From a demonstration given by Dr. Lois Bellinger of Columbia University. Photo by Martha Holmes.)

chimpanzee (Figure 10.19) joins two sticks to reach food which is otherwise inaccessible.

The initial attack on such problems by animals and young children is usually of the overt trial-and-error variety. One stick is used, then the other until the food is touched. Sometimes the sticks are fitted together, yet the subject does not realize that joined sticks provide a means of solution.

☐ An unusually bright chimpanzee studied by Wolfgang Köhler reacted to the two-stick problem in much the manner described above until, with apparent suddenness, it saw the relation between solution of the problem and the joined sticks.[58]

"Sultan, as before, pushes one stick with the other toward the objective, and as this pseudo-solution does not satisfy him any longer, he abandons his efforts altogether, and does not even pick up the sticks when they are both again thrown through the bars to him. The experiment has lasted over an hour, and is stopped for the present, as it seems hopeless, carried out like this. As we intend to take it up again after a while, Sultan is left in possession of his sticks; the keeper is left there to watch him.

"Keeper's report: 'Sultan first of all squats indifferently on the box, which has been left standing a little back from the railings; then he gets up, picks up the two sticks, sits down again on the box, and plays carelessly with them. While doing this, it happens that he finds himself holding one rod in either hand in such a way that they lie in a straight line; he pushes the thinner one a little into the opening of the thicker, jumps up and is already on the run toward the railings, to which he has up to now half-turned his back, and begins to draw a banana toward him with the double stick.' "

This behavior was repeated on several occasions after Köhler was called to the scene. □

Insightful learning like that just described is possible only in situations where various aspects of the problem are presented simultaneously. Such situations make it easier for the subject to "put two and two together." He can look over the situation and grasp the relation between different aspects, like the stick, the bars, and the food beyond the bars. Indeed, it is through their ability to learn by observing, instead of merely by doing, that some of the higher organisms, including human beings, may be aided by observing the performances of others. Thus monkeys and chimpanzees have solved problems, without overt trial-and-error, by watching others solve them. It is said, therefore, that they learn by imitating. Such learning is so important for human beings that it warrants special attention here. ■

LEARNING BY IMITATION

Although higher organisms may learn a great deal by observing and attempting to copy the performances of others, they must first *learn to imitate*. Also, if imitation is to be possible, the example must utilize activities *already in the observer's repertoire*.

Learning to imitate is illustrated by the following experiment with forty-two first-grade children.

□ One child (the leader) was told which of two small boxes to open. When he opened it,

● **10.19**

Chimpanzee Joining Sticks So That Food May Be Reached. Finding that food is inaccessible with one stick, the chimpanzee picks up the two sticks, fits them together, and pushes the combined sticks toward the food. (From the film, "Monkey into Man," by Huxley and Zuckerman. Courtesy, Walter O. Gutlohn.)

a piece of candy was found. Another piece in the box was to be left there. The other child (the imitator) was rewarded with the second piece of candy if he opened the same box as the leader. He was not rewarded if he went to the other box. In any test, both children stood within the test room at a place marked "Start." On the first test, the children were told: "Here are two boxes, there and there. Here is a piece of candy. You are to find the candy. He gets the first turn. Then you get a turn. If you don't find it the first time, you will get another turn." The leader always had his turn, then the imitator. The position of the candy varied, of course, from one box to the other in a random order. Twenty per cent of the children imitated on the first trial. Some or all of the 80 per cent who went to the other box may have done so because, seeing the leader get candy out of a box, they reasoned that there would be no more in that box. After an average of three trials, the second child copied the performance of the first child. When the situation was changed, so that the children were confronted by four boxes arranged at the corners of an imaginary square, 75 per cent of the subjects imitated. This demonstrated that they generalized, or transferred to a different situation, the tendency to imitate that they had learned in the first situation. Other children were taught *not* to imitate. They were rewarded for not doing what the leader did. Their nonimitative tendency transferred 100 per cent to the new situation.[59]

In this experiment it is noteworthy that the children given an opportunity to imitate already had within their response repertoire the basic activities required. They could all walk toward a box, open it, and lift out what was in it. A child who could not already do these things would obviously fail to imitate. This point, quite obvious here, is perhaps not so obvious, although even more important, with regard to skills of far greater complexity, like learning to dismantle and reassemble a watch or some other complex device. □

Learning of many athletic, industrial, and professional skills is today facilitated by moving picture demonstrations of skilled performance. The effectiveness of such demonstrations, as in the illustrations just given, depends upon their use of basic skills already present in the observer.

Regardless of how the subject responds while witnessing an actual or a movie demonstration of a complex skill, the sample performance has at least two decided advantages over a pure trial-and-error approach.

(1) It shows the correct performance, thus enabling the learner to save time and effort which might otherwise be wasted in making incorrect approaches. Suppose, for example, that you were a native of Central Australia who had never seen or heard of a bicycle — that you had not the least idea what the entire device or its various mechanisms were for, but you were shown a moving picture of a man riding a bicycle. Then, although you would be far from acquiring skill in riding, you would at least know that the device was for transportation, that one sits on a certain part rather than another, and that moving it requires pushing the pedals with the feet. Human beings are often called upon to learn industrial skills just as foreign to their past experience as cycling is to the past experience of the native.

In such instances, seeing a skilled performance saves a great deal of time which would otherwise be spent in trial and error.

(2) Observing a skilled performance not only gives general orientation like that described, but it also gives the observer certain insights at the start which, if he ever acquired them during practice, might come only after a long process of trial and error. ■

LEVELS OF COMPLEXITY

Many complex skills, both motor and verbal, involve an integration of simpler skills. Some involve successively higher stages of integration as learning proceeds. They are, for this reason, referred to as *habit hierarchies*.

Take typing, for example. One first learns to hit the correct keys. These learned responses may be designated *letter habits*. After habits of striking the correct keys have progressed to the point where the individual is fairly proficient, he finds that he is developing *word habits*. Letters like T, H, and E, instead of eliciting noticeably separate responses, arouse a single response. The individual looks at the word "THE" or thinks it, and the separate responses seem to take care of themselves. After a while, *phrase habits* appear. Common phrases like "Very sincerely yours" are typed without the typist paying attention either to the separate letters or to the separate words.

Habit hierarchies are also quite evident whenever messages are to be sent or received in code, as in telegraphy. Indeed, psychologists have long been interested in telegraphy and much research has centered upon the most efficient methods of teaching it. There has also been a lively interest in the course of progress in learning to send and receive telegraphic messages.[60]

After complicated skills have been practiced for a long while, they tend to run their course automatically. There are many examples of this in everyday life. Think of the concentrated attention that one must give to riding a bicycle for the first time. One is aware of movements made in balancing the vehicle, in guiding it, and in working the pedals. After considerable practice, however, these balanc-

● 10.20

Apparatus Used for Mirror Drawing. The subject is required to trace the star-shaped pathway with a stylus, moving in a clockwise direction and attempting to avoid contact with the sides of the path. In the apparatus illustrated, each time the side is touched, an electrical contact is made and an electric counter records the error. The time taken to trace the star is also recorded. What make the task a difficult one is that the subject does not see the path, except in a mirror, which of course produces a near-far reversal to which adjustment is required. Any entrance into one of the notches in the pathway is counted as an error. The full pathway is shown at the left. Sometimes a subject has great difficulty in getting out of a notch. One must do the opposite of what the mirror image seems to indicate, or be "stuck." (After Snoddy)

ing, steering, and pedaling activities take place automatically — one does not have to think of them. He may daydream or engage in a conversation while riding. Eventually, he rides with as little thought as when he walks. ■

TRANSFER

Learning one skill often influences the acquisition of other skills. This influence may be such that the acquisition of one type of performance facilitates learning of another. The influence of earlier learning on later learning may, on the other hand, be such that acquisition of one skill interferes with acquisition of another. In the first instance we have positive transfer effects, frequently referred to as "transfer of training" or "transfer of learning." In the second instance we have a negative transfer effect, called "negative transfer" or "habit interference."

Bilateral transfer

One of the simplest examples of positive transfer effects is found in experiments showing improvement in performance with one side of the body as a result of practice with the other side. This is *bilateral transfer*, sometimes also referred to as *cross-education*.

A mirror-drawing apparatus like that shown in Figure 10.20 is often used in the laboratory to demonstrate bilateral transfer. The general procedure is described under the figure. Experiments using this and other problems have shown that practice with the right hand improves performance with the left.

☐ Two equivalent groups are customarily used, a control and an experimental group. Both groups are given one trial with the left hand. One of these (the control group) does nothing further for the time being. The other (experimental group) is given a large number of trials, say fifty, with the right hand. After this

● **10.21**
A Monkey Doing a Learning-to-Learn Test. The monkey has just lifted the cylinder and is getting a raisin out of the recess below it. Had he lifted the cube, he would have forfeited the reward. A screen would have dropped, preventing response to the cylinder. On the next trial, the cylinder might appear in the same place, or at the left, depending upon a chance order of positioning. After the stimulus tray is arranged, the screen rises, signaling the time for another response. A one-way vision screen prevents the monkey from seeing the experimenter and possibly getting a clue as to the position of the reward. (After Harlow)

training period is completed, both groups are given a further trial with the left hand. The procedure just described may be represented in this fashion.

Control Group

Left hand   (rest period)   Left hand

Experimental Group

Left hand (Practice with right hand) Left hand

After this procedure has been followed through, the improvement in performance made by the control group is subtracted from the improvement made by the experimental group. The difference indicates the amount of improvement in the left hand resulting from practice with the right. A control group is made necessary by the fact that the second trial with the left hand, because of what was learned in the first trial, would show some improvement, even if no training with the right hand occurred.

In one investigation of transfer in mirror drawing, the error scores of the control group dropped 55 per cent, without intervening practice with the right hand, while those for the experimental group dropped 76 per cent. Thus the transfer from the right-hand practice to performance with the left hand was, from the standpoint of errors, about 21 per cent. Time scores for the control group dropped 46 per cent. Those for the experimental group dropped 82 per cent. Thus the transfer in terms of time was 36 per cent.[61] □

Learning of one activity sometimes facilitates the learning of another that is similar to it in certain respects. We see one example of this in studies on development of *learning sets,* or "learning how to learn."

Learning how to learn

Higher organisms, including monkeys, chimpanzees, and human beings, often achieve an understanding of learning situations such that when they encounter comparable situations they know what to do.

A situation used in experiments with monkeys is like that in Figure 10.21. There are two objects and under one of them is a reward, in this case a raisin. The correct object changes position from right to left in accordance with a chance sequence, hence the animal must learn which object is correct. In other words, a position habit will not reward him consistently. Let us suppose that the cylinder is correct. If the subject lifts this he gets his raisin. But if he lifts the cube he gets nothing for the trial. One might think that, after discovering the raisin under the cylinder, the monkey would lift this on the next trial; or that, not finding it under the cube, he would lift the cylinder next time. However, there is the position to be considered. Finding the raisin under the right-hand object, he might associate it with that position, which would be incorrect. Moreover, he might have a preference for one object of the pair. Actually, it takes many trials before the subject "catches on" and consistently lifts the cylinder. The learning curve for the initial discrimination (the lowest curve in Figure 10.22) shows how gradually this is acquired. It suggests that the animal acquires the discrimination on a typical trial-and-error basis.

After the first discrimination habit has been mastered, a new problem is presented. Perhaps the two objects are now a pyramid and a triangle, with the latter hiding the raisin. This problem is learned much more readily than the last one. Then two more objects are presented — say a large cube and a small one, with the small one correct. This is learned even more readily than the preceding problem. New pairs of stimulus objects are used until, finally, the monkey needs only one trial to learn what he is to do. What he does on the first trial gets him the raisin, or it doesn't. On the second trial, however, he reacts by lifting the object that he lifted before (if this was rewarded) or by lifting the other object (if his first trial was unrewarded).

At the beginning of such a series of problems the second trial is correct only about 50 per cent of the time (see lowest curve in Figure 10.22). This percentage rises as training continues so that, after 300 problems have been solved, it reaches the level of 97 per cent or better (see second trial in each curve from the bottom up in Figure 10.22). Some monkeys eventually get to the stage where the second trial is always correct.[62]

Sudden learning like that which occurs in the later stages of such discrimination problems as we have described suggests the presence of insight. It is as if the subject "catches on," as if it understands what the experimenter is requiring of it.

Somewhat similar learning sets are developed when the stimuli to be discriminated remain the same from test to test, but the one that has been correct in one test is incorrect in the next. That is, each successive experiment involves a reversal of what was required in the preceding one. Under these circumstances, the animal starts off as before —

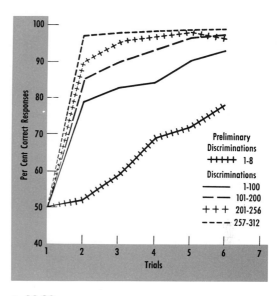

● 10.22

Discrimination Learning Curves on Successive Blocks of Problems. Note the steady improvement in the lower curve and the sudden mastery indicated in the upper ones. The first trial would, by chance, yield 50 per cent correct responses. The second trials from below up, are worthy of special attention. They begin at the 52 per cent level and finally reach about the 97 per cent level. (From H. F. Harlow, "The Formation of Learning Sets," *Psychol. Rev.,* 1949, 56, p. 53.)

gradually getting to the point where the cylinder, let us say, is always lifted, regardless of its position. In the next experiment, however, the cylinder is wrong — there is no reward under it. Now the cube is correct. This is often a disturbing situation and many more trials than in the initial learning may be necessary to "unlearn" the "cylinder habit." In short, there is a negative transfer effect. After the reversal has been learned, the cylinder is again correct. This reversal may be learned much more readily than either the initial discrimination or the first reversal. Successive reversals are then learned more and more readily.[63]

Acquisition of learning sets has been demonstrated in numerous animals, ranging from rats to man, but infraprimates have, in general, learned comparable sets much more slowly and have achieved a lower level of efficiency in using them.[64]

Simulated to real situations

It is often advantageous in real-life situations, as in flight training, to give preliminary practice with a training device that simulates the real thing, i.e., a so-called synthetic trainer. But training of this kind is advantageous only if there is positive transfer from the simulated to the real task. If there is negative transfer, the preliminary training hinders later acquisition. If there is no transfer, one might as well omit preliminary training. It sometimes happens, however, that there is negative transfer or no transfer during initial stages of the shift from the simulated to the actual task, yet progress in attaining skill on the real task is faster than it would have been without the preliminary training. This represents a saving in overall training time and also a saving in equipment, for the latter is not tied up as long as it otherwise would be (in training novices). The following experiment illustrates transfer that is at first negative, yet advantageous from the standpoint of overall saving in time and equipment.[65]

□ A simulated and a real task were devised so that both were identical from the standpoint of movement patterns and operations required. Eleven unskilled navy men were trained to control the movements of a small trolly, using information provided by the trolley, but via a cathode-ray tube. Movement of the trolley along a track was controlled by appropriate movements of a stick operated with the thumb. A comparable group of twelve navy men learned to control the actual trolley, also through thumb-operated stick movements. In both groups, each subject was required to move the trolley from its initial position to an indicated target as fast as possible, then to stay on target for two seconds. The score on each run was the number of seconds required to get the trolley to the target, plus the two seconds on target. There were ten trials daily. The experimental group, with the simulated task, was trained for three days, then shifted to the real task. The control group,

on the other hand, was trained for four days with the real task. □

As shown in Figure 10.23, the experimental group was at a disadvantage immediately after shifting to the real situation. Whereas they had been doing nearly as well as the control group, with a mean score of about five seconds, their score on the first transfer trials went to approximately ten seconds. That is, they now required twice the time to accomplish their task. In five trials, however, they were doing as well as before, and as well as the control group was doing after a total of thirty-five trials. There was thus a considerable saving despite the initial disadvantage.

Transfer in verbal learning

Transfer of verbal skills often occurs. When comparable lists of nonsense syllables are learned one after the other, there is a gradual reduction in the trials required to learn successive lists. It is as if the subjects, like those of the discrimination experiments discussed above, are learning how to learn this type of material. Somewhat similar results are obtained with school children memorizing poems, digits, and other verbal materials. They learn similar materials with greater facility than children without the previous training. Where dissimilar materials are learned, however, transfer is negligible. Thus, children who memorize one kind of material usually do not memorize another kind any better than they would have without the previous training. Where improvement does occur, it is attributable to a carry-over of procedures and attitudes.[66] ■

BASES OF TRANSFER

Where transfer occurs, either in motor or verbal learning, it comes from (1) *similarity of contents*, (2) *similarity of techniques*, (3) *similarity of principles*, or (4) *a combination of these*.

• *Similarity of contents.* Parts of old habits may be "run off" as a response to new situations, perhaps with minor modifications.

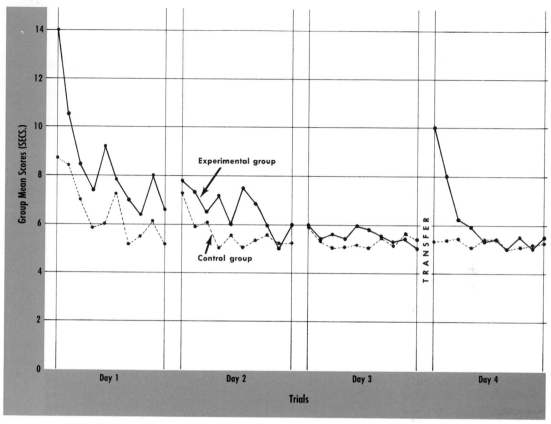

● **10.23**

Transfer from a Simulated to a Real Task. The tasks are described in the text. Note that there were ten trials daily for a total of four days. Time scores of the control group, working at the real task, were at first lower than those of the experimental group. After three days, the latter group was shifted from the simulated to the real task. Observe that their time scores went up, indicating the presence of negative transfer effects. Within five trials, however, this group was doing as well as before and as well as the control group was doing after 35 trials on the real task. (From M. Hammerton, "Transfer of Training from a Simulated to a Real Control Situation," *J. Exper. Psychol.*, 1963, *66*, p. 452.)

Thus, after learning items T S Q N A F P L J it is easy to learn T S Q N A F L J R Z because most of the items are learned already. A person familiar with several card games will learn the rules of another readily since many of the new rules are like those he already knows, i.e., a Queen takes a Jack; there are only four Aces in the deck, and so on. After one has learned to drive one car, he soon masters the controls of another. The brake is still under the right foot, a clockwise movement of the wheel steers the car to the right. In school subjects one also finds similarity of contents. Indeed, almost everything we learn

in school is conveyed to us through words and other symbols learned earlier. Without this "common content," how could we hope to learn history, biology, physics, and other subjects? There is transfer from mathematical skills to mechanical engineering skills, because both involve the same symbols and symbolic relations. Transfer from one language to another occurs if the symbols and grammatical constructions are alike. There is very high transfer from Spanish to Portuguese because of this similarity; and there is a certain amount of transfer from English to French because many words are similar.

• *Techniques.* There are courses in how to study which aim to teach the student how to organize his learning so as to make him maximally efficient. Any transfer from such courses is a transfer of study techniques.

Transfer in terms of techniques also occurs if, having learned the scientific approach to problems in one subject, the student applies scientific procedures to problems in other fields. Likewise, if the student takes a course in formal logic and thereafter thinks more logically, or tests his thinking in terms of logic, the procedures of formal logic have been transferred. Occasionally, a student who has learned in mathematics to formulate a problem by letting x equal this, y that, and so on, applies the same type of formulation to comparable problems in everyday life.

A word of caution is, however, in order. Having taken a course in how to study, in scientific method, in logic, in mathematics, or any other subject, does not guarantee that transfer will occur. The teacher with his eye on transfer will do well to give practice exercises in which transfer is called for. That is, he will teach how to transfer the methods to practical situations. Transfer, even though possible, does not always take place automatically.

• *Principles.* Transfer of principles is not always clearly different from transfer of techniques, because the use of a technique may involve the application of principles.

□ An experiment which clearly involves transfer of principles is illustrated by the following: Children were confronted with a series of doors on which geometric figures appeared. There was also a figure above each door. The upper and lower figures were changed from trial to trial. In every trial, however, one door had a matching figure above it. Opening this door revealed a toy. Thus the principle to be learned was: "The correct door is always the one whose figure matches the one above it"; or, "none of the wrong doors have figures which match those above." After having learned this problem with figures, many children learned, without any further training, new problems in which colors were used. Having learned the principle with figures, they

applied it to the color problem. Transfer was 100 per cent.[67]

A study of puzzle-solving in human adults showed that, when subjects were taught the principle involved in solution of one problem, they solved, without any error, new puzzles which involved the same principle. Those who did not learn the principles involved failed to show much transfer.[68]

In one of the best-known experiments on transfer of principles, a group of boys was given instruction in principles of refraction, while another (comparable) group received no such instruction. Both groups were then called upon to hit an underwater target with darts. This they accomplished with approximately equal success. But when the target was shifted to a new position, the boys with a knowledge of the principles of refraction made a much more rapid readjustment than did those with no knowledge of these principles. The investigator concluded that generalization, or application of principles to new situations involving the same principles, had occurred.[69] □

Formal discipline

Studies of transfer have failed to support the contention, once quite prevalent, that training in certain subjects, such as Latin and mathematics, serves to strengthen particular psychological functions. This doctrine, known as that of "formal discipline," has often been used to justify inclusion in the curriculum of studies which, although having no apparent practical value for certain students, are said to be useful in "improving memory," in "improving judgment," in "strengthening the scientific intellect," or in "giving elasticity to mental functions." The evidence from experimental investigations shows that transfer, where it occurs, is due to similarity of contents, of techniques, or of principles, not to development of particular psychological faculties or functions.[70]

When we say that a subject like Latin does not, any more than some other subject, increase one's intellectual capacities, we are not saying that studying it is a waste of time. It is exacting, and some people like to master exacting subjects, even when they see no practical outcomes. But it has also been maintained, apparently with justification, that the study of Latin improves one's English vocabulary and makes the many English words with Latin derivatives much more meaningful than they would otherwise be. Much of the Latin idiom is lost in translation, so that a student who wishes to feel and think with the Romans can do it better by reading Latin than by reading translations. The same is also true of Greek, as well as modern languages. But we must again call attention to the fact that transfer, although possible, does not necessarily occur. Students who were taught geometry in the traditional manner improved slightly in reasoning ability in relation to non-geometrical problems whereas a group that was taught geometry in such a way as to emphasize critical thinking showed marked transfer to other reasoning situations.[71] Similarly, the study of Latin does not necessarily improve the student's English vocabulary. It does so, however, when attention is given to the Latin derivation of English words and how to recognize Latin roots when they are present.[72]

Habit interference

Many errors made in the early stages of learning are responses transferred, inappropriately, from previous habits. Sometimes we experience great difficulty in eliminating these inappropriate responses. Since "carry-over" from earlier training is usually a mixture of useful, useless, and interfering responses, we can see that whether transfer is positive or negative depends upon whether one's learning as a whole is aided or hindered by previous training. In discussing transfer from a simulated to a real situation, we saw that there was at first interference, but that this was soon dissipated. A review of the literature on motor skills shows that negative transfer effects are usually of a transitory nature.[73]

When we come to thinking and reasoning (Chapter 13) we shall see that many of the errors, or false tries at solution, are carried over from what we have learned in other problem situations, but are inappropriate to meet the new situation. They send our thinking in the wrong "direction" and thus interfere with solution.

We see habit interference in everyday life. The person who has learned to drive a car with a left-hand drive has unusual difficulty in learning to drive one with a right-hand drive. Anybody who has habitually guided a sled with his feet experiences a certain amount of interference when he learns to guide a plane. Pushing the rudder bar with the right foot sends a sled to the left, but it sends a plane to the right. Some flyers have found themselves in difficulty because their training plane differed in certain respects from the plane they were finally called upon to fly.

□ ". . . a pilot, in attempting to correct for undershooting a field, pulled back on the throttle and pushed the stick forward, resulting in a nose dive into the ground. This incorrect pattern of adjustment was due to the fact that the pilot was flying a plane in which the controls were placed differently from those in the plane in which he was trained. He was used to advancing the throttle with his right hand and pulling back the stick with his left hand; and the 'left-hand-back, right-hand-forward' habit pattern transferred itself automatically, to the pilot's astonishment and resulting distress."[74] □

Habit interference in verbal activities also occurs at times. After the end of the year, you may continue for some time to write the previous year on your checks, and you may continue to write May after June has arrived. Likewise, after your telephone number or that of a friend has been changed, you may continue for a time to try to use the former number. Students are sometimes "tripped up" by the construction or sound of new words so that negative transfer occurs.[75] Here is an example. When asked to define "recapitulation," some said that it meant "recovery" (from recapture), some "refinancing" (from recapitalizing), and some "renewed life" (from recuperation).

Negative transfer, like positive, occurs on the basis of similar content, techniques, or principles, but it involves interference rather than facilitation. The contents, techniques, or principles which make for negative transfer are opposed to those required by the new situation. ■

• SUMMARY

Living organisms are modified by inherent growth processes (maturation) and also by what happens to them and what they do (learning). The learning process differs from maturation in that it requires stimulation and activity. Learned modifications differ from sensory adaptations in being permanent, or relatively so, rather than transient. The things that we learn (acquire) have a wide range of complexity. Among the simplest acquisitions are: habituations, as when organisms become accustomed to something not previously tolerated; conditioned responses; and elementary skills, such as putting on our clothes. The most complex skills are those which involve problem-solving on a symbolic level, as with words and numbers. The skills of higher mathematics are of this nature. Indeed, reasoning is referred to as a higher learning process.

Conditioned responses are simple habits. Many were initially reflexes elicited by *un-conditioned* stimuli. An example is salivation elicited by food in the mouth. Conditioning has occurred whenever some previously ineffective stimulus arouses such a response — as when ringing a bell produces salivation. The bell is in this case a *conditioned* stimulus and salivation a *conditioned* response. In so-called *classical* conditioning we have the sort of situation just described.

Responses often occur without application of an external stimulus. They are *emitted*. Scratching an ear, pecking, and pressing a lever exemplify such responses. In emitting them, the organism is, so to speak, operating upon its environment, hence the term *operant* behavior. Reinforcing an operant response, as by following it with food, increases its frequency. An increased rate of response is the evidence that conditioning has occurred. Conditioning along these lines is said to be *instrumental* because the response is instrumental in obtaining reinforcement.

Studies of classical conditioning have revealed that more rapid conditioning occurs when the conditioned stimulus precedes the unconditioned stimulus (and unconditioned response) by a brief interval. Stimuli resembling the conditioned stimulus in certain respects may also elicit the conditioned response — the principle of *stimulus generalization*. When two somewhat similar stimuli are presented, and only one of them is reinforced, *discrimination* develops. Now only the stimulus that was followed by reinforcement is effective. Repeated presentation of the conditioned stimulus without reinforcement produces *experimental extinction* — the response weakens, the conditioned stimulus loses its effectiveness. After an interval, however, there may be *spontaneous recovery* — a return of the previously extinguished response. The conditioned response often differs from the original response to the unconditioned stimulus — it may be abbreviated, as when the dog at first struggles when shocked but finally does no more than lift the shocked foot. *Anticipatory responses* may also occur. *Higher-order conditioning* can be obtained, as when a bell that has come to elicit salivation is substituted for food in developing a second conditioned response. This is an example of *secondary reinforcement* as well as second-order conditioning. In one form of instrumental conditioning an anticipatory response serves to escape shock. It is thus instrumental in avoiding the punishment. This is sometimes also referred to as *avoidance conditioning*.

Operant conditioning is instrumental, yet it differs from the instrumental conditioning just described in that there is no unconditioned stimulus — or at least none known to the investigator that he can use to elicit the response. The organism must emit the response — initiate it without experimental control — before it can be conditioned. The experimenter does, however, arrange certain contingencies — for instance, the sort of reinforcement that the response, once emitted, will bring. Thus, in pressing a lever, the contingency is food. Studies of operant conditioning have shown that reinforcement following *any* response may condition it so that it occurs at an increasing rate.

In *reward training*, where pressing a lever or pecking at a disc is followed by reinforcement with food, various reinforcement schedules may be used, and with somewhat different effectiveness regarding the rate of responding. Food may come at every response or it may come intermittently. Intermittent reinforcement may occur at fixed intervals (say, every minute), at fixed ratios (say, every fifth response), or at variable intervals or variable ratios. The highest rate of responding is found with variable intervals or ratios, for the animal then does not know after what interval, or after how many responses, reinforcement will come.

Complete removal of reinforcement is followed by a slower and slower rate of responding. Spontaneous recovery may occur after an interval, as in classical conditioning. Continued absence of reinforcement finally produces experimental extinction. Secondary reinforcement is also found in operant conditioning, as when a click associated with food becomes an effective reinforcing stimulus and a chimpanzee works for poker chips which he can later exchange for food. Some attention was given to verbal reinforcement in human operant conditioning. The potency of operant conditioning procedures in shaping behavior is especially evident in training which involves reinforcement of successive approximations to a desired response.

Escape training is an operant procedure which also has some of the aspects of classical conditioning. An electric shock produces escape movements. That is where the similarity lies. However, of many things that the subject may do, one and only one turns off the shock. This response is emitted. It is reinforced by cessation of the punishment. Like the response of reward conditioning, this response grows in frequency until, finally, it takes precedence over all other responses and is made immediately after the shock comes on.

Although they may have much in common with conditioned responses, skills are obviously more complex. In studying acquisition of skills, we disturb the organism's adjustment, then observe its success in achieving a readjustment. Mazes are widely used for this purpose.

Learning curves not only give a graphic record of the progress of learning, but they are useful for comparative purposes. Increasing proficiency is indicated by a decrease in time, errors, or excess activity — or by an increase in correct responses. These changes are plotted as a function of trials. As examples of typically human skills investigated in the laboratory we have referred to tracking (both compensatory and pursuit) and to such verbal skills as reciting memorized material.

Both animals and human beings solve detour problems, puzzle boxes, and tool-use problems by an overt trial-and-error attack; but human beings are more likely to solve them by implicit trial and error and by observation. While animals below man sometimes solve such problems by grasping significant relations (using insight) and by copying the performances of others (imitating), they are more likely to use overt trial and error. Even where animals do learn problems by using insight and by imitating others, human beings solve problems of much greater complexity than the animals can solve on these bases.

Acquisition of complex skills may be facilitated by observation of skilled performance. This does not mean that the skills are learned by imitation alone; it means only that observation of skilled performance may short-circuit, as it were, some of the overt trial and error that occurs in learning.

Both motor and verbal skills have different levels of complexity. We are often required to learn relatively simple habits and then to combine them into habits of increasing complexity. Typing, telegraphy, and many other activities of everyday life are habit hierarchies. It is noteworthy that, as higher-order habits develop, the simpler habits tend to become more automatic, which means that we are decreasingly aware of their presence.

There is much evidence that learning of some skills facilitates the acquisition of others which involve similar contents, techniques, or principles. This is a positive effect, generally referred to as positive transfer.

Negative transfer effects, which are usually referred to as negative transfer or habit interference, are often found in motor and verbal learning. These effects are likely to occur when the contents, techniques, or principles already learned are the reverse of those required in new learning and when familiar situations require new responses. ∎

• SELECTED READINGS

Braun, J. R. (Ed.), *Contemporary Research on Learning.* D. Van Nostrand, 1963. A book of readings.

Brazier, M. A. B., *The Central Nervous System and Behavior.* Josiah Macy Jr. Foundation, 1959. This book contains an excellent pictorial section (Magoun, Darling, and Brazier), a chapter on Pavlov (Gantt), and a chapter on Bechterev (Yakovlev). A chapter by Liddell, Olds, and Sperry deals with later developments in this area.

Cofer, C. N., and B. S. Musgrave (Eds.), *Verbal Learning and Verbal Behavior,* McGraw-Hill, 1961; and *Verbal Behavior and Learning,* McGraw-Hill, 1963. The proceedings of two conferences, with original papers and discussions.

Daniel, R. S. (Ed.), *Contemporary Readings in General Psychology* (2nd ed.). Houghton Mifflin, 1965. Readings 16, 17, 18, 39, and 53.

Gagné, R. M., *The Conditions of Learning.* Holt, Rinehart and Winston, 1965. A general survey designed to show how the psychology of learning can be used in improving education.

Grose, R. F., and R. C. Birney (Eds.), *Transfer of Learning.* D. Van Nostrand, 1963. A book of readings.

Kimble, G. A., *Hilgard and Marquis' Conditioning and Learning.* Appleton-Century-Crofts, 1961. A revision of the earlier book which gives a broad survey of research and theory.

Melton, A. (Ed.), *Categories of Human Learning.* Academic Press, 1964. The papers contributed to a symposium by fifteen leaders in the field of learning.

Munn, N. L., *The Evolution and Growth of Human Behavior* (2nd ed.). Houghton Mifflin, 1965. Chapters 4 and 7, on learning in animals and children.

Skinner, B. F., *Cumulative Record* (enlarged ed.). Appleton-Century-Crofts, 1961. This contains reprints of many of Skinner's most significant studies. The beginning student will be especially interested in and will profit from reading his Sigma Xi lecture, which appears on pages 100–131. Teaching machines are discussed in this book, as are many other applications.

Staats, A. W. (Ed.), *Human Learning.* Holt, Rinehart and Winston, 1964. A series of papers extending conditioning principles to complex behavior.

11

Foundations of Learning

*T*he scope of learning in animals and human beings has been surveyed. Now we are ready to examine the learning process more closely, and with special reference to such questions as *why* and *how* learning occurs. There is a great deal of information relevant to these questions, even though it is not yet possible to answer them completely. Much is known about sensory contributions, the participation of the brain, the importance of motivation, and the relative economy of different learning procedures. Theories of learning are attempts to systematize and interpret the information already available, then to extend our knowledge by formulating relevant hypotheses and testing them.

This chapter, then, provides an introduction to certain facts and principles which have an important place in theoretical discussions of the learning process. We shall also see the practical value of applying some of these principles in studying and teaching.

From what has been said about conditioned responses, motor and verbal skills, problem-solving, and various aspects of transfer (positive and negative) one might wonder how such a wide variety of acquisitions can be subsumed under a single term, such as *learning*. Despite their apparent diversity, however, all of these have two features in common: all of them involve *modifications of the organism*, and all are *dependent upon what happens to us as individuals*.

Except when "bad" habits are acquired, the learning process is adaptive. It helps the organism adjust to its environment. Learning *not* to do certain things also aids adjustment, as when we cease responding to irrelevant aspects of the environment (habituation) and when we learn to refrain from doing things that are painful or injurious. But in order to aid in adapting the organism, all of these must be retained, and this is possible only when a relatively permanent modification has occurred.

The individualistic origin of learned responses is evident when we consider that the modifications involved are produced by the effects upon an organism of changes in stimulation, as well as the effects of activity, of practice, of special training, of observation, or of a combination of these. It is important to recognize these foundations of learning for the reason that unlearned modifications of behavior also occur. This is especially so during the early months and years of human life. These modifications have already been discussed as changes resulting from natural growth processes, or *maturation*. We have pointed out elsewhere that such modifications are largely due to heredity. Responses resulting from maturation are fundamentally alike in all members of the species (as in the case of reflexes), whereas those which have a learned origin are different from one individual to another (as in the case of skills, discussed in the preceding chapter.)

Learning is, at base, a stimulus-response function. Without external stimulation mediated by the sense organs, there could be no learning. For this reason, attention is directed to sensory contributions in habit formation and to the sensory control of habits once they are formed. Learning is also dependent upon nervous functions. Such functions are important in the acquisition of responses and also in the subsequent control of these. The cerebral cortex is a central nervous structure of particular importance in this respect, especially when complex learning is involved. It is necessary, therefore, to consider both the sensory (peripheral) and central neural contributions to learning. One important theoretical issue focuses upon what is known about sensory and central neural contributions. This is the issue of whether learning is primarily peripheral or primarily central. That is to say, of whether it is basically a matter of acquiring responses to stimuli (developing S-R connections), or of acquiring brain modifications (or "ideas") which serve to interpret the stimulating situation and to initiate relevant responses. This issue will enter later theoretical considerations.

From what has already been said about reinforcement, both primary and secondary, it is apparent that motivation plays an important role in learning. For this reason we examine some representative studies on motivation and learning. Emphasis is given to the motives which facilitate human learning.

Even when we are highly motivated, the efficiency of our learning is not necessarily maximal. There are different ways of learning and some of these are more economical, in expenditure of time and effort, than others. A large amount of research in psychological laboratories, and in classrooms and industrial plants as well, has had as its aim the discovery of economical learning procedures. The present chapter therefore considers some of the most important outcomes of such research.

The chapter concludes with a discussion of selected theoretical issues and a recapitulation of some important principles of learning. ■

SENSORY CONTRIBUTIONS

A problem of particular interest is the relative importance of our various senses in habit formation. Verbal learning, as everyone knows, is practically nonexistent in people who are born both blind and deaf, unless, as in the case of Helen Keller, the tactual sense is somehow used to represent what normally comes through sight and sound. Acquisition of motor habits, on the other hand, does not show such dependence upon any particular avenues of stimulation.

The blind learn to find their way around on the basis of touch and hearing, but vision would of course greatly facilitate their learning. They also learn to avoid obstacles (see Figure 1.10, p. 22) which are presented to us visually, but to them only through hearing. In learning to avoid these obstacles when blindfolded, we would also use the auditory sense. Likewise the deaf person may learn to respond in situations where the rest of us use auditory cues. He learns to respond to them through his visual sense (lip reading) and his tactual sense (frequencies and intensities of vibration being sensed with the finger tips).[1]

The contribution of the senses to the acquisition of a relatively simple motor skill is illustrated by an experiment on white rats.[2] In this experiment, large groups learned an elevated multiple-T maze (see Figure 11.1). Some learned with all of their senses intact. Others were blind. Still others were deprived of vision and other senses at the same time. The error curves for the various groups are shown in Figure 11.1 and discussed in the legend. These curves reveal that learning is retarded to the degree that a rat is deprived of its sensory functions. This is not surprising in view of the fact that these are its only avenues for obtaining information about the maze.

Similar results are obtained with rats trained under conditions in which external cues are rendered ineffective through experimental controls, rather than by operations on the sense organs. The animals are deprived of visual cues by running them in total darkness; of auditory and olfactory cues from outside of the maze by rotating the whole structure to different positions from trial to trial; and of olfactory cues within the maze by interchanging units of the maze pathway between one trial and the next. As in the case of operated animals, the retardation in learning is directly related to the extent of sensory deprivation.[3] ■

LEARNING AND THE BRAIN

The importance of the brain for learning is unquestioned. Although conditioned responses may in some instances develop on a brain-stem level, the formation of a maze habit, or any skill of greater complexity, requires the participation of cerebral mechanisms. Earlier discussions (pp. 53–54) called attention to the relation between the size and complexity of the brain and the level of an organism's learning ability. This relationship holds for organisms at different levels of evolution and also for the individual organism as it grows from birth to maturity. In this connection look

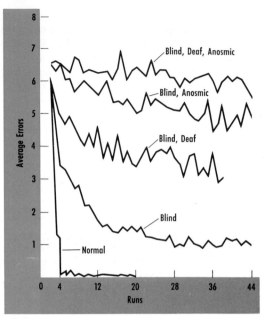

● **11.1**

Maze Learning and Sensory Deprivation. The investigator used a fourteen-unit elevated multiple-T maze, one section of which is illustrated. The rat is approaching a choice point — a left turn here leads toward the goal; a right turn, into a dead end. The latter is the type of error represented in the learning curves. Some rats (normal) had all of their senses intact and they soon eliminated errors. Others were blind, deaf, and anosmic (i.e., without the sense of smell). Note that these rats learned very little. With vision, hearing, and smell gone, the only senses which might have helped them were touch and kinesthesis (the muscle sense). In this kind of maze, however, touch does not provide enough information to be helpful. Kinesthesis, while important in the control of habits once they are learned, is also of little help in learning a maze of this kind. The blind and anosmic rats learned a little more than those that were also deprived of hearing. In forty-four trials, however, their performance did not improve beyond the level of 4–5 errors per trial. Blind-deaf rats had smell as the primary source of information; that this was helpful is shown by a curve falling, irregularly, to the level of 3 errors per trial. Rats deprived of vision alone showed steady improvement down to the level of one error. This level was reached by the twenty-eighth trial. Note, however, that rats with all of their senses intact (the normal group) were making almost no errors after the fourth trial. (After C. H. Honzik, "The Sensory Basis of Maze Learning in Rats," *Comp. Psychol. Monogr.,* 1936, *13,* No. 64.)

again at the graph (p. 110) showing how a human brain grows in size as the individual approaches maturity, a period during which there is a marked increase in the complexity of what can be learned and the readiness with which it is learned.

Most of the research on learning and the brain has centered around the question: Is

the entire cerebrum involved, with no region participating more than any other, or are different learning functions localized in different regions? The answer is far from simple. It depends among other things, on the organism involved and what is being learned.

Lashley attempted to answer this question, at least for rats, by removing brain tissue and observing the subsequent effect on maze learning.[4] In some rats he removed as little as 1.5 per cent of the cerebrum. Lesions of this size had little or no effect. With more extensive lesions, involving up to 80 per cent of the cerebrum, there was a decided retardation in learning ability. This was not evident for simple maze problems. However, as shown in Figure 11.2, a maze with eight blind alleys proved extremely difficult for animals with large lesions. Error scores in this maze increased as the magnitude of the lesions increased. The correlation between these two variables was .84.

Although error scores varied with the size of the lesion, they did not vary with its location. For instance, a 30 per cent lesion produced approximately the same number of errors regardless of whether it was located in a posterior, anterior, or lateral region of the cerebrum. Such findings led Lashley to conclude that, so far as maze learning in rats is concerned, the *amount* rather than the location of the damage is what counts. This is referred to as a *mass action* effect.

Mass action could be explained in different ways. One of these is to suppose, as Lashley did, that different parts of the brain are *equipotential* — that the brain as a whole contributes something of importance for learning and that, with respect to this, its different parts participate equally. However, certain brain structures, even in as low a mammal as the rat, have rather specific sensory functions. One part is especially concerned with vision, another with hearing, and so on. Therefore it may be that removing one area is followed by loss of sensitivity to visual details of the maze; removing another, by loss of sensitivity to sounds; removing still another, by loss of olfactory sensitivity. Removing a larger area would thus interfere with more senses — would eliminate more sensory cues. But why should the same amount of destruction in different areas of the cerebrum have equivalent effects? The answer could be as follows: With a small lesion destroying vision, let us say, the rat still has its other senses. With a lesion of equal size, but which eliminates olfactory sensitivity, there is still the combination of remaining

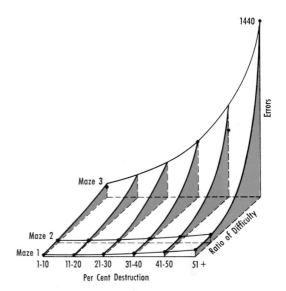

● **11.2**

Relation Between the Extent of Cerebral Lesions and Learning. Separation of the three curves at their base indicates the relative difficulty of the three problems for normal animals. The abscissa shows the per cent of the cerebral cortex destroyed. The number of errors made in learning the respective problems is represented by the height (ordinate) of the graph. Maze 1 was the least and maze 3 the most complex. (From K. S. Lashley, *Brain Mechanisms and Intelligence*, University of Chicago Press, 1929.)

senses. One might conclude, therefore, that the combination of senses minus vision is equivalent to the combination of senses minus olfaction. The same argument might apply even if the lesions were sufficiently large to destroy more than one sense. That is, with vision and hearing gone, the rat still has olfaction and touch; with olfaction and touch gone, it still has vision and hearing — and the combination of what is intact is equivalent regardless of the specific senses involved.[5] However, this interpretation is not entirely satisfactory. In the first place, as indicated earlier, some senses (vision, olfaction) are more important for maze learning than others. In the second place, Lashley has shown that removing vision peripherally (by taking out the eyes) is much less disruptive than removing it centrally (by destroying the visual cortex).[6] Lashley attributed the greater loss from brain lesions than from peripheral injury to a disturbance, not only of sensory functions but also, and more importantly, of the integrative functions of the cerebrum as a whole.

However we interpret such results, it must be remembered that they were obtained with rats and limited to maze learning. They do not necessarily hold for all animals and for all kinds of habits. Recent studies have shown, moreover, that Lashley's results may apply only to caged rats trained in an alley maze. Free-ranging rats subjected to a highly stimulating environment and tested in situations requiring perceptual learning did not show the mass action effect. The retardation which followed lesions depended upon where these were localized.[7]

Lashley and others have shown that the learning of sensory discriminations is definitely dependent upon localized brain areas. Discrimination of visual shapes, for example, fails to develop if the visual cortex is removed. Destruction of nonvisual areas, on the other hand, does not prevent the animal from learning the visual discrimination, although it may make for slower learning, possibly through interference with integrative processes. What this may mean, in the last analysis, is that brain lesions, wherever located, lower an organism's vigilance.[8]

The dependence of particular sensory discriminations upon specialized areas of the cerebrum becomes increasingly evident as we go up the scale from lower mammals to man. A dog with both temporal lobes removed still responds to loud noises, but a man with comparable lesions is completely deaf.[9] Likewise, a dog whose occipital lobes have been destroyed can still differentiate between light and dark, but a man with comparable lesions is completely blind.[10] Motor functions are also localized (see pp. 59–60). Thus running or other activity involved in learning utilizes the motor cortex more than any other region. Again, there is more dependence upon the motor cortex in man than in other animals. Although human beings may to some extent recover their motor functions after lesions in the motor cortex, animals do this much more

readily.[11] Beyond these specific sensory and motor contributions, which are so important for learning, we see, at the human level, a localization of linguistic functions, or of neural links essential for these functions, such as those of the speech area. Localization is also evident in aphasia (p. 60).

Experiments on rats and monkeys, as well as observations of test performances in human beings with brain lesions, have led some to conclude that control of higher learning processes — such as require recall of past experience, insight, and reasoning — is localized in the anterior regions of the frontal lobes; that is to say, at the front of these lobes. The evidence is that lesions in these areas disturb such processes more than lesions of comparable size elsewhere in the brain. This is clearly true when both frontal regions are destroyed. However, the facts are subject to conflicting interpretations. One of these is that injuries to the brain, and perhaps frontal lesions particularly, have such general effects as lowering vigilance, making the organism less attentive, making it more distractible, or, in general, decreasing its motivation. If this interpretation should be substantiated, it would effectively refute the idea that special learning processes are localized in (or especially dependent upon) the frontal regions.[12] ∎

THE ROLE OF MOTIVATION

In research on learning it is almost axiomatic that adequate reinforcement must be provided. The hungry animal must receive food; the thirsty one, water; or the punished or confined animal must escape. Such reinforcement is obviously necessary where learning of skills is concerned. It is not so obviously an aspect of conditioning; but even here, as we pointed out earlier, reinforcement of some kind seems necessary. Instrumental conditioning provides reinforcement in that the organism's response brings food or escape. Classical conditioning may also involve reinforcement in this sense. True, the unconditioned stimulus (UCS) follows the conditioned stimulus (CS) at a given interval, whether or not a conditioned anticipatory response occurs. It is possible, however, that the CS arouses an expectation of the UCS, perhaps a tension of some sort, and that the appearance of the UCS relieves this, thus providing reinforcement of the CS. But this would not be true for simultaneous presentation of CS and UCS, nor for the UCS–CS sequence (backward conditioning) — neither of which, however, is particularly effective in developing conditioned responses.

☐ A strong claim for nonreinforced learning comes from experiments on so-called sensory preconditioning where the mere pairing of two stimuli brings about an association. After repeated pairing of the two stimuli, one is subsequently used as a conditioned stimulus. Finally, the stimulus paired with it earlier, but never used in the conditioning situation, is shown to be effective in arousing the conditioned response.[13] But even here, one could argue that whenever one stimulus repeatedly follows another after a specified interval, the coming of the second stimulus provides reinforcement for the tension or "expectation" induced by onset of the first. The equivalence of the "sensory-preconditioned" and the conditioned stimuli could thus be envisaged in terms of reinforcement. One difficulty with such an interpretation, however, is that the "expectation" of the second stimulus is itself a product of learning — but reinforced by what?

A more convincing demonstration of nonreinforced conditioning is to be found in a recent experiment with twenty-three kittens.[14] These were divided into a control group of twelve and an experimental group of eleven animals. To control hereditary differences as much as possible, the groups were derived from split litters, a procedure described earlier (p. 26). The kittens were tested one at a time in a rotating wheel-like cage, which turned like the rotating drum of the apparatus in Figure 6.1 (p. 153). The investigator's aim was to see whether he could condition the animals to turn the cage when a 1,000-cycle tone came on, yet without reinforcing this response in any way.

It was necessary, at first, to discover if there was any initial response to the tone. Two tests per kitten involved turning on the tone while the animal was inactive. Not one of the twenty-three animals turned the cage in these tests. Now the experimental group was given a series of test periods. During these, the experimenter turned on the tone as soon as he saw the cage moving. This procedure continued until each kitten had accumulated thirty cage-turning responses. The control group also accumulated thirty cage-turning responses, but none of these was followed by tone. A kitten usually continued turning; so not only the occurrence of turning, but also its duration, was measured. In successive groups of ten responses, the durations for the experimental group averaged 4.89, 5.87, and 8.49 seconds. For the control group, the corresponding averages were 4.07, 4.61, and 4.97 seconds. We see, then, that the duration increased in the experimental group (by 3.60 seconds) and did not change much in the control group (0.9 seconds). This difference suggests that the experimental procedure was conditioning the kittens. But the best indication came from twenty subsequent test sessions. In each of these the tone was turned on after a kitten had been quiet for 30 seconds or more. The same procedure was followed for both groups and the question to be answered was whether the experimental kittens would turn the cage significantly more, in response to the tone, than the control kittens turned it. This they did. The experimental group had an average of 38 cage-turning responses to only 7 for the control group. This difference, a statistically reliable one, is taken to indicate that "contiguity of stimulus and response is a sufficient condition for learning." One possible interpretation, however, is that the kittens were in an operant-conditioning situation in which they learned *to turn on the tone* by rotating the cage. This interpretation is discounted by the investigator for various reasons, particularly because there was no evidence that the tone itself had any reinforcing properties initially, as food does when the rat presses a lever, and because the total responses, number of test periods, and frequency of responses per test period during the training phase did not differ for the two groups, as they would be expected to do in operant conditioning. ☐

The issue of nonreinforced learning, even at such an elementary level as conditioning, is a crucial one in learning theory and we will return to it near the end of this chapter. It may be noted at this point, however, that the sort of training involved in the preceding examples is quite inefficient. Learning occurs much more quickly and with greater stability when obvious reinforcement is a part of the procedure. Thus, even though conditioning without reinforcement may have been demonstrated, the fact remains that reinforcement is normally an important contributor to efficient learning. The following discussions provide evidence in support of this conclusion. They also show the relative effectiveness of different kinds and degrees of reinforcement.

● **11.3**

The Effect of a Food Reward on Maze Learning in Rats. Observe that the rapidity of learning, and the level of achievement, varied with motivation and reward. The limited learning by hungry, nonrewarded and less-hungry, rewarded rats may be attributed to the incentive value of escape from the maze. Time scores for these groups actually increased during the course of the experiment, while those for the hungry, rewarded group decreased in the normal manner. (From E. C. Tolman and C. H. Honzik, "Introduction and Removal of Reward, and Maze Performance in Rats," *Univ. Calif. Publ. Psychol.*, 1930, *4*, p. 246.)

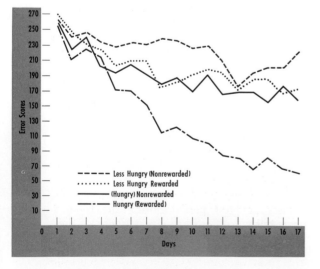

Rewards in animal learning

Learning of hungry rats which found food at the end of a maze was compared, in one investigation, with the learning of rats which were hungry and found no food, and with the learning of rats which were not hungry and found food.[15] As illustrated in Figure 11.3 the hungry-rewarded group showed normal progress toward mastery of the maze habit, while the other groups exhibited little progress.

When hungry rats ran the maze without finding a food reward, and food was later introduced, there was a sudden drop in the time and error curves. Maze performance in the absence of food suggested that little or nothing was being learned. But when food was introduced at the tenth trial, performance soon approximated that of a group rewarded continually over a long period.[16] Such sudden improvement suggested that the unrewarded rats had been learning something, even though they had not previously shown evidence of it — a phenomenon referred to as *latent learning*. Latent learning is discussed in more detail near the end of this chapter, in the context of learning theory.

Withdrawal or delay of reward,[17] or change to a less preferred reward, after performance has reached a high level of efficiency, all lead to less efficient maze running.[18]

Motivation and human learning

Laboratory investigations of human learning sometimes use primary reinforcers (like food) but they more often resort to secondary reinforcers (like money or recognition).

• *Monetary rewards.* It is well known that money may motivate human learning. An illustration of the effectiveness of monetary rewards is provided by an experiment on the learning of an elevated finger maze by sixty blindfolded boys. Three groups having equivalent chronological and mental age were used. Members of the first group received no reward other than that which might come from satisfaction in learning the maze; members of the second group received a material reward (a penny) at the end of each trial; and members of the third group received a verbal reward, such as

"Good," "Very good," or "Let me see if you can make even fewer mistakes this time."

The no-reward group learned slowly, the verbal-reward group somewhat faster, and the material-reward group fastest. The average number of errors in the last five trials was: no reward, 2.6; verbal reward, 2.3; and material reward, 1.7. Statistical analysis shows that although these differences are small, there is a very low probability that they are due to chance.

In a further experiment, utilizing the same maze but different boys, a quarter was given for every trial without error. Although not many perfect performances occurred, and few quarters were thus received, this condition led to the fastest learning of all.[19] In an experiment on visual discrimination learning there was no significant difference in the error scores of nine-year-old boys given either one cent or fifty cents for each correct response and required to forfeit the same amount for each error.[20] A correct response was always signaled by the lighting of red bulbs. It is interesting to note that a group given this information and no reward had fewer errors than either of the reward groups. The investigators think that the monetary reward groups may have regarded the monetary transactions as a secondary task and that this interfered with their discrimination learning. In the maze experiment, a monetary reward was given at the end of every correct trial. There was nothing taken back for errors, as there was in the discrimination experiment. It may well be, then, that the failure of the higher pay to make any difference in the discrimination experiment resulted from this complication. In any event, it is evident that one cannot make any general statement about the effectiveness of monetary rewards in learning.

• *Punishment and reward.* Numerous experiments on learning in rats and human subjects have compared the effects of punishment and reward, the punishment usually being a mild electric shock. In most of these studies, involving a variety of learning situations, shock for errors has been more effective, in combination with reward, than reward alone.[21] However, the effect of punishment is not clearly indicated. If punishment is given for incorrect responses, it leads to more rapid elimination of these responses than occurs without it. However, under certain conditions, punishment for correct responses, which are also rewarded, leads to more rapid fixation than occurs without it.[22]

Punishment, or the "annoyance" produced by it, tends to make the learner more cautious and more sensitive to the stimuli associated with a response, whether correct or incorrect. It develops attitudes of anticipation like those already considered in the discussion of conditioning. As one investigator put it, "Annoyers do not act on learning in general by weakening whatever connection they follow. If they do anything in learning, they do it indirectly, by informing the learner that such and such a response in such and such a situation brings distress, or by making the learner feel fear of a certain object, or by making him jump back from a certain place, or by some other definite and specific change which they produce in him."[23]

• *Praise and reproof.* What is the relative effectiveness of praising good performances and reproving poor ones? One of the best studies on this question was done with 160 fourth- and sixth-grade girls. Four groups, matched in arithmetical ability and in age, were used. The task was that of solving as many as possible of thirty arithmetic problems in a given time limit (fifteen minutes). Five comparable groups of problems were used, one on each of five trials, given one day apart. The reproved group, regardless of how well it did, was asked to come to the front after each day's work and face the class. It was then "bawled out" for its mistakes, careless work, and failure to improve. This group actually had no knowledge of how many problems it had solved correctly in the time limit. The praised group, regardless of how well or how badly it performed, was brought before the class each day and complimented on its fine performance. The ignored group, while it heard the praise and reproof administered to the other groups, was not referred to during these periods. A control group, working in a separate room, was neither praised nor reproved. It did not observe the treatment of the other groups, nor was it given any suggestion concerning the status of its own performance.[24] The average scores of all four groups were initially the same — about twelve problems solved correctly. On the second day, both the praised and the reproved groups gave comparable performances solving an average of slightly over sixteen problems. From this point on, however, the praised group improved and the reproved group grew worse. Neither the ignored nor the control group showed any consistent improvement.

• *Rivalry and recognition.* Most members of our society tend to put forth effort when competing with others, and when they know that social recognition will come to those who achieve. This was demonstrated in a piece of research in the classroom in which groups of children did addition problems in five consecutive daily sessions. Some groups did the problems under conditions in which no rivalry and no recognition for achievement were involved. Comparable groups did the same problems, but under conditions involving intergroup competition. After each day's session, the children of the winning group held up their hands so that other children could see them. Not only this, but their names were placed on the blackboard. The results were quite clear-cut. Both the rivalry and the no-rivalry groups started at approximately the same level of performance, with a score of 4. Thereafter, the rivalry group improved gradually, attaining a score of better than 8 after five sessions. The no-rivalry group, on the other hand, raised its average score to approximately 5 and stayed at that level.[25]

It should be recognized, of course, that intense rivalry may have disruptive effects on performance, and thus interfere with learning. More is said about this in a later discussion (Chapter 17) of learning in group situations, where rivalry is often involved.

• *Knowledge of results.* Another term for this is *information feedback*. Motor skills are not generally acquired without the learner knowing something, at least, about the effectiveness of his efforts. The importance of information feedback is neatly shown in an experiment with the device illustrated in Figure 11.4.

By proper manipulation of both handles at once, the subject could move the spot of light onto the bullseye. He was given a score

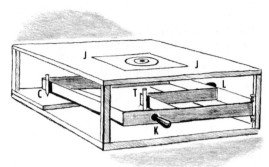

• **11.4**

Two-Hand Coordination Apparatus. The subject was instructed to move handles K and L in such a manner as to throw a spot of light from the torch T upon the bull's-eye of the target, J.J. Too small a movement of K caused the spot to move too far to the left. The performance was registered on a sheet of paper at C. A score of 10 was given for a bull's-eye, 9 for the next ring out, and so on. The outermost ring scored 1 and a miss, 0. The subject was required to move both hands just once at each trial. Therefore, he was not allowed to explore to locate the target. (From J. L. Elwell and G. C. Grindley, "The Effect of Knowledge of Results on Learning and Performance," *Brit. J. Psychol.*, 1938, 29, p. 41.)

based upon how close he came to the bullseye. After preliminary practice, two groups were trained, one with the light off so that no knowledge of accuracy would be possible, and the other with the light on so that accuracy in hitting the target would be known. Subjects working without knowledge of results failed to show any improvement. They also became exceedingly "bored" with the whole procedure. On the other hand, those who knew the accuracy with which they hit the target, improved rapidly as practice continued. When knowledge of results was withdrawn, this was followed by a deterioration in performance.[26] Numerous experiments on a wide variety of skills add support to these findings.[27]

Subjects in one experiment of this nature tried to keep a wavering needle on the zero mark for as long a period as possible.[28] This is of course a compensatory tracking problem (p. 320). Subjects could see when the needle deviated very much from the zero point, hence there was some visual knowledge of results.

However, a visual signaling system was arranged so that small increments of cumulative time on the target could also be indicated. In addition, an auditory signaling device was installed so that a subject wearing headphones could hear clicks which indicated his level of success in staying on the target. One group (high-level knowledge of achievement) received this additional visual and auditory feedback throughout each ninety-second trial. Another group (low-level knowledge of achievement) had no information feedback during any trial except that naturally present in watching the needle. At the end of each trial, however, they were told their score for that trial. Learning curves for these groups are shown in Figure 11.5. It is quite evident that the greater information resulted in more efficient performance.

Information feedback augmented by clicks or other supplementary information is clearly helpful in the acquisition of a tracking skill. From a practical standpoint, however, one may ask whether this additional information should reveal that the subject is *on target*, that he is *off target*, or that he is *off target in a particular direction*. A further investigation[29] was designed to discover the most advantageous of these possibilities. A visual tracking task was involved. The control group received only the normal visual information provided by the display itself. This group acquired the skill much more slowly, and achieved a poorer level of final performance, than three experimental groups provided not only with the normal visual information, but also with auditory feedback. These wore headphones in which clicks were heard. One group heard the clicks while on target, one while off target, and the third while off target to the right (clicks in right ear) and while off target to the left (clicks in left ear.) The results, shown in Figure 11.6, indicate that the most advantageous arrangement for augmented feedback in this kind of task is one which indicates merely when the subject is *off target*. The investigators point out that the information that one is off target emphasizes errors and facilitates their correction. It is apparently of no further advantage to have clicks indicating the direction of the error.

Improved performance with knowledge of

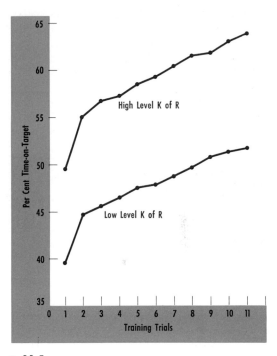

• **11.5**

Knowledge of Results in Compensatory Tracking. The low knowledge-of-results group had no more visual information feedback than could be gained by watching the needle. The subjects were told their time-on-target scores after each trial. The other group had additional auditory and visual feedback during each trial. This illustration does not include data on transfer, which were also in favor of the group with the greater knowledge of results. (From A. F. Smode, "Learning and Performance in a Tracking Task under Two Levels of Achievement Information Feedback," *J. Exper. Psychol.*, 1958, *56*, p. 300.)

results has three principle explanations: (1) good motivation is fostered, in that subjects working with information feedback usually find the task more interesting than it would otherwise be, hence work at it enthusiastically and try to improve their performance; (2) because the individual knows when he is making errors, he can attempt to correct them, and his improved performance shows the extent to which he is successful in doing so; (3) if successful acts can be identified, efforts may be

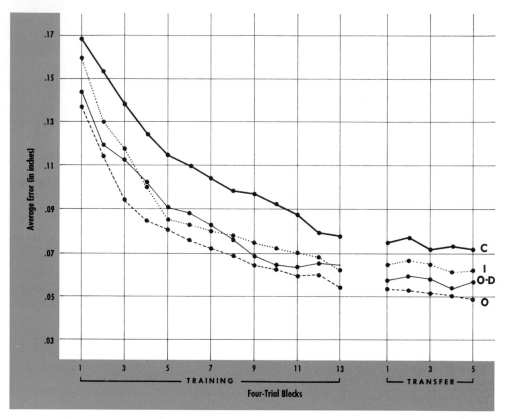

● 11.6

Information Feedback and Tracking Skill. These curves show the average tracking error as a function of successive blocks of trials, with each trial of thirty seconds duration. The control group (C), trained only with visual feedback normal to the situation, exhibited the poorest performance, both in training and in transfer trials. Three experimental groups, given auditory feedback (clicks heard through earphones) to augment the feedback normally present, differed in their performance level. The best performance occurred in the group given information indicating simply that they were off target (O). Group O-D, with directional off-target information, performed at a somewhat poorer level. On-target information (group I) was least effective in augmenting the customary visual feedback. (From A. C. Williams and G. E. Briggs, "On-Target Versus Off-Target Information and the Acquisition of Tracking Skill," *J. Exper. Psychol.,* 1962, *64,* p. 521.)

made to repeat them. The latter advantage is quite evident in athletic skills, where particular arm or leg movements are more easily identified than the relatively small movements made in tracking. ■

INTENTIONAL VERSUS INCIDENTAL LEARNING

The intention to learn is a clearly important motivational factor in learning motor skills; in acquiring verbal skills like reading, writing, and arithmetic; and in gaining knowledge of complex subjects. But do we also learn incidentally; that is to say, without intending to do so? It appears that we do, at times, acquire a certain amount of information this way. On the other hand, it is difficult to prove that any learning is completely unmotivated. We confronted this problem in discussing latent learning (p. 344) and also the topics of sensory preconditioning and contiguous conditioning (p. 343). Here we discuss some relevant research on incidental learning. Theoretical implications are considered near the end of this chapter.

Incidental acquisition

Many examples could be cited of failure to learn when the intention to do so is absent. The teacher reading a list of words which his students are to recall does not necessarily learn the list himself. A person who read the morning prayer provided by the Episcopal Church an estimated 5,000 times over a period of twenty-five years was unable to recite it without the prayer book before him.[30] One often finds himself reading a lesson with "his mind elsewhere." He then realizes that he has been reading without learning anything of what he reads. In the next chapter we shall see that the reason why so many people have difficulty recalling names is that they take a passive attitude — have no intention to recall them — while being introduced. The intention to learn is of even greater importance in acquiring complex skills, either verbal (as in reciting a poem) or motor (as in playing a piano). One would learn very little while merely "going through the motions."

Several experiments, in which subjects were mechanically guided through performances instead of initiating their own responses, have shown that complete learning of a skill does not occur on this basis alone. Guidance sometimes aids in the acquisition of a skill, but sometimes fails to have any effect.[31]

Experimental studies on incidental versus intentional learning have shown that, in general, the latter is much more efficient.[32] In a typical experiment of this nature, students read nonsense syllables to other students who had been instructed to learn the lists. A subsequent test of recall showed that the readers, while they learned some of the words, did not do nearly as well as those who had been asked to learn them.[33] However, subsequent research has revealed complicating elements in such an experiment. For example: Was the significant variable indeed the fact that the listeners intended to learn and the readers did not? Was significance attached to the fact that the two groups were doing different things — one listening and the other reading? And, did the readers learn less because reading interfered with learning while listening facilitated it?

□ An experiment designed to disentangle these variables used three comparable groups. Group I was instructed to learn numbers which appeared, one by one, in a controlled-exposure apparatus. This was an intentional-learning group in the usual sense. Group II was given the same numbers, but instructed only to circle corresponding numbers on a coded matrix, a different matrix for each repetition of the list. Members of this group thought that they were helping the experimenter find the best way to code numbers. This was an incidental learning group in the usual sense. Group III was asked both to circle the numbers on the matrix and to learn them. This group therefore had the same orienting task (circling numbers) as the second group, but also the intention to learn the numbers. Within each of the three groups cited, there were three subgroups which varied in the rate at which the numbers were presented to them — i.e., at 2-second, 3-second, and 6-second intervals. All were subsequently tested to see how many numbers had been learned. The amount learned was generally in favor of the first group, learning intentionally by the usual procedure. However, the differences between the intentional and incidental groups performing the same orienting task depended upon the rate of presentation of the numbers. At relatively fast rates (2 and 3 seconds between) there was no significant difference; but, at the slower rate (6 seconds between), the difference was significantly in favor of intentional learners — whether or not they performed the orienting task.[34]

Other investigations have revealed further complications. For example, it has been shown that the nature of the orienting tasks and of the materials to be learned has much to do with determining whether or not intentional learners are superior to incidental learners.[35] □

A frequent criticism of experiments on incidental learning is that the incidental learners may, without instructions from the experimenter, set themselves the task of learning the material. In some instances, members of the incidental group have reported the presence of such self-induced motivation.[36] Even when orienting tasks like those involved in the above experiments are used, these do not preclude the possibility of such motivation.

A related question is that of whether learning can take place without awareness. If an individual learned something incidentally, but did not know it at the time, we could say that he learned unconsciously, or without being aware that he was doing so.

Learning and awareness

One does not learn complex skills without being aware of it; but how about such relatively simple things as acquiring conditioned responses and associating one word with another? Research has focused on elementary acquisitions of this kind.

Investigators of classical conditioning differ on the role of awareness. Some believe that they have conditioned subjects who were unconscious of what was going on; others have found no evidence for conditioning without awareness.

☐ Normal subjects learned a maze and, at times, sucked lollipops while red or green lights flashed on and off.[37] Instructions were designed to direct attention toward the maze problem and make the subjects unaware of the fact that their salivary responses were being conditioned to the lights. Control subjects went through the same procedure but were given information to the effect that their salivation was being conditioned. This group did not condition as readily as the other, a finding with various possible interpretations. One does not know, for sure, that the uninformed subjects were unconscious of the fact that they were being conditioned; hence it would be hazardous to assume that they were unaware and conditioned more readily because of this. The findings might mean that the informed subjects were too attentive to the conditioning procedures and that this interfered with acquisition. It has often been reported that quicker conditioning occurs when attention is directed elsewhere, but this does not necessarily mean that there is *no* awareness of what is going on.

In another experiment,[38] students who learned words while eating lunch — with the understanding that the effect of learning on digestion was being studied — were later found to secrete more saliva in response to lunch-related words than to a control list. These students were conditioned, but were they actually unaware of the fact that this was happening? One cannot be certain that they were.

If the above subjects were conditioned without awareness, one might have to conclude that salivary conditioning is an exception to the rule, for investigations involving other responses favor the view that awareness is a necessary condition.

With the focus directly on the awareness issue, recent investigators have questioned their subjects at some length. After the conditioning sessions are over, the subjects tell what they thought was happening. In this way it is possible to split the data in terms of awareness and unawareness.

In one such study, also on classical conditioning, nonsense syllables (CS) were presented with pleasant words (UCS).[39] The aim was to see whether this association of syllables with pleasant words would lead the subjects to rate the nonsense syllables as pleasant. A similar procedure was followed with nonsense syllables and unpleasant words. After the conditioning sessions were over, the subjects rated the syllables on a seven-point pleasantness-unpleasantness scale. Control subjects, seeing these syllables for the first time, also rated them. On the basis of answers to questions about awareness, the experimental subjects were divided into an aware and an unaware group. Interestingly enough, the aware group rated the syllables as pleasant or unpleasant in terms of their conditioning. The unaware group did not show this effect. Their responses were essentially like those of controls. In short, there was no evidence of conditioning without awareness. ☐

So much for classical conditioning, insofar as it has been studied from the standpoint of awareness. But how about instrumental conditioning? Perhaps we should expect awareness to be especially important, since what the subject does is followed by rewards or punishments. In operant conditioning, the subject himself initiates the responses. Is he aware of what he is doing? More important, is he aware of the contingency between what he is doing and what follows? The experiments below are examples of operant conditioning. One, lacking an adequate control, suggests the possibility of unconscious conditioning. The other experiment shows no evidence of conditioning without awareness.

□ We have already described (p. 312) an experiment in which the experimenter said *Mm-hmm* as reinforcement for the subject's use of plural words.[40] As the experiment proceeded, the subjects increased their use of plural words. Following withdrawal of reinforcement, experimental extinction occurred. Out of fifteen subjects in this experiment, only one reported that he was aware of the experimenter's attempts to shape his behavior by reinforcing plural words. Other experiments of a similar nature have been reported, with essentially the same outcome, but these have been subjected to critical attack on the grounds that subjects were not questioned sufficiently about their awareness and that there were no adequate control groups.[41] For example, there should have been a control group given reinforcement but unrelated to particular verbalizations.

The operant conditioning of motor responses in relation to awareness was investigated with large groups of female students who were told that they were contributing basic data for a "woman in space" project.[42] Each girl entered a spherical "pressure chamber" where the temperature was 105° F and the relative humidity 85 per cent. Various tasks occupied the subject while she sat in front of an air shaft which, at intervals, delivered ten-second streams of cool air. She was observed through a porthole with one-way vision. After viewing the subject's actions for five minutes, the investigator decided which action would be reinforced with cool air. In some cases this was tapping with the right foot; in others, touching the chin with the right hand; in still others, pressing the lips together; and so on. Control subjects were given the same treatment, including an equal number of reinforcements, but no particular act was reinforced. After the conditioning sessions were over, each of the experimental sub-

jects answered various questions designed to determine the presence or absence of awareness. Less than 50 per cent were aware of the contingency between their acts and the stream of cool air. These subjects, who were able "to verbalize mediational steps that intervened between the experimental variables and the changes in their behavior" increased the frequency of the reinforced responses as the experiment proceeded. The unaware group did not show this outcome. Their reactions were like those of the control group. The conclusion: no conditioning here without awareness. □

We have described only a few experiments relevant to the issue of awareness in learning. A symposium[43] on this and a recent review of the literature[44] leave the impression that if learning occurs without awareness, it has not yet been demonstrated in an unequivocal fashion. Most of the evidence fails to support the idea that learning occurs without awareness. But one should not overlook the possibility that awareness may be essential for some acquisitions and not for others.

The question of learning while asleep is also relevant to this issue, for if one learns anything while in reality asleep, he is learning it without awareness.

The question of sleep learning

The possibility that a person might learn while sleeping is an intriguing one and writers of science fiction, like Huxley[45] in his *Brave New World*, have given the possibility a great deal of attention. This is also of considerable interest from a practical standpoint. Devices and procedures designed to facilitate learning during sleep are widely advertised.

If it were possible to learn while asleep, the student could turn on a recorded lecture, a list of foreign verbs, or any other lesson, and set it to repeat at intervals while he slept. Thus he could learn during a period which, at least from an academic standpoint, is wasted. That is the practical side. But what about the theoretical? Learning during sleep would be incidental — or at least passive in the sense that it does not involve the subject's conscious attention. It might, at first, appear also to be unmotivated. But the student does have the intention to learn — before he goes to sleep — and motives do not necessarily disappear during sleep. Freud regarded even dreams as motivated.

In view of these interesting possibilities, it may be disappointing to discover that sleep learning is without adequate experimental verification. Several studies have seemed to find evidence for it, but they were inadequately controlled. The chief criticism is that they presented no convincing evidence that their "sleep learners" were really asleep during the entire period of presentation.

In an investigation[46] designed to correct the shortcomings of earlier studies, the experimenter turned on the recording (ten one-syllable words) only when electroencephalograms (EEG's) showed that the subjects were asleep. It often happened that a subject began to wake up (indicated by an alpha EEG, p. 58) while the recording was on. In this event, the experimenter promptly turned the record off. It was turned on again only when the sleep EEG returned. The experimental group comprised nine men who had served in other sleep experiments and were thus adjusted to the experimental situation. They were required to choose from a list of fifty words the words that had been played during sleep. In this test, however, they did no better than controls — subjects who had no experience of any kind with the test words. The general conclusion from this and other tests of sleep learning was that subjects do not learn while asleep.

It is perhaps worth noting that the positive results of earlier studies — perhaps of learning while in a state of drowsiness — were for the learning of relatively simple material. There is no doubt, moreover, that a comparable group of wide-awake subjects would exceed the performance of any group attempting to learn while asleep, or while in a state of drowsiness. ■

THE RELATIVE ECONOMY OF DIFFERENT LEARNING PROCEDURES

Assuming that the subject is well motivated, what are the best procedures to be followed in developing proficiency? Is it better, for example, to concentrate practice periods, or to distribute them, with a short or long interval between? Within a given practice period, is it better to give just one trial, or to give a number of trials? What is the most economical interval to introduce between practice periods — one hour, six hours, or a day? In learning verbal or motor skills, is it better to go over the material again and again, without a recitation or rehearsal, or is it better to introduce recitation or rehearsal periods at intervals during the original learning? If so, what proportion of the learning time should be given to reading, and what proportion to recitation? In learning a poem, a maze, or any other serial habit which may be broken up into parts, is it better to learn it a part at a time, or is it better to go over the whole thing from beginning to end at each trial? These are the chief questions with which discussions of economical learning are concerned. A great amount of research, involving animals and men, children and adults, and motor and verbal materials, has been concentrated on such questions.

Distribution of effort

Here we actually have two problems: (1) what is the optimal amount of work per practice period — i.e., between rest periods? One might study for 15 minutes, 30 minutes, or 60 minutes before taking a rest. (2) Given a certain work unit, what duration of rest is most effective? If one is to study for 30 minutes at a time, for example, should he rest 5 minutes, 10 minutes, 15 minutes, or longer between each study period?

Variations in the unit amount of work and in the length of the rest period, singly and together, both influence the progress of learning. However, the optimal work unit or rest interval, or the optimal combination of these, varies a great deal for different tasks, for different subjects, and for different degrees of motivation. We can illustrate this by describing three experiments in which there were (1) different amounts of work, (2) different durations of rest, and (3) different combinations of work and rest.

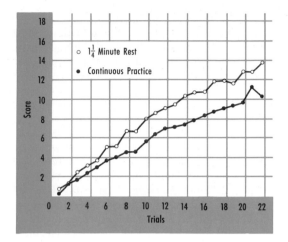

• 11.7

Learning as Influenced by the Rest Interval . Observe that the group with continuous practice did not, after the second trial, reach the performance level of the group given 1¼-minute rest intervals. The score was the number of syllables correctly anticipated (recalled without prompting). With the anticipation method, one syllable is given, and the subject tries to recall the next. If he fails to do so within a fixed period, the syllable is given, and he attempts to recall (anticipate) the next, and so on, until the last syllable is reached. (From S. T. H. Wright and D. W. Taylor, "Distributed Practice in Verbal Learning and the Maturation Hypothesis," *J. Exper. Psychol.*, 1949, 39, p. 529.)

• *Amount of work per period with the rest period constant.* Three comparable groups of college students were given six practice periods of, respectively, one, two, and four minutes on a pursuitmeter (p. 320). The rest interval in each case was three minutes. Comparisons were based on the percentage of the time in each practice period that the stylus was on the target. In all six trials the percentages for the two-minute group were higher than those for the other groups. This was true despite the fact that the two-minute group had a total of only twelve minutes of practice as compared with twenty-four minutes for the four-minute group.[47]

• *Constant amount of work with variation in the duration of rest.* In a study on the influ-

ence of different durations of rest, each work unit (trial) comprised 20 exposures of a list of 18 nonsense syllables. The group with massed learning had continuous practice for 22 trials; but other groups were given a rest of, respectively, 8, 3½, 2, and 1¼ minutes between trials. Figure 11.7 represents the learning of these 18 nonsense syllables by the group with no rest and the group with a 1¼-minute rest. The longer rest periods were all more economical than zero rest, but not more so than this shortest rest period.[48]

• *Work and rest periods independently varied in learning the same task.* This type of experiment is illustrated by a study which required students to pick up, turn over, and replace small cylindrical blocks in four rows of fifteen holes each (see Figure 11.8). Each subject's score was the number of blocks that he turned over. The design of the experiment is shown in Table 11.1. Observe that, with work constant at 10 seconds, rest periods of 10 and 30

• 11.8

The Minnesota Rate of Manipulation Test. As described in the text, the examinee must pick up, turn over, and replace the small cylindrical blocks, being timed while he does so. (Courtesy, Dr. Kenneth Clark)

■ **TABLE 11.1   Design of the Experiment**

Group	Work period	Rest period	Number of subjects
1	10 sec.	10 sec.	24
2	10 sec.	30 sec.	24
3	30 sec.	10 sec.	24
4	30 sec.	30 sec.	24

From G. A. Kimble and E. A. Bilodeau, "Work and Rest as Variables in Cyclical Motor Learning," *J. Exper. Psychol.*, 1949, *39*, p. 151, Table I.

seconds were used. With work constant at 30 seconds, 10- and 30-second rest periods were again used. This experimental design enabled the experimenters to discover which is a more important determiner of efficiency in performing the task, the amount of work or the duration of rest. It also indicated which combination of work and rest brings the most efficient learning. The results are summarized in Figure 11.9. Note that the 10-second work period yields higher average scores than the 30-second work period. We can thus say that a 10-second work period, for this task, is more economical than the 30-second work period. The 10-second work period is superior with a rest period of either length, so we can also say that the amount of work is a more significant variable than the rest period. But the efficiency of performance *does* also vary with the rest period. Observe that with either work unit, the 30-second rest is more economical than the 10-second rest. The most economical combination of work and rest is a 10-second work period and a 30-second rest.[49]

The most effective work unit for any task, as well as the most effective interval of rest, must, as we have already said, be determined for the particular task and subjects concerned. Indeed, it has been shown that here, as in experiments on details of intentional versus incidental learning, many variables influence the effectiveness of a particular procedure.[50]

Sometimes a practical situation arises which, despite its poor economy in other respects, may make practice with few rest periods (massed practice) more desirable than prac-

tice with relatively frequent rest periods (distributed practice). Suppose, for example, that skilled workers could be turned out with fewer lessons if their lessons were shortened, or came after a longer interval, but that skilled workers were needed in a hurry. Let us say that a certain skill is acquired in 50 standard lessons when lessons are given five times daily, and in only 30 when they are given one day apart. Distributed learning thus saves 20 lessons. With massed practice, however, a worker acquires the skill in 10 days; with distributed learning he acquires it in 30 days. Economy in time to get skilled workers, therefore, might dictate massed learning even though workers would need 20 trials in addition to those required if learning were distributed over a longer period.

● **11.9**

Learning as Influenced by Amount of Work and Duration of Rest Periods. The label 10–30 means a ten-second work period with a thirty-second rest between periods. This combination gave the highest scores (average number of blocks turned over and replaced). Note that both ten-second work groups reached a higher level of performance than either of the thirty-second work groups. With both work units, the thirty-second rest period yielded the higher scores. (From G. A. Kimble and E. A. Bilodeau, "Work and Rest as Variables in Cyclical Motor Learning," *J. Exper. Psychol.*, 1949, *39*, p. 153.)

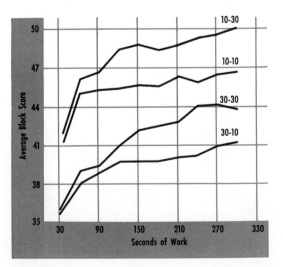

There is another practical consideration which might make a certain degree of massed learning better than distributed learning. Some individuals take a long time to "get down to business" in studying or other kinds of learning. These would waste a large proportion of each interval before accomplishing anything, hence, they might accomplish more if they worked for a longer period at a time.

Why distributed learning is economical

There are various reasons why distributed learning is generally more economical than massed learning. These reasons will be considered with respect to (1) the work unit, and (2) the rest period.

• *The length of the work unit.* If this is prolonged, fatigue may set in, thus offsetting the effectiveness of one's efforts. Everyone has experienced the "lost motion" of trying to study, or to accomplish anything else, while fatigued. A short work unit, moreover, usually produces better motivation than a long one. Extra effort is induced, as in a short sprint. But a large work unit induces us to save ourselves for the "long pull" ahead.

• *The rest period.* A rest period, like a short work unit, reduces fatigue and leads to improved motivation, but it has additional advantages. Once we stop work there is apparently a perseveration of neural processes aroused by our activities.* Such perseveration perhaps underlies the "running of a tune through the head." According to one theory, perseveration "consolidates" what has been learned. A rest period is thus assumed to be advantageous because intense external stimulation ceases and allows internal consolidation to occur.[52]

There is evidence supporting the view that organisms resist (are refractory to) early repetition of an act. This "reactive inhibition," as it is often called, may be a further reason for the relative ineffectiveness of massed learn-

ing. Rest periods obviously reduce the necessity for such repetition.[53]

One other factor may be of even greater importance than those already mentioned as favoring rest periods in learning. This is the tendency for incorrect associations (errors) to be forgotten faster than correct ones. We would expect such differential forgetting, the reason being that erroneous responses receive no positive reinforcement. But how does this bear upon the effectiveness of rest periods? The answer is that without a rest, forgetting cannot so readily occur. With an interval between trials, forgetting occurs, with the incorrect associations being weakened much faster than the correct ones. If the incorrect associations weaken faster than the correct ones there is of course a relative advantage to the latter when practice is resumed after the interval.[54]

We see, then, that fatigue, poor motivation, restricted perseveration, resistance to early repetition of an act, and hindrance to differential forgetting of correct and erroneous responses may all contribute to the lessened efficiency of massed as compared with distributed learning.

Recitation

The value of recitation versus mere reading has been investigated for memorizing a variety of verbal materials. The best-known study is one in which large groups of children from several grades memorized nonsense syllables and brief biographies.[55]

Some children put 100 per cent of their time into reading the material. A comparable group put 80 per cent of its time into reading, and 20 per cent into reciting what it had read. Another group, comparable with the others, put 60 per cent of its time into reading and 40 per cent into reciting, and so on, down to the group which put only 20 per cent of the time into reading and 80 per cent into reciting. The outcome was quite clear: the larger the percentage of recitation, up to the limit indicated, the greater the efficiency of learning. In this instance the largest amount of recitation was 80 per cent.

In a more recent investigation with fifth-

---

* This does not mean that the individual is rehearsing the material during the rest period. In fact it has been shown that rest periods are as advantageous in animal as in human learning. It is not likely that a rat, for example, would be implicitly rehearsing what it has been learning.[51]

and sixth-grade children memorizing nonsense syllables, arithmetical facts, a difficult English vocabulary, and spelling, almost all the various distributions of reading and recitation used were better than reading without any recitation. The results of both studies make it clear that recitation contributes to efficiency in memorizing.[56]

Why recitation should be more efficient than mere reading is fairly clear. In the first place, reading with the knowledge that one must soon recite what he is reading is conducive to good motivation — to what some have called "the will to learn." We have seen that intentional learning is often more efficient than incidental learning. In the second place, a recitation tells us how well we are progressing. It gives a better knowledge of results than could occur from passive reading. Every time we reproduce something read there is a reward element introduced, and every time we fail to reproduce an item there is an effect somewhat comparable to punishment for incorrect responses. In the third place, one must eventually recite the material — so the person who recites is practicing the sort of reproduction he aims to achieve.

Whole versus part learning

Perhaps the least generally applicable of the learning principles mentioned is that which refers to learning by parts as compared with learning by wholes. In part learning the individual concentrates on one portion of the material, or on one aspect of a skill, at a time. He masters the parts separately and then combines the separate habits so that the whole performance can be accomplished. The whole method, on the other hand, calls for concentration on the entire task at one time, without separate attention to subsidiary activities.

A vast amount of research in the laboratory, classroom, and industrial plant has been concentrated on determining the relative efficiencies of part, whole, and combination part-whole methods. These studies have involved a variety of tasks, such as maze learning, compensatory tracking, and memorizing verbal materials. Maze studies have involved rats, children, and adults. The tracking studies

used male college students. Both children and adults have learned verbal material under each of the various procedures mentioned above.

The general procedure in maze studies is as follows: The maze is divided into, let us say, four parts. As the subject gets to the end of one part he is introduced to the entrance of the next. The *part* group learns part one, then part two, then part three, and finally part four. It then receives further training, this time running the maze from beginning to end. This continues until the criterion of learning has been reached, which might be three successive trials without error. The *whole* group, comparable with the other, is trained on the entire maze from the start. A group may be included which learns by a *progressive part* method. That is to say, it learns part one, then runs part one and part two together. After learning this much, the subject runs parts one, two, and three as a unit. Finally it is running the whole maze.[57]

When verbal materials are used, the procedure is similar. Verses or other sections of a poem may be learned separately or within the whole. They may also be learned by a progressive part method.[58]

In one tracking study, the task was tridimensional.[59] There were three meters, each representing a different direction of movement, and the subject's task was to keep each indicator at zero position. He attempted to do this by moving a stick left — right, front — back, and clockwise-counterclockwise. Here again, the subject might learn one of these controls at a time or the entire pattern of control from the outset. He might also learn by the progressive part procedure. The effectiveness of a given training procedure is here evaluated through the transfer of skill to tasks involving different levels of complexity. In this particular study, better results were obtained with the whole and the progressive part methods than with the pure part method.

Research on part versus whole learning has had no outcome justifying a generalization that the whole method, the part method, or some combination of whole-part methods is most economical. Even with the same kind of material, the results have not all been in favor of one particular procedure. An excellent statement of the general outcome of research in this field has been given in Woodworth and Schlosberg's *Experimental Psychology:*

☐ "The net result of all the experimental studies of whole and part learning is something like this: the parts are easier to learn and the learner is often happier and better adjusted to the task if [he] begins with the parts. But he finds that putting the learned parts together requires much additional work. In the end he may have saved time and energy by commencing with the parts — or he may not — much depending on the size of the total 'lesson' and on his technique and patience. In a practical situation there is something to be said for the flexible plan of starting with the whole but watching for difficult spots that may call for special attention"[60] ■

THEORETICAL CONSIDERATIONS

Learned behavior and conditions which facilitate or hinder its acquisition have been described. But a mere descriptive account provides too limited a view of the learning process. Concerned primarily with facts, it disregards many issues of great interest, particularly questions relating to processes which must intervene when the organism is stimulated and a learned response occurs. As we said at the beginning of this book, psychologists are interested in stimulus-response aspects of behavior, but they are also interested in the organism that responds, the O of the S-O-R formula (p. 23). Thus, much attention is given to what is happening in O when it is stimulated and a response evoked.

We said earlier that theories are attempts to systematize what is already known about some field of investigation and to fill the gaps in our knowledge by further investigation. If a theoretical scheme (or model) is correct, then it enables us to predict, and to verify our predictions, concerning things at present unknown. To paraphrase an earlier quotation (p. 28) from James B. Conant, science involves "series of concepts and conceptual schemes" that are "fruitful of further experimentation and observations." The most useful theories

of learning are those which have clearly defined concepts and that generate hypotheses which may be tested experimentally. Some deal with the learning process in all of its phases, while others concentrate on particular aspects, such as neurological foundations or mathematical interpretations of the acquisition process.

Neurological theories of learning are focused on what happens in the nervous system when learning occurs, and the sort of modification which enables an organism to retain what it has learned. These theories deal with such questions as whether this modification is in the cell body, the synapse, or some special integration of nerve cells — some sort of "cell assembly."[61] Then there are such questions as whether the modification is structural (involving interconnections through new growth of nerve fibers), or chemical, or even electrical. Although this is a very active area of research, the final answers to neurological questions are not yet evident.

A complete understanding of the learning process would require explanation on several levels. By "explanation" is meant a detailed description of what is involved. Suppose, for instance, that we had enough information to say what changes in specified neural tissues occur while the organism is learning. Explanation on this level, however complete, would have very limited value out of context — that is, without information on concomitant aspects of the learning situation, such as the stimulating circumstances, the motivation of the organism, and so on. We would also need to know such things as *what* was being learned, how the stimulus-response aspects were interrelated spatially or temporally, and how the activities in progress produced the underlying neural changes, whatever their nature might be. Generally speaking, psychologists are more interested in explanation at the stimulus-response level than they are in neural explanations. That is, they seek a complete explanation of what organisms learn in particular situations and of how they learn. The question *how* is concerned not so much with neurophysiological questions as it is with the essential stimulus-response and motivational conditions involved in learning.

The question "*What* does an organism learn?" is deceptively simple. Take a rat in the maze, for example. One will answer, without thinking much about it, that the animal learns the maze — that it learns to find its way from the entrance to the exit. However, one theoretical envisagement of the learning process[62] says that the rat learns *responses*, which, as learning occurs, are automatically elicited by stimuli associated with the maze pathway and its surrounding stimulus-complex, such as directional sounds and odors. Another theory would have it that the animal is learning the *significance* of stimuli, and responding to them in terms of its *expectation* or *anticipation* of the consequences of responding to them in particular ways.[63] To put it crudely, the first theory views the animal pretty much as a robot whose responses are triggered by stimuli, while the second theory views it as a perceiving and knowledgeable creature. The issue boils down to this: Are learned responses elicited by stimuli as reflexes are elicited, or does their arousal depend upon such intervening implicit processes as perceptions, insights, and what the organism *knows*?

The clearest instance of the learning of a response, as such, is found in classical conditioning, where a more or less isolated action, rather than an integrated series of movements, is required. Salivation in response to a bell, or an eyeblink elicited by light, are good examples of this. In instrumental conditioning and problem-box learning the responses could be elicited directly by external stimuli, or they could be mediated by intervening variables, such as expectancies. As learning situations become more complex, there is an increasing

likelihood that, instead of being elicited automatically, responses will be influenced by implicit processes, or what one theorist called "cognitive* maps" and "means-ends expectancies."[64] Let us see how these opposing views of what is learned may be tested.

What is learned in the maze?

Viewed from the response-learning standpoint, maze learning by rats is *serial learning* or *response chaining*. These terms suggest that what the rat learns in such situations is a series of responses with each response providing stimulation for the next. At a particular choice point, the significant stimuli could come from previous movements; that is, from muscle tensions and other proprioceptive cues. They could come from something in the maze itself — intra-maze cues like odor, roughness, and sounds made by pattering feet. Or they could come from the extra-maze environment — from directional illumination, sounds, or odors. If this habit indeed involves serial learning, the subject learns to make the appropriate turns in response to successive stimuli or stimulus combinations. Thus, as stated above, the various turns would be reeled off automatically much as conditioned salivation comes in response to a bell.

Viewed from the opposing standpoint, the maze habit is something other than a chain of responses. It involves an element of knowledge as to what is going on. Those who hold to this interpretation say that the rat *learns a place* — the place where food is, the place

* From *cognition*, which means perceiving, knowing, or discerning.

● **11.10**

Performance on an Open Alley Maze. The same rat varies its route from trial to trial. It is always going to the same place, but its responses are not stereotyped. (From J. F. Dashiell, "Direction Orientation in Maze Running by the White Rat," *Comp. Psychol. Monogr.*, 1930, No. 7.)

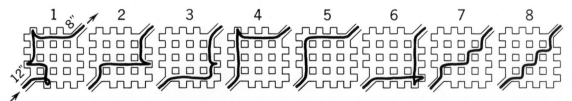

where escape is possible, and so on. According to this view,[65] it does not learn to respond automatically to a sequential arrangement of stimuli. Rather, the animal learns what the stimuli mean. It learns their significance as guideposts. It learns "what leads to what."[66]

There is indeed a great deal of evidence that, at least in some maze situations, rats learn a place rather than (or in addition to) a series of specific responses set off by particular stimuli. In a maze like that shown in Figure 11.10, where several equally short paths to food are open, the subject takes sometimes one path and sometimes another.[67] When short cuts are introduced into a maze, rats frequently take the shorter path.[68] Moreover, when they have learned to run through a maze with metal walls, which is then filled with water, they swim through it.[69] They follow the correct path despite the fact that swimming requires different responses than does running.

Actually there is no clear answer to the general question, "Does the rat learn specific responses to stimuli or does it learn a place?" The reason for this is that rats sometimes learn responses, sometimes a place, and sometimes both.

In a single-unit T-maze (Figure 11.11), rats learned a response or a place, depending upon the circumstances in which they found themselves; but even in learning a place they were dependent upon a specific form of stimulation that was associated with it.[70]

□ The rat ran along the elevated pathway from the starting place to the food cup. The stem leading to the choice point was shifted to the opposite side of the choice arm when the rat was to enter from that direction. The two arms beyond the choice point, each of which had a food cup at its farther end, were interchanged, thus varying olfactory or other intramaze stimuli which otherwise might serve as cues. The maze itself was in a room so constructed that there were no extra-maze directional cues except those which the investigator introduced for experimental purposes. Two such cues were introduced; a small light at each end of the goal arm at a distance six inches beyond the food cup.

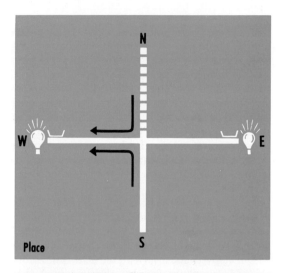

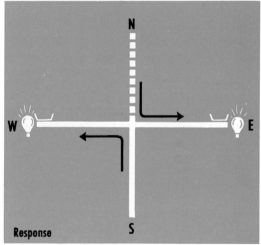

● 11.11

Place and Response Learning at a Choice Point. This was an elevated pathway. The broken line represents the fact that the entrance unit was at times shifted to that position. The place-learning rats went west, making a right turn when coming from N and a left turn when coming from S. Another place-learning group went to the east. The response-learning rats always made a left turn, which sent them to E when coming from N and to W when coming from S. Another group was trained to make a right turn every time. Food cups are shown schematically at E and W positions, with light bulbs beyond them. (After Scharlock)

There were four groups of twenty rats each. These had comparable preliminary training and were equated in other ways. During preliminary training it was found that some had a preference for a right, and others for a left turn. These were equally represented in each group. In the experiment proper, a rat was trained to turn in the opposite direction from its preference. Each subject was given four trials per day, spaced at least ten minutes apart. Training continued for seven consecutive days.

Two groups were trained to *make a specific response* (right for some rats, left for others) and to make the same response whether they entered from the N or S direction. In each set of daily trials, a rat entered two times from N and two times from S. Each animal that was to learn a right turn was thus fed at E when it came from S and at W when it came from N. Two other groups were trained to *learn a place*, W in the case of some and E in the case of others. A rat from either of these groups would, in always going to the same place, have to make a right turn if coming from one direction and a left turn if coming from the other. Thus a rat trained to go to E would need to make a right turn when coming from S and a left turn when coming from N.

Of the two *response* groups, one had a light near each food cup — and the other had a light at only one food cup — always at E for one animal and always at W for another. With two lights, the animal, whether it was turning always right or always left, was also going always toward a light. With only one light, a right-turning rat sometimes approached a light and sometimes went away from it.

Of the two *place* groups, one had a light at each end and the other had it only at one end — the end where the food was always found. Animals of the two-light place group were required to go to the same place, regardless of the direction from which the maze was entered, but since there was a light at each end, they had no extra-maze guidance as to where the food was. Of course they had no intra-maze guidance either — because the units were interchanged from trial to trial as already described. The one-light place group

did have extra-maze guidance. This is because a light was always at the place where food was found and not in the other direction. □

Generally speaking, the performance of response groups was superior to that of place groups. The two-light response group (always making the same turn and running toward a light) gave the best performance. Next came the one-light response group (making its turn sometimes toward and sometimes away from the light). In third place was the one-light place group (always with a light near the food place). The two-light place group (a light near the food place and also in the opposite direction) learned very little. We might have predicted such an outcome from the fact that animals of this group had no cue especially associated with the food place.

A further test with the one-light place group showed that these animals were indeed responding to the light and not to the food place itself. The light was moved from six inches beyond the food cup to twenty inches beyond it. Given another run under these circumstances, fourteen of the twenty ran off the end of the maze and landed on the floor. Four fell into the food cup and two stopped just in time.

The investigator concludes that "place performance and response performance are both based on learned discriminations, the cues supporting the former being primarily visual and those supporting the latter primarily proprioceptive."[71]

From other experiments, it appears that whether or not the animal is a "place learner" depends upon prior maze experience.[72] It may be that highly experienced rats develop a *set* for spatial exploration, thus facilitating place learning. As one writer puts it, the "maps" of naïve rats may be "narrow and confined" in comparison, hence lead them to depend more upon the acquiring of responses to particular stimulus aspects of the situation. It thus appears that "the rat in a maze is neither a mechanical automation nor a sagacious geometer surveying spatial relations. For naïve animals, at least, it appears that the truth lies somewhere between the two theoretical extremes."[73]

How does learning occur?

The answer to this question may well depend upon *what* is being learned. Psychologists who hold that there is basically only one kind of learning are those who, like Pavlov (p. 296), stress the idea that it is essentially a matter of developing S-R connections of the type observed in acquisition of conditioned responses. This is a relatively simple type of explanation. Such an approach, as we suggested at the beginning of this chapter, is sometimes referred to as *peripheralist*. That is to say, it emphasizes such outer aspects of the learning process as muscular reactions elicited by sensory stimuli. It plays down the possible role of the central nervous system in controlling learned behavior, an aspect stressed by the so-called *centralists*.

It should come as no surprise that it is the centralists who lay particular emphasis on insight, understanding, cognitive maps, and expectancy. These are complex processes which depend to a large extent on the involvement of the central nervous system, and particularly of the brain. Nor should it be surprising to learn that these are the same theorists who believe in more than one kind of learning process. For those referred to as peripheralist, there is basically one learning process, the development of S-R connections. Centralists, on the other hand, regard this as only one kind of learning — in fact, the simplest kind. Tolman[74] believed that there are at least six kinds of learning, conditioning being one of these. Now it seems that there are really two kinds of conditioning, classical and operant, each requiring its own explanation.[75] So we see that no agreement has been reached on this issue.

• *Hull's theory.* What is perhaps the best-known theory of how learning occurs is that of the late Professor Clark L. Hull (Figure 11.12).[76] This theory assumes that there is basically only one kind of learning. Hull developed an elaborate, logical, well-organized theory to deal in a most comprehensive way with learning and behavior. What Hull's theory postulates, basically, is that learning involves the acquisition of stimulus-response associations. Hull felt that when we have discovered how learned responses come to be as-

• 11.12

Professor Clark Hull (1884–1952). The curve partially visible on the blackboard is illustrative of Professor Hull's efforts to obtain quantitative data and treat them mathematically. Reaction potential ($_sE_R$) is shown decreasing as a function of extinction trials. $_sE_R$, which signifies "the strength of the tendency to respond," is itself regarded as a function of, among other things, habit strength ($_sH_R$) and drive (D). The simplest expression of this relationship is given by the equation, $_sE_R = D \times {}_sH_R$. For other factors which influence reaction potential, see the discussion on pages 132–136 in E. R. Hilgard, *Theories of Learning* (2nd ed.), Appleton-Century-Crofts, 1956. The quoted phrase is from Hilgard, page 132.

sociated with the stimuli which arouse them, we will perhaps be able to extend this knowledge to embrace all learning of whatever complexity. Knowledge, for example, might involve complicated acquired responses of brain mechanisms to relevant stimuli, internal or external.

Hull's theory is too detailed and complicated for adequate treatment at an elementary level. However, some of its essential aspects can be stated briefly.

☐ Repetition of stimulus-response associations, under conditions in which the organism's relevant drives are reduced by its activities, results in the gradual strengthening of S-R connections. That is to say, "The process of habit formation [accumulation of habit strength] consists of the physiological summation of a series of discrete increments, each increment resulting from a distinct receptor-effector conjunction closely associated with a reinforcing state of affairs."[77] Reinforcement may be *primary*, as when the hunger drive is reduced, or *secondary*, as when a stimulating situation associated with drive reduction serves as an incentive in itself.[78]

To the question, "What does the organism learn?" Hull thus answered that it learns S-R (or receptor-effector) connections: to respond to stimuli which training has made effective. To the question "How does it learn?" he answered that it learns through the gradual accumulation of habit strength, which accumulation depends upon the activation of receptor-effector processes in close contiguity with reinforcing conditions. Habit strength, defined as "a precise dynamic relationship between afferent and efferent neural impulses," is the most important intervening variable of Hull's system.[79] There are several others, but we cannot deal with them here. Although the aspects of this system that we have described are retained in modified versions, some other details have needed to be changed in view of the outcomes of research designed to test their soundness. ☐

Hull's learning theory is in many respects more comprehensive than any other, and it has stimulated more research. Hull himself realized that aspects of the theory would need modification as the testing of hypotheses derived from it made new information available. Such modification is taking place, largely at the hands of Professor Kenneth Spence, and the theory is now sometimes referred to as the Hull-Spence theory.[80]

• *Contiguity theory.* One important difference between Hull's attempt to explain how learning occurs and similar efforts by certain other theorists lies in the role attributed to reinforcement. Hull, as we have seen, regarded reinforcement (primary or secondary) as an essential condition. According to this view

there is *no* learning without reinforcement. The opposing theoretical position is that reinforcement, while having a great deal to do with the *efficient use* of what has been learned, is not essential to the acquisition process.

Guthrie,[81] for example, said that S-R contiguity (the simultaneous or near-simultaneous occurrence of a stimulus and a response) is sufficient to establish an association. There are, in fact, some findings which give a certain amount of support to such an assertion, especially with respect to acquisition of relatively simple associations. We have already discussed some relevant findings: sensory preconditioning (p. 343),[82] contiguous conditioning (p. 343),[83] incidental learning (p. 348).[84] Learning sometimes occurs in a single trial, as if all that was necessary to establish the S-R association took place through the sheer contiguity of S and R.[85] Associations between verbal units (words, nonsense syllables) has also been demonstrated under conditions which suggest that contiguity was solely responsible. Sometimes, however, what appears to be a purely contiguous association turns out, on closer examination, to have rather subtle motivational undercurrents. Thus, at the conclusion of an experiment on "association by contiguity," the investigators point out that their subjects, associating verbal items, were required to learn *something*, and this was perhaps motivating in itself. They say, "Whether or not associative learning would occur if pairs were presented to S without requiring auxiliary learning is not handled by the present experiments."[86]

While Tolman is not classed as a contiguity theorist, he did argue for nonreinforced learning. He believed that there was evidence for this in the experiments on latent learning.

☐ In a typical latent learning experiment there are three equivalent groups of hungry animals. One of these (the rewarded group) receives food whenever it gets to the exit of a maze. Another (nonrewarded group) is subjected to the same training conditions except that it receives no food at the end of the maze. It is fed outside of the maze, sometime after the day's run. Under these conditions, the rewarded group exhibits a steady reduction in errors (and time) as the daily trials continue.

See Figure 11.3 (p. 344). The nonrewarded group exhibits some learning, but the learning curve levels off by about the tenth or eleventh trial and there is no further progress. The third group, up to this point, is treated exactly like the nonrewarded group. Then, beginning with the eleventh trial, food is found at the maze exit. What happens now is that the learning curve drops, within one or two trials, to the same level as that of the group rewarded since the experiment began, a group that has had twelve rewarded trials.[87]

Such a sudden improvement suggests that the animals had acquired information which they did not utilize until (after the tenth day) it became advantageous for them to do so. That they acquired this information without reinforcement from food is obvious. But what about other possible sources of reinforcement? Some reinforcing conditions may be present in the maze situation. If the animal has an exploratory drive (curiosity), the satisfaction of this would itself provide reinforcement. Being removed from the maze, as well as returning to the home cage, might also be reinforcing. Any hindrance to the rat's ongoing activity, such as running into a blind alley and having to turn around to get out, might serve as negative reinforcement. The fact that hungry nonrewarded animals show some improvement in performance can be accounted for in such ways, and also by the fact that they were acquiring information about "what-leads-to-what," which they later utilized when rewarded with food. □

We see, therefore, that the latent learning phenomenon provides no clear proof of unreinforced learning. If this phenomenon could be obtained without any kind of reinforcement at all, it would then provide support for the idea that contiguity is a sufficient condition for learning, or at least for acquiring information. One would then have to suppose that, in wandering through the maze pathway, the animal just happened to notice certain stimulating circumstances (and associations between these and particular turning responses) and also that it retained this information in usable form, even though it had no reason at the time, for doing so.

Contiguity is essential for learning. None of the theories question that. The only issue is whether it is sufficient, in and of itself, without reinforcement. It appears, from what we have said about it, that contiguity may be sufficient to account for something relatively simple, like so-called contiguous conditioning (p. 343), but that learning at higher levels of complexity requires reinforcement.

While we are on the subject of how learning occurs, a somewhat different theoretical approach should be called to the reader's attention. This is a mathematical approach.

• *Mathematical learning theory.* One well-known mathematical theory, the "statistical model" of Professor Estes, begins with the proposition that learning is explicable in terms of probability. The situation in which learning occurs is "represented by a set of S stimulus elements and the effective stimulation on any trial is represented by a randomly drawn subset of elements."[88] What this means is that there are many stimuli (or aspects of the learning situation) to which the organism might respond (in the sense of noticing them) and that it responds to these indiscriminately at first. Possible overt responses in the given situation are many. In a bar-pressing situation, for example, the rat may paw the side of the cage, run along the floor, scratch himself, sniff at various locations, and so on. It is assumed by Estes, however, that particular responses, in a given situation, have a certain probability of occurrence, and that this probability rises as training proceeds. Thus, "in the operant conditioning situation, the momentary probability of the bar-pressing response is the theoretical dependent variable."[89] Moreover, the "relations between response probabilities and experimentally defined response measures are derivable by application of probability theory."[90]

With respect to the acquisition process itself, it is assumed that, on any trial, "all stimulus elements sampled by the organism become connected to the response reinforced on that trial." As training proceeds, the reinforced response "receives an increment in probability"[91] and at the same time there is "a compensating decrease in the probability of other responses."[92]

Although the term "reinforcement" is used by Estes, his is not necessarily a reinforcement theory because its basic principles would apply equally well if contiguity should turn out to be a sufficient basis for learning. If this were so, it could be said that stimulus elements which the organism samples (which it notices, for example) become connected to the response that is contiguous with them. There is much more to this theory than one could describe in a elementary textbook, but the foregoing indicates its basic aspects. In certain respects it is not essentially different from Hull's theory, which, as we have seen, also looks upon learning as a gradual strengthening of S-R connections. Both theories are able to predict the shape of the acquisition curve for relatively simple habits.

Statistical learning theory has stimulated several investigations of *probability learning*, the results of which may be regarded as providing some support for it. On each trial, the subject is confronted with a two-choice situation. Perhaps there are two levers; one is to be pressed. The problem is like a guessing game in that the subject must decide which one to press. Sometimes one lever yields a reward, sometimes the other. If reinforcement of a particular lever were 100 per cent, the subject would soon learn this and then press it always. But reinforcement is less than 100 per cent. One group of subjects is, let us say, given reinforcement 70 per cent of the time for pressing one lever and 30 per cent of the time for pressing the other. Another group is reinforced 80 per cent for one and 20 per cent for the other. And so on, with other probabilities of reinforcement. According to statistical learning theory, the learning curve for each group will rise to a level of accuracy which matches the probability of reinforcement. Thus the final accuracy of the 70 per cent reinforcement group will approximate 70 per cent; that of the 80 per cent group, 80 per cent; and so on.

Several experiments with rats and human subjects have brought outcomes in accordance with the above predictions.[93] There are certain training situations, however, which yield results contrary to those predicted.[94] One can

therefore expect that the theory will be modified in an attempt to make it more generally applicable.

• *Some basic conditions.* It remains to be seen whether learning of every degree of complexity can be reduced to a common basis and explained by any single theory. If there is basically only one kind of learning, then we may look for one set of principles capable of explaining every acquisition. On the other hand, if there are basically dissimilar learning processes, we shall need a somewhat different model to explain each. In any event, it seems at the present time that learning theory, in one way or another, must take cognizance of three important principles: namely, contiguity, reinforcement, and repetition.

We have seen that contiguity is an *essential* aspect of learning, whether or not it is ever sufficient in itself to explain the process. Reinforcement (primary or secondary) is generally conceded to be important for *efficient* learning, even though there are alleged instances of learning without reinforcement. Repetition (trials, practice periods, pairings of S and R) is usually required, even though learning sometimes occurs in a single trial. The latter may happen when the stimulus involved is intense (vivid) and the consequences of response are painful, as when the child touches a hot stove. Under emotional circumstances we sometimes learn an association in an instant, even the name which goes with a certain face. We may learn a performance, moreover, by imitating someone, and with only one demonstration. This may be true if we already have the component skills and need only integrate them in the demonstrated fashion. In most learning, on the other hand, a certain amount of repetition is necessary. This is sometimes referred to as the principle of *exercise*, or of *frequency*. The basic idea is that, in order to strengthen a stimulus-response association, one must repeatedly present the learning situation. Several investigations have, however, shown that mere repetition is ineffective.[95] We saw this in attempts to develop skills without knowledge of results.

Except in rare instances, if learning is to

occur, one must repeat *in close contiguity*, the *stimulating circumstances*, the *responses elicited* by these, and the *associated reinforcement*, whether primary or secondary. When this combination occurs repeatedly, the usual result is greater frequency, magnitude, or fixation of the reinforced responses. Responses not followed by positive reinforcement or those negatively reinforced tend to drop out, to be extinguished. This principle holds even though reinforcement may be intermittent.

Much of the current research on learning is centered on the theoretical issues that we have discussed. The results of current experimental studies of these problems are bound to have important implications not only for learning theory but also for other aspects of psychology, such as perception, motivation, individual differences, personality, and the field of applied psychology, including education. ∎

• SUMMARY

Learning is a modification of behavior resulting from what happens to the organism, or from what it does, rather than from the growth processes which characterize its race. Unlearned reactions are, by contrast, racial in origin and their development in the individual is a maturational process. Although learning and maturation are basically different processes, the level of maturation places limits upon what is or can be learned.

Since learning is a stimulus-response affair, sensory processes are of great importance for the learner. In acquiring any skill, the organism uses all of its senses that are relevant to that skill. Nevertheless, some skills are primarily visual, others primarily auditory, and so on. Experiments on sensory deprivation show that as more senses are rendered ineffective, there is a corresponding decline in learning ability. Rats deprived of vision, hearing, and smell are unable to learn complex mazes, apparently because their other senses do not provide sufficient information about the maze pathway. One of these senses, kinesthesis, is important in controlling habits once they are formed.

All but the simplest forms of learning require participation of the cerebrum. Maze-learning ability in rats is reduced by cerebral lesions, but the detailed findings are subject to different interpretations. The mass-action theory supposes that the entire cerebrum participates in learning and that the amount of tissue destroyed, rather than its location, is of major importance. One conception of mass action supposes that different parts of the cerebrum, so far as maze learning is concerned, are equipotential. That is, that each part contributes equally to this habit. Another interpretation is that lesions of the same size in different regions of the cerebrum disturb different combinations of senses, and that one combination is no more important than another. However, it can be shown that brain damage does more than disturb sensory processes — it interferes with integrative, or associational processes as well. The mass-action concept has also been questioned on the grounds of its generality, even in rats. When they are reared in a highly stimulating environment and tested in maze situations which require observational learning, operated rats do not show mass-action effects alone. The location of the lesion as well as its size is important.

In the learning of sensory discriminations and special motor skills, particular sensory or motor regions of the cerebrum must be intact. These localized sensory and motor regions become increasingly important as the human level is approached. The higher learning processes, such as recall memory and reasoning, may also depend to a large extent upon localized brain tissues, those in the frontal regions. This again, is a controversial issue. Frontal lesions might interfere with higher learning processes because these are localized in the frontal lobes or only because frontal injuries, more than those in other parts of the brain, disrupt the vigilance that is so important in these complex forms of learning.

Motivation is an important, possibly an essential aspect of all learning. Experimental studies have emphasized such incentives as material rewards (food, money), praise, and social recognition. The relative effectiveness of different incentives depends upon the particular learner and also, to some extent, upon what is being learned. Knowledge of results adds to the efficiency of learning because it motivates and also because it facilitates repetition of correct responses and the correction of errors.

Intentional learning is usually superior to incidental, or passive, learning. The intention to learn is essential for acquisition of complex skills. When incidental learning does occur, important factors are: what is being learned, how the learner has been instructed, and the rate at which material to be learned is presented. The role of awareness in learning is a controversial issue. Some psychologists believe that learning can occur while the learner is unconscious of what is going on. This would be a clear instance of incidental learning. There is contrary evidence, however. We have described some experiments in which only those who were aware learned anything. Related to this issue is that of so-called sleep learning. In experiments which seemed to demonstrate learning while the subjects were asleep, it now appears that the subjects may have been intermittently asleep and awake, or only drowsy. Even so, they were learning very simple material, and material that would have been learned more efficiently if they were awake and alert.

Distributed learning is generally more economical than massed learning. One possible reason is that, during a rest period, errors are forgotten faster than correct responses. Recitation is more economical than a mere reading of what is to be learned. One important reason is that recitation provides knowledge of how well, or how poorly, one is doing. Whole learning is sometimes more economical than part learning and sometimes not, depending upon the learner and the length and difficulty of what is being learned.

Theorists attempt to integrate what is already known about the learning process and to fill the gaps in our knowledge by generating, from their theoretical models, hypotheses (or predictions) which may be tested experimentally. Learning theories are particularly concerned with *what* is learned (information, responses, or both) and with *how* learning occurs. The question of what is learned has been tested with rats in maze situations. Here the more specific issue is whether the animals merely learn S-R connections (responses elicited more or less automatically by stimuli) or whether they learn a place (a location associated with food and represented implicitly by something analogous to a map showing what leads to what — a so-called cognitive map). Rats apparently do not resolve the issue for us, because it appears that they sometimes learn a response and sometimes a place. They may even learn both concurrently. The issue of how learning occurs is also a difficult one to answer. For a complete explanation of how learning takes place we would need detailed description of what happens at various levels — neural, motivational, stimulus-response, and even mathematical, in that stimulus and response probabilities are involved.

One of the most comprehensive theories (that of Hull) focuses upon the question of how S-R connections get established. It assumes, on the basis of a great deal of experimental evidence, that reinforcement (primary or secondary) is essential. Like all other theories, it looks upon contiguity as an essential condition, although not (in contrast with certain other theories) as a sufficient condition. It was Hull's hope that, from the explanation of S-R connections, we might eventually explain even the most complex acquisitions in terms of the same principles. His theory is undergoing refinement and modification as research generated by it makes new information available.

Certain other theories take issue with Hull's, chiefly with respect to *what* is learned and the role of reinforcement in learning. Tolman's theory, for example, stresses "cognitive maps," as against S-R connections, and takes the stand that at least some learning takes place without reinforcement. In acquiring information, for instance, contiguity is regarded as a sufficient basis. We have seen, in fact, that there is some evidence for purely contiguous learning of relatively simple associations (sensory preconditioning, contiguous conditioning). Tolman stressed the evidence from latent learning experiments. Our discussion of some representative experiments indicated that although latent learning no doubt occurs, there is a good possibility that reinforcement of a relatively subtle kind is involved. There is a good possibility, in fact, that there is more than one learning process and that each will require an explanation somewhat peculiar to itself. Sensory preconditioning and some other relatively simple acquisitions may require only the repetition of contiguous relationships. Other types of acquisition may require repetition of contiguous S-R associations and reinforcement at the same time. With the limited information now available it would be hazardous to attempt to predict the final outcome of such theoretical issues.

Mathematical learning theory takes its departure from certain mathematical concepts. Estes' statistical theory, the only mathematical model that we mentioned, attempts to account for learning on a probabilistic basis, i.e., in terms of probability theory. Probability applies to the stimulating circumstances (the chances that particular aspects of the total stimulus-complex will be noticed by the organism), to the organism's response repertoire (which response, out of all possible responses, will occur), and to the chances that a particular set of stimulus elements will be noticed at the same time that a response occurs and is reinforced. Although Estes uses the concept of reinforcement, it is not a necessary part of his theoretical model. The theory might apply equally well if a contiguous occurrence of S and R should turn out to be all that is essential for learning. One prediction from this theory is that organisms will learn to discriminate in terms of the probabilities of reinforcement. The outcomes of some experiments support this prediction. Other experiments have shown that modifications in the theory are necessary before it can be applied to every two-choice situation involving probability learning.

In our discussion of learning theory we have seen that every theory, in some way, takes cognizance of three important variables — contiguity, reinforcement, and repetition. ∎

REFERENCES AND NOTES FOR THIS CHAPTER ARE IN THE APPENDIX.

• SELECTED READINGS

Beach, F. A., D. O. Hebb, C. T. Morgan, and H. Nissen, *The Neuropsychology of Lashley.* McGraw-Hill, 1960. This includes Lashley's papers, to which we have referred in this chapter.

Deese, J., *The Psychology of Learning* (2nd ed.). McGraw-Hill, 1958. Chapter 12 deals directly with theoretical issues.

Estes, W. K., S. Koch, K. MacCorquodale, P. E. Meehl, C. G. Mueller, Jr., W. N. Schoenfeld, and W. S. Verplanck, *Modern Learning Theory.* Appleton-Century-Crofts, 1954. The theoretical systems of Hull, Tolman, Skinner, Lewin, and Guthrie are discussed.

Hilgard, E. R., *Theories of Learning* (2nd ed.). Appleton-Century-Crofts, 1956. A broad survey of all current theories.

Koch, S. (Ed.), *Psychology: A Study of a Science,* Vol. 2. McGraw-Hill, 1959. See the chapters by Tolman, Guthrie, and Estes on their learning theories; also Logan's chapter on the Hull-Spence theory.

McGeoch, J. A., and A. L. Irion, *The Psychology of Human Learning* (2nd ed.). Longmans, Green, 1952. Although several chapters are relevant, Chapters 5 (distribution of learning), 7 (the law of effect), and 8 (the role of frequency) will be particularly helpful.

Melton, A. W. (Ed.), *Categories of Human Learning*. Academic Press, 1964. See the discussions by Estes (probability learning) and Postman (incidental learning).

Mowrer, O. H., *Learning Theory and Behavior*. Wiley, 1960. An attempt to synthesize the vast amount of information on learning. This is for the student who wishes to dig deeply into the area that we have barely touched upon in this chapter.

Woodworth, R. S., and M. R. Sheehan, *Contemporary Schools of Psychology* (rev. ed.). Holt, 1964. The discussions of associationism, behaviorism, and gestalt psychology present, in a concise manner, some of the major theoretical approaches to learning.

12

Remembering and Forgetting

So far our discussion of the learning process has emphasized acquisition. Now, in turning to memory, we give special consideration to the retention and recall of what has been learned.

Remembering is retaining, although not necessarily with awareness of what has been retained. Even if awareness is necessary for learning (p. 350), many acts, once learned, are performed automatically without our being conscious of what we are doing. This is especially true of motor skills. Underlying motor skills there is also memory; but it is memory in the sense of neural retention, without involvement of processes which one can verbalize. Retention without awareness is sometimes referred to as "biological memory."

Without memory in at least the biological sense there could be no learning. On each trial the organism would, so to speak, "start from scratch." Instead of this there is, as we have seen, a more or less progressive change as training or practice continues. The organism responds to a previously neutral stimulus, there are more correct responses, a task is performed with a decreased expenditure of energy.

Here we are not so directly concerned with biological aspects of retention as we are with memory on a more or less symbolic level. At this level memory is evidenced by such things as recalling something in its absence (perhaps mediated by so-called memory images), recognizing that a particular object or event has been experienced before (sometimes referred to as a "feeling of familiarity"), reciting a poem that one has memorized (memory involving obvious verbal mediation), and consciously performing some verbal or motor activity after witnessing another's performance.

Learning, retaining, recall, recognition, and forgetting are clearly interdependent processes. Whatever makes for good learning is advantageous because it facilitates retention in all of its aspects. Conversely, poor learning is generally followed by quick forgetting. In fact we can think of forgetting as the obverse of retention.

Remembering and forgetting vary in degree. To all appearances we may retain (or forget) some knowledge or some skill completely, partially, or not at all. We say "to all appearances" because it is impossible to prove that anything once learned is ever completely forgotten.

If you were asked to describe your earliest experience, you would recall events that, seemingly, had been completely forgotten before you began to probe the remote past. Your memories would most likely go no further back than your third or fourth year, although there are some authentic instances of memories going back to the first year.[1]

Memory for something may be complete, it may be partial, or it may, as far as appearances go, be negligible. In the latter instance, however, forgetting may still not be complete. Suppose, for example, that you learned a poem as a child. You may be able to recall it completely, reciting it word for word, just as you did as a child. Perhaps you cannot recall the poem, even partially, but you can recognize it as one learned in childhood. Among many other poems which you did not learn, it appears familiar. Perhaps you cannot even recognize the poem. But since you learned it as a child, the chances are that you will be able to relearn it with a saving in the repetitions required. That is to say, you memorize it now much more readily than you memorize poems of comparable difficulty which you never before learned. In this event there is some retention, small as it may be.

Evidence of memory comes, then, from several sources. An organism may reproduce some motor performance, it may relearn with a saving in time and effort some response which it cannot perfectly reproduce, it may respond in terms of some stimulus which has been present but which is absent at the time (like looking for a lost object), and it may select from a random assortment of objects some object shown to it previously. When language is present there may also be verbal evidences of memory.

THE MEMORY TRACE

While awake we are constantly being bombarded by more potential information than we can grasp, or retain. There are various selective (or limiting) factors. We are not interested in everything presented to our senses and, even if we were, our sensory and neural mechanisms could not process so much information. It is as though available information were filtered in various ways before transmission to the neural mechanisms which might retain it.[2]

☐ One aspect of this filtering process is illustrated in the "span of attention" or "span of perception" experiment. Suppose, for example, that you are told to look at a screen, and also that you are asked to report what you can of the material flashed upon it. Now twelve items (words, letters, digits, or forms) are exposed for, let us say, 100 milliseconds (1/10 sec.). Like most other subjects, you will be able to remember only four or five of the exposed items. However, you will perhaps be aware of seeing more than this. Some interesting research, the details of which cannot be dealt with here, has demonstrated that, although only four or five items get into "permanent memory storage," there is a "short-term memory" for more items than are in the memory span.[3] This lasts for approximately 270 msec. (a little more than 1/4 sec.). Immediately after exposure, the short-term storage begins to fade. It fades until, after about 1/4 sec., only four or five items remain. These are retained on a relatively permanent basis.

The fading memory trace in short-term visual memory is revealed through a sampling procedure in which the subject reports designated items, after short intervals, rather than attempting to recall the whole. Whether this trace is visual (in the form of a visual image which fades) or represented by some weakening neural process is not evident. ☐

Whenever we retain anything more or less permanently, there must be a correlated change of some kind in the nervous system. This is often referred to as a "memory trace," "a neurogram," or an "engram." The word "engram" is probably the most general term that may be used for the intervening variable which makes retention possible. This is because it does not imply anything about the anatomical or other characteristics of the nerve cells or neural integrations involved. In an earlier discussion of the associative functions of the cerebral cortex we referred to the idea that engrams are modifications analogous, in some ways, to the molecular changes in a magnetic tape which allow us to play back what was recorded. Pavlov's model (Figure 10.1) of what takes place when conditioned responses are acquired assumes that new neural connections are formed. Essentially the same idea has been held by some to account for verbal associations, as when a student learns that the French equivalent of *man* is *homme*. This is no doubt a gross oversimplification; moreover, other neural theories, while stressing new connections in the cerebral cortex, involve models of far greater complexity, even including the idea that reverberating circuits (see p. 50) carry the memory traces.[4]

Some theories of the engram go beyond neuroanatomy to the biochemistry of nerve cells. These are sometimes referred to as "molecular theories of memory." One of these, based on research with planaria and rats, gives particular attention to the idea that "memory storage" is dependent upon RNA (ribonucleic acid) metabolism.[5] However, as two recent reviewers have pointed out, the results alleged to support the RNA theory could be interpreted in two different ways.[6] Thus:

☐ (1) "RNA molecules, like many other types of molecules, are important constituents of the nervous system whose structural and functional state may change dramatically during a learning experience, but they do not function as permanent memory traces."

Or (2) "RNA molecules do have a unique role in the nervous system, that of serving as the final engram of experiential memory, the permanent memory trace."

However, "a comprehensive theory of the structural basis of memory must also consider the function of the entire neuron, with consequent emphasis on the reciprocal relationships between the cell body and the synapse, as well as the complex functional interrelationships between neurons." ☐

Although neural theories of the engram stress the interrelationships among neurons, they do not preclude the possibility that RNA or other biochemical aspects are important. As an example of neurological theorizing, the following statement by an eminent neurologist is interesting.

☐ "Memory involves the making of an impression by an experience, the retention of some record of this impression and the re-entry of this record into consciousness (or behavior) as recall and recognition. . . .

"The human brain is composed of some 10 billion nerve cells, more or less alike, which interact in various ways. Each cell contributes to behavior, and presumably to mental activity, by firing impulses or failing to fire. All the phenomena of memory must be explained in terms of the temporal and spatial patterns of these discharges.

"If experience is to modify behavior, the activity of neurons connected with an experience must alter their subsequent activity patterns. Two general questions regarding the neural trace must be asked, and both can be given a reasonable, if not a certain, answer today. The first is: Does memory depend on a continuing activity or on some static residue, some structural alteration, left behind by past activity? Is a river the water flowing in it or the channel the water cuts? The answer today is tending strongly toward the latter. The second question is: Is the structural trace (or dynamic process) for each memory located in a particular region, or are memory traces suffused through the brain in some way? Are memories marks placed on violin strings or are they wave trains playing over these strings? The latter would imply dynamic memory, but the trace would still be structural, like the wiggled groove on a phonograph record. Whether the trace is localized or diffuse, its exact nature is a third, if somewhat subsidiary question. Current investigations suggest that there are multiple patterns of local traces rather than a single well-localized one, but the nature of the trace is almost pure guess."[7] ☐

In speaking of an engram, therefore, one refers in the most general way to whatever it is that underlies memory. This discussion is also relevant to forgetting because, when we forget, the trace must have been obliterated, or else rendered ineffective by something which interferes with its expression in behavior.

In view of our ignorance of what actually takes place in the nervous system when we learn, some investigators prefer to make no assumptions about neural traces. With respect to the *man-homme* association, for example, they are satisfied to speak of the *associative strength* of the connection, by which they mean merely that, as practice continues, there is an increasing probability that, given the stimulus *man*, the response *homme* will follow.[8] They are perfectly satisfied to leave speculation about the nature of neural traces to neurologists and biochemists.

Our discussion of the memory process begins with nonverbal evidence of retention. ■

NONVERBAL EVIDENCE OF RETENTION

In animals (and in children before language develops) there is no evidence of retention except through nonverbal behavior. This evidence comes from *reproduction of* a performance learned some time earlier, and from the ability of the organism to *relearn* a skill in fewer trials, with fewer errors, or in less time than in learning it originally.

Reproducing a motor performance

Suppose, for example, that a rat or a human being has learned a maze to the criterion of three trials in succession without error. The next day, or a week or a month later, we may wish to see whether the habit has been retained. If the subject can traverse the maze for three trials without error, we say that it remembers perfectly — that there has been no forgetting.

Some rats have retained simple problem-box habits perfectly for as long as a month. Still higher organisms may retain such habits for months or years. It is probable that human beings have better retention than any other organism. Prolonged practice on tracking skills (see p. 320) has been followed by perfect retention after as long a period as two years.[9] On the other hand, an especially difficult tracking task, also practiced extensively, exhibited some decrement after only six months.[10] Where a decrement does occur, it can usually be overcome with relatively little further practice. These skills, learned in the laboratory, are hardly comparable with most of the skills of everyday life. You may not have ridden a bicycle for many years, yet will still be able to do so. In the case of a skill like typing, however, some decrement is to be expected, especially with respect to speed.

How long we retain a motor habit perfectly depends to a large degree on how much we have practiced it. Skills like eating with a knife and fork, buttoning and unbuttoning clothes, and writing are practiced so frequently that, even if something should prevent us from practicing them for many years, they would be retained without noticeable loss.

The almost perfect retention of motor skills over long periods has led some to suppose that such skills are necessarily better retained than verbal skills. That this is not so has been demonstrated in experiments where predominantly verbal activities (memorizing nonsense syllables) and predominantly motor activities (learning mazes) have received equal repetition. Under these circumstances, retention of motor skills is no better than retention of verbal ones.[11]

It has been argued in this connection, however, that human maze performance involves verbal elements and hence that the investigators were comparing one verbal skill with a motor skill which was to a great extent verbal. Pursuitmeter learning (p. 320) is probably less verbalized than maze performance, and more recent research has shown that, after equal practice, retention of this motor skill is far superior to retention of nonsense syllables.[12] This seems to support the point about verbalization. In developing pursuitmeter skills, however, the subject seems to be learning one instead of several things. The motor task is unitary and highly integrated. A list of nonsense syllables, by comparison, consists of several things to be learned. It is piecemeal, or loosely organized. One might expect the more unitary task to show a greater resistance to disintegration during a period of no practice,

hence have superior retention. But what happens when motor and verbal tasks are both closely integrated? A study involving operation of switches versus memorization of nonsense syllables arranged in a pattern corresponding to the switches was designed to answer this question. Retention of the motor habit was superior, but not significantly so.[13]

The conclusion that one may draw from these studies is that motor skills acquired in the course of everyday life are retained better than verbal skills because many of them are overlearned as compared with verbal skills, and also because they are better integrated. Still another reason for better retention of motor skills in everyday life is perhaps the fact that most of them are learned under better motivation than are most verbal skills. One would expect, in short, that equally practiced, equally integrated, and equally interesting motor and verbal skills would be equally well retained.

Relearning as evidence of memory

Suppose that retention is not perfect. Some forgetting has occurred. But how much? The amount retained can be measured by the *savings method*, a method used with animals as well as human beings.

In order to discover the degree of retention (or forgetting), we require that the task be relearned to the same criterion as that originally involved. Thus, if the maze was learned to the point where it could be traveled three times in succession without error, it is relearned to the same criterion. We then compare the original performance with the relearning performance.

Suppose, for example, that a rat required twenty trials to learn a maze and only five trials to relearn it some time later. The saving is fifteen trials, or 75 per cent of the trials originally required. The rat has forgotten 25 per cent. In one maze-learning experiment with rats, there was a saving in trials and time to relearn which averaged 90 per cent after two weeks, 88 per cent after four weeks, 85 per cent after six weeks, and 73 per cent after eight weeks.[14]

Subjects may learn verbal materials until they can be recited without error. Weeks, months, or years later, the material may be partially forgotten. By relearning it to the criterion of one perfect repetition, and comparing the repetitions required with those originally involved, the amount or percentage of retention can be determined.

☐ A saving in time and effort required for learning may occur even when the material was originally not learned to the point where it could be recalled, and even where there was no evident attempt to memorize it. This is illustrated by an experiment in which a psychologist read certain Greek passages to his child between the ages of fifteen and thirty-six months, and several years later required the child to memorize them. Some of the passages were learned at the age of eight and a half years and others at the age of fourteen years. In each instance the repetitions required to memorize the material read to the child were fewer than those required to memorize new passages of equal difficulty. The average number of repetitions required at eight and a half years was 317 for learning the passages presented earlier and 435 repetitions for learning the new passages, a saving of 27 per cent. Hearing the passages in childhood, although it did not produce recall, led to a saving of 27 per cent when learning to the point of recall was later required. The materials learned at fourteen years yielded a saving of only 8 per cent. Thus, the effects of earlier experience with the Greek passages apparently grew weaker with time.[15] ■

THE DELAYED REACTION

Tests of delayed reaction are used to obtain evidence of recall in animals and infants. The ability to respond in terms of an absent stimulus in a delayed-reaction test signals the emergence of an elementary symbolic process. This point receives further elaboration in the following discussion.

In the original experiment on delayed reactions in animals the apparatus represented in Figure 12.1 was used.[16] The subject was first trained to associate a lighted compartment with food and an unlighted compartment with an

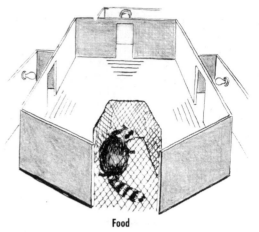

Food

● **12.1**
Hunter's Delayed-Reaction Apparatus. This particular form of the apparatus was used with raccoons. The animal in the release box could be stimulated by the lights. It was required to associate a light, appearing in any one of the three doors in a chance order, with the presence of food. An electric shock was administered whenever the animal attempted to enter an unlighted chamber. Food was obtained at the front of the apparatus whenever the correct chamber had been entered. In the training series the release box was raised while the light was still on. After the association between a lighted compartment and food had been thoroughly established, the light was turned off before release. The animal was now required to remember in which compartment the light had appeared. If it continued to go to the previously illuminated compartment, a longer delay between turning off the light and raising the release cage was instituted. The time of delay was gradually increased until the animal could no longer remember which compartment had been illuminated.

electric shock. The lighted compartment varied in position in a random sequence from trial to trial so that the problem could not be learned merely by going to the middle door, to the right-hand door, to the left-hand door, or to the three doors in any particular sequence. If it learned this part of the problem at all, the subject did so on the basis of response to the light.

After the subject came to select the lighted compartment at every trial, the delayed-reaction tests were instituted. The light was turned on in a compartment, but turned off before the animal was released. In order to respond to the previously lighted compartment, it was now necessary to remember in which compartment the light had been. If the interval between turning off the light and release was one minute, and the animal consistently went to the previously lighted compartment in a series of trials, it was credited with remembering for one minute — or, more specifically, recalling after one minute. The delay could then be increased until a marked inaccuracy of performance occurred.

Rats and dogs did not respond correctly after an interval of even a few seconds unless they kept their heads turned toward the correct compartment. This motor set — involving muscle tensions — enabled them to respond correctly. Raccoons and children, on the other hand, did not need to maintain a motor set. They moved around in the release box and, after it was raised, turned and proceeded toward the correct compartment.

In rats and dogs there was no evidence of response to an absent stimulus. Although the light was off, kinesthetic stimuli associated with the fixed position of the body were present to guide them. The raccoons and children, on the other hand, maintained no motor set — hence, they had neither the light nor kinesthetic stimuli for guidance. Controls showed that no other external stimuli were acting as cues. The investigator thus concluded that the raccoons and children were guided by some implicit process which represented the absent light. This he called a *symbolic process*. He defined the symbolic process as "any process which is a substitute, which can arouse a selective response, and which can be recalled if it ceases to be present."

In the case of raccoons and children, something inside of the organism — presumably some sort of memory trace — substituted for the light. Its function was selective because it guided them to the previously lighted compartment — not to any or all compartments. The engram was presumably not functioning

while the raccoons or the children were turning in this direction and that, but it was reinstated after an interval.

Rats and dogs, although they failed to exhibit the symbolic process in this situation, have given ample evidence of it in later research, with simplifications of the original technique.[17]

Current research on delayed reaction in animals and children utilizes a more direct method than that described. It is more direct in that the subject does not first have to be trained to associate a particular isolated stimulus (like the light) with food. For example, a monkey sits a short distance from the experimenter. Two cups are placed before it, one to the right and one to the left, or one near and one more distant. While the animal watches, the experimenter slips a piece of lettuce under one of the cups. The animal is now removed from the situation, perhaps taken to another room. Some time later it is returned to the experimental situation and released. If it goes directly to the food cup, the monkey is allowed to eat the lettuce and is credited with a correct response. If the correct cup is selected trial after trial, despite the fact that both cups smell alike, that the food appears under one cup at one time and another at another time, and that no other external cues as to the correct cup are available, we are forced to conclude that the animal remembers under which cup it saw the food placed some minutes or hours before.[18] Stimulation provided by the experimenter's placing of the food must leave an engram which later serves as a substitute for the actual stimulation. More about the nature of this symbolic process is suggested by a further experiment.

Monkeys ate lettuce if they found lettuce after seeing it placed under a cup, but they preferred bananas to lettuce. "What would the monkeys do," the experimenter asked, "if they saw a piece of banana placed and found lettuce when they returned to the situation?" When they found the lettuce under these circumstances, the monkeys usually refused it. They left it where they found it and walked away. Sometimes they examined

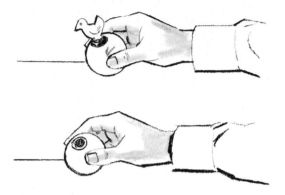

● **12.2**
A Memory Test for Infants. The infant is shown that a chicken pops out as the ball is squeezed. Then another ball, similar in appearance but with no chicken, is substituted. Recall of the chicken is indicated if the child shows surprise at its absence or looks inside the ball for it. Not until infants are nearing their first birthday do they show much ability in performing this test. Even then they can remember for no longer than one minute. That is to say, after one minute has elapsed since they last saw the chicken, they no longer give signs of remembering it. By the age of two years, however, most children remember for fifteen minutes or more. (After Bühler and Hetzer)

the vicinity as if looking for the missing banana. Temper tantrums were occasionally exhibited. Children behaved in a somewhat similar fashion when a nonpreferred reward like a chocolate drop was substituted for a jelly bean. Sometimes, however, they asked where the chocolate had gone.[19]

Various relatively simple delayed-reaction tests have been devised for use with children. These are variations of the direct method. One such test,[20] used with babies, is illustrated in Figure 12.2. The *Stanford-Binet Intelligence Scale* (pp. 119–120) has a test requiring the child to find an object that it had previously seen being hidden. Still another test used in research with children asks them to find a cookie that has been hidden under one of three identical plates.[21] The child sees the cookie placed; then, sometime later, it must remember the location of the plate that hides

it. Of course the child is given a series of tests, with the cookie shifting from plate to plate in accordance with a random schedule.

The period of delay after which recall can occur tends to increase from lower mammals to human beings. In the latter, it increases during the growth period. An infant of one year may remember for only a few minutes, a child of five years for a month or more. Older children and adults may recall a particular event years later. No doubt this improved recall as children get older is partially due to neural maturation. But familiarity with objects and the development of language are important contributing factors. As a vocabulary is acquired, words help to bridge the gap between an event and the occasion for recalling it.

Delayed matching in terms of a sample also tests recall in animals and children. Subjects are presented with a sample (Figure 12.3) and later required to identify it among a variety of other items. The monkey is first trained to lift an object in order to obtain food. Several objects are used in this way. Then he is taught to lift an object resembling whatever sample he has been shown. A triangle is shown and then removed. Several seconds or minutes later the animal is confronted with a triangle and several other forms. In order to be scored correct, he must now lift the triangle and not touch the circle, square, or other objects presented with it. A circle, let us say, is then shown. Later it is presented with other forms. Now the circle must be lifted and the triangle and other objects left untouched.[22]

When children are used in such experiments, they may be instructed to "find the form like the one I showed you a few minutes ago." They must then point to the form or other object resembling the sample.[23] ■

VERBAL RECALL

Delayed reaction tests, while useful in gauging the recall memory of animals and infants, are too simple for use with older children and adults. Recall at these levels is tested by using nonsense syllables, words, digits, or

● **12.3**
Delayed Matching from Sample. In the delayed matching-from-sample test, the object at the left is first shown by itself. It is then removed and the forms to the right are shown. To recognize which of these forms was seen earlier, the subject must remember what the original form was. Sometimes the forms are all of the same shape but different in color. At other times they may differ in both shape and color. Then the subject must remember not only the shape of the sample but its color as well. (Photos, courtesy H. F. Harlow)

more complicated verbal or symbolic materials.

The simplest type of recall test with verbal materials is found in memory span tests. The subject may be presented with a series of digits gradually increasing in length. Each list is given only one presentation. When the auditory memory span for digits is tested, the digits are read off by the tester. As soon as the end of the series is indicated, the subject tries to repeat the digits vocally or in writing. Thus as the experimenter reads, "0 4 1 6 2 8 5," the subject attempts to reproduce these numbers in correct order.

The first series may have four digits, the next five, the next six, and so on up to a series of a dozen, as in the following sample, which you may use to test your own or another's memory span.

7152
16529
531584
9152693
86103279
726394105
6574398961
40315806296
374691705824

The memory span for digits is the longest group of digits one can recall in correct order, regardless of the length of the series read to him. He may recall the entire series until he gets to six or seven; but he may get eight out of the list of a dozen. His span for that presentation is then eight. The span will differ somewhat from presentation to presentation, so an average of several tests is often taken.

When the visual memory span for digits is measured, the subject is shown the digits, one at a time, perhaps in the window of an apparatus like that illustrated in Figure 12.4. He then recalls them orally or in writing.

The memory span as ordinarily tested is larger than the perceptual span already discussed (p. 371), because the items are presented serially and the subject is allowed more time to observe them. There are large variations in memory span, depending upon the individual, age, and the type of material used. For example, the average span for auditory presentation and vocal recall of digits is four between four and five years, five between six and eight years, six between nine and twelve years, and seven beyond twelve years.[24]

When familiar objects are presented, one at a time, and named by the child as they

● 12.4
A Memory Drum. The material to be memorized appears in the slit. One of a series of nonsense syllables rotating on the drum is shown. (Courtesy, Ralph Gerbrands)

appear, his memory span is about five at five years and eight at thirteen years.[25]

Learning lists of items

If a list of items, like the nonsense syllables below, is to be memorized, they may be read from beginning to end until the subject feels that he can recall the entire list, or they can be learned by the *anticipation method.* That is, JEK may be exposed and the subject guesses (anticipates) the next syllable. If he responds with SUT, he is credited with a correct anticipation, SUT is exposed, and he anticipates the next item. This is continued until every syllable is correctly anticipated.

JEK
SUT
DOX
LIF
GAJ
SEK
BAF
CIV

As learning of such a list continues, the frequency of SEK in response to GAJ increases. In other terms, we may say that there is an increasing probability that the response SEK will follow the response GAJ. This is what investigators mean when they say that the *associative strength* of the connection between GAJ and SEK has increased.

The reader will doubtless have noted that the anticipation method involves a recitation procedure, as described on page 355.

Recall of Paired Associates

Suppose that the following pairs of English words and transliterated Russian equivalents were shown, one pair at a time, and you were asked to learn the Russian associate of each English word:

SKULL	CHEREP
EYE	GLAZ
SKIN	KOZHA
BRAIN	MOZG
FOOT	NOGA
HEAD	GOLOVA
MOUTH	ROT
BONE	KOST
HAIR	VOLOS
BACK	ZAD

After one repetition of the list of associates, you might be given the first members of the pairs in a changed order and asked to recall their associates. You might recall a few of the Russian words after this single presentation, but you would not recall all of them. After each successive repetition of the pairs, however, you would probably recall more associates. Finally, you would be able to recall the Russian equivalent of every English word.

The anticipation method is also applicable here and, again, there is an increasing probability, as learning continues, that, for example, the item HEAD will elicit the response GOLOVA.

Recalling narratives

Children and adults read or hear narratives which they later attempt to recall, either orally or in writing. Recall after a single reading is like a test of memory span, although connected rather than disconnected material is involved. When the narrative is read or heard repeatedly and a recall is required after each repetition, we have something like the typical memory experiment in which increased retention occurs as a function of repetition. A learning curve may be plotted for such data. Sometimes, however, recall is required at intervals of minutes, hours, days, or weeks, after a single presentation of the narrative. This is to see how forgetting proceeds, and whether or not distortions are introduced as a function of time and repeated recall. A still further variation of memory experiments with narratives is to have one individual read or hear the narrative, then tell it to another who, in turn, tells it to still another, and so on. In this way, changes introduced as the story passes from one to another, as when rumors pass from mouth to mouth, or legends are handed down, may be investigated.

In one extensive investigation involving the above procedures, university students read stories, then attempted to reproduce them.[26] For example, a student read the following story twice, then engaged in other activities for fifteen minutes. Here is the original story followed by his reproduction after the fifteen minutes.

ORIGINAL STORY

The Son Who Tried to Outwit His Father

A son said to his father one day: "I will hide, and you will not be able to find me." The father replied: "Hide wherever you like," and he went into his house to rest.

The son saw a three-kernel peanut, and changed himself into one of the kernels; a fowl coming along picked up the peanut and swallowed it; and a wild bush-cat caught and ate the fowl; and a dog met and caught and ate the bush-cat. After a little time, the dog was swallowed by a python, that, having eaten its meal, went to the river and was snared in a fish-trap.

The father searched for his son and, not seeing him, went to look at the fish-trap. On pulling it to the riverside, he found a large python in it. He opened it, and saw a dog inside, in which he found a bush-cat, and on opening that he discovered a fowl, from which he took the peanut, and breaking the shell, he then revealed his son. The son was so dumbfounded that he never again tried to outwit his father.

REPRODUCTION

The Son Who Tried to Outwit His Father

A son one day said to his father: "I will hide, and you will not be able to find me." His father replied: "Hide wherever you wish," and went into the house to rest.

The son saw a three-kernel peanut, and changed himself into one of the kernels. A fowl saw the peanut and ate it. Soon afterwards a bush-cat killed and ate the fowl, and then a dog chased and finally killed and ate the bush-cat. After a time a python caught the dog and swallowed it. Soon after its meal, the python went down to the river and was caught in a fish-trap.

The father looked for his son, and when he could not find him, he went to the river to see whether he had caught any fish. In his fish-trap he found a large python which he opened. In it he found a dog in which was a bush-cat. On opening the bush-cat, he found a fowl, in which he found a peanut. He opened the peanut, and revealed his son.

The son was so dumbfounded at being discovered that he never tried to outwit his father again.

Observe that the reproduction retains the theme of the story and the succession of events. However, certain words, like the "wild" bush-cat, are omitted entirely; synonyms for others, such as "wish" in place of "like," are given; and some words — and ideas — are added which were not in the original. For example, the original does not say that the fowl was killed and eaten by the bush-cat "soon after" the fowl ate the peanut. All it says is that the bush-cat caught and ate the fowl. After successive repetitions of such materials, each recall gives more and more details and, in general, accurate reproduction is approximated. But when successive recalls by the same individual occur without any further presentation of the original, increasing distortion of details is introduced.

Some of the investigator's conclusions from his analysis of a mass of such data are: (1) "accuracy of reproduction, in a literal sense, is the rare exception"; (2) "the general form, or outline, is remarkably persistent, once the first version has been given"; (3) "style, rhythm, precise mode of construction . . . are very rarely faithfully reproduced"; (4) " . . . omission of detail, simplification of events and structure, and transformation of items into more familiar detail, may go on almost indefinitely"; and (5) "in long-distance remembering, elaboration becomes more common in some cases . . . and there may be increasing importation or invention . . . aided by the use of visual images."

☐ When the individual reads or hears a narrative, then tells it to another, and that one tells it to still another, and so on, the theme may be retained, but there is usually a marked distortion of details. The following reproduction of "The Son Who Tried to Outwit His Father" illustrates the point. It was obtained from the twentieth person who had heard the story chain-fashion so to speak:

A small boy, having got into some kind of mischief, wished to hide himself from his father. He happened to be standing under a tree, when an acorn fell to the ground, and he immediately determined to hide himself within it. He accordingly concealed himself within the kernel. Now a cat chanced to be passing along that way, and when she saw the acorn, she forthwith swallowed it. Not long afterwards a dog killed and ate this cat. Finally the dog himself was devoured by a python.

The father of the boy was out hunting one day when he met the python, and attacked and slew it. On cutting the beast open, he discovered the dog inside it, and inside the dog the cat, and inside the cat the acorn. Within the acorn he found his long-lost son. The son was overjoyed at seeing his father once more, and promised that he would never again conceal anything from him. He said that he would submit to the punishment he deserved, whatever his crime might be. ☐

Reproduction of forms

In Figure 12.5 are shown two figures and their reproduction after they had been observed for one minute. An experiment on the memory of college students for such forms was conducted along the lines of the experiment on narratives. Successive repetitions of presentation and reproduction brought an increasingly faithful reproduction of the original. However, successive reproduction after only one presentation brought omissions, additions and inaccuracies reminiscent of those found when narratives were repeatedly recalled. The main outline or general schema was retained. For example, if a man was pictured, the reproduction was of a man, although one markedly different from the original. One tendency which stands out in such reproductions is that the reproduction becomes increasingly conventional. This is also true when, as in the case of narratives, the picture is passed on, chain-fashion, to a number of subjects, each of whom reproduces it from memory and then shows his reproduction to another.[27]

Testimony

Many studies have been made of the ability of children and adults to describe or otherwise report events witnessed just once. The situation is somewhat like that of testifying about accidents or other events while in a courtroom. Still or moving pictures may be used. Sometimes, however, a carefully rehearsed scene is enacted before the group, without any knowledge on their part that it is acted, and without any expectation, either, that they will be called upon to testify concerning the event.

Thus, while Erle Stanley Gardner was addressing a class on the subject of legal evidence, at the University of California at Los Angeles, "a woman burst into the room and rushed at him shouting, 'You got my brother hung!' She then unsuccessfully attacked him with a pointed can opener before being escorted from the room by the regular instructor . . . who planned the stunt to dramatize the great variance of eye-witness accounts to the same event. . . ."[28]

COCK AND SWAN
Original

COCK AND SWAN
Drawing from memory

● **12.5**

Reproduction of Form. This is typical of experiments on memory for form. The subject was shown the original drawing; after the drawing had been removed, he was asked to reproduce it. Observe that the general features, or themes, have been retained but that certain details have been changed or omitted. (After experiments in the book *Remembering*, by Sir Frederic Bartlett.)

Descriptions of still pictures, movies, scenes enacted, or actual events are in most instances grossly inaccurate, and they become increasingly so with a lapse of time between the original experience and the reproduction. With respect to the above incident, thirty-four students were asked to describe the woman's complexion. Three said "dark," two "ruddy," one "medium," five "fair," seven "pale," three "heavily powdered and made up." and thirteen said they did not know. Actually, she was fair, had freckles, and wore no makeup.*

Sometimes the subject is given a list of statements or questions concerning the scene witnessed. He then attempts to say whether the statements are true or false, or to answer the questions. Recall in these terms also shows much inaccuracy. The type of inaccuracy is often related to the way in which the question is framed.

Inaccuracy of recall, under circumstances like the above, has several possible bases. (1) Observation is perhaps incorrect in the first place, leading to omission of certain details and the addition of others. (2) Interests, attitudes,

and expectations of the observer may influence both observation and recall. (3) Unintentional elaboration or exaggeration may be involved, as in the recall of narratives already considered. (4) As time has elapsed, there may be actual forgetting of details that were witnessed correctly at the time. Moreover, when forgetting occurs, there is a tendency to fill in gaps. Anything which seems reasonable in the light of what is remembered may be "recalled." This is one basis of the exaggeration mentioned above. (5) The individual may be misled by suggestions. When asked, "Did the man have on a dark or a light tie?" he may answer "light" or "dark," even though the man wore no tie. Any or all of these shortcomings may be responsible for the omissions and errors so often involved in courtroom testimony. They are also relevant with respect to rumor, which is discussed in Chapter 17.

Eidetic imagery

Sometimes, especially in children under six years of age, testimony is exceptionally accurate — almost as accurate, in fact, as if the child could still see a picture after it has been removed. Indeed the child often reports that he *does* still see the picture. These exceptionally accurate "memory images" have

* Psychology has played a big part in the understanding of legal processes. *On the Witness Stand*, by Hugo Münsterberg (McClure, 1908), was a pioneer contribution to this field.

● 12.6

Recall in Terms of Reduced Cues. If you fill in the missing parts — arms and face — mentally, you are recalling (or perceiving) in terms of reduced cues. (Courtesy, Shuron Continental)

been called *eidetic*, a term which suggests that they possess the clarity of hallucinations.*

The most common test of eidetic imagery is to present some very detailed picture, then remove it and ask the child to describe what he sees, or to answer questions concerning it. The eidetic child seems to project the picture on any convenient surface and to describe what he sees. Acoustic as well as visual images are sometimes reported.[29] A child with acoustic eidetic imagery will repeat long lists of digits after hearing them once. A colleague once told me how an eidetic child looked at the desk while a list of a dozen or so digits was being read to him, then "read" the list off forwards and backwards while still looking at the desk.

Eidetic imagery is rarely present in older children and adults. Something akin to it per-

* In hallucinations the individual sees, hears, or feels things that are not actually present, yet he believes them to be present. The person with an eidetic image, even though it may be as clear as an hallucination, does not necessarily believe it to be a perception of things actually present.

haps exists in people who report a "photographic memory," like a student who told me that, after reading an assignment, she could see the material before her and "read" it again in imagination.

The role of stimuli in recall

In discussing the delayed reaction, we pointed out that the subject recalls an absent stimulating situation. This does not mean, however, that recall is without stimulation. The point is that the part of the situation that the subject recalls is absent. But some relevant stimulation is necessary for recall. Thus, in the experiment with raccoons, the light recalled was not present at the time, but the experimental situation with its three compartments, the hunger of the animal, and other extraneous yet associated stimulating factors were present. In an entirely different external situation, or in the same external situation when not hungry, the animal in all probability would not recall the light.

• *Stimuli for recall may be external or internal.* You may see a redhaired girl, and the redness of her hair may make you recall a childhood sweetheart whose hair was red. You may smell the odor of some flower that once grew in your home garden, then recall the garden. These, and innumerable examples that one might give, illustrate recall elicited by an external stimulus.

But you may have a stomach-ache and recall the green apples you ate as a child. You may be nauseated for some reason and recall that trip across the Atlantic during which you were violently seasick. These instances illustrate recall elicited by internal stimuli.

• *Recall of one experience often leads to recall of another.* This phenomenon is sometimes referred to as *free association*. When we indulge in free association, we may recall many early experiences which we have not recalled for years. The success of psychoanalysts in getting better recall of childhood experiences than normally occurs comes from their use of free association. They have their patients "think out loud" and sometimes keep them at it during séances spread out over months or years.

● **12.7**

Test for Recognition Memory. Look at these faces for one minute; then turn to page 604 of the Appendix and see how many you recognize. (Courtesy, Adelaide College of Education)

• *Reduced cues.* Any fraction of some previously experienced situation may, by itself, lead to recall of a whole experience. This phenomenon is variously referred to as *redintegration, recall in terms of reduced cues, or response to minimal cues.* As illustrated in Figure 12.6, our redintegrative ability enables us to recall (or perceive) a whole situation in terms of significant parts. To use our previous illustration — red hair, the odor of a perfume, the sound of footsteps, or any other single aspect of some friend — may lead to complete recall, not only of a friend, as such, but also of former experiences to which she contributed. In delayed reaction the present stimuli apparently serve to redintegrate the absent ones so necessary to the correct response. ■

RECOGNIZING

Recognizing is much easier than recalling. This is why examinations of the matching and multiple-choice variety are easier than completion tests, in which blanks are left to be filled in, or essay examinations covering the same material. When the student has all the material before him, he does not have to recall it. His task is merely to differentiate between the familiar and the unfamiliar, or what has been experienced before and what is new.

In the typical experiment on recognition memory, a subject is shown nonsense syllables, words, forms, or other simple materials. He is given one or more complete presentations, the items usually being presented one at a time as in experiments on recall. The items involved in these trials are then presented among new items, the new and the old being mixed up in a random order. Now the subject must indicate which of the items appeared originally.

You may try this test yourself. Examine each of the faces in Figure 12.7, allowing yourself one minute for the whole group. Then turn to page 604, and record the number of every face that you recognize as having been in the first group.

So-called *false recognition* is another

example of response to reduced cues. We may "recognize" a person as our friend because of some similarity to the friend, such as hair-color, walk, build, or dress. Some aspect of former stimulation involving our friend leads us to recall him, and at the same time to identify the present person with the one recalled. The feeling that one has been in a certain place before or that he has done or said something before, even though he knows that this is the first time, has a similar basis. It is often referred to as the *déjà vu* experience. Something in the present situation or present behavior may be identical with, or very much like, something that occurred previously. This present aspect of former stimulation or activity leads us to recall the original experience and we incorrectly identify it with the present one. ■

RETENTION AND ORIGINAL LEARNING

Any activity which produces a poor memory impression obviously yields poor retention. The poorly motivated subject learns little, and, as we see when he is tested for retention later, he retains little. But even where motivation is good, the most economical method of learning usually yields the best retention.

We have already considered how distributed practice and recitation facilitate learning. Now we see that they also improve retention.

Distributed versus massed practice

Thirty-two college students memorized lists of nonsense syllables to the point where they could recall the list perfectly. They learned comparable groups of syllables by the distributed practice and massed practice methods. Some lists were recalled after an interval of ten minutes, and others after an interval of twenty-four hours. The same lists were then relearned to the original criterion — namely, one perfect repetition. The results were quite clear-cut. After every interval, the average recall score for distributed practice was higher than the recall score for massed practice, despite the fact that learning with distributed practice involved fewer repetitions. There was a suggestion, too, that the difference in favor

of distributed practice became greater as the interval between original learning and recall increased. In terms of repetitions required to relearn, distributed practice was again better than massed practice. As in the case of recall, this was true after each interval between learning and relearning. Although the above discussion refers to group averages, most individuals also recalled more and relearned faster when practice was distributed.[30]

These results were quite clearly in favor of distributed practice, but some other investigations on verbal and motor learning have shown that retention after distributed practice is not always better than retention after massed practice.[31] Much depends upon the nature of the learning task and the sort of distribution used. Generally speaking, however, it appears that massed practice seldom, if ever, leads to better retention than distributed practice. Thus, from a purely practical standpoint, the student will be wise to distribute his learning time. He may or may not gain by doing this, but he will probably not have poorer retention than if he had used massed practice.

Recitation

We have already described an experiment[32] in which the most efficient learning (immediate recall) of nonsense material occurred with 80 per cent recitation. It is interesting to observe, therefore, that retention after four hours was best for the percentage of recitation which had already proved most efficient in learning. The retention scores for nonsense syllables are shown in Figure 12.8.

Speed of learning

It has often been claimed that slow learners retain better than fast learners, who of course require fewer repetitions to learn, but this is a difficult question to investigate and the outcome varies with methods of investigation. One method favors the slow learner by giving him as much time as he wants, hence an opportunity to overlearn. Another method favors the fast learner. This sets a given learning period that is equal for both

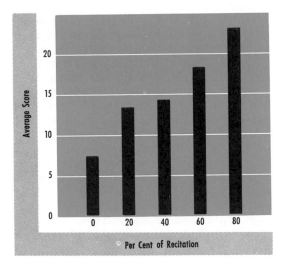

• 12.8
Retention of Nonsense Syllables as a Function of Recitation. Note that the retention score increases with each increment of recitation. (Data from A. I. Gates)

the fast and slow learners. Obviously, the fast learner will learn more in the time allowed, hence have more to retain. Consequently his retention score will be higher than that of the slow learner. When overlearning is prevented (by withdrawing each item as soon as it is learned) and the amount learned is equated (by terminating the learning session as soon as a certain number of items are learned), the fast learners still have better retention.[33] It is possible, however, that the fast learner, even though he learns only the items acquired by the slow learner, has them impressed upon him more strongly; that is, they may have greater *associative strength* for him than for the slow learner. Using a statistical technique too elaborate to describe here, it is possible to compare the retention by fast and slow learners of items having equal associative strength for each at the end of the learning period. When this is done, fast and slow learners retain the material equally well.[34]

What does this mean? It means that, in a situation where every variable except retention *per se* is held constant, fast learners retain as well, but no better than, slow learners. In

the uncontrolled situations of everyday life, fast learners retain *more* than slow learners only when they learn more, or learn it better.

The slow learner, however, may obtain a relative advantage by overlearning.

Overlearning

Suppose that a given number of practice periods is required to memorize some material so that you can recall it correctly just once. What would be the advantage, if any, of having extra practice? Ebbinghaus and several later investigators have found that there are decided advantages to be derived from extra practice — or what is referred to as *overlearning*.

The value of overlearning for retention is illustrated by an experiment in which adult subjects learned lists consisting of twelve monosyllabic nouns. They learned with different amounts of repetition beyond that required for the first perfect recall.[35] The criterion of learning was one perfect repetition of the list. Having half again as many repetitions as were required to reach the criterion was designated 50 per cent overlearning. Having twice the number of repetitions required for learning was 100 per cent overlearning. Thus, if four repetitions allowed the subject to reach the criterion of learning, six repetitions would constitute 50 per cent overlearning, and eight repetitions 100 per cent overlearning.

Different groups learned comparable lists of nouns, with 0, 50, or 100 per cent overlearning. Recall and relearning occurred (in different groups) at intervals of one, two, four, seven, fourteen, and twenty-eight days. Figure 12.9 shows the retention curves for recall when overlearning was 0, 50, and 100 per cent. Somewhat similar results were found in the case of repetitions saved during relearning. It is quite clear from these data that larger amounts of overlearning bring larger degrees of retention.

A later investigation followed the same experimental design, but involved mazes instead of words.[36] The results were in fairly close agreement with those already indicated. In this study, however, 200 per cent overlearning was also introduced. The results show quite clearly that diminishing returns occur as

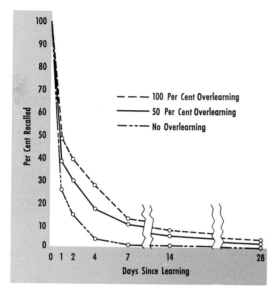

● 12.9

Retention as a Function of Overlearning. Note that after an interval of one day there was 26 per cent retention for 0 overlearning, 38 per cent for 50 per cent overlearning, and 49 per cent for 100 per cent overlearning. Taking the results as a whole, the increase from 50 to 100 per cent overlearning (a 33 per cent increase in the number of repetitions) brought less than a 33 per cent increase in retention. Thus diminishing returns were evident. This fact is apparent in the curves. Note that there is a wider space between the 0 and 50 per cent than between the 50 and 100 per cent curves. (After Krueger)

overlearning is increased. For example, an increase of 100 per cent overlearning (100 to 200) brought an increased retention which averaged less than 50 per cent.

Reminiscence

In all of the experiments so far considered, the material was learned completely before retention was tested. A list of nonsense syllables, for example, was learned to the point where it could be recalled with an accuracy of 100 per cent. Suppose, however, that it had been learned to an accuracy of only 70 per

cent. Quite obviously, there can be no better retention than 100 per cent of something completely learned, but it is conceivable that a person who learned something so that he could give a performance that was 70 per cent accurate might perform later with an accuracy greater than 70 per cent. Indeed, there are many experiments which show that this is the case. Better retention of *incompletely* learned material after a rest interval than immediately after learning has been found in experiments with children, human adults, and animals, using both motor and verbal skills.[37]

Improved retention after an interval has been called *reminiscence*. It is illustrated graphically in Figure 12.10, which represents the retention of an incompletely learned list of nonsense syllables by college students.

Reminiscence is perhaps related to the phenomenon of better learning and retention after distributed than after massed effort and also to the well-established fact that interrupted activities are recalled more frequently than completed activities.[38] The explanation

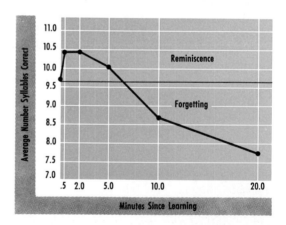

● 12.10

The Phenomenon of Reminiscence. Observe that the average score immediately after practice was approximately 9.5 syllables. The score rose to almost 10.5 at intervals of .5 and 2 minutes. Even after 5 minutes, the score was still better than that immediately after practice stopped. After longer intervals, however, forgetting became evident. (After L. B. Ward)

of these apparently related phenomena is not clear. It is possible that rehearsal of the material during an interval accounts for some reminiscence, but this still occurs when rehearsal is prevented by having the subjects perform some other activity during the interval. It is also found in situations where rehearsal could not occur — for example, in rotary pursuit learning[39] (Figure 10.14) and in maze learning by rats.[40] Perseveration and consequent consolidation of the memory trace could conceivably account for some reminiscence; but the fact that it occurs when other activities intervene rules out perseveration as a necessary basis. The explanation stressed in recent discussions is one already mentioned in connection with distributed learning — the marked tendency for incorrect, hence interfering, associations to drop out during a rest period.

Reminiscence is, of course, only a temporary improvement in retention. It is followed by a more or less rapid loss, such as occurs after completed learning. ■

FORGETTING

Forgetting is the loss, permanent or temporary, of the ability to recall or recognize something learned earlier. In certain instances it may be described as negative retention. A retention curve drops as a function of time. Such curves are customarily used to represent the course of forgetting. If forgetting were plotted directly, in terms of the amount forgotten as a function of time, the curve would rise rather than fall. For comparison of retention and forgetting curves based upon the classical experiments of Ebbinghaus, see Figure 12.11.

Ebbinghaus memorized many lists of nonsense syllables by reading them through until one perfect repetition was possible. He relearned certain lists twenty minutes after he had memorized them. Other lists were relearned a day after, some two days after, and so on. Some of the intervals used, and the savings in time to relearn, appear in the figure. About 47 per cent was forgotten in twenty minutes, 66 per cent in one day, 72 per cent in two days, 75 per cent in six days, and 79

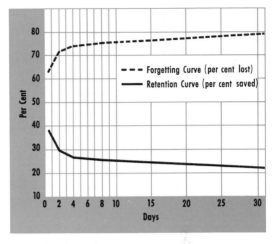

● **12.11**
Retention and Forgetting Curves for Nonsense Material. Two curves are shown to illustrate the fact that retention is the obverse of forgetting; or, that forgetting is "negative retention." (Data from Ebbinghaus)

per cent in thirty-one days. Thus the forgetting of nonsense syllables was at first rapid (47 per cent lost in twenty minutes) and then slow (only 32 per cent more lost in a month).[41]

Later investigators, using many subjects and averaging the results, have verified the general trend of the forgetting curve found by Ebbinghaus for nonsense syllables — i.e., a relatively high rate of forgetting at the outset. In general, however, these investigators have found less overall forgetting than Ebbinghaus reported. One recent study showed only a 12 per cent loss after twenty minutes as compared with the more than 40 per cent loss found by Ebbinghaus.[42]

□ There are several reasons for such differences. Ebbinghaus used only one subject, himself. Individual differences could thus account for some of the discrepancy between his results and those obtained with other subjects, especially since the data for many were, in later experiments, averaged. Perhaps of greater importance is the fact that Ebbinghaus learned thousands of syllables in the course of his experiments. This being so, it is quite likely that many syllables learned in earlier experiments interfered with later learning and retention, thus making for more rapid forgetting than would occur in the case of subjects learning (and later relearning) only one list. Such interlist interference has been avoided in recent research by having each subject learn only one list, then relearn it after an interval. This means, of course, that a different group is represented in the relearning at each interval. The list is learned, let us say, by 100 subjects. Twenty of these relearn after 20 minutes, 20 after one day, 20 after two days, 20 after five days, and the remaining 20 after a week. Under these conditions, forgetting is much less, at any interval, than Ebbinghaus found.

Forgetting also varies with the method used to test it. The above comparisons were based upon the relearning (or saving) method. Had the subjects merely been asked to recognize the syllables (to identify them in a list including many others), little or no forgetting would have been evident. In a recent investigation with college students, all syllables of a 12-syllable list were recognized after an interval of 20 minutes and there was an insignificant loss after one and two days.[43]

Another retention test requires the subject to anticipate the first syllable of the list, then the next, and so on, until all can be repeated without prompting. In the study referred to above, this method uniformly yielded lower mean retention scores than the recognition method. For example, 8.90 as compared with 12.00 after 20 minutes, and 6.80 as compared with 11.90 after one day.

Quite evidently, then, one cannot make a general statement about the course of forgetting — he must specify, among other things, the method used to test it. □

Ebbinghaus demonstrated, and others have verified the finding that meaningful materials (words, poems, narratives) are more easily learned, unit for unit, than nonsense syllables. Even among nonsense syllables there are some with greater meaning than others. Thus YIL has more meaning than XUY. Syllables with high meaning value are usually learned more readily than those with little or no meaning. But what about forgetting? Is there a difference between the forgetting of meaningful and of meaningless material?

Experiments on short-term memory[44] have focused upon the retention, after 0–18 seconds, of nonsense syllables and of words having different degrees of meaningfulness. An item is presented, the subject counts so as to prevent rehearsal, and after three seconds he attempts to recall the item. Other subjects recall it after six seconds, still others after nine seconds, and so on. The results of such experiments are quite clear-cut. Common words are retained with little or no loss, even after the 18-second interval, while nonsense syllables are almost completely forgotten. Groups of three unrelated words are forgotten almost as quickly as nonsense syllables.[45]

These results were obtained with single items or groups of items presented only once. But how about lists of items to be memorized, and recalled, in serial order? With respect to these, the answer is not as clear-cut as for a single presentation. One difficulty encountered here was discussed in relation to slow and fast learning, where we pointed out that the associative strength of the memorized items must be considered. When few repetitions are required (as in the case of meaningful material), the items have relatively low associative strength, hence may be forgotten readily. On the other hand, material that is learned more slowly may build up a high degree of associative strength, thus facilitating retention. This difficulty may be overcome by using materials of different meaning value, but arranging the experimental conditions so that they have equivalent associative strength at the termination of the memorizing sessions. Under these conditions there is no difference in retention. Nonsense syllables with different meaning values are retained equally well.[46] The same holds for nonsense syllables compared with words.[47]

Failure to find a difference in retention as a function of meaning runs counter to everyday observation. However, one must remember that what is involved in these experiments is rote learning of a more or less artificial character. In daily life, the more meaningful aspects receive much support from many activities.

When complicated material is learned, especially material involving insight and the understanding of principles, there is a quite positive relation between meaning and retention. With insight (or understanding), early forgetting is seldom found. For example, college students learned various puzzles (match tricks) either by memorizing the solutions or by memorizing the principles involved. The majority of those who memorized without understanding the principles exhibited marked and rapid forgetting within a month. On the other hand, most of those who learned the principles had almost perfect retention when tested later at intervals of up to one month.[48]

WHY DO WE FORGET?

There is no single nor simple answer to this question. Many variables are involved in forgetting and some are difficult to explain.

One should note at the outset that what appears to be forgetting may occur because there was no impression, or an inadequate one, in the first place. This was discussed in relation to errors of omission in testimony. By the same token, much that we learn incidentally is poorly retained because there was only a weak impression. We often fail to remember names because we pay little or no attention when we hear them. Inability to remember what happened during an exciting or disturbing event is likewise due, in part at least, to inattention. This type of "memory loss" is sometimes referred to as *anterograde amnesia*. It is in contrast with forgetting of what occurred before the disturbing event, or *retrograde amnesia*. This should not be confused with retroactive inhibition, which involves an interference by new learning with what was learned earlier.

Experimental extinction in conditioning is also followed by a loss that, in certain ways, resembles forgetting.

But suppose that learning has actually occurred, that there has been no emotional upset, and that experimental extinction has not been attempted. Why, even under these circumstances, does forgetting occur? That is the question to which we now address ourselves.

The time variable

It is commonly assumed that lapse of time in itself is responsible for forgetting. According to this view, the memory trace, unless it is used, gradually deteriorates. Beyond a certain plausibility, however, this explanation finds little scientific support. Perhaps the strongest support comes from general observations such as the following:

☐ "The child who has normal vision for the first two years of life or thereabouts and then becomes blind loses all the effects of visual learning; at maturity he is indistinguishable from the congenitally blind. . . . Early visual learning, therefore, is reversible; forgetting can occur by disuse. Clinically, however, it is known that if the human subject has had vision long enough its effects do not disappear. If the child does not become blind until the age of four or five, the learning becomes more "ingrained" and disuse has little or no effect; in these circumstances, the subject never becomes like the congenitally blind."[49] ☐

One difficulty with such evidence is that nonvisual activity may itself have weakened the memory traces. Moreover, as will become apparent later, memories which were apparently lost may be recovered by appropriate stimulation, including direct stimulation of the cerebral cortex. It is thus possible that the early visual engrams, although not evidenced in performance, are still present.

Other observations suggest that time may be a factor in forgetting only because of the activities which occur in time. It has been demonstrated quite clearly that sleep and other forms of relative inactivity slow down the forgetting process.

Sleep

Two subjects memorized lists consisting of ten nonsense syllables before a period of (1) normal daily activity or (2) sleep. Retention was tested after one, two, four, and eight hours of either waking activity or sleep. Under each of these conditions different lists of nonsense syllables were learned and recalled, but they were all of comparable difficulty. Each duration of sleep yielded better retention than a comparable duration of waking. After the successive intervals of sleep, the percentages of nonsense syllables recalled were: 70, 54, 55, and 56. There was, as we see, no further forgetting after the one-hour interval of sleep. The comparable percentages for waking were: 46, 31, 22, and 9. The longer the interval of waking, the more forgetting occurred. These findings have been verified in later research. The investigators concluded that "forgetting is not so much a matter of the decay of old impressions and associations as it is a matter of the interference, inhibition, or obliteration of the old by the new."[50]

The fact that forgetting occurs during sleep, even though it occurs less rapidly than when we are awake, is of course no basis for discrediting the idea that interpolated activity rather than time itself causes forgetting. Although one is not learning new activities while asleep, the nervous system is active.

Relative inactivity

The subjects of the experiments on sleep did not go to sleep immediately, although they tried to do so. It has since been claimed that if it were possible to put the subject "into a dreamless sleep immediately after learning, so that no new experiences would have an opportunity to interfere with, inhibit, or obliterate the old, a perfect retention might be expected."[51] The same writers point out that, "Because of the dangers of drugs, anesthetics, and other methods of inducing unconsciousness quickly, no one has thus far attempted to realize these conditions with human S's, but with animals the case is different."[52] The animals used for a test of the activity theory of forgetting were cockroaches. These were selected because they could be rendered inactive without the use of drugs or other agents which might have deleterious effects on the nervous system. The method of rendering them inactive after learning had occurred was extremely simple. They were placed in a state of tonic immobility or animal hypnosis by inducing them to crawl between layers of tissue paper. Sheets of tissue paper were placed in a box which could be entered through a cone. The inducement to enter was escape from

bright light. While in contact with the sheets of tissue paper the cockroach was perfectly motionless. When the period of inactivity was to be terminated, the animal was removed from the tissue paper and tested for retention.

What the cockroach was trained to do was to avoid the shaded area at the end of the box shown in Figure 12.12. Its natural response was to run toward the shaded area at the end of the alleys. But when it ran into this area, the animal received an electric shock through the floor. When it failed to move toward the shaded area, it was pushed. Gradually the cockroach learned to avoid shock by swerving around the end of the glass partition and returning without entering the shaded area. Each animal was trained until it turned around the partition, instead of entering the shaded area, for nine out of ten trials. Control groups were normally active during rest intervals. The intervals, for different groups, varied from ten minutes to twenty-four hours. Retention was measured in terms of the savings in trials and in the number of shocks administered during relearning.

The results of this experiment are summarized in Figure 12.12, which shows the saving score (retention) of the dark-avoidance habit for the inactive and control groups over intervals up to twenty-four hours. It is apparent (1) that the inactive group retained very much more than the active group, and (2) that whereas the inactive group showed no further loss of retention between two and eight hours, the active group retained less as further time elapsed.[53]

These results of course favor the view that it is not time *per se* that makes us forget, but what happens in time. Later we will have something to say about the effects of events (such as new learning) which come between original learning and the time of recall. But we first consider the fact that people sometimes forget because they want to and sometimes because appropriate stimulation is lacking.

Repressive forgetting

Like Scarlett O'Hara in *Gone With the Wind*, we may dispose of unpleasant events by saying, "I'll think of that tomorrow." When

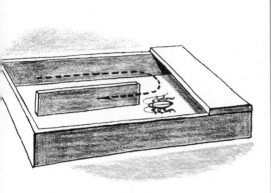

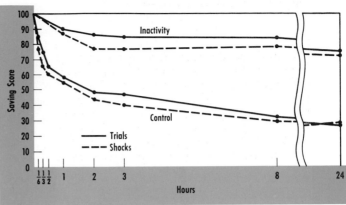

● 12.12

Learning Box and Relearning Curve for Cockroaches. The box had a shaded area which attracted the cockroaches, but they were trained to avoid this area by following the path indicated. Entrance into the shaded area brought an electric shock. The curves show the savings in trials-to-relearn, and the shocks administered for errors, after each of the indicated intervals. It is quite evident that inactive animals retained the avoidance habit much better than did controls. This was true for the savings in both trials and shocks. (After H. Minami and K. M. Dallenbach, "The Effect of Activity upon Learning and Retention in the Cockroach," *Amer. J. Psychol.*, 1946, 59, p. 2.)

tomorrow comes, with its own events, the unpleasant thought may, as it were, be crowded out. This is *repression*. We discussed earlier (p. 279) the case of a man who, in trying circumstances, forgot his identity. Repression was involved, but the memory defect itself, an example of functional neurosis, is designated *retrograde amnesia*. We read about such functional amnesia quite often in the press.

According to Freud, the mere forgetting of names, of appointments, or of duties to be performed is motivated rather than accidental.[54] Freud's view receives some support from such everyday experience as this: a person accepts an invitation to a dinner party and is chagrined, the day after it is over, to learn that he forgot to go. Such forgetting is inexcusable. It is quite evident to his would-be hostess that he really didn't want to attend her party.

An interesting thing about all such instances of motivated forgetting is that it may be temporary. The memory trace, whatever its nature, is apparently intact. The man with retrograde amnesia, for example, may regain what was lost. The forgetful person recalls the invitation when attention is called to it. Quite evidently, then, forgetting under such circumstances involves some sort of interference with recall, not a loss of the engram. A psychoanalyst, through free-association and dream analysis, may elicit recall of many events which were apparently forgotten. Hypnosis is often conducive to recall of the apparently forgotten, including memories which go back to early childhood.[55] Likewise, under the influence of sodium pentathol (the "truth drug") a patient may recover memories which were previously inaccessible.

Although it is evident that much forgetting is motivated, that interference rather than loss of the memory trace is involved, and that it is possible under certain circumstances to recover the memories which were apparently lost; the basic factors involved are not known. What is of special interest to us here, however, is the fact that forgetting may occur even though the memory trace still exists.

The need for stimulation

Some forgetting may occur because the appropriate stimuli for recall are absent. You may be oblivious to some earlier experience. It may not have been recalled since childhood. Yet, suddenly, you recall it. Upon noting the circumstances, it is apparent that an odor, a

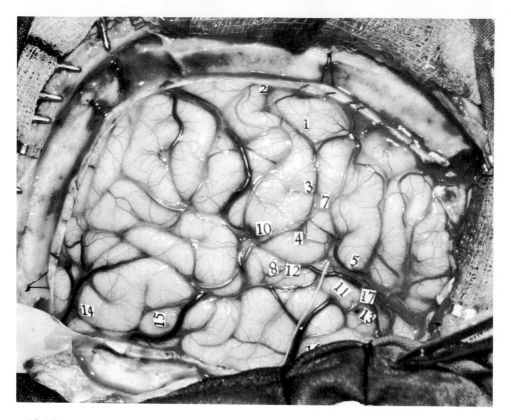

The Right Cerebral Cortex during Electrical Stimulation. This is the cortex of a 26-year-old woman. It was exposed during an operation to alleviate epileptic seizures. The numbered tickets mark the points which, when electrically stimulated, produced sensory, motor, or so-called psychical responses. The latter include interpretive illusions and recall of previous experiences, referred to in the text. (From W. Penfield, *The Excitable Cortex in Conscious Man,* Thomas, 1958, p. 27.)

name, or some other stimulus is responsible. The effectiveness of free association may be attributed to the fact that it arouses verbal stimuli which, in turn, activate recall of seemingly forgotten events.

A dramatic illustration of how stimuli may arouse memories that were apparently lost is reported by the noted brain surgeon, Wilder Penfield.[56] In the course of operating upon the brain to alleviate certain forms of epileptic seizure, he stimulated various points on the cerebral cortex with a weak electric current. In some regions, as noted earlier (pp. 58–59), there were reports of visual, auditory, or other experiences — as experiences of the moment, like seeing light flashes, hearing music, and so on. But when Penfield stimulated certain points in the associative temporal cortex,

memories rather than immediate experiences were reported. When a certain point (11 in Figure 12.13) was stimulated, one patient said that she heard a mother calling her boy; not now, but years ago. She was told that stimulation would be repeated, but it was not. There was no report. Then the same point was stimulated again. Now there was a further report about the voice calling, and certain details of earlier experience were added, such as the observation that this was taking place in a lumber yard. Stimulated at another point nearby (12 in Figure 12.13), the patient recalled still another childhood experience. Stimulation of a point toward the frontal lobe (point 13) produced memories of voices and also of seeing circus wagons. Still another point (17) elicited memories of an office in which the patient had worked as a stenographer and also memories of watching a play. Penfield believes that these incidents would never have been recalled "without the aid of the stimulating electrode."

Such results do not mean that the engram is localized in the bit of brain tissue right under the electrode. Penfield points out that electrical stimulation actually interferes with "local cortical function." However, the local stimulation sets up impulses which, upon being carried to other regions, and perhaps becoming involved in relevant neural circuits, serve indirectly to revive the memories reported. As we said earlier, there is still much speculation about the nature of memory traces and their localization. In this connection, it would be well to read again the quotation about engrams (p. 372). On Penfield's views concerning cortical localization, in this instance of motor functions, refer again to the footnote statement on page 60.

Regardless of the nature of the memory trace, it is quite evident that we sometimes forget because the stimuli for recall, for activation of the trace, are lacking.

Obliterating memory traces

Although there is no conclusive evidence that a memory trace deteriorates as a function of time (or disuse), we do know that certain conditions can obliterate it. One of these is the electroconvulsive shock (ECS, for short) that is used in the treatment of mental patients (p. 286) and also involved in numerous experiments on learning and retention in rats. These clinical observations and experimental studies show conclusively that ECS produces amnesia for the events which immediately precede it. Patients forget (apparently forever) the preparations just preceding the shock and, in some cases, even the trip into the hospital. Nor do they recall the shock itself.[57] Experiments with rats have shown that ECS administered shortly after each trial greatly retards learning.[58] Given after a habit has been learned, it is followed by poorer retention than in a control group shocked only on the leg.[59] How ECS interferes with retention is not known. Some animal research

suggests that it is the convulsion as such that produces this effect, not the passage of an electric current through the brain.[60] It has been claimed that the electric current (or associated conditions, such as temporary anoxia) destroys brain cells. A view more widely held is that a memory trace needs to consolidate, to get set, and the electric current, the convulsion, the anoxia, or some other condition associated with ECS, interferes with this. To quote Woodworth and Schlosberg's *Experimental Psychology*, "anything learned or experienced just before the shock may be irretrievably lost because its traces were not sufficiently established."[61]

An emotional shock may have somewhat comparable effects on retention, presumably because it also interferes with consolidation of the memory trace. This is borne out by general observation of amnesia for events just preceding emotional upset and also by the following experiment:

☐ College students, working one at a time in a small lighted darkroom, were given several repetitions of a list of nonsense syllables, after which they recalled as many syllables as they could. Following this recall they were sometimes given jokes to read, none of which was highly mirth-provoking. They were then asked to recall the syllables again. At other times, and quite unexpectedly, they were given a marked emotional upset after recalling a list of syllables just presented. The back of the chair collapsed, an electric shock was felt in the arms, scrap metal fell from the ceiling to the floor, a pistol shot rang out, and the lights went off, producing total darkness. All of this happened simultaneously. As soon as the commotion ceased, the subject was again asked to recall all of the syllables that he could remember. With the emotion-provoking situation interpolated between first and second recalls, retention was decreased more than under the control condition. In some individual cases there was a very large decrease. After experiencing the situation described, one subject forgot every syllable in the list.[62] ☐

An important cause of forgetting in everyday life and in laboratory experiments with human subjects is conflict between what has been learned and subsequent learning. One interferes with recall of the other. With respect to retention, there is negative transfer. When the learning of one habit interferes with retention of a subsequent habit, we have an example of forgetting produced by *proactive inhibition*. Of greater overall significance, however, is forgetting caused by interference with retention of the first habit by the learning of a second habit. Interference on this basis is *retroactive inhibition*.

Proactive inhibition

Proactive inhibition may be demonstrated by an experiment designed as follows: There are two comparable groups, the experimental and the control. The experimental group learns a list of nonsense syllables (list A) and then another list of nonsense syllables (list B). The control group, on the other hand, learns list B without having first learned list A. It can be demonstrated that the control group learns list B to the criterion more rapidly and with fewer errors than the experimental group. But what of retention, which is of major interest to us here? In a test of retention for list B, the control group is again ahead. The learning of list A by the experimental group interferes not only with the learning of list B but also with retention of it.

The poorer retention of list B by the group that had first learned list A could perhaps be attributed to differences in the associative strength of the list B syllables for the experimental and control groups. It could also be attributed to the intrusion, while recalling list B, of syllables from list A. For instance: list A has the syllables DAX, RIK, etc; list B has the syllables SEK, LAK, etc. In recalling list B, the subject who has already learned list A may erroneously recall DAX or RIK. This is especially possible if the syllables in the two lists have a degree of similarity.[63]

There is a further example of proactive inhibition by intrusion, one that is closer to everyday life. The author is copying a quotation. He looks at the source, then at the paper on which he is writing. As he recalls what he has just read, he occasionally substitutes a word from his own vocabulary for the word that he read. Thus, the printed page says: "The human brain is composed of some 10 billion nerve cells, more or less alike, which interact in various ways. . . ." What he writes is: "The human brain *has* some 10 billion *neurons*, more or less alike, which interact in *numerous* ways. . . ." It is this kind of proactive inhibition that makes it incumbent upon those who quote others to check, word for word, what has been copied.

A similar process is perhaps involved in falsification such as occurs when we repeat a story with additions, give erroneous testimony, or introduce changes in reproductions of drawings. In each instance, there may be intrusions from earlier experience which interfere with, or supplant, particular features that we are trying to recall or reproduce.

Retroactive inhibition

Experiments on retroactive inhibition provide further evidence for the widely held view that much forgetting comes from the effects of activity interpolated between original learning and recall. In a typical experiment on retroactive inhibition, a large group memorizes a list of nonsense syllables, list A. On the basis of this performance, the subjects are separated into two groups with the same mean score. One group (experimental) then learns another list of nonsense syllables, list B. While they are doing this, the control group rests or, to prevent rehearsal of list A, sings, tells stories, or does something else unrelated to learning nonsense syllables. After the experimental group has learned list B, both groups recall as much as they can of list A. The general design of the experiment is as follows:

Experimental Group	*Control Group*
Learns List A	Learns List A
Learns List B	Rests
Recalls List A	Recalls List A

What happens under these circumstances is that the recall score for the experimental group is usually much lower than that for the control group. This applies rather uniformly to individual scores as well as to group averages.

Thus learning list B obviously interferes with the retaining of list A.

Retention is poorer when new learning comes soon after original learning than when it comes later. This is demonstrated by an experiment with 1000 school children.

☐ The children were separated into groups equated for age, sex, and other nonexperimental factors. Some children studied twenty-five verbs and then recalled all they could after twenty-one minutes and after twenty-four hours. The experimental group studied a list of nouns for seven minutes of the interval. Some of the experimental group studied the nouns immediately after studying the verbs, others studied them following a rest of four minutes, and still others following a rest of eight minutes. Thus, the interpolated learning came at different intervals after learning. The control group sang familiar songs during the entire twenty-one-minute period.

Retention scores averaged 121 for controls and between 50 and 69 for experimental groups. The lowest retention scores within the experimental group were made by those who had interpolated study immediately after learning. The longer the rest period between learning and interpolated study, the higher the retention scores. Retention after twenty-four hours showed little loss for the control group, but a large loss for the experimental group. Again, the earlier the new learning, the poorer the retention.[64] ☐

Various investigations have shown that there is also a relation between the degree of forgetting and the *similarity* of the interpolated activity to that involved in original learning. With a very high degree of dissimilarity (as between memorizing words and singing), there is relatively little retroactive inhibition. With a high degree of similarity (as between memorizing nonsense syllables and memorizing other nonsense syllables), there is usually a large degree of retroactive inhibition. Within these extremes the relationship between degree of similarity and degree of retroaction is a complicated one which we need not consider here.

To say that forgetting is due to retroactive inhibition, wholly or in part, does not, of course, explain it. The question, "Why does interpolated learning interfere with retention?" needs to be answered. There are a number of probable reasons. One is that learning new material leads to unlearning of the old, especially in the sense that the new responses supplant the old.[65] Another reason, also given to explain why Ebbinghaus forgot more than other subjects in comparable experiments (p. 387), is that items learned formerly tend to intrude themselves during tests of retention. Ebbinghaus, it will be recalled, had learned many lists, whereas subjects in the more recent studies learned and relearned only one list. It has been demonstrated, in fact, that subjects recalling a list of nonsense syllables after the interpolation of another list are often bothered by intrusions from the interpolated material. They give items from the interpolated list in place of the items they are trying to recall.[66] But even when the interpolated items are not overtly recalled, there may be implicit conflict from them which interferes with recall of the initial material. Still another reason often given for poor retention after interpolated learning is that this interferes with perseveration, with reverberating circuits, or, in more general terms, with the setting or consolidation of the original memory trace. The same principle has been invoked (see p. 355) to account for the superiority of distributed over massed practice. This idea cannot be discounted entirely, although there are some difficulties with it, including our ignorance of what memory traces are like, the fact that similar interpolated material is more disturbing than dissimilar material, and the observation that even after a long interval (during which consolidation of the trace should have occurred) interpolated material still produces interference.[67] It is likely that unlearning, intrusions, and interference with consolidation of the memory trace are all involved to some degree. Early interpolation may interfere with retention primarily because it disturbs the consolidation process. Later interpolation may do so, not by disturbing consolidation, but by causing the individual to unlearn earlier material or to confuse the new material with the old, as in the case of interlist intrusions.

In view of the above, how can we answer the question, "Why do we forget?" One must say that the forgetting of different habits, and forgetting in different situations, may require different explanations. Lapse of time (or disuse of the memory trace) could be responsible for some forgetting, but this has not been demonstrated in a conclusive manner. Time itself is of course important only because it provides the opportunity for things to happen. Improved retention following relative inactivity (including sleep) suggests that activities which occur after learning are more responsible for forgetting than the lapse of time as such. This view is supported by studies showing that the interpolation of new learning tends to weaken retention of the old (retroactive inhibition). Such is especially evident when verbal habits, like recall of lists of nonsense or verbal materials are involved. Some explanations of retroactive inhibition, such as presence of inter-list intrusions, could apply only to such habits. It has been demonstrated that earlier learning may, by interfering with new learning, weaken retention of the latter (proactive inhibition). Some forgetting depends upon a poor original impression. Some depends upon the desire to forget and some on absence of relevant stimulation. There is also an obliterating effect upon the memory trace from emotional upset. Electroconvulsive shock is conducive to forgetting, presumably because it obliterates memory traces. Numerous as these reasons are, there are perhaps still other reasons why we forget. ■

MEMORY TRAINING

Almost everybody would like to improve his memory. Some want to remember names and faces better. Salesmen would like to remember "selling points" better. Public speakers would like to remember their speeches — or at least remember outlines — so that they could avoid reading them. Students would like to remember better the important points of a lecture or an assignment. They would like to be able to read lists of French verbs, say, and remember them without a large amount of study. And they would like to have more suc-cess in recalling the foreign equivalents of English words, or vice versa. It is not surprising, therefore, that the development of mnemonic systems has a long history, and that, even today, thousands of people buy courses whose authors promise improved memory.[68]

Of course all of us use various devices to remember things that are ordinarily difficult to retain. To quote a *Scientific American* writer,

☐ "Everyone uses mnemonic devices — ways of memorizing bits of information by associating them with things that are easier to remember. In the U.S. the most familiar of these devices is surely the rhyme beginning: "Thirty days hath September. . . ." Another well-known mnemonic device is: "Every good boy does fine" (for EGBDF, the lines of the musical staff).

The same principle can also be applied, with ingenious variations, to the memorizing of numbers. Such tricks come easily to mathematicians. When Bertrand Russell visited New York in 1951 he told a newspaper columnist that he had no difficulty in recalling the number of his room at the Waldorf-Astoria — 1414 — because 1.414 is the square root of 2."[69] ☐

Mnemonic courses facilitate remembering, not by developing some hypothetical entity called "memory," as a muscle might be developed by exercise, but by teaching people to utilize various devices which facilitate learning and recall. In the last analysis, whatever success is achieved by those who adopt such devices comes from an increased efficiency of learning or the acquisition of some crutch which facilitates recall.

If you follow principles like those involved in any memory system, you may improve your "memory"; but, if such improvement does occur, your "memory" will return to its former efficiency (or should we say, inefficiency?) whenever you fail to use the principles. Sheer memorizing of something, with the idea that it will improve memory as exercise improves a muscle, is a waste of time. This was amply demonstrated in an experiment on college students.[70] One group which simply memorized various materials showed no improvement later in memorizing similar materials. On the other hand, a group which learned to apply efficient principles of learning while memorizing did show an improvement in later memorizing. The improvement came because principles learned while memorizing one set of material were applied to memorizing the other. This is an example of transfer resulting from application of principles. Some of the principles involved in this experiment and a few additional ones are summarized below in the form of rules that one might consider when embarking on a learning task.

(1) Have the intention to learn. Suppose, for example, that you are introduced to Mr. Flynn. The person introducing him says, "I would like you to meet Mr. Flynn." You will probably say, "How do you do," "Pleased to meet you," or something similar. You may not even have listened to the name. You may have listened, but without hearing it correctly. Your poor memory for names may therefore be attributed to failure, in the first place, to learn the name.

(2) If you have the intention to learn, you will also pay close attention to what is before you. If it is important for you to remember Mr. Flynn's name, you will probably listen attentively as the name is spoken.

(3) Use imagery to the fullest possible extent. Try to get a photographic impression of Mr. Flynn which may be revived later. Notice his eyes, his hair, how he is dressed, and so on. If he has a particular accent, that may help you to recall. Some systems advise picturing him doing something ridiculous, the more ridiculous the image the better.

(4) Tie up what you are learning with other things. That is to say, develop as many associations as possible. William James once said:

□ "In mental terms, the more other facts a fact is associated with in the mind, the better possession of it our memory retains. Each of its associates becomes a hook to which it hangs, a means to fish it up by when sunk beneath the surface. Together they form a network of attachments by which it is woven into the entire tissue of our thought. 'The secret of a good memory' is thus the secret of forming diverse and multiple associations with every fact we care to retain. But this forming of associations with a fact, what is it but *thinking about* the fact as much as possible? Briefly, then, of two men with the same outward experiences and the same amount of mere native tenacity, the one who THINKS over his experiences most, and weaves them into systematic relations with each other, will be the one with the best memory."[71] □

Individuals sometimes marvel at how an expert in some field can read a new book in a couple of hours and retain what they could retain only after a course of intensive study. The reason for the expert's "better memory" is, of course, his background in the field. He has, as it were, many hooks on which to hang what he reads. The newcomer to the field must "start from scratch."

Most memory "systems" give major emphasis to association. Some of these advise one to memorize a list of logically related words. First this list is mastered thoroughly, so that it can be said forward and backward, and the word in any position (sixth, forty-first, and so on) can be recalled without hesitation. Then each new thing to be remembered is, as it were, "hooked" onto one of these words or placed in the appropriate "file." If a list of "selling points" is to be memorized, for example, the first is associated with the first word in the list and the second with the second word, and so on. The key words, being so thoroughly retained, are recalled quite readily. In being recalled, they tend to bring the respective "selling point" with them.

In stressing association, most memory systems utilize the idea of getting vivid, even ridiculous associations, in addition to those provided by the system itself.[72]

(5) Rhythm is an aid to retention. This has been shown in several laboratory researches and it is exemplified in the theme songs of radio advertising, and in rhymes such as, "Winston tastes good like a cigarette should." The writer learned the multiplication table in a sort of sing-song and this no doubt helped it stick. There are decided limits, however, to the application of rhythm in learning.

(6) Distribute your learning as much as possible. If it can be avoided, do not cram.

You may "get by" the next day, but chances are that you will not retain very much over longer periods.

(7) Where possible, rehearse or recite. We have already pointed out the advantages of recitation compared with passive reading.

(8) Rest, or better still, sleep after you have studied. From what we know about the obliterating effect of interpolated activities, it is poor practice to study one subject immediately after another. There should at least be a pause in which any study is avoided. ■

• SUMMARY

Remembering is retaining. Retention is mediated by neural modifications, the anatomical and physiological details of which are not yet known. Such modifications are referred to as memory traces, neurograms, or more simply as engrams.

Before language develops, memory is evidenced by: reproduction of a motor performance; the relearning of a habit with a saving in trials, errors, or time; and delayed reaction. Ability to do delayed reactions indicates the presence of recall memory, an elementary symbolic process. It is symbolic because an engram of some kind represents (is a symbol for) what is recalled. The interval between removal of a critical stimulus and successful recall increases as we ascend the animal scale. It also increases in the individual from infancy to maturity. Bridging the time interval is greatly facilitated when verbal symbols are acquired.

Verbal recall is studied in a variety of ways. Special attention has been given to the memory span, the memorizing of item lists by various procedures, recall of narratives, reproduction of forms, testimony, and eidetic imagery. All of these involve recall and, with respect to some of them (narratives, testimony), we noted errors which have significance in such aspects of everyday life as transmission of rumors and inaccurate testimony. In recall of narratives, pictures, and events, the theme is usually retained, but the details change, some being omitted and others added. When eidetic imagery is present, recall may be unusually accurate, much as in so-called photographic memory.

Any fraction of some former stimulating situation may be sufficient to elicit recall of the whole situation. This is response in terms of reduced cues. Another name for it is redintegration.

In recognizing, we differentiate the familiar from the unfamiliar. This is easier than recall. False recognition shows the influence of reduced cues.

Procedures which facilitate learning are also conducive to good retention. Distributed learning and recitation exemplify this principle. Although overlearning aids retention, there are diminishing returns from large amounts of it.

Under ordinary circumstances, fast learners retain more than slow learners. This is because they learn more in the same learning period and because they overlearn. But when the associative strength of what is learned is held constant, fast and slow learners retain equally well.

Forgetting, in an ultimate sense, is failing to retain — a loss of the memory trace. On the other hand, forgetting may occur even though the memory trace remains. This is evident in repressive forgetting, an extreme form of which is functional retrograde amnesia. Forgetting sometimes occurs because stimulation adequate to activate the memory trace is absent. Recall of what has apparently been forgotten may be facilitated by hypnosis, use of sodium pentathol, and direct electrical stimulation of certain regions in the temporal cortex. Some "forgetting" may also be attributed to absence of a memory trace (or a poor one), as in anterograde amnesia.

Experimental studies show that forgetting is at first rapid, then relatively slow. Although there may be some deterioration of the memory trace with time (with disuse), this has not been demonstrated conclusively. There is much evidence, on the other hand, that forgetting is produced, not by time *per se*, but by what happens in time. For example: the least amount of forgetting occurs after inactivity and sleep; the greatest amount, after interpolation of activities between original learning and tests of retention. The latter effect (retroactive inhibition) is greatest when the new learning comes soon after the original and when it involves similar, but not of course identical, material. Earlier learning may also interfere with learning and recall of what is learned later. This is the phenomenon of proactive inhibition. In retroactive and proactive inhibition we have further examples of negative transfer effects. These effects are sometimes rather obviously due to the intrusion, into what is being recalled, of items learned earlier. Sometimes there may be conflict without actual intrusion. With respect to retroactive inhibition, there is also the possibility that interpolated learning interferes with perseveration and consolidation of the memory trace. Moreover, in learning interpolated material, a subject may, to some extent, unlearn the original material. There is at present no reason for concluding that any one of these factors operates to the exclusion of the others.

Memory training does not develop a "memory" faculty, it merely increases the efficiency of learning. Using the principles involved — intending to learn, using imagery, associating — will improve one's "memory"; but, whenever he fails to apply them, his "memory" will be no better than it was before. ■

REFERENCES AND NOTES FOR THIS CHAPTER ARE IN THE APPENDIX.

• SELECTED READINGS

Bartlett, F. C., *Remembering*. Cambridge University Press, 1932. A classic experimental study which deals with social as well as individual aspects.

Daniel, R. S. (Ed.), *Contemporary Readings in General Psychology*. Houghton Mifflin, 1965. Readings 20–22: Young's paper on memory systems in the brain, Miller's on information and memory, and Whalen's on accuracy of testimony.

Ebbinghaus, H., *Memory*. Columbia University Press, 1913. The pioneer scientific study of memory, first published in German in 1885.

Filloux, J-C., *Memory and Forgetting*. Walker, 1963. A brief, interesting, and largely philosophical treatment which emphasizes the contributions of French psychologists.

McGeoch, J. A., and A. L. Irion, *The Psychology of Human Learning* (2nd ed.). Longmans, Green, 1952. See Chapter 10 for additional information on retention and forgetting.

Melton, A. W. (Ed.), *Categories of Human Learning*. Academic Press, 1964. See the chapters by Underwood (rote verbal learning) and Postman (short-term memory).

Miller, G. A., *Psychology: The Science of Mental Life*. Harper and Row, 1962. Chaps. X, XI have interesting discussions of recognizing, identifying, and other aspects of memory.

Morgan, C. T., *Physiological Psychology* (3rd ed.), McGraw-Hill, 1965, pp. 546–555, on chemistry and the memory trace.

Postman, L., "The Present Status of Interference Theory," Chapter 7 in C. N. Cofer and B. S. Musgrave, *Verbal Learning and Verbal Behavior*. McGraw-Hill, 1961.

Riley, D. A., "Memory for Form," in L. Postman, *Psychology in the Making*. Knopf, 1962. An historically oriented study.

Underwood, B. J., and R. W. Schultz, *Meaningfulness and Verbal Learning*. Lippincott, 1960. This is concerned especially with factors which determine the meaningfulness of trigrams and other such items.

Weinland, J. D., *How to Improve Your Memory*. Barnes and Noble, 1957. A psychologically sound treatise on improving recall of names and factual material.

Woodworth, R. S., and H. Schlosberg, *Experimental Psychology* (rev. ed.). Holt, 1954. See Chapter 23 for an excellent survey of experimental research on memory.

13

Thinking

*T*hinking involves manipulation of symbols which represent past experience. When we think of something, the symbol may be a word for it, a gesture which represents it, an image of it, or some less obvious substitute, like muscle tension which has come to have meaning in terms of past experience. Kinesthetic imagery has often been suggested as an aspect of the thought processes. Who has not seemed to be on the verge of recalling something, yet without any word or clear image of what he seeks? The vague inner tension which appears to exist under such circumstances may well be kinesthetic. But engrams may also serve a symbolic function without being externalized in verbal or gestural expressions and without the arousal of images.

We think with what we retain from past learning; but we also, through our thought processes, learn things that we did not know before. The inventor puts together bits of information relevant to the problem before him and he comes up with something new. The atomic scientists, following the same general procedure, could predict the atomic explosion before it had ever occurred. Thinking about what was already known to them taught them something not known before. The fact that we may learn by thinking has led psychologists to refer to thought as a "higher learning process."

Thinking is typically a sequential arousal of symbols. We think of one thing; that starts us thinking of another; that of still another, and so on. In this way we manipulate and rearrange, as it were, the various aspects of the world which have fallen within the range of our experience. Except when we "think out loud," this process is carried on implicitly. Words are unspoken and the gestures are so abbreviated as to escape notice. The images are by their very nature implicit.

In this chapter our chief concern is with the kind of thinking called *reasoning*. Reasoning is distinguished from mere *thinking of* something, because it involves a *sequence* of symbolic activities. When you *think of* something, you are of course calling up symbols which, like those aroused in the delayed reaction experiments, enable you to respond in terms of absent stimuli. This aspect of the thought processes is synonymous with *recall*.

Reasoning also differs from what has been called *reverie*, or free association of ideas. This is because, in reasoning, what we recall and the sequence of associations involved are controlled. In reverie, the associations are random, as they would most likely be if I should ask you to say every word which comes to mind. In reasoning, however, the "associations begin in a problem, and end in its solution."[1] The nature of the problem gives us a directional *set*. It produces selective rather than indiscriminate recall. Suppose instead of asking you to say every word that comes to mind, I should ask you to say the names of animals. Then you would have an "animal set." Your associations would concern animals, and nothing else. In reasoning, the set comes from the problem. If the problem is how to get the car started, we think of things that might be wrong with the car, not of unrelated things.

Reasoning is distinguished from the type of thinking called *fantasy* by being more realistic than the latter. Typical forms of fantasy are dreaming and daydreaming. Dreaming is often directed toward the solution of a problem — but the solution is usually unrealistic. Sometimes the dream is a symbolic wish-fulfillment, as claimed by Freud. You would, let us say, like to spend a winter in Florida. In the dream you buy your ticket, get on the train, see the landscape passing by, alight at a fashionable seaside resort, and so on, even though there is, in reality, no chance of your being able to make the trip. The dream fulfills your wish, but only symbolically.

Sometimes the dream fantasy looks like an attempt to explain some sort of present stimulation. You dream, for example, that you are hanging by your hands from a skyscraper, you see the street way below with its toy-sized people and vehicles, your fingers are slipping, and you scream for help, perhaps waking yourself. Then you find that you are lying on your back with your arms stretched back in an awkward position, caught under the end of the bed. You are actually in a predicament, but not the predicament symbolically represented. The writer once dreamed that he was trying to escape from hell, but woke to find his feet on a hot radiator. The dream fantasy often, so to speak, seeks a way out of difficulties.

Daydreams are essentially like dreams. The fantasy is again usually unrealistic. If you are not able to meet your financial obligations, for example, you may imagine yourself winning thousands of dollars in a contest, digging up buried treasure in your garden, or receiving a legacy from some rich uncle. You may, on the other hand, lay definite plans to solve your problem. You may think of getting a job that pays a larger salary, of selling some of your property, or of doing some extra work in spare hours. If these are realistic solutions — solutions probable of accomplishment — we say that you have been reasoning, rather than that you have been daydreaming. ■

EVIDENCE FOR REASONING

Some ancient writers referred to man as "the reasoning animal" and at the same time implied that other organisms do not reason. We now know that man is not the only reasoning animal. Reasoning is evident in lower mammals like the rat. But how do we know? What is the evidence? Our discussion of the evidence will serve three purposes: (1) to tell how we know that animals can reason, (2) to demonstrate how the same problems may be used to compare animal and human reasoning, and (3) to indicate something of the nature of reasoning itself — especially in its elementary stages.

Looked at from one standpoint, reasoning is combining past experiences in order to solve a problem which cannot be solved by mere reproduction of earlier solutions. Rats, as we know, are good at learning mazes. They acquire a series of responses which leads them to the food; or, as some would say, they learn where the food is. In any event, there is no evidence here of reasoning. It is conceivable that the rat is responding directly to stimuli without the mediation of symbolic activity. Suppose, however, that we teach the animal two different habits as illustrated and explained in Figure 13.1, then confront it with a new problem — one that can be solved only if both habits are combined. If an untutored solution is achieved, if the problem is solved more or less suddenly, by "putting two and two together," we must credit the animal with at least a modicum of reasoning ability.

In a variety of tests like that illustrated, rats have indeed shown that they can put two and two together. They first learn how to get onto or off one table (by climbing or sliding down a ringstand). They learn to obtain food by climbing a ringstand to another table and running along the proper pathway. But they have never descended from the first table, run across the floor, and climbed the ringstand to the second table. In the crucial test, in which this is the only way to reach the food, some rats solve the problem. After a certain amount of random activity on the first table, they slide down the ringstand, run across the floor to the other ringstand, climb it, and run to the food. The ringstand climbed is the one involved in the particular animal's early training.[2]

The behavior of some rats in this test resembles the insightful problem-solving discussed in the context of learning processes.

A somewhat comparable test has been used with children. The subjects were between four and eight years old, but insightful behavior was not shown by children under five.[3]

Reasoning at a higher level of difficulty than that just described calls for more than insightful observation. It requires discovery of a relationship between otherwise disconnected events — that is to say, a principle or a generalization. Animals and infants cannot tell us the principle, of course, but we can discern from their behavior whether or not they have discovered it.

As an example of this type of reasoning test let us take the *double-alternation problem*. This has been used with animals ranging from

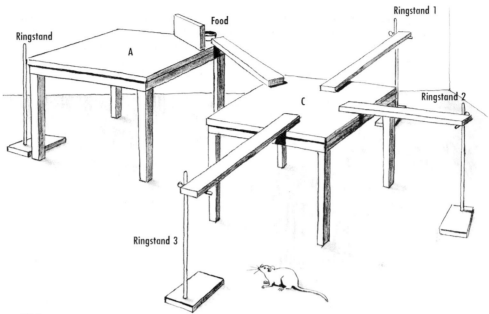

● **13.1**

A Reasoning Test for Rats. A rat is first allowed to explore the room, the ringstand, and table A, reached by climbing the ringstand. The partition around the food blocks off this region. Preliminary exploration continues for a few days so that familiarity with every aspect of the situation may develop. Table C is then added and an elevated pathway is run from it to the food. Three other paths, each reached by a ringstand, are connected with C as illustrated. Any one of these ringstands and pathways leads, via C, to the food. Learning to run from any part of the room, up a ringstand and onto table A is Experience I. It does not enable the rat to reach the place where food will appear in the actual reasoning test. After addition of C and the new ringstands and paths, the animal is trained to climb one of the three ringstands and traverse the path which runs from it to C, and from C to the food. This is Experience II. The test of reasoning comes when the rat is placed at A. Its problem is to reach the food. It has learned to descend a ringstand (part of Experience I), and it has learned to climb, let us say, ringstand 3 and proceed from that point to C, and then to the food (Experience II). But it has never before descended the original ringstand and gone to ringstand 3. Will the rat bridge this gap? If it does so without further training, one may conclude that it has combined the two separate experiences. (After N. R. F. Maier, "Reasoning in White Rats," *Comp. Psychol. Monogr.*, 1929, No. 6, p. 23.)

rats to monkeys and with human beings at various age levels from infancy to adulthood. The most common form of double-alternation test utilizes what is called a *temporal maze*, to distinguish it from the spatial mazes with which we are already familiar from our study of maze learning. In a temporal maze, as the name implies, the animal makes different turns in the same place at different times instead of always the same turn, as in spatial mazes.

Animals and young children are often tested in temporal mazes with open alleys, but older children and adults may be tested with a stylus form of the same pattern, as illustrated in Figure 13.2. A two-box double-alternation test (Figure 13.3, p. 405) has also been used with younger children. But, whichever version we use, the problem is similar — i.e., to make a series of responses such as *right, right, left, left* (*rrll*), or the reverse.

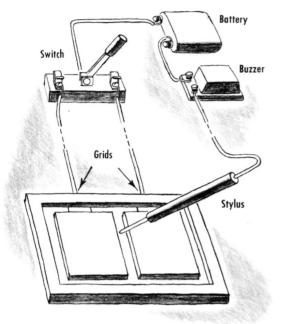

Switch
Battery
Buzzer
Grids
Stylus

● 13.2
A Stylus Form of Hunter's Double-Alternation Temporal Maze. The stylus is shown in the central alley near the choice point. As he moves toward the bifurcation at the top, the subject must decide whether to go to the right or the left. The buzzer sounds whenever he makes the wrong choice. For further explanation, see the text.

After walking (or tracing) the central alley, the subject is required to turn right the first time, right next, then left, and finally left again. Four trips constitute one trial. A rest follows. Each correct turn brings a reward, although in the case of adults this is perhaps no more than the knowledge that a correct response has been made. Each incorrect turn may bring an electric shock or, in the case of human subjects, a buzzer or some other signal that an error has been made. After a wrong turn, the subject must retrace until the correct alley is reached.

☐ Note that the apparatus is bilaterally symmetrical, and that there are no external differential cues to guide the subject. If a dim light flashed on whenever a right turn was to be made and a bright light whenever a left turn was required, these lights would serve as differential cues. We would have a mere discrimination problem. The correct turn would be made in terms of the brightness of the light at the end of the central alley.

Suppose that no lights were present, but that the right and left turns were made in different places within the apparatus. Then we would have the type of maze considered earlier and referred to as a *spatial maze* because the turns differ spatially. Differing in spatial position, they provide different visual, auditory, olfactory, tactual, and kinesthetic cues to which the respective turns may become conditioned. Making the correct turns in this type of maze, whatever their sequence, would provide no proof of reasoning. In the *temporal maze* used in reasoning tests, however, each turn occurs in the same place, at the end of the central alley. In short, a temporal rather than a spatial sequence is learned. Moreover, all external conditions are identical, regardless of whether the turn required at any moment is right or left.

But how about kinesthetic cues; those associated with muscle tensions? One might think that these would provide cues for the required turn. If the sequence were *rlrl* instead of *rrll*, this might be true. Having turned to the right in one trial might produce muscle tensions which would persist until the animal reached the same point again. These cues might become conditioned to a left turn. Likewise, muscle tensions persisting after the left turn might serve as conditioned stimuli for a right turn. But in the *rrll* sequence, no such guidance is possible. After having turned right the first time, the animal might have muscle tensions which would guide it to the right again. On the third trip, however, the same muscle tensions would have to guide the animal to the left. Muscle tensions from just having gone to the left would then have to guide to the left again. In a continuation of the sequence, the same tensions would have to guide the animal to the right. In other words, the same muscle tensions would at some stages have to guide the animal in one direction and at other stages in another direction. Such a dual guidance by the same stimuli in close temporal succession is impossible. The only satisfactory explanation of *rrll* responses in the temporal maze is that the animal somehow "figures out" the proper sequence.[4] □

Human subjects usually formulate this problem verbally. They attack it in an overt trial-and-error fashion at first, but soon begin to test out this or that hypothesis. The correct hypothesis is sometimes hit upon rather suddenly. A subject may seem to be making no progress — then a correct sequence occurs. Following this he says something like "Oh, I get it. You go two times to the right and two times to the left." He often reports that he tried out and tested various other hypotheses before hitting upon the correct one.

White rats, the lowest animals tested with the temporal maze, have not learned the problem in its usual form, even in one thousand trials. But some learned the solution by other means. They first learned the separate turns in different T-shaped boxes. Then the *rr* sequence was taught in one box and the *ll* sequence in another. Transferred to the temporal maze after such training, a few of the rats eventually learned the *rrll* sequence. When required to continue after the *rrll* series, they responded *lllll*. . . . Rats thus failed to continue the sequence.[5]

Raccoons, on the other hand, have learned the sequence in the temporal maze directly — that is, without preliminary training in other mazes — and have continued the sequence for two additional turns, making the response series *rrllrrrr*. This shows a much better grasp of the problem than occurs in rats. Monkeys have done better still. In a special form of the problem, they have learned an *rrllrrll* sequence, then extended the series to eight additional turns, their total series of responses being *rrllrrllrrllrrll*.[6]

Human performance on double-alternation tests improves as the adult level is approached and it also correlates with intelligence as measured by standardized tests. One of the most extensive studies[7] used the apparatus illustrated in Figure 13.3.

□ Thirty-one children between the ages of two and six years were confronted with two boxes placed side by side, each with a lid.

● **13.3**
An Apparatus to Study Reasoning in Children. The child obtains candy when he opens the correct box. As described in the text, the candy is placed twice in the right-hand box, then twice in the left-hand box, and so on, for a series of eight trials. The child must discover the correct sequence. (From W. S. Hunter and S. C. Bartlett, "Double Alternation in Young Children," *J. Exper. Psychol.*, 1948, *38*, p. 559. Photo, courtesy S. C. Bartlett.)

Upon being brought into the room the child was asked, "Would you like to play this game?" If he said he would, he was allowed to examine the apparatus and open and close the lids. The experimenter said, "I'll put candy in the boxes." Then, "Shall we begin?" Both of the experimenter's hands were put into the boxes, but one left a very small piece of candy in what was, for that trial, the correct box. This was done in accordance with a scheme unknown to the child. The candy was placed in a given box in accordance with the sequence *right, right, left, left*. On the first trial, for example, the candy was in the right-hand box. On the next it was also in the right-hand box. On the next it was in the left-hand box, and so on. What the child was to learn — what he was to figure out in terms of his success or failure on particular trials — was the sequence followed by the experimenter. But he was told nothing about this. All he knew, until he learned further details through reasoning, was that candy could be obtained by opening lids. If he made an incorrect response, the child of course found no candy. In order to get it he had to reach into the other box. Each time the sequence had been run through, the child had a brief rest period. Then the sequence was repeated. The child continued until he achieved three successive errorless sequences.

Two out of eight three-year-olds solved the problem described. All of eleven four-year-olds solved it. The number of trials required for solution decreased with age, as one might expect. The youngest child who solved the problem by verbalizing was five years old. Children who did this showed that their reasoning process was somewhat as follows: "I know now: two times and two times" or "They go one, and then in the same, and then in the other."

In another investigation with children a card form of the test was used.[8] Five playing cards were placed face down before the subject, four of them with black figures and the other with red. The red card was alternated from the left to the right of the spread, in an *llrr* sequence. Each time the cards were placed before the child, he was to turn one over. If this was red, it was of course correct. A test was terminated when the child had been given thirty trials, or when he had turned over the red card in two successive *llrr* sequences. There were forty children in each of the age groups 6 to 12 years. The correlation (rho) between C.A. and number of correct responses was .77. M.A. correlated .59 with correct responses.

Normal adults learn double-alternation problems much more readily than children. In one study the average number of errors was thirty for children and sixteen for adults.[9] □

The process which underlies ability to learn the double-alternation problem is not known. However, a recent study with college students, in which they learned a verbal-conditioning version of the problem, leads to the conclusion that they "remember previous events at least far enough back to discern the pattern."[10] The difficulty that rats have in learning double alternation is attributed to poor "immediate memory." However, even granting that immediate memory is important, discerning the pattern is also necessary, and this is

where reasoning, as such, enters the situation.

In addition to showing that animals as well as men can reason, the studies we have reviewed indicate that reasoning is not necessarily verbal. However, three things are essential. In order to reason, an organism must (1) retain aspects of earlier experience, (2) recall these when occasion arises, and (3) combine them in such a manner as to solve problem situations. Most animals can retain, but mammals alone have shown evidence of recall — as in the delayed-reaction test (pp. 374–376). We have seen that mammals from rats to men may, upon occasion, achieve the higher level, reasoning. ■

THINKING MACHINES

It is interesting to observe that the "electronic brains" or "thinking machines," about which we hear so much today, have retentive and associative functions built into them. There are memory devices (punched cards, magnetic tapes, or electronic tubes) which store in coded form the information fed into the machine. Then there are devices for giving the machine access to the "memories" relevant to a problem and for collating these in such a manner as to provide a solution.[11]

Apart from the fact that "reasoning" done by "thinking machines" is merely computational, there are other major differences between the most complex of these and a thinking organism. Take, for instance, the problem of finding the area of a right triangle. As shown in Figure 13.4, we may consider the area of such a triangle as one-half that of a rectangle whose area is the base times the height of the triangle. A child who is taught this may transfer the solution to similar triangles in different dimensions. A "thinking machine" could answer the same problem, and do so rapidly, when given it in suitable form. But the process would be entirely routine.

Before a "thinking machine" could begin to calculate anything, even the area of a right triangle, the procedure to be followed would need to be programmed, step by step, somewhat as in the legend of Figure 13.4. To quote George A. Miller, whose example we have borrowed:

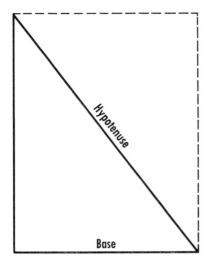

Hypotenuse

Base

● **13.4**

Finding the Area of a Right Triangle. It is possible to find the area of any right triangle with only the base and hypotenuse given, by following the algebraic steps: (1) $h + b = v$, (2) $h - b = w$, (3) $v \times w = x$, (4) $\sqrt{x} = \pm y$, (5) $y \times b = z$, (6) $z/2 = $ area. On the other hand, as Wertheimer pointed out in his *Productive Thinking*, there is a way to teach this problem which gives more insight. Observing that the triangle is one-half of a rectangle of the same height and base, the learner can solve this problem more simply, and with greater understanding and transfer value, by finding the altitude with the Pythagorean theorem (the square on the hypotenuse equals the sum of the squares of the other sides), the area of the rectangle from the base and altitude, and the area of the triangle by halving this. (After G. A. Miller, "Information and Memory," *Scientific American*, August 1956, 42.)

□ "The machine is able to perform arithmetical operations such as addition, subtraction, multiplication, division, and the extraction of roots. Instruction for the machine consists in writing a "program" — like the series of steps [in the figure] except that the computer's program must be even more explicit and detailed, with even less hint of the basic strategy. Computing machine engineers have their hearts set on some day designing machines

which will construct programs for themselves: that is, given the strategy for handling a problem, the machine will understand the problem well enough to create all the appropriate operations or subroutines required to solve it. The desirability of such a development is obvious. In the first place, at present it takes many hours of drudgery to write the detailed instructions for all the steps a computer must take. Then, after the instructions have been written, they must be stored in the machine in some easily accessible form. In a large machine the number of subroutines may run into thousands; it might actually be more economical to equip the machine with the ability to create them on demand rather than to build the necessary storage and access machinery. In other words, in a very elaborate computer it would be more efficient to store rules from which subroutines could be generated than to store the routines themselves."[12] □

One would not give as simple a problem as that illustrated to a computing machine. It is much more easily solved with one's own brain. However, enough has been said to emphasize the fact that, despite current interest in "electronic brains" or "thinking machines," none has yet even approached the versatility of a human brain.[13]

There is obviously much more to thinking than one finds in a rat solving elementary reasoning problems, a monkey discovering the principle of a double-alternation problem, or an electronic computer finding the answer to a complex mathematical problem. Some of the differences in the thinking of rats, monkeys, and machines will become increasingly evident as human reasoning is discussed. ■

THE REASONING PROCESS

Reasoning does not occur unless there is a difficulty, or unless a question has arisen for which there is no ready answer. It is quite possible that the rats and other animals used in our experiments on reasoning reasoned then for the first time in their lives. It is quite possible, too, that they never again reasoned after psychologists finished the experiment. In order to induce these organisms to reason, it was necessary to confront them with problems which could not be solved by mere reproduction of former solutions, by conditioning, or by overt trial and error.

In man, also, reasoning is only initiated by situations which cannot be met in a routine manner. We may go for hours or even days without reasoning, especially if our work is so routine that habitual modes of response enable us to meet, in a more or less automatic way, every situation that arises. As soon as habitual modes of response fail, however, reasoning is likely to begin. Some problems of everyday life which initiate reasoning are how to get certain things done, how to make something go that has stopped, how to get food, how to pay our bills, how to get where we want to go, and how to avoid distressing situations. Being human, we also express curiosity about aspects of the world. We want to know what certain things are for, and why certain events occur. An average child of three years is already puzzled by objects, situations, and events not directly related to its personal adjustments.

In their investigations of human reasoning, psychologists have, for the most part, used relatively artificial situations in which verbal, numerical, or graphic symbols predominate. Sir Frederic Bartlett, who regards thinking as "a high-level form of skilled behavior, requiring signs and symbols for its expression," has drawn attention to what he calls "thinking within closed systems."[14] Here certain information, or evidence, is given and the thinker's task is to "fill up gaps in the evidence." The following is an example:

A, By   *Horrible*

Given these three scraps of information, the subject is asked to fill the gap. Some fill it in any old way. Some indulge in flights of fancy. But the serious thinker looks for a logical scheme, one that makes some sort of sense. So he may interpolate the words:

Can, Door, Every, Floods, Gunners

His solution, therefore, is: each word must be longer, by one letter, than the preceding, and must begin with the next letter of the alphabet.

Some problems call for extrapolation. The information given might be:

A, GATE, NO, I, DUTY, IN, CAT, BO, EAR, O, TRAVEL, ERASE, BOTH, GET, HO, FATE

ERASE
FATE

The subject is told: "from the group of words above, complete the vertical arrangement indicated by the two words 'erase' and 'fate,' taking 'erase' as the middle word in the column. Not all the words given need be used." Confronted with this problem, individuals adopt various strategies. A few, observing that "fate" has one letter less than "erase," that "duty" also has one letter less, and so on, and that an alphabetical sequence of initial letters may be arranged. They achieve the following solution:

A
BO
CAT
DUTY
ERASE
FATE
GET
HO
I

More information from which to extrapolate may be given — for example,

DUTY
ERASE
FATE

When this is done, the solution given above is, of course, much more readily obtained.

Other reasoning problems used by Sir Frederic Bartlett involve what he calls "adventurous thinking," thinking with a larger element of freedom than in the examples cited.[15] The thinking of scientists, artists, and novelists falls in this general area.

Three reasoning problems which come closer to situations of everyday life than those described above are shown in Figure 13.5. Solve them, noting at the same time, if you can, how the solution was achieved. Then check your answers by referring to the Appendix. Some of these problems enter into the ensuing discussions of the reasoning process.

Hypotheses

You will doubtless have noticed that, once the problem was given, and you accepted the task of solving it, suggestions began to occur to you. These are known as *hypotheses*. Quite often they occur as questions. You say, "Must the whole match be used for the side of a triangle?" "Will it work if I cross the matches?" And so on.

Let us illustrate from a problem of everyday life. Suppose that your car stops all of a sudden without apparent cause. You ask, "What's the matter?" "Could it be that I have run out of gas?" You may check the truth of the hypothesis that you have run out of gas by looking at your gas indicator or, if you don't trust that, by examining the gas tank. These are what we might call *explicit* methods of testing your hypothesis; but you might test it *implicitly* by recalling that you filled the tank only yesterday, that you have traveled so many miles since then, and that it could or could not be empty — unless the gas tank has sprung a leak or someone has syphoned off some gasoline. Failing to find the tank empty, you get another suggestion; "Is the gas line choked?" You then check that possibility. So one possible explanation after another occurs to you until, providing you do not run out of relevant hypotheses beforehand, one of them is found correct. If your knowledge of automobile motors is limited, you may run out of suggestions very soon. You must then call in an expert, one who has many more symbolic representations of motors and things that might go wrong with them than you have.

Hypotheses involve recall of past experience. They are always limited by what one already knows about the situation involved.

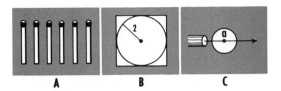

● **13.5**
Some Reasoning Problems. A. Problem: to make four equilateral triangles. **B.** Problem: to find the area of the square. **C.** Given: an inoperable stomach tumor situated at *a*, and rays which destroy organic tissue at sufficient intensity. Problem: how to destroy the tumor with these rays, yet without injuring the surrounding healthy tissue. For answers, see the Appendix. (After Duncker)

The more facts he can recall about the situation, the more he is likely to formulate hypotheses and the better these are likely to be.

Those who claim that education should teach people to think rather than cram facts into their heads often overlook the dependence of thinking upon facts with which to think. We should be taught facts, especially those that are relevant to situations which we are likely to meet, and we should also be taught to think more efficiently.

Hypotheses are usually evaluated before being accepted or rejected. Dewey calls this the *rational elaboration of ideas*. We may accept the first hypothesis that comes to us or we may bring relevant knowledge to bear upon it. Evaluation in the light of other knowledge at our disposal sometimes leads to rejection, then to a groping for some other suggestion. Thus, we realize that, in terms of how much gas we had in our tank yesterday and the number of miles we have traveled, our gas could not have been used up. Then we think of other possibilities.

Sometimes an objective test of our hypotheses is necessary. Our critical evaluation of an hypothesis, like that of the empty gas tank, for example, may convince us of its correctness. In many instances, however, especially in scientific reasoning, it is necessary to prove the correctness of an hypothesis by objective or experimental means. It often happens that hypotheses generally accepted as reasonable are found to be false when tested experimentally.

Direction

Recall in reasoning, as we have already seen, is directed rather than random. The nature of the problem, as one conceives it, gives a more or less definite trend to what is recalled. If our car has stopped running, we recall things about cars. Our inferences concern cars and what we know can happen to them. We are not likely to recall things that are completely irrelevant. The inferences that we make are related more or less closely to the problem as we conceive it.

It often happens, however, that our inferences, while generally bearing on the problem, follow an inadequate direction in other respects. There are many examples of this in everyday life. A man in his early forties, say, begins to have dizzy spells, and jumps to the conclusion that his heart has gone bad. He begins to think of cleaning up his affairs in case he should drop dead. He limits his exercise and his eating. Finally, he convinces himself, or someone else convinces him, that he should have a physical examination. The doctor finds nothing wrong with his heart, but asks some questions about his eyes. Then the patient recalls for the first time that he finds it easier to read if he holds the paper at arm's length, that he experiences difficulty in reading small print on labels, and that his dizziness comes when he suddenly looks from a near to a more distant object, or vice versa. None of these things occurred to him before because the idea that there must be something wrong with his heart sent him thinking in the wrong direction. A checkup with the oculist shows that the patient needs bifocals in place of his present glasses. He makes the substitution and his dizziness eventually disappears.

• **Delusions and directions.** Certain delusions of the mentally ill are attributable to reasoning in wrong directions. In so-called monomaniacs, for example, the direction of associative processes gives bizarre interpretations to the most innocent events.

☐ "Has she a tired look? — it is proof of adultery; a gay manner? — she comes from a rendezvous. A look, a movement of the eyebrows, lips, or fingers are so many telltale signs; the same with smiles or tears. Should she utter the name of the supposed lover, the sound of her voice leaves no doubt; should she repeat it often, it is to accustom herself to hear it in public without blushing; if she ceases to mention him, the motive can be guessed. In the street, the jealous man thinks that the passers-by are laughing at him; ceaseless allusions are made to his misfortune; he is taken for a complaisant husband. His wife's footsteps on the parquet floor are so many signals to her lovers and compose a telegraphic alphabet that he can successfully interpret. . . .

"Mme. X . . . studies minutely the letters that she receives. Punctuation marks or spelling mistakes give rise to numerous interpretations. Her father writes to her: 'We desire your cure. She observes that the stop is of an unusual size; it must read: 'We desire your cure to stop.' (Nous ne désirons *point* ta guérison.) Another woman imagines that her husband is announcing the intention of leaving her by putting two five-centime stamps on a letter instead of a ten-centime one. A look, a smile, a gesture, the shouts and songs of children, the coughing or spitting of a neighbor, the whispers of passers-by, pieces of paper found in the street, a door opened or closed, a mere nothing, serves as a pretext."[16] ☐

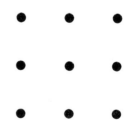

• **13.6**

The Nine-Dot Problem. Connect these dots by drawing four straight lines without taking the pencil from the paper and without retracing. The solution is given in the Appendix.

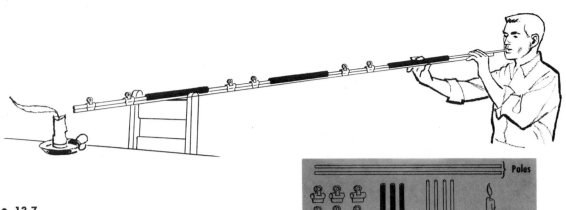

● 13.7
Maier's Candle-Blowing Problem. Problem: Given these poles, clamps, and tubes, blow out the candle from a distance of eight feet.

● *Direction in problem-solving.* The disadvantage of getting the wrong direction and the advantage of getting the right direction in problem-solving has been investigated in the laboratory. How the wrong direction or wrong set may interfere with solution is illustrated by the problem indicated in Figure 13.6. One is required to connect the nine dots by drawing four straight lines without taking the pencil off the paper and without retracing.

In attempting to solve this problem, you make one inference after another, and all are relevant in that they concern the nine dots and the instructions. Any inference which concerns the nine dots, but fails to conform with the instructions, is rejected almost as soon as suggested. You have a set, in other words, that is related to the dots and to the instructions. But you may also have a set not involved in the instructions — that is, the set which makes you keep all lines within the limits of the area bordered by the dots. As long as your thinking is thus fixated, you cannot solve the problem. Every inference will prove inadequate. But when you think of the possibility that lines may go outside of the area within the dots, you have the right direction. The solution may still be far off, but at least you will make inferences more in keeping with the requirements of solution. Eventually, you may hit upon the solution illustrated in the Appendix.

Following a certain line of thought to the exclusion of others, as in the above example, often seriously interferes with problem solution.* The importance of shifting direction is illustrated by an experiment with college students.

One of the problems used in this study called for blowing out a lighted candle from a distance of eight feet with nothing but the materials illustrated in the lower part of Figure 13.7. The problem was given to one subject at a time. In a control group of 206 students (working without instructions about the mode of attack), 48 per cent solved the problem within the time allowed. An experimental group of 178 students received a preliminary twenty-minute lecture in which the following advice was given and elaborated:

1. Locate a difficulty and try to overcome it. If you fail, get it completely out of your mind and seek an entirely different difficulty.

2. Do not be a creature of habit and stay in a rut. Keep your mind open for new meanings.

3. The solution-pattern appears suddenly. You cannot force it. Keep your mind open for new combinations and do not waste time on unsuccessful efforts.

* In an interesting article on problem-solving, its author says: "There is truth to William James's statement that habit is the 'fly-wheel of society,' but one might add that habit can be the flypaper of society. The direct availability of a habitual mode of response may make it much harder to break with habit and approach a problem afresh. . . . If insight is the essential element in intelligent problem-solving, fixation is its archenemy."[17]

The problem was solved within the time limit by 68 per cent of this group — 20 per cent more than in the group that received no instructions about changing direction.

In an experiment done to check these results, 169 subjects attacked two problems of equal difficulty, one before and one after receiving the above instructions. Here the effect of instructions about changing direction doubled the number of individuals achieving a solution.[18]

One difficulty in getting the proper direction is an inability to *reconstruct* the situation implicitly. Take, for example, the problem of the area of the square (p. 409). If this problem is completely novel, we must implicitly move the radius until it touches an edge. If we do this, the answer occurs in a flash. We see that the radius of the circle is one half of the side of the square. The match problem is solved, or well on the way to being solved, as soon as we implicitly place the matches into a tridimensional figure.

□ Professor Wertheimer studied thinking in children, observing them under various kinds of classroom instruction. What impressed him was the routine or "blind" nature of much that is taught, and the inflexibility of much of the thinking that results. He decried the "emphasis on mechanical drill, on "instantaneous response,' on developing blind, piecemeal habits." "Repetition," he said, "is useful, but continuous use of mechanical repetition also has harmful effects. It is dangerous because it induces habits of sheer mechanized action, blindness, tendencies to perform slavishly instead of thinking, instead of facing a problem freely."[19]

What Wertheimer was arguing for is the sort of thing stressed in the above experiments on direction in thinking — that is, looking at a problem in different ways, to seek new meanings, and to look for new combinations. The case of Gauss, the great mathematician, was cited by Wertheimer to illustrate the value of flexibility in thinking.

When Gauss was six years old, his school teacher gave the class a problem in arithmetic, asking, "Which of you will be first to get the sum of $1 + 2 + 3 + 4 + 5 + 6 + 7 +$

$8 + 9 + 10?$" Shortly afterwards, while the others were still busy figuring out the answer, Gauss raised his hand and said, "Here it is." Members of the class were doubtless saying "1 plus 2 is 3, and 3 is 6, and 4 more is 10," or something like this. Surprised by the child's quick answer, the teacher is reputed to have said, "How the devil did you get it so quickly?" We know the method that Gauss used (indeed he had hit upon the gist of a very important mathematical theorem) but we do not know exactly what he replied. According to Wertheimer, from whom the above has been paraphrased, Gauss probably said something like this: "Had I done it by adding 1 and 2, then 3 to the sum, then 4 to the new result, and so on, it would have taken very long; and trying to do it quickly, I would likely have made mistakes. But you see, 1 and 10 make 11, 2 and 9 are again — must be — 11! And so on! There are 5 such pairs, 5 times 11 make 55."[20] The theorem is, sum $= (n + 1)\frac{n}{2}$, and it of course applies as well for odd as for even-numbered series. □

How to achieve such flexibility of thinking is the problem. It occurs readily enough in a genius, who has the relevant information. But what about the rest of us? Such flexibility requires teaching for understanding, or insight, at the same time that necessary drill is given. Several investigations have shown that this is possible in the schoolroom, even among children who do not have the mental caliber of a Gauss.[21]

The area problem of Figure 13.4 (p. 407) is another example of teaching for understanding instead of using rote methods. ■

LANGUAGE AND THOUGHT

The view has often been expressed that thinking is "restrained speaking," "subvocal talking," or "implicit language activity." Reasoning can, however, occur without language. This was illustrated earlier by experiments on animals.

Even where language does exist, a certain

amount of thinking is probably nonlinguistic. We may, for example, think about things for which we do not have names. In such instances we often have an image, visual or otherwise, of the thing thought about. Some psychologists have claimed that thinking can occur without involving either words or images.

After recognizing these limitations on the view that thinking is merely implicit language activity, we must admit that the symbols which represent most of the world are language symbols (verbal, gestural, or written), and that most of our thinking appears to be an internal manipulation of such symbols.

That thinking is closely tied up with inner speech is suggested by attempts to analyze thought processes. Try to analyze your everyday thinking and you will find that words are everywhere evident. It usually appears that, in thinking, you are talking to yourself. Children often do their thinking out loud for everyone to hear it — until they learn that it is customary, and usually worthwhile, to keep one's thoughts to oneself.

☐ Thinking is often associated with activities of the speech mechanisms, especially of the tongue and throat in people who can hear, and of the fingers in deaf mutes. In one study with hearing subjects, electrodes were placed on the tongue or underlip and connected with a sensitive galvanometer, an instrument which records electrical impulses (action currents) associated with nerve and muscle activity. When the subject imagined counting one-two-three, the indicator, which had been at rest, showed three marked series of excursions. Thus action currents were coming from the tongue or lips. Instructions like "imagine telling your friend the date," "recall a song or poem," "multiply certain numbers," and "think of eternity," brought action currents very similar to those involved in actually saying the words.[22]

Action currents are obtained from the hands of deaf mutes during thought.[23] Sometimes the activities of the hands are of sufficient magnitude to be detected with the naked eye. In one study, deaf mutes and normal subjects were asked to multiply mentally, divide mentally, and so on. Under these conditions, 80

● 13.8

The Disc Problem. From two to six discs are placed at *A*, arranged in order of size, with the larger (or largest) at the bottom. The problem is to move these discs to other circles so that, eventually, all are at *B* in their original order. However, only one disc at a time may be moved, it must never be placed over a smaller disc, and the task must be accomplished in the fewest possible moves. (After P. H. Ewert and J. E. Lambert, "The Effect of Verbal Instructions Upon the Formation of a Concept," *J. Gen. Psychol.,* 1932, *6,* pp. 400–413; and R. M. Gagné and E. C. Smith, Jr., "A Study of the Effects of Verbalization on Problem Solving," *J. Exper. Psychol.,* 1962, *63,* pp. 12–18.)

per cent of the deaf mutes had action currents in the hands. Only 30 per cent of the hearing subjects showed such responses. The reason for hearing subjects exhibiting action currents in the hands at all may be that they often use, or have used, their hands in making calculations — with or without using a pencil or chalk. The average magnitude of the responses obtained from the hands was about four times larger for the deaf-mute than for the hearing subjects. ☐

Thinking is more than talking to oneself — more than mere implicit verbalizing. There is no doubt of that. Nevertheless, verbalizing while trying to solve a problem is often advantageous. In an experiment utilizing the discs and other materials[24] shown in Figure 13.8, subjects who were required to verbalize while attempting to solve the problem learned more quickly and with fewer incorrect moves than those not required to verbalize. Those instructed to verbalize had to say aloud why they made each move as they made it. Nothing was said to the other subjects about verbalizing, although one group was told to try to give a rule for the solution. According to the investigators, requiring the subjects "to verbalize during practice has the effect of making them think of new reasons for their moves, and thus facilitates both the discovery of general principles and their employment in solving successive problems."[25] ■

IS THINKING NECESSARILY MOTOR?

According to the so-called *central* theory of thinking, we think with our brains alone. This is contrasted with the *peripheral* or *motor* theory, which claims that a person thinks with his whole body. The latter is better designated a *central-peripheral* theory, since it allows for the fact that engrams essential to thinking are somehow stored in the brain and that much of the integration involved is attributable to brain functions.[26] However, it emphasizes motor activities. Those of the vocal and gestural mechanisms have already been mentioned. One can also demonstrate that eye movements and other muscular activities are integrally involved in, or are at least concomitant with, the thought processes. For example, eye movements during attempts to imagine an object are often very similar to those made in the original examination of it.[27] Eye movements during recall also are often similar to those made in the original reading of what was recalled.[28] But other muscles may also be involved in thinking. One investigator found that thoughts of lifting a weight with the right hand were correlated with action currents in the biceps of the right arm.[29]

Findings like the above support the idea that thinking involves the whole body as well as the brain. But they do not allow us to conclude that motor activities, even those of the vocal musculature, are in themselves the thought processes, or that they are essential aspects of thinking. A good argument could

be made to the effect that these motor activities are secondary, or merely incidental. It is conceivable that one could think on a purely central basis, without activity in his tongue, eyes, or other muscles.

□ A medical experiment with d-tubocurarine (curare), a drug which paralyzes the muscles without affecting the nervous system, lends support to the view that thinking can occur as a purely central process.[30] In this experiment, a healthy 34-year-old medical doctor was given a gradually increasing amount of d-tubocurarine until every muscle of his body was paralyzed. By speaking as long as he was able to do so, and thereafter by prearranged muscular movements in answer to questions, the subject kept in communication with the experimenters until paralysis was complete. A drug was then introduced which led to gradual recovery. Four hours elapsed from the time the first dose of the paralyzing drug was given until the counteracting drug was injected. Electroencephalograms taken throughout this period were normal, even at the time of complete paralysis of the skeletal musculature. Thus the drug had no apparent central effect. What is of special interest to us here, however, is the fact that thought processes were reported to be normal. In the subsequent report of his experiences, the subject indicated that he was fully conscious and thinking even when completely paralyzed. □

Although the subject of the above experiment reported no disturbances of his thought processes, it is conceivable that tests would have indicated limitations in the scope or flexibility of thinking. If this were so, we would have evidence that the motor mechanisms, while not essential, are at least contributory.

One cannot, in any event, overlook the essential contributions of the cerebral cortex, both as a repository of engrams and as an integrating mechanism. We have already (pp. 61, 342) referred to the significance of the frontal lobes in this connection.

Even when thinking is viewed from the standpoint of the central processes and motor mechanisms involved, we must recognize the importance of external stimuli in initiating and perhaps to some extent controlling it. The reader may recall, in this connection, the discovery (pp. 174–175) that conditions of relative isolation from external changes in stimulation often produce marked distortions of the thought processes. ∎

CONCEPTS

A concept is a process which represents the similarities in otherwise diverse objects, situations, or events. Concepts are products of reasoning and, once developed, play an important role in further thinking. A large proportion of the words in any complex language represent concepts. Words such as "tree," "dog," "liquid," "beauty," and thousands of others in our language, represent common aspects of things that are in many respects quite different one from another.

In a sense, concepts are condensations of past experience. They bring together in a single idea, so to speak, what has been learned about properties of many different things. Take, for example, the concept *tree*. This concept is foreign to certain Australian tribes. The native speaks of particular objects, like the jarrah, the mulga, and the gum, but he has no word to represent what is common to them.

The development of concepts requires two processes known respectively as *abstracting* and *generalizing*. Sometimes the two cannot be separated clearly, but each of them is at least implied whenever a concept is formed.

Abstracting is observing the similarity of otherwise different things. The individuals who first invented the concept *tree* must have observed that trees, regardless of how much they differ, still have something in common. Likewise, the child, in acquiring the concept *tree*, or understanding the word "tree," must make similar observations. The child's first experience with a tree may be with a magnolia, with which he hears the word "tree" associated. But later on, the child hears the same word attached to the pine, an object of quite different appearance. Later still, he hears the oak called a tree. After a series of such experiences with a variety of trees, the child may see, let us say, a willow, which has never

before been called a tree in his presence. If he designates this as a tree, the child must have observed something of what the willow has in common with other trees. But he must also have put aspects of previous experience together with the present experience and reached the conclusion that this, being like the others in certain respects, is in the same category. Deriving a principle from varied experiences in this way is generalizing. A person might abstract without generalizing, but he could not achieve an adequate generalization, or concept, without first abstracting.

One should not gather the impression, from what we have just said, that the processes of abstracting and generalizing are necessarily deliberate, or even carried on consciously. In animals and human infants, our only evidence of abstraction and generalization comes from observation of similar reactions to different situations having a common characteristic. Looking at it from another angle, all we know is that different situations are equivalent from the standpoint of the reactions aroused and that this equivalence depends upon something which these situations, despite their diversity, have in common. We do not know whether the subjects deliberately analyze the situations, nor whether they are conscious of similarities and relations. ∎

EXPERIMENTS ON CONCEPT FORMATION

Concepts have been developed, under experimental conditions, in a variety of organisms ranging from rats to men. A typical procedure with animals and infants is as follows:

☐ The subject is confronted with two forms and required to discriminate between them. These may be, for example, a triangle and a circle. Using a discrimination procedure (p. 13), a response to the triangle is rewarded and a response to the circle is either not rewarded or punished. These figures are switched from side to side in a chance order so that the problem may be solved only by discriminating the visual stimuli. When the triangle is being selected with an accuracy approaching 100 per cent, a square, or some other figure, is substituted for the circle. This is to discover if the subject is responding negatively to the circle or positively to the triangle. Continued correct performance indicates the latter. Usually, the subject does continue to select the triangle. We then replace the circle and *invert* the triangle. When we do this, most animals respond as if confronted by a new problem. Accuracy of response drops from around 100 to around 50 per cent. It is apparent, in such instances, that what was being discriminated was a particular pattern of black and white, not a triangle *per se*. Monkeys and children have continued to select the inverted triangle. For these subjects, the inverted triangle and the original one were apparently equivalent. The subjects must have reacted in terms of triangularity, three-sidedness, or some other abstracted property which triangles have, regardless of their position. Animals which fail to make this transition abruptly may be trained to respond to properties which otherwise dissimilar triangles possess. In one study, rats learned to respond to a large variety of triangles (small, large, upright, inverted, apex to right, apex to left) as equivalent; but over 1,000 trials, with frequent substitutions of triangles, and further training, were required. In each trial the only constant aspect of the positive situation was the presence of some sort of triangle. All other concomitants varied. Finally some animals responded positively to triangles different from any of those involved in training. They made a transfer, for example, to right-angled, equilateral, and outlined triangles. It is evident that these rats had learned to abstract triangularity, the only characteristic involved in all of the different kinds of triangles. The abstracted characteristic may have been three-corneredness, three-sidedness, or the like.[31] □

Generalizing, and the development of concepts somewhat more complicated than in the experiments on triangularity, is illustrated by the materials in Figure 13.9. Here the child learns that each shape has its own name, such as MEF, TOV, YOP, and ZIL. It also learns, however, that both MEF and TOV are VIC's; YOP and ZIL, DAX's. Finally it learns that all of these shapes, despite their differences, are alike in being XIP's. All of forty-five five- to seven-year-olds learned the first step. That is to say, they selected, from various blocks, the blocks with specific names. All but three also learned the second step. When asked for a VIC, they gave either MEF or TOV; when asked for a DAX, they gave either YOP or ZIL. The next step, however, was especially difficult and only twenty-two attained it within the limits of this experiment. A successful child could select a MEF, TOV, YOP or ZIL when asked for it. From a large assortment of shapes, he could pick out all the XIP's. And, when asked to remove the VIC's, he could take back MEF and TOV. Problems like this are comparable to calling a certain thing a worm, an animal, and also living matter. Many of our concepts are similarly hierarchical. They start with specific things and become increasingly inclusive.[32]

Another problem on concept formation is illustrated in Figure 13.10. Using a controlled-exposure apparatus to present one picture at a time, the experimenter asked the subject to name each picture as it occurred. Each picture had a nonsense name, as illustrated, but all figures possessing a common characteristic had

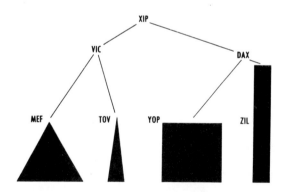

● 13.9

A Generalization Problem. After learning the specific names for each block, the child then learns that MEF and TOV are both VIC, that YOP and ZIL are both DAX, and that all the VIC and DAX blocks fall under the broader classification, XIP. Control tests used blocks of different dimensions but the same general shape. (From L. Welch and L. Long, "The Higher Structural Phases of Concept Formation of Children," *J. Psychol.*, 1940, 9, 61.)

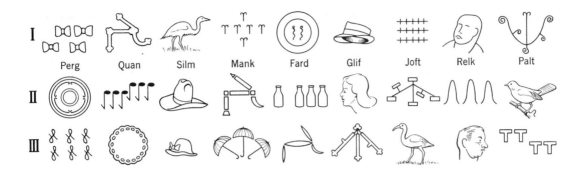

● **13.10**
Materials Used for Heidbreder's Experiment on Concept Formation. The terms *Perg, Quan,* etc., represent concepts rather than particular pictures. What is *Perg* in the second line? In the third? (After E. Heidbreder, "The Attainment of Concepts," *J. Psychol.,* 1947, 24, p. 95.)

the same name. For example, the pictures in the first row had, respectively, the following names: *Perg, Quan, Silm, Mank, Fard, Glif, Joft, Relk, Palt.* Look at the first picture in the second series. What is its name? Its name is *Fard.*

The subjects of course saw only one figure at a time and none was labeled. Moreover, they thought that the experiment was on memory. Their initial set, at least, was to memorize, not to abstract and generalize. Whenever the subject failed to respond in time, or said the wrong name, he was prompted. The experiment continued until each picture in sixteen strips like those illustrated was correctly named. With the material illustrated, you can test yourself on abstracting the common features of all the *Fards*, all the *Pergs* and so on. The results of the experiments using this type of material need not concern us here.[33]

Tests of concept formation are often used in clinical psychology to discover something about the mental functioning of the patient. His reactions may also indicate whether he is psychotic, whether brain damage is present, and other aspects of his disorder. Two tests that are widely used for such purposes may be seen in Plates 8 and 9 (facing page 432). How they are administered is described in the legends.

One can recognize that the *Object-Sorting Test* is one of concept formation, for the subject's task is to group different things which

have some common attribute. Some of the most frequent bases of grouping are: *use* (tools, eating utensils, edibles), *situation* (dinner setting, tools in a tool box), *color* (silver, brown, white), *form* (oblong, round), *double occurrence* (pairs — two lumps of sugar, two forks), and *material* (wood, metal).[34]   Children, schizophrenics, and patients with brain injuries tend to group the objects on a very *concrete* basis, such as the reds together, or matches and candle together. Normal adults group on the basis of concrete aspects, but they are able to transcend the obvious similarities or associations and group on the basis of such abstract relations as "tools," "pleasure-giving objects," and so on. When an individual assumes this conceptual approach, "the presented articles are not taken as *individual* things, but as representative of a category. The subject deliberately disregards, abstracts from, the concrete singularity of the presented article."[35]

The *Vigotsky Test,* as illustrated and described in Plate 9, also elicits different degrees of conceptualization, from concrete to highly abstract.[36] Concrete responses are revealed by such acts as putting together objects of the same shape, all of the same size, all of the same height, or all of the same color. An intermediate level of conceptualization would be putting all blocks with corners together. The highest level of conceptual response, however, is to place all of the large tall blocks together in one group, all of the large flat blocks together in another group, and so on. The test could of course be changed to call for some other classificatory scheme, such as colored-flat, colored-tall, or green-flat-circular.

Teaching concept formation

Some investigators have sought to facilitate concept formation by discovering the best method of teaching individuals to proceed from the concrete to the abstract. In one such study, Chinese characters were used. These lend themselves to such research because each written word has within it a symbol which gives the "essence" of what it refers to. Thus several words, that are in most respects quite different, all have a common symbol which represents something which all have in common. For example, the symbol 木 is the word for wood. The following are the words for, respectively, table, bed, frame, tree, and forest: 檯牀架樹林: All are wood, so the symbol 木 appears in every word. Likewise the symbol for soil 土 appears in the words for land 地, grave 墳, dust 塵, and ditch 壕.

□ In the research on facilitation of concept formation, college students were shown Chinese characters like the above and, two and one-half seconds after each character was presented, a nonsense sound representing the characteristic which it had in common with certain others in the series was also presented. Thus all having the element 氵 were *oo*, all having the element 歹 were *yer*, and so on. Characters having the common element were mixed with others having a different common element.

The subjects were not told that they were doing an experiment on concept formation, abstracting, or generalizing. Until they learned otherwise as a result of their experience, all thought that they were doing a memory experiment. They were merely asked to name the element (*oo*, *yer*, etc.) as the complex Chinese character containing it was presented.

Eventually it "dawned" on most of the subjects that the different *oo* characters, for example, were linked by a common factor — the 氵 embedded in each of the Chinese characters. The investigator says that "indi-vidual concepts usually came into consciousness very gradually. Erroneous first impressions were either discarded or transmuted into the correct form by a continuous development. Trial and error plays, if not a dominating, at least a very great rôle in the process."[37]

Various training procedures were used with different groups and each varied from the others in the readiness with which it produced conceptual responses. There was no difference in the efficiency of starting with simple characters and going to complex ones, on the one hand, and starting with complex characters and going to simple ones on the other. Nor was there any advantage to teaching the concepts out of their context — that is, by presenting the naked common elements. In identification with new complete Chinese characters, the individuals who had the concepts given them in naked form had to learn to discriminate them from the whole character. In this test, which is the sort of thing required in everyday life, neither those who had the concepts given them nor those who evolved them through trial-and-error learning had an advantage. A combination method in which naked characteristics were given, mixed in with the series of complete characters, was better than any other mentioned above. The most efficient method of all was to present the entire character, but with the common element redrawn in red so that it stood out or attracted attention. □

Regardless of the precise method used, it is essential that the principle of *dissociation by varying concomitants* be followed if an adequate concept is to develop. This principle has been stated as follows: "What is associated now with one thing and now with another tends to become dissociated from either, and to grow into an object of abstract contemplation."[38] Thus, if the concept of triangularity is to develop, the triangularity must appear in different particular situations; if the concept *oo* is to develop, the character 氵 must appear now in one context and now in another; if the child is to develop an adequate concept *dog*, the word *dog* must be associated with white creatures, black ones, brown ones, large ones, small ones, smooth ones, rough ones, and so forth. The concept would never develop so long as only one dog, or one type of dog, was associated with the term *dog*.

Individual strategies

So much for methods of presenting instances from which concepts may be derived. But how about concept formation from the standpoint of the learner? How does he come by his concepts? How does he learn that different items belong in the same category? In many instances, and especially in the categorizing of animals and infants, this process is a more or less passive one. That is to say, "The features common to a class of objects summate their impressions on the observer who thus gradually acquires a picture in which the common features stand out strongly while the variable characters are washed out."[39] In other instances there is an active search process. The individual develops the hypothesis that items having certain characteristics belong in the same category. He then tests this hypothesis by noting whether each new instance does or does not belong to the category.[40] Thus the child's hypothesis that all four-legged animals are dogs is supported when he hears one four-legged animal after another called "dog" but he must discard it when he hears a certain four-legged animal called "cat" or "horse."

Adults confronted with complex categorizing tasks take a quite evident problem-solving attitude. In attempting to discover the concept involved and in evaluating each new instance from the standpoint of whether or not it supports the hypothesis, various strategies may be adopted, some of which are more efficient than others. This was illustrated in a comprehensive investigation of categorizing behavior in college students.[41]

As an example of the type of materials used in this investigation, see Plate 10. The strategy described in the legend to this plate may be called "holist" because the subject takes the entire initial card (three circles and a triple border) as the basis of his tentative concept. Then he modifies this in terms of subsequent instances.

Another strategy may, by contrast, be designated "partist." The subject using this strategy bases his initial concept on only part of the first card — let us say, "three black circles." The next card of the illustration (one red cross and a double border) is a negative instance, hence not at all informative. It tells nothing about the adequacy (or inadequacy) of the "three circle" concept. The next card (green circle and triple border) is informative. The experimenter indicates that this is a positive instance. Now the subject must give up the "three circle" hypothesis in favor of another. If he remembers former cards — which might be quite a task if many have preceded — he may hypothesize that "any circle" is the concept sought. This must be discarded, in turn, when a green circle with double border is shown and designated as a negative instance.

In general, the holist strategy is the more effective of those described. This is because the holist's hypothesis "is modified at each step to incorporate the information gained from the instances he has encountered. He need never recall either his past hypotheses or the relation between these. *For his present hypothesis is a current summary of all these.* Only when he must recover from an error is recourse to memory necessary." However, the partist "must fall back on memory or the record" whenever something is shown which weakens or invalidates his hypothesis.[42]

Whether they use a whole or part approach, or shift from one to the other, as some subjects do, the participants in experiments like the above show other differences in strategy. Some adopt what has been called a "conservative strategy." They proceed cautiously and systematically, focusing on one feature at a time. Suppose, for example, that the first card has three red circles within a double border and that the concept to be discovered is "red circles." The next card has two red circles within a double border and is positive. Our methodical subject gets from this instance the information that three figures are not required. The next card has three green circles within a double border and it is negative. Our subject notes, from this instance, that he needs to retain red in the concept. Next he is shown three red crosses in a double border and informed that this is negative. From this is gained the knowledge that circle is relevant. Now he is given a card with three red circles and a single border. The card is positive, so he notes that two borders are not necessary. The problem is solved. The concept is "red circles." Every bit of information has been used in an efficient manner. Thus the concept has been achieved with a minimal amount of information.

Instead of concentrating on one feature at a time in the manner described, some subjects adopt a gambling strategy. They jump to conclusions. The first card, let us say, has three red circles and a double border and the concept is "three figures." The next card perhaps has three green crosses in a single border and the subject is told that it is positive. He concludes immediately that the concept is "three figures."[43] This is correct. He gambled and won. But suppose that the concept, involving the same cards, had been "three *colored* figures." The next card, let us say, has three black squares within a triple border and is of course designated as negative. Now the subject must change his tactics. He must think back to the earlier cards and develop a new hypothesis by comparing these with the new instance. The conservative strategy, while it involves minimal risk of developing wrong concepts, is sometimes given up in favor of the gambling strategy. This is especially true when a limited number of instances is to be given, or when time is limited and the concept has not yet been achieved.

Concept formation in everyday life

Many situations in everyday life do not involve such obvious common elements as those of the experiments described above. Human beings not only acquire concepts by observing common elements and figuring out relationships, but they learn them by asking questions about things which puzzle them and getting answers in return. The child hears his parents talking about having time to do a certain chore, about its being time to go to bed, about something happening in time, and so on. Puzzled, he asks what time is. His parents may have great difficulty in explaining time, but what

they tell the child leads to formation of a concept of *time*, adequate or inadequate. Take the concept *life*, as a further example. This may have both an observational basis and a basis in interrogation of elders. The child observes dead and living animals, and he observes, perhaps, that the living ones move and the dead ones do not. But concepts of *life* and *death* on this basis alone are likely to be far from adequate. Upon helping to bury the dead animal, the child may ask, "When is he going to wake up?" "Does he like being down there?" or, "How is he going to get out?" You then realize how limited the child's concept really is. You perhaps explain that animals once dead never wake up, and that they do not know anything, so can neither like nor dislike being buried. This process of observing, questioning, and getting answers goes on for years before the child has concepts of life and death which come close to those held by adults.

☐ One method of finding out what concepts children already have is that of questioning them. Several investigators have used this method to discover how particular concepts develop with age and experience. The child is asked, for example, "Do you know what it is to be alive?" A reply to this question brings further questions.

Thus, a boy of eight years was asked, "Is the sun alive?" to which he answered, "Yes." Asked, "Why?" he replied: "It gives light. It is alive when it is giving light, but it isn't alive when it is not giving light." Asked, "Is a bicycle alive?" the child replied: "No, when it doesn't go, it isn't alive. When it goes, it is alive." To the question, "Is a mountain alive?" the child answered, "No." The query, "Why not?" brought the reply, "Because it doesn't do anything." It is obvious that for this child the concept *life* means ability to move or do something. By way of comparison, let us take the more mature concept of a twelve-year-old boy similarly questioned. The boy said that he knew what it meant to be alive. He was then asked, "Is a fly alive?" He said, "Yes," and, upon being asked, "Why?" he replied, "If it wasn't alive it couldn't fly." To the question, "Is a bicycle alive?" the boy replied, "No." "Why not?"

brought the reply, "Because it is we who make it go." Further questioning verified the fact that this boy attributed life to anything that could move of its own volition.[44]

Using a standardized questioning procedure and standardized objects, investigators have studied the development of the "life" concept in thousands of school children.[45] Animism, or the attributing of life to inanimate objects, is usually found to go through stages somewhat like those already suggested. At first a child attributes life to *anything in good condition.* Broken objects, for example, are excluded. Life is later attributed only to *objects which move.* Later still, it is attributed only to *objects which move spontaneously* or, as suggested above, of their own volition. The concept is still further refined when it is applied only to *plants and animals.*

There is no definite correlation between age and stages of concept formation. Bright children may develop the more adequate concept earlier than other children, but they probably go through comparable stages in achieving it.[46] There is, however, some question about the universality of this process. White, Indian, and Negro children in American schools respond in the manner described above.[47] But somewhat different results have been found in China[48] and in a South Sea Island group.[49] This discrepancy has, however, been attributed to the fact that the latter investigations used procedures different from those of the other studies.

An interesting outcome of research on animism is the discovery that many college students have apparently failed to outgrow animistic concepts. It is not uncommon, for example, to find students maintaining that a lighted match is alive or that the sun is alive because it gives forth energy. The lowest incidence of animism has been found in biology students.[50] □

Of course there are many other concepts relating to our world which come to us gradually as we manipulate aspects of the environment, observe, and ask questions. There are, for example, concepts of duration, number, magnitude, order, causality, and conservation of matter. These and other concepts, so basic

to logical and scientific thinking, have been investigated in great detail, principally by Piaget and his associates at the University of Geneva. Volumes have been written about these studies and we can do no more, here, than to bring them to the reader's attention and to indicate something of their general nature.[51]

As they grow from early childhood to maturity, children develop concepts of orderly relationships, as revealed by such tests as that illustrated by Figure 13.11. They also develop the understanding which makes them see that twelve objects remain twelve when colored differently, when of different shape, and when arranged in different spatial patterns; that a ball of modeling clay retains its magnitude and weight when it is squashed into a pancake or

● **13.11**

The Flowing Liquid Test. Above the stopcock is a colored liquid. The child manipulates the stopcock so as to let a certain amount of liquid into the glass below. She notes how the upper and lower levels vary, the upper falling as the lower rises. The test of her understanding is the arrangement, in proper sequence, of cards showing what the respective levels would be if the upper vessel were gradually emptied. (From the research of Barbel Inhelder, of Piaget's laboratory. The photograph appeared in M. Mead, "Towards More Vivid Utopias," *Science,* 1957, 126, p. 960.)

rolled into a cylinder; and so on for other aspects of their world which have the attribute of remaining constant in certain respects while changing in others. Take, for example, the clay illustration. According to Piaget, the conservation-of-mass concept here represented is not fully appreciated until children are eleven or twelve years old. The two- to four-year-old thinks of the clay as having become greater in amount when transformed so as to cover a larger surface. By age seven or eight, the child realizes that the process is reversible, that the pancake may become a ball again, but he still does not appreciate that its mass is constant during this transformation. A year or two later, he appreciates the constancy of mass but still does not conceive of the weight as unchanged. Finally, at around twelve years, the concept of constant size, weight, and volume is fully developed.[52] Other investigators have differed with Piaget with respect to the ages of this and similar conceptual developments, some finding particular concepts present at earlier age levels than in his studies.[53] It is rather generally agreed, however, that such concepts go through various stages of development before adult levels of understanding are approximated.

There is no doubt that many adult concepts are inadequate from the standpoint of the scientist or the philosopher. But, inadequate as they may be, our concepts give us an advantage in thinking about our world and ourselves which would be lost if we spoke and thought about particulars only. ∎

CREATIVE THINKING

Many of man's creative works develop gradually, as if by a process of trial and error. One of the first attempts at developing a locomotive, for example, was a boatlike structure with a sail and wheels which ran on tracks. Next, a horse running on a treadmill was used for motive power. Then a horse pulled the carriages along the tracks. The steam-driven vehicle which followed had many obvious defects — it was so uncertain in action, actually that a horse-drawn "train" raced it. There were then gradual refinements of locomotives,

leading up to our present streamliners. Despite the obvious trial-and-error progress here represented, there were many inspirations which made successive steps in the development of the locomotive possible. And so it is with all creative work. There is an evident need to produce something different, then attempts to produce it, followed, quite often, by significant insights.

There is currently much interest in creativity — from the standpoint of what creative thinkers are like (intellectually and as persons) and from the standpoint of the creative process itself.* Studies of creative intelligence have used specially designed tests to measure differences in originality, imagination, and related processes. Some of the findings have been factor-analyzed in an effort to discover the "basic ingredients" of creativity.[54]

Recent studies of creative intelligence have distinguished two kinds of productive ability — *convergent* and *divergent*. These abilities may be exhibited in various areas, such as dealing with pictorial material, handling numbers, utilizing symbols such as words, and so on. Abilities of the convergent class are those used in bringing together otherwise divergent things. In the symbolic area, this might be exemplified by the arranging of a given set of words into a certain number of classes, with every word included in one or another class. Divergent production abilities, on the other hand, are those in which one starts from a specific item or group and makes as many further things as possible. Thus, given two straight lines and a curved line, one is called upon to make as many combinations as possible in a stated period. Or, given the numbers 2 3 4 5 6, he makes as many equations as he can. The first of these examples is from the figural, or pictorial, area; the second, from the symbolic area.[55] It has been claimed that divergent production abilities are particularly important in

* There is also a great deal of current interest in the years of man's greatest creativity. Actually, the age of maximum creative accomplishment varies with the individual and the field in which creation occurs. See H. C. Lehman, *Age and Achievement*, Princeton University Press, 1953; and "The Chemist's Most Creative Years," *Science*, 1958, 127, 1213–1222.

creative thinking. For creativity in mathematics and certain other fields, divergent production of a symbolic variety is called for. On the other hand, creativity in the visual arts and inventive pursuits requires divergent production of the figural variety.[56]

The personality of creative individuals (architects, artists, composers, novelists, and others) has also been studied with tests, principally of such things as artistic judgment, independence, and self-feelings. These studies have shown, among other things, that especially creative people, as compared with ordinary individuals, are more "vigorous and have available to them an exceptional fund of psychic and physical energy"; live "more complex lives, seeking tension in the interest of the pleasure they obtain upon its discharge"; and have "more contact . . . with the unconscious — with fantasy, reverie, the world of imagination."[57] This is of course just the sort of outcome that one might expect from general contact with creative people.

What is of most interest to us here is not so much the intelligence or personality of creative individuals as the process involved in creative problem-solving. Several political theorists, artists, and scientists have either analyzed their own thinking or had the products of their thought analyzed by others in an attempt to discover something of the creative process. It is generally agreed, as a result of these studies, that creative thinking often passes through three or four, more or less definite stages. These are: (1) *preparation*, (2) *incubation*, (3) *inspiration* or *illumination*, and (4) *verification* or *revision*.[58] Henri Poincaré, the great French mathematician, who also wrote about the process of creative thinking, experienced these stages. In Figure 13.12, he is pictured solving a mathematical problem.

Preparation

All education is, of course, a preparation for creative thinking, although we may not use its products creatively. Specialized education, like training in medicine, is preparation for creative thinking along special lines. The doctor's education gives him the information (symbolic processes) which prepares him for possible creative thinking in medicine. The inventor of electrical devices must have preparation along electrical lines. Einstein's concept of relativity would never have occurred to him had he not first learned advanced physics and mathematics.

In addition to this general preparation for possible creative thinking, one needs specific preparation for specific problems. Thus, a doctor confronted by some especially difficult medical problem may have to consult other authorities about various aspects of the general problem before being able to reach a conclusion concerning it. Even in preparing a term paper, which may at times be a creative activity, you must first acquaint yourself with relevant facts concerning the topic about which you are to write. A comparable "soaking-up" of facts is the required preparation for any creative work.

Preparation for creative thinking often includes attempts to relate facts in various ways. There is much trial and error. Perhaps there is pacing of the floor or biting of fingernails. You attempt to write your term paper; you may write something, tear up what you have written, and start over again, only to tear that up in disgust. Edison remarked that much of his inspiration was actually perspiration, referring, perhaps, to this sort of preparational activity.

Incubation

This stage of creative thinking is characterized by absence of overt activity, and in many instances even by absence of thinking about the problem. Sometimes, however, certain ideas concerning the problem recur. Poets and artists report the following details about their incubation periods:

The idea smoulders in my mind until completed.

I have an idea in the back of my mind for a long time, sometimes a week or two. I don't think constantly about it, but it keeps coming back.

I often carry an idea around for several weeks before I make a picture, though some-

● **13.12**

The Four Stages of Creative Thought. These drawings illustrate what is described by Poincaré as follows: "For fifteen days I strove to prove that there could not be any functions like those I have since called Fuchsian functions. I was then very ignorant; every day I seated myself at my work table, stayed an hour or two, tried a great number of combinations and reached no results. One evening contrary to my custom, I drank black coffee and could not sleep. Ideas rose in crowds; I felt them collide until pairs interlocked, so to speak, making a stable combination. By the next morning I had established the existence of a class of Fuchsian functions, those which come from the hypergeometric series; I had only to write out the results, which took but a few hours.

"Then I wanted to represent these functions by the quotient of two series; this idea was perfectly conscious and deliberate, the analogy with elliptic functions guided me. I asked myself what properties these series must have if they existed, and I succeeded, without difficulty in forming the series I have called theta-Fuchsian.

"Just at this time I left Caen, where I was then living, to go on a geologic excursion under the auspices of the school of mines. The changes of travel made me forget my mathematical work. Having reached Coutances, we entered an omnibus to go some place or other. At the moment when I put my foot on the step the idea came to me, without anything in my former thoughts seeming to have paved the way for it, that the transformations I had used to define the Fuchsian functions were identical with those of non-Euclidean geometry. I did not verify the idea; I should not have had time, as, upon taking my seat in the omnibus, I went on with a conversation already commenced, but I felt a perfect certainty. On my return to Caen, for conscience' sake I verified the result at my leisure." (From H. Poincaré, "Mathematical Creation," as edited and presented by J. R. Newman in *Scientific American*. Drawings by Stanley Meltzoff.)

times longer. I got ideas in Santa Fe last summer to do now. The ideas recur from time to time while I am occupied with other things.[59]

This is a period of no obvious progress. Some creative thinkers intentionally put all thoughts of their problem in the background after preparing themselves. Some go for a stroll, read light literature, engage in a game of golf, or perhaps sleep.

The stage which follows incubation has led some to assume that, while the creative thinker turns his attention elsewhere, his problem is being solved unconsciously. This would be difficult, if not impossible, either to prove or disprove. It is likely that associational activities initiated by attempts to solve the problem continue to some degree. We see some evidence of this in connection with dreams. The individual may give up his problem and go to bed, only to have aspects of it appear in his sleep. There is no reason to believe otherwise than that the associational processes would continue in a similar manner were he to remain awake and engage in other activities. This continuance of associational activities, once started, has already been referred to as *perseveration*.

Inspiration

Most creative thinkers claim that their creative ideas, following the period of incubation, come to them suddenly. The significant ideas may occur at any time, sometimes even while the thinker is dreaming.

In writing creatively you have doubtless been discouraged by an evident lack of progress, when suddenly the material seemed to organize itself, the relevant ideas came copiously and rapidly, and what had been obscure became clear. One will recognize that this process resembles the process of insight during other forms of learning activity. It is often, as in those instances, preceded by a certain amount of trial and error.

Trial-and-error activity, however, is usually considered part of the preparation rather than the incubation stage of creative thinking. Several creative thinkers have pointed out that their trial-and-error activity apparently led

nowhere, and that it was only after they put the problem aside that inspiration came.

We should not overlook the insights which sometimes occur when there is no evident problem. In science, and in other areas of creative endeavor, it often happens that the individual whose background has prepared him for it discovers something he is not looking for.* The discovery of penicillin by Sir Alexander Fleming is a good illustration.

While talking with Pryce, a colleague who had dropped in to see him, Sir Alexander began to examine some Petri dishes containing old cultures of staphylococci. As Maurois describes the subsequent event:

☐ Several of the cultures had been contaminated with mould — a not unusual occurrence. "As soon as you uncover a culture dish, something tiresome is sure to happen. Things fall out of the air." Suddenly he stopped talking, then, after a moment's observation, said, in his usual unconcerned tones: "That's funny. . . ." On the culture at which he was looking there was a growth of mould, as on several of the others, but on this particular one, all around the mould, the colonies of staphylococci had been dissolved and, instead of forming opaque yellow masses, looked like drops of dew.

Pryce had often seen old microbial colonies which for various reasons had dissolved. He thought that probably the mould was producing acids, which are harmful to the staphylococci — no unusual occurrence. But, noting the keen interest with which Fleming was examining the phenomenon, he said: "That's how you discovered lysozyme." Fleming made no answer. He was busy taking a little piece of the mould with his scalpel, and put-

---

* This is sometimes referred to as "serendipity," a word coined by Horace Walpole (*The Three Princes of Serendip*) to "denote the faculty of making lucky and unexpected 'finds'." The three princes were "always making discoveries, by accident and sagacity, of things they were not in quest of."[60] The story itself may be found in T. G. Remer (Ed.), *Serendipity and the Three Princes*, University of Oklahoma Press, 1965. It should be emphasized that serendipity is preceded by preparation. As an editorial writer in *Science* has said, "Serendipity is a bonus to the perceptive, prepared scientist, not a substitute for hard work."[61]

ting it in a tube of broth. Then he picked off a scrap measuring about one square millimetre, which floated on the surface of the broth. He obviously wanted to make quite sure that this mysterious mould would be preserved.

"What struck me," Pryce says, "was that he didn't confine himself to observing, but took action at once. Lots of people observe a phenomenon, feeling that it may be important, but they don't get beyond being surprised — after which they forget. That was never the case with Fleming. I remember another incident — One of my cultures had not been successful, and he told me to be sure of getting everything possible out of my mistakes. . . ."

Fleming put the Petri dish aside . . . He showed it to one of his colleagues: "Take a look at that," he said, "it's interesting — the kind of thing I like; it may turn out to be important." The colleague in question looked at the dish, then handed it back with a polite: "Yes, very interesting." But Fleming, in no way discouraged by this manifestation of indifference, temporarily abandoned his investigation of the staphylococci, and gave himself entirely to studying the surprising mould.[62] □

Verification or revision

Inspiration is sometimes the final stage in creative thinking. In most instances, however, it is necessary to evaluate, test, and perhaps revise, the idea that comes to us. Is it logical? We can at times determine whether an idea is logical by casting it into syllogistic form and testing it by the laws of formal logic. Very often, however, it is necessary to carry out controlled observations which will prove whether or not an inspiration is correct, or workable, or needs revision.

This is the method followed by scientists. Likewise, the inventor must show that his ideas work in practice as well as in his blueprints. Indeed, the scientist, inventor, and artist frequently find that their inspirations need considerable modification before their creative work is satisfactory.

The inspiration is, so to speak, only a prelude to further intensive work. It is one thing for the person to get the idea for a picture, a novel, a poem, an invention, or a theory, and quite another to paint the picture, write the novel, write the poem, produce the invention, or formulate, test, and verify the theory. ■

• SUMMARY

Thinking is manipulating the world internally, using modifications of the organism which represent the things that produced them, i.e., symbolic processes. The term *thinking* covers such activities as thinking of (or recalling) something; reverie, or free association; fantasy, or daydreaming; and reasoning, or implicit problem-solving. We have given major attention to the latter process.

The existence of reasoning in animals ranging from rat to man is clearly indicated by results obtained with several learning problems. These are problems which could not conceivably be learned without the use of symbols.

One type of reasoning problem gives the subject two separate "experiences" and then confronts him with a problem he can solve

immediately only by combining these experiences. Rats have solved simple problems of this nature, and so have children five years of age and older.

One form of the double-alternation problem utilizes a temporal maze in which the subject is required to make a related series of reactions, for example, to follow a right-right-left-left sequence, without differential sensory cues to guide him. The ability to solve double-alternation problems and to extend the sequence beyond that involved in training increases as we go up the scale from rat to man. In children, ability to solve the double-alternation problem begins at about three years and increases with age. The problem is quite readily learned by adults, the subject often saying, "*right, right, left, left,*" as he responds.

In all reasoning, three things are requisite: retention, recall, and recombination of what is recalled. So-called thinking machines have such processes built into them, but their computing is dependent upon a detailed programming of routines to be followed. Their activities resemble human reasoning only in its elemental aspects.

When confronted by problems or difficulties which cannot be met in a routine manner, human beings formulate hypotheses about the cause of their difficulties or the solutions of their problems. This is the most important step in human reasoning. Hypotheses are formulated on the basis of past experience, and they are limited in scope and relevance by the limitations of experience. Before accepting or rejecting our hypotheses we usually evaluate them, either by further implicit activity or by carrying out an actual check on their applicability.

Our associational processes in reasoning are directed by the nature of the problem, as we conceive of it. The problem gives us a set, or determining tendency, which facilitates recall of certain items and inhibits recall of others not relevant to the situation. Sometimes, despite this general directional tendency, we are hindered by limitations which we place on our own thinking. We accept the first inference that comes to mind, perhaps, and let our thoughts go in the direction suggested. Delusions often have such a basis. The reasoning process is more efficient when we change direction frequently, seeking new inferences when the one we have does not work.

Much of human thinking involves subvocal talking. Evidence for this view comes from such observations as the following: children "think out loud" before they learn to think subvocally, organs involved in speech give rise to action currents while a person is thinking, action currents come from the fingers while deaf-mutes are engaged in thought, and eye movements similar to those involved in reading a passage may occur when the individual is thinking of it. There are also action currents from other relevant muscle groups, as from the biceps while a person thinks of an activity in which these muscles are involved.

Despite all such motor concomitants of the thought process, thinking still occurs during complete paralysis. This was brought out in the experiment with curare. It suggests that, while thinking normally involves the vocal and other motor mechanisms, it can occur on a purely central basis, i.e., in the brain.

The brain is involved in thinking in at least three ways: it contains modifications (engrams) which represent past experience, it mediates recall, and it activates and integrates the various activities of the vocal and other mechanisms normally involved.

Many of the terms used in thinking represent common properties of things that are diverse. These are conceptual terms, and the ideational processes which underlie them are called concepts. Acquiring concepts requires that the individual discriminate the common properties of different objects — that he discern similarity amid diversity. This is the process known as abstracting. In order to develop a concept, it is also necessary that the individual generalize — that he relate the similarities in such a manner as to derive a generalization like "all objects having these properties are trees."

The general method followed in concept formation is dissociation by varying concomitants. Research on concept formation in adults, using Chinese characters, suggests that the most efficient method of teaching individuals to abstract and generalize is that of presenting total situations with the common elements emphasized. The common properties of many situations which call for concept formation are by no means obvious, and the individual must "figure them out." Individuals confronted by difficult concept (categorizing) problems use different strategies, some of which are more efficient than others. Many concepts are learned by asking questions. Children's concepts, at first very inadequate, gradually approach those of their elders.

Creative thinking is especially evident in the productions of such people as scientists, inventors, artists, and poets. Productions may be divergent or convergent, with the latter type of most importance in creative thinking.

Much trial and error underlies most creative work. Inspirations, insights, or illuminations are its spectacular aspects. Analysis of creative thinking by the thinkers themselves, and by others, has led to the conclusion that four stages are more or less clearly evident. These are: preparation, the gathering of relevant information and attempts to organize it; incubation, a period of relative inactivity, perhaps with recurrence of ideas about the problem, but no evident progress; inspiration, the sudden illumination, or "aha" experience; and verification or revision, the testing and evaluation of the idea, inference, or hypothesis, either by implicit processes or by actual experiment. The last stage is not always present, but it is essential in research and in certain inventive pursuits. ■

REFERENCES AND NOTES FOR THIS CHAPTER ARE IN THE APPENDIX.

• SELECTED READINGS

Anderson, C. A., and D. P. Ausubel (Eds.), *Readings in the Psychology of Cognition.* Holt, Rinehart and Winston, 1965. Most of the papers reprinted here deal with topics discussed in this chapter.

Anderson, H. H. (Ed.), *Creativity and its Cultivation.* Harper, 1959. A series of papers. Those by Guilford, Hilgard, and Stoddard are relevant to our discussion.

Bartlett, F. C., *Thinking: An Experimental and Social Study.* Allen and Unwin, 1958. Some ingenious experiments on aspects of thinking and an excellent discussion of creative thinking.

Berlyne, D. E., *Structure and Direction in Thinking.* Wiley, 1965. A systematic analysis of thinking and its relation to other forms of behavior.

Dulany, D. E., R. L. DeValois, D. C. Beardslee, and M. R. Winterbottom, *Contributions to Modern Psychology* (2nd ed.). Oxford University Press, 1963, Chapter 5. Five papers on thinking and imagination.

Flavell, J. H., *The Developmental Psychology of Jean Piaget.* Van Nostrand, 1963, Chapter 10. Piaget's experiments on spatial concepts are discussed.

Mandler, J. M., and G. Mandler, *Thinking: From Association to Gestalt.* Wiley, 1964. An original paperback.

Mowrer, O. H., *Learning Theory and the Symbolic Processes.* Wiley, 1960. Chapter 6 deals with learning, thought, and insight.

Piaget, J., *The Language and Thought of the Child.* Meridian Paperback, 1955 (originally published in 1926). Also see the Piaget bibliography in the Flavell reference, above.

Thompson, R., *The Psychology of Thinking.* Penguin Books, 1959. A paperback survey of work on thinking in animals and humans.

Wertheimer, M., and Michael Wertheimer, *Productive Thinking* (rev. ed.). Harper, 1959. An updating, by Wertheimer's son, that is based upon papers left by his father.

Whorf, B. L., *Language Thought, and Reality.* Wiley, 1956. Papers selected and edited by J. B. Carroll, whose introduction is a fascinating account of a most interesting man. The basic idea throughout the several papers that are relevant to our present discussion is that language shapes man's concept of reality and also his thinking. The papers on thinking in primitive communities (p. 65), the relation of habitual thought and behavior to language (p. 134), and language, mind, and reality (p. 246) are especially worth reading.

14

Communication and Language

- LIMITATIONS OF ANIMAL COMMUNICATION
- LINGUISTIC ORIGINS
- SPEECH MECHANISMS
- LEARNING TO SPEAK
- THE COMMUNICATION PROCESS
- THE MEANING OF WORDS
- NONVERBAL COMMUNICATION
- SUMMARY

Communication is an integral feature of interaction between organisms. It occurs whenever the behavior of one organism acts as a stimulus for the behavior of another. Sometimes the behavior of one organism is informative. It may indicate that danger approaches, that food is to be found in a particular place, or, at a level of much greater complexity, that a friend is expected to reach New York on Wednesday. In its barest essentials, communication goes something like this: The behavior of one organism acts as a stimulus. The second organism, because of the inborn makeup of its nervous system, or because of neural changes that have resulted from learning, responds appropriately to the stimulation provided. At the human level, stimulation may be transmitted through various intermediaries, including telephone wires or cables, not to mention deliverers of the message. Even so, the fact remains that a message is understood only because the stimulation involved arouses appropriate processes in the recipient. In short, there is no transfer of information except in such terms.

Most human interaction involves language, which may be defined in the simplest terms as *communication with gestures or with spoken or written words.* Speech symbols (gestural, spoken, or written) are conventionalized, which is to say, bound by rules. They involve stimuli which signify something that is understood, more or less, by both the person who initiates them and the person for whom they are intended. A message "gets across" because the sender encodes his message according to custom and the receiver decodes it in the same terms.

It is well to recollect, in this connection, what has already been said about symbolic processes. Linguistic stimuli are symbols in that they represent something other than themselves. When one wishes to convey a message, in conversation or otherwise, he encodes it, so to speak, in the signals he has learned to make. The recipient decodes the message. He reacts to the symbols in terms of the meanings he has learned to attach to them. This encoding and decoding process is usually quite automatic, unless the code used is a secret one that must be deliberately deciphered.

Speech sounds and gestures, as well as written words, are therefore not *just* sounds, or movements, or scratchings on paper. They are symbols that represent objects or events with which communication is concerned. One who knows the language reacts to them as having conventional meanings. He knows the code, hence he can decode them. The printed symbol, HAT, is generally accepted as meaning a certain kind of headgear. "You "get" what is encoded because you know the convention. But take the following symbol: HAŠESAH.[1] What is printed provides visual stimulation. But no message is transmitted, for the simple reason that you have not learned what this stimulation means. It happens to be Mayan. Thus it arouses no appropriate symbolic counterpart in you, such as a student of this ancient language might have. In short, you cannot decode whatever "message" might be said to be imbedded in the word.

Communication at an elementary level involves no more than the stimulation of one animal by another in such a manner as to produce a similar response in the latter. Thus the chirping of a cricket, or the croaking of a frog, starts up similar activity in others. At a somewhat higher level of complexity, communication may have a signaling function. A response in one animal may signal danger to its companions. One antelope, say, raises its tail, and the others, reacting to this reflex as signaling danger, depart hurriedly from the vicinity. At a still higher level, one animal stimulates another to do something positive, like going in search of food or helping it do something. Communication at this level is sometimes assumed to involve language. We will see, however, that language in its fully developed form is a purely human accomplishment.

Some will doubtless question the statement that only human organisms communicate linguistically. They will point to the parrot that "talks," or to the dog that learns to "speak" for a cooky. This chapter answers them by calling attention to the very real differences between animal and human communications, differences which do not justify application of the term "language" to the former.

Human beings at times communicate as animals do. Communication may involve signals, even reflex ones, as when somebody screams and people look or rush in that direction. On the other hand, most human communication is mediated by language. Some is nonverbal, as when conventionalized gestures rather than words are used. More of it is verbal, involving spoken, written, or printed words.

We begin with so-called animal language. This discussion brings out the basic characteristics of linguistic as compared with other forms of communication. Attention is then focused upon vocal mechanisms and the ways in which they produce speech sounds. Acquisition of verbal skills is considered next. Then we examine basic speech functions and some informational aspects of language. The processes within the organism that underlie the meanings of words — or which, in a sense, link the name with what it represents — are also considered. Finally, we outline some nonverbal forms of communication in man. ■

LIMITATIONS OF ANIMAL COMMUNICATION

All but the simplest animals, through their own behavior, stimulate the behavior of others of their kind. They do this sometimes by exuding odors, sometimes by emitting sounds, and sometimes by assuming postures. These acts are essentially reflex, as are the responses to them. Certain odors may signal that a female is sexually receptive. Vocalizations may have a similar function. Birds, for example, vocalize to call a mate, to challenge an enemy, or to proclaim their territorial rights.[2] The howler monkey vanquishes its enemies by literally "howling them down."[3] By assuming a certain posture the baboon warns others not to approach his food or his females. A female chimpanzee, by assuming a mating posture, may divert the otherwise dominant male from a food supply, thus getting more of it for herself.[4] Indeed, books have been written about these and other ways in which animals communicate with each other.

The "language" of the bees

A highly elaborate form of communication occurs in bees. It is so elaborate as to have been called the "language" of the bees.[5]

Upon returning to its hive from a success-ful foraging trip, the bee brings with it nectar and pollen. The latter, by itself, may signal the kind of flower visited, possibly through its odor. But more is signaled by a dance which the bee performs. If the food source is nearby, the dance assumes a circular pattern. A more distant source is signaled by a dance which, in its pattern, resembles a figure eight. The bee runs forward, circling now to the right and now to the left. Meanwhile its tail end wags from side to side. The rapidity of circling and tail-wagging signals the distance of the food source. The direction in which the bees must go is indicated by the direction of the run between turns.

How bees decode such information is not definitely known, although certain details have been discovered. For one thing, other bees imitate the dance of the informant, no doubt instinctively. Then they, too, fly off in the proper direction.

Remarkable as it is, there are marked limitations in this communication between bees. As one commentator says, "You and I can have endless conversation about all sorts of subjects, but bees are able to discuss one thing only — food and where to find it."[6]

Communication among chimpanzees

Communication at a much higher level of complexity — at a higher level because it seems

● 14.1

Communication in Chimpanzees. Top: Bula touches Kambi near the mouth and turns her head toward the grill. Middle: Bula's hand is on top of Kambi's, pushing it down toward a rope. Bottom: Bula and Bimba pull together. (From M. P. Crawford, "The Cooperative Solving of Problems by Young Chimpanzees," *Comp. Psychol. Monogr.*, 1937, 14, No. 2, p. 59.)

to be *intentional** rather than reflex, and because it has *symbolic significance* approaching that of human communication — is found in chimpanzees. Take, for example, an experiment on cooperative behavior. Chimpanzees were taught, one at a time, to pull in a box containing food. Then the box was made too heavy for an animal to pull it in unaided. Now there were two ropes (Figure 14.1) and, in order to get the food, cage-mates were required to pull the two ropes at the same time. This was quite a problem. One animal pulled, found that the food box would not budge, then gave up. The other animal pulled, and also failed to obtain the food.

After special training, which called for joint pulling on command, the animals learned to pull at the same time. Finally, without the experimenter's command, the chimpanzees took up the ropes and, by watching each other, pulled in unison. Sometimes, however, one animal was more eager than the other. His problem, then, was how to get his partner to cooperate. It is here that gestures approximating language came into play. One animal solicited cooperation by putting its hand on the partner's shoulder and turning it around, or by touching it in various ways. When successful, these motions oriented the partner toward the rope. The observer of such behavior cannot escape the impression that the chimpanzee is all but saying, "Help me do something."[7]

If the chimpanzee pointed at the rope or handed it to the partner, this could be even more effective, providing, of course, that the partner knew enough to perceive the significance of such acts. Chimpanzees never have been known actually to point, nor to solicit cooperation more directly than by turning another animal in a relevant direction. They come very close to language, yet can do no

* We qualify this statement by saying "*seems to be* intentional" because there is never any absolute proof of intention. A human being can of course tell us that he intends to do a certain thing (whether or not he actually does it) and he can tell us that he did or did not intend to do something that he has done (like committing a crime), but the limitations of animal communication are such that we can do no more than infer the presence of intentions.

more than signal the need for help, in the most general way.

In an experiment in which chimpanzees developed a morphine addiction, the addicted animal sometimes took the experimenter's hand and pulled him toward the dispensary. There, at times, the chimpanzee handed him the syringe and bent over to receive an injection. Here again, the best the animal could accomplish was to say, in effect, "Do something for me."[8]

In short, a chimpanzee's behavior cannot tell another in detail *what to do*. Nor can it in any way *describe* an object or an action.

Teaching a chimpanzee to "talk"

An orangutan[9] and a chimpanzee[10] have been taught to say a few words. However, their accomplishment is far from true speech.

The "talking" chimpanzee, trained by Keith and Cathy Hayes, and subject of the latter's book, *The Ape in Our House*, is shown in Figure 14.2. She was treated as a child and called "Viki." At the beginning Viki made no sounds beyond those which chimpanzees normally make when excited. She did not babble. Except when emotionally aroused, she was silent. The initial problem, therefore, was to get her to make nonemotional sounds. This seemed hopeless. Efforts to induce Viki to "speak" for her milk by making sounds were also, at first, in vain. Accordingly, milk was withheld in the hope that Viki would "say" something. But Mrs. Hayes and Viki looked at each other, or at the milk, and Viki made no sound. When the milk was about to be taken away, Viki let out worried little "oo-oo's," typical reflex vocalizations. For making such sounds, emotional though they were, she was given a sip of milk. In the excitement over getting milk, Viki made some reflex barking sounds, and was given more milk. Then, as her appetite wore off, she was silent again. When urged to "speak," she said nothing. The threatened departure of Mrs. Hayes brought more "oo-oo's," and more milk was given. And so it went.

Viki was not speaking on command. Noises were, so to speak, "tricked out of her." This continued for five weeks. Then with face

● 14.2
Teaching Viki to Say "Mama." By pressing her lips together, as illustrated, and moving them as she made the "ahhh" sound, Mrs. Hayes eventually taught her to say something approximating "Mama." As the lips began to move without aid, touching with a finger was sufficient. Finally Viki said "Mama" without help, although she did so only when commanded, or under obviously relevant circumstances, as when it would bring a reward. (Courtesy, The American Philosophical Society)

contorted, and obviously with great effort, Viki began to make a sound like "*ahhh*." When she did so, she reached for the milk. Now, at long last, it appeared that she was vocalizing intentionally. Viki then made the "*ahhh*" sound when she was asked to speak, and also initiated it herself in "asking" for things.

Now that Viki was vocalizing on an apparently intentional basis, the next step was to try to teach her to say words. The first of these was "Mama." Manipulation of the mouth as she said "*ahhh*" was necessary. However, as described in the legend of Figure 14.2, this could finally be dispensed with, and Viki said "Mama" without help. The word "Papa" was acquired after she had learned to imitate a "Bronx cheer." The word "cup" was a combination of the sounds "k" and "p," one quickly following the other. Viki also learned to click her teeth, signifying that she wanted to go for a ride.*

Although Viki learned a few words, we are not justified in crediting her with language. When parrots, chimpanzees, or other animals learn to "speak," they do so only under human tuition. Without this tuition, and the patterns set for them by their trainers, like the movements Viki was induced to make by human manipulation of her lips, they never acquire anything resembling speech. To call Viki's few acquired vocalizations "speech" would, in any event, be purely academic. The sounds did not, and probably never would, function like speech. As one writer has pointed out, after reviewing the extensive literature on "animal language," animals do not use their acquired vocal skills to communicate as human beings do. Their vocalizations are stereotyped and closely tied to the situations in which they were conditioned. They are used only in the presence of human beings; not to communicate with another animal. Even more significant is the fact that no animal combines its acquired vocalizations, as words are combined, to form phrases and sentences. It is also noteworthy that animal vocalizations refer to the present (or possibly the future as in anticipation of milk), but never to the past.[11]

When animals learn to respond appropriately to speech, as many do, they are influenced by the pitch, loudness, or pattern of sounds — not by their symbolic content, nor their meaning in a human sense. Perhaps the best example of this was given by Thorndike, who trained cats to run to a box when he said, "I must feed those cats." After this conditioning had been accomplished, he said, "My name is Thorndike." The cats ran to the box as before. They did this, also, when he said, "Today is Tuesday." In fact, any vocalization that he used had an equivalent effect.[12]

The role of insight

Even when animals learn to vocalize with apparent intent, as Viki did, they still lack insight into the significance of the sounds

* Unfortunately, the experiment was ended with Viki's death from what seemed to be a virus infection.

they are making. This difference between animals and human beings is interestingly exemplified by the blind and deaf Helen Keller. One morning during her seventh year, Helen patted Miss Sullivan's hand and pointed to running water, signifying in this way that she wanted its name. The word w-a-t-e-r was spelled out on her hand in the manual alphabet. Later, while filling a cup at the pump, Helen had the word w-a-t-e-r spelled out again. This time the cold water was overflowing on her hand, and the spelling of the word at the same time had a remarkable effect. This is described by her teacher, Miss Sullivan:

☐ "The word, coming so close upon the sensation of cold water rushing over her hand, seemed to startle her. She dropped the mug and stood as one transfixed. A new light came into her face. She spelled "water" several times. Then she dropped to the ground and asked for its name and pointed to the pump and trellis, and suddenly turning round she asked for my name. I spelled "teacher." Just then the nurse brought Helen's little sister into the pump-house and Helen spelled "baby" and pointed to the nurse. All the way back to the house she was highly excited, and learned the name of every object she touched, so that in a few hours she had added 30 new words to her vocabulary."[13] ☐

Helen had discovered that *everything has a name*. After this, she began "to see the world in a new light." She had "learned the use of words, not merely as mechanical signs and signals, but as an entirely new instrument of thought."[14]

Where are animals lacking?

It is somewhat of a mystery why animals fail to develop languages in the human sense and why, under human tuition, an animal as intelligent as a chimpanzee fails to achieve insight into the significance of words. The difficulty does not appear to lie in the vocal mechanisms. Parrots and chimpanzees, for example, have a wide vocal range and even do a fairly good job of imitating human vocalizations.

Some writers feel that a necessary prelude to development of speech is the vocal play, or babbling, in which human infants engage. They feel that, since animals do not vocalize spontaneously, but only in a reflex manner when emotionally aroused, an important stepping stone to language is missing.[15]

The absence of vocal play could itself be due to the failure of animals to develop anything corresponding to the human speech area (p. 61), a region of the left motor cortex which controls speech movements.[16]

A deficiency that is every bit as important as absence of babbling or the lack of a motor speech center is the low level of symbolic functioning in animals. Symbolic processes were discussed earlier in relation to the delayed-reaction test. There we observed that, whereas some animals recall absent stimuli after a delay, human beings do much better on such tests — recalling after a longer delay and under conditions of greater complexity. Such recall is possible because persisting neurological changes, referred to earlier as engrams, can be reactivated when a proper new stimulus situation arises. As we said in earlier discussions, the reactivation of such "neural traces" is basic to all symbolic processes that an individual acquires.

The prelinguistic symbolic processes of animals and children seem to possess "all the functions of language except the social characteristic of interstimulation and response." True language, it may be maintained, "grows out of the symbolic processes used by some animals in the solution of the types of problems represented in the delayed-reaction experiment."[17] What this means is that the symbolic processes of animals are insufficiently evolved to make the transition from nonlinguistic to linguistic symbols. The reason perhaps lies in their brain structure, especially the small proportion of the brain that is given over to functions of association, as compared with sensorimotor duties.* The frontal lobes, which are so prominent in man, and possibly of particular significance for symbolic functions, are also much less pronounced in animals. This is true even at the chimpanzee level.

* See in this connection, the earlier discussion of association areas in the cerebral cortex (pp. 60–62).

Such deficiencies as we have mentioned are doubtless interrelated. That is to say, the absence of vocal play, and a low level of symbolic functioning, are tied in with such features of the animal brain as its smallness; its associative insufficiency, particularly in the frontal regions; and its lack of specialized motor structures corresponding to the motor speech area in man.

In stressing symbolic processes at the level of recall (as in the delayed-reaction experiment), we must not overlook one other extremely important fact: the use of language requires much more than ability to recall. It requires insight and reasoning as well. It calls for the sort of understanding that came to Helen Keller when, in a flash, she discovered that things may be represented by names and when she followed up this insight by seeking the name of everything around her.

Nor must we overlook the fact that our remote forbears didn't merely discover language. They *invented it*. In fact they invented many languages, in different parts of the world, apparently in complete independence of each other.

Each individual has a relatively easy task. Instead of starting from scratch as the earliest men must have done, he is handed a language ready made. All he has to do is learn it, difficult as this may be for some. ■

LINGUISTIC ORIGINS

How man made the transition from nonlinguistic to linguistic communication is unknown. This "whole day of creation" or "whole chapter in evolution," as one philosopher has called it, is perhaps forever beyond our comprehension.[18] The reason is that primitive men, although they left relics of their tools and other implements, and paintings on the walls of caves, could not, until writing itself was invented, leave any information about their speech. However, absence of information on the earliest forms of verbal behavior and how they were invented has not prevented scholars from theorizing. There are, in fact, many theories about the origin of speech, but this is not the proper place to consider them in detail. It will be sufficient for our purposes to sketch two interrelated theories which psychologists have put forth, not with the implication that these are correct, but only to indicate a line of reasoning that receives some support from what is known about human learning today.

☐ It may be said at the outset that the only essential condition for the development of a new language is isolation of a group of individuals with no ready-made means of communication. One way or another, they will soon acquire means of communicating with each other.[19] One speech theory comes from Judd, who calls attention to the fact that children sometimes chance upon (or invent) expressions and then use them to represent objects. For example, one child was heard calling pebbles *pocos*, a term which did not come from its environment, hence must have been made by chance (or invented) and then adopted to represent pebbles. Judd says:

"When the world was young, the opportunity for inventing new words must have been unlimited. Even in that far-away age, however, the inventor's task was less than half accomplished when he emitted the new sound. Before he could regard his task as complete, he must induce his neighbors to use the sound as he had used it."[20]

The other theory, proposed by Thorndike, stresses chance associations between babbling sounds (say *ug*) and objects perceived at the same time. Thorndike says:

"Consider a child of early man playing with a large shell. . . . Let us take the state of affairs least favorable to connecting the sound *ug* with that shell. . . . Let his prattling possibilities consist of a thousand syllables all equally likely to occur in any one situation or in any other. Then the chance that he will utter *ug* as he puts a pebble in the shell as 1 in 1000 if he prattles at all."[21]

Should the child, out of all these possibilities, happen to make the *ug* sound, more will be needed to establish this as representative of the shell (or pebble, or act of dropping the latter). The *ug*-shell association will need considerable strengthening, otherwise some new sound, or none at all, will next time accompany dropping of the pebble into the shell. In this connection, Thorndike says that, "there are forces which tend to cause progress away from purely miscellaneous vocal play. First of all the child who puts one pebble in the shell is likely to put another in then and there. His enjoyment of the act makes him repeat it, that is, strengthens its connection with the mental set in which he did it first. Now that mental set happened at that time to evoke also the vocal play of saying *ug*, and the confirming reaction which the enjoyment of the manual play set in action tends to spread or scatter so as to strengthen also the connection of the situation with the utterance. . . . In the second place, saying *ug* to the shell and pebble may be itself enjoyable and the connection may thereby be strengthened. Consequently, the probability that the child will drop a second pebble is substantial and the probability that he will utter *ug* therewith if he utters anything is far above 1 to 1000."[22]

Note that both of these theorists refer to *children* vocalizing. This is perhaps because children, more than adults, engage in random vocalizations. Here, as earlier (p. 435), we observe an emphasis upon babbling as a significant stepping stone to speech.

Whether the first words were chanced upon, or invented, by children or adults, there was still the problem posited by Judd: namely, that of having the sounds adopted by others as symbols for the objects (or events) which they represented for the discoverer. It is unlikely, unless they had unusual insight, that adults would have taken over the sounds from children. It is possible that preverbal adults themselves engaged in spontaneous vocalizations — that they prattled to themselves and that associations like those suggested by Thorndike took place at the adult level. But how did such sounds receive acceptance from the group, so as to become conventional symbols for the things represented? No doubt prestige was an important factor. It is not uncommon today for people to adopt some saying or gesture because the person who initiates it has prestige. ☐

Once man attained the idea of using sounds to represent objects or events, there must have been a marked acceleration of verbal behavior. A human child today, after it begins to talk, soon adds new words at a rapid rate. Helen Keller, when verbal insight came to her, began a greatly accelerated linguistic development. In the case of primitive man, the initial idea, however it occurred, was probably followed by the *invention of* or *search for* new vocalizations to represent the various facets of his world.

Gestures probably have an origin corresponding, in many respects, to the beginnings of speech. Whether conventionalized gestures preceded or followed speech, or whether they developed concurrently, is a controversial point — again, one that is apparently beyond solution.

It is rather generally agreed that writing followed the development of speech. Its special virtue is that "it makes possible the transmission of cultural acquisitions in a manner much more extensive and permanent than that rendered possible by either gestures or vocalizations, which depend, of course, upon personal contacts."[23]

The first written language that we know anything about used pictures to represent objects or events. In time the representations became increasingly sketchy, as in Figure 14.3. Quite often, only a fragment of the original picture was retained to represent the object. Then, even this departed more and more from the original. A word (or letter) now bore little or no resemblance to the picture from which it originated. The representations had indeed become symbolic. This process was notably important in that it fostered the association of sounds with written symbols. Except in a few instances, as when the sound *buzz* might be used to represent what makes it, sounds bear no resemblance to the things represented.* Pictures do bear a resemblance. But with neither the written nor the spoken sign resembling what was symbolized, it was a relatively short step to the use of written symbols as representing sounds, or vice versa. Thus the written symbol for *eye* also repre-

---

* This is known as *onomatopoeia*, and it is involved in a theory of speech origins which supposes that the first words were sounds like those made by the objects represented.

● **14.3**

From Picture to Letter. The Egyptian hieroglyph for owl looked very much like this bird. It was, in fact, a stylized picture. Successively, in the Egyptian, Phoenician, and Greek, it approximated our letter M. The significance of this transition, discussed in the text, is that pictures, which came to represent objects without looking anything like them, could be used to represent sounds, finally being combined as letters into words which, graphically and orally, represent objects and situations.

sented the sound *i*. Take, as a further example, the letter M, already illustrated. This originated in the Egyptian picture of an owl. The spoken word for owl began with the sound *m*. Finally the M, now not looking at all like an owl, came to represent the sound *m*.

The final stage in the evolution of writing came when the separate "M's," "i's," etc., were combined in the same order as the sounds of oral speech to form written words.

This very short sketch of the antecedents of man's verbal behavior prepares us to examine his speech mechanisms and to describe how speech sounds are produced. ■

SPEECH MECHANISMS

Speech involves many motor skills. It requires that the diaphragm, the lungs, and the muscles of the chest as well as the vocal cords, mouth, tongue, and lips (Figure 14.4) be manipulated in ways which are very complex. The motor skill aspect would be even more apparent if we had to activate these structures with our hands, as a violinist, say, manipulates the strings and bow of his instrument. Beyond motor skill there are such factors as the sort of information which the vocalizations transmit and, related to this, their meaning for the person who produces them and the one who listens. These aspects are considered later.

The mechanisms described in Figure 14.4 are of course under nervous control. Messages are, as it were, "encoded" by the brain and sent, via the motor speech area, the brain

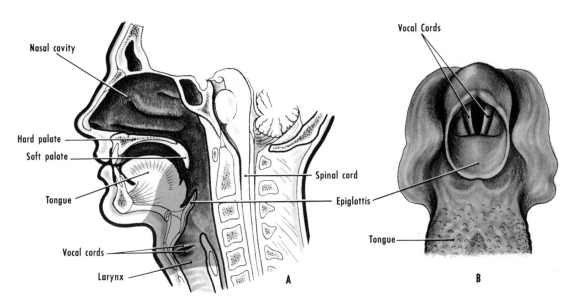

Nasal cavity

Hard palate

Soft palate

Tongue

Vocal cords

Larynx

Spinal cord

Epiglottis

A

Vocal Cords

Tongue

B

● **14.4**

Speech Mechanisms. The *vocal cords* are two membranes stretched across the interior of the boxlike *larynx* at the level of the Adam's apple. They add "voice" to what we say. Without them speech is only a whisper. The vocal cords vibrate in response to air forced up the windpipe by the lungs, which act in the manner of a bellows. With the cords tightly drawn, there is rapid vibration and tones have a high pitch. With the cords under less tension, lower tones are produced. The opening between the vocal cords is called the *glottis*. With this wide open, through relaxation of the vocal cords, there is no more than whispering. This is also true when the larynx is removed. The pitch of tones may also be raised or lowered by raising or lowering the larynx itself. Tonal quality is modified by resonance cavities within the chest, head, and nose — as when a person speaks with a "nasal twang." Vowel sounds are produced by the vocal cords with relatively little obstruction or modification by other speech mechanisms. Consonants, on the other hand, are produced by various changes imposed upon the expelled air. Fricative consonants, like *th, sh,* and *z,* are so named because friction resulting from lips, tongue, teeth, and palate is required to produce them. In making these sounds one can note how this is done. There are also explosive consonants, like *p, t,* and *ch.* One can observe, in making these sounds, why they are designated explosive. Consonants like *m* and *n* involve the nasal cavities, hence are said to be nasal.

stem, and peripheral nerves, to the vocal musculature. The role of cerebral association areas in speech was described when we discussed the various aphasias (pp. 60–61). It is well, too, to recall what was said earlier (p. 52) about feedback. Feedback from the auditory receptors, as when we hear ourselves speak, is also of the utmost importance for speech. Experiments in which the auditory feedback is delayed produce stammering, stuttering, and, as mentioned earlier (p. 202), a great deal of frustration. We will see presently that auditory feedback is a necessary condition in the development of babbling, an early step in learning to speak. Kinesthetic feedback is likewise important, but perhaps to a lesser degree than the auditory.

An infant's initial vocalizations are reflex reactions, apparently under the control of internal stimuli. Such reflex sounds are, so to speak, the basic ingredients of human speech. It is out of these, as well as others that make their appearance as the infant matures, that the words of the language are built. The child's motor task is to combine such sounds in ways which make them have representative significance for himself and those who listen to him. That is, he must learn to encode a message — and also to decode similar messages initiated by others.

□ Observations of the earliest sounds made by infants demonstrate that, although more than forty distinguishable sounds (*phonemes*) are recognized and listed in the International Phonetic Alphabet, the neonate uses only eight.[24] Five of these are vowel sounds. The sound *a* as in cat accounts for about 90 per cent of all the initial utterances. In a group of forty babies under ten days old this was the only vowel sound used by all. The other four vowels, used by some, were *i* as in fit, *e* as in set, *u* as in up, and *oo* as in food. There is also a sound made by pressure of air against the closed glottis. The two recognizable consonants are *h* and *l*. Gradually the infant adds to the initial phonemes so that eventually all those found in the adult are present. One investigator,[25] tape-recording the vocalizations of his own infant periodically

during the first two months of life, "found all of the speech sounds that the human vocal system can produce, including French vowels and trills, German umlaut and guttural sounds, and many that are describable only in phonetic symbols."

Different languages of course utilize phonemes differently. A particular language emphasizes some and does not use others. In acquiring speech, therefore, the infant bases his utilization of phonemes on the pattern characteristic of his culture. But before he combines these in meaningful ways, he repeats them in the manner known in our culture as babbling. □

Although speech is learned, there is always the limiting factor of maturation. The increasing range of phonemes as the infant gets older is probably due to maturation of vocal mechanisms. Babbling may be delayed until the third month or later because the motor cortex is not sufficiently developed. Even after words are spoken, we observe limitations which are usually attributed to immaturity of the vocal mechanisms — for example, the inability of an infant to say "*l*ight" instead of "*y*ite." No doubt maturation and learning play interdependent roles in speech development; so interdependent, in fact, that it is often impossible to disentangle their respective influences. ▪

LEARNING TO SPEAK

One may look upon the infant's initial vocalizations (phonemes) as operants which, if and when they are reinforced, "gradually assume forms which produce appropriate consequences in a given verbal community." These "unpatterned vocalizations," these "raw responses from which verbal behavior is constructed" are not produced by any known stimuli. In terms of our earlier discussion of operants (p. 307), they are "emitted."[26]

Since we cannot control the stimuli which underlie these early vocalizations, we must, if we are going to reinforce them, wait until they occur. It has been suggested, however, that such vocalizations become, in time, self-reinforcing.

The infant of course hears the sounds that he makes and, through kinesthetic feedback, perhaps also senses their motor aspects. It is thus possible for him to engage in a form of self-stimulation that may be rewarding in and of itself. Secondary reinforcement may also supplement whatever reinforcement is inherent in the vocalizations *per se*. This might come initially from the mother's voice. In caring for the infant's needs she usually speaks to him. Through this association with feeding, changing diapers, and so forth, her voice perhaps becomes a secondary reinforcer. Then, through the process of stimulus generalization (p. 304), the infant's own voice may acquire the properties of a secondary reinforcer. After this, the sounds that he makes, as well as those of the mother, may have reward value. They perhaps "sound good" to the baby.[27]

Babbling

An important stage in learning to speak is marked by the transition from indiscriminate vocalizing to babbling, where a particular vocalization is repeated, as in *lal-lal-lal*. Babbling may appear as early as the third month. It is a prevalent response by the fifth or sixth month. Among the repetitive sequences, one is likely at this time to hear such combinations as *ma-ma*, *lul-lul*, *a-bah-bah*, and *da-da-da*. It

is notable that only human beings engage in such vocal play — a point elaborated upon earlier. Also of considerable interest is the fact that deaf infants, although they make sounds, do not babble.[28]

On the surface, babbling is a form of self-imitation. But how is it established? According to one widely accepted theory, it is a conditioned sequence, with the sounds made by the infant himself serving as conditioned stimuli for their repetition.[29] The theory supposes that some sort of stimulation, presumably internal, leads to emission of the initial response, such as *da*. Then, once the *da* response is made, it becomes an external stimulus, the sound "da." Since the response and the associated sound occur close together in time, this contiguity may be all that is needed to make the sound a conditioned stimulus for the response, thus producing the sequence *da-da-da.* . . . This possibility is presented in Figure 14.5.

Our diagrams take no cognizance of reinforcement, although there is the additional possibility that each sound emitted by the baby reinforces the response which produced it. That is to say, circular connections like those described "may be strengthened by the rewarding value of the child hearing himself produce a sound similar to that produced by his mother."[30]

● **14.5**
The Reflex Circle Concept of Babbling. The child, in making the sound "da," stimulates himself in two ways. He hears himself say "da" and at the same time kinesthetic impulses from the vocal musculature feed into his nervous system. Finally a reflex circle (left) is established, with the sound "da" serving as a stimulus for its re-arousal. The diagram at the right amplifies this process and it is further elucidated in the text. (After F. H. Allport)

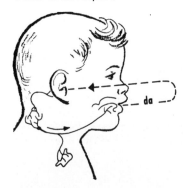

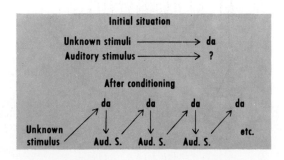

● 14.6

Learning a Word. By association with the sound emitted by an infant, an object may come to be represented by that sound. (After F. H. Allport)

When the baby starts a chain of vocalizations like *da-da-da* . . . this runs its course until fatigue sets in, or until some other stimulus initiates a different reaction.

Acquiring words

The next important step in learning to speak is copying (or attempting to copy) the verbalizations of others. Having learned to imitate himself, the child now attempts to copy others. If someone says "da," for example, the child who has learned to imitate his own "da" may copy this response. If the word happens to be "door," or "doll," the child, if he attempts to copy it at all, will do the best he can, which may well be "da." A closer approximation comes in time. The trial-and-error process involved in learning to say words as others say them was described earlier (p. 321).

Acquiring the motor skills of speech is one thing; learning the meaning of what is said is another. This is true even though skill and the appreciation of meanings may, to a certain extent, develop concurrently.

At an elementary level, the acquisition of word meanings may be accounted for on a conditioning basis. The child says "da-da," let us say, and the father appears. This happens a few times, perhaps with unusual attention (picking up the child, fondling him, etc.), and

shortly, the father, or anyone resembling him, is represented by the vocalization "da-da." The situation may be diagrammed as in Figure 14.6. At this stage of development, anything presented repeatedly while the infant is emitting a particular vocalization may come to be represented by the latter. The psychologist, John B. Watson, arranged for a milk bottle to be brought whenever his child said "da-da." Subsequently the milk bottle became "da-da" and "da-da" apparently *meant* the milk bottle.[31]

A child's first word is usually spoken by the end of the first year. But, as in every other aspect of behavior, there are wide individual differences. Biographical studies — those made by parents or relatives in close contact with a child — report the first words as early as eight months in some children and as late as twenty months in others.[32] Many of a large group of gifted children, according to parental reports, spoke their first word at an average age of eleven months.[33] However, some of the same group did not speak until they were two to three years old. One would expect to find such differences, because speech is especially sensitive to social conditions, which of course differ greatly from one home to another. It has been found, for example, that *only children*, probably because they receive unusual attention from their parents, are usually accelerated in speech development.[34] Children reared in

■ TABLE 14.1   Number of Words Spoken and Number of Different Words Used per Three Hours (approximately) by Nursery-school Children

Age in months	Number of children	Total number of words spoken		Total number of different words used	
		Range	Mean	Range	Mean
24–29	11	236– 729	402	60–142	94
30–35	20	99–1,967	763	32–298	153
36–41	22	396–1,990	1,296	111–394	254
42–47	26	332–3,084	1,772	117–552	309

Adapted from A. T. Jersild and R. Ritzman, "Aspects of Language Development: The Growth of Loquacity and Vocabulary," *Child Development*, 1938, 9, 243–259. Reproduced by permission of the Society for Research in Child Development.

institutions, on the other hand, are usually retarded in this respect. Socio-economic conditions are also important. Generally speaking, the higher the socio-economic level of the parents the earlier their children speak.[35] There is of course also the possibility that hereditary differences are partially responsible. However, even apart from the fact that they may contribute a superior heredity to their offspring, parents in the upper socio-economic levels tend to spend more time playing with them and reading to them. When this happens, development of speech is likely to be accelerated.

After the first word is spoken, others soon follow. The growing vocabulary of the child may be observed by listening every moment that he is awake. Every word may then be recorded. Several such observations have been carried out. In the early stage of speech development this is relatively easy. But as the child moves over a wider territory and his vocabulary assumes larger proportions, recording every word that he speaks becomes impractical. Many parents have started out with the idea of jotting down a child's every word, only to give up in despair as words began to come so fast that they couldn't keep up with them. Another method is to sample the vocabulary at various times and age levels and to pool the results for many children. One study[36] in which this was done with nursery-school children ranging in age from two to four years, yielded the results shown in Table 14.1. Each period of observation lasted only three hours. No doubt a longer period of observation, under a variety of circumstances, would have yielded much larger vocabularies. Of course it is necessary, as in this case, to differentiate between the total number of words spoken (i.e., the child's loquacity) and the number of *different* words spoken (his vocabulary). Both increase with age. Observe that some two-year-olds were using as many as 142 different words in a three-hour period and that, by the fourth year, some of them were using 552 different words.

Some words are used as if they were sentences. For example, a child may say "mama" in such a manner as to give it the meaning, "Mama, come here." Words used in this way are often referred to as "word sentences" or "holophrases."[37] The vocabulary is usually quite extensive (one hundred words or so) before a child combines words into phrases and sentences. The average length of phrases in two-year-olds is two words. By the age of five years, the average is about five words.[38]

Analysis of verbal behavior

The first words acquired are usually nouns. This is to be expected in view of the fact that the most obvious aspects of an infant's environment are objects. At eighteen months, when the vocabulary averages 145 words, about

80 per cent of them are nouns. Nouns continue to predominate. Next to nouns, the most prevalent words are verbs. Adjectives come next.[39]

As a child begins to pick up the rules of syntax, the parts of speech come to have a frequency more in line with their relative usage in his cultural group. But even before children construct their sentences grammatically, they operate on a syntactical rather than a purely random basis. Of course many word combinations are imitated *in toto;* hence we have no indication, from them, that rules of grammar are being followed implicitly by the child. However, when the child generates sentences on his own, and makes mistakes, we then have some indication of the rules he may have followed, perhaps unconsciously.[40] And *there are rules.* Thus the child may say, "Where did daddy went?" or "What you say?" or "It breaked. Get it together like this are." These are obviously not random verbalizations. Children gradually learn to make their speech approximate the syntax of adult speech, even when new words are used. It has been suggested that "learning of inflectional and syntactical skills is akin to concept formation," and that "its rate of occurrence may well be governed by such variables as number of instances, amount of feedback, ratio of positive to negative instances, reinforcement contingencies, and all of the other variables pertinent to concept formation."[41]

□ Skinner's analysis of verbal behavior distinguishes between verbal habits in terms of their functions rather than their grammatical classification.[42] He distinguishes, for example, between what he calls *mands* and *tacts,* and he sees a somewhat different origin for each.

The term *mand* has been adopted by Skinner to designate words, phrases, or sentences which have an element of demand or request — like "Up," (meaning, "Lift me up,") "Give me," or "Go!" It is noteworthy that mands are emitted, presumably under the influence of some internal motivating condition. They are reinforced by the favorable response of the person addressed. Although mands are regarded as operants (as emitted rather than externally elicited responses) external stimuli

may come to provoke them, as in the case of a child who, seeing candy in a window, asks for some.

Tact is a term invented to represent verbalizations which name, symbolize, or represent aspects of the environment. The term suggests the idea of "making contact with" the things or events represented. To quote Skinner: "In very general terms we may say that behavior in the form of the tact works for the benefit of the listener by extending his contact with the environment, and such behavior is set up in the verbal community for this reason."[43] The origin of a tact may be envisaged somewhat as follows: A doll, let us say, is presented. The child at first has no name for it. He hears the word "doll" or is perhaps urged to say it himself. He may, as in our earlier illustration (p. 440), say "da," the best that he can do. But this response is reinforced by what follows — excitement, praise, fondling, and so on. Gradually, through what appears to be a trial-and-error process (p. 321), the child develops enough skill to say the word in a manner completely acceptable to those around him. The names that we have for aspects of our world and the phrases and sentences that we use to convey information about them conform to Skinner's concept of the verbal tact. □

Although words are learned in ways already described, many are acquired in other ways. People point at things while naming them. They hand the child various objects and name them while doing so. The child asks for the names of things, as Helen Keller did in the incident cited earlier. Names are picked up from overhearing conversations, from being read to, and from formal education in the classroom. The meaning of many words that are new to the child is learned through their verbal context.[44]

In this process, there is what was previously referred to (p. 328) as "learning to learn." The child is soon "using language in order to learn language." Indeed, language becomes so much a part of the individual and everything he does that its general utility is taken for granted. As one noted psychologist put it, "teaching of the ability to use language correctly and with grace is probably as general a 'training of the mind' as it is possible to carry out," and "in a most important sense, the development of language in an individual is the growth of the human mind in that person."[45]

Word usage is often taken as "the mark of a man." Common use of words like "square, pad, cool, crazy-man, real gone, far out, the most, and chick" indicate affiliation with a particular social type, while words like "embolism, lacerated, determine, antibiotic, and superficial" suggest something quite different. It has been shown in numerous experiments that "individual differences in word usage relate not only to obvious differences such as these but also to subtle differences in the ways people learn, perceive, and interact socially."[46] We will see some examples in Chapters 16 and 17 of how language influences perceptual processes and social interactions.

Nothing has been said about the meaning of words beyond the fact that the object named may be considered the "meaning" of the word used to represent it. But there is of course much more to meaning than this. Many words are conceptual in nature. They represent not particular things, but categories — like animals, people, trees, and houses. These words and meanings are taken over

ready-made in some instances. In others they are acquired through a reasoning process in which abstracting and generalizing (p. 415) play an important role. Quite obviously, many conceptual words (like *life*) are used, even by adults, with only a limited understanding of what they mean.

The problem of word meanings receives further attention as we discuss the communication process. ■

THE COMMUNICATION PROCESS

Communication involves a chain with at least three major links — a sender, a communication channel, and a receiver. The sender encodes a message. That is to say, he puts what he wants to communicate into the appropriate signals. These may be puffs of smoke, drumbeats, dots and dashes, or some other conventional representations of letters, words, or numbers. Thus encoded, the signals are transmitted via a communication channel — for instance, air, wires, or printed pages. When a person receives such signals, he decodes (transforms) them to get the message. Thus the person who witnesses a deaf-and-dumb sign message translates the gestures into words; the reader of a Braille message transforms into words what he feels with his fingertips. The reader of this page, although he may not realize that he is doing so, actually translates the printed signs into words. If the signals are carried by conventionalized sound-wave patterns, like those in Figure 14.7, the receiver likewise decodes them to get a spoken message.

Telephone engineers are naturally interested in the encoding, transmission, and decoding of messages, and especially the most efficient ways of transmitting information. It should not be surprising, therefore, to learn that investigators at the Bell Telephone Laboratories and other research centers have introduced a type of study, under the rubric *information theory*, which involves the detailed analysis, often mathematical, of all aspects of the transmission process. What may be surprising, however, is that information theory has extended its influence far beyond

● **14.7**
Representation of the Auditory Stimulus. The words encoded here are "Joe took father's shoe bench out." (From J. C. R. Licklider, D. Bindra, and I. Pollock, "The Intelligibility of Rectangular Speech Waves," *Amer. J. Psychol.*, 1948, 61, 2.)

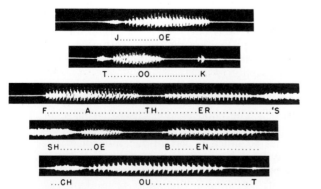

the practical issues of transmitting information over cables or telephone wires.*

It should perhaps be made clear at the outset that this type of study uses the term *information* in a highly restricted sense. The term has reference only to the encoding, transmission, and decoding of signals in a message. There is, for example, no attempt to deal with what a message means to the recipient. The word *democracy,* let us say, could be encoded, transmitted, and decoded perfectly, but still mean different things to different people, depending upon their particular background. Information theorists are concerned with meaning indirectly, however. Suppose that a message becomes distorted during

---

* Information theory has had broad ramifications in various fields of science. In neurology it has influenced concepts of how receptors encode information, how the neurons transmit this to the brain, and how the brain decodes it. In the general area of automation it is influencing the design of the so-called electronic brains. A chess-playing machine has been invented and some success has been achieved in designing machines to translate languages. In the general field of linguistics (the scientific study of languages) this approach has focused attention upon certain statistical (or probabilistic) characteristics of language structure, such as the greater probability that one letter will be followed by a certain specified letter than by others. Examples of this occur later in the text. In psychology, the information theory approach has influenced research on learning and the thought processes as well as the area under discussion here, where linguistics and psychology overlap. The present discussion attempts no more than a sketch of this approach to communication in its broadest outlines. The details are formulated in mathematical terms which we shall not attempt to present, but which the interested reader may find in such references as the following: C. E. Shannon and W. Weaver, *The Mathematical Theory of Communication,* University of Illinois Press, 1949; H. Quastler (Ed.), *Information Theory in Psychology,* Free Press, 1955; C. Cherry, *On Human Communication,* Wiley, 1957; and F. Attneave, *Applications of Information Theory in Psychology,* Holt-Dryden, 1959. Also see W. N. Locke and A. D. Booth, *Machine Translation of Languages,* Wiley, 1955; and " 'Brain' Translates Russian," *Science Newsletter,* June 27, 1959, p. 406. This cites the need for participation of editors after the machine has finished. An analysis of human skill in terms of information theory is presented by E. R. F. W. Crossman, "Information Processes in Human Skill," *Brit. Med. J.,* 1964, 20, 32–37. Also, in the same journal (pp. 3–7), see Kay's article on human learning with reference to information theory.

transmission — due to humming in telephone wires, static on radio, poor picture or sound transmission on television, or even typographical errors or smudging on a printed page. In this event, the receiver might lose the meaning intended because he failed to get the signals clearly. Distortions of any sort which are irrelevant to, or interfere with transmission of messages are referred to by information theorists as *noise.*

The information approach has another peculiarity beyond its failure to consider meaning, and this is basic to the entire undertaking. It is the idea that information reduces uncertainty in the mind of the receiver. Let us suppose that you pronounce a letter of the alphabet and I hear you, but not well enough to make it out. In this event, I can do no better than guess that it was any one of the twenty-six letters. The only thing I know definitely is that you spoke. It is clear that my uncertainty here is a function of the number of possibilities. If you had merely tossed a penny, my uncertainty as to whether you would say "heads" is much less than my uncertainty in the above example, namely a function of two rather than of twenty-six possibilities. Thus "the word information relates not so much to what you *do* say, as to what you *could* say. That is, information is a measure of your freedom of choice when you select a message."[47]

The bit

When there are only two possible messages — like "heads" or "tails," "yes" or "no," "true" or "false," "good" or "bad" — it is said that the selection of one of these transmits a unitary amount of information, or one *bit.** This does not have the usual meaning of "bit," as "a small piece." It has meaning here only in terms of how much one's uncertainty is reduced by selection of the alternative. One bit is thus any amount of information which reduces uncertainty by one-half. Saying "yes" when one could have said either "yes" or "no" reduces uncertainty by half, or provides one *bit* of information. In fact the number of bits

---

* An abbreviation of *binary digit,* the 1 or 0 so widely used to encode information in computers.

Sign	1st	2nd	3rd	Solution
A	1	1	1	
B	1	1	0	
C	1	0	1	
D	1	0	0	
E	1	1	1	
F	1	1	0	
G	1	0	1	
H	1	0	0	

● **14.8**

Some Features of Information Theory. In the text we have said that information reduces uncertainty. This fact, together with an understanding of the *bit* as a unit of information, is illustrated here. Note that there are eight consecutive letters, A through H. As the experimenter, I have in mind, let us say, the letter C. The subject is asked to discover the letter I have selected with the fewest possible guesses. If he adopts the most efficient strategy, he will begin by asking something like this: "Is it among the upper four?" The answer I give is, of course, "Yes." He has, in this move, reduced his uncertainty by half. Thus he has one bit of information. Now, if he is wise, he will ask something like: "Is it one of the upper two?" The answer being "No," he has reduced the preceding uncertainty (upper or lower pair) by half. Another bit has been gained. Only one more bit is necessary to solve the problem. He gets this by asking, for example: "Is it the third?" The answer is "Yes" and his information is complete. Had he asked, "Is it the fourth," and been told "No," he would still have known just as certainly that the third letter was correct. By asking questions at random, the individual might get the answer quickly or he might not. The chances are that a random guess would yield less than one bit, as defined in information theory. The bit, as we said in the text, is a contraction of "binary digit." Such digits, as illustrated here, are often used to code information. *Yes* could be encoded by 1, *No* by 0; *True* by 1, *False* by 0; *On* by 1, *Off* by 0; and so on. Morse code (dot-dash) and punched card systems of storing information also use binary encoding. (From C. Cherry, *On Human Communication*, Wiley, 1957, pp. 170–171.)

in a communication is defined as the logarithm to the base 2 of the number of possibilities from which the choice might be made. With four possibilities, the transmission of one provides two bits of information, with eight possibilities, three bits, and so on. By looking up 26 in a $\log_2$ table we find that the hearing of one letter of the alphabet, as in our earlier example, would give us 4.7 bits — providing that the speaker is as likely to use one letter as any other. The concept of information as reduction of uncertainty, and the use of the bit as an index of this, is amplified in Figure 14.8 and the accompanying legend.

Statistical characteristics of language

We have said that the above considerations apply if all possible signals have an equal probability of occurrence. It is an interesting fact, however, that linguistic sequences have contingent probabilities. Putting it otherwise, the appearance of one letter depends to a certain extent upon the letter that preceded it. Thus there is a greater probability that *u* will follow *q* than that *l*, or *p*, or *x* will follow it. By the same token, if *q* is in an English message, *u* will almost certainly follow. In this event, the appearance of the *u* adds little or no information beyond that given by *q*. The same considerations apply to words. Some are used much more frequently than others. In fact the appearance of any word in a message is highly predictable from a knowledge of those which preceded it. It is unlikely that the word *dear* will be followed by *water*, *snake*, or *sky* but very likely that it will be followed by words such as *Sir*, *Madam*, *friend*, or a person's name.

Information theorists and other students of linguistic behavior are therefore very much interested in the statistical characteristics of language. For one thing, if the probability of occurrence of certain sequences were known, this could also enter the mathematical formulas which represent the informational aspects of communication. The search for knowledge concerning these aspects of our language has revealed some interesting facts.

☐ If all twenty-six letters of the alphabet were put in a hat and drawn blindly, one at

446

a time, with what had been drawn replaced, we would get some such sequence as the following: rxkhrjffbzl. This is zero approximation to the contingent probabilities of English sequences and it doesn't look at all like English. But suppose we draw one letter and have an individual use it in a word, then select the following letter in this word, again having another person use it in a word, and so on. By this procedure we obtain a first-order approximation to the sequential characteristics of English.* To make this point clearer, let us suppose that the letter *p* was drawn. The person to whom we gave it wrote the word *pin*. We have *p* and *i*. The letter *i* is given to another person who, let us say, writes the word *life*. This gives us *p*, *i*, and *f*. The person given *f* perhaps writes *fall*, which adds *a* to our sequence. This procedure gives us some such series as *pifaota . . .* , which is obviously more like English than our

* There are as yet no probability tables for letter or word sequences, hence the present method. There are, however, other ways of getting the same kind of data. These are discussed in the previously mentioned books on information theory.

first example. For a second-order approximation, we take two letters at a time. Suppose that the letters selected first are *g* and *l*. Our first subject, instructed to use these in a word, writes *gland*. The next subject is given the letters *a n* and asked to use this combination in a word. Suppose he says *anvil*. The next subject is given *v i* and perhaps writes *vipers*. The next subject gets *p e* and may write *peach*. And so on, with the next subject being given *a c*. This will give us a sequence like *glanviac. . . .* Following this general procedure, but taking three letters at a time, then four letters, one comes to the point finally, when he has something much more recognizable as English, even though it is scrambled. The following passage, with a space introduced between each approximation to a word, represents a third-order letter approximation: *in no ist lat whey cratict froure birs grocid pondenome of demonstratures.*[48] □

The same general procedure may be followed with words instead of letters. One word is selected. A subject makes a sentence involving this word. The next word in his

● **14.9**

The Statistical Structure of English. The first line, obtained as described in the text, shows zero approximation to statistical properties of word sequences in English. Approximation to English is successively closer in the lower lines until, in the bottom one, we have an example from actual English text. (From G. A. Miller and J. A. Selfridge, "Verbal Context and the Recall of Meaningful Material," *Amer. J. Psychol.*, 1950, *63*, pp. 184–185.)

byway consequence handsomely financier bent flux cavalry

abilities with that beside I for waltz you the sewing

was he went to the newspaper is in deep and

tall and thin boy is a biped is the best

saw the football game will end at midnight on January

they saw the play Saturday and sat down beside him

the history of California is largely that of a railroad

sentence is given to another subject, and so on. In higher approximations, word pairs triads, and so on, may be given for the start of a new sentence. One such investigation yielded many sequences, from which we have chosen the examples in Figure 14.9. From the top down, they represent zero to fifth-order approximations of English word sequences. The last line is not an approximation, but taken from an actual text.

Redundancy

Another interesting feature of linguistic communication, related to what we have just been discussing, is known as *redundancy*. In everyday language, this refers to the tendency to indulge in verbiage — to use more words than are necessary to convey our message. In the preceding sentence, for example, the words following *verbiage* are redundant. Then, why write them? The justification in this instance is that for some readers, they make the point of the first part of the sentence clearer than it would otherwise be. Generally speaking, however, redundancy is frowned upon. It is believed that one should get his point across in as few words as possible.

In information theory, on the other hand, the term *redundancy*, like *information* itself, is used with a special meaning, within the context of the idea that information reduces uncertainty. This special use of the term is not unlike its general use except that it places redundancy in a somewhat more favorable light.

Linguistic sequences, as we have just observed, contain certain letters (like *u*) which almost inevitably follow other letters (like *q*). Thus, with *q* in the message, *u* is excess baggage. Redundancy is almost 100 per cent. Nevertheless, if *q* should be garbled in transmission (due to noise), the presence of the *u*, as well as the general context of the message, might enable one to fill in the missing letter. Many letters are, of course, less redundant than *u* in the example cited. The letter *h* follows *t* with a high frequency, but so do *a*, *i*, *o*, and other letters, although probably not *k* or *x*. The same principle applies to words and phrases. Their sequential probabilities in-

troduce redundancy, but this reduces uncertainty in cases where noise interferes with transmission. *Dear*, before *Sir* is redundancy of this kind, as is *Sincerely* after *Yours*.

It has been claimed that redundancy in English is about 50 per cent — that "about half of the letters or words we choose in writing or speaking are under our free choice, and about half are really controlled by the statistical structure of the language, although we are not ordinarily aware of it."[49] One learns this structure (quite often as rules of good usage) when he acquires the letters and words and phrases of the language.

Even apart from the redundancy in linguistic sequences, that introduced on a purely individual basis has certain merits. One may use more words than are essential to get a message across, but at the same time this increases the probability that it will actually make the intended impression. Thus, "a magnetic storm can garble the telegram 'I love you' into 'I hate you' but the message could be sent as 'I love you, darling'."[50] In this event the word "darling," although redundant, guards against such a marked error in transmission as to change the overall meaning of the message.

Without involving ourselves in the mathematical details of information theory we have outlined its major concepts and shown something of what it reveals about linguistic communication and the structure of our language. An important topic with which information theory does not deal will now receive attention. This is the problem of meaning. ■

THE MEANING OF WORDS

One of the greatest impediments to effective communication is the fact that many of the words used are insufficiently conventionalized in meaning. Words which merely denote, or "point to," an object do not give us too much trouble. Take the word *pencil*. It means much the same thing to all of us and has little meaning beyond "an elongated object containing lead and used in writing." Connotative words, on the other hand, are often troublesome. This is because, in addition to signifying particular objects or events, they can have additional implications. As an example of this the word *pig* will serve. It represents what we might otherwise call a *hog*, but it, like *hog*, has also come to signify unclean, greedy, and obese. What is worse, it is sometimes applied to human beings!

Certain other connotative words are much more troublesome than those which designate an object. These include words like *equality*, *freedom*, and *democracy*. The meanings of words in this category are especially difficult to pin down. Moreover, they are often used with connotations which their origin does not justify. Our difficulties with them are highlighted in international communication. Sometimes the intended meanings cannot be translated readily into another language. Even when words are translated, the interpretation placed upon them may be different from our own. For example, an English-speaking member of the United Nations "says 'I assume'; the French interpreter renders it 'I deduce'; the Russian interpreter 'I consider'. — By that time the assumption idea has gone with the wind!"[51] Problems of this nature fall within the general area of *semantics*, "the systematic study of meaning."

☐ Lewis Carroll, in *Through the Looking Glass*, tells how Alice ran into a problem with semantics:

". . . There's glory for you!"

"I don't know what you mean by 'glory,' " Alice said.

Humpty Dumpty smiled contemptuously. "Of course you don't — till I tell you. I meant 'there's a nice knock-down argument for you!' "

"But 'glory' doesn't mean 'a nice knock-down argument,' " Alice objected.

"When I use ·a word," Humpty Dumpty said in a rather scornful tone, "it means just what I choose it to mean — neither more nor less."

"The question is," said Alice, "whether you *can* make words mean so many different things."

"The question is," said Humpty Dumpty, "which is to be master — that's all." ☐

The semantic problem also receives attention in George Orwell's *Animal Farm*, where the commandment "All animals are equal" is finally changed to read, "All animals are equal but some animals are more equal than others."

It is easy to give examples of semantic difficulties but quite another matter to arrive at solutions. In general, there are three facets to linguistic meanings: (1) a word's meaning as derived from its history, (2) its meaning to the individual in terms of his own experience, and (3) the bodily process which represents the relation between words and the things (or events) that they symbolize. Let us consider each of these in turn.

Cultural and personal origins

It is always interesting to learn where a word came from and how its meaning grew (or changed) with the passage of time. When he learns a particular word, however, the individual usually knows nothing of its history. Much of its potential meaning is therefore lost upon him. One writer puts it this way: "Every word is a heritage from the past, and has derived its meaning from application to a countless number of particulars differing among themselves either much or little. When now I utter such a word, I throw at the listener's head the entire residue of its previous applications. . . . In uttering a word, the speaker necessarily offers to the listener the whole range of its meaning."[52] This does not imply, of course, that the speaker himself necessarily knows the full range of a word's meaning.

Despite the broad historical meaning that a term may have, both the speaker and the listener are limited in their understanding of it by their individual pasts. To the child who was given a milk bottle every time he said "da-da" (p. 441) this expression came to mean something quite different from what it means to a child whose conditioning has associated "da-da" with a certain man. We have cited a very simple case. Moreover, the first child will later learn the "proper" meaning of *da-da*. But many denotive meanings are acquired on this level. The actual meaning acquired depends, as in this example, upon the patterns set by the child's elders. These are carriers, although in a limited sense, of the historical meanings of words. Moreover, there is much more to it than this, as we indicated earlier in discussing how a child acquires words and how, in time, he uses particular words to categorize aspects of his world, like *dog, life,* and so forth. Also, as a person grows older, he learns the meanings of words from their context, and from dictionaries, which define them in terms of other words.*

In acquiring words which categorize aspects of our world — particularly words like *capitalist, unionist, Republican, Democrat,* and *oriental* — we often acquire a semantically erroneous tendency. This is the tendency to assume, for example, that orientals are a class, and that any oriental is like every other oriental, any capitalist like every other capitalist, and so on. Korzybski was particularly concerned with such problems in what he called "general semantics."[53] The sort of difficulty involved is well illustrated by the following quotation from S. I. Hayakawa, also a leader in general semantics.

□ "In spite of the fact that my entire education has been in Canada and the United States and I am unable to read and write Japanese, I am sometimes credited, or accused, of having an "Oriental mind." Now, since Buddha, Confucius, General Tojo, Mao Tse-tung, Syngman Rhee, Pandit Nehru and the proprietor of the Golden Pheasant Chop Suey House all have "Oriental minds," it is hard to imagine what is meant. The "Oriental mind," . . . is purely and simply a fiction. Nevertheless, I used to note with alarm that newspaper columnists got paid for articles that purported to account for Stalin's behavior by pointing

* Many scientific words are coined as knowledge develops — words such as *radium, x-ray, neuron, synapse, penicillin,* and *cybernetics.* Then, too, the scientist sometimes redefines terms so as to give them more limited meanings in scientific discourse than in everyday life. Examples are words like *energy, information,* and *intelligence.* There is also a disposition in scientific circles to "pin down" the meaning of a word so that it denotes no more than the operation required to reveal the phenomenon in question. A purely operational meaning of intelligence therefore is merely "what one measures with an intelligence test."

out that since he came from Georgia, which is next to Turkey and Azerbaijan and therefore "more a part of Asia than of Europe," he too had an 'Oriental mind.' "[54] □

The solution, of course, is to be much more discriminating in our use of conceptual terms than we normally are. One important aim of general semanticists is to make people more cautious in their use of words.

The meaning of meaning

What is the meaning of "meaning?" Put otherwise, what is the nature of the engram which links a symbol and the object symbolized? We know that word meanings are learned. It is generally agreed, also, that meaning must be somehow represented in the nervous system. Beyond this, however, there is nothing but theory.[55] Some theories stress subjective processes. For example, one such theory claims that an image represents the object named. Other theories look for behavioral forms of representation. Thus Osgood[56] stresses the idea that meaning is mediated by "some fractional part of the total behavior elicited by the significate." In other words, the meaning of *dog* for me is represented by abbreviated forms of such reactions to dogs as stroking them, pushing them away from me, jumping back from them, and being afraid of them. Thinking of certain actions and objects, as well as words, is associated with action currents in the muscles involved (p. 413). What the above quotation implies is that such highly abbreviated reactions, if aroused in the past by an object (or event), may come to represent it within the organism. Our discussion of the completely paralyzed man (p. 414) may have some relevance here. According to the present theory, words and events could have no meaning to him during his paralysis, unless, possibly, they were emotional meanings mediated by his autonomic nervous system. The data offer no evidence on this point.

Before theories of meaning can be evaluated one must have some way to measure a word's meaning and to represent it in quantitative terms. Osgood and his collaborators have taken a step in this direction. It involves a technique called the "semantic differential."

The semantic differential

We are already familiar with something very much like the semantic differential. The procedure is similar, in some respects, to that used to discover the feelings associated with a particular emotion, such as fear. One may recall, from the discussion on page 193, that fear was described as unpleasant, tense, and so on. This was the meaning of fear to the individual who offered the report. Likewise, facial expressions of emotion (p. 194) were rated on a scale with pleasant at one extreme and unpleasant at the other.

In using the semantic differential to represent word meanings, one asks the subject to rate a word within various dimensions, like *weak-strong,* *angular-rounded,* *rough-smooth,* and so on. Each dimension covers a seven-step scale, as indicated in Figure 14.10. Here we see what the adjective *polite* means in terms of such semantic analysis. Note how it is rated with respect to each dimension. Also observe that two groups of college students gave the word a very similar semantic profile. For all of them it meant rounded, strong,

● 14.10
The Meaning of "Polite." Observe how closely two separate groups of college students agree in the meaning that they attach to the word "polite." This illustrates one use of the semantic differential, described in the text. (After C. E. Osgood, "The Nature and Measurement of Meaning," *Psychological Bulletin,* 1952, *49,* pp. 197–237.)

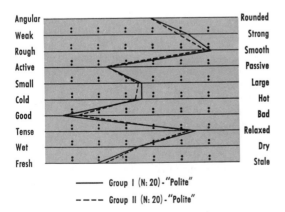

———— Group I (N: 20) - "Polite"

– – – – Group II (N: 20) - "Polite"

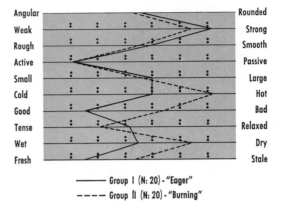

———— Group I (N: 20) - "Eager"

– – – – Group II (N: 20) - "Burning"

● 14.11
Semantic Differentiation of Two Adjectives. One can see that to the twenty students here represented, "eager" and "burning" are alike in some dimensions of meaning but different in others. (After C. E. Osgood, "The Nature and Measurement of Meaning," *Psychological Bulletin,* 1952, *49,* pp. 197–237.)

smooth, active, and so on, to approximately the same degree. One is not to conclude, however, that *polite* means no more than these things, even to the subjects of this experiment. Osgood himself says that this procedure pins down only part of a word's meaning. In Figure 14.11 it may be observed that the adjectives *eager* and *burning* have certain meanings in common (strong, active) and others in which they differ (bad-good, dry-wet.)[57]

Analysis of data obtained with the semantic differential shows that three major factors are involved. These have been designated *activity,* *potency,* and *evaluation.* The activity factor includes such dimensions as fast-slow, active-passive, and excitable-calm. Within the potency factor are included such dimensions as hard-soft, masculine-feminine, and strong-weak. Evaluation involves dimensions like good-bad, kind-cruel, and beautiful-ugly.[58]

The semantic differential represents the first systematic effort to quantify word meanings. One of its weaknesses has already been mentioned — it does not embrace every aspect of meaning. A related weakness is that it places more emphasis upon the emotive or feeling aspects of meaning than upon the referent

● 14.12

Gestures Which Encode Verbal Information. In many situations where oral signals may not be heard, a conventional "hand talk" has been adopted. These pictures show some of the signals used at the American Stock Exchange. Top: A clerk signals an order to buy 700 shares. The same finger combination given with a downward sweep would be an order to sell 700. Bottom: A specialist flashes a ⅜ bid (bent fingers) and ½ offered (upright finger). Signals range the alphabet and give fractions down to 1/64. (Courtesy, Peter White and *The New York Times Magazine*.)

of a word. Thus the word *dog* refers to an animal with certain categorized features, and it means this to any two persons with the same cultural background. Nevertheless, one may rate it on the semantic differential as active, the other as passive; one as good, the other as bad; one as weak, the other as strong; and so on, these meanings in each case depending upon personal experience.

Despite its limitations, the semantic differential has been useful in many areas of research, including aesthetics, attitude measurement, and mass communications. According to Osgood and his collaborators, "there is nothing surprising about this. Meaning is one of the most significant pivotal variables in human behavior, and even a crude and very provisional measure of it, such as the semantic differential now is, readily finds uses."[59] ■

NONVERBAL COMMUNICATION

Any stimulus can be said to communicate something to the person who responds to it. However, the term *nonverbal communication* refers to transmission of culturally significant information without using words.

Nonverbal communication seems of small importance, compared with verbal communication, until we look into it closely. Then we discover that it is extremely prevalent, subtle, and informationally efficient. In many instances, as the authors of a recent book on this subject have shown, a nonverbal act may convey meanings that words are not adequate to convey; also, where words may be adequate, if we use enough of them, the nonverbal act conveys the same information much more quickly.[60] All that we attempt in the following discussion is to suggest the extensiveness of nonverbal communication and to give a few examples.

Gestures provide a good starting point. But we must exclude gestures which have the same significance as words — like the gesticulations of a person "speaking" the deaf-and-dumb language, and the stock exchange clerk signaling an order (Figure 14.12). These motions are *verbal* — that is, hand talk. They are ways of expressing words which would otherwise be encoded vocally, or in writing. And they are conventionalized to the same extent that vocal and written expressions are.

Nonverbal gestures, while they do not represent words, must also be conventionalized. If they were not, they would lack communicative significance. Any well-acted pantomime conveys meaning because it uses gestures, in their appropriate setting, with which we are all familiar. In every society there are many conventional gestures. Some of these are stylized in the dance, as in Bali, Japan (Kabuki), and Hawaii (hand motions). Isolated examples are gestures like head-nodding, head-shaking, nose-thumbing, thumb-jerking on the highway, traffic signals with the hand, and others of the kind illustrated in Figure 14.13. Most people in a given culture know when such gestures are appropriate, how to make them, and what they signify when seen. And we should not, in this connection, overlook such vocal yet nonverbal signs as "wolf whistles" and "Bronx cheers."

In addition to the gestures which have conventionalized significance only within a particular culture, there are others of almost universal significance. Some emotional expressions, but not all of them (p. 191), are of such a nature. This is quite evident when one looks at the photographs in Edward Steichen's *The Family of Man.*[61] There we see that certain situations in the life of all men arouse similar expressions — smiling in happiness, embracing in love, weeping at loss of loved ones, and dancing in exuberance. In their respective settings, these expressions are nonverbal avenues of communication.

Another feature of gestures that is worth our attention is their use as an adjunct to verbal communication, not only in public speaking and acting but also in ordinary conversation. Here they may be used to punctuate what is said, or to give added emphasis. Some national groups notably use their hands as well as their mouths while communicating.[62] Most of us do this to a certain extent, but not always in a conventionalized manner. The conventionalized use of such adjuncts to speech is seen in pointing, slapping the forehead with the palm of the hand, snapping the fingers, and pounding the table with the fist to emphasize a statement.

How one walks may have communicative significance. A person may walk "as though he is master of all he surveys" or he may walk

● **14.13**
Nonverbal Communication. Do you "get the message" encoded in each of these gestures? If not, see the explanation in the Appendix.

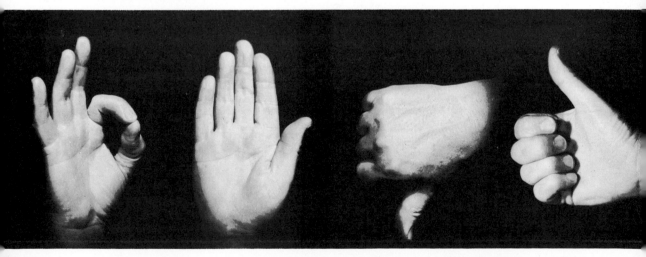

in a manner which indicates utter despair. He may have an effeminate gait, although what this signifies is not always certain. Sailors and farmers often have their gait as an unintentional "trademark." The sound of an individual's footsteps may also serve as a sign of his imminent appearance.

More removed from gestures, we have such nonverbal signs as "the old school tie," the Phi Beta Kappa pin, the sort of clothes a person wears, the kind of car he drives, whether he eats lunch at a restaurant or carries a tin lunch box. Often what is signified by such signs is social status. Status of a sort is also signified by wearing beards in a predominantly beardless society, or a certain kind of jacket and long sideburns.

A recent book calls attention to additional aspects of what its author calls the "silent language." He particularly notes the utilization of time in nonverbal communication — as when, in our own culture, being late for an appointment is taken as a sign of disrespect, and keeping a person waiting in your outer office for an hour may signify his unimportance, if not an intentional insult.[63] ■

• SUMMARY

Animals have neither gestures nor sounds which are sufficiently conventionalized and flexible to warrant the claim that there are animal languages. Even the chimpanzee, almost human as it is, has no language. Some chimpanzees come close to language in their efforts to get others to help them. But the best they can do is no more specific than a gesture implying, "help me do something." The chimpanzee taught a few words learned these only after intensive training. When animals learn words, these have very limited significance, they are not combined as words normally are, and there is no effort to use them in communicating with other animals.

Language involves conventional signals. Conventionality is crucial, for both the initiator and the recipient of a message must understand the rules that apply, otherwise nothing is communicated. Words are symbols, as are gestures, used for linguistic communication. Encoding, decoding, and appreciation of their meaning require the use of symbolic processes.

The question of why man alone developed language has been the basis of much speculation. The following are probably of great importance in this connection: the size of his brain, the preponderance of associative tissue, and the presence of Broca's speech area. Related to such features of the brain are man's high level of insight and his tendency to engage in spontaneous vocalizing. We pointed out, in the latter connection, that animals do not vocalize except when emotionally aroused.

Although human beings invented language, how they did so is unknown to us. Theories mentioned in this chapter stressed the idea that chance vocalizing in the presence of an object may have led to adoption of the same sound to represent the object. After someone had achieved the insight that objects could be represented by sounds, the development of language must have undergone marked acceleration. Attention has been called to the evolution of writing, which began with pictures and ended with symbols which represented the sounds of speech.

The vocal cords add voice to what would otherwise be whispers. Verbal habits are complex motor skills which involve, in addition to the vocal cords, the diaphragm, the tongue, the lips, and other structures of the mouth and throat. The nervous system is of basic importance in this connection, for messages are encoded in the brain and then transmitted to the vocal musculature via the motor speech area, the brainstem, and peripheral nerves. Feedback is also important. This comes from hearing oneself speak and from kinesthetic impulses originating in the peripheral motor mechanisms.

The initial vocalizations are operants. They are reinforced by the reactions of others to them and also, possibly, by the resemblance of the auditory feedback to sounds made by the mother. Babbling, generally regarded as an important stage in the development of speech, is apparently a conditioned response, with the self-initiated sounds becoming stimuli for their repetition.

Objects presented while an infant is vocalizing may be represented later by particular vocalizations, as in the case of *da-da* and the milk bottle. After having learned to imitate his own sounds, as in babbling, the child attempts to copy sounds made by others. With increasing maturation and practice, these sounds come to approximate those of adults.

Verbal behavior may be analyzed from the standpoint of grammar (parts of speech and syntax) and from the standpoint of how it functions in communication. With regard to its functions, Skinner has invented the terms *mand* and *tact*. Mands are such functions as demanding or requesting. Tacts name objects or events and impart information. Although early mands and tacts are conditioned reactions, later acquisition of such functions is based, among other things, upon the fact that language is used to learn more language.

Information theory is concerned with the communication process, but it uses the term *information* in a highly restricted sense; viz., as reduction of uncertainty. An amount of information which reduces uncertainty by half is called one *bit*. A message may be inadequately transmitted, even garbled, by extraneous factors referred to, in general, as *noise*. Redundancy is the inclusion in a message of noninformative items. The sequential structure of English involves a high degree of redundancy. Given a certain letter or word (or a sequence of letters or words), the next unit in a message is to a large degree statistically determined. Thus it is possible, in terms of sequential probabilities, to compose combinations of letters (or words) which, while they are meaningless, resemble English.

Although very much concerned with the transmission of messages, information theory pays only indirect attention to meaning. The latter aspect of communication falls in the general area known as semantics. There are three basic problems here.

One semantic problem has to do with the cultural history of word meanings. The point made is that neither the speaker nor the listener is necessarily aware of the full historical meaning of what is said.

The second semantic problem involves the question of how an individual acquires word meanings. This occurs in various ways. At the beginning, an infant is conditioned so that the sounds made mean the objects or events for which they stand. Later he learns many meanings from verbal contexts, in listening and reading. The learning of concepts (or of categories) is an important part of this process.

The third semantic problem — what processes within the organism represent the meaning of words — has not been solved. Some theories stress images. Others present the idea that responses made to an object are somehow retained in abbreviated form as a link between that object and its name. One thing is certain — that the ultimate basis of meaning is represented in the nervous system.

The semantic differential is used to define word meanings in terms of how they are rated in certain polar dimensions — like weak-strong, good-bad, active-passive. Not all of a word's meaning is represented in this way. Nevertheless, the semantic differential has proved itself a useful instrument in research.

Nonverbal communication is of course communication without words. Much of it utilizes gestures, but we have called attention to a distinction between gestures which represent letters (as in the deaf-mutes' language) and gestures which, while conventionalized, have no such reference. Pointing would be an example of the latter. Clothing and other objects may also have communicative significance. ▪

REFERENCES AND NOTES FOR THIS CHAPTER ARE IN THE APPENDIX.

• SELECTED READINGS

Attneave, F., *Applications of Information Theory.* Holt, 1959. This is a summary of basic concepts, methods, and results.

Brown, R., *Words and Things.* Free Press, 1958. An interestingly written survey of work on language and related topics.

Cherry, C., *On Human Communication.* Technology Press of the Massachusetts Institute of Technology and Wiley, 1957. Reissued in 1964 as a paperback. Information theory and semantics as well as other aspects of communication.

Cofer, C. N., and B. S. Musgrave, *Verbal Behavior and Learning.* McGraw-Hill, 1963. Chapter 5, "The Acquisition of Syntax," by R. Brown and C. Fraser, is particularly relevant in the present context.

Hayakawa, S. I., *Our Language and Our World.* Harper, 1959. A selection of articles on various phases of general semantics.

Lenneberg, E. H., *New Directions in the Study of Language.* M. I. T. Press, 1964.

Lewis, M. M., *How Children Learn to Speak.* Basic Books, 1959. This traces the development of speech.

Mann, J., *Frontiers of Psychology.* Macmillan, 1963. Chapter 4 discusses psychological implications of communications (information) theory.

Munn, N. L., *The Evolution and Growth of Human Behavior* (2nd ed.). Houghton Mifflin, 1965. See Chapter 12 for a more detailed discussion of the development of speech in children.

Osgood, C. E., G. J. Suci, and P. H. Tannenbaum, *The Measurement of Meaning.* University of Illinois Press, 1957. The nature of the semantic differential and its application in several fields.

Osgood, C. E., "Psycholinguistics," in S. Koch (Ed.), *Psychology: A Study of a Science,* Vol. 6. McGraw-Hill, 1963.

Skinner, B. F., *Verbal Behavior.* Appleton-Century-Crofts, 1957. Verbal responses treated as operants.

Whorf, B. L., *Language, Thought, and Reality.* Wiley, 1956. Several papers in this collection of Whorf's writings (edited by J. B. Carroll) are of interest here in that they show a relation between language and thought processes.

15

Knowing Our World

*E*verything that we know of the world around us comes from the impingement of stimuli on sense organs and the resulting activation of receptors, nerve fibers, and brain cells. This is true whether experience is direct, as in watching a sunset or hearing a symphony, or indirect, as in looking at pictures, reading, or listening to descriptions of what we have not ourselves experienced. Likewise, everything that we do is dependent, in the last analysis, upon information encoded in messages from our receptors.

Receptors have been referred to as "gateways to knowledge," and with good reason. The most important of these "gateways" are of course our visual and auditory receptors, but receptors in the skin, the nose, and the mouth are also significant avenues of information about the world around us. In addition to these senses, concerned primarily with stimuli originating in the external environment, there are three others which bring information about one's own body and its position in space. We are already quite familiar with one of these, the kinesthetic sense, since it was referred to as providing information feedback during the learning and performance of motor skills. Another, the static sense, is concerned with equilibrium. The kinesthetic and static senses play an important part, not only in telling one about the position of his limbs and the orientation of his body as a whole, but also in facilitating general body coordination. The organic sense was mentioned in discussing the visceral components of emotional experience. This sense also underlies such experiences as nausea, stomach cramps, and bladder tensions.

Each sensory process involves a succession of events beginning with stimulation of receptors. Resulting receptor activities encode messages for the brain. These coded messages are conveyed as nerve impulses. They go to centers in the spinal cord and/or brain stem. They are then relayed to the cerebral cortex. The meaning of nerve impulses — the sensory information that they provide — depends upon their point of origin (in which receptor they were initiated) and their destination in the cerebral cortex. When nerve impulses reach their destination they are decoded and integrated with other information. The outcome is information about the world and one's own body. What we do about this information is also dependent upon nerve impulses, in this instance impulses going from the brain or spinal cord into the muscles and glands.

In this chapter we are concerned more with input than with output — more with knowing than with doing — hence emphasis is given to reception, to related neural events, and to the information which these provide. Such information is no doubt a limited representation of the world around us, and it is not always free from error (as will be apparent when illusions are discussed), but it is all the information that we have.[1] ■

SENSORY STIMULATION

A stimulus is anything inside or outside of the body which initiates activity of some kind. Sensory stimuli are those which activate the sense organs. There are many aspects of the environment, however, which fail to stimulate us. We cannot be aware of these aspects, except through instruments which record their presence, or through the reactions of other organisms sensitive to them. This is because we have no receptors attuned to such features of the environment. Visual stimuli, for example, are light waves which range in length from about 400 to 760 millionths of a millimeter. Wavelengths above and below these limits are ineffective visually. Similarly, the range of auditory stimuli is limited. Sound waves of about 20 to 20,000 cycles (double vibrations per second) stimulate our auditory receptors and arouse corresponding experiences of pitch, but frequencies outside of this range are without effect. Some animals have a more extended auditory range than we do. Dogs, for example, respond to frequencies which we cannot hear. A dog whistle cannot be heard by us because its frequency is above the range to which human receptors are attuned. Our olfactory (smell) receptors are attuned to certain chemicals in gaseous form. The gustatory sense (taste) is also stimulated chemically, in this instance by liquids.

Receptors in the skin are attuned to mechanical and thermal stimulation, giving information about the tactual properties of one's immediate environment. Kinesthesis depends upon stimulation provided by movements in muscles, tendons, and joints. The stimuli are pressures and pulls on these structures. Static sensitivity is aroused by stimulation associated with movements of the head and the body as a whole. Such movements activate receptors in the equilibratory mechanisms of our inner ear. The stimuli for organic sensitivity are gases, tissue changes, and chemical activities associated with gastric and other internal processes.

☐ Although all animals are to some degree attuned to their environment, some have no receptors and many have receptors very different from our own. The whole body of an amoeba is responsive to light, to contacts of various kinds, and to chemicals. No part is more sensitive, or differently sensitive, than any other part. Since specialized receptors are lacking, the amoeba is sensitive to its environment only in a very limited way. Take light, for instance. Only its brightness, direction, and movement are effective. The characteristics of light which in higher animals give rise to perceptions of color, shape, depth, and other details of the visual world are lost on an amoeba because it has no receptors attuned to them. The same situation exists with respect to other features of the world. Although an amoeba is sensitive to mechanical vibration applied more or less directly to its body, it is insensitive to weak vibrations carried through the air, hence it is completely deaf. This is because it lacks auditory receptors. The amoeba is generally responsive to chemical stimuli in contact with its body, but it possesses no specialized chemical senses — no taste or smell.

An amoeba also lacks nervous mechanisms. Certain effects of stimulation are conducted to the part which moves, but conduction is diffuse. Since there are no specialized moving organs (effectors), any part may become a pseudopod and reach out or contract in response to stimulation.

Receptors, nerve cells, and effectors evolved together. Many lower organisms have muscle cells which respond directly to stimulation. One touches such a cell, for example, and it contracts. Animals somewhat higher in the scale have definite receptors and definite muscle cells and the two are functionally in contact. Now stimulation of a receptor activates a muscle cell through the receptor's nervelike projections. In still higher forms of animal life, receptors and effectors are connected via an intervening neural link. This link becomes increasingly complex until, at the vertebrate level, it forms the spinal cord and brain (central nervous system) with their incoming and outgoing branches (peripheral nervous system). At some point in this development the brain becomes sufficiently complex to mediate awareness of the surrounding world as well as to interconnect receptors and effectors. Thus we not only make overt responses to light, but we also *see* colors and other visual aspects of our surroundings. ☐

The neural structures and functions which mediate sensitivity were described in Chapter 2. It would be a good idea, at this point, to review the relevant parts of that chapter.

VISION

Light is thought of as being composed of electromagnetic waves, waves of radiant energy emanating from a source, usually the sun. We said earlier, in discussing stimulation, that the eye is attuned to only a relatively narrow range of wavelengths. The range is from slightly below 400 to slightly above 700 millionths of a millimeter, as suggested by the spectrum in Plate 11. White light is a mixture of all wavelengths; but when it is broken down into various wavelengths with a prism (Figure 1.1, page 8, and Plate 12), we see that the shorter waves underlie the experience of violet and the longer waves the experience of red.

Intermediate wavelengths give rise to blue, green, and yellow. These colors, and variations of them, are referred to as *hues*.

Colors also vary in *saturation*; that is to say, in their richness or purity. Thus a red may be very red, or only reddish, as in the case of pink. Differences in saturation are produced by mixing varied wavelengths. A mixture of all wavelengths produces a completely unsaturated color, i.e., white or gray. The saturation of any color can be reduced by mixing it with white. To increase the saturation of a hue, we reduce the wave band to the point where it approximates a monochrome. Thus, the most saturated red is obtained by transmitting only a narrow band of wavelengths in the red region of the spectrum.

What we see also has an aspect commonly referred to as *brightness*, although physicists refer to it as *luminance*. Differences in brightness (luminance) are related primarily to the amount of displacement (amplitude) of light waves. This determines their energy level. It is necessary to point out, however, that *seen* brightness and brightness as measured with photometric instruments may differ considerably. There are various reasons for this discrepancy. One reason (see Plate 13) is that the human eye is more sensitive to the middle range of wavelengths than to those at either end of the spectrum. Another reason for the discrepancy between physical intensity and perceived brightness is that the latter depends on visual adaptation. In the light, our eyes become *light adapted*; in darkness, or conditions of low illumination, they become *dark adapted*. When we enter a motion-picture theater during the daytime, our eyes are light adapted, so everything in the theater appears dark, and we have a hard time seeing the seats and people. After a short time in the theater we begin to dark adapt, so everything gradually brightens. If we return to daylight after an hour or so in the unlighted theater, we are almost blinded by the glare. Very quickly, however, our eyes adapt and the glare disappears. Such variations in the perceived brightness of our surroundings depend upon changes in the sensitivity of the eye and they occur even when the physical intensity of light has

● 15.1

Intensive Aspects of Light Are Influenced by Context. Both circles reflect an equivalent amount of light, yet one is seen as darker than the other. You can see that the gray circles are physically equivalent by placing over each figure a screen which shows only the circles, or a part of them. With their context removed in this way, the two grays appear identical. The experienced intensity of light is so greatly influenced by contextual aspects that a distinction is sometimes made between colors seen as unattached to any surface (*aperture or film* colors) and colors attached to surfaces (*surface colors*). By covering the grays with an aperture, we abstract them, as it were, from a particular surface and surround. They were then comparable with aperture colors. Colors seen through a film, or a fog, are similarly abstracted from their surroundings. On the other hand, the gray circles in their light or dark surround, the red of a fabric, or the yellow of a flower are on surfaces and in particular contexts which influence our perception of their characteristics. It is therefore becoming customary, in technical discussions, to make a distinction between the experienced intensity of color as such (i.e., aperture or film color) and color in varied contexts (i.e., surface color). The term *brightness* is reserved for the former and the term *lightness* for the latter. Thus the circles as they appear in this figure differ in lightness. When covered with a screen so as to remove their contexts, the circles are seen to be equally bright. In principle, the same would apply were our circles red, blue, or some other color.

not changed. Still another reason why physical intensity fails to indicate the experienced brightness level is illustrated in Figure 15.1. What our eyes receive from the two gray circles is reflected light. A physicist will tell us that the light reflected from these circles is the same. From this we might expect the circles to look identical. But this expectation is not confirmed. Anybody looking at the circle surrounded by black will tell us that this is brighter than the other. However, if we look at a restricted part of either circle, through a tube (or both at the same time through apertures separated by the proper distance), we observe that they appear alike. Our observation, under these circumstances, corresponds with the physicist's statement that the reflectances of the circles are equal. Thus, the setting in which an object appears may influence our perception of its brightness. This fact has led certain psychologists and physicists to make a distinction between color in the abstract and color associated with surfaces, and to use the term *lightness* rather than brightness in referring to the intensive aspects of the latter.[2] The legend of Figure 15.1 explains this distinction. Since the following pages deal with vision in its basic aspects, the term *brightness* will be used to represent experienced intensity.

The relations between hue, saturation, and brightness may be represented by a color solid, as illustrated in Plate 14. Hues of neutral brightness and maximum saturation are located on the circle where the two cones join. Note that the order of the hues on this *color circle* is the order observed in the spectrum. It is as though the spectrum were curved to form a circle. However, the ends of the spectrum are represented as if joined by purple, a color which does not appear in the spectrum, but which may be produced by mixing light from the red and violet regions. Brightness is represented by a line running through the center of the solid from black to white with neutral gray at the midpoint. This gradation is referred to as a *black-white continuum*. The most highly saturated hues are shown as equivalent in brightness to neutral gray. As the brightness value of a hue increases (approaches white) or decreases (approaches black), the color tends to become less saturated. The least saturated colors are those at either end of the solid and also those anywhere within the solid that are represented as close to the black-white axis, or

gray. For practical purposes, a color may be specified rather accurately in terms of the three dimensions of this model; that is, in terms of its hue, its saturation, and its brightness.*

Color mixture

The colors that we experience in everyday life are often mixtures, in various combinations, of the hues represented on the color circle. It should be interesting at this point, therefore, to consider some of the ways in which colors are mixed.

Retinal color mixture is obtained by rotating colored discs, as shown in Plate 15. Discs differing in color are locked together and placed on the shaft of the motor. As the discs rotate, each point on the photosensitive surface of the eye is stimulated now by one color and now by another. If the succession is too slow, a marked flicker occurs. As the mixer speeds up, flicker disappears and a uniformly distributed resultant becomes apparent. This is sometimes a gray and sometimes a hue, depending upon the components.

☐ When two complementary colors, like the blue and yellow of our illustration, are mixed in appropriate proportions, a uniform gray results. Which colors can be mixed in this way to produce gray is evident from the color solid. Complementary hues are opposite each other on the color circle. A straight line from one to the other passes through the center, the midpoint of the black-white continuum. This represents the fact that, by mixing complementary colors, we obtain gray or, to put it otherwise, a complete loss of saturation. Our example involved a blue-yellow mixture, but similar results are obtained by mixing blue-green with red, purple with green, and so on. If the component hues differ in brightness, the mixture has a brightness that is intermediate.

When we mix two complementary mixtures — for example, by rotating blue, yellow, blue-green, and red discs together in the proportions which produced gray — we again get gray. That is to say, if 120° of yellow and

* The Munsell Color System exemplifies this, although its terminology is different from that given here.

240° of blue gave gray, and 180° of blue-green and 180° of red also gave gray, then a mixture comprising 60° yellow, 120° blue, 90° blue-green, and 90° red also produces gray. This is because we are, in effect, missing two grays. If the original grays differed in brightness, the resulting mixture is intermediate in brightness.

When non-complementary hues are mixed in the manner described for complementaries we obtain a very different result. Instead of gray we get another hue. This falls between the component hues, as represented on the color solid. Look again at the color circle represented in Plate 14 where the two cones come together. Suppose that blue and green are mixed. The resultant is blue-green. With a mixture of blue and red, the resultant is violet or purple, depending upon the amount of blue. Mixing yellow and red produces orange. In each instance, the brightness of the mixture lies between the brightnesses of the component hues. □

Retinal color mixture is additive. Another type of additive mixture is produced with overlapping lights, as illustrated in Plate 17. Observe, here, that yellow results from a mixture of red and green light. Similar results may be obtained when one eye is stimulated with red light and the other with green. A special stereoscopic device is used. With this device, and while the subject is fixating a bright light backed by a white screen, a certain red filter is placed in front of one eye and a certain green filter in front of the other.* What the subject then sees is a patch of red, a patch of yellow, and a patch of green. The yellow is seen where the red and green overlap, much as in the overlapping circles of Plate 17. This is *binocular* color mixture.[3] We shall see later that special interest attaches to the fact that yellow can be produced in this way from red and green. Note, however, that the resemblance of this to additive production of yellow by overlapping lights is only superficial. The latter can be observed as readily with one eye as with two. In binocular mix-

ture, on the other hand, one eye is stimulated with red and red is all that can be seen with that eye. The other eye, stimulated only with green, can see only green. It is only when both eyes are stimulated simultaneously, one with red and one with green, that yellow is perceived.

In *subtractive* color mixture (Plate 16), yellow and blue pigments are combined to produce green. The artist obtains green in this way. Green is produced by such a mixture because: (1) yellow pigment absorbs all wavelengths except those for yellow and green, (2) blue pigment absorbs all wavelengths except those for blue and green, and (3) blue and yellow cancel, leaving green.

Which colors are regarded as primary is thus seen to depend upon how the colors are mixed. In retinal color mixture we use red, green, yellow, and blue. In mixing lights additively, we use only three so-called primaries — red, green, and blue. Yellow is not regarded as primary because we can produce it with red and green. In binocular color mixture, too, we obtain yellow from a mixture of red and green light. In mixing pigments, on the other hand, the primary colors are said to be yellow, blue, and red. Green, it will be recalled, is obtained by mixing yellow and blue.

It is interesting to observe that there are certain conditions which will generate a wide range of hues from only two colors, red and green. A demonstration of this, arranged by Dr. Edwin H. Land of the Polaroid Corporation, is pictured in Plate 18. There are various possible explanations of such demonstrations. Although Land[4] interprets them as meaning that fewer than three primary hues are required to produce the whole range of color experiences, others view them as "neither more nor less than stunning illustrations of simultaneous induction or contrast mechanisms."[5] Simultaneous induction, or contrast, is discussed below (page 464). It should also be noted that sometimes several hues are seen when interlocked black and white discs are rotated at slow speed on a color mixer. There is, as yet, no satisfactory explanation of this phenomenon.[6]

We shall return to the question of primary colors when theories of color vision are dis-

---

* Eastman Kodak's wratten filter #29 (red) and #58 (green).

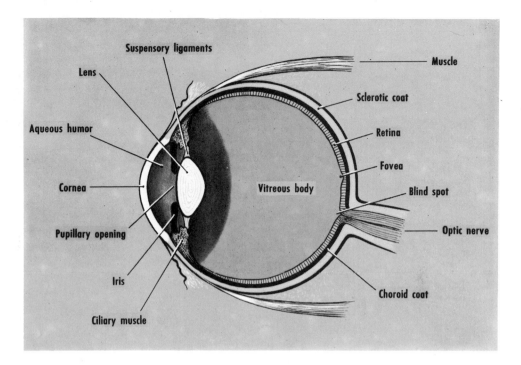

Labels on figure: Suspensory ligaments, Lens, Aqueous humor, Cornea, Pupillary opening, Iris, Ciliary muscle, Muscle, Sclerotic coat, Retina, Fovea, Blind spot, Optic nerve, Choroid coat, Vitreous body

● 15.2

A Cross-Section of the Human Eye. Light rays entering the eye pass through the tough glassy cornea, a watery liquid known as the aqueous humor, the pupil, and the lens. The pupillary opening varies in size, depending upon the intensity of light. These variations are brought about through reactions of the iris, which thus serves a function comparable with that of the diaphragm on a camera. To focus light rays, the curvature of the lens needs to change from time to time. This adjustment, known as accommodation, is carried out automatically through changes in the ciliary muscle and the suspensory ligaments. After passing through the jelly-like vitreous body, light rays produce an image on the retina. Clearest vision is in the fovea, an especially sensitive depression. Nearby is the blind spot, the point at which nerve fibers leave the retina. The walls of the eye comprise the tough outer covering known as the sclerotic coat; an intermediate, heavily pigmented layer known as the choroid coat, which keeps out all light except that which comes through the pupil; and the retina, which is an extremely complex photosensitive mechanism for translating photic stimulation into nerve impulses.

cussed. It will be observed, then, that the most widely accepted and factually supported theory posits three primary colors — red, green, and blue.

After-images and simultaneous contrast

When the eye is stimulated intensely, as by the flash of a clear hundred-watt lamp in a darkroom, a positive after-image of the stimulus is seen. In the case of a lamp, the yellow filament may be observed as if projected on the wall. One may also see this image after closing his eyes.

Positive images are due to continuation of receptor and neural processes after the stimulus has gone. They have the same color and brightness that existed when the stimulus was present. However, the positive after-image, even of an intense light, seldom lasts more than a few seconds. In everyday life we seldom experience positive after-images.

When the positive after-image of a light disappears, the negative after-image takes its place. This after-image is complementary to the stimulus in both hue and brightness. Thus, if the filament is bright yellow, the negative after-image is dark blue.

Negative after-images are sometimes referred to as examples of *successive contrast*, to distinguish the phenomenon from that of *simultaneous contrast*, where the external stimulus and the complementary hue co-exist, but in neighboring regions of the visual field.

Simultaneous contrast is often used in stage lighting. Yellow light at the edge of the stage makes gray shadows on the stage appear bluish and it makes blue objects appear more blue. The latter effect is similar in some respects to the effect produced by looking at a blue area after you have been fixating yellow. The blue of the after-image is, as it were, mixed with the blue before you, and this makes for a more highly saturated color. Artists who paint so-called realistic pictures must take this phenomenon into active consideration. For example, such painters correctly represent shadows on a yellow, sunny snow scene as blue.

Structures and functions

The millions of light-sensitive cells which actually receive and are stimulated by radiant energy initiate nerve impulses. Collectively these and other neural and non-neural elements make up the inner coat of the eyeball known as the *retina* (Figure 15.2). In order to perceive the shapes of objects it is necessary that an accurate image of them be cast on the retina, just as it is necessary for a good image to be focused on the film in a camera if we are to obtain a clear picture. Indeed, as we examine the structure of the eye we note many obvious similarities between its structures and those of a camera. There is a light-tight "box" with a sensitive "film" at the back and an aperture at the front fitted with a lens system which can be adjusted to bring to a focus objects at various distances. One dissimilarity is that a focus is achieved in the camera by moving the lens forward and back while the eye performs this function by altering the power of the lens. This it does by changing the curvature of the lens surfaces. The image on the retina, like that on the film of a camera, is inverted. When a special system of lenses inverts the image before it reaches the eye, it appears on the retina right side up. Then the world is seen as upside down.[7]

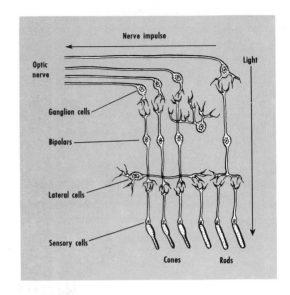

● **15.3**

The Human Retina. The rods and cones face away from the front of the eye. As indicated by the arrow, light must pass through the neural elements of the retina in order to stimulate them. When it reaches a layer of pigment in close proximity to the rods and cones, it stimulates their tips, arousing nerve impulses. These impulses pass to the bipolars and then to the ganglion cells of the optic nerve, which carries them to the brain. Most of the cones, as illustrated, have their own "private" paths to the brain, whereas two or more rods usually share the same pathway. It has been estimated that there are about 137 million rods and cones in each normal eye. (After Bartley)

The legend accompanying the diagrammatic representation of the eye indicates the functions of its various structures.

The most important structures of the retina are diagrammed in Figure 15.3. These consist of the visual receptors, called *cones* and *rods*, and their nerve connections.

Nerve impulses initiated when light stimulates the retina are carried by the optic nerve, via the thalamus, to the cerebral cortex. They terminate in the occipital lobe. The visual area in the right cerebral hemisphere receives impulses from the right half of each eye, and that in the left cerebral hemisphere from the

PLATE 8

An Object Sorting Test. This is the males' form of the Gelb, Goldstein, Weigl, Scheerer Object Sorting Test. The items are not arranged in the standardized pattern with which an administration begins. The subject is asked to select any item, then to place with it all the articles which in his opinion go with it. He may be asked to group articles with one that the examiner selects, or to group *all* articles which belong together. When the test is used for diagnostic purposes, the patient may be asked to arrange new groupings and also to say why the objects in a grouping arranged by the examiner belong together. (After K. Goldstein and M. Scheerer, "Abstract and Concrete Behavior: An Experimental Study with Special Tests," *Psychol. Monogr.,* 1941, 53, No. 239.)

PLATE 9

The Vigotsky Test. This is Hanfmann and Kasanin's adaptation of a test devised by Vigotsky. The nonsense syllable on each block is turned under during the test. Blocks belonging to the same category have the same syllable. Thus those that are both tall and large, irrespective of shape or color, belong to the LAG category; tall and small, to the MUR category; flat and large, to the BIK category; flat and small, to the CEV category. To start, one block is turned over to show its category. The subject then is asked to select from among all of the blocks the ones which go with the sample. Suppose, now, that the sample is the green triangular block. The subject responding on a concrete basis might select either another green block or another triangular one. The experimenter turns up the one selected to show that it does not belong to the proper category. By this procedure the subject learns the proper classification of each block, which is achieved only when single concrete properties of the blocks are disregarded and sorting is done in terms of both height and size. (Courtesy, C. H. Stoelting)

PLATE 10

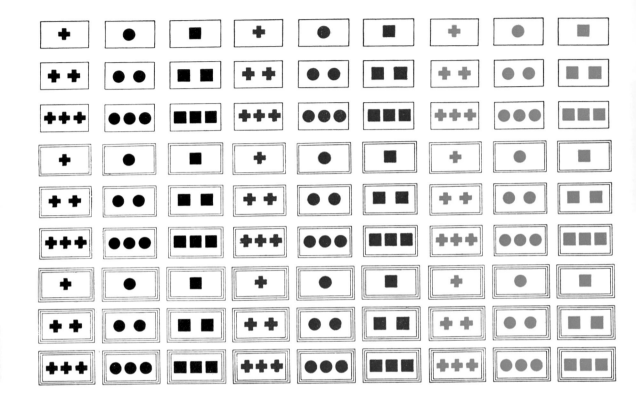

Concept Formation Cards. This set of eighty-one cards is presented one at a time and the subject is not allowed to see earlier cards in the series. Any one of the cards might be shown in a given instance. The subject is required to discover the concept that the investigator has in mind. Let us suppose it is "any circle with a triple border." To exemplify this concept, the card with three black circles and a triple border is shown. The subject might hypothesize, on the basis of this sample, that the correct concept is "three black circles with three borders." Let us suppose he is then shown a card with a red cross and a double border and told that this *does not* exemplify the concept. Next he may be shown a card with a green circle and a triple border and told that this *does* exemplify the concept. The experiment proceeds in this manner until the concept is correctly stated and the subject shows that he can, in each instance, tell whether a particular card is an exemplar of the concept. (Adapted from J. S. Bruner, J. J. Goodnow, and G. A. Austin, *A Study of Thinking*, Wiley, 1956.)

PLATE 11

The Range of Wavelengths Correlated with Vision.
One millimicron (mμ) is a thousandth of a micron and
one micron (μ) is one thousandth of a millimeter. Thus
one millimicron is a millionth of a millimeter.

700 Mμ 600 Mμ 500 Mμ 400 Mμ

PLATE 12

Use of a Prism. This shows how different components of white light are separated to produce
the visible spectrum.

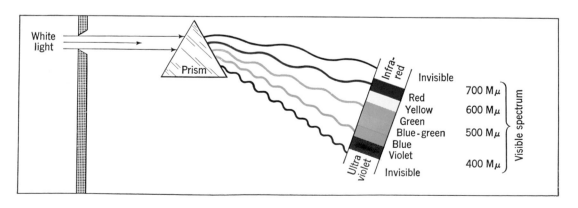

PLATE 13

Wavelength Sensitivity. Percent of light as: (a) transmitted by red glass, (b) reflected by green leaf, (c) utilized by the eye. Relative sensitivity is shown in the luminosity curves. Daylight sensitivity is greatest for about 550 Mμ; night sensitivity (dark adaptation), for about 510 Mμ. Percentages represent the energy of each wavelength transmitted or reflected. Peak sensitivity is arbitrarily said to be 100 percent.

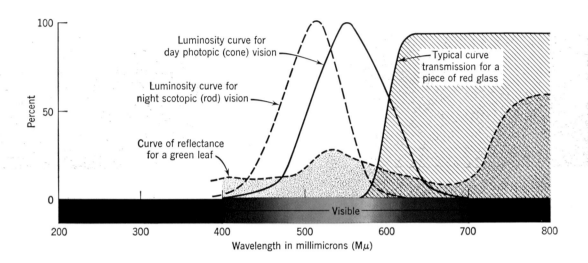

Luminosity curve for day photopic (cone) vision

Luminosity curve for night scotopic (rod) vision

Typical curve transmission for a piece of red glass

Curve of reflectance for a green leaf

Percent

100

50

0

Visible

200   300   400   500   600   700   800

Wavelength in millimicrons (Mμ)

PLATE 14

A Color Solid. The relation between hue, brightness, and saturation is shown by conceiving of the range of colors as varying, in a tridimensional solid, around the white-black axis. Mid-gray is represented as in the exact center. The most saturated hues, at any brightness level between white and black, are represented as on the outside of the solid. Hues decrease in saturation as the white-black axis is approached.

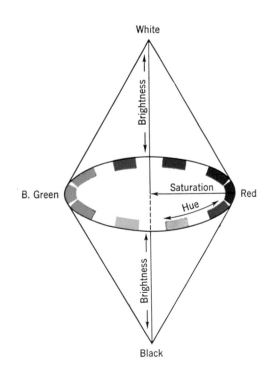

White

Brightness

B. Green

Saturation

Hue

Red

Brightness

Black

PLATE 15

A Color Mixer. This is a small electric motor the shaft of which is adapted to hold the discs shown. As the discs are rotated rapidly, the two colors seem to merge so that a single color is seen. (Courtesy of Ralph Gerbrands.)

PLATE 16

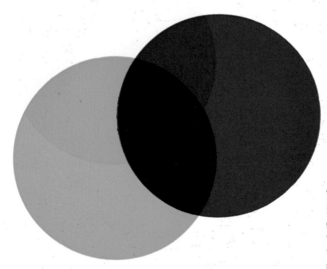

The Subtractive Primaries. Observe that yellow and blue here produce green, whereas in retinal color mixture they produce gray. Note also that a mixture of all subtractive primaries yields black, whereas in Plate 17, representing additive primaries, a mixture of all three yields white.

PLATE 17

Additive Combination of Colors. Three projectors arranged to throw red, green, and blue spots of light, partly overlapping, on a white screen. Such combination of red and green light, called additive mixture, produces yellow. Additive combination of red, green, and blue makes white. (By *LIFE* photographer F. W. Goro, © *Time*, Inc.; from "Color," *LIFE*.)

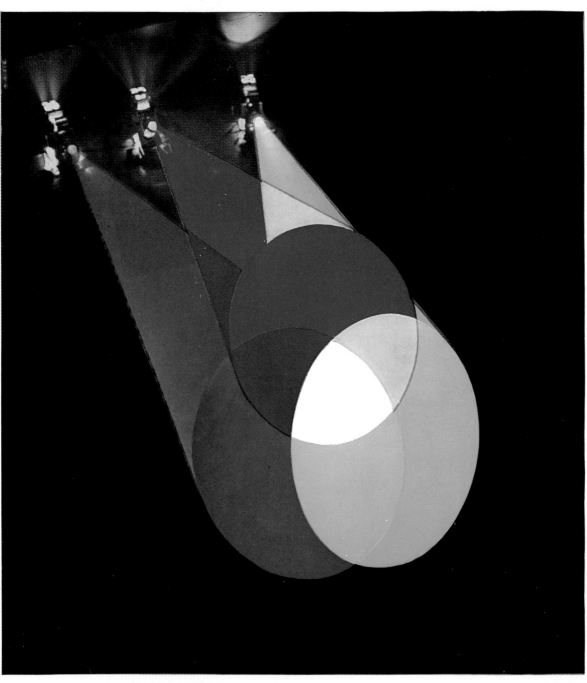

PLATE 18

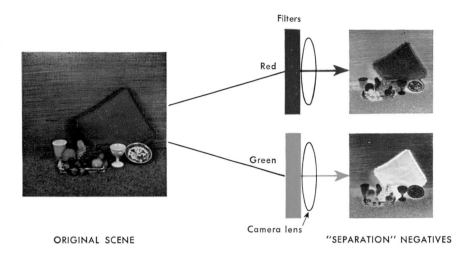

Filters

Red

Green

Camera lens

ORIGINAL SCENE

"SEPARATION" NEGATIVES

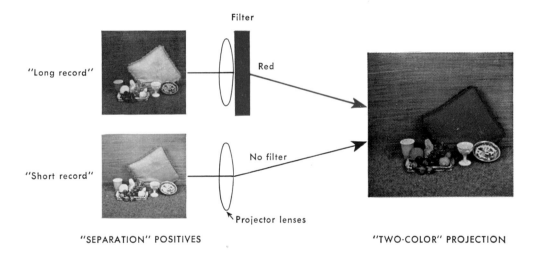

Filter

"Long record"

Red

"Short record"

No filter

Projector lenses

"SEPARATION" POSITIVES

"TWO-COLOR" PROJECTION

One of the Land Demonstrations. The original scene is photographed twice, once with a red filter over the lens and once with a green filter. Note differences in the shading of the two black-white "separation" negatives which result. One (the red) is taken with the long wavelengths as a light source, the other with shorter wavelengths. These are sometimes referred to, accordingly, as the "long record" and "short record," as in the lower reproductions of the positives made from them. (It is interesting to observe in passing that somewhat similar results are obtained by using longer and shorter wavelengths, which differ much less than in the case of the red and green of this demonstration.) When the long record is projected on a screen through a red filter and the short record through a green filter — or through no filter at all (as illustrated) — the original scene appears in almost its complete color range. In this illustration, of course, it was necessary to use the three subtractive primaries to show what Land obtained with basically only two colors.

PLATE 19

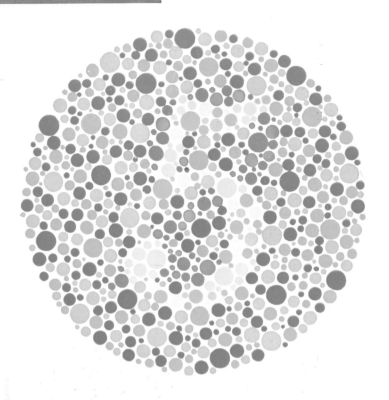

Chart for the Detection of Color Blindness. A person with red-green blindness sees the figure 2. The person with normal color vision sees the figure 5. If you observe closely, you will notice that the discs which make up the 5 differ from the background in hue, but that their brightness differs in a random manner over a wide range and is not distinguished from the brightness of discs outside of the figure. This random arrangement of discs with respect to brightness makes it impossible for an individual who is red-green blind to see the number. Look again. You may notice that certain discs of different brightness from the others are arranged systematically to form a figure of some kind. It is a 2. You will have difficulty in tracing it; your set for hue may make it impossible for you to do so. However, the individual who cannot see the hues, but who is especially set for brightness, cannot help seeing the 2. (Copied by permission from Ishihara's "Series of Plates Designed as Tests for Color Blindness," Tokio, 1920.)

PLATE 20

Color Zones of the Retina. These were located as follows: With one eye closed and the other fixating a point in the center of the perimeter arm, the subject observed, in the corner of his eye, the color of a small disc that is moved by the experimenter from the extreme periphery of the arm inward, or from the center of the arm outward. Moving outward, the disc reaches a point where its color is no longer seen. Moving inward, a corresponding point is found where the color reappears. These points are located on the major axes of the eye — up-down, nasal-temporal — and intermediate axes.

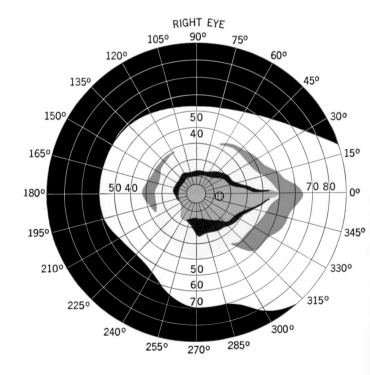

left half of each eye. If the visual cortex of the right hemisphere is destroyed, the right half of both eyes becomes blind. Total blindness resulting from cortical injury could occur only if the visual areas were destroyed in both cerebral hemispheres.

When light stimulates the rods and cones of the eye, chemical processes are started and these are accompanied by electrical changes. Such electrical voltage shifts may be picked up and amplified for observation by the apparatus illustrated in Figure 15.4. The resulting record, known as an *electroretinogram*, has been studied in great detail.[8] This study has revealed that there is a somewhat different response to different wavelengths and to photopic and scotopic conditions.

Electrical impulses (action currents) aroused by retinal stimulation may also be picked up from the optic nerve. We have already seen a picture of them (Figure 2.11, p. 47), which shows that their frequency is correlated with increases in light intensity. Impulses of greater complexity may be recorded at the optic thalamus and, in the form of an electroencephalogram (EEG), at the occipital cortex. These so-called brain waves were discussed in Chapter 2.

□ It is worth while to note, at this stage of our discussion, a fact that is of great importance for theories of color vision. This was taken up earlier (p. 47), but needs reiterating. It is the fact that if a nerve cell is excited at all, it is excited to its maximum extent (all-or-nothing principle) and that any difference in the experience aroused thus depends upon (1) how many fibers are activated, (2) the frequency of discharge in particular fibers, and (3) where the impulses go. The number of fibers activated and the frequency of discharge in each is determined by the intensity of stimulation and, in the case of vision, this underlies brightness differences. Where impulses begin determines, to a major degree, where they go. Thus impulses beginning in the retina lead to differential excitation of neurons in the occipital cortex of the brain. This results in color vision. □

• *Color blindness.* Animals that have no retinal cones are color blind. They respond to

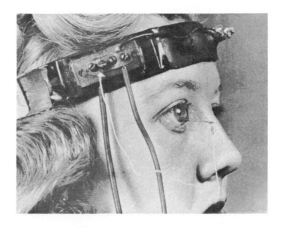

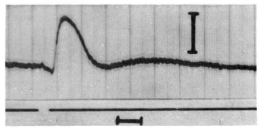

● **15.4**
The Electroretinogram. On the subject's eye is a specially fitted plastic contact lens containing a tiny electrode which makes contact with the cornea. In the head band is a neutral electrode which makes contact with the forehead. The two heavy leads go to an amplifier and a delicate recording mechanism. When light enters the eye, electrical currents are generated in the retina. These are transmitted, via the corneal electrode, to the amplifying and recording mechanism, from which records like the one above are obtained. This is an electroretinogram, usually shortened to "ERG." ERG's have been observed from animal eyes for almost a century, but invention of the contact lens electrode by Dr. Lorrin Riggs of Brown University has facilitated recording of such responses from the human retina. Recent research has shown that ERG's vary in certain respects, depending, among other things, on whether the eye is light- or dark-adapted. The ERG shown here is from a dark-adapted subject. The short vertical line denotes 500 microvolts; the short horizontal line, 0.1 second. (Courtesy, Lorrin Riggs and the *A.M.A. Archives of Ophthalmology.*)

wavelength differences as to grays. For example, if such an animal is differentiating colors which are to us green and red, and we change the brightness value of the red so that it matches that of the green, the animal no longer discriminates. This is because, to it, the two stimuli are now identical. An animal with adequate cones, however, would not be disturbed by this change. It would continue to respond to the wavelength difference. It would respond to one stimulus as "green" and the other as "red," much as we normally do, despite the fact that these stimuli have equal brightness.[9]

Human color blindness is usually attributed to some defect in the cones or in their neural connections. The person with normal vision is able to perceive all colors from a mixture of three primaries. It is generally assumed that he has at least three different types of cones. It is believed, furthermore, that these mediate, respectively, red, green, and blue. Yellow, as we said earlier, is not primary. Some individuals are totally color blind, hence presumably lack cones, as in the animals mentioned above. Such individuals are quite rare. The most prevalent form of color blindness is commonly referred to as *red-green blindness.* This is because those who have this anomaly confuse red and green when these hues have equivalent brightness.

There are many tests of color blindness, but one of the most convenient is the Ishihara Test, from which Plate 19 has been reproduced. Indeed, the most widely used tests of color blindness involve series of charts comparable to that illustrated. Some charts are designed so that the color-blind see a figure and those with normal vision see nothing but a random assortment of color patches. Others are devised so that those with normal color vision see a figure while the red-green blind see only a random assortment of patches.

• *Color zones.* Cones are most thickly concentrated in the fovea, which contains no rods. From the fovea outward, i.e., toward the periphery of the retina, cones decrease in number but rods increase. This underlies the fact that rather than being equally sensitive to all colors over its entire surface, the retina has zones of sensitivity. As illustrated in Plate 20, a certain

• **15.5**

The Blind Spot. Close your left eye and fixate the cross with your right eye, holding the book before your face at a distance of about four inches. If you see the square under these conditions, move the book slightly closer to or farther away from your eye. When the book is at an appropriate distance, there will be a complete, perceptually filled-in blank where the square previously appeared.

region is completely color blind and another red-green blind. Moreover, as indicated on the chart, one small area in each retina is completely, or almost completely, blind. This is known as the *blind spot.* As shown in the cross-section of the eye (p. 463), it is where the optic nerve leaves the retina. (You can demonstrate the existence of your own blind spot by following the instructions in the legend to Figure 15.5.) The color zones and blind spot were located by using a *perimeter* (Figure 15.6) and following the procedure described in the legend of Plate 20.

Under constant conditions of illumination, the results obtained in measuring peripheral color vision are, in general, as follows: all colors are seen in the center of the visual field. As the red or green test object is moved from the center outward, however, it reaches a region where it is no longer observed as red or green. Yellow and blue are observed over a more extended area, but these also drop out. One of them sometimes drops out before the other. Beyond the region where blue and yellow are no longer seen, the observer still sees gray and white.

Outside of the yellow-blue zone of the retina, as measured under high illumination, there are probably few, if any, cones.

• *Color theory.* While it is definitely established that the cones mediate color vision, very little is known about how they do it. There are many theories, each attempting to explain color phenomena in terms of activities within the cones, or within the nervous system. However, no theory accounts for all of the phenomena of color vision, and at the same time conforms with the facts of stimulation, physiology, and neurology.[10]

☐ The simplest tenable theory supposes that there are three kinds of cones, and that these, while overlapping considerably in their range of wavelength sensitivity, have peak sensitivities for respectively, the red, green, and blue regions of the spectrum. We have already observed that mixtures of different pairs of these hues may be used to produced all other colors, including yellow. As recently as 1964, two groups of scientists working independently, discovered that there are indeed three kinds of cones in the retina.[11] Studying the absorption spectrum of individual cones, they found that there are three types with maximum absorption in, respectively, the blue, green, and yellow-red regions of the spectrum. This is taken to offer further support for a three-component theory of color vision such as that proposed in 1801 by Thomas Young and further developed by Ludwig von Helmholtz.

The Young-Helmholtz theory not only accounts for the three-component mixtures described earlier, and for the binocular production of yellow, but also for negative after-images. The latter are assumed to arise from differential stimulation of the three types of cones. For example, wavelengths in the red region maximally stimulate and fatigue the *red* cones, but leave the blue and green cones relatively unaffected. Stimulation with achromatic light (as when we look at a white or gray surface) now activates the blue and green cones more than the red. What we have, in effect, is the resultant of a mixture of blue and green, or white minus red — i.e., blue-green. Other negative after-images are similarly explained. Yellow appears after stimulation with blue because it corresponds with a mixture of red and green, or white minus blue.

It has often been thought that a person with red-green blindness must lack the cones which mediate red and green. If this were so, the Young-Helmholtz theory would be placed in a tenuous position, for yellow is assumed to be the resultant of the red and green processes.

● **15.6**
A Perimeter. The subject is fixating a central spot in the arc of a Brombach perimeter. By turning the perimeter arm to other positions, any point on the retina may be stimulated. A colored disc, to be discriminated "out of the corner of the eye," is moved inward or outward on the perimeter arm. Its carrier is seen at the subject's right. (Courtesy, American Optical Company)

How then could a person who lacks these still see yellow? It now seems apparent, however, that persons with red-green color blindness do have the cones which mediate red and green. The difference between these and people with normal color vision is that they have low sensitivity for certain regions of the spectrum. But note this very important point: if the red-green blind have both "red" and "green" cones, the cortical terminations of these receptors may be in the respective regions as in normal persons. Thus an intensity of light sufficient to activate the defective "red" and "green" cones may arouse impulses which, when they reach the cortex, give rise to the experience of yellow. Recall, in this connection, the observation that stimulating one eye with red and the other with green (binocular color mixture) arouses an experience of yellow which must be attributed to a fusion process at the level of the cerebral cortex. The same sort of fusion may allow the red-green blind to see yellow when appropriately stimulated.[12]

The Young-Helmholtz three-component theory has much to support it, as we have seen. But recent electrophysiological research on single ganglion cells of the retina (see Figure 15.3, p. 464) has led to a revival of interest in a four-component theory proposed, in its original form, by Hering.

The four color components of Hering's theory (red, green, yellow, and blue) are reducible, it is claimed, to opposing pairs (red-green and blue-yellow). Two types of cones are posited, one type to mediate the red-green and the other the blue-yellow components. Red, for example, is assumed to arouse one kind of process in the red-green cones while green arouses the reverse process. Blue and yellow are assumed to produce similarly antagonistic responses in the blue-yellow cones.

Physiological details in support of this theory have been lacking, but there is now evidence that impulses aroused in the retina by short-wave and long-wave stimulation have opposing effects when they reach the retinal ganglia. Short wavelengths activate a ganglion cell at their onset, whereas long wavelengths activate it at their termination. The responses thus elicited are referred to respectively as "on" or "off" responses. This finding has led one investigator to conclude that color vision is "at least a two-stage process, consistent with the Young-Helmholtz theory at the receptor level and with the Hering at the level of the optic nerve and beyond." This would mean that "three-color information is somehow processed in the retina and encoded into two-color on-off signals by each of the color-sensitive retinal ganglion cells for transmission to the higher visual centers."[13]

What we have said reflects some current thinking on the question: How do we see color? But investigators in this area, where physics, physiology, and psychology converge, are by no means satisfied that they have, as yet, found a complete answer to this important question. □

• *The rods and their functions.* There are, as we have seen, no rods in the fovea, and there are relatively few immediately surrounding it. Rods increase in number as the periphery of the retina is approached.

Rod vision is solely achromatic. If you slowly decrease the illumination on the spectrum in Plate 11, the sensitivity of your cones will gradually decrease and, when a sufficiently low illumination is reached, all hues will disappear, leaving only a series of grays. This is the point at which your cones stop functioning. At a still lower illumination, the fovea, containing cones only, becomes blind. Then you can see only with the peripheral retina — out of the "corner of your eye." Under conditions of light adaptation, your cones are highly sensitive; but under conditions of dark adaptation they become completely insensitive. Your vision is then purely peripheral, and purely rod vision. Under these circumstances brightness, but not hue, is perceptible. This shift from cone to rod vision is responsible for the *Purkinje phenomenon*, named after the scientist who first described it. It is a shift in the relative brightness value of the yellow-red and blue-violet regions of the spectrum. For example, as illustrated in Plate 13, yellow is brighter for daylight (photopic) vision and blue is brighter for night (scotopic) vision.

You can observe the Purkinje phenomenon by looking at a varicolored garden or carpet as darkness falls. Note that the brightest colors under conditions of good illumination are yellow and red. As darkness falls, however, these become less bright. Green and blue, which are relatively dark in daylight, now become brighter than yellow and red. This is why we see the green leaves of a rosebush long after the red roses have disappeared. Under these conditions, we perceive the shape and brightness of the leaves but not their hue.

The sensitivity of the eye becomes possibly as much as a hundred thousand times greater in complete dark adaptation than in light adaptation. This increased sensitivity to light is due to changes which take place in the rods. That dark adaptation is a function of the rods rather than of the brain is shown by the fact that one eye can be dark adapted while the other is being light adapted.

While the eye is in darkness there is increasing concentration of a photochemical substance in the rods. Because it has a purplish color, this substance is referred to as *visual purple*.

People who do not readily become dark adapted are relatively blind under conditions of low illumination such as exist at night. They are said to be *night blind*.

□ A key factor in night blindness is vitamin A.[14] This vitamin plays an important part in the synthesis of visual purple, hence a certain amount is needed for good dark adaptation. It is interesting to note, in this connection, that the ancient Egyptians recognized the existence of night blindness and used liver, preferably raw, as a remedy. We now know that liver is a rich source of vitamin A, as are certain fruits and vegetables.

Army and Navy personnel who must see well at night are fed a diet rich in vitamin A. This enables them to adapt readily to the low night illumination. Sometimes the diet is supplemented with doses of vitamin A. You should not assume, however, that a person with no vitamin A deficiency will see better at night by taking additional amounts of vitamin A.

It takes about forty minutes to become completely dark adapted, yet this adaptation is lost within a few minutes when one looks at brightly illuminated objects, like charts and instrument boards. One then becomes *light adapted*.

Light produces a photochemical reaction which bleaches the visual purple and thus reduces its sensitivity. This being so, how can one who must look at charts, instrument boards, and the like, keep his dark adaptation so as also to respond readily to objects with low illumination?

One solution is to use red light, which has only a negligible effect on the dark adapted rods. Thus a convenient way to keep dark adapted while at the same time carrying on activities which require response to illuminated objects is to wear special tight-fitting red goggles. Since the goggles admit only red light, the rods do not lose their adaptation. One takes the goggles off when he steps out into

• 15.7
A Test of Visual Acuity. The degree of your acuity is measured by how small a separation you can see at a specified distance and with a specified intensity of illumination. The ability to observe a small separation of objects on the retina depends on the lens and refractive media of your eye, but it also depends on the separation of receptive fields in the retina. This is a part of the Landolt broken ring test.

the darkness and puts them on again before he goes into the light.

When such goggles are used, charts must of course be drawn in colors other than red, for red markings cannot be distinguished through red filters.[15] □

• *Acuity.* The closer two impressions may be on your retina, and still be seen as two, the greater your visual acuity. As intensity of illumination increases, acuity also increases. For example, observe the broken rings in Figure 15.7 under different intensities of illumination, but keeping the figure at a constant distance, say, six feet from the eye. You will observe that the smallest visible separation decreases as the intensity of illumination increases. Acuity is poorest under low illumination, when the rods alone are functioning. Under conditions of constant illumination, it becomes poorer as the periphery of the retina is approached. For example, fixate an object to the side of the figure and look at the latter "out of the corner of your eye." You will observe that a larger separation must now occur in order to be visible. Given good illumination, acuity is at its maximum in the fovea — that is to say, in direct vision.

Separate points or lines, in order to be differentiated, must activate different receptor mechanisms. This is more likely to occur in the fovea than elsewhere for two reasons: (1) there are more receptor cells in the fovea than elsewhere, and (2) most of these have separate pathways to the brain, whereas those outside of the fovea (the rods) often share a common pathway. Even though two of those which share the same pathway are activated, the effect on the brain is as if only one were stimulated. Thus, in order to produce differentiation, lines or points need to be farther apart on the periphery of the retina than in the foveal region.[16]

• *Flicker.* When a light flashes on and off at a sufficiently slow rate, we see the separate flashes. As the flash rate is speeded up — that is, the interval between flashes shortened — a frequency is reached where separate flashes are no longer evident. Flicker occurs. With a further increase in the frequency of flashes, a stage is eventually reached where it appears that we are stimulated by a constant light. The separate flashes of your sixty-cycle electric light are seen neither as separate nor as flicker. It appears that the light is constant. The frequency of flashes required to produce such a fusion is known as the *critical flicker frequency*, or *c.f.f.*

This frequency, related as it is to visual acuity, is a function of light intensity, among other variables. It is low with a low light intensity and high with a high light intensity.

☐ The critical flicker frequency differs somewhat from one person to another and this difference is now known to be related to cir-

culatory and other physiological conditions of the individual. It has also been used as an index of neural interaction within the retina. As we have already suggested, the retina is an intricate mechanism comprising not only the rods and cones, but also lateral neurons, bipolar cells, ganglion cells, and other neural structures. There is no evidence of interaction between retinal neurons in the foveal region, with its many cones, each connected by a "private wire" to the brain. Whatever interaction occurs must take place in the brain. But the rods are so interconnected that some sort of interaction at a retinal level is to be expected. Several experiments have shown, in fact, that the effects of stimulating different groups of rods summate (p. 44) so as to produce results different from those obtained with one group alone. For example, four small flashing discs on the peripheral retina had a c.f.f which was 2.5 flashes per second higher than when only one flashing disc of the same intensity was used. The effect was as if there had been an increased intensity of stimulation. In the fovea, one or four discs had approximately the same c.f.f., showing that here there was no summation.[17] ■

● **15.8**

The Limits of Human Hearing. Observe that the range of frequency for the piano is from 28 to 4096 cycles. (After an illustration in the Encyclopaedia Britannica film, "Fundamentals of Acoustics.")

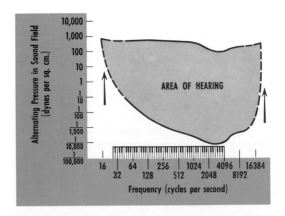

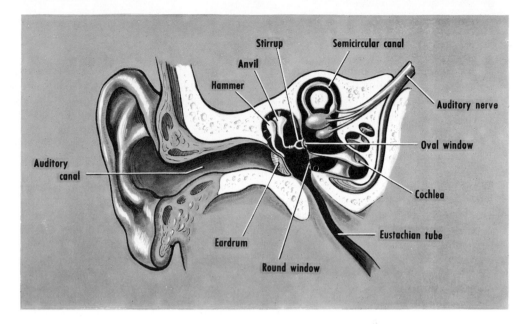

● 15.9

A Diagrammatic Cross-Section of the Human Ear. Sound waves travel through the *auditory canal* until they strike the *tympanic membrane* (eardrum). Vibration of this membrane activates the attached *hammer* and, through it, the *anvil* and *stirrup*. Attached to the hammer is the *tensor tympani,* a muscle that adjusts the hammer and tympanic membrane for different intensities in such a manner as to prevent injury to the latter. The stirrup, which also has a muscular attachment, presses against the *oval window.* Its movements press the membranous window in and out. Movements of the oval window cause waves to travel up the *vestibular canal* and back down the *tympanic canal* of the *cochlea.* Both canals, shown in detail in Figure 15.10, are filled with liquid. A push of the stirrup is compensated for by an outward bulge of the round window, which appears at the lower extremity of the tympanic canal. Withdrawal of the stirrup causes an inward bulge of the round window. Observe that the *auditory nerve* has two branches. One of these, the vestibular, connects with the semicircular canals and serves the static (equilibratory) sense. The other branch, the cochlear, is auditory in function.

HEARING

Waves set up by vibrating bodies are transmitted through air to the eardrum. In the ear they arouse certain mechanical activities which stimulate nerve fibers. When the impulses thus elicited get to the brain, we hear.

The *pitch* of a sound is determined primarily by the *frequency* of air waves, that is the number of waves per second. Thus the note middle C is correlated with a frequency of 256 cycles per second. Lower frequencies produce tones of lower pitch; higher frequencies, tones of higher pitch. Observe in Figure 15.8 that frequencies toward which the human ear is attuned range between approximately

20 and 20,000 cycles per second, and that the ear is most sensitive to frequencies between 2000 and 5000 cycles per second. This means that sound waves within this frequency range need less intensity (sound pressure) to make them audible than do waves of higher and lower frequency. The *loudness* of a sound is a function primarily of the sound pressure that activates the eardrum. This is correlated with the *amplitude* of the sound wave, i.e., the degree of displacement of the vibrating body from the resting position. Think, for instance, of the maximum displacement of a tuning fork prong or vibrating harp string. Vibrating bodies usually vibrate complexly. The harp string, for example, vibrates as a whole, in

thirds, in fourths, and so on, all at the same time. The *complexity* thus involved determines the *timbre* or tonal quality of a sound. Thus a harp and a horn playing the same note sound different.

While *tone* is the auditory effect of periodic sound vibrations, as described above, *noise* is the auditory effect of irregular (aperiodic) sound vibrations.

Before we can hear, sound waves must activate the ear mechanisms and give rise to nerve impulses which travel to the cerebral cortex. For this reason, psychologists study the structures and functions of the ear itself as well as the auditory pathways and their interconnections with various brain structures.

The gross anatomy of the ear is illustrated in Figure 15.9, which also shows the semicircular canals and the vestibular branch of the auditory nerve, neither of which has anything to do with hearing. We will consider the latter structures when the static sense is discussed.

The auditory sense organ is the *cochlea*, essentially a single long liquid-filled canal which ascends, then descends. This is illustrated in

Figure 15.10, A and B. In B the cochlea is represented as uncoiled. The place at which the canal reverses its direction is the *helicotrema*, situated at the apex of the cochlea. The entire structure is coiled in the form of a spiral with two and one-half turns. Separating the two large canals of the cochlea is a ledge of bone and other tissue. It contains two thin membranes which enclose a small channel known as the *cochlear canal*. It is in this that the true auditory receptors are located.

A cross-section of the uncoiled cochlea is represented in Figure 15.10, C. Here we see the relation of the three canals to each other. The cochlear canal is separated from the vestibular by *Reissner's membrane*, and from the tympanic by the *basilar membrane*. On the basilar membrane is the *organ of Corti*, the hair cells of which project up into the liquid which fills the canal. These cells connect with nerve fibers which run along the center of the cochlea and then out into the cochlear branch of the auditory nerve. The *tectorial membrane* is above the hairs, whose upper ends project into it.

● **15.10**

The Cochlea. A, the cochlea, coiled as it is in position in the inner ear. **B**, the cochlea partly extended and sectioned to show the internal structure. **C**, the cochlea in cross-section, showing the organ of Corti, and hair cells.

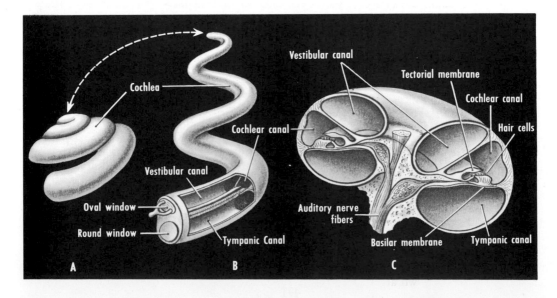

The basilar membrane is set in motion whenever a disturbance occurs in the ascending (vestibular) and descending (tympanic) canals. This motion has been characterized as a traveling wave or bulge. Different portions of the basilar membrane are apparently attuned to different frequencies, so that, when a given frequency activates the ear, the corresponding part is bulged to a greater degree than other parts.[18]

The basilar membrane itself is a harplike structure with fibers ranging in length from short to long. Fibers are shortest at the base of the cochlea, where most of the bulk is merely connective tissue. They become progressively longer as the apex (which has very little connective tissue) is approached. The region containing short fibers is near the stirrup, i.e., at the base of the cochlea. This is the place of maximal response to high frequencies. The part of the cochlea containing the longest fibers is, as we said, near the apex (the helicotrema). This portion responds maximally to low frequencies.

Activity of the basilar membrane moves the organ of Corti, the hair cells of which are induced to bend. This bending excites the ends of nerve fibers associated with the hairs. Hair cells are activated to the greatest degree, presumably, in the region of the basilar membrane in which maximal disturbance is taking place.

Nerve impulses aroused by the hair cells of Corti travel to the thalamus, where synaptic connections are made with fibers running to the temporal lobe of the cerebrum. Each ear is connected with both sides of the cortex. Thus, loss of one temporal lobe does not produce complete deafness in either ear. Loss of both temporal lobes in man produces complete deafness. Some animals, however, continue to respond to noise after the entire cerebrum has been removed. In such instances it is apparent that the thalamic connections are sufficient for response to noise.[19]

Theories of hearing

Theories of hearing attempt to fit together the facts of auditory experience on the one hand, and what is known about the structures and functions of the auditory mechanisms on the other. They are particularly concerned with the physiological events which intervene from the moment the ear is stimulated until the moment we hear a tone of a particular pitch. Loudness, timbre, and other aspects of auditory experience also receive attention. However, as in the case of vision, we have several theories and there is as yet no single generally accepted explanation of all the facts which an adequate theory needs to encompass. Two different yet supplementary theories are worthy of attention. These are the place and the volley theories.

• *Place theory.* This was presented in its original form by Helmholtz, who thought that the fibers of the basilar membrane resonate to external frequencies somewhat like wires in a piano. In its present form the place theory supposes that each region of the basilar membrane is especially attuned to a certain frequency of vibration. Thus, a particular narrow region of the basilar membrane is supposed to react maximally to a certain frequency, although other parts are also to some extent activated. Our experience of pitch would depend upon the part of the basilar membrane which gives the maximal response to a vibration frequency. It is generally supposed, however, that impulses aroused in different regions of the basilar membrane go to different regions of the auditory area of the cerebral cortex. Thus, the cortical region affected would be the most immediate correlate of a particular pitch experience.

Although its fibers do not vibrate in the manner of wires in a harp or piano, the basilar membrane does respond differentially to different frequencies.[20]

There is also evidence, although somewhat conflicting, that exposure of an animal's ear to loud sounds of high pitch destroys the basal regions of the cochlea, where the short fibers — those assumed by the place theory to function for high pitch — are located. Low tones of great intensity produce widespread rather than localized damage to the basilar membrane.[21]

According to the place theory, loudness depends on how much of the basilar membrane is activated. Two tones of the same

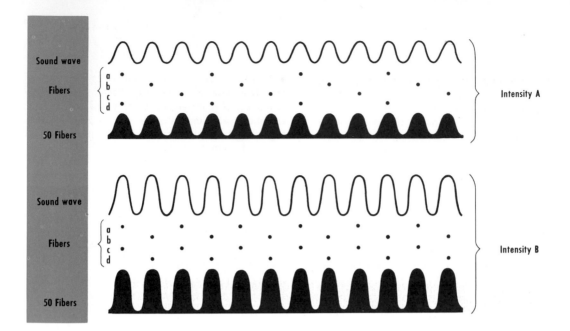

● 15.11

The Volley Principle. In the upper figure note that, for each condensation of the sound wave, some fibers, say 50, respond. Fiber *b* responds at every third condensation starting with the second, and so on. Although no one fiber responds at each condensation, all respond in synchrony with the external frequency. The mound at the bottom represents the sum of all impulses aroused by each condensation. Note that there is a mound for every condensation, because each condensation is assumed to produce its own spurt of neural activity. The frequency of these spurts or volleys is said to be the physiological basis of pitch. The lower figure shows a sound wave of the same frequency as above, but of greater amplitude. Fibers *a, b,* etc., react to every second instead of only to every third condensation. In effect, the frequency of volleys is unchanged, but more impulses are added to each volley. The mounds at the bottom are spaced like those above, but their height is greater. (From E. G. Wever, "Hearing," in Boring, Langfeld, and Weld's *Introduction to Psychology,* Wiley, 1939.)

frequency and intensity would activate the same range of fibers. Moreover, the same particular fibers would be activated maximally. If the two tones of like frequency differed in intensity, however, the range of fibers activated would be greater in the case of the greater intensity, even though the fibers maximally activated would be the same. Thus, according to the place theory, pitch depends upon the place maximally activated, and loudness upon the spread of disturbance in either direction from the place most involved.

● *Volley theory.* It has been observed in research by Wever and Bray[22] that frequencies up to about five thousand cycles per second are somehow transmitted by the auditory nerve,

even though no single fiber responds more frequently than one thousand times per second (as determined by an absolute refractory period of .001 second). This suggests that nerve fibers work in squads. A particular group of fibers would be discharged by one wave but not by the next. Some fibers in the group, because of their greater excitability, would discharge more often than others[23] This is an excellent example of the fact that the external physical energies of stimuli act upon receptors in such a way as to initiate "coded" impulses in the nerves that carry information to the brain.

Despite wide differences in the excitability of different fibers in the auditory nerve, there would be a spurt of impulses involving some fibers with every wave. Thus, for a tone of three thousand cycles per second, there would be a spurt of activity in the auditory nerve every three thousandths of a second, with different groups of fibers responding each time, and some fibers, because of greater excitability, contributing to more of the spurts than others. Pitch, according to this theory, is thus dependent upon the frequency of *volleys*, not the frequency carried by the individual fibers.

Loudness is accounted for by supposing that, with an increase in the intensity of stimulation more impulses occur in each spurt. We have already seen that an increase in the intensity of stimulation causes more nerve fibers to respond and also leads to a more frequent response in each fiber. Thus, a wave of increased amplitude might activate one hundred instead of fifty fibers; and fibers which had been responding only five hundred times per second might now respond seven hundred times per second. The total effect would be to produce more impulses per volley, without changing the frequency, or temporal spacing, of the separate volleys. This is illustrated in Figure 15.11.

At the present time it seems apparent that both the volley and place principles are involved in hearing, with the volley factor playing a major role in mediating frequencies up to around five thousand cycles and the place factor a major role in mediating higher frequencies. Although there is much to be learned about how these principles operate, especially in producing complexities of hearing, both appear necessary.[24] ■

STATIC SENSITIVITY

If stimulation of all other senses were eliminated, static sensitivity would still make it possible for us to know whether we were right side up or upside down, falling or going up, spinning or standing still, moving forward or backward, or to the right or left.

The receptors which mediate static sensitivity are in the nonauditory labyrinth, which, as illustrated in Figure 15.12, has three semicircular canals and two small sac-like chambers

● **15.12**

The Nonauditory Labyrinth. This contains a liquid called *endolymph*. Each canal is roughly at right angles to the others. Rotating the head clockwise or counterclockwise activates *a*; tilting it to the front or back, *b*; and tilting it to the right or left, *c*. The swelling (*ampulla*) at the base of each canal contains the *crista*, whose projecting hairlike structures are bent by the motion of the endolymph. As the head turns to the right, the liquid in *a* lags, causing these structures to bend to the left, or vice versa. Similarly, "hairs" in canal *b* are bent in the upward or downward direction and those in *c* in the right or left direction, depending on the direction of rotation. The *vestibule* at the base of the canals comprises the *utricle* and *saccule*, which contain hairlike structures weighted on the ends with calcium particles (*otoliths*). These respond to rectilinear motion — that is, movement in the up-down direction (as in an elevator), the forward-backward direction (as in a car, or the right-left direction. Because the otoliths lag in adjusting to motion, their "hairs" bend in the opposite direction. Nerve impulses are aroused by movements of "hairs" in the semicircular canals and the labyrinth. These reach the brain via the vestibular branch of the auditory nerve. This was illustrated in Figure 15.9.

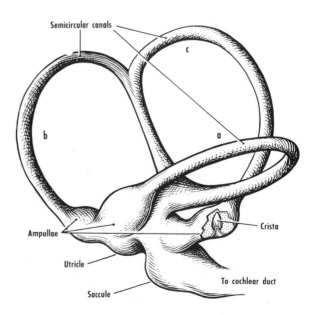

Semicircular canals

c

b

a

Ampullae

Crista

Utricle

To cochlear duct

Saccule

(saccule and utricle), known jointly as the vestibule.

Under most conditions of everyday life, our semicircular canals and vestibules are stimulated simultaneously. Impulses which come from the separate structures are coordinated in the cerebellum. They play a major role in maintaining the tonus of muscles and the equilibrium of the whole body. Coordination of impulses from these mechanisms enables the cat to land on its feet, regardless of the position from which it is dropped.

Rotary movement on the horizontal plane elicits compensatory head and eye movements. These result from reflex neural connections between the semicircular canals, brain, and eyes. The head and eyes drift, as it were, in the direction of movement and then snap back.

Rapid oscillatory eye movements (*nystagmus*) are particularly noticeable after rotation on the horizontal plane. If you observe someone who has been rotated several times and just stopped, you will notice that his eyes make quick back-and-forth movements. They "drift" in the direction in which he has been moving, then "snap" in the opposite direction. This is known as *post-rotational nystagmus*. Absence of post-rotational nystagmus arouses a suspicion that the semicircular canals or their connections are defective. In acrobats, flyers, ballet dancers, and others whose activities stimulate the semicircular canals a great deal over a long period of time, however, post-rotational nystagmus may be absent or of very brief duration. Experiments on animals and human subjects in the laboratory have shown that such nystagmus may be eliminated by repeated rotation, yet without impairment of static sensitivity.[25]

The dizziness which follows rotation is also reduced by training in rotation, probably, in part at least, because the eye movements are reduced. This dizziness, as well as nystagmic movements, can easily be induced by rotating an environment of black and white stripes without stimulating the semicircular canals at all. Thus, while there is normally a close relation between static sensitivity and eye movements, this is not a necessary relation. Under such circumstances as we have described, one kind of activity may occur without the other.

☐ Unusual stimulation of the semicircular canals and vestibule is conducive, in many people, to a malady known in general as *motion-sickness*. People who get seasick, airsick, carsick, or swingsick can, at least in part, blame their static mechanisms. Animals and human beings without active labyrinthine mechanisms do not get motion-sick.

Why some people with good labyrinthine mechanisms are susceptible to motion-sickness while others are not is an unsolved problem. It is possible, as we shall see, that organic as well as static sensitivity is an important cause of motion-sickness.[26]

Tests of susceptibility to motion-sickness are utilized in the selection of airborne military personnel. The tests involve prolonged subjection to motion in long swings, elevators, rotating chairs, and the like. Some subjects grow pale, begin to perspire, and end by being ill, while others stand the tests without any signs of sickness.

Most people who experience motion-sickness get over it as the trip continues. This probably means that their static mechanisms have in some way become adapted to the unusual movement. After leaving a plane or boat, many people feel that the ground is unsteady and that buildings are swaying in various directions. Such phenomena are often experienced by people susceptible to motion-sickness.

Today the drugs dramamine and Bonamine may be used to reduce the incidence of motion-sickness. How they do this is not definitely known.[27]

Some deaf-mutes have congenitally defective inner ears (both cochlear and vestibular mechanisms). They do not experience motion-sickness and they have little idea as to which way is up when they swim under water with their eyes closed. ■

KINESTHESIS

Any normal individual with eyes closed can touch his nose, ear, or any part of his body with a high degree of accuracy. He can move his limbs in various ways and know their position from moment to moment. He can, by lifting objects, discern their relative weights. He can go directly to the familiar light switch in complete darkness, walk along the street without paying attention to what his legs are doing, carry on a conversation without thinking of the muscular movements involved, and, if he is an experienced aviator, fly "by the seat of his pants," giving no attention to the manipulation of controls. Likewise, the typist types without looking at or thinking of her fingers, the knitter knits without looking at her knitting needles, and so on. Many of these movements are carried out in the most automatic and stereotyped manner. If we turn our attention to them, they are often disrupted, as in the case of the centipede in this little poem.

> The centipede was happy quite
>   Until a toad, in fun,
> Said, "Pray, which leg goes after which
>   When you begin to run?"
> That worked her mind to such a pitch,
> She lay distracted in a ditch,
>   Considering how to run.

The automaticity of such behavior and its independence of vision are made possible by receptors in the muscles, tendons, and joints.

The kinesthetic receptors are subjected to pressure, or release of pressure, as muscles, tendons, and joints are moved. As a consequence, nerve impulses are sent to the brain, providing information concerning the position of the limbs. Other impulses are sent back to the muscles, tendons, and joints, thus stimulating further activity Through this feedback mechanism, motor activities act as stimuli for their own rearousal, or for the arousal of other motor activity. This is why kinesthetically controlled habits can proceed so automatically.

☐ Few people realize their dependence on kinesthesis unless they are afflicted with *tabes dorsalis* or observe others so afflicted. This disease (sometimes caused by syphilis) involves destruction of tracts (see Plate 2, tracts for the muscle sense) which carry impulses from our kinesthetic receptors to the brain. When these tracts are disrupted at any level, all kinesthetic sensitivity below that level is, in effect, destroyed. Impulses come into the spinal cord

as before, but they now have no pathway to the brain. The individual thus affected sways considerably when his eyes are closed, cannot lift his foot onto the curb without looking at it, walks with a peculiar (tabetic) gait, and if the destruction is high in the cord, cannot touch his nose or ear with his eyes closed without extensive exploration. If the destruction is in the brain itself, the individual has little success in repeating such words as "electricity" and "episcopal." Phrases like "black bug's blood" are especially difficult. Even ordinary speech becomes "thick" and, in very serious cases, almost unintelligible. ■

SMELL

Smell (olfaction) is very important in the adjustment of many lower animals. It might be of greater importance in everyday human life than it actually is but for the fact that our visual and auditory senses serve us so well.

Although unimportant as compared with vision and audition, olfactory sensitivity plays a more or less subtle part in many of our experiences and activities. The "taste" of substances is largely smell. Olfaction puts us on guard when foodstuffs are unfit to eat. When food smells good, on the other hand, we eat it with increased relish. Smell may be one factor which enables babies to select appropriate foodstuffs in the cafeteria feeding situation (p. 166). In an experiment with hosiery of exactly the same quality, but lightly scented with narcissus in some cases and unscented in others, six times as many women preferred the narcissus-scented stockings as preferred the others, yet only two out of the two hundred and fifty subjects suspected that any of the stockings had been scented.[28] Perfumers emphasize the potency of their wares in attracting the male to the female, while soap manufacturers warn that offensive odors will prevent us from "making friends and influencing people."

In order to arouse olfactory experience, substances must be disseminated in gaseous or vaporous form. When the nostrils are completely filled with an odoriferous liquid, no olfactory experience is elicited, but when the

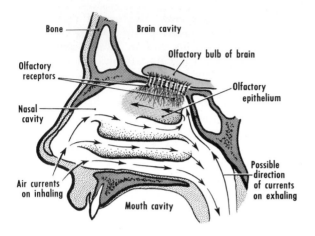

Bone

Brain cavity

Olfactory bulb of brain

Olfactory receptors

Olfactory epithelium

Nasal cavity

Possible direction of currents on exhaling

Air currents on inhaling

Mouth cavity

● 15.13

A Cross-Section of the Nose. The olfactory receptors (shown in gold) are long threadlike structures leading from the *olfactory bulbs* down into a small area at the extreme top of the nasal cavities. At their lower ends, on which small hairs or cilia appear, the olfactory cells are embedded in the *olfactory epithelium*. Note that this is above the main current of air going from nostrils to lungs. Only eddying currents reach the receptors. This is why sniffing helps to identify a weak odor. Nerve fibers run from the olfactory bulbs into part of the limbic system (see Figure 6.5, p. 161). They connect there with a very complex network of neurons.

liquid is removed and sniffed in the ordinary way, its odor becomes quite apparent. Some substances, such as ammonia, arouse a *common chemical sense* as well as smell. They irritate the tissues of the nostrils, and sometimes even produce painful effects.

The olfactory receptors are shown diagrammatically in Figure 15.13 and discussed in the legend. How they are stimulated is not known. Two possibilities have been suggested. One of these, the traditional theory, assumes that odorous substances give off gaseous particles which stimulate the olfactory receptors chemically. The other possibility is suggested by the fact that chemists often identify gases in terms of their different absorptions of infrared (heat) radiation. Our whole body is a source of such radiation. The theory assumes

that olfactory receptors radiate a variety of wavelength bands and that different odoriferous vapors, upon entering the nostrils, absorb different bands. If they did so, the respective receptors would lose energy. This heat loss could arouse nerve impulses and the brain might interpret these as odors.[29] So far it has not been possible to obtain crucial evidence with which to evaluate these theories.

People vary a great deal in their sensitivity to odors. Some have no olfactory sensitivity, an abnormality known as *anosmia*. Moreover, everybody's sensitivity to certain odors is much greater than to others. We smell musk when only minute quantities of the substance are present. Certain other substances have a weak smell, even when we sniff them.

Everyone has experienced olfactory adaptation. Even the most obvious odors weaken and finally disappear if we are constantly subjected to the substance that gives rise to them. It is interesting to observe, however, that adaptation to one odor does not necessarily bring adaptation to others. ■

TASTE

That the "taste" of familiar substances is in reality smell is easily demonstrated. With his nostrils blocked to prevent air from reaching the olfactory receptors, a subject has little or no success in recognizing substances placed on his tongue. Place a drop of lemon juice on his tongue, and he says merely that it is "something sour." A drop of Coca-Cola may elicit the response "bittersweet." Quinine is identified merely as bitter. As soon as the nostrils are opened, however, lemon juice is identified as lemon juice, a cola drink as such, and quinine as quinine.

Experiments have shown that there are actually only four fundamentally different tastes; that all true tastes are salt, sour, sweet, bitter, or combinations of these.

Although taste and smell are the primary contributors to what commonly passes as "taste," other senses sometimes play an important role. The characteristic "feel" of a substance in the mouth may be important. Some substances (like chili and mustard) actually arouse experiences of prick or burn, suggesting that common chemical sensitivity is activated. Other substances merely feel smooth or rough, suggesting cutaneous involvement. It is well known, furthermore, that certain substances "taste" quite different at different temperatures. There is a marked difference, for example, between cold and hot coffee and between cold and warm Coca-Cola.

It is common knowledge that one taste may blend with or cancel another. Thus, we have bitter-sweet and other blends. On the other hand, sweet substances in sufficient concentration may mask bitter.

Adaptation also occurs. After eating candy, an otherwise sweet-tasting fruit (grapefruit, pineapple, strawberry) may taste excessively sour, apparently because our sensitivity to sweetness has been rendered dull by the preceding stimulation.

In order to arouse gustatory sensitivity, substances must be soluble. The reason for this is quite evident when we observe the nature of gustatory receptors. These are below the surface of the tongue and substances must seep down to them before stimulation occurs.

The tongue has a number of slight elevations (papillae), the most evident of which are those aligned in the form of a chevron toward the back (Figure 15.14). These, the *circumvallate papillae*, contain taste cells especially sensitive to bitterness. The *fungiform papillae*, evident along the sides and tip of the tongue, also contain taste cells. Those at the tip of the tongue are especially sensitive to sweetness, those at the sides to sourness, while others scattered all over the tongue except at the center are sensitive to saltiness. The center part of the tongue toward the front is not sensitive to any gustatory stimuli. Some papillae contain no taste cells.

The taste receptors proper are in *taste buds* at the sides of the circumvallate and fungiform papillae. These buds, because of the peculiar arrangement of their taste cells, were once referred to as "taste onions." The location of taste buds within the circumvallate papillae is also illustrated in Figure 15.14.

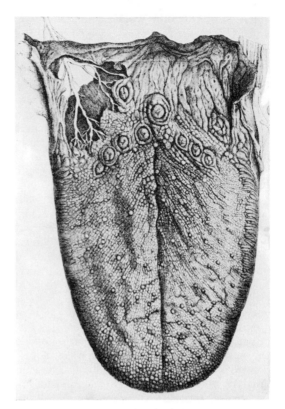

● **15.14**

Taste Receptors. The nerve shown at the upper left goes to the brain. The larger circular-appearing cells near the top of the tongue, shown in greater detail in the cross-section drawing, are the circumvallate papillae. Note that each taste cell has its own nerve fiber, but only one in each taste bud is represented here. Each bud also has many more cells than can be shown in the diagram. (Drawing from Warren and Carmichael, after Wenzel.)

This drawing gives some idea of the structure of the taste cells and their neural connections. Each of the papillae contains several taste buds, and each of these has several taste cells. We can now see why substances must be in liquid form to stimulate the taste receptors. They must get into the crevices of the papillae, seep into the pore of a taste bud, and then reach the taste cells.

Nerve fibers at the base of the taste cells carry impulses over the nerves, shown in Figure 15.14, to the brain. Studies of electrical potentials in isolated gustatory nerve fibers suggest that there are at least three kinds of fibers.[30] The subjects were cats. All fibers that were studied gave a response to acid (sour) placed on the tongue. Some of these also responded to salt, but not to sugar or quinine. Others also responded to quinine, but not to sugar or salt. No fibers responded to sugar. A particular taste may of course depend upon a given pattern of discharge in different fibers. Other senses may also be implicated, as pointed out earlier. ■

ORGANIC SENSITIVITY

Organic sensitivity is sensitivity of the visceral and other internal organs of the body cavity. The viscera include the stomach, intestines, internal sex structures, and kidneys. Nonvisceral inner structures are the throat, lungs, and heart. Activities of the internal organs excite sensory fibers, sending nerve impulses into the central nervous system. Reception of these impulses in the brain underlies organic sensitivity.

Many experiences, most of them rather vague, are associated with the activity of internal structures. Some of these are thirst, hunger, nausea, bladder and intestinal tensions, sexual cravings and thrills, suffocation, and the feeling of fullness. In several instances these feelings have been reduced to the kinds of sensitivity found in the skin; such as feelings of dryness, pressure, warmth or coldness, and pain. Thirst, for example, is associated with dryness in the throat; hunger is associated with pressures and pains resulting from stomach contractions; and nausea is reducible to aches and pains as well as dizziness.

Organic sensitivity is usually stressed in discussions of physiological drives, but it is given relatively little attention from the standpoint of experience. In fact, one will gather from our discussion of hunger, thirst, and sex (pp. 163–172) that these organic activities contribute much more to motivation than to experience.

Some of the nausea and other symptoms associated with motion-sickness are perhaps attributable to visceral disturbances. When the body is moved suddenly upward, as in an elevator, or on a wave, there is a lag in the movement of the visceral organs as a result of their inertia. Pulls are thus exerted on the membranes which keep the intestines in position. Pulls are exerted in the opposite direction when the body sinks suddenly. Such pulls, when applied during an abdominal operation, cause nausea and vomiting.[31] It thus appears that visceral tensions may have a role in production of motion-sickness. On the other hand, motion-sickness exists only in individuals with intact labyrinths. Since those without labyrinths do not become motion-sick, even when subjected to visceral tensions, such tensions cannot be the sole cause of motion-sickness. ■

THE SKIN SENSES

All complex cutaneous experiences, such as itch, burn, roughness, smoothness, stickiness, wetness, and vibration, are reducible to one or more of the following: cold, warm, pain, and pressure. It is now generally accepted that these four are primary skin experiences.

☐ You can easily demonstrate for yourself that there are four distinct skin senses. To observe them you need only touch point after point on your skin with the cold or warm tip of a nail or similar metal object, with the end of a coarse hair, and with the tip of a needle. As the cold object is applied, some points on the skin will respond with a "flash" of cold, while others merely yield a pressure experience. The points which give the cold experience are called *cold spots*. Some other points, when stimulated with a warm stimulus, will respond with a "flash" of warmth. These are designated *warm spots*. Touching various points on the skin with the end of a coarse hair will arouse pressure experiences. If pressure on the hair is light, "tickle" or contact will often be elicited. Still heavier pressure will arouse what has been called "neutral pressure." As the intensity of stimulation is increased, more of the stimulated points will respond with some sort of pressure experience. Heavy pressure with a blunt object will elicit experiences characterized as "dull pressure." The points which respond to stimulation with a hair are called *pressure spots*. When stimulated with the point of a needle, most points on the skin give a "prick" or "pain" experience. These are called *pain spots*. ☐

Research on cutaneous sensitivity utilizes techniques much more refined than those just described. An area is mapped (Figure 15.15) so that the investigator knows beforehand which points are to be stimulated. He may stimulate the same points several times with the same or with different stimuli. The apparatus itself is specially designed to provide constant and measurable stimulation with respect to area, pressure, and temperature. A widely used method of studying pain sensitivity is to expose a small area of the skin to radiant heat.[32] Electrical stimulation is also used.[33]

Almost all of the body surface is thickly covered with pain spots. Pressure spots are also widely distributed. Many of these are located just above the hair follicles (see Figure 15.15). Others are found on hairless regions like the palms and soles. Cold and warm spots occur less frequently than pain and pressure spots, and a given area of the skin often yields many more cold than warm spots.

When the cold, warm, pressure, and pain spots were discovered, physiologists and psychologists tried to locate correlated receptors. They found that the skin does indeed contain a variety of structures which might serve as specialized receptors. Some of these structures are illustrated in Figure 15.16 and their involvement in cutaneous sensitivity is discussed in the legend.

The pressure and temperature senses show rapid adaptation to stimuli. When constant pressure is applied to a pressure spot, sensitivity gradually decreases until nothing at all is

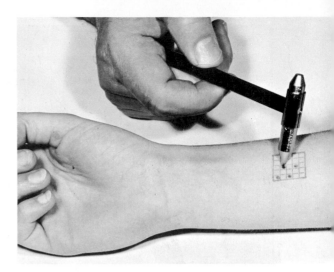

● **15.15**
Mapping Skin Sensitivity. The instrument used here is a temperature cylinder, chilled to locate cold and warmed to locate warm spots. In careful research, there is a better control of temperature and pressure than this common laboratory instrument provides, cold water of constant temperature running through the stimulator and warmth being maintained electrically. A more refined exploration of the skin may also be undertaken with a binocular microscope, which makes each hair seem as large as a telegraph pole.

felt. Everyday examples of pressure adaptation are obvious. One ceases to feel his clothing soon after putting it on, the ring on his finger might as well be nonexistent as far as pressure sensitivity is concerned, and his glasses are not felt to be pressing on the bridge of his nose. Temperature adaptation is also more or less commonplace. The cold air feels less cold after we have been out of the house a few minutes, and the warm air of the house seems less warm after we have been subjected to it for a while. If both hands are placed in lukewarm water after one has been in very cold and the other in very warm water, the lukewarm water feels very warm to the cold-adapted hand and quite cool to the warm-adapted one.

Localization

If somebody touches you anywhere on the body while your eyes are closed, you unhesitatingly name the general region touched. You know, for example, whether the stimulus has

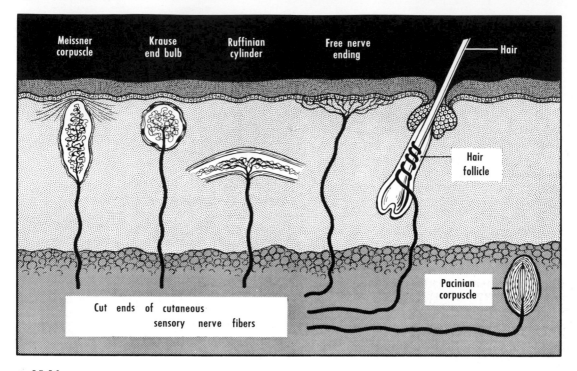

Labels on figure: Meissner corpuscle · Krause end bulb · Ruffinian cylinder · Free nerve ending · Hair · Hair follicle · Cut ends of cutaneous sensory nerve fibers · Pacinian corpuscle

● **15.16**

Diagrammatic Representation of Some Cutaneous Structures. *Meissner's corpuscles* mediate light pressure on hairless regions. *Hair follicles,* with their associated nerve fibers, as illustrated, are also pressure receptors. In addition, light pressure activates some *free nerve endings.* Other free nerve endings are pain receptors. These have thinner fibers and carry nerve impulses at a lower velocity than those which respond to light pressure. Heavy pressure reaches the subcutaneous tissues, where *Pacinian corpuscles* are found. *Krause end bulbs* and *Ruffinian cylinders* were once thought to be receptors for, respectively, cold and warm. But when cold and warm spots were located, cut out, and examined histologically, there was no evidence of such receptors (see reference 34). Free nerve endings were found. Throughout the skin, moreover, there are networks of microscopically fine blood vessels. It has therefore been posited (by Nafe) that sensitivity to warm and cold is based, respectively, upon the dilation and contraction of such blood vessels (see reference 35). According to this (vascular) theory, the pattern of excitation sent to the brain by receptors stimulated by contracting muscles of the blood vessels underlies the experience of cold. The opposite reaction (dilation) is assumed to send a pattern of excitation which arouses the experience of warmth. One difficulty with this theory, however, is that many more cold than warm spots are located on the skin. There are other theories, but it sufficient to observe, at this point, that the Krause end bulbs and Ruffinian cylinders have no known sensory functions. (Illustration adapted from Warren and Carmichael.)

been applied to your right or left hand, your forehead or chest, your abdomen or back. You may be able to report the finger touched, or even the point on a particular finger. The accuracy of such localization is investigated in two general ways.

Tactual-kinesthetic localization requires the subject to make overt localizing movements — he is required to touch the spot stimulated by placing the point of a stylus or pencil on it. The accuracy of tactual-kinesthetic localization depends on two factors: (1) the subject must know where he has been touched, and (2) he must be able to make muscular reactions of sufficient delicacy to touch the point that he knows has been stimulated.

Localization improves a great deal with practice, but the improvement may be due, wholly or in part, to greater accuracy of muscular movement. It does not necessarily follow, in other words, that knowledge of the point stimulated has improved just because the subject can now touch it more accurately. As a matter of fact, the subject often reports from the outset that he knows perfectly well where he has been touched, but that he has difficulty in guiding the pencil point to this spot. If we allow him to do so, he may move the pencil around on the skin until the stimulated spot is reached. Even when such exploration is not permitted, however, the place touched usually differs from the place stimulated by only a centimeter or two. With practice, the error may be reduced to a few millimeters.[36]

Tactual localization may also be studied without requiring the subject to make overt localizing movements. He may indicate on a photograph of his arm the place just stimulated. This allows him to localize visually and it removes the error introduced by trying to guide a pencil point to the stimulated spot. A still better method is to mark the actual arm with the points to be stimulated, have them numbered, and require the individual to indicate by number the point just stimulated. This type of experiment is conducted under low illumination and stimulation is lightly applied, the aim being to leave no impression on the skin which the subject might see. The error of localization under such conditions is relatively small and, like tactual-kinesthetic localization, it is reduced with practice.[37]

Localization on other parts of the body is not as accurate as on the hand or forearm. In general, the error of localization decreases as one goes from relatively immobile parts of the body, like the thighs or back, to highly mobile parts, like the fingers.

How do we recognize so accurately the region stimulated? The answer usually given is that each region of the skin has a somewhat different feel and that this *local sign* enables us to recognize it. Much discussion has centered on the question as to whether these signs are inborn or acquired. The fact that tactual localization without overt localizing

movements improves with practice suggests that we may learn to locate points of stimulation in terms of their different "feel," but it does not, of course, explain why different regions "feel" different. The question is, however, by no means settled.

The two-point threshold

How close together may two points of contact be, yet be clearly discriminated as two? The answer depends, primarily, on the region stimulated. If your back is stimulated, sometimes with one point and sometimes with both points of an aesthesiometer, as illustrated in Figure 15.17, the points will need to be about 70 mm. apart before you can tell whether one or both have stimulated you. On your fingertip, however, the threshold is very low. When the points are two millimeters apart, you will have no difficulty in telling when you have been stimulated by one point and when you have been stimulated by two. Reduce the

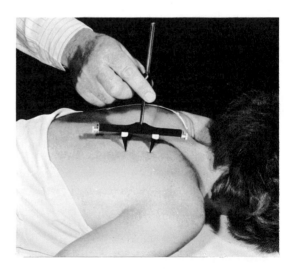

● **15.17**
Using an Aesthesiometer. The instrument is being used on the subject's back to measure the two-point threshold. It is customary to start with a separation that is easily discriminated and gradually reduce it, or to start with a separation that is not discriminated and gradually increase it. Both methods may be used and the results averaged.

separation of the points to less than one millimeter, however, and you will not be able to distinguish between application of one point and application of two.

The two-point threshold, like the error of localizing a single point, is smallest on the most mobile parts of the body. It improves a great deal with practice, but there is probably an irreducible threshold for each region. For instance, the threshold on the back might be reduced by practice, but it is doubtful whether it could ever be reduced to, let us say, five millimeters. The problem is much like that of visual acuity, where the smallest discriminable separation of two points of light depends upon the smallest distance between receptors. The distance between cutaneous receptors is smaller on the tip of the finger than on the middle of the back. Thus, no amount of training could be expected to reduce the two-point threshold of the back to the same threshold found for the fingertip. ■

• SUMMARY

All that we know of the world around us and about our own bodies comes from the decoding by the brain of messages carried to it from receptors by impulses traveling over nerve fibers. The messages are initiated by sensory stimuli — light waves, air vibrations, mechanical pressures, and chemical properties of the environment. Basically, the messages carried by nerve fibers are all alike. This is because all that the stimulus does is to release energy already in the fibers. When it responds at all, a nerve fiber responds completely. Because of this all-or-none response, the only way in which a message about the qualitative aspects of stimulation may be coded is in terms of an impulse's: (1) place of origin — the receptor stimulated — and (2) its destination in the brain. Thus an impulse from a visual receptor always goes to a particular place in the cerebral cortex. An impulse from an auditory receptor, although just like one from a visual receptor, goes to a different place. The brain thus decodes the message, i.e., gets information as to its auditory or visual nature, in terms of the place activated. While impulses originating in the ears bring information as to the auditory qualities of an object and those originating in the eyes bring information concerning its visual qualities, a succession, or combination, of such impulses brings additional information.

Information about the intensive aspects of stimulation is coded in terms of the number of nerve impulses entering a particular region of the cerebral cortex. A more intense stimulus does two things: (1) it increases the number of impulses per second (the frequency of the nerve impulse), and (2) it activates more fibers at the same time. The brain reacts to these messages in such a manner as to make us aware of differences in brightness, loudness, pressure, and so on.

What we see is dependent upon (1) the light transmitted to our eyes, either directly or by reflection, (2) the physiological and neural reactions of the eye and cortex to light which falls upon the retina, and (3) our interpretation of these reactions, which of course involves nonvisual as well as visual regions of the brain.

The appearance of abstracted (aperture or film) colors corresponds more closely with what we know about the stimulus aspects of color than does the appearance of objects or surfaces, i.e., surface colors. (This was illustrated and described in Figure 15.1.) The apparent intensity of surface colors, both achromatic and chromatic, is referred to as *lightness*. *Brightness* (luminosity) is used to refer more specifically to the apparent intensity of aperture colors.

Chromatic vision varies in *hue* and *saturation*, as well as in brightness (or lightness). Hue is what we commonly call "color" — for example, red and green. It is correlated with the wavelength of light. Saturation refers to the amount of color and it is correlated with the complexity of light waves.

Brightness differences may be represented by the black-white continuum. Color differences are often represented by a color circle. The spectrum is bent, as it were, to form a circle, but with purple, a nonspectral color obtained by mixing red with blue or violet, bridging the gap between red and violet. The black-white continuum and color circle are combined in the color solid, one form of which is a double cone. Brightness is represented in this solid as varying from white at one end of the vertical axis to black at the other. Neutral gray takes the intermediate position. This position is the level of the color circle, or base of the two cones. Hues are represented here as at their greatest saturation, or purity. This represents the fact that the most highly saturated colors are of intermediate brightness. As brightness increases or decreases, the color is represented as having shifted above or below the brightness midpoint, and thus as having moved inward toward the vertical axis of the figure.

Some hues are referred to as "primary" because they cannot be derived from mixtures. The "additive" primaries are red, blue, and green. Yellow is not regarded as primary because it can be produced by combining red and green (mixing colored lights, binocular color mixture). Mixing all three of the additive primaries produces white, or gray. Mixtures of pigments are subtractive. The subtractive primaries are yellow, blue, and red. In subtractive mixtures, green is obtained by mixing yellow and blue.

Retinal color mixture is additive and it may be accomplished with discs rotated so that the retina is stimulated successively by each of two or more hues. Mixtures of complementaries (such as red and blue-green and yellow and blue) produce gray. Retinal mixture of noncomplementary hues yields colors that are intermediate on the color circle. Thus red and blue mix to give purple. In all retinal color mixtures, the brightness falls between the brightnesses of the components.

After-images may follow removal of a visual stimulus. Positive after-images are sometimes experienced immediately after the stimulus is removed, as when a light is turned off

and we still see the filament without a change in color. The hue of negative after-images is complementary to that of the stimulus color. Simultaneous contrast occurs when objects close to a color take on the complementary hue, as when gray on a background of blue appears yellowish.

The human eye is in some respect comparable to a camera. Both focus an image on a photosensitive surface. In the case of the eye, this is the retina with its photosensitive receptors, the rods and cones. Retinal stimulation is followed by an electrochemical change which, when recorded and amplified with suitable instruments, is represented in the electroretinogram. When the rods and cones are activated, nerve impulses pass across the bipolar neurons, on to the optic ganglia, and then along the optic nerve. When they reach the thalamus they are relayed to the visual cortex (in the occipital lobe). Half of the fibers of each optic nerve cross (in the optic chiasma) to the other side. Fibers from the right half of each eye go to the right occipital cortex. Likewise, those from the left half of each eye terminate in the left occipital cortex. Brightness depends upon the number of nerve fibers activated by a stimulus and the frequency of discharge in these. Experience of hue depends upon activation of cones.

Animals without cones are color blind. Total color blindness in human beings is extremely rare. The most common type of color blindness involves difficulty in discriminating red and green.

It can be demonstrated with a perimeter that the central (foveal) region of the retina is sensitive to all hues and that there is a peripheral region sensitive only to blue and yellow. Vision outside of the blue-yellow zone is achromatic.

The Young-Helmholtz theory is based upon the idea that there are three kinds of cones maximally sensitive to, respectively, the blue, green, and red regions of the spectrum. Yellow is assumed to depend upon an interaction of the red and green processes. This theory receives support from additive color mixture, what is known about negative after-images, and the recent discovery that there are three kinds of cones with maximal absorption in the blue, green, and yellow-red regions of the spectrum. From the ganglion cells, however, color information may be transmitted to the brain in terms of a fourfold code somewhat resembling that posited by the Hering theory.

Rods mediate achromatic vision and make vision under conditions of low illumination possible. They contain a light-sensitive substance (visual purple) which bleaches when exposed to light and which recovers in darkness.

As twilight approaches, the yellow-red region of the spectrum, the brightest in daylight, becomes relatively less bright. On the other hand, the blue-green region, not very bright under daylight conditions, becomes the brightest region. This shift (the Purkinje phenomenon) is explained by the differential sensitivity of cones and rods to portions of the spectrum, and to the dropping out of cone vision as darkness comes on.

The fovea contains only cones, packed tightly together. Its visual acuity — its differentiation of fine details, such as separation of two points, or lines close together — depends upon the densely packed cones and upon the many cones having individual connections with optic nerve ganglia. Peripheral acuity, dependent mainly on the rods, is poorer than in the fovea.

Flicker is produced by alternating light flashes. The frequency at which these flashes fuse to give an impression of steady light is the critical flicker frequency (c.f.f.). This becomes higher as light intensity increases.

The chief facts about audition are these: pitch is correlated with the frequency of sound waves, loudness with their amplitude, and timbre with their complexity. Noise differs from tone in that the sound waves correlated with noise are irregular, or aperiodic. The range of frequencies to which human ears are attuned is from about twenty to twenty thousand cycles per second.

Sound waves carried to the eardrum make it vibrate. Vibration is carried to the oval window of the cochlea by three small bones in the middle ear. As the oval window of the cochlea vibrates, liquid in the two outer canals is set in motion. This motion causes a bulge to travel up and down the basilar membrane, the lower part of the middle (or cochlear) canal. Movement of the basilar membrane causes small hairs in the structures above it to bend. Nerve impulses are aroused which travel over the auditory nerve to the brain.

The cochlea responds differentially to different frequencies, its base making a maximal response to high frequencies, and its apex a maximal response to low frequencies.

The place theory of pitch supposes that each part of the basilar membrane is so attuned that it responds maximally to only one frequency. Thus, the place in the basilar membrane maximally activated, and the place in the brain to which impulses from this maximally activated region go, would determine what pitch was heard. Loudness, according to this theory, is associated with the spread of excitation, a more intense stimulus affecting more of the basilar membrane than a weaker one. The volley theory supposes that the frequency of volleys of nerve impulses coming into the auditory cortex determines the pitch of a sound and that the number of impulses per volley determines loudness.

The present situation with respect to auditory theory is that a combination of the place and volley principles is required.

Static sensitivity comes from activation of the semicircular canals and vestibule by, respectively, rotary and rectilinear motions of the body.

Kinesthetic sensitivity depends upon activation of receptors in the muscles, tendons, and joints. It is of special interest that, because of these receptors, muscular activities provide the stimuli for their own rearousal or for the arousal of other muscular activities. Kinesthetic feedback underlies the automaticity of our well-established habit patterns.

Smell plays a subtle role in everyday life, especially in its contribution to what commonly passes for "taste." Olfactory receptors are located high up in the nostrils and are stimulated only by substances in gaseous form.

Taste, as such, consists of four primary qualities, namely salt, sour, sweet, and bitter.

The taste receptors are small buds located in the walls of certain of the papillae of the tongue. In order to stimulate cells in the taste buds, substances must be soluble. The "taste" of many substances is largely olfactory and cutaneous.

Organic sensitivity is that associated with functioning of the internal organs. It includes hunger, thirst, sexual cravings and thrills, and bladder and intestinal tensions. Some organic sensitivity, at least, is reducible to complex patterns of pressure, pain, and temperature sensitivity.

The primary skin senses, once referred to in combination as the sense of touch, are pressure, pain, cold, and warmth. Sensitivity to light pressure is mediated by hair follicles, Meissner's corpuscles, and free nerve endings. Heavy pressure involves the deep-lying Pacinian corpuscles. Pain sensitivity is mediated by free nerve endings, those at the ends of relatively thin fibers. No specialized receptors for temperature sensitivity have been located. Complex cutaneous experiences like vibration, stickiness, dryness, wetness, smoothness or roughness, and heat are due to simultaneous arousal of two or more of the primary skin senses. ■

REFERENCES AND NOTES FOR THIS CHAPTER ARE IN THE APPENDIX.

• SELECTED READINGS

Bedichek, R., *The Sense of Smell*. Doubleday, 1960. A naturalist's account of olfactory sensitivity in animals.

Békésy, George von, *Experiments in Hearing*. McGraw-Hill, 1960. A presentation of the author's experiments on hearing.

Buytendijk, F. J. J., *Pain: Its Modes and Functions*. University of Chicago Press, 1962.

Gardner, E., *Fundamentals of Neurology* (4th ed.). Saunders, 1963. Chapters 11 and 12 describe the neural connections between the receptors and the cerebral cortex. Of special interest to premedical students.

Geldard, F. A., *The Human Senses*. Wiley, 1953. Chapters 6–15 provide a great deal of additional detail on the topics covered in this chapter.

Graham, C. H. (Ed.), *Vision and Visual Perception*. Wiley, 1965. The psychological and physiological bases of vision.

Koch, S. (Ed.), *Psychology: A Study of Science*, Vol. 1. McGraw-Hill, 1959. See the chapters on auditory theory (Licklider) and color theory (Graham).

Morgan, C. T., *Physiological Psychology* (3rd ed.). McGraw-Hill, 1965. Chapters 5, 6, 8, and 9 deal with the senses.

Mueller, C. G., *Sensory Psychology*. Prentice-Hall, 1965. An excellent brief survey.

Neff, W. D. (Ed.), *Contributions to Sensory Psychology*. Academic Press, 1965. Papers on auditory, static, and visual processes.

Stevens, S. S. (Ed.), *Handbook of Experimental Psychology*. Wiley, 1951. Here are some very technical discussions of hearing (Licklider, Békésy, and Davis), taste and smell (Pfaffman), cutaneous senses (Jenkins), and the static sense (Wendt).

Woodworth, R. S., and H. Schlosberg, *Experimental Psychology* (rev. ed.). Holt, 1954. Chapters 10–12 will take the reader beyond our relatively elementary account of hearing and the other senses, but without the highly technical detail of the Stevens reference.

16

Attending and Perceiving

Attending and perceiving are closely related processes. Indeed, certain phenomena grouped under the heading of attention and under the heading of perception are identical. What one psychologist discusses as fluctuation of attention, another discusses as fluctuation of perception. One psychologist asks, "How many things can we attend to at once?" while another asks, "How many things can we perceive at once?" In certain other instances the two processes are clearly distinguishable. Attending often precedes perception. It anticipates, as it were, the perception to come. But attending does not, of course, guarantee that perception will follow. One may listen for the expected call that fails to come. He may look, but fail to see what he is looking for. Another difference between attending and perceiving is that the former does not in itself determine the organization or meaning of perceptual experience. The same situation may be perceived differently by all who attend to it. It may be meaningful for all, but have a somewhat different meaning for each, depending upon past experience.

From the standpoint of perception, attending has aptly been called a "preperceptive attitude" — a "reaction of expectancy and exploration,"[1] or "an anticipatory perceptual adjustment."[2] This readiness to be stimulated, or to perceive, is the aspect of attending which interests us most in the present context.

Although attending involves a readiness to perceive, it is not a readiness to perceive indiscriminately. We neither notice nor expect to notice everything. Attending is, in fact, highly selective. Our receptors are bombarded continually by innumerable stimuli, but relatively few of these produce effects of which we are aware, or which change our behavioral adjustments. One reason for this is that the channels of communication between the receptors and the cerebral cortex have a limited capacity for transmitting information. As we suggested earlier (p. 371), it is as if a filtering mechanism were interposed between the receptors and the cortex to select some information and block the rest.[3] Regardless of the sort of mechanism which operates, it appears that whatever information is necessary for the task at hand, or relevant to the needs or interests of the individual at the moment, is most likely to be coded and get through. Novel events are also likely to get the right-of-way. There is further selectivity at the cortical level. Information reaching this level is attention-provoking or not, depending upon such factors as activity in progress and information already available.[4]

Novel or unexpected events of great intensity *do* get the right-of-way, as already suggested. It is as though they forced their way into one's attention. He responds to them involuntarily, even reflexly. Attending is more selective in so-called voluntary and habitual attending. Voluntary attending occurs when we are looking for something, or striving to note the chief points in a lecture. Habitual attending is typified by such more or less permanent sets as those which predispose us to attend to things of particular interest to us. Think, for example, of the doctor set to hear the telephone and his wife set to hear the baby. Think of the male's readiness to notice a beautiful girl and the female's readiness to notice a handsome male. Think of our periodically recurring interest in food and drink. Think of our readiness to perceive good in the actions of our friends and evil in the actions of our enemies. Think of the naturalist's observation of plants and bugs which we fail to notice. Think of the attitude of alertness which characterizes a class as soon as a topic such as sex is mentioned by the instructor. ■

SOME ASPECTS OF ATTENDING

There are four very evident standpoints from which the attentive process may be viewed. *First,* it involves *receptor adjustments.*

Second, there is a more or less general *postural adjustment. Third,* the attending individual is aware of *muscle tensions* or related feelings of effort, especially if the process of attending is of long duration. Finally, the process is

● **16.1**
A Puzzle Picture. Can you see the motorcycle policeman? Once you have seen him, his presence is obvious. If you see him immediately, try this on someone else. If you cannot find him after a good search, look at page 605.

characterized by an *increased clearness*, a bringing out of detail, in whatever is attended to. Some of these aspects of attending are readily observed in ourselves or in others.

Look at the puzzle picture in Figure 16.1 and search for the hidden motorcycle policeman.[5] Note, before you start, that no such person is clearly, or perhaps in any way, apparent. While carrying on the search, which is obviously a process of attending, you adjust your head and eyes, there is a change in general body posture, muscle tensions are involved, and various changes take place within your nervous system. You are perhaps not aware of many such changes. When you finally discover the policeman, you will observe that he stands out from everything else. He will probably stand out so obviously that you cannot thereafter fail to see him.

Many of the adjustments involved in attending can best be observed in someone else. Ask somebody who had not already seen Figure 16.1 to search for the policeman. Note the eyes scanning the picture; note the generally alert posture; note changes in posture, or in positioning of the book, which enables the picture to be observed from various angles. Observe whether the muscles of the face are more tightly drawn as unsuccessful exploration continues. Quite frequently there are emotional reactions during such a search. The subject may be frustrated by inability to discover what he is looking for, and may become exasperated. On the other hand, he may become generally relaxed after discovery.

Similar receptor, postural, and emotional reactions are often observed in students when the teacher is trying to "put across" some idea not easy to grasp.

Receptor adjustment

As already suggested, gross receptor adjustments in visual attending are readily observable. The head and eyes turn toward the object to be observed, and there is either a continued fixation or a scanning process. Rapidly changing adjustments of head and eyes may be seen in the observers of a tennis match as the ball goes from one player to another.

Devices for photographing eye movements and recording the duration of fixations are often used to discover the "attention value" of different parts of a page and of different aspects of an advertisement. It is assumed that those portions which attract the eyes most often and for the longest continued fixation periods have the highest attention value.[6] Eye movements and successive fixations involved in a woman's scanning of a man are illustrated in Figure 16.2. Figure 16.3 shows how eye movements and fixations may actually provide a record resembling the major features of what is viewed, in this case a picture.

□ The pupil of the eye dilates when interesting visual stimuli, like pictures of partially nude figures, are presented.[7] Measurements of pupillary size in response to these, as compared with control pictures, such as landscapes, reveal increases as great as 18–20 per cent. These pupillary changes are related to the emotion-provoking function of the pictures. They may be interpreted as reflex responses controlled by the hypothalamus and the sympathetic division of the autonomic nervous system (see pp. 49–50). Similar pupillary reactions are observed during emotional arousal. We cannot conclude, therefore, that the pupils dilated in order to see better.* □

When the dog "pricks its ears," we have just as obvious a receptor adjustment as that of turning the head and eyes. Some animals not only erect their ears, but also turn them in directions conducive to better reception of sound waves. The hard-of-hearing in former days moved their ear trumpets in a somewhat similar fashion, for the same purpose. We cannot move our ears, but we do move our heads to facilitate reception. This is especially evident in the person who has only one good ear.

* This is not to deny the claim of Darwin and others that pupillary dilation during emotion has evolved because of its utility to the emotion-provoked organism.

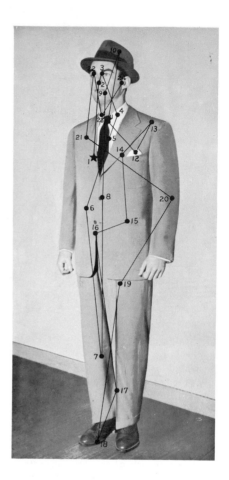

● 16.2
Plotting of Eye Movements. An eye-movement camera was used here to photograph the location, duration, and sequence of a woman's fixations as she looked at a man. The dots indicate fixations, numbered in order of occurrence. First the woman fixated the man's chest, then her eyes swept to his face, from there to his left eye, then to his collar, etc. Data for a group of ninety-eight women whose eye movements were studied in the same way showed that fixations on the face predominated (32 per cent of the total fixation time). Fixations on the collar and tie came next (22 per cent). Courtesy of the copyright owners, Marshall Field & Company, and *LOOK*. For the method used, see H. Brandt, *The Psychology of Seeing*, Philosophical Library, 1945.)

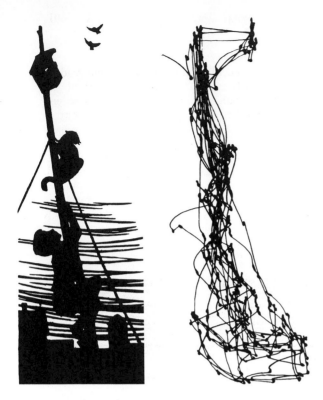

● **16.3**

Eye Movements in Looking at a Picture. The photograph at the right was made by reflecting a beam of light from one eyeball onto sensitized paper. It shows how normal eye movements trace the general pattern of what is being observed, in this case the silhouette drawing shown at the left. (Courtesy, Professor A. L. Yarbus, USSR Academy of Science and *Scope Weekly,* Physicians News Service, Inc.)

He turns his head to bring it in the direction of the sound waves; he may even cup his hand behind it. A finer receptor adjustment associated with hearing involves a muscle of the middle ear (the *tensor tympani*). This muscle produces a change in the tension of the eardrum to adjust it for sounds with different intensities. The adjustment apparently protects the ear from being injured by low tones of great intensity.[8]

Changing the position of the nose and sniffing are obvious receptor adjustments. Touching a substance with the tip of the tongue and moving it around in the mouth so that it falls near the tip, back, or side are likewise receptor adjustments.

Postural adjustment

This form of adjustment is especially evident when one stoops, as in looking at something on the ground, when one crouches on the starting line, and when one strains forward in his seat. Attentive postures may be continued for long periods without tiring the person, so long as what he is attending to is intrinsically interesting. The dog pointing and the cat with its paw in position to catch a mouse about to emerge from a hole are good examples of attentive posture.

Muscle tension

This is involved in any postural adjustment, but it is at times more subtle than general observation would indicate. For example, when efforts are made to distract subjects working at (attending to) a task, the expected decrease in efficiency often fails to appear. But frequently there is clear evidence of increased attention to compensate for the distraction. Associated with this compensatory process is increased energy expenditure, some of which is attributable to heightened muscle tension.

□ Six subjects were given a task in which they were required to press appropriate keys as each of a series of letters was exposed. There were ten keys, somewhat comparable to the keys of a typewriter. These were numbered from 1 to 10. The letters exposed were L M N P S T V X Y Z. They were exposed upon red, yellow, or green backgrounds. As a letter appeared, the subject was required to look at it, note the color of the background, look at a code just below, translate the letter (in accordance with the code) to one of the first ten letters of the alphabet, then press the key whose number corresponded to the number of that letter of the alphabet. Pressure brought automatic exposure of a new letter. Unknown to the subjects, there was attached to each key a device through which the amount of pressure exerted could be recorded. The aim of the experiment was to see whether the amount of pressure would change when attempts were made to distract the subject by introducing noise. The average pressure exerted under conditions of quiet was tested, both before and after noise had been introduced. This pressure under conditions of quiet was compared with the average pressure during noise.

All subjects exerted more pressure under noise conditions than under conditions of quiet. The average pressure exerted just before noise was introduced was 305 grams. Under noise conditions it rose to 438 grams. In a period of quiet which followed noise, the average pressure was 292 grams. The amount of work accomplished did not differ significantly under conditions of noise and quiet. Heightened attention to the task, with which the muscular exertion was associated, apparently compensated for the distracting influence of noise.[9]

Another example of muscle tension during the act of attending comes from an experiment in which the thickening of each of four muscle groups was measured (1) while the subjects were listening for a click known to be barely audible, and (2) while they were listening for a click known to be quite obviously audible.[10] Subjects were required to press a key as soon as the sound was heard. They attended more closely while expecting the weaker than while expecting the louder sound. Concomitant with this additional effort was a greater thickening of the muscles whose tension was recorded. □

Muscle tensions are involved in yet another way in the act of attending. When one has been asked to attend to something, and especially when he has been asked to attend to a variety of specified details, he is likely to repeat the instructions, either aloud or silently. Even when he repeats them silently, his tongue, throat muscles, and perhaps other muscles of his body are thrown into action. Action currents generated in this way were discussed in Chapter 13.

Attending and clearness of perception

As we have already pointed out, attending to some aspect of the environment or to some bodily process is followed by a clearer perception than previously existed. Part of this increased clarity, this bringing-out of details, is due to receptor adjustment. While reading these words, you are only vaguely, if at all, aware of your surroundings. But suppose you now attend to a piece of furniture in front of you or to the side of you. Its image may have been falling upon your eye while you were reading, but it either elicited no conscious reaction or, at best, only a vague perception. Now, if you fixate upon it, the lens of your eye adjusts so as to bring it into better focus on your retina. This makes it clear and its details distinct.

Although receptor adjustment plays a part in clarifying perception, it is not solely responsible. One may have a perfectly clear retinal image, yet — especially if he is preoccupied with his thoughts — fail to have a corresponding visual perception.

Postural adjustments and muscle tensions also fail to tell the whole story. The student in a classroom may be in a posture of rapt attention, but, when called upon by the teacher to recite on what has just been said, he may reveal that his thoughts have been far away from the classroom situation.

Are there independent central controls?

The receptor and neural adjustments so far considered are largely peripheral phenomena, even though they must also involve the central nervous system and, in particular, the cerebral cortex. Is there, however, a purely central attending process? Can we attend with our cerebral cortex independently of peripheral activities? It would be easy to answer this question if we could find some way to measure brain functions without at the same time evoking receptor and postural changes. The problem is similar to that already discussed in the chapter on thinking, where the question was raised as to whether thought can occur without peripheral activities. There we cited the case of a completely paralyzed man (p. 414) who apparently retained an awareness of what was happening around him and was still able to think.[11] Presumably, therefore, his attentive process was operating on a purely nonmuscular basis. Postural contributions were eliminated, but the subject's receptors were still functioning. Because of this we

● **16.4**
A Reversible Configuration. If you fixate the center, or any other part of this figure, you will note that now one aspect, now the other stands out. At one moment, for example, you see the black figure as though on a white background; the next moment you see the white figure as though on a black background. The frequency of such figure-ground fluctuations can be influenced by trying to hold one as long as possible. The figure will change, despite your effort to hold it, but it will very likely change less often.

cannot claim that he exhibited a purely central attentiveness.

Some perceptual phenomena do suggest the possibility of an independent central attending process. Take, for example, the fluctuations which occur in hearing when the sound of a watch fades out or reappears; and in vision when a dim star seems to come and go. Reversible configurations like the one in Figure 16.4 are also relevant. Some hypnotic phenomena likewise suggest the presence of centrally maintained sets either to attend or not to attend to stimulation. Thus a hypnotized subject may be rendered apparently inattentive to painful stimulation. Teeth have been pulled and operations performed under hypnosis, yet without there being any evidence

of pain. On the other hand, if the subject is told that a pencil is a red-hot object, he will show all of the signs of being hurt as it is placed on his skin. Phenomena like these suggest some sort of central control which is independent of receptor and postural activities. But, because receptor and/or postural changes may be involved, such evidence must be regarded as inconclusive.

Experimental investigations focused upon this issue have sometimes yielded data in support of a purely central attending process, but the evidence is equivocal.[12] Thus, while central adjustments are intimately involved in attending, there is as yet no conclusive evidence that they are ever independent of receptor and postural adjustments.

Some of the central neural correlates of attention are being revealed by research on cerebral activities concomitant with the act of attending. ■

THE SEARCH FOR NEURAL CORRELATES

There is much neurophysiological support for the concept of attending as a preperceptive act — as a getting ready to perceive. Some of this support is very recent. It has long been known that attention to visual and other stimuli, and even to one's own thought processes, tends to suppress the alpha rhythm, described earlier (pp. 58, 200) in our discussion of electroencephalograms (EEGs). There is evidence that it is the *act of attending*, and not external stimulation as such, that flattens the alpha rhythm.[13] Similar findings have appeared in research with cats and monkeys.[14] We know from these observations that the EEGs of an attentive organism differ from those of an inattentive one and it has been surmised from this that the flattening of the alpha rhythm in man, and of comparable rhythms in animals, is associated with a readiness of the cerebral cortex to react to incoming impulses. Recent studies on the reticular formation of the brain stem (pp. 52, 159) appear to substantiate this notion. We pointed out in an earlier discussion (p. 159) that the reticular formation is activated from below (through collaterals from

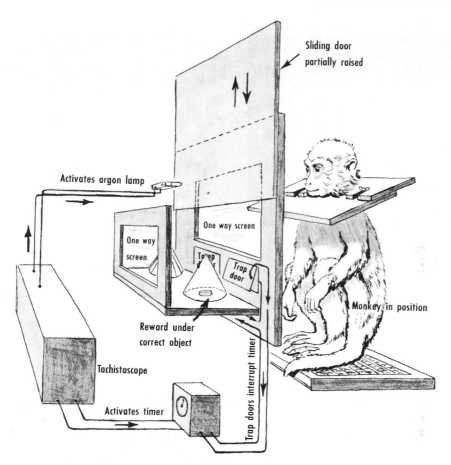

Sliding door
partially raised

Activates argon lamp

One way screen

One way
screen

Trap
door

Trap
door

Monkey in position

Reward under
correct object

Trap doors interrupt timer

Tachistoscope

Activates timer

● 16.5

Monkey Discriminating Tridimensional Objects. Monkeys were first trained to discriminate between white tridimensional objects which differed in shape. The above pair comprised a cone and a twelve-sided pyramid. One object of a pair, in this case the cone, had a food reward under it. The right-left position of the correct object was varied randomly. After looking through the screen, the animal reached for an object via the appropriate trap door. If this response was correct, toppling the object gave access to the reward. If it was wrong, the sliding door was lowered and no reward was obtained for that trial. The animal viewed the objects against a dark background. During initial training the objects were given unlimited exposure. In later tests, however, they were exposed momentarily during a flash of the argon lamp, the exposure time being determined by a tachistoscope, a device about which more will be said later (p. 509). Each exposure was preceded by an auditory alerting signal. This caused the monkey to watch for the stimuli, exposed two seconds later. When the flash came, the subject, after making his observation, opened the trap door and, if correct, secured his reward. As expected, the reaction time was slower and the discriminations increasingly inaccurate as the exposure time was shortened. But what is of special interest in terms of our present discussion is the fact that the same subjects, when stimulated with a mild electric current within the reticular formation, were consistently faster and more accurate than under control conditions. The implanted electrodes do not appear here. (From J. M. Fuster, "Effects of Stimulation of Brain Stem on Tachistoscopic Perception," *Science,* 1958, *127,* p. 150.)

the projection pathways) and also from above (by impulses originating in the cerebral cortex). Activated by ascending impulses, the reticular formation discharges diffusely to the cortex, alerting it for the reception of sensory information. Descending impulses may also activate the reticular formation in such a manner that there is a feedback to the cerebral cortex. However, these impulses sometimes have an inhibitory effect, as will become apparent shortly.

We have already discussed the relatively new technique (pp. 160–162) of implanting electrodes at various places within an animal's nervous system so that neurons can be stimulated electrically, or electrical potentials picked up from them while they are activated. These techniques have also been used to study interactions between the reticular formation and the cerebral cortex. In most of these studies the subjects have been cats and monkeys. One finding that is highly relevant to the above discussion is the observation that when the reticular formation is electrically stimulated the animal becomes alert. At the same time there is a decrease in amplitude of the resting brain rhythm — a result comparable to the flattening of the alpha rhythm during attention in man. This of course gives added support to the view that the reticular formation is an alerting mechanism. But what is of even greater significance is the finding that discrimination and speed of reaction in monkeys is improved during electrical stimulation of the reticular formation. For details of this experiment, see Figure 16.5. These results suggest that this electrical stimulation of the reticular activating system made the animals more attentive to external stimulation than they would normally be.[15] Another investigation, this time with cats, involved electrodes implanted in various regions of the auditory cortex.[16] Although activity was recorded at some of the electrodes whenever an auditory stimulus was presented, activity at others seemed contingent upon the cat showing obvious signs of attending to the stimulus — signs like turning its head, looking at it, or appearing to listen. The authors therefore concluded that some "neural processes responsible for attention play an important role in determining whether or not a given acoustic stimulus proves adequate." In view of other evidence, it would not be surprising to find the reticular formation implicated in this result.

Descending fibers that feed into the reticular formation may have a great deal to do with the selectivity of attending — i.e., attentiveness to certain stimuli but not to others, as in our examples of mental set. As suggested earlier (pp. 159–160), impulses coming from the cerebral cortex itself may activate the reticular formation in such fashion that an alerting feedback occurs, comparable with that associated with ascending impulses which originate in the receptors. This might occur when, for example, the organism looks and listens even though relevant external stimulation is absent. It would be an instance of what was referred to earlier as "voluntary attending." Although descending impulses may have this sort of alerting function, some of them apparently have an inhibitory effect. This is suggested by experiments[17] in which cats had recording electrodes implanted in the cochlear nucleus — the part of the brain stem to which impulses come from the cochlea and from which they are shunted to upper levels of the brain, including the thalamus and cerebral cortex. When clicks were made near the cat's ear, there was a quite evident increase in the amplitude of the recorded response of the cochlear nucleus, as shown in Figure 16.6, upper and lower records. But when the same clicks were made while a fish odor was being sniffed, or while the cat was looking at mice in a glass jar, the spike that was formerly evident disappeared. In short, when the cat was not attending to something else, the cochlear nucleus responded to an auditory stimulus, but when attention was elsewhere it failed to respond. Whenever the extraneous attention-demanding stimulus was removed, the cochlear nucleus again responded to the clicks. Evidently, then, there is some neural mechanism associated with attention which is selective — which blocks one kind of input when another is of greater significance to the organism. Although there was nothing in the experiment that we have described which would indicate how this blocking occurred — i.e., the neural

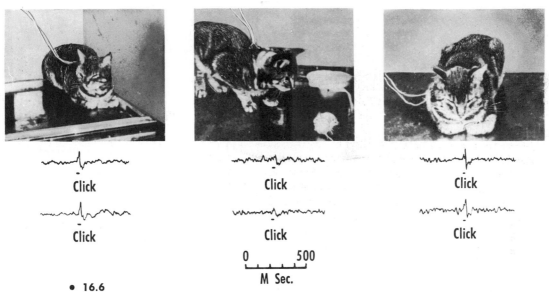

● 16.6

Responses of the Cat's Cochlear Nucleus. The cochlear nucleus of the resting cat gave a marked response (spike) every time the click was presented (first and last pictures). However, when white mice in a jar were presented, the cat assumed attentive postures (middle picture) and the neural response to the click was either greatly reduced, as illustrated, or completely absent. (From R. Hernández-Peón, H. Scherrer, and M. Jouvet, "Modification of Electrical Activity in Cochlear Nucleus during 'Attention' in Unanesthetized Cats," *Science*, 1956, *123*, p. 332.)

mechanism responsible for it — there is other research[18] which shows that electrical stimulation of a certain part of the reticular formation has a comparable effect upon sound-induced potentials from the cochlear nucleus. It appears possible, then, that impulses descending from a portion of the cortex preoccupied with one kind of stimulation may activate the reticular formation in such a manner as to block irrelevant sensory input. ■

DETERMINERS OF ATTENTION

There has been a large volume of research on the attention-getting value of different aspects of external stimulation. The findings, as one might guess, have proved extremely valuable in the field of advertising. An advertiser's problem is to sell his product, but before he can induce you to buy it, he must call your attention to it and to the reasons for preferring it to other products. As you turn the pages of a magazine, scan the newspaper, listen to your radio, or watch television, there are many things more interesting than observing what an advertiser has to say about his wares. Hence, he must literally force you to attend. Any advertisement which produced involuntary attention, and then caused you to hold your attentive set, would be most effective. Successful advertisers use external stimuli which will "catch your eye" or "get your ear," and at the same time tap your motives.

External determiners

Among the important external determiners of attention are the nature, location, intensity, size, color, motion, repetition, and novelty of the stimulating conditions.

By the nature of visual stimulating conditions we refer to such things as whether a picture is that of a woman, an animal, or a product to be sold. By the nature of auditory stimulation we refer to such things as a narration, singing, or orchestral music. It has been shown, among other things, that pictures attract attention more readily than words; that a picture with human beings in it tends to attract attention more than a picture of inanimate objects alone; and that a particular rhyming auditory passage attracts attention better than the same passage presented as a narrative.

The best location of a visual stimulus from the standpoint of attention-getting is directly in front of the eyes. Where this is not possible, there are still certain positions that are better than others. Research in advertising has discovered the attention value of various positions, not only within a magazine, but also on a given page. This research has utilized eye-cameras like those already mentioned.

Intensity is exemplified by a brilliantly lighted sign or the blaring of a loud-speaker. As you read this **sentence,** you can hardly escape noticing the word printed in bold type. You probably noticed it as soon as you turned to the page. Here we have not only intensity, but contrast. The heavy black letters, because of their relative intensity, stand out from surroundings. Intense odors, tastes, pressures, and pains, especially when they represent a sudden change from previous stimulation, also elicit attention.

The size of a stimulus is of obvious importance, but again contrast is an important aspect. If all of the LETTERS on this page were printed in capitals, the capitalized word in this sentence would have no greater attention-getting value than any other word; if all were printed in small type, the word with small type would have no advantage. Generally speaking, a large advertisement will get more attention than a small one, especially when the latter is surrounded by other material. But an extremely small advertisement in the center of a page that is otherwise blank is a strong determiner of attention.

Some colors are more agreeable than others, and advertisers make use of this fact. Reds and blues play a large part in color displays because of their agreeableness. But here again, contrast is important. The word in gold

was no doubt noticed long before you read this paragraph. It would not matter what the color had been. Color advertising derives some of its attention-getting value not so much from the colors or color combinations used as from the fact that, being colored, it stands out from the black and white which characterizes most of the other material in the magazine.

Other things being equal, a moving object is more attention-demanding than a stationary one. This is true for animals. Many an animal is safe from others so long as it keeps still, but as soon as it moves, it is pounced upon. The large neon signs typical of Broadway illustrate the value of moving stimuli. These also utilize another distinctive phenomenon, to be considered shortly.

Repetition is a factor of great importance in drawing attention to some aspect of our environment. When a stimulus is repeated several times, we may eventually notice it, although we failed to do so at first. Despite the value of repetition in calling attention to a stimulus, continued repetition beyond a certain point may bring diminishing returns. We may eventually become so accustomed to the situation that it ceases to be noticed. Advertisers get around this by introducing change, and especially novelty.

Most of us attend to anything that is novel. Sounds, smells, and tastes to which we are accustomed may go unnoticed, whereas a strange sound, smell, or taste is immediately noticed. Strange animals and unusual dress or furnishings attract attention because of their novelty. Use of novelty to attract attention is but another example of contrast. Anything that is novel derives this property through its contrast with what is customary. To put it in other terms, either a familiar item in novel surroundings or a novel object in familiar surroundings is usually attention-getting.

Internal determiners

External factors are potent to the degree that they tap, as it were, our continuing sets, i.e., the internal determiners, which were referred to in the discussion of habits of attention. These determiners stem from motives.

If the individual is motivated by hunger, he is much more likely to notice the smell of cooking food or to see the picture of steak on a magazine page than if he has just had a good meal. The sexually deprived male is much more likely to notice females than is the sexually satiated one.

Advertising agencies and other organizations concerned with mass persuasion have become interested in probing unconscious motives, as revealed by projective tests and psychoanalysis, so that they can capitalize on these "internal determiners of action."* This attempt to manipulate human beings by "getting at them below their level of awareness" is the subject of Vance Packard's well-known book *The Hidden Persuaders.***

It bears repeating that, in many respects, attending is one process and perceiving another. Attending may or may not be followed by perception. When it is, however, the perceptual process itself demands analysis. ∎

BASIC ASPECTS OF VISUAL PERCEPTION

Visual perception involves an extremely complex series of events over and beyond those already described in discussing visual reception. In that discussion we were considering elementary visual processes, often referred to as visual *sensations*, and the question before us was how the intensive and wavelength characteristics of light are sensed by the organism — how they arouse experiences of brightness and color. What we perceive, however, is not just white, gray, black, or hues, but *objects* having various achromatic or chromatic char-

---

* See E. Dichter, *Handbook of Consumer Motivations*. McGraw-Hill, 1964.
** This type of persuasion is different from that which attempts to influence the buyer by stimulating him so weakly that he is unaware of the fact that he has been stimulated. Such stimulation is below the threshold of visual perception. Another word for threshold is *limen*; hence this sort of influence is said to be *subliminal*. Actually, as several studies have shown, the effectiveness of subliminal advertising is doubtful.[19] It is worthy of note, in any event, that a threshold is ordinarily determined by statistical means, and that one can not always know when a presentation is slightly above or slightly below the threshold.

acteristics. Nor do we merely perceive objects. We perceive situations in which objects stand out against backgrounds. That is, we perceive *figure-ground* relationships. Some rather obvious examples have already been given of how the background (or context) of figures may change their lightness (p. 460), their hue (p. 464), and what they appear to be, as in fluctuating figure-ground relationships. We turn our attention now to some other basic perceptual phenomena.

It is interesting to observe, at the outset, that visual perception requires stimulus change. The environment must, so to speak, lack homogeneity. If the eye looks into a homogeneously lighted sphere, there is an impression of inpenetrable fog, close at hand. Quite frequently, what appears to be a blackout is reported. Subjects report "Foggy whiteness, everything blacks out, returns, goes. I feel blind. I'm not even seeing blackness. This differs from the black when lights are out."[20] According to the investigator, "It may be conjectured that the perceptual mechanism has evolved to cope with a differentiated field, and, in the absence of differentiation, there is a temporary breakdown of the mechanism." When a hue, such as red, is introduced into the homogeneous field, the colored fog gradually changes to gray.[21] Introduction of a figure into the previously homogeneous field changes the appearance of the fog. A figure-ground relationship develops, and the foglike background is seen as closer or more distant.

Normally the eye scans what is before it and, even though the object does not move, there is movement of its image across the retina. Even when called upon to look steadily at an object, the subject cannot hold his eyes perfectly still. They move, despite his efforts to keep them steady; thus the retinal image is far from stationary. What would happen, however, if the retina were stimulated by a stabilized or "stopped" image? The eye itself cannot be immobilized without deleterious effects. However, means have been found to make a viewed target move in perfect unison with eye movements, thus making its retinal image stand still. One method is to attach a small mirror to a contact lens on the eye and have the target figure reflected from this to a

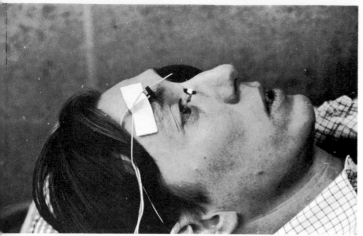

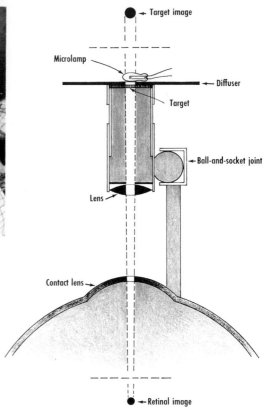

← Target image

Microlamp

← Diffuser

Target

← Ball-and-socket joint

Lens

Contact lens →

← Retinal image

● **16.7**

Stabilizing Retinal Images. As described in the text, this device provides images which move as the eye moves. Such stabilized or "stopped" images give rise to perceptions which fade and reappear instead of having the stability of images perceived under normal conditions. (Photo, courtesy *Scientific American* and Dr. Roy M. Pritchard. Diagram of the optical system redrawn from *Canadian Journal of Psychology*, 1960, *14*, p. 69.)

screen on which the subject views it through a special optical system.[22] Thus the target moves as the eye moves, so that its image stands still on the retina. A simpler method, illustrated in Figure 16.7, attaches the entire optical system to a contact lens on the eye.[23] With either procedure, what happens is that, within a few seconds, a stabilized image fades. If the target is a line, it fades and disappears completely within a few seconds. Target figures of greater complexity also fade and disappear, but often with one part going at a time. If the figure is a triangle, for example, one side or the base will fade out, or two sides, or the base and a side, before the entire figure disappears. Regeneration of the figure also occurs in time, often with fragments reappearing before the entire figure is re-established. Then it disappears again. A circle that is half blue and half white becomes completely achromatic, first with a brightness difference between the two halves, then as a uniformly gray area. These are just a few of the phenomena associated with a stabilized retinal image.

There are many others, and efforts are being made to explain why a stabilized image should produce such perceptual effects. There is no clear answer as yet; but we need only note, in this context, that visual perception normally involves, indeed requires, stimulus change.

The visual experiences associated with a homogeneously illuminated environment and with a stabilized retinal image are no doubt dependent, in the last analysis, upon the nature of our visual receptors and the structure and physiological functions of our nervous system. The same is true of certain illusions which all of us experience. These appear to be independent of previous relevant experience, hence we may regard them as "primitive organizations" of perception; that is, organizations imposed upon us by the nature of stimuli and the way in which our sensory and neural mechanisms are constructed. It is interesting to observe, in this connection, that animals, children, and primitive people behave as if the stimulating properties of some of these situations were the same for them as for us.

Visual illusions

Illusions are "false" perceptions. When we experience an illusion, we experience certain things which fail to correspond with the situation as objectively measured. Illusions should not, however, be confused with hallucinations.*

• *The Müller-Lyer illusion.* This is illustrated in Figure 16.8. You, in common with all other normal adults, will say that the vertical line in A looks shorter than that in B. Children old enough to indicate the nature of their experience give a comparable report. Some animals react as though they also see what we see. The following experiment with chickens illustrates the procedure and outcome of such an experiment.

□ Two lines of obviously different length to the experimenter and, as it turned out, of obviously different length to the chickens, were presented in a discrimination apparatus. The shorter line appeared on the right side of the discrimination chamber in some trials, and on the left side in others, the side being alternated in a chance order. The longer line always appeared on the opposite side to the shorter one. The chickens were trained to discriminate between them by approaching the shorter line and avoiding the longer. Whenever they approached the shorter line, they received food. Approaching the longer line brought punishment in the form of an electric shock. After several hundred trials (the number differing

* Hallucinations may also be thought of as inaccurate perceptions, or, as some prefer to say, dreamlike images which are mistaken for objectively measurable external phenomena. They differ from illusions in certain important respects. In the first place, although we all experience illusions, few of us ever have hallucinations. While normal people sometimes experience them, hallucinations are usually confined to the mentally ill and those under the influence of drugs. In the second place, illusions always have a clearly apparent external stimulus. Hallucinations sometimes occur when there is no apparent objective stimulus. In the third place, the same situation arouses the same illusion in all subjected to it. That is why we class it with primitive organizations. On the other hand everybody who has an hallucination under particular circumstances has a different hallucination. When one person sees red devils, another may see snakes, or dragons, or executioners.

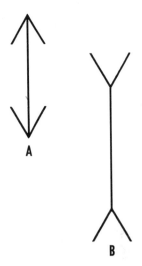

● 16.8
The Müller-Lyer Illusion. Which vertical seems longer from apex to apex, A or B? They are actually the same length.

from one chicken to another), discrimination reached an accuracy of from 80 to 90 per cent. The difference in length of the lines was then gradually reduced. Moreover, changes in the figures were made so that the chickens would not be disturbed later by introduction of arrows. It is important to note that the changes introduced could by no means be considered training for perception of the illusion, for they introduced no illusory effects. Finally, two lines of equal length, but each bounded by arrows as in the illustration, were introduced. Most animals continued to discriminate (as accurately as they had discriminated the shorter line), the line that to us appears shorter. It was, of course, possible that they were reacting to the overall length of the figure (including ends of arrows) rather than to the horizontal lines as such. That this was not the case was shown by control experiments. When the overall length of the figures was made the same, by decreasing the length of the line whose arrows flanged outward (the negative figure), there was a marked tendency to choose this, the figure previously avoided. Since the central line of this figure was now actually shorter than that of the other, although the overall length of

The Effect of Apparent Distance on Size. The two rectangles are of exactly the same size, yet the one seen on the horizon appears larger than that in the foreground. It is worthy of note that, "the effect would be much greater in viewing a truly three-dimensional scene, where binocular and other cues would enhance the impression of depth. Conversely, the effect can be increased by viewing the picture with only one eye, because the impression of the two-dimensional surface of the page can be somewhat reduced." (From I. Rock and L. Kaufman, "The Moon Illusion," *Science*, 1962, *136*, p. 1029.)

the figure was the same, it suggests that the chicks had really been responding to the central line all along.[24] □

The Müller-Lyer illusion is just one of many that psychologists have studied. There would be no point in mentioning more of these except two that are of particular interest, as well as being commonly experienced by all of us. One of these is the moon illusion. The other is the illusion of apparent motion.

• *The moon illusion.* Everyone has observed that the moon looks relatively small at its zenith and that, as it approaches the horizon, it appears to grow larger. Note, in this connection, that the retinal image formed by the moon on our retina remains constant throughout this change in the moon's apparent size. Why, then, do we perceive such a change? The answer to this question has puzzled philosophers and astronomers from ancient times. Ptolemy, the second-century astronomer of Alexandria, explained the illusion in this way. He pointed out, first of all, that the images of the overhead and horizon moon have the same optical size. He noted, in the second place, that the horizon moon is seen across a terrain whereas the overhead moon is seen through empty space. He called attention to the fact that objects viewed along a terrain seem farther away than objects at the same distance viewed through empty space. Ptolemy then concluded that the horizon moon looks larger than the zenith moon because it is seen as more distant. That is to say, when objects have retinal images of the same size and one is judged as farther away, the latter is perceived as larger.

□ We see an example of this in Emmert's law about the size of an after-image projected upon surfaces at different distances. If the reader will look at some object, say a white disc on a black background or vice versa, long enough to obtain a clear after-image, he may demonstrate this law for himself. The image projected upon a sheet of paper nearby is small. Projected on the ceiling, it is large. It will be perceived as of intermediate sizes when projected at distances between those mentioned. The retinal image, of course, is constant in size throughout, yet the perceived figure is larger when viewed, as it were, at a greater distance. □

Observe, also, that the black rectangle in Figure 16.9 looks larger when seen in a context simulating distance than when viewed as if close by. Here we have something resembling a terrain between the observer and the object. It should be pointed out, however, that the significance of terrain is not to make the object (moon, rectangle, or whatever one is viewing) larger by comparison with objects in the same apparent vicinity. The moon looks larger than a house when viewed in the same context, but it looks equally as large seen across a calm sea or a flat desert. Thus it is the perceived distance as such which makes us see it as larger on the horizon than high in the sky. These facts, and others revealed by recent research with simulated moons studied under laboratory conditions, provide support for Ptolemy's explanation of the moon illusion.[25] There is evidence, also, that having to raise the head (or eyes) to view the zenith moon

may contribute to our perception of it as smaller than the horizon moon.[26]

• *Illusions of apparent motion.* We all experience the illusion of movement when we look at a motion picture, yet few realize what is really taking place. A succession of still pictures (Figure 16.10), projected one after the other at a suitable rate, gives us the illusion that movement occurs. This illusion is known as the *phi-phenomenon*. We see it not only in the movies but also in many electrical advertising signs. The red arrow which appears to move from one position to another does not really move. Two arrows in different positions are flashed on one after the other. Likewise, the greyhound on the bus signs does not really move. We see it running because different positions of the body involved in running are successively lighted at appropriate intervals.

The phi-phenomenon is often studied experimentally by using an apparatus which allows presentation of two or more lights, one after the other.[27] Such an arrangement of lights is: ◯   ◯. Experimental research has shown that, in order to get the illusion, one must present the lights at an appropriate brightness, size, distance apart, and temporal interval. If the size, brightness, and distance between the lights are held constant, and you view the situation from a fixed distance, the timing factor may be clearly demonstrated. If there is too long an interval between flashes, you see one light go on and then the other. There is no apparent movement. If the interval between flashes is too short, you see two lights flashing at approximately the same time. However, if one flash follows the other at an appropriate interval (the interval depending upon the space between the lights, their size, and their brightness), you see a light move from one position to the other. That is to say, you see not two lights, but one that appears to move across the space where no light actually exists.

□ This illusion is not confined to human adults. Children and animals behave as though influenced by it. The following experiments with cats and guinea pigs are especially interesting.

The animal is clamped into a holder, but

● 16.10

Successive Frames from a Motion Picture. What is projected upon the screen is merely a series of still pictures like these, each slightly different from the preceding one. Observe, for example, the position of the right knee in successive frames. The perceived motion is an illusion. In commercial motion pictures a sequence of events somewhat as follows takes place: a shutter cuts out all projected light, and a new frame with a slightly different picture on it moves into place. The shutter opens and an unmoving picture is projected on the screen. A shutter cuts across this still picture while it remains in position, thus increasing the frequency of flickering interruptions and producing less perceptible flicker. The shutter once again cuts across the field, and a new frame moves up, stops, and is held still. The whole sequence is then repeated for that picture. Thus, there is never any objective movement on the screen itself, which would be seen only as a blur, but rather one sees in a moving picture the most beautiful example possible of synthetic movement.

with its head free to move. Its eyes face the inside surface of a rotating cylinder covered with alternate vertical black and white stripes. As these stripes move by in a clockwise (or left-right) direction, the animals exhibit typical right-left head movements (head nystagmus). Thus their eyes follow a stripe momentarily and then return to the original position. Under normal conditions the nystagmic movements are elicited only when stripes are present and when these are actually moving. Human beings react in a similar manner to such stimulation.[28]

So far we have described the reaction to actual movement of the striped pattern. However, the same reaction occurs when the stripes do not actually move, but are flashed on in successive positions. This successive presentation of the stripes is produced by use of stroboscopic illumination. The whole inside of the apparatus is dark, except at intervals when the light flashes on. The cylinder moves all the time, but the stripes can stimulate the eye only during a flash determined by the stroboscope. The flashes are synchronized with the moving drum in such a manner that the eye is stimulated by stripes which appear in first one position, then another, without perceptible real movement. This resembles the successive frames of a movie film with intervals of darkness between. Now the animal still acts as though it were being stimulated by moving stripes. These results "seem significant in suggesting that the capacity for apparent movement vision is a fundamental aspect of mammalian vision and is not, as has been implied by some theories, a perceptual capacity based primarily upon some process of learning or acquired perceptual interpretation." The same results are obtained when the cerebral hemispheres are removed. This shows that the phenomenon, at least in guinea pigs and cats, is mediated by mechanisms in the brain stem or retina or both. □

It has been clearly demonstrated that the illusion of apparent motion is not based upon eye movements, for, with two sets of lights, like those referred to but with one set above the other, an observer simultaneously sees one light moving from right to left (above) and one moving from left to right (below). That is, he perceives movement in two different directions at the same time, something which would be impossible if movement of the eyes from one position to the other were necessary. Nor is the phi-phenomenon due to images. If a light moved across the space between the two positions, we might have after-images of it. Since it does not actually move, there are no after-images representing intermediate stimulation. The phenomenon is apparently dependent upon some rather stereotyped reactions of our visual receptors, or nervous system, or both, to the stimulus relationships involved.[29]

Perceptual constancy

The Müller-Lyer illusion, the moon illusion, and the phi-phenomenon illustrate that what one perceives does not always correspond with what is before him. The so-called constancy phenomenon is a further illustration of this fact, although it perhaps has a quite different explanation. It is the tendency to perceive objects as constant, even though they stimulate us in a variety of ways.

Size constancy is easily demonstrated. Look at some familiar object, say a coin, a pencil, or a book. Hold it close to your eyes. Does the object look smaller as you move it away (thus providing a retinal image of rapidly decreasing size) and larger as you move it closer? The chances are that it does not. It will look smaller only when it is moved much farther away than the length of your arm. *Brightness* (or lightness) *constancy* is illustrated by looking at a familiar object and failing to see its brightness change while changes in illumination are introduced. One can illuminate a piece of coal until the amount of light entering the eye is greater than that received from a white shirt, yet the coal will still appear black and the shirt white. *Form constancy* is exemplified every time we perceive a plate as round when, because of its position with respect to the eye, the image is actually elliptical. Likewise, the square table top is continually seen to be the same square, although, as we look at it from different positions, the image on the retina undergoes a variety of changes. These constancy phenomena are taken into consideration when the artist wishes to create an impression of reality. For example, if he draws a square table top as square from a position in which it is actually impressed upon the retina as a diamond, it looks unnatural to us. He must draw it as a diamond for us to see it as a square.[30]

Relative constancy of perceived objects has obvious utility to the organism. Think of the confusion that would exist if we were to respond to every aspect of our world in terms of its visual image alone. Objects would be seen to shrink or enlarge as the retinal image varied in size, to change their brightness or color as corresponding retinal changes occurred. But, within certain limits, we see things as we "know" them to be, despite what the retinal picture alone would tell us. Everything else we know tells us that they are constant.

Consider size constancy again. Although an object is perceived as being of the same size despite a decreasing retinal size, there is a distance beyond which the object *does* seem to shrink in size. What we do, however, is to perceive it not as smaller, really, but *at a greater distance.** Therefore, there must be some sort of compromise between seeing a thing as constant in size (when near) and as smaller in size when far from us. This is, of course, not an explanation of size constancy. We still need to know whether the tendency to make such a compromise is inborn or acquired, or based upon some interrelation of inherent and learned tendencies. If it is learned, we are certainly not aware of the cues that we use in seeing things as constant under certain circumstances and as changing under others. It is interesting to observe, however, that size constancy is greatly dependent upon the context in which an object is viewed. Laboratory experiments have been performed which reveal size constancy in certain contexts and its absence when there has been nothing but the size of the retinal image of the object to go by. That is to say, with context removed, the size of the retinal image determines the perceived

---

* In the case of the moon illusion, of course, the size of the retinal image remains constant and our perception of the horizon moon as more distant than the zenith moon gives us the illusion that it is larger.

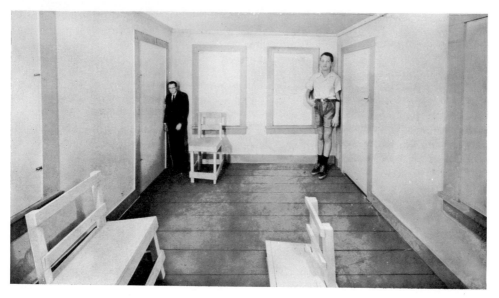

● **16.11**

How Our Eyes Can Deceive Us. When the man and the boy change places, the man looks very large and the boy looks very small. The room (see one like it in the Appendix, p. 605) is actually very much distorted, yet it seems normal as viewed here. (Photographed by Eric Schaal, *Life,* © Time, Inc.)

size of the object.[31] In unusual contexts, moreover, known sizes are greatly distorted. An example of this is seen in Figure 16.11. Here, also, we have something of distorted shape (a room) that is perceived as normal. Shape constancy is greatly dependent upon what we know about the objects perceived, and their relationships to other objects. In changed contexts, shape constancy may also disappear. Similarly with brightness constancy. Brightly illuminated coal in an otherwise completely black room takes on a silvery appearance instead of maintaining its blackness. Likewise, a white object, viewed under conditions in which its context and recognizable characteristics are lost, also fails to show brightness constancy. Instead of retaining its whiteness, it becomes grayish in appearance, and a darker gray as illumination is reduced.[32]

Up to this point we have emphasized visual processes. But one should not get the idea that illusions are confined to visual perception. There are also tactual illusions.[33] Moreover, some illusory experiences occur in auditory localization and in the field of static sensitivity. These are discussed later in this chapter, in the context of space perception. It is reasonable to suppose, moreover, that constancy phenomena exist in other senses besides vision, even though, to the writer's knowledge, psychologists have not yet described any. ■

PRIMITIVE GROUPING

Among the basic aspects of perceiving, and cutting across the visual, tactual, and auditory senses, is a tendency for separate things to fall into meaningful configurations. As an elementary example of this, take these dots:

●●   ●●   ●●   ●●

Even though you may never have seen this particular pattern of dots before, it has a certain degree of organization or meaning for you.

You see the dots, not as so many dots, but as four pairs of dots. You probably noticed the grouping before you observed the number of dots. Moreover, the same general configuration (gestalt) would remain if these were white dots on black; if they were small squares instead of circles; if they were red, or yellow, or blue; and, in fact, if they were any visual objects that one might imagine.

The grouping is therefore independent of the particular parts (the dots, etc.) which serve to represent it.

Even outside of vision, the same grouping would remain. Thus, eight taps with a pencil, eight blasts on a trumpet, or almost any eight auditory stimulations imaginable, would produce the same perceptual configuration if presented in pairs with a perceptible time interval between each pair. Likewise, the essential aspect of the configuration would be retained if one were to arrange points of stimulation on the skin with a large enough distance between each of the paired points (and the pairs of points) to make them discriminable. You would experience four groups of paired points.[34]

The dot example is but one of many used to illustrate primitive groupings. Indeed there are various kinds of perceptual groupings, and several principles involved in their determination have been enunciated by gestalt psychologists who, as we pointed out earlier (p. 32), have been particularly interested in perceptual organization. Our illustration will suffice, however, to indicate the general nature of this approach, which is dealt with more adequately in books on perception.[35]

Most, if not all, of the perceptual phenomena discussed so far are greatly dependent upon the nature of our receptors and related neural mechanisms. That is to say, they are imposed upon us more by the way we are made than by what we have learned, even though learning no doubt has some influence in the case of constancy phenomena. Our ability to perceive *differences* in size, brightness, weight, and other aspects of the perceptual world is also largely determined by the structure of our sensory and neural mechanisms. These place definite limitations on the intensity of stimulation required for detection (the *absolute threshold*) and also on how small a difference can be detected (the *difference threshold*). It is with the latter that we will now be concerned. ■

PERCEIVING DIFFERENCES

How much must two stimuli differ before you can notice the difference? The answer depends on several things. Small differences, unless you are set to observe them, may pass unnoticed. They are, so to speak, below the threshold of discrimination. Let us assume, however, that you are set to observe small differences. Then the answer to our question depends upon (1) the relative size, intensity, etc., of the stimuli to be compared, (2) the sense stimulated, and (3) the manner in which the stimuli to be compared are presented to the subject.

If three candles are burning in a room and you add one, there will be a perceptible increase in the illumination of the room. As a matter of fact, the change will clearly be perceptible. It will be far above the threshold. However, if one hundred candles are burning and you add one, there may be a just perceptible or just noticeable difference (j.n.d.) in illumination. Suppose, now, that two hundred candles are burning and we add another. No matter how much you are set to perceive a small difference in illumination, you will not perceive the change. It will be below the threshold of discrimination. Likewise, one pound added to two or three pounds (or subtracted from two or three pounds) will lead to a clearly perceptible change in weight. The object will feel heavier or lighter, as the case may be. Add one pound to one hundred, however, and the difference in weight will not be noticed.

In an old psychology text[36] there is a description of an experiment carried out on a frog. The frog sat in water the temperature of which was gradually increased until it reached the boiling point. However, the animal failed to move. It was boiled alive without ever having made an effort to escape. Why? Because the increase in temperature was so gradual (was such a small proportion of the preceding temperature) that the frog could not at any moment sense an increase in temperature.

These simple illustrations suggest that, whether or not a difference in intensity is discriminated depends upon the ratio of the change in stimulus intensity to the intensity of stimulation existing prior to the change. In other words, whether one discriminates a difference between the intensity of stimulus *a* and stimulus *b* (or a difference in the correlated experiences *a* and *b*) depends upon what proportion the change from *a* to *b* is of *a*. This is known as *Weber's law*, so named because Weber, a German physiologist, whose work was referred to in Chapter 1 (pp. 7–8), first formulated it.*

□ In experimental investigations of Weber's law, one stimulus intensity is held constant and referred to as the standard intensity. We then determine what stimulus intensity can be just barely discriminated from the standard intensity. If Weber's law applies, the increase required is a constant fraction of the standard intensity. This fraction is referred to as the *constant*(*C*). When Weber's law applies, the j.n.d. may be found by using the formula $\triangle S/S = C$, where S is the standard stimulus intensity, $\triangle S$ the change in S required to produce a j.n.d. in intensity, and C the constant ratio.

If one candle added to one hundred produced a just noticeable difference in brightness, S would be 100; $\triangle S$, 1; and C, 1/100. Suppose that this ratio applied generally to brightness discrimination; then, how many candles would need to be added to five hundred in order to produce a j.n.d. in brightness? The answer is one to every hundred, or five. The increase (or decrease) must be one-hundredth of the preceding intensity, the standard intensity.

The Weber ratio (*C*) varies, depending upon the kind of sensitivity being measured. It is much smaller for visual than for auditory intensity, roughly 1/100 as compared with 1/5. It differs, also, with the range of intensities involved, being constant only within an intermediate intensity range.

* This general area of research is known technically as *psychophysics*. It deals with the relations between experienced intensity and physical intensity. The methods used to study these relationships are known as *psychophysical methods*.

There are several psychophysical methods, each of which yields a somewhat different ratio.[37] One of these, the method of just noticeable differences, will serve to illustrate how a visual j.n.d. for length of lines could be measured.

The subject is presented with two lines at a time, one of which is always the standard. He is asked in each case to say which of the two lines is the shorter. A standard line of 10 inches, say, is presented with each of several comparison lines. The standard line appears an equal number of times on the right and the left. When the subject sees a particular length as shorter than the standard about 75 per cent of the time, we say that the difference in length is the just noticeable (or the threshold) difference.

The standard length, let us say, is seen as shorter than a line of 10.5 inches 95 per cent of the time, as shorter than a line of 10.4 inches 87 per cent of the time, as shorter than a line of 10.3 inches 83 per cent of the time, as shorter than a line of 10.2 inches 80 per cent of the time, as shorter than a line of 10.1 inches 75 per cent of the time, and as shorter than a line of 10.09 inches 70 per cent of the time. In this case, unless a finer determination were desired, we would assume that 10.1 minus 10.00, or .1, is the threshold difference. The Weber ratio in this case is 1/100. □

The psychophysical methods have been used to develop the decibel scale of loudness (see Glossary), a scale used by physicists and sound engineers as well as psychologists. These methods have also been found useful in many other fields, including those of educational, social, business, and industrial psychology. They are useful whenever we wish to determine how much difference in something must be present before people can notice it. If some practical situation requires that certain differences be perceived, we make sure that the differences are well above the threshold of discrimination. ■

SET IN PERCEIVING

Although we have already considered attentive sets as predispositions to perceive, we have not dealt with them from the standpoint of how they can determine *what* is perceived. Sets of a relatively simple nature are aroused in the laboratory by instructing subjects so that they expect certain things to appear. How such instructional sets influence what is perceived will be considered presently. Sets of far greater complexity are those which each of us carries around with him in the form of prejudices, interests, values, and other such motivational aspects of his personality. Some of these, and their influence on perception, were dealt with in earlier chapters. After considering instructional sets we will draw together relevant material that is scattered through preceding chapters, then survey briefly some related experimental investigations. These deal with perceiving as a function of motivational sets, such as the personal values which an individual brings to an experimental situation.

Instructional sets

In laboratory experiments involving instructional sets the material to be perceived is ambiguous in that it is capable of inducing different perceptions. It is customarily presented for a very short interval — one too brief for the subject to make out all details. An instrument quite often used in such experiments is the tachistoscope, one form of which appears in Figure 16.12. The chief feature of any tachistoscopic device is that it enables an investigator to control the exposure time with great accuracy.

In one experiment of this general nature, different observers perceived different things, depending upon what they were led to expect.[38] Ambiguous figures like O——O , ⌒ , and ✳ were exposed, one at a time, for a brief interval. After each exposure, the subject made a reproduction of what he had seen. When subjects had been told that the figure O——O would be like a pair of glasses, they perceived something like this: ⊂○—○ Other subjects who saw the same figure under similar conditions, but who expected a dumbbell, drew reproductions like this: ⊂——⊐ If the subject had been told that he would see something like barbells, his drawing would probably have been more

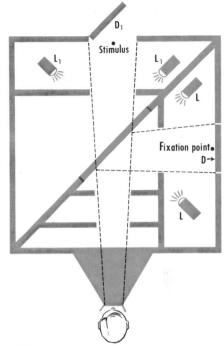

● **16.12**

One Type of Tachistoscope. Before exposure of the material to be perceived, the subject sees the fixation point on the diagonal lucite plate (gold), which acts like a half-silvered mirror, when the lights *L* are on. The stimulus material is placed on the hinged door at D_1 and this is closed. Now, as the other lights L_1 go on for the controlled exposure period, lights *L* go off, and the stimulus material is visible for the exposure period decided by the experimenter. The lamps are mercury argon tubes which have special advantages for this kind of research. This tachistoscope is a modification of earlier ones by Dodge (mirror tachistoscope). (After J. G. Merryman and H. E. Allen, "An Improved Electronic Tachistoscope," *Amer. J. Psychol,* 1953, 66, pp. 110–114.)

like the stimulus than it was when he was told that he would see something like glasses, or like a dumbbell. The second of the above figures was seen as ⌒ or ⌣ depending upon the expectancy that, respectively, a canoe or a kidney bean would appear. Likewise, depending upon the instructional set, the third figure was perceived as a ship's wheel (✳) or sun (✳).

A certain expectancy may be built up, during the course of an experiment, yet without specific verbal instructions like those above.

This expectation may also influence perception. In one such study the subjects were asked to judge which of two figures, the right or the left, constituted the more perfect geometrical design.[39] They had four seconds to examine each of eleven pairs. The subjects of the experimental group were shown a series in which the right-hand figure was always more symmetrical, while the control group was shown a series in which either the right-hand or the left-hand figure was more symmetrical. Thus the experimental group had a set for selecting right-hand figures and the control group had no such set. The crucial test of how this difference in sets might influence perceptual judgment came when a twelfth pair was presented. This comprised a square and a rectangle, with the square on the left. Although in no way ambiguous, these figures were so slightly different that close scrutiny would be necessary in order to say which was the square, hence the more perfectly symmetrical. Interestingly enough, the experimental group, with its "right-hand set," selected the rectangle in 81.2 per cent of the judgments. The control group, with no positional set, selected this figure in only 12.5 per cent of the judgments.

Motivationally determined sets

In earlier discussions we saw that such conditions as hunger and the desire to achieve may influence what individuals perceive in relatively unstructured situations. The picture on page 238 was perceived differently by those with and those without experimentally aroused achievement motivation. In discussing personality tests (pp. 273–274) we saw that a T.A.T. picture (or a Rorschach inkblot) brings different interpretations, depending upon motivational factors in the perceiver. In the ambiguous picture, for example, the person who regards his world as a threatening place will perceive signs of threat, like attackers, or "forces of evil." In the Rorschach test he may perceive bugs, or blood, or human beings "crushed by the forces of nature." The person with a different outlook will perceive none of these things.

This influence of motivational sets upon perception is by no means confined to vision.

Ambiguous sounds, or sounds at too low an intensity to be perceived for what they really are, likewise arouse different interpretations, and these may also stem from differences in motivational backgrounds. The same would be true if ambiguously shaped objects were felt by different subjects.[40]

The reader may recall, as relevant to the above, what was said earlier (p. 410) about direction in thinking. There a man misinterpreted his wife's actions and perceived the sounds of her footsteps as signals to her lover. The motivational set was jealousy. Other emotional states may likewise influence perception, as Shakespeare recognized.

> Or in the night, imagining some fear,
> How easy is a bush supposed a bear!
> *Midsummer Night's Dream*

Many of our motivational sets are based upon habit and these also influence what we perceive. The entomologist, being an expert on insects, perceives organisms which completely escape our observation. Likewise, an astronomer perceives much more in the heavens than those of us with no such habitual interest, even though we, also, may be gazing at the sky through a telescope.

Social psychologists have been particularly concerned with the relation between interests, attitudes, values, and other personality variables, and how the individual perceives aspects of his social environment. It has been said, for example, that,

☐ "perceptual readiness effects the dual requirements of coping with an environment — directedness with respect to goals and efficiency with respect to the means by which the goals can be attained. It is no matter of idle interest that a religious man picks up perceptually things that are relevant to his interest more easily and more quickly than other things, and at the same time this efficiency continues to reflect what is likely to occur in his surroundings. What it suggests is that once society has patterned a man's interests and trained him to expect what is likely in that society, it has gained a great measure of control not only on his thought processes, but also on the very material on which thought works — the experienced data of perception."[41] □

There is no doubt that an individual develops interests, attitudes, and values which lead him to expect, and hence to perceive, aspects of his environment which others fail to perceive. He finds in his environment the things that he is looking for, the sorts of things which conditioned him in the first place. By the same token, he tends to overlook, and sometimes actively avoid, aspects of the environment that are not consonant with his interests.

□ Despite the evidence of motivationally derived sets and their influence on perception in situations of everyday life, efforts to demonstrate them experimentally have been beset with difficulties. In one relevant experiment the subjects were first differentiated on the basis of their responses to the *Allport-Vernon* Study of Values* (p. 276).[42] This test, as we said earlier, rates individuals in terms of their predominant values — religious, economic, scientific, political, and so on. Thus the person who scores highest with respect to the items having to do with religion is rated as "religious"; the person scoring highest on political items is rated as "political," and so on. Now it is quite obvious that certain words in our language are "religiously toned" — words like *sacred, prayer,* and *reverent.* Others are "politically toned" — words such as *dominate, govern,* and *citizen.* What the investigators wanted to find out, therefore, was whether the "religious person," as indicated by the test, would perceive religious words more readily than, say, the politically, economically, or scientifically toned. Accordingly such words were exposed, one at a time in mixed-up order, in a tachistoscope. A word was shown three times at an exposure duration of .01 second. If the subject failed to name it correctly, it was exposed three more times, now with a duration of .02 second. This procedure was continued, with exposure times increasing by .01 second, until the word was correctly named. Then another word was exposed. This continued until a subject had

* This was the original version of the test, now the *Allport-Vernon-Lindzey Study of Values.*

named six words each in the areas of religious, economic, aesthetic, political, scientific, and social interests. Results were in the anticipated direction. Words in the area of a subject's major interest were usually recognized sooner, i.e., with fewer exposures, than other words. But there was a serious flaw in this experiment, which other investigators were quick to point out — the fact that a person usually has a larger vocabulary in the field of his major interest than in other fields. The "religious man," for example, knows more religious than political words. Knowing more religious words, or being more generally familiar with them, he might be expected to recognize such words for this reason, over and beyond any readiness, as such, to perceive what is religiously toned. The same principle might hold for other values. One possible solution to this methodological difficulty would be to use words which, regardless of their religious, economic, or other overtones, are equally familiar to all subjects. In an investigation involving this sort of control, the differences noted in the earlier research largely disappeared.[43]

One experiment in this general area seemed to demonstrate that its subjects had an unusual resistance to perceiving tabooed words such as *whore, bitch,* and *belly.*[44] When these were presented tachistoscopically, as in the above experiments, they were named more slowly than other words. But here again, serious objections were raised, one of which is that tabooed words are less familiar in everyday life than other words. Hesitancy to say such words, even when they were perceived, was possibly another contributing factor.[45] □

Long as our discussion of perceiving as a function of set has been, we have by no means mentioned every facet of this highly interesting topic. It appears, in general, that so long as one is working with relatively simple sets established in the laboratory, the results are clearly in support of the view that set influences what is perceived. Clinical data (T.A.T., Rorschach) and many observations from everyday life also support this view. But when attempts are made to subject some of man's most significant and complex sets to laboratory investigation, the variables are so complex and difficult to control that the experimental outcomes are far from clear-cut.■

PAST EXPERIENCE AND MEANING

Set is largely determined by past experience. The only aspects that are not so determined are those which stem rather directly from biological motives like hunger, thirst, and sex. But past experience gives us more than a set to perceive certain things. It determines, in large measure at least, the *meaning* of what we perceive. The exceptions to this are spatial meanings associated with inborn sensory and neural structures, already discussed as "primitive organizations." These underlie aspects of visual perception. The present discussion is confined to meanings that the individual has acquired.

The meaning of an object, situation, or event is in most instances dependent upon how it has stimulated us in the past and how we have previously reacted to it, emotionally and otherwise. Consider, for example, the perceptions which an apple may elicit at different stages of our perceptual development. Before we are old enough to eat an apple, one is perhaps rolled toward us in play. If this occurs sufficiently often, the apple means "something to play with." If balls have also been rolled toward us, the apple may be regarded as a ball. The apple is perhaps identifiable in terms of shape, size, weight, and color. Since all of these aspects stimulate us simultaneously, they may become associated so that any one or a combination of them arouses symbolic processes representing the others. Thus, something with a similar color arrangement and shape (say a picture of an apple) might arouse perceptual experiences somewhat like those aroused by a real apple. After we have eaten an apple, its taste is also associated with its other characteristics. The taste not only enables us to identify the substance as apple, but also may arouse imagery representing other things previously associated with the taste of apple. Moreover, the apple now means something to eat, not merely something to play with. As we learn about Adam and Eve, drink apple cider, eat apple pie, take part in apple dunking contests, learn about apple tree swings, and make love under apple trees, the object "apple" comes to have increasingly rich meaning. Any one of an apple's properties may arouse rich perceptual experience. This does not mean, of course, that we always perceive all of an object's meaning. The point is that we *may* perceive it, in terms of any experience formerly associated with it.

New situations are often fitted, as it were, into the individual's experiential background. Thus, a little girl who saw a caterpillar for the first time called it "a kitty bug." Another who was used to statues of the "Holy Mother" called the Nelson statue in Trafalgar Square "a Holy Daddy." A boy whose father taught in a college building with a clock tower interpreted every other building with a clock tower as a college. Upon further contact with objects and situations, each of us brings his interpretations more in line with reality.

Here are further illustrations of the fact that, in perceiving the new, we utilize our background of earlier experience.

□ People born blind because of cataracts sometimes gain their vision during childhood or later, by having their cataracts removed. For these people, objects presented visually for the first time have very limited meaning.[46] A face known to the patient through touch is not recognized by sight alone. It becomes recognizable in terms of vision only after the person has both felt and looked at it. As another example, let us suppose that the person who has been blind and has merely felt the difference between a ball and a cube is shown these objects. He sees that the two objects are different but he cannot identify them as a ball and a cube until he has an opportunity both to see and to feel them at the same time.

A chimpanzee reared in darkness for periods ranging from seven months to over a year, and then taken into the light, also failed to perceive visually what had been known to it through its other senses. Take, for example, the feeding bottle. The animal had held it in her hands and smelled and tasted its contents. But, when she saw it for the first time, she failed to respond to it as a milk bottle. Indeed

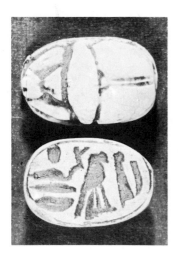

● 16.13

How Many Objects Can You Identify? Although the objects actually differ in size, none of them is longer, or wider, than three inches. After you have identified as many as you can, check your identifications with those on page 605 and with the identifications made by other students. How would you explain the differences?

she made no response to it at all. If the bottle touched her face, however, it aroused the usual reaction to a familiar bottle. She grasped it and sucked. More than thirty feedings in the light were necessary, however, before the chimpanzee recognized the bottle visually; i.e., protruded her lips toward it when it came into view.[47] □

The same object often has quite different meanings to different persons. Look at Figure 16.13 and see how many objects you can identify. Then compare your identifications with those of fellow students. In each instance, you, and others, receive exactly the same external stimulation, yet an object has much meaning for some and little or no meaning for others. Some objects, moreover, have different meanings for different persons, depending upon relevant past experience.

• Reduced cues. As perceptual experience grows, parts of situations come to elicit the same response formerly aroused by the entire situation. This is the *redintegrative* process, the tendency to respond in terms of reduced cues, an aspect of which was considered in the discussion of remembering (pp. 383–384).

Reading provides a good example. Our eyes fixate briefly on a word — too briefly to take in all of the details — yet we grasp the meaning of the word. This is why typographocal errors like those involved in this sentence often pass unobserved, unless one is locking for them. How many were there?

Many people in our culture have little difficulty in identifying A in Figure 16.14 from the cues given. On the other hand, relatively few identify B. The reason is that few have had relevant experience with what is pictured.

A   B

● 16.14

What Objects Are Here Represented? Can you fill in the gaps? See page 605. (After Street)

Only those who have observed a photographer kneeling with a graflex camera are able to see the photographer taking a picture. Even some who have had such experience have perhaps had it so infrequently that the cues provided do not arouse the appropriate perception.

• *Context.* We have already seen that context, the general setting in which objects appear, has a marked influence upon their perceived shape, size, and brightness. There are further illustrations of this in many situations of everyday life, some of which aid in the identification of objects or events, while others hinder such identification. Indeed, the statement that perception is influenced by the total situation applies quite generally. When we enter a motion picture theater in the middle of a film, it is usually difficult to perceive what is going on — to get the thread of the story — unless we know what has preceded. If we know this, then what is seen and heard at the moment takes on added meaning. It is likewise difficult to identify a piece of music, even a popular song, when one hears only a brief portion, taken out of its context.

Camouflage provides an extreme instance of how context may be changed so as to hinder identification. A simple illustration of this is shown in Figure 16.15. Here, as in other forms of camouflage, the object to be identified is concealed by changing its surroundings. Sometimes, of course, an object may itself be changed to resemble its surroundings. A soldier in the jungle may, for example, wear a helmet with green leaves painted on it so as to conceal his presence from aerial observers.

With the possible exception of a few illusions, like the Müller-Lyer (p. 501), the influence of context is dependent upon past experience in perceiving. In terms of what we

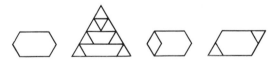

● **16.15**
How Context May Conceal a Form. Try to locate the first form in the figures at the right. (After Gottschaldt)

have learned about them, we expect to find familiar things in certain contexts. When the context is changed, perception is hindered. ■

VISUAL DEPTH AND DISTANCE

The apparent size, position, distance, and depth of objects which reflect light onto the retina are judged in terms of a variety of cues, some physiological and some psychological.

The retinal image, unless very small, is curved to conform to the curvature of the eyeball. But this curvature is of the same nature as the curvature that we might impose upon a photo by bending it. It involves no real depth.

If there is no depth in the retinal image of objects at different distances from the eye, how do we perceive the third dimension?

It is well to recognize, at the outset, that there is no inner person which looks at the image on the retina. Nor is the image transmitted, as a picture, to the brain. What happens is that the light pattern on the retina arouses nerve impulses which find their ultimate locus in the visual area of the cerebral cortex. There is reason to believe that the pattern of such impulses is correlated with the retinal pattern in some orderly way, yet without having the characteristics of a picture. It is the reaction of the cerebral cortex to this pattern of stimulation rather than a person's reaction to the image on his retina, which gives him his perception of the external world.

Although the retinal image is without depth, there is nevertheless some correlation between certain of its aspects and the "surfaces, slopes and edges of the world" about us. Likewise, although there is no picture transmitted to the cerebral cortex, the cortical pattern is a counterpart of that on the retina.[48]

In Figure 16.16 an artist has portrayed the typical visual field of one eye. His picture is flat, yet the spacing of the horizontal lines is so arranged as to give the impression of a floor, or something of the kind, receding into the distance. The artist has not drawn a picture of anything in particular, yet he has a spacing arrangement which correlates with, or is a counterpart of, an actually receding space.

Photographs as well as drawings illustrate similar principles. Thus, in Figure 16.17, the apparent size of the clods of earth, their detail, and the shadows cast by them are correlates of what was photographed; they give us, when we look at the picture, an impression of increasing distance.

Patterns of nerve impulses traveling to the brain doubtless correlate in some way with the retinal image, and thus with aspects of the external world. They are not replicas of the things perceived, nor do they picture them, yet they mediate appropriate responses to the tri-dimensional aspects of space.

Psychologists are particularly interested in the cues which allow us to perceive depth and distance. The retinal image itself may contain several such cues, as we have already suggested. Some of these are as effective when we use one eye as when we use two, hence we say that they are *monocular*. A cue which necessarily involves both eyes is designated *binocular*. Cues depending upon correlates in the visual image are designated *psychological*, while those arising from the structure and movements of the eyes are called *physiological*.

A question which arises in connection with all of these is whether or not we must learn to interpret them. The question is by no means settled. Some psychologists maintain that, at least to a certain extent, our perceptions of space are *given* to us directly by visual cues, even from the beginning of life.[49] Recent research involving a visual cliff (Figure 16.18) shows that, at least by the time they are able to crawl, infants avoid going over a visual "drop off." They must therefore have some perception of depth, or of distance.

Some maintain that visual cues come to have meaning only as we learn about the world through our other senses. They claim that we learn to interpret these cues through associated tactual and muscular processes. Thus it is claimed that an object comes to look round because it *feels* round; to look nearer than another because the muscular effort in reaching it is less than in reaching the others.[50] This is not an "either-or" proposition, however, for innate organizations and acquired meaning may both be involved. It has been shown (pp. 500–506) that certain primitive organizations as

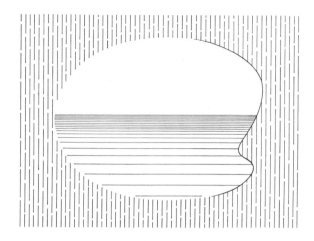

● **16.16**

The Typical Field of One Eye. Note the impression of increasing distance given by lines of decreasing separation. (From J. J. Gibson, *The Perception of the Visual World*, Houghton Mifflin, 1950, p. 68.)

● **16.17**

A Textural Gradient. Observe how the clods of earth seem to become smaller, closer together, and less detailed, the farther they are away from the camera (or the eye). (From J. J. Gibson, *The Perception of the Visual World*, Houghton Mifflin, 1950, p. 60.)

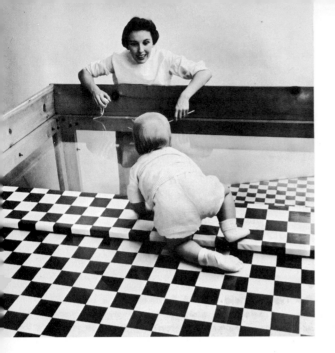

● 16.18
Infant on a Visual Cliff. The infant crawled along a heavy sheet of glass toward his mother. Underneath was a textured piece of linoleum. Halfway across, however, the linoleum dropped 3½ feet below the surface of the glass. In a group of thirty-six infants 6½ to 14 months old, only 8 per cent ventured beyond the visual drop-off. The others either crawled in the opposite direction or refused to proceed, even with coaxing from their mothers. Similar results have been found in testing a variety of animals, among them goats, kittens, rats, and chickens. (See R. D. Walk and E. J. Gibson, "A Comparative and Analytical Study of Visual Depth Perception," *Psychol. Monogr.*, 1961, *75*, No. 15. Photo by William Vandivert from Eleanor J. Gibson and Richard Walk, "Visual Cliff," *Scientific American*, April 1960, p. 65.)

well as habit factors contribute to our knowledge of the world around us.

Psychological cues

Since the psychological cues are just as effective whether we use one or both eyes, they are also classified as *monocular.* Among them are the following, all represented by correlates in the retinal image: size of image, interposition, linear perspective, aerial perspective, shadows, and relative movement.

• *Size of image.* The retinal image is larger for nearby than for distant objects. If the distance is sufficiently great, so that size constancy (p. 504) is not involved, we perceive the object as smaller, hence as more distant when its retinal image is smaller. But we must be acquainted with the actual size of the object. Any particular kind of bird is of a fairly constant size, hence when the image is small, we judge the bird to be at a greater distance than when the image is large. In the case of unfamiliar objects, however, the size of the retinal image is of little or no help. Take clouds, for example. These could be of almost any size. What we see might be a large cloud far up or a small cloud near the earth.

• *Interposition.* This is a rather obvious distance cue. The object represented in the retinal image as partially obscuring our view of another object is of course judged to be closer. The essential cue is related to the contour lines of the overlapping objects.[51] The object whose contour is continuous at the point of overlapping is seen as closer; the object whose contour is lost at the point of overlapping is seen as more distant. Note in Figure 16.19 that the upper rectangle has continuous contour lines at *c*, hence looks closer. At *d*, however, its contour line is lost while that of the lower rectangle is continuous. Now the lower rectangle seems nearer.

• *Linear perspective.* The decrease in the size and separation of objects as they become more

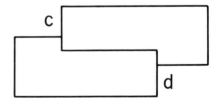

● 16.19
The Interpositional Cue. This figure is ambiguous. At *c* the lower rectangle appears more distant; at *d* the upper rectangle. (From P. Ratoosh, "On Interposition as a Cue for the Perception of Distance," *Proc. Nat. Acad. Sci.*, 1949, *35*, p. 258.)

● 16.20

How Many Depth or Distance Cues are Represented in This Drawing? Observe that the road seems to go down hill, then up as it recedes into the distance. At the top it seems to go down again. What other tridimensional cues are evident? (Adapted from H. Buckley, *Perspective*, London, Sir Isaac Pitman and Sons, Ltd., 1947; and J. J. Gibson, *The Perception of the Visual World*, Houghton Mifflin, 1950, p. 139.)

distant is often used by artists to represent distance. Lines converging as the horizon is approached give the impression of increasing distance. Trees, telephone poles, and other objects are decreased in size as they recede into the distance. The upper part of the picture always represents the horizon; the lower part the ground, or floor, nearby. The decreasing size of the clods of earth in Figure 16.17 (p. 515) as they approach the upper region of the picture is also illustrative of linear perspective.

• *Aerial perspective.* When we do not know the actual distance of objects, an important cue is provided by the clearness of perceived detail. A mountain, a building, or any other object which stands out from its surroundings seems closer on a clear day than on a smoky or foggy one. In fact any familiar object seems closer when we can make out its details. This is exemplified every time we use binoculars or a telescope, or take photographs with a telescopic lens. It is likewise illustrated by the clods of earth already referred to. The nearer ones are pictured in greater detail than those more distant.

All psychological factors so far considered are given interrelated representation in Figure 16.20. Observe that the road seems to go down hill, then up. This is because the rate at which the lines are converging in the lower part of the picture changes. The decreased *rate* of convergence near the end of the fence represents an uphill slope while the *continued convergence* of these lines represents increasing distance. Nearby objects fill more of the picture, as they would the retinal image. Interposition is represented by the fact that some buildings partially obscure others. Aerial perspective is, in a sense, also represented. The nearby trees and buildings, for example, show more detail than those pictured as in the distance. In a fog or haze, less detail would be evident and these objects would be perceived as at a still greater distance.

• *Shadows.* Depth cues also come from shadows. Note in Figure 16.21, for example, that the impression of depth may actually be reversed if the picture is turned upside down, thus making the shadows slope in the opposite direction.

● **16.21**

The Influence of Shadows on Depth Perception.
This is a volcano crater in Rabaul. Turn the
picture upside down, however, and a mound is
perceived instead of a crater. *Life* once printed
a picture of the moon inverted, in which the
craters appeared to be mounds. Photographers
often obtain a marked enhancement of depth in
buildings and other objects by an appropriate
arrangement of shadow. (Photo from Whites
Aviation, Ltd.)

● *Movement cues.* The relative movement of
objects is sometimes important in judging distance. Other things being equal, the object
which seems to move by us rapidly is judged
to be closer than that which moves by slowly.

If we ourselves are moving, objects nearby
seem to go past in the opposite direction to
that in which we are traveling, but distant objects appear to move with us.

There is evidence that individuals with
only one eye depend upon clues derived from
head and eye movements as well as movements
in the environment. This is especially true
for judgment of near distance, as when returning a spoon to a sugar bowl.

Some movie cartoons utilize a combination of psychological cues, including relative
movement, to give a very realistic impression
that one is viewing a tridimensional picture.

Physiological cues

Here we have three generally recognized
cues: accommodation, convergence, and retinal
disparity. The first is monocular, the second
may be monocular or binocular, and the third
is binocular.

● *Accommodation.* The lens changes its curvature (accommodates) as we fixate nearby objects. This adjustment of the lens is mediated
by the ciliary muscle and suspensory ligaments
(Figure 15.2, p. 463) and it is thus possible
that resulting nerve impulses provide the brain
with cues as to the relative distances of the
object fixated.

● *Convergence.* The eyes converge (turn inward) more when one fixates nearby objects
than when he fixates those at a greater distance.
These reactions are controlled by muscles attached to the eyeball, hence nerve impulses
generated in the course of this adjustment
might serve as distance cues. The same turning
movements are made when a person has only
one eye. But convergence is of doubtful value
as a spatial cue unless the objects fixated are
fairly close.[52]

● *Retinal disparity.* Each eye gets a somewhat
different picture of the same object or situation. In looking at an object the right eye sees
around the right side a little more than does
the left eye. On the other hand, the left eye
sees a bit farther around to the left. This difference in the view obtained with each eye is
referred to as *retinal disparity.* That it provides
important cues concerning depth is well known
to anybody who has viewed pictures through
a stereoscope.

The principle of the stereoscope is illustrated in Figure 16.22. Observe that the right
eye sees only the picture taken with the camera
on the right, and the left eye only that taken
with the camera on the left. The partition
prevents either eye from being stimulated in
any way by the noncorresponding picture. The
function of the prisms is to throw the disparate
images on the same regions of the retina which
would be stimulated if the original scene were
viewed by the two eyes under normal circumstances. The tridimensional image, produced by some fusion process in the brain, is
projected, as it were, along the dotted lines.
These lines are illustrated as extensions of the
lines from prisms to retina.

The well-known Viewmaster accomplishes
the same result without the use of prisms. A
stereo camera takes two pictures simultaneously

one from the position of each eye. In looking through the Viewmaster, or a comparable viewer, we place the right-side picture over the right eye and the left-side picture over the left eye, with the result that an extremely realistic depth effect is produced.

☐ You have perhaps observed another application of the retinal disparity principle, for it is sometimes used in store-window advertising and in motion pictures. The pictures used are printed in two colors, usually red and blue. Instead of being printed as separate pictures, however, they are superimposed. But what would be seen with the right eye is printed in red and what would be seen with the left eye in blue. You now look at the still picture, or movie, through spectacles having a red and a blue filter. The red filter over the left eye prevents you from seeing the red picture (appropriate for the right eye). Likewise, the blue filter over the right eye enables you to see the red picture but not the blue one (appropriate for the left eye). Under these conditions you observe depth, much as in a stereoscope. The result is so realistic in movies of a man pitching a ball toward the camera that most members of the audience "duck, as the ball comes toward them." It appears that the ball leaves the screen and is about to hit one between the eyes. These representations of the retinal disparity principle are known as *anaglyphs*.

A similar principle is involved in the so-called "3-D" movies shown in theaters. In these pictures, however, two separate images, one for each eye, are projected upon a special metallic screen. In coming from the projecting lenses, the light from each picture is polarized in a different direction. The light from one picture vibrates in one direction; that from the other, in a different direction. Looking at the screen without special glasses, the viewer sees confused double images. But his polaroid glasses provide filters for the respective eyes which allow only the appropriately directed vibrations to pass through. Thus the right eye sees only what was photographed with the right-hand lens of the camera and the left eye only what was photographed with the left-hand lens. The result is a marked impression of tri-dimensionality.

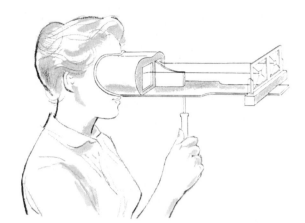

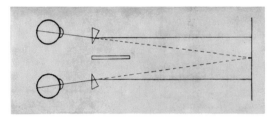

● 16.22
The Principle of the Stereoscope. Observe that the prisms of the stereoscope throw the images toward the outer part of the retina, where they would fall if the object were straight ahead. The subject then sees the picture, with depth, at a point between the actual pictures, the point where the dotted lines meet. The small partition prevents the right eye from viewing the picture designed for the left eye and the left eye from viewing the picture designed for the right eye. Some modern stereoscopic devices for viewing 3-D colored transparencies are described in the text.

Cinerama produces depth effects in a very different manner from that described. A very wide, curved screen leaves much of the picture in peripheral vision and judgments of depth come from interpretation of what we have referred to as "psychological cues." ☐

Depth perception based upon retinal disparity can be demonstrated in children as young as one year.[53] A doll, for example, is seen between us and the screen. The child with polaroid glasses reaches for the doll where we see it, hence must have "3-D" vision.

Whether three-dimensional vision is inborn or based upon acquired interpretations is not known. It seems likely, however, that it is another example of "primitive organizations" like the geometrical illusions, primitive groupings, and illusions of motion discussed earlier in this chapter.

The principles of stereoscopy have many military uses. Stereoscopic cameras take reconnaissance pictures which make it possible to tell not only that a building stands at a particular spot, but also its height, and many other characteristics. Visual range-finding instruments likewise make much use of retinal disparity and the stereoscopic vision based on it. ■

AUDITORY SPACE PERCEPTION

Our ears provide us with relative cues to the *distance* and *direction* of objects (that is, sound sources), but judgments based upon these cues are in most instances quite crude, especially as compared with judgments based on visual cues.

Distance

If a sound is familiar, we can usually judge its distance in terms of loudness, since we associate increasing distance with decreasing loudness. Complexity is another possible distance cue. The sound of an airplane motor is far less complex at a distance than when it is nearby. When it is close, we hear a great variety of sounds; at a distance, however, only the low hum is audible. Likewise, the relatively faint higher overtones of musical instruments become inaudible with distance. Nearby sounds also have greater volume than more distant ones. The boom of a cannon a few yards away seems to fill all space. From a distance of several miles, however, the same boom appears to take up relatively little space. Moreover, it is heard as but one of several sounds. It does not drown out everything else.

Direction

Our ability to locate sound sources is partially dependent upon previous knowledge.

We know, for example, that those traffic sounds are coming from the road over there, that the airplane is overhead, and that the cheering comes from the stadium. Vision also provides us with cues which aid in auditory localization. We hear a woodpecker, for instance. Looking up in the trees and seeing the bird pecking, we locate the source of the sound. It happens, of course, that vision sometimes deceives us. We "hear" sounds issuing from the mouth of the ventriloquist's dummy because we see its mouth moving at the same time as words are spoken. Likewise, we seem to see and hear an actor speak on the screen, even though the loudspeaker may be several feet above, below, or to the right or left of his mouth.

Under such circumstances as the above, only one ear is necessary for localization. All we need do is hear and recognize what we hear. When previous knowledge and vision are eliminated, however, two ears are necessary. This is because we are not able to localize sounds in terms of auditory cues alone unless they stimulate each ear differently.

In a typical experiment on auditory localization the subject sits with closed eyes, his head in the center of what is, in effect, a large sphere. This is illustrated in Figure 16.23.

□ A click may be presented at any position on the surface of the sphere. As soon as he hears the click, the subject must name or point to the place from which the click came. His error of localization is measured in degrees. We find that he is able to localize the click fairly well so long as it is at a different distance from each ear. When it appears at *a*, the click is much closer to the right ear than to the left. The subject usually says that it is directly to the right. Suppose that the click is presented at *b* — that is, to the front on the left side. It is closer to the left ear than to the right. Again the subject is quite successful in localizing the source of the click. Suppose, however, that we present the click directly in front at a position equidistant from the two ears — that is, at *c*. Now the subject may say that it is up, back, down, to the front, or in any position in the median plane, which cuts through the head directly between the ears.

His accuracy of localization within this plane is no better than could occur by chance. This is because, at every position, the ears are stimulated identically. □

What differences in stimulation at the ears are provided by a sound to the right or left of the median plane? There are three important possibilities. These are: (1) a difference in time of arrival of the sound wave at the ears; (2) a difference in the phase of the cycle activating each ear; and (3) a difference in the intensity of the stimulus at the ears. The sound wave, of course, reaches the nearer ear first; it may be in a different part of its cycle when it strikes the nearer ear than when it strikes the farther ear, and it may have a greater intensity at the nearer than at the farther ear.

Under conditions of everyday life, time, phase, and intensity differences are often simultaneously present, and we may use now one and now another, or all three combined, in localizing unfamiliar and unseen sounds. When the locus is familiar, or the sound source is seen, these cues are not necessary, and they are probably not used. When a noise, such as a click, is involved, time is the most important clue as to direction. But when a tonal stimulus is involved, phase also becomes important, especially if the sound wave is of low frequency, hence relatively long. A long wave has a better chance of stimulating the two ears in different parts of its cycle than a short wave. One ear may be stimulated by the crest (condensation), and the other by the trough (rarefaction). In the case of high frequencies, or short waves, on the other hand, one ear may be stimulated by the crest of one wave and the other ear by the crest of the next wave. As far as phase is concerned, this is equivalent to stimulating both ears with the crest of the same wave. Experiments have shown that some individuals localize in terms of phase differences, while others do not.

Intensity is an important cue only at relatively high frequencies, above five thousand cycles per second. This is because intensity is not greatly reduced by small differences in the distance of a sound source from the ears. Significant differences in intensity are asso-

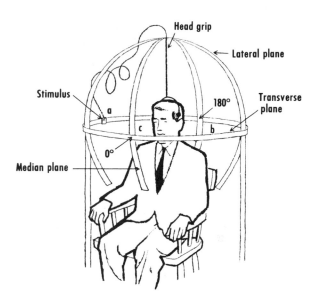

● **16.23**

Schema Illustrating a Situation Involved in Auditory Localization Experiments. The subjects may localize by naming the position of the sound or by pointing to it. For further explanation, see the text.

ciated, rather, with the shadow of the head. A sound wave coming from the right must pass around the head to get to the left ear. Long waves (those of low frequency) bend easily and show little loss of amplitude. On the other hand, short waves (those of high frequency) are so greatly reduced in amplitude that the sound may be thirty decibels louder at the nearer than at the farther ear. When complex sound waves are involved, this bending around the head not only reduces their loudness, but it also decreases their complexity. Timbre is thus different at the two ears and may provide a localizing cue.

A so-called *pseudophone* has been devised which reverses stimulation at the two ears.[54] A tube conveys to the left ear sound waves which would normally stimulate the right ear, and to the right ear those which would normally stimulate the left. If the eyes are closed, sounds actually coming from the right are heard coming from the left, and vice versa. If the eyes are open, however, the sounds are properly localized. This is because visual cues take precedence over auditory ones.

It is only under laboratory conditions that we are able to present one localizing cue while holding the others constant, and thus discover the relative importance of each.

In any complex situation, some sounds appear near and some distant; some appear to the right, some to the left, and some straight ahead. Not only this, but certain sounds move in relation to other sounds or appear against a background of constant sounds. Radio engineers have had some success in reproducing such *stereophonic effects* by radio. One method is to place two microphones on a dummy, one microphone in the position of the right ear and the other in the position of the left ear, maintaining the actual distance which separates the ears. The right-hand microphone is connected to the right earphone of a listener in another room. The left-hand microphone is likewise connected to the left earphone. Now someone walks toward or away from the dummy, around it, and so on, while talking. The listener with earphones has the illusion that someone is walking toward him, around him, and so forth.[55] Similar stereophonic effects are sometimes produced in movie theaters. Several sound tracks may be used, each recorded from a sound source in a different position, and each with its loudspeaker appropriately located in the theater.

Musical programs have been broadcast in such a manner as to utilize stereophonic effects and stereophonic records have become commonplace. In each instance, there is a simultaneous pickup from differently placed microphones, and a playback from differently placed loudspeakers. The principles are similar to those of the above-mentioned experiments. ■

INTERSENSORY CONTRIBUTIONS

What one perceives of space involves contributions from several senses, separately at times but often complexly integrated. Visual and auditory information have been stressed in our discussions. Nevertheless, it has been neces-

sary to recognize (p. 515) that perceiving the depth of seen objects may be dependent upon earlier tactual and kinesthetic experiences. In discussing certain aspects of distance perception (p. 518), it was learned that cues from the muscles which move the eyes and others which change the curvature of the lens may play an important role. We were referring, in this connection, to kinesthetic cues. The interplay of vision and hearing was cited (p. 522) in describing how visual cues may take precedence over the auditory in "auditory localization." Two other senses also provide information which helps us locate sources of stimulation not in contact with the body surface. One of these is olfaction. Although more useful to animals like the dog than to us, it does facilitate the localizing of odorous objects — as when a skunk is in the vicinity or something is burning. Temperature is the other sense which provides spatial information. This is limited to such relatively simple things as locating the direction of a draft, or of warmth.

The tactual and kinesthetic senses, often in combination, tell us about the size and shape of objects that we handle without looking at them. This sort of information has important application in some work situations, as will be seen when human efficiency is discussed. Tactual-kinesthetic information is of course crucially significant to the blind. Earlier discussions of tactual-kinesthetic localization (pp. 481–484) are relevant here, even though concerned only with locating stimulations applied to the skin — in practical situations, with locating a cut, an insect bite, or an itch.

Our discussion of static sensitivity (pp. 475–477) dealt with mechanisms involved when we discern the direction of body movement — up, down, right, left, forward, back, clockwise, or counter-clockwise. This is also relevant in the context of space perception, because much information that is important for spatial orientation comes from the static sense. Normally, this is combined with other information, especially visual and kinesthetic. It is the combination of these three senses which makes it possible for a cat to land upright when dropped. These senses do not serve us as well in this sort of situation. Never-

• **16.24**

Perceiving the Upright. The room and the chair can be tilted to any desired position. In this test, the room has been tilted, and the subject has been asked to adjust her chair so that she is upright. Visual cues make her think that she has changed to the upright position even though, as indicated by the arrow, she has not done so. When blindfolded, however, she relies on the pull of gravity without being confounded by the visual environment. Then, as the arrow shows, she adjusts her chair to the upright position almost exactly. (From H. A. Witkin, "The Perception of the Upright," *Scientific American*, February 1959, pp. 50, 52, 53. Photos by David Linton.)

theless, they do facilitate our locomotor activities. When visual cues are absent — as in some diving and flying operations — one is thrown back almost entirely upon his static sense. This alone can tell him, whether he is upright or upside down. We do not mean to imply, however, that this is an infallible guide. The need to use instruments in "flying blind" suggests that it is not too dependable as a means of spatial orientation.

An interesting series of experiments has demonstrated that perception of one's position in space is to a measurable degree dependent upon visual surroundings.[56] Some of these experiments used the apparatus illustrated in Figure 16.24. With this the body as a whole could be tilted forward or backward or to the right or left. Likewise, the entire visual environment of the subject, who was supported more or less rigidly in the padded chair, could be tilted in the same direction, either with or independently of the body. Individuals differed greatly in their reactions. But most of them had the impression, when the room alone was tilted, that they had themselves changed position. On the other hand, the body could be tilted, in a visually upright environment — the environment also moving so as to correspond — without this body-tilting movement being perceived.

The apparatus was constructed so that the subject could readjust the visual surroundings and also his own position. Such readjustments were accomplished with varying degrees of success, some subjects doing well and others poorly.

What is of special interest to us here is this further demonstration of the interplay of different senses in space perception. In a dark room or a completely foggy environment — that is to say, with no visual detail to guide him — one's static sense, combined with tac-tual and kinesthetic stimulation, might be expected to tell him whether he was upright, or tilted. In the latter instance, if he were sitting in a chair, there would be unusual pressure against his side — for example, the right side in a tilt to the right. In a tilted visual environment, however, such cues may be ineffective because the visual ones predominate, a finding reminiscent of the already-mentioned predominance of visual cues in localizing sounds. ■

• SUMMARY

Attending and perceiving are in some respects indistinguishable, but we have concentrated upon attending conceived of as a pre-perceptive set — an anticipatory perceptual adjustment. The role of the reticular formation in alerting the organism and in facilitating selective attention has been discussed.

The act of attending involves receptor adjustments, postural adjustments, muscle tensions associated with the latter but not always overtly observable, and central neural adjustments, including those of the reticular formation and cerebral cortex. Central neural adjustments are generally considered to be integrally involved in receptor and postural functions, but controversy has centered around the idea that there may at times be a central control independent of, or in addition to, the peripheral adjustments. The possibility of such a central control must be recognized, but research has so far failed to provide conclusive evidence of it.

Determiners of attention may be differentiated into two broad but somewhat related groups — namely, external and internal. To the degree that they contrast with their surroundings or with what is customary, external stimulus patterns gain in attention-getting value. Internal determiners are continuing sets which stem from motives.

Experiments with a homogeneous visual environment show that it produces fogginess with loss of visual detail in figures. These experiments demonstrate the importance, for normal perception, of nonhomogeneity, with its figure-ground relationships. Stabilized (stopped) retinal images reveal that stimulus change is an essential aspect of visual perception. When the image is stabilized, so that exactly the same rods and cones are continually stimulated, the perceived object fades and disappears, sometimes piece by piece. It also returns, as a whole or piecemeal, only to disappear again. Colored objects lose their hue under similar circumstances.

Some aspects of perceptual experience appear to be inborn rather than learned. Among such "primitive organizations" are geometrical illusions, the illusion of apparent motion (phi-phenomenon), and apparently natural groupings (or configurations). Recent research has brought the moon illusion into prominence and we have discussed some observations which suggest that the horizon moon looks larger than the zenith moon (even though their retinal images have the same size) because the former is perceived as more distant than the latter. It looks more distant because it is seen across a terrain instead of through empty space.

The constancy phenomena further illustrate the fact that what one perceives is not directly determined by the size (or shape, or brightness) of the retinal image. We have seen that objects retain their perceptual size, within limits, even though the size of the retinal image changes; that objects retain their perceived shape, again within limits, even though the shape of the retinal image changes; and that objects retain their brightness despite marked changes in illumination. The familiarity of objects, and their context (their relation to other aspects of the environment) plays an important role in perceptual constancy.

In order to perceive stimulations as different, the difference between them must bear a certain ratio to their actual magnitude or intensity. This is the essence of Weber's law. If you are to discriminate an increase in brightness, the increase in intensity of light must be about one-hundredth of the intensity that you started with. This increase is necessary to bring the difference above the threshold of discrimination, or to produce a just noticeable difference (j.n.d.) in brightness. In hearing, taste, and the other senses, different ratios apply. In every field of perception, they apply only to the middle range of intensities, they vary somewhat from one individual to another, and they vary under different experimental conditions. Similar ratios apply to certain aspects of the environment other than intensity — for example, judging the length of lines. One of the methods used to obtain Weber ratios is that of just noticeable differences.

An instructional set facilitates perceiving of items relative to the set. So also do motivational sets which the individual himself brings to a situation. The research on values and perception of related words has so far had no clear outcome.

Past experience is especially important in determining the meaning of what we perceive. Any familiar object has acquired a variety of meanings because of its association with other objects and events in the past. Thus, perception of an apple is eventually possible in terms of any one of its aspects (such as color, odor, taste), and any one of these is likely to arouse symbolic processes which represent former experiences or activities in which apples have played a part. Growth of meaning is also related to our tendency to interpret the new in terms of the old. Think of the girl who called the caterpillar a "kitty bug" when she saw one for the first time. That the same object may have different meanings for different individuals, even though it stimulates them identically, can be illustrated by use of any object not familiar to all. The influence of set in perceiving is another example of the role of past experience, for the set is itself usually determined by what has happened previously.

If we had to examine every object or situation carefully before perceiving it, we should be greatly handicapped in reacting to our environment. What we do, characteristically, is to react in terms of reduced cues. Some aspect of former experience, or some part of a present familiar object or situation, arouses symbolic processes which, as it were, "fill out" the experience.

Although the image on the retina lacks depth, it contains certain cues, correlated with aspects of the external world, which enable us to discern depth and distance. Some of these cues are monocular, requiring only one eye. Among monocular cues are those designated as psychological. Whether these cues give us any aspects of space perception prior to experience or wheher we must learn to interpret them is an unanswered question. It appears likely that a certain amount of "primitive organization" is supplemented by acquired interpretations.

Important among psychological cues are the following, all of them monocular: retinal size, interposition, linear perspective, aerial perspective or clearness of detail, shadows, and relative movement.

Among the physiological cues of depth are accommodation of the lens (monocular), convergence (monocular and binocular), and retinal disparity (binocular). Accommodation and convergence are of doubtful value except at short distances. Retinal disparity, however, is of obvious importance. It is illustrated experimentally by use of the stereoscope, anaglyphs, and other so-called "3-D" pictures. In each instance, two slightly different pictures, usually taken with lenses separated by the same distance as the eyes, are fused to produce a tridimensional effect simulating what we see with both eyes.

Depth perception based upon retinal disparity is perhaps another of the "primitive organizations" referred to earlier. It may be clearly demonstrated in children as young as one year.

A sound source equidistant from the ears gives no auditory clue as to its location. When the source is at a distance from one ear different from that from the other, however, the wave (1) reaches the nearer ear first, (2) may lead in phase at the nearer ear, and (3) may be more intense at the nearer ear. These differences enable us to localize the source, but the significance of a particular clue depends on the nature of the sound wave. Time is important for localization of noises, phase for localization of tones, and intensity for localization of high tones.

Space perception, rather than being visual, or auditory, is an intersensory affair. In many instances it is, so to speak, audiovisual. But other senses also provide spatial information: olfaction, the temperature sense, and the static and kinesthetic senses. When visual cues are in conflict with auditory or static cues, the visual may predominate. Examples were seen in auditory localization and in perceiving the body position in a tilted visual environment.

REFERENCES AND NOTES FOR THIS CHAPTER ARE IN THE APPENDIX.

• SELECTED READINGS

Allport, F. H., *Theories of Perception and the Concept of Structure.* Wiley, 1955. A very critical and thorough discussion.

Bartley, S. H., *Principles of Perception.* Harper, 1958. A good survey of much of the experimental research in this general area, including the senses as such.

Daniel, R. S. (Ed.), *Contemporary Readings in General Psychology.* Houghton Mifflin, 1965. Readings 14 (Riesen, "Arrested vision") and 15 (Ittelson, "The involuntary bet"). On brain dynamics in relation to perception, see also Sperry's chapter in E. Hutchings, Jr., *Frontiers in Science,* Basic Books, 1958, pp. 48–60.

Dember, W. N., *Psychology of Perception.* Holt, 1960. An excellent treatment of measurement in perception as well as the outcomes of experimental research on the influence of set, motivation, and other processes. See especially Chapters 9 and 10.

Dulany, D. E., Jr., R. L. DeValois, D. C. Beardslee, and M. R. Winterbottom, *Contributions to Modern Psychology* (2nd ed.). Oxford University Press, 1963, Chapter 3. The papers by Hernández-Peón *et al.,* Köhler, and Wallach are particularly relevant.

Gibson, J. J., *The Perception of the Visual World.* Houghton Mifflin, 1950. A more detailed presentation of the view that visual space perception is based upon external correlates of space.

Graham, C. H. (Ed.), *Vision and Visual Perception.* Wiley, 1965. See the chapters on perception.

Hochberg, J. E., *Perception.* Prentice-Hall, 1964. A fairly detailed introduction, excellently illustrated.

Morgan, C. T., *Physiological Psychology* (3rd ed.). McGraw-Hill, 1965. Chapter 7, on visual perception.

Munn, N. L., *The Evolution and Growth of Human Behavior* (2nd ed.). Houghton Mifflin, 1965. Chapter 9 traces the development of perceptual processes and also deals with some special problems, including inverted vision.

Vernon, M. D., *The Psychology of Perception.* Penguin Books, 1962. An excellent brief review of the subject.

Woodworth, R. S., and H. Schlosberg, *Experimental Psychology* (rev. ed.). Holt, 1954. See especially Chapters 25–27 dealing with, respectively, perception of form, visual space perception, and attention

17

Social Behavior

We begin our existence as *asocial* beings. Those who have close contact with a newborn baby know how impervious it is to social influences. One can neither communicate with it nor influence its behavior, except by such things as placing a nipple in its mouth or "burping" it to stop its crying. A month or more elapses before the infant begins to respond in a truly social manner. Its social development starts with such elementary acts as responding differently to human and nonhuman sounds, smiling when smiled at, and crying to be picked up. Gradually the child learns to imitate simple acts, to speak, and to acquire the interests and attitudes fostered by his parents and others concerned with his care. For some months after birth, the infant pays little or no attention to others of his own age. Even at the age of two years, he tends to play alone, even in the presence of other children. By the age of four or five, however, the child may be engaged in such complex interactions as cooperating with other children, dominating or submitting to them, competing with them, and forming friendships with one or more.[1] Social interactions increase in complexity throughout childhood and adolescence. When the adult level has been reached, the initially asocial being has become enmeshed in a complex web of social interrelationships, including social-class affiliations, occupational ties, family responsibilities, and so on. It is no wonder that man has been categorized as "the social animal."

It is interesting to note a rather obvious fact, and this is that the initially asocial being may be socialized in innumerable directions. We had something to say about this in discussing social aspects of motivation, and again in considering social aspects of the development of personality. One has only to look at the characteristic social behavior of different societies to see what a different "social animal" can develop as different social influences are focused upon the growing child.

Man is so preeminently a social organism that any discussion of human behavior which neglected the social aspects would be seriously deficient. But we have not been completely negligent. In Chapter 1 we considered social psychology as a branch of behavioral science. The chapters on intelligence, motivation, personality, learning, communication, and perception each dealt with aspects of social psychology. The emphasis in preceding discussions, however, has been on the influence of social conditions upon the psychological processes under consideration. Except in the chapter on communication, there has been little attention to the interaction process as such. We now move to correct this deficiency.

Social interaction takes many forms. An elementary instance occurs when the behavior of one organism is stimulated by that of another, as when one animal bares its teeth and the other runs. Imitative behavior, which has already been discussed from the standpoint of how it aids in the learning of simple skills (p. 325), is more complicated than the example just given in that the imitatee sets a pattern which the imitator copies, or attempts to copy. However, the behavior of greatest interest to us in this chapter involves reciprocal stimulation and response. That is to say, behavior in which one organism stimulates another and is, in turn, stimulated by the other's reaction. Thus the animal that runs in response to the bared teeth of another may, by the act of running, stimulate the other to chase it.

Among the topics to be discussed in this chapter are elementary forms of interaction which characterize the social life of animals, some of which carry over into human social behavior; the status characteristics of human society and the roles that persons play in their social dealings; the behavior of small groups as studied experimentally; group pressures on individual judgment; problems involved in communication of the kind designated as rumor; and broader aspects of social life, including crowd behavior and social movements. In several of these discussions we will also be concerned with problems of leadership.

This is a very broad field which only a course in social psychology could really cover. All that we shall attempt, therefore, is to spotlight a few major issues and representative experimental investigations. The function of this chapter is thus to provide preliminary orientation in the area of social psychology. ■

ELEMENTARY SOCIAL BEHAVIOR

A prime necessity for social behavior is the proximity of two or more organisms. Nevertheless, individuals may be drawn together for nonsocial reasons. And when they are together, they may still not interact. Of many examples that might be given, consider the swarming of insects around a lamp. These organisms are positively phototropic. Their makeup forces them to fly to a source of light. They are individually drawn to this region, and the aggregation is thus purely incidental. Whether the insects influence each other's reactions while in the vicinity of the light is problematical.

At the level of bird life there are further complications. Physiological and climatic changes activate each bird to migrate to its accustomed location. In migrating, however, flocks are formed in which a particular bird may take the lead and in which the behavior of each bird is influenced by that of others. It is in this fashion that behavior becomes social. In schools of fish and in herds of mammals the same sort of interaction is observed.[2]

To take a further example of how animals may congregate for other than social reasons, think of the various mammals that come together around a water hole in some such place as the African veldt. What brings them together is thirst and the proximity of a water hole. Once there, however, they interact in numerous ways — for example, by mating, fighting, and protecting their young.

It is perhaps unnecessary to point out that all vertebrates and many invertebrates are born into a social situation in which they receive care from one or both parents and in which they interact with their parents and others. Indeed, numerous naturalistic studies of social life in the animal world are largely preoccupied with such forms of interaction as mating, care and education of the young, and family organization.

Imprinting and socialization

One of the most obvious observations about social behavior is that those of a kind usually stay together — that they have a seeming attachment to (or preference for) others like themselves. It is also clear that this sort of association begins very early in life. We say a "seeming" attachment, however, because the association is not necessarily with organisms of the same species. Consider, for example, such socialization as is evident when ducklings or other young animals follow their mothers around.

Under normal circumstances, ducklings and goslings follow their mother soon after hatching, perhaps stimulated by her movements, her vocalizations, or both of these. There is nothing very remarkable about this following behavior, and it would receive no more than passing mention were it not for the fact that, under certain circumstances to be described shortly, the same behavior may be elicited by models, or by almost any perceptible object which moves, including a human being, as illustrated in Figure 17.1. Konrad Lorenz, the German student of animal behavior shown in the illustration, coined the word "imprinting" to designate this sort of attachment of young animals to members of their own or other species, or to models.[3] In one of his most interesting demonstrations of imprinting, Lorenz took a group of goslings that had been imprinted upon him, and a group that had been imprinted upon their mother. They were intermingled and placed under a box. The mother and Lorenz stood nearby. Then, as the mother moved away, the box was lifted and Lorenz walked in another direction. The outcome was quite clear, for the goslings imprinted upon Lorenz followed him and the others followed their mother.[4]

It became evident that imprinting upon a substitute for the mother usually occurs only during the first day, and even then only

● **17.1**

An Example of Imprinting. These goslings, which had been isolated from their mother, have learned to follow a human being — in this case Konrad Lorenz, the famous naturalist. (Photo by Thomas D. McAvoy, *Life*, © Time, Inc.)

if the bird has been out of contact with its own mother. Under normal conditions this "critical period" is probably that in which the bird is imprinted upon its mother and other members of the brood.

Once the duckling has come to follow its mother, or anything else on which it is imprinted, the attachment is irreversible. That is, a bird imprinted on a human being does not subsequently imprint upon its mother, or a model, even when opportunities are given for it to do so. The original attachment thus persists. Moreover, it generalizes to other activities, including sexual approaches toward the imprinting object.[5]

Imprinting has aroused much interest. Investigators have observed something compara-

ble in numerous animals, including sheep.[6] Some have undertaken laboratory investigations designed to reveal the detailed nature of this phenomenon. One such investigation is described in Figure 17.2 and the accompanying legend, which also summarizes the outcomes.[7]

Some of the interest in this social behavior stems from the possibility that it may have relevance for our understanding of initial stages in human socialization. One investigator[8] says that a child will not develop normally unless it has "a certain amount of attention and handling during a critical period of its infancy. This period is doubtless not as sharply defined as the imprinting period in birds, but it may lie within the first six months of life." The reader will no doubt recall, in this connection, our earlier discussion (p. 173) of the so-called need for affection in infants and the attachments of infant monkeys (p. 174) to mother substitutes. All such studies appear to have much in common, but whether the resemblance is superficial or real remains to be discovered.

Imprinting is generally conceded to be a learned response, but of a somewhat special kind. The investigator whose work we have illustrated regards it as

□ ". . . a rigid form of learning, differing in several ways from the usual association learning which comes into play immediately after the peak of imprintability. In other words, imprinting in our experiments results in the animal learning the rough, generalized characteristics of the imprinting object. Its detailed appreciation of the *specific* object comes as a result of normal conditioning — a process which in the case of these animals takes a much longer time and is possible days after the critical period for imprinting has passed."[9] □

Other aspects of socialization have already received attention. We indicated in earlier chapters how basic drives come to be expressed in socially approved ways, and how the child develops a concept of self (ego) and a conscience (supergo).

An aspect of socialization not yet discussed is social status. Even in animal groups, there may be struggle for status, with some individuals finding that they can dominate others. We say "dominate" because such individuals may satisfy their needs at the expense of others and, in face-to-face situations, induce submissive behavior. A good example of such a social relationship is the so-called dominance hierarchy.

Dominance hierarchies

The fact that barnyard hens are socially organized was first called to scientific attention by Schjelderup-Ebbe, a Norwegian investigator.[10] He observed that after a group of chickens had been together for some time, a pecking order became established. The most dominant chick pecked all others in the group and was pecked by none in return. The next in line pecked all other chicks except the most dominant, which of course pecked it. This social order was extended downward until, at the bottom of the hierarchy, there was a chick pecked by all and pecking none. A pecking order observed in a repetition of some of Schjelderup-Ebbe's experiments is represented in Figure 17.3.[11]

The pecking order is learned, but how long it takes for a stable hierarchy to develop depends upon the number of chickens involved. One study showed that it took 36 weeks for a group of six to develop a hierarchy like that illustrated.[12] In general, the dominant chicken is the largest, speediest, most aggressive, and most intelligent as measured by tests of learning ability.[13] This chicken learns that it can win every fight. The one at the bottom of the social ladder finds that it loses every fight. The others, after weeks of fighting, learn which to peck and which to avoid, if possible. As one would expect, the introduction of a new member of the group disrupts the established order. A new hierarchy then develops.

Studies of mammals (including mice, rats, and dogs) show that dominance relations based on fighting are quite common, but that a perfect straight-line dominance like the pecking order of hens is rare.[14]

● **17.2**

An Experiment on Imprinting. The decoy duck (male mallard) moving around the circular runway is fitted with a loud speaker and emits the man-produced sounds "gock, gock, gock, gock, gock." During the imprinting period (usually less than one hour) the duckling is taken from a box in the incubator and allowed to make a certain number of turns around the runway before being returned. At a later time, in tests for imprinting, it is released halfway between a male and a female decoy model four feet apart. The male is the same one that was used during the imprinting period. One minute is allowed for the duckling to respond to either decoy, then sound is turned on in both. The "male" makes the sounds described. The "female" gives the call of a real female. Various responses are recorded — to silent and calling models, stationary and moving models, and so on. If the duckling gives a positive response to the male decoy in all such tests, imprinting is said to be complete (100 per cent). With different groups of ducklings, imprinting is attempted at different times. In general, the results show that imprintability improves until it reaches its peak at 13–16 hours after hatching. Then it declines rapidly. At its peak, imprintability is represented by an average score of approximately 85 per cent. For these birds, tested under the conditions described, the "critical period" is toward the middle of the first day after hatching. (From E. H. Hess, "Imprinting," *Science,* 1959, 130, p. 134.)

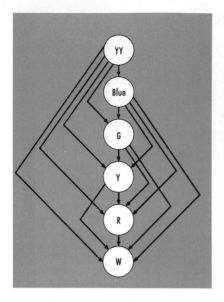

● **17.3**
A Dominance Hierarchy. Observe that YY pecked on all others, Blue pecked on all but YY, and W was pecked by all. This straight-line dominance took thirty-six weeks to develop. All of the birds represented here are barnyard roosters. (Diagram from C. Murchison, "The Experimental Measurement of a Social Hierarchy in *Gallus Domesticus,*" *J. Gen. Psychol.,* 1935, 12, p. 22. Photo © *Life.*)

The author of a book on aggression says that children of three years and older who have not learned to avoid strangers tend to

☐ ". . . engage in considerable playful aggressiveness. In many children this is a standard method of getting acquainted with a new child. If unchecked or unsupervised it should theoretically lead to a dominance order based on fighting. From the viewpoint of the cultural ideal of our society, it is desirable that no strong relationships of dominance and subordination be built up between children. No one wants his child to be at the bottom of a dominance order and become the child who is always picked on."[15] ☐

There are doubtless many situations where something approximating a dominance hierarchy based upon fighting (or fear and intimidation) develops among human beings. Notorious examples are found in teen-age gangs.[16] By and large, however, the individual's status in a human group is based upon something more subtle than physical domination — for instance, money or education. In some countries, social status rests upon one's origin. Tradition is also influential.[17] With respect to this, Lady Bowley's prayer, designed for the "lower classes," comes to mind.

O let us love our occupations,
Bless the squire and his relations,
Live upon our daily rations,
And always know our proper stations.
Charles Dickens in *The Chimes*

☐ Interesting as comparisons of dominance behavior in animals and men may be, one needs to observe due caution. The similarities that exist are no more than suggestive. Nevertheless there are some who note the dominance hierarchy in hens, then expostulate on international affairs with this as a basis. Thus a distinguished zoologist, writing on the topic of "The peck order and international relations," had this to say: ". . . much can be said for an established order of dominance and subordination, whether within groups of non-human animals or among nations. There is growing evidence that well organized flocks [of hens], in which each individual knows and is fairly well resigned to its particular social status, thrive better and produce more eggs than do similar flocks that are in a constant state of organizational turmoil. Similarly among nations, relative quiet exists when the international order of dominance is fairly firmly established and generally accepted. . . . Sooner or later, however, on the international stage as among our groups of mice, or fish, or hens, or other animals, a subordinate always seriously challenges the alpha individual or nation. Although the challenger may be beaten back, often many times, eventually alpha rank is taken over by a new despot, and the cycle starts again."[18]

But this writer renounces the peck order solution of international problems by saying, "in so far as any international organization, formal or informal, is based primarily on the hierarchy of power, as are the peck orders of the chicken pens, the peace that follows its apparent acceptance will be relatively short and troubled. Permanent peace is not to be won by following the precedents established by the dominance orders of vertebrate animals."[19] □

Analogies like these are interesting to contemplate, but human societies are different in many important respects from those of animals, even the higher ones. There will be ample evidence of this as we proceed with our discussion of human social behavior. ■

COMPETITION AND COOPERATION

One of the most widely observed effects of a group situation on the individual organism is called *social facilitation*. It is often competitive in nature; cooperative behavior is a much higher development.

Social facilitation

This term is applied when an organism does more in a social situation than when alone. For example, fish eat more when in a group than when eating alone. Ants which dig their nests excavate more dirt, per unit of time, when they work in the group than when they work by themselves.[20] Rats tested alone and in group situations eat and drink more in the latter. It has been shown, however, that facilitation of eating and drinking occurs only when the situation is competitive — when rats have to take turns at a water spout or when there is a limited supply of food.[21] Social facilitation is also evident in children.[22] Its presence in small adult groups is discussed later.

One can observe competition in many organisms and, as higher levels of animal life are approached, cooperation also enters the scene. These processes are worthy of a more detailed discussion.

In highly organized insect societies, like those of bees and ants, there is no competition. A seeming cooperation is universally observable. Every animal contributes to the common good by performing its special tasks. But this is a cooperation of necessity. Because of its makeup and the situation in which it finds itself, each individual is destined to perform certain tasks and no others.[23] At the vertebrate level of life, however, there is much greater "individual freedom." Here an organism is less bound, socially, than is an ant or bee. It competes with others for the necessities of life, thus may eat and drink more in a group situation.

A truly cooperative type of behavior — one not predetermined biologically, as in insects — is sometimes observed in laboratory experiments with rats and higher mammals. Naturalists have reported many examples of "mutual aid" among animals ranging from birds to the higher apes,[24] but we will confine our attention to some typical laboratory investigations.

Experiments on cooperative behavior

Something suggesting cooperative behavior emerged in a situation in which rats operated a lever to get pellets of food.

□ After the lever-pressing response was established, the experimenter placed the lever and the food trough at opposite ends of the experimental box. This meant, of course, that the operator had to travel a short distance before

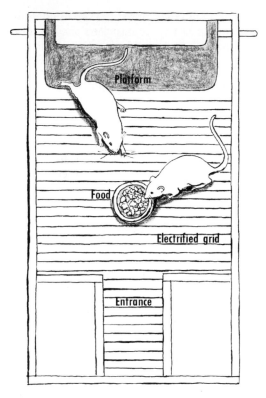

● 17.4
Device Used to Study Cooperative Behavior in Rats. The floor was electrified. Pressure on the platform turned off the shock, which remained off until pressure was released. The food crock always contained a plentiful supply. Each rat first learned, individually, to eat food from the crock; then, when the floor was electrified, to turn off the current by stepping on the platform. Finally, rats were paired, as illustrated. Would they learn to cooperate, with one depressing the level while the other ate? This cooperative solution did occur, as described in the text. (Adapted from W. J. Daniel, "Cooperative Problem Solving in Rats," *J. Comp. Psychol.*, 1942, 34, p. 362.)

he could get his reward. The next step was to place three appropriately conditioned rats in the same box. In this situation the operator usually failed to get his reward. When the food trough was reached, another animal had already eaten the pellet. Initially all three ani-

mals did some pressing, and the operator, upon reaching the trough, fought with the others for food that was no longer there. Finally, one rat found a solution. It pressed the lever several times in rapid succession, so that there was usually some food left when it reached the trough. On the other hand, its associates eventually learned that they needn't work at all. They stayed near the food trough and ate food pellets as these became available. A "class society" consisting of one worker and two parasites thus emerged. We cannot say, however, that one rat actually cooperated with the others. The worker had merely solved its own problem — how to get food in this situation. Benefit to the others was purely incidental.[25] □

An apparently genuine example of cooperative behavior occurred in another rat experiment, one not involving competition.[26] The general situation is illustrated and described in Figure 17.4. Observe that an animal could eat without getting a shock if its partner remained on the platform while it ate. At first the rats either ate at the same time, both getting a shock while doing so, or they sat on the platform together with neither of them getting anything to eat. In the case of some pairs, however, cooperation eventually developed. Their behavior became directed toward each other. One rat fed while the other was on the platform, then the latter made various responses toward the feeding animal, such as biting its tail or pulling on it until this animal returned to the platform. Eventually the rats shuttled back and forth, both getting food and both avoiding most of the shock.

Cooperative behavior of a high order has been demonstrated in chimpanzees. In an experiment already described (p. 432), pairs of chimpanzees learned to pull together so that food was brought within reach. When one member of a pair failed to get needed cooperation, it touched the other animal on the shoulder, turned it around, and, in fact, seemed to be "saying" something like "Help me." Similar results were found in a situation of still greater complexity.[27] Here two chimpanzees were in separate cages. Each cage contained two colored panels — for example, one cage a yellow and a red panel, the other a green and a blue. Food became available only when the panels were operated in a given sequence — say, *yellow, green, red, blue*. This meant that one subject, after pushing *yellow*, had to wait until its partner pushed *green*. This animal, in turn, had to wait until *red* was pushed. When *blue* was pushed, both got the reward. Some chimpanzees watched the partner and solicited when he was slow to respond. They reached through the bars, turned him in the right direction, or pushed him. However, there was no pointing toward the correct panel.

Cooperative behavior in human beings is of course greatly facilitated by pointing and by speech. In a situation somewhat resembling the chimpanzee experiment, one preschool child got the other to help her by pointing or by saying, "Look at that," or "Pull that string."[28] Another experiment on cooperation in children[29] required each subject to put a stylus in the corresponding hole at the same time, as in Figure 17.5. When each child put his stylus in the proper hole, a jelly bean was

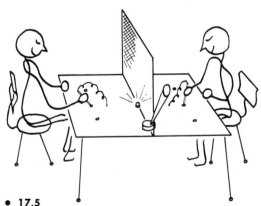

● **17.5**
Reinforced Cooperation. When both styli were placed in the holes almost simultaneously, a jelly bean fell into the cup. Without any verbal instructions as to what they were to do, the children learned to time their responses with sufficient closeness (.04 sec.) to bring reinforcement. (From N. H. Azrin and O. R. Lindsley, "The Reinforcement of Cooperation Between Children," *J. Abn. Soc. Psychol.*, 1956, 52, p. 101.)

delivered. This contingency was soon learned. However, there was only one jelly bean each time and this in itself constituted a problem. The question arose as to which child should have the jelly bean. Since it was not too easy to divide one jelly bean, the dilemma was settled verbally, usually by a decision to alternate — "The first jelly bean is mine, the next is yours," or something comparable. This sort of cooperation foreshadows the "deals" which follow childhood and which play so important a part in human affairs at every level of activity.

The preceding discussion of elementary forms of social behavior has served three purposes. In the first place it has given explicit meaning to the term "social interaction." Secondly, it has demonstrated some of the techniques used by psychologists and others to investigate social behavior in animals and children. Finally, it has provided a background against which we can project our discussion of social interaction in adult human society. ■

STATUS AND ROLE

An individual's *status* is his position in a social system. In a barnyard, this is simply a matter of relative position in the pecking order. Human society is so complex, however, that status varies, depending upon the particular angle from which we view it. From a broad political standpoint, there is the status of President, cabinet member, congressman, governor, and so on. Overall, our society has a discernible "class structure." We speak of a person's status as being, for example, *upper, middle*, or *lower class.** Overlapping this structure, but with a somewhat intellectual reference, a person may be referred to as "highbrow," "lowbrow," or somewhere in between these levels. Another frame of reference is socio-economic. One's status, from this standpoint, may be *professional, business, skilled laborer*, and so on. Some have a degree of status as "white-collar workers." There

* Vance Packard's *The Status Seekers* (McKay, 1959) is concerned with what we are discussing, but from the standpoint of the devices which individuals use to enhance their status.

are frequently status implications in being of a certain race, nationality, or religion. Within a much narrower scope are such statuses as *infant, child, adolescent, college student, female, wife,* or *parent.* There are also status positions within small established groups, such as a club or athletic team.[30]

But there is much more to status than we have suggested. With a given status there is usually a certain "style of life." Class status, for example, has associated with it certain so-called "status symbols," involving the kinds of cars driven and clothes worn. Class status is also related to the educational level attained and to the content and manner of speech.[31] According to Kinsey, such differences extend into the sex life.[32] Of greater interest, from a psychological standpoint, is the fact that different statuses require the playing of different roles.

The analysis of social behavior from the standpoint of roles is worthy of special attention. There are many definitions of the term *role* and there have been many theoretical discussions and practical applications, such as role-playing in psychotherapy and in the training of business and industrial leaders. Here we can consider no more than a few basic aspects of this concept.[33]

The role played by an actor has no reference to his status, except that of "actor." In everyday life, on the other hand, role and status are inseparably linked. As one writer has so succinctly phrased it, "the term *role* centers around the organized *actions* of a person coordinate with a given status or position."[34] This writer and others have pointed out that the person in a particular status situation is expected to act in certain ways and, in turn, expects others to reciprocate.

Acquiring roles

An important aspect of every instance of role acquisition is learning "to put oneself in the place of others" — to *identify* with them — and, as Robert Burns put it, "to see oursel's as others see us!"

A child learns to identify by role-playing, copying the behavior of others, and receiving instructions as to the proper behavior for "little

girls," "little boys," and so on. The little girl plays with her dolls — now in the role of mother, now that of doctor or nurse. She may also take the part of her doll in conversation, as when, after telling her "baby" to stay in its crib, she steps into the other role and says, "But Mummy, I don't want to stay in my crib." A comparable process is often involved in the development of conscience. A boy may even step into the role of father and admonish himself for doing what his father has forbidden.

In time we normally become adept at changing from one role to another, as each new situation arises. In each instance, the role is one dictated (in part, at least) by status. Thus the teacher plays a different role in the classroom from the one he enacts on the golf course, or in his home. In the classroom a student, in accordance with the teacher's status and his own, expects the former to lecture, for example, while he takes notes, and to give examinations while he answers them. If the teacher is also a graduate student, he will, on appropriate occasions, play the student role. And so it is with the many interlocked roles which people play in everyday life. As one's situation (and his status) changes, he may be said to assume different roles. Some would say that he exhibits different "selves," for there is a very close relation between one's self (p. 255) and the well-established roles of his everyday life.[35]

The shift from one role to another, or the actions involved in a particular role, are usually not calculated, nor is an individual necessarily aware of his role-playing, as a stage actor is. But there are instances, as everyone knows, where a person "tries to make an impression," and so obviously that we refer to his behavior as an "affectation" or to him as "affected." In most instances, however, each of us becomes so conditioned as to play appropriate roles unthinkingly.

An interesting sidelight on the interplay of status and roles is the modern tendency (in our society) to upgrade roles of low status by giving them a face-saving label. Thus the janitor may become a "custodian" and the street cleaner a "sanitary engineer."

In addition to well-established roles there are others that may be thrust upon us. The hero's role is often of such nature. In a group situation where there are problems calling for solution, an individual emerges as the leader. Some of the OSS tests described in an earlier discussion (p. 269) involved leaderless groups that were given a problem to solve. In these tests, individuals were observed to see what role each would play. Roles which emerge in such face-to-face situations are dealt with in later discussions.

Role conflicts

Although each of us plays multiple roles in this complex society of ours, role conflicts, when they exist, seldom bother us. The person whose religious affiliations are in conflict with a role he plays in everyday life tends to rationalize the discrepancy, so that the inconsistency that others may observe causes him little concern. During the last war, by contrast, many young men experienced an intense conflict between their role as followers of the "Prince of Peace" and their role as loyal citizens of a country at war. This role-conflict could not be solved by any such formula as "Praise the Lord and pass the ammunition."

Studies of behavior in situations involving disaster have shown that, under such conditions, one role may take priority over others with which it is now (perhaps for the first time) in conflict. Following a disastrous explosion in Texas City, for example, people whose duty it was to stay on the job and fight the fire rushed to their families instead, to see if these were safe, or to help them. A clergyman, who started to aid in rescue work, realized that it was more important for him to comfort the families of those who were killed, so he resolved to fill the latter role.[36] What is involved in all such situations is a conflict not merely of roles, but at the same time, and from a somewhat different slant, a conflict of obligations and loyalties.

One sometimes assumes roles, or roles are thrust upon him, which are not in harmony with his opinions, attitudes, or beliefs. Thus a man became deacon of a church while actually agnostic in his beliefs. He did this for various reasons, including the social advantages

of such status in the community. As most people do, however, he found "good" excuses for his inconsistency. This type of conflict, especially with reference to behavior in a social setting, has been extensively investigated in recent years.

When an individual is aware of a discrepancy or inconsistency between the roles that he assumes, between a particular role and the situation in which he finds himself, or between opinions, beliefs, or attitudes, he is likely to do something which reduces the inconsistency. This is the essence of Festinger's cognitive dissonance theory.[37] Dissonance is another word for inconsistency; cognitive dissonance (from *cognition*, for "knowledge") is a dissonance known to the person, an inconsistency or discrepancy of which he is aware. Dissonance may be reduced in various ways, some of which have already been discussed. The person may change his opinion, belief, or attitude to make it more consonant with the role he plays. He may give up one role that is in conflict with another, or which does not fit a change in circumstances. He may rationalize (p. 243) the inconsistency away. Discrepant or inconsistent elements in the conflict situation may be forgotten, as in our examples of repressive forgetting (p. 390). Or dissonance may be reduced in various other, often more subtle ways. Festinger's theory is an attempt to formulate hypotheses dealing with various aspects of cognitive dissonance, hypotheses that can then be tested by observation of behavior in situations of everyday life or by appropriately designed experiments.

One test of cognitive dissonance theory came in a study of a prophet and her followers. She had prophesied a catastrophe that failed to occur. How did she and her followers reduce the discrepancy between prophecy and reality? They did attempt to reduce it, of course, but they did it in devious ways, some of which were predicted.[38] One of these ways was to claim that God, because of the "impressive faith" of the prophets' followers, had cancelled the catastrophe.

☐ An experimental test of certain implications of cognitive dissonance theory was carried out with college students. These implications were as follows: "If a person is induced to do or say something which is contrary to his private opinion, there will be a tendency for him to change his opinion so as to bring it into correspondence with what he has done or said." Also, "The larger the pressure used to elicit the overt behavior (beyond the minimum needed to elicit it) the weaker will be the above-mentioned tendency."[39] The experimental test strongly supported these predictions.

Subjects were required to carry through an exceedingly boring and meaningless task for two hours. After completing it, each subject was privately requested to aid the investigator by telling other potential subjects that the task was an interesting and enjoyable one. Control subjects were offered nothing for doing this. Others were offered either $1 or $20. Some refused. However, sixty subjects (twenty in each group) cooperated. Subsequently they rated the enjoyableness and other aspects of the task on a scale from −5 to +5. This was an indication of their private opinion of the task after they had carried through their assignment. As predicted, the control subjects rated the task in the minus direction (the mean being −.45); the subjects given $1, hence not highly pressured, rated the task in the positive direction (1.35); and the subjects given $20 rated the task in the minus direction (−.05). The last-mentioned group did not have a significantly different opinion from that of the control group. What this means, perhaps, is that the individual willing to lie for $20 feels that anyone offered such an amount would do the same thing. He does not feel a need to change his opinion. On the other hand, the individual who gets only $1 may persuade himself that, after all, the task was not as boring as it first appeared. This justifies his falsehood at such a low price.

It is also interesting to note that when the subjects were finally told the nature of the experiment and asked to return the money, they were all willing to do this. ■

STUDYING BEHAVIOR IN SMALL GROUPS

Early experimental studies with small groups of human subjects dealt with social facilitation, the phenomenon already referred to as evident in animal behavior. The human subjects of experiments in this area engaged in activities like crossing out letters (e.g., every *e* on a page), tapping as fast as possible, and adding or multiplying. Sometimes they worked alone and sometimes as members of a co-working group. The latter was not, however, a cooperating group. We will discuss such groups later.

In one type of comparison, more subjects made their highest scores in the group situation — as compared with that in which they were merely working by themselves. Another type of comparison revealed a higher average output in the group than in the isolated situation. Further research of this nature showed the facilitating effect of group activity to be due, in large measure, to conscious or unconscious rivalry. For example, when individuals working in groups were told that their scores *would not be compared*, the facilitating effect of group situations failed to appear. In other experiments each person worked alone, but was told that his score *would be compared* with the scores of others working at the same time in separate rooms. Now the amount accomplished did not vary from that found in a group situation. This resembles in some ways the animal studies in which social facilitation was reduced to "competitive effort."[40]

☐ Studies like the above also demonstrate certain adverse effects of group situations, especially when competition is keen. There are individuals who become flustered and uncoordinated under group conditions, hence do more poorly than when working alone. An example of this can be seen in the simulated horse race where wooden horses on individual tracks are pulled with strings wound onto fishing reels. At the signal, an individual starts winding on his reel as fast as possible. In a practice situation, working alone and noncompetitively, there is normally a smooth performance. But in the "horse race," under keen competition to have one's horse come in first, there is often a marked incoordination, such as reversing the reel and tangling the line.[41]

Another adverse effect often noted in comparisons of individual and group performance is an excess of errors under the latter condition. This is prone to show up in arithmetical work. Thus the speed-up in a group situation may be offset by a lower quality of work than when individuals work alone. □

Current research on small groups is not so much concerned with the output and quality of performance as with the nature of social interaction; i.e., with interpersonal relations. We are ready to consider now some typical studies in this general area, which is often referred to as "group dynamics," a term introduced by Lewin (p. 226) to stress the dynamic as opposed to static characteristics of groups. This viewpoint is well represented by his statement that,

□ "The essence of a group is not the similarity or dissimilarity of its members, but their interdependence. A group can be characterized as a "dynamical whole"; this means that a change in the state of any subpart changes the state of any other subpart. The degree of interdependence of the subparts of members of the group varies all the way from a "loose" mass to a compact unit."[42] □

Many methods are used to study interpersonal relations, but we confine our attention to four. The first of these is a *social field analysis* of the type which led Lewin to speak of "group dynamics" before this term came to be more generally applied. Next we illustrate how intergroup relations may be studied by sociometric procedures. We then describe a method now widely used to record interaction in small groups while it is in process, the procedure referred to as *interaction process analysis.* Finally, we consider studies of collective problem-solving, some of which compared the efficiency of different communication networks.

Social field analysis

This involves concepts which defy an adequate brief discussion. Nevertheless we give these concepts in essence and then discuss their use by Lewin in analyzing a relatively simple situation, involving only a husband and his wife.[43] The concepts in question are *life space, social field,* and *locomotion.*[44]

Life space refers to the individual and his environment *as perceived by him.* Lewin and others have pointed out that there is a marked difference between the environment (geographical) as a physical scientist might view it and the environment (psychological) as the behaving person views it. We had such a distinction in mind when we said in an earlier discussion (p. 95) that two individuals in the same objective environment could be in very different environments psychologically.

The *social field* has reference to other people, or to what was referred to earlier as the "social environment." However, Lewin's concept of social field involves not only the actual presence of other persons, but also their symbolic presence, as when thinking of your mother's reaction to what you are contemplating either encourages or discourages you from going ahead with your plans. In the following example of social field analysis, the wife pictures her husband as doing certain things even though he is not present. Although absent, he is still part of her social field, as this is conceived of by Lewin. The life space includes the social field (as the individual perceives it) as well as the broader environment (again as the individual perceives it.)

In ordinary terminology *locomotion* is merely moving from place to place. As Lewin uses the term, it includes symbolic (expected, anticipated, intended, imagined) locomotion as well as an objective change of position.

Now we are ready to consider the marriage problem represented in Figure 17.6. This provides a good example of social field analysis.

□ The complete outer boundary of each diagram represents the limits of the individual's life space at the moment; i.e., Time 1 and Time 2 as indicated. The inner regions are conceived of, not as different parts of objective space, but as possibilities of action, even at the symbolic level, as when a person reaches a decision, moves from one attitude to another, and so on. First the life space of the husband Ⓗ is analyzed; then that of his wife Ⓦ . In the first diagram we see the respective positions of Ⓗ and Ⓦ . In terms of their situation as Ⓗ views it (including what he knows, or thinks he knows

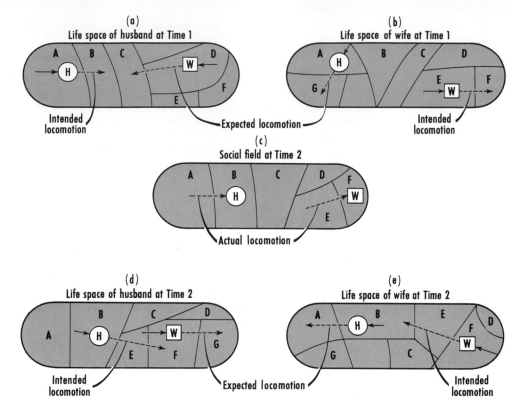

(a)
Life space of husband at Time 1

Intended locomotion

Expected locomotion

(b)
Life space of wife at Time 1

Intended locomotion

(c)
Social field at Time 2

Actual locomotion

(d)
Life space of husband at Time 2

Intended locomotion

Expected locomotion

(e)
Life space of wife at Time 2

Intended locomotion

● **17.6**

A Marriage Problem. These diagrams represent the life space of, respectively, a man and his wife, as conceived by Kurt Lewin and described in the text. (From K. Lewin, *Field Theory in Social Science*, Harper, 1951, p. 196.)

about ☐W☐), he intends, let us say, to move from region A to region B. It is assumed, here, that the social analyst has enough information about Ⓗ and his situation to predict this. Likewise, in view of the situation as Ⓗ perceives it, he expects his wife to move from D to C. All of this is represented in diagram *a*. Diagram *b* involves a comparable analysis from the wife's point of view, that is to say, from the standpoint of her own life space. Again it is assumed that enough is known about these two people to fill in the details which represent this. Note that her life space shows a marked contrast with that of her husband. It is quite differently structured. Moreover, her expectation, in terms of what she knows (or thinks she knows) about her husband is that he will move from A to G. She intends to move from region E to region F. Actually, as shown in diagram *c*, Ⓗ does move to B (which means that he may reach a

certain decision, change from one attitude to another, or even move physically from one place to another — a different house, for example). Likewise, ☐W☐ is shown in the same diagram as having moved to F.

Referring to this situation, Lewin says, "Neither husband nor wife had expected their partner to behave as he or she actually did. Obviously, the next step will depend largely on how each will react to this surprise, how each will interpret the conduct of the other, or, more generally speaking, how each will 'perceive' the new situation.

"The husband who has expected his wife to move from D to C and now sees her moving in the opposite direction, to F, may interpret this to mean that his wife has 'changed her mind.' In this case he may expect her next move to proceed in the same direction, namely toward G [as in diagram *d*]. Furthermore, the behavior of his wife is likely to change for him the meaning of C, that is, the cognitive structure of the situation. The wife who sees her husband move to B rather than G may perceive this to be an excursion to an activity which would be completed in a certain time after which he would return to A [diagram *e*]. She therefore decides to join her husband in B, whereas her husband, having a different perception of the situation [diagram *d*], intends to move on to F, which he perceives as being closer to his wife.

"Obviously, husband and wife will soon be in trouble if they do not 'talk things over,' that is, if they do not communicate to each other the structure of their life spaces with the object of equalizing them."[45] ☐

Enough has been said about social field analysis to illustrate how it goes at the task of trying to understand and predict social interaction. To an investigator well versed in its use, this type of analysis no doubt helps to clarify his thinking about the intricacies of particular interaction problems. Lewin and others have found it of practical value in industrial and other situations.[46] What we can get out of this discussion is an appreciation of the fact that interactions are not based upon the objective facts alone (as, say, a motion picture, even with sound track, might portray them), but upon how they are perceived (or interpreted) by interacting individuals, each in his own way. This type of analysis is an attempt to unravel a basic human relations problem, but a problem that is extremely difficult to study. Beyond individual relationships, as in the relatively simple illustration that we have used, the same sort of problem arises in intergroup relations — labor and management's views of each other; the Russian view of the United States and its aims, and its view of them and their intentions.

Sociometric procedures

The sociometric study of interpersonal relations also has reference to how interacting individuals view each other, but in a somewhat more limited sense than the approach already considered. There are several procedures, but they have in common the fact that individuals are asked to nominate, from among other members of their group, the member with whom they would most (or least) like to live, go on a mission, or carry out some project.[47] The individual who nominates is assured that his selections are confidential. Among a group of children, for example, each might be asked to tell, in private, the name of the child he would most like to have with him on a hike, or to share his tent. Military personnel, on the other hand, may nominate members of their group to accompany them on a combat mission. College students have been instructed to "Indicate the person whom you would most like to have as a loyal friend" and to "Name the person with whom you would most like to attend a formal affair." Sometimes the individual merely selects the person whom he would *most* or *least* like to have associated with him in one or more activities; other procedures require him to rank members of his group from the most to the least preferred.

The *sociogram* is a graphic representation of interpersonal preferences. It shows the status of each member of the group in terms of his acceptance or rejection by other members. A somewhat simplified sociogram for a group of ten persons is shown in Figure 17.7. Observe, for example, that A and B are attracted to each other — i.e., each chooses the other. I chooses G, E, and F, but is, in turn, chosen only by G. The numbers represent votes received, as described in the legend. E, who received more votes than anybody else, is the "star." J, who received no votes, is an "isolate."

Sociometry of the kind described has been widely used to select individuals for certain group projects, to discover isolates with a view to improving their social relations, to identify leaders, and to study group morale, which is likely to be high when members of the group are mutually congenial, as in the case of A, B, and D of our illustration.

Since the usual sociometric analysis lacks precise quantification, efforts have been made to improve upon it. One example is an extensive study of social relations and morale in nine fraternity groups at Syracuse University.[48] The procedure and the quantification of results

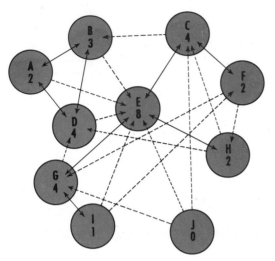

• 17.7

Sociogram of a Group of Workmen. Each person, represented here by a letter, was asked to vote for the three men most desired as working companions. Numbers represent votes. Thus *E* received 8 votes and *J* received none. Solid lines represent mutual choices. *A* and *B*, for example, voted for each other. Broken lines indicate one-way choices. *J*, for instance, voted for *E*, *G*, and *C*, but none of them selected him. The person voted for by *most (E)* is designated in sociometric research as a "star." *J*, on the other hand, selected by no one, is an "isolate." (From N. R. F. Maier, *Psychology in Industry*, 3rd ed., Houghton Mifflin, 1965, p. 141.)

are too detailed for adequate presentation here. Nonetheless, the general approach can be indicated.

Cognizance was taken of the fact that an individual might select different associates, depending upon his psychological need at the time. For example, a need for moral support in a difficult situation, for someone to have a good time with, or for someone to confide in. Therefore, each student made his nominations with reference to particular needs, which were indicated and elaborated upon by the investigator. The data were gathered in private interviews during which each student was assured that the investigator would hold his selections in strict confidence. He was asked not to tell anybody else about them. A

normal distribution curve (Figure 17.8) was shown, but without the names that appear in our figure, the meaning of which will soon be indicated. The curve was explained and the student asked to think of it as representing all males he had ever known. The subsequent instructions were:

☐ "Let us suppose that among your acquaintances there are people with whom you like to maintain a loyal friendship. You may be uncertain as to why you are attracted to such persons, but you know that being in their company on almost any occasion tends to give you a good feeling."

The interviewer then pointed to the curve and said: "Choosing from this group of people and *with this situation in mind, who BEST fits this description?* That is, with what person would you most like to maintain a loyal friendship? What is his name?"[49] ☐

The answer may have been, "Egan." Egan's name was then put at the extreme right of the curve, as illustrated. Following the same general procedure, it was ascertained that Adams *least* fitted the description, that Clark

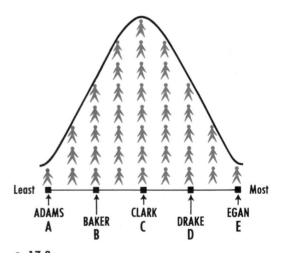

• 17.8

Normal Curve with Anchoring Points. The use of this figure has been described in the text. Clark is in the position designated "average." (Modified from E. F. Gardner and G. G. Thompson, *Social Relations and Morale in Small Groups*, Appleton-Century-Crofts, 1956, pp. 32–33.)

would be *average*, that Drake would fall half
way between Clark and Egan, and so on. All
of this was to establish reference points so that
the student could rate his fraternity brothers
in a comparable fashion.

Without going into the details of the
procedure, we can note that each fraternity
brother was placed in one of eight categories,
defined by divisions on each side of the midpoint of the distribution curve, as indicated in
our figure. It was in terms of these segments
that scores (ratings) were assigned. Thus Bill
Smith, being placed in the same segment as
Egan, would be scored 8 and John Jones,
falling in the same segment as Adams, would
receive a score of 1.

With their data quantified in this way,
the investigators were able to obtain information on how well an individual's social needs
are satisfied within his fraternity, the social-
relations status of particular fraternity men,
and the level of morale in one fraternity as
compared with another. Sociometric data were
also studied in relation to such outside indices
as general satisfaction or dissatisfaction with
fraternity accomplishments on the campus.

This refinement of sociometric procedure
has been demonstrated to have value in studying one type of small group, namely, a fraternity. It will no doubt be extended to other
small groups, possibly in industry and the
armed services.

Interaction in process

Interaction process analysis focuses upon
individuals interacting in a temporary problem situation, hence it deals with interaction
that is much more casual than that discussed
in the preceding sections. This approach has
revealed some interesting facts about interaction during cooperative problem-solving.

Observations are carried out in a laboratory setting, with a small group of students
working in a room while being observed
through a one-way vision screen. Each member of the group is informed that reactions
are to be observed and that a sound recording of everything said will be made.[50] The
general situation is shown in Figure 17.9.

● **17.9**
Observing and Recording Interaction in Process.
Observers are trained to record interaction in
terms of the following twelve categories: shows
solidarity, shows tension release, shows agreement, gives suggestion, gives opinion, gives
information, asks for information, asks for opinion, asks for suggestion, shows disagreement,
shows tension, shows antagonism. The subjects
are being viewed through a one-way vision
mirror. In this instance the task is a chess problem. (Courtesy, Dr. Robert F. Bales)

Observers who are trained for their task
use a code to record every act (verbal or otherwise) on the moving tape of a special recording device. Thus the acts of each individual
(and their timing) are recorded. The code
involves twelve response categories which investigators have found to be adequate for the
purpose. These categories are listed in the
legend to Figure 17.9.

Different observers show a high degree of
correspondence in what they record. The
reliability of the data obtained has thus been
established.

The standard task was to resolve a problem in human relations. Each member was
given an identical written report of the facts
in the case, but without knowing that his
partners had the same information. These reports were read prior to the beginning of the
group session and returned before it began.

The nature of the interactions taking place in such a session as we have described, as well as an idea of how trained observers categorize different individual acts, may be gathered from the following:

☐ *Member 1:* I wonder if we have the same facts about the problem? [Asks for opinion.] Perhaps we should take some time in the beginning to find out. [Gives suggestion.]

Member 2: Yes. [Agrees.] We may be able to fill in some gaps in our information. [Gives opinion.] Let's go around the table and each tell what the report said in his case. [Gives suggestion.]

Member 3: Oh, let's get going. [Shows antagonism.] We've all got the same facts. [Gives opinion.]

Member 2: (Blushes) [Shows tension.][51] ☐

The relative frequency of the twelve types of interaction, derived from twenty-four dif-

• **17.10**

Types of Acts Studied in One Type of Research with Small Groups. Observe that the act "gives opinion" comprises about 30 per cent of the total acts in the type of conference group with which we are concerned. About 56 per cent of the total reactions may be classified as attempts at problem-solving. These are: *gives suggestion, gives opinion,* and *gives information.* (From R. F. Bales, "How People Interact in Conferences," *Scientific American,* 1955, 192, 33.)

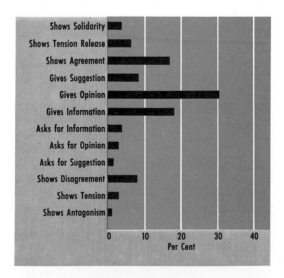

ferent groups which varied in size from two to seven members, is shown in Figure 17.10. This comparison is based upon problem-solving of the sort described above.

One interesting outcome of investigations like that described is what they reveal about leadership in such small problem-solving groups. A member's talkativeness is one important leadership variable. Two others are ratings by the group members of each individual's task-ability (how well they think he contributed) and his likeability.

It has been found that relatively few individuals rate high on all three variables. More have high ratings for talkativeness and task-ability and a lower rating for likeability. This type of leader is referred to as the "task specialist." Still more familiar is the "social specialist," the individual who rates high on likeability but relatively low on the other variables. A person who is high on talkativeness, but low on task-ability and likeability, is referred to as an "overactive deviant." He attempts to dominate rather than lead. Then, of course, there are those who rate low in all three respects — the so-called "underactive deviants," or "scapegoats."[52]

☐ What we have described is actually an oversimplified version of the findings on leadership in small groups. It has been observed that while some individuals rather generally exhibit the same sort of leadership in differently composed groups, in groups of different size, and in groups focused on different kinds of problems, others show considerable variability from one setting to another. Some lead in certain situations and not at all in others. In short, observation of behavior in small groups, as one investigator has put it, "strongly supports the contention that leadership is not an attribute of personality or of character. It is a social role, the successful adoption of which depends upon a complex of abilities and traits. But even more, the adoption of a leadership role is dependent upon the specific situation. The same individual in the same group may alternate between the roles of leader and follower as the group goal changes. Most frequently the individual is propelled into a position of leadership by virtue of his capacity for interpersonal contribution in a specific situation."[53] □

Here we have focused upon the method known as *interaction process analysis,* and illustrated how it is used to study the emergence of leadership in small problem-solving groups. What has been emphasized is the interaction process — not the efficiency of group versus individual problem-solving, nor the question of how group problem-solving can be most efficient. We now consider collective problem-solving from these standpoints.

Collective problem-solving

Outcomes of studies on differences between collective and individual problem-solving have varied, depending upon the nature of the problems, the amount of information available to each individual, and the composition of the groups. In the above studies on interaction process analysis, every individual had all of the information available. The main advantages of this group situation were: (1) some individuals had more ideas than others, and (2) any individual's ideas were subject to criticism from others. Any idea thus received an evaluation which the individual (working alone) might not have given it.

Various problems have been used to compare collective and individual performance. In some studies the group has achieved more, or better, solutions; in some, the individual; and in others there has been no difference.[54]

An approach that is quite different from most is one which compares individual and group learning of a maze problem.[55]

□ The maze used in this study had twenty pairs of brass boltheads which were arranged vertically on a black panel. One bolthead of each pair was wired to a small lamp which lit up when contact was made. This, the correct bolthead, varied from right to left as the subject proceeded from lower to upper pairs. The maze was placed in front of the individual working alone, or the group, and the experimenter pointed to the first pair. The subject said whether the right or the left bolthead was correct. Then the next pair was indicated and responded to. This continued to the twen-

tieth pair. Then, as the experimenter contacted the selected bolthead in each pair, the subject could observe his successes and failures. This procedure continued for six trials. In the group-learning situation, the experimenter acted as with the individual working alone. However, the bolthead to be selected was determined by a vote. Upon indicating a pair, the experimenter said, "How many say right?" then "How many say left?" The choice of the majority was taken as the response for that pair.

On the first trial, the mean number of errors was 9.56 for those who worked alone. The group error score was 9.94. From this trial on there was consistently greater improvement in the group situation. By the sixth trial the group error score was 1.12, as compared with 5.30 for individual learners.

Why group learning was superior is not revealed by the experiment; but the investigator points out several things which may have produced this outcome.

"The group member might obtain immediate reinforcement or inhibition of his own responses by observing their agreement or disagreement with the responses of an associate whose superiority he accepted. He might perceive anticipatory cues in the behavior of the associate prior to his own responses and be guided accordingly. Or he might delay his own response just long enough to observe the way the associate was going to respond and respond similarly; this would be feasible to some extent in the group situation, since the responses of the members tended to be quite asynchronous in the early trials and at difficult choice-points.

"The individual in the group would have another set of cues and another kind of reinforcement not available when learning alone. He would have the responses of the group as a whole. By hesitating in his own responses, he could be guided by the group responses at uncertain choice-points; and where he responded directly, the group response would provide him with an immediate check on the correctness of his own response. Since the group would be more often right than the average member, this check would be an advantage, and the responses which conformed to the group response would be to some extent reinforced by observation of this conformity. Involved in this reinforcement might be the phenomenon known conventionally as group pressure."[56]

The possibility that social facilitation was responsible for group superiority was tested in a parallel experiment, the results of which failed to support this hypothesis. Another experiment demonstrated that imitation was involved, since subjects located in the best positions to profit from the performances of superior learners had lower error scores than those not so advantageously placed. □

Our discussion of collective problem-solving so far has dealt with problems involving information that is equally available to every subject, whether working in a group or alone. But how about problems which require a pooling of information, only part of which is known to each individual? Under these circumstances, several heads are obviously better than one. This may also be true when solution calls for creativity and some individuals in a group are more creative than others.

The so-called brainstorming procedure is a group discussion designed to generate creative ideas.[57] Its originator (an advertising executive) claims that brainstorming produces more ideas than come to individuals working alone. But an experimental investigation[58] with Yale University students has shown that this is true only if each individual is compared with a group (of four in this case). When the comparison is between four individuals working alone (nominal group) and a comparable group of four individuals working as a group (actual group), the former have more ideas and better ones. It has nevertheless been claimed that "The theory underlying brainstorming seems, in the light of available evidence, to be sound. The general purpose is to produce intercommunication of as wide a range of ideas as possible. The main procedural rule is that criticism and evaluation of both one's own ideas and those of others are to be withheld (until some time later). A 'free-wheeling' attitude is encouraged as is also 'taking off' from other persons' ideas."[59] In the negative research with college students, there was apparently a tendency for the brainstorming procedure to *inhibit* creative thinking. Moreover, the subjects often fell into similar trains of thought, thus reducing the number of unique ideas. It may be argued, of course, that college students are more sensitive to criticism by their peers and thus greater conformists than business men. On the other hand, it has been demonstrated that special training of college students in brainstorming techniques leads to significant increments in creative problem-solving.[60] It has been claimed, in this connection, that individuals working alone are relatively conservative and that the brainstorming situation is conducive to ideational risk-taking. A recent review of the research on risk-taking, however, shows that some studies support and others fail to support this viewpoint.[61]

Whenever individuals have specialized information and attempt to solve a problem by pooling it, there are communication problems.[62] This fact led to the following relatively simple investigation.[63] In a given experiment there were five subjects, each with information that the others did not have. This appeared on a card containing five symbols of which those in Figure 17.11 are typical. Note that six symbols were involved in the problem. One

	Six Symbols Used: ○ △ ◇ □ + ✳					
Trial No.	Symbol Missing From:					Common Symbol
	White	Red	Brown	Yellow	Blue	
1	△	◇	✳	○	□	+
2	◇	○	□	△	+	✳
3	+	✳	□	△	◇	○
4	□	◇	△	✳	+	○

● 17.11
Typical Symbols Used in Experiments on Communication Networks. It will be seen that each subject, in a given trial, had one symbol missing. This was different for each of the five subjects. The missing symbol was, in each case, replaced by one which they all had in common. (From H. J. Leavitt, "Some Effects of Certain Communication Patterns on Group Performance," *J. Abn. Soc. Psychol.*, 1951, *46*, p. 40.)

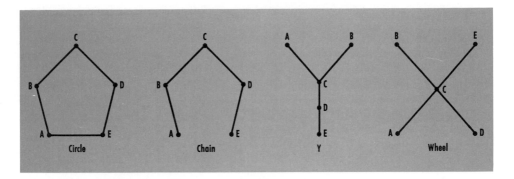

● 17.12

Some Communication Networks. As described in the text, each individual could communicate only along the channels represented by solid lines. In the wheel pattern, for example, nobody could communicate with anybody else except through C. (From H. Leavitt, *Managerial Psychology,* University of Chicago Press, 1958, p. 42.)

subject, designated "White," had the triangle missing and his five symbols included a cross. "Red" had no diamond, but his card contained a cross. The asterisk was missing from "Brown's" card, which also had a cross. Thus every card included among its five figures one that was common to all. The problem was: "which is the common figure?" Quite obviously, the members of a group had to share their special information.

In separate experiments, with different subjects each time, the five communication networks shown in Figure 17.12 were tested. In the circle, any individual could give information to the person next to him. This was done by writing on a slip of paper and passing it along the communication channel symbolized by the connecting line. In this way, information passed around the circle until some subject named the common figure. In the wheel, on the other hand, A could pass information to C, but to nobody else. C could pass it on to B, E, or D as he saw fit. These could pass it on only by sending it back to him.

The outcome of this experiment was quite clear. A wheel network was consistently shown to be most efficient and a circle least efficient. The wheel groups, for example, obtained correct solutions in the shortest time, required the fewest total number of messages, and made the fewest errors.

The individual in the center of such a network has a position of leadership from the start. Upon receiving information he can decide where it will do the most good, hence where to send it next. This no doubt contributes to the greater efficiency of the wheel network.*

We now continue our study of interpersonal relations in small groups. Again leadership is involved, but it is imposed upon the group rather than emerging from within it. ■

THE STUDY OF "SOCIAL CLIMATES"

One of the most widely known types of experimentation in the general area of "group dynamics" is that in which small groups are subjected to different kinds of leadership and their subsequent behavior analyzed in terms of group productivity, morale, and attitudes of members toward the leader and each other.[64] Experiments of this nature have been carried out with boys formed into after-school clubs

* These results cannot be generalized to all situations. Communication networks in business and industry involve special problems, and each must be evaluated in terms of specific situations. The investigator whose research we have discussed has written a book dealing with these special problems. See H. Leavitt, *Managerial Psychology,* University of Chicago Press, 1958.

for specific projects requiring group participation. In one set of experiments, for example, papier mâché theatrical masks were made. Several groups, each composed of five ten-year-old boys, were used. The groups were equated in terms of socio-economic status and other variables, including previous interpersonal relations, as determined sociometrically. Leadership was given by adults who were trained to lead in three ways — authoritarian, laissez-faire, and democratic, as called for by the experimental design. The leadership was so designated, not in terms of political structures thus categorized, but from the standpoint of the specific roles assumed by the leaders. The *authoritarian leader*, for example, determined all policies, dictated the nature of every project, and criticized, but refrained from active participation. The *laissez-faire leader* was a leader in name only. Each member of the group was given complete freedom to do anything he wished and the adult neither participated nor gave information, unless it was requested. The *democratic leader* called for a discussion of policies. He suggested possible goals and procedures, but these were actually selected as an outcome of group discussion. This type of leader also participated as a member of the group and commented upon activities from time to time, but in an objective or "fact-minded" manner. Each group worked on similar projects under different kinds of leadership and the same adult rotated from one group to another, in each case assuming the leadership role which the design of the experiment called for. Thus, in a particular experiment, one group might begin with a democratic leader, six weeks later work on a comparable project with an authoritarian leader, then, after another six weeks, change to a comparable project with a laissez-faire leader. Another group would reverse this process, beginning with an authoritarian leader. The rotation procedure assured that each club would work under each kind of leadership, and with a different leader each time a change occurred.[65]

The "group climate" or "group atmosphere" differs considerably depending upon the sort of leadership involved. Little of a favorable nature can be said for laissez-faire leadership as compared with the other two types, hence we will compare only the democratic and autocratic "climates." In some respects the autocratic situation tended to be superior — the boys who accepted it submissively worked for longer stretches, and of course got more done. But this was only while the leader was present. When he absented himself "the boys in democracy kept right on working . . . while in autocracy when the leader left, the boys stopped working as if glad to be relieved of the task they 'had' to do."[66] There appeared to be more originality in the democratic situation, as well as less hostility (toward the leader and other boys) and less aggression.

Recent research along similar lines has verified the findings described and has revealed additional details.[67] One of these is the fact that authoritarian leadership is conducive to apathy in some groups and aggressive resistance in others. We see in Figure 17.13 that the detailed outcomes of an imposed autocracy differ, depending upon the passive or aggressive reaction to it. Note, for example, that groups reacting aggressively to autocratic leadership were more discontented than those reacting passively. They also made more demands for attention and asked for more information. On the other hand, both the passive reactors and the democratic groups engaged in more work-minded conversation than the aggressive reactors. Other comparisons will be evident in examining the figure.

EFFECTS OF GROUP PARTICIPATION

An important thing to be learned from the experiments on "social climates" is that a situation which provides opportunities for individuals to become involved in what is going on, that is, to participate in decisions as well as actions, has decided advantages over one which produces either apathy or aggressiveness. Two practical examples can be cited. The first has to do with the relative effectiveness of a lecture and a group discussion; the other shows how group participation in decision-making may influence industrial output.

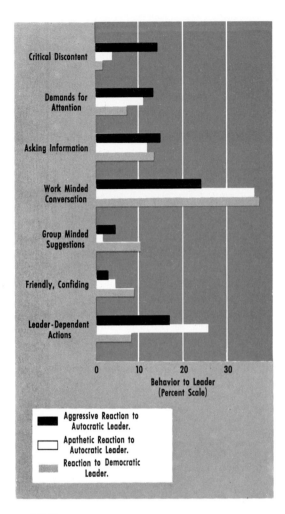

● **17.13**
Reactions to Three Kinds of Leadership. Those subjected to autocratic leadership responded aggressively or apathetically, with resulting differences in specific reactions. Reactions to democratic leadership are also shown. (Derived from R. K. White, in E. E. Maccoby, T. M. Newcomb, and E. L. Hartley (Eds.), *Readings in Social Psychology*, 3rd ed., Holt, 1958, p. 501.)

Lecture versus group discussion

During the last world war choice cuts of meat were scarce, hence it was decided to see whether housewives could be induced to make greater use of less preferred animal organs, like beef hearts, kidneys, and sweetbreads. Accordingly, the following pilot study was undertaken by Lewin and his associates for the Food Habits Committee of the National Research Council.[68]

Three Red Cross groups were given a 45-minute lecture on the need to aid the war effort by using such products, their nutritional value, how to overcome the odors associated with cooking them, how to make them palatable, and so on. Recipes were distributed and the lecturer told how she prepared these "delicious dishes" and how well they were received by her family. This was the lecture approach.

Three comparable groups were subjected to the "group-decision" approach. After some details were given, such as the need to utilize such food, and its nutritional value, a discussion designed to produce group participation was started. The women were induced to discuss the problems which "housewives like yourself" might experience in using such food and how they might overcome these. During this session the various remedies and recipes given in the lectures were introduced, but only as the discussion turned in these directions.

Early in each meeting the women who had previously used the meats indicated this by raising a hand. At the end, all who would be willing to try them during the next week indicated this by a show of hands.

The investigators checked later to see which of the women who had not previously used these meats did so during the week following the lecture or discussion. The outcome is illustrated in Figure 17.14.

A similar advantage of group decision as against lectures has been found in the case of other products — for example, increased use of powdered milk. Group decision has also been more advantageous than individual instruction.* in persuading mothers to give their infants cod liver oil and orange juice.[69]

---

* This does not mean that class discussion should replace lectures in a classroom, even if this were practicable. What we are concerned with here is the relative effectiveness of lecture and discussion in inducing people to make decisions and follow them with appropriate action.

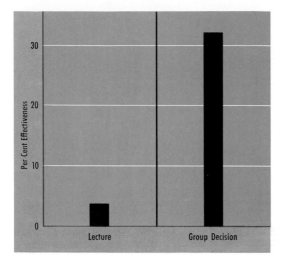

• **17.14**
The Relative Effectiveness of Lecture Versus Discussion. Of those who had never before served the foods involved in this experiment, about 3 per cent served them after hearing a lecture and about 32 per cent after group discussion. (From K. Lewin, "Group Decision and Social Change," in E. E. Maccoby, T. M. Newcomb, and E. L. Hartley, *Readings in Social Psychology*, 3rd ed., Holt, 1958, pp. 197–219.)

Lewin attributes the superiority of group decision to several factors. The most important of these is no doubt the individual involvement which group discussion brings, as compared with the relative passivity which characterizes lectures and individual instruction.

An example from industry

The problem investigated was how to overcome decreased production which followed a change in work procedures. Women workers in a pajama factory were paid in terms of work units, with the standard level of efficiency being 60 work units per hour. When it was necessary to transfer operators to new jobs, rated in a comparable fashion with their former ones, there was usually a drop in efficiency. This represented a decrease of 10 or more work units per hour. During the re-training period a bonus compensated for what would otherwise be a loss in pay. Nevertheless, the work rate usually failed to return to its former level. Many women became discouraged and either gave up trying to improve, or left the job.

The investigators, interpreting this situation from the standpoint of group dynamics, regarded it as an outcome of resistance to change.[70] They felt that resistance might be reduced by procedures similar to those just described. Accordingly, women to be transferred were formed into separate groups, each of which was introduced to the change-over in different ways. Only two of the procedures that were used (the least and the most effective) will be described. They involved, respectively, *no participation* in the decision to change (control group), and *total participation* in this decision.

Members of the nonparticipating group were subjected to the usual factory routine in which the change-over was introduced with a statement that it was necessary to meet competitive conditions and that a new piece rate was being set, a rate explained by the time-study man. The participation procedure was very different. Workers met in small groups. The need to reduce costs was dramatically illustrated by having the women examine two garments which, despite a large difference in cost of production, they could not distinguish. Under these conditions, many suggestions were made by the members and a plan of operation was approved by the group.

The difference in outcome between these approaches is graphically demonstrated in Figure 17.15. Note that the control group made little recovery after the change-over, whereas the experimental group not only reached the former level of 60 units per hour, but exceeded this by a large margin. There was also general satisfaction with the job in the latter group, and no turnover during a subsequent period of observation.

Enough of this experiment and its outcome has been described to indicate that, here again, the group dynamics approach successfully supplanted the usual procedure. ■

GROUP PRESSURES ON INDIVIDUAL JUDGMENT

We are all subjected to group pressures — daily, in fact, from the time of birth for as long as we live. Socialization, referred to so frequently in earlier discussions, is one example of this. In adult life we are also influenced, sometimes positively and sometimes negatively, by what others in our immediate vicinity are doing and saying. As a result, we may change our tastes, our attitudes, our opinions, and our judgments.

The two experiments to be described here show how even a small temporary group may influence the perceptual judgments of one of its members.

The autokinetic experiment

The first experiment involves what has been called an *autokinetic effect*. If you were put into a completely dark room and a small fixed spot of light were exposed, you would see it move in different directions as though it were moved here and there by the experimenter. This illusory movement is the autokinetic effect.

A subject entered the dark room with the experimenter, who pointed to a response key and said: "When the room is completely dark, I shall give you a signal READY, and then show you a point of light. After a short time the light will start to move. As soon as you see it move, press the key. A few seconds later the light will disappear. Then tell me the distance it moved. Try to make your estimates as accurate as possible."[71]

Two seconds after a subject pressed the key, a shutter closed and the light disappeared. Then another trial was given. One hundred judgments were obtained from each subject. With isolated subjects working in this way, the investigators established individual norms. Although there was no actual movement, each subject settled down, after a time, to judgments which, while they differed from those of other individuals, were more or less stable for him. Thus one subject reported an average movement of 7.5 inches, another of 2 inches, and

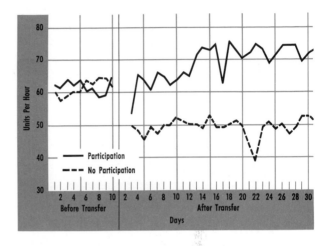

● 17.15

Effects of Participation and Nonparticipation in Decision Making. Whereas both groups had comparable production records (60 units per hour) prior to transfer, the nonparticipation group decreased its efficiency and did not return to the former level, while the participation group, after a brief decline, actually increased its efficiency. (After L. Coch and J. R. P. French, "Overcoming Resistance to Change," *Human Relations,* 1948, I, p. 522.)

still another of .5 inch, as indicated at the left of Figure 17.16.

To test for a group influence, the same subjects were subsequently placed in the darkroom together. Now they heard each other's reports, with the result illustrated in the graph. One can see that, in three successive sessions, their judgments converged. Two were influenced to raise their estimates slightly. One lowered his until it conformed with that of the others. This happened in other groups, but not always with changes as marked as in the case of the last-mentioned subject.

Some subjects were tested in the group situation for three sessions, then alone. These carried the former judgment into the individual situations, as illustrated in Figure 17.17. The group influence, which became apparent early in the first session, led to a marked similarity of judgment and, as one might well expect, this carried over to the last session,

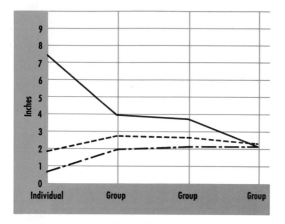

● **17.16**
Individual Conformity to Group Norms. These are the averages for three individuals. In the initial series, where each reported the amount of movement individually, there was marked divergence. In a succession of tests with the three reporting in each other's presence, there was the illustrated funneling effect. Finally, all were giving similar reports. (From M. Sherif, "A Study of Some Social Factors in Perception," *Arch. Psychol.,* 1935, No. 187, p. 33.)

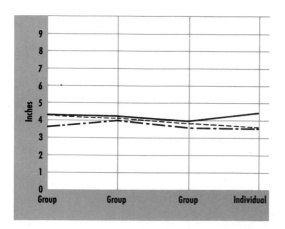

● **17.17**
Effects of Earlier Group Experience on Individual Judgments. Compare this figure with Figure 17.16. This one shows an absence of the funneling effect often found when individuals are first tested alone. (From M. Sherif, "A Study of Some Social Factors in Perception," *Arch. Psychol.,* 1935, No. 187, p. 33.)

where the individual gave his judgment in isolation.

Later research[72] suggests that some of this group effect is due to the way a subject views (or structures) the situation. Although the movement is purely subjective, and there is therefore no correct answer to the question "How far did the light move?" one usually assumes that movement has actually occurred and that his judgment, as compared with the judgments of others, must be faulty. Therefore he tends to make a correction. This was confirmed in a repetition of the above experiment with college women. In some of the later experiments, however, the subjects were told that movement was illusory and that nobody was necessarily more accurate than anybody else. Each subject was paired in the darkroom with another who was, so to speak, "fixed." The latter had been instructed to give reports within a certain narrow range regardless of what she actually experienced. Now the convergence of reports observed in earlier experiments did not so often appear. In a group of ten naïve subjects tested in this way, only four showed the usual convergence, and these either forgot about the illusory nature of the movement or did not believe what they had been told concerning this.

One against a majority

The second type of group-pressure experiment that we wish to consider differed in cer-

 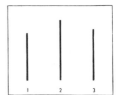

● **17.18**
Sample Cards from the Judgment Experiment. The first line was shown and covered. Then the individual was to say which of the lines on the second card equaled it in length. (From S. E. Asch, "Studies of Independence and Submission in Group Pressure," *Psychological Monographs,* 1956, 70, No. 416, p. 7.)

tain important respects from the one just described. First, it dealt with a real difference — a difference in the length of lines (Figure 17.18) — rather than an illusory one, hence actual errors could be measured and their magnitude compared for the different conditions of the experiment. Second, as illustrated in Figure 17.19, it involved a larger group and a more natural situation than that in the first type of study. Finally, it placed the individual in a situation in which there was a decided discrepancy between the evidence of his senses and what other members of the group were reporting. This was because (unknown to him) each of the others had been instructed to give the correct line on certain trials and, on all other trials, to respond unanimously by naming a certain incorrect line. The correct estimates were interpolated so as to mislead the subject. Estimates were given, in order, by individuals 1 to 7. Table 17.1 makes the situation very clear. There

were eighteen trials. On the first of these the standard line was 10 inches long. The comparison lines were (1) 8¾ inches, (2) 10 inches, and (3) 8 inches. The correct line was obviously No. 2, and the group, beginning with the first member and proceeding in succession to the subject, and one beyond him, all gave this as their estimate. On the next trial, the line was 2 inches long. Now, in order, the comparison lines were 2, 1, and 1½ inches. Again there was unanimity, all in this case designating No. 1. On the third trial, however, the other members of the group unanimously gave a response that was incorrect. The line was 3 inches long; the three other lines were, in order, 3¾, 4¼, and 3 inches long. The correct line was No. 3, but everyone except the naïve subject said that it was No. 1. The error was thus ¾ inch. On the next trial the group again differed from the naïve subject. On the next they agreed with him. And so on, as shown in Table 17.1.

● 17.19

The Group Pressure Situation. As described in the text, all but a naïve student had been instructed to give unanimously incorrect judgments about the length of lines on cards as shown in Figure 17.18. Reports started with man 1 and ended with man 7. The naïve subject (6) found his judgments to be in conflict with those of the group. (Courtesy, *Scientific American*.)

Some subjects found this a disturbing experience. To use the investigator's words: "one individual found himself suddenly contradicted by the entire group, and this contradiction was repeated again and again in the course of the experiment. . . . He faced, possibly for the first time in his life, a situation in which a group unanimously contradicted the evidence of his senses."[73] Very few subjects suspected the nature of the experiment. Data for those who did were discarded.

The investigator sought to discover how individuals in such a situation would react. Would they resist — sticking to what *they* perceived to be true — or would they yield to the majority? As the reader can perhaps anticipate, there were marked individual differences. In a group of fifty subjects, about 25 per cent reacted in complete independence of what others said. The remainder showed varying degrees of change in the group-sug-

gested direction. The subjects of a control group gave their judgments in writing and without a group influence. They averaged 0.8 errors. On the other hand, those subjected to group pressures, as described, averaged 3.84 errors. The range was from 0 to 11 errors, out of a possible 12.

Even those subjects who had no errors were at times disturbed. Some became "doubt ridden and these experienced a powerful impulse not to appear different from the majority."[74] [The reader might refer, in this connection to what was said earlier (p. 184) about the urge to conform and also (p. 537) about cognitive dissonance.] After each subject had completed the experiment, he was told that he had been misled, and why.

Other experiments of this nature placed two naïve subjects in the group. Some included a member instructed to agree with the naïve subject. Under both of these conditions,

■ **TABLE 17.1   Lengths of Standard and Comparison Lines**

Trial	Length of standard line (in inches)	Comparison lines (in inches)			Correct response	Group response	Majority error (in inches)
		1	2	3			
1	10	8¾	10	8	2	2	—
2	2	2	1	1½	1	1	—
3	3	3¾	4¼	3	3	1 *	+ ¾
4	5	5	4	6½	1	2 *	— 1.0
5	4	3	5	4	3	3	—
6	3	3¾	4¼	3	3	2 *	+ 1¼
7	8	6¼	8	6¾	2	3 *	— 1¼
8	5	5	4	6½	1	3 *	+ 1½
9	8	6¼	8	6¾	2	1 *	— 1¾
10	10	8¾	10	8	2	2	—
11	2	2	1	1½	1	1	—
12	3	3¾	4¼	3	3	1 *	+ ¾
13	5	5	4	6½	1	2 *	— 1.0
14	4	3	5	4	3	3	—
15	3	3¾	4¼	3	3	2 *	+ 1¼
16	8	6¼	8	6¾	2	3 *	— 1¼
17	5	5	4	6½	1	3 *	+ 1½
18	8	6¼	8	6¾	2	1 *	— 1¾

* Starred figures designate the erroneous estimates by the majority. (From S. E. Asch, "Studies of Independence and Submission in Group Pressure," *Psychol. Monogr.*, 1956, 70, No. 416, p. 6.)

as might be expected, the influence of the majority was greatly reduced. In research designed to discover the influence of the size of the majority lined up against a single person it was discovered that the average amount of yielding (average departure from accuracy) becomes greater as the majority increases from one to four, but then remains about the same as more persons are added to the group.[75]

Brainwashing

The experiments that we have described dealt with relatively simple attempts to apply group pressures. So-called brainwashing is an extreme effort in the same direction. As the Chinese Communists are reported to have practiced this during and after the Korean War, it included the pitting of individual beliefs against what appeared to be overwhelming contrary evidence. Take, for example, the germ-warfare propaganda that was designed to turn prisoners against their own countrymen:

□ "Of particular importance were the germ-warfare confessions extracted from a number of Air Force officers and enlisted men. The Chinese made a movie of one or two of the officers giving their testimony to the 'international' commission which they had set up to investigate the problem and they showed the movie in all the camps. Furthermore, one or two of the officers personally went from camp to camp and explained how United Nations forces had used these bombs; this made a powerful impression on many men who had, until then, dismissed the whole matter as a Chinese propaganda project. The great detail of the accounts, the sincerity of the officers, the fact that they were freely going from camp to camp and did not look as if they were then or had previously been under any duress made it difficult for some men to believe that the accounts could be anything but true."[76] □

There was much more to this brainwashing procedure, including enforced group discussions in which the leaders kept the focus on Communist ideas, or on ideas derogatory to the United States and the United Nations. Moreover, the individual prisoner was cut off from any sort of communication from outside which would lend support to beliefs already held. Under such pressures, some prisoners, including the above-mentioned officers who supported the germ-warfare story, became indoctrinated in the desired direction. There were social pressures of other kinds, like punishing the group in retaliation for individual misdeeds and rewarding a desired response while punishing others. Such background conditions as isolation from loved ones and semistarvation were also contributing factors. We cannot discuss the whole issue of brainwashing, but it is cited as a form of group pressure applied in a real-life situation. ■

THE STUDY OF RUMOR

Rumor may be defined as "an unverified report or account of an event that circulates chiefly by word of mouth."[77] The account may have an element of truth, but it is almost certainly inaccurate, especially if much detail is involved. The rumor that Professor X dropped dead in the classroom (if this actually happened) is a mere statement of fact and not as likely to suffer distortion as the rumor, for instance, that the faculty is contemplating a "clamp-down" on fraternities. In the latter instance there are no student witnesses to what the faculty is considering, student interests are involved, various possibilities of action may enter the story, and it could well be a complete fabrication.*

Rumors are especially evident in times of public crisis (war, famine, natural catastrophe) when human welfare is involved and when, quite often, reliable information is lacking. Take, for example, what followed the bombing of Pearl Harbor.

□ "The affair was important because of the potential danger it represented to all of us, and because its aftermath of mobilization affected every life. It was ambiguous because no one seemed quite certain of the extent or

* The reader not yet acquainted with Lady Gregory's one-act play, "The Spreading of the News," will get both enjoyment and some insight into the transmission of rumors from reading it.

reasons for, or consequences of the attack. Since the two conditions of rumor — importance and ambiguity — were at a maximum, we had an unprecedented flood of what became known as 'Pearl Harbor rumors.' It was said that our fleet was 'wiped out,' that Washington didn't dare to tell the extent of the damage, that Hawaii was in the hands of the Japanese. So widespread and so demoralizing were these tales that, on February 23, 1942, President Roosevelt broadcast a speech devoted entirely to denying the harmful rumors and to reiterating the official report on the losses."[78] □

While it is possible to make field studies of rumor, the process itself can best be studied under the controlled conditions of a laboratory. The reader may recall that some studies described in earlier chapters are relevant in this context. There were those dealing with memory for stories (pp. 378–380). A subject read the story and then told it to another, who told it to still another, and so on, until several had relayed it. We pointed out how the story became greatly abbreviated, with many details dropped, some details added, and other details distorted in various ways. This was not a study of rumor. It dealt with mem-

● **17.20**

A Picture Used in Experiments on Rumor. Typical reports are reproduced in the text. Only the person who started a "rumor" actually saw the picture. (From G. W. Allport and L. Postman, *The Psychology of Rumor,* Holt, 1947, p. 71.)

ory. But memory is important in the transmission of rumors. We also studied the inaccuracies which creep into testimony (pp. 380–381). Here our focus was on an individual who witnessed an event, then testified about it. This is comparable in some respects to the transmission of a rumor, for what the original observer tells another, in getting the rumor started, is subject to the same kinds of error that we described in the case of testimony. Moreover, what any person perceives of the story, as told to him, and what he passes on to the next person, is also subject to errors of testimony.

While these studies on memory and accuracy of testimony are relevant in the present context, and lead us to expect comparable inaccuracies in rumors, the latter have been subjected to specific investigation with small groups, usually of college students. Only one such study can be considered here.

The experiment took place before an audience from which six or seven volunteers had been selected to serve as subjects. After they had left the room, a picture was projected, such as the one shown in Figure 17.20. It was visible to all in the audience, but not to each subject as he returned to the room, since a partition blocked his view. When the first subject entered, a member of the audience previously selected for this purpose, described what was on the screen. He had been asked to describe twenty details of the picture. After this, the next subject was admitted. He stood beside the first, who described from hearsay what was on the screen. After this, the first subject took a seat in the audience while the second subject told the third about the picture. This procedure continued until all the subjects had been told, and had been given an opportunity to tell about the pictured event. A record was kept of everything said.

The observer's description was usually quite detailed and it had a high degree of accuracy. But the story became less detailed and increasingly inaccurate as it went from one subject to another. Take, for example, the report of this subject, who was first to hear the story: "This scene is on a streetcar or a train. There are seven adults and one child.

There is a woman sitting in one seat holding a baby and there is an elderly chubby man sleeping. Two of the adults are a colored man in a zoot suit and a white man having an argument. The white man has a razor in his hand. There are four ads, one is for "Lucky Strikes," one is for some soap, one for some sort of hotel."[79]

This report is less than half as long as the original and it includes several inaccuracies, which the reader may check for himself by examining the picture. The subsequent reports become progressively less detailed and increasingly erroneous. Take, for example, the fifth and sixth reports from the particular session we are describing:

"This is a trolley car with seven persons on it. There is a woman with a baby. Somebody is flashing a razor. There are some signs and some colored people."

"Picture of a trolley car with seven people. There is a woman with a baby. There are some colored people. Someone is flashing a razor blade."[80]

Two processes are evident in these experimental studies and in detailed rumors of every kind. The first process has been called *leveling.* This is the reduction of details. The other process, known as *sharpening,* is evident when, as certain details drop out (leveling), others are increasingly emphasized, or made more pointed. Emphasis upon the razor, which is finally "flashing," is an example. There is also a sharpening of the color angle, even to the extent that there are "some colored people" instead of one. It was not unusual for subjects to tie together the razor and the colored aspect, by having the colored man threaten the white man with the razor.

The latter illustrates another feature of rumors, the process of *assimilation* — "the powerful attractive force exerted upon rumor by the intellectual and emotional context existing in the listener's mind."[81] How does the report of a colored man threatening with a razor illustrate assimilation? For one thing, it is a prejudiced view of Negroes that they carry razors. Another prejudiced view is that Negroes are hot-headed. Thus a prejudiced person hearing the story in question may fit it into the framework of his prejudices, making

it more understandable, more plausible, or more consistent with what he already knows, or thinks he knows, about the persons or situations with which a rumor deals.

Assimilation is also very evident in the transmission of humorous stories. One forgets most of the jokes he hears, but those which "ring a bell" in terms of his interests — sexual, medical, legal — are likely to be retained, and repeated whenever he has a listener.

There is a close affinity between the origin and transmission of rumors and the origin and transmission of legends. The latter are generally assumed to have had a basis in fact; but there is no doubt that the original details have been greatly reduced (leveled), that certain details have been greatly emphasized (sharpened) and that legends (including particular details) have persisted because of the support that they give to values which the group wishes to perpetuate. Any story not so assimilated could not long persist.

BROADER ASPECTS OF COLLECTIVE BEHAVIOR

We have confined our discussion, in the main, to research on small groups, and to experimental research at that. But how about social behavior in large groups? Nothing very specific has been said about the behavior of crowds or the development of social movements. To discuss these broader aspects of social life in detail would require at least another chapter and would take us too deeply into sociology and social psychology. What follows, therefore, is only a brief introduction for those who may wish to pursue these topics on their own initiative.

Crowd behavior

The term "crowd" needs some clarification, for, as Figure 17.21 indicates, it covers groups of various kinds. However, all have in common the fact that there is a temporary aggregation, with the individuals who compose it focused in a particular direction. In a mob, behavior may be directed toward destroying

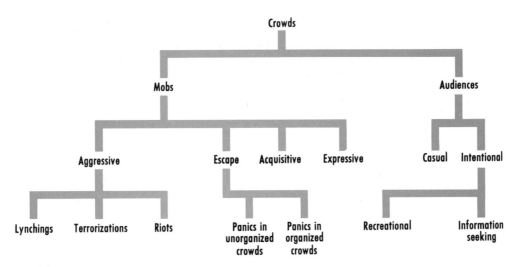

• 17.21

A Classification of Crowds. This classification is given, not with the idea that anybody should memorize it, but to indicate the broad meaning of the word "crowd" as used by sociologists and social psychologists. Roger W. Brown uses this as the organization of his chapter on "Mass Phenomena" in Lindzey's *Handbook of Social Psychology*. We have omitted two varieties of crowds which Brown gives as subdivisions of lynching mobs. (From Gardner Lindzey, *Handbook of Social Psychology*, Addison-Wesley, 1954).

a building, lynching a person, or escaping from the scene of a disaster, but in an audience attention is focused on a speaker or a performer and there is little or no action from the group. What we shall be chiefly concerned with in the following discussion is mob behavior.

Historically there have been widely different interpretations. One has emphasized the group itself, as though this were independent of the individuals who compose it. The other interpretation has emphasized the behavior of the individual who finds himself in a crowd.

The first of these interpretations is particularly associated with the name of Gustave Le Bon. In his book, *The Crowd*, Le Bon speaks of the crowd as having a "group mind," which supersedes the minds of the individual participants.[82] For illustrative material he draws largely upon aggressive mobs of the French Revolution. He notes that the individual in such a crowd is "swept up" so that he loses his individuality. The crowd is viewed as irrational and uncivilized. A participant,

no matter how rational he might be as an individual, and no matter how civilized, is reduced to a bestial level of action. Le Bon said, in fact, that this person "descends several rungs in the ladder of civilization." Other proponents of a "collective mind" have dealt with organized groups like political parties and nations rather than crowds.[83] Those who today speak of the "Russian mind," the "French mind," and the "Southern mind" are either speaking in a purely figurative manner or under the influence of group mind concepts.

The opposing concept stresses the behavior of individuals (acting as individuals) but with recognition of the fact that an individual's behavior changes in certain respects when he finds himself in the presence of other people. One influential advocate of this viewpoint is Floyd H. Allport, whose *Social Psychology* did much to further its wide acceptance.[84] Allport asked such questions as "What happens to the group mind when the individuals go their separate ways?" He pointed out that the person in a crowd acts as an *individual*, and that he may react even *more so*; by which he meant that there is a permissiveness about a crowd situation that may induce the individual to react in a less inhibited way than when he is in other situations. The individual would normally not *think* of looting a store, let alone do it. But when others are looting he may join them. The idea that "everybody's doing it" and the feeling that *he* cannot be singled out and punished for his acts are in part responsible for this change. A similar interpretation may be placed on lynching.

A great deal has been written about the heightened suggestibility of individuals in crowd situations. It is not uncommon to find writers speaking, in this connection, of "mass hypnosis" and "mass hysteria."[85] The reader may recall from an earlier discussion (p. 17) that hypnosis, an extreme form of suggestibility, has at times been linked with hysteria. Some have used the concept of social facilitation (p. 533) to account for certain features of crowd behavior. Many writers have stressed man's imitativeness (p. 177), which, as we said in an earlier discussion, is a common social habit (coenotrope) acquired early in life.[86] Imitation is often invoked to account for uniformities of behavior in panics. The individual, seeing others run, may unthinkingly copy their behavior. Another interpretation of the same phenomenon is that every individual, being similarly motivated to escape, does what others are doing without necessarily imitating the others.[87] In any event, the behavior is that of individuals (as Allport maintains) and there is no need for the concept of a collective mind.

Some crowds are led and others leaderless. The emergence of a leader is of considerable importance, for he focuses attention and brings unanimity to what might, without him, be unconcerted action. He often sets the goal and the ways to accomplish it. His influence may, of course, be either constructive or destructive.

Social movements

It has been said that a social movement is people "going somewhere."[88] As the term is customarily used, it refers to large masses who are more or less rapidly changing their way of life, or some aspect of it. Another designation is "mass movement." Such movements may be economic, political, or religious. Sometimes they are all of these combined. Take, for example, the abolitionist movement which preceded the Civil War.

A social movement may involve a relatively small segment of the population (like the religious movement known as "The Kingdom of Father Divine"),[89] or it may involve many or even most members of an entire nation, like the Nazi movement in Germany.

Nazism will serve as an illustration of how a social movement develops, and of how dependent it is upon leadership.

All social movements begin with dissatisfaction. The group involved feels that "the times are out of joint." Germany, for example, had been beaten in war. There was economic chaos. Moreover, the Versailles Treaty "aroused unequivocal and furious resentment among the people. It was a final insult to the hard-won German nationalism." Germans expressed such sentiments as: "We prefer to sacrifice everything and fight to the last man rather than accept as cowards a peace that is against our honor."[90] For these reasons, and others that need not concern us in this discussion, there was widespread insecurity, unrest, and hopeless frustration. There was a felt need for leadership. It was here that Hitler entered.

The Nazi movement began in a small way. As Cantril puts it, in his *The Psychology of Social Movement*,[91] "In 1919, a handful of disgruntled men were holding weekly meetings in a run-down Munich beer hall. They discussed the plight of Germany, the remedies needed, the possibilities of Germany's rebirth. Like so many other groups of that period, they formed a political party. By 1933, this apparently insignificant band of beer-mug philosophers had been transformed into a mass movement that swept its leader into power."

Hitler emerged as the leader of this small group, and finally of the German nation, because his program and his personal characteristics, at least as these were revealed to the masses, held out some hope of resolving their individual frustrations.

What were the characteristics which gave Hitler leadership? And why did he, rather than someone else, assume this role? It was because "he was astute enough to guess what would be an appealing program, because he so clearly saw the weaknesses of his enemies, and because he possessed the capacity, the energy, the oratorical ability, the cunning, and the apparent sincerity to convince others and to organize among his followers a political instrument of enormous efficiency. He concentrated his attacks on enemies that were either weak or disorganized. Domestic enemies, such as the Jew or the Communist, were liquidated before opponents from industry or the army were taken on; small countries were swallowed up before the bout with England and France was risked. . . ."[92]

To frustrated and disillusioned people, the picture of Germany as a nation of supermen must have been especially appealing. Their membership in the so-called Nordic race, and their symbols and slogans, welded them into a closely knit ingroup. Consolidation was fostered by giving them outgroups to hate — Jews and the Marxists. Frustrated people tend to look for scapegoats, and here they were. After Hitler gained sufficient power, he controlled the mass media of communciation — press and radio. Thus his program could be promulgated in the broadest possible way and without opposition.

Hitler's role as *Der Führer* was enhanced by his "almost hypnotic" influence over the crowds which heard him speak. As the following statement by a psychological observer of his speeches points out, this was a two-way process.[93] Hitler not only got a response, but he was quick to capitalize on this feedback.

☐ "His audience at a mass meeting was carefully selected: tickets of admission were obtainable at local Party headquarters and were generally given only to those who had already demonstrated sympathy for Nazism. These were the people, therefore, who possessed the predispositions that were likely to make them respond enthusiastically to Hitler's words. The audience generally awaited Hitler's arrival for many hours, and in the interim they listened to dull speeches by Party hacks. As a result,

Hitler's opening words released temporary tension that had been gradually mounting within them. At the outset his voice was scarcely audible through the hall: people had to strain to grasp his sentences and to become accustomed to his Austrian accent. He himself looked subdued and weary. Suddenly a phrase or an idea would evoke some applause that was not necessarily engineered by a claque. Hitler then seemed stimulated by his listeners. He would begin to grow excited and would repeat the same thought in almost identical fashion. If the audience ever grew a trifle restless, their 'leader' would rather quickly abandon his theme and grope for one that would produce cheers for Nazi principles and practices and jeers for those of his enemies." ☐

The personal qualifications and tactics that we have cited served to broaden Hitler's leadership. Finally his role changed from that of leader to that of dictator. Now the people had no choice.

This sketch of the Nazi movement and Hitler's rise to power serves to re-emphasize something that was said earlier (p. 544) about leadership — the situation and the characteristics of the leader are integrally related. Without the stage being set for a role such as Hitler's, he might have been a complete nonentity. On the other hand the stage could have been set, there could have been a role to play, but someone with the necessary qualifications could have been missing. The fact that this type of leader led Germany to disaster is beside the point of this discussion.

How did individual Germans become involved in the Nazi movement? They were the frustrated ones, each frustrated in his own spheres of interest. Hitler offered a way out. He specifically addressed himself to interest groups (professional, industrial, and so on), and he played upon their hopes and fears. But once the movement had assumed immense proportions and the individual not only saw Nazis all around him but had Nazi principles and promises drummed in his ears via radio, and placed before his eyes in print and on the screen, he found himself in the midst of great social pressures. Members of his own family — via the Nazi Youth Movement — were also part of this. We saw in an earlier discussion (p. 553) that an individual against a unanimous majority, in even a small temporary group, may have his judgments subverted by this pressure. Our discussion of "brainwashing" (p. 555) is also relevant. It should be remembered, also, that some highly respected and influential non-Germans were persuaded by Hitler's acts and words that Nazism was the "wave of the future." The individual German could not openly resist, unless he wished to lose everything, possibly even his life. Finally, in accordance with the cognitive dissonance concept (p. 537), one would predict that, having conformed to save his skin, a man's views would move toward those his actions were supposed to represent.

Nazism is but one social movement. Every movement has its unique setting and a leadership attuned to the peculiarities of the situation. A religious movement, for example, may have in common with Nazism only the fact that it begins with a desire for change and involves leadership attuned to the desires of those who are dissatisfied. ■

• SUMMARY

Newborn human beings are asocial. Except in reflex ways, as in sucking, they do not give evidence of perceiving or interacting with those around them. By the age of one month or a bit later they respond differentially to human and nonhuman aspects of their environment, and they soon begin to exhibit such social responses as ceasing to cry when picked up and smiling when smiled at. New social responses develop so that the growing child becomes increasingly socialized, competitive, cooperative, and so on, depending upon the culture in which he develops.

As the foregoing implies, social behavior is an interaction of two or more individuals. Sometimes it is one-way, with one organism being stimulated by the other, as in socialization and imprinting. The latter, a relatively simple instance of one-way interaction, is evident in goslings and other birds, as when the recently hatched bird follows its mother, or a mother substitute. There is a critical period during which this learning occurs. In goslings it occurs during the first day. Once formed, the response is persistent and irreversible.

Most of the behavior dealt with in this chapter involves reciprocal (two-way) interactions. One organism stimulates another and is stimulated (in turn) by the resulting behavior. In other words, there is social feedback. We see elementary examples in the dominance relations of animals, in social facilitation, and in competitive and cooperative behavior. Our discussions of comparative social behavior demonstrated some resemblances between animals and human beings and suggested that caution is necessary in interpreting our social life as comparable with, for example, the dominance hierarchy of barnyard hens.

Status in human societies refers to the individual's relative position in the group structure. Familiar status designations are: upper class, middle class, and lower class. Socioeconomic status is represented by such terms as "professional" and "unskilled." Status designations are always relative to the social setting. Role and status are closely related, since the individual of a particular status is expected to behave in ways which are more or less specified by his position. The status of "father," for example, brings with it a number of obligations and responsibilities in the family situation. Each of us plays many roles in his daily life. These are learned, from infancy on, as each takes his place in various groups.

We have considered some examples of role conflicts and, in this connection, the theory of cognitive dissonance. The basic assertion of this theory is that when an individual is aware of dissonance (discrepancy) between opinions, briefs, attitudes, roles (or between any of these and actual situations), he is motivated to reduce the dissonance. Reduction may be achieved in various ways — rationalization, selective forgetting, giving up dissonant elements, and so on. Some implications of this theory were considered and we described how one of these was tested experimentally.

One important approach in the study of small groups is "social field analysis" or what is known, in broader terms, as "group dynamics." It stresses such concepts as *life space, social field,* intragroup *tensions, resistance to change,* and so on. An individual's life space is, in general, his perception of his world, himself, and others. The social field represents other persons, whether actually or symbolically present. The term "locomotion" is used in its usual sense and in a special sense — as a shift in attitude, or making a decision. Overall emphasis is on the "subjective" world — the world as perceived by the individual in terms of his own interests and problems — rather than the objective world as viewed in terms of physical science. The husband-wife interaction discussed in this chapter exemplifies the "group dynamics" approach to interpersonal relations and other aspects of group behavior. Other examples dealt with "social climates" and participation in decision-making.

Sociometric procedures are used to study interpersonal relations, but they do not probe as deeply as social field analysis. There are several different sociometric techniques. All require members of a group to nominate, or rate, other members for certain preferred positions. Persons are asked, for instance, to indicate whom they would "most like" or "least like" to have as a "roommate." Those selected by none are "isolates" and those selected by all are "stars." A refinement of the usual procedures utilizes the normal curve concept and requires individuals to nominate their peers in terms of specific needs, such as for loyal friendship. This method has been used in fraternity situations to obtain information on, for example, morale and leadership.

Studies of interaction in process involved small problem-solving groups and a twelve-item classification of acts which individuals were observed to make — acts like asking for information, giving an opinion, and showing tension. The item "gives opinion" was most frequently observed and comprised about 30 per cent of the total number of acts. In discussing this type of study we emphasized leadership and, in doing so, pointed out that this depends upon both the situation and the personal characteristics of the individual who leads — a point reiterated in the later discussion of social movements and their leaders.

Group learning, as compared with learning by an individual working alone, is sometimes better and sometimes poorer, depending upon what is to be learned, and on the particular situation and procedures. Group learning of a bolthead maze was superior to individual learning. Social reinforcement and imitation of superior learners were involved, but social facilitation was not evident. Where the information is parcelled out to different individuals, collective problem-solving is the only kind. However, its efficiency depends upon the nature of the "communication network." In our illustration, a wheel network was most effective and a circular network least effective. "Brainstorming" was also mentioned. It appears of doubtful value unless preceded by special training.

Different kinds of leadership imposed upon groups are conducive to the creation of corresponding social climates. In most respects, democratic leadership is superior to other types. Laissez-faire is least effective. When subjected to autocratic leadership, some individuals react aggressively and others with apathy. Their reactions to the leader differ accordingly.

Group decision-making is more effective than lectures and the imposition of change. This was illustrated in the food-acceptance study and the study concerned with changing to new work methods in a factory.

Experiments on group pressures have involved judging the extent of illusory movement (autokinetic effect) and reporting on the actual length of lines. Both experiments demonstrated group-instigated changes in judgment. The latter experiment pitted one naïve individual against a majority that was instructed to give false reports. About 25 per cent of the naïve subjects completely resisted such pressure, although some were disturbed by it. The others conformed to varying degrees. Brainwashing involves extreme group pressure.

Rumors, unverified stories transmitted verbally, are prevalent during crises, and particularly when facts are unavailable or ambiguous. An experimental investigation of rumor was described and the concepts of leveling, sharpening, and assimilation were discussed. *Leveling* is the reduction in details as a story passes along. *Sharpening* refers to the pointing-up of certain details and their relative importance in the story as other details drop out. By *assimilation* is meant the reception given the story, in terms of prevailing beliefs, prejudices, and so on. This predisposition to accept, or reject, or modify the story is an important determining factor in the leveling and sharpening process.

There are various kinds of crowds, including sub-classifications of mobs and audiences. The concept of a "crowd mind" has particular relevance to mob behavior, where individuals often act in a manner different from what is customary when they are alone, or in other situations. Opposed to the crowd mind concept is that which conceives of the person in a crowd situation as an individual reacting to a particular type of social situation. He may be reacting even more individualistically in this situation because of his social conditioning and a realization of the fact that his behavior cannot so readily be singled out for criticism.

Social movements occur when people are dissatisfied with their way of life. As an example we described Nazism and Hitler's rise to power as its leader. Every social movement has its special background and leadership comes from individuals whose personal characteristics are consonant with the situation.

REFERENCES AND NOTES FOR THIS CHAPTER ARE IN THE APPENDIX.

• SELECTED READINGS

Berkowitz, L. (Ed.), *Advances in Experimental Social Psychology*. Academic Press, 1964. Original studies on aspects of social psychology.

Cartwright, D., and A. Zander (Eds.), *Group Dynamics: Research and Theory* (2nd ed.). Harper and Row, 1960. Reprinting of studies on aspects of group behavior.

Collins, B. E., and H. Guetzkow, *A Social Psychology of Group Processes and Decision-Making*. Wiley, 1964.

Klineberg, O., and R. Christie (Eds.), *Perspectives in Social Psychology*. Holt, Rinehart and Winston 1965. A series of original papers on various aspects of social psychology.

Koch, S. (Ed.), *Psychology: A Study of a Science*, Vol. 6. McGraw-Hill, 1963. Authoritative essays on various aspects of human social behavior.

Lambert, W. W., and W. E. Lambert, *Social Psychology*. Prentice-Hall, 1964. A brief survey which includes various aspects not covered in this chapter.

Lewin, K., *Field Theory in Social Science*. Harper, 1951. Selected papers on group dynamics.

Lindzey, G. (Ed.), *Handbook of Social Psychology*. Addison-Wesley, 1954. An almost encyclopedic two-volume account written by leaders in their respective fields.

Maccoby, E. E., T. M. Newcomb, and E. L. Hartley, *Readings in Social Psychology* (3rd ed.). Holt, 1958. Many studies discussed in this chapter are reprinted in this book.

Munn, N. L., *The Evolution and Growth of Human Behavior* (2nd ed.). Houghton Mifflin, 1965. Chapter 15 deals with social development in children.

Sluckin, W., *Imprinting and Early Learning*. Aldine, 1965. A review of research and theory which includes implications for social psychology.

Southwick, C. H. (Ed.), *Primate Social Behavior*. Van Nostrand, 1963. Reprints of important studies.

Thibaut, J. W., and H. H. Kelley, *The Social Psychology of Groups*. Wiley, 1959. A theoretical approach.

White, R. K., and R. Lippitt, *Autocracy and Democracy*. Harper and Row, 1960. Experiments on social climates.

18

Working Efficiently

A machine is efficient to the degree that output approaches input. The efficiency of an electric generator, for example, is gauged by how much energy it produces compared with the energy necessary to run it.

Human efficiency is not as easily defined as that of a machine, and it is not as easily measured. Generally speaking, however, we consider one person more efficient than another if he accomplishes more in the same time, or with the same expenditure of energy. From a slightly different angle, this is equivalent to saying that if two individuals achieve the same output, and one does it more quickly or more easily, the latter is more efficient.

We are mainly concerned in this chapter with efficiency in everyday work, a topic dealt with more comprehensively in the course designated *Industrial Psychology*. Problems of efficiency similar to those existing in industry are also found in the armed services. The motivation for doing psychological research in industry and the armed services is primarily to utilize human resources more effectively. However, the methods used to obtain information are no less scientific than the "ivory tower" research done in a university.

Early experimental psychologists stayed very close to academic laboratories. As we observed in Chapter 1, their investigations were focused upon conscious experience. They frowned upon attempts to make psychology a science of behavior, or to turn its attention to practical affairs. Their task, as they saw it, was merely to understand the human mind — not to increase human efficiency, facilitate human adjustment, or improve human relations. They made important discoveries about psychological processes, but what was of even greater significance for the advancement and application of psychology was the attitude that they injected into what had previously been mental philosophy. This was the attitude that the mental processes of man are susceptible to the same sort of scientific attack that the natural scientist focuses upon the world about him. In this vein, they demonstrated the need for impartial investigation, for systematic procedures, and for controlling such factors as stimulation and physiological conditions. It is by the utilization of the scientific attitude and scientific methods of investigation that psychologists make their most important contributions to industry and other areas of everyday life.

Efficiency in industrial and military occupations depends upon a number of things, the most important of which are: (1) *Aptitude for the tasks involved*. Aptitude is important for efficiency in that it influences the speed with which a new task is learned and also the level of skill finally attained. (2) *The characteristics of the machines, instruments, or other devices used by the worker*. These should be designed with the limitations of the worker in mind; then he can utilize them with maximum efficiency. (3) *The effectiveness of training*. Some procedures are conducive to more rapid learning, better retention, and a higher level of proficiency than others. (4) *Motivation and conditions of work*. Inducing the worker to put forth his best efforts is a complex problem involving incentives and optimum working conditions. (5) *Agents of impairment*. These include fatigue, injurious drugs, and various other substances and conditions which interfere with efficient work.

Aptitudes are considered first. Many of these have been investigated, including scholastic, artistic, musical, medical, legal, clerical, and mechanical aptitudes. Some mention will be made of the last of these, but our emphasis will be on principles and procedures which underlie all aptitude testing. ■

APTITUDES

Aptitude is inferred from relative levels of achievement. If individuals given comparable opportunities to acquire a skill differ in the ease of acquiring it, or if they differ in the level of proficiency attained, we say that they differ in their *aptitude* for that particular work.

Aptitude is more or less specific. An individual may have good aptitude for one line of work and not for others. He may do well in scholastic pursuits, yet have little aptitude for mechanical work. We *might* make a mechanic out of him, but it would require unusual time and effort, and, at best, he might be a poor mechanic as compared with others we could have chosen. On the other hand, there are some people who have a wide range of aptitudes. Some good scholars, for example, are also good mechanics, good athletes, and so on.

Before the coming of scientific psychology, aptitudes were assessed in a hit-or-miss fashion. Advice to individuals about the vocation they should enter was based upon intuition, upon hunches. Employers worked on a similar basis. They took in those they thought might succeed and dropped them if they did not. The scientific method of dealing with such problems is to study the requirements of the job, design tests which measure individual differences in the abilities required, try out such tests to see how accurately they predict success in the particular occupation, then use those with predictive value as a basis for vocational advice and selection. Following this general procedure, psychologists have devised and standardized aptitude tests for a wide variety of occupations. Quite often the individual is given a battery of separate tests, each measuring some ability relevant to a particular occupation. His performance is then rated in terms of how closely it approximates the needed aptitude pattern.

◻ Certain aspects of many aptitudes are inborn. Some individuals have longer and more dexterous hands than others. When it comes to such skills as typing, making watches, playing the piano, and perhaps carrying out certain surgical procedures, these will have an advantage over those with short stubby fingers and awkward hands — the so-called "hamhanded." Some people, because of the way they are constituted, can respond more quickly than others. In certain kinds of work these have an advantage over those who are constitutionally slow to react. Some are perhaps naturally stronger than others, hence better fitted for jobs requiring heavy work. But inborn characteristics do not tell the whole story. There is no doubt that earlier acquisitions, including interest in a certain line of work, are also of great importance. You may have dexterous fingers, yet no interest at all in becoming a watchmaker. If you do enter such an occupation, a person with less innate ability but greater interest than yours, may well outdistance you.

Thus, in saying that one person has greater aptitude than another for some job, we neither imply that the aptitude is inborn nor that it is acquired. It is in all probability dependent upon both our heredity and what we have learned. In a practical situation we have before us an individual whose aptitudes, whatever their origin may have been, are already established. ◻

From what we have already said, it is perhaps clear that aptitude and present ability do not mean the same thing. You may have no present ability to fly a plane, but you may have a high degree of aptitude for flying — which means that your chances of being a successful flyer are good, provided you receive the proper training. The chief value of aptitude testing is, in fact, that it enables us to pick out from those who do not yet have the ability to perform certain skills those who, with a reasonable amount of training, will be most likely to acquire the skills in question, and acquire them to a desirable level of proficiency.

Aptitude and intelligence

Performance on intelligence tests is sometimes indicative of aptitude for certain lines of work. In fact the use of intelligence tests in both world wars was for the purpose of selecting, from the millions drafted, those who would be most likely to profit from specialized forms of training. Selectees in World War II were given an opportunity to train as pilots only if they made higher than a certain score on specially devised intelligence, aptitude, and information tests.

■ **Table 18.1   Mean AGCT Scores and Range of Scores for Various Civilian Occupations**

Occupation	Mean standard score	Range of scores
Lawyer	127.6	96–157
Engineer	126.6	100–151
Teacher	122.8	76–155
Bookkeeper	120.0	70–157
Radio repairman	115.3	56–151
Salesman	115.1	60–153
Machinist	110.1	38–153
Mechanic	106.3	60–155
Plumber	102.7	56–139
General painter	98.3	38–147
Truck driver	96.2	16–149
Farmer	92.7	24–147
Miner	90.6	42–139

Selected from a much more extensive table in T. W. Harrell and M. S. Harrell, "Army General Classification Test Scores for Civilian Occupations," *Educ. Psychol. Measmt.*, 1945, 5, 231–232.

A suggestion of the limits of intelligence in individuals employed in various kinds of activity ranging from unskilled to professional work is given by the data in Table 18.1. This table is based on AGCT scores (p. 126). The individuals tested were those selected for the armed services, hence some professions, including medicine and dentistry, are not included. Only a few representative occupations are listed here. Note, moreover, that the scores given are neither raw scores nor I.Q.'s. They are derived from standard scores (see p. 82). Bookkeepers had a mean score of 120. However, some bookkeepers had a score as low as 70 and some as high as 157. Although the scores decrease as one goes from lawyer to miner, there is a wide range of scores at every level. There is thus much overlapping from

one occupation to another. Some miners, for example, make higher scores than some lawyers and engineers.[1]

One occupational use of AGCT scores is suggested by the following facts. More than 90 per cent of officer candidates who had an AGCT standard score of 140 and over actually became officers. As Figure 18.1 shows, the percentage of successful candidates decreased as the test scores decreased. Of those with scores under 110, only 50 per cent passed the officer training course.

Generally speaking there is a minimum intelligence level required for success in certain occupations, including those in the armed services. If the individual's intelligence were below the minimum for a given occupation, he would be advised against entering that occupation. If it were above the minimum, we would then measure other aptitudes relevant to the occupation in question.

● **18.1**

Predicting Success of Officer Candidates from Their Grades on the AGCT Test. This chart shows the per cent passing the officer training course and receiving a commission. (After Boring)

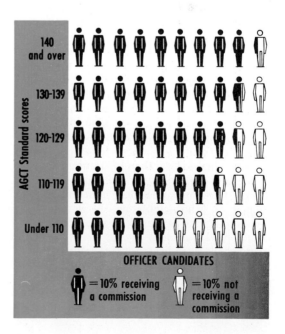

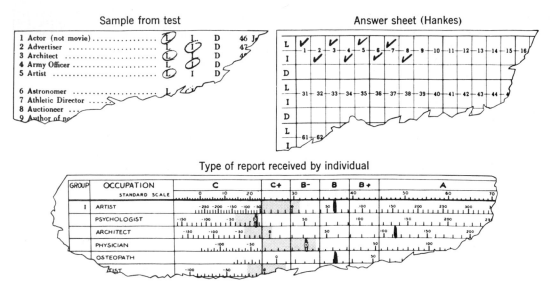

Sample from test   Answer sheet (Hankes)

Type of report received by individual

● 18.2

The Strong Vocational Interest Blank. In filling out this blank, a small piece of which is shown, the individual encircles (or checks on a special answer sheet) his like (L), indifference (I), or dislike (D) for each of a wide range of occupations, amusements, sports, and so on. Responses are scored with keys designated "artist," "architect," etc. There are separate blanks and scoring keys for men and women. The key for a particular occupation (and sex) is based upon the predominant reactions to the blank of people who have achieved success in that occupation. Note that the report received by the individual who fills out the blank gives him a grade for each occupational interest pattern. Here the grades are B for artist, C for psychologist, A for architect, B— for physician, and B for osteopath. (Courtesy, Engineers Northwest)

In selection of individuals for certain jobs, a minimum intelligence score is sometimes set. In the case of officer candidates a standard AGCT score of 110 was finally required. All who failed to reach it were denied officer training. This score was actually higher than the minimum needed by officers, but it is customary in many occupations to set the critical score at a higher level than the minimum.

There is the danger, of course, that some are on this basis prevented from entering an occupation who might succeed despite their low intelligence score. But what those concerned with selection try to do is to set a score which, as indicated by preliminary experimentation, will give the highest percentage of potentially successful individuals, without eliminating too many who might succeed.

Intelligence is seldom, however, the sole basis for guidance and selection. Interests are very important, as are specific aptitudes. We will now consider the relation between aptitude and interests, then take up the nature and measurement of specific aptitudes.

Aptitude and interests

One of the best single indicators of possible success in certain occupations is the way in which the interests of candidates compare with those of people who are successful in these occupations. It is, of course, possible for a person to be interested in something, like being a mechanical engineer, yet have little or no aptitude for mechanical engineering. Nevertheless, in selecting a group to be trained in this, or any other occupation, the interest inventories are very useful. This is because interest and aptitude are both related to success in acquiring and utilizing skills.

One widely used interest inventory is the *Strong Vocational Interest Blank*, some details of which are described in the legend to Figure 18.2. Strong[2] found that those who succeed in a particular occupation have a pattern of likes, dislikes, and indifferences which differs from that of those who are successful in certain other occupations. A person whose pattern of interests closely coincides with that of successful architects has a leaning, at least, in the direction of being a good architect. The person whose interests are represented in Figure 18.2 rates A for interest in architecture and only C for interest in psychology. His interests are thus predominantly like those of architects and not much like those of psychologists. His architectural leaning does not guarantee, of course, that he will succeed in this occupation, but it suggests the probability that he will like the work and succeed in it better than in occupations where his interests do not lie.

Another widely used interest inventory is the *Kuder Preference Record.*[3] This pro-

vides information on vocational and personal interests, as indicated in Figure 18.3. One form may also be scored for particular occupations. In this respect it is similar to the *Strong Vocational Interest Blank.*

The *Kuder Preference Record* arranges various possible activities into groups. *Visiting a museum, visiting an art gallery,* and *browsing in a library* make one such group. One responds to such items by indicating which activity he would like most and which he would like least. After the responses to many such groups are scored, a profile like that illustrated is obtained.

Interests provide useful information for the individual who wants to select a vocation and also for those looking for persons who are best fitted for particular lines of work. Such information is of limited value, however, unless one also knows about the person's intelligence, special aptitudes, and personality. He may be interested in an occupation, but have little or no aptitude for it. Or he may be interested and have aptitude, but lack the type of personality that is necessary in such

● **18.3**

Profile Based on the Kuder Preference Record. Observe that the person whose profile is presented here is interested predominantly in outdoor activities, work of a mechanical nature, and artistic pursuits. The respective percentiles (see p. 77) are roughly 70, 75, and 79. This person also prefers familiar (stable) situations to new ones, and situations characterized by friendly relations to those involving social conflict. (Courtesy, Science Research Associates)

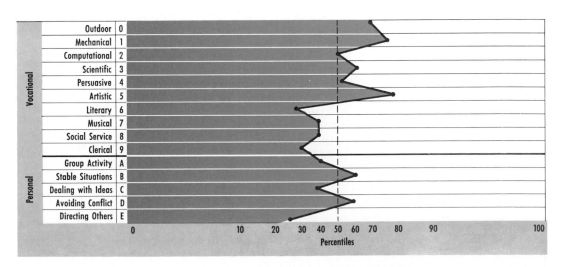

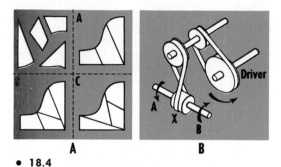

• **18.4**

Pencil-and-Paper Tests of Mechanical Aptitude. In item A, from the Minnesota Paper Formboard, the examinee is required to indicate whether the pieces in the upper left-hand corner, when fitted together, produce A, B, or C. The test has sixty-four such items, most of which are much more complicated than this one. Item B is from the *Mechanical Reasoning Test* devised by Bennett, Seashore, and Wesman. For every such item, the examinee makes a response requiring mechanical judgment. Here he is asked, "If the driver turns in the direction shown, which way will the pulley at X turn?" He indicates his judgment by marking A or B on the answer sheet. (The Psychological Corporation)

work. These are not the only considerations of importance in vocational guidance and selection, but they are cited merely to indicate that information about interests, while important, is not enough.

Tests of special aptitudes

Some of these are of the pencil-and-paper variety while others are manipulatory. Figure 18.4 illustrates two of the former, a paper formboard and a mechanical reasoning test. The paper formboard[4] emphasizes perception of spatial relations. In some respects it is like the tests which Thurstone used to measure the spatial relations factor in intelligence (p. 129). Items in the mechanical reasoning test[5] tap the understanding that comes from observing and working with machines, whether in physics courses or in the activities of everyday life. Tests of this nature are widely used to select persons fitted for a variety of mechanical occupations, including that of airplane

pilot. Manipulatory tests take many forms. One of these, the Minnesota Rate of Manipulation Test, has already been described (Figure 11.8, p. 353). It calls for gross manual activity. Two other manipulatory tests are illustrated and described in Figures 18.5 and 18.6. The first provides a measure of finger dexterity; the second, of eye-hand coordination.

Tests like those described are often used in batteries rather than singly. Suppose that one is looking for a position with prospects of success and he approaches the United States Employment Service (USES) or some comparable agency. In this event he will probably be asked to take a group of tests designed to measure a large number of aptitudes.[6] The test battery used by the USES includes an intelligence test and factored items like those of the Thurstone tests (p. 129), which measure verbal and perceptual abilities. It also includes tests more directly oriented toward specific occupational skills. There are, for example, tests of manual dexterity, precision of movement, and speed of coordinated reactions. The battery has fifteen subtests designed to measure "10 aptitudes which, in varying degrees and combinations contribute to occupational success." Different *aptitude patterns* are required in different occupations. Here are a few examples:

☐ Pattern GV —intelligence and verbal ability. Certain critical scores are set for such occupations as creative writing and journalism.

Pattern GN — intelligence and numerical ability. Critical scores are set for such occupations as accounting.

Pattern GNSF — intelligence, numerical ability, spatial ability, and finger dexterity. Critical scores are set for metal machining and mechanical repairing.

Pattern NSM — numerical ability, spatial ability, and manual dexterity. Critical scores are set for heavy metal structural work, plumbing, and wood construction. ☐

After an individual has taken the test battery, his test profile is compared with the minimum scores required in twenty different occupations. Thus, if his scores equal or exceed those that make up the GNSF pattern,

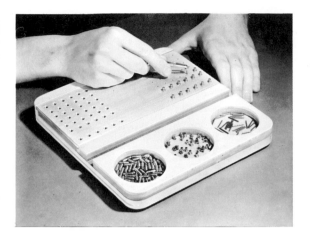

● **18.5**
Small Parts Dexterity Test. This is more specifically a test of finger dexterity. The examinee is timed while he picks up pins with the tweezers and inserts them into small holes, places small collars over the pins, puts small screws into threaded holes, and screws them down. It is in manipulating these items that finger dexterity is especially involved. (The Psychological Corporation)

he may be advised to obtain appropriate training and take up some occupation involving mechanical repair work. But scores achieved on aptitude tests are not the sole basis for such decisions. The vocational counselor also takes into consideration the individual's interests, his personality, his previous work experience, and other relevant factors not covered by the test battery.

These examples show the nature of general aptitude batteries and also how the outcomes of test administration may be used in vocational guidance and in selecting people best fitted for certain occupations. But the reader may well ask: "On what basis are test items selected?" "How does the psychologist know which separate abilities and ability patterns are required in a particular occupation?" "How does one find the minimal intelligence, the minimal finger dexterity, or the minimal reasoning ability, singly or in combination, which a particular job requires?" The following discussion is designed to answer such questions.

● **18.6**
The School of Aviation Medicine Complex Coordinator. Developed for the selection of aircraft pilots, this device uses a simulated cockpit. As illustrated, the examinee sits with one hand grasping the stick and his feet on the rudder bar. The panel has parallel sets of bulbs — three groups of thirteen pairs each. In one row of each pair is a red light which stays in position when the lights come on. As the stick is moved from the central position to the left, green bulbs light up successively to the left in the lower top row. As it is moved to the right, they light up successively to the right. Similarly, lights in the vertical column move as the stick is moved toward or away from the operator; in the lower rows, as the rudder bar is operated. When the red light in each of the three positions is matched with a green light, the red lights shift to new positions and the procedure is repeated. This continues until 40 settings, of three red lights each, have been matched. The time required to perform the whole series of operations is recorded. (Air Force Photo)

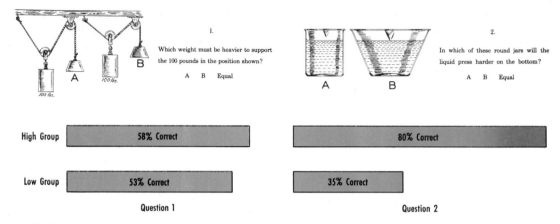

● 18.7

Item Validity. Both test items look good. They have "face validity." Moreover, they are about equal in difficulty, being answered correctly by 56 to 58 per cent of those to whom they were administered. But observe that the group rated high in mechanical comprehension did not do much better on Item 1 than the group rated low in mechanical comprehension. Item 2, however, clearly differentiated the high and low groups; hence it was judged a valid item for selecting those with mechanical comprehension. (The Psychological Corporation)

Devising aptitude tests

Although there are many tests designed to measure specific aptitudes, the particular pattern relevant to a specified occupation must be experimentally determined. In the Second World War, the United States Army Air Force psychologists did not have ready-made tests for selection of pilots, bombardiers, and navigators. It was necessary to devise suitable tests.

Psychologists in the Bureau of Aeronautics of the Navy Department also had to develop their own tests. The U.S. Employment Service, confronted with selection problems in still other areas, devised the test batteries already described.

Psychologists in business and industry can sometimes use tests already available, but for most jobs there are no ready-made aptitude batteries. Thus, in selecting people for particular jobs, the psychologist may have to adapt tests already in use, combine these into suitable batteries, or perhaps devise completely new tests. In any event, he must ascertain experimentally whether use of the tests im-

proves selection sufficiently to justify the time and expense involved in administering, scoring, and evaluating them. An item, or combination of items, may look reasonable, yet contribute little or nothing to the selection process. Compare, for example, the two test items in Figure 18.7. On the face of it, we might judge either to be a good test of mechanical comprehension. Nevertheless one differentiates those with poor mechanical comprehension and the other does not.

How do we know that one item measures mechanical comprehension and another does not? In the example given, the score on the total test of mechanical comprehension was used to select a high and a low group. Each item was then evaluated in terms of how well it alone differentiated these groups. An item which does not differentiate is worthless. It does not "pull its weight in differentiating people in the desired way,"[7] hence it is dropped from the test. Each part of a well-standardized test is subjected to an *item analysis* of this sort.

But, one may ask, how do you know that the test as a whole is really related to mechanical skill? One cannot know at the outset. A test may be internally consistent — i.e., all items in it may differentiate — yet the test may not measure what it purports to measure. Many tests have been developed to predict success in particular fields and then it has been found that they do not predict. This is the problem of *validity*, to which we will turn shortly.

Actually, the development of an aptitude test or battery requires a series of steps, of which the determination of validity is the final one. These steps are as follows:

(1) Analysis of the job for which the tests are to be used; (2) tentative selection and arrangement of items which appear to measure the psychological processes disclosed by the job analysis to be important for that job; (3) development of a standardized method of administration and scoring; (4) administration of the tests to a large and representative group of individuals from the population on which they are finally to be used; and (5) analysis of results to discover whether the tests are good predictors of success in the occupation for which they are designed, i.e., whether they are valid.

• *Job analysis.* Regardless of whether an aptitude test is devised for vocational guidance or for vocational selection, the first thing that the psychologist usually does before designing it is to make a detailed analysis of the psychological processes required in successful performance of the job in question. Before designing their tests of flying aptitude, psychologists went aloft with experienced pilots, bombardiers, and navigators. While aloft, they observed the performance of the pilot, bombardier, or navigator. Some of them went through the training process themselves, paying particular attention to the kinds of abilities they were called upon to use. After gathering information on the requirements of the job in this and other ways, they were then ready to design batteries of aptitude tests for pilots, bombardiers, and navigators. Similarly, psychologists have gone into industry and observed skilled performance or learned the performance themselves.

• *Tentative selection of test items.* After a

job analysis has been completed and some insight into the nature of the processes required has been gained, the psychologist then selects tests from those already available or devises tests to measure these processes. Suppose a certain level of intelligence, of finger dexterity, of steadiness, or of interest in the occupation seems important, then he may try out any of the tests already developed to measure these factors. And if the individual's past experience, his social obligations, and similar biographical data appear to be important, then the psychologist may try out biographical inventories already available. He also may have to devise tests that are entirely new.

After tests have been selected from those available, or special tests have been devised, the next move is to try them out and see how well they work in practice.

• *Development of a standardized procedure for administration and scoring.* We have already (pp. 71, 126) shown how important it is that psychological tests be given and scored in the same way for every individual tested. Anyone who uses a micrometer in a novel fashion or who reads off the measurements in some manner of his own choosing might just as well not use an accurate measuring device at all. His readings would certainly not agree with those taken by somebody who knows how to use a micrometer. Likewise, in the attempt to measure anything, a standardized procedure must be used. Usually, in preparing any sort of psychological test, it is necessary to try it out on a few individuals to see the best procedure to follow, how best to score it, and so on. If it is a pencil-and-paper test, requiring answers to questions, one has to do some preliminary testing with it to weed out ambiguous items and items which do not differentiate between the possession or nonpossession of the qualities which the test is intended to measure.

• *Administration to a large representative group.* Because a test seems to measure the processes which a job analysis suggests are important for a particular job, and because it is standardized in administration and scoring, one cannot assume that it is necessarily a good test. He must check to see whether it really does select the kinds of individuals needed.

During the First World War some psychologists decided, on the basis of a crude job analysis, that a pilot needs, above all else, to be a quick reactor and to be able to "keep his head" under conditions of stress. So they and the military authorities of the countries concerned decided, quite arbitrarily, that any candidate for pilot training who failed to reach a specified speed of simple reaction, and who changed his breathing and his hand-tremor more than a certain amount when a shot was fired unexpectedly, or an ice-cold cloth slapped unexpectedly on his head, could not be a good prospect for pilot training. This proposition seemed so reasonable (it had such "face validity") that several Allied countries used these tests to pre-select pilots. Hundreds of prospective pilots were told that their reactions were too slow or their emotional reactions too unstable for them to succeed as pilots. Then some investigators checked up to see whether there was actually any correlation between simple reaction time and tremor on the one hand, and skill as a pilot on the other. They found the correlations negligible. This being the case, as many good pilots were being eliminated as poor ones and as many poor ones were being selected as good ones. Those in charge of selecting pilot material would have been just as well off without using these reaction time or tremor tests.[8]

Tests must be evaluated by trying them out on a group representative of a particular occupation. There are several technical considerations in selection of this group, for it must be representative of a normal population, and so on — but we must waive this discussion in an introductory course.

In devising selection tests for pilots, the psychologists in the Army Air Forces and Bureau of Aeronautics of the Navy Department gave their tentatively selected tests to thousands of prospective pilots and then allowed these individuals to enter training, *regardless of scores made on the tests*. In this way they could determine what would have happened had they eliminated those scoring below certain possible critical levels.

• *Evaluation of test results.* To evaluate test results in terms of actual performance in an occupation, that is, to determine their validity, one must have *criteria* — that is, indices or standards of success. In the case of pilots, the criteria might be ground-school grades, time taken to reach the solo, passing or failing, success in combat (such as number of planes shot down) and so on.

In the case of workers in a certain occupation, the criterion might be how quickly the requisite skills are learned, the average daily output, how many accidents the individual has, or how long he stays on the job before being fired or quitting to get another job. In the case of life insurance salesmen, the criterion might be how much insurance is sold. One must decide beforehand, of course, which of these things he wishes to predict by use of his test. The test might predict one criterion better than another. Different test batteries might be needed for different criteria.

One method widely used to discover the relation between the test results and the criterion has already been described — that of correlating one with the other. A high positive correlation indicates that success on the test and success in terms of the criterion selected go together.

One criterion in which those who had to select pilots were particularly interested was that of passing or failing the course. Anybody who entered training and failed to become a pilot was, of course, wasting his own time, wasting the time of his instructors, wasting government money, and wasting equipment. There was thus a determined effort to eliminate such waste by selecting a group most of whom would pass.

When such an arbitrary all-or-none criterion as pass-fail is used, the usual correlation techniques discussed earlier will not work. Other techniques must be used. Nevertheless, the selective value of the tests may be illustrated graphically. In Figure 18.8 are the pass-fail data for approximately 153,000 young men who took a battery of selection tests and then entered pilot training.[9] The battery of tests included several like those already discussed in preceding pages, including the complex coordinator (Figure 18.6, p. 571).

The candidates' aptitude rating, in terms

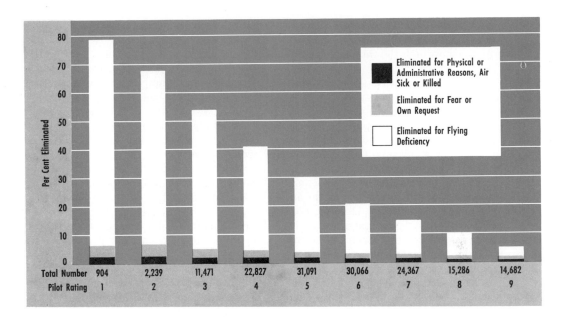

● 18.8
Per Cent Eliminated from Primary Pilot Training. This covers each pilot rating in fifteen pilot classes totaling 153,000 cases. The overall elimination rate was approximately 25 per cent. (Staff Psychological Section, "Psychological Activities in the Training Command, AAF," *Psychological Bulletin*, 1945, 42.

of overall test scores, is given at the base of the graph. The highest aptitude rating is 9, and the lowest is 1. About 80 per cent of those who made the lowest aptitude rating failed, as compared with only 5 per cent of those who made the highest rating.

In short, job analysis indicated which traits play an important role in aviation. Tests were assembled which appeared to measure such traits. These were tried out to determine their validity. Those with little or no predictive value were discarded. Finally there emerged a test battery, each item of which was valid.

☐ There was, at the time, no factor analysis of the large number of tests involved. But such factor analysis has now demonstrated that relatively few factors are being measured by a large group of tests like those used in selecting pilots. Most of the overall performance on thirty-one tests requiring movement reac-

tions could be accounted for by three factors designated, respectively, as *Fine Control Sensitivity* (the "ability to make fine, highly controlled adjustments at some critical stage of performance"), *Multiple Limb Coordination*, and *Response Orientation* ("rapid directional discrimination and orientation of movement patterns").[10] Fine Control Sensitivity is measured to a relatively high degree by eight different tests, including the complex coordinator; Multiple Limb Coordination by six tests, also including the complex coordinator; and Response Orientation by eight different tests. It is thus apparent that the same goal could be accomplished with a relatively small number of tests, each test in the battery being one which, to the highest degree, measures a particular factor. This is pointed out not to criticize the work of World War II aviation psychologists, for their job had to be done with all speed, but to illustrate again the value of factored as compared with hit-or-miss tests. ■

EFFICIENCY AND EQUIPMENT DESIGN

No matter how high the individual's aptitude level may be, his efficiency is also a function of the machines or other instruments with which he works. Think, for example, of how human efficiency was increased by invention of the lever, the wheel, steam power, and so on. Machines which increase man's efficiency are continually being invented. It is interesting to observe, however, that equipment is often so poorly designed that it fails to take full advantage of the characteristics of the individuals who must operate it. Here we consider the fact that such equipment may be designed, or redesigned, to fit perceptual and motor aptitudes, thus increasing the efficiency of performance.

Engineers have often designed equipment for appearance, convenience, or physical efficiency without recognizing that the persons who must operate it are limited in their perceptual and motor aptitudes and capacities.

● **18.9**
Device Used in the Training of Astronauts. The instructor, from his control panel, can present instrument changes requiring appropriate reactions from the trainee, in this instance, astronaut John H. Glenn, Jr. (Courtesy of the National Aeronautics and Space Administration.)

More specifically, they have failed to determine which of the various possible designs human beings can operate most efficiently.

Human operators as limiting factors in the design of machines and instruments have but recently entered the sphere of science. This field of investigation is known in Great Britain as *Ergonomics*, from *ergon* (work) and *nomos* (law). However, this embraces more than the design of machines. It also takes into consideration the entire environment of the worker, something which we will discuss later.[11] In the United States, the area of investigation involving the design of machines and other equipment with limitations of the operator in mind is known as *Psychological Engineering* or *Human Factors Engineering*.[12]

One of the latest developments in this general area is the design of equipment for astronauts. Beyond the problem of providing the human operator with a small piece of environment in which he can function adequately from a physiological standpoint, a spacecraft must be designed so that its passenger (or passengers) can operate it effectively.

☐ "The central job of engineering psychology is to adapt the human operator to the spacecraft that he operates. In order to be able to perform this function, the engineering psychologist must analyze the nature of the astronaut's job into its components, relate these components to the inherent limits of the astronaut himself, and then indicate where redesign of the space vehicle may be necessary. In performing these functions the engineering psychologist usually formulates his analysis in terms of communications theory, which can, with equal facility, be applied both to man and machine. . . . In space flight it is necessary for the machine to communicate with man and for man to communicate with the machine. The machine communicates to the astronaut by means of a series of dials and signals that are designed by engineers for just this purpose. Man communicates with the machine by the use of various levers, wheels, and other methods of control, also devised by the engineer. Both man and the machine have certain inherent limitations that must be taken into account if they are to communicate successfully with each other and thus insure the efficient functioning of the complex unit of which they both form a part."[13] □

What the engineering psychologist looks for especially are sensory and perceptual limitations (as in the reading of instruments and detection of signals) and motor limitations (with reference to dexterity, coordination, and speed of reaction). With respect to space travel, there are additional problems. Isolation and monotony may have deleterious effects upon the operator. In this connection, refer again to our discussion (p. 174) of the effects of environmental restriction upon human adults. The ability to withstand fatigue, so that performance is not impaired by a long vigil, is

another problem. Something will be said about this later in the present chapter.

Training also plays a significant role in preparing the astronaut for his job, as it does in preparation for all kinds of complex performance. Training devices which simulate those that must be operated in the actual flight are used (Figure 18.9). The operator is trained (or overtrained) to make his performance more or less automatic, even under conditions of stress. In these and other ways, "the engineering psychologist seeks to anticipate all contingencies by appropriate modification of machine design, and in this manner adapt the machine to the peculiarities of the human operator."[14]

The engineering psychologist is well versed in psychological theory and he has a back-

● **18.10**

Per Cent of Error in Reading Dials. Note that the figures, indicators, and unit intervals are comparable, but that there are wide variations in the percentage of incorrect readings depending on the type of dial used. (After R. B. Sleight, "The Effect of Instrument Dial Shape on Legibility," *J. Appl. Psychol.*, 1948, 32, p. 177.)

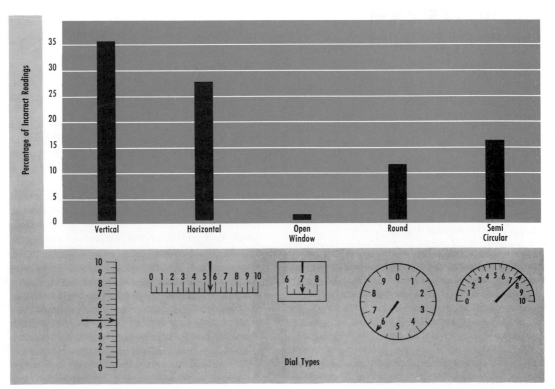

ground of factual information about human sensitivity and human behavior; but this has little more than an orienting value when he is confronted by such questions as that of which instrument is conducive to the most efficient human performance under specified conditions. There is only one effective way to answer such questions. That is to carry out properly designed experiments involving the equipment under consideration.

Utilizing perceptual aptitudes

As one example of experimental psychology in engineering design, take readability of dials. In Figure 18.10 are shown five dials, all with the same numbers, the same pointers, and approximately equal units. Any one of these dial types might appear on a speedometer or altimeter. But which will be read with least error by the average person who must use it? Research involving a constant exposure time of .12 second demonstrated that the open-window dial is most and the vertical dial least accurately read. The results are presented graphically in Figure 18.10 (top). Other things being equal, one would expect a person to read most accurately an open-window type of dial.[15]

Using similar experimental procedures, psychologists have investigated such related problems as the best spatial arrangements of particular dials in complex situations such as exist in airplane cockpits, submarines, ships, and many industrial machines. The aim in each case has been to reduce errors (and accidents) by discovering, and then utilizing, the most foolproof arrangement of such instruments. Also, instruments have themselves been redesigned (Figure 18.11) so as to conform more closely to the perceptual tendencies of those who must read them.

Another problem is the design of control knobs which will be confused with one another as little as possible. One study carried out by psychologists working for the Armed Services compared the degree of confusion between twenty-two differently-shaped knobs, which were to be distinguished purely by touch. Out of the twenty-two knobs, eight (Figure 18.12) were found which individuals never confused,

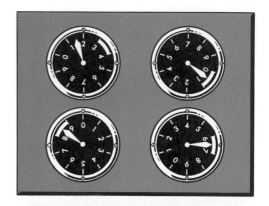

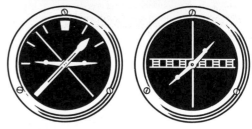

● 18.11

Dial Design for Increasing the Accuracy of Perception. Compare the arrangement of dials with indicators pointing in different directions (top) and that in which the indicators point in the same direction when everything is as it should be. Obviously the latter will be more easily and more accurately read. Then compare the two indicators at the bottom. Most horizon indicators show the horizon tilting, as at the left. It is more meaningful to show the plane tilting, and the correct adjustment as righting it. This is shown at the right. (Adapted from an article by E. L. Van Dusen; courtesy, Colliers.)

tactually, one with another. When operation of a variety of controls in the dark, out of sight, or even within the field of vision is required, such knobs should be used.[16]

□ A great deal of research is being done on auditory signals, as in the use of flybar in aviation. Flybar is a system of auditory signals which indicate to the pilot when he is performing incorrectly, the direction of error, and the amount of error with reference to keeping the plane straight, right side up, and at the correct altitude. An auditory signal which enabled subjects to fly a Link instrument trainer for aircraft pilots on a straight and level course involved the following three indications: "(1) a 'turn' signal that could be made to appear to sweep from right to left or vice versa, by reason of an intensity shift between the two ears; (2) a 'bank' signal that could be made to appear to tilt by means of a change in pitch of the carrier tone during each sweep; (3) an 'air speed' signal that took the form of a 'beep' at a rate that varied from 2 to 22 per second. This three-in-one signal was reported to be realistic and easy to interpret."[17]

Much work is also being done in attempts to improve the intelligibility of intercommunication system, like the telephone and loud speaker, especially under combat conditions where masking noises are often present. □

Operative efficiency

Still another problem in the field of adapting machines to human aptitudes is that of designing the equipment to be operated in such a manner as to speed the learning process and to achieve the highest possible level of work efficiency. One study focused upon operation of a hand wheel (crank), such as appears on many machines, including antiaircraft equipment. The task was like that required in pursuit tracking. That is, proper operation of the hand wheel kept a movable pointer in alignment with a stationary one. What the experimenter sought to discover was the most effective combination of such factors as speed of turning, gear-ratios, size of the

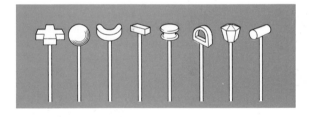

● **18.12**

Knobs Employed in a Study of Shapes for Use in Coding Aircraft Controls. Each of the blindfolded subjects was seated before a turntable containing vertically mounted plastic knobs as illustrated. A knob of a certain shape was presented to the subject, who felt it for one second. The turntable was then rotated to a predetermined point, and the subject subsequently felt knob after knob until he thought that he recognized one of the same shape as the sample. The eight shapes shown below the photograph are those which were never confused with the others. (From W. O. Jenkins, "The Tactual Discrimination of Shapes for Coding Aircraft-Type Controls," in M. L. Blum, *Readings in Experimental Industrial Psychology*, Prentice-Hall, 1952, pp. 235, 240.)

hand wheel, and its weight. He found, among other things, that a heavy hand wheel, as compared with a light one, smooths and increases the accuracy of tracking.[18] Acquisition of tracking skills was discussed earlier (pp. 319–320).

What psychologists in this field are attempting is to design equipment which takes fullest cognizance of human talents and weaknesses. As one writer says, "For many years playwrights have constructed plays to fit the specific talents of individual actors and actresses to bring out their best performance. So in the area of manipulative behavior, which is such an important factor in our modern civilization, it is possible to construct machines which will yield optimal results with a large number of workers."[19] ■

TRAINING FOR MAXIMUM EFFICIENCY

Regardless of our aptitudes and the adequacy of the devices with which we work, few of us perform as efficiently as we might. Our accomplishments fall short of what is possible. Even a student who obtains top grades might well achieve the same result in less time by using better study methods, thus giving himself more time for extracurricular activities. And the best housewife, by organizing her work systematically, so as to save unnecessary steps, might well find more leisure for other things.

Time and motion study

Taylor, the first recognized "efficiency expert" or "time study man," worked in a steel mill. Here, by selecting men best fitted for the job, by teaching them a certain way of doing it, and by utilizing their desire for more income, he increased the daily loading rate from sixteen to fifty-nine tons. This saved the mill $75,000 or more per year.[20] Careful analysis of the motions utilized in various kinds of work was first undertaken by the Gilbreths, an industrial engineer and his wife, a trained psychologist.* Gilbreth[21] first turned his attention to brick-

* These are the parents of the twelve children of the popular book and film, *Cheaper by the Dozen*.

laying. Here he found that the eighteen movements customarily involved in laying a brick could be reduced to five. Men who learned his method laid 350 bricks per hour as compared with the usual 120 bricks. This improvement involved a more appropriate arrangement of bricks, scaffolding, and other materials and also the elimination of waste motions in laying the bricks. As a further example of how time and motion study improved the efficiency of a relatively simple industrial operation, observe the two methods of work illustrated in Figure 18.13. The original method, probably hit upon in a blind, trial-and-error fashion, made it possible for the worker to solder-coat five blocks per minute. The new method, worked out by an "efficiency expert" and taught partly by demonstration, almost doubled the worker's output.

Every industrial operation requires its own investigation and, from our standpoint, only the principles and the general results of applying them need concern us.

A worker at any job usually learns it either through (1) his own untutored efforts, or (2) by copying the traditional way, as demonstrated by a trainer or other workers. The latter does not necessarily constitute the best or most efficient way. It may be no more than the stereotyped outcome of the trial-and-error activity of earlier workers. The first step aimed at increasing efficiency, therefore, is to study the worker at his job.

There are great individual differences in output and the investigator may compare the performances of those with good and poor production records, noting differences in aspects of their work behavior. He may learn the job himself, as many industrial psychologists have done. While learning, he can look for better ways of doing the job and also for ways of improving instruction. Sometimes he records the worker's performance so that it can be studied later in detail. Slow-motion movie techniques are often used, with a clock having a large second hand also in the picture, so that movements can be timed easily.

Time and motion study may have any of a variety of aims, but one of the most important of these, from the standpoint of the

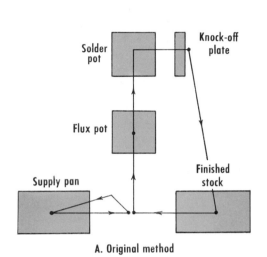

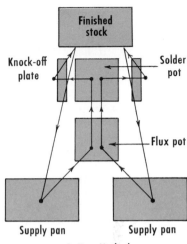

● 18.13

Comparison of an Inefficient and an Efficient Method of Performing an Industrial Operation.
In the original work pattern, both hands (represented by dots) were used, but the left
merely reached into the supply pan. The other hand performed essential operations. In
the new methods, however, both hands simultaneously reached the supply pans, each
carried a block to the flux pot, each to the solder pot, each to the knock-off plate, and
each to the stock pile. (After Morgensen)

present discussion, is to discover the best, or
most efficient, behavior patterns. There may
be more than one efficient way of doing things,
and this can also be discovered through research. Knowing that a particular pattern of
work is more efficient than others, one can
teach it to beginners, or even to experienced
workers whose performance could be improved.
As we pointed out in an earlier discussion (p.
550), however, changing work methods may
lead to labor difficulties unless the workers participate in decisions concerning these.

□ Psychologists working to improve the efficiency of the Armed Forces are not confronted with labor problems. Organized labor,
however, has often resisted time and motion
study for fear that it will make automatons of
workers, endanger their health, or throw many
of them out of work. The issue is well stated
in the following quotation from a chapter
dealing with training in industry: "Industrial
workers are working in a world of pay rates,
union rules, complexly determined attitudes
toward management, seniority rights, and other
personal, social and economic factors that determine how they will respond. . . ."[22] Such problems are often dealt with at length in books on
industrial psychology, industrial sociology, and
management and labor relations. Sometimes
management as well as labor has resisted these
methods and sometimes both labor and management have welcomed them. Another issue
is, of course, the factor of individual differences.
In some instances, what may be an efficient
procedure for one worker may not be efficient
for another, but whether or not this is so depends upon the situation involved, and the
possibility must be investigated experimentally.

There are without question many social
problems in the introduction of new industrial
procedures, especially when the aim is to do
no more than increase production.

Many industrial operations can be carried on more efficiently by automation than by
manpower, and this also poses social problems.

Quite often one operator at a control panel replaces a large work force. How the increasing use of automation will affect employment is uncertain. It has been pointed out, however, that "Automatic methods are applicable only to a limited range of manufacturing and office procedures. All work involving personal attention must remain largely unaffected, and even in highly mechanized factories human operatives are likely to continue for a long time to be the most economic means of carrying out many assembly and inspection operations. Indeed, the need for men and women to inspect products may substantially rise since automatic processes often cut down the amount of inspection that can be done by an operator in the course of actual production.

"Furthermore, even where new machinery effects a substantial saving of operators for a given output, the increase of maintenance and servicing work can often absorb many who would otherwise be redundant, and the tendency for output to rise and the fact that the automatic methods open up possibilities of manufacture not present with older methods, are likely to increase available jobs still more. There seems no justification, therefore, for the fear that the introduction of automatic methods will cause widespread unemployment. Indeed the reverse seems more likely."[23] □

Industrial psychologists are of course interested in all aspects of industrial work, including automation and its effects on the worker. Engineering psychology is also concerned with automation, as attested to by the preceding quotation, which came from a leader in ergonomics. But our chief concern in the present instance is to illustrate how scientific methods used to study other aspects of human adjustment may be applied to industrial work. Increased output is only one aspect. Other important problems relate to reduction of waste and the prevention of accidents, outcomes which contribute not only to greater efficiency but also, indisputably, to the welfare of all. Take, for example, the disc-cutting study illustrated in Figure 18.14. We are not interested, of course, in disc-cutting as such — an operation that might as well be done by automation

— but in the procedure used to study it and in how the findings were applied.

It was found that, unless a certain pattern and timing of foot movements was used, discs were broken. Moreover, it was difficult to teach the correct pattern to workers before it was known in detail. Even the experienced and efficient workers could report no more than that, when the cut was satisfactory, their foot movements had "the right feel." How to give this "feel" to trainees was the crux of the problem. When the proper pattern had been discovered the findings were used as follows:[24]

□ "Enlarged instructional posters with analytical notations were prepared both for "correct" and "incorrect" patterns and for various types of damage to the product which were shown to be reflected in the action pattern. Individual action patterns of each operator were kept in folder form also so that operators could note their progress. By careful use of the recorder at timely intervals with both the trainees and experienced operators and by interpreting the foot action patterns in terms of the standard, it was possible to reduce the training time of new operators and to improve the quality and quantity of performance of some employees already on the job." □

Learning curves based on various aspects of the individual's output showed that "Training time was effectively reduced. At 8 weeks the production performance percentage of the trainees was better than that of old operators who had the same average amount of experience by the 'pick up' method."[25] There were additional advantages, including a reduction in breakage of the expensive disc-cutting wheels.

Training

Training for maximum efficiency involves much more than finding the correct behavior pattern for a particular operation. The worker must be taught. Thus the teacher and his methods become important. It is here that the principles of economical learning discussed in Chapter 11 come into play. The learner must be adequately motivated, which includes hav-

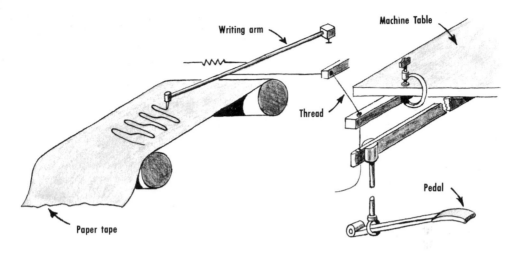

● **18.14**

Schematic Drawing of a Recorder Attached to a Disc Cutoff Machine. The pedal is oper-ated by the worker in cutting thin discs from tungsten rods. The operation involved is as follows: "The operator pushes the rods through guides into stops with a hand lever, he operates a pedal with the left foot which controls the cutoff wheel as it is applied to the rods. As soon as he cuts through the rods he lifts his foot, the wheel rises, and immediately after it has cleared the stops a backward jerk of the right hand actuates ejector or knock-out pins which knock the severed discs into the stream of water. Im-mediately after the ejection of the discs the rods are pushed back into the stops and a new cut is taken." The diagram shows how a paper tape and a writing arm were attached to the foot pedal so as to record the speed, form, rhythm, and pressure pattern of the foot. The pattern shown approximates that obtained from a good, experienced operator. (Illustration and quotation from L. G. Lindahl, "Movement Analysis as an Industrial Training Method," *J. Appl. Psychol.*, 1945, 29.)

ing a knowledge of results. One strong point in the study just considered is that, by looking at records of his performance, the trainee could observe the results of his efforts and note where improvements were needed. In addition to being adequately motivated and informed of his progress, the worker should be given distributed training. We have seen that greater progress in learning is made when practice periods are separated by rest pauses. It has also been observed that if a learner is first ac-quainted with the overall pattern that he is to learn, he is in a better position to master the constituent operation. This is the problem of whole-versus-part learning. Great improve-ments in production have also been made by training those who must teach, so that their approach to the teaching situation is conducive

to good motivation and so that the beginner will use the most adequate learning procedures. A graphic example of this improvement is given in Figure 18.15.

The learning of some skills is facilitated, in initial stages, by use of audio-visual devices like film strips and sound motion pictures which match verbal instructions with pictorial representations of the correct responses. Ex-perimental studies by psychologists working for the Office of Naval Research have shown that, in teaching recruits to tie knots, two principles increase the effectiveness of films.[26] One of these is that verbal instructions should precede the action to which they refer — so as to call attention to significant aspects of what will be seen. The other is that the film should picture learning situations from the viewer's

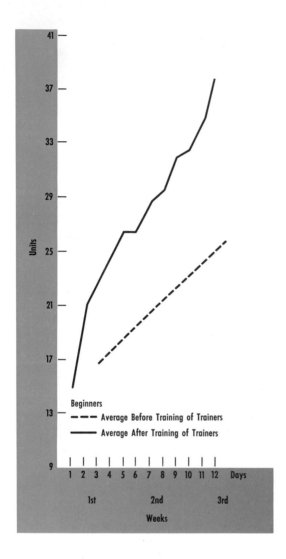

Units

Days

1st   2nd   3rd

Weeks

Beginners
- - - Average Before Training of Trainers
—— Average After Training of Trainers

● 18.15
Learning Curves of Employees Before and After Their Instructors Were Trained for Their Teaching Jobs. This study, by Alex Bavelas, of Massachusetts Institute of Technology, involved a stitching operation. Observe that the beginners taught by trained instructors made a much faster improvement and achieved a higher level of proficiency than beginners taught by instructors not especially trained for their job. (From N. R. F. Maier, *Psychology in Industry*, 3rd ed., Houghton Mifflin, 1965, p. 404; through the courtesy of A. Bavelas.)

angle. Compare, for example, the views in Figure 18.16. It is quite evident that instructions pictured from the learner's viewing angle, as in the photograph at the right, are easier to follow than those which do not involve this feature. ∎

CONDITIONS AND MOTIVES

The adjustment of human beings to their work environment, including other workers and the management, is exceedingly complex. We limit our attention, however, to three aspects of efficient work: (1) the external environment, (2) compensatory reactions to distracting elements in this environment, and (3) motivating conditions and related *esprit de corps*, or worker morale.

The external environment

Optimal environmental conditions vary with what one is doing and also with the person himself. It is obvious, for instance, that people doing work which requires fine visual discrimination need more illumination than those whose work is less visually demanding. Improving the work environment, by increasing illumination and distributing it better, by providing better ventilation, and by reducing noise, usually increases output. Sometimes there is increased production when music is introduced.[27] It is interesting to note, however, that greater efficiency subsequent to such environmental changes may be, at least in part, motivationally mediated. As a prominent industrial psychologist has recently said, "Good lighting is cheerful and stimulating. Undoubtedly, some of the improvement in production which results from proper illumination is attributable to the favorable attitude which is created by pleasant surroundings."[28] Likewise, "The influence of controlled ventilation on attitudes and job satisfaction obviously affects all types of workers, and a favorable attitude of employees toward the management is an indirect benefit which should not be overlooked."[29]

Thus environmental improvements may produce a work increment for various reasons.

 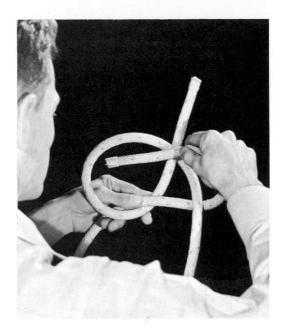

● 18.16

Illustrating the Principle That Tasks Should be Presented From the Learner's Viewpoint.
At the left we see how the sheet bend knot would look if tied while the learner faced
the demonstrator in the usual way. This sort of demonstration is significantly less effective than that pictured at the right. Here the task is presented as it would look to the
person tying the knot himself. How could this principle be applied to teaching knots to
Boy Scouts without the use of films? (Photographs, courtesy Dr. S. M. Roshal.)

Sometimes they lead directly to improved
sensory and motor functioning and sometimes
they have their effect, wholly or in part,
through improved morale.

Compensatory reactions

Suppose that you were working in a quiet
environment and noises were suddenly introduced. What would this do to your output?
The chances are that you would at first be
distracted; that you would find it hard to give
full attention to what you were doing; and that
your output would suffer. If you were well-
motivated, however, you would probably try
to overcome the distraction by concentrating
— by paying closer than normal attention to
what you were doing. Then your output might
recover, or even exceed, its former level. In this
event we would say that you had compensated,
or even overcompensated, for the distraction.
Eventually, the noises would no longer distract. In this event we would say that you

had become *adapted* to them, although the
term, used in this context, is different from the
sensory adaptation discussed earlier (pp. 294,
469). It would perhaps be better to say that
you have learned to ignore the noises.*

What has been said about noises also
applies to other distracting stimuli — like uncomfortable clothes, strong lights, or moving
objects in peripheral vision. We can compensate for, and eventually learn to ignore, almost any noninjurious distracting situation.
This is, of course, a further illustration of psychological homeostasis (p. 155) as well as
habituation (p. 295).

Laboratory investigations have shown
that, while compensating for distraction in the
ways indicated, the subject shows increased
muscular tensions and a slightly increased
energy expenditure (as measured by calories
consumed).

* We do not have in mind here an intensity of
noise which actually injures the auditory mechanisms, as mentioned on page 473.

One may recall the experiment discussed earlier (p. 492), in which subjects pressed harder on typewriter keys when distracting noises were introduced than when there was no distraction. Another experiment of a similar nature required subjects to add columns of figures under conditions of quiet and under conditions involving auditory distraction.[30] Noise sometimes preceded and sometimes followed the quiet condition. Introduction of noises at first decreased the number of correct additions per work period. Gradually, however, output returned to the level associated with quiet conditions.

When noises were first introduced, and during the compensatory period thereafter, there was a marked increase in muscular activity, as indicated by action currents. This is illustrated in Figure 18.17. Note that muscular responses decreased until, by the twelfth day, they had almost reached the level associated with conditions of quiet. Another interesting outcome of this study concerned the distribution of muscular tensions. When noise was first introduced, the tensions were diffuse, in-

volving all four limbs. Finally they were centered primarily in the right arm, which was used to write the answers.

Another outcome of this experiment was the increased energy consumption which distraction precipitated. Special physiological apparatus through which the subjects breathed, and which collected the expired air, indicated how much oxygen they had taken from the atmosphere. Since the amount of oxygen required to release each energy unit (calorie) is known, it was possible, from these measurements, to discover how many more calories per minute were being consumed under distracting as compared with quiet conditions. Mental work like adding does not require much energy, as compared with hard physical labor; nevertheless the amount is measurable, and it is measurably increased by distraction. As in the case of muscular tensions, however, energy consumption is eventually reduced to the level associated with work under conditions of quiet. This reduction in oxygen consumption is correlated with the reduction in muscular tension, thus the extra energy may be that utilized in producing the excess muscular tensions.

The subjects in such laboratory experiments as we have described are usually well motivated. This perhaps accounts, in part at least, for their ability to learn to ignore distracting conditions. The poorly motivated person, on the other hand, is likely to complain about distractions. He may even use them to rationalize poor performance, like the student who says that his low grades are due to noises in the dormitory, or library, or to the fact that his roommate or neighbors persist in playing records when he wants to study. The well-motivated person either learns to ignore such conditions, or he finds some other place to work.

Motivation

We have already pointed out certain motivational advantages of improved working conditions. Here we wish to emphasize that, among other things, there is a greater incentive to work efficiently when the worker feels that the management is interested in him as a

● **18.17**

Average Magnitude of Action Potentials on Successive Days Under Quiet Working Conditions and Under Noise Distraction. The curves show the average number of deflections per second for all four muscle groups. (From G. L. Freeman, "Changes in Tension-Pattern and Total Energy Expenditure During Adaptations to 'Distracting' Stimuli," *Amer. J. Psychol.*, 1939, 52, p. 358.)

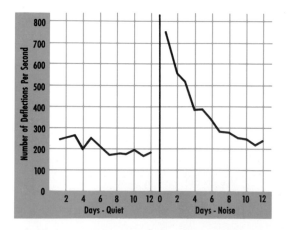

person than when he sees himself as a mere cog in the industrial machine.

☐ An experiment carried out at the Hawthorne Works of the Western Electric Company over a number of years seemed to show that increased pay, shorter hours of work, improved lighting and ventilation, rest pauses, and refreshment periods were inducing girls to increase their output of electric relays. Each time a new incentive was introduced, production went up. However, when the girls were returned to the original working conditions, their output not only failed to drop to former levels, but it continued to improve. The conclusion finally forced upon the investigators was that the girls were motivated not so much by external incentives as they were by increased morale related to the fact that they were selected for the experiment and that the company was apparently interested in them as individuals. Moreover, common interests and attitudes relating to their experiment gave the girls an *esprit de corps* which went beyond that usually found in industrial situations.

Capitalizing on the findings of this experiment, the company introduced an interview system whereby each employee could air his criticisms to, and talk about personal problems with, a person who would listen and report to the management, but without divulging names. Better morale was thereby introduced because the workers felt that the management was interested in them.[31] ■

FATIGUE

Fatigue "is a blanket term for many different effects of work — all of those effects which are harmful or deleterious, and which are a function of the duration and amount of effort, but which are recoverable through rest."[32] Only two aspects of fatigue will be considered here. These are: (1) the work decrement, and (2) feelings of tiredness or exhaustion.

The work decrement

Muscular fatigue, as indicated by a decreased capacity for work, is easily demonstrated with some form of ergograph. One such instrument is illustrated in Figure 18.18. As described in the legend; the weight is lifted to the maximum extent at first. Then performance deteriorates, down to the point where the weight cannot be lifted at all. But if we offer a new incentive, like money, this will often induce the individual to continue pulling at the weight. Thus the energy in the muscles is not entirely depleted. Substituting a lighter weight may also be followed by further action. Introducing rest pauses at intervals slows the work decrement, or even prevents it if the pauses are appropriately spaced.[33]

The impairment of an isolated muscle group, as in the ergograph experiment, is hardly representative of that which occurs in complex everyday activities. Everyday work may involve the whole organism and it is seldom as repetitive as pulling a weight in response to the stroke of a metronome. Various psychological processes may come into play and compensatory reactions may prevent a decrement, or at least delay its occurrence. In everyday activities, moreover, fatigue may be revealed in other ways than in a simple quantitative decrement. We do not merely do *less* work as fatigue comes on, but the quality of work is also impaired.

At Cambridge University a group of psychologists made an intensive study of fatigue under complex working conditions.[34] Their experiments were done with a special cockpit[35] (Figure 18.19) resembling a Link Trainer, such as that used for aircraft pilots. The work was comparable, in certain respects, to that required of a pilot on a long flight. While sitting at the Cambridge Cockpit, the subject was required to respond to a large number of signals. These were variously located within the cockpit; they were complicated in that their sequence as well as their color, location, and other characteristics had to be discerned and reacted to; and they were not simply repetitive. In responding to these signals, the subject manipulated various levers and switches. All responses had to be timed in an appropriate fashion with the signals — not just individually, but in relation to each other.

Some subjects worked for many hours

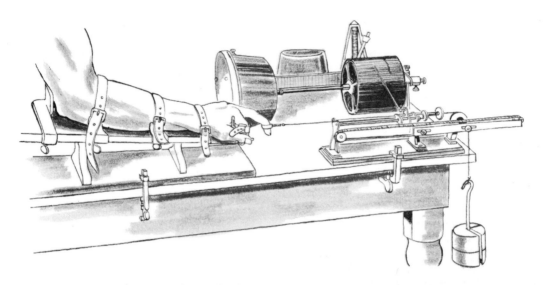

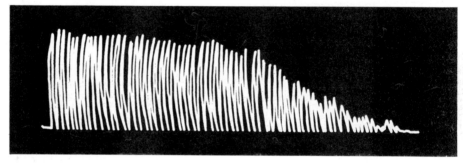

● **18.18**

An Ergogram and the Ergograph Used to Record it. The subject, after being strapped to the ergograph as pictured, pulls the weight as far as possible at each tick of a metronome. Every pull is recorded by a mark on the revolving kymograph drum. Note that the extent of the pull gradually decreases until, finally, the finger seems incapable of further action. (Ergogram after Yochelson and ergograph after Mosso, as used in J. F. Dashiell, *Fundamentals of General Psychology*, 3rd ed., Houghton Mifflin, 1949, p. 644.)

without fatigue, especially when, at fifteen-minute intervals, they could learn how they were doing. When fatigue did occur, it had various manifestations, the most outstanding of which were as follows: (1) A widening indifference to signals which required action. At first, when a signal indicated that the plane was off course, the subject was alert and made the proper compensatory adjustments. Gradually, under conditions of fatigue, he became indifferent, either ignoring the signals or waiting until they were of greater magnitude than

before.* (2) The correct reactions were often made at the wrong time, usually too late for

* We have here a decrement in what is often referred to as *vigilance*, although this term now has a somewhat technical meaning with reference to the detection of faint, infrequent, and irregular signals such as a radar operator is required to observe in watching his screen for ships or planes. Vigilance in this restricted sense has been investigated extensively by psychologists with the aim of discovering its nature and the conditions which improve or weaken it. See, in this connection, the excellent brief review by Broadbent, whose definition we have paraphrased.[36]

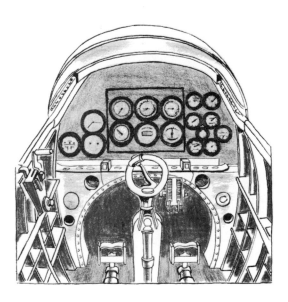

● **18.19**
The Cambridge Cockpit. The various dials signaled what the subject had to do in order to keep his "plane" on course, at the proper altitude, appropriately fueled, and so forth. His task, as one can see, was partly perceptual and partly motor. (After Dashiell, from D. R. Davis, "Pilot Error: Some Laboratory Experiments," *Appl. Psychol. Res. Unit, Med. Res. Council,* Great Britain, 1948.)

accurate performance. Incorrect reactions occurring at the right time were not so prevalent. (3) Time estimates were off, sometimes as much as 200 per cent. (4) Flurry, or panic, often occurred. In a "tight spot," the subject used one control or the other indiscriminately, something which in real life might well have led to disaster. This would be comparable, in a sense, with stepping on the accelerator instead of the brake of a car, or shifting to the reverse instead of the drive position. (5) The cockpit had an indicator which, if the subject responded to it, gave him more gasoline. Under conditions of fatigue, subjects sometimes forgot this indicator and, for them, the experiment came to "an inglorious end." (6) With the onset of fatigue, bodily discomfort came into prominence. The subjects said that they were tired, that their muscles ached, and so forth.

(7) Complaints about the apparatus began to appear. The levers or switches were said to be "sticky," "sloppy," or ineffective in other ways. And (8) the previously silent operator began to sigh and, eventually, to show such signs of temperament as swearing violently.

In the early stages of fatigue, a person does not know that his performance is deteriorating. He thinks that he is doing as well as he ever did. Later, when he realizes, or admits to himself that he is fatigued, he can perhaps make various compensatory adjustments, like paying closer attention to what he is doing and using greater caution.*

Feelings of fatigue

Continued mental or physical work often brings reports of experienced fatigue, of weariness, or even exhaustion. The person says that he feels fatigued. These feelings, because of their subjectivity, cannot be measured. However, the individual can rate their intensity on a scale of, say, 1 to 5, with 1 representing no fatigue, and 5 a maximum level. When this is done, and the degree of felt fatigue is compared with actual output, there is often no relationship.[37] Output may remain at a high level even though experienced fatigue, as rated, is increasing. Laboratory studies suggest, in general, that the feeling of fatigue begins earlier and runs a more rapid course than the work decrement. But well-motivated subjects in the laboratory are more likely to continue working at a high level, despite feelings of fatigue, than are workers in, say, a factory situation. What one usually does when he feels fatigued is to slow down, or take a rest.

ALLEVIATING FATIGUE

Feelings of fatigue as well as impairment of performance may be lessened by strong

---

* Alcohol, another agent of impairment, has similar effects. The intoxicated person, when he realizes his condition, may compensate by paying close attention to his movements — sometimes in such an obvious way as to make himself appear even more ridiculous. There are definite limits to such compensations, however, and the person soon gives up the struggle.

motivation, knowledge of results, rest pauses, and the use of certain drugs.

Motivation

We have been faced repeatedly, in this chapter, with the fact that performance varies with motivation. Increased output under improved working conditions was attributed, at least in part, to improved motivation, or worker morale. The subject who seemed completely fatigued in the ergograph experiment was capable of further work when given an incentive to continue. And the effects of distraction were seen to be less if the subject was well motivated. There is thus no doubt that the more strongly a person is motivated to do what he is doing, the greater his ability to delay the work decrement and the less likelihood that he will feel fatigued. Think, for example, of how fatigued one can become while reading an uninteresting assignment, yet show no fatigue, a few minutes later, in reading an interesting detective story; how fatigued he can become while writing some letter which he is obliged to write, and how quickly the fatigue is overcome as he begins a love letter; or how tired he is while doing some heavy work that he has to do, yet how quickly he recovers when invited to play an interesting game of tennis.

Knowledge of results

With knowledge of how we are doing, the task is more interesting and we are more likely to continue than if no knowledge of results is available. This was brought out in our discussion of the learning process (pp. 346–348). One interesting outcome of the experiments with the Cambridge Cockpit was the fact that knowledge of results counteracted the work decrement. Providing they had periodic information on how well they were doing, some subjects worked for many hours at a stretch without showing fatigue. Nor was there any "delayed fatigue," such as sometimes occurs after prolonged work.[38] Similar results were found in studies on long-continued reading in which the subjects were high-school and college students, working for hourly remuneration and the advancement of science.

☐ The earlier of two such investigations required students to read continuously over a period of four hours.[39] During this time, eye-movements were recorded electrically. Evidence of a reading decrement was sought in such aspects of reading as blinking, fixations, lines read, and regressive movements (returning to a word previously fixated). Subjects had no knowledge of results. Under these conditions a decrement began to appear during the first half-hour of reading and became more pronounced as reading continued. Words, lines and whole paragraphs were sometimes skipped.

In the second of these investigations,[40] the reading period was extended to six hours, but the task was made more interesting than before. Interest was added by inserting comprehension tests at intervals in the reading matter. These contained multiple-choice items concerning what had just been read. There was no rest pause. The reader encircled the answers and went on to the next reading matter. Under these conditions there was no evidence of a reading decrement. The eyes continued to function as well at the end of six hours as at the beginning. This was undoubtedly due to good motivation provided, in part, by a knowledge of results. With comprehension tests inserted, the subjects had a reason for reading every line, they had something interesting to look forward to at intervals, and the confidence with which they could answer the test items gave them some knowledge of how well they were doing. Tests gave them a further incentive — to try to improve on previous tests.

It was not uncommon for subjects to complain about the length of the test, to wish that they were through with it, to get annoyed, or to say that they felt tired. But they succeeded in overcoming these feelings, hence their performance failed to show a decrement.[41] If the reading matter had been exceedingly interesting, and if it had been read for pleasure instead of for an hourly wage, even the feeling of fatigue might have been absent. Think of the many people who read a long novel at a single sitting without any apparent fatigue! ☐

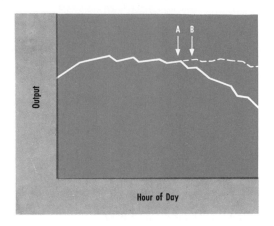 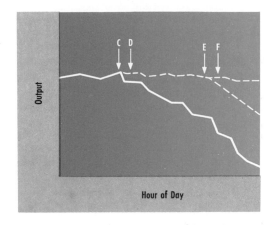

● **18.20**

Typical Industrial Output During Daily Work. The heavy line shows the typical output per work hour during an eight-hour day, with a rest pause at noon. At A the curve begins to drop. If a rest pause is introduced here, or at B (if the worker knows that it is coming), output may be expected to conform to the dotted line. Likewise, a rest pause might be introduced at C or D. Should output show a further drop, despite this pause, another might be introduced at E or F. (From H. E. Burtt, *Applied Psychology*, 2nd ed., Prentice-Hall, 1957, p. 438.)

Rest pauses

It is sometimes difficult to convince people that, by taking a rest now and then, and thus working less time, they can get more accomplished. Nevertheless, it is a well-established fact, both for laboratory studies of fatigue and for industrial work, that the judicious use of rest is conducive to increased output.[42]

The typical output, from hour to hour, in an industrial situation involving complex motor work is shown in Figure 18.20. There is usually a slight rise in output (a warm-up) during the first hour, then a gradual decline toward the midday luncheon hour. After lunch there may be an increase in output, over that present before the rest. Then there is usually a decline to the lowest point for the day, the hour just before quitting time. These variations in output exist despite the fact that workers take unauthorized rest pauses, like going to the washroom. When scheduled rest pauses are introduced, they are more effective than those which the worker takes on his own initiative. This is because they can be so arranged as to forestall the slump in output.

The best duration and schedule of rest pauses must, of course, be worked out for each situation. In general, however, the most effective rest pause is one which, as illustrated, comes at about the place where output normally declines.

Another factor of importance, moreover, is what the worker does during the rest pause. Here is an excellent example, based upon the experience of an industrial plant which introduced a fifteen-minute rest in the middle of a two-hour work period. Workers who walked about during the rest period increased their efficiency by 1.5 per cent; those who drank tea, by 3.4 per cent; those who listened to music, by 3.9 per cent; those who had an unspecified type of rest, by 8.3 per cent; and those who relaxed in a chair, by 9.3 per cent. It is obvious that those who had a more complete rest improved their performance most.[43]

There are at least four reasons why rest pauses are so effective. In the first place, they facilitate recovery from physiological fatigue. We see this most clearly in the ergograph experiment, where a particular muscle group is, so to speak, isolated for observation. The harder and longer a muscle works, the longer the rest required for recovery. This is because, without rest pauses, energy in the muscle is more quickly and extensively depleted and waste products cannot be eliminated.[44] In the second place, the knowledge that a rest pause is near spurs the individual to keep up his effort. Without a scheduled rest pause, he tends to slow down in anticipation of later fatigue. In the third place, rest pauses relieve boredom. Finally, the fact that an employer has instituted rest pauses suggests that he is interested in the worker's welfare. This is conducive to improved morale, the factor which played so important a part in the Hawthorne experiment and which has been suggested as contributing to higher output following environmental improvements like better illumination and ventilation.

Sleep

Sleep is the form of rest most conducive to prevention of fatigue and to recovery from it. Studies have shown that, while it is possible for some people to go for very long periods (even 200 hours) without sleep, yet keep up their efficiency in brief laboratory tests, they achieve this result through exceptional compensatory efforts.[45] The "cost" of this accomplishment is reflected in irritability and other emotional responses. In long tests, however, lapses occur in vigilance and in other aspects of performance (see Figure 18.21).[46]

Many adults feel fatigued and show impaired performance if they do not get from seven to eight hours of sleep per day. But there are great individual differences, and each individual must decide for himself, in terms of his efficiency and well-being, how much sleep he needs.[47] Some people find that they can take a brief nap during the day and that this makes it possible to work longer at night without becoming drowsy.

With respect to the effect of prolonged work, as well as the loss of sleep, it has been said that brief *lapses*, rather than a continual slowing down or continual increase in errors, are most critical. Thus, "Crudely speaking, a man is not like a child's mechanical toy, which

goes slower as it runs down. Nor is he like a car engine which continues normally until its fuel is exhausted and then stops dead. He is like a motor which after much use misfires, runs normally for awhile, then falters again, and so on."[48]

Drugs

Two drugs are especially helpful in alleviating fatigue. One of these is caffeine, common sources of which are coffee, tea, and cola drinks. The other is benzedrine, a drug which is often ·useful in emergencies.

• *Caffeine.* Ergographic studies (see p. 588) and several experiments on work of greater complexity have supported the widespread belief that caffeine counteracts fatigue.[49]

☐ The most extensive of these studies involved an elaborate but necessary check on all important variables, including attitudes which, as we have seen (p. 24), are of the utmost importance in research on drugs. Pure caffeine was administered in capsules, in doses of two, three, or six grains.[50] Control capsules, indistinguishable in taste or in any other way from those containing caffeine, were also used. Neither the subject, nor the assistant who administered the various tests, knew whether or not a capsule contained caffeine. By using pure caffeine given in capsules, the investigator not only removed the suggestion factor, but also any effects due to sugar, cream, and other substances commonly present in a cup of coffee.

The subjects (ten men and six women) were engaged, with pay, for a period of forty days. Most of their time each day was spent in the laboratory. Before beginning the experiment, each subject signed an agreement to regulate his daily living in specified ways, including complete abstinence from alcohol, coffee, tea, and other specified beverages. He undertook to swear on oath, if need be, that he had conformed to the contract in every respect.

A carefully worked out schedule guided the conduct of the experiment. The three doses, the control doses, the various tests, times of eating, of resting, and so on, were scheduled in such a way that, finally, the effect

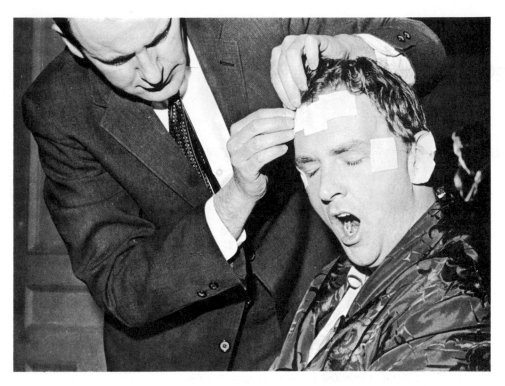

● 18.21

Acute Sleep Loss. This is Peter Tripp, a disc jockey, after almost 200 hours without sleep. During this period he was under constant supervision. Electrodes to measure his brain waves (EEG's) are being attached to his head. Others have stayed awake for as long as 100 hours while being studied by physiologists and psychologists. Some of the most spectacular outcomes of long sleepless periods are delusions and hallucinations, such as hearing voices when nobody has spoken. Increased irritability and subtle changes in perceptual and motor activities are also observed, although these do not always appear. In a brief test, the subject can usually marshal his resources so as to compensate for his fatigue — he pays closer attention and exerts more than normal effort. It may thus appear that his lack of sleep has caused no deficit. However, a very extensive investigation, involving sleep loss of up to 97 hours, and longer periods of continuous work than usual, has disclosed that there may be marked impairment of vigilance, speed of reaction, and memory. This was shown in research carried out by a team of psychologists at the Walter Reed Army Institute of Research. In tests of vigilance, the subjects were required to watch for certain signals and to listen for others. As the period of observation increased, and as the amount of sleep deprivation grew longer, there were lapses, so that signals were missed. Impairment was also observed in other psychological functions. The lapses took the form of drowsiness, with a corresponding decline in EEG alpha amplitude. When the subject set the pace of what he was to do, there was a tendency to slow down, but when the experimenter set the pace, so that a slow-down could not occur, there was an increase in the frequency of errors. The investigators point out that similar deficits are found in oxygen deficiency and fatigue. For further details, see the text. (From H. L. Williams, A. Lubin, and J. J. Goodnow, "Impaired Performance with Acute Sleep Loss," *Psychological Monographs*, 1959, No. 14; UPI photo.)

of a particular amount of caffeine could be ascertained. Everything was arranged, that is, so that caffeine was the only independent variable.

The various tests measured such variables as speed of reaction, speed of tapping, speed and accuracy of typewriting, color-naming, and calculating. In addition, there were tests of muscular steadiness. One such test is illustrated in Figure 18.22. The subjects kept daily records which indicated the quantity and quality of their sleep as well as their general health during the experiment.

Quite generally, the performances following administration of caffeine were superior to those which followed the control doses. Caffeine in any of the amounts given increased the rate of tapping, facilitated color-naming, improved the speed and accuracy of calculation, and increased the accuracy of typing. With respect to speed of typing, however, the small dose had an accelerating and the large dose a

● **18.22**
A Steadiness Test. The subject holds a metal stylus in a small hole and attempts to do this so steadily that it does not touch the side. Whenever a contact is made, this is recorded electrically. This type of test is used extensively in studying the effect of smoking, alcohol, and various drugs on muscular steadiness. The task is increased in difficulty by using smaller holes.

retarding effect. The intermediate dose had no effect. In the case of reaction time, only the large dose proved stimulating. The only uniformly deleterious influence of the caffeine was on hand-tremor. All doses made the subjects less steady. Sleep was disturbed in some subjects but not in others. When this occurred, the largest dose was usually responsible.

Beyond its demonstration of the stimulating effect of caffeine on various activities, this investigation also revealed some time effects. The effect on motor activities was usually present within an hour after taking caffeine. On associative processes, like color-naming and calculating, the effect came more slowly. It was usually not evident within two hours. Data from the ergographic experiments and from physiological studies, suggest that caffeine works directly on muscle tissue and that this may account for its relatively quick effect upon muscular activities.

The investigation also demonstrated two other interesting relationships. One of these is the fact that having recently eaten reduces the stimulating effect of caffeine. Thus a cup of black coffee* with meals is not as stimulating as a cup taken on an empty stomach. The other fact is that the stimulating effect of caffeine differs somewhat with body weight. In a heavy person, the stimulation is not as great as in one who is thin. Apparently the "amount of the substance ingested per unit of tissue affected" is important for caffeine stimulation.[51] ☐

A study on tea[52] revealed results somewhat comparable with those on caffeine. An average cup of tea contains roughly 1.5 grains of caffeine. The "lift" commonly alleged to follow a cup of tea may come from this caffeine, but it could also come from the carbohydrates in the sugar which some people add. It might even come from the suggestion that a cup of tea "peps" one up. Only an elaborate study like that on caffeine could reveal exactly why tea alleviates fatigue. The same is true with respect to cola drinks, which contain sugar as well as caffeine and other ingredients and

* An average cup of strong black coffee contains between three and four grains of caffeine.

which may also have their potency increased by the suggestion that they alleviate fatigue.

• *Benzedrine.* Psychological research on benzedrine confirms the view that it counteracts fatigue. But this research also discloses certain dangers from indiscriminate use. One investigation involved 180 subjects.[53] It was carried out under conditions in which the subjects did not know when the tablets they swallowed contained benzedrine and when they contained lactose. This study demonstrated that any statement about the psychological effects of benzedrine must be qualified in various ways. The general effect of the drug was to accelerate. This was especially true when thinking was not required. It is interesting to note, moreover, that the size of the dose was important. A large dose (20 mgm) was usually followed by poorer performance. About forty-five minutes had to elapse before acceleration again became evident. The chief general effect of benzedrine was to improve the subject's feelings, whether or not his performance was improved. The investigators say,[54]

□ "It should not be supposed that the ingestion of benzedrine is a guarantee of marked change in *ability* to "think," remember, do manipulative tasks, or function at a markedly increased level of efficiency, either in general or in specific ways. . . . it is rather to be supposed that there is a generally favorable reaction in mood, feeling tone, or affective attitude and that this reaction, in combination with various degrees of stimulation in a physiological sense, favors performance on tasks which call for alertness, persistence and freedom from fatigue. This statement, however, is subject to the qualifications, indicated by the effects which have been discussed repeatedly — namely, a temporary period of lessened efficiency, actual retardation, and perhaps even "confusion" for a variable period of time after ingestion, especially when the dose is heavy." □

The investigators point out, moreover, that the amount of benzedrine which an individual can take without its having deleterious effects varies from one individual to another and can only be discovered by experiment. It is not wise, therefore, to take this "unaccountable,

paradoxical, sometimes harmful, generally fatigue-reducing drug" except under the direction of a physician.[55] ■

OTHER APPLICATIONS OF PSYCHOLOGY

Our study of factors which influence the efficiency of work has provided an opportunity to observe how psychological facts and procedures may be put to practical use. One should not imagine, however, that applications of psychology are focused wholly, or even predominantly, on industrial and military problems. Increasing the worker's output is only one of many applications. Even more important is the psychological adjustment of the worker. It is increasingly recognized that good adjustment, while an aim in itself, is also conducive to efficient work.

Many applications of psychology were described, more or less incidentally, throughout this book. It became apparent that intelligence tests are useful in schools and in industry. Educational applications were particularly evident in discussions of learning, memory, and the thought processes. Books on educational psychology are largely concerned with such applications.[56]

Medical schools often recognize medical applications of psychology by requiring courses in this area. There is much in psychology that is of value to medicine, and several books on medical psychology have been written.[57] The discussions in this book which are especially relevant to medicine are those dealing with emotional behavior, motivation, personality, and the sensory and neural functions of the organism. That branch of medicine known as *psychiatry* makes considerable use of psychological tests and other psychological procedures and research techniques. Indeed clinical psychologists and psychiatrists, working in institutions and public agencies, often join forces in their attempts to improve the psychological adjustments of those under their care.

Legal psychology[58] involves applications in crime detection, in the alleviation of delinquency, and in courtroom procedure. Use of the lie detector is another application of psychology. Evaluation of testimony involves other applications. Testimony is evaluated in terms of what is known of man's memory and of his sensory and perceptual processes. An earlier discussion showed the inaccuracy which creeps into much testimony. But testimony is also evaluated in terms of what is known about sensitivity. Anybody who remembers what he studied in the chapters on sensory processes will know that a person who testifies that he saw certain hues under starlight is either lying or deluded; and he will also know that one cannot be sure, in terms of hearing alone, whether a sound originates from behind or in front of him.

Business psychology[59] involves applications of psychological facts and procedures to market research, advertising, salesmanship, and selection of employees.

In addition to applications in such fields as we have mentioned, there are many others; in the rearing of children,[60] in the training of animals,[61] in coaching athletes,[62] in adjusting the aged,[63] and so forth.

Quite often the facts of psychology are themselves applied, as in the case of courtroom testimony or the introduction of illumination suited to the acuity required for a particular type of work. What is usually more important, however, is the use of psychological procedures. A practical situation is often unique and the facts of psychology, which may have been gathered in a laboratory, are not directly applicable. It is then that procedures must be put to work. What the psychological investigator brings to such a situation is his knowledge of how to design an experiment which will reveal relevant facts, how to carry the procedure through, and how to evaluate and apply the facts when he has them. ■

PSYCHOLOGY AND HUMAN AFFAIRS

Increasingly, as psychological knowledge is systematized, the approach to each new problem, whether in the laboratory or in a practical situation, will become more clearly predictable than at present. We will use insight more and trial and error less in attempting to discover the solutions to human problems. We are, of course, far behind the other sciences in this respect. Our "laws of human behavior" are not as clearly defined as the laws of physics, of chemistry, or of physiology or genetics. We have not gone very far yet in developing equations from which, given certain known conditions, we can predict the unknown, as the astronomer can predict the appearance of a comet or the atomic physicist an explosion of predictable proportions. Some psychologists agree with those who claim that human behavior will never be completely predictable. The reason they give is that there are too many variables over which we have no control. Others think that psychology will gradually approach the stage where it can predict behavior just as other events in nature are predicted. These psychologists seek to discover laws in behavior. They hope to achieve an overall systematization of psychological knowledge. By starting with relatively simple behavior, in relatively simple animals like the white rat, they are making progress in this direction. But none of them claims that we shall have, in the foreseeable future, a system to embrace every aspect of human behavior.

We can now predict many particular things about human behavior. We can, for example, predict that, other things being equal, increasing motivation will improve output; rest pauses will facilitate learning; and a certain kind of instrument display will reduce accidents. We cannot, however, predict with any degree of assurance such complexities as the personality, or character, or achievements of a particular human infant, even when we know his parents, his environment, and the routine of his training. However, we may expect, in the future, to be able to predict and even control events of greater complexity than is at present possible. This is because rapid advances are being made in the scientific study of the social conditions which influence individual development and human interaction. James B. Conant, former president of Harvard University, has said that "Powerful tools are in the process of being forged by the scientists who study man as a social animal," and that "These tools can be used to further or to destroy certain types of behavior and certain social patterns."[64] Whether the methods of which he speaks will be used to improve human beings and their interrelations, or to debase them, is an issue which we must eventually face and which it may be the lot of the psychologist, in cooperation with other social scientists, to solve. This takes us into the field of "value judgments" and back, in a sense, to philosophy and religion. The problem is like that of whether our knowledge of atomic energy is to improve our way of life or destroy us; whether we are to create a world of automatons or a world of free men, with personal responsibility and an appreciation of the rights of those who differ from them.[65]

Psychology is playing an increasingly important role in human relations at the international level, particularly in the areas of prejudice, race relations, and the resolving of international tensions.[66]

How psychologists shall use the knowledge and the methods at their disposal is covered, in the United States, by a carefully developed and quite elaborate code of ethics which is comparable, in many respects, to the code of ethics which serves as a guide in the practice of medicine.[67] This is a fairly recent development and it indicates that psychologists are giving careful attention to their responsibilities in their relations with those who seek their services. ■

• SUMMARY

Efficiency is gauged in terms of the degree to which output approaches input. One person is more efficient than another if he accomplishes more in the same time and with the same energy expenditure. This chapter has focused upon ways in which the efficiency of human work may be increased. It has, however, also dealt with related factors, such as worker morale, and with certain applications of psychology to business and the professions as well as to industry.

Efficient performance is based, first of all, upon aptitude — the capacity to learn readily and achieve a high level of skill in some specific area of human activity. Aptitude tests are designed to measure a sample of performance and, upon the basis of this, to predict possible future success. Some tests of special aptitudes are of the pencil-and-paper variety while others require actual manipulation of test materials. Many jobs require a certain group of aptitudes — or aptitude factors. For most occupations one can specify a minimal intelligence level. Interests are always relevant, since the individual is more likely to succeed in occupations which interest him than in those which do not.

Aptitude tests for use in vocational guidance or selection must be standardized and evaluated for particular occupations. An important feature of the standardization procedure is to determine the relation between test performance and criteria of success in an occupation. These may be pass-fail criteria, grades, how long it takes to learn the job, or some measure of success — like work output. An aptitude test is said to be valid to the extent that it enables the investigator to predict such outcomes.

Although aptitude for the job is an important aspect of efficient performance, the design of equipment is also important. Just as man added to his efficiency by inventing such machines as wheels and levers, so the customary machines may often be redesigned to produce further increases in efficiency. Fitting the machine to man is necessary to a maximal degree in designing spacecraft for astronauts, but engineering psychology is also concerned with the design of everyday industrial equipment. Instruments, instrument displays, and operating equipment are of focal interest in this connection. Our discussion has illustrated the fact that certain instruments and instrument displays may be perceived more readily and more accurately than others in common use. The knobs on controls to be distinguished and operated by hand may be confused, hence investigators have discovered experimentally which shapes are easily differentiated. In this way one may make maximal use of the sense of touch, thus increasing efficiency and reducing errors which are conducive to accidents. Similarly, through experimental investigation, the other aspects of machines may be made more efficient in operation. The efficiency with which a hand-operated wheel may be manipulated, for example, is a function of its design, including its weight.

Even the person with a high level of aptitude for the job, and using a machine designed in terms of engineering psychology, may improve his learning and his ultimate proficiency through the adoption of good training procedures. These involve, first of all, a clear-cut presentation of what is to be learned. We have shown how time and motion study methods offer a means of discovering efficient behavior patterns for the job in question. When an efficient pattern is known, it may be taught. Without such a pattern, workers are likely to pick up inefficient work patterns. After the most efficient pattern has been discovered, there are further gains from using economical teaching methods. These are applications of methods discussed in the chapter on conditions of learning — introducing rest periods, using a whole before a part approach, and providing knowledge of results. When visual methods are used, as in the case of motion pictures or other demonstrations, the auditory description should precede the visual presentation, which should itself approximate, as closely as possible, the situation as the learner views it.

Improving the worker's environment usually increases output. The explanation of this fact is, however, not always clearly apparent. Improving illumination, for example, may increase output because it increases the worker's visual acuity, because it improves his morale, or because of both factors. It is for this reason that our discussion of work conditions in relation to output also stressed motivational factors. When distractions are present, the well-motivated worker tends to compensate by paying closer attention to the job or by increasing his effort. In this way his output may be maintained at a high level. The physiological cost of such compensation is evidenced through muscular tension and increased oxygen consumption. This is similar in many ways to the homeostatic phenomena discussed in the chapters on motivation. The importance of motivation for industrial efficiency was also illustrated by reference to the increased output which sometimes occurs when workers feel that the management is interested in their welfare.

Fatigue, as a factor which interferes with efficiency, was considered from two aspects — the work decrement and feelings. The nature of a relatively simple work decrement was illustrated by referring to the ergograph experiment. The Cambridge Cockpit experiment provided an illustration of fatigue in relation to complex psychomotor performance, where performance may be impaired in many ways. This experiment revealed many symptoms of fatigue, beginning with decreased vigilance and culminating in emotional outbursts. Feelings of fatigue may be rated for intensity on, for example, a five-point scale. There is, however, no clear relation between the intensity of such feelings and the magnitude of the work decrement. Quite often the work output remains at a high level despite reports of increasing weariness.

Factors of importance in alleviating fatigue are: motivation, knowledge of results, rest pauses, sleep, and certain drugs, of which only caffeine and benzedrine have been mentioned. Poor motivation is conducive to an early decrement in performance as well as complaints of weariness. Knowledge of how well one is doing tends to alleviate fatigue through its contribution to motivation. This was illustrated in the Cambridge Cockpit experiment and also in the experiment in which students read for as long as six hours without visual fatigue. Rest pauses, appropriately placed, may slow down or prevent a work decrement. What one does during the pause is, however, also important. The most complete rest comes from sleep, but relaxation in a chair provides the best practical rest pause under work conditions.

Prolonged loss of sleep lowers efficiency by producing lapses in vigilance and disrupting other aspects of performance.

Caffeine stimulates psychomotor and mental activities, yet without undesirable side effects, except in some persons whose sleep may be disturbed. Benzedrine in small amounts stimulates motor activity. In larger amounts it may have a temporary retarding effect. Its chief general effect is to increase alertness. But this and other effects differ a great deal from one individual to another, hence benzedrine should not be taken indiscriminately.

Psychology has been applied in many areas in addition to industrial work. Some applications in business, in the professions, and in personal adjustment have been suggested. While the facts revealed by psychological investigation are often applicable to business, industrial, and professional situations, the procedures of psychology are more widely applicable than many of its facts in that they may be used to discover the answers to almost any problem involving aspects of human behavior.

In the development of general laws, psychology is much more limited than such sciences as physics and chemistry, which deal with events much simpler than human behavior. Nevertheless, psychology has made great strides in the development of principles and methods and the discovery of facts which find useful application in various aspects of everyday life. It is also entering the realm of world affairs, and psychologists are concerned with the safeguarding of human values as further advances are made in the prediction and control of human behavior. ■

REFERENCES AND NOTES FOR THIS CHAPTER ARE IN THE APPENDIX.

• SELECTED READINGS

Anastasi, A., *Fields of Applied Psychology.* McGraw-Hill, 1964. A comprehensive and clearly written review of applications in various areas, including that of engineering psychology and other professions.

Chapanis, A., W. R. Garner, and C. T. Morgan, *Applied Experimental Psychology.* Wiley, 1949. Good for information on the utilization of human resources in industry. Includes a great deal on instrument design.

Floyd, W. F., and A. T. Welford, *Fatigue.* London: Lewis, 1953.

Floyd, W. F., and A. T. Welford, *Human Factors in Equipment Design.* London: Lewis, 1953.

Karn, H. W., and B. v. H. Gilmer, *Readings in Industrial and Business Psychology* (2nd ed.). McGraw-Hill, 1962.

Klineberg, O., *The Human Dimension in International Relations.* Holt, Rinehart and Winston, 1964. An excellent discussion of the psychological backgrounds of war and peace.

Maier, N. R. F., *Psychology in Industry* (3rd ed.). Houghton Mifflin, 1965. A good general review of industrial applications of psychology.

McCormick, E. J., *Human Factors Engineering.* McGraw-Hill, 1964. A readable survey of research in this area.

Mundel, M., *Motion and Time Study* (3rd ed.). Prentice-Hall, 1960. A systematic treatment of this topic.

Viteles, M. S., *Motivation and Morale in Industry.* Norton, 1953. This deals with almost every aspect of industrial motivation. The author's earlier books, although in some respects outdated, include discussions of much of the basic material from the psychological laboratory which has relevance for industrial psychology. These books are: *Industrial Psychology,* 1932, and *The Science of Work,* 1933, both published by Norton.

Welford, A. T., *The Ergonomics of Automation.* London: Department of Scientific and Industrial Research, 1960. Also see the papers by Welford and others in the conference report, *Ergonomics in Industry,* London: Her Majesty's Stationary Office, 1961. Both contain interesting illustrations of psychological engineering in British industries.

APPENDIX

ANSWERS AND SOLUTIONS

Figure 3.2, page 70:

Correct answers are: 4,1.

Figure 5.5, page 124:

Correct sequence of pictures is: D, F, C, A, E, B.

Figure 5.7, p. 127:

Correct answers: C, E, E, B, D, A, A, D, A, E.

Figure 7.1, page 191:

Left column: sorrow, surprise, grief
Right column: delight, horror

The situations were: (left) her team lost, surprise party, members of family drowned; (right) conversing with a senator, encounter with masked figure while crossing a field.

A

F

C

G

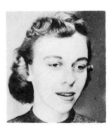

H

E

B

I

D

Figure 7.3, page 194:

The order should be, from unpleasant to pleasant: A, F, C, G, H, E, B, I, D.

Figure 12.7 Photographs for recognition memory test

Indicate by number which of these faces appeared on page 383. Then turn back to that page and check your accuracy. (Photographs used through the courtesy of Adelaide College of Education.)

Figure 13.5, page 409:

A. The six matches should be arranged as illustrated here:

B. The area of the square is 16 units.
C. The tumor is treated by rays coming from different directions but coming to a focus at the tumor.

Figure 13.6, page 410:

Begin at the top left and follow the arrows.

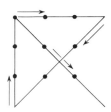

Figure 14.13, page 453:

From left to right, the signals mean: okay, stop, squelch him, give me a ride.

Figure 16.1, page 490:

The darkened area shows the location of the motorcycle policeman.

Figure 16.11, page 506:

An exterior view of a distorted room similar to that shown on page 506, showing how it is constructed to create the deceptive illusion. (Photographed for *Life* by Eric Schaal. © Time, Inc.)

Figure 16.13, page 513:

Left to right: scarab, sand dollar, trilobite

Figure 16.14, page 513:

Man on horseback; man taking picture with graflex camera.

GLOSSARY

Our glossary defines all technical terms used in this textbook, but the meanings given are only those relevant to the present subject matter. Many terms have additional meanings, relevant to other contexts. For these, and for definitions of additional psychological terms which the student may encounter in his outside reading, the following dictionary will prove especially helpful: H. B. English and A. C. English, *A Comprehensive Dictionary of Psychological and Psychoanalytical Terms,* David McKay, 1958. James Drever's *A Dictionary of Psychology* (revised by H. Wallerstein), Penguin Books, 1964, is a good inexpensive source of definitions.

ability   Present skill, as in riding a bicycle or reciting a poem. Contrasted with *capacity*, in that it refers to what an individual *does* do rather than what he might do if given appropriate training.

abnormal   *Ab* (away from), hence diverging from the normal.

abscissa   The horizontal (or *x*) axis of a graph.

absolute threshold   The weakest effective intensity of stimulation.

absorption curve   One which shows the degree to which different wavelengths of light are absorbed or reflected by an object like a green leaf.

abstracting   Discerning the common elements in situations which are otherwise different.

abstract thinking   Thinking in terms of concepts and general principles, as contrasted with thinking of specific things.

accommodation   Changes in the lens mechanism of the eye which focus it for different distances.

achievement motive   Ego involvement such that the person desires to make a good impression on others by positive accomplishment.

achievement test   A test which, as distinguished from aptitude and intelligence tests, measures what has been accomplished in specific areas, as in mathematics, history, or French.

achromatic   A (without) *chroma* (color), hence without hue, as in a black and white picture.

ACTH   (Adrenocorticotropic hormone) The hormone from the anterior pituitary which stimulates the adrenal cortex.

acquired   Developed or learned during an individual's lifetime.

action current   An electrical disturbance which traverses the nerve fiber after stimulation. Also, electrical voltage shift accompanying other activity of living cells.

activity cage   One with a device to record the running or other activity of an organism placed within.

activity cycle   Rhythmic fluctuations of activity, as in the two-hour hunger and four-day sex rhythms of rats.

acuity   Ability to distinguish small stimulus differences, as the smallest difference between two points or two intensities of stimulation. Sharpness of sensitivity.

adaptation   Adjustment. Sensory adaptation involves a change in the characteristics of experience as a result of prior stimulation, as when we gradually see more clearly in a darkened room or taste something as especially sour after eating sweets.

addiction   An uncontrollable or compulsive habit, as in the taking of drugs.

adjusted learning   The situation is arranged so that fast and slow learners acquire equal amounts and without the chance to overlearn.

adjustment   Accommodating or fitting oneself to circumstances, as when we say that an animal is adjusted to its environment or that a student is adjusted to, or gets along well with, the group in which he finds himself.

adolescence   From the Latin *adolescere*, meaning to approach maturity. It begins at puberty and ends with adulthood.

adrenal gland   An endocrine gland, about the size of a pea, located above each kidney. The central part (medulla) secretes adrenin (adrenalin), and noradrenalin, while the outer part (cortex) secretes cortisone.

adrenalin (adrenin) A secretion of the adrenal medulla. Also see **noradrenalin**.

aerial perspective Clearness of details under different atmospheric conditions. Objects with clear details appear nearer.

aesthesiometer An instrument for stimulating and measuring skin sensitivity. The two-point aesthesiometer measures acuity of tactual discrimination.

aesthetic preference A preference based upon feeling, as in the case of pleasantness or unpleasantness commonly used in judgments concerning art.

affective process One which underlies or involves feeling or emotion.

afferent Sensory (leading in).

after-image One which follows removal of the external stimulus.

aggression Hostility which may involve actual attack or pushing around of other people.

alarm reaction Referred to by Selye, in his concept of stress, as a "generalized call to arms of defensive forces in the organism."

alcoholic psychosis Mental illness brought on by use of alcohol.

alerting mechanism One which makes the organism attentive to things and events.

alexia Word blindness, as when an individual who has learned to read can no longer understand the meaning of visual symbols. In the case of congenital alexia, difficulty in learning to read attributed to inborn factors.

all-or-nothing principle A nerve fiber, or muscle fiber, if it responds at all, responds completely.

alpha rhythm An electrical brain rhythm, involving about 10 fluctuations per second, recorded when the eyes are closed and the brain relatively at rest.

ambivalence Being pulled in opposite directions, as in both loving and hating the same person.

ambivert One who has neither pronounced introvert nor extravert characteristics; a person between these extremes.

amnesia Loss of memory, as after a blow on the head or an emotional upset.

amnion The inner embryonic membrane.

amnionic fluid That which surrounds the organism within the amnionic sac.

amplitude The extent to which a vibrating body is displaced from the resting position.

ampullae The enlargements at the base of the semicircular canals.

amygdala Sometimes referred to as the amygdaloid complex, this area of the limbic system is involved in the control of emotional behavior. Electrical stimulation has the effect of enraging an animal, while destruction has a taming effect.

anaglyphs Pictures in two colors which, when viewed binocularly with suitable filters, give a tridimensional effect.

androgens The male sex hormones (testosterone).

anecdotal method The collection of stories about the doings of animals and babies.

anesthesia Partial or total loss of sensitivity, especially used in relation to skin sensitivity, as when one's sense of pain is dull or absent.

animal hypnosis See **tonic immobility**.

animal magnetism What Mesmer believed hypnosis to be.

animism Attributing life to inanimate things.

anosmia Loss of olfactory sensitivity.

anterograde amnesia Forgetting of what took place during or after a disturbing event, presumably because what was happening made no impression. See **amnesia** and compare with **retrograde** amnesia.

anthropomorphism The attributing of human traits to animals.

anticipation method. In memory experiments, one item is given and the subject attempts to recall the next, and so on, until the whole list can be recalled without prompting.

anticipatory response One in terms of a present stimulus which signals a stimulus to come, an expectant response.

anvil Small bone in the middle ear located between the hammer and the stirrup.

anxiety Apprehension, dread, uneasiness. The emotion stems from fear, but it is more a fear of what might happen, or what has happened, than of a clearly apparent fear-provoking situation. An important term in psychiatry with shades of meaning which differ depending upon the school of psychoanalysis.

anxiety neurosis   Mental illness characterized by anxiety with insufficient cause.

aperture colors   Otherwise known as *film* colors. Color *as such* without reference to any object or surface.

aperiodic   Without a rhythm, or cycle.

aphasia   Literally, without speech. A disorder involving loss of linguistic meaning, such as loss of the ability to understand what is heard or what is read. Motor aphasia is loss of the ability to articulate.

apparent motion   See **phi-phenomenon.**

appetite   Readiness to eat, but sometimes also used with reference to sex, as in so-called sexual appetite.

aptitude   The capacity to learn readily and achieve a high level of skill in some specific area, such as music, mathematics, or mechanics. Contrasted with *ability* in that it refers to potential rather than actual accomplishment.

aqueous humor   Watery substance behind the cornea of the eye.

Army General Classification Test (AGCT)   Used to measure intelligence and aptitude for various aspects of military service.

aspiration   Striving to reach a certain level of performance, hence the term *level of aspiration.*

ascending paths   Those rising to the brain from lower levels of the nervous system.

assertiveness   The tendency to master, to "push," or to be aggressive.

assessment   Evaluating an individual with respect to his various traits. See **holistic assessment.**

assimilation   To absorb, or adapt to one's own needs or purposes. With reference to rumor, the reception and modification of a story in terms of the recipient's beliefs, prejudices, or values.

association   The function of relating, bringing together, or connecting. *Association neurons* connect other parts of the nervous system; the *association experiment* is one in which the subject recalls items previously connected with or related to the stimuli presented.

associative strength   The strength of an S-R association as measured by the frequency with which a given stimulus elicits a particular response. Thus the stimulus word *white* more often brings the response *black* than the response *green* (is more likely to bring the response *black* than *green*). We can say, therefore, that the *white-black* terms are more strongly associated (or have greater associative strength) than the terms *white-green.*

asthenic physique   Thin, slender, ectomorphic.

ataxia   Muscular incoordination.

athletic physique   Muscular, strong.

attending   Getting ready to perceive, as in listening or looking, or defining the center of clearness in perception. Focusing of sense organs sometimes involved.

attitude   A predisposition to react in a certain way, a readiness to react, a determining tendency.

audiogenic seizure   A behavior disorder, resembling an epileptic attack, but produced by auditory stimulation, usually of a very high pitch.

audiovisual   Involving both hearing and sight.

audition   Hearing.

auditory labyrinth   Part of inner ear concerned with hearing.

auditory localization   Evidenced by ability to name or point to positions from which sounds emanate.

authoritarian   An authoritarian is one who acts in a dictatorial fashion in his relations with others. We have used the word as an adjective, especially with respect to the role of a leader in social situations. Thus, the authoritarian leader is one who dictates what others must do, thus creating what Lewin has called an "authoritarian climate" within the group. This is in contrast to situations (climates) calling for group decision. See **democratic leadership.**

autocorrectivism   See **homeostasis.**

autogenous   Self-initiated or self-taught.

autokinetic effect   The apparent drifting movement of a small fixed spot of light in a dark room.

automation   The use of machines to replace men in the control of industrial and other operations.

autonomic nervous system The relatively independent system, comprising the sympathetic and parasympathetic systems, which regulates the various inner organs of the body, like the heart, stomach, and glands.

aversion A tendency to avoid, to dislike.

avoidance training Where the organism avoids punishment by making an appropriate anticipatory response. Compare **escape training**.

axon That part of the neuron which carries the nerve impulse away from the cell body and into the end-brush. The motor axon carries the nerve impulse into the muscle fiber; the sensory axon into synaptic connections with the dendrites of a motor or an association neuron.

babbling The repetitive vocalizations of a baby, as if in self-imitation.

ballistocardiograph There are different kinds of ballistocardiographs, but these have in common the fact that they record heart activity indirectly, through movements of the body (very delicately balanced on a stabilimeter-like table) that are produced by the propulsive force of the flow of blood. One such instrument was used to study emotional stress. Figure 7.8 reproduces some of the ballistocardiograph tracings obtained in this experiment. Compare **electrocardiogram**.

Bard-Cannon theory The idea that the feeling aspect of emotion as well as the pattern of emotional behavior is controlled by the hypothalamus.

barriers The more or less insurmountable obstacles which interfere with need-satisfaction. They may be environmental (social or non-social) or within the individual. Barriers function psychologically only when the individual recognizes their existence.

basal age The mental age (M.A.) credited for passing all items of the Stanford-Binet Test at the level just prior to that at which some items are failed.

basal ganglia Nerve-cell groupings (gray matter) at the base of the cerebrum, principally involving the thalamus, hypothalamus, and midbrain.

basilar membrane Membrane at the base of the cochlear canal which has an important function in hearing.

beats Periodic fluctuations in loudness produced by two tones of closely similar frequency.

behavior Anything that an organism does or says.

behaviorism A school of psychology which stresses an objective, natural-science approach to psychological problems. Observations are confined to behavior. Conscious experience, because of its subjectivity, is considered outside the scope of a scientific psychology.

behavior tests Those which rate or otherwise measure observed reactions to actual life situations.

bel Unit of loudness, 10 decibels. The logarithm to the base 10 of the higher intensity to a standard intensity (.0002 dynes per square cm.). This standard intensity is taken as representative of the threshold intensity which, as such, is subject to fluctuation in repeated tests.

belittling A compensatory reaction in which the individual increases his own self-esteem by disparaging what others do, or have done.

benzedrine A drug which, among other effects, induces wakefulness.

Berkeley Growth Study A longitudinal study of mental growth carried on at the University of California in Berkeley.

bilateral Involving both sides. As applied to transfer, it means that what is learned with one side of the body (one hand or foot) is in some measure transferred to the other side.

bimodal Refers to a frequency distribution with two modes.

binary digit A digit system utilizing only the symbols 0 and 1. Used in information theory and in so-called digital computers, where, for example, 0 is zero, 1 is one, 10 is two, 11 is three, 100 four, 101 five, and so on.

Binet-Simon scale The forerunner of other individual intelligence tests like the Stanford-Binet. It was developed in France by Binet and Simon.

binocular Involving both eyes at the same time.

biographical method Tracing the development of behavior by recounting incidents which occurred at various age levels. Also referred to as the *life history* method.

biological memory Sheer retentivity underlying recall and other aspects of memory. See **engram**.

biosocial Involving the interplay of biological and social influences.

bipolar cells Cells with two poles, as in the case of those in the retina which connect synaptically with both the rods (or cones) and the ganglion cells of the optic nerve.

bit A contraction of "binary digit." It has a meaning peculiar to information theory, where it is used to represent an amount of information (not necessarily small) which reduces uncertainty (the alternatives relevant to a situation) by one-half. Also see **binary digit** and **information theory**.

black-white continuum The discriminable series of grays ranging from black at one end to white at the other.

blaming others Excusing oneself for failure on the grounds that others are responsible.

blind spot Under certain conditions a portion of the otherwise uninterrupted visual field is missing, due to the lack of receptors where the optic nerve leaves the eye.

Bonamine A drug used to alleviate, among other things, motion sickness.

borderline intelligence Between two classes, as between moron and average.

brain A term which embraces the large mass of nerve tissue above the spinal cord, including the brain-stem, cerebellum, and cerebral hemispheres.

brain stem The part of the brain which would remain if the cerebral hemispheres and cerebellum were removed. However, some neurologists do not include the thalamus and corpus striatum as part of the brain stem, but refer to them as basal ganglia. See **basal ganglia**.

brain-storming A term coined to represent a group problem-solving situation where members of the group contribute any ideas which seem relevant to them. It is a special kind of situation, functioning under certain rules designed to foster creative ideas.

brainwashing Inducing people to modify their attitudes and behavior in certain directions through various forms of social pressure and, perhaps, physical torture.

brightness The intensity aspect of light; the visual dimension represented by the black-white continuum. The term is also used to represent a high level of intelligence, in contrast with dullness.

Broca's area A region in the left motor area of the cerebral cortex which plays an important, if not crucial role in the articulation of speech sounds. Named after Broca, who discovered it.

cafeteria feeding Allowing the organism to choose its own diet from a wide assortment of foodstuffs.

caffeine Fatigue-alleviating drug in tea, coffee, and cola drinks.

capacity Similar to aptitude. It implies potential, as compared with actual, accomplishment. The individual's capacity to learn some skill, for example, might be inborn; it might depend upon prior learning; or it might, and probably would, depend upon a combination of these.

cardinal number One of the principal numbers, such as one, two, three, four, and so on.

case history Assembling of data which reconstructs an individual's past, the aim being to understand his problems and aid in his adjustment.

catatonic A form of schizophrenia (or a person with schizophrenia) characterized by such symptoms as extreme negativism and holding of bizarre postures.

categorizing Placing different items in a particular category (class) in terms of some common property or in accordance with some principle. See **concept formation**.

cell-assembly concept Hebb has postulated that psychological processes are mediated by associations of neurons arranged, functionally, into closed circuits, or cell-assemblies. It is further postulated that these assemblies become established as the young organism interacts with its environment; i.e., as an outcome of early experience.

cell body The compact central portion of a neuron; that is, the neuron exclusive of its projections.

central nervous adjustment Adjustment involving the brain and spinal cord without necessary involvement of the receptors and effectors.

central nervous system The brain and spinal cord.

central theory Theory which stresses central nervous adjustment as that is defined above.

centralist One who emphasizes the role of central neural processes (or ideas) in the control of behavior.

cerebellar ataxia Muscular incoordination resulting from injury to the cerebellum.

cerebellum Brain structure, connected to the brain stem via the pons, whose function is primarily that of motor coordination.

cerebral cortex The greatly invaginated outer layer of cerebral gray matter and the center for many complex neural adjustments.

cerebral hemispheres The two structures, joined at the corpus callosum, which together comprise the cerebrum.

cerebrotonia Temperament characterized by such features as restraint, shyness, hypersensitivity, and reflection.

cerebrum The cerebral hemispheres.

character Personality viewed from the standpoint of the ethical or the moral, as in the case of honesty; ordinarily has reference to relatively fixed traits.

chlorpromazine One of the more potent tranquilizing drugs.

cholinesterase A chemical substance (enzyme) which plays an important role in the transmission of nerve impulses.

chorea A more or less widespread jerking or twitching of muscles. Distinguished from a tic in that it involves more than one muscle or muscle group.

choroid coat The middle, pigmented layer of the eyeball, whose prime function is to exclude light.

chroma See saturation.

chromatic vision Vision which involves hues, as in a technicolor picture.

chromosomes Structures within the nucleus of a cell which contain the hereditary determiners, or genes.

chronic Persisting over a long period.

chronological age Actual age from birth.

chronoscope A device with which speed of reaction is measured. A signal is given, the chronoscope starts, and the subject's reaction stops it.

ciliary muscle Muscle which regulates the curvature of the lens, hence focuses the eye for clear vision.

circumvallate papillae Structures toward the back of the tongue which contain receptors; generally credited with mediating bitter tastes.

classical conditioning As in the experiments of Pavlov and Bechterev, where the unconditioned stimulus followed the conditioned stimulus whether or not the animal responded to the latter.

clearness An aspect of attending, in that what we attend to becomes clear, or comes into focus. See attending.

client-centered therapy The client does most of the talking, makes his own diagnosis, and finds a solution with minimal guidance from the counselor. See nondirective therapy.

clinical procedure Having to do with the diagnosis and treatment of an individual case.

clinical psychology Concerned with diagnosis and psychotherapy of the milder behavior disorders, like speech defects, school difficulties, and neuroses. Many clinical psychologists work in collaboration with psychiatrists, especially where more serious behavior disorders, like the psychoses, are involved.

cochlea Coiled structure of the inner ear which contains the receptors essential for hearing.

cochlear microphonics Electrical currents produced by the cochlea during auditory stimulation.

cochlear nucleus Part of the brain stem which receives impulses from the cochlea.

code As used in this book, a system of symbols (like Morse code or Braille) for transmitting information. See encoding and decoding.

coefficient of correlation A statistic which represents the degree of relationship between two variables, or how closely variations in one series of measurements are concomitant with variations in another, paired series.

coenotrope   A common habit, one which most members of a group have acquired. Distinguished from many habits in that the latter tend to differ from one person to another, and from instincts, in that these are inborn rather than acquired.

cognitive dissonance   One's awareness of a conflict, or discrepancy, as between his attitudes and his behavior, or his behavior and the situation in which he finds himself.

collective behavior   Group behavior, behavior of interacting individuals.

cold spot   A point on the skin which is especially receptive to stimuli with a lower temperature than the skin itself.

color blindness   A weakness or defect in sensitivity to hue, as in the case of red-green blindness, where the individual has difficulty in distinguishing red and green from grays of the same brightness level.

color circle   The various hues of the spectrum arranged systematically in a circular pattern, usually with purple, a nonspectral color, linking the red and blue. In such a scheme, either the hues or words representing them may be used.

color mixture   Mixing two or more colors. Retinal, by rotating overlapped discs; light, by overlapping areas of differently colored light; binocular, by presenting one color to one eye and a different color to the other eye with a stereoscopic device. The mixture of different color pigments is a somewhat different sort of color mixture, as described in the text. Compare **subtractive color mixture.**

color solid   A symbolic tridimensional figure which represents brightness (or luminance) on the central axis, hue on the periphery, and saturation from the center toward the periphery. Sometimes referred to as a double *color cone* or double *color pyramid.*

color vision   Response to the wavelength properties of light, i.e., what we experience as hue.

color weakness   See **color blindness.**

color zones   Regions of the retina which are especially sensitive to particular wavelengths of the visible spectrum.

common chemical sense   A nonspecialized sensitivity of the body to chemical irritants.

common social motive   One widespread within a particular cultural group and which originates in social influences to which children are subjected. Distinguished from a motive which has its origin in the physiological makeup of the organism.

communication   A form of interaction in which the behavior of one organism acts as a stimulus for the behavior of another. In verbal communication, a spoken (or written) word serves as the stimulus to arouse relevant symbolic processes in the hearer (or reader). It is often said, in this instance, that information has been transmitted from one person to the other.

communications theory   See **information theory.**

comparative psychology   Often used as synonymous with animal psychology. More strictly, the comparison of behavior at different levels of development in order to discover development trends — as in the evolution of intelligence from, say, ant to man.

compensation   Counterbalancing some change (such as a lowering of temperature) or some defect (such as a feeling of inferiority). The term has somewhat different implications depending upon the different schools of psychoanalysis.

compensatory movement   Movement such that a balance is reestablished, as when the speed of a car is regulated so that the speedometer does not go far above or below, say 50 miles per hour, or when, losing his balance, the individual regains it. The first example is an instance of compensatory tracking. See **tracking.**

complementary colors   Any two which, when mixed, produce a gray.

complex   An emotionally-toned group of ideas.

complex coordinator   An apparatus used to select pilots which requires rapid, coordinated adjustments to complex arrangements of stimuli.

complex indicators   Indicators of a complex, like repeating the stimulus word, becoming confused, or taking a long time to react.

complex learning processes   Those calling for use of symbolic processes, as in reasoning.

compulsion An irresistible urge to perform some act, such as stealing, lighting fires, or repeating a ritual.

concept An idea or conclusion based upon a generalization such as "anything burning is hot."

concept formation Learning to respond in terms of concepts.

conception Fertilization of the ovum.

conceptual Pertaining to concepts, as in conceptual (or abstract) thinking.

concrete thinking Thinking in terms of particular things (like pears, apples, bananas), in contrast to thinking in terms of categories (like fruit). The latter is abstract (or conceptual) thinking.

condensation A coming together or fusing. The coming together of air particles in a sound vibration. The fusion of ideas, as in a dream, where one object or situation symbolizes, or represents, several others.

conditioned response A response aroused by some stimulus other than that which naturally produces it, like salivation in response to a tone, or, as in operant conditioning, a response that has become more frequent under reinforcing conditions.

conditioned stimulus One which, through presentation with ·another stimulus which naturally arouses a response, itself comes to arouse the response, or some aspect of it.

conditioning Sometimes used as synonymous with learning. More specifically, the process through which conditioned responses are developed.

cone Receptor for color vision.

configuration See **gestalt**.

conflict The tension or stress involved when satisfaction of needs is thwarted.

congenital Present from birth, but not necessarily inherited. Congential syphilis, for example, is not inherited but contracted through contact with the mother. Congenital idiocy, on the other hand, is sometimes the result of an hereditary defect in the nervous system and sometimes the result of a defective prenatal environment.

conscience A self-attitude assumed by the individual when he fails to conform to the moral or ethical ways of his group, or when he is tempted to behave in ways other than the approved ways; the superego.

conscious experience Experience of which the individual is aware, as distinguished from *past experience*, of which he may or may not be aware at the moment. Conscious experiences may be considered as those which the individual can verbalize, or describe, such as sensory experiences and feelings.

consciousness Awareness, the sum total of subjective experiences at any moment.

conservation concept A child is said to have achieved this when he recognizes that objects may go through various transformations without changing their volume or weight, as when a ball of clay is pressed into different shapes. This applies, similarly, to conservation of number.

consolidation Bringing together, unifying, or interrelating different things.

constancy phenomenon The tendency for brightness, color, size, or shape to remain relatively constant despite marked changes in stimulation.

constant factors Those held constant in an experiment, as distinguished from the independent variable.

construct Basically an inference concerning things or processes underlying the observable. Motives, for example, are constructs. Many theoretical terms in science are constructs. The *id*, the *subconscious* regarded as a region of the mind, and *insight* are psychological constructs.

context The general setting in which an event occurs, the surroundings.

contiguity Being together in space (spatial contiguity) or time (temporal contiguity).

contiguous conditioning Conditioning through mere association; that is, without evident reinforcement.

contingent probability Probability dependent upon some preceding event, as when use of a particular letter (or word) determines to a certain degree what will follow in a word (or sentence). Thus in English *q* is almost always followed by *u*.

contrast An effect brought about by the simultaneous or successive proximity of different stimuli.

control group One comparable with the experimental group in all respects except the condition under experimental investigation.

controlled Varied or held constant, according to certain specifications, by the investigator.

conventionalized In accordance with established rules, as in the case of grammar and etiquette.

convergence The turning inward of the eyes, as in fixating a nearby object.

convergent production In thinking, the bringing together into one class of things that are otherwise different. Compare **divergent production**.

cornea The transparent front portion of the eyeball.

corpus callosum A large structure which unites the cerebral hemispheres.

corpus striatum Literally, the striped body. It is so named because the internal capsule, which passes through it, has a striated (striped) appearance. Some of the basal ganglia are in the corpus striatum. It appears to be concerned primarily with motor functions; injuries located in it are associated with certain forms of chorea, suggesting that it may play an important role in smoothing motor activities, in their integration. See **internal capsule**.

correlation A relationship between variables such that changes in one are accompanied by changes in the other, either positively (as when weight tends to increase with height) or negatively (as when increasing weight tends to go with decreasing speed of locomotion).

cortex Bark, outer layer, as in respect to the cortex of the adrenal gland and the cerebral cortex.

Corti, organ of Structure above the basilar membrane of the inner ear which contains hair cells important in activating the auditory nerve.

cortical Having reference to the cortex.

cortical localization The attributing of a certain function to some particular region of the cerebral cortex, like hearing in the temporal lobe.

cortical rhythm See **brain waves**.

Cortisone One of the hormones secreted by the adrenal cortex.

co-twin control The use of identical twins to control the hereditary contribution to behavior. One twin is subjected to experimental conditions while the other is not.

covert See **implicit**.

cranial nerves Those emerging from the cranium (skull). The twelve pairs of nerves connected with the brain stem, including the auditory, olfactory, and optic nerves.

creative thinking Thinking with novel, in contrast with routine, outcomes.

cretinism An abnormality of structure and behavior which results from insufficient thyroid secretion during early growth.

cristae Small structures in the ampullae of the semicircular canals whose hairs are bent by rotary motion.

criteria Those standards against which tests are validated — like grades or sales records.

critical cut-off score The score an individual must achieve in order to be admitted to a certain job, a school, or a branch of the Armed Services. The minimum acceptable score.

critical flicker frequency (c.f.f.) The frequency of light flashes necessary to eliminate flicker and to produce an uninterrupted experience of brightness.

critical period This has special reference to imprinting. It is the period of maximum imprintability or, as sometimes used, the period before and after which imprinting is difficult or impossible to obtain. See **imprinting**.

critical ratio The difference between two means divided by the standard error of the difference.

cross-education Otherwise known as *bilateral transfer*.

cross-sectional method One of the developmental methods. It involves the comparison of groups of individuals at different age levels. Contrasted with the longitudinal method, where the same individual is observed as he grows older.

crowd A temporary group of people interacting with each other, and having some common focus of attention. An audience has many of the features of a crowd, but it is usually more passive. Many kinds of crowds are recognized, such as aggressive crowds, lynching crowds, acquisitive crowds, and so on. The latter are often referred to more specifically as mobs bent on aggression, lynching, or looting.

cueing function A stimulus is said to have such a function when it produces guidance concerning an appropriate response. We have used the term with respect to motivation, where a particular drive state (like hunger) makes an organism especially responsive to food and food-related stimuli, like the odor of milk. Here it could be said that both the internal drive stimuli and the external food-related stimuli have cueing functions.

culture Traits, implements, beliefs, and practices which characterize a particular group of people.

curare A drug which has a paralyzing effect on muscles.

cutaneous Pertaining to the skin.

cut-off score See critical cut-off score.

cycle Rhythm: in auditory stimulation, one full double vibration, often recorded in number of such vibrations per second.

cytoplasm Jellylike substance which surrounds the nucleus of a cell.

dark adaptation Increasing visual sensitivity which is a function of time in darkness, or in low illumination.

daydreaming Fantasy engaged in while awake.

decibel (db) One tenth of a bel, the unit of loudness. See bel.

decode To translate signals so that they convey a message. Thus dots and dashes are translated into words. It is sometimes said that the cerebral cortex "decodes" the nerve impulses which reach it in such a manner as to give them particular meanings (visual, auditory, and so on.)

decrement Decrease, diminution, decline.

déjà vu The feeling that a new situation is familiar — that one has been there before.

delayed matching in terms of a sample Technique whereby the subject is shown a sample object and is required, after a delay, to select it from an assortment of new objects.

delayed-reaction experiment A stimulus is presented and removed before the organism is released. This stimulus may be a light in one of three doors, the organism having been trained to respond to the lighted one. After an interval the situation is again presented, but without the differentiating stimulus; in our example, the light. If the organism now responds as it did formerly, by going to the door in which the light had appeared, and if it does this consistently in a series of tests with the light in different positions, we say that it has demonstrated ability to perform this delayed reaction. What bridges the gap must be something in the organism which represents the stimulus (say, the light) during its absence. This is a *symbolic process*. See symbolic process.

delta rhythm A brain rhythm (see electroencephalogram) characteristic of sleep — relatively slow and of large amplitude.

delusion A false judgment or conclusion, as when a mentally ill person believes that people are putting ground glass in his food.

dementia praecox The name formerly given to schizophrenia. It means "youthful insanity."

democratic leadership That which uses group discussion as a basis for action. It is said to establish a *democratic group climate*.

dendrite Part of the neuron which carries the nerve impulse toward the cell body.

density Degree to which something is concentrated. Auditory density refers to the seeming compactness of sound.

dependent variable The variable (some aspect of behavior or experience) which goes with (depends upon) changes in the independent variable. For example, speed of reaction as dependent upon the intensity of the stimulus to which the response is made.

depression A low point, such as low spirits. As applied in abnormal psychology — a melancholy mood, a feeling of hopelessness, an attitude of dejection. In serious cases, a symptom of grave mental illness.

deprivation A lack of something which the organism needs, as when a hungry animal is deprived of food, or a thirsty one of water.

depth perception Perceiving depth (tridimensionality) or distance.

depth psychology That which probes into the motivational or so-called *dynamic* aspects of personality, especially those of which an individual is not aware or, in Freudian terminology, of which he is *unconscious*.

descending paths Tracts beginning at upper levels of the nervous system and terminating at lower levels.

determiners of attention The various conditions which influence attentiveness — like the *size* of a stimulus or the *interest* of an individual in what is before him. The former would be an external and the latter an internal determiner.

determining tendency An attitude predisposing the organism to react in a certain way.

deterrent Something which repels the individual, as contrasted with an incentive, which attracts him.

detour problem One in which the organism must approach the goal indirectly, by a roundabout way.

development Growth, as when an organism approaches maturity. Also used to represent growth of language, of understanding, or of some skill. Development resulting largely from hereditary factors is often referred to as *maturation*. This may be contrasted with development resulting largely from the learning process.

developmental psychology The study of psychological development. Also referred to as *genetic psychology*.

deviation I.Q. A statistically derived I.Q. of the same order as a standard score. In contrast with the conventional I.Q. (M.A./C.A. × 100), it is determined by the standard deviation of the distribution of M.A. scores at a given age level and the deviation of the individual score from the mean of this distribution.

dexterity Skillfulness, expertness, versatility. The person who uses both hands equally well is said to be ambidextrous, to possess ambidexterity.

diastolic blood pressure That associated with the dilatation of the ventricles of the heart. It is lower than the systolic pressure, associated with heart contraction.

difference threshold The smallest perceptible difference between two stimuli. See **just noticeable difference (j.n.d.)**

differential aptitude test A special test, based upon factor analysis, which measures several aptitudes at the same time. Abbreviated DAT.

differential conditioning Conditioning in which the organism discriminates between stimuli, giving a conditioned response to one and not to the other which has been paired with it.

differential forgetting Selective forgetting, especially of erroneous responses faster than correct ones.

differential response One that is discriminatory.

differentiation The change from generalized to specific structures or functions as when what was once a budlike structure becomes a hand with its integral mechanisms. Also used as synonymous with discrimination as when what was once reacted to as a whole, or in a nondescript way, is reacted to in terms of its constituent parts. *In conditioning*, the change from an overall response to a specific response (like lifting the foot instead of merely struggling) or responding differently (differentially) to two tones which were at first each reacted to in the same way.

digit span The memory span for digits. See memory span.

direction set A continuing attitude or assumption which leads the associations of the thinker to follow a certain line.

direction of conditioning The tendency for the conditioned response to be congruent with the total situation, or with the needs of the organism. For example, it is salivation and not pricking up the ears which comes to be associated with a sound presented with food.

directional cues External stimuli which provide guidance as to the direction of food, escape, and so forth.

discrimination Responding differentially, as when an organism makes one response to a reinforced stimulus and another response to a stimulus that is not reinforced.

disparity, retinal The difference in the retinal images when an object is viewed with the left and with the right eye.

displacement Emotional; anxiety focused

upon something other than its real cause. Also aggression toward a person or object other than the one causing the anger — e.g., the man, angry with his wife, who "picks on" a child, an underling, or even an inanimate object (kicking or breaking it). The anger (or aggression) is then said to be *displaced*.

dissociation Separation of ideas or of responses normally associated; like being unable to recall one's name; being able to write, yet without awareness of what one is writing; having two or more different personalities, e.g., Dr. Jekyll and Mr. Hyde.

dissociation by varying concomitants The individual confronted by many different things (like different kinds of dogs) comes to overlook (dissociate) the differences and to discern something which all, despite their differences, have in common. Basic to development of concepts.

dissonance Lack of harmony. Incongruity. See **cognitive dissonance**.

distraction Having attention diverted from what one is doing.

distributed effort Learning with small units of work and/or interpolated rest periods. Contrasted with massed learning, where the individual works continually until the skill is mastered.

divergent production In thinking, starting with one, or a few, items, the individual gives as many instances or makes as many rearrangements as possible. Compare **convergent production**.

docility Tameness.

dominance In heredity, a trait is said to have dominance when it depends upon the presence of one gene (the dominant) which suppresses the effects of its partner (the recessive). Cortical (hemispheric) dominance refers to the dominance of one side of the brain (usually the left) in control of handedness and speech.

dominance hierarchy A social situation in which one organism dominates all below it, the next all below it, and so on down to the organism that is dominated by all. A pecking order in barnyard hens.

dominant gene See **dominance**.

dorsal columns Nerve tracts toward the back of the spinal cord.

double-alternation problem One in which the organism is required to make a *rrll*, or some comparable sequence of turns, in a temporal maze.

dramamine A drug used to alleviate motion sickness.

dreaming The fantasy which, as distinguished from that of daydreams, takes place while one is asleep.

drive A physiological condition which impels the organism to become active. Distinguished from a motive in being initially indiscriminate, without an appropriate direction.

drive reduction Alleviating tensions associated with drives.

dual personality What is apparently two persons in one, as in Dr. Jekyll and Mr. Hyde.

duct glands Those with ducts which secrete outside of the blood stream, as in the case of such secretions as tears and saliva.

ductless glands Glands which pour their secretions into the blood stream. The endocrine glands.

duplicity theory The theory (now accepted as fact) that there are two kinds of visual receptors, the rods for achromatic and the cones for color vision. See **rods** and **cones**.

dynamics This term is used in psychology to refer to the underlying and changing bases of behavior such as motives. A dynamic approach is one which deals with change (or with changing forces), as in group dynamics. See **group dynamics**.

dynamometer An instrument with which we measure the force exerted in the performance of some act. A hand dynamometer measures strength of grip.

dysrhythmia Disrupted rhythm, as in the EEG's of epileptics.

ectomorphy Dimension of body build characterized by predominance of skin and nervous mechanisms.

educational psychology The field having to do with application of psychology to educative processes, such as the teaching of the school subjects.

effectors Muscles and glands considered as responding organs.

efferent neuron That which terminates in a muscle or gland; which carries motor impulses.

ego The individual's conception of himself. Also, in psychoanalysis, that part of the personality which, as an outcome of reality-testing, restrains the expressions of the id.

ego-defensive Compensatory, as in maintaining self-esteem under conditions which threaten it.

ego-involvement Being personally wrapped up in some person or situation, as when the parent feels that his child's triumphs or defeats are his own, or that his own performance in some situation will raise or lower his status in the group.

eidetic imagery Imagery of such clearness that the objects represented appear in some respects to be present. Similar to hallucinations but believed to be normal in many children at early age levels.

Electra complex A term used by Freud to represent the erotic attachment of a daughter for her father, with concomitant jealousy of the mother. This attachment may be repressed and disguised in various ways. See **complex**; also **Oedipus complex**.

electric potentials See **action currents**.

electric-shock therapy Also referred to as electroconvulsive therapy (abbreviated ECT) and electroshock therapy. Attempting to relieve such symptoms as extreme depression by passing a weak electric current through the brain from electrodes applied to the scalp. Passage of the current through the brain produces widespread convulsions.

electronic brain A highly complex machine, utilizing electron tubes, which stores and utilizes information in such a manner as to suggest some of the functions of the human brain. A "thinking machine."

electrocardiogram A record of the various phases of heart activity derived from electrical concomitants of this activity.

electrodermal changes Changes in the electrical conductivity of the skin.

electroencephalogram (EEG) A record of electrical rhythms associated with some brain activities. Recorded with an *electroencephalograph*.

electroretinogram A record representing electrical changes in the retina.

embryo, human The human organism between the second and eighth weeks of life, before which it is known as an ovum and after which it is known as a fetus.

emitted response Coming without an external stimulus, i.e., spontaneously.

emotion A condition underlying such experiences and actions as occur in fear, rage, and the other so-called emotions. In its most obvious manifestations it is an acute condition characterized by disruption of everyday experiences and activities.

emotional maturity Being grown-up emotionally, not being swayed by childish motives. Sometimes referred to as *social maturity*.

encapsulated end-organs Skin receptors enclosed in a capsule-like structure.

encoding Transforming a message into a code (or set of signals) from which it can subsequently be translated to convey information. For example, putting a message into Braille, into electrical impulses as in Morse code, and so on. See **decode**.

end-brush The branching fibers at the end of an axon.

endocrine glands Those which pour their products (hormones) directly into the blood stream. The ductless glands.

endolymph Liquid contained in the semicircular canals and vestibule of the inner ear.

endomorphy The dimension of body build characterized by predominance of fat, especially in the abdominal region.

engram Altered state of living tissue responsible for memory. Sometimes used as a synonym for *neurogram*.

enuresis Bed-wetting.

environment Everything which surrounds the units of inheritance. There is the *intracellular environment* (that within the cell), the *intercellular environment* (that involving the effect of cell upon cell), the *prenatal external environment* (that surrounding the embryonic or fetal organism), the *internal environment* (that within the organism, such as the blood), and the *exter-*

nal environment, which is what we usually think of as *the environment,* and which includes the *social* or *cultural environment* as well as the purely physical, like light and air. *Psychological,* in terms of what it means to the individual.

eosinophils The cytoplasm of some white blood cells (the granular leucocytes) contains granules which stain with the red die, eosin. The leucocytes thus stained are called *eosinophils. Eosinophilia* is an increase and *eosinopenia* a decrease in their number.

epilepsy Disorder characterized by convulsions and loss of consciousness.

equilibrium See **static sense.**

ergogram Graph showing work output as a function of continuous exercise of a restricted muscle group.

ergograph Instrument for studying fatigue of a restricted muscle group.

eroticism Sexually derived pleasure. The Freudians extend the term to cover pleasures derived from anal and oral as well as genital stimulation.

escape training This occurs in the situation where, by making a certain response (i.e., pressing a lever), the organism terminates punishment. Compare **avoidance training.**

estrin A secretion from the ovaries which plays an important role in female sexual development, including the sex drive.

estrogens. Hormones from the ovaries. See **estrin.**

Eustachian tube A tube connecting the middle ear with the throat and which has much to do with maintaining normal air pressure in the middle ear.

excitability Property of organisms which enables them to respond to stimulation.

exercise, in learning. Repetition of learning activity.

experience Used to represent what has been referred to above as *conscious experience* (like awareness of the world about us) and also to represent what has happened to an organism in the past, in the sense of *past experience.*

experimental extinction Elimination of a learned response by arousing but failing to reinforce it.

experimental introspection Describing one's experiences under controlled conditions of the laboratory.

experimental method Variation of environmental, physiological, or attitudinal factors in order to observe dependent changes in aspects of experience and/or behavior.

experimental neuroses Behavior disorders produced experimentally, as when an organism is required to make a discrimination of extreme difficulty and "breaks down" in the process.

experimental psychology Experimental investigation of psychological problems.

explicit Directly expressed, observable, objective. Overt.

exploratory drive The urge to explore, to examine or to probe in strange situations. Perhaps comparable, in apes and men, with curiosity.

external ear The outer ear as far in as the eardrum.

external environment The environment which surrounds the individual, that external to him.

external response A response of the musculature which is readily observed without instruments, like walking, typing, or speaking.

extinction, experimental Eliminating a learned response by arousing but failing to reinforce it.

extraversion Term which represents the tendency to be outwardly expressive, as in talking a lot, being excessively active, and engaging in social activities. The other extreme from introversion.

extravert Person with a high degree of extraversion.

face validity Apparent validity as distinguished from statistically established validity.

facial vision Alleged ability of blind people to avoid obstructions through tactual stimulation of the face by air currents.

facilitation Process of making something possible of accomplishment or easier than it might otherwise be. *Neural* — making the passage of impulses across a synapse occur more readily.

factor analysis A statistical procedure aimed at discovering the constituent irreducible traits in what is complex, as in the case of intelligence or personality.

factors Component or constituent parts or conditions. In intelligence or personality, the constituent aspects revealed by factor analysis.

false recognition Seeming to recognize or to remember somebody or something actually seen for the first time. French, *déjà vu*.

fantasy Imagery that is more or less coherent, as in dreams and daydreams, yet without due regard to reality.

fatigue Diminution of work output as a function of repeated activity (the *work decrement*); also the feeling of tiredness associated with continued activity, inadequate sleep, etc.

fear An emotion characterized by unpleasant feelings, tension, and, where possible, avoidance or flight. There is also marked involvement of the autonomic nervous system.

feeblemindedness A level of intelligence represented by an I.Q. of 70 or less.

feedback The return of impulses to a control center where they play a part in further control, as in the case of impulses produced by muscular activity returning to the brain, informing it of the posture of the muscles, and thus contributing to further control of these muscles. It is comparable, in a sense, with the functions of a governor on a steam engine, which feeds back the information that more or less steam is needed.

feeling Affective experience reported by the individual as pleasantness, unpleasantness, excitement, calm, tension, sadness, happiness, and so forth.

fertilization Impregnation of the ovum.

fetal infant One born prematurely during the late fetal period.

fetal period Human; from the beginning of the third month until birth.

fetus Human; organism in the womb during fetal period, i.e., from the beginning of the third month until birth.

fiber tract A bundle of nerve fibers.

figure and ground Where one part of a situation is seen as a shape with the rest of the situation as background, like an airplane seen against the sky.

film color Hue seen as such without reference to its being a surface or other characteristic of an object. Also known as *aperture color*; observed as through an aperture which prevents the color being seen in context. Contrasted with *surface color*.

fissure of Rolando The long central fissure (groove), running downward from the top of the right and left cerebral hemispheres and separating the frontal from the parietal lobe.

fissure of Sylvius Groove beginning in the lower frontal region of each cerebral hemisphere and running toward the back. It separates the frontal and temporal lobes.

fistula A tube inserted into an opening in the body. As we used the term, a tube through an opening in the stomach so that liquid could be inserted directly.

fixated response One that has been so firmly established that it is difficult to eliminate. See **fixation**.

fixation The becoming firm or stable or inflexible of some aspect of behavior — like the firm acquisition of some habit. Used in abnormal psychology to refer to the retention to a later age of some infantile trait, like oral eroticism.

fixed-interval reinforcement A schedule which makes the reward available at the end of consecutive intervals; say every 20 seconds. See **reinforcement**.

fixed-ratio reinforcement A schedule which rewards the last of each of a given series of responses; say, every fifth or every tenth response regardless of the intervals involved. See **reinforcement**.

flicker Intermittent flashes, as when illumination, or a picture on the screen, alternates rapidly between light and dark.

flight of ideas An incoherent succession of ideas such as often occurs in mania, where the person's verbalizations go off on any tangent which suggests itself.

fluctuation of attention, or of perception Periodic changes in clearness, as when what was figure becomes ground, and vice versa, and what was heard is no longer heard.

flybar A particular system of auditory signals

which indicates to the pilot when he is performing incorrectly, the direction of error, and the amount of error with reference to keeping the plane straight, right side up, and at the proper altitude.

force of habit Habits which might have been changed persist with such force that the person seems "in a rut." There is strong motivation to hold onto habits already present rather than to change them.

forebrain In animals which walk on all fours, the foremost part of the brain; in man, the uppermost brain. The embryonic forebrain gives rise to the cerebral hemispheres and thalamus.

forgetting Loss of ability to recall; extinction of what has been learned.

formal discipline The doctrine, now rather generally discredited, that the study of certain difficult subjects like mathematics and Greek improves the intellect more than the study of other subjects in the curriculum. These subjects were assumed to "discipline the mind." Actually, diligent study of mathematics, Greek, and similar subjects often provides skills of value in other studies.

formboard A test device which calls for fitting blocks of various shapes into their proper holes, or into proper relationship, one with the other.

fovea A small depression in the retina which is also the area of sharpest vision. It contains only cones.

foveal vision That involving the fovea.

fraternal twins Distinguished from identical twins in that they have different hereditary characteristics and may also differ in sex. Derived from different ova.

free association of ideas Letting thoughts or words come as they may, as contrasted with controlled association, where certain directive tendencies are introduced.

free-floating anxiety Anxiety focused upon nothing in particular.

free nerve endings Branching ends of afferent fibers which are not embedded in receptors. Contrasted with the encapsulated nerve endings also found in the skin. They mediate pain and some aspects of pressure sensitivity.

frequency, as a factor in learning. The idea that, other things (including motivation) being equal, the more often a response is made to a situation the greater· the tendency for this situation to arouse it in the future. Same as *principle of exercise.*

frequency distribution A distribution of data showing the number of times (frequency) that each consecutive score is made.

frequency principle This is based upon the observation that, within certain limits, an increased intensity of stimulation increases the number of impulses which travel along a nerve fiber in any given time interval. Within limits, then: *An increased intensity of stimulation produces more frequent nerve impulses.* This is the frequency principle. It is assumed to underlie the intensive aspects of experience — brightness, loudness, and so on. But also see the **frequency theory of hearing,** which attempts to correlate the frequency of nerve impulses not with an intensive aspect of hearing (loudness), but with a qualitative aspect (pitch).

frequency theory of hearing Here pitch is assumed to depend upon a correlation between (1) the frequency of sound waves (cycles per second) and (2) the frequency of impulses in the auditory nerve. But we saw in the text that this theory could not account for frequencies above 1000 cycles per second. According to the frequency principle of neural activity (see **frequency principle**), loudness rather than pitch would depend upon the frequency of nerve impulses. This frequency would be correlated with amplitude of the sound wave (sound pressure) rather than with the number of cycles per second. The frequency theory of hearing attempts to avoid this difficulty by supposing that the frequency of nerve impulses accounts for pitch and the number of activated nerve fibers for loudness. In the volley theory (which is a modified frequency theory) loudness is accounted for in terms of both the frequency in individual fibers and the number of fibers responding (or the total number of impulses reaching the cortex at any time). See **volley theory.**

frigidity Extremely weak sexual motivation in women.

frontal lobes Those at the front of the brain, just behind the forehead.

frustration State of an organism resulting when the satisfaction of motivated behavior is rendered difficult or impossible.

frustration tolerance Ability to withstand a great amount of frustration without developing inadequate modes of response, like "going to pieces" emotionally, or becoming neurotic.

fugue Literally, a flight. Applied to neurotic behavior involving some episode (leaving home, a crime) which the individual, when he recovers, is unable to recall.

functional autonomy The tendency of habits to continue even though the motivation which led to their acquisition is no longer present. Different from *force of habit* in that the original motivation has ceased to exist.

functional disorders Those with no known organic basis; dependent upon prior experience rather than structural defects.

functional psychology The school which argued, against the structuralists, that psychology should concern itself with what the processes of mental life do, and not merely with their conscious "structures," like sensations, images, and feelings.

fundamental tone The lowest heard in a complex of tones, as when a wire is vibrated.

fungiform papillae Structures at the sides and tip of the tongue which contain taste receptors.

Galton whistle Device for testing the upper limit of auditory sensitivity.

galvanic skin reflex (GSR) Lowered resistance of the skin to passage of an electrical current following emotional and other forms of stimulation. Recorded with the psychogalvanometer.

ganglion A nerve cell. Plural, **ganglia**. Groups of nerve cells.

ganglion cells Retinal cells of the fibers whose axons become the optic nerve.

gastrointestinal Pertaining to the stomach and intestines.

general intelligence The overall intelligence of a person as represented by his general flexibility of adjustment. The term was also used by Spearman (in his concept of *g*) to represent an alleged general ability, or capacity, which expresses itself through special skills, like the social, mathematical, mechanical, and so forth. Sometimes related to the individual's ability to deal with abstractions.

general paresis See **paresis**.

general psychology The study of psychology in the large without emphasis on animals, children, adults, or special processes like the sensory processes, learning, etc. Often used to mean an introduction to the problems, methods, and principles as represented in textbooks for the beginner.

generalization A general conclusion, theory, hypothesis, or concept based upon certain facts or observations.

generalized response An overall as compared with a specific response.

generalizing Reasoning in such a way as to arrive at a generalization.

general adaptation syndrome A term coined by Selye to represent certain compensatory (homeostatic) reactions of organisms to organic and mental stress. By *syndrome* is meant a particular group of symptoms characterizing a disease or other condition, in this case characterizing adaptation to stress. According to Selye, the anterior pituitary and the adrenal glands are important factors in this syndrome (abbreviated G.A.S.).

genes Determiners of inheritance located within the chromosomes.

genetic method Studying development by observing the growth of an organism continuously or through comparison of stages.

genetic psychology Psychology which studies the evolution or growth of psychological processes, using the genetic method.

genius A person with exceptionally high intelligence. The person is said to approach this level if his I.Q. is 140 or above. Also an individual with some very unusual talent or ability that is recognized by society.

gestalt Form or configuration.

gestalt psychology The school which disparages the analytic approach to experience and behavior, and argues for emphasis upon wholes, which, gestalt psychologists say, are more than the sum of their parts. In learning, this school emphasizes insight as opposed to trial-and-error; in perception it stresses the organizations, which appear to be independent of past experience, such as figure-ground relationships and the phi-phenomenon. The word *gestalt* is often translated as *configuration* or *form* and the school is sometimes referred to as *configurational*, i.e., as emphasizing configurations rather than their constituent parts.

gifted Persons with special talents. Used also to represent individuals with an I.Q. of 130 or above (i.e., Terman's gifted children).

glands Secreting organs, like the tear glands (duct) and the adrenal glands (ductless, or endocrine).

glottis The opening between the vocal cords, at the upper end of the windpipe.

glycogen Sugar released by the liver.

goal objects Incentives to motivated behavior.

goal orientation Behavior directed toward a goal.

gonads Sex glands; ovaries in females and testes in males.

graphology The attempt to assess personality and character through handwriting.

grasping Reflex gripping of an object with the hand such as occurs in infancy; also the later-appearing prehensile variety, where the individual reaches for and takes hold of an object.

gray matter Neural substance of the spinal cord and brain composed largely of cell bodies; the cerebral cortex is almost entirely gray matter.

gregariousness The tendency to associate with others.

grooming Exploring the skin and hair for foreign objects, as practiced by monkeys and apes.

group behavior Activities characteristic of congregations of organisms, such as family behavior, crowd behavior, and behavior of an audience.

group dynamics A term used by followers of Lewin and others to represent the study of underlying features of group behavior, such

as field forces, motives, and the like. It is concerned with group change rather than with static characteristics.

group mind concept The idea that something emerges in a group situation which is more than the reactions of individuals as such. This is referred to as the "group mind" or the "collective mind."

group tests Those designed to be administered to more than one individual at a time.

group therapy Having the patient discuss his problems with others and with the psychiatrist or counselor, all of whom meet in a group.

guidance Used to differentiate vocational guidance from vocational selection. In guidance, the individual is given advice concerning vocations for which he may best be fitted.

guided performance The organism is put through some performance to be learned rather than left to its own resources.

gustation The sense of taste.

gustatory Pertaining to taste sensitivity.

habit An acquired mode of behavior, such as a motor or verbal skill, a way of doing things, or a way of thinking. The learning process is sometimes referred to as *habit formation*.

habit hierarchy A complex learned response (like typing) which involves an integration of simpler habits (like letter habits, word habits, etc.).

habit interference Otherwise known as *negative transfer*, where the acquisition of one habit interferes with the later learning of another.

habit strength Hull's $_sH_R$, the strength of an acquired association between a stimulus and a response. The strength of the S-R connection may be gauged in terms of the frequency of the response to S, its magnitude, the probability of its occurrence, and so on.

habitual Derived from what one has learned; also, customary. Habitual set, for example, is a customary or usual set derived from earlier experience.

habituation Gradual elimination of responses not called for by a situation, as when an infant is no longer startled by (or when he becomes accustomed to) lights, sounds, strangers, and other aspects of his everyday environment.

hallucinations False perceptions which differ from one individual to another (as distinguished from illusions, which are typically alike in all) and which have the appearance of reality. For example, one alcoholic sees red devils coming at him, another sees snakes, another hears accusing voices, and another feels bugs crawling on his skin.

hammer Small ossicle of the middle ear, attached to the eardrum.

handedness The tendency to use one hand predominantly, as in the right-handed or the left-handed.

hebephrenic A variety of schizophrenia characterized by silliness.

helicotrema An opening in the basilar membrane at the apex of the cochlea, where the ascending and descending canals connect.

Helmholtz theory of audition The auditory theory which correlates pitch with the region of the basilar membrane maximally activated by a sound frequency. Also known as a *place theory, piano theory,* or *resonance theory.* (For Helmholtz theory of vision, see **Young-Helmholtz theory of vision.**)

hereditary Referring to that which is inherited, or dependent upon the genes.

heredity What is passed on from parents to offspring biologically through the genes. *Social heredity* refers to nonbiological transmission of habits and ideas, through cultural contacts.

Hering theory In addition to the rods (for black-white vision) two types of cones are posited — red-green and blue-yellow. The components of each rod and cone are assumed to be opposed. Thus red light is said to activate the red-green cones in a manner opposed to that of green light. Similarly for blue and yellow light and the blue-yellow cones.

hierarchy Organization of habits, concepts, or the like, in which simpler components are combined to form increasingly complex integrations.

hieroglyphic writing The type of picture writing used by the Ancient Egyptians, where a picture (sometimes quite abbreviated) represented an object or perhaps merely the syllable or sound which, with others, composed a word.

higher-order conditioning Stimuli which have already been made effective through conditioning are used to condition further responses, in much the same way as unconditioned stimuli are used.

hindbrain In animals which walk on all fours, the back part of the brain; in man, the lowest part. Gives rise embryologically to the cerebellum, pons, and medulla.

histogram A series of rectangles representing a frequency distribution. The height of each rectangle indicates the frequency of a particular score — i.e., the number of times that this score occurred.

holist strategy Proceeding in accordance with an inference, hypothesis, or principle based upon all available information, as in experiments on categorizing (concept formation), where all relevant stimuli (possible cues) rather than only some of them are utilized. Compare **partist strategy.**

holist assessment Emphasis upon the entire person functioning in social situations; contrasted with a piecemeal or analytic approach in terms of traits.

homeostasis The compensatory mechanism whereby a constant state is maintained. Physiologically exemplified by sweating and other processes which maintain a constant body temperature when the external temperature is high. *Psychological homeostatis* may be illustrated by maintaining one's self-respect (in the face of failure) through such compensatory devices as rationalizing, blaming others, etc. It is also exemplified when the output of a fatigued person is maintained at a high level through closer attention or increased effort.

horizontal plane That which, like the horizon, runs at right angles to the vertical.

hormones Chemical products of the endocrine glands, like adrenalin and estrin.

hue The characteristic of visual experiences related especially to the wavelength characteristic of light waves — e.g., red, green, yellow, and blue; i.e., *color* in the everyday sense of the word.

human nature Those overall characteristics of human beings which depend upon their inheritance of human genes. Biological as distinguished from acquired nature.

hunger Motivation and experience associated with delayed satisfaction of the need for food.

hunger pangs Otherwise known as *hunger pains*, the painful contractions of the stomach musculature during intense hunger.

Huntington's chorea A progressively extending chorea of hereditary origin and with mental deterioration. See **chorea.**

hybrid An organism resulting from a sperm and ovum differing in one or more gene pairs, like *rw*, or *Bb*. Also the result of a cross between two species, e.g., the mule resulting when a horse and a donkey are crossed.

hydrocephalic Pertaining to excess fluid in the brain which causes the skull to become greatly enlarged and which interferes with normal brain development, usually leading to feeblemindedness.

hyper- Above.

hypnosis A trance-like state brought on through suggestion that the individual is to relax his muscles, sleep, and carry out various acts under the control of the hypnotist. Literally a "nervous sleep."

hypo- Below.

hypoglycemia Lower than normal blood-sugar level.

hypothalamus The under side of the thalamus, containing neural mechanisms which play an important role in emotion, sleep, and other physiological functions.

hypotheses Ideas, suppositions, tentative conclusions.

hypothyroidism A condition in which there is a less than normal secretion of the thyroid hormone, thyroxin.

hysteria General term for functional disorders characterized by anxiety without sufficient cause, and such forms of dissociation as amnesia, fugue, functional anesthesia, functional paralysis, and multiple personality.

id Freudian term representing the uncon-scious (or subconscious) primitive urges which underlie behavior.

idea The term is variously used, but always with reference to some implicit representation of things or relationships; synonymous with what we have called *symbolic processes*. It may mean something of which one thinks — like getting the idea to look up something in a book — or an image, as when a person thinks of his mother. Concepts may also be referred to as "ideas."

identical twins Those derived from the same ovum; thus they are genetically similar.

identification The process whereby an individual becomes ego-involved with persons or things — their problems are his problems; criticizing his school is criticizing him.

idiot Person in the lowest intelligence bracket — with an I.Q. lower than 25.

illusion Name given to a perception which is considered as mistaken because it does not agree with some other experience, such as objective measurement, which is taken as more fundamental.

image An implicit (internal) representation of past experience; in optics, the figure of an object formed by light rays; in sensory psychology, the impression which remains after an external stimulus has been removed, i.e., a *positive* or *negative after-image* in vision.

imagery The reviving of past experiences implicitly, i.e., in the form of images.

imbecile Person in the middle range of feeblemindedness, with an I.Q. between 25 and 50.

imitation Copying (perfectly or imperfectly) some act that has been witnessed.

immobility, tonic Remaining perfectly still, as in a "death faint" or in what is otherwise called "animal hypnosis."

impairment Deterioration of function, decreased efficiency.

implicit response One not directly observable but inferred from relevant facts. Brain processes are implicit because we do not observe them directly; thought processes are, for the same reason, said to be implicit. Contrasted with *explicit*, or directly observable.

impotence Want of strength or vigor, as in

sexual impotence where sexual vigor is lacking. In females the term *frigidity* is more often used.

imprinting   A learning process observed in some birds, and possibly other animals, that occurs with extreme rapidity and at an early "critical stage" of development. It involves the socialization of an instinctive response, such as following a moving object. In our example, the subjects were goslings. The imprinting object would normally be the mother. In her absence, however, the goslings came to follow a man, or a model of a goose. Imprintability reached a maximum during the first day after hatching. Responses acquired in this way are apparently persistent and irreversible. Thus, the gosling imprinted upon its mother never follows a man (or model) and vice versa.

incentive   An end or object of motivated behavior. That which is sought after — like food, a sex object, or money. Contrasted with *deterrent*. Could also be a consummatory act, e.g., to copulate, urinate, exercise, or play.

incidental learning   Sometimes referred to as *passive learning*, i.e., learning incidentally, without trying. Also see **latent learning.**

independent variable   The variable manipulated by the experimenter — e.g., the intensity of light, the hunger of an animal, or the presence or absence of a rest-pause in learning.

index of differentiation   One representing the discrepancy between a personal attitude (expressed in a projective questionnaire) and an overt attitude (as revealed in direct responses to questions).

individual differences   Deviations of individuals from the average or from each other.

individual tests   Those administered to one person at a time.

infant   Generally speaking, a child who is relatively immature. Although the period of infancy is not very clearly defined, it is usually taken to cover the first two years.

inference   Suggestion, guess, hypothesis, or judgment based upon certain data but not directly evident, as the inference (to be tested) that one's car has stopped because it is out of gas.

inferential   Based upon inference.

information   Knowledge, however acquired, including such things as clues in problem-solving and cues in a learning situation. However, this term has a very different meaning in information theory, where it means reduction of uncertainty in a particular situation. The measure of this is the *bit*. See **bit** and **information theory.**

information theory   Not really a theory, but a system for studying the communication process. It involves the detailed analysis, often mathematical, of all aspects of the process, which involves the encoding, transmission, and decoding of signals. It is not concerned, in any direct sense with the meaning of a message, i.e., with what it means to the receiver. Of all possible signals which might be transmitted, relative to a particular message, those which reduce uncertainty by one-half are assumed to convey one *bit* of information. See **bit, redundancy,** and **noise.**

information feedback   See **knowledge of results** and **feedback.**

infrahuman   Below the human level.

infraprimate   Below the primate level; i.e., the level which includes tarsiers, lemurs, marmosets, monkeys, apes, and man.

infra-red   Below the frequency of red light, or of greater wavelength (over 700 millimicrons).

ingroup   The group to which one belongs. One's family is an ingroup, as is one's club or one's nation.

inhibit   Check, hold back, or prevent.

inhibition   The complete or partial arrest of an activity or process.

innate   Inborn, or inherited.

inner ear   The innermost part, which contains the cochlea and the semicircular canals.

innervation   The nervous activation of some organ. See **reciprocal innervation.**

insanity   Legal term for mental illness of such severity that the individual cannot be held responsible for his acts. The psychiatric term is *psychosis*.

insight   Sudden understanding, as when one "sees through" a situation or "gets the idea." Also inferred from sudden improvement in learning.

inspiration Similar to insight; a sudden grasping of the solution to a situation, the sudden occurrence of an idea. Dealt with as a stage in creative thinking.

instinct A descriptive term for a complex, unlearned, adaptive response; or an unlearned pattern of reflexes. If the adjustment were learned, the behavior pattern would be called a habit.

instinctive Originating in instinct.

instructional set One that is verbally induced, as in telling a subject that he will see pictures relating to animal life, or that he is to respond to red but not to green.

instrumental conditioning That in which the conditioned response is instrumental in achieving some end, like obtaining food or escaping punishment.

instrumentation Learning which involves the invention or utilization of instruments, as when a chimpanzee solves a problem by joining sticks and using them.

insulin A secretion from the Islands of Langerhans (in the pancreas) that is necessary for carbohydrate metabolism. An undersecretion is responsible for diabetes and the related symptoms. Hyperinsulinism (an oversecretion of insulin) can produce hypoglycemia. See **hypoglycemia.**

insulin shock therapy Injection of insulin in sufficient quantity to produce a coma, from which the patient recovers through administration of glucose. Used in treating certain psychotic conditions.

integrate To bring together diverse things so that they form a functional whole.

integration A bringing together in some meaningful or workable relationship; the process of coordinating, as in *neural integration.*

integrative process The process of integrating, as when the cortex brings together different kinds of information (visual, auditory, and so on) so that the resulting reaction is consonant with the circumstances that exist.

intelligence Flexibility or versatility of adjustment, especially exemplified in ready adjustment to new situations.

intelligence quotient In its original meaning, the ratio of a subject's mental age (as determined by a standard comparative test)

to his actual age, and multiplied by 100 — i.e., M.A./C.A. × 100. But also see **deviation I.Q.**

intensity The *quantitative* as contrasted with the qualitative aspect of stimulation or experience; for example, the magnitude, amount of pressure, or amplitude of a sound wave, as distinguished from its frequency; the brightness of a color as differentiated from its hue.

intensive Having to do with intensity. Quantitative.

intention The aim or purpose to do something.

intentional Done with intent, purposefully.

interaction process analysis Analysis of small-group behavior in terms of twelve categories — viz., shows solidarity, shows tension release, shows agreement, etc.

intercellular Between cells.

interest An attitude favorably disposing one toward some object, situation, or idea.

intergroup relations Relations of one group with another.

internal capsule A bundle of fibers (white matter) lateral to the thalamus. This comprises the descending (motor) fibers, including the pyramidal tracts. Also see **corpus striatum.**

internal environment That within the organism, especially as represented by characteristics of the blood.

internal stimuli Those originating within the organism.

interpersonal relations Relations of individuals interacting with each other. For example, the relations which exist between husband and wife, employees and management, and so on.

interpolated activity That which, as in the retroactive inhibition experiment, comes between the original learning and recall, or relearning.

interposition A monocular (and psychological) cue in visual space perception involving the overlapping, or partial obscuring, of objects as seen.

intersensory Involving more than one sense.

interstimulation A reciprocal social relation where what one person does stimulates another, whose behavior in turn serves as a stimulus. Observed in any conversation, where what one person says is the stimulus for a reply from the other and that for a further response from the one who initiated the conversation.

interval scale   Like that of the temperature scales, where the intervals are equal, but there is an arbitrary zero point.

intervening variable   An event inferred to occur within the organism between the moment of stimulation and that of response in such a way as to determine or influence the response. This could be an inferred neural response (such as neural inhibition) or some psychological response (like the expectation that the act will have certain consequences).

intracellular   Within the cell.

intramaze cues   Those within the maze itself.

intrasensory   Within the same sense.

introspection   Looking inward, so to speak, and describing one's experiences.

introversion   A tendency to be overly concerned with one's thoughts, to be inwardly reflective or introspective rather than overtly expressive. The opposite pole from extraversion.

introvert   One with high degree of introversion.

invagination   Turning or folding inward, as on the surface of our cerebrum.

involuntary   Without intention, without personal control.

involutional melancholia   Psychosis sometimes associated with the menopause (involution) and characterized by depression.

iris   The flat circular muscle which controls the amount of light admitted to the retina. It is situated in front of the lens and is responsible for the eye's color.

irradiation   Spreading of the effects of stimulation such as Pavlov assumed to underlie stimulus generalization in conditioning.

Ishihara test   A series of charts designed to detect the color weak or color blind.

isolate   A person who, in a sociometric study, is chosen by nobody. He stands alone in a sociogram.

J-curve   A frequency curve often found when data are plotted for situations in which one is expected to conform. Instead of resembling a normal distribution, the plot is one in which most individuals are represented to the left and fewer and fewer toward the right. The graph thus looks like a reversed J (Ⴑ). Our example in this text dealt with conformity in children's attitudes. Public expressions of attitude gave a J-curve, while private opinions (as revealed projectively) gave something closer to a normal curve.

James-Lange theory   The theory that the feeling aspect of emotion is an experience of bodily changes, like the activities of the viscera and of the skeletal muscular structures.

job analysis   Studying a job in such a way as to discover its components and its psychological and other requisites.

just noticeable difference (j. n. d.)   The smallest discriminable (or perceptible) difference between stimuli.

kinesthesis   The muscle or movement sense, mediated by the receptors in the muscles, tendons, and joints. See **proprioception**.

knee jerk   A reflex kick of the foot following a blow on the tendon just below the knee cap.

Krause end-bulbs   Structures in the skin assumed at one time to mediate sensitivity to cold.

Kuder Preference Record   An inventory designed to discover the degree of interest that an individual has in various areas of everyday life — like the mechanical, the scientific, and the social.

kymograph   Apparatus designed to record variations in activity as a function of time. The most common form is a rotating drum containing a strip of smoked paper on which marks are made by a recording stylus.

laissez-faire situation   One in which each individual does as he pleases. Its relevance here is with respect to the study of social climates, one of which was laissez-faire. Compare **authoritarian, democratic**.

language   Communication through conventionalized gestures, or spoken or written symbols.

larynx The upper part of the windpipe — a cartilagenous box containing the vocal cords; the "voice box."

latency The period of apparent inactivity between the time that the stimulus is presented and the moment that a response occurs.

latent learning That not evident to the observer at the time when it occurs. It is inferred from later performance in which learning is more rapid than would be expected without an earlier acquisition of relevant information. See **incidental learning**.

lateral plane From side to side, including the positions right, down, left, and up.

learning A more or less permanent modification of behavior which results from activity, special training, or observation.

learning curve Changing skill or ability, plotted as a function of trials, or practice.

learning sets Learning "know-how"; learning how to learn. Exemplified when an organism learns each successive problem (of equal or greater difficulty than earlier ones) in fewer trials.

lens A structure behind the iris of the eye which is involved in changing the focus of light on the retina. Known as the **crystalline lens**.

leptosome Thin, slender, asthenic, ectomorphic.

lesion Damage, injury. A brain lesion is some injury to the brain tissue.

lethargy Inertness, apathy, lack of motivation.

leucotomy See **lobotomy**.

leveling Reduction in the content of a rumor as it passes from mouth to mouth. The mentioning of fewer items.

level of aspiration The level of performance which the individual desires to reach, or which he feels that he can achieve.

libido According to Freud, sexual energy — an erotic force motivating behavior.

lie detector Device for recording changes in respiration, blood pressure, and the electrodermal response while the person is questioned about some crime or asked to give associations for relevant and irrelevant words.

life goal What one wishes to become; his ambition.

life space The individual and his environment at any moment, as he perceives it. See **topology**.

light adaptation Adjustment to light, as when one comes out of a dark theater into the light.

lightness The experienced visual intensity of surfaces, or objects. Contrasted with brightness (or *luminance*), which refers to film or aperture colors.

limen See **threshold**.

limbic system A system of subcortical structures (part of the old brain) which appears to play an important role in certain forms of physiological motivation, including physiological aspects of emotion. According to Joseph B. Brady and Bradford N. Bunnell, writing in 1960, "The components of this group . . . are still not very well agreed upon but generally include the hippocampus, pyriform lobe, cingulate gyrus, septal region, amygdala, thalamus, and hypothalamus." See R. H. Waters, D. A. Rethlingshafer, and W. E. Caldwell (Eds.), *Principles of Comparative Psychology*, McGraw-Hill, 1960, pp. 374–375. The only components of the limbic system discussed in our text are the amygdala, the septal region, the thalamus, and the hypothalamus.

linear perspective Perception of the distance of objects through an apparent convergence of lines and a decrease in size with increasing distance.

linguistic Having to do with language.

lobes Main divisions of the human brain, like the frontal and temporal lobes.

lobotomy The cutting of fiber tracts in the brain. *Prefrontal lobotomy* involves cutting of tracts between the thalamus and the tips of the frontal lobes.

local signs Differential experiences, aroused by stimulation in different regions, which enable the individual to tell where he has been stimulated and give him a clue to space perception.

localization *Auditory*, designating the position from which a sound originates; *cortical*, the presence of areas especially adapted to mediate particular functions, for instance the occipital area for vision or the temporal for hearing; *tactual-kinesthetic*, touching a point on the skin that has been stimulated while the person is blindfolded.

locomotion Moving from one place to another. In Lewin's topological psychology it also refers to imagined or anticipated change, and even to change in attitude or change in status.

longitudinal study A study which follows the same individual from early to later age levels. Contrasted with cross-sectional studies, in which different groups represent each age level.

loudness The intensity aspect of auditory experience, scaled in decibels.

love A feeling of attachment or affection for some person or thing, not necessarily sexual.

luminance Brightness.

luminosity A term used as synonymous with brightness. The *luminosity curve* represents the brightness value of light of different wavelengths.

maladjustment Adjustment that is faulty, poor, inadequate, abnormal, See **adjustment; abnormal.**

mammals Animals that carry their young in the uterus and suckle them after birth.

malingering Feigning sickness or disability.

mand The function of certain words is that of demanding or requesting something. A word, phrase, or sentence serving this function is called by Skinner a *mand*, from *demand*.

mania An exceptionally excited state found in manic-depressive psychosis.

manic-depressive psychosis A grave functional mental illness characterized by periods of mania and depression which alternate in different ways depending upon the person afflicted.

manipulation Moving things around, as with hands or mouth.

manual Pertaining to hands — manual dexterity or skill and manual labor refer to functions performed primarily with the hands. The manual alphabet used by the deaf and dumb is a system of signs made with the hands.

mass action In *behavior*, movement of the organism as a whole; in *cerebral cortex*, contribution of the cortex as a whole to some process, as in maze learning where an overall integrative contribution is important.

mass activity Overall activity, generalized.

mass media Communication media like newspapers, magazines, radio, and television.

mass movement A change, or attempted change, in social life that involves many people. Large numbers of people going in a new social direction, as in the case of the Nazi movement in Germany.

massed learning Learning without interpolated rest periods.

mastery motive The urge to be assertive, to stand out in the crowd, to be dominant.

maternal drive The urge to care for the young.

maternal instinct An unlearned, stereotyped pattern of caring for the young which is found in some animals.

maturation Development depending solely upon biological conditions which characterize the race, as distinguished from learning which, although it is somewhat dependent upon the level of maturation attained, requires exercise, practice, or observation of the performance of others.

maturity Full biological development, as when one reaches adulthood. However, the term is also used in respect to emotion (emotional maturity) and social independence (social maturity). In these instances it means that the person has "grown up" emotionally and socially. Thus even an adult might be emotionally or socially immature. See **emotional maturity** and **social maturity.**

maze Often used in the study of learning. Device with a more or less complex pathway having blind alleys in which the subject can get lost, or at least expend unnecessary time and energy.

mean, arithmetic The average score; the sum of the scores divided by the number of cases.

meaning The significance of something to the subject; such as its use, its origin, its association with other things.

mechanical comprehension test Designed to measure one's familiarity with and understanding of mechanical facts and principles.

median The middlemost score in a series arranged in rank order.

median plane That which cuts vertically between the ears.

medical psychology Methods and procedures of psychology having applications in the field of medicine and aspects of medicine relevant to psychology.

medulla Part of the brain stem immediately above the spinal cord, concerned primarily with vital functions like breathing.

Meissner's corpuscles The so-called touch corpuscles in the skin which are believed to be receptors for light pressure.

memory Retention of what has been learned. It is evidenced by later recall, or reproduction, recognition, or relearning with a savings. Also see biological memory and engram.

memory drum A rotating drum designed to expose, one unit at a time, and for a controlled interval, what is to be memorized.

memory span The maximum number of items (words, syllables, digits) recalled after a single presentation, whether auditory (auditory memory span) or visual (visual memory span).

memory trace A term representing the neural modification inferred to underlie memory. An engram.

menopause The end of menstrual or reproductive life.

mental In its original sense, pertaining to *the mind.* Now used with reference to the adjustments of organisms to their environment, and especially those adjustments which involve symbolic functions and of which the individual is aware.

mental age (M.A.) The degree of intelligence exhibited by an individual in relation to others of his age group. He is said to have an M.A. of 8, for example, if he does on standardized intelligence tests what the average child of 8 can do. His actual age (C.A.) might be greater or less than his M.A.

mental hygiene Concerned with the preservation of mental health. Emphasis is given to child training and to education concerning normal methods of adjustment.

mental philosophy Branch of philosophy dealing with psychological problems.

mental set An implicit readiness to perceive some particular thing, like the geologist's readiness to notice rock formations of which others are oblivious.

mental tests General term sometimes used for all psychological tests, and especially for those measuring intelligence.

mesmerism Early name for hypnosis, as practiced by Mesmer.

mesomorphy Tendency toward muscularity.

microcephalic A person with an especially small head, usually at the idiot level of intelligence.

midbrain The middle embryonic brain structure which gives rise to various mechanisms concerned with eye and ear reflexes.

millimicron One millionth of a millimeter.

mind A general term representing the sum-total of all intelligent behavior, including memory, thought, and perception. Often used as synonymous with conscious experience.

minimal cues abbreviated aspects of a total situation, reduced cues, hints.

Minnesota Multiphasic Personality Inventory (M.M.P.I.) Statements pertaining to aspects of personality are placed in one of three categories; *True, False,* or *Cannot Say.* Answers are then evaluated in terms of psychiatric categories.

Minnesota Paper Formboard A test of mechanical aptitude which requires the subject to tell which bits go together to make up each of a series of patterns.

mirror-drawing Tracing a star or other figure which is seen only in a mirror. Used to study learning, especially transfer of skill from one hand to the other.

mob A large number of people showing great excitement and bent on some antisocial act, such as looting or lynching. Not always distinguished from *crowd* which, however, is not necessarily so highly excited and antisocial.

mode In statistics, the most frequent score of a series.

molar study One which focuses on meaningful units of behavior and experience rather than relatively minute (molecular) details.

See **holistic** and **phenomenology**.

molecular study One that stresses the analysis of larger units of behavior and experience into minute details (habits into constituent reflexes and neural concomitants, perceptions into sensations, or receptor and neural processes). Contrasted with molar studies in this respect — although the line cannot always be sharply drawn. See **molar study**.

monetary incentive The inducement to work for money as a reward.

mongoloid Feebleminded person resembling a mongolian.

monochromatic light Light that is relatively pure, approximating a single wavelength, e.g., a pure red.

monocular cues Those obtainable with one eye, as distinguished from binocular cues.

monomaniac Mentally deranged person with a fixed idea or a "one-track mind."

morale Signified by individual or group perseverance in performance of the work at hand. Also a cheerful, or confident, or satisfied attitude.

mores The group ways, social customs.

moron The highest grade of feeblemindedness, represented by an I.Q. ranging from 50 to 70.

motion sickness Nausea and other effects brought on by movement, as in an airplane (airsickness), a boat (seasickness), etc.

motion study Studying in detail the movements involved in an industrial, military, or athletic activity with a view to eliminating waste motion.

motivation The inner control of behavior as represented by physiological conditions, interests, attitudes, and aspirations.

motive An impulsion or urge to attain some goal-object (like food when hungry) or some goal (such as being an engineer). Similar to *drive* except that, in the case of a drive as such, there is no clearly defined incentive.

motor area The region of the cerebral cortex, just in front of the fissure of Rolando, which controls voluntary motor activity.

motor development Development of such activities as reaching, grasping, crawling and walking.

motor end-plate End of efferent or motor nerve fiber at the point of contact with a muscle fiber.

motor neuron Nerve cell and fiber (efferent) which carries impulses to the motor organs (muscles and glands).

motor set A muscular readiness to respond.

motor speech area Region, in the left frontal lobe, which controls speech. Destruction of this area is followed by motor aphasia. Otherwise known as Broca's area.

Müller-Lyer illusion A line of a given actual length is made to appear longer or shorter by the addition of lines, such as enclosing arrowheads or arrowheads extending outward from its end.

multiple-choice problem The subject is confronted with doors, keys, or other objects which, at each setting, differ in number and position. He selects one in each setting and, if this is correct, it is related to the others in terms of some principle, such as the middlemost, the second from the right end, and so on.

multiple-choice test Any test in which statements or questions are given, each followed by two or more alternatives from which the subject must select the most appropriate. Thus: Psychology is the scientific study of: (1) organisms, (2) behavior, (3) the soul.

multiple personality The same person expresses several personalities. One person with two personalities (*dual personality*) is exemplified by Dr. Jekyll and Mr. Hyde. Some people have been known to express as many as four personalities.

Munsell color system A system of charts in which colors are designated in terms of hue, chroma (saturation), and value (lightness, brightness, or luminance).

muscle tensions Tightening of muscles; or a shift in muscle tonus.

myelin sheath The fatty covering of some nerve fibers. Also called a **medullary sheath**.

nasal retina Inner half, toward the nose.

natural selection theory The idea (Darwin's) that variation naturally occurs in structure and behavior, and that, in the struggle for existence, those having the most adaptive characteristics will survive and reproduce their kind.

naturalistic observation Observation in the field without manipulation of the situation by the experimenter.

needs Requirements for optimal adjustment to the environment, like the need for food, water, and so on.

negative after-image A visual image that has the complementary hue of the stimulus.

negative conditioning Conditioning in which the individual learns not to make an accustomed response.

negative correlation Correlation of less than zero, as when one series of paired measurements decreases while the other increases.

negative reinforcement Punishment or reproof, especially in relation to learning.

negative transfer Habit interference, as when learning one skill makes it harder to learn another.

neonate The newborn infant. Any organism that has just recently been born.

nerve A bundle of nerve fibers.

nerve fiber A threadlike structure, extending from the cell body of a neuron, which transmits the nerve impulse.

nerve impulse A successive release of energy along a nerve fiber.

nerve net A network of nerve fibers in which there are no synapses and the impulse thus goes indiscriminately through all fibers.

nervous breakdown A blanket term referring to the onset of a neurosis or psychosis.

nervous system General term referring to all neural structures and mechanisms.

neural circuits The courses followed by nerve impulses in tranversing various parts of the nervous system.

neural facilitation The continuance of a nerve impulse through the contributions of other impulses which follow in rapid succession (*temporal facilitation*) or converge upon the synapse from different directions (*spatial facilitation*). The term *summation* is also used.

neural groove The primitive precursor, in embryonic development, of the tube which becomes the spinal cord and brain. See **neural tube.**

neural inhibition A blocking of nerve impulses such as may occur at synapses.

neural trace See **engram.** Also referred to as a **neurogram.**

neural tube A tube, with three vesicles at its forward end (upper in man) which develops into the spinal cord and brain structures.

neurasthenia A functional behavior disorder characterized by abnormal fatigue and bodily complaints. Means literally, a *nerve weakness.* One of the neuroses.

neuromuscular Any function involving interaction between neurons and muscles is said to be neuromuscular.

neuron A nerve cell and its fibers.

neurosis A functional behavior disorder which, while troublesome, is seldom sufficiently severe to require institutionalization. Also referred to as a psychoneurosis.

neurotic Pertaining to neurosis. Sometimes used to designate a person who has a neurosis. Also, as in **neurotic behavior,** behavior involving the symptoms found in a neurosis.

neutral gray That at the center of the black-white continuum — of average or median brightness (or luminance).

new brain The cerebral cortex and related structures which appeared relatively late in evolution.

night blindness Unusually poor visual sensitivity under low illumination, a result of slowness or absence of dark adaptation.

noise Auditory result of aperiodic vibrations. This term is also used in information theory and related areas to represent anything which interferes with transmission of a message (distortion in the communication channel) as well as any diverting or confusing element in what is received. An ambiguous message involves noise in this sense. In a categorization experiment where, say, the elements of importance to the development of a concept are size and brightness, the irrelevant inclusion of hue would lead to the designation of hue as a "noisy attribute."

nonauditory labyrinth The semicircular canals and vestibule.

nondirective therapy Otherwise known as "client-centered." It is characterized by relatively little direction or suggestion from the therapist. Insight as to the nature of the problem and its solution is not given directly by the therapist but must come from the client himself.

nonsense syllables Combinations of three or more letters which do not make sense, which have little or no meaning for the subject. See **trigram**.

nonspecific projection system This is made up of collaterals from the ascending nerve paths. Whereas the specific projection fibers from these paths go on to the thalamus and then synapse with fibers going to the so-called projection areas of the cerebral cortex, the fibers of the nonspecific system enter the reticular formation, activating it and alerting the organism. See **ascending paths, reticular formation,** and **thalamus**.

nonstructured Subject to various interpretations, like inkblots. *Structured situations* tend to produce sterotyped outcomes.

nonverbal communication Communication without words — by gestures, pictures, the wearing of certain uniforms, and so on.

noradrenalin A secretion of the adrenal medulla (along with adrenalin) and apparently also of nerve-endings in the sympathetic nervous system. According to Hall (*The Functions of the Endocrine Glands,* Saunders, 1959), this recently discovered hormone is particularly involved in the maintenance of normal bloodpressure levels.

norm Having reference to normal in terms of average.

normal Approximating the average.

normal personality As conceived statistically, the average or the most usual. Generally speaking it is characterized by pursuit of worth-while goals and the enjoyment of life.

normal probability curve The so-called chance curve, which is symmetrical (more or less bell-shaped) with most of the measurements bunching up near the middle and the rest tapering off toward the two extremes.

normative study One which establishes norms, such as the average or median age at which children stand alone, walk, say their first word, and so on.

nucleus Essential part of a nerve cell, containing the chromosomes. **Neural,** a clearly marked cluster of cells within the central nervous system.

nurturance Parental attention or control.

nymphomania Unusually strong sexual desires in a woman.

nystagmus Oscillating movements of the eyes.

objective approach One that is social, in that all can confirm the observation for themselves; contrasted with subjective.

objective tests Those scored with a prescribed key; may be machine scored.

observational learning Learning by looking over a situation and figuring it out. See **insight**.

observer Term used by experimental introspectionists to represent the person who observes and reports on his own experiences — i.e., the person who introspects under these circumstances. Now largely replaced by the term *subject,* which has no introspectionist connotations.

obstruction method Testing the persistence of motivated behavior under conditions where, in order to reach the incentive, the organism must submit to an electric shock or some other impediment.

occipital lobe That at the back of each cerebral hemisphere, concerned primarily with vision and related perceptual and associative functions.

occupational therapy Attempting to alleviate mental illness or other disorders by having the individual engage in interesting work — use of work for its remedial effects.

Oedipus complex A Freudian term to represent the sexual attachment of a son for his mother. This is regarded as usually repressed and disguised in various ways. Going with this complex, according to Freud, is jealousy of the father because he can have intimacies with the mother that the son is denied. Also see **Electra complex** and **complex**.

old brain The part which preceded the cerebral cortex in evolution.

olfaction The sense of smell.

olfactory bulbs The two small bulblike structures below the frontal lobes and immediately above the olfactory epithelium. They give rise to the nerve fibers which mediate olfactory sensitivity.

olfactory epithelium Cells in the upper ends of the nostrils which contain the receptors for smell.

onomatopoeic words Those which sound like the object represented, such as bow-wow for dog. According to those who hold an onomatopoeic theory of linguistic origins, our primitive ancestors imitated the sounds of natural phenomena and used these imitations as symbols representing the phenomena in question.

ontogenetic study That dealing with development in the individual organism. Compare **phylogenetic**.

operant Any response that is instrumental in producing certain consequences — like a food reward or an electric shock. It "operates," so to speak, on the environment.

operant conditioning A type of instrumental conditioning which involves the modification of an operant. A response which the organism emits is reinforced in certain ways, in accordance with certain schedules, and resulting changes in its rate of occurrence are studied. The rat's pressing a lever and the pigeon's pecking a disc are operants widely used in studies of operant conditioning. The reinforcement is usually food, although a secondary reinforcer (say a click previously associated with food) may be used.

optic chiasma The partial crossing of optic nerve fibers.

optic nerve The tract carrying all nerve impulses from the eye to the brain stem.

optic radiation The system of fibers projecting visual impulses into the occipital lobe.

oral Referring to the mouth.

oral eroticism Pleasure derived from stimulation of the mouth, as in sucking.

ordinal scale One which deals with the relative position of individuals (rank order) with respect to some characteristic, such as first, second, third, fourth. Contrasted with scales involving physical units (ratio scales). See **ratio scale**.

ordinate The vertical (or y) axis of a graph.

organ of Corti Structure on the basilar membrane of the inner ear where the energy of sound waves stimulates receptors and initiates nerve impulses.

organic Having to do with the organism, with structure as opposed to function.

organic sensitivity Sensitivity of organs within the body cavity, like the viscera.

organism The entire living creature.

osmoreceptor A type of receptor that is sensitive to the osmotic pressure of the blood. Invoked by some to account for thirst motivation.

ossicles The three small bones in the middle ear which amplify and convey sound vibrations to the inner ear.

otoliths Small grains in the labyrinth of the ear which play a role in perception of movement and maintenance of equilibrium.

outgroup The group to which one does not belong. Compare with **ingroup**.

oval window Membranous opening of the cochlea against which the ossicle known as the "stirrup" vibrates.

overcompensation More than balancing a deficiency.

overlapping distributions Those falling partly within the same range.

overlearning Learning more than is necessary for one correct performance.

overt behavior Observable by others. Social rather than private. Compare with **implicit (covert)**.

ovum The female reproductive cell; also, the fertilized organism until the time at which it attaches itself to the uterus — in man this occurs during the second week following conception.

Pacinian corpuscles Specialized end organs in the skin which are responsive to heavy pressure.

pain spots Points on the skin which, when stimulated with a sharp object, elicit reports of pain.

paired associates Words, syllables, digits, or other items learned in pairs so that, when one is given, its associate is recalled.

pancreas A large gland, situated near the stomach, which secretes gastric juices and also contains the Islands of Langerhans, which secrete insulin. See **insulin.** Only the latter is an endocrine secretion (hormone).

paralysis Loss of ability to move some part of the body.

parameter A constant, a limiting condition, to the generality of results. If a learning curve were obtained for human five-year-olds with an I.Q. of 100; then being human, age five, and 100 I.Q. would be parameters. A change in any one of these could yield a different curve.

paranoid Pertaining to a type of mental illness in which the person has delusions especially of reference, such as imagining that people are doing things to him or saying things about him.

parasympathetic nervous system The part of the autonomic system which functions in opposite relation to the sympathetic system.

paresis General paralysis of the insane, an organic psychosis usually originating in syphilitic infection.

parietal lobe That situated between the fissure of Rolando and the occipital lobe. It plays a special role in somaesthetic sensitivity.

part learning Mastering one part of a complex skill at a time, then combining the partial skills; like learning one verse of a poem thoroughly before tackling the next.

partist strategy A procedure (in experiments on concept formation) which bases inferences on parts of the situation rather than the situation as a whole (upon all possible available cues). Compare **holist strategy.**

passive learning Learning without the intention to learn, incidental learning. Also see **latent learning.**

pecking order See **dominance hierarchy.**

pencil-and-paper tests Those requiring written answers and usually scored with a key.

perceiving Discriminating, differentiating, observing, grasping the meaning of things.

percentile The rank position of an individual in a serial array of data stated in terms of what percentage of the group he equals or exceeds.

perception The process of perceiving.

perceptual constancy The tendency of aspects of our world to be perceived as constant (in brightness, color, size, etc.) despite a certain degree of change in their stimulus characteristics.

perceptual-motor habit Any skill involving overt reactions based upon perceptual cues. See **sensorimotor.**

performance tests Those requiring little or no verbal instruction or verbal response by the subject.

perimeter Instrument for mapping the color zones of the retina. The subject fixates with one eye and, as it were, discerns the stimulus "out of the corner" of his eye.

periodic vibration The oscillations come in definite cycles and give rise to tonal experiences, as distinguished from aperiodic vibrations, which give rise to noise.

peripheral adjustments Those of the sense organs and muscles.

peripheral-central theory Concept of thinking which supposes that it involves an interplay between peripheral (sensory and motor) and central (i.e., brain) processes.

peripheral nervous system The spinal and cranial nerves, including the autonomic system. The nervous system which connects the brain and spinal cord with the receptors and effectors.

peripheral retina That outside of the foveal region.

peripheral vision In the periphery, out of the "corner of the eye."

peripheralist One who emphasizes the receptor-effector contribution to behavior. Contrasted with **centralist.**

permissive attitude One which avoids direct or implied criticism of what another says or does. The attitude ideally assumed by a psychological counselor in listening to his client's recounting of experiences, even those which might bring censure from parents, teachers, or others in an authoritarian position. This does not mean, however, that the counselor approves of the conduct in question.

perseveration The continuance of a process after the stimulus has been removed, like a tune running through one's head.

persona The mask worn by an actor in ancient times to indicate his role — possible origin of the term "personality."

personal equation A term used in the early days of reaction-time studies to represent a difference in the rapidity of response of equally competent observers, as when astronomers differed in their reporting of the exact moment a star crossed a line as viewed in the telescope. See **reaction time.**

personal motives Those which originate in unique individual experience as contrasted with those that are inborn (the physiological) and those common to members of a particular culture (the coenotropes).

personal-social motives Those that are individual (rather than universal or widely prevalent) yet, in their origin and expression, dependent upon cultural and other social influences.

personality The most characteristic integration of an individual's structures, modes of behavior, interests, attitudes, capacities, abilities, and aptitudes — the whole person as others see him.

personality profile A graph which shows the scores (or percentiles) made by an individual on a series of personality tests or inventories.

perversion An act that is unnatural, not acceptable to the group.

phase *In audition,* two or more sound waves are said to be "in phase" if they go through the same cyclical fluctuation in unison, as when their crests or troughs coincide.

phenomena Any observable objects or events. A **phenomenon,** as used in psychology, means no more than something observable.

phenomenology Systematic study of immediate experience, or of the world as it appears to the observer. Contrasted with an analytic approach like that of Wundt and his followers.

phenylpyruvic feeblemindedness An enzyme necessary for the oxidizing of a substance in protein known as **phenylalanine** is missing. Consequently, phenylpyruvic acid accumulates in the tissues and interferes with normal functioning of the brain.

philosophy A general discipline concerned with the ultimate nature of the world and of man.

phi-phenomenon Apparent movement, as in motion pictures and certain electric signs.

phobias Apparently unreasonable fears, as when one fears a mouse, fears that he may be buried alive, or fears to stand on a high place.

phonemes The distinguishable vocalizations out of which speech develops — the separate vowel sounds are phonemes, as are the separate sounds in consonants. The sounds which make up the International Phonetic Alphabet.

photochemical reaction One involving chemical reactions initiated by light, as in a photographic film or in the retina.

photopic vision Vision under daylight conditions, where hues are distinguished. Vision involving the cones. Compare with **scotopic vision.**

photosensitivity Responsiveness to light.

phototropism See **tropism.**

phrenology The attempt to discern character and other aspects of personality from "bumps" on the cranium.

phylogenetic psychology That which studies development of psychological processes in organisms ranging from the lowest to the highest. It is thus concerned with psychological evolution. Compare with **ontogenetic psychology.**

physiognomy The attempt to discern personality traits, including character and aptitudes, from such facial conformations as the shape of the nose and the set of the jaw.

physiological cues Those, in space perception, which come from biological makeup, like the distance between the eyes and accommodation of the lens.

physiological drives Impulsions which stem from the biological needs of the organism, like the need for food and for sleep.

physiological limit With reference to learning, the maximum proficiency attainable in view of the individual's makeup (the maximum speed at which he can work) and the nature of the situation (the maximum number of correct responses possible).

physiological needs Those determined by our biological makeup.

pineal gland A small structure in the brain stem, opposite the pituitary gland, which Descartes thought to be the point of interaction of the soul and the body. The gland is one of the endocrines but its precise functions are still not clear.

pitch   The qualitative aspect of sounds, in terms of which they may be described as high or low.

pituitary gland   A structure at the lower end of the hypothalamus which has extremely important endocrine functions. Secretions from the posterior lobe of this gland have certain metabolic functions which are as yet far from clear. Its anterior lobe secretes hormones which play a role in sexual and general body development (giving rise to dwarfism if insufficient and to giantism if excessive). The anterior lobe also secretes hormones which play a key role in metabolic processes. Among these is ACTH. Prolactin, important in motivating maternal behavior in animals, is likewise secreted by the anterior pituitary. The pituitary is generally regarded as the pacemaker of the whole endocrine system.

place learning   Learning a place — i.e., where food is located, where to escape. Compare **response learning.**

place theory of pitch   The theory that the pitch of a sound is determined by the place in the basilar membrane maximally activated by a sound wave of a particular frequency. See **Helmholtz theory.**

placebo   Literally, something to please. A pill of no medicinal value given to a patient to please him, to make him think that he is taking medicine. Used in drug experiments to prevent subjects from knowing whether or not they have been given the drug. They all think that they are taking it, because the pills or capsules look alike, but the control subjects are getting the placebo.

plateau   A period of little or no progress followed by further learning.

play therapy   Play designed to help the patient (usually a child) release tensions or learn adequate adjustments to the situations which disturb him.

pleasantness   A feeling associated with reduced tension; objectively manifested by a tendency to seek further contact with the instigating objects or situations.

pleasure principle   The tendency of organisms to seek satisfaction of their urges.

plethysmograph   Instrument with which changes in blood supply to a part of the body, like a limb, are recorded.

pneumograph   Instrument placed around the chest, and sometimes the waist, to record respiratory changes.

polarized light   Light passed through some medium which makes it vibrate in only one direction, say vertically, or horizontally.

polydactyly   Having more than five fingers.

polygraph   Apparatus for recording several responses concurrently, as in a lie detector, where changes in respiration, blood pressure, and the GSR are recorded on a moving tape.

pons   A structure just above the medulla which connects the two lobes of the cerebellum with each other and with the cerebral hemispheres.

positive correlation   Changes in one variable are concomitant with and in the same direction as those in another, as, for example, in the relation between the level of intelligence and school grades.

post-hypnotic suggestion   After being awakened, the subject follows suggestions given during hypnosis.

postnatal   After birth.

postural changes   With reference to emotion; gross changes in bodily attitudes, like crouching, running, and striking.

post-rotational nystagmus   Oscillatory eye movements following rotation.

postural set   An overall motor readiness to respond, as in the case of a runner on the mark.

practice   As distinguished from training, a more or less blind, trial-and-error attack on a learning problem.

precocity   Development far in advance of that usually found at a given age.

preconscious   Anything which may readily become conscious is said to be in the preconscious. Thus I may become aware of some obligation at this moment of which I was oblivious a few moments ago. Pictured diagrammatically by the Freudians as a region between the conscious and the unconscious.

predisposition Being already set (in terms of heredity or learning) to react in a certain way. See **set**.

prefrontal lobotomy Cutting of fibers which go from the thalamus to the tips of the frontal lobes.

prehensile Capable of grasping with the hand. See **prehension**.

prehension Voluntary grasping of an object.

prejudice Prejudgment; an attitude or opinion prior to or independent of an examination of the facts in the case.

prenatal Prior to birth.

preparation stage In creative thinking, gathering, and attempting to integrate, relevant information.

preperceptive set Attending, as in looking or listening.

pressure spots Points on the skin which respond to pressure stimulation.

prestige High reputation, great influence, glamour.

primary colors Those which are irreducible and from the mixture of which all other hues can be produced. These hues, according to the Young-Helmholtz theory, are red, green, and blue, with yellow not a primary because it can be produced by retinal mixtures of red and green. Some theories, however, recognize yellow as primary. Also see **subtractive primaries**.

primary mental abilities The abilities disclosed by factor analysis to be the basic components of intelligence. There are differences of opinion as to the number and nature of primary abilities.

primary needs Those that are basic, like the need for food, water, warmth, and so on. Needs that are inborn, dependent upon the inherited makeup of the organism. Compare with **secondary needs**. Also see **drive**.

primary odors Irreducible odors, from which the others can be produced by mixture. The nature of these is still speculative.

primary reinforcement Satisfaction of physiological needs (or drives), like the need for food or for sleep. See **primary needs**.

primary skin senses The senses (pressure, pain, warm, and cold) which fuse to arouse cutaneous experiences of greater complexity.

primary tastes The irreducible taste experiences — salt, sour, sweet, and bitter.

primitive organization A patterning of perception prior to, or independent of, learning.

principles, in transfer. Formulations of the nature of a problem which then aid in the solution of other problems involving the same or similar principles.

prism Wedge-shaped piece of glass which splits white light to form the spectrum.

private information Subjective; that which only the experiencing individual can observe. See **introspection**.

private attitude One not overtly expressed, but sometimes indirectly revealed by use of projective procedures. See **projective methods**.

proactive inhibition A type of negative transfer observed in memory experiments and other learning situations. It occurs when an item preceding that to be learned interferes with learning of the latter, or its subsequent recall. Compare with **retroactive inhibition**. Also see **negative transfer**.

probability curve See **normal probability curve**.

probability learning The subject learns to respond in terms of the probability of reinforcement. Thus, of alternatives a and b, a may be reinforced 70 per cent of the time and b 30 per cent, in which case the subject comes to select a in approximately 70 per cent of the trials.

problem box One with latches, strings, or other devices which the subject must manipulate in an appropriate way in order to get in or out.

problem-solving Adjusting to a situation by acquiring new modes of response. The term is used especially to represent learning in which a certain amount of insight or reasoning may be displayed, as in learning a problem box or finding the solution to a verbal problem.

product-moment correlation Procedure which yields the coefficient of correlation, or r.

profile A graph which represents the variation, within an individual, from one type of performance to another, for example, his relative rank in each of several skills or on each of several personality tests.

projecting The act of perceiving one's own characteristics in another or, in fantasy, interpreting situations as though one is part of them and that they reflect one's own situation, problems of adjustment, and so on. Also see **projection**.

projection Attributing one's own motives or thoughts to others as when a cheat supposes that others cheat or that the evil which he knows exists · in himself is discerned by others.

projection areas of cerebral cortex Those to which sensory impulses are "projected" from the thalamus and from which motor impulses are sent downwards.

projection paths Those carrying nerve impulses up the spinal cord to the thalamus and subsequently to the projection areas of the cerebral cortex (see above).

projective methods Those which require the subject to interpret situations susceptible to many different interpretations, or to different perceptual organizations. A person's interpretation (of inkblots, pictures, etc.) is then taken as a projection of his personality structure.

prolactin A hormone from the anterior pituitary gland which stimulates milk secretion and contributes in other ways to maternal behavior.

prone progression In a horizontal position, as in creeping and crawling.

proprioception The type of sensitivity mediated by receptors (proprioceptors) in those organs which, through their own activity, stimulate themselves. The two proprioceptive senses are the static and kinesthetic. Proprioception is one important basis for feedback within the organism. See **kinesthesis, static sense,** and **feedback**.

protective reflex Withdrawal in response to painful stimulation.

pseudo-affective Merely simulating reactions indicative of feeling or emotion. Sham emotion.

pseudophone Instrument with which sound

stimulation of the ears is reversed, sounds normally going to the left ear now going to the right, and vice versa.

pseudopsychology False or fictitious psychology; psychological quackery.

psyche Ancient Greek word for the soul or what, today, we call the mind.

psychiatrist A medical doctor who specializes in mental (or behavior) disorders.

psychiatry Branch of medicine concerned with mental (behavior) disorders.

psychoanalysis A psychotherapy which typically involves reverie and the analysis of dreams. The patient's difficulties are interpreted for him by the analyst and he is advised what to do to alleviate them. The data made available through psychoanalytic procedure are usually interpreted in accordance with psychoanalytic theory. The original theory, that of Freud, placed great emphasis upon repressed (subconscious) sexuality. There are now several schools of psychoanalysis, some of which differ from Freud's in placing considerably less emphasis upon sexual motivation. Some of these emphasize the social as well as the biological bases of human motivation.

psychoanalyst One who is qualified to use psychoanalytical procedures in dealing with behavior disorders.

psychodrama Having mental patients act out (dramatize) situations relevant to their difficulties.

psychogalvanic response A change in electrical resistance in the skin which results, among other things, from sweat-gland activity elicited by emotion-provoking stimuli. Otherwise referred to as the galvanic skin reflex (GSR) or the electrodermal response. One of the responses involved in lie detection.

psychogalvanometer A device for recording the psychogalvanic response.

psychograph Another name for a psychological profile. It is a graph which represents the degree to which various traits differ within the individual.

psychological clinic A place to which people come for help with psychological problems.

psychological cues In space perception, those

which depend for their interpretation upon previous experience in comparable situations.

psychological environment That to which the person responds in terms of its meaning for him.

psychology The science of behavior, or of the adjustments of organisms to their environment. The study of mental life in its most inclusive sense.

psychomotor tests Those which, while based upon other psychological processes (sensory, perceptual), call for a motor reaction, such as pressing a key, holding a stylus as steady as possible, or manipulating controls.

psychoneurosis One of the milder behavior disorders otherwise known as a *neurosis*. See **neurosis**.

psychopathic personality A character disorder. The individual with this type of disorder, referred to as a *psychopath*, is defective in that he fails to observe the rules which govern conduct in his society. He has failed to develop a normal superego. He may steal, lie, murder, and commit other offenses without the qualms of conscience which other people would have under such circumstances. See **superego** and **conscience**.

psychophysical methods Those used in psychophysics as defined below.

psychophysics Quantitative measurement of the relation between experienced aspects of stimulation (brightness, loudness, etc.) and the characteristics of the stimulus, usually its intensity.

psychosis The most serious type of mental disorder. It is known legally as *insanity* and usually requires treatment in a mental hospital. The person is said to be *psychotic*.

psychosomatic medicine That branch concerned with physical disorders (like some allergies, high blood pressure, and ulcers) which originate in, or are aggravated by, emotional difficulties.

psychosurgery Brain surgery carried out to alleviate mental illness, as in the case of prefrontal lobotomy.

psychotherapy Any procedure designed to alleviate behavior disorders (mental illness, adjustment problems) by psychological means — suggestion, psychoanalysis, counseling interviews, play therapy, and so on.

psychotic Deriving from a psychosis; the person who has a psychosis; an "idea system," like the illogical (or insane) conclusion that people are putting ground glass in the food, or that the patient is God.

puberty The time at which menstruation begins in girls and seminal emission in boys. The onset of adolescence.

puberty praecox Puberty at an unusually early age.

pugnacity Wanting to fight, quarrelsomeness, aggressiveness intended to injure others.

punishment Any form of stimulation imposed upon the individual which he finds distasteful, or which he normally tries to avoid.

pupil The opening in the iris through which light enters the eye.

pupillary response Contraction or dilation of the pupil, as when light strikes the eye or is withdrawn.

Purkinje phenomenon A shift in relative brightness value as illumination changes, such as the greater relative brightness of yellow in daylight and of blue in twilight illumination.

pursuitmeter A device having a moving point with which the subject attempts to keep contact with a stylus.

pyknic physique Rotund, endomorphic body build.

pyramidal cells Those of the frontal cortex, so named because of their pyramidal shape, which give rise to voluntary motor impulses. These impulses travel downward in the *pyramidal tracts*.

qualitative Having to do with the estimation of qualities — like good, reliable, dishonest. Contrasted with measurement that is quantitative. See **quantitative**.

quality A term sometimes used to represent the most distinguishable aspects of experience — sour, blue, middle C, and so on. These are called "qualitative" aspects of experience or merely "qualities." This contrasts them with the intensive or "quantitative" aspects, such as the sourness of what is sour, the brightness of blue, the loudness of middle C.

quantify To deal with something in terms of measurable quantities, such as amount, extent, duration.

quantitative Having to do with measurable quantities. Psychophysics is quantitative in that it deals with measurable stimuli and measurable responses. Compare **qualitative**.

quantitative ability Ability to deal with numbers as in solving mathematical problems. Distinguished, in some tests, from so-called *verbal ability*, where there is facility with words and related concepts.

r The coefficient of correlation.

racial history The history of one's race. As we have used the term, our human inheritance and its evolution.

radiant energy That transmitted by radiation, such as in light and heat.

rage An intense degree of anger, often giving rise to aggressive behavior.

range The difference between the highest and lowest scores in a series.

range of hearing The number of double vibrations between the lowest (about 20 in man) and the highest (about 20,000) that can be heard.

rank difference correlation (Rho) Correlation between two series of paired measurements, each ranked according to magnitude.

rate of manipulation test One in which the individual turns over small circular blocks as quickly as possible and in a particular sequence.

rate of response Its frequency (how often it occurs) per unit of time. Studies of operant conditioning are especially concerned with changes in response rate.

rating Representing the degree to which some trait is present as judged from observation, like judging whether a child's play is very constructive, moderately constructive, or lacking in constructiveness.

ratio scale One that uses physical units, so that we can say, for example, that one person is two times as quick as another, only

one-half as strong, or one-tenth heavier. Compare **interval scale** and **ordinal scale**.

rational elaboration of ideas Evaluating inferences mentally before accepting or rejecting them.

rationalizing Finding what are apparently good reasons for actions. Making what is irrational appear to be rational. Excusing one's actions on irrational grounds. See also **sour grapes reaction**.

reaction Any movement resulting from stimulation.

reaction mechanisms The structures of the body (sensory, neural, and motor) which underlie response to the environment.

reaction potential Hull's $_sE_R$, the posited tendency of S to evoke R, considered as a function of habit strength $(_sH_R)$ multiplied by drive strength (D).

reaction time Speed of reaction.

reality principle The demands of the id (pleasure principle) are adapted to actualities in the physical and social environment.

reality-testing A term used by Freud to refer to the exploratory or probing behavior which informs the individual of the consequences of commerce with the environment. Basic to development of the ego.

reasoning Solving some problem implicitly, using symbols to represent objects or situations. Thinking one's way through a problem rather than making an overt attack upon it.

recall Revival of past experience.

recapitulation theory The theory that each individual, during his early development, recapitulates (repeats) certain stages through which his race passed in its evolution from lower forms of animal life. The human embryo, for example, has gill slits at one stage and a tail at another. It has also been claimed, without adequate foundation, that the monkey-like antics of young children are attributable to the fact that human beings passed through an ape-like period in their evolution.

receptor Specialized end organ which receives stimulation. The receptors of the eye, for example, are the rods and cones.

receptor-effector system The system which

connects receptors and effectors, which of course includes the central nervous system.

receptor set The readiness of a sense organ, like the eye or ear, to receive stimulation, as in turning the head or eyes in a particular direction to see or hear something.

recessive gene One which plays a noticeable part in the development of an organism only when paired with one like itself (i.e., not dominant).

reciprocal innervation The neural interaction which leads one member of a pair of antagonistic muscles to relax as its antagonist contracts. Thus the triceps muscle relaxes as the biceps contracts, and vice versa.

recitation As a learning procedure: trying to recall what one is memorizing, as opposed to merely reading it repeatedly.

recognition Perceiving something as having been experienced before, as being familiar.

rectilinear In a straight line.

redintegration Recalling a whole experience, or making an appropriate reaction, in terms of some fraction of the original circumstances.

reduced cues Weaker, or less evident, or only a fraction of former stimulating circumstances. Minimal cues.

redundancy In ordinary usage, this means more words than are necessary to convey a message (mere verbiage). Information theorists, however, use it in a somewhat different sense. For them, *u* after *q* is redundant in English because it is almost certain that, given *q*, the next letter will be *u*. Likewise, *yours* after *sincerely* is redundant because, with *sincerely* given, *yours* adds nothing to the message.

re-education The recovery of lost functions through special training; replacement of inadequate modes of adjustment with newly acquired habits.

reflectance The property, possessed in different degrees by various surfaces, of throwing light waves back (reflecting instead of absorbing them). See **absorption curve**.

reflex An initially unlearned response of a particular part of the body, like the knee-jerk to a blow on the patellar tendon, or contraction of the pupil in response to light.

reflex arc The essential neural mechanism in-involved in a reflex, i.e., the sensory, motor, and association neurons which provide a link between the stimulus and the response.

reflex circle A type of feedback which occurs when contraction of a muscle, through stimulation of kinesthetic receptors in that muscle, provides stimulation for a further contraction. Believed to play a part in babbling and the grasping reflex.

refraction, of light. Bending of rays, as in formation of the spectrum.

refractory period That (immediately following stimulation) during which a neuron is incapable of further excitation. This is the *absolute* refractory period. The *relative* refractory period is that, after the absolute, during which only a stronger-than-normal stimulus can excite the neuron.

regression Going back to an earlier, and usually less adequate, mode of response.

reinforcement Reduction (or satisfaction) of a drive; reward; used by Pavlov to refer to the following of the conditioned by the unconditioned stimulus, as in the case of food coming after the bell. See **negative reinforcement, primary reinforcement, secondary reinforcement, verbal reinforcement,** and **schedules of reinforcement.**

Reissner's membrane The wall between the vestibular and the cochlear canal of the inner ear.

relative movement, in distance perception. Objects that move rapidly in the opposite direction are judged to be nearer than those which move more slowly, or which seem to move with the observer.

relearning Attempting to regain a skill that has been partially or wholly lost. The savings involved in relearning, as compared with original learning, give an index of the degree of retention.

reliability of tests Their dependability as measuring instruments. This is indicated, among other things, by a high correlation between scores on a test and on a retest of the same individuals.

reliability coefficient An index of the consistency with which a test measures. Often based upon the correlation between scores obtained on the initial test and a retest (test-retest reliability). Also obtained to discover the consistency of ratings, as between two or more observers. See **reliability of tests.**

reminiscence Improved recall of incompletely learned material after an interval, as when the subject recalls 80 per cent of a list of words at the end of practice and 85 per cent after a short interval.

repression Putting unpleasant things "out of mind" or "into the unconscious."

reproducing Performing something that one has learned, like a trick, a poem, or a picture that is redrawn.

reproof As a factor in learning. Scolding or criticism.

research Critical investigation as in the pursuit of knowledge. The basic method used in the increase of scientific knowledge or scientific understanding.

resonance Vibratory response of some structure (such as a wire) to vibrations of other bodies.

respiratory changes Those involved in breathing.

response An action such as doing or saying something, commonly involving the action of a muscle or a gland.

response learning Learning to make certain movements as such, contrasted with learning to find a certain place, or to follow a certain principle.

response-response (R-R) laws Those dealing with the correlation of one type of activity with another — for example, responses on a test (test score) and performance on the job (perhaps as rated by a supervisor).

retardation Unusually slow or stunted psychological development.

retention Holding onto what has been learned so that it can be utilized later, as in recall; or, if retention is partial, in relearning.

reticular formation A network of intricately interconnected nerve-cell groupings which runs through the center of the brain stem from the level of the medulla to the lower part of the thalamus. It receives impulses through collaterals of the projection pathways (nonspecific projection system) and also from the upper brain structures, including the cerebral cortex. Its main function appears to be that of alerting the cerebral cortex in readiness for incoming information. Its lower part has an inhibitory influence on certain motor activities. See **nonspecific projection system.**

retina The innermost coat of the eye, which contains the rods and cones and is thus photosensitive.

retinal color mixture That in which the retina is stimulated in rapid succession with sectors differing in color.

retinal color zones The regions of the retina which respond to particular colors, like the center to all colors and the more remote region only to yellow and blue.

retinal disparity Slight difference between retinal images of an object viewed with, respectively, the right and the left eye.

retinal image The picture projected onto the retina by light rays; analogous to the picture projected on a photographic film.

retrograde amnesia Forgetting of things actually known before the amnesia-producing event, like forgetting the identity of the opposing player in a football game who was responsible for the blow that produced the unconsciousness. See **amnesia** and compare **anterograde amnesia.**

retroactive inhibition The partial or complete obliteration of what has been learned, which results from some more recent event — like an emotional shock or new learning.

reverberating circuits Feedback mechanisms within the nervous system, as when a nerve impulse, once started, traverses the same circuit repeatedly.

reverie A dreamlike state in which one lets his thoughts wander; a form of free association. Differentiated from daydreaming in that the associations have no recognized goal.

revolving drum A device which records an animal's running activity in terms of revolutions of the drum.

reward training Reinforcing a response (operant) so that it occurs more frequently. See **operant conditioning.**

rewards Incentives, positive reinforcements. See also **drive reduction.**

reversible configuration A picture perceived

as now one thing, now another; as in the case of the picture seen both as a vase and as two facing profiles.

rhinencephalon The "smell brain." Although this region of the upper brain stem and primitive cerebrum was once thought to be a specialized area for smell, it is now known to be also involved in motivation and emotion. Its various structures comprise what is often referred to today as the *limbic system*.

rho (*ρ*) The coefficient of rank difference correlation.

rivalry Competition between individuals, or groups, or processes.

rods Rod-like retinal structures containing visual purple and serving to mediate achromatic vision.

role The part played or the function performed by a person in a particular group situation, like the role of teacher, president, secretary.

role-playing The acting out of certain roles in simulated situations, as when a person being trained for a foreman's role in industry acts the part of foreman with others playing the part of workers.

Rorschach test A series of inkblots used as a projective personality test.

round window This is a round, membrane-covered separation of the middle ear from the tympanic canal of the cochlea; located just below the oval window.

Ruffinian cylinders Structures in the skin which were once thought to mediate sensitivity to warmth but whose actual function is unknown.

rumor Any unverified report or account of an event that circulates freely by word of mouth.

saccule A small sac-like structure making up part of the vestibule of the nonauditory labyrinth.

sadist One who gets pleasure out of hurting others.

salivary response Secretion of saliva by the parotid and other glands of the mouth.

saturation, color The degree to which color of a given hue is present, i.e., different from gray of the same brightness level. A highly saturated red, for example, is very red and a poorly saturated red only barely distinguishable from gray.

satyriasis Exceptionally strong sex drive in men.

savings method Estimating the degree of retention in terms of the reduction in time or trials to relearn as compared with the time or trials required in original learning.

scapegoating The process of finding a person or group (scapegoat) on which to blame some real or imaginary wrong. Finding a substitute object for one's aggressive tendencies, as when the man who is angry with his wife "takes it out" on his children, or employees. Also see **displacement**.

scattergram A graph which illustrates the extent to which two series of paired measurements are correlated.

science The systematic, impersonal, search for verifiable knowledge.

scientific method That which has the characteristics cited for science.

schedule of reinforcement The scheme in accordance with which an operant will be reinforced. Thus, in a lever-pressing situation, every displacement of the lever may bring a pellet of food (*continuous schedule*); the pellet may come every five seconds, regardless of how many displacements occur earlier (*fixed-interval schedule*); the pellet may come at every tenth displacement (*fixed-ratio schedule*); or the pellet may come in accordance with a varying interval or varying ratio (*variable-interval* or *variable-ratio schedule*). See **reinforcement**.

schizophrenia Literally, a splitting of the mind, or of personality. A form of mental illness characterized by extreme withdrawal from reality. Since it involves marked mental deterioration (dementia) and often appears relatively early in life (adolescence or early adulthood), it has also been given the name *dementia praecox*.

sclerotic coat The outermost covering of the eyeball.

scotopic vision Night vision, rod vision. Compare with **photopic vision**.

secondary needs Those not related to physiological makeup; for example, the need for an auto, a fashionable dress, etc.

secondary reinforcement Reinforcement through something which, while it does not satisfy a need directly, has been associated with such satisfaction. Thus a sound associated with food (primary reinforcement) may come to have reward value in itself — to serve as a secondary reinforcer.

secondary sex characters Aspects of the body which differentiate the sexes but which have no direct sexual functions, such as body build, voice, distribution of hair.

second-order conditioning The use of a conditioned stimulus as the basis for further conditioning, i.e., as secondary reinforcement.

seizures Spasms or convulsions of all or part of the body.

self The individual (the I) as represented in his own awareness, and in the setting of those things with which he identifies. The ego and its involvements.

self-assertion The motive to dominate, to master, or to stand out in comparison with others.

self-consciousness Awareness of self, especially in social relations, where such awareness may have embarrassing effects.

self-excitation Stimulation of an organ by its own activity, as in the case of muscular contractions producing stimuli which cause the muscle to contract again. See also **reverberating circuits** and **feedback**.

self-repudiation Disparagement or depreciation of the individual by himself.

selves Actions at different times suggest that different personality integrations exist within the same individual, as in the dual selves (or personalities) of Dr. Jekyll and Mr. Hyde. The normal person, since he reacts differently in different situations, is sometimes said to have a "social self," a "religious self," a "fraternity self," and so on.

semantics The study of word meanings.

semantic differential An index used in an attempt to quantify word meanings. It is based upon the rating of words in terms of such dimensions as good-bad, active-passive, and so on. What one gets, finally, is a profile which represents a word's rating on each dimension. Profiles for different words can then be compared.

semicircular canals The three canals of the inner ear which mediate sensitivity to rotation.

senescence Old age. The aged are referred to as *senescent*.

senile psychosis A mental illness associated with, but not a necessary concomitant of, old age. It may take many forms, including mania and depression.

sensation Theoretically, an irreducible sensory experience such as might exist the first time a particular receptor is stimulated — i.e., a receptor process as such, devoid of meaning.

sense organ One which, like the eye or ear, contains receptors.

sensitivity Susceptibility to stimulation.

sensitivity curve A curve showing sensitivity as a function of stimulating circumstances. In the field of visual sensitivity, a luminosity curve is of such a nature. See **luminosity**.

sensorimotor Designation of any behavior that is considered in terms of its afferent (sensory) and efferent (motor) components. Any overt act initiated by receptor processes is sensorimotor. Also see **perceptual-motor habit**.

sensorium A term sometimes used to represent the sensory structures and functions of the cerebral cortex. The sensory cortex.

sensory adaptation Adaptation of some sensory function, as in dark adaptation, where objects not observed at first gradually become visible. See **adaptation**.

sensory deprivation Being rendered incapable of using one or more senses, as when the eyes are removed or the ears plugged, or when one is placed in a restricted sensory environment.

sensory habits Those learned as aspects of sensory discrimination.

sensory neuron One connected with a receptor and responsive to sensory stimulation; otherwise known as an *afferent neuron*.

sensory preconditioning The mere simultaneity of stimuli seems to produce an association between them such that, when one becomes a conditioned stimulus the other may substitute for it — i.e., may be equivalent with it in producing the conditioned response.

septal region A part of the limbic system involved in studies of the so-called pleasure areas of the brain. Rats with electrodes implanted in this region, under conditions where lever-pressing provides weak electrical stimulation of it, soon respond at a very high rate, hence the idea that such stimulation is pleasurable. See **limbic system.**

sequential development One response develops after another in a more or less definite order, as in the case of the succession of developments (sitting, crawling, etc.) which culminates in walking.

serendipity Accidental discovery. Finding one thing while looking for something else, as in the discovery of penicillin by Sir Alexander Fleming.

serial learning Learning a sequence of responses, where one response sets the stage, as it were, for the elicitation of the next in the series. Examples are running a maze or reciting a poem.

set A readiness to perceive or to respond in some way; an attitude which facilitates, or predetermines, some outcome. See **instructional set.**

shaping behavior Molding an organism's responses, as in experiments involving successive approximation, where each further approximation to a desired response (like pecking a disc) is reinforced. The same term is sometimes applied to so-called brain-washing. See **successive approximation** and **brainwashing.**

sharpening A term used in discussing rumor. It represents the tendency to distort a story so that, while overall details drop out (leveling) certain others are brought into prominence, making the story more pointed. Thus, if the person involved in the rumor is disliked, the teller is likely to emphasize derogatory details. See **assimilation, leveling,** and **rumor.**

shock therapy The production of therapeutic convulsions by passing an electric current through the patient's head or by injecting him with large doses of insulin or convulsive drugs. Used in the alleviation of certain mental illnesses.

sigma (σ or **S.D.**) The standard deviation of a distribution. In a normal distribution, 68 per cent of all cases fall between plus and minus one sigma.

simultaneous contrast Under certain circumstances a particular hue causes nearby objects to take on the hue of its complementary — as when yellow footlights make shadows on the stage appear bluish, or make blue shadows appear to have greater blueness.

skeletal muscles Those on the outer body which, when stimulated, move parts of the skeleton, like an arm or leg.

skewed distribution A frequency distribution in which measurements are much more frequent toward one end than toward the middle. Compare **normal curve.**

skill Proficiency developed through learning. May be motor (as in riding a bicycle), verbal (as in reciting), or both (as in typing).

smell brain The part which mediates olfactory sensitivity and which, in some animals, is large in proportion to the rest of the brain.

social behavior That which is influenced by or influences the behavior of others; behavior involving interaction of individuals or groups.

social climate Used in various ways to represent such features of group activity as overall morale, feeling of togetherness or its lack, the general psychological atmosphere that prevails. Different social climates were produced in studies of small groups subjected to democratic, authoritarian, and laissez-faire leadership. The term is sometimes used as synonymous with cultural or social environment. See **social environment.**

social conditioning Learning in a social context.

social environment That involving influences from other individuals. They do not, however, need to be present in person. They may influence us through what they have written or recorded in some other way. See **social field.**

socal facilitation This is said to have occurred whenever the individual in a group situation exceeds the performance level characteristically present when he works alone. It does not necessarily mean that he is more efficient in the group situation, for he may have an increased output but make more mistakes.

social field   Sometimes used as synonymous with social environment. However, Lewin and his followers have given it a special meaning, which was involved in our discussion of social field analysis. This meaning broadens the term to include not only others present at the time, but also those symbolically present — like parents or teachers who, though absent, exert an influence, as when one thinks of what they might expect him to do under the circumstances. The "great cloud of witnesses" with which the writer of Hebrews (12:1) felt himself surrounded (the prophets, Christ) was, in this sense, part of his social field.

social heritage   What has been transmitted to us from earlier generations through social rather than biological avenues.

social intelligence   The ability to get along well in social situations.

social interaction   The interplay between individuals or groups; social behavior.

social maturity   The degree to which an individual has attained independence of parental and other adult ministrations.

social motives   Those originating in what one learns from others.

social movement   See **mass movement.**

socialization   Learning to conform to group ways; acquiring a specific culture.

sociocultural influences   Social influences derived from, or dictated by, the culture.

sociogram   A graphic representation of the results obtained with a sociometric questionnaire.

sociometric questionnaire   One dealing with interpersonal relations. For example, the person names individuals with whom he would most like to carry out certain activities and with whom he would least like to carry them out.

sociometry   See **sociometric questionnaire.**

somaesthetic   Pertaining to body feeling, or to sensitivity originating in the skin, muscles and body cavity.

somatic   Pertaining to the body.

somatotonia   Temperament characterized by such traits as marked vigor, directness of manner, competitiveness, need for action.

somatotypes   Types (or dimensions) of physique according to Sheldon's system, in which the somatotype 1–1–7, for example, is low in the endomorphic, low in the mesomorphic, and high in the ectomorphic dimension.

soul   The "psyche" of the Greeks. Originally an ethereal presence manifested in behavior and experience and synonymous with what was later called *mind;* in its later (religious) meaning, the disembodied spirit. Also closely related to our present-day concept of the self.

sound waves   Air vibrations which, when they activate auditory receptors, give rise to tones and noises.

sour-grapes reaction   A form of rationalization in which the individual expresses satisfaction that he did not do what he really wanted to do, or that the things he really wants are not worth the getting.

space perception   Perceiving or otherwise reacting to the size, distance, or depth aspects of the environment.

spatial maze   A labyrinth (the most common type of maze) in which different turns occur at different places; contrasted with a temporal maze, where different turns are made in only one place — the bifurcation at the end of the central alley.

specific hunger   Hunger for such specific foodstuffs as fat, protein, or salt.

specific nerve-energy doctrine   Old term used to describe the fact that, since receptors are specialized for particular types of energy, the nerve impulses resulting from such receptor stimulation initiate specific "coded messages" in sensory nerves which lead to specialized sensory areas of the brain.

specificity of behavior   A restricted response to a particular stimulus, especially as when withdrawing a limb instead of responding with the whole body.

spectrum   The spread of colors perceived when white light is passed through a prism. It has red at one end and violet at the other.

speech   Verbal language, as represented in talking and in writing. A form of communication.

sphygmomanometer   An instrument such as

the doctor uses for measuring blood pressure, which is part of a lie detector (or polygraph), and which is used for studying blood-pressure changes in feeling and emotion.

spinal cord The part of the central nervous system which runs up the spine as far as the medulla.

split brain One in which the cerebral hemispheres have been separated by cutting the corpus callosum.

spontaneous movement Movement without apparent stimulation. Behavior "emitted" by the organism. See **emitted response**.

spontaneous recovery Return of a conditioned response after apparent extinction.

standard deviation (S.D.) A statistical index of the variability within a frequency distribution. Also known as *sigma*.

standard error of a difference A statistical index of the probability that a difference between the means of two samples is a true difference, i.e., greater than zero.

standard error of a mean A statistical index representing the probability that a sample mean is truly representative of the true mean; i.e., that of the total population from which the sample was drawn.

standard score Obtained by finding the difference between the individual's raw score and the mean score, then dividing this by the standard deviation of the distribution.

standardization of tests Developing definite procedures and methods of scoring and evaluating tests.

Stanford-Binet Intelligence Test A widely used individual verbal test of intelligence — an American revision (by Terman and Merrill at Stanford University) of the Binet-Simon test.

star In sociometry, the person chosen by all (or most) of the group. Compare **isolate**.

startle pattern The overall and partially unlearned bodily reaction immediately following onset of sudden stimulation, like a pistol shot.

static sense That involved in maintaining equilibrium through stimulation of nonauditory receptors of the inner ear.

statistics Mathematical procedures for analyzing and interpreting groups of measurements.

status One's standing in the group. Also see **prestige**.

status symbol Something that indicates a person's status. An expensive car is, for example, taken by many as a status symbol. Low status may be symbolized by such things as wearing shabby clothing and carrying a lunchbox to work.

stereophonic effects Artificial reproduction of sounds, and presentation of these to the two ears, so that they simulate the spatial aspects of the sounds of everyday life, as in cinerama and other specialized types of motion-picture projection, as well as stereophonic records.

stereoscope Instrument with which tridimensional effects are produced by stimulating each eye with a picture representing what it would see under normal binocular conditions.

stereotyped behavior That which follows substantially the same pattern whenever it is elicited.

stigmata Signs of some disorder, like the extremely small head of the microcephalic.

stimulus Any factor inside or outside the organism, but external to the living cell-groups under consideration, which initiates activity of some kind.

stimulus generalization When a response has been conditioned to a particular stimulus, say a tone of 256 cycles, or vibration on a particular part of the skin, it is also elicited by other somewhat similar stimuli.

stirrup Small stirrup-shaped ossicle of the inner ear, attached to the oval window.

strategy The procedure adopted in an effort to achieve some goal, like the solution of a problem. See **partist strategy, holist strategy**.

stress Tension or conflict.

stress interview One designed to discover an individual's ability "to take it." He is placed on the defensive by, for example, reflections on his character.

stressor Anything producing stress, bodily or mental. See **general adaptation syndrome** and **stress**.

striatum The corpus striatum, a brain structure adjoining the thalamus, and just below the corpus callosum, which plays a role in muscular coordination.

stroboscope   A device on which a moving pattern seems to stand still, or to reverse its direction, depending upon the speed of movement and the rate at which the light with which it is viewed is flashing on and off.

structural disorders   Those with an organic basis such as destruction of nerve tissue or defective glandular functioning. Contrasted with *functional disorders*, which have no apparent organic basis.

stylus maze   A labyrinth threaded with a pencil or stylus.

subconscious   Generally speaking, what is below the level of awareness. As Freudians use this term, it refers to a hypothetical region of the mind which serves as a repository of repressed and other experiences which, while influencing behavior in important ways, seldom (if ever) come into consciousness (awareness). Experiences which readily come to awareness are said to be in the preconscious. See **preconscious**. The term *unconscious*, merely referring to that of which we are not aware at the moment, is more widely used. See **unconscious motivation**.

subject   The organism on which an experiment is performed and whose responses are the dependent variables of the experiment.

subjective   Known only to the individual himself; not directly observable by others; private. Contrasted with *objective*, or socially observable. How a pain feels to me is subjective; but my cry, since others may witness it, is objective.

sublimation   Satisfying a motive indirectly but in a socially accepable manner.

subliminal   Below the level of awareness, below the threshold of stimulation, as when an auditory or visual presentation is too weak to have an effect, or at least an effect of which the individual is aware.

substitution learning   Learning to substitute one symbol for another, as in deciphering a code.

subtractive color mixture   As in the mixture of pigments, where one component, instead of adding to another, cancels out or subtracts certain effects.

subtractive primaries   The elementary hues involved in subtractive color mixture; see **subtractive color mixture**.

subvocal speech   Talking silently to oneself, as in thinking with words.

successive approximation method   The method of reinforcing every response (operant) which approximates a desired response more closely than the one which just preceded it. Thus a pigeon may be rewarded whenever its pecking comes closer to the disc which the experimenter wants it to peck. See **shaping behavior**.

successive contrast   Negative after-imagery, where removal of red, say, is followed by an image of its complementary, blue-green. Compare **simultaneous contrast**, where the complementary color is evident (in the surrounding area) during original stimulation.

suggestion   Something which prompts an individual to react in an uncritical manner. Usually of a verbal nature, as in hypnotic suggestion. See **hypnosis**.

summation   A combining of different stimuli or processes to produce an effect greater than that possible by either alone. We have been particularly concerned with neural summation (or facilitation). One type is **spatial summation**. This occurs when impulses coming to a synapse over one or more fibers, but with insufficient intensity to cross it, are enabled to cross because other impulses (from additional fibers) also converge on the synapse. Another type, **temporal summation**, occurs when an impulse too weak by itself to bridge the synapse is enabled to cross because other impulses coming after it (in the same fiber) combine their effects with its own. Both types of summation may occur at the same time, different fibers combining their effects (spatial summation) and each being effective also in terms of the frequency of impulses coming over it (temporal summation). Also see **facilitation**.

superego   Internal control (or self-criticism) derived from parental and other early influences. See **conscience**.

supine position   Lying on the back. In respect to the hand, "with palm up."

surface colors   Those perceived as the surfaces

of objects, like a red book or a green leaf. Contrasted with *film* (or *aperture*) colors, which are perceived without reference to objects.

surface traits Those personality characteristics which are readily apparent, like an individual's sociability or his shyness.

suspensory ligaments Fibrous tissues holding the lens of the eye in place.

symbolic processes Those which represent, or can substitute for, aspects of past experience. Images and words are thus symbolic. Thought processes are symbolic in that they involve the implicit manipulation of external objects, situations, and relationships.

sympathetic nervous system The division of the autonomic system which plays a predominant role in emotion and which functions in opposition to the parasympathetic system.

synapse The junction where nerve impulses pass from one neuron to another.

synaptic nervous system One with synapses, as contrasted with a nerve net system, where impulses pass indiscriminately in every direction.

syndrome A group of symptoms characterizing a particular disorder.

syntax The order in which words, phrases, clauses, and so on are put together in the language. Rules governing sentence construction.

syringomyelia A disorder in which the pain and temperature senses are absent or defective in a particular part of the body due to disruption of the crossed ascending fibers of the spinal cord.

system of psychology A way of ordering the facts of psychology so that they have meaning in relation to each other. A theoretical model which embraces as many relevant facts as possible and serves as a framework to be filled in as new information is obtained. The various **schools of psychology** were designed to systematize psychological knowledge and point the way for further research. The newer **miniature systems** focus upon particular fields of psychology (like the field of learning) rather than attempting to embrace everything psychological.

systolic blood pressure That correlated with the contraction (systole) of the heart. Compare **diastolic blood pressure**.

T-maze A maze pathway constructed of T-shaped units. A *multiple-T-maze* has several such units.

tabes dorsalis Injury to the dorsal columns of the spinal cord, ordinarily by syphilis, and resulting in a motor incoordination known as *locomotor ataxia*.

tabetic gait A jerky gait associated with advanced tabes. Locomotor ataxia. See **tabes dorsalis**.

tabula rasa Locke's concept of the mind as analogous, initially, to a blank sheet on which experience makes its impressions.

tachistoscope Any device which exposes visual material (pictures, digits, letters, words, etc.) for brief, controlled time intervals.

tact A term used by Skinner to represent verbalizations which name, symbolize, or otherwise represent aspects of the individual's world. It comes from the idea that these verbalizations form, so to speak, a type of "contact with" the things or events symbolized. Compare **mand**.

tactual localization Touching or otherwise indicating points on the skin that the experimenter has touched while the subject is blindfolded. See **local signs**.

tactual sensitivity That of the skin, touch.

tambour-mounted cage A device which wobbles as the caged subject moves, thus providing a record of activity.

taste Specialized chemical sense whose receptors are in the tongue.

taste buds Receptors for taste stimulation on the surface of the tongue.

tectorial membrane A structure in the cochlear canal of the inner ear into which the hair cells of Corti project.

temperament Such aspects of personality as joviality, moodiness, tenseness, and activity level are referred to rather loosely as expressions of a person's temperament. The term has an emotional connotation.

temperature senses Those of warmth and cold, from which heat is perhaps synthesized.

temporal lobes   Those of the cerebrum below the fissure of Sylvius (adjacent to the temples). They contain auditory projection and auditory association areas.

temporal maze   One in which the subject is required to make different turns in the same place, like two to the right followed by two to the left. Used in the double-alternation test of reasoning ability.

tension   The state of being stretched or under pressure, as in the case of muscle contraction. Also used to represent experienced strain, as when needs are not satisfied, frustration is present, or one waits to hear the outcome of some critical event.

tensor tympani   A small muscle of the middle ear which adjusts the tension of the eardrum in response to different sound pressures.

terminal threshold   The upper limit of sensitivity, beyond which increases in intensity are ineffective. Thus, after the terminal threshold for hearing has been reached, increasing the physical intensity may hurt the ears but bring no further sound experience.

test   An examination designed to reveal the relative standing of an individual in the group with respect to intelligence, personality, aptitude, or achievement.

test battery   A group of tests combined for a particular purpose.

testimony test   The subject views a pictured or actual situation and then tells from memory what he has witnessed.

testosterone   A secretion from the testes important for the sexual development and motivation of male organisms. The male sex hormone.

thalamus   A structure between the brain stem and cerebrum which serves as a switchboard mechanism to relay sensory impulses to the appropriate regions of the cerebral cortex and which, in itself, mediates a primitive level of sensitivity and modifiability. Usually regarded as the upper part of the brain stem.

thematic apperception test (T.A.T.)   A so-called projective test which requires the subject to make up stories appropriate to a series of pictures and, from these themes, gives an indication of basic personality structure.

therapy   A procedure designed to cure or alleviate some disorder.

thinking   Manipulating aspects of past experience implicitly, as in recalling (thinking of something), daydreaming, and reasoning. In large measure, at least, a form of subvocal speech.

thirst   The experience or condition associated with inadequate intake of liquids.

thought processes   See thinking.

threshold   In the most general sense, this is the point at which an experience (or response) just barely occurs. A more specific term is absolute threshold. A stimulus of threshold strength is one which, if it were weaker, would have no typical effect. A difference threshold (or threshold difference) is one that is just barely perceptible, the just noticeable difference, or j.n.d. The terminal threshold is the upper limit of sensitivity, the point beyond which further increases in intensity have no typical effect. By "typical effect" in these definitions is meant no increment to the sense being studied. If increasing the intensity of light stimulation brings pain, that is not a visual effect, hence not typical for this kind of stimulation.

threshold stimulus   One of threshold strength. See threshold.

thwarting   Placing barriers in a person's way so that he cannot satisfy some motive, or so that he has unusual difficulty in satisfying it. Frustrating him.

thyroid gland   An endocrine gland situated near the windpipe. Its secretion (thyroxin) is important for metabolism. A marked deficiency of this hormone in early life may produce the form of feeblemindedness known as *cretinism*.

thyroxin   The secretion of the thyroid gland, or a synthesized product of the same. See thyroid gland.

tic   A nervous twitch of a muscle or muscle group.

timbre   Sound quality, as in the difference between a piano and a 'cello playing the same note. A function of the complexity of sound waves, i.e., the overtones produced.

time study   Measuring the time required to

perform certain tasks; usually combined with *motion study*.

token rewards   Secondary reinforcers, like coins or poker chips, which can be used to "purchase" primary satisfactions.

tone   Periodic sound to which a particular pitch can be assigned, as compared with noise, which is aperiodic.

tonic immobility   Animal hypnosis, an immobility of the body brought on by some sudden emotion-provoking stimulus or by certain other stimuli which render an organism motionless.

tools   Devices through which the organism extends the range of its senses, or increases its strength and dexterity in coping with its environment.

topological psychology   That which considers the behavior of the individual at any moment as a function of the attracting and repelling forces (positive and negative valences) in his psychological environment (or life space). See **social field, valences, vectors**.

tracking behavior   Behavior controlled by a moving target. In **compensatory tracking**, one attempts, through compensatory movements, to keep the "target" stationary, as when the speedometer is kept as close as possible to 50 miles per hour. **Pursuit tracking** is that in which the aim is to keep on the target (as in the pursuitmeter test). A gunner trying to hit a moving object is pursuit tracking.

training   This involves observing others who are skilled in the performance to be learned and/or following instructions. Compare **practice**.

traits   Relatively constant aspects, characteristics, or dimensions of behavior. Usually applied to personality and exemplified by such terms as introversion, dominance, sociability, persistence, honesty, etc.

tranquilizer   Anything which makes a person more tranquil, quiet, or relaxed. The so-called tranquilizers so much in evidence today are drugs which have the above effect. The more potent of these tranquilizers are used to relax the mentally ill. Milder tranquilizers are often prescribed for the release of tensions in otherwise normal people.

transfer   A carryover from one habit to another. This may be *positive* in effect, as when learning one thing facilitates the learning of something else; or its effect may be *negative*, as when one habit interferes with acquisition of another.

transmission curve   One which represents the degree to which different wavelengths of light pass through a transparent substance, like red glass.

tremor   A limited muscular spasm, like the trembling or quivering of the hand.

trial   One run through a maze, one reading of something to be memorized, and so on. A practice period.

trial-and-error   A term used to represent the apparently random, haphazard, hit-or-miss exploratory activity which often precedes the acquisition of new adjustments. It may be *overt*, as exemplified in a rat's running here and there in a maze, or *implicit*, as when one thinks of this and then that way of coping with a situation. Contrasted with planned or insightful behavior.

tridimensional vision   That involving discernment of depth or distance. Present artificially in the stereoscope or in a 3-D motion picture.

trigram   Three letters, as in what were formerly called *nonsense syllables*. Usually two consonants with a vowel between.

tropism   An unlearned orienting movement of the whole organism which causes it to move toward or away from the stimulus. Examples are a moth flying into the flame (positive phototropism) and a cockroach running toward the dark (negative phototropism).

trot reflex   A diagonal reflex which typically appears in about the fifth month of human fetal life. Stimulation of a foot, for instance, may produce a response not only of the stimulated member but of the opposite hand. Believed to be a precursor of postnatal locomotion, as in crawling and walking.

two-point threshold   The smallest discriminable distance between two points of stimulation on the skin; this differs depending upon the region stimulated. The threshold is measured with an *aesthesiometer*.

tympanic canal The descending canal of the cochlea at the lower end of which is the round window.

tympanic membrane The ear drum.

typology The attempt to classify persons into types — such as in terms of physique, temperament, and introversion-extraversion.

ultraviolet light That with a wavelength shorter than 400 millimicrons (violet), hence invisible.

unconditioned response The original, or inborn response, like salivation stimulated by food in the mouth, withdrawal from an injurious stimulus, or contraction of the pupil to light, ordinarily reflex in character.

unconditioned stimulus The stimulus which arouses an unconditioned response, as defined above.

unconscious Below the level of awareness. Compare **subconscious** and **preconscious**.

unconscious motivation Urges of which the individual is not aware.

universality The characteristic of being universal, present in all normal members of the species. Not a sure criterion of innateness because all normal members of a culture may have certain learned responses in common.

unlearned response One that, rather than being acquired (i.e., dependent upon the learning process), is inborn, innate, inherited; dependent upon maturation for its appearance.

USES test battery An aptitude battery used by the United States Employment Service to screen applicants for jobs.

utricle Part of the vestibule, just below the semicircular canals. It plays a part in static sensitivity.

vagus nerve The Xth cranial nerve. Literally, the "wandering nerve," which constitutes an important part of the parasympathetic system. It connects with most of the viscera.

valences Attracting and repelling "forces" in the individual's psychological environment.

validation Determination of the validity of tests (see below), usually with correlation procedures.

validity A test is said to be valid (or to have validity) when it actually does what it has been designed to do, such as predict success in school or in some vocation or avocation. It is valid to the degree that test scores correlate with criteria of success.

values, as aspects of personality. Things that the individual holds as good, worthwhile, or important. The aspects of life to which he gives most weight, as in the Allport-Vernon-Lindzey *Study of Values*, where the relative weight given to things economic, religious, aesthetic, etc., is discerned.

variable-interval reinforcement See **schedule of reinforcement.**

variable-ratio reinforcement See **schedule of reinforcement.**

variables What we can manipulate or measure, as in the case of independent and dependent variables in an experiment.

variability The degree to which individuals, or measurements in a frequency distribution, differ from the average. The standard deviation is a measure of variability.

vascular theory The theory that sensitivity to warm and cold is based, respectively, upon the dilation and contraction of small blood vessels in the skin.

vectors In topological (or vector) psychology, the direction of psychological forces resulting from the interplay of attracting and repelling factors (positive and negative valences) in an individual's psychological environment. See **topological psychology.**

ventral columns Large fiber tracts located toward the front of the spinal cord, i.e., toward the belly.

ventral root The location of cell bodies of the motor (efferent) division of a spinal nerve. Designated *ventral* because it is toward the front (belly) of the organism.

verbal Pertaining to language.

verbal behavior That involving language; speech, written or spoken.

verbal community The group which sets the pattern for our verbal behavior and reinforces conformity with this pattern.

verbal skills Linguistic habits, as in speaking, writing, reading, or reciting.

verbalization In relation to problem solving — figuring out the solution to a problem and putting it into words, as when the person says "the solution is to go twice to the right, then twice to the left."

verification stage In creative thinking — testing one's invention to see if it really works.

versatility Facility or ease in accomplishing a variety of things. A versatile person is one who can do many things well. The ability to vary one's approach in desirable directions instead of being stereotyped. Flexibility.

vertebrates Animals with backbones.

vesicles Bulbous cavities, like those from which the brain develops in vertebrates.

vestibule A structure at the base of the semicircular canals which functions especially in perception of rectilinear motion.

vestibular canal The ascending canal of the cochlea, at the origin of which the oval window, with adjacent stirrup, is located.

vicarious functioning The taking over of a function by some structure not ordinarily serving this purpose.

vigilance Alertness, being wide awake, paying attention.

Vineland Social Maturity Scale A rating scale for social maturity, or social independence. See **social maturity**.

viscera Organs of the body cavity, like the stomach, spleen, and intestines.

visceral afferent fibers Those which carry nerve impulses from the viscera to the central nervous system, hence sensory.

visceral reactions Stomach contractions, secretion of adrenalin, and other responses of visceral organs. Visceral reactions underlie such experiences as nausea and "butterflies" in the stomach.

visceratonia A personality dimension characterized by preoccupation with or prominence of the viscera (especially the stomach); viz., unusual enjoyment of eating.

visible spectrum That region between 400 and 700 millimicrons which is perceived by the human eye as a series of hues ranging from violet to red.

visual accommodation Change in the lens so as to focus light from sources at different distances from the eye and thus to form sharp images on the retina.

visual acuity The smallest visible separation of objects or, as measured with Snellen charts, the smallest letters perceptible from a standard distance.

visual cliff An apparent, but not actual, dropoff in a situation designed to test the depth or distance discrimination of infants. They crawl on a plate of glass, the under side of which is backed with linoleum for a certain distance. At the "cliff" the linoleum is dropped some distance below the glass, and most infants refuse to go beyond this point.

visual purple A photochemical substance in the rods, otherwise known as *rhodopsin.*

vitreous humor The transparent jelly-like substance between the lens and the retina of the eye.

vocal cords Membranes in the larynx, vibrations of which produce voiced sounds.

vocal play Vocalization as in babbling.

vocality A characteristic possessed by tones that sound like vowels.

vocalization Sound made with the vocal mechanisms; not speech, however, until it has communicative significance.

vocational guidance Directing an individual, in terms of his intelligence, aptitudes, interests, etc., as well as the job opportunities, toward the fields in which he is most likely to succeed.

vocational interest blank An inventory devised by Strong which reveals the person's *liking for, dislike for,* or *indifference* to activities associated with many vocations and avocations. The pattern of interests thus revealed is evaluated in terms of the pattern of interests of people successful in various vocations.

vocational selection Picking out, in terms of the requirements of a job, the people best fitted to do it. Selection of such people is done with aptitude tests and perhaps other selection devices, including interviews.

voice As the term was used in this text, it referred to any sound made by the vocal cords. These are voiced sounds. Whispered sounds are without voice.

volley theory The theory that the pitch of sounds (at least between 1000 and 5000 cycles) is determined by the frequency of the volleys of nerve impulses reaching the brain. These volleys are carried by groups of nerve fibers, not by a single fiber. Intensity, according to this theory, is determined by the number of impulses per volley. Also see **frequency theory of hearing.**

volume   The apparent space filled by sounds. High tones seem to be restricted spatially, while low ones seem to spread out.

voluntary   Done with intention, as compared with *involuntary* acts, over which the individual has no control.

warm spots   Points on the skin which are especially responsive to stimuli with a higher temperature than the skin.

wavelength   The distance between two corresponding positions in a wave, as from crest to crest.

waxy flexibility   Found in some forms of hysteria and in catatonic schizophrenia. The patient's arm, hand, or some other part of his body can be placed in a certain position, and it is held there for what is, at times, a considerable period. It appears that he is being molded "like wax."

Weber's law   This hold that, whether or not an increase or decrease in intensity of stimulation is discriminated depends upon the ratio of the change in stimulus intensity to the intensity of stimulation existing prior to the change.

Wechsler Adult Intelligence Scale (WAIS)   An individual test designed for adults. It includes both verbal and performance items. (Formerly called the "Wechsler-Bellevue Scale.")

Wechsler Intelligence Scale for Children (WISC)   Much like the adult scale in content but graded downward in difficulty and separately standardized for use with children.

white-black continuum   The discriminable series of grays ranging from white at one end to black at the other.

white matter   Found in the outer regions of the spinal cord and in other areas in the central nervous system which appear white. It gets its name from the prevalence of the white fatty sheath (myelin) of the nerve fibers in these areas.

whole learning   Practicing some complex skill (verbal or motor) from beginning to end instead of one part at a time.

will power   Inferred from persistence in following out some line of activity despite barriers or distracting influences and also from decisiveness in making difficult choices.

will to learn   The intention to learn.

will to power   The mastery, or self-assertive motive.

word blindness   The aphasia (otherwise known as *alexia*) in which an individual loses ability to understand the meaning of written words; or, in congenital alexia or dyslexia, is born with a brain condition which makes learning to read unusually difficult.

word deafness   Like word blindness except that the meaning of spoken words is lost.

work decrement   The decreasing output associated with repetitive work and taken as an index of fatigue.

worry   An anxious state characterized by uncertainty and unpleasantness. Also see **anxiety.**

wratten filters   Gelatin filters made by the Eastman Kodak Company for photographic and scientific purposes, as in approximating a monochromatic color in experiments involving color discrimination. The filters transmit specified wavelength bands of light.

X-chromosome   One of the sex chromosomes. The male has only one, the female two.

Y-chromosome   One of the sex chromosomes, possessed only by males.

Young-Helmholtz theory of color vision   This theory assumes that there are three primary colors (red, green, and blue) with cones especially receptive to the wavelengths of each. Yellow is assumed to result from simultaneous activation of the "red" and "green" cones.

REFERENCES

Chapter 1

The Science of Psychology

1. B. F. Skinner, *Science and Human Behavior.* Macmillan, 1953, p. 12.
2. Quoted from C. E. Kenneth Mees, "Scientific Thought and Social Reconstruction," *Electrical Engineering*, 1934, *53*, 383–384.
3. M. Super, M. Cotzin, and K. M. Dallenbach, " 'Facial Vision': The Perception of Obstacles by the Blind," *Amer. J. Psychol.*, 1944, *57*, 133–183; P. Worchell and K. M. Dallenbach, " 'Facial Vision': The Perception of Obstacles by the Deaf-Blind," *Amer. J. Psychol.*, 1947, *60*, 502–553; C. H. Ammons, P. Worchell, and K. M. Dallenbach, " 'Facial Vision': The Perception of Obstacles Out-of-Doors by Blindfolded and Blindfolded Deafened Subjects," *Amer. J. Psychol.*, 1953, *66*, 519–53. See also *Life*, Vol. 35, No. 13, Sept. 28, 1953, pp. 57–59.
4. N. Tinbergen, *Social Behavior in Animals.* Wiley, 1953.
5. H. E. Jones, *Motor Performance and Growth.* University of California Press, 1949.
6. Staff, Psychological Section, "Psychological Activities in the Training Command, Army Air Forces," *Psychol. Bull.*, 1945, *42*, 37–54.
7. J. B. Conant, *Science and Common Sense.* Yale University Press, 1951, p. 25.
8. L. Carmichael, *Basic Psychology*, Random House, 1957, p. 5.

Chapter 2

The Human Organism

1. D. Hooker, *The Prenatal Origin of Behavior,* University of Kansas Press, 1952; also see D. Hooker, *Evidence of Prenatal Function of the Central Nervous System in Man,* American Museum of Natural History, 1958.
2. T. Humphrey, "The Spinal Tract of the Trigeminal Nerve in Human Embryos between 7½ and 8½ Weeks of Menstrual Age and in Relation to Fetal Behavior," *J. Comp. Neurol.*, 1952, *97*, 143–209.
3. Hooker, *op. cit.*, 1952, p. 70.
4. L. B. Arey, *Developmental Anatomy* (6th ed.). Saunders, 1959.
5. See J. C. Eccles, "The Physiology of Imagination," *Scientific American*, September 1958, *199*, 135–146; or, by the same author, *The Neurophysiological Basis of the Mind,* Oxford University Press, 1953.
6. B. Katz, "How Cells Communicate," *Scientific American*, September 1961, pp. 211–212. Used by permission.
7. The brain weights given appear in R. H. Wheeler, *The Science of Psychology* (rev. ed.), Crowell, 1940, p. 373. There is much variability in the brain weight of human individuals; and brain-weight/body-weight ratios have no meaning at all when applied here. Even among people rated as geniuses (see Chapter 5), brain weight has varied from 1200 grams to over 2000 grams (about four pounds). For some comparisons, see A. M. Lassek, *The Human Brain*, Thomas, 1957, p. 32.
8. See A. J. Carlson and N. Johnson, *The Machinery of the Body* (rev. ed.). University of Chicago Press, 1948, p. 438.
9. R. W. Sperry, "Cerebral Organization and Behavior," *Science*, 1961, *133*, 1749–1757; and "The Great Cerebral Commissure," *Scientific American*, January 1964, 42–52.
10. C. B. Trevarthen, "Double Visual Learning in Split-Brain Monkeys," *Science*, 1962, *136*, 258–259.
11. D. A. Sholl, *The Organization of the Cerebral Cortex.* Wiley, 1956, p. 110.
12. C. S. Sherrington, *Man: On His Nature.* Cambridge University Press, 1941, pp. 223–224.
13. See the discussion by A. L. Towe and T. C. Ruch in Chapter 21 of Ruch *et al.*, *Neurophysiology*, Saunders, 1961, for further information on EEG's.
14. Examples of such reports aroused by electrical stimulation of the exposed cortex are given in W. Penfield and T. Rasmussen, *The Cerebral Cortex of Man*, Macmillan, 1950; and W. Penfield, *The Excitable Cortex in Conscious Man*, Thomas, 1958.
15. The pioneer studies in this field were carried out by Franz, a physiological psychologist. See S. I. Franz, *How the Brain Works*, University of California at Los Angeles, 1929.
16. See W. Penfield and T. C. Erickson, *Epilepsy and Cerebral Localization*. Thomas, 1941, p. 163.
17. *Ibid.*

18. On functions of the prefrontal areas, see such recent studies as: K. H. Pribram, "Neocortical Function in Behavior," in H. F. Harlow and C. N. Woolsey, *Biological and Biochemical Bases of Behavior,* University of Wisconsin Press, 1958; W. A. Wilson, M. Oscar, and H. Gleitman, "The Effect of Frontal Lesions in Monkeys Upon Widely-Spaced Delayed-Response Trials," *J. Comp. Physiol. Psychol.,* 1963, 56, 237–240; and J. M. Warren and K. Akert, *The Frontal Granular Cortex and Behavior,* McGraw-Hill, 1964. These studies and the references listed in them will indicate, among other things, the controversial nature of conclusions concerning the functions of the prefrontal cortex.

Chapter 3

Individual Differences

1. E. L. Thorndike, *The Measurement of Educational Products.* Public School Publishing Co., 1918, p. 16.
2. See S. S. Stevens, "Measurement in Man," *Science,* 1958, 127, 383–389.
3. For one attempt to define zero intelligence, see L. L. Thurstone, "A Method of Scaling Psychological and Educational Tests," *J. Educ. Psychol.,* 1925, 16, 433–451.
4. Stevens, *op. cit.*
5. Stevens, *op. cit.*
6. E. V. Berne, "An Experimental Investigation of Social Behavior Patterns in Young Children," *Univ. Iowa Stud.,* 1930, 4, No. 3.
7. M. Barker, "A Preliminary Report on the Social-Material Activities of Children," *Child Develpm. Monogr.,* 1930, No. 3.
8. P. H. Nygaard, "A Percentage Equivalent for the Coefficient of Correlation," *J. Educ. Psychol.,* 1926, 17, 86–92.

Chapter 4

How Individual Differences Originate

1. J. D. Watson and F. H. C. Crick, "Molecular Structure of Nucleic Acids," *Nature,* 1953, 171, 737–738. For an interesting discussion of the molecular model of DNA, see *Molecules to Man,* Houghton Mifflin, 1963, pp. 142–151. This is the Blue Version of this book, arranged by the American Institute of Biological Sciences.
2. Th. Boveri, as reported in H. E. Walter, *Genetics,* Macmillan, 1914, p. 32.
3. See the discussion and references in pages 311–325 of *Molecules to Man, op. cit.,* reference 1.

4. See B. Mintz (Ed.), *Environmental Influences on Prenatal Development,* University of Chicago Press, 1958; and M. F. A. Montagu, *Prenatal Influences,* Thomas, 1962.
5. For an illustration of the chromosomes from a person with mongolism, see page 377 of *Molecules to Man, op. cit.,* reference 1.
6. See the data summarized in L. Erlenmeyer-Kimling and L. F. Jarvik, "Genetics and Intelligence: A Review," *Science,* 1963, 142, 1477–1479.
7. See reference 6, in which the following studies are cited: H. H. Newman, F. N. Freeman, and K. J. Holzinger, *Twins: A Study of Heredity and Environment,* University of Chicago Press, 1937; J. Shields, *Monozygotic Twins Brought up Apart and Brought up Together,* Oxford University Press, 1962; F. J. Kallmann (Ed.), *Expanding Goals of Genetics in Psychiatry,* Grune and Stratton, 1962, in which E. Stromgren cites the work of N. Juel-Nielson and A. Mogensen. Some additional studies are cited in the Shields reference.
8. A. Anastasi, *Differential Psychology* (3rd ed.). Macmillan, 1958, pp. 295–300.
9. See reference 6.
10. From C. C. Dunn, *Heredity and Variation.* The University Society, 1932, p. 33.
11. B. E. Ginsburg and D. S. Miller, in D. Hooker and C. Hare (Eds.), *Genetics and the Inheritance of Integrated Neurological and Psychiatric Patterns.* Williams and Wilkins, 1954.
12. C. S. Hall, "Genetic Differences in Fatal Audiogenic Seizures Between Two Inbred Strains of House Mice," *J. Heredity,* 1947, 38, 2–6.
13. G. Witt and C. S. Hall, "The Genetics of Audiogenic Seizures in the House Mouse," *J. Comp. Physiol. Psychol.,* 1949, 42, 58–63.
14. R. C. Tryon, "Genetic Differences in Maze-Learning Ability in Rats," *39th Yearbook, Nat. Soc. Study Educ.,* Part I, 1940, pp. 111–119.
15. W. R. Thompson, "The Inheritance and Development of Intelligence," *Proc. Assoc. Res. Nerv. Ment. Dis.,* 1954, 33, 209–231.
16. D. O. Hebb and K. Williams, "A Method of Rating Animal Intelligence," *J. Genet. Psychol.,* 1946, 34, 59–65; M. S. Rabinovitch and H. E. Rosvold, "A Closed Field Intelligence Test for Rats," *Canad. J. Psychol.,* 1951, 3, 122–128.
17. For further examples and a general discussion of behavior genetics and individuality, see J. Hirsch, "Behavior Genetics and Individuality Understood," *Science,* 1963, 142, 1436–1442.
18. Tryon, reference 14. Also see the discussion of

polygenic inheritance in C. Stern, *Principles of Human Genetics* (2nd ed.), Freeman, 1960.

19. L. Carmichael, "The Development of Behavior in Vertebrates Experimentally Removed from the Influence of External Stimulation," *Psychol. Rev.*, 1926, *33*, 51–58; and "A Further Study of the Development of Behavior in Vertebrates Experimentally Removed from the Influence of External Stimulation," *Psychol. Rev.*, 1927, *34*, 34–47.

20. For examples, see L. B. Arey, *Developmental Anatomy* (6th ed.), Saunders, 1959.

21. M. B. McGraw, "Neural Maturation as Exemplified by the Achievement of Bladder Control," *J. Pediatrics*, 1940, *16*, 580–590.

22. W. Dennis and M. G. Dennis, "The Effect of Restricted Practice upon the Reaching, Sitting, and Standing of Two Infants," *J. Genet. Psychol.*, 1935, *47*, 17–32.

23. A. Gesell and H. Thompson, "Learning and Maturation in Identical Infant Twins," in R. G. Barker, J. S. Kounin, and H. F. Wright, *Child Behavior and Development*. McGraw-Hill, 1943.

24. H. M. Halverson, "The Development of Prehension in Infants," in Barker, Kounin, and Wright, *op. cit.*, reference 23. Also see McGraw, reference 26.

25. Halverson, reference 24.

26. M. B. McGraw, *The Neuromuscular Maturation of the Human Infant*. Columbia University Press, 1943. This monograph summarizes the findings reported in several lengthier studies, the references to which are cited there.

27. See McGraw, reference 26. This has been reissued, with slight editorial changes, by Hafner, 1963.

28. M. M. Shirley, *The First Two Years: Postural and Locomotor Development*. University of Minnesota Press, 1931.

29. L. B. Ames, "The Sequential Patterning of Prone Progression in the Human Infant," *Genet. Psychol. Monogr.*, 1937, *19*, 409–460; also see McGraw, reference 26.

30. K. Koffka, *The Growth of the Mind*, Harcourt, Brace, 1924; and M. M. Shirley, "Locomotor and Visual-Manual Functions," in Murchison's *Handbook of Child Psychology* (2nd ed.), Clark University Press, 1933.

31. See Dennis and Dennis, reference 22.

32. W. Dennis, "The Effect of Cradling Practices upon the Onset of Walking in Hopi Children," *J. Genet. Psychol.*, 1940, *56*, 77–86; and "Does Culture Appreciably Affect the Patterns of Infant Behavior?" *J. Soc. Psychol.*, 1940, *12*, 305–317.

33. *Ibid.*

34. W. Dennis and P. Najarian, "Infant Development Under Environmental Handicap," *Psychol. Monogr.*, 1957, *71*, No. 7.

35. W. Dennis, "Causes of Retardation among Institutionalized Children: Iran," *J. Genet. Psychol.*, 1960, *95*, 47–59.

36. See Dennis, reference 35.

37. See Dennis, reference 35.

38. M. B. McGraw, *Growth: A Study of Johnny and Jimmy*. Appleton-Century-Crofts, 1935.

39. W. N. Kellogg and L. A. Kellogg, *The Ape and the Child*. McGraw-Hill, 1933.

40. W. H. Furness, "Observations of the Mentality of Chimpanzees and Orang-Utans," *Proc. Amer. Phil. Soc.*, 1916, *55*, 281–290; K. J. Hayes and C. Hayes, "The Intellectual Development of a Home-Raised Chimpanzee," *Proc. Amer. Phil. Soc.*, 1951, *95*, 105–109; and "Vocalization and Speech in Chimpanzees," 16mm. Sound Film, Psychological Cinema Register, State College, Penn., 1951; C. Hayes, *The Ape in Our House*, Harper, 1951.

41. H. E. Jones, *Development in Adolescence*. Appleton-Century-Crofts, 1943.

Chapter 5

Intelligence

1. V. C. Hicks and H. A. Carr, "Human Reactions in a Maze," *J. Anim. Behav.*, 1912, *2*, 98–125; R. W. Husband, "A Comparison of Human Adults and White Rats in Maze Learning," *J. Comp. Psychol.*, 1929, *9*, 361–377; C. Lathan and P. E. Fields, "A Report on a Test-Retest Performance of 38 College Students and 27 White Rats on the Idential 25-Choice Elevated Maze," *J. Genet. Psychol.*, 1936, *49*, 283–296.

2. S. D. Porteus, *Guide to Porteus Maze Test*. Vineland: The Training School, 1924. This test has been used extensively, especially in medical areas.

3. A. S. Edwards, "Intelligence as Capacity for Variability or Versatility of Response," *Psychol. Rev.*, 1928, *35*, 198–210.

4. This hypothetical experiment is suggested by an animal investigation by D. O. Hebb and his discussion of it in his book, *The Organization of Behavior*. Wiley, 1949.

5. H. B. English, *Child Psychology*. Holt, 1951, p. 310.

6. A. Binet, as quoted in J. Peterson, *Early Conceptions and Tests of Intelligence.* World Book Co., 1925, p. 185.

7. W. Stern, as reported in Peterson, *op. cit.,* reference 6, p. 224.

8. A. Gesell and C. S. Amatruda, *Developmental Diagnosis.* Hoeber, 1941. The Northwestern Intelligence Tests have utilized many items from earlier tests by Gesell, Bayley, Psyche Cattell, and Bühler. They were developed by Dr. A. R. Gilliland and are published by Houghton Mifflin Company.

9. See especially, J. R. Wittenborn et al., "A Study of Adoptive Children. II. The Predictive Value of the Yale Developmental Examination of Infant Behavior," *Psychol. Monogr.,* 1956, *409,* 59–92, and the relevant references to earlier studies.

10. N. Bayley, "On the Growth of Intelligence," *American Psychologist,* 1955, *10,* 808.

11. P. R. Hofstaetter, "The Changing Composition of Intelligence: A Study of t-Technique," *J. Genet. Psychol.,* 1954, *85,* 159–164.

12. L. M. Terman and M. A. Merrill, *The Stanford-Binet Intelligence Scale.* Houghton Mifflin, 1960.

13. D. Wechsler, *Measurement and Appraisal of Adult Intelligence* (4th ed.). Williams and Wilkins, 1958.

14. D. Wechsler, *The Wechsler Intelligence Scale for Children.* Psychological Corporation, 1949.

15. See A. Anastasi, *Psychological Testing* (2nd ed.). Macmillan, 1961, pp. 319–320.

16. C. S. Yoakum and R. M. Yerkes, *The Army Mental Tests.* Holt, 1920.

17. "Development of Armed Forces Qualification Test and Predecessor Army Screening Tests," PRS Reports, 976, Personnel Research Section, TAGO, 1952, p. 55.

18. I. Lorge and R. L. Thorndike, *Lorge-Thorndike Intelligence Tests.* Houghton Mifflin, 1957.

19. C. Spearman, *Abilities of Man.* Macmillan, 1927.

20. L. L. Thurstone and T. G. Thurstone, "Factorial Studies of Intelligence," *Psychometric Monographs,* No. 2, 1941.

21. N. W. Kettner, J. P. Guilford, and P. R. Christensen, "A Factor-Analytic Study Across the Domains of Reasoning, Creativity, and Evaluation," *Psychol. Monogr.,* 1959, No. 8.

22. C. M. Cox, *Genetic Studies of Genius.* Stanford University Press, 1926.

23. *Ibid.*

24. E. G. Boring (Ed.), *Psychology for the Armed Services.* Infantry Journal Press, 1945, p. 227.

25. P. Frank, *Einstein: His Life and Times.* Knopf, 1947, p. 8.

26. L. M. Terman and M. H. Oden, *The Gifted Child Grows Up,* Stanford University Press, 1947. The intermediate report is *The Promise of Youth,* by B. S. Burks, D. W. Jensen, and L. M. Terman, also published by the Stanford University Press. Later reports are: L. M. Terman and M. H. Oden, in P. Witty (Ed.), *The Gifted Child,* Heath, 1951; L. M. Terman, "Scientists and Non-Scientists in a Group of 800 Gifted Men," *Psychol. Monogr.,* 1954, *68,* No. 7; and L. M. Terman, "The Discovery and Encouragement of Exceptional Talent," *American Psychologist,* 1954, *9,* 221–230.

27. L. M. Terman, "The Discovery and Encouragement of Exceptional Talent," *American Psychologist,* 1954, *9,* 221–230.

28. *Science News Letter,* January 12, 1952.

29. P. A. Witty and M. D. Jenkins, "The Case of 'B____' A Gifted Negro Girl," *J. Soc. Psychol.,* 1935, *6,* 117–124.

30. L. S. Hollingworth, *Children above 180 I.Q.* World Book Co., 1942, pp. 300–302.

31. Ruth Strang, "Psychology of Gifted Children and Youth," in W. M. Cruickshank, *Psychology of Exceptional Children and Youth.* Prentice-Hall, 1955, pp. 477–478.

32. See D. B. Tower, "Neurochemical Substrates of Cerebral Function and Activity," in H. F. Harlow and C. N. Woolsey (Eds.), *Biological and Biochemical Bases of Behavior.* University of Wisconsin Press, 1959, p. 351. A pamphlet published by the U. S. Department of Health, Education, and Welfare in 1963, entitled *Phenylketonuria,* describes diagnosis, corrective diets, etc. The authors are W. R. and S. A. Centerwall.

33. Boring, *op. cit.,* reference 24, p. 228.

34. For the experiences of a mother with a feeble-minded child and her reasons for placing the child in an institution, see P. Buck, *The Child Who Never Grew,* John Day, 1950.

35. See N. Bayley, "On the Growth of Intelligence," *American Psychologist,* 1955, *10,* 805–818, and the earlier studies cited there.

36. L. W. Sontag, C. T. Baker, and V. L. Nelson, "Mental Growth and Personality Development," *Monogr. Soc. Res. Child Develpm.,* 1958, *23,* No. 2.

37. Bayley, *op. cit.,* reference 35, p. 814.

38. Bayley, *ibid.*, p. 815.

39. Sontag *et al., op. cit.,* reference 36, p. 23.

40. K. W. Schaie, "Rigidity-Flexibility and Intelligence: A Cross-Sectional Study of the Adult Life Span," *Psychol. Monogr.,* 1958, 72, No. 9.

41. See especially, C. Fox and J. E. Birren, "The Differential Decline of Subtest Scores of the Wechsler-Bellevue Intelligence Scale in 60–69-Year-Old Individuals," *J. Genet. Psychol.,* 1950, 77, 313–317; and D. Wechsler, *The Measurement and Appraisal of Adult Intelligence* (4th ed.), Williams and Wilkins, 1958, Chapter 9.

42. See the following references: L. R. Wheeler, "The Intelligence of East Tennessee Mountain Children," *J. Educ. Psychol.,* 1932, 23, 351–370. The later study, showing a 10-point rise in I.Q., is L. R. Wheeler, "A Comparative Study of the Intelligence of East Tennessee Mountain Children," *J. Educ. Psychol.,* 1942, 33, 321–334. M. Sherman and C. B. Key, "The Intelligence of Isolated Mountain Children," *Child Develpm.,* 1932, 3, 279–290. A. S. Edwards and L. Jones, "An Experimental and Field Study of North Georgia Mountaineers," *J. Soc. Psychol.,* 1938, 9, 317–333. The canal boat and gypsy children were studied by H. Gordon. A résumé of these and other relevant studies appears in W. L. Valentine and D. D. Wickens, *Experimental Foundations of General Psychology,* Rinehart, 1949, pp. 135–143.

43. For a summary of the studies on rural-urban comparisons, see L. E. Tyler, *The Psychology of Human Differences* (2nd ed.). Appleton-Century-Crofts, 1956, pp. 327–333.

44. Q. McNemar, *The Revision of the Stanford-Binet Scale.* Houghton Mifflin, 1942, p. 38; W. S. Neff, "Socio-economic Status and Intelligence: A Critical Survey," *Psychol. Bull.,* 1938, 35, 727–757.

45. B. S. Burks, "The Relative Influence of Nature and Nurture Upon Mental Development: A Comparative Study of Foster Parent-Foster Child Resemblance and True Parent-Child Resemblance," *27th Yearbook, Nat. Soc. Stud. Educ.,* 1928, Part I, pp. 219–316. Abbreviated in Barker *et al., Child Behavior and Development,* McGraw-Hill, 1943, pp. 245–257. A M. Leahy, "Nature-Nurture and Intelligence," *Genet. Psychol. Monogr.,* 1935, 17, 235–308.

46. H. E. Jones, "The Environment and Mental Development," in L. Carmichael (Ed.), *Manual of Child Psychology* (2nd ed.). Wiley, 1954, p. 685.

47. See reference 45.

48. The figures given are based upon data in T. R. Garth, *Race Psychology,* McGraw-Hill, 1931, Chapter 5.

49. O. Klineberg (Ed.), *Characteristics of the American Negro.* Harper, 1944.

50. B. E. Fulk and T. W. Harrell, "Negro-White Army Test Scores and Last School Grade," *J. Appl. Psychol.,* 1952, 36, 34–35.

51. J. B. Miner, *Intelligence in the United States.* Springer, 1957.

52. F. L. Goodenough, "Racial Differences in Intelligence of School Children," *J. Exper. Psychol.,* 1926, 9, 388–397.

53. A. Anastasi and R. Y. D'Angelo, "A Comparison of Negro and White Preschool Children in Language Development and Goodenough Draw-a-Man I.Q.," *J. Genet. Psychol.,* 1952, 81, 147–165.

54. Miner, *op. cit.,* reference 51, p. 75.

55. E. S. Lee, "Negro Intelligence and Selective Migration," *Amer. Sociol. Rev.,* 1951, 16, 227–233.

56. Anastasi and D'Angelo, *op. cit.,* reference 53, pp. 148–149.

57. J. B. Miner, *Intelligence in the United States.* Springer, 1957, pp. 77–78.

58. Garth, *op. cit.,* reference 48, Chapter 5.

59. T. R. Garth, "A Study of the Foster Indian Children in the White Home," *Psychol. Bull.,* 1935, 32, 708–709.

60. J. H. Rohrer, "The Test Intelligence of Osage Indians," *J. Soc. Psychol.,* 1942, 16, 99–105.

Chapter 6

Motivation

1. S. Freud, *An Outline of Psychoanalysis.* Norton, 1949, p. 14.

2. M. J. Moskowitz, "Running-Wheel Activity in the White Rat as a Function of Combined Food and Water Deprivation," *J. Comp. Physiol. Psychol.,* 1959, 52, 621–625. Similar results with the running wheel have since been reported by F. R. Treichler and J. F. Hall, "The Relationship Between Deprivation Weight Loss and Several Measures of Activity," *J. Comp. Physiol. Psychol.,* 1962, 55, 346–349. Other devices (stabilimeter and open-alley maze) did not show such a relationship.

3. R. W. Greene, unpublished thesis, cited in Moskowitz, *op. cit.*

4. First described by G. H. Wang, "Relation be-

tween 'Spontaneous' Activity and Oestrus Cycle in the White Rat," *Comp. Psychol. Monogr.,* 1923, 2, No. 6.

5. E. F. Kinder, "A Study of the Nest-Building Activity of the Albino Rat," *J. Exper. Zool.,* 1927, 47, 117–161.

6. M. Sturman-Hulbe and C. P. Stone, "Maternal Behavior in the Albino Rat," *J. Comp. Psychol.,* 1929, 9, 203–237. Also see the studies on nest-building reported in H. L. Rheingold (Ed.), *Maternal Behavior in Mammals,* Wiley, 1963.

7. See E. J. Van Liere, *Anoxia,* University of Chicago Press, 1942, p. 106. A summary of the early studies of high altitude effects may be found in H. G. Armstrong, *Principles and Practice of Aviation Medicine,* Williams and Wilkins, 1939, pp. 1–5. For a brief discussion of research on effects of oxygen want, see R. A. McFarland, "The Psycho-Physiological Effects of Reduced Oxygen Pressure," Chapter VI in *The Interrelationship of Mind and Body,* Williams and Wilkins, 1939. J. R. Ullman, *Kingdom of Adventure: Everest,* Sloane, 1947, has many first-hand reports on the effects of high altitude upon the psychological processes of climbers. Some interesting experiments on adaptation of animals to carbon dioxide conditions and anoxia have been reported by Peter van Sommers, "Carbon Dioxide Escape and Avoidance Behavior in the Brown Rat," *J. Comp. Physiol. Psychol.,* 1963, 56, 584–589; and "Air-Motivated Behavior in the Turtle," *J. Comp. Physiol. Psychol.,* 1963, 56, 590–596. In both experiments the animals learned to manipulate the device so as to regain near-normal respiratory conditions.

8. Fredericq, quoted by W. B. Cannon, *The Wisdom of the Body,* Norton, 1932, p. 21.

9. *Science News Letter,* September 22, 1956, p. 180.

10. F. A. Beach, "Characteristics of Masculine 'Sex Drive,'" *Nebraska Symposium on Motivation* (Marshall R. Jones, Ed.), 1956, p. 4.

11. See E. W. Dempsey, "Homeostasis," in S. S. Stevens, *Handbook of Experimental Psychology,* Wiley, 1951; and the critical review of homeostatic concepts by J. R. Maze, "On Some Corruptions of the Doctrine of Homeostasis," *Psychol. Rev.,* 1953, 60, 405–412.

12. See S. Freud, *Three Contributions to the Theory of Sex,* as reprinted in A. A. Brill (Ed.), *The Basic Writings of Sigmund Freud,* Modern Library, 1938, pp. 610–612.

13. Clark L. Hull, *Principles of Behavior,* Appleton-Century-Crofts, 1943, p. 252.

14. A. Amsel, "A Combination of Primary Appetitional Need with Primary and Secondary Emotionally Derived Needs," *J. Exper. Psychol.,* 1950, 40, 1–14.

15. See especially W. B. Webb, "The Motivational Aspect of an Irrelevant Drive in the Behavior of the White Rat," *J. Exper. Psychol.,* 1949, 39, 1–14; C. M. Brandauer, "A Confirmation of Webb's Data Concerning the Action of Irrelevant Drives," *J. Exper. Psychol.,* 1953, 45, 150–152; W. S. Verplanck and J. R. Hayes, "Eating and Drinking as a Function of Maintenance Schedule," *J. Comp. Physiol. Psychol.,* 1953, 46, 327–333; G. R. Grice and J. D. Davis, "Effect of Irrelevant Thirst Motivation on a Response Learned with Food Reward," *J. Exper. Psychol.,* 1957, 53, 347–352.

16. K. S. Lashley, "Physiological Analysis of the Libido," *Psychol. Rev.,* 1924, 31, 196–197.

17. F. A. Beach, "Characteristics of the Masculine 'Sex Drive,'" *Nebraska Symposium on Motivation* (Marshall R. Jones, Ed.), 1956, p. 21.

18. L. Carmichael, *Basic Psychology.* Random House, 1957, p. 1956.

19. These studies were carried out by a European group of investigators (Lorenz, Tinbergen, and others) who call themselves "ethologists." See especially N. Tinbergen, *The Study of Instinct,* Oxford University Press, 1951.

20. On the reticular formation in relation to motivation, see D. B. Lindsley, "Psychophysiology and Motivation," in *Nebraska Symposium on Motivation* (Marshall R. Jones, Ed.), 1957, 44–105; H. W. Magoun, *The Waking Brain* (2nd ed.), Thomas, 1963; G. Moruzzi and H. W. Magoun, "Brain Stem Reticular Formation and Activation of the EEG," *EEG Clin. Neurophysiol.,* 1949, 1, 455–473; J. D. French and H. W. Magoun, "Effects of Chronic Lesions in Central Cephalic Brain Stem of Monkeys," *Arch. Neurol. Psychiat.,* 1952, 68, 591–604; D. B. Lindsley, L. H. Schreiner, W. B. Knowles, and H. W. Magoun, "Behavioral and EEG Changes following Chronic Brain Stem Lesions in the Cat," *EEG Clin. Neurophysiol.,* 1950, 2, 483–498; J. D. French, R. Hernández-Peón, and R. B. Livingston, "Projections from Cortex to Cephalic Brain Stem (Reticular Formation) in Monkey," *J. Neurophysiol.,* 1955, 18, 74–95; H. H. Jasper et al., *Reticular Formation of the Brain,* Little, Brown, 1958, has thirty-seven

articles dealing with various aspects of reticular functions.

21. On monkeys and porpoises, see J. C. Lilly, "Some Considerations Regarding Basic Mechanisms of Positive and Negative Types of Motivations," *Amer. J. Psychiat.*, 1958, *115*, 498–504. Numerous other studies on a variety of animals are reported in D. E. Sheer (Ed.), *Electrical Stimulation of the Brain,* University of Texas Press, 1961.

22. J. Olds, "Physiological Mechanisms of Reward," *Nebraska Symposium on Motivation* (Marshall R. Jones, Ed.), 1955, 73–139. For the original study, see J. Olds and P. Milner, "Positive Reinforcement Produced by Electrical Stimulation of the Septal Area and Other Regions of Rat Brain," *J. Comp. Physiol. Psychol.,* 1954, *47*, 419–427. A popular account appears in an article by Olds in *Scientific American,* October 1956, *193*, 105–116. Also see J. Olds, "Self-Stimulation of the Brain," *Science,* 1958, *127*, 315–324; and M. E. Olds and J. Olds, "Approach-Avoidance Analysis of Rat Diencephalon," *J. Comp. Neurol.,* 1963, *120, 259–295.*

23. See the experiments on dogs and monkeys reported in Sheer, *op. cit.,* reference 21.

24. The maze-learning study referred to in the text is reported in J. Olds, "Runway and Maze Behavior Controlled by Basomedial Forebrain Stimulation in the Rat," *J. Comp. Physiol. Psychol.,* 1956, *49*, 507–512. Brightness discrimination has also been learned with hypothalamic stimulation as reward. See R. E. Keesey, "Intracranial Reward Delay and the Acquisition Rate of a Brightness Discrimination," *Science,* 1964, *143, 702–703.*

25. See Olds and Milner, *op. cit.,* reference 22.

26. For these studies on human subjects, see R. R. Monroe, R. G. Heath, *et al., Studies in Schizophrenia,* Harvard University Press, 1954; M. A. B. Brazier (Ed.), *The Central Nervous System and Behavior,* Josiah Macy, Jr. Foundation, 1959, pp. 272–274; and M. P. Bishop, S. T. Elder, R. G. Heath, "Intracranial Self-Stimulation in Man," *Science,* 1963, *140*, 394–396.

27. B. G. Hoebel and P. Teitelbaum, "Hypothalamic Control of Feeding and Self-Stimulation," *Science,* 1962, *135*, 375–376.

28. D. L. Margules and J. Olds, "Identical 'Feeding' and 'Rewarding' Systems in the Lateral Hypothalamus of Rats," *Science,* 1962, *135*, 374–375.

29. Y. C. Tsang, "Hunger Motivation in Gastrectomized Rats," *J. Comp. Psychol.,* 1938, *26*, 1–17. See also K. W. Bash, "An Investigation into a Possible Organic Basis for the Hunger Drive," *J. Comp. Psychol.,* 1939, *28*, 137–160; and C. T. Morgan and J. D. Morgan, "Studies in Hunger. II. The Relation of Gastric Denervation and Dietary Sugar to the Effect of Insulin upon Food-intake in the Rat," *J. Genet. Psychol.,* 1940, *57*, 153–163.

30. J. P. Quigley, V. Johnson, and E. I. Solomon, "Action of Insulin on the Motility of the Gastrointestinal Tract," *Amer. J. Physiol.,* 1929, *90*, 89–98.

31. A. B. Luckhardt and A. J. Carlson, "Contributions to the Physiology of the Stomach. XVII. On the Chemical Control of the Gastric Hunger Mechanism," *Amer. J. Physiol.,* 1915, *36*, 37–46; R. D. Templeton and J. P. Quigley, "The Action of Insulin on Motility of the Gastrointestinal Tract. II."

32. C. T. Morgan, *Physiological Psychology* (3rd ed.). McGraw-Hill, 1965, pp. 375–376.

33. J. R. Brobeck, "Mechanisms of the Development of Obesity in Animals with Hypothalamic Lesions," *Phys. Rev.,* 1946, *26*, 541; N. E. Miller, "Experiments on Motivation," *Science,* 1957, *126*, 1271; J. Mayer, "Appetite and Obesity," *Scientific American,* November 1956, 108–116.

34. N. E. Miller, C. J. Bailey, and J. A. F. Stevenson, "Decreased 'Hunger' but Increased Food Intake Resulting from Hypothalamic Lesions," *Science,* 1950, *12, 256–259.*

35. See Miller, *op. cit.,* reference 33, p. 1272.

36. See reference 28.

37. See reference 27.

38. N. E. Miller and M. L. Kessen, "Reward Effects of Food via Stomach Fistula Compared with Those of Food via Mouth," *J. Comp. Physiol. Psychol.,* 1952, *45*, 555–564.

39. N. E. Miller, "Shortcomings of Food Consumption as a Measure of Hunger; Results from Other Behavioral Techniques," *Ann. N. Y. Acad. Sci.,* 1955, *63*, 141–143.

40. N. E. Miller, "Experiments on Motivation," *Science,* 1957, *126*, 1273–1274.

41. M. Kohn, "Satiation of Hunger from Food Injected Directly into the Stomach versus Food Ingested by Mouth," *J. Comp. Physiol. Psychol.,* 1951, *44*, 412–422; M. M. Berkun, M. L. Kessen, and N. E. Miller, "Hunger-Reducing Effects of Food by Stomach Fistula versus Food

by Mouth Measured by a Consummatory Response," *J. Comp. Physiol. Psychol.*, 1952, *45*, 550–554.

42. Miller, *op. cit.*, reference 40, p. 1273.

43. On this, see C. Pfaffmann, "The Pleasures of Sensation," *Psychol. Rev.*, 1960, *67*, 253–268, and the references cited by him.

44. B. Barelare and C. P. Richter, "Increased Sodium Chloride Appetite in Pregnant Rats," *Amer. J. Physiol.*, 1938, *121*, 185–188.

45. C. P. Richter and J. F. Eckert, "Mineral Metabolism of Adrenalectomized Rats Studied by the Appetite Method," *Endocrinology*, 1939, *22*, 214–224.

46. See P. T. Young, "Food Preferences and the Regulation of Eating," *J. Comp. Psychol.*, 1933, *15*, 167–176; and C. P. Richter, L. E. Holt, and B. Barelare, "Nutritional Requirements for Normal Growth and Reproduction in Rats Studied by the Self-Selection Method," *Amer. J. Physiol.*, 1938, *122*, 734–744.

47. C. M. Davis, "Self-Selection of Diet by Newly Weaned Infants," *Amer. J. Dis. Children*, 1928, *36*, 651–679; and, by the same author, "Results of Self-Selection of Diets by Young Children," *Canad. Med. Journal*, 1939, *41*, 257–261.

48. On food preferences and related processes, see P. T. Young, *Motivation and Emotion*, Wiley, 1961, pp. 156–166; and "The Role of Hedonic Processes in Motivation," *Nebraska Symposium on Motivation* (Marshall R. Jones, Ed.), 1955, especially pp. 204–232. On selection of Vitamin B_1 see especially C. P. Richter, L. E. Holt, and B. Barelare, "Vitamin B_1 Craving in Rats," *Science*, 1937, *86*, 354–355.

49. N. E. Miller, "Experiments on Motivation," *Science*, 1957, *126*, 1273.

50. A. Keys, J. Brozek, *et al.*, *The Biology of Human Starvation. University of Minnesota Press*, 1950.

51. H. S. Guetzkow and P. H. Bowman, *Men and Hunger: A Psychological Manual for Relief Workers*. Brethren Publishing House, 1946, p. 32.

52. *Ibid.*

53. W. B. Cannon, "Hunger and Thirst," in C. Murchison (Ed.), *A Handbook of General Experimental Psychology*. Clark University Press, 1934.

54. E. F. Adolph, "The Internal Environment and Behavior: Water Content," *Amer. J. Psychiat.*, 1941, *6*, 1365–1373; also see, by the same author, *Physiological Regulations*, Cattell, 1943.

55. A. V. Wolf, *Thirst*. Thomas, 1958. Also, by the same author, "Thirst," *Scientific American*, January 1956, pp. 70–76. For a review of the large amount of recent research on the psychophysiology of thirst, see L. I. O'Kelly, "The Psychophysiology of Motivation," in *Annual Review of Psychology*, Annual Reviews, Inc., 1963. The neural and glandular bases of thirst are not yet known, in detail; but our brief general statement seems warranted by the information available at present.

56. See the discussion in E. G. Walsh, *Physiology of the Nervous System*, Longmans, 1957, pp. 450–452.

57. B. Andersson and S. M. McCann, "A Further Study of Polydipsia Evoked by Hypothalamic Stimulation in the Goat," *Acta Physiol. Scand.*, 1955, *33*, 333–346. Reproduced in D. E. Dulany, R. L. DeValois, D. C. Beardslee, and M. R. Winterbottom, *Contributions to Modern Psychology*, Oxford University Press, 1958, pp. 236–239.

58. Research in N. E. Miller's laboratory, as reported by him in D. E. Sheer (Ed.), *Electrical Stimulation of the Brain: Subcortical Integrative Systems*, University of Texas, 1957, and cited in reference 49, p. 1275.

59. Miller, *op. cit.*, reference 49, p. 1275.

60. Andersson and McCann, *op. cit.*, reference 57.

61. B. Andersson and S. M. McCann, "The Effect of Hypothalamic Lesions on the Water Intake of the Dog," *Acta Physiol. Scand.*, 1956, *35*, 312–320. Also reproduced in Dulany *et al.*, *op. cit.*, reference 57.

62. C. P. Stone, "Sex Drive," in E. A. Allen (Ed.), *Sex and Internal Secretions* (2nd ed.). Williams and Wilkins, 1939.

63. F. A. Beach, "Importance of Progesterone to Induction of Sexual Receptivity in Spayed Female Rats," *Proc. Soc. Exper. Biol. and Med.*, 1942, *51*, 369–371.

64. For nontechnical discussions on ACTH, Cortisone, and related pituitary functions, see the articles by G. W. Gray and C. H. Li in *Scientific American Reader*, Simon and Schuster, 1953.

65. A. C. Kinsey *et al.*, *Sexual Behavior in the Human Female*. Saunders, 1953.

66. See especially the discussion of human gonadal functions, in R. G. Hoskins, *Endocrinology*, Norton, 1941.

67. For these and other sexual anomalies, see K.

Menninger, *The Human Mind* (3rd rev. ed.), Knopf, 1948.

68. A. C. Kinsey, W. B. Pomeroy, and C. E. Martin, *Sexual Behavior in the Human Male*. Saunders, 1948, Chapter 6.

69. F. M. Teagarden, *Child Psychology for Professional Workers* (rev. ed.), Prentice-Hall, 1946, has a good discussion of such perversions and how they develop.

70. C. P. Stone, "The Congenital Sexual Behavior of the Young Male Albino Rat," *J. Comp. Psychol.*, 1922, 2, 95–153; "The Awakening of Copulatory Ability in Male Albino Rats," *Amer. J. Physiol.*, 1924, 68, 407–424; "The Initial Copulatory Response of Female Rats Reared in Isolation from the Age of 20 Days to Puberty," *J. Comp. Psychol.*, 1926, 6, 73–83. Verification of Stone's observations is contained in studies by F. A. Beach, "Comparison of Copulatory Behavior of Male Rats Raised in Isolation, Cohabitation, and Segregation," *J. Genet. Psychol,* 1942, 69, 121–136.

71. H. W. Nissen, "Instinct as Seen by a Psychologist," *Psychol. Rev.*, 1953, 60, 291–294; also, H. C. Bingham, "Sex Development in Apes," *Comp. Psychol. Monogr.*, 1928, 165, No. 23. On the transition from stereotyped to varied sexual behavior and its relation to brain development, see F. A. Beach, "Central Nervous Mechanisms Involved in the Reproductive Behavior of Vertebrates," *Psychol. Bull.*, 1942, 39, 200–226.

72. C. S. Ford and F. A. Beach, *Patterns of Sexual Behavior*. Harper, 1951.

73. See B. P. Weisner and N. M. Sheard, *Maternal Behavior in the Rat*, Oliver and Boyd, 1933; also the studies reported in H. L. Rheingold, *Maternal Behavior in Mammals*, Wiley, 1963.

74. M. Ribble, *The Rights of Infants*. Columbia University Press, 1943.

75. Ashley Montagu, in a lecture at Springfield College, October 1958.

76. See *The New York Times Magazine*, April 3, 1960, pp. 90–94, for an illustrated discussion of the Mt. Sinai Hospital "mother bank."

77. L. J. Stone and J. Church, *Childhood and Adolescence*. Random House, 1957, p. 65.

78. See the review by H. Orlansky, "Infant Care and Personality," *Psychol. Bull.*, 1949, 46, 1–48; and S. R. Pinneau, "The Infantile Disorders of Hospitalism and Anaclitic Depression," *Psychol. Bull.*, 1955, 52, 429–452. Also see W.

Dennis and M. G. Dennis, "The Effect of Restricted Practice upon the Reaching, Sitting, and Standing of Two Infants," *J. Genet. Psychol.*, 1935, 47, 17–32.

79. H. F. Harlow, "The Nature of Love," *American Psychologist*, 1958, 13, 673–685. H. F. Harlow, "Love in Infant Monkeys," *Scientific American*, June 1959, 68–74. H. F. Harlow and R. R. Zimmermann, "Affectional Responses in Infant Monkeys," *Science*, 1959, 130, 421–432. H. F. Harlow, M. K. Harlow, and E. W. Hansen, "The Maternal Affectional System of Rhesus Monkeys," Chapter 8 in Rheingold, *op. cit.*, reference 73.

80. W. H. Bexton, W. Heron, and T. H. Scott, "Effects of Decreased Variation in the Sensory Environment," *Canad. J. Psychol.*, 1954, 8, 70–76, quotation from pp. 71–72. Also reproduced in Dulany *et al., op. cit.*, reference 57. A popular account appears in W. H. Heron, "The Pathology of Boredom," *Scientific American*, January 1957.

81. Bexton, Heron, and Scott, *op. cit.*, p. 76.

82. J. C. Lilly, "Mental Effects of Reduction of Ordinary Levels of Physical Stimuli on Intact, Healthy Persons," *Psychiat. Res. Reports*, 1956, No. 5, 1–28. Also relevant are: P. Solomon *et al., Sensory Deprivation*, Harvard University Press, 1961; and J. Vernon, *Inside the Black Room*, Clarkson N. Potter, 1963.

83. D. E. Berlyne, "The Arousal and Satiation of Perceptual Curiosity in the Rat," *J. Comp. Physiol. Psychol.*, 1955, 48, 238–246.

84. L. Festinger, "Motivations Leading to Social Behavior," in *Nebraska Symposium on Motivation* (Marshall R. Jones, Ed.), 1954, 193.

85. Berlyne, *op. cit.*, reference 83.

86. K. C. Montgomery and M. Segall, "Discrimination Learning Based Upon the Exploratory Drive," *J. Comp. Physiol. Psychol.*, 1955, 48, 225–228.

87. G. B. Kish, "Learning When the Onset of Illumination Is Used as Reinforcing Stimulus," *J. Comp. Physiol. Psychol.*, 1955, 48, 261–264.

88. G. B. Kish and J. J. Antonitis, "Unconditioned Operant Behavior in Two Homozygous Strains of Mice," *J. Genet. Psychol.*, 1956, 88, 121–129.

89. R. A. Butler and H. F. Harlow, "Persistence of Visual Exploration in Monkeys," *J. Comp. Physiol. Psychol.*, 1954, 47, 258–263.

90. H. F. Harlow, "Motivation as a Factor in the Acquisition of New Responses," *Current*

Theory and Research in Motivation, University of Nebraska, 1953, pp. 24–49. Also see H. F. Harlow and G. E. McClearn, "Object Discrimination Learned by Monkeys on the Basis of Manipulation Motives," *J. Comp. Physiol. Psychol.,* 1954, *47,* 73–76.

91. H. W. Nissen, "The Nature of the Drive as Innate Determinant of Behavioral Organization," *Nebraska Symposium on Motivation* (Marshall R. Jones, Ed.), 1954, 305. (Based on Welker's study; see reference 92.)

92. W. I. Welker, "Some Determinants of Play and Exploration in Chimpanzees," *J. Comp. Physiol. Psychol.,* 1956, *49,* 84–89.

93. Festinger, *op. cit.,* reference 84, p. 193.

94. See S. Schachter, *The Psychology of Affiliation.* Stanford University Press, 1959.

95. S. Smith and E. R. Guthrie, *General Psychology in Terms of Behavior.* Appleton-Century-Crofts, 1928, p. 238. For an example of "universal" learned behavior in rats, see N. L. Munn, *The Evolution and Growth of Human Behavior* (2nd ed.), Houghton Mifflin, 1965, p. 50.

96. Several coenotropes are listed in Warren and Carmichael's *Elements of Human Psychology,* Houghton Mifflin, 1930, p. 396, as examples of "human instinctive responses."

97. On this point, see D. C. McClelland, "Some Social Consequences of Achievement Motivation," in *Nebraska Symposium on Motivation* (Marshall R. Jones, Ed.), 1955, 41–69; and M. R. Winterbottom, "The Relation of Need for Achievement to Learning Experiences in Independence and Mastery," in J. W. Atkinson (Ed.), *Motives in Fantasy, Action, and Society,* Van Nostrand, 1958, Chapter 33.

98. See "Sex and Temperament," in Margaret Mead, *From the South Seas.* Morrow, 1939.

99. Quoted from M. Mead, *From the South Seas,* Morrow, 1939, pp. 167, 196–197.

100. An excellent review of the earlier work on level of aspiration is to be found in J. McV. Hunt, *Personality and the Behavior Disorders,* Ronald, 1944, Chapter 10. The chapter was written by Lewin, Dembo, Festinger, and Pauline S. Sears.

101. I. L. Child and J. W. M. Whiting, "Determinants of Level of Aspiration: Evidence from Everyday Life," *J. Abn. Soc. Psychol.,* 1949, *44,* 303–314.

102. See M. Sherif and H. Cantril, *The Psychology of Ego-Involvements,* Wiley, 1948.

103. For a review of earlier studies and the report of an extensive investigation with children, see B. Kutner, "Patterns of Mental Functioning Associated with Prejudice in Children," *Psychol. Monogr.,* 1958, *72,* No. 7. The anecdote about the child appears on page 45.

104. L. L. Thurstone and E. J. Chave, *The Measurement of Attitudes: A Psychophysical Method and Some Experiments with a Scale for Measuring Attitude Toward the Church.* University of Chicago Press, 1929.

105. D. D. Droba, *A Scale for Measuring Attitude Toward War.* University of Chicago Press, 1930.

106. J. W. Getzels and J. J. Walsh, "The Method of Paired Direct and Projective Questionnaires in the Study of Attitude Structure and Socialization," *Psychol. Monogr.,* 1958, *72,* No. 1.

107. *Ibid.,* p. 8.

108. Getzels and Walsh, *op. cit.,* pp. 15–30.

109. G. W. Allport, "The Functional Autonomy of Motives," *Amer. J. Psychol.,* 1937, *50,* 141–145; reprinted in G. W. Allport, *The Nature of Personality: Collected Papers,* Addison-Wesley Press, 1950, p. 78.

110. See Allport, *op. cit.,* reference 109, 1950, p. 91.

111. W. James, *The Principles of Psychology.* Holt, 1890, Vol. 1, p. 121.

Chapter 7

Feeling and Emotion

1. R. S. Woodworth and H. Schlosberg, *Experimental Psychology* (rev. ed.). Holt, 1954, p. 108.

2. E. Duffy, "Leeper's Motivational Theory of Emotion," *Psychol. Rev.,* 1948, *55,* 324–328. Also see Duffy's *Activation and Behavior,* Wiley, 1962.

3. Helen Nowlis, as reported by V. Nowlis, "The Development and Modification of Motivation Systems in Personality," in *Current Theory and Research in Motivation,* University of Nebraska, 1953, p. 127.

4. W. B. Webb, "A Motivational Theory of Emotions," *Psychol. Rev.,* 1948, *55,* 329–335.

5. W. A. Hunt, "The Reliability of Introspection in Emotion," *Amer. J. Psychol.,* 1937, *49,* 650–653.

6. Also see H. Schlosberg, "The Description of Facial Expressions in Terms of Two Dimensions" *J. Exper. Psychol.,* 1952, *44,* 229–237.

7. C. Darwin, *The Expression of the Emotions in Man and Animals*. Appleton, 1873. A new edition (with an introduction by Konrad Lorenz) was published by the University of Chicago Press in 1965.

8. R. W. Leeper, "A Motivational Theory of Emotion to Replace 'Emotion as Disorganized Response,' " *Psychol. Rev.*, 1948, *55*, 19.

9. W. B. Cannon, *Bodily Changes in Pain, Hunger, Fear and Rage* (2nd ed.). Appleton, 1929.

10. Cannon, *ibid*. On the effects of injecting adrenalin, see H. Cantril and W. A. Hunt, "Emotional Effects Produced by the Injection of Adrenalin," *Amer. J. Psychol.*, 1932, *44*, 300–307.

11. T. T. Gilman, F. L. Marcuse, and A. V. Moore, "Animal Hypnosis," *J. Comp. Physiol. Psychol.*, 1950, 99–111, and the references there cited; Hartman's article, "Playing Possum," *Scientific American*, January 1950, pp. 52–55, is also relevant.

12. See, for example, G. W. Hartmann, "A Field Experiment on the Comparative Effectiveness of 'Emotional' and 'Rational' Political Leaflets in Determining Election Results," *J. Abn. Soc. Psychol.*, 1936, 99–114. The chapter entitled "Emotions" in Minnick's *The Art of Persuasion* (Houghton Mifflin, 1957) has some interesting examples.

13. S. Freud, *Outline of Psychoanalysis*. Norton, 1949, pp. 16–17.

14. See D. C. McClelland, *Personality*. Dryden, 1951.

15. *Ibid.*, p. 466.

16. *Ibid.*, p. 466.

17. *Ibid.*, p. 467.

18. T. R. Garth, *Race Psychology*, McGraw-Hill, 1931, has a good discussion on color preferences of different racial groups; also see J. P. Guilford, *General Psychology*, Van Nostrand, 1939, p. 327. See also the rest of Guilford's discussion on affective value; and P. T. Young, *Motivation and Emotion*, Wiley, 1961, Chapter 5.

19. P. R. Farnsworth and H. Beaumont, "Suggestion in Pictures," *J. Gen. Psychol.*, 1929, *2*, 362–363; also M. Sherif, "An Experimental Study of Stereotypes," *J. Abn. Soc. Psychol.*, 1935, *29*, 371–375. Also see the comment by I. A. Richards, *Practical Criticism*, Harcourt, Brace, 1936, pp. 315–316.

20. H. Cason, "Common Annoyances: A Psychological Study of Everyday Aversions and Irritations," *Psychol. Monogr.*, 1930, No. 182; and

J. E. Moore, "Annoying Habits of College Professors," *J. Abn. Soc. Psychol.*, 1935, *30*, 43–46.

21. L. F. Shaffer, "Fear and Courage in Aerial Combat," *J. Consult. Psychol.*, 1947, *11*, 137–143. Also see E. G. Boring, *Psychology for the Armed Services*, Infantry Journal Press, 1946, p. 384.

22. S. A. Stouffer *et al.*, *Measurement and Prediction*, Vol. 4. Princeton University Press, 1950, pp. 140–142.

23. C. W. Darrow, "Quantitative Records of Cutaneous Secretory Reactions," *J. Gen. Psychol.*, 1934, *11*, 445–448.

24. J. E. Reid, and F. E. Inbau, *Lie Detection*. Williams and Wilkins, 1964.

25. W. E. Blatz, "The Cardiac, Respiratory, and Electrical Phenomena Involved in the Emotion of Fear," *J. Exper. Psychol.*, 1925, *8*, 109–132.

26. D. B. Lindsley, "Emotion and the Electroencephalogram," in M. L. Reymert (Ed.), *Feeling and Emotion* (The Second International Symposium). McGraw-Hill, 1950.

27. R. D. McDonald and K. Yagi, "A Note on Eosinopenia as an Index of Psychological Stress," *Psychosomat. Med.*, 1960, *22*, 149.

28. H. Basowitz, H. Persky, S. J. Korchin, and R. R. Grinker, *Anxiety and Stress*. McGraw-Hill, 1955.

29. M. M. Berkun, H. M. Bialek, R. P. Kern, and K. Yagi, "Experimental Studies of Psychological Stress in Man," *Psychol. Monogr.* 1962, *76*, No. 15.

30. R. D. McDonald, K. Yagi, and E. Stockton, "Human Eosinophil Response to Acute Physical Exertion," *Psychosomat. Med.*, 1961, *23*, 63.

31. Berkun *et al.*, *op. cit.*, p. 31.

32. Berkun, *et al.*, *op. cit.*, pp. 30–31.

33. For a general discussion of this relationship and a summary of the literature, see H. S. McCurdy, "Consciousness and the Galvanometer," *Psychol. Rev.*, 1950, *57*, 322–327.

34. D. W. Dysinger, "A Comparative Study of Affective Responses by Means of the Impressive and Expressive Methods," *Psychol. Monogr.*, 1931, *41*, 14–31.

35. F. H. Lund, *Emotions*. Ronald, 1939, pp. 195–198.

36. S. Wolf and H. G. Wolff, "Evidence of the Genesis of Peptic Ulcer in Man," in S. S. Tomkins, *Contemporary Psychopathology*. Harvard University Press, 1943.

37. A. F. Ax, "The Physiological Differentiation be-

tween Fear and Anger In Humans," *Psychosomat. Med.*, 1953, *15*, No. 5.

38. D. H. Funkenstein, S. H. King, and M. E. Drolette, *Mastery of Stress.* Harvard University Press, 1957.

39. H. Cantril and W. A. Hunt, "Emotional Effects Produced by Injection of Adrenalin," *Amer. J. Psychol.*, 1932, *44*, 300–307.

40. S. Schachter and J. E. Singer, "Cognitive, Social, and Physiological Determinants of Emotional State," *Psychol. Rev.*, 1962, *69*, 379–399.

41. See W. James, "What is an Emotion?" *Mind*, 1884, *9*, 189–193; "The Physical Basis of the Emotions," *Psychol. Rev.*, *1*, 516–529.

42. P. Bard, "A Diencephalic Mechanism for the Sympathetic Nervous System," *Amer. J. Physiol.*, 1928, *84*, 490; Bard, in C. Murchison, *A Handbook of General Experimental Psychology*, Clark University Press, 1934; and W. B. Cannon, "Again the James-Lange and Thalamic Theories of Emotion," *Psychol. Rev.*, 1931, *38*, 281–295.

43. See K. S. Lashley, "The Thalamus and Emotion, "*Psychol. Rev.*, 1938, *45*, 42–61.

44. J. H. Masserman, *Behavior and Neurosis.* University of Chicago Press, 1943, p. 35.

45. W. R. Hess, as reported in H. W. Magoun, *The Waking Brain.* Thomas, 1958, p. 53.

46. T. C. Ruch, "Neurophysiology of Emotion and Motivation," in T. C. Ruch, H. D. Patton, J. W. Woodbury, and A. L. Towe, *Neurophysiology*, Saunders, 1961, p. 491.

47. M. D. Egger and J. P. Flynn, "Amygdaloid Suppression of Hypothalamically Elicited Attack Behavior," *Science*, 1962, *136*, p. 43.

48. Ruch, *op. cit.*, p. 491.

49. Egger and Flynn, *op. cit.*, pp. 43–44.

50. R. S. Woodworth and H. Schlosberg, *Experimental Psychology* (rev. ed.). Holt, 1954, pp. 109–110.

51. J. B. Watson and J. J. B. Morgan, "Emotional Reactions and Psychological Experimentation," *Amer. J. Psychol.*, 1917, *28*, 163–174.

52. M. C. Sherman and I. C. Sherman, *The Process of Human Behavior.* Norton, 1929, p. 145.

53. O. C. Irwin, "The Latent Time of Body Startle in Infants," and "Infant Responses to Vertical Movement," *Child Develpm.*, 1932, *3*, 104–107; 167–169.

54. J. H. Taylor, "Innate Emotional Responses in Infants," *Ohio State University Contributions in Psychology: Studies in Infant Behavior*, No. 12, 1934, 69–93.

55. K. M. B. Bridges, "A Genetic Theory of Emotions," *J. Genet. Psychol.*, 1930, *37*, 514–527.

56. Sherman and Sherman, *op. cit.*

57. K. M. B. Bridges, "Emotional Development in Early Infancy," *Child Develpm.*, 1932, *3*, 324–341.

58. F. L. Goodenough, "Expression of the Emotions in a Blind-Deaf Child," *J. Abn. Soc. Psychol.*, 1932, *27*, 428–433. The description is paraphrased. Similar results are reported by J. Thompson, "Developments of Facial Expression of Emotion in Blind and Seeing Children," *Arch. Psychol.*, 1941, No. 264.

59. O. Klineberg, "Emotional Expression in Chinese Literature," *J. Abn. Soc. Psychol.*, 1938, *33*, 517–520.

60. H. E. Jones and M. C. Jones, "Fear," *Childhood Education*, 1928, *5*, 142–143.

61. E. R. Hagman, "A Study of Fears of Children of Pre-School Age," *J. Exper. Educ.*, 1932, *1*, 110–130.

62. J. B. Watson and R. Raynor, "Conditioned Emotional Reactions," *J. Exper. Psychol.*, 1920, *3*, 1–4.

63. See especially W. E. Blatz and D. A. Millichamp, "The Development of Emotion in the Infant," *University of Toronto Studies: Child Development Series*, 1935, No. 4; and F. L. Goodenough, *Anger in Young Children*, University of Minnesota Press, 1931.

64. R. A. Spitz, "The Smiling Response: A Contribution to the Ontogenesis of Social Relations," *Genet. Psychol. Monogr.*, 1946, *34*, 57–125.

65. C. Bühler, *The First Year of Life.* Day, 1930.

66. A. T. Jersild, F. V. Markey, and C. L. Jersild, "Children's Fears, Dreams, Wishes, Daydreams, Pleasant and Unpleasant Memories," *Child Develpm. Monogr.*, 1933, No. 12.

67. See especially O. H. Mowrer and R. R. Lamoreaux, "Fear as an Intervening Variable in Avoidance Conditioning," *J. Comp. Psychol.*, 1946, *39*, 29–50; M. A. May, "Experimentally Acquired Drives," *J. Exper. Psychol.*, 1948, *38*, 66–77; N. E. Miller, "Learnable Drives and Rewards," in S. S. Stevens (Ed.), *Handbook of Experimental Psychology*, Wiley, 1951, 432–472; and R. L. Solomon and E. S. Brush, "Experimentally Derived Conceptions of Anxiety and Aversion," *Nebraska Symposium on Motivation* (Marshall R. Jones, Ed.), 1956, 212–305.

68. C. Landreth, *The Psychology of Early Childhood*, Knopf, 1958, p. 381.

69. J. A. Taylor, "A Personality Scale of Manifest Anxiety," *J. Abn. Soc. Psychol.*, 1953, *48*, 285–290.

70. See, for example, K. W. Spence, I. E. Farber, and H. H. McFann, "The Relation of Anxiety (Drive) Level to Performance in Competitional and Noncompetitional Paired-Associates Learning." *J. Exper. Psychol.*, 1956, *52*, 296–305.

71. A. Anastasi, N. Cohen, and D. Spatz, "A Study of Fear and Anger in College Students Through the Controlled Diary Method," *J. Genet. Psychol.*, 1948, *73*, 243–249.

72. N. S. Endler, J. McV. Hunt, and A. J. Rosenstein, "An S-R Inventory of Anxiousness," *Psychol. Monogr.*, 1962, *76*, No. 17.

73. G. Mandler, J. M. Mandler, I. Kremen, and R. D. Sholiton, "The Response to Threat: Relations among Verbal and Physiological Indices," *Psychol. Monogr.*, 1961, *75*, No. 9.

74. As described by J. P. Scott, *Aggression*. University of Chicago Press, 1958, p. 48.

75. *Ibid.*, p. 49.

76. *Ibid.*

77. See reference 71.

78. H. Meltzer, "Student's Adjustments in Anger," *J. Soc. Psychol.*, 1933, *4*, 285–309.

79. See A. H. Rifkin, "Violence in Human Behavior," *Science*, 1963, *140*, 904–906. The report of a conference which summarizes the views and suggested solutions of several psychologists, psychoanalysts, and anthropologists. Also see A. H. Buss, *The Psychology of Aggression*, Wiley, 1961; and L. Berkowitz, *Aggression*, McGraw-Hill, 1962.

80. L. Berkowitz, "The Effects of Observing Violence," *Scientific American*, February 1964, pp. 35–41.

81. R. H. Walters, E. L. Thomas, and C. W. Acker, "Enhancement of Punitive Behavior by Audio-Visual Displays," *Science*, 1962, *136*, 872–873.

82. R. W. Washburn, "A Study of Smiling and Laughing of Infants in the First Year of Life," *Genet. Psychol. Monogr.*, 1929, *6*, 397–539.

83. S. H. Britt, *Social Psychology of Modern Life* (rev. ed.), Rinehart, 1949, p. 270. See also, A. Rapp, "A Phylogenetic Theory of Wit and Humor," *J. Soc. Psychol.*, 1949, *30*, 81–96.

84. J. Levine, "Responses to Humor," *Scientific American*, February 1956, *194*, 31.

85. F. A. Moss, T. Hunt, and K. T. Omwake, *Social Intelligence Test*. Center for Psychological Service, 1930.

86. From Levine, *op. cit.*, reference 84, p. 31.

87. H. Iisager, "Factors Contributing to Happiness among Danish College Students," *J. Soc. Psychol.*, 1948, *28*, 237–246.

88. G. Watson, "Happiness Among Adult Students of Education," *J. Educ. Psychol.*, 1930, *21*, 79–109.

89. G. W. Hartmann, *Educational Psychology*. American Book Co., 1941.

90. S. M. Jourard, *Personal Adjustment*. Macmillan, 1958, p. 235. Also see E. Fromm, *Man for Himself*, Rinehart, 1947, especially pp. 96–107.

91. See especially P. Mullahy, *Oedipus Myth and Complex*. Hermitage, 1948.

92. W. McDougall, *Social Psychology* (13th ed.). Luce, 1918, p. 97.

93. F. H. Allport, *Social Psychology*. Houghton Mifflin, 1924, p. 239.

94. K. M. B. Bridges, *The Social and Emotional Development of the Pre-school Child*. Kegan Paul, 1931, p. 49 (American edition, Harcourt, Brace).

Chapter 8

Conflict and Adjustment

1. S. Rosenzweig, "An Outline of Frustration Theory," in J. McV. Hunt (Ed.), *Personality and the Behavior Disorders*. Copyright 1944 by the Ronald Press Company, p. 385.

2. K. Lewin, *A Dynamic Theory of Personality*. McGraw-Hill, 1935, Chapter III. This is a brief introduction, first published in Murchison's *Handbook of Child Psychology* (2nd rev. ed.), 1933, Chapter 14.

3. See reference 2 and N. E. Miller, "Experimental Studies of Conflict," in J. McV. Hunt (Ed.), *Personality and the Behavior Disorders*, Ronald, 1944, Chapter 14.

4. N. L. Munn and E. P. Johnson, *Student's Manual to Accompany Psychology*. Houghton Mifflin, 1956.

5. N. R. F. Maier, in his *Frustration* (McGraw-Hill, 1949), defines frustration as behavior that has lost its goal-direction. Although this very limited definition is not generally accepted, Maier's book should be read for its valuable discussion of reactions to what others would call "extreme" frustration. Among these are aggressions, regressions, delinquency, and fixations.

6. For a critical discussion of the frustration-aggression hypothesis and its variations, see A. H. Buss, *The Psychology of Aggression*, Wiley, 1961, and the references cited by him.

7. W. E. Leonard, *The Locomotive God.* Appleton-Century-Crofts, 1927.

8. See E. Bagby, *The Psychology of Personality.* Holt, 1928, pp. 44–46.

9. See M. H. Erickson, "Experimental Demonstrations of the Psychopathology of Everyday Life," *Psychoanal. Quart.,* 1939, 8, 338–353.

10. As quoted on pp. 214 and 215 of P. T. Young's *Motivation of Behavior,* Wiley, 1936.

11. H. Selye, *The Stress of Life.* McGraw-Hill, 1956, p. 311.

12. *Ibid.,* p. 31.

13. *Ibid.,* p. 87.

14. *Ibid.,* pp. 180–181.

15. S. Wolf and H. G. Wolff, "Evidence of the Genesis of Peptic Ulcer in Man," Chapter X in S. S. Tomkins, *Contemporary Psychopathology.* Harvard University Press, 1943. Also see A. J. Sullivan and T. E. McKell, *Personality in Peptic Ulcer.* Thomas, 1950.

16. W. L. Sawrey and J. D. Weisz, "An Experimental Method of Producing Gastric Ulcers," *J. Comp. Physiol. Psychol.,* 1956, 49, 269–270. Also see W. L. Sawrey, J. J. Conger, and E. S. Turrell, "An Experimental Investigation of the Role of Psychological Factors in the Production of Gastric Ulcers in Rats," *J. Comp. Physiol. Psychol.,* 1956, 49, 457–461.

17. J. V. Brady, "Ulcers in 'Executive' Monkeys," *Scientific Monthly,* October 1958, pp. 89–95. Also J. V. Brady, R. W. Porter, D. G. Conrad, and J. W. Mason, "Avoidance Behavior and the Development of Gastroduodenal Ulcers," *J. Exper. Anal. Behav.,* 1958, 1, 69–72.

18. Quoted by Dunn in pp. 185–186 of S. S. Tomkins, *Contemporary Psychopathology,* Harvard University Press, 1943. A review of several studies dealing with peptic ulcer as a psychosomatic disorder appears in N. Cameron, *Personality Development and Psychopathology: A Dynamic Approach,* Houghton Mifflin, 1963, pp. 688–689.

19. For a good general discussion of psychosomatic disorders, see Cameron, *op. cit.*

20. L. Freeman, *Fight Against Fears.* Crown, 1951.

21. J. Knight, *The Story of My Psychoanalysis.* McGraw-Hill, 1950. "Knight" is a pseudonym.

22. *Psychosomatic Medicine,* published by the American Psychosomatic Society, Baltimore, Md.

23. V. E. Fisher, *Autocorrectivism.* Caxton Press, 1937.

24. G. R. Bach, "Young Children's Play Fantasies," *Psychol. Monogr.,* 1945, 59, No. 2.

25. D. C. McClelland, *Personality.* Dryden, 1951, pp. 370–371.

26. S. Freud, *An Outline of Psychoanalysis.* Norton, 1949, pp. 54–55. See also Freud's *A General Introduction to Psychoanalysis,* Part II. Garden City Publishing Co., 1943.

27. W. Dement and N. Kleitman, "The Relation of Eye Movements During Sleep to Dream Activity: An Objective Method for the Study of Dreaming," *J. Exper. Psychol.,* 1957, 53, 339–346. Also, N. Kleitman, "Patterns of Dreaming," *Scientific American,* November 1960, pp. 82–88.

28. D. R. Goodenough, A. Shapiro, M. Holden, and L. Steinschriber, "A Comparison of 'Dreamers' and 'Nondreamers': Eye Movements, Electroencephalograms, and the Recall of Dreams," *J. Abn. Soc. Psychol.,* 1959, 59, 295–302.

29. Many such studies are to be found in the *Psychoanalytic Review.* Karpman's study of *Gulliver's Travels* (1942, 29, 26–45; 165–184), for example, leads the analyst to conclude that Swift was neurotic, psychosexually infantile, and preoccupied with excretory functions. Also see J. Riviere, "The Unconscious Phantasy of an Inner World Reflected in Examples from English Literature," *Int. J. Psychoanalysis,* 1952, 33, 160–172.

30. D. McClelland, J. W. Atkinson, R. A. Clark, and E. L. Lowell, *The Achievement Motive.* Appleton-Century-Crofts, 1953. Also see the study by S. Epstein, "The Measurement of Drive and Conflict in Humans: Theory and Experiment," in *Nebraska Symposium on Motivation* (Marshall R. Jones, Ed.), 1962.

31. McClelland, *op. cit.,* reference 25, pp. 116–118.

32. Published by Whittlesey House (McGraw-Hill), 1946.

33. Cameron, *op. cit.,* reference 18, p. 418.

34. Cameron, *op. cit.,* reference 18, p. 418.

35. R. R. Sears, "Experimental Studies of Projection: I. Attribution of Traits," *J. Soc. Psychol.,* 1936, 7, 151–163.

36. J. R. Patrick, "Studies in Rational Behavior and Emotional Excitement: II. The Effect of Emotional Excitement on Rational Behavior of Human Beings," *J. Comp. Psychol.,* 1934, 18, 153–195.

37. O. H. Mowrer, "An Experimental Analogue of 'Regression,' with Incidental Observations on 'Reaction Formation,'" *J. Abn. Soc. Psychol.,* 1940, 35, 56–87.

38. R. G. Barker, T. Dembo, and K. Lewin, "Frustration and Regression: An Experiment with

Young Children," *University of Iowa Studies in Child Welfare*, 1941, *18*.

39. P. Rosenzweig, "Need-Persistive and Ego-Defensive Reactions to Frustration as Demonstrated by an Experiment on Repression," *Psychol. Rev.*, 1941, *48*, 347–349. A fuller account appears in *J. Exper. Psychol.*, 1943, *32*, 64–67.

40. B. Zeigarnik, "Über das Behalten von erledigten und unerledigten Handlungen," *Psychol. Forsch.*, 1927, *9*, 1–85.

41. T. G. Alper, "Memory for Completed and Incompleted Tasks as a Function of Personality: An Analysis of Group Data," *J. Abn. Soc. Psychol.*, 1946, *41*, 403–421; A. G. Glixman, "Recall of Completed and Incompleted Activities Under Varying Degrees of Stress," *J. Exper. Psychol.*, 1949, *39*, 281–295. A statistically significant difference was found only in the latter study.

42. I. P. Pavlov, *Lectures on Conditioned Reflexes*, Vol. 1, International, 1929. See especially Chapter XXXVI.

43. J. A. Dinsmoor, "A Discrimination Based on Punishment," *Quart. J. Exper. Psychol.*, 1952, *4*, 27–45.

44. J. H. Masserman, *Behavior and Neurosis*. University of Chicago Press, 1943; R. E. Watson, "Experimentally Induced Conflict in Cats," *Psychosomat. Med.*, 1954, *16*, 340–347; J. Wolpe, "Experimental Neurosis as Learned Behavior, *Brit. J. Psychol.*, 1952, *43*, 243–268.

45. P. E. Lichtenstein, "Studies of Anxiety. I. The Production of Feeding Inhibition in Dogs," *J. Comp. Physiol. Psychol.*, 1950, *43*, 16–29.

46. Q. F. Curtis, "Experimental Neurosis in the Pig," *Psychol. Bull.*, 1937, *34*, 723.

47. J. H. Masserman and C. Pechtel, "Neuroses in Monkeys: A Preliminary Report of Experimental Observations," *Ann. N. Y. Acad. Sci.*, 1953, *118*, 408–411.

48. C. J. Warden, *Animal Motivation Studies*. Columbia University Press, 1931.

49. J. A. Dinsmoor, "Abnormal Behavior in Animals," Chapter 10 in R. H. Waters, D. A. Rethlingshafer, and W. E. Caldwell, *Principles of Comparative Psychology*. McGraw-Hill, 1960.

50. S. W. Cook, "Production of 'Experimental Neurosis' in the White Rat," *Psychosomat. Med.*, 1939, *1*, 293–308.

51. S. W. Bijou, "A Study of 'Experimental Neurosis' in the Rat by the Conditioned Response Technique," *J. Comp. Psychol.*, *36*, 1–20.

52. W. J. Griffiths, Jr., "The Production of Convulsions in the White Rat," *Comp. Psychol. Monogr.*, 1942, *17*, 13.

53. Curtis, op. cit., reference 46.

54. See the various sections in Cameron, *op. cit.*, reference 18, which deal with conflict as a basis of human behavior disorders.

55. J. Barcroft, *The Brain and Its Environment*. Yale University Press, 1938, p. 96.

56. See especially E. Jacobson, "Electrophysiology of Mental Activities," *Amer. J. Psychol.*, 1932, *44*, 677–694; L. W. Max, "An Experimental Study of the Motor Theory of Consciousness," *J. Gen. Psychol.*, 1935, *12*, 159–175; and *J. Comp. Psychol.*, 1937, *24*, 301–344.

57. J. H. Bair, "The Acquirement of Voluntary Control," *Psychol. Rev.*, 1901, *8*, 474–510.

58. Muscle control, practiced quite often by physical culturists, exemplifies this isolated movement of muscles. See Maxick's *Muscle Control*; or *Body Development by Will Power*. Ewert, Seymour, 1913.

59. J. V. Basmajian, "Control and Training of Individual Motor Units," *Science*, 1963, *141*, 440–441.

60. D. B. Lindsley and W. H. Sassaman, "Autonomic Activity and Brain Potentials Associated with 'Voluntary' Control of the Pilomotors (*mm. arrectores pilorum*)," *J. Neurophysiol.*, 1938, *1*, 342–349.

61. R. Menzies, "Conditioned Vasomotor Responses in Human Subjects," *J. Psychol.*, 1937, *4*, 75–120.

62. W. S. Hunter and C. V. Hudgins, "Voluntary Activity from the Standpoint of Behaviorism," *Acta Psychologica*, 1935, *1*, 114. Also in *J. Gen. Psychol.*, 1934, *10*, 198–204.

Chapter 9

Personality

1. G. W. Allport and H. S. Odbert, "Trait-Names: A Psycho-Lexical Study," *Psychol. Monogr.*, 1936, No. 211.

2. R. B. Cattell, *Description and Measurement of Personality*. World Book Co., 1946, pp. 466–571.

3. L. L. Thurstone, "The Factorial Description of Temperament," *Science*, 1950, *111*, 454–455.

4. C. Bühler, *The First Year of Life*. John Day, 1930.

5. See R. Spitz, "The Smiling Response: A Contribution to the Ontogenesis of Social Relations," *Genet. Psychol. Monogr.*, 1946, *34*, 57–125.

6. Bühler, op. cit.; A. Gesell and H. Thompson, Infant Behavior: Its Genesis and Growth, McGraw-Hill, 1934.

7. See reference 4.

8. See reference 4.

9. A. Gesell, and F. L. Ilg, Child Development: An Introduction to the Study of Human Growth. Harper, 1949, especially pp. 31–32.

10. A. T. Jersild, Child Psychology (5th ed.). Prentice-Hall, 1960, pp. 310–311.

11. S. Freud, An Outline of Psychoanalysis. Norton, 1949, pp. 16–17.

12. M. Ribble, The Rights of Infants. Columbia University Press, 1943; R. A. Spitz, "Hospitalism: An Enquiry into the Genesis of Psychiatric Conditions in Early Childhood," in O. Fenichel et al., The Psychoanalytic Study of the Child, International Universities Press, 1945.

13. W. Dennis and P. Najarian, "Development Under Environmental Handicap," Psychol. Monogr., 1957, No. 7.

14. H. L. Rheingold, "The Modification of Social Responsiveness in Institutionalized Babies," Monogr. Soc. Res. Child Develpm., 1956, 21, 3–48.

15. G. W. Allport, Pattern and Growth in Personality. Holt, Rinehart and Winston, 1961, p. 78.

16. See Harlow's chapter in H. L. Rheingold (Ed.), Maternal Behavior in Mammals, Wiley, 1963.

17. W. H. Sewell, "Infant Training and the Personality of the Child," Amer. J. Sociol., 1952, 58, 150–159.

18. R. R. Sears, E. E. Maccoby, and H. Levin, Patterns of Child Rearing. Row, Peterson, 1957.

19. Ibid., p. 389.

20. See C. Kluckhohn, H. A. Murray, and D. M. Schneider, Personality in Nature, Society, and Culture. Knopf, 1953.

21. G. W. Allport, Personality. Holt, 1937, p. 102.

22. Sears et al., op. cit., reference 18.

23. H. F. Hooker, "A Study of the Only Child in School," J. Genet. Psychol., 1931, 39, 122–126.

24. H. E. Jones, "Order of Birth in Relation to Development in the Child," in C. Murchison (Ed.), A Handbook of Child Psychology. Clark University Press, 1931. Also see H. L. Koch, "Attitudes of Young Children Toward their Peers as Related to Certain Characteristics of their Siblings," Psychol. Monogr., 1956, 70, No. 19.

25. E. R. Guthrie, The Psychology of Human Conflict. Harper, 1938, p. 128.

26. C. G. Jung, Psychological Types. Harcourt, Brace, 1923.

27. L. R. Marston, "The Emotions of Young Children: An Experimental Study of Introversion and Extroversion," University of Iowa Studies: Studies in Child Welfare, 1925, 3, No. 3.

28. A. R. Root, "A Short Test of Introversion-Extraversion," Person. J., 1931, 10, 250–253.

29. C. A. Neymann and G. K. Yacorzynski, "Studies of Introversion-Extraversion and Conflict of Motives in the Psychoses," J. Gen. Psychol., 1942, 27, 241–255.

30. E. M. L. Burchard, "Physique and Psychosis: An Analysis of the Postulated Relationship Between Bodily Constitution and Mental Disease Syndrome," Comp. Psychol. Monogr., 1936, No. 13.

31. W. H. Sheldon, S. S. Stevens, and W. B. Tucker, The Varieties of Human Physique, Harper, 1940; W. H. Sheldon and S. S. Stevens, The Varieties of Temperament, Harper, 1942.

32. R. W. Parnell, "Physique and Performance," Brit. Med. J., August 1954, 491–496. Also see R. W. Parnell, Behavior and Physique, Williams and Wilkins, 1958.

33. See the discussion in C. M. Harsh and H. G. Schrickel, Personality, Ronald, 1950, p. 375.

34. D. W. Fiske, "A Study of Relationships to Somatotype," J. Appl. Psychol., 1944, 504–519.

35. A. Keys et al., Human Starvation. University of Minnesota Press, 1950, Vol. 1; see p. 153.

36. Parnell, op. cit., reference 32, 1954, p. 492.

37. J. E. Horrocks, The Psychology of Adolescence (2nd ed.). Houghton Mifflin, 1962. Also see S. Fisher and S. E. Cleveland, Body Image and Personality, Van Nostrand, 1958.

38. R. G. Hoskins, Endocrinology. Norton, 1941.

39. For one such case, see L. P. Thorpe and W. W. Cruze, Developmental Psychology. Ronald, 1956, p. 121.

40. The OSS Assessment Staff, The Assessment of Men. Rinehart, 1948.

41. Ibid., p. 114.

42. Ibid.; quotations from p. 133.

43. Ibid., p. 141.

44. Ibid.; abridged from pp. 209–210.

45. Ibid., p. 462.

46. E. L. Kelly and D. W. Fiske, The Prediction of Performance in Clinical Psychology. University of Michigan Press, 1951.

47. See E. L. Kelly and L. R. Goldberg, "Correlates of Later Performance and Specialization in Psychology: A Follow-up Study of the Trainees As-

sessed in the V. A. Selection Research Project," *Psychol. Monogr.*, 1959, 73, No. 12.

48. OSS Assessment Staff, *op. cit.*, p. 71.

49. R. R. Sears, "Influence of Methodological Factors in Doll-Play Performance," *Child Develpm.*, 1947, 18, 190–191.

50. From S. J. Beck's report on a case in H. A. Murray, *Explorations in Personality.* Oxford University Press, 1938, pp. 687–689.

51. M. R. Hertz, "Rorschach: Twenty Years After," *Psychol. Bull.*, 1942, 39, 538.

52. J. E. Bell, *Projective Techniques.* Longmans, Green, 1948, especially pp. 139–149.

53. L. L. Thurstone, "The Rorschach in Psychological Science," *J. Abn. Soc. Psychol.*, 1948, 43, 474. For other critical studies of the Rorschach test, see G. F. King, "A Theoretical and Experimental Consideration of the Rorschach Human Movement Response," *Psychol. Monogr.*, 1958, No. 458; and J. F. Okarski, "Consistency of Projective Movement Responses," *Psychol. Monogr.*, 1958, No. 459.

54. H. A. Murray, *Explorations in Personality.* Oxford University Press, 1938. The complete test is obtainable from the Harvard University Press, Cambridge, Massachusetts.

55. J. P. Guilford, *An Inventory of Factors STDCR.* Sheridan Supply Co., 1940.

56. S. R. Hathaway and J. C. McKinley, *The Minnesota Multiphasic Personality Inventory* (rev. ed.). University of Minnesota Press, 1943.

57. G. W. Allport, P. E. Vernon, and G. Lindzey, *A Study of Values: A Scale for Measuring the Dominant Interests in Personality* (3rd ed.). Houghton Mifflin, 1960. Based on E. Spranger, *Types of Men* (translated from 5th German edition of *Lebensformen*), Stechert, 1928.

58. K. Menninger, *The Human Mind* (rev. ed.). Knopf, 1937, pp. 138–139.

59. H. W. Frink, *Morbid Fears and Compulsions.* Moffat, Yard, 1918, p. 165.

60. For a detailed report of this case, see C. H. Thigpen and H. Cleckley, "A Case of Multiple Personality," *J. Abn. Soc. Psychol.*, 1954, 49, 135–151. Also in *Three Faces of Eve*, by the same authors; McGraw-Hill, 1957.

61. For a review of the various schools of psychoanalysis, see especially G. Murphy, *Historical Introduction to Modern Psychology* (rev. ed.), Harcourt, Brace, 1949; or R. S. Woodworth and M. R. Sheehan, *Contemporary Schools of Psychology* (3rd ed.), Ronald, 1964.

62. C. Rogers, *Counseling and Psychotherapy*, Houghton Mifflin, 1942; and *Client-Centered Therapy*, Houghton Mifflin, 1950.

63. Quoted from C. Rogers, *Counseling and Psychotherapy*, Houghton Mifflin, 1942, pp. 272–273; 420–421.

64. A book under the editorship of C. R. Rogers and R. D. Dymond presents a series of coordinated studies on *Psychotherapy and Personality Change.* It was published in 1954 by the University of Chicago Press.

65. See especially J. W. Klapman, *Group Psychotherapy.* Grune and Stratton, 1946.

66. J. L. Moreno, *Psychodrama.* Beacon House, 1946.

67. L. J. Karnosh and E. M. Zucker, *A Handbook of Psychiatry.* Mosby, 1945, pp. 115–116.

68. F. J. Kallmann, *The Genetics of Schizophrenia*, Augustin, 1938; and, by the same author, *Heredity in Health and Mental Disorder; Principles of Psychiatric Genetics in the Light of Comparative Twin Studies*, Norton, 1953.

69. See N. Pastore, "Genetics of Schizophrenia," *Psychol. Bull.*, 1949, 46, 285–302. Other critics are cited by S. Arieti in *American Handbook of Psychiatry*, Basic Books, 1959, pp. 484–486.

70. Much of this work is summarized in R. G. Hoskins, *The Biology of Schizophrenia*, Norton, 1946.

71. These are discussed by H. E. Himwich in "Psychopharmacologic Drugs," *Science*, 1958, 127, 59–72.

72. A brief summary of the most widely held theories is to be found in C. Landis and M. M. Bolles, *Textbook of Abnormal Psychology* (rev. ed.). Macmillan, 1950, pp. 371–373.

73. Himwich, *op. cit.*, reference 71, p. 60.

74. *Ibid.*

75. W. Freeman and J. W. Watts, *Psychosurgery* (rev. ed.). Thomas, 1950. Landis and Bolles, *op. cit.*, reference 72, p. 390; see also pp. 391–395 for a discussion of comparable results obtained in the Columbia-Greystone project, which involved a new operation known as *frontal topectomy.* Also see J. F. Fulton, *Frontal Lobotomy and Affective Behavior*, Norton, 1951, and J. M. Warren and K. Akert, *Frontal Granular Cortex and Behavior*, McGraw-Hill, 1964.

76. M. F. Robinson and W. Freeman, *Psychosurgery and the Self.* Grune and Stratton, 1954.

77. L. F. Shaffer and E. J. Shoben, Jr., *The Psychol-*

ogy of Adjustment (2nd ed.). Houghton Mifflin, 1956, pp. 384–590.

Chapter 10
The Learning Process

1. See the writer's The Evolution and Growth of Human Behavior (2nd ed.), Houghton Mifflin, 1965, Chapter 5, for a discussion of the evolution of learning ability in animals.

2. According to Carleton S. Coon, in his The Story of Man, Knopf, 1954, Homo sapiens, the only surviving human species, "finished his long infancy as a species" some 35,000 years ago. Other types of men were extinct by that time.

3. See G. Wallas, Our Social Heritage. Allen and Unwin, 1921, pp. 16–17. Published in the United States by Yale University Press.

4. W. H. Thorpe, Learning and Instinct in Animals (2nd ed.), Methuen, 1963, has an extensive discussion of habituation.

5. I. P. Pavlov, Conditioned Reflexes (trans. by G. V. Anrep). Oxford University Press, 1927, p. 395.

6. M. A. B. Brazier (Ed.), The Central Nervous System and Behavior (Trans. 1st Conference), Josiah Macy, Jr. Foundation and National Science Foundation, 1959. This is a fine source of historical data on conditioning. It contains over a hundred photographs relating to early work in this area. Recent research with implanted electrodes implicates the reticular formation. For a review of this work, see V. Rowland, "Conditioning and Brain Waves," Scientific American, August 1959, 89.

7. W. A. Bousfield, "Lope de Vega on Early Conditioning," American Psychologist, 1955, 10, 828.

8. There is a vast literature here. Some examples of conditioning in animals without a cortex (snails, worms, frogs, etc.) are to be found in the writer's The Evolution and Growth of Human Behavior (2nd ed.), Houghton Mifflin, 1965. On conditioning in decorticate mammals, see R. B. Bromiley, "Conditioned Responses in a Dog after Removal of Neocortex, J. Comp. Physiol. Psychol., 1948, 41, 102–110. On the controversial issue of spinal conditioning, see T. Pinto and R. B. Bromiley, "A Search for 'Spinal Conditioning' and for Evidence that it can Become a Reflex," J. Exper. Psychol., 1950, 40, 121–130; and R. A. Dykman and P. S. Shurrager, "Successive and Maintained Conditioning in Spinal Carnivores," J. Comp. & Physiol. Psychology, 1956, 49, 27–35.

9. See N. L. Munn, "Learning in Children," in L. Carmichael (Ed.), Manual of Child Psychology (2nd ed.), Wiley, 1954; The Evolution and Growth of Human Behavior (2nd ed.), Houghton Mifflin, 1965, pp. 226–228; and the studies by G. H. S. Razran and others, summarized in his "The Dominance-Contiguity Theory of the Acquisition of Classical Conditioning," Psychol. Bull., 1957, 54, 1–46.

10. V. M. Bechterev, General Principles of Human Reflexology. International, 1932. See also the chapter on Bechterev in Brazier, reference 6.

11. The terms classical and instrumental come from E. R. Hilgard and D. G. Marquis, Conditioning and Learning, Appleton-Century Crofts, 1940. The revised edition by Kimball (1961) retains this distinction.

12. The following references deal with the question of the best CS-UCS interval under various conditions, and also backward conditioning of certain responses. H. M. Wolfle, "Conditioning as a Function of the Interval Between the Conditioned and the Original Stimulus," J. Gen. Psychol., 1932, 7, 80–103. G. A. Kimball, "Conditioning as a Function of the Time Between Conditioned and Unconditioned Stimuli," J. Exper. Psychol., 1947, 37, 1–15. Also see the data in A. Spooner and W. N. Kellogg's "The Backward Conditioning Curve," Amer. J. Psychol., 1947, 60, 321–334. In conditioning finger withdrawal in sixty college students, these investigators found a far greater percentage of conditioned responses when shock followed the buzz by a half-second interval than when it was simultaneous with the buzz or followed by a one-second interval. Their results for a zero interval (simultaneous conditioning) and shock before the buzz (backward conditioning) led them to question whether conditioning was actually present under these conditions. However, Razran's review of the literature on backward conditioning shows that it has often been obtained. G. H. S. Razran, "Backward Conditioning," Psychol. Bull., 1956, 53, 1–34. R. A. Champion and J. E. Jones, "Forward, Backward, and Pseudoconditioning of the GSR," J. Exper. Psychol., 1961, 62, 58–61, discuss this general problem as it relates to the GSR, and present evidence of backward conditioning.

13. See especially Brazier, reference 6, pp. 365, 367.

14. This is nicely demonstrated in an old film by Culler, entitled "Motor Conditioning in Dogs." It is distributed by C. H. Stoelting Co., 424 N. Homan Avenue., Chicago.

15. M. J. Bass and C. L. Hull, "The Irradiation of a Tactile Conditioned Reflex in Man," *J. Comp. Psychol.*, 1934, *14*, 47–65.

16. See G. A. Kimble, *Hilgard and Marquis' Conditioning and Learning*, Appleton-Century-Crofts, 1961, for discussions of eyelid conditioning. One of the most recent studies, with a bibliography including researches since 1961, is W. E. Vandament and L. E. Price, "Primary Stimulus Generalization Under Different Percentages of Reinforcement in Eyelid Conditioning," *J. Exper. Psychol.*, 1964, *67*, 162–167.

17. H. A. Schlosberg, "A Study of the Conditioned Patellar Reflex," *J. Exper. Psychol.*, 1928, *11*, 468–494. Another study in which the patellar reflex was conditioned is G. R. Wendt's "An Analytical Study of the Conditioned Knee Jerk," *Arch. Psychol.*, 1930, *18*, No. 123.

18. C. Shagass and E. P. Johnson, "The Course of Acquisition of a Conditioned Response of the Occipital Alpha Rhythm," *J. Exper. Psychol.*, 1943, *33*, 201–209. Brazier, reference 6, describes some later studies. That the conditioned modification is small and unstable is suggested by the study reported recently by R. Albino and G. Burnand, "Conditioning of the Alpha Rhythm in Man," *J. Exper. Psychol.*, 1964, *67*, 539–544.

19. See J. M. Notterman, W. N. Schoenfeld, and P. J. Bersh, "Partial Reinforcement and Conditioned Heart Rate Responses in Human Subjects," *Science*, 1952, *115*, 77–79: Also, refer to the study by P. J. Lang, J. Geer, and M. Hnatiow, "Semantic Generalization of Conditioned Autonomic Responses," *J. Exper. Psychol.*, 1963, *65*, 552–558. Reference is made here to an unpublished Indiana doctoral dissertation by R. W. Shearn, which deals with operant conditioning of heart rate.

20. See A. A. Gerall and J. K. Woodward, "Conditioning of the Human Pupillary Response as a Function of the CS-UCS Interval," *J. Exper. Psychol.*, 1958, *55*, 501–507. This deals with earlier research and also points out some complicating considerations.

21. W. J. Brogden, E. A. Lipman, and E. A. Culler, "The Role of Incentive in Conditioning and Extinction," *Amer. J. Psychol.* 1938, *51*, 109–117; R. L. Solomon, L. J. Kamin, and L. C. Wynne, "Traumatic Avoidance Learning: The Outcomes of Various Extinction Procedures with Dogs," *J. Abn. Soc. Psychol.*, 1953, *48*, 291–302.

22. See N. L. Munn, "The Relative Effectiveness of Two Conditioning Procedures," *J. Gen. Psychol.*, 1939, *21*, 119–136.

23. B. F. Skinner, *Science and Human Behavior.* Macmillan, 1953, p. 65.

24. *Ibid.*

25. E. L. Thorndike, "Animal Intelligence: An Experimental Study of the Association Process in Animals," *Psychol. Monogr.*, 1898, *2*, No. 8. Reprinted in *Animal Intelligence*, Macmillan, 1911; see pp. 48–56.

26. B. F. Skinner, " 'Superstition' in the Pigeon," *J. Exper. Psychol.*, 1948, *38*, 168–172; also see W. H. Morse and B. F. Skinner, "A Second Type of 'Superstition' in the Pigeon," *Amer. J. Psychol.*, 1957, *70*, 308–311. Both are reprinted in D. E. Dulany, R. L. DeValois, D. C. Beardslee, and M. R. Winterbottom, *Contributions to Modern Psychology* (2nd ed.), Oxford, 1963.

27. B. F. Skinner, " 'Superstition' in the Pigeon," *J. Exper. Psychol.*, 1958, *38*, 171.

28. J. Anliker and J. Mayer, "An Operant Conditioning Technique for Studying Feeding-Fasting Patterns in Normal and Obese Mice," *J. Appl. Physiol.*, 1956, *8*, No. 6.

29. C. B. Ferster and B. F. Skinner, *Schedules of Reinforcement.* Appleton-Century-Crofts, 1957.

30. See reference 29.

31. B. F. Skinner, *Science and Human Behavior.* Macmillan, 1953, p. 104.

32. R. Bugelski, "Extinction With and Without Sub-Goal Reinforcement," *J. Comp. Psychol.*, 1938, *26*, 121–134.

33. J. B. Wolfe, "Effectiveness of Token-Rewards for Chimpanzees," *Comp. Psychol. Monogr.*, 1936, *12*, No. 5.

34. B. F. Skinner, "How to Teach Animals," *Scientific Monthly*, December 1951, pp. 26–29.

35. J. T. Cowles, "Food-Tokens as Incentives for Learning by Chimpanzees," *Comp. Psychol. Monogr.*, 1937, *14*, No. 5.

36. J. Greenspoon, "The Reinforcing Effect of Two Spoken Sounds on the Frequency of Two Responses," *Amer. J. Psychol.*, 1955, *68*, 409–416.

37. See the film "Motivation and Learning," by N. E. Miller and G. Hart, distributed by The Psychological Cinema Register, Pennsylvania State University, University Park, Pa.

38. E. R. Guthrie and G. P. Horton, *Cats in a Puzzle Box.* Rinehart, 1946.

39. A nice illustration of this appears in the film, "Reinforcement in Learning and Extinction" (K. C. Montgomery, R. J. Herrnstein, and W. H. Morse), distributed by McGraw-Hill Text-Film Department.

40. B. F. Skinner, *The Behavior of Organisms*. Appleton-Century-Crofts, 1938.

41. *Ibid.*, pp. 339–340.

42. R. Pierrel and G. Sherman, *Barnabus, The Barnard Rat Demonstration*. Barnard College, 1958. An article about this rat, together with nine photos, appeared in the *New York Times*, February 19, 1958. These are also reproduced in R. W. Lundin, *Personality: An Experimental Approach*, Macmillan, 1961.

43. K. Breland and M. Breland, "A Field of Applied Animal Psychology," *American Psychologist*, 1951, *6*, 202–204.

44. B. F. Skinner, "Teaching Machines," *Science*, 1958, *128*, 971.

45. *Walden Two* was published in 1948 by Macmillan. It has recently been reissued in a paperback series.

46. B. F. Skinner, *Science and Human Behavior*, Macmillan, 1953.

47. K. Dunlap, *Habits: Their Making and Unmaking*. Liveright, 1932. For a later study and a review of earlier literature, see M. Smith, "Effectiveness of Symptomatic Treatment of Nail-biting in College Students," *Psychological Newsletter*, 1957, *8*, 219–231.

48. E. R. Guthrie, *The Psychology of Human Conflict*. Harper, 1938.

49. See M. C. Jones, "The Elimination of Children's Fears," *J. Exper. Psychol.*, 1924, *7*, 382–390; and A. T. Jersild and F. B. Holmes, "Methods of Overcoming Children's Fears," *J. Psychol.*, 1936, *1*, 75–104.

50. Methods of treating enuresis, together with a critical review of the extensive literature, will be found in S. H. Lovibond, *Conditioning and Enuresis*, Pergamon Press, 1964.

51. *Ibid.*, pp. 85–93.

52. A recent review of research on latent learning appears in Kimble's revision, *Hilgard and Marquis' Conditioning and Learning, op. cit.*, reference 16, pp. 226–234.

53. V. C. Hicks and H. A. Carr, "Human Reactions in a Maze," *J. Anim. Behav.*, 1912, *2*, 98–125; R. W. Husband, "A Comparison of Human Adults and White Rats in Maze Learning," *J. Comp. Psychol.*, 1929, *9*, 361–377; C. Lathan and P. E. Fields, "A Report on a Test-Reset

Performance of 38 College Students and 27 White Rats on the Identical 25-Choice Elevated Maze," *J. Genet. Psychol.*, 1936, *49*, 283–296.

54. E. C. Tolman and D. B. Nyswander, "The Reliability and Validity of Maze Measures for Rats," *J. Comp. Psychol.*, 1927, *7*, 446.

55. R. G. Farr, M. K. Dey, and E. Bloch, "The Airplane Control Test, *Percept-Motor Skills*, 1956, *6*, 78.

56. G. H. Miles and D. Lewis, "Age and Handedness as Factors in the Performance of a Complex Pursuit Task," *Proc. Iowa Acad. Sci.*, 1956, *63*, 569–575.

57. B. J. Underwood and R. W. Schulz, *Meaningfulness and Verbal Learning*. Lippincott, 1960. This includes tables showing the meaningfulness of nonsense syllables and similar items. The first such study was made by J. A. Glaze, "The Association Value of Non-Sense Syllables," *J. Genet. Psychol.*, 1928, *35*, 225–269. This was followed by a study by W. C. F. Krueger, "The Relative Difficulty of Non-sense Syllables," *J. Exper. Psychol.*, 1934, *17*, 145–153. Later, more comprehensive studies are those of E. J. Archer, "A Re-Evaluation of the Meaningfulness of Possible CVC Trigrams," *Psychol. Monogr.*, 1960, No. 497; and C. E. Noble, "Measurements of Association Value (a), Rated Associations (a'), and Scaled Meaningfulness (m') for the 2100 CVC Combinations of the English Alphabet," *Monogr. Suppl. Psychol. Rep.*, 1961, *8*, 487–521.

58. See especially W. Köhler, *The Mentality of Apes*. Harcourt, Brace, 1925.

59. N. Miller and J. Dollard, *Social Learning and Imitation*. Yale University Press, 1944, pp. 122–131.

60. F. S. Keller, I. J. Christo, and W. N. Schoenfeld, "Studies in the International Morse Code: V", *J. Appl. Psychol.*, 1946, *30*, 265–270, and earlier studies cited there.

61. P. H. Ewert, "Bilateral Transfer in Mirror-Drawing," *Ped. Sem.*, 1926, *33*, 235–249.

62. H. F. Harlow, "The Formation of Learning Sets," *Psychol. Rev.*, 1949, *56*, 51–65; and, with J. M. Warren, "Formation and Transfer of Discrimination Learning Sets," *J. Comp. Physiol. Psychol.*, 1952, *45*, 482–489.

63. See Harlow, *op. cit.*, reference 62; and A. J. Riopelle, "Transfer Suppression and Learning Sets," *J. Comp. Physiol. Psychol.*, 1953, *46*, 108–114.

64. See the discussion of learning sets in various

organisms from lower vertebrates to man, in N. L. Munn, *The Evolution of Growth of Human Behavior* (2nd ed.), Houghton Mifflin, 1965.

65. M. Hammerton, "Transfer of Training from a Simulated to a Real Control Situation," *J. Exper. Psychol.*, 1963, 66, 450–453.

66. L. B. Ward, "Reminiscence and Rate of Learning," *Psychol. Monogr.*, 1937, 49, No. 220. Also see J. A. McGeoch and A. L. Irion, *Psychology of Human Learning* (rev. ed.). Longmans, Green, 1952, pp. 306–309.

67. K. E. Roberts, "The Ability of Pre-School Children to Solve Problems in Which a Simple Principle of Relationship is Kept Constant," *J. Genet. Psychol.*, 1932, 40, 118–135.

68. G. Katona, *Organizing and Remembering*. Columbia University Press, 1940.

69. C. H. Judd, "The Relation of Special Training to General Intelligence," *Educ. Rev.*, 1908, 36, 28–42.

70. E. L. Thorndike and R. S. Woodworth, "The Influence of Improvement in one Mental Function upon the Efficiency of Other Functions," *Psychol. Rev.*, 1901, 8, 247–261; 384–395; 553–564; J. B. Stroud, "Experiments upon Learning in School Situations," *Psychol. Bull.*, 1940, 37, 777–807.

71. G. Ulmer, "Teaching Geometry to Cultivate Reflective Thinking: An Experimental Study with 1239 High School Pupils," *J. Exper. Educ.*, 1939, 8, 18–25.

72. R. I. Haskell, doctoral thesis cited by E. R. Hilgard, *Introduction to Psychology* (2nd ed.), Harcourt Brace, 1958, p. 268.

73. E. A. Bilodeau and I. McB. Bilodeau, "Motor Skills Learning," in *Annual Review of Psychology*, 1961, 261–268.

74. N.R.C. "The Psychology of Learning in Relation to Flight Instruction," C.A.A. Division of Research: Report No. 16, June 1943.

75. W. B. Johns, "The Growth of Vocabulary Among University Students with Some Consideration of Methods of Fostering It," *J. Exper. Educ.*, 1939, 8, 89–102.

Chapter 11

Foundations of Learning

1. R. H. Gault, "Recent Developments in Vibro-Tactile Research," *J. Franklin Instit.*, 1936, 221, 703–720.

2. C. H. Honzik, "The Sensory Basis of Maze Learning in Rats," *Comp. Psychol. Monogr.*, 1936, 13, No. 64. For an extensive summary of the research on sensory control in the rat, see N. L. Munn, *Handbook of Psychological Research on the Rat*, Houghton Mifflin, 1950, Chapter 6.

3. Honzik, *op. cit.*, and experiments cited on pp. 192f. of the Munn reference.

4. K. S. Lashley, *Brain Mechanisms and Intelligence*. University of Chicago Press, 1929.

5. See W. S. Hunter, "A Consideration of Lashley's Theory of the Equipotentiality of Cerebral Action," *J. Gen. Psychol.*, 1930, 3, 455–468.

6. C. B. Finley, "Equivalent Losses in Accuracy of Response after Central and Peripheral Sense Deprivation," *J. Comp. Neurol.*, 1941, 74, 203–237. K. S. Lashley, "Studies of Cerebral Function in Learning: XII. Loss of the Maze Habit after Occipital Lesions in Blind Rats," *J. Comp. Neurol.*, 1943, 79, 431–462. For a summary, see N. L. Munn, *op. cit.*, reference 2, pp. 213–225.

7. On the effects of early experience, see D. G. Forgays and J. W. Forgays, "The Nature of the Effect of Environmental Experience in the Rat," *J. Comp. Physiol. Psychol.*, 1952, 45, 322–328; R. H. Forgus, "Early Visual and Motor Experience as Determiners of Complex Maze-Learning Ability under Rich and Reduced Stimulation," *J. Comp. Physiol. Psychol.*, 1955, 48, 215–220; B. Hymovitch, "The Effects of Experimental Variations on Problem Solving in the Rat," *J. Comp. Physiol. Psychol.*, 1952, 45, 313–321. The brain-damage studies are those of H. C. Lansdell, "Effect of Brain Damage on Intelligence in Rats," *J. Comp. Physiol. Psychol.*, 1953, 46, 461–464; and C. J. Smith, "Mass Action and Early Environment in the Rat," *J. Comp. Physiol. Psychol.*, 1959, 52, 154–156.

8. K. S. Lashley, "Cerebral Function in the Pattern Vision of the Rat," *Psychol. Bull.*, 1931, 28, 221–222. On the vigilance interpretation, see G. H. Shure and W. C. Halstead, "Cerebral Localization of Intellectual Processes," *Psychol. Monogr.*, 1958, 72, 13, 19, 23–24.

9. See E. Culler and F. A. Mettler, "Conditioned Behavior in a Decorticate Dog," *J. Comp. Psychol.*, 1934, 18, 291–303.

10. D. G. Marquis, "Effects of Removal of the Visual Cortex in Mammals, with Observations on the Retention of Light Discrimination in Dogs," *Proc. Assoc. Res. Nerv. Ment. Dis.*, 1934, 13, 558–592.

11. See the data summarized in N. L. Munn, *The Evolution and Growth of Human Behavior* (2nd ed.), Houghton Mifflin, 1965, pp. 110–113.

12. S. G. Klebanoff, J. L. Singer, and H. Wilensky review the relevant literature in "Psychological Consequences of Brain Lesions and Ablations," *Psychol. Bull.*, 1954, *51*, 1–41; B. Milner, "Intellectual Functions of the Temporal Lobes," *Psychol. Bull.*, 1954, *51*, 42–62; and the final citation in reference 8 have more recent data on cerebral lesions in man. On functions of the frontal lobes, see also, J. M. Warren and K. Akert (Eds.), *Frontal Granular Cortex and Behavior*, McGraw-Hill, 1964.

13. W. J. Brogden, "Sensory Pre-Conditioning," *J. Exper. Psychol.*, 1939, *25*, 323–332. Also, D. R. Hoffeld, S. B. Kendall, R. F. Thompson, and W. J. Brogden, "Effect of Amount of Preconditioning Training Upon the Magnitude of Sensory Preconditioning," *J. Exper. Psychol.*, 1960, *59*, 198–204. This also gives a good bibliography on this phenomenon. R. J. Seidel, "A Review of Sensory Preconditioning," *Psychol. Bull.*, 1959, *56*, 58–73, is another good source of additional information.

14. W. J. Brogden, "Contiguous Conditioning," *J. Exper. Psychol.*, 1962, *64*, 172–176.

15. E. C. Tolman and C. H. Honzik, "Introduction and Removal of Reward, and Maze Performance in Rats," *Univ. Calif. Publ. Psychol.*, 1930, *4*, 257–275.

16. Reference 15; and E. C. Tolman, "The Determiners of Behavior at a Choice Point," *Psychol. Rev.*, 1936, *45*, 1–41. This reviews and interprets the relevant research. Also see C. Buxton, "Latent Learning and the Goal Gradient Hypothesis," *Contrib. Psychol. Theor.*, 1940, *2*, No. 2.

17. Tolman and Honzik, *op. cit.*, reference 15; see especially pp. 262–263. R. H. Bruce, "The Effect of Removal of Reward on the Maze Performance of Rats," *Univ. Calif. Publ. Psychol.*, 1930, *4*, 203–214.

18. M. H. Elliott, "The Effect of Change of Reward on the Maze Performance of Rats," *Univ. Calif. Publ. Psychol.*, 1928, *4*, 19–30. On delay of reinforcement, see the studies by Wolfe, Perin, and Grice, summarized in Munn, *op. cit.*, reference 2, pp. 388–395.

19. L. B. Abel, "The Effects of a Shift in Motivation Upon the Learning of a Sensori-Motor Task," *Arch. Psychol.*, 1936, No. 205.

20. L. B. Miller and B. W. Estes, "Monetary Reward and Motivation in Discrimination Learning," *J. Exper. Psychol.*, 1961, *61*, 501–504.

21. See P. T. Young, *Motivation and Emotion*, Wiley, 1961, pp. 490–496, for a review of the relevant literature.

22. E. C. Tolman, C. S. Hall, and E. P. Bretnall, "A Disproof of the Law of Effect and a Substitution of the Laws of Emphasis, Motivation, and Disruption," *J. Exper. Psychol.*, 1932, *15*, 601–614; K. F. Muenzinger, "Motivation in Learning: II. The Function of Electric Shock for Right and Wrong Responses in Human Subjects," *J. Exper. Psychol.*, 1934, *17*, 439–448; K. F. Muenzinger and H. Newcomb, "Motivation in Learning: III. A Bell Signal Compared with Electric Shock for Right and Wrong Responses in the Visual Discrimination Habit," *J. Comp. Psychol.*, 1935, *20*, 85–93; H. Gurnee, "The Effect of Electric Shock for Right Responses on Maze Learning in Human Subjects," *J. Exper. Psychol.*, 1938, *22*, 354–364.

23. E. L. Thorndike, *Human Learning*. Appleton-Century-Crofts, 1931, p. 46.

24. E. B. Hurlock, "The Evaluation of Certain Incentives Used in School Work," *J. Educ. Psychol.*, 1925, *16*, 145–159.

25. E. B. Hurlock, "The Use of Group Rivalry as an Incentive," *J. Abn. Soc. Psychol.*, 1927, *22*, 278–290.

26. J. L. Elwell and G. C. Grindley, "The Effect of Knowledge of Results on Learning and Performance," *Brit. J. Psychol.*, 1938, *29*, 54. See also S. J. Macpherson, V. Dees, and G. C. Grindley, "The Effect of Knowledge of Results on Learning and Performance: II. Some Characteristics of Very Simple Skills," *Quart. J. Exper. Psychol.*, 1948, *1*, 68–78; and "III. The Influence of the Time Interval Between Trials," *ibid.*, pp. 167–174.

27. For a review of the literature, see E. A. Bilodeau and I. McD. Bilodeau, "Motor-Skills Learning," *Annual Review of Psychology*, 1961, pp. 250–259.

28. A. F. Smode, "Learning and Performance in a Tracking Task Under Two Levels of Achievement Information Feedback," *J. Exper. Psychol.*, 1958, *56*, 297–304.

29. A. C. Williams and G. E. Briggs, "On-Target Versus Off-Target Information and the Acquisition of Tracking Skill," *J. Exper. Psychol.*, 1962, *64*, 519–525.

30. E. C. Sanford's experience, as reported in F. C. Dockeray and G. G. Lane, *Psychology*

(2nd ed.), Prentice-Hall, 1950, pp. 158–159.

31. See the data summarized in J. A. McGeoch and A. L. Irion, *The Psychology of Human Learning* (2nd ed.), Longmans, Green, 1952, pp. 287–290. Also see H. Gleitman, "Place Learning," *Scientific American*, October 1963, pp. 120–121, for a description of a somewhat different type of "putting-through" experiment.

32. E. Neimark and L. J. Saltzman, "Intentional and Incidental Learning with Different Rates of Stimulus-Presentation," *Amer. J. Psychol.*, 1953, 66, 618–621; see especially p. 618.

33. J. G. Jenkins, "Instruction as a Factor in 'Incidental' Learning," *Amer. J. Psychol.*, 1933, 45, 471–477.

34. I. J. Saltzman, "The Orienting Task in Incidental and Intentional Learning," *Amer. J. Psychol.*, 1953, 66, 593–597; and Jenkins, *op. cit.*, reference 33.

35. L. Postman, P. A. Adams, and A. M. Bohm, "Studies in Incidental Learning: V. Recall for Order and Associative Clustering," *J. Exper. Psychol.*, 1956, 51, 334–342. See also the earlier studies of this series listed on p. 342 of the reference.

36. See Reference 33, p. 474.

37. G. H. S. Razran, "Attitudinal Control of Human Conditioning," *J. Psychol.*, 1936, 2, 327–337.

38. G. H. S. Razran, as reported in *Science News Letter*, January 7, 1950, pp. 6–7.

39. N. E. Spear, B. R. Ekstrand, and B. J. Underwood, "Association by Contiguity," *J. Exper. Psychol.*, 1964, 67, 151–161.

40. J. Greenspoon, "The Reinforcing Effect of Two Spoken Sounds on the Frequency of Two Responses," *Amer. J. Psychol.*, 1955, 68, 409–416.

41. See W. S. Verplanck, "The Control of the Content of Conversation: Reinforcement of Statements of Opinion," *J. Abn. Soc. Psychol.*, 1955, 51, 668–676; and the later critical studies of N. H. Azrin, W. Holz, R. Ulrich, and I. Goldiamond, "The Control of the Content of Conversation through Reinforcement," *J. Exper. Anal. Behav.*, 1961, 4, 25–30, and Paul, Eriksen, and Humphries, reference 42.

42. G. L. Paul, C. W. Eriksen, and L. G. Humphries, "Use of Temperature Stress with Cool Air Reinforcement for Human Operant Conditioning," *J. Exper. Psychol.*, 1962, 64, 329–335.

43. C. W. Eriksen (Ed.), *Behavior and Awareness.* Duke University Press, 1962.

44. P. London and D. Rosenhan, "Personality Dynamics," in P. R. Farnsworth (Ed.). *Annual Review of Psychology*, 1964, pp. 466–468.

45. A. Huxley, *Brave New World.*

46. W. H. Emmons and C. W. Simon, "The Non-Recall of Material Presented During Sleep," *Amer. J. Psychol.*, 1956, 69, 76–81. For a critical review of the earlier studies, see C. W. Simon and W. H. Emmons, "Learning During Sleep?" *Psychol. Bull.*, 1955, 52, 328–342.

47. R. C. Travis, "Length of Practice Period and Efficiency in Motor Learning," *J. Exper. Psychol.*, 1939, 24, 339–345.

48. S. T. H. Wright and D. W. Taylor, "Distributed Practice in Verbal Learning and the Maturation Hypothesis," *J. Exper. Psychol.*, 1949, 39, 527–531.

49. G. A. Kimble and E. A. Bilodeau, "Work and Rest as Variables in Cyclical Motor Learning," *J. Exper. Psychol.*, 1949, 39, 150–157.

50. A long series of experiments by Underwood bear upon this problem. One of the most recent, with reference to some of the earlier studies, is B. J. Underwood, "Ten Years of Massed Practice on Distributed Practice," *Psychol. Rev.*, 1961, 68, 229–247.

51. See the data on rats in Munn, reference 2.

52. See R. S. Woodworth and H. Schlosberg, *Experimental Psychology* (rev. ed.). Holt, 1954, pp. 765–767.

53. See J. A. McGeoch and A. L. Irion, *The Psychology of Human Learning* (2nd ed.). Longmans, Green, 1952, pp. 176–177.

54. See K. S. Lashley, "A Simple Maze with Data on the Relation of the Distribution of Practice to the Rate of Learning," *Psychobiol.*, 1918, 1, 353–368. For research on the faster dropping out of errors in verbal material during distributed practice, see C. I. Hovland, "Experimental Studies in Rote-Learning Theory: IV. Comparison of Retention by Massed and Distributed Practice," *J. Exper. Psychol.*, 1940, 26, 568–587.

55. A. I. Gates, "Recitation as a Factor in Memorizing," *Arch. Psychol.*, 1917, 6, No. 40.

56. G. Forlano, "School Learning with Various Methods of Practice and Rewards," *Teachers College Contrib. Educ.*, 1936, No. 688.

57. See, for example, L. A. Pechstein, "Whole Versus Part Methods in Motor Learning," *Psychol. Monogr.*, 1917, 23, 2.

58. See McGeoch and Irion, op. cit., reference 53.

59. Briggs, G. E., and J. C. Naylor, "The Relative Efficiency of Several Training Methods as a Function of Transfer Task Complexity," J. Exper. Psychol., 1962, 64, 505–512.

60. R. S. Woodworth and H. Schlosberg, Experimental Psychology (rev. ed.). Holt, 1954, p. 786.

61. D. O. Hebb, The Organization of Behavior. Wiley, 1949, pp. 60–78. This was the first presentation of Hebb's neurological theory, involving the concept of developing cell-assemblies.

62. C. L. Hull, Principles of Behavior, Appleton-Century, 1943; and A Behavior System, Yale University Press, 1952.

63. E. C. Tolman, Purposive Behavior in Animals and Men, Appleton-Century, 1932.

64. E. C. Tolman, Behavior and Psychological Man. University of California Press, 1958. See especially selections 13 and 19.

65. E. C. Tolman, "Cognitive Maps in Rats and Men," Psychol. Rev., 1948, 55, 189–208. This and other relevant papers by Tolman are reprinted in Tolman, reference 64.

66. Tolman, the preceding references.

67. J. F. Dashiell, "Direction Orientation in Maze Running by the White Rat," Comp. Psychol. Monogr., 1930, No. 7.

68. C. H. Honzik, "Maze Learning in Rats in the Absence of Specific Intra- and Extra-maze Stimuli," Univ. Calif. Publ. Psychol., 1933, 6, 99–144; D. L. Wolfle, "The Effect of Continuous Interchange of Alley Sections on the Maze Pattern of Rats," J. Comp. Psychol., 1935, 19, 91–106.

69. D. A. Macfarlane, "The Role of Kinesthesis in Maze Learning," Univ. Calif. Publ. Psychol., 1930, 4, 277–305.

70. D. P. Scharlock, "The Role of Extramaze Cues in Place and Response Learning," J. Exper. Psychol., 1955, 50, 249–254.

71. Scharlock, op. cit., p. 253.

72. See the review by F. Restle, "Discrimination of Cues in Mazes: A Resolution of the 'Place-vs.-Response' Question," Psychol. Rev., 1957, 64, 217–228; and H. Gleitman, "Place Learning," Scientific American, October 1963.

73. Gleitman, op. cit., reference 72, p. 122.

74. E. C. Tolman, "There is More Than One Kind of Learning," Psychol. Rev., 1949, 56, 154.

75. With respect to this, see the discussion in Chapter 4 of G. A. Kimble, Hilgard and Mar-

quis' Conditioning and Learning, Appleton-Century-Crofts, 1961.

76. See Hull, the sources cited in reference 62.

77. C. L. Hull, Principles of Behavior. Appleton-Century-Crofts, 1943, p. 102.

78. Hull, op. cit., made a distinction between primary and secondary motivation and stressed the importance of both. A recent review of research on secondary reinforcement is that of J. Myers, "Secondary Reinforcement: A Review of Recent Experimentation," Psychol. Bull., 1958, 55, 284–301. The readings in R. C. Birney and R. C. Teevan, Reinforcement, Van Nostrand, 1962, are also relevant.

79. Hull, op. cit., reference 77, p. 404.

80. F. A. Logan, "The Hull-Spence Approach," in S. Koch (Ed.), Psychology: A Study of a Science, McGraw-Hill, 1959, Vol. 2. Also see K. W. Spence, Behavior Theory and Conditioning, Yale University Press, 1956; and F. A. Logan, Incentive, Yale University Press, 1960, for theoretical outgrowths of Hull's system.

81. E. R. Guthrie, "Association by Contiguity," in S. Koch (Ed.), Psychology: A Study of a Science, McGraw-Hill, 1959, Vol. 2. Also see V. Voeks, "What Fixes the Correct Response?" Psychol. Rev., 1945, 52, 49–51; and, by the same author, "Postremity, Recency, and Frequency as Bases for Prediction in the Maze Situation," J. Exper. Psychol., 1948, 38, 495–509. Also Voek's "Formalization and Clarification of a Theory of Learning," J. Psychol., 1950, 341–362.

82. Brogden, reference 13.

83. Brogden, reference 14.

84. See references 32–35.

85. B. B. Hudson, "One-Trial Learning in the Domestic Rat," Genet. Psychol. Monogr., 1950, 41, 99–145.

86. N. E. Spear, B. R. Ekstrand, and B. J. Underwood, "Association by Contiguity," J. Exper. Psychol., 1964, 67, p. 161.

87. See Buxton, op. cit., reference 16.

88. W. K. Estes, "The Statistical Approach to Learning Theory," in S. Koch (Ed.), Psychology: A Study of a Science, McGraw-Hill, 1959, Vol. 2, p. 399.

89. Ibid.

90. Ibid.

91. Ibid.

92. Ibid.

93. See especially W. K. Estes and J. H. Straughan, "Analysis of a Verbal Conditioning Situation in Terms of Statistical Learning Theory," J.

Exper. Psychol., 1954, 47, 225–234. Also see references 88 and 94.

94. C. N. Uhl, "Two-Choice Probability Learning in the Rat as a Function of Incentive, Probability of Reinforcement, and Training Procedure," J. Exper. Psychol., 1963, 66, 443–449.

95. E. L. Thorndike, "Watson's Behavior," J. Anim. Behav., 1915, 5, 452–467. See also the information summarized in the writer's Animal Psychology, Houghton Mifflin, 1933, pp. 342–344.

Chapter 12

Remembering and Forgetting

1. G. J. Dudycha and M. M. Dudycha, "Childhood Memories: A Review of the Literature," Psychol. Bull., 1941, 38, 668–681. Also see the study by S. Waldfogel, "The Frequency and Affective Character of Childhood Memories," Psychol. Monogr. 1948, No. 291. A detailed evaluation of this study appears in I. M. L. Hunter, Memory: Facts and Fallacies, Penguin Books, 1957, pp. 125–131.

2. See D. E. Broadbent, Perception and Communication. Pergamon, 1958. The filtering of information is also discussed in Broadbent's Behavior, London: Eyre and Spottiswoode, 1961, pp. 198–200.

3. G. Sperling, "The Information Available in Brief Visual Presentations," Psychol. Monogr., 1960, 74, No. 11; and E. Averbach and A. S. Coriell, "Short-Term Memory in Vision," Bell. Syst. Tech. J., 1961, 40, 309–328. Or see the summary of these studies by Sperling and Averbach in C. Cherry (Ed.), Information Theory, London: Butterworth's, 1960.

4. See discussions of the memory trace in D. O. Hebb, The Organization of Behavior, Wiley, 1949.

5. See W. Dingman and M. B. Sporn, "Molecular Theories of Memory," Science, 1964, 144, 26–29.

6. Dingman and Sporn, op. cit., pp. 27, 28.

7. R. W. Gerard, "What is Memory?" Scientific American, September 1953, 118–126. Quotation from pp. 118–120.

8. Various indicators of associative strength are discussed in R. S. Woodworth and H. Schlosberg, Experimental Psychology (rev. ed.), Holt, 1954, pp. 43–71.

9. See E. A. Fleishman and J. F. Parker, Jr., "Factors in the Retention and Relearning of Perceptual-Motor Skill," J. Exper. Psychol.,

1962, 64, 215–226; also the review by E. A. Bilodeau and I. McD. Bilodeau, "Motor Skills Learning," Annual Review of Psychology, 1961.

10. M. Hammerton, "Retention of Learning in a Difficult Tracking Task," J. Exper. Psychol., 1963, 66, 108–110.

11. J. A. McGeoch and A. W. Melton, "The Comparative Retention Values of Maze Habits and of Nonsense Syllables," J. Exper. Psychol. 1929, 12, 392–414. See also P. W. Van Tilborg, "The Retention of Mental and Finger Maze Habits," J. Exper. Psychol., 1936, 19, 334–341.

12. H. J. Leavitt and H. Schlosberg, "The Retention of Verbal and Motor Skills," J. Exper. Psychol., 1944, 34, 404–417.

13. F. Van Dusen and H. Schlosberg, "Further Study of the Retention of Verbal and Motor Skills," J. Exper. Psychol., 1948, 38, 526–534.

14. C. A. Tsai, "Comparative Study of Retention Curves for Motor Habits," Comp. Psychol. Monogr., 1924, 2, No. 11.

15. H. E. Burtt, "An Experimental Study of Early Childhood Memory," J. Genet. Psychol., 1937, 50, 187–192.

16. W. S. Hunter, "The Delayed Reaction in Animals and Children," Behav. Monogr., 1913, 2, No. 1.

17. See N. L. Munn, Handbook of Psychological Research on the Rat, Houghton Mifflin, 1950, pp. 272–278, for a summary of this research.

18. O. L. Tinklepaugh, "An Experimental Study of Representative Factors in Monkeys," J. Comp. Psychol., 1928, 8, 197–236. H. F. Harlow, H. Uhling, and A. H. Maslow, "Comparative Behavior of Primates: I. Delayed Reaction Tests on Primates from the Lemur to the Orangutan," J. Comp. Psychol., 1932, 13, 313–344.

19. Tinklepaugh, op. cit., 231–232.

20. C. Bühler and H. Hetzer, Testing Children's Development from Birth to School Age, Farrar and Rinehart, 1935; and H. Hetzer and S. Wislitsky, "Experimente über Erwartung und Errinnung beim Kleinkind," Zsch. f. Psychol., 1930, 118, 128–141.

21. M. Skalet, "The Significance of Delayed Reactions in Young Children," Comp. Psychol. Monogr., 1931, 7, No. 4.

22. B. Weinstein, "Delayed Matching from Sample in Monkeys." A film distributed by the University of Wisconsin and Coronet Films.

23. Skalet, op. cit., reference 21.

24. A. S. Starr, "The Diagnostic Value of the

Audito-Vocal Digit Memory Span," *Psychol. Clin.*, 1923, *15*, 61–84.

25. E. W. McElwee, "Further Standardization of the Ellis Memory for Objects Tests," *J. Appl. Psychol.*, 1933, *17*, 69–70.

26. F. C. Bartlett, *Remembering*. Cambridge University Press, 1932.

27. *Ibid.*

28. An experiment by W. W. Houts, reported in *Science News Letter*, July 31, 1954.

29. More detailed discussions of eidetic imagery will be found in the following references: H. Klüver, "Eidetic Imagery," in C. Murchison (Ed.), *A Handbook of Child Psychology* (2nd ed.), Clark University Press, 1933; N. L. Munn, *The Evolution and Growth of Human Behavior* (2nd. ed.), Houghton Mifflin, 1965, pp. 349–350; and T. X. Barber "The Eidetic Image and 'Hallucinatory' Behavior: A Suggestion for Further Research," *Psychol. Bull.*, 1959, *56*, 236–239.

30. C. I. Hovland, "Experimental Studies of Rote Learning Theory: IV. Comparison of Retention Following Learning to Same Criterion by Massed and Distributed Practice," *J. Exper. Psychol.*, 1940, *26*, 568–587.

31. See B. J. Underwood, "Ten Years of Massed Practice on Distributed Practice," *Psychol., Rev.*, 1961, *68*, 229–247; and Fleishman and Parker, *op. cit.*, reference 9.

32. A. I. Gates, "Recitation as a Factor in Memorizing", *Arch. Psychol.*, 1917, *6*, No. 40.

33. A. L. Gillette, "Learning and Retention: A Comparison of Three Experimental Procedures," *Arch. Psychol.*, 1936, No. 198.

34. B. J. Underwood, "Speed of Learning and Amount Retained: A Consideration of Methodology," *Psychol. Bull.*, 1954, *51*, 276–282.

35. W. C. F. Krueger, "The Effect of Overlearning on Retention," *J. Exper. Psychol.*, 1929, *12*, 71–78.

3. W. C. F. Krueger, "Further Studies in Overlearning," *J. Exper. Psychol.*, 1930, *13*, 152–163.

37. See the following reviews: L. Carmichael (Ed.), *Manual of Child Psychology* (2nd ed.), Wiley, 1954, pp. 425–430; and N. L. Munn, *Handbook of Psychological Research on the Rat*, Houghton Mifflin, 1950, pp. 292–293.

38. B. Zeigarnik, "Über das Behalten von erledigten und unerledigten Handlungen," *Psychol. Forsch.*, 1927, *9*, 1–85. Translated in W. D. Ellis, *A Source Book of Gestalt Psychology*, Harcourt, Brace, 1938; and abbreviated in L. W. Crafts, *et al.*, *Recent Experiments in Psychology* (2nd ed.), McGraw-Hill, 1950, pp. 64–73.

39. Unpublished data from M. H. Graves, reported in G. A. Kimble and N. Garmezy, *Principles of General Psychology*, Ronald, 1963, p. 156.

40. M. E. Bunch and W. K. Magdsick, "The Retention by Rats of an Incompletely Learned Maze Solution for Short Intervals of Time," *J. Comp. Psychol.*, 1933, *16*, 385–409; A. C. Anderson, "Evidences of Reminiscence in the Rat in Maze Learning," *J. Comp. Psychol.*, 1940, *30*, 399–412.

41. H. Ebbinghaus, *Memory* (trans. by Ruger and Bussenius). Teachers College, Columbia University, 1913.

42. L. Postman and L. Rau, "Retention as a Function of the Method of Measurement," *Univ. Calif. Publ. Psychol.*, 1957, 217–270.

43. *Ibid.*

44. L. R. Peterson and M. J. Peterson, "Short-Term Retention of Individual Verbal Items, *J. Exper. Psychol.*, 1959, *58*, 193–198.

45. B. B. Murdock, "The Retention of Individual Items," *J. Exper. Psychol.*, 1961, *62*, 618–625.

46. B. J. Underwood and J. Richardson, "The Influence of Meaningfulness, Intralist Similarity, and Serial Position on Retention," *J. Exper. Psychol.*, 1956, *52*, 119–126.

47. Postman and Rau, *op. cit.*

48. G. Katona, *Organizing and Remembering*. Columbia University Press, 1940.

49. D. O. Hebb, *A Textbook of Psychology*. Saunders, 1958, p. 147.

50. J. G. Jenkins and K. M. Dallenbach, "Obliviscence During Sleep and Waking," *Amer. J. Psychol.*, 1924, *35*, 605–612.

51. H. Minami and K. Dallenbach, "The Effect of Activity Upon Learning and Retention in the Cockroach," *Amer. J. Psychol.*, 1946, *59*, 2.

52. *Ibid.*, p. 2.

53. This experiment was done by Minami and Dallenbach, *op. cit.* Their data for overactive groups, which showed no retention, are not mentioned, the reason being that irritability and fatigue induced by the enforced activity in a treadmill interfered with relearning ability as well as retention.

54. S. Freud, *Psychopathology of Everyday Life*. Originally published by Macmillan but reprinted in 1951 as a Mentor Book. In the latter edition, see pp. 70–90.

55. See the data on hypnosis and recall in J. A. McGeoch and A. L. Irion, *The Psychology of Human Learning* (2nd ed.), Longmans, Green, 1952, pp. 362–363; and the discussion and references in R. W. White, *The Abnormal Personality* (2nd ed.), Ronald, 1956, pp. 349–350. On sodium pentathol, see p. 68.

56. W. Penfield, *The Excitable Cortex in Conscious Man.* Thomas, 1958.

57. See White, *The Abnormal Personality, op. cit.,* pp. 540–542.

58. C. P. Duncan, "The Retroactive Effect of Electroshock on Learning," *J. Comp. Physiol. Psychol.,* 1949, *42,* 32–44.

59. See the data summarized in N. L. Munn, *Handbook of Psychological Research on the Rat,* Houghton Mifflin, 1950, pp. 443–449.

60. P. B. Porter and C. P. Stone, "Electroconvulsive Shock in Rats under Ether Anesthesia," *J. Comp. Physiol. Psychol.,* 1947, *40,* 441–456.

61. R. S. Woodworth and H. Schlosberg, *Experimental Psychology* (rev. ed.). Holt, 1954, p. 773.

62. L. M. Harden, "Effect of Emotional Reactions upon Retention," *J. Gen. Psychol.,* 1930, *3,* 197–221.

63. For a more detailed discussion of the extensive literature on proactive inhibition, see J. Deese, *The Psychology of Learning* (2nd ed.), McGraw-Hill, 1958, pp. 256–269. Also see B. J. Underwood, "Interference and Forgetting," *Psychol. Rev.,* 1957, *64,* 49–60. The illustration on page 53 summarizes and interrelates the data of several studies on proactive inhibition.

64. F. J. Houlahan, "Immediacy of Interpolation and Amount of Retention," *J. Educ. Psychol.,* 1941, *32,* 37–44.

65. A. W. Melton and W. J. von Lackum, "Retroactive and Proactive Inhibition in Retention: Evidence for a Two Factor Theory of Retroactive Inhibition," *Amer. J. Psychol.,* 1941, *54,* 157–173; and G. E. Briggs, "Retroactive Inhibition as a Function of the Degree of Original and Interpolated Learning," *J. Exper. Psychol.,* 1957, *53,* 60–67.

66. See especially A. W. Melton and J. M. Irwin, "The Influence of Degree of Interpolated Learning on Retroactive Inhibition and the Overt Transfer of Specific Responses," *Amer. J. Psychol.,* 1940, *53,* 173–203; and J. A. McGeoch A. L. Irion, *The Psychology of Human Learning* (2nd ed.), Longmans, Green, 1952, pp. 404–467.

67. See the discussion in Deese, reference 63, pp. 260–262.

68. For example: R. H. Nutt, *How to Develop a Good Memory,* Simon and Schuster, 1941; J. Brothers and E. P. F. Eagan, *Ten Days to a Successful Memory,* Prentice-Hall, 1957; J. D. Weinland, *How to Improve Your Memory,* Barnes and Noble, 1957.

69. M. Gardner, "Mathematical Games," *Scientific American,* October 1957, p. 130.

70. H. Woodrow, "The Effect of Type of Training on Transference," *J. Educ. Psychol.,* 1927, *18,* 160–171.

71. W. James, *Psychology* (Briefer Course). Holt, 1908, p. 294.

72. See G. H. Estabrooks, "A Handy Memory Trick," *J. Genet. Psychol.,* 1927, *34,* 617.

Chapter 13

Thinking

1. H. C. Warren and L. Carmichael, *Elements of Human Psychology.* Houghton Mifflin, 1930, p. 307.

2. N. R. F. Maier, "Reasoning in White Rats," *Comp. Psychol. Monogr.,* 1929, No. 6.

3. N. R. F. Maier, "Reasoning in Children," *J. Comp. Psychol.,* 1936, *21,* 357–366.

4. W. S. Hunter, "The Behavior of Raccoons in a Double Alternation Temporal Maze," *J. Genet. Psychol.,* 1928, *35,* 374–388.

5. W. S. Hunter and J. W. Nagge, "The White Rat and the Double Alternation Temporal Maze," *J. Genet. Psychol.,* 1931, *39,* 303–319.

6. L. W. Gellermann, "The Double Alternation Problem. III. The Behavior of Monkeys in a Double Alternation Box-Apparatus," *J. Genet. Psychol.,* 1931, *39,* 359–392.

7. W. S. Hunter and S. C. Bartlett, "Double Alternation in Young Children," *J. Exper. Psychol.,* 1948, *38,* 558–567.

8. A. Hodges, "A Developmental Study of Symbolic Behavior," *Child Develpm.,* 1954, *25,* 277–280.

9. L. W. Gellermann, "The Double Alternation Problem. II. The Behavior of Children and Human Adults in a Double Alternation Temporal Maze," *J. Genet. Psychol.,* 1931, *39,* 197–226.

10. J. W. Schoonard and F. Restle, "Analysis of Double Alternation in Terms of Patterns of Stimuli and Responses," *J. Exper. Psychol.,* 1961, *61,* 365–367. Quotation from page 367.

11. See P. De Latil, *Thinking by Machine,* Houghton

Mifflin, 1957; Editors of *Scientific American*, *Automatic Control*, Simon and Schuster, 1955.

12. G. A. Miller, "Information and Memory," *Scientific American*, August 1956, 42–46. Reprinted in R. S. Daniel, *Contemporary Readings in Psychology*, Houghton Mifflin, 1965, pp. 110–115.

13. On this issue, see A. Newell and H. A. Simon, "Computer Simulation of Human Thinking," *Science*, 1961, *134*, 2011–2017; and U. Neisser, "The Imitation of Man by Machine," *Science*, 1963, *139*, 193–197.

14. F. C. Bartlett, *Thinking: An Experimental and Social Study*. Allen and Unwin, 1958, p. 198.

15. Bartlett, *op. cit.*, pp. 97–200.

16. E. Rignano, *The Psychology of Reasoning*. Harcourt, Brace, 1923, pp. 326–327. Quotation used by permission of Harcourt, Brace and World, and Routledge & Kegan Paul.

17. M. Scheerer, "Problem Solving," *Scientific American*, April 1963, p. 128.

18. N. R. F. Maier, "An Aspect of Human Reasoning," *Brit. J. Psychol.*, 1933, *24*, 144–155.

19. M. Wertheimer, *Productive Thinking*. Harper, 1945, p. 112.

20. *Ibid.*, p. 90.

21. A. Luchins, "Mechanization in Problem Solving: The Effect of Einstellung," *Psychol. Monogr.*, 1942, *54*, No. 6. Also see Z. P. Dienes, *An Experimental Study of Mathematics Learning*. Hutchinson, 1963.

22. E. Jacobson, "Electrophysiology of Mental Activities," *Amer. J. Psychol.*, 1932, *44*, 677–694.

23. L. W. Max, "Experimental Study of the Motor Theory of Consciousness: IV. Action Current Responses in the Deaf During Awakening, Kinesthetic Imagery and Abstract Thinking," *J. Comp. Psychol.*, 1937, *24*, 301–344.

24. P. H. Ewert and J. E. Lambert used this problem in "The Effect of Verbal Instructions Upon the Formation of a Concept," *J. Gen. Psychol.*, 1932, *6*, 400–413.

25. R. M. Gagné and E. C. Smith, Jr., "A Study of the Effects of Verbalization on Problem Solving," *J. Exper. Psychol.*, 1962, *63*, 12–18. Quotation from p. 18.

26. For a comparison of these theories, see J. F. Dashiell, *Fundamentals of General Psychology* (3rd ed.), Houghton Mifflin, 1949, pp. 588–590.

27. E. Totten, "Eye Movements During Visual Imagery, *Comp. Psychol. Monogr.*, 1935, *11*, No. 3.

28. P. H. Ewert, "Eye Movements During Reading and Recall," *J. Gen. Psychol.*, 1933, *8*, 65–84.

29. Jacobson, *op. cit.*, reference 22.

30. S. M. Smith, H. O. Brown, J. E. P. Toman, and L. S. Goodman, "The Lack of Cerebral Effects of d-Tubocurarine," *Anesthesiology*, 1947, *8*, 1–14.

31. P. E. Fields, "Studies in Concept Formation: I. The Development of the Concept of Triangularity in the White Rat," *Comp. Psychol. Monogr.*, 1932, No. 9; "Studies in Concept Formation: IV. A Comparison of White Rats and Raccoons with Respect to their Visual Discrimination of Certain Geometrical Figures," *J. Comp. Psychol.*, 1936, *21*, 341–355. K. U. Smith, "Visual Discrimination in the Cat: II. A further Study of the Capacity of the Cat for Visual Figure Discrimination," *J. Genet. Psychol.*, 1934, *46*, 336–357. C. C. Neet, "Visual Pattern Discrimination in the Macacus Rhesus Monkey," *J. Genet. Psychol.*, 1933, *43*, 163–196. G. Andrew and H. Harlow, "Performance of Macaque Monkeys on a Test of the Concept of Generalized Triangularity," *Comp. Psychol. Monogr.*, 1948, *19*, No. 3. N. L. Munn, B. Steining, "The Relative Efficacy of Form and Background in a Child's Discrimination of Visual Patterns," *J. Genet. Psychol.*, 1931, *39*, 73–90.

32. L. Welch and L. Long, "The Higher Structural Phases of Concept Formation in Children," *J. Psychol.*, 1940, *9*, 59–95; "A Further Investigation of the Higher Structural Phases of Concept Formation," *J. Psychol.*, 1940, *10*, 211–220; L. Welch, "The Genetic Development of the Associational Structures of Abstract Thinking," *J. Genet. Psychol.*, 1940, *56*, 175–206.

33. E. Heidbreder, "The Attainment of Concepts," a series in *J. Gen. Psychol.*, 1946, *35*, 173–223, and *J. Psychol.*, 1947, *24*, 93–138; 1948, *25*, 299–329; 1948, *26*, 45–69; 193–216; 1949, *27*, 3–39, 263–309.

34. K. Goldstein and M. Scheerer, "Abstract and Concrete Behavior: An Experimental Study with Special Tests," *Psychol. Monogr.*, 1941, *53*, No. 239.

35. *Ibid.*, p. 83.

36. The original test was developed by Vigotsky. His *Thought and Language*, one chapter of which is devoted to this test, has been translated by Hanfmann and Vakar and published by Wiley, 1962.

37. C. L. Hull, "Quantitative Aspects of the Evolution of Concepts," *Psychol. Monogr.*, 1920, No. 123, p. 85.

38. W. James, *Psychology* (Briefer Course). Holt, 1908, p. 251.

39. R. S. Woodworth, *Experimental Psychology,* Holt, 1938, p. 801.

40. See reference 39 and also a recent experimental comparison of these processes by H. A. Podell, "Two Processes of Concept Formation," *Psychol. Monogr.,* 1958, No. 468.

41. J. S. Bruner, J. J. Goodnow, and G. A. Austin, *A Study of Thinking.* Wiley, 1956.

42. *Ibid.,* p. 133.

43. *Ibid.,* p. 87.

44. J. Piaget, *The Child's Conception of the World.* Harcourt, Brace, 1929, pp. 196, 202.

45. R. W. Russell and W. Dennis, "Studies of Animism: I. A Standardized Procedure for the Investigation of Animism," *J. Genet. Psychol.,* 1939, *55,* 389–400; R. W. Russell, Studies in Animism: II. The Development of Animism," *J. Genet. Psychol.,* 1940, *56,* 353–366; R. W. Russell, "Studies in Animism: IV. An Analysis of Concepts Allied to Animism," *J. Genet. Psychol.,* 1940, *57,* 83–91.

46. W. Dennis, "Piaget's Questions Applied to a Child of Known Environment," *J. Genet. Psychol.,* 1942, *60,* 307–320.

47. W. Dennis and R. W. Russell, "Piaget's Questions Applied to Zuni Children," *Child Developm.,* 1940, *11,* 181–187; W. Dennis, "Animism and Related Tendencies in Hopi Children," *J. Abn. Soc. Psychol.,* 1943, *38,* 21–36.

48. I. Huang and H. W. Lee, "Experimental Analysis of Child Animism," *J. Genet. Psychol.,* 1945, *66,* 69–74.

49. M. Mead, "An Investigation of the Thought of Primitive Children with Special Reference to Animism," *J. Royal Anthrop. Instit.,* 1932, *62,* 173–190.

50. W. Dennis, "Animistic Thinking Among College and University Students," *Scientific Monthly,* 1953, *76,* 247–250.

51. See J. Piaget and B. Inhelder, *The Child's Conception of Space,* Routledge, 1956; and B. Inhelder and J. Piaget, *The Growth of Logical Thinking From Childhood to Adolescence,* Basic Books, 1958.

52. On the conservation concept, see Inhelder and Piaget, *op. cit.*

53. See especially M. D. S. Braine, "The Ontogeny of Certain Logical Operations: Piaget's Formulation Examined by Nonverbal Methods," *Psychol. Monogr.,* 1959, *73,* No. 5, and other references cited there.

54. See especially N. W. Kettner, J. P. Guilford, and P. R. Christensen, "A Factor-Analytic Study Across the Domains of Reasoning Creativity and Evaluation," *Psychol. Monogr.,* 1959, No. 479, and the earlier studies referred to in this monograph.

55. J. P. Guilford and R. Hoepfner, "Current Summary of Structure-of-Intellect Factors and Suggested Tests," *Reports from Psychological Laboratory of the University of Southern California,* December 1963.

56. J. P. Guilford, P. R. Merrifield, and A. Gershon, "Some Primary Abilities in the Areas of Nonverbal Divergent Production," *Science,* 1962, *136,* 326.

57. A brief account of this research is given in F. Barron, "The Psychology of Imagination," *Scientific American,* September 1958, pp. 151–166.

58. G. Wallas, *The Art of Thought.* Harcourt, Brace, 1926, Chapter IV. For a general summary, see E. D. Hutchinson, "Materials for the Study of Creative Thinking," *Psychol. Bull.,* 1931, *28,* 392–410.

59. C. Patrick, "Creative Thought in Poets," *Arch. Psychol.,* 1935, No. 178, pp. 30, 31; and "Creative Thought in Artists," *J. Psychol.,* 1937, *4,* 53.

60. Quoted from W. R. Benét, *The Reader's Encyclopedia.* Crowell, 1948, p. 1012.

61. P. H. A., *Science,* 1963, *140,* 1177.

62. From A. Maurois, *The Life of Sir Alexander Fleming.* Dutton, 1959. The quotation is from p. 125. By permission of E. P. Dutton & Co., Inc., and Jonathan Cape Limited. The film, "Scientific Method," Encyclopedia Britannica Films, dramatizes Fleming's discovery.

Chapter 14

Communication and Language

1. Translation (according to B. L. Whorf, *Language, Thought, and Reality,* Wiley, 1956, p. 188) is "causes by drilling."

2. W. Craig, "The Voices of Pigeons Regarded as a Means of Social Control," *Amer. J. Sociol.,* 1908, *14,* 86–100. Also see K. Lorenz, *King Solomon's Ring,* Crowell, 1952; and W. H. Thorpe, "The Language of Birds," *Scientific American,* October 1956, pp. 129–138.

3. C. R. Carpenter, "A Field Study of the Behavior and Social Relations of Howling Monkeys," *Comp. Psychol. Monogr.,* 1934, *10.*

4. See R. M. Yerkes, *Chimpanzee: A Laboratory Colony,* Yale University Press, 1943, p. 86.

5. K. von Frisch, *The Dancing Bees*. Harcourt, Brace, 1955. A popular account appears in A. Krogh, "The Language of the Bees," *Scientific American*, August 1948, pp. 19–21: and H. Kalmus, "More on the Language of the Bees," *Scientific American*, July 1953, pp. 60–64. Bees also transmit information through the sounds they make. On this, see A. M. Wenner, "Sound Communication in Honeybees," *Scientific American*, April 1964, pp. 116–124.

6. C. Cherry, *On Human Communication*. Wiley, 1957, p. 18.

7. M. P. Crawford, "The Cooperative Solving of Problems by Young Chimpanzees," *Comp. Psychol. Monogr.*, 1937, *14*, No. 2.

8. S. D. Spragg, "Morphine Addiction in Chimpanzees," *Comp. Psychol. Monogr.*, 1940, *15*, No. 7.

9. W. H. Furness, "Observations on the Mentality of Chimpanzees and Orangutans," *Proc. Amer. Phil. Soc.*, 1916, *55*, 281–290.

10. K. J. Hayes and C. Hayes, "The Intellectual Development of a Home-Raised Chimpanzee," *Proc. Amer. Phil. Soc.*, 1951, *95*, 105–109. Also, C. Hayes, *The Ape in Our House*, Harper, 1951.

11. See J. A. B. de Haan, "Animal Language in Relation to that of Man," *Biol. Rev.*, 1929, *4*, 249–268.

12. E. L. Thorndike, *Animal Intelligence*. Macmillan, 1911.

13. See Helen Keller's *The Story of My Life*. Doubleday, 1903, p. 315.

14. E. Cassirer, *An Essay on Man*. Yale University Press, 1944, p. 35.

15. S. K. Langer, *Philosophy in a New Key*. Harvard University Press, 1942.

16. The most extensive published study on Broca's area and its significance in speech is to be found in W. Penfield and L. Roberts, *Speech and Brain Mechanism*. Although the speech area is often cited as located on the left side of the brain for *right-handed* persons, these investigators find it on that side regardless of which hand is preferred.

17. W. S. Hunter, *Human Behavior*, University of Chicago Press, 1928, p. 329.

18. Langer, *op. cit.*, p. 83.

19. O. Jesperson, *Language: Its Nature, Development, and Origin*. Holt, 1930.

20. C. H. Judd, *The Psychology of Social Institutions*. Macmillan, 1926, p. 195.

21. E. L. Thorndike, "The Origin of Language," *Science*, 1943, *98*, 4. Also in *Selected Writings from a Connectionist's Psychology*. Appleton-Century-Crofts, 1949.

22. *Ibid.*, p. 4.

23. N. L. Munn, *The Evolution and Growth of Human Behavior* (2nd ed.). Houghton Mifflin, 1965, p. 384.

24. O. C. Irwin and H. P. Chen, "Development of Speech During Infancy," *J. Exper. Psychol.*, 1946, *36*, 431–436. See also O. C. Irwin, "Infant Speech," *Scientific American*, September 1949, pp. 22–24.

25. C. E. Osgood, *Method and Theory in Experimental Psychology*. Oxford University Press, 1953, p. 684.

26. B. F. Skinner, *Verbal Behavior*. Appleton-Century-Crofts, 1957, p. 31.

27. O. H. Mowrer, "On the Psychology of 'Talking Birds' — A Contribution to Language and Personality Theory," in Mowrer's *Learning Theory and Personality Dynamics*, Ronald, 1950; see especially p. 707.

28. See the letter quoted in Mowrer, *op. cit.*, p. 707.

29. This is Holt's reflex circle theory. See E. B. Holt, *Animal Drive and the Learning Process*, Holt, 1931, pp. 37–38.

30. N. E. Miller and J. Dollard, *Social Learning and Imitation*. Yale University Press, 1941, p. 277.

31. J. B. Watson, *Behaviorism*. Norton, 1930, pp. 208–209.

32. W. C. Olson, *Child Development*. Heath, 1949.

33. L. M. Terman *et al.*, *Genetic Studies of Genius: Mental and Physical Traits of a Thousand Gifted Children*. Stanford University Press, 1925.

34. See D. McCarthy, "Language Development in Children," in L. Carmichael (Ed.), *Manual of Child Psychology* (2nd ed.), Wiley, 1954, for a good discussion of the origins of speech and especially for data on the "first word"; and E. A., Davis, "The Development of Linguistic Skill in Twins, Singletons with Siblings and Only Children from Age Five to Ten Years," *Institute of Child Welfare Monogr. Ser.*, 1937, No. 14.

35. See McCarthy, *op. cit.*, pp. 587–588.

36. A. T. Jersild and R. Ritzman, "Aspects of Language Development: The Growth of Loquacity and Vocabulary," *Child Develpm.*, 1938, *9*, 243–259. Another study, using a method of estimating the vocabulary, is that of M. E. Smith, "An Investigation of the Development of

the Sentence and the Extent of Vocabulary in Young Children," *Univ. Iowa Stud. in Child Welfare*, 1926, *3*, No. 5.

37. I. Latif, "The Physiological Basis of Linguistic Development and of the Ontogeny of Meaning," *Psychol. Rev.*, 1934, *41*, 55–85; 153–176; 246–264.

38. See Smith, *op. cit.*, reference 36.

39. M. M. Nice, "The Development of the Child's Vocabulary in Relation to Environment," *Ped. Sem.*, 1915, *22*, 35–64; F. M. Young, "An Analysis of Certain Variables in a Developmental Study of Language," *Genet. Psychol. Monogr.*, 1941, *23*, No. 1. Also see McCarthy, *op. cit.*

40. See R. Brown and C. Fraser, "The Acquisition of Syntax," in C. N. Cofer and B. S. Musgrave, *Verbal Behavior and Learning.* McGraw-Hill, 1963.

41. From Charles N. Cofer's comments on the Brown and Fraser paper, referred to in reference 40, p. 198.

42. Skinner, *op. cit.*, reference 23.

43. B. F. Skinner, Verbal Behavior. Appleton-Century-Crofts, 1957, p. 85.

44. For further details concerning this process, see N. L. Munn, *The Evolution and Growth of Human Behavior* (2nd ed.), Houghton Mifflin, 1965, pp. 391–393. An extensive critical review of Skinner's *Verbal Behavior*, which regards his approach as too limited in scope, has much to say about the many ways in which verbal responses are acquired. This review, by N. Chomsky, appears in *Language*, 1959, *35*, 26–58.

45. L. Carmichael, *Basic Psychology*, Random House, 1957, pp. 182, 193.

46. J. C. Nunnally and R. L. Flaugher, "Psychological Implications of Word Usage," *Science*, 1963, *140*, 775–781. Quotation from p. 775.

47. W. Weaver, "The Mathematics of Information," in *Automatic Control* (A Scientific American Book), Simon and Schuster, 1955, p. 100. In the same book, see also, G. King, "What Is Information?" Much of this is based upon the pioneer investigations of C. E. Shannon, "Prediction and Entropy in Printed English," *Bell Syst. Tech. J.*, 1951, *30*, 50–64.

48. Weaver, *op. cit.*, p. 102.

49. Weaver, *op. cit.*, pp. 105–106. A more detailed discussion of redundancy based upon the statistical structure of English and an experiment showing the constraints imposed by different numbers of preceding letters in a selection is to be found in N. G. Burton and J. C. R. Licklider, "Long Range Constraints in the Statistical Structure of Printed English," *Amer. J. Psychol.*, 1955, *68*, 650–653.

50. G. King, "What Is Information?" in *Automatic Control*, Simon and Schuster, 1955, p. 87.

51. Stuart Chase, in the Foreword to B. L. Whorf, *Language, Thought, and Reality.* Wiley, 1956, pp. vii-viii. His information comes from E. S. Glenn, "Semantic Difficulties in International Communication," first published in *ETC*, A Review of General Semantics, and reprinted in S. I. Hayakawa (Ed.), *Our Language and Our World,* Harper, 1958.

52. A. H. Gardiner, *The Theory of Speech and Language*, Oxford University Press, 1932, p. 35.

53. A. Korzybski, *Science and Sanity*, Institute of General Semantics, 1933.

54. S. I. Hayakawa, "How Words Change Our Lives," in R. Thruelsen and J. Kobler (Eds.), *Adventures of the Mind.* Knopf, 1959, p. 249. Also see, by the same author, *Language in Thought and Action.* Harcourt, Brace, 1949.

55. These are discussed in various books, including C. K. Ogden and I. A. Richards, *The Meaning of Meaning,* Harcourt, Brace, 1923 (reissued in Harvest Books, 1959); C. E. Osgood, G. J. Suci, and P. H. Tannenbaum, *The Measurement of Meaning,* University of Illinois Press, 1957, Chapter 1; and R. Brown, *Words and Things,* Free Press, 1958, Chapter 3.

56. Osgood *et al., op. cit.*, p. 7.

57. C. E. Osgood, "The Nature and Measurement of Meaning," *Psychol. Bull.*, 1952, *49*, 197–237.

58. C. E. Osgood and G. J. Suci, "Factor Analysis of Meaning," *J. Exper. Psychol.*, 1955, *50*, 325–338. Also see Osgood *et al., op. cit.*, Chapter 2.

59. Osgood, *et al., op. cit.*, p. 329.

60. J. Ruesch and W. Kees, *Nonverbal Communication: Notes on the Visual Perception of Human Relations.* University of California Press, 1956.

61. Published in 1955 by The Museum of Modern Art, New York.

62. A study of such gestures has been made by D. Efron, *Gesture and Environment.* King's Crown Press, 1941.

63. E. T. Hall, *The Silent Language.* Doubleday, 1959. Although this book emphasizes the utilization of time as a means of nonverbal communication, it is also concerned with other nonverbal, yet communicative, aspects of a culture.

Chapter 15
Knowing Our World

1. We can make no pretense of knowing what "really exists" beyond the limits of our skin; or, for that matter, within it. This is a problem that has puzzled many learned men. Writing more than a hundred years ago, a physiologist said: "It may well be, that sensation consists in the sensorium receiving through the medium of the nerves, and as a result of the action of an external cause, a knowledge of certain qualities or conditions, not of external bodies, but of the nerves of sense themselves." This was J. Müller, as quoted by W. M. O'Neil, in "Basic Issues in Perceptual Theory," Psychol. Rev., 1958, 65, 348–361.

2. D. Katz, The World of Colour, Kegan Paul, 1935. H. Helson, "Fundamental Problems in Color Vision: I. The Principle Governing Changes in Hue, Saturation and Lightness of Non-Selective Samples in Chromatic Illumination," J. Exper. Psychol., 1938, 23, 439–476; and, with V. B. Jeffers, "II. Hue, Lightness and Saturation of Selective Samples in Chromatic Illumination," J. Exper. Psychol., 1940, 26, 1–27. Also see R. M. Evans, An Introduction to Color, Wiley, 1948.

3. S. Hecht, "The Binocular Fusion of Colors and its Relation to Theories of Color Vision," Proc. Nat. Assoc. Sci., 1928, 14, 237–240.

4. E. H. Land, "Color Vision and the Natural Image, Part I," Proc. Nat. Acad. Sci., 1959, 45, 115–129; "Part II," ibid., pp. 636–644; "Experiments in Color Vision," Scientific American, May 1959, 84–99.

5. See G. L. Walls, " 'Land! Land!' " Psychol. Bull., 1960, 57, 29–48; and L. M. Hurvich and D. Jameson, "Color Vision," Annual Review of Psychology, 1960, 11, 99–130. The quotation is from the latter reference, p. 105.

6. This is discussed in M. A. Wenger, F. N. Jones, and M. H. Jones, Physiological Psychology, Holt, 1956, pp. 219–220.

7. See the discussion and references cited in N. L. Munn, The Evolution and Growth of Human Behavior (2nd ed.), Houghton Mifflin, 1965, pp. 290–298.

8. Two extensive reviews of the research are to be found in E. P. Johnson, "The Character of the B-Wave in the Human Electroretinogram," A.M.A. Archives of Ophthalmology, Part II, 1958, 60, 565–591; and L. A. Riggs, "The Human Electroretinogram," ibid., pp. 739–754.

9. See the discussion of color vision in animals in Munn, op. cit., pp. 98–100.

10. A good review of the various color theories appears in F. A. Geldard, The Human Senses, Wiley, 1953.

11. These findings are reported in the following: W. B. Marks, W. H. Dobelle, and E. F. MacNichol, Jr., "Visual Pigments of Single Primate Cones," Science, 1964, 143, 1181–1183; and P. K. Brown and G. Wald, "Visual Pigments in Single Rods and Cones of the Human Retina," Science, 1964, 144, 45–52. Also see G. Wald, "The Receptors of Human Color Vision," Science, 1964, 145, 1007–1016.

12. This interpretation, a modified version of the views of Leber (1869) and Fick (1879), is presented by Graham and Hsia as one outcome of their research on color blindness. See Y. Hsia and C. H. Graham, "Spectral Luminosity Curves for Protanopic, Deuteranopic, and Normal Subjects," Proc. Nat. Acad. Sci., 1957, 43, No. 11, 1011–1019; and C. H. Graham and Y. Hsia, "Color Defect and Color Theory," Science, 1958, 127, 675–682.

13. See E. F. MacNichol, Jr., "Three Pigment Color Vision," Scientific American, December 1964, pp. 48–56. Quotation from p. 56. This study reviews results on ganglion-cell research as well as that on cones. For an updated version of the Hering theory, see L. M. Hurvich and D. Jameson, "An Opponent-Process Theory of Color Vision," Psychol. Rev., 1957, 64, 384–404.

14. S. Hecht and R. E. Williams, "The Visibility of Monochromatic Radiation and the Absorption Spectrum of Visual Purple," J. Gen. Physiol., 1922, 5, 1–33. See also G. Wald, "Visual Systems and the Vitamins A," in H. Klüver (Ed.), Visual Mechanisms, J. Cattell Press, 1942, pp. 43–71.

15. N.R.C., Psychology for the Fighting Man. The Infantry Journal, 1943, Chapter III.

16. See S. H. Bartley, Vision: A Study of Its Basis. Van Nostrand, 1941, Chapter IV.

17. See, for example, R. Granit, "Comparative Studies on the Peripheral and Central Retina: I. On Interaction Between Distant Areas in the Human Eye," Amer. J. Physiol., 1930, 94, 41–50. For other relevant data on retinal interaction, see E. D. Adrian and R. Mathews, "The Action of Light on the Eye: III. Interaction of Retinal Neurones," J. Physiol., 1928, 65, 273–298; C. H. Graham, "The Relation of Nerve Response and Retinal Potential to Number of

Sense Cells Illuminated in an Eye Lacking Lateral Connections," *J. Cell. Comp. Neurol.*, 1932, 2, 295–310.

18. George von Békésy, "Current Status of Theories of Hearing," *Science*, 1956, 123, 779–783; and "The Ear," *Scientific American*, August 1957, pp. 66–78. Also see the chapter by Békésy and Rosenblith in S. S. Stevens (Ed.), *Handbook of Experimental Psychology*, Wiley, 1951; and George von Békésy, *Experiments in Hearing*, McGraw-Hill, 1960.

19. C. C. Bunch, "Auditory Activity after Removal of the Entire Right Cerebral Hemisphere," *J. Amer. Med. Assoc.*, 1928, 90, 2102.

20. By Hallowell Davis and associates. See Chapter 13 in S. S. Stevens and H. Davis, *Hearing: Its Psychology and Physiology*, Wiley, 1938.

21. For a review and evaluation of this research, see E. H. Kemp, "A Critical Review of Experiments on the Problem of Stimulation Deafness," *Psychol. Bull.*, 1935, 32, 325–342.

22. E. G. Wever and C. W. Bray, "The Nature of Acoustical Response: The Relation Between the Sound Frequency and Frequency of Impulses in the Auditory Nerve," *J. Exper. Psychol.*, 1930, 13, 373–387.

23. E. G. Wever, *Theory of Hearing*, Wiley, 1949.

24. Wever, *op. cit.*, p. 435.

25. See the summary by G. R. Wendt, "Vestibular Functions," Chapter 31 in S. S. Stevens (Ed.), *Handbook of Experimental Psychology*, Wiley, 1951, especially pp. 1215–1216.

26. See Wendt, *op. cit.*, pp. 1206–1208.

27. Again see Wendt's discussion.

28. D. A. Laird, "How the Consumer Estimates Quality by Subconscious Sensory Impression," *J. Appl. Psychol.*, 1932, 16, 241–246.

29. L. H. Beck and W. R. Miles, "Some Theoretical and Experimental Relationships Between Infrared Absorption and Olfaction," *Science*, November 28, 1947, 511. See also, by the same authors, "Infrared Absorption in Field Studies of Olfaction in Honeybees," *Proc. Nat. Acad. Sci.*, 1949, 35, 292–310.

30. C. Pfaffman, "Gustatory Afferent Impulses," *J. Cell. Comp. Physiol.*, 1941, 17, 243–258. See also his chapter on taste and smell in Stevens, *op. cit.*, reference 9.

31. K. Lenggenhager, "Die Genese der Luft-, See- und Eisenbahnkrankheit in neuen Licht," *Schweiz. med. Woch.*, 1936, 17, 354–357.

32. H. G. Wolff and S. Wolf, *Pain*. Thomas, 1948, pp. 4–7.

33. E. S. Siker, M. Swerdlow, and F. F. Foldes, "An Earlobe Algesimeter: A Simple Method of Determining Pain Threshold in Man," *Science*, 1954, 120, 273–274.

34. K. M. Dallenbach, "The Temperature Spots and End-Organs," *Amer. J. Psychol.*, 1927, 39, 402–427. This paper discusses earlier experiments of a similar nature and verifies them.

35. J. P. Nafe, "The Pressure, Pain, and Temperature Sense," in C. Murchison (Ed.), *A Handbook of General Experimental Psychology*. Clark University Press, 1934, pp. 1049–1058. For a critical evaluation of this theory, see W. L. Jenkins, "A Critical Examination of Nafe's Theory of Thermal Sensitivity," *Amer. J. Psychol.*, 1938, 51, 424–429. See also Nafe's reply, *ibid.*, pp. 763–769.

36. S. Renshaw, "The Errors of Cutaneous Localization and the Effect of Practice on the Localizing Movement in Children and Adults," *J. Genet. Psychol.*, 1930, 38, 223–238.

37. N. L. Munn, "Tactual Localization Without Overt Localizing Movements and Its Relation to the Concept of Local Signs as Orientation Tendencies," *J. Exper. Psychol.*, 1937, 20, 581–588.

Chapter 16
Attending and Perceiving

1. H. Piéron, *Principles of Experimental Psychology*. Harcourt, Brace, 1929, pp. 65–68.

2. F. C. Paschal, "The Trend of Theories of Attention," *Psychol. Rev.*, 1941, 48, 383–403.

3. D. E. Broadbent, *Perception and Communication*. Pergamon, 1958.

4. See Broadbent's filter and information-flow model in reference 3. A brief presentation of this model appears in A. M. Treisman, "Selective Attention in Man," *Brit. Med. Bull.*, 1964, 20, 12–16.

5. Suggested by an illustration in S. I. Franz and K. Gordon, *Psychology*, McGraw-Hill, 1933, p. 405.

6. H. Brandt, *The Psychology of Seeing*. Philosophical Library, 1945.

7. E. H. Hess and J. M. Polt, "Pupil Size as Related to Interest Value of Visual Stimuli," *Science*, 1960, 132, 349–350.

8. See S. S. Stevens (Ed.), *Handbook of Experimental Psychology*. Wiley, 1951, pp. 1077, 1133.

9. J. J. B. Morgan, "The Overcoming of Distraction and Other Resistances," *Arch. Psychol.*, 1916, No. 35.

10. G. L. Freeman, "The Spread of Neuromuscular Activity During Mental Work," *J. Gen. Psychol.*, 1931, *5*, 479–493.

11. S. M. Smith, H. O. Brown, E. P. Toman, and L. S. Goodman, "The Lack of Cerebral Effects of d-Tubocurarine," *Anaesthesiology*, 1917, *8*, 1–14.

12. G. A. Talland, "Inter-Senory Perceptual Set," *Brit. J. Psychol.*, 1959, *50*, 231–234.

13. H. Jasper, "Reticular-Cortical Systems and Theories of the Integrative Action of the Brain," in H. F. Harlow and C. N. Woolsey (Eds.), *Biological and Biochemical Bases of Behavior*. University of Wisconsin Press, 1958. On pages 42–43 there is a review of the relevant studies by Berger, Adrian, Mathews, and others.

14. These findings are summarized by H. W. Magoun, *The Waking Brain*, Thomas, 1958, pp. 64–78. Also D. B. Lindsley, "The Reticular System and Perceptual Discrimination," in Jasper *et al.* (Eds.), *Reticular Formation of the Brain*, Little, Brown, 1958, pp. 519–532.

15. J. M. Fuster, "Effects of Stimulation of Brain Stem on Tachistoscopic Perception," *Science*, 1958, *127*, 150.

16. D. H. Hubel, C. O. Henson, A. Rupert, and R. Galambos, "'Attention' Units in the Auditory Cortex," *Science*, 1959, *129*, 1279–1280.

17. R. Hernández-Peón, H. Scherrer, and M. Jouvet, "Modification of Electrical Activity in Cochlear Nucleus during 'Attention' in Unanesthetized Cats," *Science*, 1956, *123*, 331–332. Also in D. E. Dulany, R. L. DeValois, D. C. Beardslee, and M. R. Winterbottom, *Contributions to Modern Psychology* (2nd ed.), Oxford University Press, 1963, pp. 103–107. For another interpretation of these findings, in terms of reactions of muscles in the middle ear, see A. Hugelin, S. Dumont, and N. Paillas, "Tympanic Muscles and Control of Auditory Input During Arousal," *Science*, 1960, *131*, 1372–1373.

18. M. Jouvet, E. Berkowitz, and R. Hernández-Peón, mentioned in Dulany *et al.*, *op. cit.*

19. J. V. McConnell, R. L. Cutler, and E. B. McNeil, "Subliminal Stimulation: An Overview," *American Psychologist*, 1958, *13*, 229–242.

20. W. Cohen, "Spatial and Textural Characteristics of the Ganzfeld," *Amer. J. Psychol.*, 1957, *70*, 403–410. The quotations are from page 407.

21. W. Cohen, "Color Perception in the Chromatic Ganzfeld," *Amer. J. Psychol.* 1958, *71*, 390–394.

22. L. A. Riggs, F. Ratliff, J. C. Cornsweet, and T. N. Cornsweet, "The Disappearance of Steadily Fixated Test Objects," *J. Opt. Soc. Amer.*, 1953, *43*, 495–501.

23. R. M. Pritchard, W. Heron, and D. O. Hebb, "Visual Perception Approached by the Method of Stabilized Images," *Canad. J. Psychol.*, 1960, *14*, 67–77, and R. M. Pritchard, "Stabilized Images on the Retina," *Scientific American*, June 1961, pp. 72–78.

24. C. N. Winslow, "Visual Illusions in the Chick," *Arch. Psychol.* 1933, No. 153. See also C. J. Warden and J. Baar, "The Müller-Lyer Illusion in the Ring Dove, (Turtur risorius)," *J. Comp. Psychol.*, 1929, *9*, 275–292.

25. This discussion is based on the material in I. Rock and L. Kaufman, "The Moon Illusion," *Science*, 1962, *136*, 953–961, 1023–1031.

26. E. G. Boring "The Moon Illusion," *Amer. J. Physics*, 1943, *11*, 55–60.

27. M. Wertheimer, "Experimentelle Studien über das Sehen von Bewegungen," *Z. f. Psychol.*, 1912, *61*, 161–265.

28. K. U. Smith, "The Neural Centers Concerned in the Mediation of Apparent Movement Vision," *J. Exper. Psychol.*, 1940, *26*, 443–466. K. U. Smith and W. E. Kappauf, "A Neurological Study of Apparent Movement Vision in the Cat," *J. Gen. Psychol.*, 1940, *23*, 315–327.

29. S. H. Bartley, *Vision. Van Nostrand*, 1941, Chapter VII. Neural mechanisms in the illusion of movement are also discussed by P. A. Kolers, "The Illusion of Movement, "*Scientific American*, October 1964, pp. 98–106.

30. For a more adequate discussion of constancy phenomena, see L. Postman and J. P. Egan, *Experimental Psychology*, Harper, 1949, pp. 148–155; and S. S. Stevens, in Boring, Langfeld, and Weld's *Foundations of Psychology*, Wiley, 1948, pp. 229–237. Some relevant researches are R. H. Thouless, "Phenomenal Regression to the Real Object," *Brit. J. Psychol.*, 1931, *21*, 339–359; *ibid.*, *22*, 1–30; and E. Brunswik, "Distal Focusing of Perception: Size Constancy in a Representative Sample of Situations," *Psychol. Monogr.*, 1944, No. 254. The latter reference has an extensive bibliography of early work by Brunswik and others.

31. See A. H. Holway and E. G. Boring, "Determinants of Apparent Visual Size with Distance Variant," *Amer. J. Psychol.*, 1941, *54*, 21–37; also relevant is W. Lichten and S. Lurie, "A New Technique for the Study of Perceived

Size," *Amer. J. Psychol.*, 1950, *63*, 280–282.

32. See the discussion by J. E. Hochberg, *Perception*, Prentice-Hall, 1964, pp. 50–51; also D. O. Hebb, *A Textbook of Psychology*, Saunders, 1958, p. 186.

33. Aristotle's illusion is one of these. If the index and middle fingers are crossed and a pencil is placed between the crossed fingertips, one feels two pencils. E. B. Titchener discusses this in the qualitative student's manual of his *Experimental Psychology*, Macmillan, 1902. On illusions of tactual movement, see S. H. Bartley, *Principles of Perception,* Harper, 1958, pp. 268–273.

34. M. Wertheimer, "Laws of Organization in Perceptual Forms," in W. D. Ellis, *A Source Book of Gestalt Psychology.* Harcourt, Brace, 1938, pp. 71–88.

35. A good discussion of spatial organization will be found in W. N. Dember, *Psychology of Perception*, Holt, 1960, pp. 161–169.

36. E. W. Scripture, *Thinking, Feeling, Doing* (2nd rev. ed.), Putnam, 1907, p. 91.

37. The psychophysical methods, and some laboratory exercises calling for their use, are presented in R. S. Woodworth and H. Schlosberg, *Experimental Psychology* (rev. ed.). Holt, 1954, Chapters 8 and 9; S. S. Stevens, and E. H. Galanter, "Ratio Scales and Category Scales for a Dozen Perceptual Continua," *J. Exper. Psychol.*, 1957, *54*, 377–411; and S. S. Stevens, "Measurement and Man," *Science*, 1958, *127*, 383–389.

38. L. Carmichael, H. F. Hogan, and A. A. Walter, "An Experimental Study of the Effect of Language on the Reproduction of Visually Perceived Form," *J. Exper. Psychol.*, 1932, *15*, 73–86.

39. L. Immergluck, "The Role of Set in Perceptual Judgment," *J. Psychol.*, 1952, *34*, 181–189. Reproduced in E. L. Hartley and R. E. Hartley, *Outside Readings in Psychology* (2nd ed.), Crowell, 1957, pp. 77–86.

40. B. F. Skinner, "The Verbal Summator and a Method for the Study of Latent Speech," *J. Psychol.*, 1936, *2*, 71–108; W. W. Grings, "The Verbal Summator Technique and Abnormal Mental States," *J. Abn. Soc. Psychol.*, 1942, *37*, 529–545. Also see J. E. Bell, *Projective Techniques,* Longmans, 1948, Chapter 4. A tactual-kinesthetic test might use such materials as the Twitchell-Allen tri-dimensional ceramic forms, although this test is also used visually. See D. Twitchell-Allen, "A 3-Dimensional Apperception Test: A New Projective Technique," *American Psychologist*, 1947, *2*, 271–272. Distributed by The Psychological Corporation.

41. J. S. Bruner, "Social Psychology and Perception," in E. E. Maccoby, T. M. Newcomb, and E. L. Hartley (Eds.), *Readings in Social Psychology* (3rd ed.). Holt, 1958, p. 94. Bruner's article, especially written for this volume, is an excellent résumé of the highly controversial studies mentioned here. They are also dealt with, at greater length, by F. H. Allport, *Theories of Perception and the Concept of Structure*, Wiley, 1955, Chapter 13.

42. L. Postman, J. S. Bruner, and E. McGinnies, "Personal Values as Selective Factors in Perception," *J. Abn. Soc. Psychol.*, 1948, *53*, 142–154.

43. R. L. Solomon and D. H. Howes, "Word Frequency, Personal Values, and Visual Duration Thresholds," *Psychol. Rev.*, 1951, *58*, 255–270; and D. H. Howes and R. L. Solomon, "Visual Duration Threshold as a Function of Word Probability," *J. Exper. Psychol.*, 1951, *41*, 401–410.

44. E. McGinnies, "Emotionality and Perceptual Defense," *Psychol. Rev.*, 1949, *56*, 244–251.

45. For a discussion of the idea of "perceptual defense," as involved in reference 44, see F. H. Allport, *op. cit.*, reference 41; and D. Howie, "Perceptual Defense," *Psychol. Rev.*, 1952, *59*, 308–315.

46. For a critical discussion of such findings and for revelant references, see M. Wertheimer, "Hebb and Senden on the Role of Learning in Perception," *Amer. J. Psychol.*, 1951, *64*, 133–137.

47. See A. H. Riesen, "Arrested Vision," *Scientific American*, 1950, *183*, 16–19.

48. These two paragraphs are based upon J. J. Gibson's discussion in his *The Perception of the Visual World*, Houghton Mifflin, 1950. See especially pp. 8–9.

49. See Gibson, *op. cit.*, Chapter 2, for a discussion of these theories.

50. This view is presented by F. L. Goodenough, *Developmental Psychology*, Appleton-Century-Crofts, 1934, pp. 138–139.

51. P. Ratoosh, "On Interposition as a Cue for the Perception of Distance," *Proc. Nat. Acad. Sci.*, 1949, 257–259.

52. On accommodation and convergence, see the account by R. S. Woodworth and H. Schlosberg,

Experimental Psychology (rev. ed.), Holt, 1954, pp. 475–480.

53. B. Johnson and L. F. Beck, "The Development of Space Perceptions: I. Stereoscopic Vision in Preschool Children," *J. Genet. Psychol.,* 1941, *58,* 247–254. This study gives the earliest age as two years, but Professor Beck has since informed the writer that one-year-olds have made similar reactions.

54. P. T. Young, "Auditory Localization with Acoustical Transposition of the Ears," *J. Exper. Psychol.,* 1928, *11,* 399–429.

55. For a fuller description of this work by Steinberg and Snow, see S. S. Stevens and H. Davis, *Hearing: Its Psychology and Physiology,* Wiley, 1949, pp. 181–183.

56. H. A. Witkin, "Perception of Body Position and of the Position of the Visual Field," *Psychol. Monogr.,* 1949, *63,* No. 7. The importance of visual factors was further investigated by H. A. Witkin and S. Wapner, "Visual Factors in the Maintenance of Upright Posture," *Amer. J. Psychol.,* 1950, *63,* 31–50.

Chapter 17

Social Behavior

1. See N. L. Munn, *The Evolution and Growth of Human Behavior* (2nd ed.), Houghton Mifflin, 1965, Chapter 15, for a survey of the research on which these observations are based.

2. See J. P. Scott, *Animal Behavior.* University of Chicago Press, 1958, pp. 17–18.

3. K. Z. Lorenz, "The Companion in the Bird's World," *Auk,* 1937, *54,* 245–273; here he speaks of imprinting as a conditioned reaction (p. 262). Also see, by the same author, *King Solomon's Ring,* Crowell, 1952, Chapter 11.

4. This is shown in a film entitled "Action and Reaction" (one of a series called "John Kieran's Kaleidoscope"), distributed by Almanac Films, 516 Fifth Ave., New York.

5. One of the earliest descriptions of what is now called "imprinting" was given by William James, based upon the earlier observations of D. A. Spalding. See W. James, *Principles of Psychology,* Holt, 1890, Vol. II, p. 396. Craig found that pigeons fed by hand from the time of hatching become fixated upon the hand so that copulation with it is attempted and the normal outlet is neglected. See W. Craig, "The Voices of Pigeons Regarded as a Means of Social Control," *Amer. J. Sociol.,* 1908, *14,* 86–

100. Still other, earlier examples of what has come to be called "imprinting" are cited by Hess (see reference 7).

6. An example is given by Scott, *op. cit.,* p. 179. E. H. Hess, reference 7, lists several species of birds known to be imprintable, as well as two mammals, the sheep and guinea pig.

7. E. H. Hess, "Imprinting," *Science,* 1959, *130,* 133–141. Another report of this research, also by Hess, is " 'Imprinting' in Animals," *Scientific Monthly,* March 1958, 81–90.

8. Hess, *op. cit.,* reference 7, p. 90.

9. Hess *op. cit.,* reference 7 (1959), p. 141.

10. T. Schjelderup-Ebbe, "Social Behavior of Birds," in C. Murchison (Ed.), *Handbook of Social Psychology.* Clark University Press, 1935.

11. C. Murchison, "The Experimental Measurement of a Social Hierarchy in *Gallus Domesticus,*" *J. Gen. Psychol.,* 1935, *12,* 3–39.

12. Murchison, *op. cit.,* pp. 21–22.

13. On intelligence in relation to the pecking order, see D. Katz and A. Toll, "Die Messung von Charakter und Begabungsunterschieden bei Tieren," *Zsch. f. Psychol.,* 1923, *93,* 287–311.

14. See Scott, *op. cit.,* pp. 172–176.

15. J. P. Scott, *Aggression.* University of Chicago Press, 1958, p. 118.

16. See especially F. M. Thrasher, *The Gang,* University of Chicago Press, 1927; and W. F. Whyte, *Street Corner Society,* University of Chicago Press, 1943.

17. See in this connection the discussion by Kimball Young, *Social Psychology* (3rd ed.), Appleton-Century-Crofts, 1956, pp. 502 ff.) on prejudice and status in race relations.

18. W. C. Allee, *The Social Life of Animals,* Abelard-Schuman Limited, 1958, p. 204.

19. *Ibid.,* p. 204.

20. See the work of J. C. Welty (on fish) and S. C. Chen (on ants) as reported in Allee, *op. cit.,* pp. 98–102.

21. H. F. Harlow, "Social Facilitation of Feeding in the Albino Rat," *J. Genet. Psychol.,* 1932, *41,* 211–221; E. W. Rasmussen, "Social Facilitation in Albino Rats," *Acta Psychol.* (Hague), 1939, *4,* 295–304; R. H. Bruce, "An Experimental Analysis of Social Factors Affecting the Performance of White Rats," *J. Comp. Psychol.,* 1941, *31,* 363–377.

22. C. Leuba, "An Experimental Study of Rivalry in Young Children," *J. Comp. Psychol.,* 1933, *16,* 367–378.

23. A good reference here is W. M. Wheeler,

Ants, Their Structure, Development and Behavior, Columbia University Press, 1913. An Ann Arbor Science Paperback by W. Goetsch, *The Ants,* 1957, also deals with social behavior.

24. Examples are given in F. Alverdes, *Social Life in the Animal World,* Harcourt, Brace, 1927. Also see the discussion by D. O. Hebb and W. R. Thompson, in G. Lindzey, *Handbook of Social Psychology,* Addison-Wesley, 1954, pp. 540–543.

25. This experiment is shown in a film by O. H. Mowrer: "An Experimentally Produced Social Problem in Rats," distributed by the Psychological Cinema Register, Pennsylvania State University.

26. W. J. Daniel, "Cooperative Problem Solving in Rats," *J. Comp. Psychol.,* 1942, *34,* 361–368.

27. M. P. Crawford, "Cooperative Solution by Chimpanzees of a Problem Requiring Serial Responses to Color Cues," *J. Soc. Psychol.,* 1941 *13,* 259–280.

28. D. L. Wolfle and H. M. Wolfle, "The Development of Cooperative Behavior in Monkeys and Young Children," *J. Genet. Psychol.,* 1939, *55,* 137–175.

29. N. Azrin and O. R. Lindsley, "The Reinforcement of Cooperation Between Children," *J. Abn. Soc. Psychol.,* 1956, *52,* 100–102.

30. For a general survey of status, see S. S. Sargent and R. C. Williamson, *Social Psychology* (2nd ed.), Ronald, 1958, Chapter 5.

31. A good reference is T. R. Sarbin, "Role Theory," in G. Lindzey, *Handbook of Social Psychology,* Addison-Wesley, 1954, Vol. I.

32. A. C. Kinsey, W. B. Pomeroy, and C. E. Martin, *Sexual Behavior in the Human Male.* Saunders, 1948, Chapter X.

33. For further information, see A. Bavelas, "Role Playing in Management Training," *Sociatry,* 1947, *2,* 183–191; and N. R. F. Maier, *Principles of Human Relations,* Wiley, 1952, Chapters 4 and 5.

34. See Sarbin, *op. cit.,* p. 225.

35. On this, see Sarbin, *op. cit.,* pp. 248–255. From Gardner Lindzey, *Handbook of Social Psychology,* Addison-Wesley, 1954.

36. These and similar instances are cited in L. M. Killian, "The Significance of Multiple-Group Membership in Disaster," *Amer. J. Sociol.,* 1952, *57,* 309–313.

37. L. Festinger, *A Theory of Cognitive Dissonance.* Row, Peterson, 1957.

38. L. H. Festinger, H. W. Riecken, and S. Schach-ter, *When Prophecy Fails.* University of Minnesota Press, 1956.

39. L. Festinger and J. M. Carlsmith, "Cognitive Consequences of Forced Compliance," *J. Abn. Soc. Psychol.,* 1959, *58,* 203–210. Quotation from pp. 209–210.

40. These experiments, by F. H. Allport and J. F. Dashiell, are described in the latter's chapter, "Experimental Studies of the Influence of Social Situations on the Behavior of Individual Human Adults," in C. Murchison, *Handbook of Social Psychology,* Clark University Press, 1935.

41. N. Triplett, "The Dynamogenic Factors in Pacemaking and Competition," *Amer. J. Psychol.,* 1898, *9,* 507–533.

42. K. Lewin, *Resolving Social Conflicts.* Harper, 1948, p. 84.

43. K. Lewin, *Field Theory in Social Science,* Harper, 1951, Chapter IX.

44. See the preceding book by Lewin and also R. W. Leeper, *Lewin's Topological and Vector Psychology: A Digest and a Critique,* University of Oregon, 1943.

45. Lewin, *Field Theory in Social Science, op. cit.,* p. 197.

46. Many such investigations have been carried out by the Survey Research Center for Group Dynamics, originally set up at the Massachusetts Institute of Technology by Lewin and later moved to the University of Michigan. Some of the studies are reprinted in D. Cartwright and A. Zander, *Group Dynamics: Research and Theory* (2nd ed.), Row, Peterson, 1960.

47. J. L. Moreno, *Who Shall Survive? Foundations of Sociometry, Group Psychotherapy and Socio-Drama* (rev. ed.). Beacon House, 1953.

48. E. F. Gardner and G. G. Thompson, *Social Relations and Morale in Small Groups.* Appleton-Century-Crofts, 1956.

49. Gardner and Thompson, *op. cit.,* p. 33.

50. R. F. Bales, "Task Roles and Social Roles in Problem-Solving Groups," in E. E. Maccoby, T. M. Newcomb, and E. L. Hartley, *Readings in Social Psychology* (3rd ed.). Holt, 1958, pp. 437–447. Also see, by the same author, "How People Interact in Conferences," *Scientific American,* 1955, *192,* 31–35.

51. Bales, *op. cit.,* reference 50, p. 439.

52. Bales, *op. cit.,* p. 447.

53. C. A. Gibb, "The Principles and Traits of Leadership," *J. Abn. Soc. Psychol.,* 1947, *42,* 269. Also in P. Hare, E. F. Borgatta, and

R. F. Bales (Eds.), *Small Groups*, Knopf, 1955, pp. 87–95.

54. A pioneer study in this area is that of M. E. Shaw, "A Comparison of Individuals and Small Groups in the Rational Solution of Complex Problems," *Amer. J. Psychol.*, 1932, *44*, 491–504. Generally speaking, the groups solved more problems. However, a repetition of the study by Marquart showed that the average performance of three individuals working alone and three working as a group did not differ. Thus, individual for individual, the group situation was not superior. See D. I. Marquart, "Group Problem Solving," *J. Soc. Psychol.*, 1955, *41*, 103–113. On the other hand, studies by Lorge and his collaborators, using a different kind of problem, have shown collective problem-solving to be superior. See I. Lorge, J. Tuckman, L. Aikman, J. Speigel, and G. Moss, "Problem-Solving by Teams and by Individuals in a Field Setting," *J. Educ. Psychol.*, 1955, *46*, 160–166. Also see the review by C. P. Duncan, "Recent Research on Human Problem Solving," *Psychol. Bull.*, 1959, *56*, 397–429.

55. H. Gurnee, "Group Learning," *Psychol. Monogr.* 1962, *76*, No. 13.

56. Gurnee, *op. cit.*, p. 10.

57. A. F. Osborn, *Applied Imagination* (rev. ed.). Scribner, 1957.

58. D. W. Taylor, P. C. Berry, and C. H. Block, "Does Group Participation When Using Brainstorming Facilitate or Inhibit Creative Thinking?" *Admin. Sci. Quart.*, 1958, *3*, 23–47.

59. J. W. Thibaut and H. H. Kelley, *The Social Psychology of Groups*. Wiley, 1959, p. 267.

60. See A. Meadow and S. J. Parnes, "Evaluation of Training in Problem Solving," *J. Appl. Psychol.*, 1959, *43*, 189–194.

61. B. E. Collins and H. Guetzkow, *A Social Psychology of Group Processes in Decision-Making*, Wiley, 1964. Pages 42–45 discuss group problem-solving from the risk-taking angle. Also relevant is N. Kogan and M. A. Wallach, *Risk Taking*, Holt, Rinehart and Winston, 1964.

62. A. Bavelas, "Communication Patterns in Task Oriented Groups," *J. Acoust. Soc. Amer.*, 1950, *22*, 725–730. Reprinted in D. Cartwright and A. Zander, *Group Dynamics* (2nd ed.), Row, Peterson, 1960.

63. H. J. Leavitt, "Some Effects of Certain Communication Patterns on Group Performance," *J. Abn. Soc. Psychol.*, 1951, *46*, 38–50. Reprinted in Maccoby et al., *op. cit.*, reference 50, pp. 546–563.

64. K. Lewin, R. Lippitt, and R. K. White, "Patterns of Aggressive Behavior in Experimentally Created 'Social Climates,'" *J. Soc. Psychol.*, 1939, *10*, 271–299.

65. See R. K. White and R. Lippitt, "Leader Behavior and Member Reaction in Three 'Social Climates,'" Selection 28 in Cartwright and Zander, *op. cit.* Also, R. Lippitt and R. K. White, "An Experimental Study of Leadership and Group Life," in Maccoby, *et al.*, *op. cit.*, reference 50, pp. 496–511.

66. R. K. White and R. Lippitt, in Cartwright and Zander, *op. cit.*, reference 62, p. 541.

67. Lippitt and White, in Maccoby *et al.*, *op. cit.*, reference 50, pp. 501–506.

68. K. Lewin, "Group Decision and Social Change," in Maccoby, *et al.*, *op. cit.*, reference 50, pp. 197–219.

69. *Ibid.*, pp. 204–207.

70. L. Coch and J. R. P. French, "Overcoming Resistance to Change," *Human Relations*, 1948, *I*, 512–532. Reprinted in Maccoby et al., reference 50.

71. See M. A. Sherif, "A Study of Some Social Factors in Perception," *Arch. Psychol.*, 1935, No. 187. Also discussed in detail in M. A. Sherif and C. W. Sherif, *An Outline of Social Psychology* (rev. ed.), Harper, 1956.

72. H. G. Sperling, "An Experimental Study of Some Psychological Factors in Judgment," unpublished Master's thesis described by S. E. Asch, *Social Psychology*, Prentice-Hall, 1952, pp. 487–492.

73. S. E. Asch, "Effects of Group Pressure Upon the Modification and Distortion of Judgment," in Maccoby *et al.*, *op. cit.*, pp. 174–183. A more detailed report is given in S. E. Asch, "Studies of Independence and Submission in Group Pressure," *Psychol. Monogr.*, 1956, *70*, No. 416. For a briefer presentation see, by the same author, "Opinions and Social Pressure," *Scientific American*, 1955, *193*, 31–35.

74. Asch, in Maccoby *et al.*, *op. cit.*, p. 177.

75. See S. E. Asch, *Social Psychology*. Prentice-Hall, 1952, pp. 473–484.

76. E. H. Schein, "The Chinese Indoctrination Program for Prisoners of War: A Study of Attempted 'Brainwashing,'" *Psychiatry*, 1956, *19*, pp. 149–172. Reprinted in Maccoby *et al.*, *op. cit.*, pp. 311–334. Quotation from p. 318.

77. H. B. English and A. C. English, *A Compre-*

hensive *Dictionary of Psychological and Psychoanalytical Terms*, David McKay, 1958, p. 470.

78. G. W. Allport and L. J. Postman, "The Basic Psychology of Rumor," *N. Y. Acad. Sci.*, Series II, 1945, 8, p. 61.

79. G. W. Allport and L. Postman, *The Psychology of Rumor*. Holt, 1947, pp. 81–82.

80. Allport and Postman, *op. cit.*, p. 82.

81. Allport and Postman, *op. cit.*, p. 100.

82. G. LeBon, *The Crowd: A Study of the Popular Mind*. T. Fisher Unwin, 1896.

83. See W. McDougall, *The Group Mind*. Putnam, 1920.

84. F. H. Allport, *Social Psychology*. Houghton Mifflin, 1924.

85. For a good discussion of suggestion and hypnosis from this standpoint, see S. E. Asch, *Social Psychology*, Prentice-Hall, 1952, Chapter 14. Also see Cantril, reference 89, pp. 64–77.

86. Imitation was stressed by G. Tarde, *The Laws of Imitation*. Holt, 1903. However, this interpretation of behavior has not been widely accepted.

87. See, for example, Peterson's interpretation of such so-called "imitative" behavior. J. Peterson, "Imitation and Mental Adjustment," *J. Abn. Soc. Psychol.*, 1922, 17, 1–15.

88. S. S. Sargent and R. C. Williamson, *Social Psychology* (2nd ed.). Ronald, 1958, pp. 192, 523.

89. This religious movement is discussed in H. Cantril, *The Psychology of Social Movements*. Wiley, 1941.

90. Quoted by H. Cantril, *The Psychology of Social Movements*. Wiley, 1941, p. 218.

91. Cantril, *op. cit.*, p. 210.

92. Cantril, *op. cit.*, p. 269.

93. L. W. Doob, *Social Psychology*. Holt, 1952, pp. 308–309.

Chapter 18

Working Efficiently

1. N. Stewart, "AGCT Scores of Army Personnel Grouped by Occupations," *Occupations*, 1947, 26, 5–13: T. W. Harrell and M. S. Harrell, "Army General Classification Test Scores for Civilian Occupations," *Educ. Psychol. Measmt.*, 1945, 5.

2. E. K. Strong, *Vocational Interests of Men and Women*. Stanford University Press, 1943.

3. G. F. Kuder, *Revised Manual for the Kuder Pref-erence Record*. Science Research Associates, 1958.

4. D. G. Paterson *et al.*, *Minnesota Mechanical Ability Tests*. University of Minnesota Press, 1930.

5. Distributed by The Psychological Corporation, New York City.

6. B. J. Dvorak, "The New USES General Aptitude Test Battery," *J. Appl. Psychol.*, 1947, 31, 372–376.

7. Test Service Bulletin No. 51 (December 1956), The Psychological Corporation.

8. N.R.C. Committee on Selection and Training of Air-Craft Pilots, *An Introduction to Aviation Psychology*. C.A.A. Research Bulletin, No. 4, 1943.

9. Staff Psychological Section, "Psychological Activities in the Training Command, AAF," *Psychol. Bull.*, 1945, 42, 46. Also P. H. DuBois (Ed.), *The Classification Program*, AAF Aviation Psychology, Prog. Res. Report No. 2. Government Printing Office, 1947.

10. E. A. Fleishman, "Dimensional Analysis of Movement Reactions," *J. Exper. Psychol.*, 1958, 55, 438–453.

11. See for example, *Ergonomics in Industry*. London: Her Majesty's Stationery Office, 1961.

12. Division 21 of the American Psychological Association is the Society of Engineering Psychologists.

13. From J. Mann, *Frontiers in Psychology*. Macmillan, 1963, pp. 29–30.

14. Mann, *op. cit.*, pp. 31–32.

15. R. B. Sleight, "The Effect of Instrument Dial Shape on Legibility," *J. Appl. Psychol.*, 1948, 32, 170–182.

16. W. O. Jenkins, "The Tactual Discrimination of Shapes for Coding Aircraft-Type Controls," in P. M. Fitts (Ed.), *Psychological Research in Equipment Design*. Government Printing Office, 1947, pp. 199–205.

17. From P. M. Fitts, "Engineering and Equipment Design," in S. S. Stevens (Ed.), *Handbook of Experimental Psychology*. Wiley, 1951, p. 1313.

18. H. Helson, "Design of Equipment and Optimal Human Operation," *Amer. J. Psychol.*, 1949, 62, 473–497.

19. Helson, *op. cit.*, p. 497.

20. F. W. Taylor, *Principles of Scientific Management*. Harpers, 1911.

21. F. B. Gilbreth, *Motion Study*. Van Nostrand, 1911.

22. D. Wolfle, in S. S. Stevens (Ed.), *Handbook of*

Experimental Psychology. Wiley, 1951, p. 1284.

23. From A. T. Welford, *The Ergonomics of Automation.* London: Her Majesty's Stationery Office, 1960, p. 16.

24. L. G. Lindahl, "Movement Analysis As An Industrial Training Method," *J. Appl. Psychol.,* 1945, 29, 424.

25. Lindahl, *op. cit.* p. 436.

26. Research by J. v. Zuckerman and S. M. Roshal, as reported in E. R. Hilgard, *Introduction to Psychology.* Harcourt, Brace, 1953, p. 250.

27. For a good recent discussion of the effects of environmental changes on work output, see D. H. Fryer and E. R. Henry, *Handbook of Applied Psychology,* Rinehart, 1950, Vol. I, Chapter 2, Sections 10, 11; T. A. Ryan and P. C. Smith, *Principles of Industrial Psychology,* Ronald, 1954, Chapter 12; and N. R. F. Maier, *Psychology in Industry* (3rd ed.), Houghton Mifflin, 1965, Chapter 18.

28. Maier, *op. cit.,* p. 604.

29. Maier, *op. cit.,* p. 610.

30. G. L. Freeman, "Changes in Tension-Pattern and Total Energy Expenditure During Adaptation to 'Distracting' Stimuli," *Amer. J. Psychol.,* 1939, 52, 354–360.

31. F. J. Roethlisberger, *Management and Morale,* Harvard University Press, 1941, has a good digest of these experiments. They are reported more fully in F. J. Roethlisberger and W. J. Dixon, *Management and the Worker,* Harvard University Press, 1940.

32. Ryan and Smith, *op. cit.,* p. 287.

33. For a summary of the relevant research, see E. S. Robinson, "Work of the Integrated Organism," in C. Murchison (Ed.), *Handbook of General Experimental Psychology,* Clark University Press, 1934; and A. G. Bills, *General Experimental Psychology,* Longmans, Green, 1934, Chapter XXI.

34. This research has been reported by Sir Frederic Bartlett in "Fatigue Following Highly Skilled Work," *Proc. Royal Soc.,* 1943, B131, 247–257.

35. After Dashiell, from D. R. Davis, "Pilot Error: Some Laboratory Experiments," *Appl. Psychol. Res. Unit. Med. Res. Council,* Great Britain, 1948.

36. D. E. Broadbent, "Vigilance," *Brit. Med. Bull.,* 1964, 20, p. 17.

37. See especially A. T. Poffenberger, *Principles of Applied Psychology.* Appleton-Century-Crofts, 1942, p. 111.

38. F. C. Bartlett, *The Mind at Work and Play.* Beacon Press, 1951, p. 53.

39. A. C. Hoffman, "Eye-Movements During Prolonged Reading," *J. Exper. Psychol.,* 1946, 36, 95–118.

40. L. Carmichael and W. F. Dearborn, *Reading and Visual Fatigue.* Houghton Mifflin, 1947.

41. *Ibid.,* p. 370.

42. For a good summary of the relevant literature, see H. E. Burtt, *Applied Psychology* (2nd ed.), Prentice-Hall, 1957, pp. 435–439.

43. From E. G. Boring (Ed.), *Psychology for the Armed Services.* Infantry Journal Press, 1946, p. 182.

44. On this point, see the discussion in G. L. Freeman, *Physiological Psychology,* Van Nostrand, 1948, pp. 466–473.

45. A. S. Edwards, "Effects of the Loss of 100 Hours of Sleep," *Amer. J. Psychol.,* 1941, 54, 80–91.

46. H. L. Williams, A. Lubin, and J. J. Goodnow, "Impaired Performance with Acute Sleep Loss," *Psychol. Monogr.,* 1959, No. 484.

47. See especially the survey on sleep, provided by S. H. Bartley and E. Chute, *Fatigue and Impairment in Man.* McGraw-Hill, 1947, Chapter 13. Also see I. Oswald, *Sleeping and Waking,* Elsevier, 1962; and N. Kleitman, *Sleep and Wakefulness* (rev. ed.), University of Chicago Press, 1963.

48. D. E. Broadbent, "Variations in Performance Arising from Continuous Work," *Conference on Individual Efficiency in Industry.* Cambridge, England: Med. Res. Council, 1955, p. 2, as quoted in reference 46.

49. Also summarized in Bartley and Chute, *op. cit.*

50. H. L. Hollingworth, *The Influence of Caffeine on Mental and Motor Efficiency.* Science Press, 1912.

51. *Ibid.,* p. 164.

52. W. C. Stanley and H. Schlosberg, "The Psychophysiological Effects of Tea," *J. Psychol.,* 1953, 36, 435–448.

53. G. P. Carl and W. D. Turner, "The Effects of Benzedrine Sulfate (*amphetamine sulfate*) on Performance in a Comprehensive Psychometric Examination," *J. Psychol.,* 1939, 8, 165–216; "Temporary Changes in Affect and Attitude Following Ingestion of Various Amounts of Benzedrine Sulfate," *J. Psychol.,* 1939, 8, 415–482; "A Further Report on Benzedrine Sulfate: Psychophysical Effects and Supplemen-

tary Results from a Fifth Experimental Group," *J. Gen. Psychol.,* 1940, 22, 105–191.

54. Carl and Turner, *op. cit.,* p. 215.

55. See Boring, reference 43, p. 223.

56. There are many books on educational psychology. Among the most recent of these are: L. M. Smith and B. B. Hudgins, *Educational Psychology,* Knopf, 1964; and H. Sorenson, *Psychology in Education,* McGraw-Hill, 1964.

57. M. H. Hollender, *Psychology of Medical Practice,* Saunders, 1958. Also see W. Dennis (Ed.), *Relation of Psychology to Medicine,* University of Pittsburgh Press, 1950; G. K. Yacorzynski, *Medical Psychology,* Ronald, 1951; A. Anastasi, *Fields of Applied Psychology,* McGraw-Hill, 1964, pp. 518–546.

58. H. E. Burtt, *Legal Psychology,* Prentice-Hall, 1931; C. Whitmer, "Psychology in Law," in J. S. Gray (Ed.), *Psychology in Use,* American Book Co., 1951. Anastasi, *op. cit.,* pp. 547–575. Also see H. Toch (Ed.), *Legal and Criminal Psychology,* Holt, Rinehart & Winston, 1961.

59. E. K. Strong, *Psychological Aspects of Business,* McGraw-Hill, 1938; D. H. Fryer and E. R. Henry, *Handbook of Applied Psychology,* Rinehart, 1950, Chapter VIII; H. W. Hepner, *Psychology Applied to Life and Work* (3rd ed.), Prentice-Hall, 1959, Part V; Anastasi, *op. cit.,* pp. 251–336.

60. B. v. H. Gilmer, *How to Help Your Child Develop Successfully.* Prentice-Hall, 1951.

61. B. F. Skinner, "How to Teach Animals," *Scientific Monthly,* December 1951, 26–29.

62. C. R. Griffith, *Psychology and Athletics,* Scribner, 1928; and, by the same author, "The Physical Educator," in Fryer and Henry, *op. cit.,* Section 99, pp. 658–664.

63. J. E. Birren, *The Psychology of Aging.* Prentice-Hall, 1964. A brief survey is that of A. T. Welford, "The Study of Aging," *Brit. Med. Bull.,* 1964, 20, 65–69. On a prevalent problem of old age, see M. P. Lawton and F. G. Lawton, *Mental Impairment in the Aged,* Philadelphia Geriatric Center, 1965.

64. J. B. Conant, *Science and Common Sense.* Yale University Press, 1951, p. 345.

65. G. Murphy, *Human Potentialities,* Basic Books, 1958; A. H. Maslow (Ed.), *New Knowledge in Human Values,* Basic Books, 1959.

66. See O. Klineberg, *Human Dimension in International Relations.* Holt, Rinehart and Winston, 1964.

67. American Psychological Association, *Ethical Standards of Psychologists.*

Index of Names

Numbers below 657 refer to pages on which an author's contribution is discussed or on which his work is cited as a suggested reading. Numbers above 657 refer to the page on which an author's contribution is identified and its source given.

Index of Subjects